HANDBOOK ON THE GEOGRAPH
AND FINANCE

RESEARCH HANDBOOKS IN GEOGRAPHY

Series Editor: Susan J. Smith, *Honorary Professor of Social and Economic Geography* and *The Mistress of Girton College, University of Cambridge, UK*

This important new *Handbook* series will offer high quality, original reference works that cover a range of subjects within the evolving and dynamic field of geography, emphasising in particular the critical edge and transformative role of human geography.

Under the general editorship of Susan J. Smith, these *Handbooks* will be edited by leading scholars in their respective fields. Comprising specially commissioned contributions from distinguished academics, the *Handbooks* offer a wide-ranging examination of current issues. Each contains a unique blend of innovative thinking, substantive analysis and balanced synthesis of contemporary research.

Titles in the series include:

Handbook on Geographies of Technology
Edited by Barney Warf

Handbook on the Geographies of Money and Finance
Edited by Ron Martin and Jane Pollard

Handbook on the Geographies of Money and Finance

Edited by

Ron Martin

Professor of Economic Geography, Director of Research and Fellow of St Catharine's College, University of Cambridge, UK

Jane Pollard

Professor of Economic Geography, Centre for Urban and Regional Development Studies and School of Geography, Politics and Sociology, Newcastle University, UK

RESEARCH HANDBOOKS IN GEOGRAPHY

Cheltenham, UK • Northampton, MA, USA

Published by
Edward Elgar Publishing Limited
The Lypiatts
15 Lansdown Road
Cheltenham
Glos GL50 2JA
UK

Edward Elgar Publishing, Inc.
William Pratt House
9 Dewey Court
Northampton
Massachusetts 01060
USA

Paperback edition 2018

A catalogue record for this book
is available from the British Library

Library of Congress Control Number: 2016957229

This book is available electronically in the **Elgar**online
Social and Political Science subject collection
DOI 10.4337/9781784719005

ISBN 978 1 78471 899 2 (cased)
ISBN 978 1 78471 900 5 (eBook)
ISBN 978 1 78897 772 2 (paperback)

Typeset by Servis Filmsetting Ltd, Stockport, Cheshire
Printed and bound by CPI Group (UK) Ltd, Croydon CR0 4YY

Contents

Contributors

Dr Manuel B. Aalbers
Department of Geography
KU Leuven, Belgium

Professor David S. Bieri
Global Forum on Urban and Regional Resilience
Virginia Tech, USA

Professor (Emeritus) Dick Bryan
Department of Political Economy
The University of Sydney, Australia

Professor Brett Christophers
Department of Social and Economic Geography
Uppsala University, Sweden

Professor Gordon L. Clark
Smith School of Enterprise and the Environment
University of Oxford, UK

Dr José Corpataux
Institut de Sociologie, Switzerland

Professor Olivier Crevoisier
Institut de Sociologie, Switzerland

Professor Kavita Datta
School of Geography
Queen Mary University of London, UK

Dr Adam D. Dixon
School of Geographical Sciences
University of Bristol, UK

Dr Sabine Dörry
School of Geography and the Environment
Oxford University Centre for the Environment
University of Oxford, UK
Luxembourg Institute of Socio-Economic Research (LISER)
Maison des Sciences Humaines, Luxembourg

Professor Gary A. Dymski
Leeds University Business School
University of Leeds, UK

Dr Mia Gray
Department of Geography
University of Cambridge, UK

Professor Dr Britta Klagge
Department of Geography
University of Bonn, Germany

Professor Janelle Knox-Hayes
Department of Urban Studies and Planning
Massachusetts Institute of Technology, USA

Dr Stephan Köppe
School of Social Policy, Social Work and Social Justice
Geary Institute
University College Dublin, Ireland

Dr Ginevra Marandola
Department of Economics
University of Bologna, Italy

Professor Ron Martin
Department of Geography and St Catharine's College
University of Cambridge, UK

Dr Peter North
Geography and Planning
School of Environmental Sciences
University of Liverpool, UK

Dr Peter O'Brien
Centre for Urban and Regional Development Studies (CURDS)
Newcastle University, UK

Professor Luca Papi
Department of Economic and Social Sciences
MoFiR (Money and Finance Research Group)

Professor Andy Pike
Centre for Urban and Regional Development Studies (CURDS)
Newcastle University, UK

Dr Marc Pilkington
Department of Economics
Université Bourgogne Franche Comté, France

Professor Jane Pollard
Centre for Urban and Regional Development Studies (CURDS)
School of Geography, Politics and Sociology
Newcastle University, UK

Dr Michael Pryke
Geography Department
Faculty of Social Sciences
The Open University, UK

Dr Michael Rafferty
The University of Sydney Business School
The University of Sydney, Australia

Dr Lena Rethel
Department of Politics and International Studies
University of Warwick, UK

Professor Emma Sarno
Department of Human and Social Sciences
University of Naples L'Orientale, Italy

Dr Beverley A. Searle
School of the Environment
University of Dundee, UK

Dr Mimoza Shabani
School of Business and Law
University of East London, UK

Professor Timothy J. Sinclair
Department of Politics and International Studies
University of Warwick, UK

Dr Enid Slack
Director, Institute on Municipal Finance and Governance
Munk School of Global Affairs
University of Toronto, Canada

Professor Peter Sunley
School of Geography and Environment
University of Southampton, UK

Dr Thierry Theurillat
Laboratory Technics, Territories and Societies (LATTS)
University of Paris-Est, France

Dr Thomas Wainwright
School of Management
Royal Holloway University of London, UK

Dr Duncan Wigan
Department of Business and Politics
Copenhagen Business School, Denmark

Professor Dariusz Wójcik
School of Geography and the Environment

Oxford University Centre for the Environment
University of Oxford, UK

Dr Godfrey Yeung
Department of Geography
National University of Singapore, Singapore

Professor Alberto Zazzaro
Department of Economics and Statistics
CSEF (Center for Studies in Economics and Finance)
University of Naples Federico II, Italy
Department of Economic and Social Sciences
MoFiR (Money and Finance Research Group)
Università Politecnica delle Marche, Italy

Mr Bryan Zhang
Cambridge Judge Business School
University of Cambridge, UK

Acknowledgements

I would like to thank Matthew Pitman at Edward Elgar for originally suggesting the topic of the Geographies of Money and Finance for one of the publisher's Research Handbooks. Producing such a Research Handbook is really too much for one individual, and I was delighted when Jane Pollard accepted my invitation to join forces on the project. Her knowledge about the geographies of money, her attention to detail, and her constant good humour, have all been crucial to the completion of the book. I have enjoyed working with Jane immensely. Of course, compiling a Research Handbook such as this, always a lengthy task, depends critically on the cooperation and patience of the many contributors: our heartfelt thanks to them all for taking part in this project. My interest in the geographies of money and finance was first aroused in the late-1980s, and several cohorts of students attending my second year economic geography lectures at Cambridge endured my ramblings on the subject. Little did any of us know then just how profound and catastrophic an impact ever-increasing financialisation would come to have two decades later. I've always found academic life itself to be a rollercoaster, with its highs and lows. I have been fortunate, however, to have had the unswerving encouragement and confidence of my wife, Lynda: to her I dedicate this book.

RLM

I would like to thank everyone involved in the preparation of this book, our authors, Editor, Matthew Pitman, and all the production staff at Edward Elgar. Thanks to Ron Martin for asking me to edit this with him; many years and months later, we are – I am happy to report – still friends. I also owe a debt of gratitude to all the Undergraduate, Masters and PhD students who have taken and helped to teach my courses on money and have keenly debated questions around money and finance. To my colleagues at Newcastle in CURDS and the School of Geography, Politics and Sociology who have created such a congenial, good humoured and supportive environment, a big thank you. Neill Marshall most especially has been a friend and mentor and contributed so much to my and others' work on money and finance. Much of this volume took shape while I was a Visiting Professor in the Urban Planning Department at the Luskin School of Public Affairs at UCLA and in the Center for Place, Culture and Politics at CUNY. I would like to thank Evelyn Blumenberg, Brian Taylor, Ruth Wilson Gilmore, Mary Taylor and all the staff at UCLA and CUNY for making that possible. Special thanks to Diane and my extended family and friends for their support, you know who you are. Finally, I want to acknowledge my Dad who died during the production of this volume. He was a principled, fearless, compassionate man who made me laugh and taught me so much.

JSP

For Lynda, for her steadfast support and encouragement over many years.

For my parents, Lilian Pollard and John Brian Pollard, for their love, strength and support.

1. The geography of money and finance

Ron Martin and Jane Pollard

1.1 INTRODUCTION: THE CASE FOR A GEOGRAPHY OF MONEY

The aim of this Handbook is to make the case for the necessity – conceptual, empirical and political – to think spatially about the constitution and expressions of money and financial systems: in short to make the case for a geography of money. A key tenet of the Handbook is that taking space and place seriously is essential to understanding the constitution, operation and organization of money and financial systems, institutions, agents and markets. For economic geographers such thinking is by no means new (Harvey, 1973, 1982; Corbridge et al., 1994; Leyshon and Thrift, 1997; Martin, 1999), although the dynamics of money and finance have, for too long, appeared 'offstage' (Clark, 2006: 84) relative to long(er) standing concerns of production, work, technological change, competition, agglomeration and urban and regional economic development. Beyond the discipline of Geography, and notwithstanding the ground-breaking work of Viviana Zelizer (1979), however, much of the social sciences have encountered matters financial as 'largely the (self-appointed) preserve of (financial) economists, wrapped in a forbidding mantle of technicality that warned outsiders of finance's inherent complexity' (Christophers, 2015: 189). More recently, however, a burgeoning body of work on money and finance in Sociology, Anthropology, Development, Management and Political Science, has been inspired by the growing social and cultural visibility of financial logics, practices and institutions in contemporary life.

The chapters in this Handbook reflect some of this proliferating interest in money and finance, but more than this, they also articulate some of what is at stake in developing a more sophisticated understanding of the spatialities of money and finance. The role of financial logics, institutions and practices in producing and distributing a series of devastating, and ongoing, economic and political upheavals – most recently in the shape of the subprime crisis of 2007–08 – demonstrates the urgent necessity to move beyond narratives of 'inherent complexity' to better understand the economic, social, political and cultural relations of money and power that shape livelihoods and patterns of international, urban and regional development.

What do we mean when we talk about a more sophisticated understanding of the spatialities of money and finance? One part of this involves appreciating the constitutive, and not merely expressive, significance of geography. These chapters go much further than simply recognizing that money and finance are arranged and instituted in particular geographical forms, that financial logics, practices, markets and institutions are located and 'happen somewhere'. Instead they argue that spatiality is integral to money, in the forms it takes, the organizations through which it is institutionalized, the ways in which it deconstructs, reassembles and distributes assets, liabilities, risk and indeed, conceives of time and space.

Relatedly, an important element of thinking spatially is to acknowledge and understand the world in its variegation and complexity, as opposed to the world represented in the neoclassical parables of *homo economicus*, perfect information and frictionless flows of capital to the highest rate of return. Such an acknowledgement and commitment is essential; geography can help reveal the sociality and politics of financial relations otherwise depicted as 'technical', 'neutral' or simply 'economic'. More than this, spatial thinking is part and parcel of understanding money and finance holistically, as incorporating economic, social, political, environmental, and cultural issues.

The chapters in Part I of the Handbook are concerned with some of the conceptual issues involved in thinking about the geography of money. One of the primary features of the history of money is the recurrent tendency for the emergence and inevitable subsequent bursting of 'asset bubbles', what Kindleberger (1978) famously referred to as 'manias, panics and crashes'. According to Kindleberger, financial crises have a distinctive temporal pattern, in terms of how originate, develop and then end. But as **Dymski and Shabani (Chapter 2)** argue, bubbles and crashes are also spatially constituted. They interrogate three contrasting definitions of asset bubbles – those based on ideas of equilibrium, those empirically defined, and those rooted in heterodox concerns with economic processes and outcomes in real-time settings. Their key argument is that while economists are increasingly incorporating asset bubbles into their analyses of financial crisis, they 'are interested in commonalities in experience across space, and thus conduct analyses implicitly *in* space, but not *of* space'. As such, econometric modelling of asset bubbles serves to invisibilize the importance of space by reducing it to merely a 'site' of infection or contagion. This impoverished conception of space serves a broader theoretical and methodological purpose; spacelessness enhances the generalizability of mainstream models. So, even as recent financial crises and their asset boom and bust characteristics have spawned a myriad of opportunities for modelling crises and contagion – usually oriented around transaction costs, missing information and the institutional limits of markets – such approaches decline to 'place' asset bubbles, to interrogate the territorialized differentiation of how firms, households, investors and consumers connect with different circuits of capital (see Benner et al., 2010), or to interrogate how these territorializations shape both cause and consequence.

So, what would a more spatially sophisticated and realistic conception of an asset bubble look like? Dymski and Shabani endorse a geographical political economy that argues that asset bubbles come into being in given places because of spatially uneven market and income structures and, in turn, their interaction with wider, uneven flows of goods, services, credit, and capital. In essence, and connecting to broader work on the subprime crisis (e.g. Aalbers, 2009), this spatialized understanding requires an interrogation of the links between the local and the global and a recognition of the variegation of crisis and its contingent, developing spatial outcomes.

The financial crisis of 2007–08 also informs the discussion by **Christophers (Chapter 3)**, which deploys a political economy framework to trouble another orthodox parable, namely the idea of 'market discipline' which conceives markets as institutions that crystallize information into prices, act as regulators and check risk taking behaviour. Christophers argues that 'market discipline' had, at best, a tenuous relationship with banking reality prior to the financial crisis of 2008 and, in its aftermath, has even less relevance. The chapter develops this argument by examining the shifting nature of pre- and post-crisis relations between three key groups of actors, commercial banks and financial institutions, central banks and states. Christophers delineates a post-crisis geographical political economy of money and finance that is marked by a reordering of relationships between these different institutional actors. He notes the growing power of banks deemed 'too-big-to-fail' (TBTF) and interrogates the shifting spatiality of 'the market' deemed to be disciplining such institutions in the aftermath of the crisis.

As such, Christophers delineates some emerging contours of a new political economy of money, one marked by some very different geographies to its predecessor and a more central role for nation states in managing markets. These contours chart the growth and political power of transnational institutions deemed TBTF – beyond market discipline – and their reliance on 'geographically-specific re-couplings' with relevant nation states, notably the US and Great Britain, able and willing to effect their bailouts and to secure the conditions of their political and economic reproduction. This new political economy is one in which, Christophers argues, the materiality of central and commercial banks and states – vis-à-vis markets – has deepened and become more visible. An important question raised here, and reflected in many other chapters, concerns the politics of governing financial institutions and relations; if 'market discipline' is of declining relevance to institutions deemed TBTF, then who or what is disciplining such institutions?

Corpataux, Crevoisier and Theurillat (Chapter 4) focus on exploring some of the conditions in which investors and entrepreneurs can and are becoming increasingly disconnected from each other. They argue that financialization is an intrinsically spatial phenomena in that it is a form of producing and then exploiting the mobility of capital. Financial markets, while appearing ever more remote from the workings of 'real' economies of machines, buildings and infrastructure, are profoundly significant in shaping uneven development. Drawing on research in Switzerland, the chapter explores various spatial, institutional and functional disjunctures between the workings of financial markets and the real economy. In terms of corporate governance, for example, they chart some of the institutional and regulatory changes needed to convert real into financial capital, changes that produce and enhance the liquidity and mobility of financial capital that, in turn, allow the separation of the investor and the entrepreneur. Such institutional changes have ushered in a system of exceptional capital mobility that allows for strategies of quick exit and little commitment. Investment strategies can be detached, quantitative and decontextualized, products of Markovitz's (1959) portfolio theory that encourages the diversification of risk through investment in non-correlated assets. A key argument here is that 30 years of enhancing the mobility of capital has meant that the distance – functional, spatial, social or otherwise – between investors and their investments has been growing.

How are such shifts territorialized? And with what consequences? Corpataux, Crevoisier and Theurillat argue that this growing distance between investors and their investments is manifest in the concentration and centralization of investment decisions, epitomized in the growth of global cities. One corollary of this centralization and concentration is the takeover of regional banking institutions and a reduction in regional capacities for monetary creation. Another is the 'short circuiting' of the traditional boundaries and hierarchies of local, national and international governance. The resulting spatial hierarchy is bifurcated between a network of global cities that compete on the basis of attracting investment flows and a 'mosaic' of territories competing in terms of innovation and cost reduction.

The mobility of capital in different and changing forms is a theme that animates the chapters by Dick Bryan, Michael Rafferty and Duncan Wigan and Michael Pryke. **Bryan, Rafferty and Wigan (Chapter 5)** interrogate what they term the 'deconstruction and reconstruction of capital' as constitutive for understanding the changing spatialities and temporalities of capital. Using David Harvey's (1973) work on absolute, relative and relational space, they explore how financial markets are creating forms of relative and relational capital that generate complex, opaque geographies of obligation that defy absolute forms of measurement. Their analysis points not just to the changing scales of finance, but also its changing forms. Thus, they explore how financial derivatives deconstruct 'things' into constituent elements before blending and reconstructing different elements into a single measureable unit that can be traded. This ability to deconstruct and then reconstruct all manner of spatio-temporal forms of capital poses insuperable challenges to ideas about knowability, control, measurement and pricing. Financial transactions connect and blend different times, spaces and risks, transcending ideas about linear time and 'national' and 'offshore' jurisdictions. This appreciation of the changing forms and possible spatialities of capital have profound implications and open up different ways of thinking about how we understand capital and its classic institutional forms like 'the corporation', which is now being deconstructed and reconstructed into tradable constituent parts.

In similar vein, albeit from a different theoretical orientation, **Pryke (Chapter 6)** argues that space is not simply an inert backdrop or passive flatland, but is actively entangled in market practices. His chapter is centrally concerned to use some of the lessons of the 2008 crisis to produce a more spatially sensitive understanding of money. Again, the idea that financial innovation *is* spatial innovation figures prominently. Pryke argues for a topological understanding of space that is supple enough to comprehend how financial risks can be imagined and assembled from assets around the globe. Aided and abetted by mathematical models and visualization software, mortgages in cities like Baltimore can be 'reduced to code' and traded internationally. Such an understanding transcends metaphors of 'flows' and 'circulation', with implications for authorities tasked with regulating these time-spaces. National regulatory authorities are faced with financial innovations that not only generate new connections and linkages, but also new risks that generate radical uncertainty and unpredictability. Risk is always much more than a statistical attribute of data and as such, finance is never merely 'technical'; its politics must always be interrogated. While the software and modelling create new instruments and combinations, the brute materiality of finance strikes when these markets unravel, as they did in 2008 to devastating effect.

1.2 MONEY, THE SPATIAL ORGANIZATION OF FINANCIAL SYSTEMS AND UNEVEN GEOGRAPHICAL DEVELOPMENT

The contributions gathered in Part II of the book are all concerned, in one way or another, with how the operation – and, indeed, the very spatial organization – of financial systems (their institutions and markets) shapes the geographies of socio-economic development. The tendency for capitalism to develop unevenly across space has long attracted the attention of geographers. Over the years, various theoretical and conceptual frameworks have been advanced for understanding this tendency and its effects. We know much about how the forces of competition and technological change drive a constant process of 'creative destruction' in which new firms, new jobs, new products, new skills and new technologies drive out and render obsolete old ones, thereby producing perpetual instability of economic landscapes (see, for example, Harvey, 2006; Cooke et al., 2011). We know much about how this instability involves an ongoing tension between forces making for the spatial agglomeration of economic activity on the one hand, and their geographical dispersal on the other, and how these forces have themselves become increasingly global in scope, operation and consequences (see Scott, 2006, 2011).

Yet, it is probably no exaggeration to say that, for the most part, our theories of uneven geographical development have not assigned much explicit recognition or integration of the roles that financial markets and institutions play in this process. Certainly finance rarely figures as a key determinant in the models and analyses of agglomeration, innovation, clustering, production networks, governance, and the like around which much of the recent work in economic geography and regional studies has centred. But access to finance is of crucial importance to the investment and disinvestment decisions of firms, their capacity to innovate, and their merger and acquisition strategies. How financial institutions allocate funds to firms, economic activities, and hard and soft infrastructures exerts a key influence over economic development and economic growth. Likewise, firms vary significantly in the power they are able to exert over financial institutions when seeking capital. Thus the geography of financial systems – how banking systems, capital markets and the institutions involved are spatially organized, and the rules and practices by which such systems allocate funds across space – and the geography of economic and social development – the spatialities of investment, disinvestment, innovation, employment, infrastructure housing and per capita incomes – are inextricably interrelated (see Figure 1.1). Regional development drives a demand for finance for investment which is funded (or not, as the case may be) by the financial system, which allocations and reallocations of funds in turn shape the pattern and form of regional development. The chapters in this section of the book explore and identify the nature of this interrelationship.

Firms can raise capital for new investment, expenditure on new R&D, on new product development, takeover, merger or acquisition, and other activities requiring finance, from various sources. The conventional sources have been loans from banks, retained profits, and capital raised by issuing shares. Retained profits and bank loans have traditionally been major sources of finance for small, privately owned firms unwilling or unable to raise funds via a public listing on a stock market. A bank loan immediately links a firm into the banking system more generally, and into the wider financial system as a whole, given banks will have other opportunities for lending and/or investment, and that the interest rates charged on a loan will be influenced by the bank rate set by the central bank of the country concerned, and that this rate in turn will reflect that central bank's monetary policies. The use of retained profits will, of course depend on the performance of the firm and its other obligations, as well as conditions in the wider financial marketplace (such as interest rates). For larger firms and corporations that are publicly listed on stock markets the main source of new capital will be via the issuance of new shares to private and institutional investors (such as pension funds). Equities entail dividend payments by the firms concerned, and of course the value of a company's shares will depend not only on the company's performance (in particular its declared profits), but also on the movements on

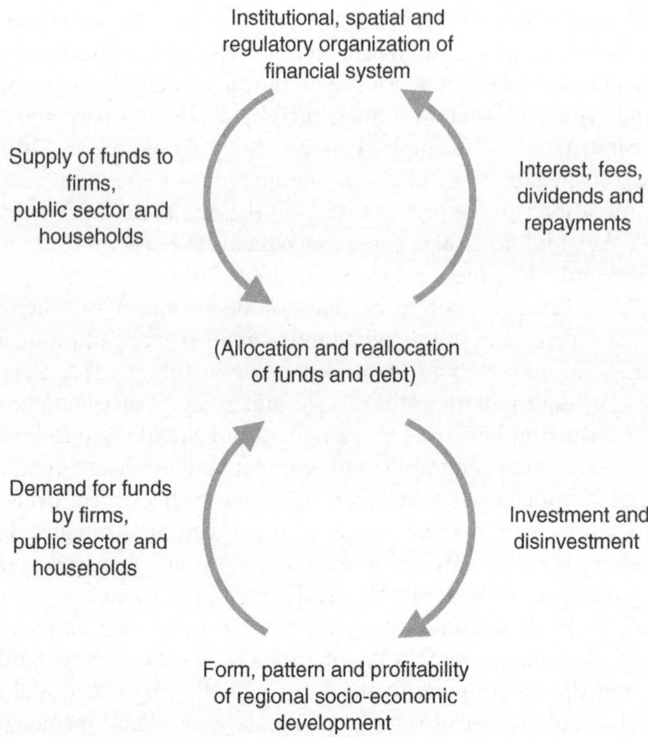

Figure 1.1 The intersection and interdependence of the financial system and regional socio-economic development

stock markets more generally, movements that may have nothing to do with the company in question but which reflect wider market sentiments, global economic conditions, and economic and political shocks of various kinds.

Over the past thirty years or so, other capital circuits have come into existence which provide firms with alternative sources of funds, such as venture capital, private equity and crowdfunding. Venture capital is intended – at least in principle – to provide forms of finance for new, early-stage and emerging growth companies, particularly in high-risk sectors and activities that cannot easily raise funds by issuing debt or borrowing from banks. Private equity is a source of investment capital from institutions and high-net-worth individuals for the purpose of investing and acquiring equity ownership in companies. Although often trumpeted as supporting and fostering the new and small firm sector, especially in high-technology, a not inconsiderable proportion of venture capital finds its way into management buy-out and buy-ins, even mergers and acquisitions, and in lower-risk sectors of activity such as retailing. Private equity firms raise funds and manage these monies to yield favourable returns for their shareholder clients, typically over a short time horizon. In recent years both of these new circuits of finance for companies have expanded beyond their individual home nation borders and have gone global. The phenomenon of 'crowdfunding' provides a novel Internet-based platform through which small, often 'alternative' businesses can raise finance from a myriad of individuals, each typically committing only a small sum in return for an attractive rate of return (Langley, 2016). It offers a source of funds for business that operates outside conventional and institutionalized financial markets.

But at the same time as these developments have been occurring, in many countries banking systems themselves have undergone or have begun to undergo historic processes of restructuring, centralization and concentration, involving reductions in the number of independent banks and a shift towards a more branch-based banking model. This process happened in the UK as early as the nineteenth century, but is a more recent, and still ongoing, development in countries like Germany and Italy. And while this has been happening, many larger banks have gone global, establishing branches worldwide and operating on a truly global scale, seeking out the most profitable investment and projects, and using securitization to bundle loans with different degrees of risk into debt instruments that can be traded on global financial markets.

How the financial system interacts with and shapes uneven geographical development is thus inextricably bound up with the changing institutional and spatial organization of the financial system itself. In her 'stages of banking development' theory of the spatial evolution of the financial system, Dow (1999) used post-Keynesian monetary economics combined with Myrdalian ideas of centre-periphery uneven development to argue that the spatial structure and organization of financial systems are intimately bound up with their economic and institutional development. Thus, the increasing concentration of a banking system into just a few major banks, if accompanied by the spatial concentration of the main offices and high order functions of those banks into a major financial centre, can lead to or exacerbate a core–periphery pattern of regional development dominated by the region hosting that financial centre. Funds and savings will tend to flow from the peripheral regions to the core region where opportunities for liquidity, investment and financial returns are highest. How far and under what conditions and terms funds flow back to the periphery then becomes a key factor affecting economic development and growth there.

According to conventional theory, provided financial markets work freely and smoothly, and there are no information barriers or frictions, the spatial structure and organization of a financial system should have no material effect on the geographical allocation of loan and investment capital: distance should not be a factor influencing the spatial flow of funds. This issue has attracted increasing interest from researchers, both in the United States and in Europe. The balance of evidence suggests that even though credit scoring of firms has become increasingly codified and automated, and information can now be easily gathered and communicated electronically, physical distance continues to matter in banking and that most loans and related services provided to small businesses are made by financial institutions close to those businesses (Peterson and Rajan, 2002; DeYoung, Glennon and Nigro, 2006; Alessandrini et al., 2009; Udell, 2009; Brevoort and Wolken, 2009; Cerqueiro, Degryse and Ongena, 2009). Under such conditions, whether the financial system is spatially centralized or decentralized may then assume key importance for the form and pattern of uneven geographical development.

Klagge, Martin and Sunley (Chapter 7) develop this argument conceptually, and then explore it empirically by comparing the UK and Germany, the former having a well-established branch banking model and a highly spatially centralized financial system (in London), the latter a much more decentralized system, with numerous local banks and several financial centres (see also Klagge and Martin, 2005). The evidence, particularly with respect to venture capital, where regular contact between the investee firm and the investor institution is important, suggests that the more decentralized market in Germany results in a more even distribution of investment across regions: in the UK, in contrast, the geography of venture capital investment is regionally uneven and biased towards London and the South East, where the majority of venture capital institutions are also located. There is also evidence for the UK that at times of financial crisis and recession, peripheral regions are more likely to suffer from credit rationing by banks (Degryse, Matthews and Zhao, 2015).

While physical distance may be the most obvious measure of 'proximity' between banks and customer firms, it is not necessarily the most meaningful or relevant, particularly when either the bank or its customer firms have multiple geographical locations. Especially in the provision of credit, when a bank has multiple branches, the concept of 'distance' becomes complex. The bank's branches may play different roles in providing services to borrowers, with one branch serving as a point of personal contact with a firm seeking a loan, another housing the decision makers who approve or deny the loan, and yet another which has responsibility for loan monitoring operations (Brevoort and Wolken, 2009). Similarly, for firms with multiple locations, it is not necessarily clear which location in the most relevant for obtaining financial services. Each location may play a role, and the importance of each may differ according to the nature of the financial service being sought. Thus 'distance' can be a complex, multidimensional relational concept. Drawing on earlier work (for example, Zazzaro, 1997; Alessandrini, Croci and Zazzaro 2005), **Papi, Sarno and Zazzaro (Chapter 8)** make a distinction between 'operational distance', the physical distance between a bank and its customers, and 'functional distance', defined as the distance between a bank's decision-making centre and the bank's branch. Functional distance thus captures the spatial remoteness between the different hierarchical layers of a banking organization. Using network analysis techniques, and focusing on the Italian banking system, they show that the overall interconnectedness of geographical credit markets has significantly increased over time, whether measured at the regional or provincial level. They go on to demonstrate that within this process, there has been a growing and marked centralization of the system within a few northern Italian banking centres to the detriment of the southern credit markets and regions. Their study highlights the importance of the concept of distance, especially that of functional distance, in shaping the relationships between banks and local borrowers, and how this has worked in recent years to intensify the country's core–periphery financial and banking divide, with adverse consequences for the small business sector in the south of the country.

For large firms, of course, apart from retained profits, the main source of finance for expansion and growth is often the public stock market, that is by issuing shares, stocks and bonds. Historically, in the early days of industrialization, manufacturing firms used retained profits or bank credit for their development and expansion. But with the emergence of large corporations in the twentieth century, and their need to raise large amounts of capital for investment, national stock markets assumed a key role as a source for such funding. Again, historically, this suggests a certain geography of reliance on stock markets, with those regions and localities specializing in large-scale manufacturing being much more linked into the stock market than other regions. National stock markets – or sometimes regional ones where these exist – thus became the conduits for steering capital from investors, wherever these were located, into the industrial base of particular regions.

Although stock markets have become globalized in their operations and interrelationships, a 'home bias' by investors nevertheless seems to have persisted, and even a financial centre bias (whereby firms near a nation's financial centre are more likely to participate in stock markets than are provincial firms – see Wójcik, 2009). One issue that has remained under-explored, however, is the relationship between innovative firms and the stock market. According to **Wójcik (Chapter 9)**, there are several interrelated questions here. Are more innovative firms more likely than less innovative ones to use stock markets to raise capital? Or put another way, do stock markets tend to promote more innovation by firms? Are innovative service sector firms just as likely to use stock markets as manufacturing firms? Using cross national data, Wójcik finds empirical support for these hypotheses. And what do stock markets imply for the geographies of innovation? While the venture capital market has developed to direct capital to innovative SMEs, large innovative firms (whether manufacturing or service based) may prefer to use stock markets. And venture capital markets often function as a feeder to stock markets. The presence of a large and thriving stock market may thus help to promote innovation in an economy, and thence may influence how this new economy develops geographically. As Wójcik asks: how far and in what ways do particular production systems and financial systems co-evolve (he mentions Silicon Valley and NASDAQ in the US)? Even more prosaically, if a local high-tech cluster produces its own stock market index of leading local firms, does this help to attract capital into the area (Cambridge, UK, has one such index, which is regularly compared to – and outperforms – the FTSE on the London stock market).

Of course, local and regional development is not just about the activities of firms, and how those activities are financed. It also involves investment in the public infrastructures that facilitate those activities, in the social infrastructures that support and attract workers and their families – especially housing – and in the public services on which both business and households depend. In fact, investment in infrastructure, of all kinds, is now widely recognized as key to economic growth and development at all spatial scales. The demand for new and improved infrastructure appears to be almost insatiable. But at the same time, its financing has become a major challenge (Della Croce and Gatti, 2014). As western advanced economies have shifted to neoliberal economic policies, in which privatization of public sector assets and latterly restrictions on public spending imposed as part of a new politics of 'fiscal prudence' (austerity), have taken hold, so states have sought other means of financing investments in key infrastructures. As **O'Brien and Pike (Chapter 10)** argue,

> the result is that governments and private actors are exploring – and in some cases being compelled – to adopt (more) financialized practices and mechanisms in an attempt to leverage new capital . . . The financialization of infrastructure, which has a distinct geography concentrated on urban and suburban areas . . . is a growing feature of an increasingly financialized global economy.

Whether it be the use of various kinds of public–private partnerships (PPPs),whereby a national or local government enters into a contract with private sector organizations to build and manage infrastructure (roads, airports, hospitals, etc.), which the national or local government then rents back, or outright privatization of existing or private provision of new infrastructures (possibly with state guarantees or underwriting), infrastructure has become a distinct asset class for private, institutional and some sovereign wealth fund investors. As such, the financing of local, regional and city infrastructures is becoming increasingly interwoven with global financial institutions, flows and markets. But, as O'Brien and Pike show, using the UK, USA and Australia as examples, this process is unfolding in different ways in different countries, and even between different localities and cities within them.

And it is not just public infrastructure that is undergoing a major transformation in terms of funding. Other dimensions of public spending, such as on local services and utilities, are also facing increasing pressures. In almost all advanced countries, local governments and public bodies have responsibilities for delivering key social and related services that help to underpin local economic performance and social reproduction, from healthcare to education, from environmental services to police and fire services. Different countries have evolved different models for delivering and financing such activities, involving different funding arrangements as between the central state and local state authorities – in essence, different degrees of devolution of revenue-raising (essentially local taxes) and revenue-spending powers **(Slack, Chapter 11)**. Some countries, such as Denmark, Japan and to a lesser extent the United States, have long had a relatively high degree of local devolution of tax-raising powers. Others, such as Spain, France and Italy, have been moving progressively towards greater devolution. The United Kingdom stands in quite marked contrast, in not only having a low level of decentralization, but in having become more centralized (see Table 1.1).

At the same time that a process of fiscal devolution has occurred in many countries, state-sponsored institutional investors – commonly referred to as sovereign wealth funds (SWFs) – have grown in number. As **Dixon (Chapter 12)** shows, there are now perhaps as many as 60 or more of these SWFs, commanding assets of around $6 trillion. Widely viewed as a new and distinct class of actor in global financial markets, SWFs fall into three main types, in terms of the sources of their funds: resource commodity-revenues, balance of payments surpluses, and fiscal surpluses. Sovereign wealth funds can also be found in quite different types of political-economic regime, from social democracies (such as Norway) to command economies (such as China) to autocracies (such as some Middle Eastern oil states). While some SWFs may be more of a status symbol than a necessary policy tool, as Dixon argues, SWFs can influence socio-economic development in significant ways, whether by covering state pension obligations or by investing

Table 1.1 Proportion of total local tax revenue raised by local government (per cent)

Country	1975	1995	2012
United States	14.7	13.2	15.2
Spain	4.3	8.5	9.9
Denmark	30.4	31.9	26.9
France	7.6	11.0	13.2
Italy	0.9	5.4	16.4
Japan	25.6	25.3	24.7
Germany	9.0	7.4	8.2
United Kingdom	11.1	3.7	4.9

Source: OECD (2015) *Tax Policy Analysis*.

in companies, infrastructure and property. Through their involvement in global financial markets SWFs can influence the movement of funds across space, both within and between nations. Both through their investments, both direct and indirect, in companies, public infrastructure projects and (mostly urban) property, both at home, and abroad, SWFs can significantly reinforce or reconfigure the geographies of economic development. The complexity of the overseas investment of these SWFs is only now beginning to emerge, and while they can provide much-needed capital for local businesses and projects, their investment has not been without concern, for example over their implications for the loss of local ownership or security of local strategic infrastructures and utilities.

One of the primary arenas for the impact of finance on the socio-economic landscape has been housing. Indeed, as **Aalbers (Chapter 13)** argues, the twentieth century could well be called the 'century of the mortgage market'. During the course of that century, across the leading OECD nations the share of mortgage loans in banks' total lending activity roughly doubled, from 30 to 60 per cent. The rising demand for home ownership, not just as social necessity but increasingly as a household investment vehicle (especially as a pension asset), and the steady and seemingly ineluctable increase in house prices, all fuelled the expansion of the mortgage market, and traditional mortgage institutions (Sassen, 2009). What historically had been a 'locally originating, locally distributed' model of mortgage lending had become a 'locally originating, globally distributed' model (Wainwright, 2009; Martin, 2011), linking housing and the geographies of urban development into the flows and forces of the global financial system more widely (Aalbers, 2009). Those geographies, furthermore were uneven: in the United States, for example, the housing and subprime mortgage boom was not a universal phenomenon, but one concentrated in particular cities and states, such as Nevada and Florida, often associated with large-scale speculative housing developments. Thus when the housing bubble burst, in 2007, as a result of escalating numbers of mortgage repayment defaults, the collapse and credit squeeze induced recession this triggered were likewise geographically uneven (Immergluck, 2011; Martin, 2011; Walks, 2013). Not dissimilar geographically uneven effects of this housing mortgage boom and bust cycle have been experienced in other countries, such as Spain (particularly along its Mediterranean coast) and Ireland (especially around Dublin). Thus the global financial crisis was not only a regionally uneven process in its origins, but also in its socio-economic effects.

As **Searle and Köppe (Chapter 14)** go on to show, the mortgage crisis links directly to the wider issue of household debt. They document how household debt has risen dramatically in many countries over recent decades, to reach almost $30 trillion in some 22 OECD countries by the eve of the financial crisis in 2007. The relaxation of financial constraints on banks and mortgage institutions in the 1980s and 1990s, together with low interest rates in the 2000s, have resulted in an historic increase in both secured and unsecured debt in the household sector. And this increase in household debt is part of a more general rise in debt across other major sectors of the socio-economy (non-financial corporate, financial, and government). The geographies of debt have not been that extensively studied, but the financial crisis has revealed just how important these geographies can be, both in fuelling inflationary bubbles (in housing especially), and when these bubbles burst (Walks, 2014). Not only has housing debt become inextricably bound up with the financial system as a whole, and with the latter's globalization; increasingly, housing is being seen not just as a social necessity, but as an asset invested in order to build up capital resources to be deployed for both consumption (for example, through equity release) and welfare purposes, especially retirement pensions. In some advanced states, asset-backed welfare is increasingly being used to supplement or even replace traditional state welfare provision, and housing provides just one such key asset. This development raises a number of issues. For one thing, households have a vested interest in ever-rising house prices, since the increase in the capital value of a house offers greater potential income in case of emergencies, and most importantly in the form of equity which can be realized to help fund retirement (and/or to pass on to other members of the family). The geographies of house price inflation take on an obvious relevance in this context, and these geographies will reflect underlying processes of wage growth, and housing demand and supply, which in their turn will be shaped by patterns of regional and local economic growth and development. But at the same time spatial variations in house prices and housing costs will influence the geographies of affordability, household debt, and welfare. The rise of 'credit capitalism' signals a new phase, and certainly a new major mechanism, of uneven regional development, driven by households' access to and use of credit and the circulation and refinancing of the debt so generated.

The growth of 'credit capitalism' has been paralleled by a growing crisis of what many have called 'pension fund capitalism' (Clark, 2000). One of the most striking post-war developments in the advanced economies was the dramatic expansion of the pension fund industry, a development that transformed the financial structure and institutions of modern capitalism. Not only was this expansion associated with the growth of the public sector, the employees of which enjoyed generous final retirement benefits, but also with the growth of company pension schemes. Largely an Anglo-American phenomenon, but copied elsewhere in different variants, the growth of company pension plans and funds accompanied the growth of the large company and corporation. For much of the post-war period, when virtually full employment and steady economic growth obtained, corporate sector pension fund assets comfortably exceeded the demands made on them by retiring employees. New institutional structures arose to manage and govern the huge pension funds involved, and, inevitably, those institutions and the flows of monies they invested and managed on behalf of the company sector developed distinct geographies, being articulated by institutions in national financial centres. There is then a complex geography to pension fund capitalism, which may involve and produce spatially uneven outcomes (see for example, Martin and Minns, 1995; Sunley, 2000; Monk, 2009).

Yet it is precisely this system of pension fund capitalism that has come under increasing strain, indeed crisis. According to **Clark (Chapter 15)** 'company-sponsored pension benefit systems have had their day'. He argues that 'pension fund capitalism' has been undercut by the transformation of corporate form and functions, and that the long-term decline of employer-sponsored benefit systems matches the transformation of managerial capitalism, including the relative decline of manufacturing, the spatial and functional dissembling of production systems, and the tensions involved in allotting profits between shareholder returns and workers' pension benefits. Added to such issues, demographic ageing has meant that the outgoings from pension funds often exceed incomings from company and workers' contributions, so that many corporate pension funds (and indeed public sector funds) have gone into deficit. Further, increased stock market volatility in recent years has dented the investment returns to pension funds. It would be premature indeed to announce the end of 'pension fund capitalism': in the UK for example, a new law means that every employer must automatically enroll workers into a workplace (defined contribution) pension scheme (provided they are aged between 22 and State pension age, earn more than £10,000 a year, and work in the UK). But fundamental changes are firmly underway in the form and structure of the pension fund industry that will almost certainly have major implications. As Clark argues, these changes raises key issues about employee decision-making, and crucially, about income distribution and inequality, and hence about the geographies of socio-economic development. Hitherto, relatively little attention has been directed to the geographical impact of pension fund systems (though see, for example, Botts and Patterson, 1987; Monk, 2009) yet it is clear that their sheer scale as a financial circuit, their close dependence on the geographies of economic growth and development, and their impact back on those geographies, all call for closer scrutiny and analysis.

1.3 SPACES OF FINANCIAL AND MONETARY REGULATION

The history of modern capitalism is also a history of the development of regulation, of systems and architectures of rules, principles and laws intended to govern and stabilize the functioning of the economy, ranging for example from competition and company law, to employment law, to trading agreements and policy, to taxation, to rules prescribing the operation of banks and financial markets. Regulatory rules and principles have their own geographies or 'landscapes', their own 'spaces'. Those spaces can be local, national or global, and can vary not only in their geographical coverage or jurisdiction, but in their geographical (un)evenness. There can be complex multiple layers and scales to a regulatory system. Nowhere is this more evident than in the regulation of finance and financial institutions. Given the fungibility and mobility of money – the ease with which it can be converted from one form into another and moved from place to place – and hence its inherent instability as a store of value, a means of exchange and as a social relation, it is not surprising that historically both national and subnational authorities have introduced regulatory structures intended to control financial activity without overly hindering the basic functions and importance of money in the economy.

The history of financial regulation is long and well documented. In many nations, responsibility for overseeing financial markets and financial services has evolved over centuries, and in many instances the shifts and changes that trace out that evolution have been as much in response to major crises, economic upheavals and political events, as to the march of incremental adjustments and additions. And while different nations have developed their own internal regulatory systems, these have long interacted with and been influenced by the evolution of international systems of monetary cooperation, financial standards and regulatory practices, which themselves have their specific geographies.

The Gold Standard is one case in point. The Gold Standard was a way to solve the instability and disruptions to international capital markets caused by the collapse of the bimetallic system: it was a response to the failure of countries to agree on steps to sustain international bimetallism. Most countries went onto the Gold Standard between the 1870s and the first decade of the twentieth century. However, as Eichengreen and Flandreau (1994) show, geographically the Gold Standard had several core–periphery distinctions. It did not revolve simply around the City of London, but evolved out of the British, French and German zones of global economic influence, and as a consequence had three main centres, London, Paris, and Berlin, corresponding to a complex geography of 'peripheries'. The geographical spread of the Gold Standard, as an international monetary system, was shaped by countries' level of economic development, the magnitude of their reserves relative to world specie markets, whether those reserves were concentrated at a central bank, and by the presence or absence of imperial ties. What some regard as the world's most successful international monetary arrangement appears to have worked automatically, requiring little more than a resolve on the part of the involved countries to keep their own Gold Standards in good working order (Selgin, 2013). The institutional setup consisted of nothing other than the sum of these national Gold Standard arrangements: there was nothing in it akin to the International Monetary Fund or Special Drawing Rights or other such centralized and bureaucratic facilities. But it nevertheless performed a regulatory function, in that it kept international exchange rates from fluctuating beyond very narrow bounds, and thereby encouraged the growth of international trade and investment. However, just as Britain's adoption of the Gold Standard had led to its geographical diffusion across large swathes of the international economy, so Britain's abandonment of the standard in 1931 quickly led to its almost universal abandonment.

Its successor, the post-war Bretton Woods system of international monetary regulation, set up in 1944, was far more institutionalized. The Bretton Woods agreement saw the establishment of two new international regulatory institutions, the IMF and the World Bank, and a system of monetary management and fixed exchange rates, with all currencies linked to the US dollar, which in turn was linked to gold. To prevent speculation against currency pegs, capital flows between countries were severely restricted. This system was accompanied by nearly a decade and a half of rapid economic growth amongst the more advanced countries, and a relative paucity of economic recessions and financial crises. Its success depended in large part on the economic prosperity and leadership of the United States, which acquired considerable geopolitical power and influence as a result. The IMF and World Bank also to a large degree came under the influence of – and some would say, served the interests of – the US. Certainly these two institutions came to have their fierce critics, not least for their perceived domination by the rich world. At the level of international regulation, the post-war financial system was controlled by the United States. But in the end it proved too inflexible to deal with the rising economic position of Germany and Japan, coupled with the declining economic power of the US and its reluctance to adjust its domestic economic policies to maintain the gold peg. When President Nixon abandoned the link to gold in 1971, the fixed exchange rate system disintegrated. The period since has seen repeated financial instability, with countries involved in what has been a 'race to the bottom' in terms of deregulating their domestic financial systems as part of a more general shift to a neoliberal stance towards economic policy and economic management.

The wave of domestic financial deregulation began in the 1970s but gathered pace in the 1980s and 1990s. Most countries up to that time had developed various legal controls and strictures governing the activities of banks and other financial institutions. Arguably, the United States had acquired one of the most complex of all domestic regulatory landscapes, with Federal and state layers of regulation and supervision (see Komai and Richardson, 2011). As Viner, writing back in the mid-1930s put it, this development was

> rooted in the country's history, in its regional diversities, and local loyalties. Its persistence is due to the support it derives from state jealousy of encroachments on state autonomy, from agrarian and small-town jealousy of the metropolitan areas, and from the nation-wide fear of undue concentration of financial power in the great metropolitan centers, and especially fear of Wall Street domination. (Viner, 1936: 112)

This statement was made barely three years after the introduction of the Glass–Steagall Act of 1933, in response to the collapse of a large portion of the American commercial banking system earlier that year. Among other things, this Act introduced the separation of bank types according to commercial and investment activity. This Act remained in operation until its repeal in 1999. Other key Acts that defined distinctions and demarcations between banks and other financial institutions had been abolished in the 1980s. And the restrictions on inter-state banking, that had been in force for decades, were removed in 1994.

Financial deregulation has been no less dramatic in the UK. Over the course of the 1980s and 1990s, the established practices in the London Stock Exchange (the historical separation between stockbroking and market-making functions) were abolished (by the Financial Services Act of 1986 – so-called 'Big Bang'), the separation between investment banking and retail banking removed, legislation passed to allow building societies to demutualize and become banks, and barriers to foreign ownership of British financial institutions were removed. These changes, made by the Thatcher governments, were basically intended to make the UK financial services sector, and the City of London especially, more competitive.

There is no doubt that the wave of deregulation, in the USA, UK and elsewhere, over the 1980s and 1990s helped spur the dramatic growth in finance and banking on global markets and in the major financial centres like New York and London. Finance became viewed as *the* engine of economic growth, even as itself the driver of a new form of capitalism, a 'new world order'. Thus speaking in mid-2007, Gordon Brown, the UK Chancellor of the Exchequer claimed that as a result of the City of London's 'remarkable achievements', aided by the 'light touch regulation' he had pursued as Chancellor, the British economy had entered 'an era that history will record as the beginning of a new Golden Age' (Brown, 2007). A year earlier the Conservative leader, David Cameron, had sounded no less triumphant, proclaiming the 'victory of capitalism, privatization and liberalization' and attaching the credit for Britain's finance-based and City-focused success to the 'critical Conservative decisions' that the Tories had taken when they were in government. It was, he argued, their historic deregulation of banking and the City of London in the 1980s, especially Big Bang in 1986, that had 'injected an enterprising spirit' into the City and the economy as a whole (Cameron, 2006).

As it turned out, of course, the celebratory tone of these self-congratulatory encomia proved to be a hostage to fortune. The collapse of Northern Rock Bank in the UK in November 2007, and of Lehman Brothers in the US less than a year later in September 2008, were just two of the many bank failures that marked the most severe financial crisis for 80 years, a crisis that emphatically undermined any presumption about the pre-eminent driving role of financial services within the economy and which instead has cost taxpayers dear in bailouts to keep the banking system afloat. The cause of the global financial crisis was obviously not simply due to the neoliberal obsession with deregulation. But the more permissive regulatory landscape that had emerged over the 1980s and 1990s was undoubtedly a major contributing factor. The dramatic advances in telecommunications technologies and the ingenuity of financiers and financial institutions to dream up ever more sophisticated financial products, instruments and practices enabled money to escape what weak regulatory structures there were. At the same time, weak regulatory and conduct authorities failed to detect the spread of fraudulent practices within the financial services sector, such as mis-selling financial products and fixing inter-bank interest rates. While there has since been some tightening up of regulatory structures, and banks have been fined and compelled to hold larger capital reserves, governments have stopped short of more rigorous control and oversight (in the UK, for example, the new Financial Conduct Authority dropped its promised enquiry into banking culture and standards only a few months after it was launched).

How the changing landscapes of financial regulation shape the operation of financial systems across geographical space is thus a key issue for enquiry, and is the subject of the chapters that form Part III of the book. In his chapter, **Bieri (Chapter 16)** examines the process of financial regulation as part of the larger process of regulatory governance of the economic system as a whole. As he argues, financial regulation (like all economic regulation) is a deeply path-dependent process, in the double sense that at any one time the regulatory architecture that is in force reflects the cumulative legacy of its past development, and in that every action in a regulatory regime creates a financial reaction the consequences of which, both spatial and non-spatial, tend to have lasting effects on the configuration of activity in the financial sector and the real sector alike. Thus the trajectory of spatial economic development and the advancement of the monetary-financial system should be seen as a joint historical process, with regulation playing a key linking causal role. Using this conceptual framework, this chapter shows how different regulatory regimes shape the international and interregional flow of funds across space. The structure of the regulatory system influences in important ways the roles played by the various components of the monetary-financial system (financial instruments, financial markets, and monetary and financial intermediaries) in promoting the mobility of funds among the various sectors of the space economy. This chapter illustrates how shifts in the political economy of financial regulation have created new geographies of the flows of funds – a set of spatial circuits that are characterized by a rapid evolution in bank complexity. Focusing on the US banking sector before and after the recent crisis, it is shown how the interplay between structural changes in financial intermediation and shifting regimes of US banking regulation gave rise to a distinct unevenness of spatial capital flows and depository agglomeration – a combination that ultimately co-determined the spatial impact of the fall-out from the financial crisis. Overall, this chapter develops the case that money and finance are non-neutral with regard to space principally because the institutional arrangements of financial regulation matter for how the spatial economy evolves.

In her chapter, **Dörry (Chapter 17)** seeks to define and elaborate the notion of 'regulatory space', and how such spaces interact with the evolving nature of financial systems, institutions and practices. As these systems, institutions and practices have become ever more integrated globally, and ever more sophisticated technologically, so they have rendered regulation ever more difficult. The globalization of money and financial markets challenges the effectiveness and territoriality of national-level systems of regulation, while at the same time enabling money flows to escape to exploit gaps and differences in those national regimes: global flows of mobile finance can 'touch down' in chosen places to exploit the regulatory environments that best match their 'needs' and from where those monies, and financial practices, technologies, and instruments on which they rely are injected back into the global financial system. The rise of so-called 'offshore financial centres' over recent decades illustrates this constant search by financial institutions – and high-net-worth individuals – for gaps and holes in the regulatory landscapes of money. These offshore centres take various forms, but their primary purpose is to attract incomes and earnings of individuals and companies by offering low or even zero taxes, financial secrecy and a range of services intended to benefit the 'shell subsidiaries' that such individuals and companies typically use for this purpose. These have the outward appearance of being legitimate, but are just empty shells that do nothing but manage money while hiding its ownership. The Tax Justice Network (2012) estimated that perhaps as much as US$21–$32 trillion of assets and profits is sheltered from taxes in unreported tax havens worldwide, though other estimates put the sum at around US$8 trillion. But even that lower figure implies that large sums of tax revenue are being lost to the countries where the individuals and companies are based, revenues that could contribute to public expenditure and welfare in the countries concerned. The Panama Papers scandal that broke in 2015 testifies to the scale of the use of these 'offshore' havens. A huge leak of some 11.5 million documents containing confidential information on more than 200,000 offshore companies involved with one of the world's most secretive companies, the Panamanian law firm Mossack Fonseca, show just how widespread the abuse of offshore tax havens is. Among its lists of companies are more than 110,000 incorporated in the offshore centre of the British Virgin Islands, nearly 50,000 in Panama itself, and around 15,000 in each of the Bahamas and the Seychelles. A number of well-known banks were among these lists. What is clear is that tax avoidance or evasion is occurring on a global scale, and despite the outcry by national governments in response to the Panama Papers leak, the reality is the issue can only be solved effectively by regulatory measures agreed at an international level. However, the construction of a supranational regulatory space seems a long way off.

While attention has understandably focused on these 'offshore' gaps in the regulatory landscape of money and finance, and the role they have played in the development of financial products and circuits intended to escape national tax regimes, as **Wainwright (Chapter 18)** argues we should not lose sight of the fact that national governments themselves have been re-regulating their onshore spaces in an attempt to mimic offshore financial centres, to create what in effect are 'onshore–offshore' spaces. By introducing 'light-touch' regulation, secrecy guarantees and other such inducements, governments have used various 'liberalization' concessions to attract mobile corporate profits and funds, as well as personal wealth, into their jurisdictions, and thereby boost their financial services industry. In the US, states such as Delaware and Nevada allow shell companies, whose owners are not identified, thereby providing cover for foreign cash. Britain is perhaps even worse. London runs a network of some of the worlds' largest offshore havens, the remnants of the British Empire. To be sure these places are partly independent. But their lax financial legislation is approved in London. And London acts as a hub for sucking up the unregulated monies, of the handling of them, from this network of offshore centres. Under the aegis of the City of London Corporation, the independent body that represents London-based financial institutions and financiers, London itself operates in effect as an onshore–offshore centre. However, using empirical evidence on the growth of asset-backed securities (ABS) markets, and ideas from emergence theory, Wainwright shows how this onshore–offshore phenomenon has permeated European financial space more widely. European financial centres have developed onshore–offshore havens modelled on the earlier activities of the offshore centres found on numerous small island economies. A desire by the financiers involved with the growth of ABS and other special purpose vehicles (SPVs) to domicile assets close to European centres, combined with the recognition by governments of the usefulness of securitization as a financial mechanism that could lower costs to corporate borrowers and potentially fund growth, and the design of bespoke regulation aimed at facilitating these products and activities, have resulted in the legitimization of these onshore–offshore markets. No longer can 'offshore' financial space be equated with the well-known list of small island economies. Nor can offshore space be viewed as being isolated from wider financial networks involving the world's main financial centres. Traditionally 'offshore' activities have become integrated within onshore spaces to create new 'hybrid' spaces driven by and consistent with new financial products.

Perhaps understandably, most of the literature on the instabilities of the global financial system – and indeed much of financial geography literature – has focused on developments and weaknesses in western financial centres, and to some extent on emerging market countries, and much less attention has been directed at the problems and challenges facing banking and finance in transition economies, like those of Eastern Europe and China. From an institutional and regulatory perspective, these countries have been developing their own 'hybrid' varieties of capitalism, involving among other things a blurring of the boundaries between private and public (state) property rights. In his discussion, **Yeung (Chapter 19)** documents the case of the restructuring and re-regulation of Chinese banking. As he argues, 'mainstream' (that is western) theories of banking and finance may not be applicable to the Chinese economy. Although China has been adopting some of the organizational forms and imperatives of market capitalism, it does not yet have a functioning market-based system of banking, and the state still exerts a powerful influence and regulatory control over the economy. Banking in China exhibits features typical of a transitional economy, with some of the world's largest joint-stock banks co-existing with former state-owned banks, city commercial banks, and hundreds of thousands of rural cooperative institutions. Since the early-2000s, China has been embarked on a mission to improve the efficiency, governance and monitoring of this complex system of banks, with the task being overseen by the China Banking Regulatory Commission (CBRC) established in 2003. As Yeung reveals, the CBRC is essentially performing a balancing act between ensuring the long-term viability of the banking industry and the financial security of the general public. While the CBRC's regulatory reforms have helped to promote and underpin the country's rapid economic growth over the past two decades, problems of moral hazard have continued to characterize the Chinese banking system, whereby non-performing loans taken out by local government officials and state-owned enterprises are expected to be bailed out by the central government, and investments are expected to be safe under the CBRC's regulations. At the same time, the levels of debt within the Chinese financial system, and within its economy as a whole, have risen substantially in recent years. A substantial part of this debt has gone to fund infrastructural projects and a housing development bubble, with the latter resulting in the co-existence of high prices and a huge inventory of unsold property, not just in the major cities of the eastern seaboard, but also in third and fourth tier cities, where at the time of writing property price deflation is already evident (*South China Morning Post*, 2016). China's debt–GDP ratio has risen to exceed that of leading western countries such as the USA and Germany and local government debt stands at an all-time high (over 50 per cent of total government debt). Sensing the dangers of this rise, the Chinese government has introduced new restrictions on local government debts, as well as new regulations on the shadow banking sector that has also grown in recent years. What the case of China illustrates is the regulatory tensions and challenges created by the transition of a system long dominated by state-ownership and underwriting to one increasingly exposed to market-based operations and instabilities.

In **Chapter 20, Marandola and Sinclair** switch attention to the role and regulation of credit rating agencies. These are private organizations that charge banks, financial and non-financial corporations, and local, provincial and national governments, for evaluating their creditworthiness in the form of 'credit ratings' or assessments of the credit risk of a prospective debtor, predicting their ability to repay the debt. Credit ratings are ubiquitous in financial markets, and since they determine the ease with which, and the cost at which, organizations and governments can raise credit in financial markets, they can exercise considerable influence over the geographies of credit flows in the global economy. For example, countries such as Australia and Canada, typically rated at AAA, can raise credit more easily and cheaply compared to countries such as Greece and Venezuela (both rated CCC). Yet, as Marandola and Sinclair argue, credit rating agencies pose an interesting puzzle for the legitimacy of global regulation. As profit-seeking firms, they lack a formal element of coercion. They do not set legal rules that borrowers are forced to observe, yet they are able to wield considerable power in shaping financial landscapes. There have been repeated calls from firms, governments and financial regulators to hold credit rating agencies accountable for their activities. Yet this demand for accountability has not had much effect on how these agencies operate. Attempts to regulate credit agencies have not proved particularly effective. In essence, there seems to be a major and persistent 'accountability gap' (Kerwer, 2004), a gap that is the more disturbing given that just three such agencies – Moody's, Fitch, and Standard & Poor's, all US-based – dominate the global financial system. Being of US origin, these big three have been criticized for being unable to adapt their standards and assessment benchmarks to different economies and regions, showing a tendency to underrate non-US businesses. Marandola and Sinclair discuss a number of ways in which this accountability gap might be closed and credit rating made more effective, including a greater critical self-awareness of the potential systemic and longer-term impact of their activities (to counterbalance the overwhelming emphasis on short-term rent seeking), and an organizational architecture based on regional and national communities of agencies, in which geographical proximity would facilitate communication and sharing of norms and best practices among members.

Taken together, the chapters in this section of the book point emphatically to the importance of the regulatory landscape for understanding the evolution, expansion and operation of financial markets. The geographies of money and the geographies of regulation are inextricably intertwined, each influencing the other. Regulatory structures condition the spatial flows of money, while financial innovation – of both products and institutions – allows money to escape or circumvent regulatory structures. Regulatory arrangements have failed to keep pace with financial innovation. In fact, even worse, the deregulation of financial markets that has taken place across much of the globe over the past three decades itself helped to stimulate a wave of financial innovation that culminated in the global financial crisis of 2007–09. As nation states and international bodies now struggle to reinstate (some degree of) regulatory control over financial systems, public confidence in banks, financial institutions and financiers is at an all-time low. Little wonder then, that various alternative monies and financial circuits have emerged that operate outside the conventional financial system. These too have taken on their own geographies.

1.4 NEW AND EMERGING MONEY SPACES

Money, as Harvey (1982: 245) reminds us, is not merely an expression of wealth, but rather 'the very incarnation of social power'. As such, money – its forms, institutions, movements and distribution – is always intensely political, always a source for contestation, struggle and innovation. Financial crises typically produce the conditions for an intensification of such struggles and innovations and spawn new and different thinking about money and how it is and should be organized. The recent crisis has focused attention again, not only on regulatory failures and weaknesses, but more broadly on the centrality of money to everyday life and on how the economy and society 'work' and are controlled.

The chapters in this section explore, in different ways, some new and emerging geographies of money that are shaped by an unease with the status quo. Such explorations typically return us to some very basic questions about money, values and social relations that have long occupied social theorists of money. For starters, what is money? Social theories of money have long stressed the contradictory dualities of money. For Georg Simmel (1978: 277), money is 'the most perfect representation' of the tendency to reduce quality to quantity, an impersonal, indiscriminate medium that morphs complex economic and social relations into a quantity, a price. The corollary of this reduction and quantification is that, 'we do not ask what and how, but how much' (Simmel, 1978: 259). For Marx (1973: 221), this reduction was alienating and corrosive because money, as 'the god among commodities', dissolved personal and community ties and became 'the *real community*' (Marx, 1973: 225). Yet money, as Viviana Zelizer's (1989) work reminds us, is simultaneously particular, social, laden with meaning and ritual, and often gendered. For all money's powers of rationalization, homogenization and absolute interchangeability, its sociality stubbornly persists. For Zelizer (1989: 347–348), 'values and sentiments reciprocally corrupt money by investing it with moral, social and religious meaning'. Money, be it in commodity form or as state promise, is inseparable from ideas of obligation, reciprocity, domination, authority and commitment that tie people together through space and time.

Thinking about new and emerging geographies of money thus entails juggling this duality, while also looking beyond questions of 'how much' to revisit broader normative questions about values, economic and otherwise. What forms of money represent appropriate stores of value and means of circulation? Who can and should issue money? What is the geographic reach of different monies? In what ways is money tied up with concerns about growth (or the lack of) and sustainability in different places? These are by no means new questions. Money has long been central to thinking about values, pecuniary and otherwise. Thinking about money, its forms, its institutions and its mobilities, has been integral to the political strategies of Utopian, environmental and other social movements keen to challenge the hegemony of capitalist markets. The 2008 crisis has, not surprisingly, spawned new international protest movements like *Occupy* – that cite the greed and corruption of 'the 1 per cent' as central to the production and reproduction of wider patterns of social and economic inequality – while also intensifying the search for forms of financial institutions and innovations that make some claims to fulfilling broader socially and economically useful objectives.

Knox-Hayes (Chapter 21) takes the events of 2009 as her starting point and juxtaposes the unfolding of the financial crisis in the US and Europe with the Copenhagen meeting of world leaders, activists and other civil society groups that was designed to generate an international response to climate change. For Knox-Hayes, these financial and environmental crises are inextricably linked. Climate change, biodiversity loss, resource depletion and ecological degradation are all the results of human production and, more specifically, the productivity (or not) of capitalism. Financial and environmental crises are fundamentally rooted in a crisis of production and representation of value over time and space. Knox-Hayes thus explores the hitherto neglected relationship between the generation of value through socio-economic and socio-natural circuits of capital, drawing on recent developments in financial markets designed to price environmental goods and services. She revisits and extends our understanding of spatial and temporal dynamics of circuits of capital by exploring the possibilities and limits of how financial markets are being used to price environmental goods and services. On the plus side, environmental finance can be conceived as producing a 'parallel economy', one in which the use of externality pricing is intended to balance the environmental impact of production and to possibly extend the value of environmental resources over future space and time. So, for example, carbon markets can raise awareness and make explicit hitherto unaccounted costs of burning fossil fuels and encourage high emitters to either become more efficient or go out of business. Such results are inevitably spatialized; emission reduction in one place can be tied to clean energy production elsewhere, with material and discursive benefits. The flip side of environmental finance, however, is a deepening of the logics and practices of financialization. The very mobility of say carbon credits, and the process of translating environmental resources and stresses into financial representations, allows the spatial and temporal separation of the sale/purchase of the carbon credit and the material reality of emissions. Financial representations of the environmental world can just as easily mismanage resources and ultimately can produce financial crises.

In his exploration of the recent proliferation of alternative, complementary and community currencies, **North (Chapter 22)** takes us to some different fringes of financial markets. Local currencies vary along a spectrum of social, technological and geographical difference. For example, are they convertible (or not) with bank-created fiat money or instead perhaps calibrated around time? Do they have a physical form or are they entirely electronic? Are they conceived as 'local' to particular geographic areas, or, like Bitcoin, seen as potentially global? And for whom and for what ends are they created? North reveals some of the myriad rationales behind their conception, from survival strategies, alternative ways of living and the sharing economy, to re-claiming and re-embedding money in more convivial, cooperative local communities, through to wider critiques of value, growth and environmental sustainability.

Struggles over how, and by whom, money is labelled, represented and appropriated feature prominently in **Datta's (Chapter 23)** examination of the vast and rapidly growing flows of transnational migrant remittances. Such flows have attracted growing policy interest, not least when their growth is juxtaposed against declining or at best fluctuating overseas development assistance (ODA) and foreign direct investment (FDI). But how are such flows to be conceptualized? Geography, again, is integral to understanding differences in the uses and meanings of money and indeed in how different individuals and communities conceive, experience and live the material and emotional relations between money, work and caring. In some senses remittances can be viewed as 'alternative' forms of finance that follow migration patterns and meet basic human welfare needs around different parts of the globe. Yet the interest of the World Bank, Wall Street, other national and financial intermediaries and Development Economics also lends weight to suggestions that remittances are now conduits for the formalization and extension of circuits of 'poverty capital' (Roy, 2010). As such, remittances can be seen as a new opportunity for mainstream financial institutions, alongside neoliberal discourse about the creation of migrant-investor subjectivities and a discursive and political shift to explore how remittances can be used not merely to support consumption, but rather as forms of investment.

As Datta's chapter investigates the complex economic and social resources and aspirations behind remittances, **Rethel (Chapter 24)** interrogates the possibilities and limits of Islamic finance. Islamic finance houses a diverse, emerging set of principles and practices about debt, credit and risk that make claims to be based on risk sharing, fairness and social responsibility. Another attractive element of Islamic finance is its emphasis, in principle if not always in practice (Pollard and Samers, 2007), on profit and loss sharing. Beyond the mutual financial interests that bind financial intermediaries with the firms and projects they invest in, there is the wider aspiration in Islamic finance that the financial economy and the 'real' economy of good ideas and making things stay closely integrated; the speculative excesses of finance that have seen the explosive growth of derivatives markets – out of all proportion with the growth in global commodity trade – is frowned upon in Islamic finance. As with all 'alternatives', however, questions of definition and differentiation from 'the mainstream' are everywhere. These relate to different conceptions of what Islamic finance is and should be, and, more prosaically, how Islamic finance can co-exist with some of the geographies of regulation explored in Part III. Rethel explores three competing 'imaginary landscapes' of Islamic finance and their jostling for position in Malaysia, the US and the UK. These imaginaries vary from a form of 'business as usual' through to more radical visions that position Islamic finance as an 'alternative' and more moral and responsible form of finance than that responsible for the 2008 crisis.

For all the growing interest in Islamic finance, the 2008 financial crisis has generated interest in other 'alternatives' to the traditional banking sector. **Gray and Zhang (Chapter 25)**, explore another one of these in the form of crowdfunding. Depending on how it is defined, crowdfunding has been around for a long time, but its recent growth is associated with new Internet technology platforms and ongoing disquiet with traditional banks and capital markets. Crowdfunding enables individuals and organizations to provide capital to firms, ideas and projects. As is true of local currencies, remittances and Islamic finance, however, on closer examination crowdfunding is a concept that houses a diversity of motivations and practices, from supporting new creative projects or local charities through to financing new tech start-ups. Again, this alternative raises all manner of questions, conceptual and political. How should crowdfunding be conceptualized? What is the size, scope and nature of crowdfunding? Who and where are the investors and recipients? Is crowdfunding simply replicating existing circuits of capital or opening up new streams of finance for entrepreneurs and communities? What is crowdfunding doing to existing geographies of capital?

Finally, **Pilkington (Chapter 26)** explores the foundation of Bitcoin, a new form of digital money launched in October 2008 by a pseudonymous person or persons calling him/herself or themselves Satoshi Nakamoto. Bitcoin is distributed in a peer-to-peer database of electronic signatures and its most powerful innovation is a 'Blockchain', an electronic register of all the Bitcoin transactions authenticated by a network of computers. Bitcoin are finite – their creation rests on computing power and cryptographic technologies premised on the impossibility of factorizing prime numbers – and represent a largely untraceable and anonymous way of moving money. One of the most disruptive properties of Bitcoin is its signaling of a world of new peer-to-peer technologies that allow the transfer of credit without the need for nation states and banking and other financial intermediaries as we currently understand them. Bitcoin is stateless (and designed as finite so that it cannot be debased by nation states), does not rely on conventional payment systems and intermediaries and was born in the aftermath of the financial crisis amidst distrust and revulsion of the status quo. Again, what are the limits and possibilities of Bitcoin? In what contexts are such developments democratizing, or, as several high profile cases thus far suggest, an opportunity for criminality and yet more tax avoidance? What can we say of its efficacy given that it requires no national regulatory authority or promise and privileges peer-to-peer transactions over those routed through conventional intermediaries? How are existing regulators and financial intermediaries responding to its threat but also its possibilities in terms of securing their own proprietary variants of Blockchain technology? Bitcoin is further evidence, if any were needed, of the growing problems that new technologies generate for nation states and international bodies struggling to reinstate confidence and control in financial systems and institutions. It also provides a fascinating glimpse into the relations between money, space, values, technology, identity, regulation and trust. Like other technologies, such as writing and the advent of double-entry bookkeeping, Bitcoin has the potential to change how we think about and use money.

1.5 A CONCLUDING COMMENT

According to Cohen (1998: 21) a geography of money itself requires a clear analytical distinction between physical and functional notions of space – the former being tied to location and place, the latter to 'networks of transactions and relationships'. Put another way, monetary geography has to do with 'spaces of flows' rather than a 'space of places', and requires a 'flow-based model' of financial relations in which '[t]he dimensions of currency space are more accurately measured not by the standard coordinates of longitude and latitude but by supply and demand, the behaviour and decisions of diverse agents, including governments, in the global marketplace for money' (Cohen, 1998: 21).

The network idea is indeed vital for understanding the spatial organization of money and finance. There is a very real and significant sense in which money space is a complex system of networks of financial flows, transactions and relationships. This point was in fact emphasized well over a half a century ago by the French economic historian

Francois Perroux. He coined the phrase 'monetary space', 'seen more easily in terms of a "network" of payments' (Perroux, 1950: 97–98). Today such networks – for there are multitudes of such webs – are organized and integrated through electronic information systems which compress both time and space.

This focus on networks resonates closely with the so-called 'relational turn' in human and economic geography, in which the interactions between agents, firms, institutions and social groups define both the nature of geographic space itself, and the meaning and relationship between the places in which those agents, firms, institutions and groups are located. Yet such a conception does not negate the importance of place, of location, far from it: the nodes on any network matter. The more so if certain nodes dominate the network. In the global financial system, a handful of global financial centres (typically metropolitan capitals or major cities) control and shape the flows of money in the specific networks concerned (be they investment banking, securities trading, foreign exchange trading, insurance and so on). Money tends to flow to these and other key nodes, to be collected and managed there: there is an ineluctable 'lumpiness' in the spaces of money (a bit like the tendency for liquid mercury to form globules – Clark, 2005). The flows of money help to constitute and give meaning to these places, whilst the latter articulate those same flows and hence the importance of those places in their respective networks. Further, money does not flow equally, or equally easily, to other nodes (cities and regions) on those networks: relational dependencies, hierarchies and asymmetries typify monetary spaces. Together, the various chapters in this Handbook are all concerned with conceptualizing or analyzing these complex relational geographies of finance and money. And taken together they not only point to the growth of interest in this exciting area of research, but also, hopefully, provide inspiration for the future work that needs to be undertaken.

REFERENCES

Aalbers, M.B. (2009), 'The globalization and Europeanization of mortgage markets', *International Journal of Urban and Regional Research*, **33**, 389–410.

Alessandrini, P., M. Croci and A. Zazzaro (2005), 'The geography of banking power: the role of functional distance', *Banca Nazionale del Lavoro Quarterly Review*, **LVIII**, 129–167.

Alessandrini, Pietro, M. Fratianni and A. Zazzaro (2009), *The Changing Geography of Banking and Finance*, Dordrecht: Springer.

Benner, C., C. Berndt, N. Coe, E. Engelen, J. Essletzbichler, J. Glassman, J. Glückler, M. Grote, A. Jones, R. Leichenko, D. Leslie, P. Lindner, M. Lorenzen, B. Mansfield, J. Murphy, J. Pollard, D. Power, E. Stam, D. Wòjcik and M. Zook (2011), 'Editorial: emerging themes in economic geography: outcomes of the Economic Geography 2010 Workshop', *Economic Geography*, **87**, 111–126.

Botts, H.A. and J.G. Patterson (1987), 'Pension fund investments: an initial geographic assessment', *The Professional Geographer*, **39**, 416–427.

Brevoort, K.P. and J.D. Wolken (2009), 'Does distance matter in banking', in Pietro Alessandrini, Michele Fratianni and Alberto Zazzaro (eds), *The Changing Geography of Banking and Finance*, Heidelberg, Springer, pp. 27–56.

Brown, G. (2007), Mansion House Speech, London, 20 June.

Cameron, D. (2006), 'The New Global economy', Speech at the Euromoney Conference, London, 22 June.

Cerqueiro, G., H. Degryse and S. Ongena (2009), 'Distance, bank organization structure and lending decisions', in Pietro Alessandrini, Michele Fratianni and Alberto Zazzaro (eds), *The Changing Geography of Banking and Finance*, Heidelberg, Springer, pp. 57–74.

Christophers, B. (2015), 'The limits to financialization', *Dialogues in Human Geography*, **5** (2), 183–200.

Clark, G.L. (2000), *Pension Fund Capitalism*, Oxford: Oxford University Press.

Clark, G.L. (2005), 'Money flows like mercury', *Geografiska Annaler*, B, **87** (2), 99–112.

Clark, G.L. (2006), 'Setting the agenda: the geography of global finance', in Sharmistha Bagchi-Sen and Helen Lawton Smith (eds), *Economic Geography: Past, Present and Future*, London: Routledge, pp. 83–93.

Cohen, Benjamin (1998), *The Geography of Money*, Ithaca: Cornell University Press.

Cooke, Phillip, Bjorn Asheim, Ron Boschma, Ron Martin, Dfana Schwartz and Franz Tödtling (eds) (2011), *Handbook of Regional Innovation and Growth*, Cheltenham, UK and Northampton, MA, USA: Edward Elgar Publishing.

Corbridge, Stuart, Ron Martin and Nigel Thrift (eds) (1994), *Money, Power and Space*, Oxford: Blackwell.

Degryse, H., K. Matthews and T. Zhao (2015), 'SMES and access to bank credit: evidence on the regional propagation of the financial crisis in the UK', CESifo Working Paper No. 5425.

Della Croce, R. and S. Gatti (2014), 'Financing infrastructure – international trends', *OECD Journal – Financial Market Trends*, **2014** (1), 123–138.

DeYoung, R., D. Glennon and P.J. Nigro (2006), 'Borrower–lender distance, credit-scoring, and the performance of small business loans', FDIC Centre for Financial Research, Working Paper 2006–04.

Dow, S. (1999), 'The stages of banking development and the spatial evolution of financial systems', in Martin, R.L. (ed.), *Money and the Space Economy*, Chichester: John Wiley, pp. 31–48.

Eichengreen, B. and M. Flandreau (1994), 'The geography of the Gold Standard', Discussion Paper 1050, London: Centre for Economic Policy Research, London School of Economics.

Harvey, David (1973), *Social Justice and the City*, London: Edward Arnold.

Harvey, David (1982), *The Limits to Capital*, Oxford: Blackwell.

Harvey, David (2006), *Spaces of Global Capitalism: Towards a Theory of Uneven Geographical Development*, London: Verso.

Immergluck, Daniel (2011), 'The local wreckage of global capital: the subprime crisis, federal policy, and high-foreclosure neighborhoods in the US', *International Journal of Urban and Regional Research*, **35**, 130–146.

Kerwer, D. (2004), 'Making global regulators accountable: the case of credit rating agencies', Working Paper 11, School of Public Policy, Munich Technical University.

Kindleberger, Charles (1978), *Manias, Panics and Crashes: A History of Financial Crises*, 5th edition (Kindleberger, C.P. and Aliber, R.Z, 2005), New York: John Wiley.

Klagge, B. and R.L. Martin (2005), 'Decentralised versus centralised financial systems: is there a case for local capital markets?', *Journal of Economic Geography*, **5**, 387–421.

Komai, A. and G. Richardson (2011), 'A brief history of regulations regarding financial markets in the United States, 1789 to 2009', NBER Working Paper 17443, National Bureau of Economic Research, Cambridge, MA.

Langley, P. (2016), 'Crowdfunding in the United Kingdom: a cultural geography', *Economic Geography*, **92**, 301–321.

Leyshon, Andrew and Nigel Thrift (1997), *Money/Space: Geographies of Monetary Transformation*, London: Routledge.

Markovitz, Harry (1959), *Portfolio Selection: Efficient Diversification of Investments*, London: John Wiley.

Martin, R.L. (ed.) (1999), *Money and the Space Economy*, Chichester: John Wiley.

Martin, R.L. (2011), 'The local geographies of the financial crisis: from the housing bubble to economic recession and beyond', *Journal of Economic Geography*, **11**, 587–618.

Martin R.L. and R. Minns (1995), 'Undermining the financial basis of regions: the spatial structure and implications of the UK pension fund system', *Regional Studies*, **29**, 125–144.

Marx, Karl (1973), *Grundrisse*, Harmondsworth: Penguin.

Monk, A.H.B. (2009), 'The geography of US pension liabilities and fund governance in the United States', *Environment and Planning A*, **41**, 859–878.

OECD (2015), *Tax Policy Analysis*, retrieved on 11 October 2016 from www.oecd.org/ctp/tax-policy/.

Perroux, F. (1950), 'Economic space: theory and applications', *Quarterly Journal of Economics*, **64**, 89–104.

Peterson, M.A. and R.G. Rajan (2002), 'Does distance still matter? The information revolution in small business lending', *Journal of Finance*, **57**, 2533–2570.

Pollard J.S. and M. Samers (2007), 'Islamic banking and finance: postcolonial political economy and the decentring of economic geography', *Transactions of the Institute of British Geographers*, **32** (30), 313–330.

Roy, Ananya (2010), *Poverty Capital: Microfinance and the Making of Development*, London: Routledge.

Sassen, S. (2009), 'When local housing becomes and electronic instrument: the global circulation of mortgages – a research note', *International Journal of Urban and Regional Research*, **33**, 411–426.

Scott, Allen (2006), *Geography and Economy*, Oxford: Clarendon.

Scott, A.J. (2011), 'A world in emergence: notes toward a resynthesis of urban-economic geography', *Urban Geography*, **32**, 845–870.

Selgin, G. (2013), 'The rise and fall of the Gold Standard in the United States', *Policy Analysis*, **729**, 1–24.

Simmel, G. (1978), *The Philosophy of Money*, London: Routledge and Kegan Paul.

South China Morning Post (2016), 'China property bubble bound to burst', *South China Morning*

Post, 3 February, retrieved on 11 October 2016 from www.scmp.com/business/article/1909119/china-property-bubble-bound-burst-say-experts.
Sunley, P. (2000), 'Pension exclusion in grey capitalism: mapping the pensions gap in Britain', *Transactions of the Institute of British Geographers*, **25**, 483–501.
Tax Justice Network (2012) *The Price of Offshore Revisited*, retrieved on 11 October 2016 from www.taxjustice.net/cms/upload/pdf/The_Price_of_Offshore_Revisited_Presser_120722.pdf.
Udell, G.F. (2009), 'Financial innovation, organisation, and small business lending', in Pietro Alessandrini, Michele Fratianni and Alberto Zazzaro (eds), *The Changing Geography of Banking and Finance*, Dordrecht: Springer, pp. 15–26.
Viner, J. (1936), 'Recent legislation and the banking situation', *American Economic Review*, **26** (1), 106–119.
Wainwright, T. (2009), 'Laying the foundation for a crisis: mapping the historico-geographical construction of residential mortgage backed securitization in the UK', *International Journal of Urban and Regional Research*, **33**, 372–388.
Walks, R. (2013), 'Mapping the urban debtscape: the geography of household debt in Canadian cities', *Urban Geography*, **34** (2), 153–187.
Walks, R. (2014), 'Canada's housing bubble story: mortgage securitization, the state, and the global financial crisis', *International Journal of Urban and Regional Research*, **38** (1), 256–284.
Wójcik, D. (2009), 'Financial centre bias in primary equity markets', *Cambridge Journal of Regions, Economy and Society*, **2** (2), 193–209.
Zazzaro, A. (1997), 'Regional banking systems, credit allocation and regional economic development', *Economic Appliqué*, **1**, 51–74.
Zelizer, V. (1979), *Morals and Markets: The Development of Life Insurance in the United States*, New York: Columbia University Press.
Zelizer, V. (1989), 'The social meaning of money: "special monies"', *The American Journal of Sociology*, **95** (2), 342–377.

PART I

THE CASE FOR A GEOGRAPHY OF MONEY

2. On the geography of bubbles and financial crises

Gary A. Dymski and Mimoza Shabani

Challenge magazine interview with Charles Kindleberger ("Crashes, Crises, and Moral Capital"), published July 1, 1991, concluded with the following question-and-answer sequence:
Q: "What is your closing advice?"
A: "An MIT physicist, Robley Evans, has promulgated a carefully worded law: 'Everything is more complicated than most people think.' Should one be a monetarist or a Keynesian? A good economist, like Adam Smith, was both, each under appropriate circumstances."

2.1 INTRODUCTION

This chapter explores the academic literature on the geography of asset bubbles. It represents a response to two important interventions in academic geography journals. In 2011, Ron Martin observed in the *Journal of Economic Geography* that "we [geographers] know relatively little about the spatial logics of financial bubbles and crashes . . . both macro and micro dimensions." His concern stemmed from the fact that the flurry of crises in recent years had "received little or no economic-geographical study" (Martin, 2011: 613), despite "new pressure to devise analytical frameworks that provide better insight into the origins and determinants of price and speculative bubbles, especially within housing but also more generally, with a view to explaining why some countries seem far less prone to such bubbles than others." Martin concludes with the hope that "geographers could make a significant contribution to such studies." Three years later, Muellerleile et al. (2014) wrote in *The Professional Geographer* about "the disciplinary challenges to influencing mainstream debates over financialization and the recent financial crisis and the recurring lament that economic geography 'misses the boat' by failing to significantly impact key scholarly and policy issues."

Given the occurrence of bubbles and crises across the global map in the past six years, one might guess that a white-hot debate would be raging between geographers and economists over the links between financial and economic crises and asset bubbles – and indeed, over the very definition of "bubble." But nothing of the sort has happened. One explanation, proposed by Muellerleile et al. (2014), is that economic geographers have not been able to "isolate a disciplinary core" which might serve as a rallying point in dialogues with economists. We focus here on a second, complementary root cause of this apparent anomaly: while asset bubbles have increasingly been incorporated into analyses of financial crisis, academic discourse using rigorous econometric methods to identify asset bubbles has invisibilized geographic considerations. The economists developing this literature are interested in commonalities in experience through time and across space: they focus on repetitive patterns, abstracting from the peculiarities of when and where these events occurred. Thus this chapter argues that while interest in bubbles has grown, courtesy of recent financial crises, econometric models looking to interrogate them have de-spatialized any understanding of their characteristics by looking for commonalities across bubbles, in essence developing models *in* space but not *of* space.

This chapter goes on to argue, contrary to this established literature, that "placing" asset bubbles and crises is the only way to fully grasp their causes and consequences. In integrated economies with developed divisions of labor and well-organized institutions for investment, lending, and saving, asset bubbles arise systematically: they are commonplace, not rare. We establish this argument on the basis of cross-border accounting balances. This way of understanding asset bubbles suggests that whether they are readily deflated or instead grow to problematic and unsustainable peaks depends on local market and income structures and on cross-border flows of all kinds. So understanding asset bubbles – and their role in the uneven growth of income, wealth, and debt – requires an examination of the geographic political economy which has generated them (or failed to generate them), thereby creating new layers of losers and winners in residents', enterprises', and financiers' struggles for sustenance, security, and gain.

We begin by defining asset bubbles, and examine the fissures between different schools of academic thought regarding these phenomena. We then review the chronological trajectory of the scholarly literature on asset bubbles, and show how and why economists' investigations have systematically sidelined space as an analytical element. Finally, we propose an alternative spatial political economy approach to asset bubbles, and explain how it can restore a geographic focus to the examination of asset bubbles.

2.2 THREE DEFINITIONS OF BUBBLES

Three approaches to bubbles can be identified. The first approach builds upon the idea of market equilibrium: bubbles arise when asset prices have risen systematically higher than the values implied by their underlying fundamentals (Allen and Gorton, 2012). What constitutes 'fundamentals,' in turn, depends on the asset class in question: for example, for equity shares and bonds issued by a firm, fundamentals consist of the discounted present value of expected net profits (cash-flows); for foreign-exchange futures, the anticipated future state of the economies whose currencies are being bought and sold. For economists committed to theoretical models of market equilibria and rational agents, explaining why bubbles arise presents a difficult challenge, since prices should reflect only fundamentals in competitive markets. Explaining 'bubbles' in the sense of this definition, then, requires one or more divisions from the conditions required for competitive market equilibria.

The second definition is entirely empirical: a bubble arises when an asset price rises above its prior historical norm. If this asset is closely linked to another empirical variable, then a bubble can be identified by comparing the trajectory of these two variables across time. An example is the ratio of single-family housing prices to average household income. Investigating the convergence or deviation of data series underlying such ratios permits the use of time-series econometric techniques (in particular, unit-root tests) to determine whether such price-deviations have occurred.

The third definition focuses on the contingent aspects of economic processes and outcomes in real-time settings. For Minsky, to take the most prominent example, an asset bubble exists when there is both an unsustainable higher-than-average return to holding an asset, and a surge of above-trend purchases of the asset in question (Minsky, 1986:

71, and Minsky, 1990). What makes this growth unsustainable is not, as in the neoclassical vision summarized above, the discovery of a gap between the current price and a fundamentals-based price; rather, it is that asset positions must be financed. And as more agents take on debt to purchase more of the asset in question, what justifies their purchases is a continually rising asset price. Sooner or later, the spiral of rising debt and rising asset prices will collapse. Fundamentals do not enter into the equation; when a serious gap arises between the cost of financing a position in an asset and the return from holding it, the balance-sheet positions of those holding the asset become unsustainable and the bubble collapses. The focus in this approach, then, is not on a price gap, but on financing processes and their occasional breakdown.

2.3 FISSURES IN THE LITERATURES ON ASSET BUBBLES AND FINANCIAL INSTABILITY

The approaches to bubbles defined above have emerged in the past four decades because of the increasing frequency of sizable asset bubbles, and of the episodes of financial instability and crises with which they have been linked. This has offered rich terrain for research rooted in the fields of economics, geography, and regional studies, among others. Interchanges among scholars in these different fields – and even among scholars using different methodologies within the same field, in the case of economics – have been rare. Even the terminology used to investigate these phenomena have differed systematically – between fields.

A key-word search of the Web of Science database reveals the scope of the problem. Of 110 articles incorporating "bubble" or "bubbles" as topic words in six leading mainstream economics journals between 1981 and 2014, only two also included "spatial" or "geographic."[1] Of 47 articles incorporating "bubble" or "bubbles" in four leading heterodox economics journals, only one also included "spatial" or "geographic". Of 130 articles in the latter set of journals incorporating "financial instability" or "financial fragility" or "Minsky" as topic words, none include "spatial" or "geographic" as topic words. Finally, of 156 articles in these heterodox journals and 113 articles in these mainstream journals incorporating "financial crisis" or "financial crises" in this time period, none include "spatial" or "geographic" as topic words. By contrast, in a sample of ten regional studies and geography journals, the terms "spatial" or "geographic" appeared as topic words in half the articles with any of the above topic words.[2]

Figures 2.1–2.3 illustrate these fissures graphically. Figure 2.1 counts all instances of the use of "bubble" or "bubbles" in mainstream economics, heterodox economics, and regional studies-geography journals (as listed in endnotes 3 and 4). Note that the mainstream journals initiated "bubble" as a topic word – but the number of articles peaks in the 2001–05 period. The use of "bubble" as a topic word picks up in the heterodox and regional/geography journals in the post-crisis period. Half (14) of the heterodox articles with key-word "bubble" also had "financial crisis" as a key-word in the 2009–14 period; but none of the mainstream articles in this time period did (and only three of the regional/geography journals).

Occurrences of the topic words "financial instability" or "financial fragility," in turn, are depicted in Figure 2.2; and occurrences of the topic word "Minsky" in Figure 2.3.

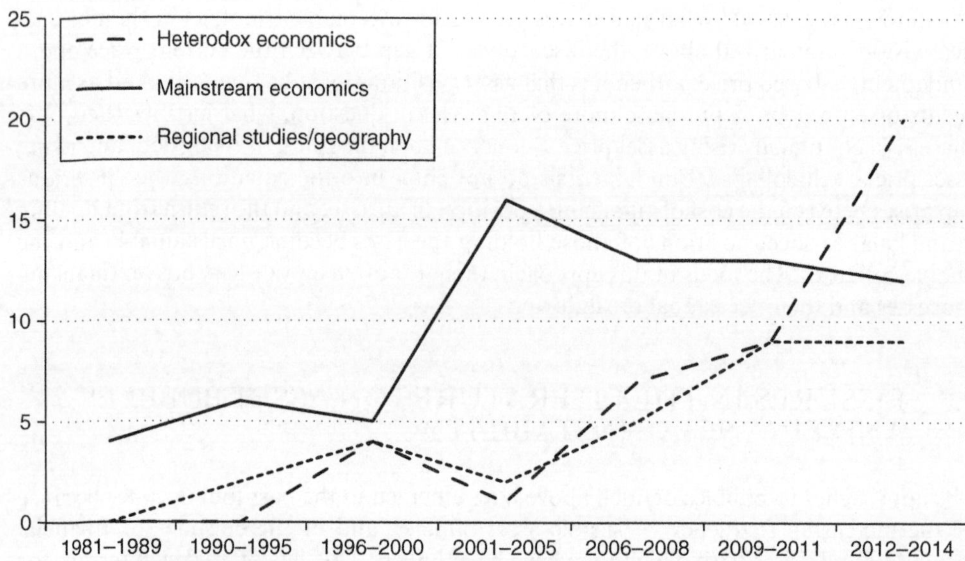

Notes: See endnotes 1 and 2 for a list of journals included in these topic-word counts. Year of publication is recorded for all data shown.

Figure 2.1 "Bubble" or "bubbles" as topic words in Web of Science, selected journals, 1981–2014

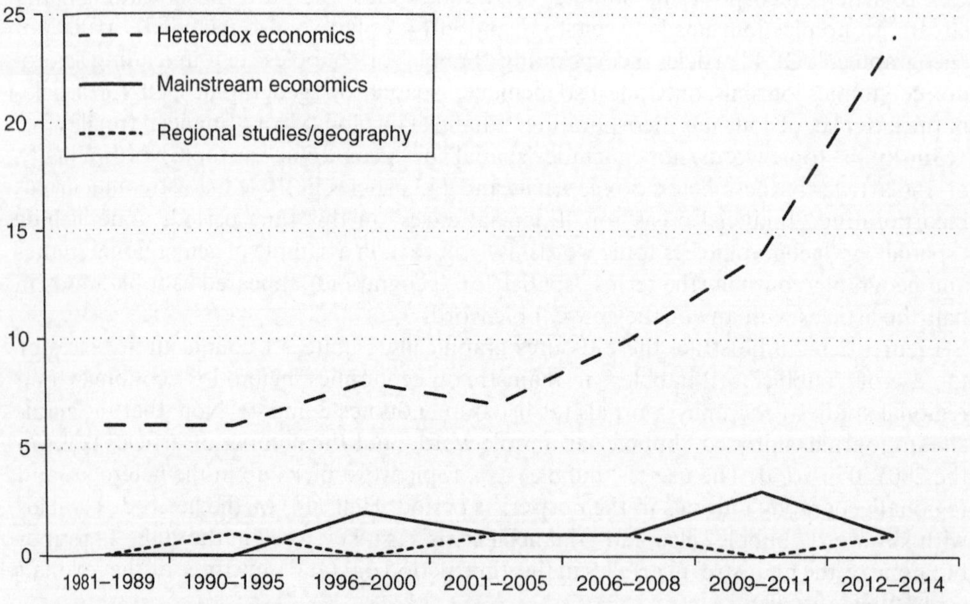

Figure 2.2 "Financial instability" or "financial fragility" as topic words in Web of Science, selected journals, 1981–2014

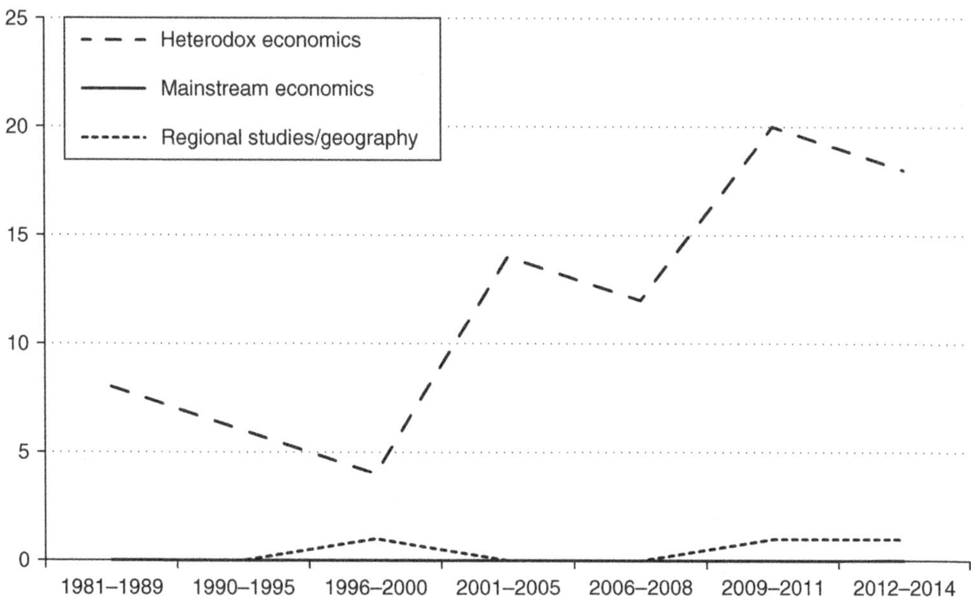

Figure 2.3 "Minsky" as a topic word in Web of Science, selected journals, 1981–2014

Minsky is chosen, of course, because of the prominent discussion of his ideas in the popular and financial press during the subprime crisis.[3] A significant number of topic-word references to both terms appear for the heterodox economics journals, with more references over time. It may not be surprising that these two terms are virtually absent as topic words in mainstream economics journals; but it surely is a surprise that they are equally absent from the regional/geography journals. Finally, Figure 2.4 depicts uses of "financial crisis" or "financial crises" as topic words. Through 2008, there are more uses of these terms in mainstream journals than in the other two categories; but this pattern reverses after that.

This topic-word overview suggests four conclusions.[4] First, mainstream and heterodox economists, almost without exception, undertake non-intersecting investigations of the same phenomena, using different terms and referring to different authorities. Second, the contrast between the equilibrium-based approach of mainstream economics and the process approach of heterodox economics is evident. The term "bubble" itself connotes the existence of a "fundamental" and distance from that fundamental. Most heterodox economists would object vehemently to this dual notion – especially the Keynesian (and for that matter Minskian) economists likely to be most engaged in research on financial crisis. The turn of heterodox articles toward use of the term "bubble" after its use as a mainstream key-word had peaked indicates that heterodox economists are tying the term in to their discussions of the financial crisis – a link that is completely absent in the mainstream journals examined here.

Third, these figures suggest that regional/geography articles track heterodox economics journals in topic-word interest in financial crisis; but the terminology used in regional/geography articles – "bubble," not "financial instability" or "Minsky" – tracks

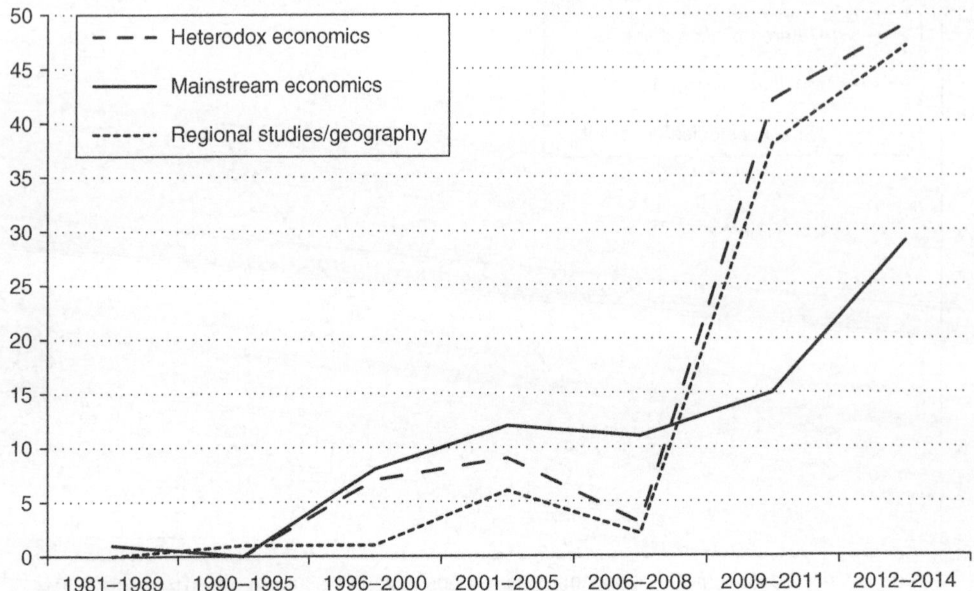

Figure 2.4 *"Financial crisis" or "financial crises" as topic words in Web of Science, selected journals, 1981–2014*

the mainstream. Fourth, economists committed to different worldviews do not ask, when given new events to explain, how space matters; they instead highlight explanatory mechanisms they have used for earlier events in other spaces and times. Theoretical frameworks, whether orthodox or heterodox, generally eradicate the particularities of space: places become just sites of infection or contagion.

2.4 AFTER THE KEYNESIAN CONSENSUS, FINANCIAL TURBULENCE: MINSKY AND KINDLEBERGER ENTER

As Figures 2.1–2.4 illustrate, this academic focus on bubbles and financial instability is of very recent vintage. In the 1950s and 1960s, the theory of efficient financial-market theory – and the companion theory of portfolio equilibrium – had been invented and integrated into macro theory.[5] Monetary theorists worked with models in which financial market prices tended toward equilibrium: that is, bubbles were ruled out by assumption.[6] As Lerner (1972) put it, since economic transactions could be regarded as "solved political problems," economic policy involved working out the technical details of the consensus models of the time.

The turbulent 1970s, however, changed all that: with the end of the Bretton Woods system, two cataclysmic oil-price shocks, and rising inflation and interest rates, financial systems came under severe pressure. Efforts to stabilize finance by market deregulation led instead to the thrift and Latin American debt crises by the early 1980s. The broad consensus on Keynesian macroeconomic policy collapsed, as did faith in the large-scale macroeconometric models providing empirical guidance for those policies.

Two leading economists, Charles Kindleberger and Hyman Minsky, argued that financial forces constituted a root cause of these tectonic institutional and economic shifts. Economic historian Kindleberger had been investigating problems of global economic interaction for decades. He suggested in *Manias, Panics, and Crashes* (Kindleberger and Aliber, 2005) that asset bubbles, both historical and contemporary, followed an overall temporal architecture. His model of the anatomy of a typical crisis was drawn explicitly from the work of Hyman Minsky:[7] "Minsky highlighted the pro-cyclical changes in the supply of credit, which increased when the economy was booming and decreased during economic slowdowns . . . led to fragility in financial arrangements and increased the likelihood of financial crisis" (Kindleberger and Aliber, 2005: 25).[8]

Some pages later, his description of a bubble conforms to the first definition set out above:

> Economists use the term bubble to mean any deviation in the price of an asset or a security or a commodity that cannot be explained in terms of the 'fundamentals.' Small price variations based on fundamentals are called 'noise.' In this book, a bubble is an upward price movement over an extended period of fifteen to forty months that then implodes. Someone with 'perfect foresight' should have foreseen that the process was not sustainable and that an implosion was inevitable. (Kindleberger and Aliber, 2005: 29)

Kindleberger insists that what he calls "the Minsky model" provides a sufficient framework for characterizing manias, panics, and crashes across time. Interestingly, however, in the text on which Kindleberger drew in distilling Minsky's model – *John Maynard Keynes* (1975) – Minsky's own characterization of his ideas is very different. For one thing, Minsky viewed Keynes's notion of fundamental uncertainty, and not probabilistic risk, as the proper framework for investment and financing behavior. For another, Minsky is focused not on the architecture of boom and bust, but on the processes involved. And a final key difference is that Minsky's entire focus is on the tension between investing in assets and financing them – what he liked to call "taking position to make position." Finance appears in Kindleberger's characterization as Minsky's theory as the point that credit supply matters in the architecture he describes; but for Minsky, the financing dimension is not an attachment to the model, it is at the heart of the model. Financial instability exists as a process precisely because firms and investors competing for profitable asset positions must increasingly turn to finance as the investment cycle unfolds – indeed, this cycle will turn once financing commitments exceed the cash-flow generated by the asset positions taken on.

This difference in view is subtle if one views both texts from the 30,000-foot level. But a closer view reveals key differences. For one thing, Minsky doesn't use the word "bubble" in this text (and uses it sparingly elsewhere in his work. Similarly, Minsky uses the word "crash" only to describe the 1929 Wall Street meltdown; and he uses the term "mania" only to describe the US's 1960s conglomerate wave. And most importantly, the term "fundamental" – in the sense indicated in our first definition of bubble, and in the above passage from Kindleberger – never appears in his work.[9] Kindleberger's text, in turn, does not use the terms "financial instability" or "financial fragility."

The magisterial work of these two authors, then, built on Minsky's core ideas, cut in two very different directions. Minsky's thesis represents a defense of a Keynesian approach to economic policy, with special emphasis on the need for coordination between central-bank intervention and countercyclical fiscal expenditures in eras of financial crises.[10] Kindleberger, to the contrary, mentions fiscal policy only as a structural feature of a nation in payments difficulty; his silence on the question of whether he is Keynesian or monetarist is deafening – something highlighted in the passage quoted at the beginning of this chapter. Kindleberger's fealty to the neoclassical definition of bubble in the context of a sweeping history of financial crises in all times and all places – and thus, not particular to any time or place – prefigures the trajectory that much work on financial crises and bubbles was soon to take.

2.5 BUBBLES IN A LANDSCAPE OF FINANCIAL INSTABILITY?

Between the year in which Minsky published his first book, 1975, and his last, 1986 (*Stabilizing the Unstable Economy*), a new non-Keynesian approach to macroeconomic theory and policy took hold of the economics profession. Minsky's defense of Keynesianism, based on the notions of financial fragility and instability, was ignored by mainstream economists, as Figures 2.2 and 2.3 illustrate. Only heterodox economists followed Minsky's lead. Why?

The answer lies in the policy and modeling activism of the macroeconomists allied with Milton Friedman's monetarist – anti-Keynesian – approach. Led by Robert Lucas, Jr., these economists built on the macroeconomic chaos of the 1970s – which, as noted, had undercut Keynesian empirical and modeling approaches – and introduced new modeling wrinkles that exploited this very chaos. The key addition was to build in the assumption of rational expectations – the notion that private-sector agents were perfectly capable of achieving their own optimal outcomes, understood government's intentions, and could offset government actions when those actions were predictable. The answer to the breakdown of government oversight and the subsequent market disorganization was: *more* market. Implanting rational expectations in a solvable intertemporal setting required the radical simplification of macroeconomic models, and the linking of whatever behavioral structure remained to market-efficiency assumptions. As Meltzer pointed out, rational-expectations models do not have unique equilibria, and those equilibria often have dynamic paths that don't converge, but can instead be explosive.

As it turned out, this very feature of rational-expectations equilibria provided a key for testing the idea of economic bubbles as a deviation from fundamental values (conventionally defined). As Flood and Garber (1980: 746) put it, "A bubble can arise when the actual market price depends positively on its own expected rate of change, as normally occurs in asset markets." These authors used newly-developed time-series methods to distinguish between the components of price reflecting underlying fundamentals, on one hand, and components of price reflecting rationally anticipated future price changes. Blanchard (1979) argued that speculative bubbles were consistent with rational expectations, and could take many forms. Almost immediately, Shiller (1981) challenged this idea of "rational bubbles," arguing that changes in stock prices were too high relative to fundamentals (changes in dividends) to be consistent with fully rational behavior; instead prices may reflect buyers' "irrational exuberance" (Shiller, 2005).

An extensive but inconclusive volatility literature quickly emerged. For it proved impossible either to generate rational speculative bubbles in rational-expectations models (Kompas and Spotton, 1989), or to definitively show that bubbles were manifestations of irrational exuberance (West, 1988).[11] As Flood and Hodrick (1990: 85) observed in a survey paper, the "analytical and statistical tools [required to resolve this issue] were inadequate." Mainstream economists wrote numerous papers examining what features of the trading environment – that is, what deviations from the conditions required for competitive equilibrium – could explain the deviation of financial-market prices from fundamentals. Proposals included less and more informed ("noise") traders (De Long et al., 1990), fads (West, 1988), herd behavior (Lux, 1995), limits on short-selling, and so on.

While the academic debate over rational equity-market bubbles was still midstream, it was paralleled by academic and policy debates over a cascade of crises and market crashes: the 1982 Latin American debt crisis, the 1982–89 US thrift and oil-patch bank crisis, the 1987 stock-market crash, the junk-bond crash, the commercial real-estate bubble and crisis of the late 1980s and early 1990s, the Tokyo real-estate and equity-market bubbles and subsequent crashes in Japan, and many episodes of exchange-rate volatility, among the principal episodes. These events were linked to the deregulation of banking and finance, global-factory outsourcing, volatile commodity prices (especially petroleum), monetary-policy extremism, and to global imbalances in the neoliberal era.

Table 2.1 provides a list of identified asset price bubbles in both developed and developing countries. Even though most of the identified bubbles in this table are taken from Reinhart and Rogoff (2009) it is important to highlight that we are not reproducing their table.[12] The information provided in Table 2.1 both illustrates and demonstrates the limitations of uniform methodologies for identifying bubbles. There are many different ways to get to financial folly and one of them is the asset bubble. Reinhart and Rogoff (2009) provide a list of different crises. Along with external and domestic debt crisis, they identify the occurrence of banking crisis. They argue that such crises are linked to asset bubbles, and they associate the bursting of such bubbles with the year marking the start of the crisis.

Table 2.1 Asset price bubbles, place-based origins

Year	Country	Description
1977	Spain	Housing bubble
1987	Norway	Housing bubble and stock market bubble
1991	Finland	Housing bubble and stock market bubble
1991	Sweden	Housing bubble and stock market bubble
1992	Japan	Housing bubble and stock market bubble
1997	Hong Kong; Indonesia; Malaysia; Philippines; South Korea; Thailand	Housing bubble
1998	Colombia	Housing bubble
2001	Argentina	Housing bubble
2001	US	Dot-com bubble
2007	Iceland; Ireland; Spain; US; US	Housing bubble
2008	Hungary	Housing bubble

Sources: Reinhart and Rogoff (2009) and Scherbina (2013).

The volcanic outburst of crises altered the participants and terms of reference in academic debate about financial crises and bubbles. Banking analysts (for example, Kane, 1989) and development experts (Eaton, Gersovitz, and Stiglitz, 1986) introduced game-theoretic models in their efforts to unearth design flaws and behavioral problems that had led to too much lending for projects and assets whose returns had been systematically overestimated.[13] While these models did not focus on bubbles per se, they clearly implied that the assets financed – commodity extraction in Latin America, commercial and residential developments in the American Southwest, and so on – had been overvalued. The exchange-rate volatility of these years, in turn, gave rise to models initially focused on whether nation-states' "fundamentals" would permit them to sustain the overseas borrowing positions they had taken.[14]

These financial crises and bubbles, spread across different regions and nations, had complex geographies. But what economists picked up on was the repetition of patterns: the idea that governing explanations might be found for all the Latin American (and other) nations that had defaulted on their debt obligations. Economists were now searching for a general theory covering all the possible categories of bubbles (currency, investment, land), and all places; they were not interested in a political economic explanation for any one category and place. How might events in space be systematically related by underlying factors operating across space? In trying to answer this question, economists widened the conceptual toolkit for understanding how bubbles could emerge.[15]

The 1990s brought yet more financial crises linked to bubbles. The Mexican "tequila" crisis of 1994–95 took the form of a run on the peso just two years after the signing of the 1992 North American Free Trade Agreement. That a crisis could hit a country that had become a favored locus for capital inflows due to its financial liberalization, its renewed growth, and its openness to overseas investment, came as a shock. Indeed, this crisis created substantial interest among economists in the possibility that currency crises could be driven by small changes in investors' beliefs. This implied that such "sunspots" could have contagion effects elsewhere.

There was not long to wait. East and Southeast Asia were also favored venues for capital inflows in the early and mid-1990s. The outbreak and spread of the Asian financial crisis, like the tequila crisis, took economists by surprise. Asset prices had risen in these nations – especially urban land and equity shares – but these increases appeared as bubbles only when lending flows stopped. The spread of financial crisis linked to bubbles in yet another global region spurred a new round of papers blaming moral hazard or informational frictions for this new outbreak of crisis.[16] But the multi-country Asian crisis could be explained by the collapse of neither macroeconomic fundamentals (which had been good in Asia, pre-crisis) nor beliefs.[17] And this time, the recurring pattern of intertwined and contagious lending booms, asset bubbles, currency crises, and macroeconomic downturns opened economists' eyes to the dangers inherent in these markets' interconnections (Edison, Luangaram, and Miller, 2000).

Consider the evolution of the theoretical ideas of the influential tandem of Allen and Gale in these years. In a paper published in 1998, they acknowledged that "Empirical evidence suggests that banking panics are related to the business cycle and are not simply the result of 'sunspots.' Panics occur when depositors perceive that the returns on bank assets are going to be unusually low." However, they propose "a simple model . . . [in which] bank runs can be first-best efficient" (Allen and Gale, 1998: 1). Two years later, however, their "Bubbles and Crises" paper worries about patterns that can be observed in the past two decades' financial crises, and seeks out patterns:

> In recent crises a bubble, in which asset prices rise, is followed by a collapse and widespread default. Bubbles are caused by agency relationships in the banking sector. . . . Risk can originate in both the real and financial sectors. Financial fragility occurs when positive credit expansion is insufficient to prevent a crisis. (Allen and Gale, 2000a: 1245)[18]

Allen and Gale (2000b), in turn, show how financial contagion is likely given this pattern of interlinked asset bubbles and crisis pre-conditions.

The widespread occurrences of financial crises suggested that the positive feedback relationship between financial structure and economic growth, a hardy perennial of orthodox development thinking, might have broken down. Several groups of economists associated with the International Monetary Fund (IMF) and the World Bank – institutions whose resources were being regularly drawn upon in these episodes – pioneered the creation of a new approach: selected data-points for the years immediately before and after financial-crisis (including currency crisis, banking crisis, and so on) episodes were gathered together for each country, standardized (so that, for example, two years prior to the outbreak of crisis is regarded as year "t-2", and so on), and then analyzed, in hope of identifying common patterns across time and space. The path-breaking paper of Demirgüç-Kunt and Detragiache (1998), for example, finds that financial liberalization increases the probability of banking crisis, and that financial crises' contagion effects are large and costly. The original database used in this and other papers (Beck, Demirgüç-Kunt, and Levine, 2000), augmented by other variables, was subsequently expanded and relaunched (Beck, Demirgüç-Kunt, and Levine, 2010).

This comparative empirical approach, which treats space as a homogeneous agar plate that can give rise to specimens of a commonly occurring phenomenon, has itself grown like a virus; a large proportion of current research on financial bubbles and crises now uses the IMF database or builds on the construction of yet new cross-time, cross-sectional databases. This viral growth can be traced to two sources. One is the very plasticity of *au courant* formal models: the varieties in use among mainstream theorists – rational-expectations, asymmetric-information, game-theoretic, and so on – are all incomplete-markets models, and as such have infinite possible equilibria.[19] So nothing can be resolved through a given formalization: all models are merely illustrative, not definitive, characterizations. Second, the increasing number of occurrences of crises encourages empirical testing. This said, the data available are time series, on which only very limited, weak-power tests can be conducted, with virtually no hope of stating with confidence that any X causes any Y. At the same time, what relational statements between X and Y can be made (like the test of "fundamentals" versus "asset prices" mentioned above) are possible only by systematically controlling for variation in all variables apart from those the theorist has decided are important. The rationale for this latter approach is that it permits economists to isolate relationships across time and space so as to probe the underlying links.

2.6 THE 2000S HOUSING BUBBLE AND SUBPRIME MELTDOWN

Famously, the global financial crisis that began with the Shearson-Lehman bankruptcy in 2008 was initially centered around what is now commonly understood to have been a subprime lending boom linked to a housing bubble, underwritten by the self-dealing of a set of out-of-control, fraud-driven megabanks and shadow banks. During the build-up of the subprime bubble, very few economists saw the crisis coming, as Krugman (2009) observed in the *New York Times*' Sunday magazine.[20]

There were warning signs. Two studies – one examining California (Riddel, 1999), the other, the United Kingdom (Levin and Wright, 1997) – found evidence of bubbles in early-1990s housing markets. Zhou and Sornette, looking only at the speed of housing-market price increases and writing in an econophysics journal, found evidence of post-2000 housing bubbles, first in the UK and then in the US (Zhou and Sornette, 2003, 2006).

Soon enough, the Flood–Garber analytical machinery for identifying a bubble was used to investigate housing price bubbles in the 2000s. The task of identifying "fundamentals" was daunting. Among the reasons: housing is a non-homogeneous good, with long lead times between housing-construction decisions and realized housing supply; households have extremely variable degrees of risk aversion; housing price-changes are serially correlated; and so on. Glaeser and Gyourko calibrated a spatial equilibrium model of housing, but without determining how much "market inefficiency . . . [might explain] the persistence of high frequency price changes" (Glaeser and Gyourko, 2006: 1). Two years later, these authors (Glaeser, Gyourko, and Saiz, 2008) published a paper on housing bubbles which argues that housing supply matters: places with more elastic housing supplies should experience fewer and shorter bubbles, all things equal; however, this conclusion was only provisional. Goodman and Thibodeau (2008), in a study of speculative bubbles in US housing markets, wrote that "speculation has driven house prices well above levels that can be justified by economic fundamentals in less than half of the cities examined" (Goodman and Thibodeau, 2008: 117). Contradicting the 2008 Glaeser et al. finding, many of the cities experiencing housing bubbles – all (with the exception of Las Vegas) within 75 miles of either the Pacific or Atlantic coasts – had positive supply elasticities. Coleman, LaCour-Little, and Vandell (2008) found that economic fundamentals drove house-price dynamics in the US prior to 2004, but not thereafter; they also found that subprime lending per se was less significant in driving this change than the shift to private-mortgage issuance after this date.[21]

Post-crisis evaluations have provided further evidence of a housing bubble, but have reaffirmed the idea of housing-price shifts as a variegated map. Clark and Coggin (2011) find empirical evidence of an overall house-price bubble in the 2000s, due to the absence of cointegrating relationships between house prices and several fundamental economic variables. Kivedal (2013) also find evidence of a housing bubble in the form of explosive price increases not attributable to any fundamental factors. Montañés and Olmos (2013), in turn, find that US housing prices have not converged: some degree of price segmentation exists in the US housing market, with some evidence of a regime break after 2010.

2.7 AFTER THE SUBPRIME CRISIS: BUBBLE-DRIVEN GROWTH AS THE NEW NORMAL, OR AS THE DESTROYER OF SOVEREIGN VIRTUE?

Some themes can be detected in this moving feast of academic work on asset bubbles. First, the sequential emergence of financial crises with asset boom/bust characteristics across space, has invited a continuing cascade of models whose explanations of crises and their contagion focus on transaction costs, missing information, markets' institutional limits, or some combination of these factors.[22] The possibilities for formalization are in principal limitless.[23] By implication, even as opportunities for characterizing asset bubbles and crisis *in* space grow, there remains no imperative to incorporate the geographical or spatial aspects of these possibilities as a core explanatory element. To the contrary, spacelessness enhances generalizability for those using mainstream models.

Second, the further development of cross-section/time-series methods in econometrics, has led to new protocols for bubble detection. The synthetic construction of event-centered data series (such as, "a currency crisis under a given definition") permits empirical tests of definitions one and two (as listed above), premised precisely on the erasure of space and time (except for sequential time) from any analytical role. To pick one example, the idea is to control for the "Argentina" effect, not to examine Argentina in depth.

Third, the spread of asset-bubble related problems from equity resale markets, to cross-border lending, to housing, and finally to sovereign debt, has renewed interest in Kindleberger's temporal architecture of booms and crashes; but it has led to a different conclusion than he reached.[24] As crises mounted (and as we have seen the brief review above), more theorists proposed models which involved sequences of bubble- and debt-related events, in which an asset bubble that emerges in one area of the economy ends up provoking a crisis for the economy as a whole. Indeed, there is a marked shift from writing about asset bubbles to writing about financial crises, even among mainstream economists (Figures 2.1, 2.4).

Fourth, the quickening pace of boom–bust growth and crisis, and of scholarship about it, has had little or no effect on the mainstream/heterodox divide – a divide reflected, as we noted above, in the very definition of bubble. Heterodox theorists have developed analyses of the sequence of events described here using the analytical tools developed in the Keynesian, institutionalist, and Marxian traditions that their work has explored. While Minsky died in 1996, his framework has been a foundation-stone for these efforts. Among many works, we might single out Wray (2009) and Bellofiore and Vertova (2014) as representative of Keynesian and Marxian work. And while only a few works by heterodox authors build bridges to mainstream definitions and analyses of asset-bubbles and crises – a notable example is Rosser et al. (2012) – mainstream authors uniformly ignore heterodox work.[25]

The fifth trend in work on asset bubbles and crises is a polarization of views about how policy should respond to bubbles. One view explores the normalization of bubbles as a component of economic growth. Caballero, Farhi, and Hammour (2006) show how the US economy can be boosted by the spread and extreme valuation of speculative assets. Martin and Ventura (2012) develop a model in which investors hold a portion of their wealth portfolio in bubble assets that play no role in production and are, in principle, costless. Galí (2014) suggests that monetary policy should strike a balance between stabilizing asset bubbles and stabilizing economic growth.

The writing tandem of Reinhart and Rogoff have vigorously made an opposing argument on the basis of their 2009 volume, which parallels Kindleberger and Aliber (2005) in the scope of its treatment of asset bubbles and financial crises. This volume and these authors' ongoing series of papers, however, interpret the implications of financial crises differently than does Kindleberger. Kindleberger's 1978 book tells the story as one of chronic human failing; he emphasizes the need for lender-of-last-resort institutions capable of rescuing failing national or regional financial systems. Reinhart and Rogoff, by contrast, have increasingly emphasized, in their retelling, that financial history involves government treachery, the loading onto the public of a burden of debt originated elsewhere. They write in their 2011 paper, for example, that

> external debt surges are an antecedent to banking crises. Second, banking crises (domestic and those in financial centers) often precede or accompany sovereign debt crises. . . . Third, public borrowing surges ahead of external sovereign default, as governments have 'hidden domestic debts' that exceed the better documented levels of external debt. (Reinhart and Rogoff, 2011: 1676)

The implication is that financial crises can be contained only by taming bubbles, which must necessarily involve proper regulation and the restoration of fiscal discipline.

2.8 AN ALTERNATIVE APPROACH TO THE SPATIALITY OF ASSET BUBBLES AND FINANCIAL CRISIS

The dominant approaches to asset bubbles, to date, have incorporated space by erasing geography because it has served their deeper theoretical and policy purposes. This erasure is done in the name of Occam's Razor – don't make things more complicated than they have to be – and to focus on the consequences of imbalances *in* space – that is, in any given space, whose borders are left unspecified. To assume that the division of space into bordered areas doesn't matter, however, is an extremely strong assumption, one not justified by empirical findings.

Our first step in arguing for an explicitly spatial approach to asset bubbles is to explicitly recognize the role of borders in economic relationships. We proceed as follows. Economic assets, goods, and services can be divided along two dimensions: on one axis, those that have fixed location, and those that do not; on the other, those requiring large fixed costs, and those without them. The relationship of any contiguous bordered area with the rest of the world (ROW) – and/or with spatial subcomponents of the rest of the world – can, in turn, be characterized by the following relationship:

Earnings from selling goods and services to ROW net of what is bought from ROW =
Purchases of assets in ROW + Increase in financial reserves (currency) (2.1)

If the first line of equation (2.1) is positive, then local gains from trade are positive; net earnings can either be used to purchase assets in other spaces, or to build up cash reserves. If the first line of equation (2.1) is negative, this must be financed either by attracting capital or credit from the rest of the world, or by spending down reserves. Equation (2.1) obtains not just for nation-states, but for every spatially contiguous area. For example, a suburb of a large city exports labor to the city center, remits earnings, and uses them to purchase imported food and consumer goods. Clearly, a balance between the first line of equation (2.1) – the "current account" – and the second line – the "capital account" – is unlikely; and the smaller the spatial unit, the less likely is cross-border balance.

Now consider investment, in the macroeconomic sense of an expenditure whose intent is to increase productive capacity in a given economic unit. Investment can be financed locally or "offshore" – from outside the spatial area in which the investment is being made. Investment will be made with the intention of augmenting the production of goods and services, and increasing revenue flows. In the moment when investment is undertaken, this future production has not yet happened; its value depends on future events yet to unfold. In this sense, investment is always speculative. And when financing is obtained outside a spatial unit, the lenders or funders are necessarily supporting an asset bubble – they are devoting cash-flow in advance for revenues from a flow of goods and services that has not yet been realized. If we break any geographic area down to small subunits, it is clear that financiers will almost invariably be in one space, and investments in another. This means that to finance investment is to speculate, to participate in building up an asset bubble in one area before knowing whether the "fundamentals" will catch up in the longer run. In other words, the distinction between fundamentals and bubble growth, when considered spatially, is a false one. Investment always involves bubble growth – until the subsequent structural changes set in motion by this flow of funds are realized. The speculative and potentially bubble-like character of investment can be starkly seen in considering the developer's problem of building greenfield housing units in a formerly agricultural area.

The likelihood of an asset bubble in a given spatial area increases when capital inflows to that area are not specifically seeking to finance investment expenditure, but instead are seeking assets to buy. The difference is between providing finance for construction of a new home, and investing in one or more existing homes in a given area. In this case, an area that is identified as a good area for investment will attract capital and credit inflows seeking assets to buy; and if there is not a new stock of fixed assets to buy, the price of existing assets will be bid up. In this case, a bubble can easily arise. London real estate in the post-crisis period is a case in point: demand has far outpaced supply.

From this perspective, asset bubbles come into being because of the interactions between the market and income structures in any space, and the systematically unbalanced flows of goods, services, credit, and capital across the borders between that space and the rest of the world. Asset bubbles only draw analytical notice when the prices of assets rooted in sizable geographic areas experience huge increases relative to past levels. Financial crises linked to fixed assets in a given space then arise when systematic disjunctures arise between the borrowing commitments required to sustain investors' asset positions there, and the income available to service that debt.

At different points in space–time, the elements needed to create a bubble (an above-trend rise in asset prices) and then a crash (a trigger event leading to that trend's collapse) may come together in different combinations. The volume of savings that is able to seek out above-market returns, the limits on available supply, the availability of ready financing, the lack of availability of alternative investment options, and the existence of an exceedingly low rate of interest on safe assets all may be present in varying degrees in a given historical episode. The levels of these elements, in turn, are determined by historical patterns of colonization, urbanization, inequality, and financial-market regulation that will differ greatly from epoch to epoch and from place to place.

This spatial approach to seeing capital flows and asset bubbles is "Keynesian" insofar as it recognizes that the problem of uncertainty afflicts investment decisions at every scale of the economy, micro to macro. Those making investment decisions involving irreversible (spatially fixed) assets will attempt to reduce the possibility of asset-price declines and encourage asset-price inclines by whatever means they have available – the standardization of architecture, the homogenization and privatization of amenities and public services, applicant screening, and so on.

So a spatially explicit approach clarifies the dynamics of bubbles in real time and space. "Fundamentals" are not well summarized by simple metrics, as a breakdown of subprime measures shows. Figure 2.5 illustrates different housing-price trajectories between January 2000 and January 2012 – the overall 20-city average for the cities included in the Case–Shiller sample, Detroit, Las Vegas, and Los Angeles. All three cities shown experienced severe subprime lending crises; but Detroit's housing prices hardly rose in the mid-2000s, whereas Los Angeles's rose and stabilized, and Las Vegas's rose and collapsed. The link between increasing housing prices (an asset bubble) and the consequence (subprime crisis) cannot logically be reduced to a simple linear formula. Reality is more complex: fundamentals consist of interwoven elements and forces; what is needed is not a bubble equation, but a geographic political economy.[26]

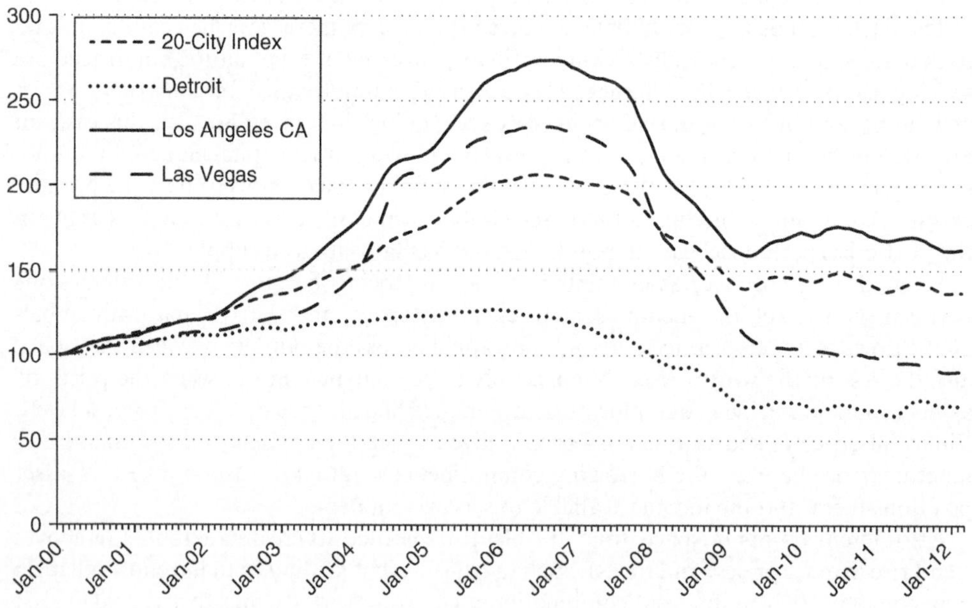

Note: January 2000 = 100 for all cities.

Figure 2.5 Case–Shiller Housing Price indices, 20-city average and 3 cities, 2000–12

2.9 TOWARD GEOGRAPHICAL POLITICAL ECONOMIES OF ASSET BUBBLES

This brings us back to the challenge posed by Muellerleile et al. (2014): what is the "disciplinary core" of economic geography? The suggestion that emerges here is geographical political economy – the study of how space matters and helps to shape economic and social outcomes, as opposed to the study of economic phenomena in space. In this aspect one needs to study the spatial distribution of financial systems in an attempt to better analyze (understand) how and why asset inflation typically emerges in particular places (and spaces) and how this inflation then diffuses spatially, through geographical contagion effects and the functioning of spaces of financial flows and markets themselves. The importance of the spatial distribution of financial systems and the institutions activities that take place within the financial markets is due to their interconnections and their close relations. It is through these strong interconnections that the contagion effect spread, as documented in the latest global financial crisis. Therefore the failure to recognize the interdependence of financial systems obscures the broader picture.

The evolving economic geography of the world we live in has been a central concern for many geographers, including David Harvey. In his 2011 volume *The Enigma of Capital and the Crisis of Capitalism*, Harvey discusses the process of uneven spatial development. He argues that because capital is a flow and not a "thing," any blockages to its circulation can slow down growth, cause investment opportunities to evaporate, and generate a full-blown crisis of overaccumulation. If growth is not restored and new opportunities to employ capital profitably are not identified, then the devaluation of capital is inevitable. Harvey (2011) describes how the process of asset value destruction in the aftermath of the latest financial crisis led to an estimated $50 trillion loss in global asset value. The spatial aspects of barriers to capital circulation and accumulation are an important element of Harvey's work. He argues that capital seeks out profitable investment outlets by circulating through seven spatially specific "activity spheres" involving "the production of new technological and organizational forms."[27] As he puts it, "capital cannot circulate or accumulate without touching upon each and all of these activity spheres in some way" (Harvey, 2011: 124).

Harvey's work does not specify the operations of the financial system per se in any depth, nor does he focus attention on its fragilities and vulnerabilities: instead, he traces the occurrence of crisis to blockages in the "activity spheres." In contrast, we argue here that the financial system is not only fragile in a Minskyian sense, but a possible source of crisis: so understanding the spatial distribution of financial-system activities is crucial for understanding not only where asset inflation arises, but also for how crises can occur. In other words, crisis tendencies can arise in financial market processes and be propagated by the activities of financial institutions.

This approach has already been signaled in some responses to the global financial crisis. Aalbers (2009) observed that the subprime crisis required a "spatialized understanding of the linkages between local and global" because it involved a collision between "Real estate [which] is, by definition, local [and] spatially fixed" and mortgage lending, which is "increasingly a global market today." The result, he argues is a crisis that is both spatially variegated and that will have myriad consequences across space as it unfolds. French, Leyshon, and Thrift (2009), in turn, showed how the subprime crisis arose in part from the mutually incompatible dynamics set in motion by processes operating at four different spatial scales: New York–London financial competition, the "insular . . . everyday geographies of money," global imbalances between China and the US, and the agency of financial media. Martin (2011), in turn, calls for this approach when he writes that "[w]e need to know much more about the geographies of asset creation and destruction" (Martin, 2011: 612–613) and the tensions between centralizing and decentralizing processes in real time and space, in the context of the global financial crisis. The analytical frame must allow conceptual space for the fact that the subprime crisis has brought asset-stripping to some cities and regions, even while others continue unscathed.

This is not to say that geographical political economy must conform to a particular methodology of inquiry. It can use conventional neoclassical tools; the *differentia specifica* is analytical attention to whether and how spatial scales might matter.[28] A number of studies of housing have indeed investigated how relations of space permeate financial flows and asset bubbles. Roehner (1999) examined the differential evolution of housing prices in different parts of Paris in the 1984–93 period. More recently, Monkkonen, Wong, and Begley (2012) study intra-metropolitan price evolution process in Hong Kong, and find that the drivers of price bubbles in the early 1990s and in the 2000s price bubbles are very different, due to changes in Hong Kong's spatial and economic structures.

2.10 CONCLUSION

In the past several years, Reinhart and Rogoff have become notorious for their argument that "this time it's [never] different." The lesson taken here is that time, place, and historical circumstance have played a large role both in determining when asset bubbles turn into asset-price crashes, and in shaping economists' discourses about asset bubbles. The Reinhart–Rogoff thesis that time and space are unimportant in understanding bubbles turns out to represent a mode of thinking about these phenomena that acknowledges geography only to erase it. This mode of thinking is embraced by economists due to their intellectual indebtedness to the ideal of economic equilibrium, which has survived their analytical recognition (due to historical experience) that market mechanisms work only imperfectly.

We have argued here that while there are insights to be gleaned from examinations of asset-bubble patterns that abstract from space (and from time), such studies implicitly make very strong assumptions about the role of space in economic growth and inequality that are warranted only in special cases – not as a general rule. In the more general case, geography is a critically important part of understanding bubbles, their formation, and their bursting. To recognize the complexity of the organization of economic activities in space, and of patterns of financial and goods flows across borders, is to embrace the fact that apparently uniform occurrences, such as the Asian financial crisis or the subprime crisis, have widely varying consequences across space and time.

NOTES

1. The "Web of Science" was selected for this keyword search because of its rigorous rules regarding "topic" words. The mainstream economics journals queried were the *American Economic Review*, the *Economic Journal*, the *Journal of Finance*, the *Journal of Housing Economics*, the *Journal of Monetary Economics*, and the *Journal of Urban Economics*. The heterodox economics journals queried were the *Cambridge Journal of Economics*, the *Journal of Economic Issues*, the *Journal of Post Keynesian Economics*, and the *Review of Radical Political Economics*.
2. The regional studies journals queried were *Regional Studies*, *Regional Science and Urban Economics*, and the *Cambridge Journal of Regions, Economy, and Society*; the geography journals queried were *Economic Geography*, *Journal of Economic Geography*, *Geoforum*, *Environment and Planning A*, *Environment and Planning D*, *Transactions of the Institute of British Geographers*, and *Annals of the Association of American Geographers*.
3. See, for example, Cassidy (2008) and Wolf (2008). It should be pointed out that the literature covered here, and the discussion of that literature, is exceedingly US-centric.
4. Similar points, using different analytical methods, are made in Dymski (2009, 2010, and 2014). The first two of these papers call for a deeper integration of thinking in regional studies and geography with that in heterodox economics; but as shown in these figures, this integration has yet to happen.
5. Tobin (1969) authored the paper that capped this process of integrating financial-market equilibrium theory with a simplified Keynesian macroeconomic model.
6. The journals listed in footnote 1 contained zero "topic-word" references to "bubble," "financial crisis," or "financial instability" in the period 1961–80.
7. These quotations are taken from the fifth edition of this text, Kindleberger and Aliber (2005).
8. The first edition of *Manias, Panics, and Crashes*, including the quotation cited here from that volume, appeared in 1978. The page numbers for these cited passages are drawn from the 2005 edition co-authored with Aliber.
9. It *is* the case that Minsky uses Tobin's "theory q", which is based on the idea of an efficient macroeconomic and portfolio equilibrium, as a short-hand investment theory. This does not, however, imply Minsky's tacit acceptance of equilibrium thinking about financial markets. For him, theory q was both a convenient short-hand and a vehicle for communicating with mainstream economists (despite his being tagged a Keynesian). The author and his doctoral supervisor, James Crotty, debated Minsky regarding this topic on several occasions, but kept no written record.
10. In Minsky (1986), he termed these, respectively, "big bank" and "big government."
11. The former impossibility is due to the logical requirements of equilibrium behavior: bubble prices require an infinite number of traders, since otherwise no buyer at the end of a buying–selling chain would want to purchase an overpriced asset, and the very possibility of a bubble would collapse (Barlevy, 2012). The latter impossibility is due to a form of the Heisenberg uncertainty problem: traders' expectations about financial prices reflect both their theory of price and their theory of expectations; but we can only know one by assuming the other, and vice versa.
12. All of the identified bubbles in Table 2.1 are taken form Reinhart and Rogoff (2009), apart from the Dot-com bubbles in 2001, which is taken from Scherbina (2013).
13. Dymski (2011) summarizes the academic and policy debates triggered by the Latin American and Asian debt crises.
14. This literature was launched by Krugman (1979).
15. Brunnermeier's survey of bubbles (2008) shows bubbles can emerge in markets with either imperfect or asymmetrically distributed information. When information is imperfect, so that all agents are unaware that market fundamentals have changed, trading prices can temporarily be too high or too low; when information is asymmetrically distributed, better-informed agents can take advantage of less-informed agents. Note that the focus on resolving how deviations from equilibrium prices can arise between rational agents precludes any need to consider what factors may explain where they do and do not occur.
16. Krugman (1998), web-published just after Korea signed an IMF agreement in December 1997, is a characteristic example.
17. Bustelo, Garcia, and Olivié (1999) provide the most comprehensive literature review of the Asian financial crisis.
18. In a pattern characteristic of papers published in mainstream journals (see Figure 2.3), there is no acknowledgement here of Minsky's origination of this term or of other heterodox contributions.
19. Geanakoplos, Magill, Quinzii, and Dreze (1990) have derived this result in a formal model; and Magill and Quinzii (1996) have extended this insight, showing that incomplete-markets models can encompass bubbles which affect equilibrium allocations.

20. Krugman attributed the problem to "mistaking beauty for truth"; the analysis set out here suggests the problem has deeper roots. Galbraith (2009) pointed out, in answer, that some economists – including the author of this chapter – did anticipate the crisis.
21. That is, the government-sponsored enterprises' (GSEs') mandate to increase housing for low-income borrowers did not cause the housing bubble. Moulton (2014) also found that the GSEs had no effect on overall mortgage lending. And Brueckner, Calem, and Nakamura (2012) found that while the growth of subprime credit is commonly supposed to be a cause of house-price escalation, their empirical results show that "subprime lending is both a consequence and a cause of bubble conditions in the housing market."
22. For example, Caballero and Simsek (2013: 2549) show that financial crises can emerge from endogenous complexity – that is, "banks' *uncertainty* about the financial network of cross-exposures . . . which can generate the possibility of a domino effect of bankruptcies."
23. This conclusion follows as a corollary of the formal proofs cited in endnote 17; it is proven rigorously in Magill and Quinzii (1996). Friedman (1971) discovered this result for infinite-horizon games: the finding that infinite sub-game perfect (Nash) equilibria can exist is termed the "folk theorem."
24. Minsky's model of financial instability itself did not provide this cross-asset-type architecture, since Minsky focused on investment financing per se. For Minsky, countercyclical public expenditure to stabilize an economy after a market meltdown was a restorative measure, even if debt-financed, not a transfer of an excess credit-supply problem from the private sector to the government sector.
25. A recent NBER paper that surveys theories of financial crises (Goldstein and Razin, 2013) has 122 references, none to heterodox authors. Minsky is not cited; he appears in the bibliography by virtue of being included in the title of a paper by Eggertsson and Krugman (2012), which in turn lists only Minsky (1986) and no other heterodox work in its bibliography. Dymski (2014) explores the foundations of the mainstream-heterodox gap in economics.
26. Cohen, Coughlin, and Lopez (2012) document that the spatial locus of housing-price bubbles varies considerably with changes in the geographic scale at which analysis is conducted.
27. These seven activity spheres, in Harvey's words, are: "technologies and organizational forms; social relations; institutional and administrative arrangements; production and labor processes; relations to nature; the reproduction of daily life and of the species; and mental conceptions of the world" (Harvey, 2011: 123).
28. An example here is McCann and Acs (2011). Their exploration of the relationship between country size, city size, and economies of scale investigates whether the importance of agglomeration – the relationship between city size and country size – has changed over time. They find that it does: "For industrialized countries, the size of a city is nowadays much less important than its level of global connectivity, whereas the size of the city is still dominant in newly industrializing countries" (McCann and Acs, 2011: 17).

REFERENCES

Aalbers, M.B. (2009), 'Geographies of the financial crisis', *Area*, **41** (1), 34–42.

Allen, F. and D. Gale (1998), 'Optimal financial crises', *Journal of Finance*, **53**, 1245–1284.

Allen, F. and D. Gale (2000a), 'Bubbles and crises', *Economic Journal*, **110**, 236–255.

Allen, F. and D. Gale (2000b), 'Financial contagion', *Journal of Political Economy*, **108**, 1–33.

Allen, F. and G. Gorton (2012), 'Churning bubbles', in D.D. Evanoff, G.G. Kaufman and A.G. Malliaris (eds), *New Perspectives on Asset Price Bubbles: Theory, Evidence, and Policy*, Oxford: Oxford University Press, pp. 13–40.

Barlevy, G. (2012), 'Rethinking theoretical models of bubbles', in D.D. Evanoff, G.G. Kaufman and A.G. Malliaris (eds), *New Perspectives on Asset Price Bubbles: Theory, Evidence, and Policy*, Oxford: Oxford University Press, pp. 41–64.

Beck, Th., A. Demirgüç-Kunt and R. Levine (2000), 'A new database on financial development and structure', *World Bank Economic Review*, **14** (4), 597–605.

Beck, Th., A. Demirgüç-Kunt and R. Levine (2010), 'Financial institutions and markets across countries and over time: the updated financial development and structure database', *World Bank Economic Review*, **24** (1), 77–92.

Bellofiore, R. and G. Vertova (2014), *The Great Recession and the Contradictions of Contemporary Capitalism*, Cheltenham, UK and Northampton, MA, USA: Edward Elgar Publishing.

Blanchard, O.J. (1979), 'Speculative bubbles, crashes and rational expectations', *Economics Letters*, **3**, 387–389.

Brueckner, J.K., P.S. Calem and Leonard I. Nakamura (2012), 'Subprime mortgages and the housing bubble', *Journal of Urban Economics*, **71**, 230–243.

Brunnermeier, M.K. (2008), 'Bubbles', in Steven N. Durlauf and Lawrence E. Blume (eds), *The New Palgrave Dictionary of Economics*, New York: Palgrave Macmillan.

Bustelo, P., C. Garcia and I. Olivié (1999), 'Global and domestic factors of financial crises in emerging economies: lessons from the East Asian episodes (1997–1999)', ICEI Working Paper No. 16/99, Complutense University of Madrid.

Caballero, R.J. and A. Simsek (2013), 'Fire sales in a model of complexity', *Journal of Finance* **68** (6), 2549–2587.

Caballero, R.J., E. Farhi and M.L. Hammour (2006), 'Speculative growth: hints from the US economy', *American Economic Review*, **96** (4), 1159–1192.

Cassidy, J. (2008), 'The Minsky moment', *The New Yorker*, February 8.

Clark, S.P. and T.D. Coggin (2011), 'Was there a US house price bubble? An econometric analysis using national and regional panel data', *Quarterly Review of Economics and Finance*, **51**, 189–200.

Cohen, J.P., C.C. Coughlin and D.A. Lopez (2012), 'The boom and bust of US housing prices from various geographic perspectives', *Federal Reserve Bank of St. Louis Review*, September/October 2012, **94** (5), 341–367.

Coleman IV, M., M. LaCour-Little and K.D. Vandell (2008), 'Subprime lending and the housing bubble: tail wags dog?', *Journal of Housing Economics*, **17**, 272–290.

De Long, J.B., A. Shleifer, L. Summers and R. Waldmann (1990), 'Noise trader risk in financial markets', *Journal of Political Economy*, **98** (4), 703–738.

Demirgüç-Kunt, A. and E. Detragiache (1998), 'The determinants of banking crises: evidence from developing and developed countries', *IMF Staff Papers*, **45** (1), 81–109.

Dymski, G.A. (2009), 'Afterword: mortgage markets and the urban problematic in the global transition', *International Journal of Urban and Regional Research*, **33** (2) (Symposium, Sociology and Geography of Mortgage Markets), 427–442.

Dymski, G.A. (2010), 'Confronting the quadruple global crisis', *Geoforum*, **41**, 837–840.

Dymski, G.A. (2011), 'The international debt crisis', in Jonathan Michie (ed.), *Handbook of Globalisation*, 2nd edition, Cheltenham, UK and Northampton, MA, USA: Edward Elgar Publishing, pp. 117–134.

Dymski, G.A. (2014), 'Neoclassical sink and heterodox spiral: political divides and lines of communication in economics' *Review of Keynesian Economics*, **2** (1), 1–19.

Eaton, J., M. Gersovitz and J. Stiglitz (1986), 'The pure theory of country risk', *European Economic Review*, **30**, 481–513.

Edison, H.J., P. Luangaram and M. Miller (2000), 'Asset bubbles, leverage and "lifeboats": elements of the East Asian Crisis', *Economic Journal*, **110**, 309–334.

Eggertsson, G.B. and P. Krugman (2012), 'Debt, deleveraging, and the liquidity trap: a Fisher–Minsky–Koo approach', *Quarterly Journal of Economics*, **127** (3), 1469–1513.

Evanoff, D.D., G.G. Kaufman and A.G. Malliaris (eds) (2012), *New Perspectives on Asset Price Bubbles: Theory, Evidence, and Policy*, Oxford: Oxford University Press.

Flood, R.P. and P.M. Garber (1980), 'Market fundamentals versus price-level bubbles: the first tests', *Journal of Political Economy*, **88** (4), 745–771.

Flood, R.P. and R.J. Hodrick (1990), 'On testing for speculative bubbles', *Journal of Economic Perspectives*, **4** (2), 85–101.

French, Sh., A. Leyshon and N. Thrift (2009), 'A very geographical crisis: the making and breaking of the 2007–2008 financial crisis', *Cambridge Journal of Regions, Economy and Society*, **2**, 287–302.

Friedman, J. (1971), 'A non-cooperative equilibrium for supergames', *Review of Economic Studies*, **38** (1), 1–12.

Galbraith, J.K. (2009), 'Who are these economists, anyway?', *Thought and Action*, 85–98.

Galí, J. (2014), 'Monetary policy and rational asset price bubbles', *American Economic Review*, **104** (3), 721–752.

Geanakoplos, J., M. Magill, M. Quinzii and J. Dreze (1990), 'Generic inefficiency of stock market equilibrium when markets are incomplete', *Journal of Mathematical Economics*, **19**, 113–151.

Glaeser, E.L. and J. Gyourko (2006), 'Housing dynamics', NBER Working Paper No. 12787, Cambridge, MA: National Bureau of Economic Research.

Glaeser, E.L., J. Gyourko and A. Saiz (2008), 'Housing supply and housing bubbles', *Journal of Urban Economics*, **64**, 198–217.

Goldstein, I. and A. Razin (2013), 'Three branches of theories of financial crises', NBER Working Paper No. 18670, Cambridge, MA: National Bureau of Economic Research.

Goodman, A.C. and Th. G. Thibodeau (2008), 'Where are the speculative bubbles in US housing markets?', *Journal of Housing Economics*, **17**, 117–137.

Harvey, D. (2011), *The Enigma of Capital and the Crisis of Capitalism*, London: Profile Books.

Kane, E.J. (1989), 'The high cost of incompletely funding the FSLIC shortage of explicit capital', *Journal of Economic Perspectives*, **3** (4), 31–48.

Kindleberger, C.P. and R. Aliber (2005), *Manias, Panics, and Crashes: A History of Financial Crises*, New York: Wiley Investment Classics.

Kivedal, B.K. (2013), 'Testing for rational bubbles in the US housing market', *Journal of Macroeconomics*, **38**, 369–381.

Kompas, T. and B. Spotton (1989), 'A note on rational speculative bubbles', *Economics Letters*, **30**, 327–331.

Krugman, P. (1979), 'A model of balance of payments crises', *Journal of Money, Credit, and Banking*, **3** (1/2), 311–325.

Krugman, P. (1998), 'What happened to Asia?', Working Paper, MIT Department of Economics.
Krugman, P. (2009), 'How did economists get it so wrong?', *New York Times*, September 6.
Lerner, P.A. (1972), 'The economics and politics of consumer sovereignty', *American Economic Review*, **62** (2), 258–266.
Levin, E.J. and R.E. Wright (1997), 'The impact of speculation on house prices in the United Kingdom', *Economic Modelling*, **14**, 567–585.
Lux, Th. (1995), 'Herd behaviour, bubbles and crashes', *The Economic Journal*, **105** (431), 881–896.
Magill, M. and M. Quinzii (1996), 'Incomplete markets over an infinite horizon: long-lived securities and speculative bubbles', *Journal of Mathematical Economics*, **26**, 133–170.
Martin, A. and J. Ventura (2012), 'Economic growth with bubbles', *American Economic Review*, **102** (6), 3033–3058.
Martin, R. (2011), 'The local geographies of the financial crisis: from the housing bubble to economic recession and beyond', *Journal of Economic Geography*, **11**, 587–618.
McCann, P. and Z.J. Acs (2011), 'Globalization: countries, cities and multinationals', *Regional Studies*, **45** (1), 17–32.
Minsky, H.P. (1975), *John Maynard Keynes*, New York: Colombia University Press.
Minsky, H.P. (1986), *Stabilizing the Unstable Economy*, New Haven: Yale University Press.
Minsky, H.P. (1990), 'The bubble in the price of baseball cards', Hyman P. Minsky Archive, Paper 94, retrieved on October 12, 2016 from http://digitalcommons.bard.edu/hm_archive/94.
Monkkonen, P., K. Wong and J. Begley (2012), 'Economic restructuring, urban growth, and short-term trading: the spatial dynamics of the Hong Kong housing market, 1992–2008', *Regional Science and Urban Economics*, **42**, 396–406.
Montañés, A. and L. Olmos (2013), 'Convergence in US house prices', *Economics Letters*, **121**, 152–155.
Moulton, S. (2014), 'Did affordable housing mandates cause the subprime mortgage crisis?', *Journal of Housing Economics*, **24**, 21–38.
Muellerleile, C., K. Strauss, B. Spigel and Th. P. Nariǹs (2014), 'Economic geography and the financial crisis: full steam ahead?', *The Professional Geographer*, **66** (1), 11–17.
Reinhart, C. and K. Rogoff (2009), *This Time is Different: Eight Centuries of Financial Folly*, Princeton, NJ: Princeton University Press.
Reinhart, C. and K. Rogoff (2011), 'From financial crash to debt crisis', *American Economic Review*, **101** (5), 1676–1706.
Riddel, M. (1999), 'Fundamentals, feedback trading, and housing market speculation: evidence from California', *Journal of Housing Economics*, **8**, 272–284.
Roehner, B.M. (1999), 'Spatial analysis of real estate price bubbles: Paris, 1984–1993', *Regional Science and Urban Economics*, **29**, 73–88.
Rosser, Jr., J. Barkley, Marina V. Rosser and M. Gallegati (2012), 'A Minsky–Kindleberger perspective on the financial crisis', *Journal of Economic Issues*, **46** (2), 449–459.
Scherbina, A. (2013), 'Asset price bubbles: a selective survey', International Monetary Fund (IMF), Institute for Capacity Development, Working Paper, WP/13/45.
Shiller, R. (1981), 'Do stock prices move too much to be justified by subsequent changes in dividends?', *American Economic Review*, **71** (3), 421–436.
Shiller, R. (2005), *Irrational Exuberance*, 2nd edition, Princeton, NJ: Princeton University Press.
Tobin, J. (1969), 'A general equilibrium approach to monetary theory', *Journal of Money, Credit, and Banking*, **1** (1), 15–29.
West, K.D. (1988), 'Bubbles, fads and stock price volatility tests: a partial evaluation', *Journal of Finance*, **43** (3), 639–656.
Wolf, M. (2008), 'The end of lightly regulated finance has come far closer', *Financial Times*, September 16.
Wray, L.R. (2009), 'The rise and fall of money manager capitalism: a Minskian approach', *Cambridge Journal of Economics*, **33**, 807–828.
Zhou, W. and D. Sornette (2003), '2000–2003 real estate bubble in the UK but not in the USA', *Physica A*, **329**, 249–263.
Zhou, W. and D. Sornette (2006), 'Is there a real-estate bubble in the US?', *Physica, A*, **361**, 297–308.

3. The geographical political economy of money and finance after the great crisis: beyond 'market discipline'

Brett Christophers

3.1 INTRODUCTION: LOCATING MARKET DISCIPLINE

The global financial crisis (GFC) which began in 2007 represented a convulsive shake-up and shake-out of the established order where much about the geographical political economy of money and finance is concerned. This chapter seeks to illustrate and make sense of some of the most striking and significant aspects of these transformations, in order to paint a picture of what this political economy broadly looks like 'after' the crisis period – albeit while recognizing the problematic nature of any such conceptual-temporal closure.

The central theme with which the chapter works, as is befitting of any political-economic account, is that of power. In and through which social fields or institutional constellations does the power to shape monetary and financial processes and outcomes flow and crystallize? To which primary forms of socio-economic relationality – relations, always power-laden, among and between markets, states, banks, classes, regulators, and so forth – do we need to refer to explain why the monetary and financial world takes the forms it does? And what predominant geographical configurations do the political-economic structures, relations and processes in question tend to assume?

In submitting answers to these questions, the chapter necessarily offers a partial take. It does not, for example, address assuredly important matters of, perhaps most notably, the monetary and financial underpinnings of contemporary global economic imbalances, which are of course very much about power of both political and economic varieties. As the international political economy literature has amply demonstrated, large current-account surpluses in China, Germany and Japan and a persistent deficit in the US are predicated upon the US's ability to continue to sell to the rest of the world financial assets denominated in the world's dominant reserve money: the dollar. This state of affairs reflects, as Schwartz (2014: 69) observes, 'the structure of political power globally and domestically in a few key countries' as much as it does 'underlying economic activity in those countries'. And it is clearly a crucial feature of the contemporary geographical political economy of money and finance, broadly conceived.

But, it is not our focus here. Partly this is because the GFC represented, in Helleiner's (2014) terms, a 'status quo' event where such imbalances and their monetary-financial infrastructure are concerned: seven years on, the US dollar remains essentially unchallenged as the world's reserve currency of choice. More fundamentally, however, the chapter focuses elsewhere because its concern is not with the specific geographies of (monetary and financial) power in terms of absolute or relative location. Rather, it interrogates transformations in the *general* spatial characteristics and *general* institutional constitution of the processes by which the economy's principal monetary and financial frameworks are produced and reproduced – wherever these processes might be located, and whatever their implications for wider 'geopolitical' shifts. If this distinction sounds rather abstract, it will become clearer as the chapter progresses. Suffice it to signal here that the chapter examines such (general) transformations as they have occurred in the (specific) geographical heartlands of the crisis: the US, the UK, and continental Europe.

Both as a way into the chapter and as a framing device for what follows, the chapter mobilizes the much-discussed idea of 'market discipline'. Why? Because, the chapter's principal argument is that the crisis, and the response to it, has entailed a decisive shift away from putative market hegemony, the 'discipline' it theoretically enacts, and the geographies associated with 'the market's' powers. The geographical political economy of money and finance has thus evolved 'beyond' market discipline.

Consider, to begin with, how financial regulation was typically figured in the pre-crisis period. 'Given the ostensible efficiency and supremacy of markets as aggregators of information, the primary purpose of regulation', notes Langley (2014: 145), was envisaged as 'enabling the so-called "market discipline" of banking that follows from the assessments of creditors and investors'. Yet what exactly is, or was, this market discipline that regulators were supposed to encourage? In short, by virtue of its superior ability to process information and crystallize it in prices, 'the market' would satisfactorily keep risk-taking in check, penalizing excess risk – for example by levying higher interest rates on gluttonous borrowers – and thus enforcing financial prudence. Actors *in* the market were disciplined *by* the market. Here, from 2001, is Andrew Crockett, the then General Manager of the Bank for International Settlements (BIS) and Chairman of the Financial Stability Forum:

> The disciplinary strength of market forces derives from the immense power of the price system to aggregate information. The views of economic agents, sharpened by profit maximising instincts, are reflected in the constellation of prices at which funds are allocated and risks exchanged. In turn, these prices are a powerful and economical mechanism to summarise and convey information about those views. Market forces can raise the cost or restrict the volume of funding for those activities with unattractive risk/return trade-offs. Together with the ultimate threat of the demise of the enterprise, these mechanisms can deter excessive risk taking. (Crockett, 2001)

For our purposes, the critical feature of such market discipline is that it entailed – at least in theory – a particular configuration of institutional forces vis-à-vis money and finance, and a particular spatial configuration at that. At the apex of the pyramid was the market itself – an unforgiving disciplinary master which, crucially, was deemed to be effectively place*less*, or at the very least not place-constrained or constraining. To be sure, different territories had different financial markets, but avowedly dwindling opportunities for straightforward geographical arbitrage evidenced the fact that prices were smoothly harmonized between them. Markets, then, were the vital scaffolding of what was now a 'flat world' (Friedman, 2007) for and of finance. General Manager Crockett made this point explicit too, insisting that as well as imposing prudence, market forces 'were instrumental in redirecting resources towards more productive uses, *both within and across borders*' (Crockett, 2001; emphasis added).

If markets were to the fore, meanwhile, all other institutional forces were – and belonged – very much in the background. More than for any other, this was the case for states and their regulatory arms – perhaps the most place-bound among the various institutional forces we shall have occasion to consider. With the market exerting its powers of discipline over potentially errant commercial actors, the state could afford to occupy a regulatory backseat. All that was required was to put in place the conditions necessary for market discipline to 'work'. Lane (1993: 54) specified these as follows:

> Financial markets must be open. Information bearing on a borrower's creditworthiness must be readily available to lenders. Markets must not anticipate that a delinquent borrower will be bailed out, which also implies that the borrower must not have access to central bank financing that would enable it to maintain an otherwise unsustainable position. Finally, for market discipline to work smoothly, the borrower must respond to market signals. Market discipline fails when these conditions are not met.

Leaving aside for now the necessity that neither bailouts nor preferential central bank funding are available – yes, alarm bells should be ringing, and yes, Lane's specification was selected specifically with the events of 2007 onwards in mind – market discipline makes relatively mild demands of regulators. Their role is reduced, as Langley (2014: 131) remarks, 'largely to ensuring information flows in transparent markets [and] providing protections against fraud'.

What, then, of those other main institutions implicated in the political economy of money and finance: namely, financial institutions in general, and banks in particular? According to the theory underlying market discipline, banks, too, were subsidiary to the market and its powers. And this applied, significantly, both to central banks and to commercial (retail and investment) banks.

As far as central banks were concerned, the guiding principle was to sit for the most part on the sidelines as markets worked themselves out, vested as such banks were 'with a primary objective of inflation targeting, and a lesser objective of financial stability' (Bowman et al., 2013: 463). The former of these objectives constituted the monetary side of central bank policy – that is, 'a relatively narrow concern with price stability' (Goodhart, 2015: 24) – and the latter, effected conventionally through acting as lender of last resort, the financial side. Most critically of all, the principal, money-oriented objective required only intermittent engagement with, or intervention in, markets. Finessing interest rates to control inflation was a matter, specifically, of intervallic 'open-market operations' (OMOs). Thus, periodically (once per week in the case of the Bank of England), the bank would open the doors separating it from 'the market', endeavouring to regulate the money supply by, for example, purchasing short-term government bonds or lending or borrowing through fixed-term repurchase agreements. Its OMOs rapidly concluded, the bank would then retreat safely to behind closed doors until next required to venture out. In the meantime, markets would continue to discipline.

The commercial banks whose reserve levels OMOs serve to adjust are also subsidiary under the 'market discipline' scenario. Granted, banks discipline one another by assessing risk levels and pricing credit accordingly, but only because markets enable – indeed, theoretically require – them to do so. Precisely because they operate *in* markets, individual banks lack the power to *move* markets in and of themselves. They are price 'takers' rather than 'makers', responding to as opposed to determining the price signalling for which markets are so lavishly lauded. For, the US, UK and (most of) Europe had undergone a crucial transition, according to the narrative of 'market discipline', from 'bank-based' to 'market-based' financial systems. Where, historically, banks had been the dominant institutions – the pivotal nodes of a relationship-based financial system largely lacking effective competition and, therefore, price signals – the growing ascendancy of financial markets had led to an increase in competition and thus more efficient price signalling, disciplining banks as a result (e.g. Boot and Thakor, 1997; Rajan and Zingales, 2003).

This chapter argues that the GFC and subsequent developments in the political economy of money and finance – including, but not limited to, the establishment response to the crisis – have thoroughly put paid to this 'market discipline' picture: partly by exposing its rather limited purchase on actual pre-crisis realities, and partly by materially transforming the roles of and relations between different primary actors in ways that render that picture even less accurate today than it was hitherto. We are today confronted, this is to say, by a new political economy of money and finance whose key contours are only just beginning to come into focus. And this new political economy, the chapter claims, is characterized by a markedly different geography. Where market hegemony encourages, in theory at any rate, placelessness, the materiality of place is writ increasingly large under the 'post-crisis' scheme of things.

The chapter develops these arguments over the course of three main sections which consider, respectively, the three main sets of institutions whose power and/or significance, nominally muted by market discipline, have been resurgent during the past half-decade. Section one examines commercial banks, and commercial financial institutions more generally; section two focuses on central banks; and section three turns the spotlight on states. However, as one would imagine, none of these types of institutions can be adequately analysed in isolation from the others (or from markets), and hence while the emphasis is on one institutional type at a time it is always more on relations than on 'internal' properties per se. Following the three main sections, a short conclusion closes the chapter.

3.2 TOO BIG TO FAIL AND TOO BIG TO DISCIPLINE: COMMERCIAL BANKS

The abundant power and significance of banks – and not just of banks in general, but of a relatively small number of huge transnational institutions – has been much in evidence and much discussed since the outset of the GFC. In this section we shall review some of the most striking such evidence, and begin to consider its implications for the contemporary geographical political economy of money and finance. First, however, a word on terminology/definition is necessary. Where this chapter refers to (commercial) 'banks', it does so in a very broad sense. In particular, it includes within this category those non-deposit-taking institutions, often grouped together under the label 'shadow banking', that have increasingly grown their share of total credit intermediation over the past three to four decades. Typically taken to include the likes of investment banks, structured investment vehicles and private-equity and hedge funds, shadow banking was recently estimated, for instance, to have grown its share of total US intermediation from below 10 per cent in the early 1970s to above 30 per cent in the decade 2004–13 (Antill et al., 2014).

In an important but often underappreciated sense, the GFC itself, in its initial US subprime-centred materialization, represented powerful evidence of the disproportionate import of big banks. When global credit markets began to freeze up in the second half of 2007 and then further deteriorated through 2008, they did so in relation to fears concerning the credit-worthiness of what was generally a relatively small number of institutions: the likes of BNP Paribas and UBS in Europe; of Northern Rock and HBOS in the UK; and, in the US, of Bear Stearns, Merrill Lynch and, of course, Lehman Brothers. That individual institutions could have such widespread ramifications speaks clearly to their systemic significance. And so, too, of course, does the fact that with the exception of Lehman, it was deemed necessary to find ways for institutions ultimately considered unviable to be rescued either by competitors (e.g. Bear, HBOS, Merrill) or by the state (e.g. Northern Rock). So significant were such institutions that, whatever their faults, they could not be allowed to fail.

From this point on the issue of 'too-big-to-fail' (TBTF) was firmly on the agenda. That particular agenda has since evinced a variety of important sub-narratives and conflicts, but of especial interest for us is the fact that being (seen as) a TBTF or – as the Financial Stability Board (FSB) identified 29 financial institutions in November 2013 – 'globally systemically important' bank (G-SIB) is now widely seen to entail being in receipt of implicit financial subsidies. The reason for this is that if potential counterparties think there is a likelihood that a bank will receive state assistance if it runs into trouble, they will be willing to lend to such a bank more cheaply than they otherwise might: there is lower risk of default, hence removing the requirement to levy a higher rate of interest. Two vitally important, linked implications flow from this. First, if banks already arguably benefitting from scale economies are further buttressed by favourable financing conditions, it becomes accordingly difficult to envision the markets in which they operate as 'competitive' in any meaningful sense of the term. Second, and partly in view of this circumscribed competitiveness, there must be a major question-mark over the extent of any 'discipline' that the market is applying vis-à-vis the institutions in question. In fact the history and future possibility of rescues flies directly in the face of the conditions deemed necessary for effective market disciplinarity. Recall Lane: 'Markets must not anticipate that a delinquent borrower will be bailed out. . .'

Perhaps more significant still is the geography of bailout, which makes the TBTF agenda an inextricably *political* agenda. To this point we have repeatedly emphasized the fact that most nominally TBTF institutions are thoroughly transnational. And, indeed, they are. Yet there is often a stark spatial mismatch here in relation to the mechanism and constituency of bailout. Consider the case of American International Group (AIG). Despite being multinational to its core, with operations in well over 100 countries, AIG was recapitalized by the US government – and behind the US government, the US taxpayer – in late 2008. The other term frequently substituted for such recapitalization or bailout – *nation*alization – is, in this sense, the more revealing. Hence, moreover, the tone and target of AIG's apologetic advertising campaign launched shortly after the US Treasury sold off its final stake in AIG in late 2012, a campaign titled 'Thank You America' (but not the rest of the world) (Irwin, 2012). Bailouts of this sort constitute just one among a wider array of recent geographically specific re-couplings of states with financial institutions that we shall have cause to consider in more detail in subsequent sections.

At the time of writing of this chapter in late 2014, TBTF remains on the agenda for a very simple reason: the fact that next to nothing has been done, in any major western territory, to redress the problem (and it is indeed regarded as a problem by virtually all stakeholders, the handful of institutions in question excepted). This lack of redress points, once more, to the power and significance of today's largest banks; for although in some territories influential voices have called for the TBTF hazard to be addressed head-on, for example by breaking up oversized institutions into smaller pieces, to date no such initiatives have borne fruit, repeatedly running instead into opposition mobilized by the financial sector itself. The power we are concerned with in this section manifests itself in this particular context, then, as the power specifically to frustrate and thwart reform.

Such power has been evidenced in recent years in connection with reform efforts ranging much more widely than TBTF matters alone. Three examples attest to the wider pattern. First, in the US, industry lobbying resulted in substantial watering-down of the key provisions of the single major piece of post-crisis finance-sector reregulation, 2010's Dodd–Frank Act (Coffee, 2011; Kane, 2012). Similarly, second, in Europe: 'Again and again', observes Bieling (2014: 357), 'the European Commission submitted legislative proposals which were diluted and delayed after intense lobbying on the part of European finance'. And third, at the wider international scale, comparable dynamics characterized the process of development of the new Basel III capital adequacy requirements for the banking sector. As Lall (2012) has shown, the months following the Basel Committee on Banking Supervision's issuing of preliminary proposals for new standards in December 2009 saw large international banks, and in particular those 'with personal links to the regulatory community' (Lall, 2012: 627), rapidly 'capture' the regulatory process. The upshot was a comprehensive failure to meet the Committee's initial objectives, with core provisions being relaxed, rendered non-binding, or delayed. More generally, as McKeen-Edwards and Porter (2013) demonstrate, the rules of global finance are increasingly coordinated by financial industry elites, often stitched together across borders into formal transnational financial associations.

Not only, in fact, did the authorities' response to the GFC do very little to correct the TBTF imbalance, but it has arguably worsened this structural problem in two important ways. The first concerns decisions taken in the midst of the crisis to allow faltering institutions from the (allegedly) TBTF ranks to be acquired by more soundly financed competitors. Ordinarily these combinations – Lloyds TSB with HBOS in the UK, and, in the US, a whole host of emergency couplings, of which three of the most prominent were Bank of America with Merrill Lynch, J.P. Morgan with Bear Stearns, and Wells Fargo with Wachovia – would have attracted close scrutiny from competition law (antitrust) authorities. They brought together accumulations of assets swelling the new entities to well above 'normal' thresholds for legal investigation. In the event, however, such scrutiny was waived; such were the exceptional circumstances, the risk of failure of one institution was perceived to outweigh any risk of market power ultimately accruing to the consolidated entity (Christophers, 2013). As such, normal conditions were relaxed and special clauses – for example, a 'national interest' clause in the Lloyds HBOS case – were invoked. The result? In the three aforementioned US cases, three enlarged institutions (Bank of America, which swallowed Merrill; J.P. Morgan Chase, which took over Bear; and Wells Fargo, which acquired Wachovia), all of which appear on the FSB's list of G-SIBs (FSB, 2013).

The second way in which responses to the GFC – or to the monetary/financial conditions arising from the crisis – have tended to aggravate the problem of TBTF banks, making the latter larger rather than smaller, is found in the realms of monetary policy.

A perceived failure of conventional monetary policy based on the raising or lowering of base interest rates saw the central banks of both the UK and the US engage in drawn-out practices of 'quantitative easing' (QE). We shall have more to say about such practices, given their provenance in the workings of central banks, in the following section. But they are pertinent here in view of their implications – which have tended not to be so widely discussed – for commercial banks.

Simply stated, such unconventional monetary policy departs from convention (in which, as we saw in the introduction, there is a place for asset purchases) in two main respects: firstly, it entails purchase of, on average, considerably longer-dated financial assets; and second, the issuers of these assets are private as well as public bodies, financial institutions prominent among them. Writing about the approach of the US Federal Reserve, Roach (2013; original emphasis) explains the fundamental underlying departure as follows: 'It [i.e. the Fed] has shifted its focus from the *price* of credit to influencing the credit cycle's *quantity* dimension through the liquidity injections that quantitative easing requires'. Ditto for the Bank of England.

In turn, one of the main outcomes of QE has been appreciation, on both sides of the Atlantic, in the value of the asset markets into which liquidity has been thereby injected. And herein lies the pivotal link to commercial banks and, for many commentators, the crux of the problem with QE – a problem acknowledged even by conservative commentators such as Roach (former Chairman of Morgan Stanley Asia). In its reliance on QE, Roach observes, the Fed is relying on so-called 'wealth effects' as 'its principal transmission mechanism for stabilization policy'; but 'wealth effects are for the wealthy'. The biggest beneficiaries of QE-induced appreciation in financial asset values are, by definition, the largest owners of such assets: among them, large, TBTF banks. This explains why Bowman et al. (2013: 478), cognizant of such banks' resistance to passing on low interest rates or to expanding lending (cf. Macartney, 2014), ask 'whether quantitative easing is above all a form of bank welfare'. As a policy nominally of financial stabilization, QE has had the perverse effect of expanding rather than contracting already-bloated TBTF balance sheets.

At the same time as governments' response to the GFC has served further to entrench the TBTF problem, meanwhile, the world of money and finance has been wracked by a series of scandals that attest equally forcefully to the power of the institutions we have been discussing in this section. Two such scandals call for particular mention. The first, which surfaced in mid-2012, concerns banks' (proven) manipulation of the London Interbank Offered Rate (LIBOR) and other influential interest rate benchmarks; LIBOR is a measure of borrowing conditions in money markets and is used as a reference/fixing point in numerous types of financial contracts across all manner of different international financial markets. The second scandal, still being investigated at the time of this writing, involves alleged manipulation of benchmark rates in foreign exchange (currency) as opposed to money/credit markets. These two scandals are of significance here insofar as they add considerable weight to the dual impression developed thus far that not only do a relatively small number of large institutions wield enormous power in today's markets, but they often operate according to norms even further removed from supposed 'competition' and 'free market' ideals.

Take, first of all, the nature of the 'markets' referenced by such benchmarks. Investigations triggered by the scandals have been valuable not just for highlighting fraudulent behaviours but for shining a light on markets hitherto relatively impenetrable to academic researchers. While popular figuring of currency and other financial markets often has them as intensely competitive spaces in which individual institutions – to use the terms favoured in this chapter – are disciplined by the market rather than vice versa, the reality is that trading activity has long been dominated by major, TBTF international banks, and that such domination appears only to be increasing. A recent investigation by three *Financial Times* journalists (Schäfer et al., 2013) found this to be decisively the case for currency markets in particular:

> In spite of its size, the foreign exchange market is run by a small group of global traders. One corner of foreign exchange – the $2tn spot market – is controlled by a group of fewer than 100 individual traders at a handful of large banks. . . . The largest four banks in foreign exchange – Deutsche Bank, Citigroup, Barclays and UBS – have amassed more than half the overall market share, up from less than 20 per cent 15 years ago.

All four, needless to say, are found on the FSB's G-SIB list.

Perhaps one of the most striking findings of the various investigations into the LIBOR scandal is that even this (legal) level of market dominance does not seem to be enough for some of the institutions in question. That is to say, unsatisfied with such an established position of power, traders at certain banks went further still and actively sought to manipulate credit-market rate benchmarks to the advantage of the institutions for which they worked – often doing so in active collaboration, furthermore, with individuals working at other, notionally 'competitor', banks. The details of these manipulations are illuminating and reveal a great deal about the sociology as well as the (adulterated) economics of the markets that were thus contorted (Ashton and Christophers, 2015). Without needing to rehearse those details here, the single most important observation one can extract from them is that traders actively sought to minimize, or even annul, the (arguably already limited level of) 'risk' and 'discipline' to which fair participation in the market exposed them and their institutions. As Vasudevan (2013: 10) has correctly argued, therefore, 'the LIBOR scandal is not about risky bets or bad judgment of rogue traders, but the deliberate strangling of market forces in the pursuit of profits'.

In sum, the events of the past six to seven years have broadly bolstered, and provided repeated substantiation of, the disproportionate significance of a small number of vast transnational financial institutions now considered TBTF; and in so doing, have supplied an ever-expanding list of reasons to ask: whatever did happen to the financial 'markets' of lore, those hallowed spaces of anonymity, competition, and disciplined price-taking? The extraordinary power of TBTF banks is indicative of a contemporary political economy of money and finance far removed from that envisioned by the discourse of market discipline. And so, too, we shall now see, is the transformed role not of commercial but of central banks.

3.3 CENTRAL BANK-LED CAPITALISM?

The core of the argument to be developed in this section is that the power and significance of central banks has been amplified no less than that of commercial banks since the onset of the GFC. In particular, central banks' relation to financial markets has transformed beyond recognition, and understanding this specific transformation is critical to understanding the political economy of money and finance today.

This is not to suggest, however, that central banks were somehow feeble, powerless creatures before the crisis began. Clearly, they were not. In fact in some respects they were, and still are, among the most powerful of capitalist institutions. Mann (2013) has made this case especially forcefully, figuring money as 'the decisive exception in capitalist liberal democracy' – 'the domain of absolute, non-democratic sovereign authority' – and 'independent' monetary authorities as, in turn, the Leviathan-like figures presiding over this exceptional domain, wielding 'virtually unaccountable power' in the process (Mann, 2013: 199). Monetary authority in capitalism, Mann avers, simply 'can never be "democratic"' (Mann, 2013: 202). Not only that, but this authority is far from free-floating, abstracted as it were from the complex social relations through which capitalism is daily constituted and reconstituted. Rather, it is authority rooted in social place, its location unambiguously signalled by Mann's reference to 'the virtually complete capture of central bank control and monetary policy decision-making by one class fraction: finance capital' (Mann, 2013: 205).

The starting-point for the following discussion, then, is not that central banks somehow lacked power pre-crisis, but that this power, and the roles through which it was exercised, was altogether more circumscribed and discrete than it has now become. We have already noted in the introduction that central banks, with their OMOs, tended to be episodic venturers into financial markets as opposed to a core, constant presence. Equally, the dual mandates – vis-à-vis monetary policy and financial stability respectively – widely bestowed on these banks were typically seen to be, and in practice usually were, separate and separable. The former, generally one of explicit inflation targeting or – in the case of the US Fed – de facto inflation control, was, moreover, privileged over the latter. This privileging of a relatively narrow, nominally-technocratic concern with price stability was critical to enabling central banks to maintain their independence – or, at the very least, the impression thereof – from the state.

All of this, however, has now, demonstrably, changed, for all of the world's major western central banks, the Bank of England, the Fed, and the European Central Bank (ECB) included. Since it is with the case of the Fed that these changes are most visible (and arguably, given the significance of that case, most material for the global political economy), the Fed will be our primary focus for the remainder of this section.

If there is one learning above all that it is crucial to take away from this discussion, it is that the Fed's role transformed during the course of the GFC – transforming, in the process, its own relation to other institutional forces. Mehrling (2011) provides the definitive account of what this transformation entailed. In the early months of the crisis, Mehrling shows, the Fed essentially fulfilled its traditional function in regard to financial stability, that is, that of acting as lender of last resort. Selling Treasury bills to fund this expanded lending, the Fed implemented it through extensions (for example, the Term Auction Facility, instituted in December 2007) of the standard discount facility through which it lends to eligible financial institutions, and facilitated it by 'accepting a wider selection of collateral from a wider selection of counterparties' (Mehrling, 2011: 121). So far, so un-extraordinary.

Subsequent to the collapse of Lehman, however, the Fed's role began to change, ultimately beyond all recognition. For one thing, to finance an even greater expansion in lending, it was required to borrow heavily from member banks, and began paying interest on reserves for the first time. But more significantly, according to Mehrling, the rapid doubling in the size of its balance sheet precipitated by this expansion entailed the Fed transitioning away from its circumscribed historic role of last-resort lender. Now, says Mehrling, it was acting as 'dealer' of last resort, 'in effect taking the collapsing wholesale money market onto its own balance sheet' (Mehrling, 2011: 122–123). As opposed to just supporting broker-dealers by lending to them, it had begun implicitly to usurp their functionality. In the process, rather than merely lending freely – the last-resort role prescribed to central banks by the traditional doyen of central banking theory, Walter Bagehot – the Fed was effectively now *insuring* freely.

To appreciate the significance and novelty of this insurance function, it is particularly important to recognize how and where the scope of the Fed's intervention changed during the course of 2009 in particular. Having initially restricted its interventions to the money markets, from March 2009 it expanded its dealings to the capital markets, firstly with the opening of the Term Asset-Backed Securities Loan Facility, and then through direct purchase of mortgage-backed securities backed by the government-sponsored enterprises Fannie Mae and Freddie Mac. As newly-installed dealer of last resort in the capital markets, claims Mehrling, what the Fed was insuring was not so much 'the payments that the debtor had promised to make but rather the market value of the promise itself' (Mehrling, 2011: 134).

This, needless to say, represents something of a leap from the conventional, pre-crisis norms of central banking, when, as Mann (2010: 610) puts it, the rote activity of inflation targeting 'uses interest rates like a thermostat, heating up or cooling down economic activity to maintain the inflation target'. A useful way to express the leap might be like this: from a predominant concern with the value of money, and with the potential for inflation to destroy that value, the Fed had arrived at a concern with the value of a wide range of markets denominated in such money. In short, and extending Mehrling's concept of dealership, we might say that the Fed was now the principal backstop for the ongoing circulation of (financial) capital: there is, after all, little point in insuring payments if the value of the markets in which those payments are made flesh is itself uninsured. And, as intimated, this trend was not just about the Fed, even if the latter was its primary exhibit. The Bank of England, ECB and Bank of Japan have all made market investments on an unprecedented scale in recent years. Indeed, describing these investors – not insignificantly, given our framing concept for this chapter of price signalling-based market discipline – as 'insensitive to prices and fundamentals when purchasing', a representative of BNP Paribas (Craig, 2014) recently reported that central banks had become 'the most important players in each of the world's four largest bond markets'. Not for nothing, then, do Bowman et al. (2013), in observing such developments go so far as to speak of the post-crisis conjuncture as potentially one of 'central bank-led capitalism'.

While this may be to overstate the case, it is nonetheless clear that the role of the Fed, in particular, now extends well beyond its erstwhile remit. As well as taking markets onto its balance sheet, it has also incorporated them – more officially – into its legislative fiat, being assigned new powers and responsibilities by Dodd–Frank, specifically in the area of so-called macroprudential policy (MPP) and specifically in relation to supervision of what the Treasury calls 'systemically important financial institutions' (that is, TBTF banks). Designed to safeguard the 'safety and soundness of the broad financial system and payments mechanism' (Baker, 2013: 114), MPP starts from the premise that the microprudential approach of endeavouring to make individual institutions (all) safe does not necessarily make the system as a whole safe.

Giving the Fed responsibility in this area was at one level simply to broaden and generalize its financial stability function. But it is hard to imagine that it will not have more far-reaching consequences. As Goodhart (2015) argues, it seems unlikely, for example, that the Fed will be able to retain its vigorously defended role/image of a merely technocratic agency charged with merely technical issues (such as operation of the aforementioned thermostat). Even if the Fed were minded to 'segment the policy area of MPP from that of its "core business" of monetary policy', Goodhart suggests, such a notional divide would surely prove untenable in a world where monetary policy and financial risk are not only increasingly interrelated but 'increasingly seen as inter-related'. 'As interest rates fall', notes Goodhart by way of example,

> individuals undertake a "search for yield." The sources of that yield may contribute to risk in ways that are not visible to market participants and not priced into assets, setting the scene for higher overall risk and financial crises. Given the potential link between interest rates and systemic risk, the Fed cannot operate monetary policy solely with an eye on inflation. (Goodhart, 2015: 23)

Nor, of course, can other 'independent' central banks. The fact that such banks increasingly 'have to care about the management of risk in the financial sector and the indicators of systemic risk, *even when deciding monetary policy*' (Goodhart, 2015: 23; emphasis added) has been palpably plain to the Bank of England, for instance, for several years. And the risk is not restricted to the financial sector, either. It is widely acknowledged that historically low interest rates have contributed to a robust, debt-fuelled post-crisis recovery in UK house prices which, at the time of this writing, shows few signs of abating. So, while the work of the Bank's interest-rate-setting Monetary Policy Committee is theoretically separate from that of its own newly-minted MPP arm (the Financial Policy Committee), with the two committees required merely to 'consider the policies of each other in discharging their responsibilities' (Tucker et al., 2013: 197), it is inconceivable that the risks related to housing markets and housing finance are not central to contemporary UK monetary policymaking. The Bank's governor essentially confessed as much when suggesting, in July 2014, that the Bank 'would be risking a dangerous housing bubble and a return to recession if it left interest rates at an all-time low for too long' (Monaghan, 2014). Yet this admission arguably amounts to (gesturing at) closing the stable door after the horse has bolted, and also elides the unspoken, maybe greater, risk associated with the alternative course of action – that of a dangerous housing crash, and perhaps also a return to recession, if and when interest rates are raised.

Central banks, this is all to argue, now find themselves at the very kernel of decision-making in respect of both monetary and financial political economy, charged with powers which, if difficult comfortably to reconcile in theory, will be harder still to co-negotiate in practice. What these tensions bring to the fore perhaps most forcefully of all, of course, is the political in political economy. If it was generally feasible prior to the crisis to figure the technocratic work of conventional monetary policymaking as being extra-political – a figuring which always defied the reality that capitalist money, and the governance thereof, is political to the very core (Mann, 2013) – then such a figuring seems altogether more challenging today. It would take some doing to persuade electorates that the housing sector and management of the risks associated with its financing is a merely 'technical' matter. Likewise the financial sector and its own systemic risk properties. As Goodhart (2015: 3) argues, for example, there are good reasons to doubt the ability of a Fed systematically fulfilling its MPP remit to maintain comfortable arm's-length autonomy from government, if only because MPP requires banks to hold additional equity capital, banks regard this as excessively costly, and those same banks – as we know – are well-positioned to lobby for political support. Hence, 'robust operation of the new mandate carries the potential for conflict'.

But this particular inflection on relations between, on the one hand, central banks now occupying an even more pivotal position in political economies of money and finance and, on the other, states, barely scratches the surface of a much deeper and wider set of issues: namely, the role of states per se in those post-crisis political economies, in relation not just to central banks but to other sets of institutional forces. If the crisis and post-crisis years have seemingly shunted markets and market forces into the background as banks of all varieties have become preeminent dealers and discipliners, where do states fit into this picture? And, given the state's spatial boundedness, with what geographical implications? These are the questions we turn to now.

3.4 THE REASSERTION OF THE STATE IN THE POLITICAL ECONOMY OF MONEY AND FINANCE

Under capitalism the state has always been intimately bound up with finance capital; and money has always been the most powerful expression of this coupling. As Mann (2013), following Ingham (2004), has observed, the very fact that both states and commercial banks create money (itself always a social relation of credit and debt), and that we neither can nor need to tell such monies apart, indelibly links the two constituencies. 'The co-circulation – and, more importantly, the indistinguishability – of privately and publicly issued debt money in modern capitalism is evidence of the complex interdependence of the state and the banking system', Mann (2013: 201) writes. Central banks exist right at this interface, occupying the resultant 'space of exception' alluded to earlier, wherein and whereby 'both the state and finance capital realise their political power' (Mann, 2013: 203). There is, moreover, one especially salient quality of the state that requires highlighting, not least because it helps explain finance capital's willingness to join forces monetarily: the fact that it is a *territorial* state with sovereign spatial power.

The decades leading up to the GFC, however, which is to say the decades of ascendance of the political economy and philosophy of neoliberalism, saw a measure of decoupling where the state-finance capital axis is concerned. To be sure, the extent of this decoupling can all too easily be overstated; neoliberalism, we now realize, was never really about the withdrawal of the state from markets (Panitch and Konings, 2009), and the speech marks put around the word 'independence' in relation to central banks – here as elsewhere – are not simply decorative. Yet, trusting in the efficiency of financial markets in particular, including disciplining finance capital-qua-institutions, states did seek to limit their supervisory role to, for instance, ensuring smooth flows of information. Perhaps more importantly still, there was a distinctive geographical decoupling occasioned by banks' increasing willingness to grow their exposure to foreign sovereign debt. In Europe, for example, Dutch, Belgian and Danish banks had all increased the share of foreign government debt in their sovereign bond portfolios to close to or above 70 per cent by the time that the sovereign debt crisis hit Europe (Gabor, 2012: 20). In the era of global market hegemony and its flat-world invocations, sovereigns and banks, the state and finance capital, had begun to drift apart – spatially as much as institutionally.

The GFC and its aftermath, though, have summarily arrested this trend. States, the rest of this section will suggest, are once again at the very epicentre of the dynamic geographical political economy of money and finance. Not only that, but the response to the crisis has frequently entailed states re-coupling with finance capital (or vice versa), albeit rarely seamlessly or entirely unproblematically.

The forceful reassertion of the state in the financial and monetary political economy was evident first of all at the height of the crisis itself, and in the forms and terms of its governance. Consider the advice that survivors of previous systematic banking failures gave to the US and the UK on rescuing their effectively insolvent financial institutions. 'Recapitalise and do it now was the lesson', but *not* through central banks. Rather: 'Recapitalisation requires a fiscal response, and that can be done only by governments' (King, 2008: 4). Yet, bank nationalization was only the most vivid expression of the state's active, multi-pronged intervention. Indeed, the vast majority of readings of the governance of the GFC, from, as Langley (2014) observes, left *and* right, posit such governance as in large part a matter of the state – for good or ill – saving capitalist markets from themselves. Helleiner's (2014: 19) reading, self-consciously 'state-centric' and focused as such on 'power and politics among and within influential states', is in many respects emblematic.

Langley's own (2014) study of the GFC's governance stands out for avowedly departing from this narrative, and demands discussion here precisely in view of this. For Langley, understanding the governance of the crisis requires, above all, understanding how it was rendered governable – as, he demonstrates, a series of relatively discrete problem-objects (e.g. liquidity, solvency, toxicity, and so forth). The resulting 'apparatuses of governance' certainly featured sovereign state institutions, Langley accepts, but they were not reducible to them; they (the apparatuses) entailed substantive transformations of sovereign techniques (monetary, financial, and regulatory); and the agency 'behind' those apparatuses was, he submits (pace Foucault), 'decentred and distributed, relational and compounded'. And yet, for all the sophistication of Langley's theoretical setup, and for all the undoubted truth in the fact that understanding the crisis does require an appreciation of how it was rendered governable, doing so does not – on this author's reading, both of the crisis and of Langley's book – ultimately require us to decentre the state, even if sovereign techniques were, indeed, transformed. Indeed if one thing leaps consistently out at the reader of the various chapters in which Langley recounts, painstakingly and compellingly, the figuring and 'fixing' of the crisis's various problem-objects, it is, perversely, the state's unwavering centrality: it looms larger than ever throughout.

That the nation-state has been central to the reconfiguration of global finance after the crisis has, unsurprisingly, had significant implications for the nature and extent of that reconfiguration. Aside from a small number of measures agreed and actioned at the international level, such as the (highly diluted) Basel III standards on capital adequacy, most regulatory and supervisory oversight remains national, and it has therefore fallen to states and their regulatory arms to try to effect change from within. In a world, however, where major transnational financial institutions are only too happy to engage in regulatory arbitrage, or at least to threaten to do so, the pressures militating against forceful, widespread reregulation are only too obvious (Rixen, 2013). 'National laws and authorities continue to dominate', observes Donnelly (2014: 981), 'with negative effects on financial stability'.

While Donnelly's concern relates specifically to stability (or the perceived lack thereof) in the banking sector, and to the state's limited ability and/or willingness to redress this situation, the GFC, in Europe at any rate, was ultimately a crisis in the finances of states themselves as much as of banks (though it is important to recognize that in some, if not all, countries, crisis in the latter played a major role in fomenting crisis in the former). One particular dimension of the crisis-related rebuilding and attempted stabilization of state finances calls for particular attention here, since it highlights precisely the geographically bounded re-coupling dynamics foregrounded above – between states on the one hand and banks, central and commercial, on the other.

Bowman et al. (2013: 470–471) usefully collate data attesting to central bank-led re-coupling. They do so for the US and the UK. For the former, they report on the 'long-position on the U.S. government' rapidly accumulated by the Fed through purchases of US government bonds. For the UK they describe a similar trend and provide striking data: of the £291.7 billion of assets acquired by the Bank of England through its specially-created Asset Purchase Facility through to March 2012, 99.9 per cent – that is, all but £400 million of corporate bonds – represented UK government bonds.

If private finance capital's geographical realignment with sovereign states has been less pronounced than this, it is no less material from a geographical political economy perspective. For, where Europeans banks' collateral management strategies had seen them increase their holdings of foreign government debt in the years leading up to the crisis, the crisis and its aftermath triggered a reversal in the form of a retreat to the domestic sphere. Beginning in 2011, there has been a marked and progressive re-domestication of private sovereign-debt holdings, particularly in those countries where international markets were seen to apply most pressure (Gabor, 2012): in the first half of 2013, Spanish banks absorbed 60 per cent of their government's net debt issuance, with the comparative figure even higher, at 75 per cent, in Italy (Unmack, 2013). With the disciplinary dictates of the international financial markets – buttressed, it is fair to say, by state and quasi-state dictates from Berlin and Brussels (Watkins, 2013) – deemed unbearable politically as well as economically, such states abruptly fell back on the 'memorable alliance' between state and (domestic) finance capital that Mann (2013) delineates, and which had been eroding somewhat during the decades beforehand.

Yet this reversion has, of course, been anything but unproblematic. And, as much as anything else, the problems encountered in countries such as Italy and Spain relate to the necessarily partial nature of this rejoining. Yes, state and finance capital have been increasingly yoked together at the national scale, but the one dimension in which such yoking has been denied is the crucial one which underpinned the historic alliance in the first place: money, and the indistinguishability of territorialized state/bank variants. To stress nationally oriented re-couplings in the wake of the crisis is, in the context of the euro and the euro area, to risk underplaying the manifold significance of that area's *extra*-national monetary framing. Blyth (2014: 249–50; original emphasis) spells out the materiality of this particular scalar incongruence:

> the Eurozone periphery is in an austerity-induced depression precisely because of the material reality of these economies being *national* economies deprived of their own printing presses. Unable to act as a national state and yet being required to bear the costs of one, they cannot inflate or devalue: all they can do is deflate internally, with very material consequences. Their bond markets are *national* markets with *national* yield spikes paid by *national* publics. Their labor markets are *national* labor markets with *national* unemployment rates.

The situation looks very different, of course, for states generating surpluses as opposed to running deficits, and especially those backed by their own currencies. We will end our discussion in this section by considering the significance of the small subset of such states which have historically concentrated surpluses into so-called 'sovereign wealth funds' (SWFs) that proceed to invest those sovereign assets in private financial markets around the world: the likes of China (with the China Investment Corporation), the Gulf States (the Gulf States' Funds), Norway (the Government Pension Fund-Global) and Singapore (Government of Singapore Investment Corporation). These SWFs are increasingly integral to the contemporary geographical political economy of money and finance.

For one thing, and at the most generic level, they arguably represent something of a blurring of the traditional lines between the state on the one hand and finance capital – understood as a class fraction – on the other. The state, here, effectively wields its own public finance-capital arm. Thus, if, as we just noted, the post-crisis period has seen states and finance capitals re-coupling geographically in parts of southern Europe, elsewhere they had already done so – SWFs are not new, even if their profile has risen dramatically over the past decade – albeit in markedly different ways and with different ends in mind.

SWFs are also demonstrably pivotal, moreover, to a major feature of today's global political economy which, as explained in the introduction, has not been explicitly dealt with in this chapter, but which demands brief mention here nonetheless. This is the question of global imbalances, with non-western surpluses counterbalancing, funding and maintaining western (and especially) US current account deficits. SWFs are clearly not responsible for such imbalances, but neither are they merely a passive symptom thereof. By choosing to invest in certain assets issued in certain jurisdictions, they serve to maintain the imbalances in question (Gieve, 2009).

Third, SWFs also played an important though often overlooked role in recent crisis 'management'. We have discussed above the fact that recapitalization of insolvent financial institutions was generally seen to demand a fiscal response in the shape of government investment, but, crucially, the state which stepped in to provide such support was not always the domestic state. As Gieve (2009: 170) notes, at least four major Anglo-American banks – Barclays, Citigroup, Merrill Lynch and Morgan Stanley – received substantial injections of foreign SWF financing in 2007 and 2008. They did so in some cases (for example, Barclays), furthermore, specifically to avoid having to rely on nationalization by domestic governments for survival, finding external state funding preferable politically as well as financially. This, in itself, makes SWFs an important object of study within post-crisis geographical political economy.

Above all else, however, and encompassing all of these various dimensions, SWFs are significant for embodying especially vividly the principal wider development that this section of the chapter has sought to emphasize: that is, the re-emergence of the state as a key actor in contemporary finance, as the hegemony of the disciplinary market appears to have somewhat faded. As Clark et al. (2013: 4) comment, SWFs 'offer states an opportunity to reassert their sovereignty and authority over the hegemonic forces of global capitalism'. Their method for doing so, of course, is, as Clark et al. also acknowledge, rather ironic – exploiting (or at least, relying upon) international financial markets precisely to insulate themselves from exposure to market vagaries, such funds representing, in part, 'tools for managing imminent and future crises' (Clark et al., 2013: 26). Yet this does not gainsay the fundamental point: SWFs can be seen as 'representatives of the global transformation of nation-state economic prospects over the past decade and the next fifty years' (Clark et al., 2013: xiii) – or of, at any rate, the transformation of the prospects of some, very important states. Active manifestations of *national*, *state* power (both words warranting emphasis), SWFs symbolize a world far removed from the borderless plane of passive price-taking figured by the discourse of market discipline with which we began.

3.5 CONCLUSION

The idea of market discipline, as we saw in the introduction, was and is very much an idea of neoliberal ilk. It places markets on a pedestal as supreme processors of information and posits that those institutions required or desiring to regulate or participate in markets can be viewed as subordinate *to* the market accordingly. In the context of financial markets, the implications were clear and not infrequently spelled out. Banks could try all they liked to dominate markets but competition would prevail. And states could safely step back from micro-management of markets since markets and the competition occurring in them, if not quite coercing individual (finance) capitals in the manner famously illuminated by Marx, were certainly robust and efficient enough to discipline them and thus keep them in their place.

This picture was always something of a caricature, of course, and the events of the recent crisis and 'post-crisis' years have demonstrated as much. States invariably played a more active role than the above gloss allowed. Banking has always had oligopolistic tendencies, which indeed have often been politically encouraged given concerns about financial instability in the event of 'excess' competition (Christophers, 2013); the active market (for example, interest rate benchmark) manipulations surfaced in investigations conducted since the crisis, moreover, were clearly in many cases present before the crisis, too. And the work of central banks has always been much more central to the political economy of money and finance than the notion of an 'independent', technocratic thermostat tinkerer suggests.

Be this as it may, however, the picture of market discipline and its attendant connotations was truer before the crisis than it is now. The crisis, and everything that has come in its aftermath, has indubitably deepened the materiality of banks – central and commercial – and states vis-à-vis markets. This, note, does not necessarily mean that states have become more powerful within the monetary and financial political economy; it means simply that their relevance, in all manner of dimensions, has been reanimated. These various reconfigurations, furthermore, have been fundamentally geographical reconfigurations, as the significance of more nationally oriented institutions has resurfaced in conjunction with a dampening of the predominance, if not the pervasiveness, of – in the shape of markets – more transnational ones.

Going forward, geographers and geographies of money and finance and of their political economies will have to grapple repeatedly with such reconfigurations. The latter are unlikely to become any less dynamic and consequential; the ways in which they work themselves out will have major implications for capitalist political economy more broadly, not least its potential for irruptions of the type which we have seen in the recent past. If, in relation to money and finance, we are to understand power and its geographies and – more ambitiously – to speak the truth to it, then understanding these reconfigurations will be essential. Power morphs, but it does not dissipate. If the world has indeed moved 'beyond' market discipline, then who or what, we must ask, is doing the disciplining now?

REFERENCES

Antill, S., D. Hou and A. Sarkar (2014), 'Components of US financial sector growth, 1950–2013', *Economic Policy Review*, **20** (2), 59–83.

Ashton, P. and B. Christophers (2015), 'On arbitration, arbitrage and arbitrariness in financial markets and their governance: unpacking LIBOR and the LIBOR scandal', *Economy and Society*, **44**, 188–217.

Baker, A. (2013), 'The new political economy of the macroprudential ideational shift', *New Political Economy*, **18**, 112–139.

Bieling, H. (2014), 'Shattered expectations: the defeat of European ambitions of global financial reform', *Journal of European Public Policy*, **21**, 346–366.

Blyth, M. (2014), 'A curious case of caveats and causes: some thoughts on the causal story of banking across boundaries', *Environment and Planning A*, **46**, 245–250.

Boot, A. and A. Thakor (1997), 'Financial system architecture', *Review of Financial Studies*, **10**, 693–733.

Bowman, A., I. Erturk, J. Froud, S. Johal, A. Leaver, M. Moran, M. and K. Williams (2013), 'Central bank-led capitalism?', *Seattle University Law Review*, **36**, 455–487.

Christophers, B. (2013), 'Banking and competition in exceptional times', *Seattle University Law Review*, **36**, 563–576.

Clark, G., A. Dixon and A. Monk (2013), *Sovereign Wealth Funds: Legitimacy, Governance, and Global Power*, Princeton, NJ: Princeton University Press.

Coffee, J. (2011), 'The political economy of Dodd–Frank: why financial reform tends to be frustrated and systemic risk perpetuated', *Cornell Law Review*, **97**, 1019–1082.

Craig, A. (2014), 'A new era in bond and currency markets'. Retrieved in October 2014 from www.bnpparibas-ip.com/central/insights-and-ideas/investment-ideas/20140224_prespectives-new-era-bond.page?l=eng&p=IP_XX-NSG.

Crockett, A. (2001), 'Market discipline and financial stability. Speech by Andrew Crockett, General Manager of the Bank for International Settlements and Chairman of the Financial Stability Forum, at the Banks and systemic risk conference, Bank of England, London, 23–25 May 2001'. Retrieved in August 2014 from www.bis.org/speeches/sp010523.htm.

Donnelly, S. (2014), 'Power politics and the undersupply of financial stability in Europe', *Review of International Political Economy*, **21** (4), 980–1005.

Friedman, T. (2007), *The World is Flat: The Globalized World in the Twenty-first Century*, London: Penguin.

FSB (2013), '2013 update of group of global systemically important banks'. Retrieved in May 2014 from www.financialstabilityboard.org/publications/r_131111.pdf.

Gabor, D. (2012), 'The power of collateral: the ECB and bank funding strategies in crisis'. Retrieved on 1 November 2016 from https://ssrn.com/abstract=2062315 or http://dx.doi.org/10.2139/ssrn.2062315.

Gieve, J. (2009), 'Sovereign wealth funds and global imbalances', *Revue d'économie financière* (English edition), **9**, 163–177.

Goodhart, L. (2015), 'Brave new world? Macro-prudential policy and the new political economy of the federal reserve', *Review of International Political Economy*, **22** (2), 280–310.

Helleiner, E. (2014), *The Status Quo Financial Crisis: Global Financial Governance after the 2008 Meltdown*, New York: Oxford University Press.

Ingham, G. (2004), *The Nature of Money*, Cambridge: Polity Press.

Irwin, N. (2012), 'AIG to America: thanks, guys!', *The Washington Post*, 31 December.

Kane, E. (2012), 'Missing elements in US financial reform: a Kübler-Ross interpretation of the inadequacy of the Dodd–Frank Act', *Journal of Banking and Finance*, **36**, 654–661.
King, M. (2008), 'Speech given by Mervyn King, Governor of the Bank of England, to the CBI, Institute of Directors, Leeds Chamber of Commerce and Yorkshire Forward at the Royal Armouries, Leeds, 21 October 2008'. Retrieved in October 2014 from www.bankofengland.co.uk/archive/Documents/historicpubs/speeches/2008/speech362.pdf.
Lall, R. (2012), 'From failure to failure: the politics of international banking regulation', *Review of International Political Economy*, **19**, 609–638.
Lane, T. (1993), 'Market discipline', *Staff Papers – International Monetary Fund*, **40** (1), 53–88.
Langley, P. (2014), *Liquidity Lost: The Governance of the Global Financial Crisis*, Oxford: Oxford University Press.
Macartney, H. (2014), 'From Merlin to Oz: the strange case of failed lending targets in the UK', *Review of International Political Economy*, **21**, 820–846.
Mann, G. (2010), 'Hobbes' redoubt? Toward a geography of monetary policy', *Progress in Human Geography*, **34**, 601–625.
Mann, G. (2013), 'The monetary exception: labour, distribution and money in capitalism', *Capital & Class*, **37**, 197–216.
McKeen-Edwards, H. and T. Porter (2013), *Transnational Financial Associations and the Governance of Global Finance: Assembling Wealth and Power*, London: Routledge.
Mehrling, P. (2011), *The New Lombard Street: How the Fed Became the Dealer of Last Resort*, Princeton, NJ: Princeton University Press.
Monaghan, L. (2014), 'Low interest rates now a threat to UK economy, says Mark Carney', *The Guardian*, 23 July.
Panitch, L. and M. Konings (2009), 'Myths of neoliberal deregulation', *New Left Review*, **57** (May/June), 67–83.
Rajan, R. and L. Zingales (2003), 'Banks and markets: the changing character of European finance', NBER Working Paper 9595. Retrieved in August 2014 from www.nber.org/papers/w9595.pdf.
Rixen, T. (2013), 'Why reregulation after the crisis is feeble: shadow banking, offshore financial centers, and jurisdictional competition', *Regulation & Governance*, **7**, 435–459.
Roach, S. (2013), 'Occupy QE', *Project Syndicate*, 25 September. Retrieved in June 2014 from www.project-syndicate.org/commentary/how-quantitative-easing-exacerbates-inequality-by-stephen-s--roach.
Schäfer, D., A. Ross and D. Strauss (2013), 'Foreign exchange: the big fix', *Financial Times*, 12 November.
Schwartz, H. (2014), 'Global imbalances and the international monetary system', in Y. Oatley and W. Winecoff (eds), *Handbook of the International Political Economy of Monetary Relations*, Cheltenham, UK and Northampton, MA, USA: Edward Elgar Publishing, pp. 69–88.
Tucker, P., S. Hall and A. Pattani (2013), 'Macroprudential policy at the Bank of England', *Quarterly Bulletin*, **Q3**, 192–200.
Unmack, N. (2013), '"Home bias" for bonds put euro zone at risk', *International Herald Tribune*, 19 July.
Vasudevan, R. (2013), '"Libor"ing under the market illusion', *Monthly Review*, **64** (8), 1–12.
Watkins, S. (2013), 'Vanity and venality', *London Review of Books*, **35** (16), 17–21.

4. The territorial governance of the financial industry

José Corpataux, Olivier Crevoisier and Thierry Theurillat

4.1 INTRODUCTION

What financial markets 'think' – in terms of sentiments and the movements of major indexes and values – has become a key component of the daily data influencing the economies of countries and regions. The social and economic development and competitiveness of regions and nations depends on bets made on financial markets as well as on the institutionalisation of exit strategies. While becoming increasingly autonomous from the real economy, financial markets have paradoxically gained an increasing control on it. Financial markets have become increasingly remote from everyday life while at the same time profoundly affecting social conditions and environment through the financialisation of State debts, city production (real estate and infrastructure), individual property (house mortgages) and the retirement system (pension funds industry).

This disjunction corresponds to a spatial form, the 'global city', a densely interconnected global network of financial centres where monetary mobility/liquidity occurs and which occupies an overhanging position above other regions, cities, and even nations. Thanks to the 'mobility/liquidity of capital' – described below as the main characteristic of financial markets – large institutional groups and other financial players that make up the 'global city' can organise the economic system from the 'top', along a logic of 'global financial networks' by combining and articulating the various attributes of places (skills, labour costs, tax benefits, weak regulation, low environmental legislation, and so on). The organisation of this integrated space where money can 'freely' circulate has gone along with the compliance of territories to financial criteria. National policy reforms have contributed to the reorientation of a range of institutions (relating to the economic, budgetary, fiscal, monetary, and even environmental spheres) in conformity with the imperatives and evaluations of financial markets. Put differently, policies have helped to increase the power of the 'global city' by shortcutting the traditional national and regional scales where social and economic compromises are elaborated.

Notwithstanding the heterogeneity of degrees of financialisation between countries (French et al., 2011; Engelen et al., 2010; Pike and Pollard, 2010), this chapter develops an interpretative and conceptual framework for understanding the emergence of the finance industry at the heart of the economy over the past three decades. Considering financial markets as institutional and geographical constructs, this framework is based upon a 'territorial approach' to the financialisation of the economy and of regions (Theurillat et al., 2008; Corpataux et al., 2009; Theurillat et al., 2010; Crevoisier and Theurillat, 2011).

First, finance and financialisation are spatial phenomena. The financial system is the main driver of the spatial foundations of capitalism (Harvey, 1982). It enables the circulation of capital between various 'circuits' or economic sectors and is at the origin of the creation of new sources of profits or 'spatio-temporal fixes' that resolve or postpone the crisis tendencies of capitalism. Second, the contemporary finance industry is at the core of the 'financialised accumulation regime' (Aglietta, 1998; Orléan, 1999; Boyer, 2000; Lordon, 2000; Chesnais, 2001) that has risen to the fore over the past three to four decades. Based on liquidity, that is the easy and fast purchase/sale of securities on the financial market, and on financial innovations, this regime has led to an accumulation of capital (or economic growth) that takes place more on financial markets than in the 'real' economy (Corpataux and Crevoisier, 2005). The disjunction of finance with the rest of the economy has to be considered in functional, institutional, time and space terms. Simultaneously, this regime has imposed management criteria that are increasingly based on financial calculation than on the provision of goods and services (Boyer, 2009; Orléan, 2011).

This chapter is divided into four sections. First, at a micro-institutional level, there is a separation between the owners of money (shareholders and fund managers) and firms. Dominant theories in modern finance are based on a financial vision that all but excludes the entrepreneur. This abstract vision of investments and of firms' activities goes along with increasingly complex circuits where opacity still remains despite/because of the involvement of various professional intermediaries. Second, at a macro-institutional scale, there is a hierarchical separation between the three spaces of money collection, of investment and of the global city. Being a space of financial control and innovation, the 'global city' has the power to selectively connect companies, sectors and regions at (very) long distances beyond national borders. Third, these various configurations, fundamentally based on the mobility of capital, are the result of a process of contradictions with the real economy as well as both of increasing autonomy and expansion of the contemporary finance system into the real economy and its geography. Based on the dominant theory of investment advocating diversification, investors make investment decisions on two basic criteria: financial risk and return. This evaluation of the economy by the finance industry has been accompanied by the creation of new financial bubbles and the gradual and selective financialisation of new economic sectors (such as infrastructure and real estate, housing debts, and so on) and of new territories (Eastern European countries, BRICs, and so on) since the mid-1980s. Finally, by systematically comparing the attributes of territories in terms of financial risks and returns and by virtue of the extraordinary fungibility and mobility of money, the finance industry can simply exercise its considerable 'exit power' to escape national or regional restrictions or controls and seek out more profitable opportunities in less intrusive locations. Our aim in this chapter is to explore these developments and their implications, both in terms of how finance has reshaped space and territory and what this reshaping implies for a renewal of theories of the geographies of the financial system.

4.2 CORPORATE GOVERNANCE: A FUNCTIONAL AND SPATIAL SEPARATION OF THE FINANCIAL INVESTOR AND THE ENTREPRENEUR

At a micro-scale, the modern finance industry has involved institutionalising a separation between professional financial investors and investment managers on the one hand, companies and entrepreneurs, on the other, a separation that has become embedded in modern portfolio theory. In this configuration, investors can withdraw their assets from companies, sectors, regions or nations at any time. By systematising the diversification of investments, modern financial institutions encourage a more distant, more abstract, and more opaque relation between investors and the companies and entrepreneurs seeking finance. What is referred to as systems of 'corporate governance' in the literature are attempts to overcome the loss of control by investors of companies which occurs because of this increasing distance and abstraction.

The Building of Capital Mobility/Liquidity: A Conceptual and Historical Approach

With the increasing power of financial markets within contemporary economies and the globalisation of financial flows, relationships between the real and financial spheres have undergone a radical change. Some writers sympathetic to or affiliated with the 'regulationist school' of economics (Aglietta, 1998; Orléan, 1999; Boyer, 2000; Lordon, 2000; Chesnais, 2001) have been quick to herald the arrival of a new financialised accumulation regime based on a financial system which has managed to impose its institutions and operational principles on the rest of the economy and society, and which has superseded the Fordist regime based on mass consumption and production. Under the preceding Fordist accumulation regime, finance was subordinate to productive industrial capital, and mainly took the form of bank credit. Indeed, the transition from administratively managed financial systems to liberalised financial systems (Aglietta, 2008) indicates an increasingly autonomous force at work within contemporary finance. To borrow the regulationists' phrase, finance might even become the 'dominant institutional form controlling the practices and pace of accumulation'.

Let us not forget, however, as Orléan (1999) has pointed out, that what defines financial markets (in contrast with real capital) is their liquidity. Real capital has little or no mobility, and consequently confines those which hold it to the social constraints of spatial proximity and fixity. Liquidity mitigates the risk that capital's immobility carries by giving capital owners the possibility of divesting themselves of their investments at any stage (Orléan, 1999; Lordon, 2000). From a geographical point of view, what is liquidity, if it is not the mobility of the property of securities (Billaudot, 2001) between increasing numbers of players who participate in the expanding space in which securities are traded? The finance industry's creation of capital mobility/liquidity gives investors the ever-available opportunity to withdraw their assets from a given place to immediately invest it elsewhere. Elsewhere is not, however, synonymous with 'anywhere': we remain permanently enclosed within the sphere of financial activities and financialised businesses.

Moreover, to go from real to financial capital, a certain number of transformations are therefore required, transformations which relate to territory (for example, borders, institutions, networks, nodes). First, it is imperative that the control of real capital through securities (equity, shares in funds, and so on) be formalised. The mobility and profitability of these activities is then encouraged by setting up an institutional framework (removal of boundaries, taxation legislation supporting transactions, and so on), technologies (financial markets are amongst the main consumers and promoters of IT and telecoms integration (O'Brien, 1992)) and, of course, specialised agents (finance sector businesses, stock exchanges, specialist media, training and research institutes, brokers, analysts, consultants, and so on). These transformations allow the financialisation of economic activities, that is the continuous evaluation of economic investments by financial markets (Orléan, 1999 and 2011). It becomes possible to compare financialised assets quickly and systematically, as well as to disengage from any part, sphere or space of the economy at very short notice.

During the last 30 years, two types of reforms have been undertaken in most countries in order to promote capital mobility/liquidity. On the one hand there are those reforms which aim to remove regulatory barriers to the free and complete movement of finance capital (for example, the removal of exchange rate controls in the UK in 1979, the partial opening up of the Japanese financial market in 1983–84, the liberalisation of the movement of capital in Europe under the Single European Act), and to thereby encourage the spatial mobility of capital. On the other hand are those reforms which aim to improve the operational and informational efficiency of the financial markets, that is which seek to encourage their liquidity and transparency as well as guaranteeing good quality public information. This is what we have termed the expansion of capital mobility/liquidity (Corpataux and Crevoisier, 2005) since the liberalisation of the movement of capital goes hand in hand with the growth of financial markets and their transactions. This mobility/liquidity has been boosted by a number of factors relating to national legislation and particularly the power of those political and economic actors in a position to lobby for and support these legislative changes: deregulation allowed capital owners to move their assets where they wished, banks to develop business in many places, competition to increase, and the costs of transactions to be lowered. Fiscal rules were redesigned in order to facilitate rapid transactions. For example, in the USA, the 'safety net' which had been implemented in the 1930s to regulate the financial system – after the 1929 stock market crash and the Great Depression – were removed completely throughout the 1990s: the McFadden Act, which prevented banks from expanding in more than one state was abolished in 1994, and the Glass–Steagall Act, which prevented banks from moving their assets into insurance and share-dealing was dismantled in 1999.

As a consequence, the growth of mobility/liquidity has encouraged the hyper-mobility of capital and the ease of exit strategies. According to Dembinski (2008), contemporary finance makes it possible to detach oneself from the issue of timescales, the various parties' commitment and the negotiation of compromises between them. The system allows detachment from these issues whilst selling and collecting capital gains. The multidimensional links which existed between the real and financial spheres during the Fordist era seem to be disintegrating, or at least undergoing a radical reconfiguration. Whatever the case may be, under this new system, investors are focused on financial profitability and are less and less involved in the economic, social and environmental aspects of their investments. Financial markets have therefore been configured so as to ensure exceptional mobility, providing, in governance terms, an exit strategy which has no parallel in the history of capital commitment. Certainly, in principle, entry into the financial market by investors does not exclude an in-depth understanding of businesses and the environments in which investments are made. However, we are arguing in this chapter that the workings of financial markets do not encourage or require a detailed or contextual knowledge of businesses and their backgrounds on the part of individual and institutional investors such as large pension or mutual funds.

Portfolio Theory: An Exclusively Financial Vision (Which Excludes the Entrepreneur)

If the free movement of capital in space and the existence of sufficiently liquid financial markets are essential prerequisites for the finance industry's development, the combination of these possibilities and the trend for portfolio diversification (see Markowitz, 1959) define modern financial theory and practice. In practice, the diversification principle – 'do not put all your eggs in one basket' – means investing in assets that have historically different evolutions, in financial terminology, in statistically non-correlated financial assets. The agent's selection procedure is increasingly down to quantitative, statistical and often automated analysis. Whilst this diversification principle can be seen as a major landmark in contemporary finance, it goes against hitherto-taught rules of financial theory, namely that portfolios should be selected on the basis of the individual risk and return calculations for each share, considered in isolation (Rainelli-Le Montagner, 2003). From a geographical point of view, this traditional principle of prudence comes down to investing your money in those activities and in those places where there are fewest risks over the long term, that is, where there are favourable stability and growth conditions.

Nevertheless, although the diversification principle seems widespread, there are still several investors who refuse to comply with it. Warren Buffett, one of the world's most successful investors of the past 30 years has resolutely avoided this strategy (Sauvage, 1999). Buffett's portfolio shows remarkably little diversification in terms of modern portfolio selection theories. Instead, he continues to invest in a limited number of companies whose 'qualities' he knows intimately and in which he often holds a considerable stake for considerable periods of time. Although his method uses quantitative criteria of good financial management, it does not ignore qualitative considerations linked specifically to the company and its environment. We have to acknowledge here the opposing nature of these two approaches and their underlying philosophy. Buffett maintains a traditional analytical approach. He is primarily focused on companies' long-term profitability (Hagstrom, 2013). This focus takes into consideration a huge range of parameters, amongst which are such issues as corporate structure, management, the competitive environment, demand levels, predicted technological developments, and so on. As Sauvage (1999) observed, Buffett manages a portfolio of industrial holdings rather than a diversified portfolio of stocks and shares.

Conversely, for those who believe in diversified portfolio management and who, moreover, believe in the efficiency of financial markets, qualitative and detailed analysis is considered of little value. Indeed, the most efficient portfolio is one that is viewed as being made up of shares which represent, on a small scale, the market structure, as it is impossible to improve on this without incurring greater risk. Advice from industry professionals and detailed analysis of listed companies are given little weight. To yield the maximum gain from the market, what is needed is a diversified portfolio which mirrors market structure (or a particular segment of the market), taking into account the level of risk which the financial market itself represents.

In short, in portfolio theory, greater attention is paid to the risk a given security represents to the portfolio than is paid to the risk that the security itself represents (Rainelli-Le Montagner, 2003). In other words, what is more important is the degree of correlation between one security and all the others than the security itself. Although this diversification strategy now seems predominant amongst financial players, it does not necessarily help these same players to build up any detailed knowledge of the businesses (or products) in which they are investing.

Increasingly Long and Complex Circuits: The Simultaneous Growth of Transparency and Opacity

Financial players have a basic need for transparency in order to make their calculations and to compare different asset classes to assess their returns and risks. Thus, using information gathered, financiers may compare investments between, say, a Russian mining company and a Swiss chemicals company, or an investment fund made up of a selection of bonds and equity with a real estate fund. Although the definition of transparency is not entirely clear-cut, it is fundamental in keeping the markets operational and liquid. All comparability presupposes, in effect, the permanent creation/construction of *transparency*, that is, comparative data in space which is both standardised and publicly available. Moreover, it is typical of market-oriented financial systems that they do not take into account close bilateral or private relationships, as these are not public and are therefore considered opaque. Varying and often contradictory forces are at play in the finance industry and are, paradoxically, sources of *opacity* for certain players. Such opacity does not encourage players to be either active shareholders or to understand better the businesses and areas in which they are investing.

Three main characteristics epitomise the dynamic of today's financial industry (Corpataux et al., 2009). First, both the increasing mobility/liquidity of capital and the principle of diversification combine to favour the internationalisation of investments. Yet the new countries in which investments are made are often less well known to investors. Second, the emergence of new investment sectors such as real estate or urban infrastructure requires new skills in comparison with those required for traditional industrial investments. Third, in common with most business sectors, finance is also undergoing a process of standardisation of its products/services whilst at the same time these same products/services become ever more innovative/complex.

Indeed, alongside the banks and institutional investors, numerous businesses are now specialising in financial engineering, expert services, rating and auditing. Financial markets require public, external and impartial evaluations based on standardised information. The industry therefore generates its own burgeoning process of development and complexity. The fluctuation between inculcating personal responsibility in each actor and also controlling them (through such notions as accountability or the use of third parties to divest oneself of responsibility (Theurillat et al., 2008)) has led to a proliferation of participants.

In summary, capital mobility/liquidity offers investors the option to pull out (exit) at any time. The implementation and widespread acceptance of the diversification principle have led to an eclectic approach to portfolios, investors, sectors, countries and financial products. The distance (whether geographic, social, technological or otherwise), between investors and the destination of their investment has become ever more stretched, creating complexity and opacity. None of this encourages those who hold capital to develop a detailed knowledge of the businesses and areas in which they are investing. They are increasingly divesting themselves of an entrepreneurial role to take on a 'purely' financial role. In brief, space, and more specifically the distance and overhanging position which is created between the financial investor, at one end of the network, and real activities at the other end, is at the heart of the today's micro-organisation of the economy. Now, let's see how these microstructures correspond to some spatial and economic macrostructure.

4.3 A HIERARCHICAL SPATIAL DIVISION: THE GLOBAL CITY AND THE REST OF THE ECONOMY

What are the spatial forms that correspond to this increasing disjunction between the entrepreneurial and the investment functions? First, the global city appears as the places where the flows of savings are transformed into flows of investment. However, the global city is much more than a mere intermediary. It is also the place where assets are evaluated, where monetary creation occurs, where financial innovations develop and where systemic effects emerge. Upstream, savings flows directly feed the global city, shortcutting traditional local financial centres. Downstream, the headquarters of large listed companies, working in close connection with financial market and players, concentrate in the global city, from where they manage their worldwide network of subsidiaries, usually without transiting through capital cities. Therefore, the traditional regionally-based spaces of accumulation that characterised the development of industrial capitalism are increasingly bypassed, and a fully new geography is emerging.

The Global City as a Space of Capital Governance and Financial Innovation

Finance, especially international finance, is now an activity that is spatially hierarchical, with jobs and decision-making powers more and more concentrated in particular urban regions. Genuine interrelated financial centres, known as the 'global cities' (Sassen, 1991), have emerged, so that local managers in a few major financial centres frequently decide on the geographic distribution of investments worldwide (see Figure 4.1). Being 'innovative and calculative milieux' (Corpataux and Crevoisier, 2016), these 'global cities' have been the sites of major financial innovation, which has accelerated in the era of liberalised finance.

For example, writing 20 years ago Martin and Minns (1995) showed that in the United Kingdom, although savings are collected throughout the nation by pension funds, financial institutions that are based mainly in the southeast of the country and especially in London invest these assets chiefly in the London Stock Exchange and only in listed companies – essentially large companies. Only a small part of these funds is reinvested in other regions of the country. Since the 1990s, the same trend is apparent in Switzerland (Corpataux et al., 2009). Pension savings are collected in a relatively uniform manner throughout the country through the spatial distribution of jobs. Savings are then managed primarily in a largely centralised manner by a few companies that are based in Zurich and Geneva. This centralisation of investment decisions has generated two major changes in investment circuits. First, the proportion of listed securities has increased to the detriment of direct, unlisted, investments, for instance in real estate. Second, portfolios have become increasingly internationalised, first by investments in foreign companies and second by investments in Swiss companies whose activities mostly take place abroad. Consequently, this new configuration favours the internationalisation of investments at the expense of the regions where savings are collected.

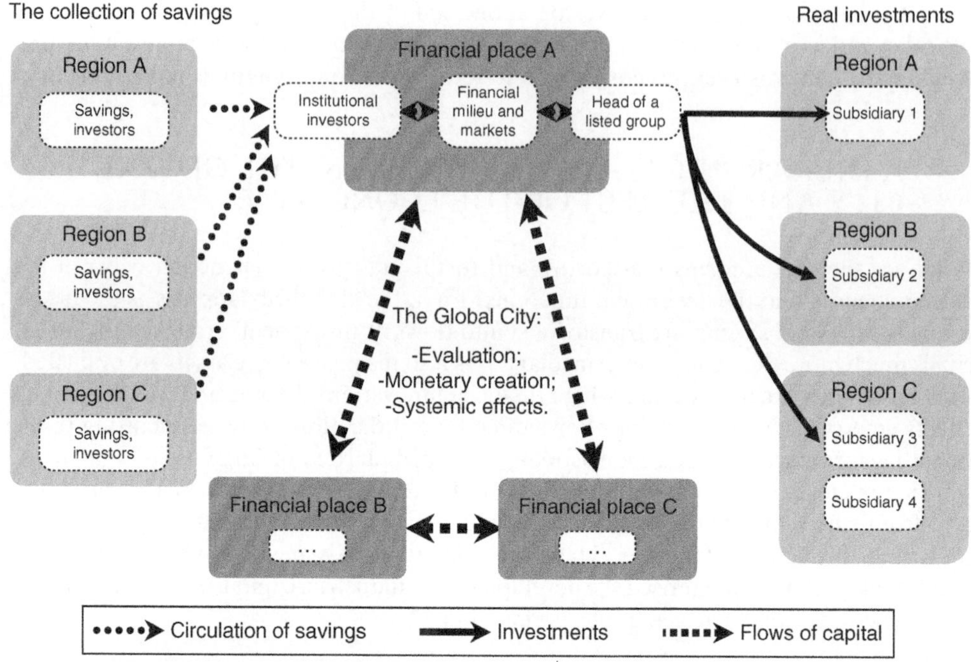

Source: Crevoisier and Theurillat (2011).

Figure 4.1 The spatial separation between savings collection and real investments spaces, and the Global City

In short, financial power is increasingly concentrated in financial markets which operate within the network of 'global cities'. Innovations in the financial sector (securitisation and other new financial products and practices, and so on), the free circulation of capital at a national and international level, and the ability of financial centres to transform companies' real assets into liquid securities for trade on the markets, put the opportunities for investment at an ever greater distance from the centres where the major financial institutions are concentrated. These innovations confer upon such centres a power of spatial arbitrage (Leyshon and Thrift, 1997) between the regional, national and international spaces of investment opportunity.

Not all spaces and actors manage to make close connections with the financial markets. Indeed, contemporary financial investment networks operate on a preferential, selective and hierarchical basis. They include and exclude certain actors, industries and locations, even when these boundaries are not static but constantly evolving. In fact, until recently, the relatively closed nature of national economies, combined with certain forms of regulation, enabled decentralised financial systems to support the various local economies within a nation in a relatively equitable manner. However, the liberalisation of financial systems has driven a process of centralisation and spatial concentration, which in its turn has led to spatial biases and exclusions in the supply of and access to investment and loan funds.

The Disappearance of Traditional Spaces of Accumulation

This process of spatial concentration and centralisation within the financial system brings into question the development and particularly the autonomy of local banking systems. According to Dow (1999), the preference for liquidity is the driving force of the spatial centralisation of financial systems. At the same time, in an increasingly competitive environment, regional banks are being bought out by larger banks, leading to a process of institutional concentration. This reduces regional monetary creation capacity (Dow and Rodriguez-Fuentes, 1997) and local, independent decision-making powers, with local bank branches acting first and foremost as a way of collecting savings which then find their way upwards and towards a nation's primary financial centre(s) (Crevoisier, 2001). Ultimately, these various elements are intensifying the stratification between 'global cities' and other regions.

This substantial change in financial channels and flows presents both places and companies with very different situations. For some, access to capital is made easier; for others, it becomes more difficult. Broadly speaking, we have on the one hand SMEs unable to access financial industry resources (Dow, 1999; Pollard, 2003; Klagge and Martin, 2005; Torrès, 2011) and unable to finance their growth without losing their independence (Crevoisier, 1997; Corpataux and Crevoisier, 2005). On the other hand we have multi-institutional, multinational and multi-local groups whose parent companies are well connected to financial milieux and which are far more able to navigate and access financial markets to raise the funds needed to develop and grow. Moreover, this boundary between large and small firms has shifted considerably as a large number of SMEs have been bought up by the larger, listed groups, a movement which makes them an active part of the financialised accumulation regime (Chabanas, 2002; Crevoisier and Quiquerez, 2005). Other methods, such as IPOs, venture capital and private equity funds, often have the same effect. The centralisation and concentration of financial systems in the global cities is both a consequence and a cause of the extraordinary space–time compression that typifies this new regime.

4.4 FINANCE IN SOCIETY: CONTRADICTIONS AND EXPANSION

Beyond the bounds of the financial industry, what are its effects on the rest of society? For Hall (2013), a large and 'mundane' literature about high finance claims that finance is separate from the real economy while asserting its presence in everyday life. For us, the question should be addressed in a different way: the autonomisation of finance means that it has its own, ever reinforcing internal logic, distinct from the real economy, while at the same time exerting a strong control on it. To address this question, we identify its impact on the rest of the economy in two stages: a finance-specific way of calculating risks and returns; and an extension of these financial criteria to new businesses, industries and nations. This expansion occurs based on a certain number of continuities, and more crucially, on the tensions and contradictions which characterise the way finance works in society.

The Space–Time of the Finance Industry's Calculations: Contradictions with the Real Economy and its Geography

When the finance industry constructs and exploits the mobility/liquidity of capital in space, it invokes specific management principles (the diversification of investments) and criteria (return and risk), with their own time and space patterns. Modern financial theory is based on managing portfolios of assets. But more recently, the goal has been to maximise return and minimise risk and to invest in assets whose evolution is not statistically correlated, as we have discussed above. However, finance is characterised by a particular conception of the notions of returns and risk, which is distinct from that used in the real, non-financialised economy (see Table 4.1). So the use of these management criteria implies specific temporalities and spatialities, which can contradict those of the real economy.

In the real economy, return characterises the accumulation of capital and the control of it over time, that is, in accordance with economic cycles, whether they be short (production cycles for example) or long (such as technological cycles). This accumulation occurs at various levels (business, industry, region, nation) which correspond to the organisation of real production, consumption and exchange. As far as the financial economy is concerned, return is modelled on a *moment-by-moment* comparison basis, monitoring the returns of other financial market investments; the process of financial market evaluation is thus continuous and invariably disconnected from production time (Orléan, 1999 and 2011), and on two levels.

First, the financial industry requires short-term financial performances, thereby dangerously shortening companies' temporal horizons. Indeed, there is a genuine risk of

Table 4.1 Comparison of investment criteria between real and financialised economy

Investment criteria	Real Economy		Financialised Economy	
	Basis of Calculation	Spatial and Temporal Factors	Basis of Calculation	Spatial and Temporal Factors
Return (Yield)	Expected future project returns	Time frame for real project, accumulation, place where project is located	Comparison with market indices (over- or under-performance)	Instantaneous and comparable profitability in a globalised, financialised channel
Risk	Industrial or technological risk or one linked to market for goods and services	Linked to where project takes place	Probability can be calculated and reduced by diversifying among asset classes and between countries where trends are uncorrelated	Creating an area mix with uncorrelated patterns and trends that is financialised

Source: Corpataux et al. (2009).

certain businesses focusing on dividends to shareholders rather than making the investments needed to maintain their innovative capacity over the long term. Financial time and production time can therefore contradict each other.

Second, a commitment to a particular industrial project involving its own specific risks and considerations is replaced by a standardised calculation and securities acquisition transaction. Long-term commitment is therefore replaced by the threat of exit, of short-term defection. Accumulation over time is replaced by mobility in space; the stakeholder is superseded by shareholder value. In the real economy, the entrepreneur's risk is hard to rationalise in the form of a calculation. The entrepreneur is taking a gamble on the future and the future is not perfectly known or knowable. This is what Keynes referred to as 'radical uncertainty'.

In financial theory, the term 'risk' is used to describe situations whose outcome cannot be fully controlled, but for which all the possible exit scenarios are known at the start and to which a probability of each occurring can be assigned, thus enabling the future to be predicted and calculated (Moureau and Rivaud-Danset, 2004). In terms of portfolio assets, the risk can be reduced by diversifying between asset classes and between nations or regions whose returns are not correlated. Diversifying means investing in different sectors, as well, perhaps, in countries with economies at varying levels of development. Diversification means taking a pick-and-mix approach to places and territories.

If the 'real' entrepreneurial risk is not calculable, share prices represent nothing other than the beliefs of financial opinion or 'sentiment'. Which brings us back to Keynes's famous 'beauty contest' analogy: actors do not act in accordance with their own beliefs, but rather in accordance with what they think that others believe. Financial actors can therefore develop increasingly autonomous representations which are increasingly disconnected, and even in stark opposition, to the real economy. From a spatial and sectoral point of view, they can therefore have representations and conventions which a priori rule out certain sectors and regions. Moreover, this mixing up of investments occurs within financialised space. A number of actors, sectors and spaces can therefore become excluded, even when financialised space (for example through globalisation) is expanding (Corpataux and Crevoisier, 2011).

In short, in the real economy, return and risk are understood in relation to the spaces and temporalities of production and economic cycles. The uncertainty around these processes is radical and its probability cannot be calculated. In financial economics, within the financialised sphere of the economy, the return/risk paradigm is like a solution to a problem in a financial engineering exercise which relies upon very specific conceptions of space and time. As the financial community continues to develop its own increasingly distinct investment criteria, representations, and behaviours, so the finance industry takes on a life of its own and develops its hold over the rest of the economy. Indeed, the current era of liberalised and global finance seems to herald a new dynamic of financial expansion, a new 'spatial fix' (Harvey, 1982), by means of which to enhance profits. This expansive drive, however, is what fuels the creation of financial bubbles.

The Permanent Creation of New Financial Bubbles and the Expansion of the Finance Network into the Rest of the Economy

Over the last 25 years, stock market-led finance has followed its own expansionary pattern. A good example of this process is the way in which, after the stock market crash of early 2000, financial actors turned to new, previously neglected sectors such as commodities, gold, oil, and so on or new sectors of the economy, such as real estate or urban infrastructure, which had, until that point, remained more or less outside of the main investment markets. This led to an increase in their stock market value and the gradual financialisation of the economy. The financial markets have subsequently focused on a succession of specific assets and sectors, even specific regions, such as emerging countries. These assets, their selection driven by speculation, are those which most involve the latest innovations within the financial sphere. The way that new actors, sectors and spaces are enrolling in the network seems particularly striking. This expansion of the financial sphere has occurred in two different ways.

One route has been via its increased involvement with household savings. Nowadays, these kinds of savings are, in effect, increasingly 'financialised'. In banking-oriented financial systems individuals would deposit their savings with a bank, which would then replace the savings with bank credits or the value of real estate. Withdrawals were protected through a system of distribution, more often than not guaranteed by the State, and the funds barely entered the financial markets, if at all. However, with the institutionalisation of collective savings (for example through funded pension and other mutual funds), and the accompanying increase in power of institutional investors, an increasingly substantial portion of these funds now enter the financial markets. Furthermore, this attraction of funds has often been facilitated by the periodic 'reformatting' of the legal and regulatory framework, in an attempt to make it more 'malleable' in line with the principles and criteria of the finance industry (for the transformation of the financial institutional framework in Switzerland, see Theurillat et al., 2008).

On the investment side of things, the involvement of financial markets in the real economy also tends to grow. Until recently, fairly large swathes of the economy managed to escape the influence of the financial markets, either because they could function independently or because they were only partially integrated into them. State-run and state-controlled businesses, as well as traditional artisan industries, and a considerable proportion of agriculture, tourism, and SMEs, continued to conduct themselves either entirely or partially according to different principles. As a result of the privatisation of the large public service industries (telecommunication, transport, electricity, and so on) in Europe at the end of the 1980s and throughout the 1990s, there was a sharp increase in the number of business quoted on stock exchanges and subject to their rules.

The upshot has been that the institutionalisation of collective savings has renewed the flow of capital into financial markets and is, in part, responsible for the dramatic growth of the financial industry over the last 30 years or so. At the same time, financial institutions, and governments, have permitted, even encouraged rising levels of household debt, typically secured against property, thereby helping to fuel asset price bubbles in housing markets. The upshot has been that many businesses and areas of activity, and increasing swathes of households, have subject to the calculations and exigencies of financial markets. This process of expansion and subjugation has also been a quintessentially uneven process geographically, both in its dynamics and its implications.

4.5 TODAY'S TERRITORIAL GOVERNANCE OF THE FINANCIAL INDUSTRY

Financial globalisation should be seen as the superimposition of two systems of governance and thus of two geographical systems: a regionally, nationally and internationally based real economy, on the one hand, and a financial economy organised into networks based around the global cities, on the other.

The Systematic Play of Somewhere Else

Real capital (machines, buildings, communication and transport infrastructures, as well as skills, and so on) has little mobility and consequently subjects its owners to the economic and social constraints of proximity. Conversely, the current structures of finance, based on the growth of financial capital mobility/liquidity, mitigates the risk that capital's immobility carries by giving capital owners the possibility of disinvestment at any stage. The growth of mobility/liquidity encourages the systematic play of 'somewhere else'. Add to this the fact that contemporary finance exclusively focuses on notions of risk and return, and we gain a better understanding of why the multidimensional links which existed between the financial and real spheres during the Fordist era have since dissolved. Financial investors are driven to concern themselves purely with financial profitability and to ignore the social and territorial consequences of their actions (Corpataux and Crevoisier, 2011).

If we liken the relationship between a business and those who own capital to a social relationship, what is striking is that in the case of the financial markets and portfolio-style management, this relationship is extremely narrow: all that seems to matter now is financial return and risk. By contrast, the social connection between owners of capital and businesses outside of the financial market always involves other issues: for example, a dependency on skilled labour, on local supplier chains and customers, dealing with environmental impacts of a company's operation, all of which are relatively dependent on place, on local context, at least in the medium term. This disconnection between financial investors and entrepreneurs is thus, in part at least, spatial and territorial in nature. Put simply, one might argue that where there is proximity and spatial fixity, there is less scope for ignoring impact on local or national society. In contrast, creating and exploiting the mobility/liquidity of capital, financial markets make it possible to invest capital over long distances, through complex and opaque circuits, which reduce the identity and the qualities of both investors and actors in the real economy to quantitative notions of financial risk and return.

Financial Globalisation and Short-circuiting the Traditional Scales of Governance

From a spatial point of view, the institutional context of financial globalisation has enabled businesses and financial actors to short-circuit the traditional operational hierarchies of the nation-state economy. According to Yeung (2002), globalisation is usually defined specifically as the capacity of certain actors to operate indiscriminately at various spatial levels. This capacity goes beyond the power to relocate certain operations here or there. It is characterised by the gradual emergence of a new operational level, whereby companies take a global approach to business optimisation, which does not follow the traditional local – national – international route. The global approach short-circuits traditional boundaries and hierarchies, and consequently places and states, not simply by having all places and nations compete against each other, but by pitting, say, the city of Kunming against France, the City of London against the Argentine peso, and so on.

According to Yeung (2002), it is necessary to understand how this hierarchy has developed throughout various periods of history. Over the last 25 years, it is the financial industry which has, to a previously unseen level, presided over the integration of major groups, their subsidiaries and their investors. We are therefore seeing an overlap between two styles of governance with entirely different spatial characteristics. On the one hand, the real economy, with businesses largely dependent on their manufacturing and market situation, has to make concessions to local and national authorities, trade unions, regulations governing working practices, health and safety and environmental regulations, and so on. The degree of mobility is relatively limited. On the other hand, finance, in a leading position thanks to its hyper-mobility and fungibility, and distanciation it has created between investors and businesses, directly connects subsidiaries to listed groups on distant stock markets and formulates its requirements in line with constantly forming speculative cycles.

A Re-examination of Traditional Social and Territorial Compromises

The social and territorial compromises made under the Fordist regime have been fundamentally called into question. Today's configuration works now unquestionably in favour of a few actors and territories and to the detriment of the rest. Effectively, over the last 25 years economic power has shifted to the financial industry, to banks, investment houses, and the managers of stock market listed companies. This can be seen as a reversal of the power relationships between these actors and local and national societies, the latter generally being obliged to subordinate their public policies in areas such as taxation, training and research, the employment market, the environment, and so on to the demands of financial calculation and rating. To put it plainly, due to the development of the financial industry, regions and nations are no longer the driving spaces of capital accumulation. This role has shifted to global financial centres. Yet a company's economic competitiveness can only be partly disassociated from the locations from which it operates. Over the last 25 years, researches into national and regional competitiveness (clusters, innovative milieux, regional production systems, and so on) have demonstrated how important local context and embeddedness can be. In fact, a major determinant of firm competitiveness is the local capacity to articulate the various resources and assets needed for development and innovation. From this point of view, it is not just firms that are competing but also, in a sense, territories. Some survive unscathed, others are put under pressure. From an economic standpoint, it is a matter of (re)producing skills, developing innovation, managing costs, developing infrastructures, and so on. From a social point of view, a harmonious employment situation, social security and so on are all shaped by a local capacity for striking a compromise. Finally, from an environmental point of view, it is local societies that are on the front line with regards the (re)production and sustainability of resources.

These territorial entities are characterised by unique organisations and specialisations which are qualitatively distinct. But at the same time, they are subject to the same non-local quantitative constraint of financial return. How will a form of competitiveness which has a significant local regional and national component be reconciled with businesses which are now mostly stock market listed companies and which cover dozens if not hundreds of sites in very diverse countries, and have ownership structures that can be highly geographically dispersed? This is a tension that now plays a major role in driving the process and pattern of geographically uneven development.

4.6 CONCLUSION

This chapter has sought to provide an integrated view of how market finance has developed during the last 30 years, its effects on the rest of the economy and society, and of how this corresponds to a new specific territorial organisation. How can we describe these forms?

To understand the connection between the real and financial spheres from a geographical perspective, we argue that corporate governance is a spatial construction between both business and financial functions which separates, distances, abstracts and hierarchically stratifies. This governance institutionalises exit strategies (Hirschman, 1970). There is now a clear division between, on the one hand, investors who are primarily concerned with investing, disinvesting and reinvesting their capital, and, on the other hand, business entities which control production and innovation. Distance is the geographical, institutional or social space which now separates the investor and the business person, the business and the territory in which it is based. This distance is made up of the financial relationships between companies, world-scale financial markets and end investors.

And finally, spatial hierarchical organisation goes hand-in-hand with the investors' ever-available opportunity to exit thanks to the liquidity of financial markets. This hierarchy defines on the one hand those tightly-knit central regions known as global cities (Sassen, 1991), and on the other hand a mosaic of territories which are increasingly subject to the management standards of global, liberalised finance. Beyond these specific (dis)connections between real and financial spheres, how can we characterise the overall evolution of the financial and economic system, the evolution of the main theories dealing with it and the corresponding space–time patterns?

In a system where banks act as intermediaries between savings and investment circuits, money can flow in two directions. First, following the neoclassic view, savings are constituted by households and then invested in companies through loans granted by banks. Second, following Keynesian theories, credits originate in agreements between bankers and entrepreneurs and then create deposits; in such a perspective, savings do not induce investment, they only weaken consumption. In one way or in the other, the spatial form of this intermediated system consists in the shortest path from savings to banks and from companies to banks, that is something like a central place pattern.

The so-called dis-intermediation process that started in the 1980s with the liberalisation of the financial sector induced the emergence of a different connection between the spaces of collection of savings and the spaces of investments: the global city. The development of information and communication technologies also played a role allowing banks, stock exchanges and other financial players to be interconnected to remote financial markets. The speeding up of transactions inside this digital space allowed the global city to become increasingly autonomous from 'real' flows. The disjunction between these two spheres is where investors and company top managers no longer focus on what is going on inside companies and on real consumer markets, but on the evolution of share prices on stock markets. Corporate governance theories and practices are the micro-fundamentals of this disjunction.

In short, the emergence of the global city has gone along with other major economic and organisational changes. The emblematic economic players are no longer industrial companies making money by producing and/or selling goods to customers, but headquarters of listed ever-growing holding companies, multinational and transnationals that achieve economic success as much from the attraction of investors – and indeed by engaging in financial activities themselves – as from their production of goods and services. This evolution has also corresponded to an additional step in the secular evolution of the financial system, where the increase in the distance between savings and investments corresponds to a growing centralisation of financial institutions and an increase in liquidity and endogenous money creation capacity (Dow and Rodriguez-Fuentes, 1997). As Dow (1999) has argued, the centralisation of the financial system in national and global cities, a process itself driven by securitisation and globalisation, has simultaneously fuelled a new phase of combined and uneven geographical development, with economic financial and often political power concentrated in and exercised from such cities to the detriment of the regions.

REFERENCES

Aglietta, M. (1998), 'Le capitalisme de demain', Notes de la Fondation Saint-Simon, No. 101, November.

Aglietta, M. (2008), *Macroéconomie Financière*, 5th edition, Paris: La Découverte.

Billaudot, B. (2001), *Régulation et croissance, Une macroéconomie historique et institutionnelle*, Paris: L'Harmattan.

Boyer, R. (2000), 'Is a finance-led growth regime a viable alternative to Fordism? A preliminary analysis', *Economy and Society*, **29** (1), 111–145.

Boyer, R. (2009), 'Feu le régime d'accumulation tiré par la finance', *Revue de la Régulation*, **5**, 2–34.

Chabanas, N. (2002), 'Les entreprises françaises des groupes vues à travers les enquêtes. Liaisons financières de 1980 à 1999', INSEE, Division Synthèse des Statistiques d'Entreprises, E2002-04.

Chesnais, F. (2001), 'La théorie du régime d'accumulation financiarisé: contenu, portée et interrogations', Article presented at the *Forum de la Régulation*, 11–12 October, Paris.

Corpataux, J. and O. Crevoisier (2005), 'Increased capital mobility/liquidity and its repercussions at regional level: some lessons from the experiences of Switzerland and UK', *European and Urban Regional Studies*, **4** (12), 315–334.

Corpataux, J. and O. Crevoisier (2011), 'Gouvernance d'entreprise et mobilité/liquidité du capital: quel ancrage territorial dans une économie financiarisée?', *Géographie, économie, société*, **13**, 387–411.

Corpataux, J. and O. Crevoisier (2016), 'Lost in space: a critical approach to ANT and the social studies of finance', *Progress in Human Geography*, **40** (5), 610–628.

Corpataux, J., O. Crevoisier and T. Theurillat (2009), 'The expansion of the finance industry and its impact on the economy: a territorial approach based on Swiss pension funds', *Economic Geography*, **85** (3), 313–334.

Crevoisier, O. (1997), 'Financing regional endogenous development: the role of proximity capital in the age of globalization', *European Planning Studies*, **5**, 407–415.

Crevoisier, O. (2001), 'Les NTIC, le développement économique et l'espace: quelques enseignements à partir du cas du secteur financier', in L. Vodoz (ed.), *NTIC et les territoires*, Lausanne: Presses polytechniques romandes, pp. 197–210.

Crevoisier, O. and F. Quiquerez (2005), 'Inter-regional corporate ownership and regional autonomy: the case of Switzerland', *Annals of Regional Science*, **39**, 663–689.

Crevoisier, O. and T. Theurillat (2011), 'Les territoires de l'industrie financière: quelles suites à la crise de 2008–2009?', *Revue d'économie industrielle*, **134**, 133–158.

Dembinski, P. (2008), *Finance: Servant or Deceiver Financialization at the Crossroad*, Basingstoke: Palgrave Macmillan: Observatoire de la finance, Geneva.

Dow, S.C. (1999), 'The stages of banking development and the spatial evolution of financial systems', in R. Martin (ed.), *Money and the Space Economy*, New York: John Wiley & Sons, pp. 31–48.

Dow, S.C. and C.J. Rodriguez-Fuentes (1997), 'Regional finance: a survey', *Regional Studies*, **31** (9), 903–920.

Engelen, E., M. Konings and R. Fernandez (2010), 'Geographies of financialization in disarray: the Dutch case in comparative perspective', *Economic Geography*, **86** (1), 53–73.

French, S., A. Leyshon and T. Wainwright (2011), 'Financializing space, spacing financialization', *Progress in Human Geography*, **35** (6), 798–809.

Hagstrom, R.G. (2013), *The Warren Buffet Way*, New York: J. Wiley.

Hall, S. (2013), 'Geographies of money and finance III: financial circuits and the "real economy"', *Progress in Human Geography*, **37** (2), 285–292.

Harvey, D. (1982), *The Limits to Capital*, Chicago, IL: University of Chicago Press.

Hirschman, A. (1970), *Exit, Voice, and Loyalty: Responses to Decline in Firms, Organizations, and States*, Cambridge, MA: Harvard University Press.

Klagge, B. and R. Martin (2005), 'Decentralized versus centralized financial systems: is there a case for local capital markets?', *Journal of Economic Geography*, **5** (4), 387–421.

Leyshon, A. and N.J. Thrift (1997), *Money/Space: Geographies of Monetary Transformation*, London: Routledge.

Lordon, F. (2000), *Fonds de pension, piège à cons? Mirage de la démocratie actionnariale*, Paris: Editions Raisons d'Agir.

Markowitz, H. (1959), *Portfolio Selection: Efficient Diversification of Investments*, London: J. Wiley.

Martin, R. and R. Minns (1995), 'Undermining the financial basis of regions: the spatial structure and implications of the UK pension fund system', *Regional Studies*, **29** (2), 125–144.

Moureau, N. and D. Rivaud-Danset (2004), *L'incertitude dans les théories économiques*, Paris: La Découverte.

O'Brien, R. (1992), *Global Financial Integration: The End of Geography*, London: Royal Institute for International Affairs.

Orléan, A. (1999), *Le pouvoir de la finance*, Paris: Odile Jacob.

Orléan, A. (2011), *L'empire de la valeur: refonder l'économie*, Paris: Seuil.

Pike, A. and J. Pollard (2010), 'Economic geographies of financialization', *Economic Geography*, **86** (1), 29–51.

Pollard, J. (2003), 'Small firm finance and economic geography', *Journal of Economic Geography*, **3** (4), 429–452.

Rainelli-Le Montagner, H. (2003), *Nature et fonctions de la théorie financière*, Paris: PUF.

Sassen, S. (1991), *The Global City*, Princeton, NJ: Princeton University Press.

Sauvage, G. (1999), *Les marchés financiers, Entre hasard et raison: le facteur humain*, Paris: Seuil.

Theurillat, T., J. Corpataux. and O. Crevoisier (2008), 'The impact of institutional investors on corporate governance: a view of Swiss pension funds in a changing financial environment', *Competition and Change*, **12**, 307–327.

Theurillat, T., J. Corpataux and O. Crevoisier (2010), 'Property sector financialisation: the case of Swiss pension funds (1992–2005)', *European and Planning Studies*, **18** (2), 189–212.

Torrès, O. (2011), 'Proxémies financières des PME. Les effets collatéraux de la financiarisation des banques', *Revue française de gestion*, **213**, 189–204.

Yeung, H.W.-C. (2002), 'The limits to globalization theory: a geographic perspective on global economic change', *Economic-Geography*, **78** (3), 285–306.

5. The map and the territory: exploring capital's new financialized spatialities[1]

Dick Bryan, Michael Rafferty and Duncan Wigan

5.1 FINANCE AND SPACE – AN HISTORICAL AND INTELLECTUAL CONTEXT

Former United States Federal Reserve Bank Chairperson, Alan Greenspan, could well be considered the grandfather of the current era of financial markets and financial regulation. His recent book, *The Map and the Territory – Risk, Human Nature and the Future of Forecasting* (Greenspan, 2013) certainly suggests a decidedly spatial agenda, but also one addressing knowledge capacities to traverse that space. The term 'the map and the territory' has become a phrase to differentiate between an abstraction or representation of something (a map), and what is being represented (a territory). In its literary form it is generally traced back to Lewis Carroll[2] and especially Victor Borge.[3] The point of that reference of course is that as with any abstraction there is always a difference between what is being represented and how it is represented.

Having expressed disappointment at the economics profession's inability to foresee the global financial crisis coming (economic forecasting was, as he concluded elsewhere 'mugged by reality'), Greenspan re-gathered his libertarian credentials and now blames the taxation of upper income earners (for eroding national savings potential) and dependence of the poor on welfare for slower rates (crowding out) of innovation and economic growth. But what makes an otherwise banal attempt at reputational repair interesting is that he also revisits earlier comments about innovation and the restructuring of US production (the 'new economy'), in particular the shift toward more service-based, intangible commodities in the world economy. He observes, for instance, that the changing composition of innovation and growth means that the majority of output growth over recent decades has been in intangibles, such that:

> The considerable increase in the economic well-being of most advanced nations in recent decades has come about without much change in the bulk or weight of the gross domestic products. . . . This means that increases in the conceptual component of GDP – that is, those components reflecting advances in real GDP in knowledge and ideas – explain almost all of the rise in real GDP. (Greenspan, 2013: 181)

Intangible assets are a form of abstract property that is increasingly coming to dominate the value of corporations in the leading sectors of the economy, and driving corporate investment. How we monitor this emergent intangible, knowledge economy is a moot point, but it is clear that the old taxonomies and theories are falling short (Oxley et al., 2008). Existing measures designed for a different, and probably simpler, process of production and circulation are looking increasingly obsolete in a world of generalized intangible capital, when a click on a website in say Sydney Australia can generate marketing sales revenues for a corporate entity holding licence rights for intellectual property of a corporation in the Cayman Islands or Ireland, with a lattice of transactions with related firms in a range of other national jurisdictions exercising financing, ownership, revenue, risk and cost sharing arrangements.

Greenspan's book title also alludes to the un-knowability and immeasurability of the changing spatial and temporal scales and speeds of economic and especially financial processes. The point Greenspan is developing here, reprising Hayek's reading of Adam Smith's invisible hand guiding markets, is that the invisible hand is not just a metaphor for collective (and here he now admits sometimes irrational) market practices, but also their complexity, inter-connectedness and thus ultimate un-knowability. Financial markets, he says are 'unredeemably (sic) opaque', and therefore beyond the knowing of individual market participants. Furthermore, the implication for regulators is that they 'can never get more than a glimpse of the internal workings of the simplest of modern financial systems' (Greenspan, 2011). When we talk about shadow banking, off-balance sheet and offshore finance, we are essentially then talking about that opacity: finance that transcends existing regulatory spaces and conceptual forms.

The implication is that even detailed knowledge of the internal operations of financial institutions and markets gives but limited access to how things are working. It requires a formal theoretical framing, but not one so heavy-handed that it pre-determines meanings. This chapter argues that it is indeed important that we are not drawn into predetermined conclusions about the nature of 'globalization' or of 'financialization', for the proposition developed in the chapter is that these processes are playing out in novel, indeterminate ways. Indeed, innovation in finance and corporate organization is blurring older industrial divisions and demarcations,[4] just as offshoreness and shadow banking blurs our conventional spatial and national regulatory taxonomies.

5.2 DIMENSIONS OF CAPITALS' SPATIO-TEMPORALITY

Economic geography, and the social sciences more generally, are not short of spatial concepts and metaphors, from spaces of flows, fixity and motion, plateaus, action at a distance, and space–time compression (Castells, 1996; Brenner, 1998; Harvey, 1990 Latour, 2005; Deleuze and Guattari, 1987).[5] In order to deal with the spatial and temporal implications of developments in finance this chapter uses David Harvey's (1973, 2006) tripartite notion of capitalist spatiality. The chapter uses Harvey's three modalities to address how the transformations wrought by finance have been as much about transforming the spatio-temporal relations of capitalism, as growing/magnifying existing ones. In this sense, the chapter seeks to show that Greenspan's claim to un-knowability can be thought of as not just as a statement about the growing scales of capital's spatiality, but a pointer towards finance's (and therefore capital's) transcendence of certain forms of spatio-temporality.

Harvey provides a tripartite division of the modalities in the way capitalist space and time can be understood:

- absolute,
- relative, and
- relational.[6]

A key to this taxonomy is that the three forms of spatio-temporality open up different forms and levels of abstraction, and that each determines what sorts of attributes and issues are in focus and how. Absolute space (and time) is fixed, geometric and linear where the world is comprised of well-defined properties of time and distance, and can be represented on an immovable (and scaleable) grid. Significantly for our engagement with Greenspan, absolute notions of space permit the production of cartographic maps and engineering practices (that is, measurable and calculable). Absolute time and space was based historically on segmenting the world into time zones and nations (or empires). It was significant, therefore, that the home of time (Greenwich in London) stood above the Admiralty and the slave docks that created colonial production chains.[7]

Relative space is, by contrast, about the different sorts of relations and spatial (and temporal) scales being measured (not just the distance between fixed objects in space per se) but the changing times taken to reach one another in physical or communicative terms. Relative space thus introduces different ways that different spatial attributes measure (map) upon what spatial scales, and this is not independent of time. As Harvey notes of relative space:

> The uniqueness of location and individuation defined by bounded territories in absolute space gives way to a multiplicity of locations that are equi-distant from, say, some central city location. We can create completely different maps of relative locations by differentiating between distances measured in terms of cost, time, modal split (car, bicycle or skateboard) and even disrupt spatial continuities by looking at networks, topological relations (the optimal route for the postman delivering mail), and the like. We know, given the differential frictions of distance encountered on the earth's surface, that the shortest distance (measured in terms of time, cost, energy expended) between two points is not necessarily given by the way the legendary crow flies over physical distance. Furthermore the standpoint of the observer plays a critical role. (Harvey, 2006: 95)

We can note in this context that the home of time in Greenwich gave way to triangulated time, determined from satellites, at the same time as the old docklands of London gave way to the skyscraper trading floors of international banks, utilizing those same satellites to transmit 'product' globally. By the 1980s, the Greenwich that mattered economically was not just Greenwich in London, but the other less conspicuous Greenwich in Connecticut: the home of hedge funds.

Relative space, then, is not about the ahistorical uniqueness of a particular location, but about the different sorts of relations between different attributes and subjectivities existing in space and across time. To pick up one of our interests, relative space creates not just different scales, but different attributes, characteristics and relationships, each with their own measurement requirements. As Harvey notes, 'relativization, it is important to note, does not necessarily reduce or eliminate the capacity for calculability or control, but it does indicate that special rules and laws are required for the particular phenomena and processes under consideration' (Harvey, 2006: 123).

Relational space is, by contrast, about the relationship of *and* between processes that are both internal and external to itself. It is, in other words, about the relations within and between different (relational and absolute) characteristics that exist in and that define their own spatial orders. These spatio-temporal relational forms thus bring different scales (absolute) and different spatio-temporal attributes (relative) together, such that a third order of relation develops. Harvey (2006: 123) notes, 'The relational view of space holds there is no such thing as space outside of the processes that define it. Processes do not occur *in* space but define their own spatial frame'. These are the opaque relations across space and time to which Greenspan refers, where space is not inherently national (where national sovereignty can be unbundled such as in the 'offshore' world and shadow banking) and time not inherently linear (where finance can change the temporal and location of activities such as in derivatives markets and offshore).

Using this tripartite framing of capital's spatio-temporality, the chapter now introduces some developments in finance and how they are being measured and understood. It is organized, following Greenspan, around the question of how we might map the new territories of finance?

5.3 MAPPING THE TERRITORIES OF FINANCE: FROM ABSOLUTE TO RELATIVE TERMS

The framing of the territory and time of finance in absolute terms has been, and remains, the dominant one. It is usually undertaken in terms of transactions between residents of territorially discrete nations, as measured over time; usually a year. Its conventional form is balance of payments data. If we start from a balance of payments taxonomy, how do we make sense of the contemporary international mobility of investment and finance? In this section we show how the ongoing priority given to this taxonomy increasingly limits the capacity to engage relative and then relational space. Five points stand out. It starts out with examples that stretch absolute spatial concepts, and then introduces examples that transcend them.

Balance of payments categories in their modern form are largely a post-war, and Keynesian taxonomy. They were formulated in a world of fixed exchange rates and tight capital controls, and the framing of those accounts conceived of the trade account (measuring physical flows across territorial borders over time) as core and the capital account (net changes in the stock of international financial and investment aggregates) as 'accommodating' – meaning that financial and investment flows would adjust to offset trade imbalances and this national 'balance' would support a fixed exchange rate (Meade, 1951; Mundell, 1962). To paraphrase Harvey (1988), it could be said that the concepts and methodology of balance of payments accounting institutionalized in the 1950s a certain 'spatial fix' of capital. It is innate to the structure of balance of payments categories that commodities, incomes, investments and finance must all be given a singular national category and linear cross-national flow. In some ways, that spatial fix approximated (to varying degrees) nation-centred patterns of accumulation that were to characterize the period (and during the Bretton Woods period were the active targets of state policy). Accordingly, from the 1950s MNC were considered as the special case (from trade as the principal form of international exchange), warranting distinctive theory and specific empirical explanation (Hymer, 1960).

With trade measured as a cross-border flow over time (for example, a year), what mattered about financial and investment flows was how the *net* investment position changed between the start and the end of the accounting period, literally to accommodate trade flows. Indeed, policy could (and under fixed exchange rates was required to) manage capital flows to give the desired change in stock.

In a world of capital liberalization and floating exchange rates, we can still measure balance of payments data, but the concern remains for the net financial position at the end of the accounting period. In this world of net balance, it matters less whether these positions are based on large or small flows during the accounting period, or even the composition of those flows, than simply their contribution to the ongoing primacy of national balance. However, the problems of measuring absolute space in a world of liberalized capital flows and the generalization of the multinational firm started to become prevalent (Turner, 1991; Julius, 1990), and we saw that playing out in several ways (IMF Balance of Payments Committee, various; Kester, 1992, 1995).

First, it is well understood that the rapid growth of cross-border transactions in finance and investment now make commodity trade appear as a quantitatively minor category[8] in international economic transactions, and the capital account (now called the financial account) of the balance of payments is far from 'accommodating'. Significantly, the national trade and financial 'balances' are also largely beyond management by national policy, even for understanding and regulating the increasingly internationalized money and banking activities. Indeed, Andrew Haldane, the Deputy Governor of the Bank of England, has noted the potential financial fragility of large international capital flows especially for smaller economies which he termed the Big Fish Small Pond problem, and noted that over the past quarter of a century the networks of international capital flows has grown more extensive and complex (Haldane, 2011: 3). We will return to networks as another framing of financial space–time shortly, but for now the point is that the balance of payments taxonomy locks in the idea that only the net positions at the end of accounting periods are what matters for finance and investment. The flows themselves, and the fact that they are growing much faster than trade, are not what matters. The priority given to net investment positions feeds into a depiction of some forms of finance as 'speculation' and 'hot money', despite increasing evidence that the distinctions between forms of international capital increasingly have less and less association with any differences in the observable behaviour of those categories (Claessens et al., 2005; Lucio and Taylor, 1999; Becker and Noone, 2009).

Second, the net international investment position shown in the balance of payments measures net flows *and* changes in the valuation/prices of foreign assets (due to exchange rate changes and mark-to-market computations of asset values such as stock market pricing). As exchange rates and stock prices have become more volatile in the last two decades, this has fed through to increasing volatility in capital account valuations, which purport to represent net flows, but which are increasingly dominated by asset pricing volatilities.

Figure 5.1 shows changes in the net international investment position for the United States, broken down into new flows, exchange rate and price valuation changes, and other adjustments. Only the bar immediately below the horizontal axis is actually new flows but, as the line representing the net figure shows, new flows explain less and less of the changes in the net investment position. What we are increasingly seeing is that cross-border 'flows' recorded in balance of payments are only a small proportion of the forces driving the statistical changes in the net investment position. Not only is it increasingly difficult to think of investment as a flow accommodating to the overriding impulses of national trade, it is increasingly difficult to think of investment and finance as a cross-border flow at all.

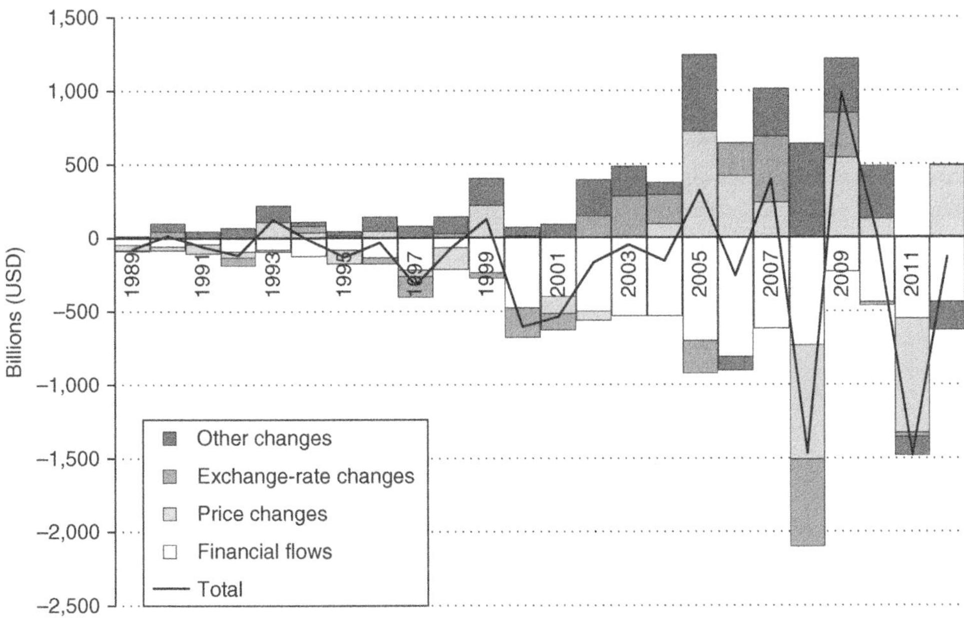

Source: Bertaut (2009), updated by authors.

Figure 5.1 Components of changes in the net international investment position at current cost, 1989–2012

The revaluations are important for re-establishing absolute space, but are not revealing anything significant about relative or relational space.

Relative space started to come to the analytical fore when trade and financial relations liberalized in the aftermath of a process of 'deindustrialization' in the old centres of advanced capitalism, the associated rise of 'emerging economies' and the growth of 'Eurofinance' markets. There became increasing awareness that the conventional (and often post-colonial) structures of post-war trade and finance were not giving sufficient detail to comprehend a changing world, either analytically or for national policy. This was the period of the rise of strategic and dynamic 'competitive advantage' (Porter, 1985) (as opposed to static and structural 'comparative advantage'), which became the new discourse for understanding global trade and finance. Mobile capital was now understood not to have an inherent nationality simply because it is located within a territory or even had a majority of its owners in that country. From a national competitive advantage policy perspective firms could 'earn' their nationality by behaving in ways that accorded with national policy goals (notably investing in high value added activities within the country). Whilst balance of payments data were still the dominant discourse, understanding relative space required more complex analysis in which space and time were now variables to be analysed rather than fixed and linear. The emerging agenda for understanding relative spaces of trade and finance became more acute as the growing structural complexity of capital flows became the predominant theme and the growing prominence of emerging markets and offshore financial centres its central insight. The policy issue was how nation states would strategize in this increasingly complex structure of relations, and find a niche of success.

Yet for so long as balance of payments data set the dominant terms of analysis, the conception of relative space would be largely constrained to observed complexity, and relational space remain almost completely inaccessible. The analytical crisis, if it can be called that, was that the development of the relative and relational spaces of finance could not be decoded (or recoded) neatly into balance of payments data, and the evidence of this crisis was that balance of payments data became increasingly incoherent. World balance of payments data, which should net to zero, were showing that the world carried a rapidly increasing deficit, with itself. This deficit could not be explained by simple 'accounting errors': it was about the rise of financial derivatives, securitization, special purpose vehicles, transfer pricing, offshore financial centres and hedge funds. The combined effect of these developments was to change the spatio-temporal attributes of trade finance and investment, and this started to show up as a sort of dark matter in balance of payments. Figure 5.2 shows the growing discrepancies in balance of payments accounting.

What emerged in the wake of this crisis of measurement and as an outgrowth of the competitiveness agenda has been growing attempts to understand developments in production, trade and finance in modes closer to Harvey's relative space and time. Central here has been network-type analysis such as Global Production Networks (GPN) along with Global Value Chain analysis (GVC) and Actor–Network theory (ANT). GPN and GVC has been in part a response to the unbundling of production and trading activities (Baldwin, 2011) and the spatial decentring of what used to be thought of as core corporate

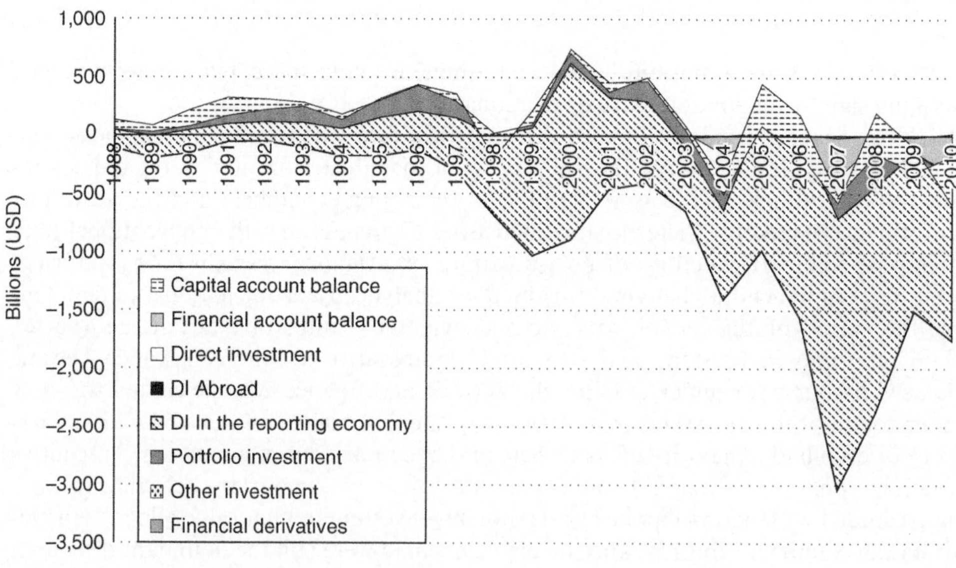

Source: IMF Balance of Payments Committee (2011).

Figure 5.2 Global balances on capital and financial accounts 1988–2010

headquarter functions (Desai, 2009). In recognition of the increasingly general character of internationalized production and trade GPN/GVC has provided more fluid and eclectic ways of conceptualizing industrial organization and trade. However, many of these newer concepts and taxonomies are themselves being challenged, notably as retaining an overly simple, linear approach to production, distribution and consumption (Froud et al., 1998), no clear engagement with labour (Bernstein and Campling, 2006a, 2006b), and of particular import here, not engaging with money and finance (Coe et al., 2014).

Although initially developed to analyse the complex interactions between humans and their non-human environments and elements, ANT attracted wider interest in the context of the blurring boundaries between individuals, organizations and nations, as well as wider social relations. In building its associational analysis ANT follows actors in networks to build what is purported to be a more open-ended account of spatial processes. But it has been critiqued for its uncritical use of data such as balance of payments and corporate accounting, which is itself 'an outcome of the boundary setting practices of the participants' (Whittle and Spicer, 2008: 616). Further, because it develops a flat ontology, and agnosticism about structure and process, 'all actors and entities are placed on the same level plane' (Dudwhalla, 2009: 2). Taken together, the problem is that network theory recognizes the problem of absolute notions of spatio-temporality but often has the effect of recreating absolute spatial forms of analysis, or at least not transcending it.

For our purpose, network-type analysis helps uncover increasing levels of detail of corporate taxation strategies and the use of offshore financial centres, which gives us access to a much better understanding the structures and dynamics of relative space. Offshore Financial Centres (OFCs) have not only grown in numbers, but are now so 'entangled' with the onshore world that it is difficult to draw distinct lines between on and offshore. For example, according to the IMF Co-ordinated Direct Investment Survey (CDIS), in 2010 Barbados, Bermuda and the British Virgin Islands received more FDI (combined 5.11 per cent of global FDIs) than Germany (4.77 per cent) or Japan (3.76 per cent). During the same year, these three jurisdictions made more investments into the world (combined 4.54 per cent) than Germany (4.28 per cent).

On a country-by-country position, in 2010 the British Virgin Islands were the second largest investor into China (14 per cent) after Hong Kong (45 per cent), and ahead of the United States (4 per cent). For the same year, Bermuda appears as the third largest investor in Chile (10 per cent). Similar data exists in relation to other countries, for example Mauritius is the top investor country into India (28 per cent), the British Virgin Islands (12 per cent), Bermuda (7 per cent) and the Bahamas (6 per cent) are among the top five investors into Russia (OECD, 2013: 17).

This sort of evidence points to detailed structures of financial flows between countries: one that could not have been imagined at the time of the post-war formation of balance of payments categories. Indeed, it also transcends the nationalist discourse of 'competitive advantage'. These data tell an important story about strategy in investing, revealing a very different version of relative space.

A further obstacle for understanding and measuring the spatiality of capital is that a guiding concept underpinning the cross-border growth of firms in balance of payments is of bilateral relationships (originally equity, but gradually including debt and other hybrid forms of capital) between national firms or financial institutions in country and separate companies in another foreign country. But that institutional form has been superseded, as MNCs have developed sophisticated and complex financing and tax minimization strategies involving a range of corporate forms (subsidiaries, SPEs, and related party entities) across several jurisdictions. Here is how a review of the measurement problems of internationalized capital noted the emerging challenge:

> The conceptual framework under which the existing data on U.S. international capital transactions are collected is that of the balance of payments, which defines international economic transactions as those between residents of the United States and non-residents (foreigners), those outside U.S. boundaries. Under this framework, data are collected on economic exchanges that cross national borders between the United States and the rest of the world. However, as U.S. financial activities have become global in nature, cross-border financial exchanges increasingly represent capital transfers among worldwide offices and branches of U.S. financial institutions, not transactions between U.S. firms and foreign firms. There is also a growing presence of foreign owned firms in U.S. domestic markets and of U.S.-owned firms in markets abroad. These developments have complicated identification of resident versus non-resident transactions. As the U.S. economy becomes increasingly internationalized, there is a blurring of the traditional distinction between domestic and international economic activities. (Kester, 1995: 3)

One response to the dilemma was to begin preparing an alternative version of balance of payments based on the nationality of ownership rather than the residence basis of traditional national accounting (Julius, 1990; Lipsey and Kravis, 1987; Kester, 1992), although national ownership accounting has proven to be of limited impact, as even competitive advantage has been surpassed in policy discourse.

Moreover, it is increasingly difficult to determine where, what form and in what direction 'capital' is 'flowing', because in a world of financial derivatives, and many other 'off balance sheet' transactions, viewing capital in absolute (flow) terms creates what Peter Garber (1998) termed an 'optical illusion' where some things are measured as cross-border flows definitionally (such as reinvested earnings in FDI), while other transactions may not create immediately measured flows because they are trading contingent claims about future risks, or are shifting rights to income, costs or other attributes in ways that avoid on-balance sheet measurement. As particle physics found as it moved towards its relative approach, through finance, capital has created a world in which where 'it' is at any point can depend on who is measuring and for what purpose. This double life of capital is most clear in hybrid finance where, in search of optimized after-tax returns, an instrument is structured so as to be treated as equity in one jurisdiction and debt in another. Here we are seeking to highlight that contemporary capital flows are less and less readily understood in terms of absolute or cartographic space, and perhaps also increasingly not in terms of Cartesian time–space principles.

The best-known recent example of this transcendence is the so-called Double Irish Dutch Sandwich. This tax planning arrangement involves the disaggregation of asset ownership, costs and revenues across multiple countries (tax jurisdictions) so that the taxation profits are minimized. In order to do this, forms of capital have to be produced (licences for intellectual property (IP) such as trademarks and patents) such that they are no longer directly attached to the parent company's (United States) tax jurisdiction (and are shifted to a low or zero tax jurisdiction like say Bermuda). Nor is this capital even located in the jurisdiction/s where the sales associated with the IP are realized (so a sales subsidiary in Ireland and the Netherlands are used as the base for European sales). Similarly, the sales have to be recorded so that they do not trigger corporate withholding taxes. The Irish and Dutch subsidiaries are structured to fix that problem.

The one remaining problem for these complex onshore and offshore arrangements is that if the US headquarters wants to repatriate the profits it would trigger the corporate tax bill. Until the US government has an amnesty for untaxed profits offshore, these companies cannot bring the money back onshore. This has seen large accumulations of cash in offshore financial centres (estimated to be around US$2 trillion). In 2013 Apple commenced a borrowing programme in US capital markets to fund an estimated $60 billion to pay for dividends and share buybacks over the following three years.

5.4 FRAMING CAPITAL'S RELATIONAL SPACE

We believe the limitation implicit in the sort of network diagram depicted in Figure 5.3 is that, although it shows the increasing complexity of finance and investment flows of relative space, it does not capture what Harvey termed relational flows. It fails to capture how the finance that is being monitored is itself transforming and changing its own relative form. Finance is less and less about direct and portfolio investments, or even about international loans, and more about liquid securities and derivative markets, in which the form of finance is constantly changing – its spatial and temporal position can change in milliseconds.

In this context, balance of payments data measuring changes in national stocks over accounting periods, rely on a limited and outmoded taxonomy of capital (its reliance on concepts of residency, cross-border flow and so on), and no matter how embellished by supplementary ownership accounts or bilateral measurement, they fail to capture the changed meaning of financial space and time. There has, accordingly, been some discussion about how capital itself is evolving.

A common theme to emerge from this discussion is that dominant concepts of money and capital are based on certain assumptions about spatial fixity, nationality and thingness of capital, which were, in part, a product of the particular historical development of capital and a related set of regulatory arrangements and practices of the post-war period (fixed exchange rates, capital controls, national and corporate accounting conventions and so on). Innovations in finance as well as in corporate organization and funding have given greater fluidity and liquidity to capital's accumulation project. One of the early motives for this innovation was precisely to bypass those regulatory arrangements that made the forms and mobility of capital comply with the post-war monitoring of absolute scale. For instance, Burn (1999: 226) suggests that the 1957 emergence of the Euromarkets in London signaled a shift in the financial market from 'one directed towards the furtherance of distinct "national" regimes of accumulation, based on a system that was almost wholly regulated, to one that is today mostly responsive to the demands of global speculation and almost wholly unregulated'.

Subsequently, developments in derivative and securities markets, transforming finance into an industry of risk trading, proved more powerful in changing our conception of capital and the identification of capital's space and time, albeit that taxation avoidance seems to be a core driver.

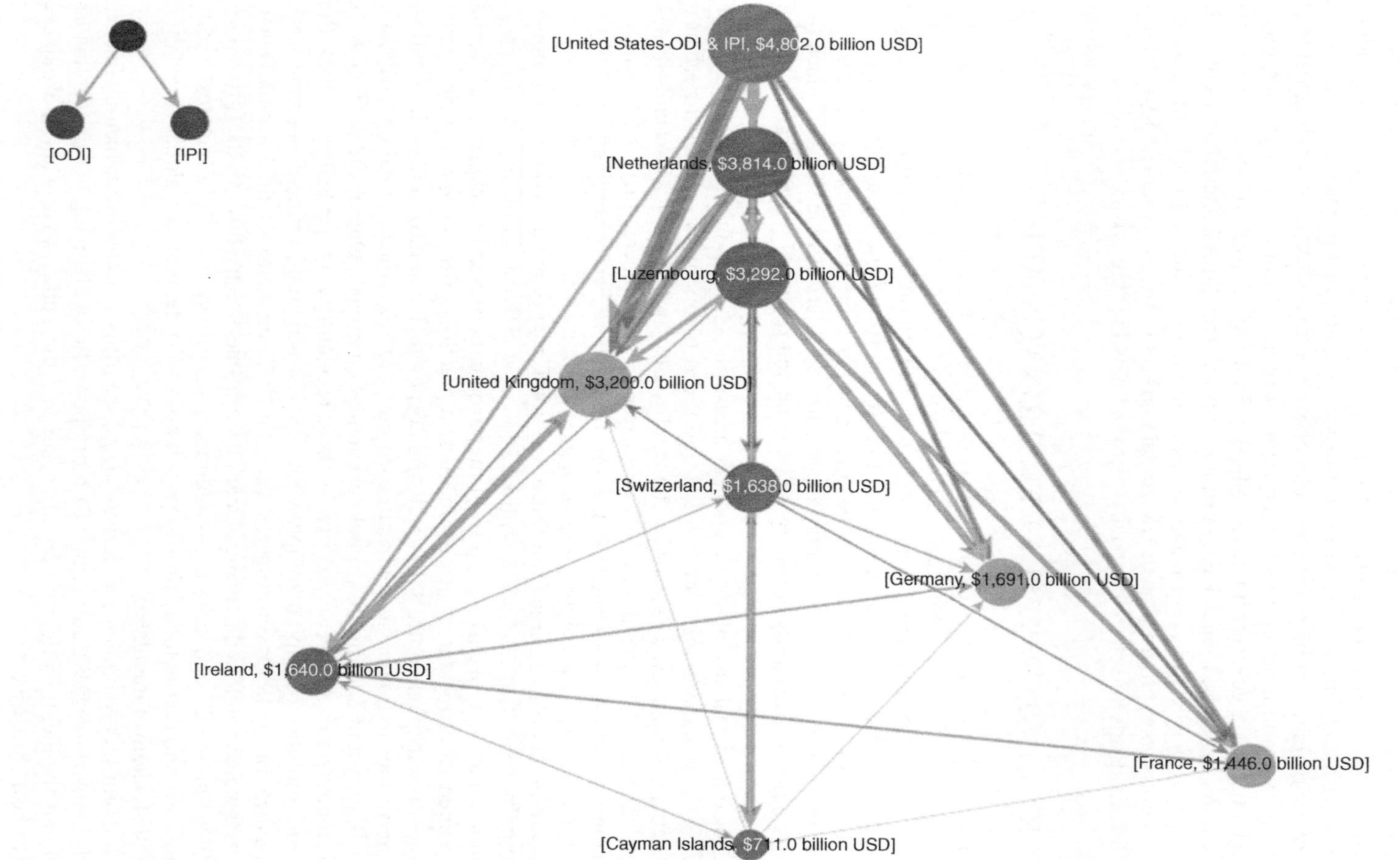

Figure 5.3 *The world's top ten capital exporting countries 2012 – international portfolio and direct investment stocks*

5.5 FINANCE AND ABSTRACT CAPITAL

Our point of emphasis here is the development of not merely new forms of capital (especially derivatives) but forms of capital that are themselves able to change their own profile to suit circumstances. The starting point was a recognition that the old, post-war taxonomy of capital (portfolio investment, direct investment, debt) was actually historically specific, even though it was being treated as theoretically ahistorical (Jones, 1987). Two statements, by two Nobel Prize winners of modern finance help make the point. First, on the role of tax arbitrage in driving financial innovation Merton Miller noted that:

> Incentives are created to transform high taxed forms of capital income such as interest or dividends into lower tax capital gains. And since the distinctions among these forms are matters of legal and accounting definitions rather than of economic fundamentals, such transformations can be confidently expected. The corporate business form is a particularly efficient engine for these and related transformations. (Miller, 1991: 272)

Then Myron Scholes, one of the developers of the theory of options pricing and a key figure in the development of the theory of financial derivatives, noted that existing taxonomies of capital are largely descriptive, and therefore historically unstable:

> Standard debt and equity contracts are institutional arrangements or boxes ... These arrangements survive only because they provide lower cost solutions than competing alternative arrangements. Competitive opportunities evolve over time with changing frictions and restrictions. . . . Time will continue to blur the distinctions between debt and equity. (Scholes, 1997: 146–147)

Innovations in finance revealed that particular forms of capital asset embody a range of risks, and that it was possible to design products to trade those risks, without trading the asset itself (creating forms of mobility or liquidity without formal motion). So whilst an asset may look like debt, a direct investment or a portfolio investment, the owner may be holding a set of risk exposures significantly detached from the risks of those assets. The incentives of owners to buy, sell and move assets therefore can less and less be read off from the attributes of the assets themselves. Another, relational, logic is at work, but balance of payments accounting (a measurement system based on absolute space and time) doesn't help.

Since the Bank for International Settlements began their Triennial survey of over-the-counter derivative markets, the notional value of derivatives contracts has grown from US$48 trillion in 1995 to US$100 trillion in 2001, US$516 trillion in 2007 and US$693 trillion in 2013 (BIS, 2013). In the face of this ostensibly startling growth, those focusing on absolute and even relative space were inclined to reflect on how these products have grown 'out of proportion' (with seemingly little relation) to the growth of production of so-called 'real' things – reinforcing the comprehension of finance as speculative and hot money. But if we consider the relational dimensions of derivatives, then a starkly different story emerges.

The relational dimension challenges the conventional categories of what constitutes ownership and control, the key criteria for determining the distinction between those balance of payments capital account categories of FDI and Portfolio investment. For example, the derivative form enables a 'decoupling' and blending of different attributes of debt and equity. As Hu and Black (2008: 666) have noted:

> the rules governing public firms presume that ownership of shares is a meaningful concept and conveys a standard package of shareholder rights ('full ownership'). Some of these rights are economic, including dividend, liquidation, and appraisal rights under corporate law. Some rights are not purely monetary, including voting rights, director fiduciary duties, rights to bring suits and inspect corporate records, access to corporate proxy machinery, and so on. Over the course of the last century, the assumption that most shareholders held full ownership mostly worked. This assumption works no longer. The derivatives revolution in finance, the growth of sophisticated, lightly regulated hedge funds, and the related growth in the share lending market now make it easy to decouple voting rights from economic ownership, and to further decompose economic ownership – for instance, by separating appraisal or dividend rights from other economic rights.

A key feature of financial derivatives is they involve deconstructing a 'thing' into a set of constituent elements or attributes, and then configure those attributes as themselves quantifiable or tradeable (Bryan and Rafferty, 2006, 2013). These attributes can then be re-framed as quantified risk and risk-trading transactions in a way that the underlying, original 'thing' may not. With derivatives, one trades in the future performance (shift in the measure) of an attribute of a thing, but without necessarily trading in the 'thing' itself. Derivatives are pure risk contracts in the sense that it is just a set of risks (with a purely monetary settlement), and no necessary underlying asset gets traded.

The effect here is to bring to the fore the relative and especially relational dimensions of the space and time within which assets (both financial and non-financial) move. Gone is the era of thinking of capital movement as bringing national balance, or even of a global pattern of capital movement *between* nations. The fluidity of derivatives means that times and locations follow a calculative logic that is internal to the derivative process itself.

5.6 RE-THINKING RELATIONAL OFFSHORE FINANCE

We have already noted that one aspect of the growth of international capital has been the spatial 'de-centring' of aspects of corporate activity, now with key headquarter functions (finance, patent ownership and legal headquarters) previously thought to be the most spatially fixed becoming much more spatially (or jurisdictionally) mobile as separate units (Desai, 2009). We would ascribe to that decentring a certain 'derivatives logic' in that attributes of the firm can be separated out from others and relocated in ways that blur clear locational identity in absolute terms.

This spatial and functional unbundling of the firm has been a critical dimension of the growth of offshore finance, enabling firms to locate financing activities closer to capital markets, in jurisdictions with lower reporting requirements, and/or at a distance from higher tax jurisdictions. This is most clearly expressed in the historical evolution of more complex global corporate structures, especially around their financial activities. Peter Garber suggests several ways that financial derivatives have been critical to this process. Financial derivatives provide firms with an:

> increased ability to separate and market risks. . . . Coupled with the existence of weak financial systems and the inherent opaqueness of derivative positions due to obsolete accounting

> systems . . . derivatives can be used to leverage financial safety nets. . . . Often, such activity must move offshore to evade detection and naturally generates a gross international capital flow. Moreover, derivatives can be used readily to evade onshore prudential regulation and capital and exchange control, thereby generating yet more measured capital flows. (Garber, 1998: 2)

Garber provides several examples how capital flows that appear to be cross-border flows of debt, can with the use of accompanying derivative transactions, actually be more akin to equity, how what appears as a portfolio flow is probably more like a direct investment and so on. A key feature of derivatives therefore is that by extracting attributes from one form of capital the former boundaries between debt and equity, long and short term, and between ownership and control have been blurring. Indeed, in terms of the capital account categories in balance of payments accounting Garber concludes that, 'Sub-account data, such as portfolio investment, equity investment, foreign direct investment, or long or short maturity fixed interest rate lending, are illusory in the presence of substantial volumes of derivatives' (Garber, 1998: 32).[9]

Indeed, financial derivatives, along with a range of complex internationally co-ordinated corporate financial structures, are the leading expressions of capital's internationality. MNCs now typically work through a myriad of financial entities, with indirect relationships such as special purpose entities (SPEs) located in several national jurisdictions, which have different regulatory or tax treatments for different financial activities. These entities may have no or very few employees, but have become key conduits, assembly points and transfer stations for capital within MNC networks which may act as a significant repository, or offshore payment factories, for key corporate assets or financing structures (Coates and Rafferty, 2007).

The financialization of the MNC has also seen a blurring of boundaries between industry and finance, and between production and circulation. These financial processes at the heart of the MNC mean that in some ways all MNCs are becoming their own hedge funds. A key conclusion for economic geography from this is that these developments are challenging our understanding of what we mean by space in the circuit of capital accumulation. As Oudekken (2005: 3–4) notes, of the regulatory changes of the 1980s finance internal to the MNC has been critical here, allowing intra-group credit on a global scale and the establishment of offshore financing companies undertaking regulatory arbitrage. He explained:

> During these decades the nature of FDI progressively changed from 'one-to-one investments' to 'chain investments', with many indirect links between related enterprises. This was equally true for equity and debt operations. . . . To optimize their financial performance further many multinational enterprises established treasuries for their worldwide group. Deregulation stimulated the development of many specific banking products like 'netting', 'pooling' and 'zero-balancing', further boosting (even on a daily basis) the gross flows between related enterprises. At the end of the decade this resulted in the development of so-called 'in-house banks' and 'payment factories' responsible for the entire financing and settlement of all payments of the entire group. Also tax-treaty shopping reached ever higher levels of sophistication in the form of 'round-tripping'. FDI was now circling around across a number of countries. This evolution of investment and financing behaviour of multinational enterprises has fundamentally changed the character of and what we mean by financial flows between related enterprises. (Oudekken, 2005: 3–4)

The problem here is that as finance has produced forms of relative and relational capital it is transcending absolute forms of measurement. In particular, the idea of bilateral exchange between two discrete nations has been rendered obsolete as transactions across jurisdictional space are often part of a multiplex of other transactions involving related and unrelated parties in several jurisdictions, which often specialize in different aspects of transfer, payment or re-badging. Consequently, current and financial account categories have less and less economic content.

A key conclusion is that finance has been an emerging process of 'deconstruction and reconstruction' of capital, which enables the spatial and temporal attributes of capital to be changed in fluid ways and on a large scale. An important implication of this process, which echoes Richard Walker's concerns about corporate geography, is that finance is contributing to a further de-centring of the corporation (at least as we thought we knew it) as the institutional subject of capital.

5.7 CONCLUSION

The chapter has explored some key spatio-temporal developments of finance in contemporary capitalism and the analytical and measurement challenges they pose. The expansion of the frontiers of finance include offshore financial centres, financial derivatives, hedge funds and special purpose entities. These developments are not merely about the changing spatial *scales* of finance, but are changing the spatio-temporal *forms* of capital. Financial derivatives are, for instance, not just a quantitative increase in the scale of finance, they are unbundling attributes of capital. They permit those attributes to be separated from the underlying and traded in their own right, without any necessary change in the ownership, location or temporality of the underlying asset. What is owned with financial derivatives are not machines and equipment, tonnes of wheat, or barrels of oil, but changes in the future financial performance of the machines, the wheat or the oil (or weather, stock price indices or exchange rates). In so doing, financial derivatives are giving new forms of liquidity, fluidity and mobility to capital. Importantly, these new abstract forms of finance not only change the spatial scale of capital. They change its temporal forms as well. For derivatives, as a whole, the relevant metric of performance is not absolute, but performance relative to, and in (temporal and spatial) relation with other forms of capital. Offshore finance, likewise, is not just, or even mostly, about capital moving globally on an expanded scale – erasing territory in its wake. Offshore finance is, as Palan (2002), Hudson (1998) and others have noted, about attributes of state sovereignty (legal sovereignty, fiscal sovereignty, and so on) being unbundled in order to re-work the functional scope of a state's engagement with the fluid and liquid forms of capital that finance has been developing.

We are now in a position to reflect on the chapter's opening comments by former Fed Chairperson Alan Greenspan, that finance is now inherently opaque and beyond measurement (and regulation). We may have some form of answer, or at least part of an answer, to Greenspan's dilemma about scale and navigation.

Using Harvey's conceptual trilemma, we can say that even in absolute forms of spatio-temporality, there will always be an issue of the relevant scale/s of measurement. However, we have argued that developments in finance have shown that capital's spatio-temporality cannot adequately be captured only in absolute forms, and that increasingly relative and relational concepts of capital are required to understand modern finance. Indeed, finance has not just transcended absolute forms of spatio-temporality, in producing a whole new generation of financial forms and institutions it is now self-conscious of that transcendence. Much of what happens in OFCs, off-balance sheet transactions, SPVs, corporate finance, shadow banking and so on is explicitly about using the differences (gaps) between absolute and relative and relational spatio-temporal forms as regulatory categories. Modern finance requires us to engage with relative and relational modalities of capital's spatio-temporality, and in finance the logic of regulating capital on absolute space is presenting capital with an active subject of (or perhaps space for) arbitrage. We showed through mapping capital flows in absolute space how those processes present a range of paradoxes regarding what is happening in global capitalism. A broad conclusion, not restricted to this chapter, is that too much of what gets represented by such forms of measurement are artefacts of corporate and national accounting, and obscures the very relational fluid nature of the processes that are occurring. Greenspan resorts to an inherent opacity of finance, but economic geography can re-pose this complexity as capital's different spatio-temporal moments.

One conclusion of this analysis therefore is that in relative but especially in relational forms of capital's spatio-temporality, the standard sorts of measurement (such as corporate and national balance of payments accounting) become increasingly difficult because they require converting inherently fluid, abstract and mobile forms of capital back into fixed, thing-like, institutional and locational forms of absolute space. This is a point Harvey himself noted; 'Measurement becomes more and more problematic the closer we move towards a world of relational space–time. But why would it be presumed that space–time only exists if it is measurable and quantifiable in certain traditional ways?' (Harvey, 1973: 96). This chapter suggests that building analysis of relational space–time will be needed to address capital's frontiers.

In the calculative and commensurative properties of financial derivatives, we can identify one way that capital is developing forms of measurement adequate to Harvey's relative and relational modalities of capital. In unbundling attributes of capital, each financial derivative market provides a financial metric relative to the same attribute of another capital in another spatio-temporal location. Taken together, where different attributes of different capitals across different temporalities are being organized and commensurated, we can start to open up access to capital's developing relative and relational spatio-temporalities.

NOTES

1. The authors acknowledge support from the 'Systems of Tax Evasion and Laundering: Locating Global Wealth Chains in the International Political Economy' (STEAL 2012–15) project funded by the TaxCapDev programme under the Research Council of Norway (#212210/H30). They also wish to thank the Nigel Douglas for research assistance in the preparation of this chapter.
2. Lewis Carroll in *Sylvie and Bruno* concluded:

> 'What do you consider the largest map that would be really useful?'
> 'About six inches to the mile.'
> 'Only six inches!' exclaimed Mein Herr. 'We very soon got to six yards to the mile. Then we tried a hundred yards to the mile. And then came the grandest idea of all! We actually made a map of the country on the scale of a mile to the mile!'
> 'Have you used it much?' I enquired.

> 'It has never been spread out, yet,' said Mein Herr, 'the farmers objected: they said it would cover the whole country and shut out the sunlight! So we now use the country itself, as its own map, and I assure you it does nearly as well.' (cited in Cep, 2014)

3. Borge wrote a short parable he titled 'Of Exactitude in Science', along the lines of Carroll:

> In that Empire, the craft of Cartography attained such Perfection that the Map of a Single province covered the space of an entire City, and the Map of the Empire itself an entire Province. In the course of Time, these Extensive maps were found somehow wanting, and so the College of Cartographers evolved a Map of the Empire that was of the same Scale as the Empire and that coincided with it point for point. Less attentive to the Study of Cartography, succeeding Generations came to judge a map of such Magnitude cumbersome, and, not without Irreverence, they abandoned it to the Rigours of sun and Rain. In the western Deserts, tattered Fragments of the Map are still to be found, Sheltering an occasional Beast or beggar; in the whole Nation, no other relic is left of the Discipline of Geography. (cited in Cep, 2014)

4. For instance, Randy Martin (2007) has noted that finance is increasingly 'inside' production, and production 'inside' finance.
5. Sheppard (2002) provides a useful survey.
6. Harvey (1973: 13) noted:

> If we regard space as *absolute* it becomes a "thing in itself" with an existence independent of matter, it then possesses a structure which we can use to pigeon-hole or individuate phenomena. The view of *relative* space proposes that it be understood as a relationship between objects which exists only because objects exist and relate to each other. There is another sense in which space can be viewed as relative and I choose to call this *relational* space – space regarded in the manner of Leibniz, as being contained in objects in the sense that an object can be said to exist only insofar as it contains and represents within itself relationships to other objects. (emphasis added)

7. Edney observed: 'Imperialism and mapmaking intersect in the most basic manner. Both are fundamentally concerned with territory. . . . To govern territories, one must know them' (Edney, 1998: 1).
8. Just to give one indicator, external assets and liabilities of the developed countries increased from 100% of GDP in 1985 to 400% in 2005 (IMF, 2010).
9. van Dool (2006) in an analysis of what he terms 'pass through' capital concludes, 'FDI figures may have nothing to do with the reporting economy'.

REFERENCES

Baldwin, R. (2011), 'Trade and industrialisation after globalisation's 2nd unbundling: how building and joining a supply chain are different and why it matters', Working Paper 17716, NBER, Cambridge, December.

Bernstein, H. and L. Campling (2006a), 'Commodity studies and commodity fetishism 1: trading down', *Journal of Agrarian Change*, **6**, 239–264.

Bernstein, H. and L. Campling (2006b), 'Commodity studies and commodity fetishism ii: profits with principles?', *Journal of Agrarian Change*, **6** (3), 414–447.

BIS (2013), 'Derivative statistics – triennial central bank survey, Monetary and Economic Department', Bank for International Settlements, Basel. Retrieved on 12 October 2016 from www.bis.org/publ/rpfx13.htm.

Becker, C. and C. Noone (2009), 'Volatility and persistence of capital flows', Reserve Bank of Australia Research Discussion Paper No. 2009–09, Reserve Bank of Australia, Sydney. Retrieved on 12 October 2016 from www.rba.gov.au/publications/rdp/2009/pdr/rdp2009-09.pdf.

Bertaut, C. (2009), 'The financial crisis and US cross-border financial flows', *Federal Reserve Bulletin*, **95**, A147–A167.

Brenner, N. (1998), 'Between fixity and motion: accumulation, territorial organization, and the historical geography of spatial scales', *Environment and Planning D: Society and Space*, **16** (4), 459–481.

Bryan, D. and M. Rafferty (2006), *Capitalism with Derivatives: A Political Economy of Financial Derivatives, Capital and Class*, London, Palgrave.

Bryan, D. and M. Rafferty (2013), 'Fundamental value: a category in transformation', *Economy and Society*, **42** (1), 130–153.

Burn, G. (1999), 'The state, the city and the euromarkets', *Review of International Political Economy*, **6** (2), 225–261.

Castells, M. (1996), *The Information Age: Economy, Society and Culture Volume 1: The Rise of the Network Society*, Oxford, Blackwell.

Cep, N. (2014), 'The allure of the map', *The New Yorker*, 22 January. Retrieved on 12 October 2016 from www.newyorker.com/books/page-turner/the-allure-of-the-map.

Claessens, S., M. Dooley and A. Warner (2005), 'Portfolio capital flows: hot or cold?', *World Bank Economic Review*, 9 (1), 153–174.

Coates, N. and M. Rafferty (2007), 'Offshore financial centres, hot money and hedge funds: a network analysis of international capital flows', in L. Assassi, A. Nesvetailova and D. Wigan (eds), *Global Finance in the New Century: Beyond Deregulation*, Basingstoke, Palgrave Macmillan, pp. 38–54.

Coe, N., K. Lai and D. Wójcik (2014), 'Integrating finance into global production networks', *Regional Studies*, **48** (5), 761–777.

Deleuze, G. and Felix Guattari (1987), *A Thousand Plateaus – Capitalism and Schizophrenia*, translated by Brian Massumi, Minneapolis, University of Minnesota Press.

Desai, M. (2009), 'The decentering of the global firm', *The World Economy*, **32** (9), 1271–1290.

Dudhwalla, F. (2009), 'What is actor network theory? What are its strengths and weaknesses as a form of sociological theory?'. Retrieved on 14 November 2016 from www.academia.edu/542543/What_is_Actor-Network_Theory?

Edney, M. (1998), *Mapping an Empire – The Geographical Construction of British India, 1765–1843*, Chicago, IL: The University of Chicago Press.

Froud, J., C. Haslam, S. Johal, J. Williams and K. Williams (1998), 'Breaking the chains: a sector matrix for motoring', *Competition and Change*, **3**, 293–374.

Garber, P. (1998), 'Derivatives in international capital flows', NBER Working Paper 6623, Cambridge, National Bureau of Economic Research.

Greenspan, A. (2011), 'Dodd–Frank fails to meet test of our times', *Financial Times* 29 March 29. Retrieved on 12 October 2016 from www.ft.com/intl/cms/s/0/14662fd8-5a28-11e0-86d3-00144feab49a.html#axzz3UXGjjgeS.

Greenspan A. (2013), *The Map and the Territory: Risk, Human Nature, and the Future of Forecasting*, London, The Penguin Press.

Haldane, A. (2011). 'The big fish small pond problem', Speech given at the Institute for New Economic Thinking Annual Conference, Bretton Woods, New Hampshire, 9 April. Retrieved on 9 November 2016 from www.bankofengland.co.uk/archive/Documents/historicpubs/speeches/2011/speech489.pdf.

Harvey, D. (1973, 1988), *Social Justice and the City*, Oxford, Basil Blackwell.

Harvey, D. (1990), *The Condition of Postmodernity: An Enquiry into the Origins of Cultural Change*, Cambridge, MA: Blackwell.

Harvey, D. (2006), 'Space as a keyword', in Harvey, D. (ed.), *Spaces of Global Capitalism – Towards a Theory of Uneven Development*, London, Verso, pp. 119–148.

Hu, H. and B. Black (2008), 'Debt, equity and hybrid decoupling: governance and systemic risk implications', *European Financial Management*, **14** (4), 663–709.

Hudson, A. (1998), 'Reshaping the regulatory landscape: border skirmishes around the Bahamas and Cayman offshore financial centres', *Review of International Political Economy*, **5** (3), 534–564.

Hymer, S.H. (1960), 'The international operations of national firms: a study of direct foreign investment', PhD Dissertation. Published posthumously, The MIT Press, 1976, Cambridge, MA.

IMF Balance of Payments Committee, Annual Reports, various. Retrieved 12 October 2016 from www.imf.org/external/bopage/bopindex.htm.

IMF (2010), Understanding Financial Interconnectedness, BOPCOM 10/23, prepared for the Strategy, Policy and Review/ Monetary and Capital Markets Departments.

Jones, C. (1987), *International Business in the Nineteenth Century: The Rise and Fall of a Cosmopolitan Bourgeoisie*, New York, New York University Press.

Julius, Deanne (1990), *Global Companies and Public Policy: The Growing Challenge of Foreign Direct Investment*, New York, Royal Institute of International Affairs, Council on Foreign Relations Press.

Kester, Anne (1992), *Behind the Numbers: US Trade in the World Economy*, Washington, DC, National Academy Press.

Kester, Anne (1995), *Following the Money: US Finance in the World Economy*, Washington, DC, National Academy Press.

Latour, Bruno (2005), *Reassembling the Social: An Introduction to Actor–Network Theory*, Oxford, Oxford University Press.

Lipsey, R. and I. Kravis (1987), 'The competitiveness and comparative advantage of US multinationals 1957–1984', *Banca Nazionale Lavoro Quarterly Review*, June (161), 147–165.

Lucio, S. and M. Taylor (1999), 'Hot money, accounting labels and the permanence of capital flows to developing countries: an empirical investigation', *Journal of Development Economics*, **59** (2), 337–364.

Martin, R. (2007), *An Empire of Indifference: American War and the Financial Logic of Risk Management*, Durham, NC, Duke University Press.

Meade, J.E. (1951), *The Theory of International Economic Policy, Volume I: The Balance of Payments*, Oxford, Oxford University Press.
Miller, Merton (1991), *Financial Innovations and Market Volatility*, Cambridge, Blackwell.
Mundell, R.A. (1962), 'The appropriate use of monetary and fiscal policy for internal and external stability', Staff Papers, International Monetary Fund, **9** (1), 70–79.
OECD (2013), *Update: Base Erosion and Profit Shifting*, Paris: OECD Publishing. Retrieved on 12 October 2016 from www.oecd.org/mcm/C-MIN(2013)7-ENG.pdf.
Oudekken, F. (2005), 'Special purpose entities and the measurement of foreign Direct investment (some further considerations)', IMF Committee on Balance of Payments Statistics and OECD Workshop on International Investment Statistics, Direct Investment Technical Expert Group. Retrieved on 12 October 2016 from www.imf.org/External/NP/sta/bop/pdf/diteg9c.pdf.
Oxley, L., P. Walker, D. Thorns and H. Wang (2008), 'The knowledge economy/society: the latest example of "measurement without theory"?', *The Journal of Philosophical Economics*, **II** (1), 20–54.
Palan, R. (2002), 'Tax havens and the commercialization of state sovereignty', *International Organization*, **56**, 151–176.
Porter, Michael (1985), *Competitive Advantage*, New York, Free Press.
Scholes, M. (1997), 'Derivatives in a dynamic environment' Nobel Lecture, 9 December. Retrieved 12 October 2016 from www.nobelprize.org/nobel_prizes/economic-sciences/laureates/1997/scholes-lecture.pdf.
Sheppard, E. (2002), 'The spaces and times of globalization: place, scale, networks, and positionality', *Economic Geography*, **78** (3), 307–330.
Turner, P. (1991), 'Capital flows in the 1980's: a survey of major trends', *BIS Economic Papers*, **30**, Basel, Bank for International Settlements.
van Dool, G. (2006), 'The problem of pass through funds and capital in transit in FDI statistics', presentation at MENA conference, Istanbul, 9 November.
Whittle, Spicer, A. (2008), 'Is actor network theory critique?', *Organization Studies*, **29** (4), 611–629.

6. 'This time it's different' . . . and why it matters: the shifting geographies of money, finance and risks

Michael Pryke

6.1 INTRODUCTION

We live in a world increasingly made through the practices and calculations of finance, as the build-up to and aftermath of the global financial crisis[1] (GFC) stand testament. Put slightly differently, the interconnectivities made through the processes of financial computation and measuring and their outcomes, are 'world making'. What follows then is a small contribution to the larger, established arguments not simply about the relevance of geography to understanding how finance works (see for example Aalbers, 2008; Christophers, 2015; French, Leyshon and Thrift, 2009; French, Leyshon and Wainright, 2011; Lee et al., 2010; Pani and Holman, 2014; Pike and Pollard, 2010; Wainwright, 2009), but how these complex financialized spatialities might be talked about and imagined. The spatial plays of the crisis have intrigued not just geographers but mainstream economists and others. Reinhart and Rogoff (2009: 240) for example ask how the subprime crisis morphed 'from a local or regional crisis into a global one?', while the Bank of England's Andrew Haldane talks of the 'changing shape and scale of the underlying topology the international monetary system' dating from the late 1970s (Haldane, 2014: 6). Geography is inescapably bound up in such observations about the spread and span as well as the intensity of modern finance, as the capture of value globally is organized through innovative connections spliced through financial markets. And it is the unexpected geographies described by the crisis and made through complex connections that mean that 'this time it is different'. This difference arguably demands a fuller appreciation not simply that 'space is not static' but that that the practices of financialization generate consequences that are perhaps better captured through financial topologies rather understood as involving an interplay of scales from the local to the national.[2] To argue this the chapter begins by setting out briefly the two distinguishing features of contemporary finance.

Financial crises are nothing new. Financial innovation, too, has a long history (Neal, 1990: 5). Yet there's something distinctive both about the recent global financial crisis and the underlying innovative practices and processes that fuelled national and international financial 'systems' since the mid-1970s. The distinctiveness stems first from the sheer pervasiveness of finance in the years prior to the crisis, a pervasiveness achieved through the multiple links forged not just within the worlds of international financial markets, but between these markets and corporations, through to everyday finance and money such as savings products, mortgages, pensions, and the like. For those within centres such as Wall Street and the City, it is as if in the decade or so prior to the crisis, money and finance became a creative feedstock fuelling a 'new' imaginary amongst market participants. Though in many respects at odds with the cold rationalities of 'finance' and clinically precise calculation, this imaginary was able to infiltrate and inform so many aspects of the everyday precisely because of the passionate belief it engendered in what a highly financialized space–time could deliver (LiPuma and Lee, 2012). Innovative tricks in international markets tied together multiple financialized space–times, as financial organizations engaged in imaginative calculations that in effect saw them connecting, storing, and exchanging ever growing multiples of what were thought to be manageable risks, rather than Knightian uncertainties.

This leads into the second distinctive feature of the crisis: the striking spatialities that emerged swiftly as the crisis unfolded (see French et al., 2009). Only when the crisis hit and promises of risk management and easy enrichment lay shattered, did the consequences of innovative connectivities dreamt up by financial organizations become apparent. The crisis thus lays bare contemporary financial innovation as a form of spatial innovation where the latter is understood as the myriad, novel, financialized connections that resulted from packaging and trading often complex finance related risks drawn from across a global playing field. The inevitable 'spatial fix' (Harvey, 1982) that shadows every crisis was given an added twist due to the seemingly improbable interconnections generated by the financial innovations that have been pushed enthusiastically into the heart of financial markets since the late-1970s. By the time of the crisis, finance was no simple servant of urban accumulation (Dymski, 2009: 434) but had become an independent, masterful conjurer of endless, innovative, and cynically profitable, linkages. Yet, to borrow from Mirowski (2013) we 'should never let a serious crisis go to waste'. Indeed the crisis presents geographers with an opportunity to 'realize the potential' of financial geography at the present moment (Lee et al., 2010; Pike and Pollard, 2010), a moment that will not last for ever.

After all, the GFC now seems merely a rude interruption. Capitalism's tendency to develop an occasional and dangerous financial lop-sidedness (Arrighi, 1994; see also Blackburn, 2008) got the better of the system, for short while at least, but now, supported by the taxpayer in the form of 'quantitative easing', the game continues and those still standing once again seek to fulfil their desire to possess the world in 'financial garb' (Buchan, 1997: 278). Equipped with the latest ICT, (still) highly leveraged hedge funds, pension funds, mutual funds, and the once triumphant but now ever so slightly more modest 'large and complex financial institutions' such as J.P. Morgan Chase and UBS[3] continue to prowl the globe in search of an edge: world stock markets from Japan to London; any number of market indices such as the Dow Jones; energy markets; bond and money markets; metals from aluminium to zinc; markets in currencies; wheat and shrimp futures; the impact of bird flu and 'mad cow' on soy and corn demand; commodity futures; the growing interest in ethanol production and its effect on the demand for sugar – all and more are scanned constantly, day-in, day-out. Everything it seems, from a shrimp to the weather, stands in line waiting to be drawn into the processes that channel and connect investment 'globally'. The materials of finance, from state of the art ICT, to research reports, to the daily sociocultural practices of interpreting and making sense of data flows that stream into dealing rooms, meld together constantly to make markets.

6.2 FROM 'FLOW' AND 'CIRCULATION' TO EMERGENT FINANCIAL TOPOLOGIES

Yet what can we make of all this, of the intensive movement and extensive interconnectivity achieved through financial flows and circulation, of that is, the spatial reach of financial market practices and their collective impact both immediately and in the near future? The 'capitalization of almost everything' (Leyshon and Thrift, 2007) goes some way but not far enough.

In the growing shadow of the GFC metaphors such as 'flow' and 'circulation' (or even 'mercury' (Clark, 2005) are found wanting; they capture neither the entangled time–spaces that accompany the dynamic traffic in financial instruments, nor do such terms help make sense of the sheer spatial disruptiveness when things go wrong. When in other words the 'interactive complexity' (Bookstaber, 2007) of modern finance and its risks becomes too much for the system to cope with. As the authors of a recent Bank of England Working Paper put it:

> An astonishing feature of the 2008 financial crisis was how quickly and extensively the relatively small write-downs in US subprime mortgages spread to a situation where only two years later governments worldwide had to provide massive support to their banking systems. In the years prior to the crisis, large banking groups had become highly interdependent across national borders through a complex web of direct claims on each other, ownership structures and other risk transfers and also through participation in common markets. Because the system was so intertwined, the financial crisis was transmitted rapidly through default chains, funding squeezes, fire-sale externalities and a rash of counterparty fear. (Garratt et al., 2011: 5)

Even as descriptors, flow and circulation join the story half-way through. They tend to omit first the formative stages where an increasingly coded landscape, amenable in turn to further mathematical calculations and imaginative socio-technical-cultural practices and processes emerge; where, to echo Andrew Haldane (2009), the changing topology of the financial network is generated in centres of mathematized time–space such as London and New York. Second, such terms fail to grasp those later moments when risks intertwine and uncertainties prove unmanageable, when 'fear', 'default', and 'funding squeezes', and the like, take hold.

To talk of fear is also a reminder that the GFC demonstrates clearly why finance is not an exclusively technical field and also why its presumed authority should be questioned. As Bill Janeway (2009: 28) put it 'modern finance theorists thought that they had tamed "risk" by treating it as a statistical attribute of time series of data. They thought that they had escaped the fundamental uncertainty that exists about the future results of present decisions. They have been proven stunningly wrong'. A significant reason why things turned out this way is because, as Janeway continues, in trying to 'emulate the most mathematically rigorous of the natural sciences' (Janeway, 2009: 31) financial economics forgot what Frank Knight pointed out many decades ago: 'the sheer brute fact that the results of human activity cannot be anticipated' (Janeway, 2009: 28). The brute fact becomes more brutal when the influence of mediating devices on human activity and human imagination is recognized. Financial markets and financial innovation do not just deal in 'time alone' (Adam, 2003: 70); like all financial innovations financial futures for example are a money culture's way of reimagining how financialized space–times may be traded. A future made through today's finance ceases to be something that can be understood as a neatly linear calendar time[4] and becomes instead highly unpredictable, 'intertwined' relational space–times.

As this suggests, whilst finance is understood here as a combination of components, there is a need to recognize the seductive qualities of our present 'money culture'. To acknowledge in other words the sensual side of finance that provides the flux enabling these components or devices to move amongst market cultures. Contemporary finance is just as much about the lure of a financialized time–space made 'malleable' by both imaginaries *and* energizing devices, as it is about the technicalities of financial modelling (which is itself dependent on imagination and narratives (see for example Morgan, 2001, 2004, 2012)). The processes of financial innovation in the build-up to the crisis suggest an agreed sense of an imagined *simultaneous future* woven into the fabric of financial innovations and markets in them; devices and imaginations fused, to draw innovative financialized future time–spaces into an actionable present – albeit uncertainly.

To argue for a more spatially aware account of financial markets, one that makes more accessible the capacity of finance to spatialize, to *generate* emergent financial topologies, new and consequential connections and adjacencies, rather than deploy an arguably less appropriate scalar imaginary, calls for a quick run over familiar terrain.

6.3 A VERY QUICK REHEARSAL: ACKNOWLEDGING THE STUFF PRODUCING UNEXPECTED SPATIALITIES

Finance gains its capacity to perform through sets of tools that enable calculative agencies (Callon, 1998: 20–23; Barry and Slater, 2002: 182). The tools aren't just social relations of finance but the range of contrivances, such as finance theory and software, that give shape and meaning to what is framed as the 'market', be this a market in foreign currencies or so-called catastrophe bonds. In brief, these various financial gadgets 'do not merely record a reality independent of themselves; they contribute powerfully to shaping, simply by measuring it, the reality that they measure' (Callon, 1998: 23); the gadgets in other words contribute to 'financially relevant activity' (to adapt Law, 2002) all too easily overlooked in more orthodox approaches to finance.[5]

The work of Beunza, Hardie and MacKenzie (2006), Callon and Muniesa (2005), MacKenzie (2001, 2003a, 2003b, 2004a, 2004b) and Hardie and MacKenzie (2007) for example argue that markets are actively made; they insist (in line with Callon's original thesis (1998)) that they are performed and that moreover this performance depends on the *materiality* of these markets – a materiality that includes finance theory itself (for example Maurer, 2005a, 2005b; Miyazaki, 2005; MacKenzie, 2009). In brief, financial markets are understood as hybrid collectives or *agencements*[6] (Callon and Muniesa, 2005; Callon, Millo and Muniesa, 2007), that is 'hybrid collectives comprising human beings as well as material and technical devices' (Callon, 2005: 4). It is through such collectives that action is achievable. In a similar fashion John Law (2002) approaches economic calculation as 'materially heterogeneous practices'. In this and in Callon's sense it is acceptable to talk of the stuff and things of markets. Expressed in terms of cultural economy, culture is already distributed through the agencement that configures the realm of possible calculations.[7] This body of work, I would argue, helps to make sense of just how a range of calculative tools at the heart of modern finance, and the calculative agencies they facilitate, enliven spatialities. To explain.

To view a financial market as an *agencement*, as a 'socio-technical combination' (MacKenzie, 2009: 21), is to recognize it as a very particular congregation of the social, cultural and the technical. The trading floors of Wall Street, of Chicago and the City are a mix of human traders and sophisticated trading technologies. The screens, the mathematics, and so on, are active material components in the making financial markets; they do not collectively form a passive backdrop to human traders (Callon, 1998: 26). Instead they are understood to help expand and stake out a terrain of possibilities for market making. And because the material equipment is consequential, as Donald MacKenzie reminds us (2009: 19), it is important to recognize that far from being inert, when drawn into the social relations of finance, the devices contribute not only to 'making the world go around' they are part of the growing tendency for 'finance' to assemble the world through which it slides and worms its various routes. The move in the build-up to the crisis by the London based hedge fund, Titian, to combine a 'fundamentals only' approach with what they described as the 'block box' approach favoured by the 'quant funds', is perhaps illustrative of this point. The fund's deliberate combination of approaches was driven by Titian's attempt to implement long and short term investment strategies tailored to allocating funds across what they saw as the four 'biggest investment themes' that would drive global markets in the near future: clean energy, water, infrastructure and natural resources. As the Managing Partner and Portfolio Manager at Titian put it:

> We apply our fundamentals-based knowledge in the segmentation and the analysis of the long and short investment themes and the positions we like, and once we've pre-selected the underlying instruments we're comfortable with, we then use models to guide us in the tactical allocation of capital across that pre-approved universe. (Fieldhouse, 2008)

If to 'trace the agencement making up an actor' (MacKenzie, 2009: 22) is one of the chief tasks that the social studies of finance sets itself, and if the technical artefacts employed help market participants to see, understand, comprehend space anew –Titian's pre-approved universe – then the spatial impact of such devices (such as Titian's moves into and out of water, resources, infrastructure) should be traced too as part of that overall goal. This is because the devices, to include the 'fundamentals only' and 'black box' approaches, for example – help assemble innovative space–times through which market action is continually enacted. Spatiality, rather than being an inactive backdrop, a passive flatland,[8] becomes entangled in market practices of financialization to impact not just outcomes but (as part of this) how we might understand how financial risks move, mutate and complicate seemingly straightforward connections between investment decisions and markets within and across national borders. For instance, such connections may quickly become problematical because the very financial instruments designed to make risks more measurable and tailored to lessen specific risks, may well themselves introduce more unknowns simply because of the density of information required to appreciate both their characteristics and the possible consequences of the interconnectivities their use might produce. The Bank of England's Andrew Haldane (2009: 17) estimates for example that 'an investor in a CDO squared would need to read in excess of 1 billion pages to understand fully the ingredients'. The regulatory system itself was after all ill-equipped to deal with such growing complexity introduced by hedge funds and the wider shadow banking system, with their emphasis on innovations such as credit default swaps and collateralized debt obligations (Pozsar et al., 2010: 1).

How well after all does 'flow' capture either, say, what is incorporated within a CDO squared, when, as a *Financial Stability Report* noted, a typical CDO could reference more than 100 residential mortgage-backed securities, each of which in turn could reference 5,000 underlying mortgages (*Financial Stability Report*, 2011: Box 1), or the sort of 'vehicular finance' described by the Bank of England's Paul Tucker, where 'SIVs (structured investment vehicles) may hold monoline-wrapped AAA-tranches of CDOs, which may hold tranches of other CDOs, which hold LBO debt of all types, as well as asset-backed securities bundling together household loans' (Tucker, 2007: 312). These are the sorts of development in finance which prompted Andrew Haldane (2009) to talk of the changing shape of the 'topology of the financial network'. Though not sharing all of the same theoretical roots as Haldane's approach to topology, the appeal to the of conceptual resource of emergent financial topologies and its employment, as it were, in amongst the *agencements* of financial markets, is an effort to redress what are often aspatial accounts offered by cultural economy and the social studies of finance. At this point it is helpful to quickly rehearse the key features of financial innovation that came to mark the decade or more leading to the GFC.

6.4 FINANCIAL INNOVATION, SPATIAL INNOVATION

As the economic historian Youssef Cassis notes:

> The almost constant arrival of new financial products since the mid-seventies has been an unprecedented phenomenon in financial history. Until then, practices, services and activity, without being entirely static, had not fundamentally changed from one generation to the next. In this respect, innovation has been the most original aspect of recent times, especially because of its impact on the international financial centres' role. (Cassis, 2006: 248)

As this quote suggests, and as is now common knowledge, innovation in financial market instruments grew at a meteoric rate from the mid-to-late-1970s. By the mid-1980s worldwide trading volume in financial futures, swaps, and mortgage-backed securities, stood at \$10,000 billion, \$100–200,000 billion, and \$150,000 billion respectively; figures for 1975 would have been 'minute' (Cooper, 1986: 2). Innovative instruments grew phenomenally from the late 1980s onwards, a growth matched only by their complexity. The significance of this growth stems from what such innovation does to linkages amongst both financial organizations within financial centres and the connectivities sewn between these centres, intermediaries, and the world outside. Financial innovation it should be remembered works along two main, often interrelated, ways. Financial innovation can refer to the engineering of a 'new' financial instrument (such as a swap or a mortgage-backed security), altering existing securities by adding innovative devices such as sophisticated options. Another related side to innovation focuses on the innovations in trading and market making designed to develop liquid markets for new instruments. For example, so-called pass-through securities – in essence, a tradeable claim on a pool loans (and at the core of the mortgage-back market) – offered an innovation in trading arrangements whereby individually untraded mortgages gained liquidity as a result of being packaged into tradeable securities. As the familiar story goes, the growth of financial innovation over the past few decades produced markets where markets previously did not exist (financial futures contracts, for example), turned the untradeable into something tradeable (mortgages, say), transforming the incommensurate into the commensurate, and sewing together objects (loans and mortgages, for instance) and places into increasingly complex connectivities.

The significance of financial innovation lies then not simply in the way the process allowed the imagining of new financial instruments and associated trading systems, but in the way that the balance sheets of a significant range of financial intermediaries, from banks to hedge funds, were complicated by these innovative connectivities (see *Financial Stability Report*, 2011; Haldane, 2009). As two Bank of England economists put it, innovations such as credit default swaps and collateralized debt obligations, and the interdependencies they produce, 'created an environment for feedback elements to generate amplified responses to shocks to the financial system. They have also made it difficult to assess the potential for contagion arising from the behaviour of financial institutions under distress or from outright default' (Gai and Kapadia, 2010: 5).

To illustrate let's take a still topical example, the piecing together of residential mortgage-backed securities (RMBS) to illustrate some of the points made so far. RMBS is less as a case of clean cut financial engineering and more of a collection of practices that reassembles the spatialities of financial risks amongst disparate agents in less than transparent ways. The starting point is simple but arguably significant (and often overlooked): to assemble a financial instrument nowadays is almost always to partake in the assembling of other instruments where the eventual distribution of risks and rewards amongst market participants is necessarily clouded but always inherently spatial. In the borderless world of abstract finance the current regulatory environment and significantly the presence of a key instrument, the financial derivative, free special purpose vehicles (such as those essential to RMBS) to choose the routes they travel untroubled by regulatory bodies for whom the task of detecting where the risks are would appear to be all but a lost cause. The routes chosen, the innovative spatialities, become clear(er) only when the overzealous calculations made within the ethereal world of abstract finance fall to earth – as exemplified in the recent subprime crisis and ensuing credit crunch, at the heart of which lie RMBS.

To reflect on the hybrid nature of the practices that work to put the flow into the flows of finance[9] is to find a starting point to conceptualize the spatio-temporalities prepared and exchanged in the making of financial markets. The mathematical formulae and the assumptions they contain about space–time, the manner in which their assumptions become entwined in the workings of modern finance as a result of the increasing centrality of financial engineering based as it is upon such mathematical expressions, on streams of data, their manipulation and presentation on the screens in financial organizations, may now all be viewed as active players in the hybrid troupe called a financial market that, all together, produce 'unimagined topologies'.[10] But are we then still talking about the same old finance, the same old connectivities, and the same old risks? And if not, then do the connectivities generated and the risks they channel suggest that 'this time it's different'?

6.5 SAME OLD FINANCE . . .?

If we attend to the make-up of markets, to the enabling financial agencements and what they assemble, then, contrary say to Paul Hirst and Grahame Thompson (1996), global finance today is not the same as say one hundred years ago. If, as Doreen Massey (2005: 85) points out, the analysis is less about *degree* – for instance, the volume of international capital flows a century ago against comparable figures for today – and more about *form* – just what are the characteristics of such flows and what components are involved in their design and movement? – then today's financial markets are revealed as different in that they work through, to use Callon's (2005: 4) words, a 'reconfigured socio-technical agencement' (hence the attraction of this concept). Such reconfiguration has effects both *within* market cultures (see for example Preda (2009); Zaloom (2003, 2006)) *and* in the worlds outside the exchanges. The capacity of finance to reconfigure space–time through processes of coding and coordination achieved through financial mathematical modelling and visualization software, for example, has altered and expanded to reflect changes in the constituent components of finance. Nowadays the markets are, Callon (1998) would say, prepared, configured, differently. The financial models, the latest forms of ICT, and so on, as well as the 'money imaginary' of the humans involved in these markets, an imaginary that weaves its way through and feeds on the possibilities of such materials, are all potentially capable of reworking the space–times drawn into financial flows, making things different, this time. And a significant part of the reason why it's different lies in the creation of new forms of connectivity and the channelling of complex risks.

. . . Same Old Connectivities, Same Old Risks?

> *So, where are the risks?* They are all around us all of the time, of course. Some will crystallize. But that need not lead to disorder. Indeed, in most circumstances, global capital markets are deep and liquid enough – having a sufficiently wide range of participants able to trade with each other, and with different risk appetites and different actual risk exposures – to absorb shocks. But history suggests that strains can appear at times. And as the system develops, *we need to be alive to whether cracks might show up in new places or old weaknesses manifest themselves in new ways*. (Paul Tucker, Executive Director for Markets and a member of the Monetary Policy Committee, Bank of England, from a speech delivered at Euromoney Global Borrowers and Investors Forum, The London Hilton on 23 June 2005, emphasis added)

> . . . *financial markets are very different today. They are more broad based and much more connected* so that these assets that were created in the US also find their way into Germany; these *assets* that were created in the US *find their way into different kinds of vehicles and different types of investment*. It's much more broad based and much more international in scope because that's the nature of the markets. (Sam O'Neal, Chairman and CEO of Merrill Lynch, interviewed in *The Banker*, October 2007, emphasis added)[11]

> We are in a minefield. *No one knows where the mines are planted* and we are just trying to stumble through it. (Drew Matus, economist at Lehman Brothers, FT, 14 August 2007, emphasis added)

The composition of financial markets is not the only way that contemporary finance differs from the past. As the above quotes suggest the *connections* between markets and territories differ, too, as do the *risks* they channel. Financial innovation is central to the new forms of connectivity that have come to characterize contemporary financial markets; such connectivity 'breeds and multiples risk' as LiPuma and Lee remarked pre-GFC (2004: 53). The 'binding and blending' that derivatives in particular enable, facilitates connectivity as such instruments are designed to price risk and blend previously separate markets (Bryan and Rafferty, 2006: 5). In their recent study of financial derivatives Bryan and Rafferty (2006) underscore the points made above when they argue that the importance of today's derivatives lies in two related spheres. First, is their role in binding, through options and futures, the present and the future. Second, and perhaps more pertinent to the arguments in this chapter, is their function of blending through swaps in particular to establish

> *pricing relationships that readily convert between different forms of asset. Derivatives blend different forms of capital into a single unit of measure.* (They make it possible to convert things as economically nebulous as ideas and perceptions, weather and war into commodities that can be priced relative to each other and traded for profits.) (Bryan and Rafferty, 2006: 12; emphasis in original)

The moves by investment banks and hedge funds say into the US Sulfur Allowances market in search of high yields in a low interest rate environment, is perhaps one example of the possibility of imagining the weather and, say, an emerging market bond as 'commensurate'. That is, blending, as a process, involves the establishment of pricing relationships across any number of entities that then makes compatible what were previously distinct and separate. Thus binding and blending are highly spatial acts, too (Pryke and Allen, 2000). Derivatives designed to deal with the risks of highly interconnected markets at the same time become the 'authors' of their own form of connectivity (LiPuma and Lee, 2004: 150). One result (particularly post Basel II) is that such financial instruments serve to delocalize risk so much so that risk becomes the 'general feature of financial activity' as Randy Martin (2007) has argued.

As the present crisis and those preceding it over the past decade or so demonstrate only too clearly, linked to computers, and the 'technologized mathematics' (Rotman, 2008) that such technology enables, innovations such as derivatives re-energize the 'idea of finance' and transport this sign into ever-increasing number, connecting financialized space–times in original ways. Innovation always has a spatial dimension and that spatiality is present because the risks around which the innovations are wrapped are always in the end 'of the world' and thus consequential. The dreaming up and design of financial innovation is increasingly virtual but as the event of a crisis demonstrates only too clearly the outcomes have a very real materiality. Financial innovation composes, recomposes, blends old and new 'objects and relations' and produces interactions that are not all present at the moment of innovation itself but surface when a crisis strikes.

If financial innovation increasingly has been focused on ways to limit risk by discovering profitable ways to channel its distribution amongst a range of financial agents, then the spatialities of this process should be part of the narrative. The 'spatial dynamics of risk' (November, 2008: 1523) in other words need to be taken into account (see also Tellmann, 2009). Such processes are core to modern finance and are central to the 'interactive complexity' (Bookstaber, 2007) of many key financial markets such as swaps. In a recent market-wise contribution to the current situation the hedge fund manager and ex-quantitative researcher and prop trader with Morgan Stanley, Richard Bookstaber brings the language of 'interactive complexity' to bear on the design of complex financial instruments and consequences that unravel when such products start to go wrong. Of immediate interest is the way he draws attention to the source of complexity introduced by such instruments as options and swaps; their structure is non-linearly related, as he says, to the 'prices of their underlying securities'. Significantly 'Observing their day-to-day movements gives no inkling of what may be in store if the market moves dramatically'. Moreover – and here there are echoes with the earlier insistence on foregrounding 'emergence' and spatialities – with swaps and other highly leveraged positions:

> the complexity arises because that leverage can link the market unexpectedly to events that are distant [in both time and space] and economically unrelated. A market can spiral out of control simply because there is some group of overextended investors who happen to have positions that for one reason or another they are forced to liquidate. These interrelationships cannot be anticipated in advance and will shift with the fortunes and market interests of the investors and speculators. (Bookstaber, 2007: 156)

Moreover, as some have argued, the way the crisis mutated falls outside of the accepted currency of risk and volatility and perhaps more accurately captured by 'turbulence' (see for example Cooper, 2010; State Street Corporation, 2009).[12]

The intensive spaces of financial market making 'perform temporal [and spatial] syntheses' to produce spatialities – rather than *flat geographies* over which financial transactions take place – that extend through an ever increasing range of entities cum investment categories such as metals, grains, stock indices, currencies, money markets, and now through derivatives, financial market making resonates through weather, floods, earthquakes – all are now on the investment radar of the asset allocators moving according to a 2005 estimate US$45 trillion (that is 150 per cent of OECD GDP)[13] around the globe.[14] The weight of this money is not simply a *flow*. The asset allocation decisions that move potentially vast sums in and out of asset classes as situations change, increasingly 'make markets' as the International Monetary Fund has recognized (IMF, 2005: 65). 'Institutional flows' certainly flow, as they are moved from one asset class to another; those within financial centres after all spend a great deal of time organizing such movement. The simple point is that the range of decision-making that informs that movement and influences asset allocation – varying as it does in terms of, say, differing liability structures, tax exposure, accounting requirements, time horizons (IMF, 2005: 70–76),[15] the emergence of new management styles – means that the complete process is not a dispassionate, smooth flow. It is a lively, unpredictable entanglement that generates financial topologies.

6.6 WHEN BALTIMORE CAME TO TOWN – TOPOLOGICALLY SPEAKING

If private finance is to remain central to 'economic growth', then the nature and qualities, the intensities, of space–times made through and enabling financial markets and the 'instruments' they trade in, all need to be part of theoretical approaches to modern finance, its workings and outcomes. As Doreen Massey wrote in her attack on aspatial globalization, 'We are constantly making and re-making the time–spaces through which we live our lives. And globalization, imagined through the lens of this conceptualization of space–time, the [financial] globalization which we are facing now, is a thoroughgoing, world-wide restructuring of those time–spaces, along particular lines' (Massey, 1999: 23). I follow Massey's influence and argue for a 'different imagining' of financialization and its accompanying creative workshop in financial innovation and 'refuse to convene the spatial under the sign of temporality' and so move towards the 'beginnings of a fully spatialized understanding' of financial innovation and its consequences. To do or to perform financial economics is to 'geo-graphize'; space–times are actively produced through practices of market making, central to which are technical artefacts – 'market devices' (Callon et al., 2007) or 'financial objects' (Muniesa, 2009), as noted earlier – and around which such practices gather in the form of *agencements* (Callon and Muniesa, 2005), and through which emergent financial topologies are generated. These topologies are not the same as the already etched networks linking Wall Street, the City – they are not existing but *emergent*. Financial topologies are emergent in the sense that outcomes are not foreseeable; what contemporary finance assembles through market making is unknowable precisely because it is such a heterogeneous mix. It is the interaction of the stuff of modern finance that makes the idea of emergent financial topologies potentially so useful.

From a geographical perspective, then, to approach the workings of finance and financialization via emergent financial topologies help to focus on the nature of interactions or connectivities that in large part can be traced back to financial centres and their official networks but are not reducible to them and, as such, topology, rather than say scale, offers a fruitful 'conceptual insight' (Amin, 2002: 386), opens up a better understanding (Allen, 2011: 318) of the dynamic, unexpected, real-time but future oriented character of financial connectivity, than is the idea of flow or an already etched in to the earth 'network'. Financial topologies emerge in an almost self-referential way through the 'connective capabilities' of technologized finance.

If 'spacing financialization' (French, Leyshon and Wainwright, 2011) is the task ahead, then the appeal of a financial topology is that it helps to grasp the interconnectivity produced through the contemporary financial markets in real time and the unexpected adjacencies that in a sense become visible only in the event of a crisis when for example the US subprime crisis turned-up in the 'fair-weather' balance sheet of Northern Rock in late 2007. Like so many other banks, Northern Rock's balance sheet had been reshaped since its conversion from a mutual-form building society to a bank in 1997 and made fragile not simply by its use of securitization and other secured borrowing (see *Financial Stability Report*, 2007: 10–12) but by the associated adoption of a model of 'initiate and distribute', in which profits in the form of fees are made from initiating and servicing loans, whilst the risks attached to loans are (supposedly) passed through the financial markets (Chick, 2008: 117). Innovative techniques such as initiate and distribute, and the manner of Northern Rock's balance sheet growth, generated risks that became apparent only when the new bank's funding possibilities seized up to reveal the long and interconnected linkages made across the globe, and through the USA subprime market in particular; when, that is, at the moment of the funding crisis the long chains of counterparty exposures and credit claims swiftly traced their way back at the moment of crisis from 'elsewhere' to the financial heart of Northern Rock, with a vengeance.

To talk of Baltimore arriving suddenly in Newcastle, is a provocation to think topologically (rather than in scalar terms) about the subprime crisis, where attention is placed on the swift movements through interconnected financial markets and the unexpected consequences. When the subprime crisis hit, the miscalculations rapidly unfurled and the risks that were thought to have been long passed through to distant financial markets were quickly and uncompromisingly folded into Northern Rock's balance sheet; in a sense, Baltimore, reduced to financial code, had come to town and it and Newcastle (and a host of other places) were made financially adjacent. Such adjacency is always latent, for wrapped up in the preparation of innovations such as RMBSs and CDOs within the confines of financial centres, is also the potential for the sudden re-orchestration of spatialities that lie geographically far beyond the world's financial citadels but spatio-temporally within their ambit. What's more, and at the risk of labouring a simple point, what is produced through financial innovation is a financialized future that quite blatantly refuses to be corralled into neat national borders and thus be amenable to the regulatory discipline of nation states. What the present crisis highlights is the creation of risky spaces that, to use Ong's phrase, do not 'follow given scales or political mappings' (Ong, 2005: 338).

To take another example from the eye of the recent storm, Lehman Brothers, like other banks, cut and sliced MBS and CDOs which in the process multiplied the connectivities alive within the innovative instruments. Lehman had a large number of CDSs (credit default swaps) relative to its balance sheet and a significant number of counterparties. This significant number multiplied pricing distortions; true Knightian distortion, as Andrew Haldane (2009, 2014) has pointed out. The spatially dispersed counterparties, each with varying risk qualities, informed the pricing uncertainties undertaken in New York. When things went wrong, as it were, the extensive geographies of 'unknown unknowns' (also known as uncertainties) turned-up seemingly from nowhere on the balance sheet of Lehman Brothers – and others. As with Northern Rock, financial innovation produced unexpected geographies of financial risk and uncertainty; this was the outcome of what Haldane referred to as the fundamental change in the topology of the financial system that had begun to be generated decades before.

The linkages between the practices within financial centres, within organizations and exchanges, *and* the world 'outside' needs to be made more explicit. Specific place based market makers generate spatialities through their market practices, that much is clear. Yet to approach finance as a technical process, that 'flows' and 'circulates', bypasses the politics of the socio-technical relations of finance, so usefully put on the agenda by Donald MacKenzie and others, and so quite often evades the question of the responsibilities that attach to making finance. Those responsibilities revolve, in part at least, around how a highly interconnected future is imagined and made through private sector markets.

6.7 TOWARD A CONCLUSION

Taken together, the above pointers suggest that in looking to find 'what's different' and 'what's the same' about the current crisis, as a recent BIS report posed the problem ahead, there is a need to recognize that through the generative capacities of innovative financial techniques, space is no mere flatland (if ever it was) but is an active ingredient in processes of financialization, understood here as novel ways to search out and extract value. Omitting space from accounts of such financial techniques is a conceptual failure, as well as a failure fully to recognize how, most notably in the event of a crisis, the seductive promises of a politics enacted through private sector financial markets, suddenly recomposed space–times with often dire consequences.

In the move from M–M, where increasingly money seems to have an endless ability to create more money, a lot happens; people and market devices combine in sometimes extraordinary combinations to seek out market opportunities, new instruments, new ways to profitably exploit risk and to try and tame uncertainty. The innovative tactics of those within financial centres play out in the worlds outside (as if this needs to be said – but actually it does); innovation is consequential and it is consequential because increasingly the techniques of innovation – coding space and time, ways of calculating, ways of seeing, ways of drawing worlds into the calculative devices and practices of financial markets – have effects. A politics of financialized space must find ways to foreground the consequences of calculation and the spatialities of financial risk that such calculation seeks to tame yet at the same time inadvertently distributes.[16] Hence the earlier emphasis placed on beginning the discussion before the flows start moving, as it were, asking what it is that puts the flow into 'flow'[17] and just what combines to make cotemporary finance.

The role of finance in geographies of political economy, as Christophers (2015) has persuasively argued, is an ongoing project. As part of this effort, financial economics must be engaged in ways that do not leave unquestioned the world-making that the circulation and imposition of such a discourse involves (see Gibson-Graham, 2006 for similar points). It's not a case of simply making corrections to the pre-crisis models; that it's just a case of the 'right mathematics and enough information' (Green, 2000: 86 cited in de Goede, 2005: 140) for such highly mathematical finance drapes the world in financial code – a 'financial garb' – in an effort to ensure that its models deliver according to its 'metrological regime'[18] (Barry, 2002: 273) (see also MacKenzie, 2001, 2003a, 2003b, 2005). To accept the world according to such technical (supposedly) apolitical finance[19] is to be shielded from the very geopolitics and social relations of financial markets and the associated power to spatialize which (should) matter (see Massey, 2010). As recent crisis and those before testify, the future is not linear, it is not simply temporal; the future imagined and enacted through the 'socio-technical combinations' of finance relies upon and produces a complex weave of spatialities, of consequential emergent financial topologies.

ACKNOWLEDGEMENTS

Many thanks to Jane Pollard for helpful comments on an earlier draft of this chapter. The chapter draws in parts on a CRESC Working Paper 24 'Speculating on Geographies of Finance'.

NOTES

1. See Christophers (2015: 210–211) for a cautionary note on the use of the term 'crisis'.
2. The engagement with topology in this chapter is exploratory and tentative and is part of the growing interest in topology more generally within geography (see for example the collection of papers in *Dialogues in Human Geography*, 2011.3: 283–318; Martin and Secor, 2014). The appeal of trying to think topologically about finance is that it offers another way to think about the geographies of finance, how these are produced and generated by the 'stuff' of finance and the consequences.

3. As Singh reported in 2010 five key LCFIs that are active in the OTC derivatives market in the United States (Goldman Sachs, Citi, J.P. Morgan, Bank of America, and Morgan Stanley) were jointly carrying almost $500 billion in OTC derivative payables exposure as of Q3, 2009. In Europe, Deutsche Bank, Barclays, UBS, RBS and Credit Suisse are sizable players. These five largest European banks had about $600–$700 billion in under-collateralized risk (measured by residual derivative payables) as of December 2008 (Singh, 2010: 5–6).
4. This particular and pervasive sense of time as a straight line within economics/financial economics is summed up in a line from the leading economist Paul Davidson 'The economic system is moving through calendar time from an irrevocable past to an uncertain and statistically unpredictable future' (1994: 17 cited in Janeway, 2009, no page number). Although see developments around non-linear systems within quantitative economics (e.g. Hommes, 2001).
5. See Sarah Hall's (2010) excellent summary of the growing interface between cultural economy and economic geography.
6. On *agencement*/assemblage see for example John Phillips (2006: 108–109).
7. See Callon's (2005) reply to reply to Danny Miller's (2005) critique of The Laws of the Markets which clarifies his approach and draws attention to the all-important idea of agencement.
8. The sense of space I wish to subscribe to is, to borrow from Massey, 'not static, not a cross-section through time; it is disrupted, active and generative. It is not a closed system; it is constantly, as space–time, being made' (Massey, 1999: 274). Debates about the production of space, the multiplicity of time–spaces for instance seem to be absent from geographies of finance, as is a sense of the 'ever-changing ways in which flows and territories are conditions of each other. It is the practices and relations which construct them both that demand address' (Massey, 2005: 99). More broadly see Murdoch (2006) for an excellent summary of the rise of relational thinking within geography.
9. See Bill Maurer (2003: 73) for similar points. As he says, when it comes to capital mobility in particular, there is a need to investigate the nature of 'movement and the objects being moved'.
10. As Brian Rotman has noted 'the computer creates complex topological surfaces, fractal functions, and iteration based entities which were previously *not only invisible but unimagined, unconceived*' (Rotman, 2008: 66; emphasis added).
11. Sam O'Neal left Merrill in late 2007 for taking the investment bank into the RMBS market in the US at the peak of the housing boom with disastrous results; Merrill reportedly lost around US$7.9 billion in mortgage-related losses. As he 'retired' rather than being 'fired' he received a reputed US$160 million 'golden parachute'.
12. 'Turbulence is not the same as volatility. It implies not only dynamic pricing activity but the arrival of statistically unlikely events – sometimes known as black swans – that signal the breakdown of fundamental assumptions. Importantly, turbulence operates on a continuum, with varying degrees of turbulence in the market over time, making it very difficult to predict. Therefore, while identifying turbulent periods isn't strictly a binary, black and white matter, it is crucial to recognize shifts in market turbulence. Turbulence can best be understood as statistical unusualness, rather than as indicative of negative performance' (*State Street*, 2009: 2).
13. These investors include insurance companies, pension funds, and investment companies including mutual funds and unit investment trusts, and hedge funds (IMF, 2005: 66–67).
14. The market in weather derivatives, for example, in the build-up to the crash attracted the attention of leading hedge funds such as DE Shaw and Co., as well as specialist hedge funds, such as Takara (now part of Renaissance Reinsurance), which were set up specifically to facilitate private investor and fund investment in weather and weather-related products. Indeed, hurricane Katrina boosted hedge fund interest in weather derivatives – trade volume was up fivefold in 2005 on the previous year (*The Economist*, 2005).
15. Even within 'hedge funds' strategies vary to include for instance 'global macro', 'equity hedge', 'high yield', 'emerging markets' and 'fixed-income arbitrage' (see IMF, 2005: 50–51).
16. Erica Pani and Nancy Holman (2014) go some way to doing this in their detailed account of Norwegian municipalities' entanglement in global finance.
17. There are some lovely points in Coutin, Maurer, and Yngvessen (2002) to help in thinking about flows and globalization – amongst others things.
18. Andrew Barry uses the notion of 'metrological regime' (Barry, 2002: 273) – making things measurable and thus calculable – to highlight the importance of measurement to framing and thus the performance of calculation. As he says 'metrology puts new objects into circulation . . . metrology creates new objects that make a difference in the world'.
19. See de Goede (2005: 121–143) for strong argument that helps to show the gradual depoliticization of financial practices in the twentieth century and the rise of 'scientific finance', particularly post 1960s, as part of this process.

REFERENCES

Aalbers, M.B. (2008), 'The financialization of home and the mortgage market crisis', *Competition and Change*, **12** (2), 148–166.

Adam, B. (2003), 'Reflexive modernization temporalized', *Theory, Culture and Society*, **20** (2), 59–78.

Allen, J. (2011), 'Topological twists Power's shifting geographies', *Dialogues in Human Geography*, **1** (3), 283–298.

Amin, A. (2002), 'Spatialities of globalisation', *Environment and Planning A*, **34**, 385–399.

Arrighi, Giovanni (1994), *The Long Twentieth Century*, London: Verso.

Barry, A. (2002), 'The anti-political economy', *Economy and Society*, **31** (2), 268–284.

Barry, A. and D. Slater (2002), 'Introduction: the technological economy', *Economy and Society*, **31** (2), 175–193.

Beunza, D., I. Hardie and D. MacKenzie (2006), 'A price is a social thing: towards a material sociology of arbitrage', *Organization Studies*, **27** (5), 721–745.

Blackburn, R. (2008), 'The subprime crisis', *New Left Review*, **50**, 63.

Bookstaber, R. (2007), *A Demon Of Our Own Design*, Hoboken, NJ: John Wiley and Sons.

Bryan, D. and M. Rafferty (2006), *Capitalism with Derivatives: A Political Economy of Financial Derivatives*, Basingstoke: Palgrave Macmillan.

Buchan, J. (1997), *Frozen Desire: Meaning of Money*, New York: Farrar Straus Giroux.

Callon, M. (1998), 'Introduction: the embeddedness of economic markets in economics', in M. Callon (ed.), *The Laws of the Markets*, London: John Wiley and Sons/Sociological Review Monograph, pp.1–57.

Callon, M. (2005), 'Why virtualism paves the way to political impotence: a reply to Daniel Miller's critique of the laws of the markets', *Economic Sociology: European Electronic Newsletter*, **6** (2) (February), 3–20.

Callon, M. and F. Muniesa (2005), 'Peripheral vision economic markets as calculative collective devices', *Organization Studies*, **26** (8), 1229–1250.

Callon, M., Y. Millo and F. Muniesa (eds) (2007), *Market Devices*, Oxford: Blackwell/Sociological Review.

Cassis, Y. (2006), *Capital of Capitals: A History of International Financial Centres, 1780–2005*, Cambridge: Cambridge University Press.

Chick, V. (2008), 'Could the crisis at Northern Rock have been predicted?: An evolutionary approach', *Contributions to Political Economy*, **27** (1), 115–124.

Christophers, B. (2015), 'The limits to financialization', *Dialogues in Human Geography*, **5** (2), 183–200.

Clark, G.L. (2005), 'Money flows like mercury: the geography of global finance', *Geografiska Annaler: Series B, Human Geography*, **87** (2), 99–112.

Cooper, I. (1986), 'Innovations: new market instruments', *Oxford Review of Economic Policy*, **2** (4), 1–17.

Cooper, M. (2010), 'Turbulent worlds, financial markets and environmental crisis', *Theory, Culture and Society*, **27** (2–3), 167–190.

Coutin, S., B. Maurer and B. Yngvessen (2002), 'In the mirror: the legitimation work of globalization', *Law and Social Inquiry*, **27** (4), 801–843.

de Goede, Marieke (2005), *Virtue, Fortune, and Faith: A Geneaology Of Finance*, Minneapolis: University of Minnesota Press.

Dialogues in Human Geography (2011), 'Article Forum 1', **1** (3), 283–318.

Dymski, G.A. (2009), 'Afterword: mortgage markets and the urban problematic in the global transition', *International Journal of Urban and Regional Research*, **33** (2), 427–442.

Fieldhouse, S (2008), 'Tackling global change: Titian's founders see opportunities in macro themes'. Retrieved on 12 October 2016 from www.thehedgefundjournal.com/node/7407.

Financial Stability Report (2007), October, 22 'Box A The funding crisis at Northern Rock', pp.10–12. Retrieved on 13 October 2016 from www.bankofengland.co.uk/publications/Documents/fsr/2007/fsrfull0710.pdf.

Financial Stability Report (2011), 'Risks from the international financial system', 29 June, pp.6–16. Retrieved on 13 October 2016 from www.bankofengland.co.uk/publications/Documents/fsr/2011/fsrfull1106.pdf.

French, S., A. Leyshon and N. Thrift (2009), 'A very geographical crisis: the making and breaking of the 2007–2008 financial crisis', *Cambridge Journal of Regions, Economy and Society*, **2**, 287–302.

French, S., A. Leyshon and T. Wainright (2011), 'Financializing space, spacing financialization', *Progress in Human Geography*, **35** (6), 798–819.

Gai, P. and S. Kapadia (2010), 'Contagion in financial networks', Bank of England Working Paper No. 383, March. Retrieved on 9 November 2016 from www.bankofengland.co.uk/research/Pages/workingpapers/2010/wp383.aspx.

Garratt, Rodney J., Lavan Mahadeva and Katsiaryna Svirydzenka (2011), 'Mapping systemic risk in the international banking network', Bank of England Working Papers (413), 1–43.

Gibson-Graham, J.K. (2006), *A Postcapitalist Politics*, Minneapolis: University of Minnesota Press.

Green, S. (2000), 'Negotiating with the future: the culture of modern risk in global financial markets', *Environment and Planning D*, **18** (1), 77–90.
Haldane, A.G. (2009), 'Rethinking the financial network', Speech delivered at the Financial Student Association, Amsterdam, April, 1–26.
Haldane, A.G. (2014), Managing global finance as a system. The Maxwell Fry Annual Global Finance Lecture, 29 October 2014, Birmingham University.
Hall, S. (2010), 'Geographies of money and finance I: cultural economy, politics and place', *Progress in Human Geography*, **35** (2), 234–245.
Hardie, I. and D. MacKenzie (2007), 'Assembling an economic actor: the agencement of a hedge fund', *The Sociological Review*, **55** (1), 57–80.
Harvey, D. (1982), *The Limits to Capital*, Oxford: Basil Blackwell.
Hirst, P. and G. Thompson (1996), *Globalisation in Question: The International Economy and the Possibilities of Governance*, Cambridge: Polity.
Hommes, C.H (2001), 'Financial markets as nonlinear adaptive evolutionary systems', *Quantitative Finance*, **1** (1), 149–167.
IMF (2005), 'Global financial stability report: market developments and issues', International Monetary Fund Washington, DC September.
Janeway, W. (2009), 'Six impossible things before breakfast', *Significance*, **6** (1), 28–31.
Law, J. (2002), 'Economics as interference', in P. Du Gay and M. Pryke (eds), *Cultural Economy: Cultural Analysis and Commercial Life*, London: Sage, pp.21–38.
Lee, Roger, Gordon L. Clark, Jane Pollard and Andrew Leyshon (2010), 'The remit of financial geography – before and after the crisis', *Journal of Economic Geography*, **9**, 723–747.
Leyshon, A. and N. Thrift (2007), 'The capitalization of almost everything: the future of finance and capitalism', *Theory, Culture and Society*, **24** (7–8), 97–115.
LiPuma, E. and B. Lee (2004), *Financial Derivatives and the Globalization of Risk*, Durham, NC: Duke University Press.
LiPuma E. and B. Lee (2012), 'A social approach to the financial derivatives markets' *South Atlantic Quarterly*, **111** (2), 289–316.
MacKenzie, D. (2001), 'Physics and finance: s-terms and modern finance as a topic for science studies', *Science, Technology and Human Values*, **26** (2), 115–144.
MacKenzie, D. (2003a), 'An equation and its worlds bricolage, exemplars, disunity and performativity in financial economics', *Social Studies of Science*, **33** (6), 831–868.
MacKenzie, D. (2003b), 'Long-term capital management and the sociology of arbitrage', *Economy and Society*, **32** (3), 349–380.
MacKenzie, D. (2004a), 'The big, bad wolf and the rational market: portfolio insurance, the 1987 crash and the performativity of economics', *Economy and Society*, **33** (3), 303–334.
MacKenzie, D. (2004b), 'Models of markets: finance theory and the historical sociology of arbitrage', *Revue d'histoire des sciences*, 407–431.
MacKenzie, D. (2005), 'Opening the black boxes of global finance', *Review of International Political Economy*, **12** (4), 555–576.
MacKenzie, D (2009), *Material Markets: How Economic Agents Are Constructed* (Clarendon Lectures in Management Studies), Oxford: Oxford University Press.
Martin, R. (2007), *An Empire of Indifference*, Durham, NC: Duke University Press.
Martin, R. and A.J. Secor (2014), 'Towards a post-mathematical topology', *Progress in Human Geography*, **38** (3), 420–438.
Massey, D. (1999), 'Imagining globalisation: power-geometries of time–space', Power-geometries and the politics of space–time, Hettner-Lecture 1998 Department of Geography, University of Heidelberg.
Massey, D. (2005), *For Space*, London: Sage.
Massey, D. (2010), *World City*, Cambridge: Polity.
Maurer, B. (2003), 'International political economy as a cultural practice: the metaphysics of capital mobility', in R. Warren Perry and B. Maurer (eds), *Globalization under Construction: Governmentality, Law and Identity*, Minneapolis: University of Minnesota Press, pp.71–97.
Maurer, B. (2005a), *Mutual Life, Limited*, Princeton and London: Princeton University Press.
Maurer, B. (2005b), 'Does money matter? Abstraction and substitution in alternative financial forms?', in D. Miller (ed.), *Materiality*, Durham and London: Duke University Press, pp.40–164.
Miller, D. (2005), 'Reply to Michel Callon', *Economic Sociology: Electronic Newsletter*, **6** (3), 3–13.
Mirowski, Philip (2013), *Never Let a Good Crisis go to Waste*, London: Verso.
Miyazaki, H. (2005), 'The materiality of finance theory', in D. Miller (ed.), *Materiality*, Durham and London: Duke University Press, pp.65–181.
Morgan, M.S. (2001), 'Models, stories and the economic world', *Journal of Economic Methodology*, **8** (3), 361–384.

Morgan, M.S. (2004), 'Imagination and imaging in model building', *Philosophy of Science*, **71** (5), 753–766.
Morgan, M.S. (2012), *The World in the Model: How Economists Work and Think*, Cambridge: Cambridge University Press.
Muniesa, F. (2009), 'The description of financial objects: a comment on Hart/Ortiz (AT 24 [6])', *Anthropology Today*, **25** (2), 26–27.
Murdoch, Jonathan (2006), *Post-structuralist Geography: A Guide to Relational Space*, London: Sage.
Neal, L. (1990), *The Rise of Financial Capitalism: International Capital Markets in the Age of Reason*, Cambridge: Cambridge University Press.
November, Valerie (2008), 'Spatiality of risk', *Environment and Planning A*, **2008** (40), 1523–1527.
Ong, A (2005), 'Ecologies of expertise: assembling flows, managing citizenship', in A. Ong and S.J. Collier (eds), *Global Assemblages: Technology, Politics, and Ethics as Anthropological Problems*, London: John Wiley, pp.337–353.
Pani, E. and N. Holman (2014), 'A fetish and fiction of finance: unravelling the subprime crisis', *Economic Geography*, **90** (2), 213–235.
Phillips, J. (2006), 'Agencement/assemblage', *Theory, Culture and Society*, **23**, 108–109.
Pike, A. and J.S. Pollard (2010), 'Economic geographies of financialization', *Economic Geography*, **86** (1), 29–51.
Pozsar, Z., T. Adrian, A. Ashcraft and H. Boesky (2010), 'Shadow banking', Federal Reserve Bank of New York, Staff Report No. 458, July.
Preda, A. (2009), *Framing Finance: The Boundaries of Markets and Modern Capitalism*, Chicago, IL: University of Chicago Press.
Pryke, M. and J. Allen (2000), 'Monetized time–space: derivatives – money's' new imaginary'?', *Economy and Society*, **29** (2), 264–284.
Reinhart, Carmen and Kenneth Rogoff (2009), *This Time is Different: Eight Centuries of Financial Folly*, Princeton, NJ: Princeton University Press.
Rotman, Brian (2008), *Becoming beside Ourselves: The Alphabet, Ghosts, and Distributed Human Being*, Durham, NC: Duke University Press.
Singh, Manmohan (2010), 'Collateral, netting and systemic risk in the OTC derivatives market', International Monetary Fund Working Paper, no. WP/10/99.
State Street Corporation (2009), 'Turbulence' in *State Street Vision Focus*, State Street Corporation: Boston, MA. September, pp. 2–4.
Tellmann, U. (2009), 'Foucault and the invisible economy', *Foucault Studies*, **6**, 5–24.
The Economist (2005), 'Weather risk: natural hedge', 29 September. Retrieved on 9 November 2016 from www.economist.com/node/4465927.
Tucker, P. (2007), 'Speech to Merrill Lynch Conference: A perspective on recent monetary and financial system developments', 26 April, *Bank of England Quarterly Bulletin*. Retrieved on 9 November 2016 from www.bankofengland.co.uk/archive/Documents/historicpubs/speeches/2007/speech308.pdf.
Wainwright, T. (2009), 'Laying the foundations for a crisis: mapping the historico–geographical construction of residential mortgage backed securitization in the UK', *International Journal of Urban and Regional Research*, **33** (2), 372–388.
Zaloom, C. (2003), 'Ambiguous numbers: trading technologies and interpretation in financial markets', *American Ethnologist*, **30** (2), 58–272.
Zaloom, C. (2006), *Out of the Pits: Traders and Technology from Chicago to London*, Chicago, IL: University of Chicago Press.

PART II

MONEY, THE SPATIAL ORGANIZATION OF FINANCIAL SYSTEMS AND UNEVEN GEOGRAPHICAL DEVELOPMENT

7. The spatial structure of the financial system and the funding of regional business: a comparison of Britain and Germany[1]

Britta Klagge, Ron Martin and Peter Sunley

7.1 INTRODUCTION

In recent years there has been growing academic and policy interest in the financing of new and small firms, which in many quarters are considered to be key sources of dynamism, innovation and job growth. There is much concern that such businesses frequently face difficulties in raising finance, in that both banks and capital markets ration or restrict the supply of much-needed start-up and expansion finance, so that these enterprises face what is often called a 'funding gap'. Further, it is also often suggested that this funding-gap problem is much more severe in economically lagging regions, especially if these regions contain no significant capital markets or major local banks of their own and are at some distance from where such markets and banks are based; that is, there are significant 'spatial proximity effects' which can militate against the supply of funds in such regions. In other words, the argument is that the spatial structure of the financial system can influence the supply of finance to firms, and thereby contribute to uneven regional development. The implication is that the more geographically centralized is a country's financial system, the more difficult it will be for firms – and especially small firms – in peripheral regions to access funds. This would seem to suggest that there might be a case for local capital markets.

An obvious counter-argument to this line of reasoning would point to the extraordinary fungibility and mobility of money, in all its forms. Surely, in what is now a truly global financial system, where digital monies can move around the world almost instantaneously, to talk of local or regional funding gaps within a country would seem misplaced. According to this viewpoint, then, a spatially centralized financial system of itself carries no adverse implications for the supply of loan or equity capital to small firms in peripheral regions: that what matters to the lending and investment decisions of centralized banks and capital markets is not the location of the firms seeking finance, but their risk–return profiles. Financial institutions themselves claim not to bias their lending and investment activity against firms and regions located away from the financial centre, and it is argued that the problem in such regions is not one of a restricted supply of finance but a lack of demand and the absence of a dynamic small firm sector in such areas. At the same time, proponents of this view will point to the positive economies of scale and scope that follow from the agglomeration of financial institutions in a major centre, resulting in efficiencies that benefit all firms and regions. In this account, therefore, there is no case for local (regional) capital markets or a more locally orientated banking system.

However, in many countries, over the past three decades or so national and even major regional financial centres have become increasingly international and global in orientation and function. The growth processes in these centres are due in large part to the expanding volume of financial transactions among global banks and currency and equity houses, and the increasing global integration of monetary flows in the context of deregulated markets, all aided by the revolution in ICT that has taken place (Grote, 2009).[2] In addition, these international financial centres function as gateways to their respective national monetary spaces, as the portals through which global financial developments and perturbations are diffused – directly and indirectly – across domestic money and capital markets. The recent global financial crisis has revealed with dramatic force how the spatial structure and operation of financial markets has changed since the early-1980s. What were once locally originating and locally distributed systems of financing – for example, mortgage finance for house purchase – have become locally originating (in the savings and investment of local individuals) but globally distributed systems in which local savings and local debt have become securitized into financial instruments and products traded on global markets far removed functionally and spatially from where those savings originated.

This twin role – as centres of capital accumulation and financial circulation, and as the hubs through and between which instabilities can be propagated and amplified – creates tensions in the operation and orientation of these centres: between their international and their national functions. Their international orientation, combined with intensifying global competition and the economies of scale and scope they enjoy, results in a concentration on large companies and huge transaction volumes. This may well have adverse implications for flows of capital to and within the regions of their national economies, particularly for the financing of new small- and medium-sized enterprises (SMEs).[3]

In this situation one might assume that smaller regional financial centres tend to fulfil a complementary function by focusing on the client groups neglected by the larger and international financial centres. For example, in the case of countries where the financial system is entirely dominated by a national 'global' centre, and where the system is highly spatially centralized, as in the UK, it is perhaps not surprising to find arguments that small businesses in the regions lack ready access to capital. This has long been a recurring issue in the UK, for example, beginning in the 1930s and resurfacing in the 1970s, at the end of the 1990s, and again in the context of the recent financial crisis. This debate has resulted in a discussion of whether regional capital markets, focusing on SMEs, should be resuscitated (Mocroft, 2001; FT.com, 2003; Handelsblatt, 2003; Huggins et al., 2003; Skidelsky et al., 2011; Merlin-Jones, 2012). In those countries where regional banks and financial centres do exist, as in Italy, Germany, and to a lesser extent the USA, there is a tension between regional and national centres, and the latter may still draw away business from the regional centres and thus erode decentralized financial systems (Bördlein, 2003; Klagge and Peter, 2009, 2011, 2012).

In this chapter we discuss this issue of the spatial organization of the financial system and the debate around regional funding gaps for business in two ways. First we offer some theoretical comments on whether and how, under different assumptions concerning the nature and operation of the financial system, the spatial structure of capital markets might effect the provision and distribution of finance to SMEs across regions. We then seek to provide some empirical light on the issue by comparing banking, venture capital and stock market structures and the regional distribution of SME funding in the UK and

Germany. The comparison between the UK and Germany is of particular interest given that numerous British policy think tank reports have suggested that the country should move towards a German model of SME finance (see for example Simpson, 2013; Boyle, 2014). At the same time, recently changes have been at work within the German system which threaten to dilute its distinctive features and move it toward a more centralized structure; while in the UK, debate has arisen around the possible case for local capital markets, a national investment bank to serve the regions, and other measures to stimulate lending to small businesses. Given that our interest is in the regional dimensions of funding for SMEs, we focus not just on banks, but also on venture and equity capital markets.

In the recent past, discussions on the existence of an equity gap for SMEs have in fact been quite intense in both countries (for example, Bank of England, 2001, 2003; Cruickshank, 2000; KfW, 2003; Nolte et al., 2002; Paul et al., 2002; Rudolph, 2003). A shortage of funds can have serious implications for SMEs: it can inhibit their formation and expansion and their rates of innovation, it can increase the danger of their insolvency, and it can hinder their growth and competitive performance. Whether a geographically decentralized financial system and venture finance market is more conducive than a spatially centralized configuration to the supply of funds to SMEs in peripheral and non-core regions is thus an important issue. We begin in the next section with some theoretical reflections on the matter.

7.2 CENTRALIZED VERSUS DECENTRALIZED FINANCIAL MARKETS: SOME THEORETICAL REFLECTIONS

The view taken on whether the spatial structure of the financial system matters for the provision of funds to SMEs depends on how the financial system is conceived. At the most abstract level of analysis, there are two main ways of conceptualizing the relationship between the monetary-financial sphere and the real economy: monetary and financial systems can be regarded as either *neutral* or *non-neutral* in terms of their effects on the economy of production. Applied to the financial sphere, conventional (neoclassical) theory assumes perfect markets, perfectly informed and rational behaviour on the part of market participants and agents, and optimal outcomes (Figure 7.1). Under this model, there can be no permanent misallocation of loanable funds and, furthermore, external funds are a perfect substitute for firms' internal funds for the purpose of financing investment.[4] The fact that external funds (obtained from banks or the capital market) are a perfect substitute for internal funds has an interesting corollary. It implies that all *profitable* investment projects (that is, projects with a positive net-present value) receive funding, and consequently that investment cannot be prevented from taking place because of a lack of funding. Should a firm's internally generated funds prove insufficient to finance a profitable investment project (taking into account the costs of financing), under such a scenario, the firm could simply turn to the financial markets to make up the deficit; and the firm would have no problem in obtaining the required funds. Risk-adjusted real rates of return on investment are therefore the sole determinants of investment.

Thus under the neutrality assumption, financial markets ensure a perfect allocation

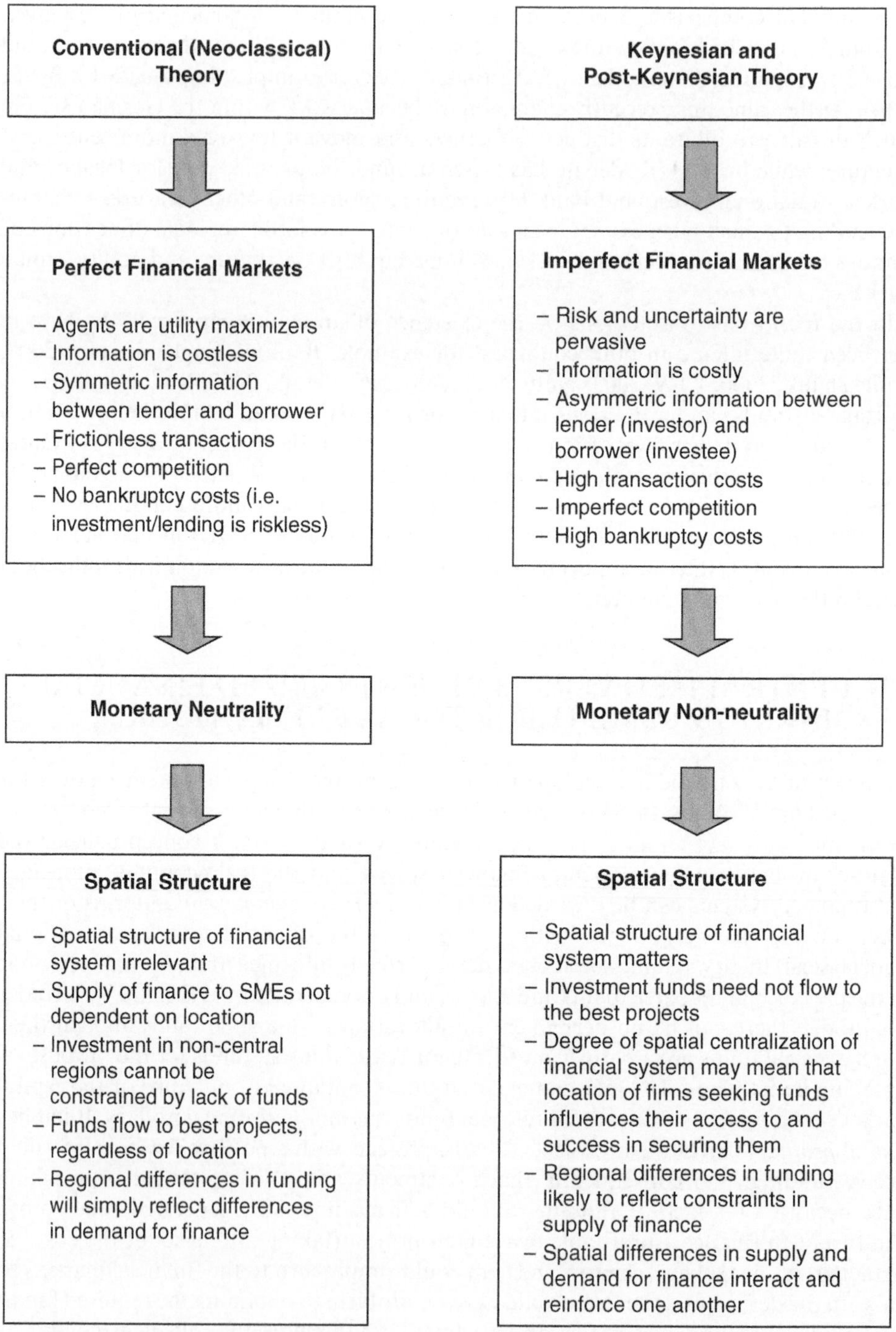

Conventional (Neoclassical) Theory

Perfect Financial Markets

- Agents are utility maximizers
- Information is costless
- Symmetric information between lender and borrower
- Frictionless transactions
- Perfect competition
- No bankruptcy costs (i.e. investment/lending is riskless)

Monetary Neutrality

Spatial Structure

- Spatial structure of financial system irrelevant
- Supply of finance to SMEs not dependent on location
- Investment in non-central regions cannot be constrained by lack of funds
- Funds flow to best projects, regardless of location
- Regional differences in funding will simply reflect differences in demand for finance

Keynesian and Post-Keynesian Theory

Imperfect Financial Markets

- Risk and uncertainty are pervasive
- Information is costly
- Asymmetric information between lender (investor) and borrower (investee)
- High transaction costs
- Imperfect competition
- High bankruptcy costs

Monetary Non-neutrality

Spatial Structure

- Spatial structure of financial system matters
- Investment funds need not flow to the best projects
- Degree of spatial centralization of financial system may mean that location of firms seeking funds influences their access to and success in securing them
- Regional differences in funding likely to reflect constraints in supply of finance
- Spatial differences in supply and demand for finance interact and reinforce one another

Figure 7.1 Two views on the financial system and relevance of its spatial structure (after Klagge and Martin, 2005)

of capital between firms and across the space-economy: investment in any given region will be independent of local savings, and local demand for finance (for loan capital or venture capital) is not constrained by local supply, but instead can access funds from anywhere in the national system. Provided new and expanding businesses requiring finance have favourable risk/return profiles, they will be able to access funds regardless of their location: the viability and potential profitability of projects – not their geographical proximity to financial centres – are the key factors determining access to capital and loans. Under these (ideal) conditions, then, there is no case for local capital markets, and there should be no sectoral or spatial 'funding-' or 'equity-gaps' in the demand for and supply of finance. In short, the spatial structure of the financial system is irrelevant.

In reality, of course, these strong assumptions are very unlikely to hold, even in a fully integrated financial system. Both new Keynesian and post-Keynesian theories of the financial system instead posit a situation of non-neutrality of money and capital markets (Figure 7.1). An important component of the New Keynesian theory, for example, is the recognition that capital markets are fundamentally different from most other markets. Finance is advanced on a promise or expectation of repayment plus a return, at some future date. Because of this temporal dimension, suppliers of capital and credit have to gather information on potential projects and debtors to evaluate the likelihood of returns to capital invested and repayment of loans made (through risk evaluation). In New Keynesian theory, information imperfections, taking the form of *asymmetric information*, interfere with this process of evaluation. The problem of asymmetric information in this context refers to the fact that the borrower may be better informed about the risk profile of an investment project than the lender or investor. The problem of informational asymmetries explains why a risk premium is attached to the use of external funds, and why this premium will vary with perceptions of risk and potential returns.

According to some authors, the link between the risk premium and asymmetric information underlies the so-called *pecking order theory* of the financial structure of firms (Myers and Majluf, 1983; Myers, 1984). Pecking order theory states that, in response to the (asymmetric-information induced) risk premia on external funds, firms' financing choices display a well-defined preference structure. Internal funds are the preferred source of finance. Next in line is debt financing, and the least favoured choice is equity financing. Another way of interpreting this idea of a pecking order of preferred forms of finance is in terms of the differences in loss of autonomy of entrepreneurial management and control that they (are perceived to) involve: internal funds involve no such loss, whereas external equity (public or private) may well entail a loss of power and control to external (share)owners. However, firms are sometimes forced or prefer to raise finance through equity because asymmetric information, or a high-risk/return ratio, or the scale of funding needed, make it impossible or less attractive to raise the quantities of external financing demanded in the form of debt finance or internal reinvested profits. Indeed, in the case of new, high-tech enterprises, there may well be a distinct preference for equity over debt. For one thing, perhaps for a while after being established such enterprises will have few if any internal profits from which to fund innovation, expansion and growth. For another, this type of firm often has a high-risk profile, and as a result may find it difficult to to obtain loan finance from banks (at least at reasonable cost). Thus, such firms may well seek other forms of funding, such a venture finance, or business angel funding, or non-mainstream sources of capital (such as crowdfunding). In the USA in the 1980s and 1990s, for example, equity was actually preferred to loans by SMEs (Frank and Goyal, 2003). Thus, the pecking order theory notwithstanding, equity finance can be of crucial significance for small firms, so that any biases or distortions that arise in its supply by virtue of the spatial structure of the capital market (public or private) could have important implications for the geographies of new firm formation and growth.

Unlike conventional theory, New Keynesian theory recognizes that financial market transactions generate frictions and that the associated transaction costs are scale-sensitive; so marginal costs fall as transaction values become larger. Information costs are considered the most important component of these costs. For individuals and firms wanting to raise funds on a centralized financial market, these costs are generated as a consequence of the need to provide the market with a steady stream of relevant information on the economic prospects of the enterprise; while for those supplying the market with funds, these information costs are incurred in the process of gathering and evaluating the information from the market in order to decide how to allocate funds. These information flows are necessary in order to address the problem of informational asymmetries and, consequently, they contribute to the efficient functioning of the market. However, the scale-sensitive character of these information costs, and transaction costs more generally, effectively excludes both small investors and small firms (and other borrowers requiring small sums) from participation in centralized financial markets.

This, at least in theory, is where a decentralized (local or regional) banking system derives its advantage. According to Zazzaro (1997), the rationale for the existence of a banking system in the economy is that banks are able to function as financial intermediaries between those savers and borrowers who are excluded from participating in the centralized financial market. Local banks are seen as being better positioned than other types of economic institution to address the problem of informational asymmetries, and the capacity to perform this role allows banks to attract savings that are not channelled to the centralized financial market.

The information gathering and monitoring functions that banks conduct on borrowers are spatially sensitive (particularly in relation to small borrowers); consequently, they are most effective when performed in close proximity to borrowers. Recent research on the relational nature of bank lending to small businesses testifies to the importance of soft, locally embedded knowledge on the part of bank loan officers (Uzzi, 1999; Uzzi and Lancaster, 2003; Agarwal and Hauswald, 2010), so that spatial proximity between local banks and local firms may be crucial:

> Loan officers at the bank branch are the real and often exclusive repositories of soft information, which is very local in nature, largely embedded in local society and the economic environment, and hardly portable. . . . In other words, soft information has a fundamental spatial dimension, which makes the geographical distribution of the banking industry, and the spatial organization of each single bank of the utmost importance for an easy and efficient access to credit for new, small and innovative, informationally opaque companies. (Papi, Sarno and Zazzaro, 2015: 4)

The geographical organization of a nation's banking system can thus play a key role in shaping the local availability of funds to small businesses. In the words, of Alessandrini and Zazzaro:

> banks operating in a region are indispensable for overcoming the isolation of those local agents who are either so small or so 'new' that transaction and information costs are usually too high to permit them to access financial centres. Thus banks operating locally are the main channel (often the only one) through which the financial needs of small and medium sized firms are met. (Alessandrini and Zazzaro, 1999: 75)

The spatial structure of the financial system may thus be of key importance (Cerqueiro et al., 2009). If the problems of asymmetric information, agency and uncertainty are themselves a function of the physical distance between firms seeking finance and institutions providing finance (see Porteous, 1995, 1999), then whether the financial system is centralized or decentralized may have consequences for the ability of firms to raise loan funds and equity capital, and hence for regional economic development and stability (McPherson and Waller, 2000). A spatially centralized system, with a single financial centre containing the main financial institutions and capital markets, could result in funds being biased to those firms within close proximity to the centre, relative to more distant firms, given that information on the former is likely to be greater and more reliable than on the latter. Thus firms in the financial core region may have a distinct market advantage compared to firms in financially peripheral regions. In fact two forms of 'closeness' or proximity have been identified as potentially important in shaping firms' access to and success in obtaining loan finance from banks: 'operational distance' (the physical nearness of an SME to a bank or bank branch) and 'functional distance' (the distance between a branch and the bank's headquarters) (Alessandrini et al., 2005, 2009). Operational proximity and functional proximity should, other things being equal, improve the information available to banks on potential borrower firms, and mitigate the 'principal–agent' problem involved in lending.

While the evidence from several countries suggests that, because of advances in technology, deregulation and increasing use of codified and score-based methods of risk assessment and due diligence, distances between small businesses and their financial services providers have been increasing, potentially giving such businesses access to a wider funding market space, geographical proximity nevertheless still matters (see the excellent survey by Brevoort and Wolken, 2009). The spatial structure of the financial system continues to be a factor shaping the funding of small business, and thus also regional development (Alessandrini et al., 2009).

In this context, several authors have expressed concern at what they see as historical trends towards organization concentration and spatial centralization in national banking systems, and the implications such trends carry for the financing of regional business. Writing a quarter of a century ago, Branson (1990) raised concerns over the implications of European financial market integration for the supply of funds for small businesses which depend on local intermediaries. He feared that small business would suffer following EU integration: 'if small local intermediaries are taken over by international banks, there is the risk that small local borrowers will be screened out of the market, at least in the short run, until a new equilibrium market structure is established' (Branson, 1990: 123). More recently, Alessandrini et al.'s (2009) study of the Italian banking system suggests that processes of bank rationalization and centralization that have emerged in Italy may well hinder the flow of investment funds to small firms in peripheral regions there.

Others, however, point to wider systemic effects of such centralization. Chick and Dow (1988) and Dow (1990, 1996, 1999), for example, develop a cumulative causation-type model of regional financial market integration in which the financial system may reinforce a core–periphery structure in an economy over the long term. Because of high liquidity preference in the periphery in the face of greater economic volatility and uncertainty, agents in the periphery prefer to hold centre-traded financial securities, which are more liquid because of the more buoyant and active financial markets in the centre. Chick and Dow argue that nationwide banks are less prepared to make credit available to agents in the periphery because they allocate loanable funds based on an implicit regional reserve ratio. The regional reserve base is diminished as funds leak out towards the centre in payment for centre goods or securities. This may perpetuate a cumulative process in which less credit means lower growth in the periphery; this in turn depresses credit demand there in the future. They also claim that historically, as the financial system has become more integrated and has developed through various stages (beginning with pure financial intermediation through to the present stage of securitization and globalization), so it has tended to become increasingly spatially centralized into a core–periphery structure.

While Chick and Dow's theory relates primarily to banking, the same logic may apply to the spatial centralization of equity capital providers and markets. Indeed, the more that financial integration promotes spatial centralization and organizational concentration of the banking system, the more likely it will be that other financial markets and institutions will follow the same process, and also agglomerate in the same financial centre (or centres). The reasons are obvious: inter-institutional linkages and trade, information networks, access to a common pool of specialized labour and expertise, and other external economies of localization. As in the case of banking, the spatial concentration of the capital market will result in flows of funds for investment out of the regions into the centre, as investors seek the liquidity and opportunities available in the central market. This raises the question whether, and to what extent, firms in the regions are as able as firms in, or near to, the centre to secure funding in the core market. Large established firms, about which there is ample market and financial information, especially if already publicly listed on the stock market, should have relatively easy access to equity on the central market, regardless of their regional location. However, new and small firms seeking equity investment are likely to face more problems. Transactions costs, unknowns and risk/return ratios are all higher for small firms, and as a consequence they may find it difficult to raise investment funds on central capital markets. And while in some countries the central capital market has introduced specialist listings aimed explicitly at the new and small business sector, these have not always been that successful. The limited capital raised on central stock markets by new and small enterprises has been one of the factors behind the emergence and growth of venture capital institutions over the past three decades.[5] Venture capitalists focus on raising (relatively modest) funds for investing in high-risk but potentially high-return new firm start-ups and expansions, and work closely with the management in their investee firms to minimize risk and help secure their success.

This 'hands-on' or 'relational' investment implies close proximity between the venture capitalist and the investee firms,[6] so that, in principle, regions away from the financial centre should be able to attract and develop their own clusters of venture capital institutions – their own specialist capital market – to support and promote the SMEs there. The claim is often made that because of the very nature and role of venture capital, this market should –

other things being equal – assume a spatially dispersed structure that corresponds closely to the pattern of demand for this form of finance. The key issue, of course, is whether other things are indeed equal. If, for various reasons, the venture capital market also assumes a centralized as against decentralized locational pattern, the proximity requirement inherent in this form of investment may mean that small firms in regions away from the centre may find it more difficult to raise risk capital. This may depress new firm formation and expansion in the regions, which then reduces the likelihood that local venture capital markets will emerge there. The result could be a situation in which the demand for and supply of venture capital across regions appears to be in equilibrium, whereas in reality this conceals underlying regional gaps (mismatches) in the allocation of venture capital (see Martin et al., 2005, for an exposition of this argument). This is in line with the post-Keynesian argument that demand and supply are not independent of one another, but rather can be mutually reinforcing (both positively and negatively) in their effects on the sectoral – and in this instance spatial – allocation of finance.

At a conceptual level, therefore, where the relationship between finance and the real economy is non-neutral, the spatial structure of the financial system – whether it is centralized or decentralized – may be of some consequence, and may result in geographical biases in the allocation of funds to firms, especially small firms, and hence contribute to uneven regional development. In the remainder of this chapter we explore this issue empirically by comparing financial markets and regional small business funding in the UK and Germany.

7.3 FINANCIAL MARKETS AND INDUSTRY IN GERMANY AND THE UK

Financial markets in Germany and the UK differ in significant ways arising from their path-dependent evolution. During the course of the nineteenth century the UK's financial system progressively moved from having a significant regionally based structure (of county and regional local banks and a system of 22 regional stock markets), to one that by the early decades of the twentieth century had become for all intents and purposes a system centralized in and operated from London. In contrast, Germany has had a 'three pillar' banking system consisting of large private banks, public banks (including Landesbanken and local savings banks, so-called Sparkassen) and cooperative banks. Despite considerable restructuring, this system has shown a resilient regional structure, and the financial system is organized around several major centres, some of which also perform some limited stock market activities. In addition, there is a government-owned development bank (Kreditanstalt für Wiederaufbau), which operates across the German regions.

A second difference is the relationship between the banking system and the 'real economy' of industry and production. In the UK, even in the 1930s concerns were expressed about the supply of loan and equity finance for small firms (as in the Macmillan Report of 1931), and the issue has resurfaced regularly ever since, as in the Radcliffe (1950), Bolton (1971), Wilson (1979) and Cruickshank (2000) Reports. In fact, over the course of the post-war period, British banks have steadily reduced the proportion of their lending to the non-financial company sector of the national economy (see Figure 7.2).

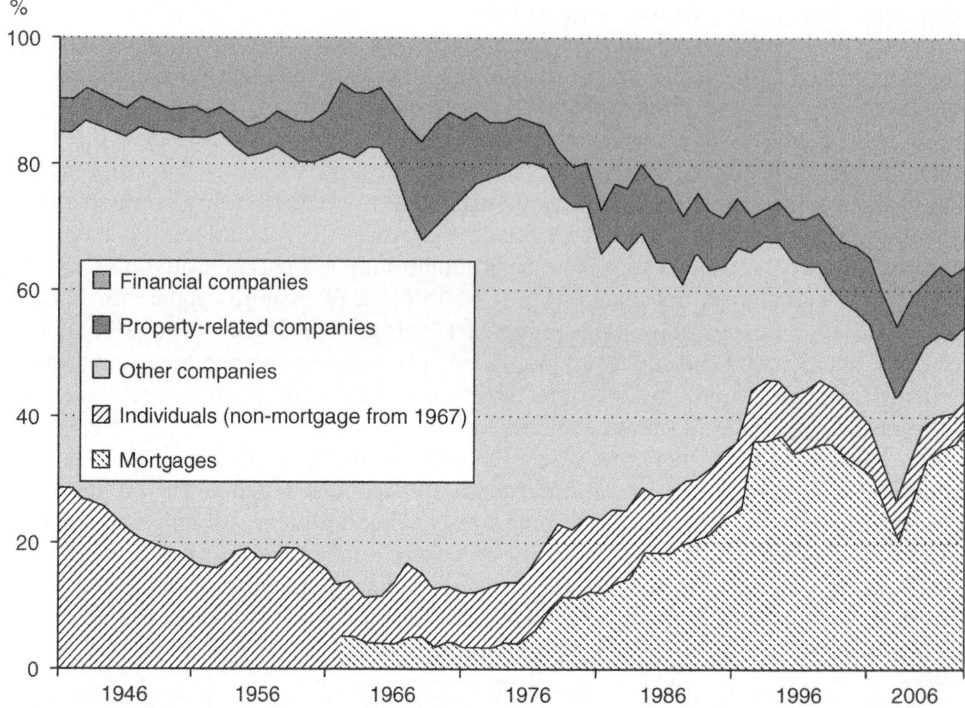

Source: Bank of England (2014).

Figure 7.2 The changing composition of UK bank lending, 1946–2013

Whereas in 1950 some 60 per cent of bank lending went into the company sector, by 1990 this had declined to below 40 per cent, and by 2010 to a mere 12 per cent. British banks have instead preferred to direct ever-increasing shares of their loans to other financial institutions and to mortgage lending. This change reflects a broader transformation in the sector over recent decades. British banking has grown enormously so that its total assets are now worth 450 per cent of nominal GDP (Bush, 2014). In many ways, it has been at the forefront of the move to a system of globalized, securitized, and over-leveraged banking which led to the financial crash of 2008. Banks in the UK securitized debt and sought profits in international derivatives markets, rather than in loan contracts with domestic business customers (Chick et al., 2013).

The situation is rather different in Germany, where loans to the non-financial firm sector accounts for 25 per cent of bank lending (6 per cent of which is mortgage lending). In total, mortgage lending is around 23 per cent of all lending, compared to 40 per cent in the UK (based on data provided by Deutsche Bundesbank for December 2014). In Germany there has traditionally been a much closer relationship between banks and industry than in the UK. In the 1990s, for example, bank credit accounted for some 75 per cent of the funds raised by the non-financial firms in Germany; however, this has fallen over the past two decades (Table 7.1). In the past, tax advantages and other regulations

Table 7.1 Share of firms' financing sources: Germany, the UK and France (per cent)

	Bank credit	Stocks	Bonds
Germany 1995	75	25	–
Germany 2010	44	50	6
UK 2010	18	68	14
France 2010	35	49	16

Source: Kaserer et al. (2011, figure 1).

Table 7.2 Indicators of enterprise finance in Germany and the UK

	Germany	UK
Capitalization of domestic publicly listed companies (per cent of GDP)		
1996	26.8	133.4
2001	55.0	141.6
2007	61.3	130.2
2012	42.1	115.5
Number of domestic publicly listed companies (end-of-year figures)		
1996	681	2,171
2001	749	1,923
2007	658	2,588
2012	665	2,179

Source: http://data.worldbank.org/indicator/CM.MKT.LCAP.GD.ZS/countries.

in Germany encouraged bank credit over equity financing (see KfW, 2003; Rudolph, 2003; Schmidt, 1999). However, the Basel II Agreement and the active promotion of stock markets, private equity and venture capital, as well as other forms of capital market financing, supported by regulatory and institutional changes, have promoted a shift from bank loans to equity. Nevertheless, German firms still rely much more heavily on bank finance than their UK counterparts, and the latter have much higher equity ratios than the former (Table 7.2).

7.4 BANK LENDING TO SMALL BUSINESS: THE UK AND GERMANY COMPARED

The relative shrinkage in bank lending to businesses in the UK has been accompanied by an increasing concentration of lending. In fact, there has been 'a remorseless process of financial centralization during the twentieth century' (Mason, 2010: 168) in which local banks have almost completely disappeared and finance is provided through the branches of a small number of large national and international banks. As a means of reducing costs in an age of digital transactions, large nationwide banks have rational-

Table 7.3 Regional shares of firm populations and new SME loan approvals (by value)

	Share of value of new loans approved (Great Britain = 100) average 2014	Share of total firm population (Great Britain = 100) 2014
London	22.5	18.2
South East	9.9	16.3
East of England	10.5	10.7
South West	12.6	10.0
North West	8.3	9.9
West Midlands	7.5	8.1
Yorkshire and Humberside	5.7	6.9
Scotland	7.3	6.3
East Midlands	8.6	6.5
Wales	4.3	4.2
North East	3.1	2.9
Great Britain	100.0	100.0

Notes: Shares of new loan approved are averages of four quarters. The total business population covers all firms including those larger than SMEs; however, SMEs account for 99 per cent of this population. Sum of regions may not equal national total due to rounding.

Source: BBA (2015).

ized their branch networks and concentrated decision-making in their head offices in London (Appleyard, 2013). The number of bank branches has been reduced from over 12,000 in 1989 to around 9,500 in 2013, so that the density of bank branches in the UK is estimated to be 150 per million population (180 including building societies) compared to 520 in Italy, 410 in France and 450 in Germany (Leyshon et al., 2008). The UK also now has one of the most concentrated banking sectors among the OECD states and the largest four banks account for 75 per cent of personal accounts and 85 per cent of business loans (Cable, 2014). There has been widespread concern that such a centralized and concentrated industry is bound to restrict the supply of capital to peripheral regions and produce a shortage of investment capital in these areas. Partly in response to this concern, in the last few years the British Banking Association (BBA) has begun to publish figures on lending to SMEs by geographical area from most of the major lenders (see Henry et al., 2014). Table 7.3 shows the supply of SME lending (new loan approvals) by region in for 2014. Some 55.5 per cent of new loan approvals in 2014 were accounted for by the four regions of London, South East, South West and East England. Further, while London's share is higher than its share of total firms would lead us to expect, for all four regions the combined share of new loan approvals is in line with their combined share of firms (55.2 per cent).

It would be tempting to conclude from these figures that worries about financial centralization are misplaced and that there is no disproportionate credit retrenchment nor shortage of lending in the peripheral regions, and that these regional variations in credit supply are simply a reflection of firm populations. However, as Degryse et al. (2015) have shown in their detailed analysis of bank lending to manufacturing SMEs in the British regions over 2004–11, the thin and centralized banking system in Britain has worked to expose the more peripheral regions to substantial variation in credit supply over the economic cycle. In their view, functional distance between bank branches and their headquarters was a key factor in SME access to finance during the recession. Their findings indicate that 'during and after the financial crisis, the distance between bank branches and headquarters plays a significant role, suggesting the presence of a "flight to headquarters" effect of banks in rebalancing their loan portfolio across different local markets in the post crisis period' (Degryse et al., 2015: 28).

There is other evidence that the financial system in the UK has become even more centralized because of the recent crash and recession. Financial employment proved more robust in London than in other second-order financial centres, where back-office employment was cut heavily (Wójcik and MacDonald-Korth, 2015). In addition, some of the regional banks, such as Northern Rock, which had followed a leverage-based model of banking were destabilized and all but destroyed by the crisis (Marshall, 2013). Together with this increasing centralization, UK banks cut back their lending to SMEs and innovative firms during the crisis. Credit rationing from 2008–9 onwards involved a significant decrease in the ability of smaller firms to access external credit, and this has recovered only slowly (British Business Bank, 2014; Lee et al., 2015). The tightening of credit has been found to disproportionately affect smaller firms. Cowling et al. (2012), for instance, find that during the recession banks became increasingly unsure about the quality of firms (see also Kitching et al., 2009).

The heterodox views of finance discussed above, in which the spatial organization of the financial system is deeply entangled with knowledge relationships, suggest that centralized banking systems are likely to magnify the effects of financial crises in peripheral regions. The argument is that without local knowledge, centralized banks find it hard to judge the credit-worthiness of firms at a distance. In a recession when risk and uncertainty increase, credit-scoring systems tend to be dominated by simple metrics and may lead to a disproportionate credit rationing in peripheral regions. According to Chick et al. (2013: 125), 'the more centralized the banking system the weaker and more volatile is the supply of credit to regions away from the financial sector due to the relatively weak knowledge base' (see also Dow and Rodriguez-Fuentes, 1997). This was precisely what Degryse et al. (2015) found in their study.

The decentralized banking system in Germany provides a stark contrast to Britain's highly centralized banking system. There is a rough, though in no way clear-cut, division of function or market between the regional banks on the one hand and large private banks on the other (see Klagge, 2010; Gärtner and Flögel, 2013). Smaller SMEs in Germany mainly rely on bank credit from their house bank, which in many cases is a local savings or cooperative bank. In contrast, larger firms more often have a close relationship with one or more private banks, Landesbanken and/or are active on capital markets. This division is a result of differences in business models and geographical structures between the different bank groups.[7]

Most private banks are headquartered in Frankfurt, and only a handful of them, namely the four largest banks (*Großbanken*), have extensive national branch networks. In contrast, the 400 savings banks and 1000 or so cooperative banks (Deutsche Bundesbank, 2015), some of them very small, have a strictly regionalized structure with headquarters all over the country and a very limited overlap of their branch networks within the two groups (Klagge and Zimmermann, 2004). As in other countries, the total number of bank branches has been declining in Germany. Bernhardt and Schwartz (2014) show that there was a decline of 12 per cent between 2003 and 2013 and that this rationalization was stronger in rural areas and in weaker regional economies. While they suggest that this does raise questions about banks' long-term personal relationships with SMEs, they argue it does not yet represent a problem in terms of credit supply. One reason for this might be that the rationalization process has been more pronounced for private banks than for local savings and cooperative banks (Klagge, 2010). As a result, there were less than 10,000 private bank branches in 2014, (excluding special-purpose banks), whereas the savings and cooperative bank sector each still had more than 11,000 branches, thus together accounting for about two-thirds of all bank branches in Germany (Deutsche Bundesbank, 2015).

Local savings and cooperative banks as well as other regional banks continue to fund small firms and some larger SMEs, and are often the only local option for firms in more peripheral regions (Gärtner, 2009). Savings and cooperative banks, in particular, constitute a stronghold of SME financing in Germany and in 2014 accounted for more than 40 per cent of all credit extended to all firms and the self-employed (Deutsche Bundesbank, 2015). This reflects both their geography and differences in their business models. Savings and cooperative banks are rather conservative and mainly operate in commercial banking at the regional level, whereas large private banks have a national and often international focus in a much wider range of both commercial and investment banking activities. Both savings banks as public entities and cooperative banks as collective entities pursue, to some extent, regional development goals in addition to a search for profits, whereas large private banks as public listed companies are subject to strong capital market and shareholder pressures.

Furthermore, there is preliminary evidence that there are differences in decision-making criteria for credit provision between large private banks, and savings and cooperative banks, which explain the latter's leading role in financing SMEs (Gärtner and Flögel, 2013). Whereas private banks tend to rely almost exclusively on standardized scoring systems when judging SME creditworthiness, there is preliminary evidence that regional banks base their credit decisions on more informal and only locally available knowledge. This means that SMEs with problematic data, but a good local reputation, can access credit (Handke, 2011). This more relational and proximity-based approach has been productive, and savings and cooperative banks have been just as economically successful as other banks – and an important source of stability, especially during the financial crisis (Gärtner, 2009, 2011).

While banks in most Western states restricted their lending because of the crisis from 2008, this was not the case for German savings and cooperative banks. Instead, and in stark contrast to large private banks, they have increased their overall credit volumes since 2007 and thus have stabilized the German economy and especially its SME sector (Gärtner, 2011; for more recent data also see Gärtner and Flögel, 2014). As we have noted, German savings and cooperative banks pursue rather conservative business models focused on commercial banking and hence they were much less affected by the financial crisis (although this is not true of the Landesbanken). Equally important is the refinancing structure of savings banks, which is not based on inter-bank markets, which almost came to a standstill following the collapse of Lehman Brothers, but relies mainly on deposits by local clients. These actually increased after 2008 as private households saw regional banks as a safe haven and shifted their assets accordingly (Klagge, 2009, 2010).

As a consequence, the availability of credit in Germany differed significantly for smaller and large firms after the financial crisis – with larger firms having more difficulty in obtaining loans than smaller firms (Abberger et al., 2009; Gärtner, 2011). Whereas smaller and more local SMEs benefitted from the strength and stability provided by regional banks, larger SMEs and internationally active Mittelstand firms with large private banks as their house banks have been confronted with very restrictive lending strategies and thus with major financing obstacles. In summary then, despite the financial crash, the decentralized banking system in Germany has by all accounts continued to provide credit to SMEs to a much greater degree than Britain's centralized and more equity-based financial system. However, the subsequent question is whether venture capital in Britain has therefore moved to play a large and significant role in SME finance across the regions.

7.5 VENTURE CAPITAL MARKETS: REGIONAL ALTERNATIVES TO BANKS?

The growth of venture capital markets across many industrialized countries in recent years is in large part a response to the problems that new, especially high-tech and innovative small firms have in raising equity on the public capital market or suitable loan finance from banks. The 'classic' form of venture capital is supposed to focus on such firms, which because of their high-risk nature, encourages venture capital investment to be 'relational' in nature, involving close, regular managerial and informational links with the investee enterprise. This implies that venture capital institutions should be located in quite close proximity to their client firms, and be well-embedded in the local business and entrepreneurial community. Thus, in theory at least, we might expect the venture capital market to be a regionally decentralized one, in the sense that, all other things being equal, the regional distribution of venture capital institutions should tend to follow the regional pattern of demand for risk equity. The comparison between the UK and Germany venture capital markets is again of considerable interest in this context.

The UK venture capital market (the second largest after that in the US), has been growing steadily since the 1980s. In 1990, UK venture capital firms invested just over £1 billion in the UK; by 2007 this had grown to £11.97 billion (with a further £19.66 billion overseas, mainly Europe and the United States). The banking crisis of 2007–08 then seriously dented activity, which in 2013 stood at £4.22 billion (with overseas investment down to £6 billion).

From its very beginning in the early 1980s, the UK venture capital industry has been overwhelmingly located in London and its close environs (Martin, 1989, 1992; Klagge and Martin, 2005). In 2005, about three-quarters of UK venture capital firms (around 170) were headquartered there, and only a few minor concentrations (typically with less than ten firms) existed outside London, most notably in Manchester, Birmingham, Leeds, Cambridge, Oxford, Edinburgh and Glasgow. For venture capital firms, one recent study finds that 85 per cent are now headquartered in London and the South, and their regional branches elsewhere in many instances remain dependent on parent head offices

Table 7.4 *Regional structure of the venture capital market in the UK: shares of national investment for selected years*

	2005	2008	2011	2014
London	35	42	44	45
South East	9	15	17	12
(South East and London	*44*	*57*	*61*	*57)*
Eastern	9	6	2	1
South West	7	2	3	5
East Midlands	16	6	3	5
West Midlands	4	5	8	7
Yorkshire-Humberside	4	6	4	8
North West-Merseyside	6	4	11	10
North East	1	1	2	0
Wales	7	1	1	1
Scotland	2	12	5	4
Northern Ireland	0	0	0	0
Total	100	100	100	100

Note: This is investment by British Venture Capital Association (BVCA) members and therefore excludes regional venture investment by overseas firms.

Source: BVCA (Annual Reports of Investment Activity).

in London. The degree of regional decentralization of the venture capital market in the UK is thus distinctly limited.

Further, the high degree of spatial centralization of these institutions in and around London has tended to impart a well-documented south-eastern bias in the regional distribution of investment (Mason and Harrison, 1991, 2002; Martin, 1989, 1992; Martin et al., 2003; Martin et al., 2005; Klagge and Martin, 2005). Since the industry emerged over three decades ago, London and the surrounding South East region have regularly attracted around 50 per cent of national venture capital investment (Table 7.4). No other region has consistently attracted as much as 10 per cent. Of course the regional economies differ in size, so this should be taken into account when comparing the geographical distribution of venture finance. However, even if regional shares of venture finance are compared to regional shares of the national stock of firms, for example, London still dominates: in recent years its share of venture capital investment has been two and half times what would have been expected based on its share of firms (see Table 7.5). Indeed the relative concentration of investment in London seems to have increased in recent years.

Given that venture capital firms tend to locate in close proximity to where there is a buoyant demand for risk capital and high rates of SME formation and growth, it is perhaps not surprising that the bulk of the venture capital market in the UK is concentrated in the economically dynamic regions of London and the South East. However, the concentration of the venture capital market in and around London also owes much to the fact that the financial system as a whole is centralized there. Many venture capital companies are linked to, or are offshoots from, other financial institutions, such as banks and investment houses. Indeed, many venture capital firms have started life as 'spin-offs'

Table 7.5 *Regional distribution of venture capital investment: averages for 1998–2002 and 2010–14*

Region	Location quotient	
	1998–2002	2010–14
London	**2.02**	**2.68**
South East	**1.17**	**1.06**
Eastern	0.70	0.51
South West	0.40	0.43
East Midlands	0.90	0.71
West Midlands	0.91	0.87
Yorkshire-Humberside	0.61	0.81
North West	0.83	0.71
North East	0.54	0.69
Wales	0.18	0.38
Scotland	**1.02**	0.34
Northern Ireland	0.15	0.06
Total	1.00	1.00

Notes: Location Quotient (LQ) defined as region's share of national venture capital investment divided by region's share of the national stock of registered businesses. Values greater than unity indicate a relative concentration of venture capital investment in the regions concerned.

Sources: BVCA.

from such institutions, or are subdivisions or branches of them. Added to this, venture capital firms draw staff from other financial institutions, and tap into the circuits of information and expertise that exist within and between such organizations. This concentration of the venture capital market in turn reinforces the high levels of demand for risk finance in London and the surrounding South East. By contrast, much of northern UK finds itself in the converse situation, with the lack of significant local clusters of venture capital markets reinforcing underlying low levels of demand in those regions, giving rise to what we referred to earlier as a 'low supply–low demand equilibrium' in these regions. Further, the lack of significant local venture capital markets in these regions – the local lack of leading venture capital firms – may well have militated against the formation of syndicated funds that might bring in non-local funds from venture capital firms located in other regions (and in London especially). In every syndication there is a need for a lead investor who plays the monitoring role: this is usually the function of the most geographically proximate investor. Thus again, the lack of local sources of venture capital can prove crucial.[8]

In the UK, solutions for the perceived SME equity gap have been sought with policies that have an explicit regional dimension. The most prominent policy scheme is the nine government-backed Regional Venture Capital Funds (RVCFs), which were established as part of a national programme in 2000 in all English regions (and a similar fund has been set up in Scotland). Managed by commercial and experienced fund managers in the respective regions, the RVCFs operated at the smaller deal-size end of the market, especially for deals of below £500,000. The scheme was not intended either to promote the decentralization of the venture capital market from London or to create regional capital markets as such. Nevertheless, whether by design or by accident, the policy has had important regional outcomes. Funds in these regions found it difficult to raise private sources of finance and as a result became more reliant on government, European Union and local authority funding, whereas the funds in the southern regions were more able to attract bank finance (for more details on these RVCFs see Sunley, Klagge, Berndt and Martin, 2005). Because of this and other policy measures, venture capital in the more peripheral regions in the UK has come to be dominated by public sector funds and intermediaries (Mason and Pierrakis, 2013). In turn, this raises serious questions about whether these investments can provide as much knowledge, advice and relational support as those in core regions (Mason and Pierrakis, 2013).

In the case of Germany, the locational geography of venture capital companies is much more dispersed and characterized by one-location firms. No one city or region dominates the industry in the same way that London and the South East do in the UK. Rather, there are five significant clusters of venture capital firms (head offices), namely around Frankfurt, Munich, Berlin, Hamburg and Düsseldorf, together with three smaller markets in the Stuttgart, Hannover and Cologne-Bonn regions. Taken together, these eight centres with neighbouring cities and communities still only account for about 80 per cent of German venture capital firms. These same eight city-regions have significant banking sectors and contain the country's six stock markets. The outcome is that venture capital investment is less spatially concentrated than is the case in the UK (Table 7.6).

Three key points seem clear. First, in both countries the spatial structure of the venture capital market follows closely that of the financial system more generally. However, it differs quite distinctly between the two. Thus in the UK, the venture capital market is highly concentrated in London and its environs, with few significant clusters of institutions in the regions. In Germany, the venture capital market is more decentralized, with significant clusters of institutions in the major regional financial centres. Second, this difference carries over to the geography of venture capital investment. In the UK venture capital investment is more spatially concentrated (in the London–South East city-region) than is the case in Germany (where several regional concentrations exist). Third, in both countries, the regional pattern of investment is consistent with the 'spatial proximity' effect that is often argued to characterize the venture capital market (see Martin et al., 2005), in that the regional distribution of investment is closely correlated with the locational geography of venture capital firms, and regions that do not have sizeable clusters of venture capital firms also tend to have shares of venture capital investment below what would be expected given their shares of firms.

What we are suggesting here is not that the UK necessarily suffers more from the existence of regional equity gaps than does Germany because of its more spatially centralized venture capital market – though the data presented here would be consistent with such a view. The basic issue in the UK is the existence of a nationwide equity gap affecting new, start-up and early expansion SMEs (especially deal-sizes below £500,000). British venture capital firms, especially in comparison with German venture capital institutions, have preferred investment in expansions, MBOs and large deals sizes, rather than in small, start-up, and early (and riskier) stages of enterprise development. However, what we are suggesting is that in combination with the high

Table 7.6 Regional distribution of venture capital investment in Germany, 1998–2002 and 2010–14

Region (Bundesland)	Location quotient	
	1998–2002	2010–14
Baden-Württemberg	**1.05**	**1.07**
Bayern	**1.21**	**1.16**
Berlin	**2.55**	**2.73**
Brandenburg	0.83	0.37
Bremen	0.81	0.70
Hamburg	**1.89**	**2.37**
Hessen	**1.34**	**1.25**
Mecklenburg-Vorpommern	0.40	0.59
Niedersachsen	0.51	0.29
Nordrhein-Westfalen	0.84	**1.05**
Rheinland-Pfalz	0.52	0.77
Saarland	0.25	0.26
Sachsen	0.78	0.39
Sachsen-Anhalt	0.52	0.32
Schleswig-Holstein	0.55	0.58
Thüringen	0.71	0.57
Total	1.00	1.00

Notes: LQ defined as region's share of national venture capital investment divided by region's share of the national stock of VAT-registered businesses (for 2001 and 2013 respectively). Values greater than unity indicate a relative concentration of venture capital investment in the regions concerned.

Source: German Venture Capital Association (BVK); Statistisches Bundesamt.

degree of spatial centralization of the venture capital market, and the similar bias of investment towards London and the South East, the orientation towards large deal sizes and established businesses in the UK may accentuate the differential access to equity by SMEs in the regions.

7.6 IS THERE A CASE FOR REGIONAL STOCK MARKETS?

The retrenchment of bank credit, and limits and struggles of venture capital, in Britain's regions have rekindled a long-running debate about the potential benefits of re-establishing regional stock markets in Britain (Huggins and Prokop, 2013). The central argument for such a move is that regional stock exchanges are more able to concentrate on smaller firms and – due to the important role of spatial proximity for these enterprises – especially on SMEs located in the same region (see Mocroft, 2001; Huggins et al., 2003). Despite the smaller size of its public equity market, the German financial system continues to have a network of regional stock exchanges and this may have some lessons for the debate.

Historically, the UK had a dense network of regional stock exchanges that had developed in tandem with industrialization during the nineteenth century. In 1914, some 22 regional exchanges existed across the UK, including exchanges in Bristol, Cardiff, Halifax, Liverpool, Sheffield, Birmingham, Bristol and Swansea. Over the subsequent decades the numbers and activities of these regional exchanges declined, and by 1973 those that remained were finally absorbed into the London Stock Exchange (LSE). Since then, the market for buying and selling stocks and shares in the UK has been monopolized by the LSE. The London exchange is primarily orientated to the market in large stock trades, so-called 'blue-chip' stocks, and to the global trading system. London itself accounts for around two-thirds of the market capitalization of the companies listed on the LSE, and London and the South East together more than three-quarters (Klagge and Martin, 2005). This reflects the dominance of London and the South East as the location for the headquarters of a very significant proportion of the UK's publicly listed companies, and many of these are the largest of the country's firms (Klagge and Martin, 2005). The bias of the LSE towards London and the South East is thus also a bias towards large companies, a feature that may actually militate against smaller firms not only in the regions but even within the London–South East core area itself.

There have been attempts to counter this 'big is better' trend, in the form of specialist markets directed at those segments not catered for by the LSE. The most notable is the setting up of the Alternative Investment Market (AIM) in 1995, which operates as a secondary tier market targeting new and small companies. However, research has found that AIM listings have also been dominated by London firms (Amini et al., 2012). These authors see this as evidence of a shortage of demand for early equity in the regions, and call for stronger links between the London market and business advice and networking organizations.

While, in 2001, the London Stock Exchange introduced a so-called 'landMARK market' as a means of strengthening relations between regional companies and investment institutions, and raising the visibility of regional investment opportunities, it failed to stimulate the re-establishment of regional exchanges. In addition, there have been several regional attempts to establish local exchanges, such as Advantage West Midlands' attempt to set up a local exchange in Birmingham in 2004 (InvestBx), but these have been unable to gain much support or momentum. By 2010 only three firms were listed on InvestBx, for example (Guthrie, 2010). Calls for regional stock exchanges have been repeated by politicians, but have met with a strongly sceptical reaction from the investment industry, which perceives the problem in terms of a lack of demand for equity, not its supply.

In some contrast again, the geographical organization of German equity markets is more decentralized. Next to Frankfurt – the national and increasingly international financial centre with the major stock exchange, the Deutsche Börse Group – there have traditionally been several significant regional financial centres in Germany with their own stock exchanges and concentrations of financial services. No one region dominates the public equity market in Germany to the extent found in the UK; and regional disparities are much less pronounced for Frankfurt-listed than for London-listed domestic companies (see Klagge and Martin, 2005; Wójcik, 2002).

In the last three decades or so, however, the system has been characterized by a consolidation and concentration of activities in Frankfurt (see, for example, Schamp,

Table 7.7 Domestic and regional firms quoted on the German regional stock exchanges, 2003 and 2014

	Domestic firms quoted on exchanges			
	Total number		Per cent regional	
	2003	2014	2003	2014
Berlin	759	866	3.4	8.4
Dusseldorf	832	648	19.6	10.3
Hamburg-Hannover	950	433	9.6	9.7
Munich	580	754	32.9	12.1
Stuttgart	864	722	7.6	9.1

Sources: Amtliche Kursblätter, and information provided by the regional exchanges for 2003 and 2014.

1999; Bördlein, 2003). While there used to be eight independent stock exchanges including Frankfurt, take-overs (of the Bremen by the Berlin market) and mergers (of the Hamburg and Hannover markets) have reduced the number of independent markets to six: Deutsche Börse in Frankfurt, and five so-called 'regional stock exchanges' (Berlin, Hamburg/Hannover, Düsseldorf, Munich, and Stuttgart). Underlying this is the fact that companies can be listed on more than one exchange, so that all stock exchanges compete with each other for companies and investors. The rise of the Frankfurt exchange is mainly due to the favourable conditions after the Second World War (primarily, the location of the country's central bank) combined with the growing importance of economies of scale and scope (Grote, 2004; Lo and Schamp, 2001).[9]

In reaction to this process, since the 1990s the regional stock exchanges have pursued niche strategies in market segments that have been neglected by Frankfurt. These strategies mainly focus on market segments that are not regionally defined (see Bördlein, 2003; Kösters et al., 2000; Neininger, 2000)[10] – despite the efforts of regional actors to use regional stock exchanges for regional-policy purposes. While the numbers and percentages of regional firms quoted on regional stock exchanges are moderate (Table 7.7), the trading volumes are rather small, particularly in comparison with other specializations. Among other things, this is because most companies are quoted on the Frankfurt market, and are traded there much more intensively.

Despite having what at least appears to be a regionally decentralized capital market system, the scope for local small firms to raise equity via their regional stock exchange is rather limited. However, regional stock exchanges can act as a stimulus or stepping-stone to a public listing for some regional SMEs. While the claim that there are a high proportion of SMEs and Mittelstand firms which are 'stock-exchange ready' (Kaserer et al., 2011), may be an exaggeration, there are certainly signs of a developing capital market culture among SMEs. More specifically, the introduction of SME bonds, so-called Mittelstandsanleihen, indicates a growing openness of SMEs towards capital market finance.

SME bonds emerged as a reaction to the credit crunch during the financial crisis, when, as we have seen, larger banks restricted their lending. First introduced by the Stuttgart exchange in 2010, they rapidly became successful, and other regional stock

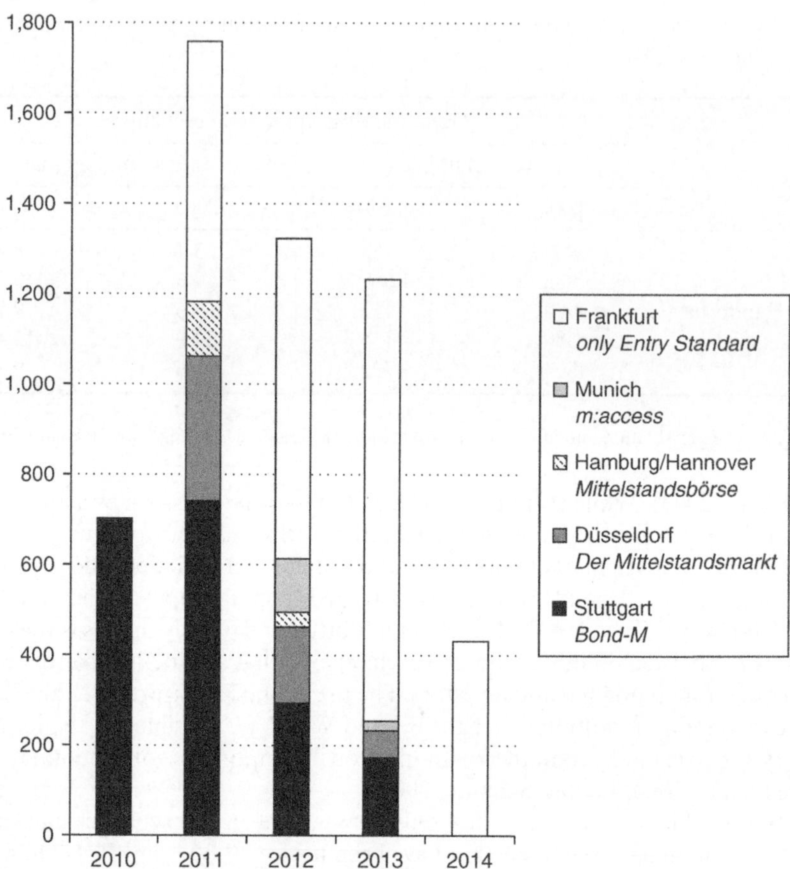

Sources: PwC, Creditreform, information provided by the stock exchange.

Figure 7.3 Volumes of SME bond issuances at German stock exchanges, in € million, 2010–14

exchanges as well as Frankfurt followed suit, resulting in more than 100 SME bond issuances with a volume of more than €5 billion by the end of 2014 (Figure 7.3), with the Frankfurt exchange being the main player in this new market. However, the recent development of the SME bond market is characterized by increasing refinancing risks and a fairly large number of defaults, and has waned somewhat since 2014 (Die ZEIT, 2015).

Despite the recent problems in the SME bond market, its development illustrates how regional stock exchanges can be important in innovating and experimenting in new initiatives in SME financing. Although bank credit undoubtedly remains the dominant financing instrument, the readiness to search for growth funding in capital markets has increased significantly among German firms (Roland Berger Strategy Consultants, 2011). This reflects, to some extent, the dynamic development of venture capital in Germany since 2009. In summary then, despite the limited role of regional stock exchanges in the direct provision of equity or debt finance to SMEs, there is evidence to suggest that these exchanges can increase the awareness and local involvement of private and regionally minded investors to build interest in capital market finance among SMEs. They have also provided a platform to strengthen and develop regional investment relationships and facilitated experimentation in niche markets and trials in new instruments, particularly bonds.

7.7 DECENTRALIZED AND CENTRALIZED FINANCIAL SYSTEMS: SOME CONCLUDING COMMENTS

Writing more than a quarter of a century ago, O'Brien (1992) argued that 'geographical location no longer holds sway in finance'. Yet, as discussions of globalization more generally have highlighted, the 'death of geography' has been much exaggerated, and location has if anything become more, not less, important. Under the pressures of global competition, deregulation and technological innovation, a wave of merger activity, consolidation and concentration has been sweeping through financial and capital markets, reshaping the monetary landscape in the process. The trend seems to be towards the spatial centralization of financial systems, institutions and flows. In this context, the issue of possible 'gaps' in the supply of capital to the real economy of production assumes heightened significance: it is perhaps no coincidence, therefore, that debates about capital and finance gaps in the SME sector and the need for local capital markets have become prominent at a time of accelerating globalization.

It is clear that capital markets do not function in a perfect, neutral way; rather, they are inherently imperfect and non-neutral. Funds do not necessarily flow to potentially profitable projects irrespective of where the latter are located. Our concern in this chapter has been whether and to what extent the spatial structure of financial systems and capital markets interacts with monetary non-neutrality to impart spatial biases to the funding of SMEs. Comparing the UK and Germany in this context is instructive, given that the former has a highly spatially centralized financial system, whereas the latter has a much more regionally decentralized system. Important differences in institutional, regulatory and corporate environment also exist between the two countries, differences that interact with the specific spatial structures of the financial system in each.[11] Interestingly, questions concerning the SME equity gap and the issue of possible regional gaps have loomed much larger in the UK, with its highly centralized financial system, than in Germany with its more decentralized system.

On the basis of the UK and German evidence (presented here and found in our earlier work – see Martin et al., 2003; Martin et al., 2005; Sunley, Klagge, Berndt and Martin, 2005), as well as the findings for other countries, such as the United States and Italy (for example, Alessandrini et al., 2009; Brevoort and Wolken, 2009; Cerqueiro et al., 2009; Degryse et al., 2015) the spatial structure and organization of the financial system is potentially of some significance. A geographically decentralized financial system with sizable and well-embedded regional clusters of institutions, networks, agents, and markets can be advantageous in at least three ways.

First, the presence of a local critical mass of financial institutions and agents – that is of a regionally identifiable, coherent and functioning market – enables local institutions, SMEs, and local investors to exploit the benefits of being in close spatial proximity. This view is supported by empirical evidence indicating that spatial proximity between financial intermediaries and SMEs facilitates contact building and information exchange and thus tends to lower transaction costs and non-cost barriers for credit and/or capital provision (Martin et al., 2003; Schmidt, Oesterhelweg and Treske, 1997). It may be that modern information and communications technologies potentially allow functional propinquity without the need for spatial proximity. But, certainly as far as new and small enterprises are concerned, the scale and nature of the risk attached to such firms, the need for detailed and regular information on their performance and activities, and the importance of fostering and supporting entrepreneurship, all put a premium on the value of close co-location of financial institutions and markets on the one hand, and client SMEs on the other. Other things being equal, a regionally decentralized system ought therefore to be more effective in matching the demand and supply of capital for SMEs. It could also improve the liquidity of their shares by gaining access to a local pool of investors interested in their region's firms.

Second, the existence of regional capital markets specializing in local firms may help to keep capital within the regions, as local investors direct their funds into local companies – and hence into local economic development – rather than investing on the central market. Recall that Chick and Dow argue that a spatially centralized financial system tends to generate a cumulative causation type of process where funds drain into the centre leaving non-core regions with a lack of capital and local firms – especially small firms not listed on the central market – with a lack of finance. This process hinders economic development, and firm formation and expansion, which in turn feed back to constrain economic development, and thence intensifies the flow of capital to the centre. While the Chick–Dow thesis is itself problematic, it does at least seek to identify possible interactions between the spatial structure of the financial system and the process of (uneven) regional development. Unfortunately, relatively little is known empirically about the spatial flows of capital and finance under different spatial configurations of the financial system: somewhat surprisingly, this remains an under-researched issue in economic geography.

Third, in a nationally integrated financial system, the case can be made for a regionally decentralized structure on the grounds that it increases the efficiency of allocation of investment between the centre and the regions. Regional markets, particularly if networked with the centre, can also fulfil an information and networking function between local SMEs and national (central) markets both by raising SMEs' awareness of financing options (especially equity), and by collecting information on regional SMEs which can then be used by national players and investors. In other words, a decentralized structure can help reduce information asymmetries and thereby increase the flow of funds from the centre to the regions.

In a decentralized system, regional stock exchanges could also function as key 'points of attachment' for other financial and related institutions and services, such as banks, accountants, lawyers, and the like, that is as the hubs for the development of regional 'financial communities' or 'ecologies', as can be seen in the case of Germany. Despite the relative neglect of regional business in most of their strategies, the regional stock markets in Germany nevertheless arguably function as 'crystallization points' for other financial actors (especially venture capital firms) and regional financial infrastructure more generally. In addition, through their association with public and quasi-public institutions (most prominently banks) they help to stimulate the local financial sector as a whole.

However, this is not to ignore the fact that regional capital markets face a number of major challenges and problems, not least that their success will depend on the economic performance and wealth of the region: economically depressed and low wealth regions may face difficulties in attracting a large enough local investor base or an adequate demand for liquidity from local businesses.[12] How regional capital markets and regional financial communities could be promoted and sustained is thus a difficult question. In the UK, the RVCFs introduced by the Labour government in 2000, which were intended to 'kick start' self-supporting regional capital markets outside of London and the South East, performed poorly.[13]

Perhaps one of the most interesting and potentially significant financial innovations in relation to SMEs, one that relies on the power of modern ICT, is that of 'crowdfunding'. This consists of online Internet platforms through which numerous individuals can lend or invest in small dynamic start-up businesses seeking short-term finance that do not wish to rely on, or have been refused support from, banks. Though most such individual investments are small, they can add up to a significant source of finance for a given firm using this system. The most striking feature of crowdfunding is the broad geographic dispersion of investors in these small early-stage projects. This would seem to run counter to the idea of, and the evidence for, the importance of spatial proximity between lenders and borrowers. In their detailed study of crowdfunding in the USA, for example, Agrawal et al. (2011) find a much-reduced influence of spatial proximity. Yet, at the same time, they find that distance still plays a role: within a single round of financing, local investors are typically the first to commit funds, and this effect seems to be driven by investors who have a personal connection or knowledge with the local entrepreneur. As the authors conclude, 'although the online platform seems to eliminate most distance-related economic frictions such as monitoring progress, providing inputs, and gathering information it does not eliminate social-related frictions' (Agrawal et al., 2011: Abstract). This appears to be consistent with other research on online activities which also shows that while many, but by no means all, distance-related frictions are reduced or eliminated, local social networks can be of importance (Blum and Goldfarb, 2006; Hortacsu et al., 2009). Thus even in the new digital age, in which new virtual circuits can easily transcend space and create financial propinquity without the need for geographical proximity, 'relational distance' in financial and monetary affairs can still be spatially constrained. While we do not claim to have provided anything like a definitive answer to our underlying question as to how far and in what ways the spatial structure and organization of a financial system shape the geographical allocation of funds to business, and particularly small business in peripheral regions, we hope we have demonstrated the need for ongoing research into this important issue.

NOTES

1. This chapter adapts, updates and revises the paper by Klagge, B. and R.L. Martin (2005), 'Decentralised versus centralised financial systems: is there a case for local capital markets?', *Journal of Economic Geography*, **5** (4), 387–421. We are grateful to Oxford University Press for permission to draw on that earlier publication.
2. There is now a large literature on change and concentration processes in the financial sector and their implications for the rise and role of major financial centres. They involve not only technological innovations in conducting financial transactions, but also regulatory and product developments in the context of increasing globalization (from a geographical perspective see e.g. Klagge, 1995; Sassen, 1991; Leyshon and Thrift, 1992; Marshall et al., 1992; Lee and Schmidt-Marwede, 1993; Martin, 1994, 1999; Schamp, 1999; Lo and Schamp, 2001). There is even a Global Financial Centres index, which ranks the major centres on a yearly basis according to various 'competitiveness' measures.
3. Land and labour costs may be driven up, and internal regional imbalance exacerbated. The economy may face risks owing to over-dependence on a single sector, and the operation of the domestic monetary policy may be compromised by the need to nurture or defend an internationally dominant financial centre. In addition, the financial sector may actually be 'parasitic', diverting valuable capital and human resources from other branches – and, we might add, other regions and cities – in the domestic economy. Dow (1999) argues that if and as a nation's financial system becomes concentrated in a single dominant centre, funds are likely to drain out of surrounding regions as investors are attracted by the greater liquidity and returns that the centre offers. She argues that the emergence and growth of a dominant national financial centre, especially if it is also a global centre, is likely to exacerbate uneven regional development within the country concerned.
4. The Miller–Modigliani theorem (1958) tells us precisely what the neutrality of money means for investment.
5. The development of venture capital goes back to the 1960s in the United States, but is a more recent phenomenon in Europe. It appeared first in the UK in the early-1980s, and then in the 1990s in Germany, France and elsewhere. Like other forms of finance, it too has become globalized.
6. For discussions of this spatial proximity aspect of venture capitalism see Thompson (1989), Martin (1989) and Martin et al. (2005). It remains a debated issue, however, though the evidence for the US and Europe tends to support the thesis that venture capital firms prefer to be near the enterprises in which they invest. Which comes first, the venture capital firms or the investee enterprises, is one of the contentious questions in this debate.
7. The *Landesbanken*, some of which were especially hard hit during the financial crisis and had to be restructured, are not explicitly included in the following analysis. Despite being owned by savings banks, their business models and behaviour have since the 1990s been based on those of the large private banks; and similar to them, they have been and still are important providers of credit to larger firms.
8. At one time the London-based venture capital firm, 3i (established after the war by the Bank of England and major clearing banks to provide funds for new and small businesses throughout the UK) had some 20 branch offices across the regions of the country. Since the company went public in the 1990s, it has dramatically refocused its activities. It has closed down many of its UK regional offices, and firmly shifted its emphasis towards being a leading global venture capital firm (with 29 offices in 14 countries).
9. The Frankfurt Stock Exchange also established the Neuer Markt in 1997, and introduced SMAX as a specialized segment for young and smaller companies in 1999. These new specialized markets raised many hopes, and capital provision to SMEs via the stock exchange through new public offerings and flotations boomed in the late 1990s. The crash of many new-economy enterprises and the crisis of the Neuer Markt in 2000/2001 brought this development to an abrupt halt. The Neuer Markt and SMAX were subsequently closed. Today, there are no specific segments for smaller or young firms; instead Deutsche Börse refers SMEs to the 'Entry Standard' established in 2005 as part of the Open Market, formerly Freiverkehr, which is much less regulated than the other two segments (Prime and General Standard). Furthermore, there are indices for small and mid caps (SDAX, MDAX), which, however, are registered under the Standard and were already established in the 1990s.
10. Such strategies included on private investors by offering favourable conditions for this group (guaranteed trading conditions, especially regarding price, extended trading hours, abolition of minimum sizes, information campaigns) and specialization in certain clearly defined segments such as for example Stuttgart's private-client segment for trading options and certifications established in 1999 (EUWAX, European Warrant Exchange).
11. Institutional differences between the UK and Germany not only concern the spatial organization of the financial system, which reflects the political organization of space (federalist versus centralist system),

but also the characteristics of the financial system regarding the preferred forms of finance (bank- versus capital market-orientation), and the preferred mechanisms of economic coordination and intervention (corporatism versus liberalism). There are developments and changes with regard to all three dimensions in both countries that complicate comparison.

12. Indeed, as the Scottish case illustrates, the presence of 'local' venture capital firms is not necessarily a panacea: Scotland's main venture capital firms (Scottish Equity Partners and penta/Pentech) do most of their investing outside Scotland.
13. The UK Coalition government in 2013 attempted to revive venture capital investment for SMEs via its Enterprise Capital Funds, which gave money directly to venture capital firms directly, but these lacked any explicit regional dimension. In addition, the Regional Growth Fund launched in 2010 has tended make large loans to big firms (such as Jaguar Land Rover).

REFERENCES

Abberger, K., C. Hainz and A. Kunkel (2009), 'Kreditvergabepolitik der Banken: Warum leiden große Unternehmen besonders?', *ifo Schnelldienst*, **62** (14), 32–34.

Agarwal, A.K. and R. Hauswald (2010), 'Distance and private information in banking', *Review of Financial Studies*, **23**, 2757–2788.

Agrawal, A.K., C. Catalani and A. Goldfarb (2011). 'The geography of crowdfunding', Working Paper 16820, National Bureau of Economic Research, Cambridge, MA.

Alessandrini, P. and A. Zazzaro (1999), 'A "possibilist" approach to local financial systems and regional development: the Italian experience', in R.L. Martin (ed.), *Money and the Space Economy*, Chichester: Wiley, pp. 71–92.

Alessandrini, P., M. Croci and A. Zazzaro (2005), 'The geography of banking power: the role of functional distance', *Banca Nazionale del Lavoro Quarterly Review*, **LVIII**, 129–167.

Alessandrini, P., M. Fratianni and A. Zazzaro (2009), *The Changing Geography of Banking and Finance*, Dordrecht: Springer.

Amini, S., K. Keasey and R. Hudson (2012), 'The equity funding for smaller growing growing companies and regional stock exchanges', *International Small Business Journal*, **20**, 1–18.

Appleyard, L. (2013), 'The geographies of access to enterprise finance: the case of the West Midlands, UK', *Regional Studies*, **47**, 868–879.

Bank of England (2001), *Finance for Small Firms – An Eighth Report*, London: Bank of England.

Bank of England (2003), *Finance for Small Firms – A Tenth Report*, London: Bank of England.

BBA (2015), 'Statistics: bank support for SMEs – 4th Quarter 2014', retrieved on 9 November 2016 from www.bba.org.uk/news/statistics/sme-statistics/.

Bernhardt, K. and M. Schwartz (2014), 'The network of Germany's bank branches is dwindling', KFW Research, Focus on Economies, Number 49.

Blum, B. and A. Goldfarb (2006), 'Does the internet defy the law of gravity?', *Journal of International Economics*, **70** (2), 384–405.

Bolton Committee (1971), *Report of Committee of Enquiry on Small Firms*, Cmnd 4811, London.

Bördlein, R. (2003), 'Die Reorganisation der deutschen "Regionalbörsen" zwischen ökonomischen und politischen Interessen', *Geographische Zeitschrift*, **91** (3–4), 156–174.

Boyle, D. (2014), *Re-Banking the UK: How to Create a Diverse Lending Infrastructure*, London: New Weather CIC.

Branson, W.H. (1990), 'Financial Market Integration, Macroeconomic Policy and the EMS', in C. Bliss and Braga de Macedo (eds), *Union with Diversity in the European Economy*, Cambridge: Cambridge University Press.

Brevoort, K.P. and J.D. Wolken (2009), 'Does distance matter in banking', in P. Alessandrini, M. Fratianni and A. Zazzaro (eds), *The Changing Geography of Banking and Finance*, Heidelberg: Springer, pp. 27–56.

British Business Bank (2014), *Small Business Finance Markets*, London: British Business Bank.

Bush, O. (2014), 'Why is the UK banking system so big and is that a problem?', *Bank of England Quarterly Bulletin*, **Q4**, 385–395.

Cable, V. (2014), 'Observations on the UK banking industry', *International Review of Financial Analysis*, **36**, 84–86.

Cerqueiro, G., H. Degryse and S. Ongena (2009), 'Distance, bank organisation structure and lending decisions', in P. Alessandrini, M. Fratianni and A. Zazzaro (eds), *The Changing Geography of Banking and Finance*, Heidelberg: Springer, pp. 57–74.

Chick, V. and S.C. Dow (1988), 'A post-Keynesian perspective on the relation between banking and regional

development', in P. Arestis (ed.), *Post-Keynesian Monetary Economics – New approaches to financial modelling*, Aldershot, UK and Brookfield, VT, USA: Edward Elgar Publishing, pp. 219–250.
Chick, V., S. Dow and C. Rodriguez Fuentes (2013), 'Good banks and bad banks, centralised banks and local banks and economic growth', *Ekonomiaz*, **84** (3), 111–127.
Cowling, M., W. Liu and A. Ledger (2012), 'Small business financing in the UK before and during the financial crisis', *International Small Business Journal*, **30** (7), 778–800.
Cruickshank, D. (2000), *Competition in UK Banking. A Report to the Chancellor of the Exchequer*, London: The Stationary Office.
Degryse, H., K. Matthews and T. Zhao (2015), 'SMES and access to bank credit: evidence on the regional propagation of the financial crisis in the UK', CESifo Working Paper No. 5425.
Deutsche Bundesbank (2015), Bankenstatistik August 2015. Statistisches Beiheft 1 zum Monatsbericht. Frankfurt: Deutsche Bundesbank, retrieved on 14 October 2016 from www.bundesbank.de/Redaktion/DE/Downloads/Veroeffentlichungen/Statistische_Beihefte_1/2015/2015_08_bankenstatistik.pdf?__blob=publicationFile.
Die ZEIT (2015), 'Junkfood für Anleger', *Die ZEIT*, 3 June 6, retrieved on 14 October 2016 from www.zeit.de/2015/23/mittelstandsanleihen-geldanlage.
Dow, S.C. (1990), *Financial Markets and Regional Economic Development: The Canadian Experience*, Aldershot: Avebury.
Dow, S.C. (1996), 'European monetary integration, endogenous credit creation and regional economic development', in X. Vence-Deza and J.S. Metcalfe (eds), *Wealth from Diversity: Innovation, Structural Change and Finance for Regional Development in Europe*, Boston: Kluwer, pp. 293–306.
Dow S.C. (1999), 'The stages of banking development and the spatial evolution of banking systems', in R.L. Martin (ed.), *Money and the Space Economy*, Chichester: Wiley, pp. 31–48.
Dow, S.C. and C.J. Rodriguez-Fuentes (1997), 'Regional finance: a survey', *Regional Studies*, **31**, 903–920.
FT.com (2003), National News – 'Call for regional stock exchanges'. *Financial Times*, 2 September., retrieved on 14 October 2016 from http://search.ft.com/s03/search/article.html?id=03092000834.
Frank, M.Z. and V.K. Goyal (2003), 'Testing the pecking order theory of capital structure', *Journal of Financial Economics*, **32**, 217–248.
Gärtner, S. (2009), 'Sparkassen als Akteure der regionalen Strukturpolitik: sind sie in strukturschwachen Regionen hinreichend erfolgreich?', *Zeitschrift für Wirtschaftsgeographie*, **53**, (1–2), 14–27.
Gärtner, S. (2011), 'Regionen und Banken: Gedanken im Lichte der Krise', *Informationen zur Raumentwicklung*, **2**, 153–167.
Gärtner, S. and F. Flögel (2013), 'Dezentrale vs. zentrale Bankensysteme? Geographische Marktorientierung und Ort der Entscheidungsfindung als Dimensionen zur Klassifikation von Bankensystemen', *Zeitschrift für Wirtschaftsgeographie*, **57** (3), 105–121.
Gärtner, S. and F. Flögel (2014), 'Call for a spatial classification of banking systems through the lens of SME finance – decentralized versus centralized banking in Germany as an example', IAT Discussion Paper 14/1, retrieved on 14 October 2016 from www.iat.eu/discussionpapers/download/IAT_Discussion_Paper_14_01.pdf.
Grote, M.H. (2004), *Die Entwicklung des Finanzplatzes Frankfurt seit dem Zweiten Weltkrieg- Eine evolutionsökonomische Untersuchung*, Berlin: Duncker and Humblot (= Untersuchungen über das Spar-, Giro- und Kreditwesen 177).
Grote, M.H. (2009), 'Financial centres between centralisation and virtualisation', in P. Alessandrini, M. Fratianni and A. Zazzaro (eds), *The Changing Geography of Banking and Finance*, Heidelberg: Springer, pp. 277–294.
Guthrie, J. (2010), 'Apathy hits plan for regional stock markets', *The Financial Times*, 25 July, retrieved on 14 October 2016 from www.ft.com/cms/s/0/ffe89560-9820-11df-b218-00144feab49a.html#axzz3nh5mt8rD.
Handelsblatt (2003), 'Regionalbörsen bringen sich in England wieder ins Gespräch', Von Felix Schönauer, *Handelsblatt*, 28 August.
Handke, M. (2011), *Die Hausbankbeziehung. Institutionalisierte Finanzierungslösungen für kleine und mittlere Unternehmen in räumlicher Perspektive*, Münster: LIT.
Henry, N., P. Sissons, P. Coombes, J. Ferreira and J. Pollard (2014), 'Tackling financial exclusion: data disclosure and area-based lending data', Report, Coventry University, retrieved on 14 October 2016 from www.coventry.ac.uk/Global/08%20New%20Research%20Section/Researchers/CCSJ/FINAL_Full%20Report.pdf.
Hortacsu, A., F.A. Martinez-Jerez and J. Douglas (2009), 'The geography of trade in online transactions: evidence from eBay and MercadoLibre', *American Economic Journal: Microeconomics*, **1** (1), 53–74.
Huggins, R. and D. Prokop (2013), 'Stock markets and economic development: the case for regional exchanges', *International Journal of Innovation and Regional Development*, **5** (3), 279.
Huggins, R., N. Emlyn-Jones and J. Day (2003), *Regional Stock Exchanges – A Viable Option for Wales and Other UK Regions?*, Cardiff: Robert Huggins Associates.
Kaserer, C., N. Kuhn and G. Fey (2011), 'Kapitalmarktorientierung und Finanzierung mittelständischer

Unternehmen', Frankfurt am Main: Commerzbank AG, Deutsches Aktieninstitut e.V. and Deutsche Börse AG.
KfW (2003), *Eigenkapital für den 'breiten' Mittelstand. Neue Wege und Instrumente.* Abschlussbericht der AG 'Eigenkapital für den "breiten" Mittelstand' unter Leitung der KfW, Frankfurt a.M., Januar 2002. Frankfurt: Kreditanstalt für Wiederaufbau.
Kitching, J., D. Smallbone and M. Xheneti (2009), 'Have UK small business been victims of the credit crunch', Mimeo, Small Business Research Centre, Kingston University, UK.
Klagge, B. (1995), 'Strukturwandel im Bankwesen und regionalwirtschaftliche Implikationen: Konzeptionelle Ansätze und empirische Befunde', *Erdkunde*, **49**, 285–304.
Klagge, B. (2009), 'Finanzmärkte, Unternehmensfinanzierung und die aktuelle Finanzkrise', *Zeitschrift für Wirtschaftsgeographie*, **53** (1–2), 1–13.
Klagge, B. (2010), 'Das deutsche Banken- und Finanzsystem im Spannungsfeld von internationalen Finanzmärkten und regionaler Orientierung', in E. Kulke (ed.), *Wirtschaftsgeographie Deutschlands*, Heidelberg: Spektrum Akademischer Verlag, pp. 287–302.
Klagge, B. and R.L. Martin (2005), 'Decentralised versus centralised financial systems: is there a case for local capital markets?', *Journal of Economic Geography*, **5** (4), 387–421.
Klagge, B. and C. Peter (2009), 'Wissensmanagement in Netzwerken unterschiedlicher Reichweite. Das Beispiel des Private equity-Sektors in Deutschland', *Zeitschrift für Wirtschaftsgeographie*, **53** (1–2), 69–88.
Klagge, B. and C. Peter (2011), 'Changes in the Germany urban system – a financial-sector perspective', *Raumforschung und Raumordnung*, **69** (3), 201–211.
Klagge, B. and C. Peter (2012), 'Knowledge management in the network mode: the case of private equity and the role of regional financial centers', *Urbani Izziv*, **23** (supplement 1), S74–84, retrieved on 14 October 2016 from http://urbani-izziv.uirs.si/Portals/uizziv/papers/urbani-izziv-en-2012-23-supplement-1-007.pdf.
Klagge, B. and N. Zimmermann (2004), 'Finanzstandort Deutschland: Banken und Versicherungen', in H.-D. Haas, M. Heß, W. Klohn and H.-W. Windhorst (eds), *IfL (Hg.): Nationalatlas Bundesrepublik Deutschland. Band 8: Unternehmen und Märkte*. Heidelberg: Springer, pp. 60–61.
Kösters, J., D. Irmen, A. Schmidt, R. Feuerbach and E. Roegele (2000), Schwerpunkt Regionalbörsen (several articles). Zeitschrift für das gesamte Kreditwesen, **53**, 820–844.
Lee, N. H. Sameen and M. Cowling (2015), 'Access to finance for innovative SMEs since the financial crisis', *Research Policy*, **44**, 370–380.
Lee, R. and U. Schmidt-Marwede (1993), 'Interurban competition? Financial centres and the geography of financial production', *International Journal for Urban and Regional Research*, **17**, 492–515.
Leyshon, A. and N.J. Thrift (1992), 'Liberalisation and consolidation: the Single European Market and the remaking of European financial capital', *Environment and Planning, A*, **24**, 49–81.
Leyshon, A., S. French and P. Signoretta (2008), 'Financial exclusion and the geography of bank and building society branch closure in Britain', *Transactions of the Institute of British Geographers*, **33** (4), 447–465.
Lo, V. and E. Schamp (2001), 'Finanzplätze auf globalen Märkten – Beispiel Frankfurt/Main', *Geographische Rundschau*, **53** (7–8), 26–31.
London Stock Exchange (2003 and 2004), Website of the London Stock Exchange, www.londonstockexchange.com.
Macmillan Committee (1931), *Report of the Committee on Finance and Industry*, Cmnd 3987, London.
Marshall, J.N. (2013), 'A geographical political economy of banking crises: a peripheral region perspective on organizational concentration and spatial centralization in Britain', *Cambridge Journal of Regions, Economy and Society*, **6**, 455–477.
Marshall, J.N., C.J.S. Gentle, S. Raybuold and M. Coombes (1992), 'Regulatory change, corporate restructuring and the spatial development of the British financial sector', *Regional Studies*, **26**, 453–467.
Martin, R.L. (1989), 'The growth and geographical anatomy of venture capitalism in the UK', *Regional Studies*, **23**, 389–403.
Martin, R.L. (1992), 'Financing regional enterprise: the role of the venture capital market', in P. Townsend and R.L. Martin (eds), *Regional Development in Transition: the British Isles in the 1990s*, London: Jessica Kingsley, pp. 161–171.
Martin, R.L. (1994), 'Stateless monies, global financial integration and national economic autonomy: the end of geography?', in S. Corbridge, R.L. Martin and N. Thrift (eds), *Money, Power and Space*, Oxford: Blackwell, pp. 253–278.
Martin, R.L. (1999), 'The new economic geography of money', in R.L. Martin (ed.), *Money and the Space Economy*, Chichester: Wiley, pp. 3–27.
Martin, R.L., C. Berndt, B. Klagge and P. Sunley (2005), 'Spatial proximity effects and regional equity gaps in the venture capital market: evidence from Germany and the UK', *Environment and Planning, A*, **37**, 1207–1231.
Martin, R.L., C. Berndt, B. Klagge, P. Sunley and S. Herten (2003), *Regional Venture Capital Policy in Germany and the UK*, London and Berlin: Anglo-German Foundation.

Mason, C. (2010), 'Entrepreneurial finance in a regional economy', *Venture Capital*, **12** (3), 167–172.
Mason, C.M. and R.T. Harrison (1991), 'Venture capital, the equity gap and the north–south divide in the UK', in M. Green (ed.), *Venture Capital: International Comparisons*, London: Routledge, pp. 202–247.
Mason, C.M. and R.T. Harrison (2002), 'The geography of venture capital investment in the UK', *Transactions of the Institute of British Geographers, NS*, **27**, 427–451.
Mason, C. and Y. Pierrakis (2013), 'Venture capital, the regions and public policy: the United Kingdom since the post-2000 technology crash', *Regional Studies*, **47** (7), 1156–1171.
McPherson, S.H. and C. Waller (2000), 'Do local banks matter for the local economy: In search of a regional credit channel', in G.D. Hess and E. van Wincoop (eds), *Intra-national Macro-economics*, Cambridge: Cambridge University Press, pp. 295–316.
Merlin-Jones, D. (2012), *Extended Lending: The Case for a State-Backed Investment Bank*, London: Civitas.
Mocroft, Tim (2001), 'Bridging the equity gap – a new proposal for virtual local equity markets', CSFI Paper Nr. 47, London: Centre for the Study of Financial Innovation.
Modigliani, F. and M. Miller (1958), 'The cost of capital, corporation finance and the theory of investment', *American Economic Review*, **48** (3), 261–297.
Myers, S. (1984), 'The capital structure puzzle', *Journal of Finance*, **29**, 147–176.
Myers, S.C. and N.S. Majluf (1983), 'Corporate financing and investment decisions when firms have information that investors do not', Working Paper 1523–84, Sloane School of Management, Cambridge, MA: MIT.
Neininger, M. (2000), 'Die Zukunft der Regionalbörsen', *Bankmagazin*, **7**, 16–18.
Nolte, B., R. Nolting and F. Stummer (2002), 'Finanzierung des deutschen Mittelstands: Private Equity als Alternative', *Sparkasse*, **119**, 344–350.
O'Brien, R. (1992), *Global Financial Integration: The End of Geography*, London: Royal Institute of International Affairs.
Papi, L., E. Sarno and A. Zazzaro (2015), 'The geographical network of bank organisations: issues and evidence for Italy', Working Paper 105, Money and Finance Research Group, Universitá Politecnica delle Marche, Ancona, Italy.
Paul, S., S. Stein and A. Horsch (2002), 'Treiben die Banken den Mittelstand in die Krise?', *Zeitschrift für das gesamte Kreditwesen*, **55**, 2–6.
Porteous, D.J. (1995), *The Geography of Finance: Spatial Dimensions of Intermediary Behaviour*, Aldershot: Avebury.
Porteous, D.J. (1999), 'The development of financial centres: location, information, externalities and path dependence', in R.L. Martin (ed.), *Money and the Space Economy*, Chichester: Wiley, pp. 95–114.
Radcliffe Committee (1950), *Report of the Committee on the Working of the Financial System*, London.
Roland Berger Strategy Consultants (2011), *Herausforderungen für Unternehmen in der Wachstumsfinanzierung im aktuellen Marktumfeld. Internationale Finanzierungsstudie 2011 – Auswertung Deutschland*, Frankfurt, Germany.
Rudolph, B. (2003), 'Finanzierungsstrukturen für die deutsche Wirtschaft', in: *Kapitalmarkt Deutschland – Erfolge und Herausforderungen*, White Paper, März 2003, Frankfurt a.M.: Deutsche Börse Group, pp. 7–12.
Sassen, S. (1991), *The Global City: New York, London, Tokyo*, Princeton, NJ: Princeton University Press.
Schamp, E. (1999), 'The financial sector and urban competition in Germany, 1970 to 1995', in E. Wever (ed.), *Cities in Perspective I. Economy, Planning and the Environment*, Heidelberg: Springer, pp. 83–98.
Schmidt, H., O. Oesterhelwegand K. Treske (1997), 'Der Strukturwandel im Börsenwesen: Wettbewerbstheoretische Überlegungen und Trends im Ausland als Leitbilder für den Finanzplatz Deutschland', *Kredit und Kapital*, **30**, 367–411.
Schmidt, R. (1999), 'Differences between financial systems in European countries: consequences for EMU', Finance & Accounting Working Paper No. 35, Universität Frankfurt, retrieved on 14 October 2016 from www.finance.uni-frankfurt.de/schmidt/WPs/wp/wp35.pdf.
Simpson, C.V. (2013), *The German Sparkassen: A Commentary and Case Study*, London: Civitas.
Skidelsky, R., F. Martin and C.W. Wigstrom (2011), *Blueprint for a British Investment Bank*, London: Centre for Global Studies.
Sunley. P., B. Klagge, C. Berndt and R.L. Martin (2005), 'Venture capital programmes in the UK and Germany: in what sense regional policies?', *Regional Studies*, **39**, 255–274.
Thompson, C. (1989), 'The geography of venture capital', *Progress in Human Geography*, **13**, 62–98.
Uzzi, B. (1999), 'Social relations and networks in the making of financial capital', *American Sociological Review*, **64**, 481–505.
Uzzi, B. and R. Lancaster (2003), 'Relational embeddedness and learning: the case of bank loan managers and their clients', *Management Science*, **49**, 383–399.
Wilson Committee (1979), *Report of the Committee on Financial Institutions*, London.
Wójcik, D. (2002), 'The länder are the building blocks of the German capital market', *Regional Studies*, **36**, 877–895.

Wójcik, D. and D. MacDonald-Korth (2015), 'The British and the German financial sectors in the wake of the crisis: size, structure and spatial concentration', *Journal of Economic Geography*, **15**, 1033–1054. doi:10.1093/jeg/lbu056.
Zazzaro. A. (1997), 'Regional banking systems, credit allocation and regional economic development', *Economic Appliqué*, **1**, 51–74.

8. The geographical network of bank organizations: issues and evidence for Italy[1]

Luca Papi, Emma Sarno and Alberto Zazzaro

8.1 INTRODUCTION

The evolution of the banking industry has always been characterized by recurrent waves of technological, regulatory and organizational changes. The frequency and impact of such changes have increased in recent years, especially in response to the global financial crisis of 2007–10.

First, a growing number of technological innovations have modified – and continue to do so – the relationships between banks and customers, the competitive advantages of banks and the role of operational (borrower-to-branch), functional (branch-to-headquarter) and interbank (borrower-to-rival banks) geographical distances in lending decisions. Examples refer to the ever-wider utilization of web-based applications for the distribution of banking products and the handling of bank–firm relationships, and the diffusion of sophisticated techniques of risk analysis based on statistical information and automated credit-scoring models.

Second, regulatory changes have removed many barriers that limited competition, increasing the ability of financial institutions to operate in further geographical and product areas. At the same time, post-crisis regulation has requested banks to comply with tougher capital requirements and risk management procedures, affecting significantly the cost structure of the banking business.[2]

Finally, in response to the new technological opportunities and regulatory constraints, important changes in the organizational and operational structures have been activated by banks during the last 25 years, with an unprecedented surge of mergers and acquisitions that resulted in two opposite spatial processes, namely the strong concentration of banking power in a few places and the increase of banks' geographical reach.

The global financial crisis has triggered a new wave of organizational and regulatory changes. The negative consequences of the recent financial and economic crisis on banks' solvency have led in many countries to a new consolidation process that is producing fewer banks and fewer bank branches. In Europe structural changes have gone in tandem with a major ongoing institutional building project (the so-called banking union), which is redesigning the overall framework of the European banking sector. In this renewed regulatory environment, it is likely that the consolidation wave that has so far been mainly characterized by a national dimension will flow beyond national borders to become a cross-country phenomenon.

All such technological, regulatory and organizational changes have had, and continue to have, significant effects on the spatial distribution of the banking industry, the geography of bank power, bank-firm relationships – especially the lending relationships with the local, small and medium enterprises – and ultimately on the spatial distribution of economic development and convergence/divergence processes across regions.

In this chapter we first discuss why and how geographical distances between the key actors of the credit market (the borrowing firm, the lending branch, the lending bank, and the rival banks) forge bank–firm relationships and interbank competition. Then, using the metrics and graph techniques for network analysis we provide evidence about the evolution of the geography of banking industry in Italy and the spatial distribution of bank power between core and peripheral regions. More specifically, in section 8.2 we discuss the role of geographical distance in banking. In section 8.3 we present the different concepts of distance and review why bank proximity should affect the provision of financial services and the extant empirical evidence on the role of distance in different realms of banking activity. In section 8.4 we summarize what it is known and what it is not known about the determinants of distances and the emergence of banking centers and peripheries. In section 8.5, using the network analysis, we investigate the changing geography of bank organizations, the spatial network of bank power and the geographical interconnectedness among bank structures in the Italian banking industry. In section 8.6 we conclude and suggest directions for policy initiatives and further research.

8.2 WHY GEOGRAPHICAL DISTANCE STILL MATTERS IN BANKING

A crucial production factor affecting bank lending decisions is the availability of accurate information about borrowers and their projects. Both the theoretical and empirical banking literature have now definitively shown that asymmetric information between borrowers and lenders and within the banking organizations prevents credit being allocated efficiently in the economy at fair terms. Credit granting necessitates the transfer of hard and soft information between borrowers and loan officers who are in charge of loan applications, and between the latter and senior managers across bank hierarchical layers, who are called upon to review the action of loan officers and, possibly, to make a final decision on certain types of loans.

Hard information consists of quantitative or easily quantifiable data that can be collected and communicated at a distance without any material loss of its intelligence content (for example, borrowers' financial statements, balance-sheet ratios, repayment records and so on). The quantity and quality of hard information available to banks depend on the legal, institutional and regulatory environment of the banking industry as well as on the advances in credit scoring technologies, regardless of their spatial organization. For example, the sharing of information about borrowers' repayment history and debt exposure through public or private credit bureaus improves the screening ability of banks, mitigating selection errors in lending (Pagano and Jappelli, 1993), borrowers' indiscipline (Klein, 1992) but also reducing the risks of information capture of borrowers by lenders (Padilla and Pagano, 1997).[3] Similarly, better accounting standards (for example, tighter accounting and reporting rules or stricter sanctions for fraudulent reporting) decrease the costs of information acquisition, thereby increasing resources devoted to selecting good borrowers, improving credit allocation and reducing the average default on granted loans (Zazzaro, 2005). Credit scoring techniques allow banks to elaborate many pieces of rough, hard information to obtain new and more accurate evidence about borrower creditworthiness and improve their lending decision-making (Petersen and Rajan, 2002).

In contrast, soft information comprises subjective knowledge accumulated over time by loan officers in the course of repeated face-to-face interactions with borrowers (for example, assessment of the quality of the firm's management, its customer relationships up and down the value chain, the ethical character and reputation of loan applicants). Soft information is not easily codifiable, storable or objectively verifiable and, as a result, it is difficult to communicate and transmit between agents at a distance (Petersen and Rajan, 2002; Berger and Udell, 2002; Petersen, 2004). Loan officers at the bank branch are the real and often exclusive repositories of soft information, which is very local in nature, largely embedded in local society and the economic environment, and hardly portable (Uzzi, 1999; Uzzi and Lancaster, 2003; Drexler and Schoar, 2014).[4] In other words, soft information has a fundamental spatial dimension, which makes the geographical distribution of the banking industry, and the spatial organization of each single bank of the utmost importance for an easy and efficient access to credit for new, small and innovative, informationally opaque companies (Klagge and Martin, 2005; Alessandrini et al., 2009c, 2009d, 2010). In this context, the geographical proximities between borrowers, the lending and rival bank branches and headquarters, impact on the costs and quality of soft information acquisition and its sound transmission flow. In addition, physical proximity reduces transportation costs for searching for prospective borrowers and lenders, for conducting bank-firm relationships in person and for the internal reviewing of loan officers' activity (Degryse and Ongena, 2005; Degryse et al., 2009b).

The different nature of hard and soft information means that different types of banks have different comparative advantages in acquiring, interpreting and using it. In general, large, hierarchical and geographically dispersed banks are in a better position to obtain and process hard information, taking advantage of economies of scale from large technology systems and extensive information datasets from the network of their branches. By contrast, they are at a disadvantage in lending to informationally opaque borrowers due to organizational frictions and the difficulties of sharing soft information across the bank hierarchical layers (Stein, 2002; Berger et al., 2005), while small local banks are better equipped to collect and assess soft information through personal and repeated interactions at the local level with local borrowers.

8.3 WHICH DISTANCE?

The literature on the geography of the banking industry and the spatial organization of banks distinguishes between three main different notions of distance: (1) the *operational* or borrower-to-branch distance; (2) the *functional* or branch-to-headquarter distance; and (3) the *interbank* or borrower-to-rival-banks distance. These notions of distance have been articulated both at the bank level, to examine the determinants of the spatial organization of banks and its effects on lending decisions, and at the geographical market level, to examine the evolution of the spatial structure of the banking industry and its impact on firms' access to credit and regional development.

Operational or Borrower-to-Branch Distance

The operational distance measures the geographical space that separates a borrower from the bank branch managing the lending relationship. In spite of advances in information and communication technology and the use of automated credit-scoring models, the borrower–branch distance remains surprisingly small: in the USA the median operational distance for credit lines was 3 miles in 2003 (Brevoort and Wolken, 2009); in Japan it was even smaller (in 2010 1.2 miles, according to Ono et al., 2013), and likewise in Europe, as results from studies conducted on single banks in Belgium, Italy and Sweden (Degryse and Ongena, 2005; Carling and Lundberg, 2005; Bellucci et al., 2013).

Consistent with the enduring importance of operational proximity for doing banking business, starting from the 1980s, banking systems in Europe and the US experienced a sharp increase in the number of branches and a wave of bank acquisitions, with large bank conglomerates spreading their presence across regions and countries through extensive webs of branches and subsidiaries. However, recent developments in the banking industry in many industrialized countries could have contrasting effects on the spatial organization of banks and the importance of operational distance. On the one hand, the new and ongoing bank consolidation process, starting in response to the global financial crisis, has reduced the number of bank branches and consequently increased the operational distance from local borrowers. In Europe, for example, the number of branches peaked at 186,256 units at the end of 2009; since then the trend has been reversed and a sharp decline has been recorded, with 163,171 branches operative at the end of 2013 (Figure 8.1). On the other hand, the increased diffusion of remote, e-banking and other Internet-related

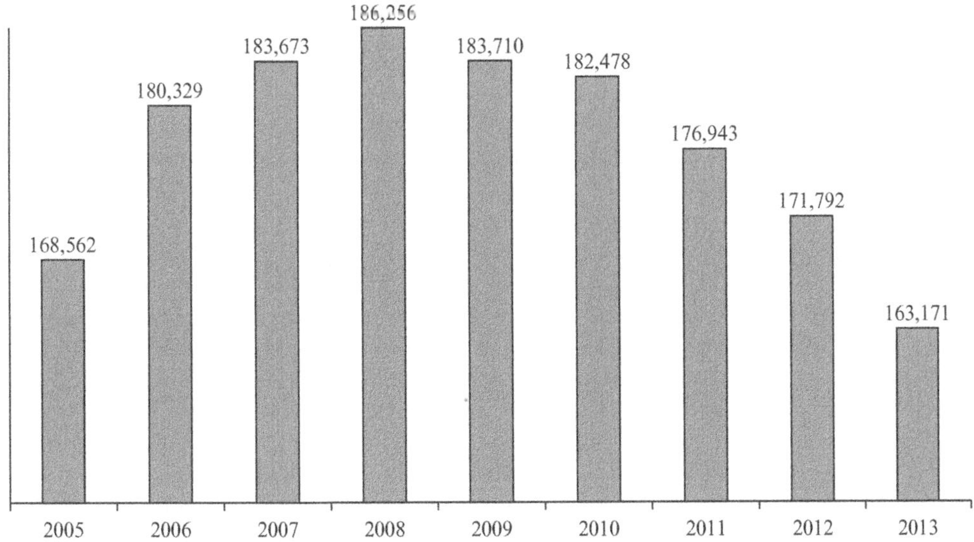

Note: Number of branches of credit institutions in the Euro area at the end of the period.

Source: European Central Bank.

Figure 8.1 *Number of branches in Euro area*

possibilities for managing lending relationships, while reinforcing the decreasing trend in the number of branches, has produced a "virtual" reduction of importance of operational proximity between borrowers and lenders (Petersen and Rajan, 2002).

As outlined above, the benefit of greater operational proximity between the contracting parties is to reduce the cost of searching, underwriting and handling loan contracts, both in terms of information and transportation costs. Consistent with this view, the choice of the main bank by firms is found to be positively influenced by their physical proximity to its bank branches (Barone et al., 2011; Ono et al., 2013). The effects of operational proximity on loan origination and loan pricing are however ambiguous, depending on whether banks tend to price discriminate borrowers spatially by location or, alternatively, whether they price loans according to marginal costs. In the former case, transportation and information cost advantages provide the bank branch that is closest to the borrowing firm with a market power against its rivals, that can be thus exploited by charging higher interest rates (Lederer and Hurter, 1986; Dell'Ariccia et al., 1999; Degryse et al., 2009a). In contrast, if banks follow a simple, non-discriminatory mark-up rule to price loans, the operational proximity of lenders should reduce interest rates and increase credit availability for nearby borrowers (Bellucci et al., 2013).

The uncertain impact of operational distance on loan terms and availability is confirmed by the empirical evidence. Petersen and Rajan (2002) were the first to provide empirical evidence of spatial discriminatory loan pricing, finding a negative relation of the ability to borrow at a distance[5] with the loan interest rates, and a positive impact on the likelihood of loan approvals. The same findings are documented by Agarwal and Hauswald (2010) who analyze the loan applications made by small businesses to a major US bank. Similarly, Brevoort and Hannan (2006) find that the probability of a bank approving a loan application in a given area increases with its spatial proximity to the customers. A negative correlation between borrower-to-branch distance and interest rate was also found by Degryse and Ongena (2005) on investigating the pricing behavior of a large Belgian bank in small business lending. To the extent that the effects of distance are significant for transactional loans and not significant for relational loans their results are consistent with the hypothesis that transportation more than information costs motivate spatial price discrimination by banks. Other studies, however, find evidence of mark-up pricing by banks in which transportation and information costs of distance are transferred to the interest rate. Knyazeva and Knyazeva (2012) show that interest rates on syndicated loans to large US firms are positively associated with the geographic distance of the borrowing firm from the lead lender or the pool of lenders. Bellucci et al. (2013) document the same relationship between distance and interest rate in the case of Italian small firms and show that distant borrowers are more likely to be credit-constrained. A similar uncertainty emerges with regard to collateral. Cerqueiro et al. (2009) find that distant loans are more likely to be secured for a sample of US firms, while this relationship is insignificant when considering a sample of firms borrowing from a Belgian bank. In contrast, Bellucci et al. (2010, 2014) document a negative correlation between distance and collateral, even after taking into account the simultaneity of collateral and interest rate decisions.

At the geographical market level, a number of studies have considered the density of bank branches per inhabitants or per square mile as a measure of the average operational distance from borrowers. Once again, the results are mixed. Using US data, Avery and

Samolyk (2004) find that the number of branches has no impact on small business lending growth in the local market, whereas the number of banks is only weakly associated with such a variable. By contrast, Bonaccorsi and Gobbi (2001) find that the density of bank branches (the ratio of branches to population) in Italian provinces is positively associated with the credit availability for local firms (particularly for small firms), whereas it is negatively associated with the share of bad loans. However, Alessandrini et al. (2009b) report that the probability of firms being credit-rationed is unaffected by the average operational distance of local branches, whereas the sensitivity of firms' investment to cash flow is weakened by the number of branches in the province per square mile, but becomes magnified if the number of branches is normalized to inhabitants. With regard to the effects of bank operational proximity on firms' innovation propensity, Benfratello et al. (2008) provide evidence that a higher bank branch density increases the probability of firms of introducing innovations in Italy. However, Herrera and Minetti (2007) and Alessandrini et al. (2010) show that the effect of branch density on firm innovation becomes statistically insignificant once controlling for other bank variables (the duration of the lending relationship or the functional distance of local banking industry) and for its possible endogeneity.

Functional or Branch-to-Headquarter Distance

A second fundamental notion of geographical distance in the banking literature is functional distance.[6] While operational distance quantifies a geographical space external to the bank, the notion of functional distance captures the internal spatial remoteness between the different hierarchical layers of a banking organization. Typically, it is measured by the distance between bank branches operated locally, where loan applications are submitted, information is collected, lending relationships are established and handled, and the bank headquarters, where the ultimate decisions about branch budgeting, loan officers' careers, lending policy and loan provisions are taken.

Recent changes in the spatial organization of economic activities emphasize the importance of functional distance for the banking industry. There is a striking trend worldwide to concentrate firms' headquarters and strategic functions in a few cities in order to take advantage of network externalities related to the knowledge and understanding of market and technological opportunities and the availability of high-quality human resources, business services and transport facilities (Klier and Testa, 2002; Storper and Venables, 2004; Strauss-Kahn and Vives, 2005; Bel and Fageda, 2008). Face-to-face buzzing and networking, access to high-skilled human resources, financial innovation and information on future trends in the economy and industries are all factors of paramount importance for the banking business (Thrift, 1994; Tschoegl, 2000; Grote, 2009). Consistently, the past and present consolidation process of banking industries in Europe and the US has produced a concentration of bank headquarters and strategic functions in a few financial centers. This has greatly increased the physical distance that separates the actual locus of control of bank lending policy from local branches, local borrowers and the local economy.

Information asymmetries and agency costs within a bank organization and "home biases" in lending policy make functional distance a major determinant of access to credit for local firms (Alessandrini and Zazzaro, 1999). Soft information is strongly embedded in the local economy and society, and can be effectively gathered only by loan officers working and living in the same neighborhoods as borrowers. This makes information about borrowers largely asymmetric within the bank organization and provides local loan officers with the opportunity to exploit this informational rent to their own benefit.

Accordingly, banks have to design costly loan reviews, officers' rotation and incentive pay systems in order to mitigate moral hazard behaviors of local officers (Udell, 1989; Hertzberg et al., 2010; Uchida et al., 2012). Asymmetry of information and interest disalignment between bank's officers and managers (shareholders) and agency costs vary with the branch-to-headquarter distance. Loan officers at distant branches of a large and geographically dispersed bank conglomerate are often only temporarily active in the local economy, coming from other regions and/or whose opportunities for career promotion will be reaped in different places. Geographical mobility incentivizes loan officers to produce short-term and easily communicable results, shying away from lending to informationally opaque (young, small and innovative) borrowers and assuming too generous an attitude toward hard information loans to well-established enterprises (Hirshleifer and Thakor, 1992; Palley, 1997; Berger and Udell, 2002). In addition, loan officers of local branches can divert time and effort from their due tasks of searching for and monitoring borrowers to lobbying senior managers at the bank headquarters for budgeting and career concerns. In this scenario, loan officers become advocates of their units and exert effort in collecting information to convince their superiors to allocate more of the firm's resources to their operating units (Dewatripont and Tirole, 1999). In contrast, loan officers at branches which are functionally proximate to the bank headquarters are often born and bred in the same area as local entrepreneurs and senior bank managers, with whom they share the same culture, values, norms and language. Their strong embeddedness in local society not only increases the opportunity to acquire information about borrowers that is not otherwise available to people external to the local society, but it also makes its transmission easier to the top hierarchical levels of the bank.

Besides information and agency problems, the geographical proximity of the "thinking head" of the bank to a region increases the sensitivity of the bank's lending policy to the needs of the local economy and to the lobbying effort of local society, introducing home and cultural affinity biases in credit allocation. In fact, internal capital budgeting and liquidity flows across bank branches and subsidiaries tend to be decided not only on the basis of local lending opportunities, but are also the result of corporate policies and the economic, social, political and cultural importance that the local economy and society have at the headquarters where the bank CEOs live and work and where budgeting decisions are taken (Meyer et al., 1992; Scharfstein and Stein, 2000; Carlin et al., 2006; Landier et al., 2009).

The empirical literature offers many consistent results supporting the importance of agency costs and home bias in geographically dispersed bank organizations. A first group of studies has documented that consolidation dealings involving out-of-region, distant banks cause a decrease in the availability of credit to small firms (Keeton, 1995, 1996; Berger et al., 1998; Peek and Rosengren, 1998; Alessandrini et al., 2008). In general, there is robust evidence for many countries that branches and subsidiaries of functionally distant banks tend to be less efficient (Berger et al., 2001; Berger and DeYoung, 2001) and shy away from small business lending and soft-information-based credit relationships

(Mian, 2006; Liberti and Mian, 2009; DeYoung et al., 2008). Furthermore, firms located in regions disproportionally populated by functionally distant banks tend to have less access to credit, a lower capacity to maintain a long-lasting bank relationship and a lower propensity to innovate (Detragiache et al., 2008; Alessandrini et al., 2009b, 2009c, 2010; Gormley, 2010; Presbitero and Zazzaro, 2011).

The existence of "home biases" in credit allocation is well documented by the literature on syndicated loans and the functioning of banks' internal capital market, showing that large and geographically dispersed banks (foreign or nationwide) exacerbate the transmission of financial shocks across regions, by moving funds from their peripheral to central (headquartered) markets (Peek and Rosengren, 1997, 2000; Cetorelli and Goldberg, 2011; Imai and Takarabe, 2011; Schnabl, 2012; Giannetti and Yafeh, 2012; Berrospide et al., 2013) and by limiting access to credit to local firms when the local economy growth rate slows down (Campello, 2002; Cremers et al., 2010). This is especially true in times of global crises, when a "flight to home" effect may explain both the decline of the banks' lending exposure to regions farther away from their headquarters (Giannetti and Laeven, 2011; de Haas and van Horen, 2013) and the restriction in access to credit suffered by firms located in regions disproportionally populated by foreign and functionally distant banks (Popov and Udell, 2012; Presbitero et al., 2014).

Interbank or Borrower-to-Rival-Banks Distance

A third concept of distance has to do with the presence and proximity of competing banks and branches in a certain area. Interbank distance and the geography of bank market power have a direct influence on credit availability to local economy and intertwine with operational and functional distance.

First, the geographical proximity of bank competitors reduces the benefits of market power coming from operational proximity to borrowers and the opportunity to discriminate them spatially (Degryse et al., 2009a). In this vein, Degryse and Ongena (2005) and Agarwal and Hauswald (2010) find that when the rivals of the lending bank are distant from the borrower the interest rate charged to that borrower is lower on average.

Second, interbank proximity affects bank information production, lending orientation and access to credit for local firms. On the one hand, the presence of a large number of banks increases the likelihood of borrowers having already been considered and correctly rejected by rival banks, thus eroding the banks' ex-ante beliefs about the applicants' creditworthiness and weakening their screening effort (Broecker, 1990; Riordan, 1993; Shaffer, 1998; Cao and Shi, 2000). Further, proximity of bank rivals facilitates the switching of borrowers from one lender to another. This reduces the possibility of the lending bank reaping the benefits of soft information production over time, undermines the incentives to make specific investments in long-lasting lending relationships, and induces the bank to increase its interest rates in the short term (Mayer, 1988; Petersen and Rajan, 1995; Ogura, 2010; Bellucci et al., 2013). In addition, the easy access to bank rivals and alternative sources of credit makes reputation costs of default less prominent, heightening borrowers' moral hazard behavior (Hoff and Stiglitz, 1997). On the other hand, a smaller interbank distance and higher competitive pressure from rivals can induce banks to support local borrowers more effectively. Local banks increase their lending to more informationally opaque borrowers on a relational basis in order to create a competitive edge with respect to their rivals and insulate themselves from pure price competition (Boot and Thakor, 2000; Dell'Ariccia and Marquez, 2004; Hauswald and Marquez, 2006). Conversely, out-of-market, functionally distant banks are forced to engage in specific local objectives in order to overcome the competition of local banks, reducing the impact of "home bias" on credit allocation and the possibility of extracting extra profits (Alessandrini and Zazzaro, 1999; Claessens and van Horen, 2009).

Third, the effects of interbank proximity depend on the types of bank rivals in the region. If the regional banking system is predominantly populated by functionally distant banks with a competitive advantage in transactional, hard-information lending, strong interbank competition in the regional credit market tends to be harmful for credit access to young, small and innovative firms: in order to find it rewarding to lend on a relational, soft-information basis, functionally distant banks ought to benefit from their market power, allowing them to extract additional future rents from investing specific resources in a lending relationship. In contrast, the market proximity of rival banks tends to promote relational lending if there is a strong presence of small and functionally close banks prepared to exploit comparative advantages in handling soft information (Presbitero and Zazzaro, 2011).

Finally, the geographical proximity of banks in credit markets may have different effects on interbank competition and bank lending orientation according to whether the same or different banks operate in different regions. This is the multimarket contact hypothesis advanced by Edwards (1955), and widely discussed in the banking literature (Heggestad and Rhoades, 1978; Mester, 1987; de Bonis and Ferrando, 2000; Fuentelsaz and Gómez, 2006; Degryse and Ongena, 2007). According to the traditional mutual forbearance argument, multiple contacts across regional credit markets facilitate tacit collusion amongst rival banks, restraining price competition and encouraging a live-and-let-live behavior (Edwards, 1955; Bernheim and Whinston, 1990). However, multiple contacts can also have pro-competitive effects (Mester, 1992), leading banks to invest in soft information and other relation-specific assets in order to create an edge to competition in some markets and limit the risk of retaliation by rival banks (Anand and Galetovic, 2006).

8.4 DISTANCE DETERMINANTS AND BANKING CENTERS

What exactly drives distances in the banking industry and the emergence, shaping and evolution of banking cores and peripheries is a crucial, though relatively unexplored, issue. In this section we provide a short review of what is known, and not known, about such matters.

What We Do Know . . .

Some recent studies have tested for the determinants of the operational distance between borrowers and lenders directly. Others have considered operational and functional distances indirectly by looking at the determinants of the geographic expansion of bank organizations.

Testing for borrower-to-branch distance

In an influential paper, Petersen and Rajan (2002) analyze data from the 1993 National Survey of Small Business Finance in the USA, and document that the average borrower-to-branch distance tripled for the lending relationships that began in the 1990s with respect to those that began in the 1970s, while the frequency of conducting bank business impersonally (phone or mail) doubled. In line with the idea that soft information is spatially embedded and hard information is spatially neutral, Petersen and Rajan also find that informationally opaque firms tend to borrow from closer lending branches, while the increasing trend in distance is explained by the productivity of bank employees in producing loans and hence by bank capacity to use hard information technologies. Consistently, bank-firm relationships conducted at a distance tend also to be conducted on an impersonal basis.

Using the same dataset, Berger et al. (2005) show that large banks have a comparative advantage in gathering and processing hard information as they lend at a greater distance and make a stronger use of impersonal ways of communication with borrowers (see also Cole et al., 2004). These results hold even after controlling for the potential endogeneity of bank–firm matches. The greater ability of big banks to lend at a distance is confirmed by Uchida et al. (2008) in the case of Japan. In addition, they show that the frequency of contacts between small banks and their borrowers is significantly higher, suggesting a greater use of soft information on the part of those banks.

Entry into geographic markets and spatial availability of banking services

Indirect evidence on spatial organization of banks and distance in credit markets comes from the studies on bank entry decisions into geographic markets and availability of banking services to local communities. A first striking result in this literature is that functional and interbank distances have a strong influence on the geographical expansion strategy of banks. At the international level, Focarelli and Pozzolo (2005) show that distance from the bank headquarters significantly and negatively affects the decision to establish a branch or a subsidiary abroad. Similarly, Magri et al. (2005) consider the activity level of banks from 22 OECD countries in Italy and find that both the number of foreign structures (branches and subsidiaries) and total assets by home (headquarters) country are negatively correlated with the distance from the host country (Italy). Buch and DeLong (2004) look at bank mergers and acquisitions and, in line with studies on entry, find that the number of cross-border bank mergers decreases with the geographical (and cultural) distance between the dealing partners and that such a negative impact increases over time.

At the national level, Chang et al. (1997) provide evidence of herding behavior in location decisions of banks, which leads to a clustering of branches across New York City census tracts. They find a positive correlation between the number of existing branches in a tract and the number of future branch openings in the same tract, thus indicating that spatial proximity to rivals produces major positive information externalities for banks. Partial confirmation of banks' herding behavior in branch openings is documented by Barros (1995) in the case of the Portuguese banking system: new banks (de novo and privatized) tend to establish their branches where incumbents hold a large share of total branches in the market. By contrast, old banks expand their geographical network of branches relatively more in markets with a small presence of incumbent banks, even if they do not seem to react to the entry of new banks. Finally, both old and new banks tend to open branches where the firm density is low, suggesting that transportation and information costs are important factors explaining banks' operational distance.

Haveman and Nonnemaker (2000) analyze the decision of savings and loan associations in California to establish branches in new geographical markets (at the county level) within the state in question. They show that the degree of multimarket contacts has an inverted U-shaped (positive) effect on the decision of multi-market (single-market) savings and loan associations to expand in a new county, suggesting that proximity to multipoint rivals can spur or deter banks from expanding geographically in order to reduce competitive pressure or to preempt warfare in other markets. An inverted U-shaped effect of multimarket contacts on entry decisions is similarly found by Fuentelsaz and Gómez (2006) for the case of savings banks in Spain. However, they also show that the number of incumbent banks in the market reduces the likelihood of a bank entering that market, consistent with the idea that, per se, potential proximity to rivals acts as a barrier to entry into new geographical markets. In contrast, the closer the bank headquarter to the new region, the more likely is the expansion of the bank organization toward that region. These findings are confirmed for Italian banks, which prove less likely to establish branches in provinces which are distant from their headquarters and their pre-entry geographical network of branches (Cerasi et al., 2000; Felici and Pagnini, 2008), and in provinces where interbank proximity is strong (Calcagnini et al., 2001).

While all the reviewed papers estimate reduced form models, there are a few studies that have considered bank branching decisions in strategic structural models of price and non-price competition. Kim and Vale (2001) consider the case of Norwegian banks from 1988 to 1995 and find that banks allow for the expected retaliatory response of rivals in their branching decisions. Similar results are documented by Carbó et al. (2009) for the case of Spanish banks between 1988 and 2002.

Finally, a number of papers have considered the availability of banking services to local communities in terms of total number of branches, branches per population or branches per square mile. Almost all these studies consistently document that the spatial distribution of branches across regions is negatively correlated with regional population density (Lanzilotti and Saving, 1969; Seaver and Fraser, 1979, 1983; Evanoff, 1988; de Juan, 2003; Alama and Tortosa, 2011), providing indirect evidence in favor of the hypothesis that operational and interbank distance are strongly influenced by average transportation and information costs.

. . . And What We Do Not Know

Starting from the pioneering study of Kindleberger (1974), an extensive literature on the emergence and evolution of international financial centers has been developed in financial economics and geography (Porteous, 1999; Gehrig, 2000; Fratianni, 2008; Grote, 2009). Much less attention has been paid to the emergence of banking centers, the uneven geography of bank power and the regional interconnectedness among bank structures at the national level.

A number of contributions in the post-Keynesian tradition have analyzed the endogenous emergence and reproduction of a spatial core–periphery structure in national banking systems (Chick and Dow, 1988; Dow, 1999; Chick et al., 2013; Crocco et al.,

2014). However, the sharp dichotomy between center and periphery does not allow these authors to explore the whole complexity of the spatial network of bank power and organizations.

Choi et al. (1986, 1996, 2003) analyzed the matrix of banks in the world's top 300 (according to *The Banker* ranking) headquartered in one of fourteen major international financial centers which are organizationally present in one of the other financial centers. They document that after a 20-year period during which the interconnectedness of international financial centers increased, in the 1990s the presence of foreign banks from one center and hosted in the others decreased significantly, with New York confirmed as the major (the most interconnected) financial center in the world, Hong Kong and Singapore that have overtaken London in terms of top foreign banks in their center, and Tokyo losing ground to other financial centers. However, the focus of these studies is the interdependence of the world's top international financial centers. In this context, the authors use the existence in the city home of a financial center of structures (representative offices, branches, subsidiaries) of banks headquartered in another financial center city as a measure of the degree of interconnection between the two centers, without investigating the properties of the banking network (centrality, density, stability) or the spatial distribution of bank organizations at the country level.

Finally, a recent strand of research has explored the characteristics of the web of aggregate, cross-border bank lending flows, as reported in the financial statistics of the Bank for International Settlements, by using the techniques and metrics of network analysis (von Peter, 2010; Minoiu and Reyes, 2011; Sá, 2013). However, since the latter studies ignore the interlinkages among bank organizations and the spatial structure of bank functional power, they cannot provide insights into the importance of operational, functional and interbank distances.

8.5 THE GEOGRAPHICAL NETWORK OF BANK ORGANIZATIONS IN ITALY

In this section we analyze the changing spatial network of banking organizations in Italy. With its predominance of small and medium enterprises and its North–South economic divide, the Italian economy represents an interesting case study to examine the spatialities of credit markets and bank-firm relationships. In addition, the structural and spatial evolution of the banking industry in Italy during the last 25 years has been broadly representative of developments experienced by many other European and non-European countries and can provide some insights into the formation of banking centers and peripheries, the uneven geographical distribution of bank power and regional banking interconnectedness.

The Italian Banking Industry

To contextualize the environment in which Italian banks operate, it is important to start from the two major structural aspects that have characterized, and continue to shape, the Italian economy. First, the predominance of small- and medium-sized enterprises

(SMEs) for which concepts such as soft and hard information, relationship and transaction lending, or bank and borrower proximity are particularly relevant in influencing credit and investment decisions. The importance of SMEs within the Italian economy emerges both in terms of workforce and value added. According to Eurostat statistics, in Italy the SMEs account for more than 80 percent of employment in the non-financial sector, versus an EU average of 67 percent. A similar gap also emerges when we consider the SMEs share of value added (67 percent in Italy versus 57 percent in the EU). This high share of SMEs contributes to explain the financial structure of Italian firms, with its relatively widespread use of debt instruments (55 percent of total liabilities in Italy versus 47 percent in the Euro area) and a high share of bank loans on total financial debt (64 percent versus 46 percent of the Euro area).[7]

The second structural aspect of the Italian economy which is important for the evolution of banking geography is the economic and social divide among the Italian regions, with southern regions still lagging well behind in terms of income and employment levels compared to central and northern regions (Figure 8.2).

During the last two decades, the above-mentioned structural aspects of the Italian economy combined with the increasing regulatory pressures on the banking industry occurring at the European and national level have contributed to shape the new geographical structure of the Italian banking system. During the same period there has been strong liberalization and harmonization of the legal, regulatory and institutional financial framework in the European Union, culminating in the completion of the European Monetary Union, and more recently in the construction of the so-called European Banking Union.

At the national level, a far-reaching overhaul of the banking sector took place in the 1990s: a new consolidated banking law was passed in 1993, paving the way to a relaxation of entry barriers into the sector, a significant liberalization of branches, wide-ranging privatization and a major wave of mergers and acquisitions.

Over the period 1992–2013 the number of banks decreased by 33 percent, from 1,025 to 684. To a large extent this reduction was due both to takeovers of troubled southern banks by northern banks and to the pressures imposed by the quest for greater efficiency in a more integrated market. Consequently, the direction of the consolidation process has brought about a loss of autonomy in the southern banking sector. Nowadays, the latter comprises only a small number of autonomous southern commercial banks, the bulk of banks being members of banking groups headquartered in the northern part of the country (Zazzaro, 2006; Giannola et al., 2013).

At the same time, to compete better on local markets, Italian banks have reduced their operational distance from customers through a significant increase in area presence by expanding their network of branches. As a result, the number of banks doing business on local markets[8] increased on average from 28 in 1992 to 32 in 2013. In Figure 8.3 we depict the variation in the number of banks by province from 1992 to 2013. In 79 provinces there was an increase in the number of independent banks (Figure 8.3, categories 3–6). This increase was exceptionally high (category 6) in Milan (+35), Turin (+22), Florence (+20) and Brescia (+19). In contrast, in 25 provinces the number of banks decreased (categories 1 and 2). A first group of provinces experiencing such a contraction is concentrated in the North-East of Italy, reflecting the consolidation process of local cooperative banks that led, in the province of Trento, to an exceptional reduction of stand-alone banking institu-

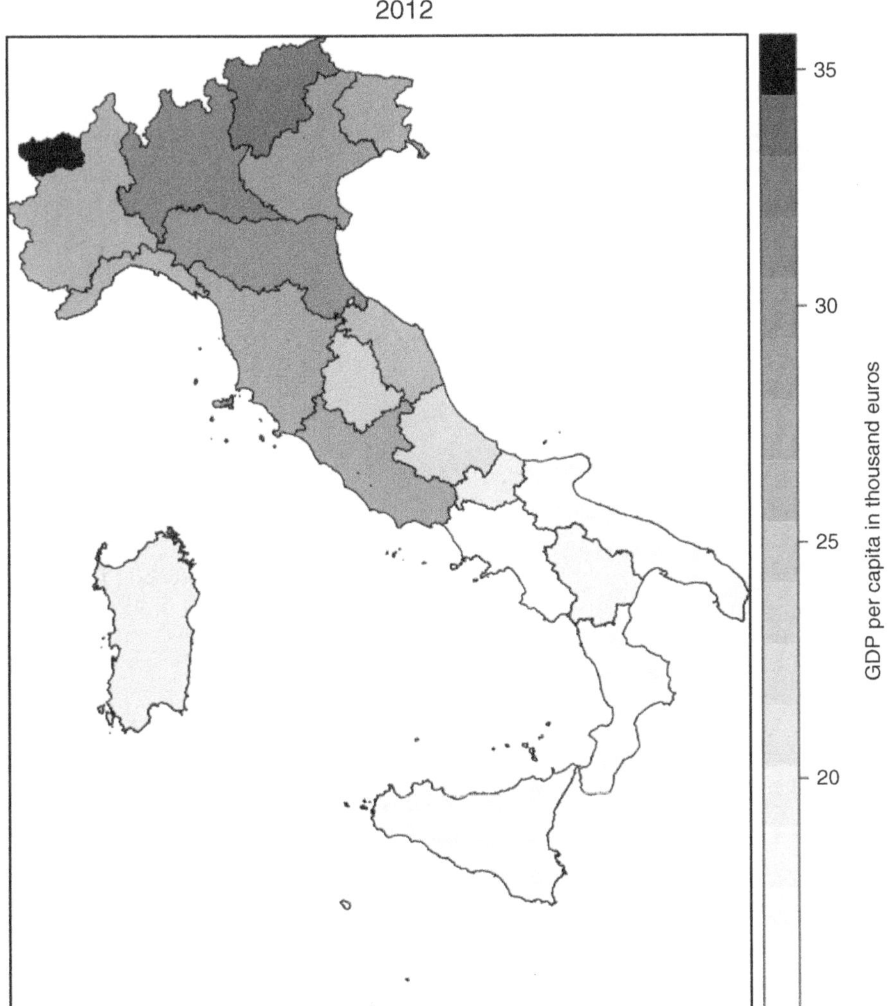

Source: Italian National Institute of Statistics (ISTAT).

Figure 8.2 GDP per capita by region

tions by 46. A decrease in the number of banks also occurred in southern provinces where many local banks were acquired by banks headquartered in the North.

The number of branches went up by more than 60 percent for the country as a whole, with the average number of branches per province increasing from 180 in 1993 to 289 in 2013. This positive trend affected all Italian provinces with the exception of three provinces in Sicily where the number of branches slightly decreased (Agrigento, Catania and Trapani; category 1 in Figure 8.4). In general, southern provinces experienced a much less marked increase in the number of bank branches than the rest of the country, such that

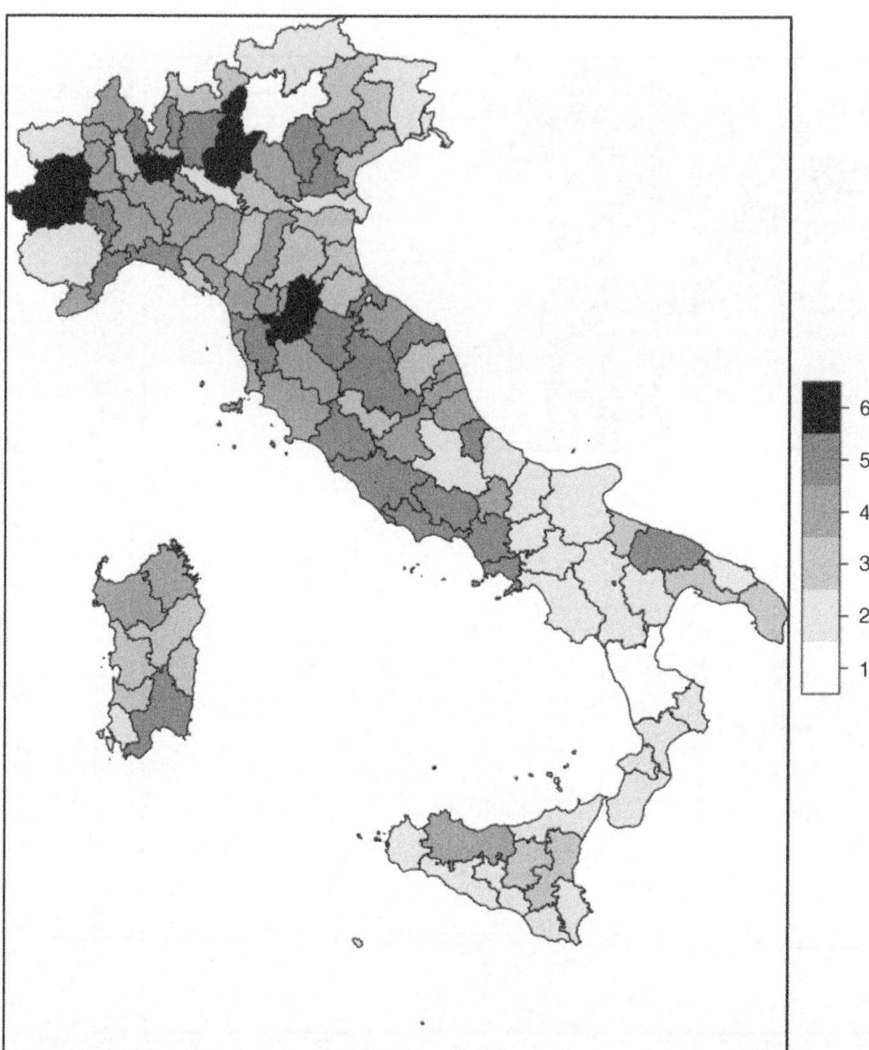

Notes: Category 1: provinces where the number of banks decreases exceptionally, Δ Banks < Q1 −1.5*(Q3–Q1) = −11, where Q1 and Q3 indicate the first and third quartile. Category 2: provinces where the variation of the number of banks is below the first quartile but not exceptionally low, −11 ≤ Δ Banks ≤ Q1 = 0. Category 3: provinces where the variation of the number of banks is between the first quartile and the median (M), 0 < Δ Banks ≤ M = 3. Category 4: provinces where the variation of the number of banks is between the median and third quartile, 3 < Δ Banks ≤ Q3 = 7. Category 5: provinces where the variation of the number of banks is above the third quartile but not exceptionally large 7 < Δ Branches ≤ Q3 + 1.5*(Q3–Q1) = 18. Category 6: provinces where the number of banks increases exceptionally, Δ Banks > 18.

Source: Bank of Italy.

Figure 8.3 Number of banks by province: variation 1992–2013

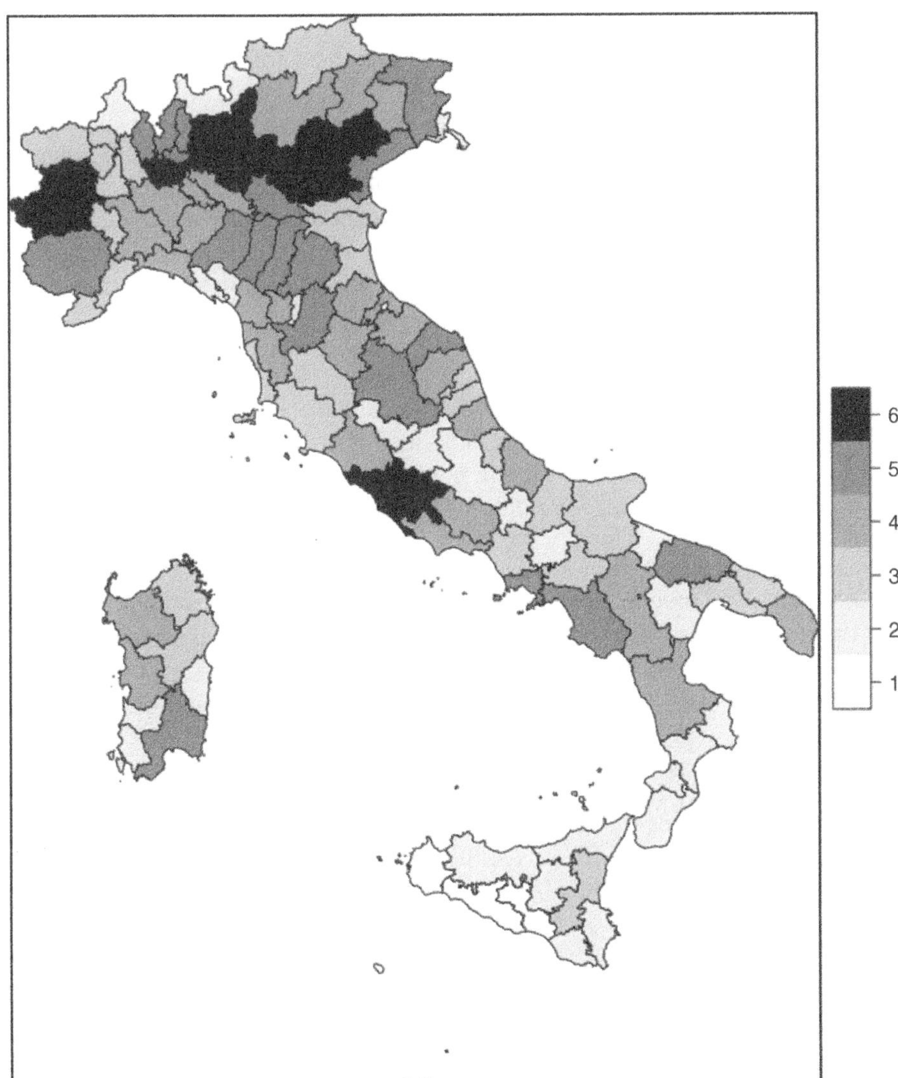

Notes: Category 1: provinces where the number of branches decreases, Δ Branches < 0. Category 2: provinces where the variation of the number of branches is below the first quartile (Q1) but not lower than zero, 0 ≤ Δ Branches ≤ Q1 = 24. Category 3: provinces where the variation of the number of branches is between the first quartile and the median (M), 24 < Δ Branches ≤ M = 42. Category 4: provinces where the variation of the number of branches is between the median and third quartile (Q3), 42 < Δ Branches ≤ Q3 = 83. Category 5: provinces where the variation of the number of branches is above the third quartile but not exceptionally large 83 < Δ Branches ≤ Q3 + 1.5*(Q3-Q1) = 171. Category 6: provinces where the number of banks increases exceptionally, Δ Branches > 171.

Source: Bank of Italy.

Figure 8.4 Number of branches by province: variation 1992–2013

the branch density significantly diverged between the North, where it is now more than six branches per 10,000 inhabitants, and the South, where there are fewer than four branches per 10,000 (Giannola et al., 2013).

Thus the process of financial consolidation in Italy has led to an increasingly passive financial integration in southern regions. This is clearly testified by the presence of out-of-region banks in the two areas. In the South, in 1986, the share of branches which had their headquarters in the rest of the country was about 16 percent. At the same time, banks from the South held a modest 1.7 percent of the active branches in the Center-North, evidencing the coexistence of two geographically segmented and functionally independent banking systems. This structure dissolved in the 1990s with the liquidation and acquisition of the Banco di Napoli, Banco di Sicilia and other major savings banks of the South by banks in the Center-North. In 2010, more than 42 percent of branches operating in the South were owned by banks headquartered outside the area and another 38 percent were attributable to banks which, whilst maintaining their headquarters in the South, were part of banking groups whose parent bank was in the Center-North. At the same time, the branches of southern banks in the Center-North shrank well below 1 percent (Giannola et al., 2013).

The recent crisis – which has hit the Italian economy more severely than most other European economies – has accelerated the bank consolidation process as a result of closures of distressed banks. As reported in Table 8.1, the number of banks decreased in Italy by 17 percent in the period 2008–13, more than in the rest of Euro area (−11 percent).[9] This decline in the number of banks also increased the concentration of the banking sector as measured by the share of the top five banks in total assets or by the Herfindahl index.

The number of bank branches, which increased steadily before the crisis (13 percent between 2003 and 2008), came to a halt with the inception of the crisis and then started to shrink markedly. In the last five years, the total number of branches has fallen by 7 percent, numbering 31,700 in 2013. This reduction was almost entirely due to the reorganization of the branch network of the top five largest banking groups that shed about 3500 branches. The overall effect has been a creeping decline in branch density with respect to the local population. At the same time, the introduction of new technologies has boosted the spatial presence of banks based on online distribution channels in favor of firms and households. In spite of the crisis, the diffusion of online banking services is on the rise everywhere, although Italy is still lagging behind other European countries in the use of Internet banking. Total users of home and corporate bank services had reached 33.9 million by the end of 2013, versus 24.9 million at the beginning of the crisis (2007) and only 1.3 million in 1997. Similar growing trends are also observable in the number of access points to the payment system (POS), or in the number of credit and debit cards.[10]

All in all, it would seem that due to the crisis, distance has recently become in some ways more relevant to bank-firm relationships, although more relevant does not translate into the same effects across different borrowers and types of services. In the next section, the information about the bank consolidation process and the decline in branch density in Italy will be combined with some measures of banking interconnectedness among Italian regions, applying the statistical tools of network analysis.

Table 8.1 *Banking sector structural and capacity indicators*

	Number of banks		Total assets to GDP (1)		Population per bank (2)		Population per local branch		Population per employee		Assets per employee (3)		Herfindahl index (4)		Five largest banks (5)	
	2008	2013	2008	2013	2008	2013	2008	2013	2008	2013	2008	2013	2008	2013	2008	2013
Italy	729	611	160	154	73	88	1751	1922	177	199	10.8	13.2	307	406	31	40
France	672	579	356	299	88	106	1625	1736	151	158	17.0	18.2	681	551	51	46
Germany	1882	1734	364	236	41	45	2077	2271	120	126	11.5	11.6	191	266	23	31
Spain	282	204	302	320	126	158	990	1362	165	213	12.2	14.6	497	757	42	56
Euro Area	5992	5248	305	241	53	57	1759	2039	146	162	13.5	14.3	686	693	44	47

Notes: (1) Total assets of domestic banks in relation to GDP (in percentage); (2) Thousands of people; (3) Thousands of euros; (4) Index ranging from 0 and 10,000; (5) Share of total assets of five largest banks.

Source: ECB.

Network Statistics

Network analysis provides tools for studying relationships (in network terminology, *links* or *edges* or *ties*) among a number of actors (*nodes* or *vertices*). It has been widely employed in economics both in theoretical and empirical research. Starting from Allen and Gale (2000), a growing number of studies have applied concepts and measures drawn from network analysis to investigate financial interconnectedness across countries and banking institutions and provide insights into the effects of financial globalization, resilience and vulnerability of banking systems to liquidity shocks and financial losses (Leitner, 2005; Nier et al., 2007, Battiston et al., 2012, Battiston and Caldarelli, 2013). As stated above, empirical research has been devoted to analyzing the network properties of international financial flows (Minoiu and Reyes, 2011; Sá, 2013) and bank exposures (Hattori and Suda, 2007), while, to our knowledge, the topological properties of domestic banking systems and the interconnectedness of local credit markets in terms of banking structures have been neglected.

The spatial organization of the banking industry, the financial interconnections among local credit markets and the geography of banking power (banking decisional centers) can be fruitfully analyzed by using networks metrics and graph techniques. In a network perspective, each geographical credit market is a *node* within a directed network (*digraph*), where *directed links* (*arcs*) model the relationships between the geographical market in which a bank has its headquarters and the markets in which it has its own branches (hereafter, the former geographical market is identified as *sender* – nodes for outgoing relationships – the latter are identified as *receivers* – nodes for incoming relationships).

Each network can be represented by a non-symmetric matrix with non-null diagonal elements, where rows correspond to senders' markets (that is, the geographical market where bank headquarters are located) and outgoing arcs, while columns correspond to receivers' markets (that is, the geographical markets where bank branches are located) and incoming arcs. In our networks, edges are weighted according to the number of branches held at the receivers' level and loops are taken into account as they refer to banks that have branches in the same province where they have their headquarters.

The metrics we use to analyze interconnectedness among geographical credit markets include measures of market centrality (*degree*, *strength* and *relative strength*) and network density (*connectivity* and *cliques*). Formally, let M_t be a matrix in which rows represent senders' vertices of outgoing arcs and columns represent receivers' vertices of incoming arcs. Each entry, $m_t = n_{ijt}$, is the total number of branches in market j owned by banks with their headquarters in market i at time t. These matrices can be transformed into their binary counterparts (adjacency matrix) A_t, where each cell a_{ijt} takes value 1 if there are banks with headquarters in i and branches in j at time t, and 0 otherwise, and all 0s on the diagonal. In detail, the descriptive statistics we use are the following.

Market centrality

Node degree and normalized node degree These indicators use information from the binary representation of a network through its adjacency matrix, and count the number of network nodes to which a node is connected by a link. In the case of directed networks, we have to distinguish incoming from outgoing arcs. Hence, we compute the *IN-Degree* (the number of incoming arcs) for each geographical market i as the number of markets $j \neq i$ from which it receives branches, and the *OUT-Degree* (the number of outgoing arcs) of a market i as the number of markets $j \neq i$ where senders' banks from i have their branches. In order to compare measures of market centrality for different geographical definitions of market (province and region), we normalize the *IN-Degree* and the *OUT-Degree* indicators by the maximum possible incoming and outgoing arcs $N-1$, where N is the total number of nodes. In formula, using the adjacency matrix A_t, the (normalized) *IN-Degree* and *OUT-Degree* of a node i at time t are, respectively:

$$IN\text{-}Degree_{i,t} = \sum_{j=1}^{N} a_{jit};\ N\text{-}IN\text{-}Degree_{i,t} = \frac{\sum_{j=1}^{N} a_{jit}}{N-1}$$

and

$$OUT\text{-}Degree_{i,t} = \sum_{j=1}^{N} a_{ijt};\ N\text{-}OUT\text{-}Degree_{i,t} = \frac{\sum_{j=1}^{N} a_{ijt}}{N-1}$$

Node strength This is the simplest weighted network indicator that captures the intensity of relationships among nodes. It is equal to the total number of connections originating or terminating in a given node, in terms of branches. More precisely, *IN-Strength* for market i is the total number of branches that i receives from other markets, whereas *OUT-Strength* for market i is the total number of branches of banks with their headquarters in that market that are located in other markets. Analytically, *OUT-Strength* and *IN-Strength* are computed by replacing the entries of matrix M_t in the above node degree formulas:

$$IN\text{-}Strength_{i,t} = \sum_{\substack{j=1 \\ j \neq i}}^{N} m_{ijt}$$

and

$$OUT\text{-}Strength_{i,t} = \sum_{\substack{j=1 \\ j \neq i}}^{N} m_{ijt}$$

Relative node strength This considers the relative importance of incoming relationships by normalizing the number of branches in market i from banks headquartered in market j by the total number of branches active in market i. Then we can compute the *Relative-IN-Strength* and the *Relative-OUT-Strength* of a market i as, respectively, the share of branches of banks external to the market i over the total branches in i and the sum of the branch shares in markets $j \neq i$ owned by banks headquartered in market i. To be precise:

$$Relative\text{-}IN\text{-}Strength_{i,t} = \sum_{j=1}^{N} \frac{m_{jit}}{\sum_{j=1}^{N} m_{jit}}$$

and

$$Relative\text{-}OUT\text{-}Strength_{i,t} = \sum_{j=1}^{N} \frac{m_{jit}}{\sum_{j=1}^{N} m_{jit}}$$

Although all these indicators are measures of market centrality, read together they also provide information about the degree of financial dependency and financial capacity of a region. In this perspective, high values of *OUT-Degree*, *OUT-Strength* and *Relative-OUT-Strength* associated to geographical area indicate the capacity of the area to produce financial services and export them to other regions. In contrast, high values of *IN-Degree*, *IN-Strength* and *Relative-IN-Strength* indicate a widespread use in that market of banking services from banks external to that area which, if accompanied by a low capacity to produce banking services, clearly suggests the financial dependency of the region.

Density of the credit market network

Network density This indicator evaluates the network connectivity globally by considering the number of links existing between geographical markets (that is, total node degree) expressed as a share of the total possible number of links (excluding loops). Let

$$L = \sum_i IN\text{-}Degree_{i,t} = \sum_i OUT\text{-}Degree_{i,t}$$

be the total number of arcs in the graph G. Then the network density is:

$$Density(G) = \frac{L}{N(N-1)}$$

Cliques A clique is a maximal complete subgraph of three or more nodes: that is, it is subgraph whose vertices are all connected with each other simultaneously. In directed graphs the reciprocity of dyadic ties is required. Hence, a digraph clique is a subgraph with three or more nodes all mutually connected to each another. In our context digraph cliques may be interpreted as geographical areas where incoming and outgoing banking power is balanced.

Network Analysis

In our analysis, we consider the 110 Italian provinces (NUTS III level) or, alternatively, the 20 Italian regions (NUTS II level) as the geographical credit markets. Therefore, provinces or regions are the nodes forming the directed network of the banking industry, which are connected with each other by the flow of branches from provinces or regions where banks are headquartered to provinces or regions where they are located. We compute the network statistics described above for all the Italian banks in 1992 (1,066 banks) and 2013 (654 banks) using information on the location of banks' headquarters and branches by provinces drawn from the Bank of Italy. In this way, we build up four different networks (and adjacent matrixes) to study how the spatial organization of the Italian banking industry has changed during the past two decades.

Credit market connectivity

The overall connectivity of geographical credit markets has significantly increased over time: the network density at the provincial level rose from 0.11 in 1992 to 0.14 in 2013 (+36 percent). Such an increase results partly from the thickening of the interregional links, but for the most part it comes from a more capillary dissemination of branches at the regional level (in particular in Veneto, Liguria, Emilia Romagna, Tuscany, Marche, Abruzzo, Puglia and Sardinia). This finds confirmation in the much higher degree of connectivity of geographical credit markets at the regional level, which has only slightly changed in the last two decades (+8.7 percent, from 0.484 in 1992 to 0.526 in 2003). In graphs reported in Figures 8.5 and 8.6, provinces and regions are ordered from the center to the periphery according to their gradually decreasing degrees. Not surprisingly, contiguous provinces are close in the graph as a consequence of stronger connections between geographically proximate markets. Southern and insular provinces confirm that they are more peripheral, with a further worsening in 2013 (Figure 8.5, panel b).

A further indication of the increasing geographical interconnectedness of the Italian banking industry comes from Figure 8.7 in which we report the nonparametric kernel density estimates of *IN-Degree* and *OUT-Degree* across provinces (panels 7a and 7b) and regions (panels 7c and 7d).

The distribution of *IN-Degree* changed significantly from 1992 to 2013: it shifts to the right, and reduces the frequency of the modal degree, especially at the provincial level (panel 7a). As a whole, these changes in the *IN-Degree* distribution suggest that in a greater number of provincial credit markets the competition from outside branches has increased during the last twenty years. In contrast, the shape of *OUT-Degree* remained more similar over time, with only the right tail slightly heavier (panel 7b) as a greater number of banks headquartered in center-northern provinces expanded their web of branches into neighboring provinces and throughout Italy.

Finally, the number of cliques, that is, the bunch of provinces that are senders and receivers to each other at the same time, greatly increased for any size from 1992 to 2013 (Table 8.2).

In addition, the size of the largest cliques increased: it was seven in 1992 for two cliques with five provinces in common ({Genoa, Rome, Milan, Turin, Vicenza, Naples, Novara} and {Genoa, Rome, Milan, Turin, Vicenza, Bergamo, Brescia}), to become ten in 2013 for two cliques sharing nine provinces ({Florence, Genoa, Rome, Milan, Padua, Turin, Venice, Verona, Vicenza, Brescia} and {Florence, Genoa, Rome, Milan, Padua, Turin, Venice, Verona, Vicenza, Bologna}). It is interesting to point out that the largest new cliques include the previous ones only partially, as some provinces like Bergamo, Novara and Naples were unable to expand their reciprocal links to other provinces. In addition, no southern province was present in the largest cliques in 2013.

Credit market centrality

Table 8.3 reports the summary statistics of our measures of credit market centrality for all the Italian provinces and regions and for the southern and center-northern areas, separately. On average, in 2013 each Italian province receives (or sends) 200 branches from banks headquartered in 15.6 different provinces, with a 110 percent increase with respect to 1992. The out-of-province branches cover 74.5 percent of the home credit market, 24

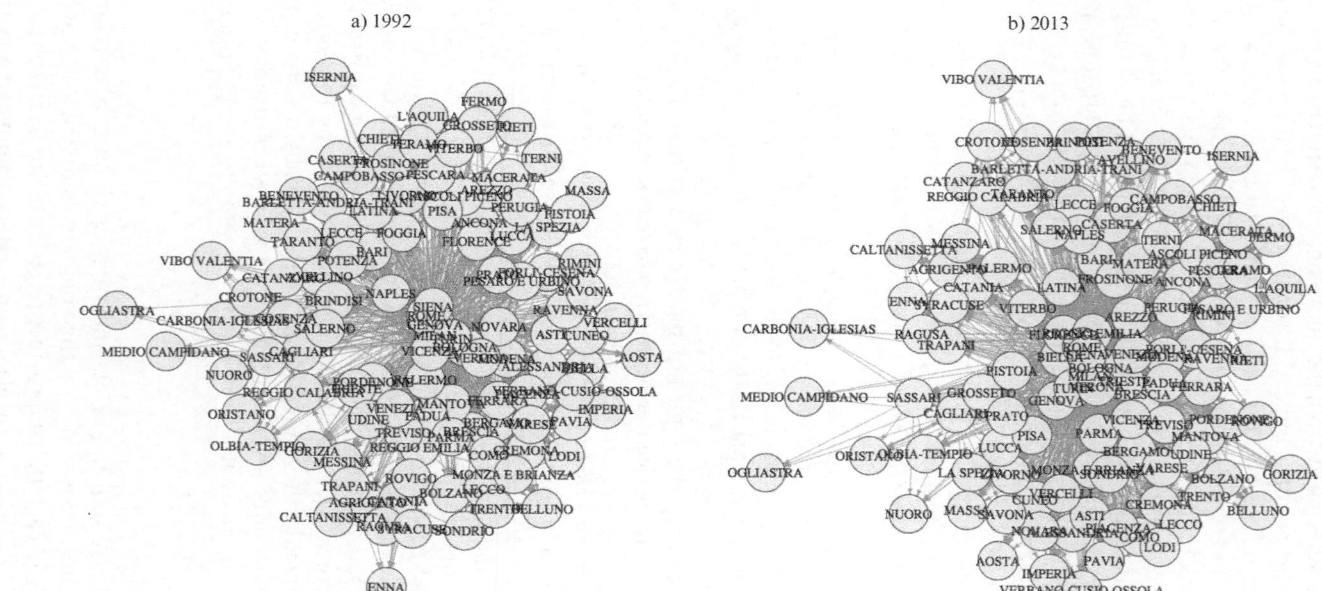

Notes: Nodes indicate provinces; directed link from a province *i* to a province *j* indicates that banks headquartered in province *i* have branches in province *j*.

Source: Bank of Italy.

Figure 8.5 Network of cross-province bank branching

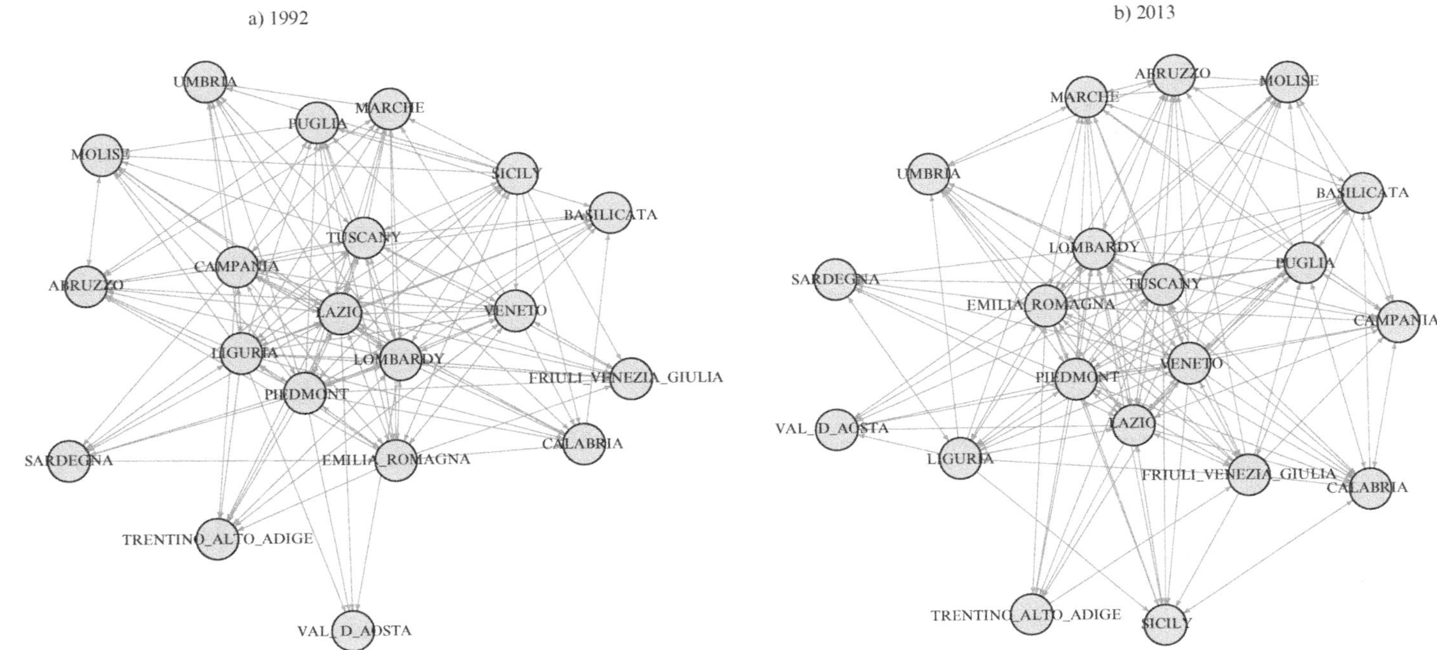

Notes: Nodes indicate regions; directed link from a region i to a region j indicates that banks headquartered in region i have branches in region j.

Source: Bank of Italy.

Figure 8.6 Network of cross-region bank branching

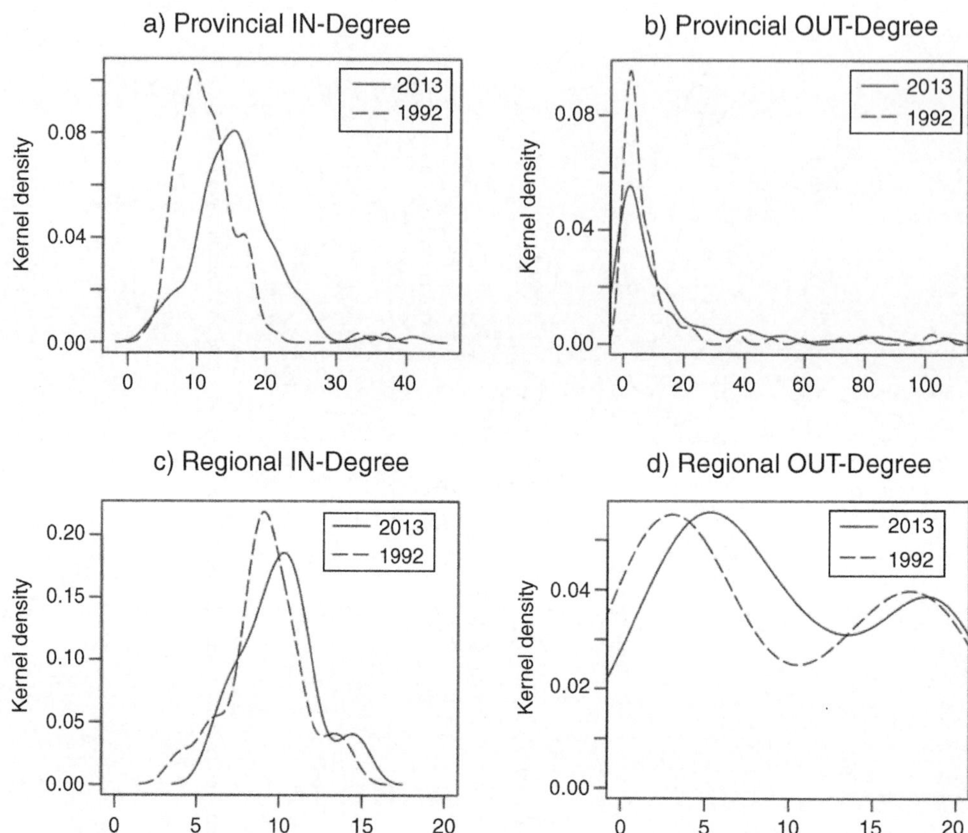

Note: The density estimates use Gaussian kernel density and bandwidth specified by Silverman's rule of thumb (Silverman, 1986).

Source: Bank of Italy.

Figure 8.7 Empirical distribution of IN-Degree and OUT-Degree indicators

Table 8.2 Number of cliques

	3 provinces	4 provinces	5 provinces	6 provinces	7 provinces	8 provinces	9 provinces	10 provinces
2013	573	805	821	589	288	95	20	2
1992	242	157	64	16	2			

Table 8.3 Network indicators: summary statistics

	Mean		Median		Min		Max		Standard Deviation	
	1992	2013	1992	2013	1992	2013	1992	2013	1992	2013
Provinces (110)										
IN-Degree	11.4	15.6	11	15	3	3	37	41	4.9	5.9
Centre-North	12.8	17.5	12	16	6	7	37	41	5.4	5.8
South	9.2	12.4	10	13	3	3	15	22	2.8	4.6
OUT-Degree	11.4	15.6	4	5.5	0	0	107	109	21.5	24.2
Centre-North	14.7	21.3	5	8	0	0	107	109	25	28.4
South	6	6	2	2	0	0	72	41	12.4	8.5
IN-Strength	94.3	199.2	73.5	140	6	16	607	1,237	86	187.3
Centre-North	107.3	240.1	84	175	20	25	607	1,237	95.2	213.9
South	72.6	130.2	53	108	6	16	314	480	62.8	99.9
OUT-Strength	94.3	199.2	14.5	24.5	0	0	1,479	4,767	232.3	559.9
Centre-North	124	286.2	19	62	0	0	1,479	4,767	276.1	688.9
South	44.5	52.6	5	4	0	0	566	570	115.6	111.2
Relative-IN-Strength	59.8	74.5	57.3	74.8	5.9	16.7	100	100	21.1	19
Centre-North	53.7	69.3	48.9	69.5	5.9	16.7	98.8	100	18.6	19.2
South	70.1	83.3	69.9	87.3	26.2	43.5	100	100	21.2	15.3
Relative-OUT-Strength	59.8	74.5	10.7	9.9	0	0	905.6	1,683.1	139.5	199.4
Centre-North	67.8	95.2	12.7	21.7	0	0	905.6	1,683.1	156.7	238.6
South	46.2	39.7	4	2.6	0	0	515.9	534.1	104.9	97.9
Regions (20)										
IN-Degree	9.2	10	9	10	4	6	14	15	2.31	2.3
Centre-North	9.6	10	9.5	10	4	6	14	15	2.6	2.7
South	8.6	10	9	10.5	6	7	11	12	1.8	1.6

Table 8.3 (continued)

	Mean		Median		Min		Max		Standard Deviation	
	1992	2013	1992	2013	1992	2013	1992	2013	1992	2013
Regions (20)										
OUT-Degree	9.2	10	5.5	8	0	0	19	19	7.35	6.74
Centre-North	11.2	12.8	13.5	15.5	0	0	19	19.0	7.9	7.1
South	6.3	5.8	4	5	1	1	17	11	5.6	3.2
IN-Strength	280.6	759.8	276	501	45	78	775	2,851	201	683
Centre-North	319.2	921.4	306	725.5	45	78	775	2,851	213.8	791.5
South	222.8	517.4	124	328.5	61	127	500	1,150	177.2	412.3
OUT-Strength	280.6	759.8	58	204	0	0	1,308	4,552	382.4	1,141.2
Centre-North	415	1186.7	368	900	0	0	1,308	4,552	437.7	1,320.6
South	79	119.5	28.5	91.5	1	1	401	329	135.6	116.2
Relative-IN-Strength	37	53.8	34.5	51.3	6.1	17.4	83.1	93	17.9	19.8
Centre-North	32.9	46.6	27.6	45.3	6.1	17.4	83.1	78.8	19.7	15.4
South	43.2	64.6	44.8	66	21.4	24	67.8	92.7	13.9	21.7
Relative-OUT-Strength	37	53.8	10.3	26.9	0	0	169.2	310.8	49.4	75
Centre-North	51	77.3	36.3	64	0	0	169.2	310.8	56.9	89.3
South	16	18.6	7.8	10.9	0.3	0.1	80	45.7	26.5	18.8

Source: Authors' calculation using Bank of Italy statistics.

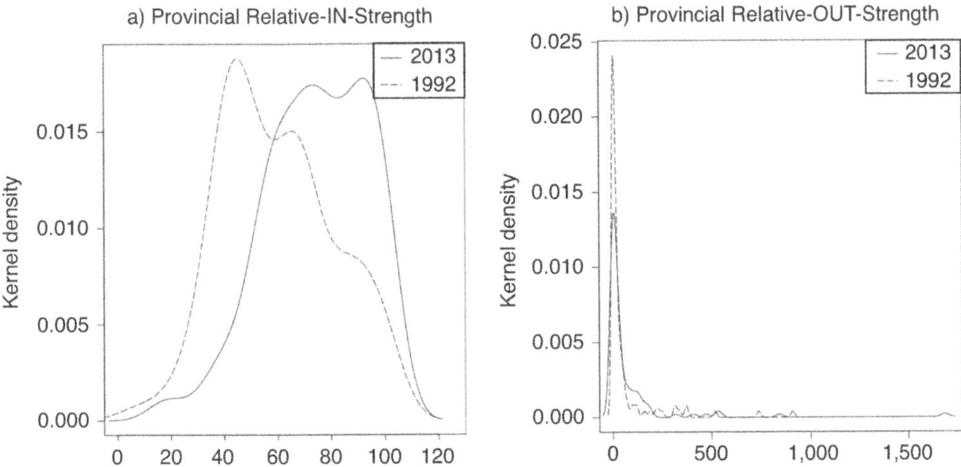

Note: The density estimates use Gaussian kernel density and bandwidth specified by Silverman's rule of thumb (Silverman, 1986).

Source: Bank of Italy.

Figure 8.8 Empirical distribution of Relative-IN-Degree and Relative-OUT-Degree indicators

percent more than in 1992. It is important to note that the range and standard deviation of *IN-Degree* are much lower than those of *OUT-Degree*, indicating that there are few provinces whose home banks export their branches all around Italy, while the import of financial services from other provinces is more uniformly distributed across nodes. The average degree of regions is much more stable over time, even if, as we expected, the normalized centrality (*N-IN-Degree* or *N-OUT-Degree*) is higher at the regional than at the provincial level.

The kernel density estimates of *Relative IN-Strength* and *Relative OUT-Strength* across provinces (Figure 8.8) indicate that the core–periphery structure of the Italian banking industry and the degree of financial dependency of many Italian provinces strongly increased from 1992 and 2013. The number of provinces whose local banking market is populated by more than 80 percent of out-of-province branches increased markedly (panel 8a), while the right tail of the *Relative-OUT-Strength* becomes much heavier, suggesting that large banks from a few provinces extended their presence throughout the country, increasing their market shares.

The centrality of southern provinces is significantly lower than that of other provinces, especially in terms of home bank branches outreaching. The two most central southern provinces (Matera and Naples) export branches in 41 and 20 provinces, respectively, and these branches belong to two main banks, Banca Popolare della Puglia e della Basilicata and Banco di Napoli, the latter being part of a banking group whose parent bank is headquartered in the North (Intesa-San Paolo in Turin). On average, in 2013 each southern province received 130 branches from outside banks, corresponding to 83.3 percent of total branches in these markets, 79 percent more than in 1992. By contrast, they sent only 52.6 branches to other provinces, with a modest 18 percent increase over 1992 which led to an extraordinary rise in net imports of branches from 28 in 1992 to 78 in 2013. In contrast, the most central provinces in the Center-North, Rome, has outgoing links with all the other 109 Italian provinces and the second, Milan, with 107 provinces. In center-northern regions the *IN-Strength* is 240 in 2013, 123 percent higher than two decades before, but the *OUT-Strength* increased from 107 to 240.

The core–periphery financial divide between the Center-North and South of Italy is even more evident if we consider the rankings of the most and the least central nodes in the provincial and regional networks (see Tables 8.4 and 8.5). In 2013, only one out of the 15 most financially connected provinces in Italy is in the South (namely, Matera) and the strength of its links is only moderate (142). As cities, Bari and Naples attract a large number of branches from other provinces and are able to export branches to other southern provinces. In fact, for only five southern provinces the number of outgoing branches is larger than the number of incoming branches while for all southern regions this difference is strongly negative.

The geographical core of the Italian banking industry is quite stable over time. It is formed by the four main provinces, namely Milan, Rome, Siena and Turin, with the largest and strongest number of outward connections in both 1992 and 2013, as well as Bologna, Genoa, Verona and Vicenza, which feature constantly among the 15 highest ranked provinces.

8.6 CONCLUSIONS

Except for a few critical voices, especially on the part of geographers, warning against the myth of stateless finance and global banking (Chick and Dow, 1988; Corbridge, 1988; Amin and Thrift, 1992; Thrift and Leyshon, 1992; Martin, 1994; Alessandrini and Zazzaro,1999), the common wisdom among scholars and practitioners in 1990s was that deregulation, advancements in ICT and the continuous development of new financial products would lead to the end of banking geography and the emergence of an internationally global banking industry. On the contrary, in the new millennium geographical and cultural distances among actors in credit markets and the spatial organization of banks are still crucial competitive strategic factors and major determinants of credit allocation. Moving from this premise, an ever growing number of studies in financial economics and geography has put the notion of distance at the center of the analysis of the evolution of the banking industry and its impact on the real economy.

In this chapter, first we reviewed the literature on the effects of geographical distances between borrowers and lenders, loan officers and bank managers, and between banks on lending relationships and interbank competition. We showed that whereas the quantity and quality of hard information depend mainly on external developments and less on spatial dimensions, soft information, being not easily codifiable and transferable, has instead a fundamentally spatial character. All this makes banks' geographical distribution and their spatial organization of paramount importance for credit access and conditions of a wide group of firms. In particular, while empirical results are mixed as far as operational distance is concerned, much clearer and more significant consequences seem to emerge from the findings involving functional distance issues, where the relevance of some

Table 8.4 *Network indicators: provincial rankings*

Highest ranked											
IN-Degree		*OUT-Degree*		*IN-Strength*		*OUT-Strength*		*Relative-IN-Strength*		*Relative-OUT-Strength*	
1992											
Rome	37	Rome	107	Milan	607	Rome	1,479	Nuoro	100	Rome	905.6
Milan	33	Milan	103	Rome	456	Milan	1,460	Olbia-Tempio	100	Milan	735.0
Bologna	21	Genoa	101	Naples	314	Genoa	653	Ogliastra	100	Naples	515.9
Treviso	19	Siena	82	Turin	311	Siena	605	Medio Camp.	100	Genoa	372.7
Turin	18	Turin	79	Varese	269	Naples	566	Carbonia-Iglesias	100	Siena	367.0
Varese	18	Naples	72	Monza	210	Palermo	501	Imperia	98.8	Cagliari	334.5
Brescia	18	Vicenza	59	Pavia	208	Turin	480	Pavia	98.1	Turin	315.4
Monza	17	Novara	49	Catania	201	Vicenza	452	Isernia	95.5	Palermo	309.7
Verona	17	Palermo	38	Florence	196	Novara	424	Oristano	95.2	Novara	247.5
Vicenza	17	Bologna	37	Bari	191	Bologna	367	Belluno	91.5	Florence	227.8
Venezia	17	Bergamo	24	Brescia	186	Bergamo	330	Brindisi	90.2	Vicenza	214.1
Padua	17	Florence	23	Bologna	180	Florence	287	Varese	89.7	Bologna	184
Udine	17	Brescia	21	Messina	179	Verona	223	Reggio Calabria	89	Cosenza	156.4
Parma	17	Verona	20	Venice	178	Padua	179	Barletta	88.2	Bergamo	119.2
Mantova	16	Mantova	17	Genoa	178	Modena	154	Vibo Valentia	88	Verona	117
2013											
Rome	41	Rome	109	Milan	1,237	Rome	4,767	Vercelli	100	Rome	1,683.1
Milan	35	Siena	107	Rome	1,092	Siena	2,311	Novara	100	Siena	838.8
Padua	27	Milan	92	Turin	794	Turin	1,658	Alessandria	100	Cagliari	534.1
Brescia	26	Reggio Emilia	87	Bologna	500	Verona	1,501	Verbano	100	Verona	532.8
Ancona	26	Bologna	83	Naples	480	Milan	1,474	Varese	100	Turin	471.1
Vicenza	25	Verona	81	Brescia	472	Sondrio	588	Imperia	100	Milan	407.2
Florence	25	Turin	74	Verona	468	Naples	570	Isernia	100	Naples	315.9
Bergamo	24	Genoa	66	Florence	450	Parma	516	Nuoro	100	Reggio Emilia	188.7
Verona	24	Biella	55	Varese	444	Vicenza	476	Olbia-Tempio	100	Ancona	181.4
Bologna	24	Vicenza	52	Treviso	404	Reggio Emilia	474	Ogliastra	100	Genoa	169.2
Turin	22	Florence	52	Monza	389	Ancona	444	Medio Camp.	100	Modena	162
Treviso	22	Parma	45	Padua	382	Modena	438	Carbonia-Igl.	100	Cosenza	154.8
Parma	22	Modena	43	Vicenza	380	Genoa	432	Pavia	99.7	Vicenza	138.4
Bari	22	Matera	41	Bari	380	Bergamo	388	L'Aquila	97.2	Parma	135.5
Varese	21	Sondrio	39	Bergamo	370	Bologna	363	Catania	95.9	Biella	125.7

Table 8.4 (continued)

Lowest ranked											
IN-Degree		*OUT-Degree*		*IN-Strength*		*OUT-Strength*		*Relative-IN-Strength*		*Relative-OUT-Strength*	
2013											
Enna	7	Enna	1	Terni	31	Enna	1	Viterbo	38.6	Barletta	0.33
Sassari	7	Aosta	0	Teramo	28	Aosta	0	Palermo	37.9	Aosta	0
Cagliari	7	Pavia	0	Gorizia	27	Pavia	0	Chieti	37.9	Pavia	0
Aosta	6	Belluno	0	Rieti	26	Belluno	0	Bologna	37.7	Belluno	0
Sondrio	6	Imperia	0	Nuoro	26	Imperia	0	Lecce	37.4	Imperia	0
Siena	6	Isernia	0	Olbia-Tempio	26	Isernia	0	Siena	37.2	Isernia	0
Benevento	6	Caserta	0	Trento	24	Caserta	0	Verona	34.8	Caserta	0
Crotone	6	Brindisi	0	Vibo Valentia	22	Brindisi	0	Padua	32.7	Brindisi	0
Nuoro	6	Vibo Valentia	0	Isernia	21	Vibo Valentia	0	Bergamo	32.4	Vibo Valentia	0
Oristano	6	Nuoro	0	Sondrio	20	Nuoro	0	Pesaro-Urbino	29.3	Nuoro	0
Olbia-Tempio	6	Oristano	0	Oristano	20	Oristano	0	Teramo	28.3	Oristano	0
Carbonia	6	Olbia-Tempio	0	Medio Camp.	15	Olbia-Tempio	0	Cosenza	26.2	Olbia-Tempio	0
Isernia	5	Ogliastra	0	Carbonia-Igl.	13	Ogliastra	0	Sondrio	23	Ogliastra	0
Medio Camp.	4	Medio Camp.	0	Crotone	12	Medio Camp.	0	Bolzano	15.7	Medio Camp.	0
Ogliastra	3	Carbonia-Igl.	0	Ogliastra	6	Carbonia-Igl.	0	Trento	5.9	Carbonia-Igl.	0
2013											
Matera	10	Aosta	0	Bolzano	68	Aosta	0	Ancona	53.7	Aosta	0
Enna	10	Varese	0	Nuoro	68	Varese	0	Teramo	53.2	Varese	0
Sassari	10	Pavia	0	Oristano	67	Pavia	0	Gorizia	53.1	Pavia	0
Olbia-Tempio	10	Belluno	0	Caltanissetta	65	Belluno	0	Brescia	51.3	Belluno	0
Bolzano	8	Imperia	0	Enna	53	Imperia	0	Pistoia	50.8	Imperia	0
Sondrio	7	Isernia	0	Biella	52	Isernia	0	Bergamo	50.1	Isernia	0
Gorizia	7	Avellino	0	Gorizia	51	Avellino	0	Crotone	47.1	Avellino	0
Vibo Valentia	7	Brindisi	0	Rieti	49	Brindisi	0	Forlì	44.7	Brindisi	0
Caltenisetta	7	Vibo Valentia	0	Medio Camp.	38	Vibo Valentia	0	Cagliari	43.5	Vibo Valentia	0
Nuoro	7	Messina	0	Carbomia-Iglesias	34	Messina	0	Biella	38.8	Messina	0
Oristano	6	Nuoro	0	Isernia	31	Nuoro	0	Siena	37.3	Nuoro	0
Crotone	5	Olbia-Tempio	0	Vibo Valentia	28	Olbia-Tempio	0	Cuneo	37.1	Olbia-Tempio	0
Medio Camp.	4	Ogliastra	0	Ogliastra	26	Ogliastra	0	Trento	32.9	Ogliastra	0
Carbonia-Igl.	4	Medio Camp.	0	Sondrio	25	Medio Camp.	0	Sondrio	20.3	Medio Camp.	0
Ogliastra	3	Carbonia-Igl.	0	Crotone	16	Carbonia-Igl.	0	Bolzano	16.7	Carbonia-Igl.	0

Source: Authors' elaboration using Bank of Italy statistics.

Table 8.5 Network indicators: regional rankings

Highest ranked											
IN-Degree		*OUT-Degree*		*IN-Strength*		*OUT-Strength*		*Relative-IN-Strength*		*Relative-OUT-Strength*	
1992											
Lazio	15	Lombardy	19	Lombardy	775	Lazio	1,308	Molise	92.7	Lazio	310.8
Lombardy	14	Veneto	19	Lazio	510	Lombardy	1,109	Basilicata	87.3	Tuscany	148
Emilia Romagna	12	Emilia Romagna	19	Campania	500	Piedmont	599	Aosta Valley	78.8	Piedmont	107.2
Campania	12	Tuscany	19	Puglia	462	Liguria	589	Puglia	72.8	Veneto	104.7
Marche	11	Lazio	19	Veneto	458	Tuscany	486	Sicily	69.1	Emilia Romagna	97.5
2013											
Lazio	14	Piedmont	19	Lombardy	2,851	Lazio	4,552	Aosta Valley	83.1	Lazio	169.2
Lombardy	13	Lombardy	19	Veneto	1,519	Tuscany	2,058	Molise	67.8	Piedmont	120.5
Tuscany	11	Liguria	19	Lazio	1,328	Veneto	1,914	Puglia	51.7	Lombardy	114.6
Marche	11	Lazio	19	Emilia Romagna	1,326	Piedmont	1,741	Liguria	47.8	Campania	80.0
Abruzzo	11	Tuscany	18	Piedmont	1,270	Lombardy	1,448	Basilicata	47.2	Tuscany	66.9

Lowest ranked											
IN-Degree		*OUT-Degree*		*IN-Strength*		*OUT-Strength*		*Relative-IN-Strength*		*Relative-OUT-Strength*	
1992											
Friuli Venezia Giulia	8	Trentino Alto Adige	4	Umbria	107	Umbria	11	Emilia Romagna	40.1	Sicily	3.3
Liguria	8	Calabria	4	Basilicata	84	Puglia	9	Tuscany	36.1	Umbria	3.0

Table 8.5 (continued)

Lowest ranked											
IN-Degree		*OUT-Degree*		*IN-Strength*		*OUT-Strength*		*Relative-IN-Strength*		*Relative-OUT-Strength*	
1992											
Aosta Valley	7	Sicily	4	Molise	61	Sardinia	7	Marche	35.7	Sardinia	1.6
Sardinia	7	Molise	1	Aosta Valley	49	Molise	1	Sardinia	24.0	Molise	0.1
Trentino Alto Adige	6	Aosta Valley	0	Trentino Alto Adige	45	Aosta Valley	0	Trentino Alto Adige	17.4	Aosta Valley	0
2013											
Trentino Alto Adige	8	Calabria	3	Basilicata	206	Abruzzo	47	Sicily	21.4	Trentino Alto Adige	1.5
Umbria	8	Trentino Alto Adige	2	Trentino Alto Adige	163	Sardinia	35	Emilia Romagna	21.0	Umbria	1.2
Sicily	6	Friuli Venezia Giulia	2	Sardinia	160	Sicily	20	Lombardy	20.7	Sardinia	0.5
Sardinia	6	Molise	1	Molise	127	Molise	1	Tuscany	19.5	Molise	0.3
Aosta Valley	4	Aosta Valley	0	Aosta Valley	78	Aosta Valley	0	Trentino Alto Adige	6.1	Aosta Valley	0

Source: Authors' calculation using Bank of Italy statistics.

kind of home bias over credit allocation is strongly corroborated by the literature. This becomes even more worrying for regional development especially in times of crisis when a "flight to home" effect might exacerbate the reduction of the banks' lending exposure to peripheral regions by functionally distant banks.

Second, we presented the much less developed literature on the determinants of the different distances in the banking industry and the formation of banking centers. A first result emerging from this literature is that functional distance has a strong influence on the spatial expansion strategy of banks in terms of both mergers and acquisitions and branch openings. In particular, interconnectedness has been mainly studied at international level explaining the dynamics of international financial centers also using the recent approach of network analysis. Much less attention has instead been paid to the evolution of the geography of bank power and interconnectedness among banks at the single country level.

Consequently, applying the metrics and graph techniques of network analysis we provided some original and new evidence concerning the evolving geographical network of bank organizations within Italy. Our analysis showed that the overall interconnectedness of geographical credit markets has significantly increased over time, whether measured at the provincial or regional level. On the one hand, this dynamic appears to have positively affected the degree of competition, yet on the other, it has contributed to make the largest cliques even bigger, bringing about a higher level of bank service concentration. Within this process, there emerges a growing and marked centrality of a few northern Italian banking centers to the detriment of the southern credit markets and regions. In other words, our analysis shows that the core–periphery financial and banking divide has even become more striking and significant over recent years. Such changes in Italian banking geography highlight the importance of the concept of distance, especially that of functional distance, in shaping the relationships between banks and local borrowers. Consequently, a sort of additional comparative advantage in favor of big enterprises over SMEs and start-ups might emerge embedded in a new type of financial constraint for local borrowers grounded on geographical issues. These spatial developments, together with the fact that young rather than small firms seem to be the main contributors to employment growth,[11] should support and suggest some policy initiatives with a view to easing financial constraints to local borrowers, especially to start-ups and young enterprises to boost economic growth. Economic policies should therefore facilitate credit access for start-ups and SMEs through various measures which are more likely to help these groups of firms, such as policy initiatives aiming to improve the collection and dissemination of firms' credit histories and economic data, or the establishment of mini-finance (like mini-bonds) markets for new companies and SMEs. These policy prescriptions should be supported by further research which might combine improvements in the collection of firm-level survey data with new statistical information on the different concepts of distance discussed above, in order to gain insights into the relationships among distance, financing conditions for firms, and economic growth.

NOTES

1. We are grateful to Jane Pollard and Ron Martin for their helpful comments and suggestions on a preliminary version of this chapter.
2. The actual impact of higher capital requirements on the real economy is a highly debated issue (Berrospide and Edge, 2010; Angelini et al., 2011; Noss and Toffano, 2014). Banks can comply with higher regulatory capital ratios by either raising additional capital or shrinking assets, by reducing credit to the economy and selling off parts of their securities portfolio. In times of crisis, banks are more likely to choose the deleveraging option instead of raising more equity capital, with costly consequences for the real economy through credit crunch and fire sales effects.
3. Consistently, empirical evidence indicates that in countries where banks can rely on well-established credit bureaus and information sharing practices bank lending amount tends to be larger and default rates lower, especially for informationally opaque firms (Jappelli and Pagano, 2002; Brown et al., 2009).
4. However, a recent study conducted on a US credit union by Campbell and Loumioti (2014) has questioned the limited portability of soft information, documenting an enduring effect of the stock of soft information accumulated over time in the bank's monitoring system by different loan officers in different branches on access to credit for borrowers, loan prices and repayment performance.
5. Petersen and Rajan (2002) do not examine the real distance between the lending office and the firm, but consider the ability to borrow at a distance as a measure of firms' information transparency. This is given by the predicted value of a regression of observed geographical distance from lenders on variables capturing public information about borrowers.
6. The expression "functional distance" was first used in the banking literature by Alessandrini et al. (2005). The same notion of distance has also been equivalently labeled in other studies as organizational, branch-to-headquarter or hierarchical distance (DeYoung et al., 2004; Jimenez et al., 2009).
7. See ECB (2014).
8. We follow the Italian Antitrust authority in identifying the NUTS III province as the main local market in banking. Until 1990, the same criterion was used by the Bank of Italy to authorize the opening of a new branch.
9. In the same period, the number of bank employees declined by 9.6%. The change in total staff differed according to banking category, with the greatest reduction among banks that downsized their branch networks (Bank of Italy, 2014).
10. The number of POS was 0.06 million in 1992, 1.18 million in 2007 and 1.53 million at the end of 2013.
11. Recent applied research has identified that young rather than small enterprises are the main contributors to employment growth (see, among others, Lawless, 2013; Criscuolo et al., 2014; Banerjee, 2014).

REFERENCES

Agarwal, S. and R. Hauswald (2010), 'Distance and private information in lending', *Review of Financial Studies*, **23** (7), 2757–2788.

Alama, L. and E. Tortosa (2011), 'Bank branch geographic location patterns in Spain: some implications for financial exclusion', Working Papers, Instituto Valenciano de Investigaciones Económicas, No. 01/2011.

Alessandrini, P. and A. Zazzaro (1999), 'A "possibilist" approach to local financial systems and regional development: the Italian experience', in R. Martin (ed.), *Money and the Space Economy*, New York, USA: Wiley and Sons, pp. 71–92.

Alessandrini, P., G. Calcagnini and A. Zazzaro (2008), 'Asset restructuring strategies in bank acquisitions: does distance between dealing partners matter?', *Journal of Banking and Finance*, **32** (5), 699–713.

Alessandrini, P., M. Croci and A. Zazzaro (2005), 'The geography of banking power: the role of functional distance', *BNL Quarterly Review*, **58** (235), 129–167.

Alessandrini, P., M. Fratianni and A. Zazzaro (eds) (2009a), *The Changing Geography of Banking and Finance*, New York, USA: Springer.

Alessandrini, P., A.F. Presbitero and A. Zazzaro (2009b), 'Global banking and local markets: a national perspective', *Cambridge Journal of Regions, Economy and Society*, **2** (2), 173–192.

Alessandrini, P., A.F. Presbitero and A. Zazzaro (2009c), 'Banks, distances and firms' financing constraints', *Review of Finance*, **13** (2), 261–307.

Alessandrini, P., A.F. Presbitero and A. Zazzaro (2009d), 'Geographical organization of banking system and innovation diffusion', in P. Alessandrini, M. Fratianni and A. Zazzaro (eds), *The Changing Geography of Banking and Finance*, New York, USA: Springer, pp. 75–108.

Alessandrini, P., A.F. Presbitero and A. Zazzaro (2010), 'Bank size or distance: what hampers innovation adoption by SMEs', *Journal of Economic Geography*, **10** (6), 845–881.
Allen F. and D. Gale (2000), 'Financial contagion', *Journal of Political Economy*, **108** (1), 1–33.
Amin, A. and N. Thrift (1992), 'Neo-Marshallian nodes in global networks', *International Journal of Urban and Regional Research*, **16** (4), 571–587.
Anand, B.N. and A. Galetovic (2006), 'Relationships, competition and the structure of investment banking markets', *Journal of Industrial Economics*, **54** (2), 151–199.
Angelini, P., L. Clerc, V. Cúrdia, L. Gambacorta, A. Gerali, A. Locarno, R. Motto, W. Roeger, S. Van den Heuvel and J. Jan Vlcek (2011), 'Basel III: long-term impact on economic performance and fluctuations', Bank of Italy, Occasional Paper, No. 87.
Avery, R.B. and K. Samolyk (2004), 'Bank consolidation and the provision of banking services: small commercial loans', *Journal of Financial Services Research*, **25** (2–3), 291–325.
Banerjee, R. (2014), 'SMEs, financial constraints and growth', BIS Working Papers, No. 475.
Bank of Italy (2014), 'Financial Stability Report', n1/2014, Rome, Bank of Italy.
Barone, G., R. Felici and M. Pagnini (2011), 'Switching costs in local credit markets', *International Journal of Industrial Organization*, **29** (6), 694–704.
Barros, P. (1995), 'Post-entry expansion in banking: the case of Portugal', *International Journal of Industrial Organization*, **13** (4), 593–611.
Battiston, S. and G. Caldarelli (2013), 'Systemic risk in financial networks', *Journal of Financial Management, Markets and Institutions*, **1** (2), 129–154.
Battiston, S., D. Delli Gatti, M. Gallegati, B.C.N. Greenwald and J.E. Stiglitz (2012), 'Liaisons dangereuses: increasing connectivity, risk sharing, and systemic risk', *Journal of Economic Dynamics and Control Services Research*, **36** (8), 1121–1141.
Bel, G. and X. Fageda (2008), 'Getting there fast: globalization, intercontinental flights and location of headquarters', *Journal of Economic Geography*, **8** (4), 471–495.
Bellucci, A., A. Borisov and A. Zazzaro (2010), 'Does gender matter in bank-firm relationships? Evidence from small business lending', *Journal of Banking and Finance*, **34** (12), 2968–2984.
Bellucci, A., A. Borisov and A. Zazzaro (2013), 'Do banks price discriminate spatially? Evidence from small business lending in local credit markets', *Journal of Banking and Finance*, **37** (11), 4183–4197.
Bellucci, A., A. Borisov, G. Giombini and A. Zazzaro (2014), 'Does collateral walk through the road? Testing the lender-based theory of collateral', Università Politecnica delle Marche, mimeo.
Benfratello, L., F. Schiantarelli and A. Sembenelli (2008), 'Banks and innovation: microeconometric evidence on Italian firms', *Journal of Financial Economics*, **90** (2), 197–217.
Berger, A.N. and R. DeYoung (2001), 'The effects of geographic expansion on bank efficiency', *Journal of Financial Services Research*, **19** (2), 163–184.
Berger, A.N. and G.F. Udell (2002), 'Small business credit availability and relationship lending: the importance of bank organisational structure', *The Economic Journal*, **112** (477), 32–53.
Berger, A.N., L.F. Klapper and G.F. Udell (2001), 'The ability of banks to lend to informationally opaque small businesses', *Journal of Banking and Finance*, **25** (12), 2127–2167.
Berger, A.N., A. Saunders, J.M. Scalise and G.F. Udell (1998), 'The effects of bank mergers and acquisitions on small business lending', *Journal of Financial Economics*, **50** (2), 187–229.
Berger, A., N. Miller, M. Petersen, R. Rajan and J. Stein (2005), 'Does function follow organizational form? Evidence from the lending practices of large and small banks', *Journal of Financial Economics*, **76** (2), 237–269.
Bernheim, D. and M. Whinston (1990), 'Multimarket contact and collusive behavior', *RAND Journal of Economics*, **21** (1), 1–26.
Berrospide, J. and R. Edge (2010), 'The effects of bank capital on lending: what do we know, and what does it mean?', Finance and Economics Discussion Series, Divisions of Research and Statistics and Monetary Affairs Federal Reserve Board, Washington, DC, June.
Berrospide, J., L. Black and W. Keeton (2013), 'The cross-market spillover of economic shocks through multi-market banks', Finance and Economics Discussion Series, Divisions of Research and Statistics and Monetary Affairs, Federal Reserve Board, Washington, DC, April, No. 2013-52.
Bonaccorsi di Patti, E. and G. Gobbi (2001), 'The changing structure of local credit markets: are small business special?', *Journal of Banking and Finance*, **25** (12), 2209–2237.
Boot, A. and A. Thakor (2000), 'Can relationship banking survive competition?', *Journal of Finance*, **55** (2), 679–713.
Brevoort, K.B. and T.H. Hannan (2006), 'Commercial lending and distance: evidence from Community Reinvestment Act data', *Journal of Money, Credit and Banking*, **38** (8), 1991–2012.
Brevoort, K.P. and J.D. Wolken (2009), 'Does distance matter in banking?', in P. Alessandrini, M. Fratianni and A. Zazzaro (eds), *The Changing Geography of Banking and Finance*, New York, USA: Springer, pp. 27–56.

Broecker, T. (1990), 'Credit-worthiness tests and interbank competition', *Econometrica*, **58** (2), 429–452.

Brown, M., T. Jappelli and M. Pagano (2009), 'Information sharing and credit: firm-level evidence from transition countries', *Journal of Financial Intermediation*, **13** (4), 787–804.

Buch, C.M. and G. DeLong (2004), 'Cross-border bank mergers: what lures the rare animals?', *Journal of Banking and Finance*, **28** (9), 2077–2102.

Calcagnini, G., R. de Bonis and D.D. Hester (2001), 'Perché le banche aprono sportelli? Un'analisi del caso italiano', in P. Alessandrini (ed.), *Il sistema finanziario italiano tra globalizzazione e localismo*, Bologna: Il Mulino, pp. 191–221.

Campbell, D. and M. Loumioti (2014), 'Monitoring and the portability of soft information', Harvard Business School Accounting and Management Unit Working Paper No. 13-077.

Campello, M. (2002), 'Internal capital markets in financial conglomerates: evidence from small bank responses to monetary policy', *Journal of Finance*, **57** (6), 2773–2805.

Cao, M. and S. Shi (2000), 'Screening, bidding, and the loan market tightness', Wharton School Center for Financial Institutions, University of Pennsylvania, No. 00-09.

Carbó, S., J. Fernandez de Guevara, D. Humphrey and J. Maudos (2009), 'Estimating the intensity of price and non-price competition in banking', MPRA Paper No. 17612.

Carling, K. and S. Lundberg (2005), 'Asymmetric information and distance: an empirical assessment of geographical credit rationing', *Journal of Economics and Business*, **57** (1), 39–59.

Carlin, W., A. Charlton and C. Mayer (2006), 'Capital markets, ownership and distance', CEPR Discussion Papers No. 5764.

Cerasi, V., B. Chizzolini and M. Ivaldi (2000), 'Branching and competitiveness across regions in the Italian banking industry', in M. Polo (ed.), *Industria Bancaria e Concorrenza*, Bologna: Il Mulino, pp. 499–522.

Cerqueiro, G., H. Degryse and S. Ongena (2009), in P. Alessandrini, M. Fratianni and A. Zazzaro (eds), *The Changing Geography of Banking and Finance*, New York, USA: Springer, pp. 57–74.

Cetorelli, N. and L.S. Goldberg (2011), 'Global banks and international shock transmission: evidence from the crisis', *IMF Economic Review*, **59** (1), 41–76.

Chang, A., S. Chaudhuri and J. Jayaratne (1997), 'Rational herding and the spatial clustering of bank branches: an empirical analysis', Federal Reserve Bank of New York Discussion Paper Series No. 9697-24.

Chick, V. and S.C. Dow (1988), 'A post-Keynesian perspective on the relation between banking and regional development', in P. Arestis (ed.), *Post-Keynesian Monetary Economics – New Approaches to Financial Modelling*, Cheltenham, UK and Northampton, MA, USA: Edward Elgar Publishing, pp. 219–250.

Chick, V., S.C. Dow and C.J. Rodriguez-Fuentes (2013), 'Good banks and bad banks, centralized banks and local banks and economic growth', **84** (3), 110–127.

Choi, S.-R., D. Park and A.E. Tschoegl (1996), 'Banks and the world's major banking centers, 1990', *Weltwirtschaftliches Archiv*, **132** (4), 774–793.

Choi, S.-R., Park, D. and Tschoegl, A.E. (2003), 'Banks and the world's major banking centers, 2000', *Review of World Economics* (*Weltwirtschaftliches Archiv*), **139** (3), 550–568.

Choi, S.-R., A.E. Tschoegl and C.-M. Yu (1986), 'Banks and the world's major financial centers, 1970–1980', *Weltwirtschaftliches Archiv*, **122** (1), 48–64.

Claessens, S. and N. van Horen (2009), 'Being a foreigner among domestic banks: asset or liability', MPRA Paper No. 13467.

Cole, R.A., L.G. Golberg and L. J. White (2004), 'Cookie-cutter versus character: the micro structure of small business lending by large and small banks', *Journal of Financial and Quantitative Analysis*, **39** (2), 227–252.

Corbridge, S. (1988), 'The asymmetry of interdependence: the United States and the geopolitics of international finance relations', *Studies in Comparative International Development*, **23** (1), 3–29.

Cremers, K.J.M., R. Huang. and Z. Sautner (2010), 'Internal capital markets and corporate politics in a banking group', *Review of Financial Studies*, **24** (2), 358–401.

Criscuolo, C., P. Gal and C. Menon (2014), 'The dynamics of employment growth: new evidence from 18 countries', OECD Technology and Industry Policy Papers No. 14.

Crocco, M., F.F. Silva, L.P. Rezende and C.J.R. Fuentes (2014), 'Banks and regional developments: an empirical analysis of the determinants of credit availability in Brazilian regions', *Regional Studies*, **48** (5), 883–895.

de Bonis, R. and A. Ferrando (2000), 'The Italian banking structure in the 1990s: testing the multimarket contact hypothesis', *Economic Notes*, **29** (2), 215–241.

Degryse, H. and S. Ongena (2005), 'Distance, lending relationships and competition', *Journal of Finance*, **6** (1), 231–266.

Degryse, H. and S. Ongena (2007), 'The impact of competition on bank orientation, *Journal of Financial Intermediation*, **16** (3), 399–424.

Degryse, H., L. Laeven and S. Ongena (2009a), 'The impact of organizational structure and lending technology on banking competition', *Review of Finance*, **13** (2), 225–259.

Degryse, H., S. Ongena and G. Tümer-Alkan (2009b), 'Lending technology, bank organization and competition', *Journal of Financial Transformation*, **26**, 24–30.

de Haas, R. and N. van Horen (2013), 'Running for the exit: international banks and crisis transmission', *Review of Financial Studies*, **26** (1), 244–285.
de Juan, R. (2003), 'The independent submarkets model: an application to the Spanish retail banking market', *International Journal of Industrial Organization*, **21** (10), 1461–1487.
Dell'Ariccia, G. and R. Marquez (2004), 'Information and bank credit allocation', *Journal of Financial Economics*, **72** (1), 185–214.
Dell'Ariccia, G., E. Friedman and R. Marquez (1999), 'Adverse selection as a barrier to entry in the banking industry', *RAND Journal of Economics*, **30** (3), 515–534.
Detragiache, E., T. Tressel and P. Gupta (2008), 'Foreign banks in poor countries: theory and evidence', *Journal of Finance*, **63** (5), 2123–2160.
Dewatripont, M. and J. Tirole (1999), 'Advocates', *Journal of Political Economy*, **107** (1), 1–39.
DeYoung, R., D. Glennon and P. Nigro (2008), 'Borrower–lender distance, credit scoring, and loan performance: evidence from informational-opaque small business borrowers', *Journal of Financial Intermediation*, **17** (1), 113–143.
DeYoung, R., W.C. Hunter and G.F. Udell (2004), 'The past, present, and probable future for community banks', *Journal of Financial Services Research*, **25** (2–3), 85–133.
Dow, S.C. (1999), 'The stages of banking development and the spatial evolution of financial systems', in R. Martin (ed.), *Money and the Space Economy*, New York, USA: Wiley and Sons, pp. 31–48.
Drexler, A. and A. Schoar (2014), 'Do relationships matter? Evidence from loan officer turnover', *Management Science*, **60** (11), 2722–2736.
ECB (2014), *Banking Structures Report*, ECB, October.
Edwards, C.D. (1955), 'Conglomerate bigness as a source of power', in G. Stigler (ed.), *Business Concentration and Price*, Princeton, NJ: Princeton University Press, pp. 331–359.
Evanoff, D.D. (1988), 'Branch banking and service accessibility', *Journal of Money, Credit, and Banking*, **20** (2), 191–202.
Felici, R. and M. Pagnini (2008), 'Distance, bank heterogeneity and entry in local banking markets', Temi di discussione (Economic working papers), No. 557, Bank of Italy.
Focarelli, D. and A. Pozzolo (2005), 'Where do banks expand abroad? An empirical analysis', *The Journal of Business*, **78** (6), 2435–2464.
Fratianni, M.(2008), 'Financial crises, safety nets and regulation', *Rivista italiana degli economisti*, **2**, 169–208.
Fuentelsaz, L. and J. Gómez (2006), 'Multipoint competition, strategic similarity and entry into geographic markets', *Strategic Management Journal*, **27** (5), 477–499.
Gehrig, T. (2000), 'Cities and the geography of financial centers', in J.J. Thisse and J.M. Huriot (eds), *The Economics of Cities*, Cambridge, UK: Cambridge University Press, pp. 415–445.
Giannetti, M. and L. Laeven (2011), 'The right home effect: evidence from the syndicated loan market during financial crises', *Journal of Financial Economics*, **104** (1), 23–43.
Giannetti, M. and Y. Yafeh (2012), 'Do cultural differences between contracting parties matter? Evidence from syndicated bank loans', *Management Science*, **58** (2), 365–383.
Giannola, A., A. Lopes and A. Zazzaro (2013), 'La convergenza dello sviluppo finanziario tra le regioni italiane dal 1890 a oggi', *Rivista di Politica Economica*, **103** (1), 145–197.
Gormley, T.A. (2010), 'The impact of foreign bank entry in emerging markets: evidence from India', *Journal of Financial Intermediation*, **19** (1), 26–51.
Grote, M.H. (2009), 'Financial centers between centralization and virtualization', in P. Alessandrini, M. Fratianni and A. Zazzaro (eds), *The Changing Geography of Banking and Finance*, New York, USA: Springer, pp. 277–294.
Hattori, M. and Y. Suda (2007), 'Developments in a cross-border bank exposure "network"', Bank of Japan Working Paper Series, No. 07-E-21.
Hauswald, R. and R. Marquez (2006), 'Competition and strategic information acquisition in credit markets', *Review of Financial Studies*, **19** (3), 967–1000.
Haveman, H.A. and L. Nonnemaker (2000), 'Competition in multiple geographic markets: the impact on growth and market entry', *Administrative Science Quarterly*, **45** (2), 233–267.
Heggestad, A.A. and S.E. Rhoades (1978), 'Multimarket interdependence and local market competition in banking', *Review of Economics and Statistics*, **60** (4), 523–532.
Herrera, A.M. and R. Minetti (2007), 'Informed finance and technological change: evidence from credit relationships', *Journal of Financial Economics*, **83** (1), 223–269.
Hertzberg, A., J.M. Liberti and D. Paravisini (2010), 'Information and incentives inside the firm: evidence from loan officer rotation', *Journal of Finance*, **65** (3), 795–828.
Hirshleifer, D. and A.V. Thakor (1992), 'Managerial conservatism, project choice, and debt', *Review of Financial Studies*, **5** (3), 437–470.
Hoff, K. and J.E. Stiglitz (1997), 'Moneylenders and bankers: price-increasing subsidies in a monopolistically competitive market', *Journal of Development Economics*, **52** (2), 429–462.

Imai, M. and S. Takarabe (2011), 'Bank integration and transmission of financial shocks: evidence from Japan', *American Economic Journal: Macroeconomics*, **3** (1), 155–183.

Jappelli, T. and M. Pagano (2002), 'Information sharing, lending and defaults: cross-country evidence', *Journal of Banking and Finance*, **26** (10), 2017–2045.

Jimenez, G., V. Salas-Fumas and J. Saurina (2009), 'Organizational distance and use of collateral for business loans', *Journal of Banking and Finance*, **33** (2), 234–243.

Keeton, W.R. (1995), 'Multi-office bank lending to small business: some new evidence', *Federal Reserve Bank of Kansas City Economic Review*, Second quarter, 45–57.

Keeton. W.R. (1996), 'Do bank mergers reduce lending to businesses and farmers? New evidence from tenth district states', *Federal Reserve Bank of Kansas City Economic Review*, Third quarter, 63–75.

Kim, M. and B. Vale (2001), 'Non-price strategic behaviour: the case of bank branches', *International Journal of Industrial Organisation*, **19** (10), 1583–1602.

Kindleberger, C.P. (1974), *The Formation of Financial Centers*, Princeton Studies in International Finance 36, Princeton, NJ: Princeton University Press.

Klagge, B. and R. Martin (2005), 'Decentralized versus centralized financial systems: is there a case for local capital markets?', *Journal of Economic Geography*, **5** (4), 387–421.

Klein, D.B. (1992), 'Promise keeping in the great society: a model of credit information sharing', *Economics and Politics*, **4** (2), 117–136.

Klier, T. and W.A. Testa (2002), 'The Great Lakes border economy', Chicago Fed Letter, Federal Reserve Bank of Chicago, July.

Knyazeva, A. and D. Knyazeva (2012), 'Does being your neighbor's bank matter?', *Journal of Banking and Finance*, **36** (4), 1194–1209.

Landier, A., V.B. Nair and J. Wulf (2009), 'Trade-offs in staying close: corporate decision making and geographic dispersion', *Review of Financial Studies*, **22** (3), 1119–1148.

Lanzilotti, R.F. and T.R. Saving (1969), 'State branch restrictions and the availability of banking services', *Journal of Money, Credit and Banking*, **1** (4), 778–788.

Lawless, M. (2013), 'Age or size? Determinants of job creation', Central Bank of Ireland Research and Technical Papers, No. 02/RT/13.

Lederer, P.J. and A.P. Hurter (1986), 'Competition of firms: discriminatory pricing and location', *Econometrica*, **54** (3), 623–640.

Leitner, Y. (2005), 'Financial networks: contagion, commitment, and private sector bailouts', *Journal of Finance*, **60** (6), 2925–2953.

Liberti, J.M. and A. Mian (2009), 'Estimating the effect of hierarchies on information use', *Review of Financial Studies*, **22** (10), 4057–4090.

Magri, S., A. Mori and P. Rossi (2005), 'The entry and the activity level of foreign banks in Italy: an analysis of the determinants', *Journal of Banking and Finance*, **29** (5), 1295–1310.

Martin R. (1994), 'Stateless monies, global financial integration and national economic autonomy: the end of geography?', in S. Corbridge, R. Martin and N. Thrift (eds), *Money, Space and Power*, Oxford, UK: Blackwell Publishers, pp. 253–278.

Mayer, C. (1988), 'New issues in corporate finance', *European Economic Review*, **32** (5), 1167–1189.

Mester, L.J. (1987), 'Multiple market contact between savings and loans', *Journal of Money, Credit and Banking*, **19** (4), 538–549.

Mester, L.J. (1992), 'A multiproduct cost study of savings and loans', *The Journal of Finance*, **42** (2), 423–445.

Meyer, M., P. Milgrom and J. Roberts (1992), 'Organizational prospects, influence costs, and ownership changes', *Journal of Economics and Management Strategy*, **1** (1), 9–35.

Mian, A. (2006), 'Distance constraints: the limits of foreign lending in poor economies', *The Journal of Finance*, **61** (3), 1465–1505.

Minoiu, C. and J.A. Reyes (2011), 'A network analysis of global banking: 1978–2009', IMF Working Paper, No. 11/74.

Nier, E., J. Yang, T. Yorulmazer and A. Alentorn (2007), 'Network models and financial stability', *Journal of Economic Dynamics and Control*, **31** (6), 2033–2066.

Noss, J. and P. Toffano (2014), 'Estimating the impact of changes in aggregate bank capital requirements during an upswing', Bank of England Working Paper, No. 494.

Ogura, Y. (2010), 'Interbank competition and information production: evidence from the interest rate difference', *Journal of Financial Intermediation*, **19** (2), 279–304.

Ono, A., Y. Saito, K. Sakai and I. Uesugi (2013), 'Does geographical proximity matter in small business lending? Evidence from the switching of main bank relationships', Hitotsubashi University, Working Paper Series, No. 29.

Padilla, A.J. and M. Pagano (1997), 'Endogenous communication among lenders and entrepreneurial incentives', *Review of Financial Studies*, **10** (1), 205–236.

Pagano, M. and T. Jappelli (1993), 'Information sharing in credit markets', *Journal of Finance*, **48** (5), 1693–1718.

Palley, T.I. (1997), 'Managerial turnover and the theory of short-termism', *Journal of Economic Behavior and Organization*, **32** (4), 547–557.

Peek, J. and E.S. Rosengren (1997), 'The international transmission of financial shocks: the case of Japan', *American Economic Review*, **87** (4), 495–505.

Peek, J. and E. S. Rosengren (1998), 'Bank consolidation and small business lending: it's not just bank size that matters', *Journal of Banking and Finance*, **22** (6–8), 799–819.

Peek, J. and E. Rosengren (2000), 'Collateral damage: effects of the Japanese real estate collapse on credit availability and real activity in the United States', *American Economic Review*, **90** (1), 30–45.

Petersen, M.A. (2004), *Information: Hard and soft*, Chicago, USA: Northwestern University.

Petersen, M.A. and R.G. Rajan (1995), 'The effect of credit market competition on lending relationships', *Quarterly Journal of Economics*, **110** (2), 407–443.

Petersen, M. and R. Rajan (2002), 'Does distance still matter? The information revolution in small business lending', *Journal of Finance*, **57** (6), 2533–2570.

Popov, A. and G.F. Udell (2012), 'Cross-border banking, credit access, and the financial crisis', *Journal of International Economics*, **87** (1), 147–161.

Porteous, D.J. (1999), 'The development of financial centers: location, information externalities and path dependence', in R. Martin (ed.), *Money and the Space Economy*, New York, USA: John Wiley & Sons, pp. 95–114.

Presbitero, A.F. and A. Zazzaro (2011), 'Competition and relationship lending: friends or foes?', *Journal of Financial Intermediation*, **20** (3), 387–413.

Presbitero, A.F., G.F. Udell and A. Zazzaro (2014), 'The home bias and the credit crunch: a regional perspective', *Journal of Money, Credit and Banking*, **46** (s1), 53–85.

Riordan, M.H. (1993), 'Competition and bank performance: a theoretic perspective', in C. Mayer and X. Vives (eds), *Capital Markets and Financial Intermediation*, Cambridge UK: Cambridge University Press, pp. 328–343.

Sá, F. (2013), 'Bilateral financial links', in T. Beck, S. Claessens and S.L. Schmukler (eds),*The Evidence and Impact of Financial Globalization*, Amsterdam: Elsevier, pp. 51–65.

Scharfstein, D.S. and J.C. Stein (2000), 'The dark side of internal capital markets: divisional rent-seeking and inefficient investment', *Journal of Finance*, **55** (6), 2537–2564.

Schnabl, P. (2012), 'The international transmission of bank liquidity shocks: evidence from an emerging market', *Journal of Finance*, **67** (3), 897–932.

Seaver, W. and D. Fraser (1979), 'Branch banking and the availability of banking services in metropolitan areas', *Journal of Financial and Quantitative Analysis*, **14** (1), 153–160.

Seaver, W. and D. Fraser (1983), 'Branch banking and the availability of banking offices in non-metropolitan areas', *The Atlantic Economic Journal*, **11** (2), 72–78.

Shaffer, S. (1998), 'The winner's curse in banking', *Journal of Financial Intermediation*, **7** (4), 359–392.

Silverman, B. (1986), *Density Estimation for Statistics and Data Analysis*, New York, NY: Chapman and Hall.

Stein, J.C. (2002), 'Information production and capital allocation: decentralized versus hierarchical firms', *The Journal of Finance*, **57** (5), 1891–1921.

Storper, A. and M.J. Venables (2004), 'Buzz: face-to-face contact and the urban economy, *Journal of Economic Geography*, **4** (4), 351–370.

Strauss-Kahn, V. and X. Vives (2009), 'Why and where do headquarters move?', *Regional Science and Urban Economics*, **39** (2), 168–186.

Thrift N. (1994), 'On the social and cultural determinants of international financial centers: the case of the city of London', in S. Corbridge, N. Thrift and R. Martin (eds), *Money, Power and Space*, Oxford, UK: Blackwell, pp. 327–355.

Thrift, N. and A. Leyshon (1992), 'In the wake of money: the city of London and the accumulation of value', in L. Budd and S. Whimster (eds), *Global Finance and Urban Living: A Study of Metropolitan Change*, London: Routledge, pp. 282–311.

Tschoegl, A.E. (2000), 'International banking centers, geography, and foreign banks', *Financial Markets, Institutions and Instruments*, **9** (1), 1–32.

Uchida, H., G.F. Udell and W. Watanabe (2008), 'Bank size and lending relationships in Japan', *Journal of the Japanese and International Economies*, **22** (2), 242–267.

Uchida, H., G.F. Udell and N. Yamori (2012), 'Loan officers and relationship lending to SMEs', *Journal of Financial Intermediation*, **21** (1), 97–122.

Udell, G.F. (1989), 'Loan quality, commercial loan review and loan officer contracting', *Journal of Banking and Finance*, **13** (3), 367–382.

Uzzi, B. (1999), 'Embeddedness in the making of financial capital: how social relationships and networks benefit firms seeking capital', *American Sociological Review*, **64** (4), 481–505.

Uzzi, B. and R. Lancaster (2003), 'Relational embeddedness and learning: the case of bank loan managers and their clients', *Management Science*, **49**(4) 383–399.

von Peter, G. (2010), 'International banking centres: a network perspective', in Bank for International Settlements, Research on global financial stability: the use of BIS international financial statistics, CGFS Papers No. 40, 71–82.

Zazzaro, A. (2005), 'Should courts enforce credit contracts strictly?', *Economic Journal*, **115** (500), 166–184.

Zazzaro, A. (2006), 'La scomparsa dei centri decisionali dal sistema bancario meridionale', *Rivista di Politica Economica*, **96** (2), 31–60.

9. Innovation and stock markets: international evidence on manufacturing and services

Dariusz Wójcik

9.1 INTRODUCTION

This chapter investigates the relationship between firms' innovativeness and their participation in stock markets. Existing research offers clues on how the capital structure of companies and decisions to go public relate to their innovativeness, but empirically it focuses almost exclusively on manufacturing. Such focus leaves a yawning research gap, considering that services account for two-thirds to three-quarters of employment in developed economies. The scarcity of research on the relationship between innovation and stock markets in the services sector is even more striking when we recall that the most recent stock market boom was centred on Internet-related companies that belong to services rather than the manufacturing sector. This chapter contributes to the existing research by analysing the relationship between innovativeness and stock market participation in both manufacturing and services firms in 32 countries.

Financial economic literature on going public and capital structure is silent on services companies in terms of theory and largely neglects them in empirical terms. The latter may be due to the fact that available statistical sources lag behind real world developments, and still offer less information on services than on manufacturing firms. The problem with the prevailing theoretical approach, in turn, is that it focuses on the features of conventionally understood innovation, such as technology and formal research and development, and lacks consideration for features typical of innovation in services, such as knowledge intensity. In these circumstances, in this chapter I turn to the intersection of economic geography and innovation studies, which tend to treat innovation in a broad fashion and attempts to conceptualise innovativeness for any type of firm, above the level of conventional, and in some respects old-fashioned distinctions between manufacturing and services. The problem here, however, is that the economic geography of innovation in general, and on innovation in services in particular, pays little attention to the going public decision or capital structure. As Pollard (2003: 429) argued "firm finance is something of a 'black-box' in economic geography, a largely take-for-granted aspect of production". Given these problems, the second general contribution of this chapter is to combine financial economics, economic geography and innovation studies in order to address the relationship between firm innovativeness and stock market participation.

The chapter uses a dataset covering nearly 100,000 companies in 30 European countries as well as the US and Japan to address the following questions:

1. What is relationship between innovativeness and stock market participation of firms in manufacturing and services, and how does it compare between the two sectors?
2. How and why does the relationship between innovativeness and stock market participation differ between countries?

To start with, the chapter demonstrates that services account for an absolute majority of listed firms in the world. This finding reinforces the agenda of research on stock market activities of services firms. In response to the core questions, I show that while stock market participation increases with high-technology intensity in manufacturing, it increases at least as consistently with knowledge intensity of services firms. In other words, the relationship between innovativeness and stock market participation is more pronounced and easier to detect for services than manufacturing. This is probably because services are a bigger and more heterogeneous category in terms of innovativeness, ranging from the icons of the information technology revolution, such as Microsoft or Google, to some of the least innovative activities, such as cleaning services (Miles, 2005). With regard to cross-country differences, the relationship between innovativeness and stock market participation is stronger in countries with a developed institutional environment of finance. It seems that in countries with less stock market-friendly institutions, innovative firms turn for financing to banks rather than stock markets. To illustrate, the relationship between innovativeness and stock market participation is strong in the US and the UK, moderate in France and Germany, weak in Italy, and insignificant in the transition countries of Central and Eastern Europe. Finally, the chapter argues that while the Internet boom was responsible for bringing large numbers of services companies to the stock market, the relationship between stock market participation and innovativeness is likely to have existed before the boom.

Beyond adding to the stock of knowledge on why companies in different sectors and countries go public, the results of this chapter are important for one principal reason. They highlight the possibility that the development of stock markets positively affects innovation (or at least certain types of it) in an economy. While the static nature of data used in this chapter does not allow an exploration of the direction of causality between stock market development and innovation, the chapter indicates new avenues for research on the impact of financial structure on economic development (Levine, 2004).

The chapter proceeds as follows. Section 9.2 defines innovativeness and stock market participation and links them using insights from financial economics, economic geography and innovation studies. This is followed by the description of methodology and data, including a measure of stock market participation. Section 9.4 presents stock market participation by country and by sector, and compares it between manufacturing and services. The following two sections address the core research questions, investigating the relationship between innovativeness and stock market participation, using bivariate and multivariate analysis. Section 9.7 concludes, offering implications and directions for further research.

9.2 LINKING INNOVATIVENESS AND STOCK MARKET PARTICIPATION

Let us define innovation in a Schumpeterian fashion as new combinations of tangible (technology) and intangible (knowledge) inputs that are economically more viable than the old ways of doing things. Such a definition covers: (1) introduction of new goods or new qualities of goods, (2) introduction of new methods of production, (3) opening of new markets, (4) finding new sources of inputs, and (5) finding new ways of organising business (Schumpeter, 1934). Innovative firms are those that carry out innovations. Companies that participate in stock markets, in turn, can be defined as those accessing public equity markets. To be sure there are different degrees of stock market participation. A company can just have its shares quoted and traded on an over-the-counter market or listed. Fuller participation involves the issuance of new shares and raising funds through the public stock market. With these broad definitions in mind, what connections between innovativeness and stock market participation can be found in the existing theoretical and empirical research?

First of all, innovative firms can be expected to have more investment and growth opportunities that make them need more capital than less innovative firms. They are less likely to satisfy their demand for capital from retained earnings and more likely to turn to external sources. External finance is costly, as external financiers will never have information that is available to corporate managers, and face adverse selection problems. According to Myers and Majluf (1984) these problems are minimised by the issuance of the safest security, the pricing of which is least sensitive to managers' private information. Thus, debt, whose risk depends primarily on the value of collateral, is issued before equity. The rights of creditors are clearer and violations of these rights easier to verify in courts than the rights of shareholders. This logic leads to the proposition of the pecking order theory, according to which firms tend to satisfy their financial needs from internal sources first, debt second, and equity in the last instance. In addition, it is plausible to expect that by using external equity firms enhance their bargaining power in relation to banks (Pagano et al., 1998; Röell, 1996). The implication of the pecking order theory is that the relationship between the use of external equity and innovativeness may be non-monotonic. Firms with moderate levels of innovation may actually use more debt than firms with no or little innovation, but as innovativeness rises above moderate levels, the use of external equity increases (Aghion et al., 2004).

The second major factor that may affect debt-equity structure, and at the same time be related to innovativeness, is the structure of firms' assets. Shleifer and Vishny (1997) argue that equity is most suitable when a company has a large share of intangible items in its assets. Intangible assets make poor collateral and have little value in case of company liquidation. This is particularly true for assets that are specialised and firm specific, that is, it would be very difficult to sell those for use in a different company (Titman, 1984). As innovative firms are more likely to be strong in know-how, patents and other intangible assets rather than tangible assets like plant or machinery, and their assets are more likely to be firm specific, they are less likely to rely on collateral-hungry banks and more on stock markets. Empirical research tends to confirm the expected positive relationship between leverage and the share of tangible assets (Harris and Raviv, 1991; Rajan and Zingales, 1995).

Beyond investment opportunities and asset structure, there are also theories that suggest that public equity markets are more efficient than banks in collecting and processing information needed to evaluate innovative firms and their projects. Subrahmanyam and Titman (1999) highlight the role of serendipitous (collected by chance, in the course of life) information in the assessment of new industries, for example, the Internet. Public equity markets rather than private financiers or banks are considered to be natural environments for the generation and use of such information. In a similar manner, Allen and Gale (1999) develop a model indicating that public equity markets are a superior source of financing for projects that attract a diversity of investors' opinions about their likely commercial success. Interpreting that model Carlin and Mayer (2003) argue that as public markets aggregate diverse views of a large number of market participants, they could be expected to be associated with speculative investments, for example, in high technology industry. In contrast, banks tend to be biased towards prudence, and ineffective in gathering and processing information in new, uncertain situations involving innovative products and processes (Morck and Nakamura, 1999; Weinstein and Yafeh, 1998).

Theories of capital structure and theories of corporate decisions to go public make no distinction between manufacturing and services. Relevant empirical studies, though still inconclusive and few in numbers, indicate a positive relationship between firms' innovativeness and their use of equity (Rajan and Zingales, 1995; Carlin and Mayer, 2003; Bartoloni, 2013). Unfortunately, they hardly ever cover services firms, and even if they do, they do not focus on the distinction between manufacturing and services (Audretsch and Lehmann, 2004; Schäfer et al., 2004). Thus, a basic question needs to be asked. Assuming a positive relationship between innovativeness and stock market participation in manufacturing exists, are there any reasons why such a relationship would not apply to services? There seems to be nothing in the nature of innovation in services in relation to manufacturing that would prevent such a relationship. To start with, even the Schumpeterian definition of innovation, originating in the times when services were incomparably less prominent in the economy, is rich enough to encompass innovation in services (Drejer, 2004). Innovation can be conceptualised as a combination of competencies and technologies, which applies to both manufacturing and services (Gallouj and Weinstein, 1997). In fact, empirical innovation studies show that innovation dynamics in some services is more similar to certain parts of manufacturing than to other services and vice versa (Preissl, 2000; Tether, 2003). Innovation in manufacturing involves increasing amounts of knowledge, while innovation in services needs to engage with applications of high technology originating in manufacturing. To be sure, important differences between manufacturing and services remain, but they do not imply no relationship between innovativeness and stock market participation in services. While innovation in services may require less formal research and development expenditures, to be innovative in a Schumpeterian competitive sense, innovative services firms need to invest in knowledge, which may be as costly as physical/tangible assets (Sirilli and Evangelista, 1998).

Innovativeness and Stock Market Participation in Space

To consider how the relationship between innovativeness and stock market participation could vary across space, we need to put innovation in context. Invaluable in this respect are the contributions from innovation studies and economic geography of innovation, which focus on the environment of innovation. This environment may be defined as "the network of institutions in the public and private sectors whose activities and interactions initiate, import, modify and diffuse new technologies" (Freeman, 1995: 5). Such innovation systems may function as national or regional innovation systems (Cooke, 1991; Asheim and Coenen, 2005). At the same time, we need to put stock market in the context of a broader financial system. Key in this respect is the distinction between bank-based and capital market-based financial systems. In the latter firms rely to a much greater degree on stock and corporate bond markets as sources of financing, while in the former they rely predominantly on bank loans, and often form long-term relationships with banks (also referred to as house-banks). The financial sector tends to be more spatially concentrated in capital market-based systems, for example in the UK, while in bank-based systems, for example in Germany and Italy, close relationships between firms and banks sustain the status of local and regional banks (Klagge and Martin, 2005). To be sure, country size and federal structure may mitigate spatial concentration even in capital market-based systems, as they do, for example in the US (Verdier, 2002). In addition, bank- versus capital market-dependency of firms varies across regions (Clark and Wójcik, 2007).

The relationship between innovativeness and stock market participation, seen through the lens of economic geography, thus becomes a question of the relationship between innovation and financial systems, including stock markets. One set of institutions of particular importance to both innovation and stock markets consists of laws and regulations. Both innovation and stock markets require strong protection of property rights, including intellectual property, and enforcement of contracts, as these assure innovators and stock market investors that they can reap the fruits of their efforts and investments (La Porta et al., 1997). Another related set of institutions is constituted by corporate governance, which defines relationships between different stakeholders in companies, and between owners and managers in particular. It has been argued that developed stock markets are accompanied by more open and fluid corporate governance, where managers are disciplined by constant valuation of companies with investors buying and selling shares, and by the market for corporate control, with hostile takeovers (Clark and Wójcik, 2007). This constant pressure from capital markets provides incentives for innovation, in addition to those resulting from competition in markets for goods and services. On the other hand, the preoccupation of stock market investors with short-term corporate performance, epitomised with attention to quarterly financial results, may detract companies from innovation that requires long-term investment and stability of management, investor and labour relations (Christopherson, 2002). As proponents of the varieties of capitalism approach put it, liberal market economies, with developed stock markets, may offer advantages for disruptive innovation, while coordinated market economies favour incremental innovation (Hall and Soskice, 2001).

The economic geography of finance also offers clues on the interaction between stock markets and innovation. First, this literature has indicated the uneven representation of different regions and economic sectors in stock markets, hinting at, though not yet exploring, the possibility that high-technology industrial clusters may be linked more closely to stock markets than other regions (Klagge and Martin, 2005; Wójcik, 2011). Specifically, Wójcik (2009) documented a financial centre bias in stock markets, whereby firms from financial centres are more likely to participate in stock markets than provincial companies. In a similar manner, stock markets may be biased towards more innovative firms. Second, research on venture capital stresses the importance of stock markets as the key exit route for venture capital investors (Chen et al., 2010; Martin et al., 2002), while venture capital industry represents a major feeder of stock markets. As such, the interactions between venture capital and stock markets are clearly important for innovation. While this venture capital – stock market complex is highly developed in the US, in Europe it has lagged behind. In fact, one of the objectives of the EU Lisbon Agenda of 2000 (Rodrigues, 2009) was to foster the integration and development of both venture capital and stock markets in Europe in a belief that this would help foster innovation. The Lisbon Agenda is also a reminder that the relationship between stock markets and innovation operates beyond the national level. Another reminder of the significance of supra-national scale is the frequency with which many innovative firms list their shares in foreign markets, thus plugging themselves to global capital markets (Wójcik and Burger, 2010).

The existing literature makes clear that the relationship between innovation and stock markets has a crucial geographical dimension. If we assume a positive relationship between innovativeness and stock market participation, then a large stock market could indicate the preponderance of innovative sectors in an economy. Moreover, it could imply that policies supporting the development of stock markets could also enhance the development of national and regional innovation systems (Tylecote and Visintin, 2007). In what follows, we will focus on two of few studies that investigate empirically the relationship between innovativeness and stock market development across countries, and which offer most specific clues to inform our hypotheses.

Starting with an assumption that financial development reduces the costs of external finance to firms, Rajan and Zingales (1998) ask whether industrial sectors that are relatively more in need of external finance develop disproportionately faster in countries with more developed financial markets. They find this to be true in a large sample of countries over the 1980s. Carlin and Mayer (2003) extend this line of inquiry, by focusing on different types of dependence on external finance, and different aspects of corporate development. Their analysis of a matrix of 15 industries in 14 countries, leads to two results essential to this chapter. First, they find a positive relationship between dependence on equity finance and research and development (R&D) intensity of an industry. Second, they demonstrate that this relationship is particularly strong in countries with high quality of information disclosure (with the quality of accounting standards used as a proxy). In a nutshell, while Rajan and Zingales claim that financial development affects the relationship between the dependence of a sector on external finance and its growth, Carlin and Mayer claim that financial development affects the relationship between the dependence of a sector on equity finance and its innovativeness. It is worthwhile noting that these and related studies assess financial development by the size of external finance (measured, for example, as the ratio of stock market capitalisation and total credit to GDP) or by the quality of institutions underpinning it, for example accounting standards or the quality of law enforcement (Demirgüç-Kunt and Maksimovic, 2002).

It is therefore a short step from existing literature to hypothesise that the legal and regulatory environment of finance is an important factor that affects the relationship between innovativeness and stock market participation. To make the hypothesis work, we need to assume that stock market financing requires a stronger institutional environment than bank financing (Tadesse, 2002). Put differently, there are certain institutions necessary for the operation of a capital market-based financial system, which are not needed for a bank-based system. At a basic level, a bank loan requires institutions that enable the lender to seize collateral in case of borrower's default. Financing via public stock markets requires laws and regulations on shareholder rights, financial and other reporting to the public, insider trading, takeovers, corporate governance, and so on. To be sure, this is not to claim that stock markets do not have significant flaws and disadvantages in relation to credit markets.

To illustrate the hypothesis, imagine an economy made of an innovative firm, with a high demand for external finance, and a non-innovative firm, with a low demand. If the economy has strong institutions supporting capital market development, according to the pecking order theory the non-innovative firm will satisfy its demand with bank loans, while the innovative firm will turn to stock market financing. If the country has weak institutional support for capital markets, the non-innovative firm will be unaffected, while the innovative firm will remain dependent on bank financing. As a result, the weaker the legal and regulatory environment of capital markets, the less likely the positive relationship between innovativeness and stock market participation is to occur.

There are two more factors that could affect the relationship between innovativeness and stock market participation. First is the role of privatisations, whereby the government brings formerly state-owned companies to stock markets. Governmental decisions about which privatised companies should and which should not be listed and traded on stock markets may have little to do with the innovativeness of these companies. In consequence, in countries where privatisations have been a major source of publicly traded companies, the relationship between innovativeness and stock market participation may be obscured. The second consideration is the Internet boom. Considering that at the peak of the Internet boom in 1999–2000 technology companies accounted for 72 per cent of IPOs in the US (Ritter and Welch, 2002), and new segments of stock markets for young innovative firms sprang up across Europe (Posner, 2005), it is possible that the relationship between innovativeness and stock market participation is affected by this episode in the recent history of stock markets. We could expect the relationship between innovativeness and stock market participation to be particularly strong in countries that experienced a strong Internet boom.

9.3 METHODOLOGY AND DATA

To analyse the relationship between stock market participation and innovativeness this chapter uses industry-level data for 47 sectors in 32 countries. The data comes from the ORBIS database by Bureau Van Dijk Electronic Publishing (BvD) and is valid for the end of September 2006. Geographical coverage consists of all 27 European Union member states, Iceland, Norway, Switzerland, as well as the US and Japan. The data covers 23 types of manufacturing and 24 types of services following NACE codes (as amended in 2001, also known as Rev.1.1. NACE codes), the principal statistical classification of economic activities within the European Union. While access to more up-to-date data from ORBIS was impossible, it should be noted that data on listed companies represents stocks of firms accumulated over decades. Between September 2006 and September 2014, the total number of listed companies in the five largest economies in the sample (France, Germany, Japan, UK and US) fell by approximately 7 per cent, with more companies exiting rather entering the stock market, due mainly to poor market performance since the US subprime crisis of 2007–08, and the following Eurozone crisis (World Bank, 2014). Hence, we believe that even if more current data were available, it would not significantly change the results.

Stock market participation (SMP) of each sector in each country is calculated as the ratio of the number of companies participating in stock markets to the number of all companies with turnover exceeding €50 million. Companies participating in stock markets are defined as those that are publicly listed or at least publicly quoted and traded. This broad definition is applied in order to cover all alternative, smaller company, and technology focused segments of stock markets. A detailed list of each country's stock market segments covered in the chapter is presented in Appendix 9.1.

To assess SMP it is crucial to carefully delimit the broader population of companies in the underlying economy, to which the set of stock market participating firms is compared. Considering all enterprises existing in an economy would fail to recognise that companies participating in stock markets are relatively large, mainly as a result of fixed costs of stock market participation such as reporting costs as well as initial and ongoing listing fees (Pagano et al., 1998; Oxera, 2006). For this reason this chapter compares the set of stock market companies to all companies with turnover in excess of €50 million, adjusted to the price level in a given country. The threshold of €50 million is used officially in the European Union to distinguish between medium and large companies. Companies are assigned to countries where they are headquartered. They are considered as stock market traded, if they are traded on any stock market in the world, not necessarily their home country market. In short, the ratio of SMP relates the number of firms that participate in stock markets to the number of all large firms in the underlying economy.

Data on the number of large companies operating in the underlying economies were collected by filtering companies with turnover in excess of €50 million out of all companies included in ORBIS. Turnover figures are based on consolidated financial statements, if available (unconsolidated otherwise), for the last financial year, for which they were available (mostly 2005). The threshold of €50 million is adjusted to the country price level, using OECD comparative price levels for 2005 (OECD, 2006).

Any analysis comparing numbers of publicly traded companies between countries runs the risk of comparing the incomparable. What counts as a publicly traded company in one country, would not necessarily be considered as such in another country. Listing rules differ between countries and between stock exchanges. Lenient listing rules can result in high and strict rules in low numbers of recorded issuers. Considering these issues, the chapter does not focus on comparing absolute figures on SMP between countries. The emphasis is instead on comparing SMP rates between sectors of companies within countries. As the definition of a publicly traded company is a constant within each country, definitional differences between countries do not matter for comparison of SMP within countries.

Finally, to capture innovativeness of each sector the chapter uses the OECD/Eurostat classification that divides manufacturing into four, and services into three groups (Eurostat, 2006). Its advantage is that it combines the traditional understanding of R&D intensity, based on technological and tangible innovations, with the concept of knowledge intensity, much more suitable to services than the traditional definition. The allocation of each manufacturing and services sector into the seven groups of the OECD/Eurostat classification is presented in Appendix 9.2. Agriculture, mining, utilities and construction firms are not classified by the OECD/Eurostat, and are excluded from the analysis. Of course, putting all economic sectors into seven categories of innovativeness, and assuming that all companies within a sector are equally innovative is a crude simplification. This is however necessary to make any comparison between manufacturing and services possible, as more objective measures such as research and development expenditure fail to capture innovativeness in the services sector.

9.4 STOCK MARKETS PARTICIPATION OF SERVICES VS. MANUFACTURING FIRMS

Table 9.1 presents the number and the structure of companies by country. The total sample consists of nearly 100,000 firms with price-level adjusted turnover exceeding €50 million, nearly 20,000 thousand of which are publicly traded. In every country there are more large firms in services than in manufacturing, and services account for 70 per cent of the total number of large firms. This simply confirms a well-known fact that services represent a lion's share of today's world economy. What has not been pinpointed before, however, is that services firms account also for a majority of publicly traded firms. Their share in the total sample equals 62 per cent, and exceeds that of manufacturing in 23 out of 32 sample countries, with the nine exceptions being seven transition countries in Central and Eastern Europe, plus Finland and Greece. In non-transition economies of Europe (all European countries in the sample, excluding the ten transition economies) there are twice as many publicly traded services firms as manufacturing firms. The observation that services constitute a smaller share of the stock market than of the underlying economy indicates a lower SMP of services firms. In fact, in all countries except for Austria, Malta, Norway, and the UK, services have a lower SMP rate than manufacturing.

Table 9.1 also reveals how SMP varies between countries. While in the total sample there are approximately four large firms for every publicly traded firm in manufacturing and five in services, in Cyprus and Bulgaria there are more publicly traded than large firms. On the other extreme, in the Czech Republic there are seventy times as many large firms as there are publicly traded firms. The absolute SMP rates differ partly because the definition of a publicly traded company differs across countries. As stressed before, how these definitions differ is irrelevant to the rest of the chapter, as it focuses on the variation of SMP within countries, not across countries.

As presented in Appendix 9.2, SMP differs greatly across sectors. Within manufacturing it ranges from recycling, as a sole sector with SMP below 0.10, through a large cluster of sectors with SMP of 0.15–0.16, to a maximum SMP of 0.65 for the manufacture of radio, television, and communication equipment and apparatus. Within services, there are several sectors with SMP below 0.10, and the maximum value of SMP is 0.80 for activities auxiliary to financial intermediation (including brokerage firms), followed by computer and related activities with SMP of 0.75. In the UK, SMP ranges from 0.20 in South East to 0.05 in Northern Ireland.

With large variation by sector, it is not surprising that SMP differs across regions and cities within countries. In the US for example, while the average SMP is 0.26, in San Francisco MSA it reaches 0.48, and in Boston MSA 0.43 compared to 0.13 in Detroit MSA. In Germany, the SMP of 0.12 in Bavaria is double that in North Rhine-Westphalia. In France the regions with the highest SMP are the capital region Île de France and Rhônes-Alpes, with Grenoble as capital. In Sweden, the southernmost region of Scania, with capital in Malmö, has by far the highest SMP of all regions including the capital region of Stockholm. Interestingly, San Francisco MSA including Silicon Valley, Munich, Grenoble, and Malmö are commonly considered the most innovative cities in their countries. While the chapter focuses on comparisons between rather than within countries, even this cursory look at within-country variation, hints at a potential relationship between SMP and the level of innovation.

Table 9.1 Large firms, publicly traded firms, and stock market participation by country

	Large firms				Publicly traded firms				SMP	
	Number		Share		Number		Share			
	M	S	M	S	M	S	M	S	M	S
Austria	328	555	37	63	36	66	35	65	0.11	0.12
Belgium	601	1,227	33	67	58	84	41	59	0.10	0.07
Bulgaria	46	137	25	75	194	122	61	39	4.22	0.89
Cyprus	3	19	14	86	24	97	20	80	8.00	5.11
Czech Republic	541	838	39	61	10	11	48	52	0.02	0.01
Denmark	222	845	21	79	55	112	33	67	0.25	0.13
Estonia	33	99	25	75	8	5	62	38	0.24	0.05
Finland	349	519	40	60	72	59	55	45	0.21	0.11
France	2,175	4,889	31	69	322	584	36	64	0.15	0.12
Germany	2,727	5,608	33	67	363	599	38	62	0.13	0.11
Greece	221	332	40	60	159	134	54	46	0.72	0.40
Hungary	170	296	36	64	16	17	48	52	0.09	0.06
Iceland	8	31	21	79	8	12	40	60	1.00	0.39
Ireland	439	1,265	26	74	25	67	27	73	0.06	0.05
Italy	2,480	3,448	42	58	124	132	48	52	0.05	0.04
Japan	3,429	7,863	30	70	1,674	1,935	46	54	0.49	0.25
Latvia	23	90	20	80	19	13	59	41	0.83	0.14
Lithuania	43	74	37	63	19	17	53	47	0.44	0.23
Luxembourg	35	201	15	85	8	32	20	80	0.23	0.16
Malta	9	20	31	69	0	7	0	100	0.00	0.35
Netherlands	805	2,132	27	73	73	144	34	66	0.09	0.07
Norway	227	521	30	70	61	179	25	75	0.27	0.34
Poland	762	942	45	55	113	100	53	47	0.15	0.11
Portugal	225	537	30	70	25	40	38	62	0.11	0.07
Romania	250	281	47	53	49	14	78	22	0.20	0.05
Slovakia	120	253	32	68	102	114	47	53	0.85	0.45
Slovenia	91	98	48	52	45	31	59	41	0.49	0.32
Spain	1,252	2,296	35	65	69	95	42	58	0.06	0.04
Sweden	458	1,191	28	72	130	244	35	65	0.28	0.20
Switzerland	334	839	28	72	115	145	44	56	0.34	0.17
UK	2,461	7,537	25	75	548	1,702	24	76	0.22	0.23
USA	8,233	23,733	26	74	2,968	5,312	36	64	0.36	0.22
Europe non-transition	15,364	34,018	31	69	2,275	4,536	33	67	0.15	0.13
EU Transition	2,079	3,108	40	60	575	444	56	44	0.28	0.14
Total sample	29,105	68,722	30	70	7,492	12,227	38	62	0.26	0.18

Notes: The table shows the number of large firms, and publicly traded firms by country, as well as their division between manufacturing (M) and services (S). Large firms are defined as those with turnover exceeding €50m, where €50m is adjusted to the price level of the country. SMP is calculated as the ratio of the number of publicly traded companies to the number of large companies. EU Transition group consists of: Bulgaria, Czech Republic, Estonia, Hungary, Latvia, Lithuania, Poland, Romania, Slovakia, and Slovenia. Europe non-transition stands for the remaining 20 European countries.

Source: ORBIS.

To summarise, the fact that the majority of firms participating in stock markets are services firms, combined with the observation that SMP varies more across different types of services firms than across manufacturing, underscores the value of including services in the study of factors affecting firms' engagement with stock markets.

9.5 INNOVATIVENESS AND STOCK MARKET PARTICIPATION

Table 9.2 presents SMP rates for all countries and Figure 9.1 depicts the results for Europe, Japan and the US, the four largest EU economies, and the four largest EU transition economies. The results suggest a positive relationship between innovativeness and SMP in manufacturing. High technology (HT) firms participate in stock markets to a higher extent than any other group of manufacturing firms in the US, Japan, and non-transition Europe. Within the latter region, Ireland is the only country where companies other than HT have the highest SMP. However, whether a company is medium-high technology (MHT), medium-low technology (MLT) or low technology (LT) does not seem to matter much for SMP. While in the US, MHT have higher SMP than MLT firms, the same cannot be said of non-transition Europe. Moreover, in the US, Japan, Germany and Italy LT firms have higher SMP than MLT firms. The observation that SMP peaks consistently at the high end of the scale of innovativeness, but does not vary significantly for moderate or lower sections of that scale, seems to support the pecking order theory (Aghion et al., 2004). When levels of innovativeness increases, firms turn first to banks, not necessarily stock markets for additional financing. It is only when level of innovation is very high that stock market financing becomes essential.

For services, in every single country in the sample, less knowledge intensive (LKI) services have the lowest SMP rate. In 24 out of 32 countries, high technology knowledge intensive (HTKI) services have higher SMP than other knowledge intensive (OKI) firms, and OKI higher SMP than LKI. As hypothesised, the relationship between innovativeness and SMP is much more pronounced for services than for manufacturing. In nearly all cases presented in Figure 9.1, HTKI services exhibit higher SMP than HT manufacturing, and LKI services have lower SMP than LT manufacturing. To be careful, we should abstain here from claiming that the relationship between innovativeness and SMP for services is stronger than for manufacturing. Such a claim would mean that a unit increase in innovativeness implies a bigger and more significant increase in stock market participation in services than it does in manufacturing. The unit of innovativeness used here is a move from one category of OECD/Eurostat classification to another, and it is not in a strict quantitative sense comparable between manufacturing and services.

Moving from a comparison between services and manufacturing to a comparison between countries, two patterns should be highlighted. Within manufacturing, transition economies do not exhibit a positive relationship between innovativeness and SMP, not even for the most innovative firms. In fact, for EU transition economies as a whole, the relationship appears reversed, whereby LT firms have the highest and the HT firms the lowest SMP rates. In addition, in transition countries evidence on the positive relationship between innovativeness and SMP is also mixed. Two potential factors may be responsible for this pattern. First, it is possible that many formerly state-owned LT and MLT firms have been brought to the stock market via privatisations, which obscures the relationship

Table 9.2 Stock market participation by country and group of activities

	Manufacturing				Services		
	HT	MHT	MLT	LT	HTKI	OKI	LKI
Austria	0.14	0.13	0.11	0.09	0.54	0.23	0.02
Belgium	0.46	0.09	0.07	0.08	0.36	0.11	0.01
Bulgaria	1.50	4.73	3.54	5.00	1.00	1.44	0.61
Cyprus	NA	NA	NA	4.67	4.00	5.50	4.75
Czech Republic	0.00	0.02	0.01	0.02	0.04	0.05	0.00
Denmark	0.42	0.26	0.20	0.21	0.36	0.17	0.03
Estonia	0.00	0.30	0.00	0.33	0.33	0.06	0.03
Finland	0.57	0.14	0.16	0.21	0.48	0.19	0.02
France	0.44	0.12	0.13	0.13	0.72	0.12	0.06
Germany	0.32	0.12	0.09	0.12	0.59	0.12	0.04
Greece	1.08	0.38	0.79	0.82	1.15	0.80	0.22
Hungary	0.00	0.20	0.03	0.09	0.18	0.14	0.01
Iceland	1.00	1.00	NA	1.00	0.67	0.47	0.18
Ireland	0.05	0.07	0.14	0.03	0.12	0.07	0.02
Italy	0.09	0.05	0.04	0.05	0.15	0.06	0.01
Japan	0.58	0.52	0.42	0.45	0.81	0.32	0.18
Latvia	NA	2.25	0.33	0.56	0.25	0.25	0.11
Lithuania	0.50	0.56	0.20	0.44	0.33	0.64	0.12
Luxembourg	0.50	0.33	0.16	0.40	0.40	0.19	0.04
Malta	0.00	0.00	0.00	0.00	0.25	0.50	0.17
Netherlands	0.21	0.08	0.07	0.08	0.21	0.11	0.02
Norway	0.82	0.29	0.12	0.20	1.35	0.44	0.09
Poland	0.19	0.10	0.21	0.14	0.58	0.17	0.05
Portugal	0.00	0.06	0.09	0.18	0.30	0.10	0.04
Romania	0.00	0.33	0.29	0.06	0.00	0.16	0.03
Slovakia	2.00	0.68	0.66	1.06	1.80	0.85	0.20
Slovenia	0.00	0.38	0.42	0.74	0.20	0.37	0.30
Spain	0.03	0.03	0.05	0.08	0.05	0.08	0.02
Sweden	0.81	0.26	0.27	0.19	0.85	0.18	0.11
Switzerland	0.44	0.36	0.42	0.24	0.32	0.22	0.07
UK	0.57	0.22	0.22	0.15	0.51	0.30	0.09
USA	0.87	0.41	0.16	0.21	0.81	0.25	0.10
Europe non-transition	0.38	0.13	0.12	0.13	0.48	0.17	0.05
EU transition	0.18	0.26	0.27	0.31	0.42	0.31	0.07

Notes: This table shows stock market participation rates by country and group of activities according to OECD/Eurostat classification. For manufacturing: LT-low technology, MLT-medium low technology, MHT-medium high technology, HT-high technology; for services: HTKI-high technology knowledge intensive, OKI-other knowledge intensive, LKI-less knowledge intensive. SMP rates are not available for countries where there are no large firms in a given group of activities.

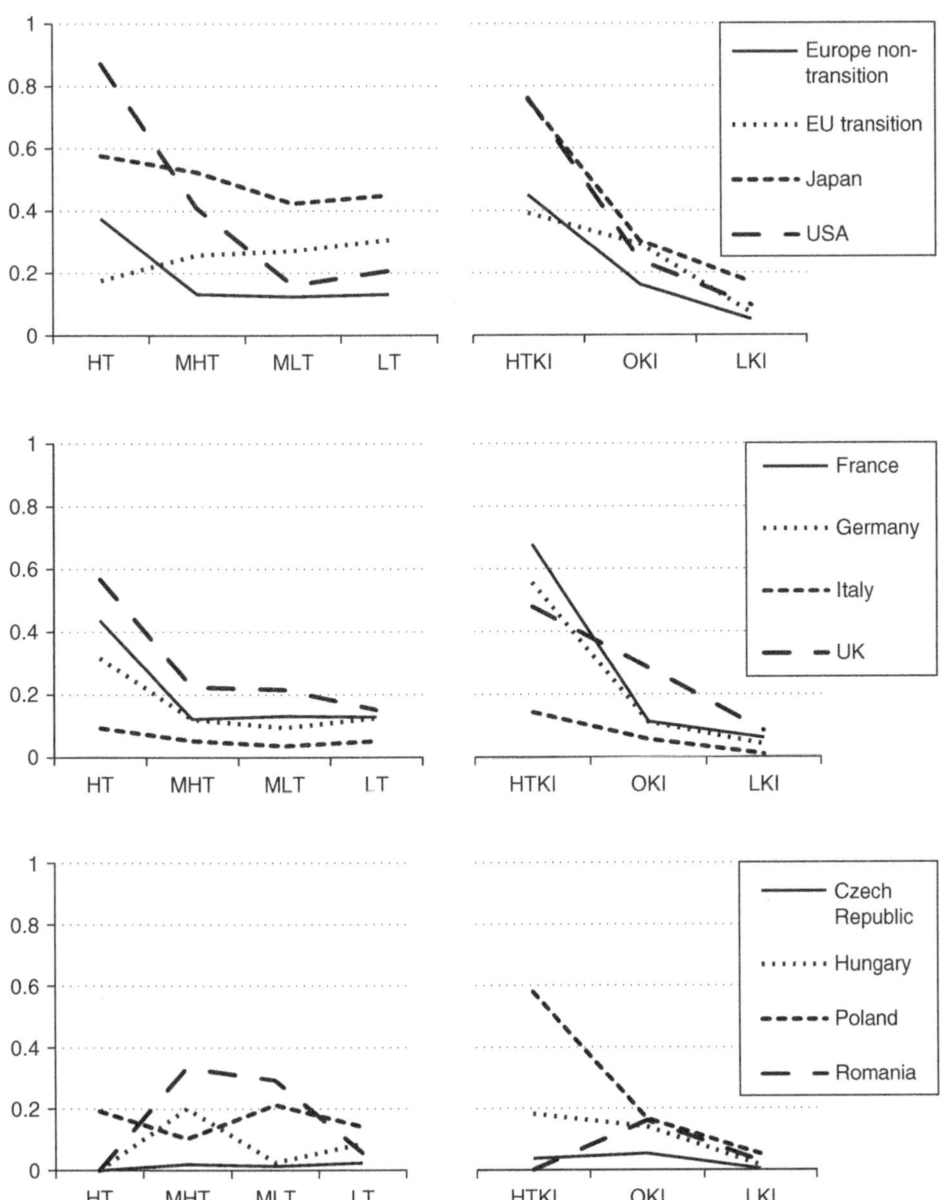

Notes: This figure depicts selected data from Table 9.2 for manufacturing (left) and services (right). It relates the decreasing level of innovativeness based on the OECD/Eurostat classification (axis x) to SMP rate (axis y).

Figure 9.1 Innovativeness and stock market participation

between innovativeness and SMP. Ljungqvist et al. (2003) estimate the share of privatisations in IPOs in 1992–99 at 50 per cent for Eastern Europe, while for Western Europe the figures range from 0.9 per cent in the UK to 12.5 per cent in Italy.

The second explanation is that the legal and regulatory environment of capital markets is relatively underdeveloped, so that even HT and HTKI firms still turn to banks rather than stock markets to satisfy their investment needs. The last explanation is consistent with the finding of Carlin and Mayer (2003) that in low GDP OECD countries (Korea, Mexico, Portugal, and Greece) the institutional environment of finance is more important for the growth of industries dependent on bank financing than it is in advanced OECD countries. This could imply that there is a threshold in the financial development. Before a country reaches the threshold, financial development increases the effectiveness and efficiency of bank financing. After the threshold is reached, financial development ceases to improve the effectiveness and efficiency of bank financing, but in turn enables and enhances successful stock market financing. Further observations from Figure 9.1 underscore the potential significance of financial development. For both manufacturing and services the UK has the strongest relationship between innovativeness and SMP, Italy the weakest, with France and Germany exhibiting moderate levels of relationship. Could different levels of financial development in these countries drive this pattern? This and related questions are explored through multivariate analysis.

9.6 MULTIVARIATE ANALYSIS

To further test the relationship between innovativeness and SMP, we move to multivariate regression analysis using the following equation:

$$SMP_{ik} = \alpha \cdot I_i + \beta \cdot Size_i + \gamma \cdot Share_{ik} + \delta \cdot (I_i \cdot LRE_k) + \phi \cdot (I_i \cdot IBoom_k) + dummies + \varepsilon_{ik} \qquad (1)$$

The equation is estimated separately for manufacturing and services and regresses *SMP* for each sector in each country on variables characterising sectors and countries. Variable I denotes innovativeness, defined in manufacturing as number 1 for LT, 2 for MLT, 3 for MHT, and 4 for HT firms; in services as 1 for LKI, 2 for OKI, and 3 for HTKI firms. We expect α to have a positive sign. *Size* is defined as the median turnover of all firms in sector i across all 32 countries for which data are available in ORBIS. According to the view that larger firms are more likely to be listed (Pagano et al., 1998), we could expect sectors with larger firms to command higher *SMP*, and β to be positive. *Share* denotes the share of a sector i in country k in the total number of firms in country k in manufacturing and services respectively. The coefficient γ is expected to have a negative sign, as there may be significant first-mover advantages in going public. Keeping other incentives equal, the smaller a sector, the more visibility and reputation a firm from that sector may gain by being public (Maksimovic and Pichler, 2001). Companies from smaller sectors would also have fewer peers to compete with for the attention of diversification-seeking investors.

The next variable is an interaction term of innovativeness and legal and regulatory environment (LRE). LRE is defined as the mean of two World Bank governance indicators: regulatory quality and rule of law both averaged over the years 1996–2006 (Kaufmann et al., 2008). These indicators encompass such issues as the flexibility of regulation that promotes private sector development, the quality of contract enforcement, and the protection of property and shareholder rights, which are vital for the development of financial markets, and stock markets in particular (La Porta et al., 1997). In other words, LRE captures the conditions conducive to the development of the financial system as a whole, and capital markets in particular. I expect SMP to grow with innovativeness in countries that have high LRE, that is, the expected sign of δ is positive. This hypothesis was explained in section 9.2, and further motivated by the bivariate analysis, which indicated that the positive relationship between innovativeness and SMP is absent or weaker for transition economies, and is particularly strong for countries with highly developed stock markets such as the US and the UK.

The following variable is interaction between innovativeness and the magnitude of the Internet boom (IBoom), and deals with the impact of the latter on the relationship between innovativeness and SMP. In the absence of data on the time of going public, I calculate the percentage increase in the number of listed domestic companies by country between the end of 1997 and the end of 2000. Here I follow Ofek and Richardson (2002) who define the start of the boom in the US as January 1998 and the end as February 2000. Given that in Europe the boom lasted a bit longer, and there were few IPOs in the remainder of 2000 after the bubble burst, the increase in the number of listed domestic companies between 1997 and 2000 should be an appropriate measure of the magnitude of the boom in terms of primary stock markets. The variable makes sense only for non-transition economies, since numbers of IPOs in transition economies could have been affected considerably by privatisations through stock market, rather than the Internet boom. If ϕ turns out positive, this would mean that *SMP* grows with innovativeness in countries that experienced strong Internet boom. As services firms constituted an absolute majority of IPOs of the Internet boom, we could expect a positive relationship between SMP and the interaction variable particularly with regard to services.

Finally, country dummies are used in the equation, with the US as the reference category, in order to account for the lack of direct comparability between SMP rates across countries. In other words, the relationships between SMP and explanatory variables are estimated in relation to country averages. Data on *size* by sector are presented in Appendix 9.2; on LRE, and IBoom by country, as well as descriptive statistics on *SMP* and *Share* are presented in Appendix 9.3. Results were estimated for the samples of all 32 countries, as well as for 22 non-transition, and ten transition economies separately. As estimations for transition economies yielded no statistically significant results for any of the coefficients, the results presented in Table 9.3 are for non-transition countries only. The maximum possible number of observations is 506 (23 sectors x 22 countries) for manufacturing and 528 (24 x 22) for services. The actual numbers are lower, since some sectors in some countries have no large firms, and no SMP rate can be calculated for them.

The variable of innovativeness behaves as hypothesized, showing a strong positive relationship with SMP. The coefficient of innovativeness loses its positive sign only for manufacturing, when the impact of I on its own seems to be overwhelmed by the impact of the interaction of I with LRE. Supporting the results of bivariate analysis, the relationship between I and SMP appears more pronounced for services than for manufacturing, with coefficients for the former four times bigger in specifications (1) to (3). As we move from a less to a more innovative category of services, SMP increases on average by 0.21–0.24,

Table 9.3 *Regression of stock market participation on sector and country variables*

	(1)	(2)	(3)	(4)	(5)	(6)	(7)	(8)	(9)
Manufacturing									
I	0.050***	0.053***	0.053 ***		−0.565***		0.086***		−0.526***
Size		−0.002**	−0.002**	−0.002**	−0.002**	−0.002**	−0.002***	−0.002***	−0.002***
Share			−0.004	−0.004	−0.004	−0.008***	−0.008***	−0.008***	−0.008***
I*LRE				0.001***	0.007***			0.001***	0.007***
I*IBoom						0.000**	0.001	0.000*	0.000
N	422	422	422	422	422	410	410	410	410
F	19.3	18.9	18.2	18.4	18.6	11.3	11.8	12.0	12.1
R sq.	0.515	0.522	0.524	0.527	0.539	0.379	0.401	0.406	0.418
Services									
I	0.210***	0.238***	0.222***		0.044		0.325***		0.799*
Size		−0.006***	−0.006***	−0.006***	−0.006***	−0.004***	−0.005***	−0.004***	−0.005***
Share			−0.011*	−0.011**	−0.011**	−0.010***	−0.009***	−0.009***	−0.009***
I*LRE				0.002***	0.002			0.003***	−0.005
I*IBoom						0.004***	−0.002	−0.002	−0.003**
N	447	447	447	447	447	417	417	417	417
F	17.9	18.3	17.9	17.9	17.2	5.0	6.7	6.5	6.4
R sq.	0.482	0.498	0.505	0.505	0.505	0.209	0.271	0.268	0.273

Notes: The table reports results of an OLS regression for non-transition countries. Independent variables are presented in appendix 2 and 3. Country dummies have been included in each equation but are not reported. Coefficients are significant at 10 per cent (*), 5 per cent (**), and 1 per cent (***) level according to t-statistics. F is significant for each equation at the level of 0.1 per cent.

so for every four to five large firms existing in the underlying economy, one more is publicly traded. An equivalent step in manufacturing implies an increase by only one publicly traded company per twenty large firms.

The coefficients of *size* are negative and significant for both manufacturing and services, what contradicts our expectations. It appears that sectors made of smaller firms tend to have higher SMP than those made of larger firms. Within HTKI services, for example, post and telecoms firms are typically bigger than R&D or computer firms, but have much lower SMP. Within LKI services hotels and restaurants are typically half the size of firms in wholesale and commission trade, but have much higher SMP. Within LT manufacturing, tobacco firms are typically five times the size of firms manufacturing dressing but are much more poorly represented on stock markets. Petroleum firms have the largest median size of all MLT sectors combined with the lowest *SMP*. As expected the share of a sector is negatively related to SMP. Manufacturing of food products and wholesale and commission trade are the largest (in terms of the number of large firms) sector in manufacturing and services respectively, and have some of the lowest SMP rates. The relationships between SMP and both *size* and share should be subject of further investigation.

The relationship between SMP and the interaction of *I* and LRE is positive, as expected, with stronger results for manufacturing than services. In specifications (5) and (9) for manufacturing, the impact of the interaction appears so strong that it gives *I*, considered on its own, a significantly negative coefficient. This seems to confirm observations from bivariate analysis. As could be seen in Figure 9.1, the relationship between innovativeness and SMP is much stronger for the US than for Japan, the latter having a much lower LRE ranking. Within EU the relationship is strongest for the UK, and weakest for Italy, the latter representing a much less friendly environment for stock market development. Finally, there seems to be no support for the existence of a strong relationship between SMP and the interaction of *I* with IBoom. The significance of the obtained coefficient for manufacturing is low, and its sign for services changes between specifications.

To test the robustness of the positive relationship between the interaction of LRE and *I* and SMP, in estimations not reported in detail, LRE in the interaction variable was substituted with the following variables: the quality of accounting standards, ownership concentration of publicly traded firms, the ratio of pension fund assets to GDP, the ratio of private equity investments to GDP, stock market capitalisation divided by GDP, and GDP per capita. For services, none of the above had a significant coefficient. For manufacturing the coefficient for accounting standards, private equity, stock market capitalisation to GDP, and GDP pc were positive, and that for ownership concentration was negative and significant. These results suggest that as the level of stock market development, however measured, increases, the propensity of highly innovative manufacturing firms relative to less innovative firms to access stock markets increases.

The nature of data, and particularly the use of a crude sectoral classification to determine the level of innovativeness across firms, calls for caution in the interpretation of results. Bearing this in mind, the multivariate analysis appears to confirm the findings of the bivariate analysis that there is a relationship between innovativeness and SMP for manufacturing and services, but the relationship for the latter is more pronounced. Second, it suggests that the relationship holds for the population of firms from non-transition countries, but not for those from transition countries. Third, the support for the role of legal and regulatory environment in shaping the relationship between innovativeness and

SMP seems to be upheld, mainly with regard to manufacturing. Fourth, SMP increases with the falling share of a sector in the economy, which seems to support the thesis on the first mover advantages in listing. Finally, the evidence on the role of the Internet boom is weak and mixed, suggesting that the relationship between innovativeness and SMP documented in this chapter is not determined by the Internet boom and burst of 1998–2000.

9.7 CONCLUSIONS AND IMPLICATIONS

The objective of the chapter was to investigate the link between stock markets and innovation, by focusing on the relationship between firms' innovativeness and their participation in public stock markets. The relationship was conceptualised using literature on capital structure and going-public decision, combined with insights from economic geography and innovation studies. This led to the conclusion that there are no reasons, why a positive relationship between innovativeness and stock market participation, which is commonly expected and partly documented in manufacturing, should not apply to services, for which it has hardly been considered before, even though services firms account for the majority of listed companies. Empirically, the chapter analysed the relationship between innovativeness and stock market participation for both manufacturing and services, using sector-level data on 47 sectors in 32 countries.

The main empirical finding is the positive and significant relationship between innovativeness and stock market participation. Strictly speaking, in more innovative sectors there are more publicly traded firms in relation to the number of large firms than in less innovative sectors. While past research has paid little attention to the link between innovativeness and stock market participation in services, in this chapter the relationship was found to be more pronounced for services than for manufacturing. In manufacturing, while the most innovative firms have by far the highest levels of stock market participation, as we move to the middle and the bottom of the scale of innovativeness, the relationship peters out. This may serve as indirect evidence in favour of the pecking order theory of finance. As level of innovativeness, and the accompanying capital needs, increase firms may turn to banks in the first instance to satisfy them. Stock market financing becomes an attractive alternative only for the most innovative, and most capital and visibility-hungry firms.

Second, the institutional environment of stock markets matters for the relationship between innovation and stock markets. The positive relationship between innovativeness and stock market participation within the EU transition countries does not hold at all for manufacturing, and is weak and insignificant for services. This may be explained with the history of privatisations, focused on state-owned companies in traditional, not very innovative sectors, obscuring the relationship in question. A complementary explanation may be the relatively weak legal and regulatory environment of stock markets in transition economies. They may all still be at a stage, where even the most innovative firms use banks, without recourse to underdeveloped stock markets. The role of institutional environment is confirmed by the results for non-transition countries. The relationship between innovativeness and stock market participation is stronger in non-transition countries with high scores in terms of legal and regulatory environment.

Third, within multivariate analysis, stock market participation was regressed on the interaction of innovativeness with the magnitude of the Internet boom, but no significant relationship was found. This does not contradict the obvious fact that the boom brought to the stock markets a myriad of services firms developing and using new information technology including Internet. It does, nevertheless, support the view that the positive relationship between innovativeness and stock market participation holds in countries where the boom was less significant, and indicates that the relationship had existed before late 1990s. It does not mean that IT-related firms have always been the most stock market savvy firms. Take Dimson et al. (2002), for example, who show that in 1900 railway companies accounted for approx. 50 per cent of stock market capitalisation in the US and the UK. At present, the OECD/Eurostat classification puts railways in the category of the least innovative services firms. The forms of innovation, and the definition of innovativeness change over time by the very nature of innovation. Companies at the forefront of economic expansion have always tended to dominate stock markets. Just as railways attained the peak of their stock market significance in the late-nineteenth century, the Internet boom of 100 years later can be seen as a wave of IT-based growth entering the stock markets. In summary, future research into the links between innovation and stock markets needs to combine the economic logic with the understanding of institutional geography and its history.

By the virtue of applying a large international dataset and giving special consideration to services, this chapter contributes to the well-established literature on the relationship between finance and development (Levine, 2004; Wray et al., 2011). The study of the relationship between stock markets and innovation is central to this literature, and has crucial policy implications. At the same time, it is very contentious. Some argue that stock markets promote innovation in ways that cannot be attained by banking sectors (for example, Michelacci and Suarez, 2004). Others remain sceptical, claiming that while financial development matters for economic growth, the structure of financial markets (stock markets versus banks) does not (Merton and Bodie, 2004). Documenting a strong relationship between innovativeness and stock market participation in both manufacturing and services in a large international sample, underscores the possibility that financial structure may indeed matter for innovation. Of course, the direction of causality between innovativeness and stock market participation cannot be analysed with data available for one point in time only. One suggestion for further research would then be to relate the level of stock market development to the change in the number and structure of firms according to their innovativeness.

Another direction for further research is to analyse the relationship between innovation and stock markets below and above the level of countries. This chapter focused on countries as the easiest starting point for testing the relationship. Country-level analysis also facilitated the use of variables for potential factors affecting the relationship, such as legal and regulatory environment. It is difficult to obtain such data on subnational regions on a worldwide basis. It does not mean, however, that no subnational analysis is possible. One specific idea would be to test the variation of SMP within countries in relation to financial centres and innovation clusters, with the expectation that both encourage a strong use of stock markets by firms, and more capital market-based local and regional financial systems. There are also research opportunities at the supra-national level. Consider, for example, the co-evolution of Silicon Valley and the NASDAQ stock market or Chinese entrepreneurs who gain experience in Silicon Valley, set up a business in China in collaboration with US venture capital firms, and then float it with the assistance of US investment banks on the US stock market (Saxenian, 2007; Zhang, 2011). Further research into such financial and production networks could uncover fascinating relationships between finance, innovation and growth.

REFERENCES

Aghion, P., S. Bond, A. Klemm and I. Marinescu (2004), 'Technology and financial structure: are innovative firms different?', *Journal of the European Economic Association*, **2** (2–3), 277–88.

Allen, F. and D. Gale (1999), 'Diversity of opinion and financing of new technologies', *Journal of Financial Intermediation*, **8**, 68–89.

Asheim, B.T. and L. Coenen (2005), 'Knowledge bases and regional innovation systems: comparing Nordic clusters', *Research Policy*, **34**, 1173–1190.

Audretsch, D.B. and E.E. Lehmann (2004), 'Financing high-tech growth: the role of banks and venture capitalists', *Schmalenbach Business Review*, **56**, 340–357.

Bartoloni, E. (2013), 'Capital structure and innovation: causality and determinants', *Empirica*, **40** (1), 111–151.

Carlin, W. and C. Mayer (2003), 'Finance, investment, growth', *Journal of Financial Economics*, **69**, 191–226.

Chen, H., P. Gompers, A. Kovner and J. Lerner (2010), 'Buy local? The geography of venture capital', *Journal of Urban Economics*, **67** (1), 90–102.

Christopherson, S. (2002), 'Why do national labor market practices continue to diverge in the global economy? The "missing link" of investment rules', *Economic Geography*, **78** (1), 1–20.

Clark, Gordon L. and Dariusz Wójcik (2007), *The Geography of Finance: Corporate Governance in the Global Marketplace*, Oxford: Oxford University Press.

Cooke, P. (1991), 'Regional innovation systems: competitive regulation in the new Europe', *Geoforum*, **23** (3), 365–382.

Demirgüç-Kunt, A. and V. Maksimovic (2002), 'Funding growth in bank-based and market-based financial systems: evidence from firm-level data', *Journal of Financial Economics*, **65**, 337–363.

Dimson, Elroy, Paul Marsh and Mike Staunton (2002), *Triumph of the Optimists: 101 Years of Global Investment Returns*, Princeton, NJ: Princeton University Press.

Drejer, I. (2004), 'Identifying innovation in surveys of services: a Schumpeterian perspective', *Research Policy*, **33**, 551–562.

Eurostat (2006), 'High tech industries and knowledge based services', *Statistics in Focus: Science and Technology*, 13/2006.

Freeman, C. (1995), 'The national system of innovation in historical perspective', *Cambridge Journal of Economics*, **19**, 5–24.

Gallouj, F. and O. Weinstein (1997), 'Innovation in services', *Research Policy*, **26**, 537–556.

Hall, Peter A. and David Soskice (eds) (2001), *Varieties of Capitalism: The Institutional Foundations of Comparative Advantage*, Oxford: Oxford University Press.

Harris, M. and A. Raviv (1991), 'The theory of capital structure', *Journal of Finance*, **46**, 297–355.

Kaufmann, D., A. Kraay and M. Mastruzzi (2008), 'Governance matters VII: aggregate and individual governance indicators 1996–2007', Policy Research Working Paper, World Bank, June 2008.

Klagge B. and R. Martin (2005), 'Decentralized versus centralized financial systems: is there a case for local capital markets?', *Journal of Economic Geography*, **5**, 387–421.

La Porta, R., F. Lopez-de-Silanes, A. Shleifer and R.W. Vishny (1997), 'Legal determinants of external finance', *Journal of Finance*, **52** (3), 1131–1150.

Levine, R. (2004), 'Finance and growth: Theory and evidence', Working Paper. Retrieved on 20 March 2015 from www.ssrn.com.

Ljungqvist, A.P., T. Jenkinson and W.R. Wilhelm (2003), 'Global integration in primary equity markets: the role of US banks and US investors', *Review of Financial Studies*, **16** (1), 63–99.

Maksimovic, V. and P. Pichler (2001), 'Technological innovation and initial public offerings', *Review of Financial Studies*, **14** (2), 459–494.

Martin, R., P. Sunley and D. Turner (2002), 'Taking risks in regions: the geographical anatomy of Europe's emerging venture capital market', *Journal of Economic Geography*, **2** (2), 121–150.

Merton, R.C. and Z. Bodie (2004), 'The design of financial systems: towards a synthesis of function and structure', Working Paper 10620, National Bureau of Economic Research.

Michelacci, C. and J. Suarez (2004), 'Business creation and the stock market', *Review of Economic Studies*, **71**, 459–481.

Miles, Ian (2005), 'Innovation in services', in Jan Fagerberg, David C. Mowery and Richard R. Nelson (eds), *The Oxford Handbook of Innovation*, Oxford: Oxford University Press, pp. 433–458.

Morck, R. and M. Nakamura (1999), 'Banks and corporate control in Japan', *Journal of Finance*, **54**, 319–340.

Myers, S.C. and N.S. Majluf (1984), 'Corporate financing and investment decisions: when firms have information that investors do not have', *Journal of Financial Economics*, **13** (2), 187–221.

OECD (2006), 'Purchasing power parities', Report. Retrieved on 20 March 2015 from ww.oecd.org/std/ppp.

Ofek, E. and M. Richardson (2002), 'The valuation and market rationality of Internet stock prices', *Oxford Review of Economic Policy*, **18** (3), 265–287.

Oxera (2006), 'The cost of capital: an international comparison', Report. Retrieved on 20 March 2015 from www.cityoflondon.gov.uk/Corporation/business_city/research_statistics/research_publications.htm.

Pagano, M., F. Panetta and L. Zingales (1998), 'Why do companies go public? An empirical analysis', *Journal of Finance*, **53** (1), 27–64.

Pollard, J. (2003), 'Small firm finance and economic geography', *Journal of Economic Geography*, **3** (4), 429–452.

Posner, E. (2005), 'Sources of institutional change: the supranational origins of Europe's new stock markets', *World Politics*, **58**, 1–40.

Preissl, Brigitte (2000), 'Service innovation: what makes it different? Empirical evidence from Germany', in J. Stanley Metcalfe and Ian Miles (eds), *Innovation Systems in the Service Economy. Measurement and Case Study Analysis*, Boston: Kluwer, pp. 125–148.

Rajan, R.G. and L. Zingales (1998), 'Financial dependence and growth', *The American Economic Review*, **88**, 59–86.

Rajan, R.G. and L. Zingales (1995), 'What do we know about capital structure? Some evidence from international data', *Journal of Finance*, **50** (5), 1421–1460.

Ritter, J. and I. Welch (2002), 'A review of IPO activity, pricing, and allocations', *Journal of Finance*, **57**, 1795–1828.

Rodrigues, Maria J. (2009), *Europe, Globalization and the Lisbon Agenda*, Cheltenham, UK and Northampton, MA, USA: Edward Elgar Publishing.

Röell, A. (1996), 'The decision to go public: an overview', *European Economic Review*, **40**, 1071–1081.

Saxenian, AnnaLee (2007), *The New Argonauts: Regional Advantage in a Global Economy*, Cambridge, MA: Harvard University Press.

Schäfer, D., A. Werwatz and V. Zimmermann (2004), 'The determinants of debt and (private) equity financing: the case of young, innovative SMEs from Germany', *Industry and Innovation*, **11**, 225–248.

Schumpeter, Joseph A. (1934), *The Theory of Economic Development*, Cambridge, MA: Harvard University Press.

Shleifer, A. and R.W. Vishny (1997), 'A survey of corporate governance', *Journal of Finance*, **52** (2), 737–783.

Sirilli, G. and R. Evangelista (1998), 'Technological innovation in services and manufacturing: results from Italian surveys', *Research Policy*, **27**, 881–899.

Subrahmanyam, A. and S. Titman (1999), 'The going-public decision and the development of financial markets', *Journal of Finance*, **54** (3), 1045–1082.

Tadesse, S. (2002), 'Financial architecture and economic performance: international evidence', *Journal of Financial Intermediation*, **11**, 429–454.

Tether, B.S. (2003), 'The sources and aims of innovation in services: variety between and within sectors', *Economics of Innovation and New Technology*, **12** (6), 481–505.

Titman, S. (1984), 'The effects of capital structure on the firm's liquidation decision', *Journal of Financial Economics*, **13**, 137–151.

Tylecote, Andrew and Francesca Visintin (2007), *Corporate Governance, Finance and the Technological Advantage of Nations*, London: Routledge.

Verdier, Daniel (2002), *Moving Money: Banking and Finance in the Industrialized World*, Cambridge: Cambridge University Press.

Weinstein, D.E. and Y. Yafeh (1998), 'On the costs of a bank-centered financial system: evidence from the changing main bank relations in Japan', *Journal of Finance*, **53**, 635–672.

Wójcik, Dariusz (2011), *The Global Stock Market: Issuers, Investors, and Intermediaries in an Uneven World*, Oxford: Oxford University Press.

Wójcik, D. (2009), 'Financial centre bias in primary equity markets', *Cambridge Journal of Regions, Economy and Society*, **2** (2), 193–209.

Wójcik, D. and C. Burger (2010), 'Listing BRICs: stock issuers from Brazil, Russia, India, and China in New York, London, and Luxembourg', *Economic Geography*, **86** (3), 275–296.

World Bank (2014), Listed domestic companies, total. Retrieved on 24 November 2016 at http://data.worldbank.org/indicator/CM.MKT.LDOM.NO.

Wray, Felicity, Neil Marshall and Jane Pollard (2011), 'Finance and local and regional economic development', in Andy Pike, Andres Rodríguez-Pose and John Tomaney (eds), *Handbook of Local and Regional Development*, London and New York: Routledge, pp. 356–370.

Zhang, J. (2011), 'The spatial dynamics of globalizing venture capital in China', *Environment and Planning A*, **43**, 1562–1580.

APPENDIX 9.1 PUBLICLY TRADED COMPANIES BY COUNTRY AT THE END OF SEPTEMBER 2006

For each country the appendix gives the total number of publicly traded companies, and a description of stock market segments included. Firms in agriculture, mining, utilities, and construction are excluded. The data were obtained from ORBIS by the BvD, and their consistency was tested by comparison to data from the World Federation of Exchanges, the Federation of European Stock Exchanges, and the websites of individual stock exchanges. In addition to the domestic segments stated, for each country the numbers include companies that are publicly traded only on a foreign exchange (for example the Irish companies traded on the Alternative Investment Market (AIM) of the London Stock Exchange, but not traded on the Irish Stock Exchange).

Austria	102	Prime and Standard segment of the Wiener Börse
Belgium	142	Eurolist and Marché Libre of the Euronext Brussels
Bulgaria	316	All companies listed on the Official and Unofficial Market of the Bulgarian Stock Exchange
Cyprus	121	All companies listed on the Cyprus Stock Exchange
Czech Republic	21	All companies listed on the Prague Stock Exchange
Denmark	167	All companies listed on the OMX Copenhagen and the First North Exchange
Estonia	13	All companies listed on the OMX Tallin
Finland	131	All companies listed on OMX Helsinki
France	906	Eurolist, Alternext, and Marché Libre of the Euronext Paris
Germany	962	Official Market and the Open Market (Freiverkehr i.e. the Regulated Unofficial market) of the Deutsche Börse
Greece	293	Big cap, mid and small cap, special financial character, and under surveillance companies at the Athens Stock Exchange, but not suspended listed companies
Hungary	33	All companies with equities category A or B traded on the Budapest Stock Exchange
Iceland	20	All companies listed on the Iceland Stock Exchange
Ireland	92	The Official List and the Irish Enterprise Exchange (IEX) of the Irish Stock Exchange
Italy	256	All segments of the Borsa Italiana i.e. Blue Chip, Star, Standard, and Mercato Expandi
Latvia	32	All companies listed on the OMX Riga
Lithuania	36	All companies listed on the OMX Vilnius
Luxembourg	40	All companies listed on the Luxembourg Stock Exchange
Malta	7	All companies listed on the official list of the Malta Stock Exchange
Netherlands	217	All companies listed at Euronext Amsterdam
Norway	240	All segments of the Oslo Stock Exchange i.e. OBX, OB Match, OB Standard, and OB New
Poland	213	All companies listed on the Main and the Parallel Market of the Warsaw Stock Exchange
Portugal	65	All companies listed on the Euronext Lisbon
Romania	63	All companies listed on the Bucharest Stock Exchange
Slovakia	216	All companies with shares traded on the Bratislava Stock Exchange

Slovenia	76	All companies on the Official and Semi-Official Market of the Ljubljana Stock Exchange
Spain	164	Companies traded on the Continuous Market and the Floor of the Bolsas y Mercados Españoles (BME-X). SICAVs and SIMs are not included
Sweden	374	All companies listed on the OMX Stockholm, the Nordic Growth Market, and the First North Exchange
Switzerland	260	Main Market, Local Caps, Real Estate Companies and Investment Companies of the SWX Swiss Exchange
UK	2,250	All companies listed on the London Stock Exchange, including the AIM
Japan	3,609	All companies traded on the Tokyo Stock Exchange, the JASDAQ, the Nagoya SE, the Osaka Securities Exchange, the Sapporo Stock Exchange, and the OTC Japan
USA	8,280	The New York Stock Exchange, the NASDAQ National Market, the NASDAQ Bulletin Board, the American Stock Exchange, and other OTC markets

APPENDIX 9.2 NACE CODES, THE OECD/EUROSTAT CLASSIFICATION AND OTHER DATA BY SECTOR

The appendix presents economic sectors and their NACE Rev.1.1. codes, as used within the European Union, as well as their OECD/Eurostat classification based on R&D intensity (Eurostat, 2006). SMP reports the ratio of the number of publicly traded companies to the number of all large companies in a given sector, calculated on the basis of ORBIS database provided by the BvD. Size is the median turnover (€m) of all firms in a sector across all 32 countries for which data are available in ORBIS. The appendix presents only these sectors for which at least one company with turnover exceeding €50m is recorded in the sample countries. This implies that categories: private households (code P95), undifferentiated goods (P96), undifferentiated services (P97), and extra-territorial organisations (Q99) are omitted. Key for the names of OECD/Eurostat groups of activities can be found at Table 9.2.

NACE code	Sector name	SMP	Size	OECD/ Eurostat
DA15	Manufacture of food products and beverages	0.15	33	LT
DA16	Manufacture of tobacco products	0.22	90	
DB17	Manufacture of textiles	0.34	22	
DB18	Manufacture of wearing apparel	0.35	17	
DC19	Tanning and dressing of leather	0.36	20	
DD20	Manufacture of wood and cork	0.15	24	
DE21	Manufacture of pulp and paper	0.16	34	
DE22	Publishing and printing	0.20	27	
DF23	Manufacture of coke, refined petroleum products, and nuclear fuel	0.16	62	MLT

NACE code	Sector name	SMP	Size	OECD/ Eurostat
DG24	Manufacture of chemicals and chemical products	0.34	42	MHT
DH25	Manufacture of rubber and plastic products	0.16	27	MLT
DI26	Manufacture of other non-metallic mineral products	0.20	26	
DJ27	Manufacture of basic metals	0.22	41	
DJ28	Manufacture of metal products	0.16	24	
DK29	Manufacture of machinery	0.25	30	MHT
DL30	Manufacture of office machinery and computers	0.57	36	HT
DL31	Manufacture of electrical machinery	0.26	30	MHT
DL32	Manufacture of radio, television, and communication eq. and app.	0.65	36	HT
DL33	Manufacture of medical, precision, and optical instruments	0.58	29	
DM34	Manufacture of motor vehicles	0.16	47	MHT
DM35	Manufacture of other transport equipment	0.22	35	
DN36	Manufacture of furniture	0.28	24	LT
DN37	Recycling	0.02	25	
G50	Sale, maintenance, and repair of motor vehicles	0.03	27	LKI
G51	Wholesale and commission trade	0.06	29	
G52	Retail trade; repair of personal and household goods	0.15	27	
H55	Hotels and restaurants	0.31	13	
I60	Land transport; transport via pipelines	0.13	22	
I61	Water transport	0.21	31	OKI
I62	Air transport	0.18	59	
I63	Supporting transport activities; travel agencies	0.10	27	LKI
I64	Post and telecommunications	0.50	32	HTKI
J65	Financial intermediation, except insurance and pension funding	0.37	13	OKI
J66	Insurance and pension funding, except compulsory social security	0.06	104	
J67	Activities auxiliary to financial intermediation	0.80	21	
K70	Real estate activities	0.20	13	
K71	Renting of machinery and equipment	0.17	27	
K72	Computer and related activities	0.75	26	HTKI
K73	Research and development	0.54	20	
K74	Other business activities	0.15	23	OKI
L75	Public administration and defense; compulsory social security	0.04	15	LKI
M80	Education	0.44	19	OKI
N85	Health and social work	0.09	18	
O90	Sewage and refuse disposal	0.22	22	LKI
O91	Activities of membership organisations	0.02	18	
O92	Recreational, cultural and sporting activities	0.29	25	OKI
O93	Other service activities	0.20	18	LKI

APPENDIX 9.3 DATA BY COUNTRY AND DESCRIPTIVE STATISTICS FOR MULTIVARIATE ANALYSIS

Panel A presents data on legal and regulatory environment (*LRE*) and Internet boom (*IBoom*) by country. *LRE* is calculated as the average of the World Bank governance indicators of the rule of law, and regulatory quality for 1996, 1998, 2000, 2002, 2004, and 2006. In other words, it is the average of 12 figures (2 indicators at 6 points in time), where each figure represents the percentile rank of a country according to a given indicator in a given year. *IBoom* is calculated as the ratio of the number of IPOs by domestic firms between the start of 1998 and the end of 2000 to the number of domestic firms listed at the end of 1997, expressed in percentage terms.
Panel B shows descriptive statistics on *SMP* and the share of a sector in the total number of manufacturing or services (*Share*). *SMP* is calculated as the ratio of the number of publicly traded companies in a given sector of a given country to the number of all companies with turnover exceeding €50m, where €50m is adjusted to the price level of the country. *Share* stands for the share of a given sector in a given country in the total number of firms in manufacturing and services respectively.

Panel A

Country	LRE	IBoom
Austria	95.0	12.9
Belgium	89.0	30.4
Bulgaria	56.0	NA
Cyprus	82.5	NA
Czech Republic	77.0	NA
Denmark	97.5	10.1
Estonia	80.5	NA
Finland	97.5	46.8
France	85.5	56.1
Germany	93.0	51.4
Greece	75.5	53.3
Hungary	78.5	NA
Iceland	92.0	NA
Ireland	95.0	16.9
Italy	75.5	43.4
Japan	82.5	14.0
Latvia	70.0	NA
Lithuania	71.0	NA
Luxembourg	97.0	16.1
Malta	84.0	NA
Netherlands	96.5	24.1
Norway	94.0	26.0
Poland	69.0	NA
Portugal	85.0	12.8
Romania	51.0	NA
Slovakia	67.5	NA

Country	LRE	IBoom
Slovenia	79.0	NA
Spain	87.0	114.8
Sweden	94.5	50.2
Switzerland	97.0	26.4
UK	96.5	34.0
USA	93.5	26.7

Panel B

	No. of cases	Min	Max	Mean	Median	St.Deviation
Manufacturing in non-transition countries						
SMP	422	0	4	0.27	0.14	0.41
Share	422	0.03	66.67	5.21	3.29	6.76
Manufacturing in transition countries						
SMP	184	0	15	0.72	0.14	1.86
Share	184	0.26	39.53	5.43	3.77	5.95
Services in non-transition countries						
SMP	447	0	13	0.38	0.12	0.96
Share	162	0.01	42.77	4.92	2.16	7.35
Services in transition countries						
SMP	447	0	12	0.45	0.06	1.37
Share	162	0.11	58.11	6.17	2.43	10.29

10. The financialization and governance of infrastructure

Peter O'Brien and Andy Pike

10.1 INTRODUCTION

The financialization of infrastructure is a growing phenomenon, encompassing the privatization of its ownership and the financing and operation of infrastructure. But while financialization – defined as the growing influence of capital markets, intermediaries and processes in economic, social and political life (Pike and Pollard, 2010) – has provided an environment for private actors to widen and deepen their engagement with public infrastructure assets and systems, the governance of infrastructure financing continues to encompass an enduring and pivotal role for the state at the national and subnational scales (O'Neill, 2013; Strickland, 2014; Ashton et al., 2014). Geography remains an integral feature of the complex processes of infrastructure financialization and its governance evident in the different legal structures, regulatory regimes and operational requirements that exist at different scales across the world and mediate how the processes unfold (Allen and Pryke, 2013).

This chapter seeks to contribute towards the growing conceptual and policy interest in the financialization of urban infrastructure. Drawing upon empirical research examining the governance of local infrastructure funding and financing, the main arguments in the chapter are twofold. First, financialization is an uneven, negotiated and messy process rather than a monolithic juggernaut rolling-out in the same way everywhere in different geographical settings; and second, the role of the state at different scales has been reinforced rather than reduced in the context of the financialization of infrastructure because of its particular, specialized nature. Infrastructure has long been viewed as a public good or service, has high capital requirements, is often associated with statutory planning, property and land ownership issues that require consideration and sometimes negotiation to resolve, and in many major infrastructure schemes there can be substantial risks during the construction phase of a project that only governments are either able or willing to bear and underwrite the costs.

In exploring the uneven geographies of infrastructure financialization and governance, it is useful, given its varied forms, to define what is meant by infrastructure. Dawson (2013: 1) offers a broad definition based on 'the artefacts and processes of the inter-related systems that enable the movement of resources in order to provide the services that mediate (and ideally enhance) security, health, economic growth and quality of life at a range of scales'. Viewed through a financialization lens, infrastructure is also increasingly seen as an alternative asset class alongside bonds, currencies, equities and so forth in the financial investment landscapc (Inderst, 2010).

Governments at all levels are taking steps to bridge the infrastructure gap between what public and private sectors currently invest in infrastructure and what investment is needed to maintain, make more efficient or build new infrastructure to address interrelated and

BOX 10.1 THE FUNDING AND FINANCING OF INFRASTRUCTURE

Funding

- Relates to the revenue sources, often collected over a number of years, which are used to pay for the costs of the infrastructure.

Examples include:

- General purpose taxation.
- User charges.
- Other charges or fees dedicated to infrastructure.

Financing

- Turns funding (i.e. the revenue sources) into capital that can be used today to build or make improvements in infrastructure. Project financing requires the predictability of funding to be in place over the lifetime of the project. Once this is in place finance (e.g. debt or equity) can be raised.

Source: Adapted from WEF (2014).

complex economic, social and environmental opportunities and challenges, particularly in urban contexts (OECD, 2014). The global financial crisis, subsequent recession and sovereign debt crisis, has led to the introduction of new capital requirements for banks and insurance companies, but increased market uncertainty has also reduced the availability of 'traditional' infrastructure finance (OECD, 2014). This situation has pushed infrastructure funding and especially financing centre stage:

> [T]he world's insatiable demand for infrastructure will require the investment of trillions of dollars over the next four decades. While infrastructure poses many challenges for governments and developers, none are as urgent or as complex as the challenges of how to finance it. (KPMG, 2012: 2)

The result is that governments and private actors are exploring – and in some cases being compelled – to adopt (more) financialized practices and mechanisms in an attempt to leverage new capital. When considering the financialization of infrastructure, it is useful to differentiate between funding and financing (Box 10.1). The funding sources for infrastructure are relatively few, and tend to be derived from taxation, user fees or other charges. Financing refers to the financial models that organize how revenue (or funding) sources are turned into capital and incurs costs in its organization by various financial institutions.

10.2 FINANCIALIZING INFRASTRUCTURE

The financialization of infrastructure, which has a distinct geography concentrated on urban and suburban areas (Graham, 2000; Ottaviano, 2008), is a growing feature of an increasingly financialized global economy. It is possible to identify distinct periods in the funding and financing of infrastructure, particularly at the local scale, which have shaped and continue to be shaped by an evolving geographical political economy, technological changes and the recent growth and extension of urbanization. At various times, public and private sectors have played different roles, and have been pre-eminent. However, there has always been a long relationship between the state, in its different guises, and the private sector, through all the various stages of the infrastructure life-cycle. In recent years, this relationship has widened, deepened and been reworked as a condition of the recent emergence of infrastructure as a new asset class.

Changing Context

An apparent shift is taking place in the nature of infrastructure funding and financing and the respective roles of the public and private sectors:

> Traditionally, infrastructure investments have been financed with public funds. The public sector was the main actor in this field, given the typical nature of public goods and the positive externalities generated by such investments. However, public deficits, increased public debt to GDP ratios and, sometimes, the inability of the public sector to deliver efficient investment spending and misallocations of resources due to political interferences have led to a strong reduction of public capital committed to such investments. As a result of this increasing public capital shortage, in the past few years, the funding of infrastructure investment in projects characterised by high specificity, low re-deployable value and high intensity of capital has increasingly taken the form of project finance. (OECD, 2014: 6)

Historically, infrastructure has been regarded as 'public works' with the state playing a pivotal role in building and maintaining public goods and public institutions that often went beyond the capability and capacity of the private sector (O'Neill, 2013; Smith, 1976). However, O'Neill (2013) argues that infrastructure is neither a public or private good. Rather, infrastructure has its own particular characteristics and plays an integral role in creating and sustaining economic success and building functional urban landscapes. The state remains an inseparable partner in particular forms of infrastructure privatization (such as utilities) through regulatory frameworks and property relationships, resulting in a more complex, uncertain and nuanced interconnection between public and private sectors in infrastructure functions, purposes, funding, financing and governance (O'Neill, 2009). Qualitative perspectives on the changing role of the state provide a deeper appreciation and understanding of the evolving but enduring presence of the state in infrastructure planning, financing and delivery, and enable close interrogation of the complex interactions that take place between public and private actors bound-up in the financialization of infrastructure governance at different spatial scales (O'Neill, 1997).

It is possible to chart specific periods when the state has played a 'senior' role in the planning, funding, financing and delivery of infrastructure. Between 1850 and the 1960s, there was a general movement in western European and American cities towards the development of centralized, monopolized, standardized and equalized infrastructure systems (Graham and Marvin, 2001; Helm, 2013), driven by prevailing Keynesian models of national state policy and demand management (Martin and Sunley, 1997). This shift was framed in the context of widening individual access to services and employment, modernization and societal progress, and was accompanied by an expansion of national state power. However, Graham and Marvin (2001) suggest that cities were different to the general trend and that modernizing and dynamic urban places, which led on (re)developing local infrastructure, experienced periodic rupture, contradiction and inequality.

According to Sleeman (1953), public infrastructure utilities are not commodities to be traded in financial markets, but are assets deemed essential to civilized life. As a mechanism that bound the state together socially and spatially (Graham and Marvin, 2001), infrastructure planning and investment was primarily undertaken by national governments, funded, in part, through debt and financed by sovereign bond issuance. Private institutional investors purchased bonds through arms-length transactions but did not directly engage in investment selection (Hebb and Sharma, 2014). As the economic, societal and technological shifts of the late 1960s and early 1970s put pressure on standardized infrastructure monopolies, liberalization and privatization began to erode the notion of the 'modern infrastructure ideal' (Graham and Marvin, 2001). Whilst it is difficult to provide accurate statistics for total infrastructure investment in the UK and other OECD member states (HoC, 2013; Vammalle et al., 2014), using UK Public Sector Net Investment (PSNI) as a proxy, total investment in the UK fell to 1.4 per cent of GDP in 2012–13 (£22 billion), down from a peak of 7.1 per cent in 1968, and is forecast to remain at approximately 1.4 per cent of GDP until 2018–19 (Figure 10.1). Since the 1980s, government investment in the UK has tended to be lower than most other advanced economies (OECD, 2012).

In an increasingly privatized and liberalized environment, some states have been displacing responsibility for financing and providing infrastructure (Clark et al., 2009; Torrance, 2008). The privatization of infrastructure sought, in part, to address what was seen as an accounting 'problem', and took the form of either outright privatization or new public procurement, such as public–private partnerships (PPPs) (Helm, 2013). PPPs enabled states to provide public service assets at a lower life-cycle cost (Wall and Connolly, 2009), whilst keeping investment off the public sector balance sheet for governments anxious about levels of sovereign debt (Spackman, 2002). Others have identified privatization and

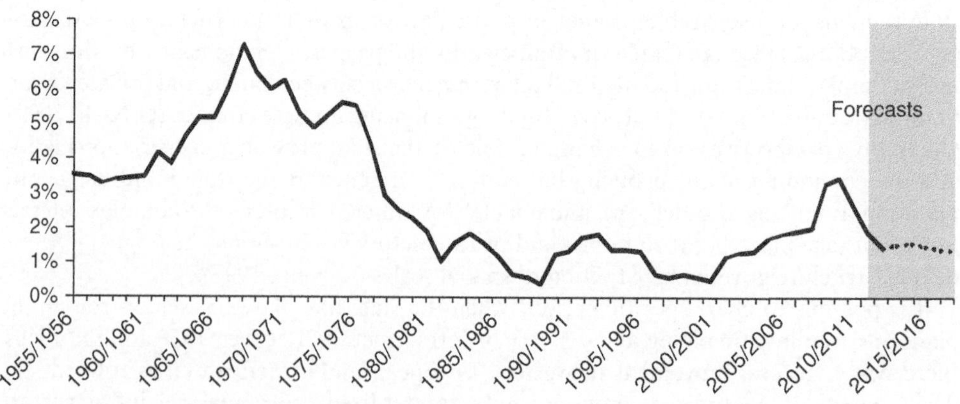

Source: House of Commons (HoC, 2013).

Figure 10.1 UK public sector net investment, % of GDP

liberalization as part of an ideological blueprint where budgetary pressures are employed as rationale for introducing smaller state settlements (Peck et al., 2013). But reflecting the continued role of the state in infrastructure funding, financing and governance, the public sector has been an integral actor in initiatives, such as PPPs, given its role as an initiator, guarantor and regulator of contracts and agreements (Martínez-Lacambra, 2013).

Private capital wielded by financial actors is discerning and increasingly seeks viable infrastructure projects that generate stable, long-term returns and presents the lowest risks within investment portfolios. This process is said to have contributed towards a splintering of the urban infrastructure system (Graham and Marvin, 2001). As infrastructure assets are bought and sold by national and international financial investors, these institutions have widened and deepened their engagement in the governance of infrastructure at the local and urban scale (Torrance, 2008). The territorial politics of city-regionalism has become increasingly nationally and internationally orchestrated (Jonas, 2013). The globalization of urban infrastructure is challenging local and regional actors to attract, embed and then extract sufficient value from private capital, so that revenues can be circulated locally for the benefit of urban landscapes and wider economic, social and environmental objectives. At a national level, global private and sovereign infrastructure investment has to navigate different regulatory regimes, which shape outcomes in different infrastructure markets. Global investment also impacts upon the ownership of strategic infrastructure assets, particularly with the growth of specialist infrastructure funds (OFT, 2010) and direct or co-investments in unlisted infrastructure companies (Inderst, 2011).

Whilst there has been an expansion of different types of PPP models (Hodge et al., 2010), particularly in the UK, the increased cost of capital has seen doubts emerge as to whether users and/or taxpayers are prepared to pay for future infrastructure investment (Helm, 2013). The private credit impasse has given rise to a new role for the state in infrastructure planning, financing and provision, particularly in underwriting investment costs (through state subsidies or guarantees) to close the gap between public and private costs of capital (Helm, 2013). Although interest rates are at a historic low, public indebtedness and politics have restricted the 'space' for governments to borrow directly from financial markets (Bailey, 2013). The irony is that the cost of private sector borrowing has always been, and will continue to be, higher than the cost for governments given the relative stability and strength of sovereign balance sheets (PwC, 2014). In specific infrastructure projects, such as Crossrail in London, where the risk to the private sector of sole financing is high given the size of the projects and the initial construction risks, the state is the critical actor in convening financial institutions and orchestrating funding, financing and governance.

Whilst the state retains a key role, national and local governments are looking to leverage additional private sector capital, using different mechanisms and practices, some of which – as we explain below – are increasingly financialized. Traditional private sector sources of infrastructure financing have been under stress since 2007–08, when fundraising fell, and the 'shadow banking sector' began to invest in infrastructure (Standard & Poor's, 2013). Fiscal constraints on government spending, coupled with new banking regulations designed to increase long-term capital investment, have focused attention on the search for an alternative asset class (OECD, 2013). Prior to the global financial crisis, institutional investors, such as banks and hedge funds, were the primary sources of long-term capital, with investment portfolios built around bonds and equities and an investment profile tied to long-term liabilities. During the last decade, there has been a shift in investment strategies, with investment in alternative assets classes, such as infrastructure, increasing (OECD 2013).

Financialization and Infrastructure as an Alternative Asset Class

In recent years, the nature and dynamism of contemporary capitalism has been shaped by debates about financialization, a process driven by the opening up of capital markets and national economies to global institutions and investors (Christopherson et al., 2013). The growing influence of capital markets, intermediaries and processes in economic and political life has seen finance bound up with and normalized through a range of everyday activities (Pike and Pollard, 2010). Financial intermediaries are now deeply ingrained within the economic geographies of individuals and communities (O'Neill, 2009). Economic geographers have called for greater attention to be paid to the impact of financialization on space and place (French et al., 2011), and for finance to be injected into conceptualizations of economic geography to provide a clear analytical framework for understanding the geography of financialized economies (Benner et al., 2011; Engelen and Faulconbridge, 2009; Lee et al., 2009; Martin, 2011, Wójcik et al., 2007). The ability of capital to create and monetize new asset classes is one of the most pervasive processes in an increasingly financialized economy (Leyshon and Thrift, 2007). Infrastructure is not immune from this development and is increasingly seen as an asset that provides long-term, income-oriented investment returns (Box 10.2) (Solomon, 2009).

BOX 10.2 THE KEY CHARACTERISTICS OF AN INFRASTRUCTURE ASSET

Infrastructure investments tend to have the following characteristics:

- Essential services for the majority of the population and businesses, either relating to physical flows in the real economy (i.e. transport, energy, broadband) or to social goods (education, healthcare);
- Government either as a direct client (via fixed term concession) or highly proximate to the transaction (through economic regulation);
- Long-term in nature (thus requiring long-term finance);
- Stable cash flows, particularly where payments are based on availability rather than demand (which is often beyond the control of a given project); charges may be linked fully or partially to inflation;
- Natural monopolies, either due to network characteristics/capital intensity or government policy; and
- Generally low technological risk.

These characteristics mean that infrastructure businesses can generally support high leverage on a long-term basis with returns that are less volatile than other investments. Some investors do not consider infrastructure a separate asset class; others consider it an alternative to (say) covered bonds or sovereign debt.

Source: Inderst (2010).

Reflecting the call for greater geographical appreciation of how financialization plays out across space, place and time, there is an uneven geography to institutional private infrastructure investment, with the drivers for, and mechanisms and practices of, finance varying between and within different countries. Amidst national and local variegations, pension and insurance institutional investors are searching for stable assets, across and within different territories that generate long-term, inflation protected returns (OECD, 2013; CBI, 2012; Llewellyn Consulting, 2013):

> [I]nstitutional investors are taking different approaches to infrastructure investing. Behind the separate investment allocation to infrastructure lies the investor decision to consider infrastructure as an asset class in its own right. Pension funds with a dedicated allocation have a target allocation to the asset class as part of the total portfolio and access the investment largely through unlisted equity instruments (infrastructure funds or direct investment). (OECD, 2013: 12)

The UK, Australia and Canada have been at the forefront of developing privately financed infrastructure investments (Weber and Alfen, 2010). Australian pension funds have pioneered institutional infrastructure investment since the early 1990s (Inderst and Croce, 2013). Canadian pension funds are home to some of the world's leading infrastructure investors, especially in 'direct investing' (*Economist*, 2012), where equity is purchased without third party fund management facilitation. The three largest Canadian pension funds, which have invested over US$31.3 billion of assets in infrastructure, possess the scale and internal institutional capacity to undertake direct investment (Preqin, 2012). In comparison, the UK led the development of new procurement models through PPPs and the private finance initiative (PFI), and has only recently begun to consider expanding pension fund investment in infrastructure (Smith Institute, 2012).

The diversity in how infrastructure is defined makes standardizing the sector as a uniform asset class problematic (Hebb and Sharma, 2014). Although governments, financial markets and investors regard infrastructure as an alternative asset class, Inderst (2011) suggests there is limited theory to support the proposition of infrastructure as a separate asset class because infrastructure is heterogeneous, with different physical pieces of infrastructure having different economic characteristics and risk and return profiles. Instead, Inderst (2011) believes that adopting a sector approach is more productive. This, however, challenges local strategies that are seeking to create efficiencies and strengthen inter-dependencies between different pieces of infrastructure through system-based models (iBUILD, 2015).

There are financial 'downsides' to infrastructure being defined as an asset class. In particular, there are high and often uncertain demands for capital, illiquid and high sunk costs, there can be a shortage of patient capital committed to returns over the long-term, and investors have to factor the transaction costs and uncertainties of engaging with different governments and regulatory institutions. There are also issues about how viable infrastructure projects are for pension and insurance funds, and whether claims about the scale, performance and potential of infrastructure investment are being over-stated. For example, there are legal restrictions on the amount of total assets that pension and insurance funds are able to invest in infrastructure (Reuters, 2013). Pension fund trustees are also required to exercise fiduciary duties and due diligence over individual investments.

The geography of finance suggests that, while financialized infrastructure investment presents an opportunity to link retirement savings to the development, success and physical vitality of cities, the underlying profit motive results in an uneven geography of investment, with improvements in some urban areas, while other places are left behind (Harvey, 2006, 2010). In a financialized climate, local actors are compelled to speculate, and embrace greater risk, in order to prosper in the global urban hierarchy. The extension and intensification of financialization in the wake of the global financial crisis (Lee et al., 2009) has compelled different places to develop innovative investment mechanisms and practices to stimulate and support urban growth and development. The result is the financialization of intensifying geographical disparities (Strickland, 2011), reinforcing the uneven geographies of finance and its impact on local and regional development prospects.

10.3 EMERGENT MODELS, PRACTICES AND GOVERNANCE IN INFRASTRUCTURE FUNDING AND FINANCING

As infrastructure becomes funded and financed in increasingly financialized ways, different practices, tools, instruments and governance arrangements are being modified or constructed in order to fund and finance local infrastructure. Local actors are determining, shaping and reshaping how financialization takes place on the ground, alongside other intermediary and capital market actors. Whilst the financialization of infrastructure is highly variegated (Strickland, 2014), a number of characteristics can nevertheless be identified between and amongst different investment practices (Box 10.3).

A variety of different infrastructure funding and financing practices have emerged in recent years, many of which blur and/or straddle traditional notions of public–private boundaries (Table 10.1). Although this analysis provides a temporal perspective, suggesting that some practices, such as grants, are 'tried and tested', whilst other models are

BOX 10.3 CHARACTERISTICS OF FINANCIALIZED INVESTMENT PRACTICES

1. The growing involvement of financial actors or intermediaries.
2. An increasing exposure of cities to – or dependence on – financial markets.
3. The increasing use of financial technologies, such as securitization.
4. A reliance on a framework of financial calculation to predict, model and speculate against the future.
5. A transformation in the purpose, function, values and objectives of government, which are being brought in line with those of financial actors and institutions.
6. An increase in public sector indebtedness and risk taking.
7. The transformation of infrastructure from a physical and productive component of the urban environment into a financial asset defined by risk and return.
8. The increasing control over infrastructure by yield-seeking surplus capital.
9. The transformation of infrastructure into an engine for economic growth and tax base expansion.
10. The highly geographically uneven ability to engage successfully – if at all – in funding or financing infrastructure.

Source: Strickland (2014).

Table 10.1 Infrastructure funding and financing practices

Temporality	Type	Examples
Established 'Tried and Tested'	Taxes and fees	Special assessments; User fees and tolls; Other taxes.
↓	Grants	Extensive range of grant programmes at multiple levels (e.g. federal national, province, state, supranational).
	Debt finance	General obligation bonds; Revenue bonds; Conduit bonds; National Loans Funds (e.g. PWLB).
	Tax incentives	New market/historic/housing tax credits; Tax credit bonds; Property tax relief; Enterprise Zones.
	Developer fees	Impact fees; Infrastructure levies.
	Platforms for institutional investors	Pension and Insurance infrastructure platforms; State infrastructure banks; Regional infrastructure companies; Real estate investment trusts; Sovereign Wealth Funds.
	Value capture mechanisms	Tax increment financing; Special assessment districts; Sales tax financing; Infrastructure financing districts; Community facilities districts; Accelerated development zones.
	Public–private partnerships	Private finance initiative; Build–(own)–operate–(transfer); Build–lease–transfer; Design–build–operate–transfer.
	Asset leverage and leasing mechanisms	Asset leasing; Institutional lease model; Local asset-backed vehicles.
Newer 'Innovative'	Revolving infrastructure funds	Infrastructure trusts; Earnback and Gainshare.

Source: Adapted from Strickland (2014).

'new and innovative', it is problematic to suggest that there has been a fundamental break between different types of practice and that the current age is one dominated exclusively by innovative and more or less financialized arrangements. Different countries and cities are deploying similar or slightly different practices (some of which are hybridized) to identify and lever in investment, and, with financial pressures and fiscal stress mounting, no options are seemingly off the table.

There are though, some subtle differences between traditional and emergent approaches to governing infrastructure funding and financing. Variations are evident when comparing the specific dimensions to individual approaches (Table 10.2). In considering the rationales for investment, for example, there has been a noticeable shift amongst policymakers towards more direct and often greater economic returns on capital and infrastructure investment. Furthermore, there is a tendency for actors seeking investment and investors themselves to favour longer time-scales for investment, and projects or programmes that can create scale and involve larger schemes in terms of size and scope. The geographies and governance of emergent approaches are also broader, encompassing multiple local

Table 10.2 Traditional and emergent approaches to governing infrastructure funding and financing

Dimension	Traditional approaches	Emergent approaches
Rationale(s)	Economic efficiency (and social equity) Market failure Managing urban (population) decline	Unlocking economic potential (e.g. GVA, employment) Releasing uplift in land and property values Market failure Managing urban (population) growth
Focus	Individual infrastructure items (e.g. bridges, rail lines, roads)	Infrastructure systems and services, interdependencies (e.g. connectivity, district heating, telecommunications) and resilience
Timescale	Short(er) 5–10 years	Long(er) to 25–30 years
Geography	Local authority administrative area	Functional Economic Area/Travel to Work Area city-region, multiple local authority areas
Scale	Targeted	Encompassing
Lead	Public sector	Public and/or private sectors (including international)
Organization	Projects	Packages of projects (or programmes)
Funding	Grant-based (e.g. from taxes, fees and levies)	Investment-led (e.g. from borrowing, grant, revenue streams, existing assets)
Financing	Established and tried and tested mechanisms and practices (e.g. bonds, borrowing and PPPs)	Innovative mechanisms and practices (e.g. value capture, asset leverage and leasing, revolving funds)
Process	Formula-driven allocation, closed	Negotiated, open
Governance	Single LA-based	Multiple LA-based (e.g. Combined Authorities, Joint Committees and Metropolitan Mayoralties)
Management and delivery	Single LA-based, arms-length agencies and bodies	Multiple LA-based, joint ventures and new vehicles

Source: Authors' research.

areas, in an attempt to provide the basis for pooling local resources, mitigating risk and co-ordinating planning and collaboration across functional economic areas. There is also growing recognition of the inter-dependency of infrastructure assets, systems and services in the sense of how specific infrastructure, such as bridges and roads, when planned and delivered in an integrated manner, can shape physical development, city environments and economic growth.

Drilling down further into financialized infrastructure funding and financing practices using UK and US examples, Strickland (2014) has identified a series of mechanisms that lie beneath individual practices and which are both increasingly shaped and, in turn, insulated from financialization (Table 10.3). In this analysis, it is possible to distinguish between those practices and mechanisms, such as grants and taxes, which feature limited, if any, financial engineering, and others, such as tax increment financing (TIF) and PPPs,

Table 10.3 Characteristics of financialized investment practices

Practice	Key Mechanisms	Financialized Characteristics	Insulation from Financialization
Grants/taxes	Grant funding (often from higher-tier government)	In UK, capital grants dependent on macroeconomic conditions. In US, states and Federal governments issue bonds, which determine available funds	Limited financial engineering Funds linked to macroeconomic performance and political choices
General Obligation Bonds (State and Local)	Issued by jurisdiction (US) that can levy a tax rate on real/personal property	Direct connection of taxpayers to financial markets Municipalities vulnerable to fluctuations in financial markets	Simple and transparent Democratic process
Revenue Bonds	Issued against specific revenue stream No recourse to general tax base Often requires ballot	Financialized engineering and creation of special purpose vehicles Policies designed to increase revenue	Cost of debt and ability to repay linked to characteristic and performance of asset
State Infrastructure Banks	Operates like a commercial bank Loans or credit enhancements Capitalized by state funds Recycle investments	State acts as financial intermediary Investors seek returns that generate profits that can be reinvested	Can help to overcome uneven geography of bank finance, and will determine location of investments
Tax Increment Financing (TIF)	In US, located in blighted area Bonds issued against future tax revenue, which incremental increases are used to service debt In UK, operates as New Development Zones or Enterprise Zones	Public sector speculation and indebtedness Dependent on asset value Public sector assumes risk Speculative (and difficult) calculation of Business Rates Borrowing against Business Rates requires appreciation of rental values and not asset value – which can leave local authorities with funding gaps and debt	Risk can be mitigated by pay as you go approach Risk mitigation through stress testing and efficient debt service profile
Asset sales	Sale or lease of assets Infrastructure maintained or operated by the private sector	Facilitates privatization, segmentation and unbundling and financialization of infrastructure	Up-front cash for public sector and avoids debt

Table 10.3 (continued)

Practice	Key Mechanisms	Financialized Characteristics	Insulation from Financialization
	Revenues from sales defined as capital receipts	Transformation from public good to revenue generation Shareholder value over public good Local government forgoes right to access revenue streams	
Self-financing expenditure	Unsupported or self-financing by local authorities borrowing (in the UK through the Public Works Loans Board – an agent of the HM Treasury, and part of the Debt Management Office (DMO))	Cost of debt is fixed to price of UK government gilts PWLB rate set by the DMO	Debt available on demand Quicker and cheaper than bonds UK Prudential Code governs PWLB borrowing by local authorities
Private Financing	Private financing or the mobilization of private finance Full divesture by public sector	Encourages the unbundling, segmentation and privatization of infrastructure: creates the conditions for privatization	Substitute for public sector investment and indebtedness
Public–Private Partnership (PPP)	Credit guarantee financing and monetization of public assets Special Purpose Vehicles created to lever in finance In US, PPPs require legislation to enable procurement and ability to issue toll revenue bonds	Explicit use of securitization Risk/transfer to private sector Uneven geography	Nominally prevents public sector indebtedness Enables public sector investment in infrastructure
Local Asset Backed Vehicle (LABV)	Form of PPP Public sector contributes land and private sector cash into LABV Assets act as collateral against future borrowing	Securitization is a key process in LABV Asset placed off balance sheet Future rental income used to leverage debt into redevelopment	Public sector already owns land Risk transferred to LABV Future asset value appreciation not essential

Table 10.3 (continued)

Practice	Key Mechanisms	Financialized Characteristics	Insulation from Financialization
European Investment Bank	Direct project loans of up to 50% of project cost Structured finance Equity/financial investment Strict compliance with EU strategic objectives	Creditors seek to generate returns on infrastructure investment EIB uses vehicles such as private investment funds Financial engineering (EIB Project Bonds) Market conditions determine availability and cost of debt	Match funding needed

Source: Adapted from Strickland (2014).

which contain explicit financialized characteristics predicated on more risky and speculative forms of development and the securitization of assets. Significantly, whether defined as traditional or emergent, all the practices have written through them deeply engrained and uneven geographies.

10.4 UNEVEN GEOGRAPHIES OF INFRASTRUCTURE FINANCIALIZATION AND GOVERNANCE

Different infrastructure funding and financing mechanisms and practices are in operation across and within different countries and cities, shaping the uneven landscape of infrastructure financialization and governance (O'Brien and Pike, 2014). Whilst there is a growing literature on the economic and governance geographies of infrastructure (see, for example, Hall and Jonas, 2014; Haughton and McManus, 2012; O'Neill, 2009, 2013; Ward, 2012; Weber, 2010), further work is required to map and explain this emergent, dynamic and fast changing field. Empirical research can strengthen conceptual understanding of the geographic significance of particular financial models, as actors in different places intensify their search for funding and financing to support infrastructure development. The following section outlines the uneven nature of these evolving arrangements, drawing upon three illustrative examples from the United Kingdom, United States and Australia where existing and new local and urban funding, financing and governance practices are evident. The analysis suggests that it is a misreading and simplistic interpretation to conclude that there has been a linear shift or transition in developed and developing countries from state to market-led approaches in the financing of infrastructure (see Table 10.4), which is at odds with the view of actors, such as the World Bank: 'Over the last 20 years, private participation in infrastructure (PPI) has emerged to address infrastructure finance and efficiency shortfalls. Private provision is now the norm in the sub-sectors of telecommunications, ports and power generation, and a growing share of land transport infrastructure' (World Bank, 2012: 5).

Table 10.4 Illustrative case study examples of uneven geographies of infrastructure funding and financing

Approach	London	UK Cities	US	Australia
1. State	Corporatist (London Underground, buses). Nationalization and standardization between 1930s and 1960s. TfL issued bonds for Crossrail finance. Austerity reducing state and city region investment.	Municipal funding and financing of infrastructure systems – led by local authorities. Nationalization and standardization between 1930s and 1960s. Possible LA Municipal Bond Agency. Austerity reducing state and local investment.	Road and water infrastructure supplied by state or local governments that raise revenues and spend on public goods or overcoming market failure. Majority of publicly owned infrastructure funded by tax revenues via bonds. Austerity and indebtedness reducing state and city investment.	Major infrastructure assets (e.g. energy) funded by governments. Many assets and systems still owned and operated by public sector. Infrastructure bonds introduced in 1990s but abandoned. Federal and state governments reluctant to borrow for direct investment in infrastructure. Austerity reducing state and local government investment.
2. Market-led	Large-scale privatization of infrastructure in 1980s and 1990s. Complex PPP and Metronet in late 1990s, but collapse of Metronet in 2010. Transport for London bought out the tube lines in the private consortia.	Expansion of PPPs and PFIs, particularly in soft infrastructure assets and systems, such as schools, waste, social and leisure services.	Most US households rely on privately-owned communications, energy and transport infrastructure. Emergent federal government interest in PPPs, which has been limited part of US infrastructure investment to date.	Privatization increased over the past 25 years. Australian variant of PPP introduced. Some notable failures such as Sydney Cross City Tunnel. Macquarie Infrastructure Model led the mobilization and securitization of earnings from once-state-owned infrastructure utilities in Australia, UK and Canada. Federal Government new infrastructure asset recycling programme. Further privatization. Increased focus on user charging.

Table 10.4 (continued)

Approach	London	UK Cities	US	Australia
3. Hybrid (state and financialized)	State or public sector guarantees for private capital (e.g. Crossrail, NL Extension). Infrastructure funds (RIFs) (e.g. London Energy Efficiency Fund). Pension and insurance fund investment (debt and equity). Sovereign Wealth Fund. Crossrail 2 funding options. TfL as a property developer to fund transport infrastructure. Fiscal decentralization.	'Business-type' City Deals. Investment-led approach. RIFs, Earn-backs, TIFs. Pension and insurance fund investment (debt and equity). Sovereign Wealth Funds. Regeneration Investment Organization seeking FDI in UK infrastructure. Fiscal decentralization.	TIFs. Mix of bonds and PPPs – e.g. Qualified Public Infrastructure Bonds as first type of bonds available for PPPs.	Interest in UK City Deals Link to proposal for Federal Government to shift from grants to incentivized models – i.e. something for something or deal-making approach. Local government seeking to introduce more value capture mechanisms. Pension and insurance fund investment (debt and equity). Sovereign wealth investment through state investment vehicles, such as Queensland Investment Co. Government to provide minimum revenue guarantees for a defined period. Call for great fiscal decentralization to states and cities.

Source: Authors' research.

The reality is rather more messy, partial and uneven. Recently, there has been a growth of mixed ownership arrangements and different infrastructure funding and financing practices and mechanisms, as government and private actors attempt to address the challenges of reduced or constrained public and private funding and finance. These practices and mechanisms are either exclusive to the state, or are market-led, whilst others are deeply financialized and hybrid in nature, in which the state *and* private capital are intertwined across different elements of the infrastructure life-cycle, from design, build and finance through to operation and maintenance (iBUILD, 2015).

United Kingdom

In the nineteenth century and early part of the twentieth century, the funding, financing and operation of UK municipal infrastructure were led by the local state directly (Helm, 2013). This process started to be rolled-back following nationalization and standardization between 1930s and the 1960s, and was further eroded by infrastructure privatization in the 1980s (Whitfield, 2010). Since the global financial crisis, local authorities have sought and been encouraged to strengthen their involvement in the planning, funding and financing of infrastructure. In the highly centralized government and governance system in the UK, there remains a limited place for local actors, however, in the implementation of the UK national infrastructure plan (RSA, 2014).

Typically, UK local authority investment in capital projects has been financed through grants and self-financing prudential borrowing from the public works loans board (PWLB). Faced with a recent reduction in central government grants, a tight squeeze on their revenue streams as part of national fiscal consolidation and a highly centralized system controlling their ability to tax and spend, but coupled with an increase in the cost of PWLB loans, local authorities have been considering turning to the bond markets for infrastructure finance. Aside from the bonds that were issued in 2012 by Transport for London (TfL) to finance the London Crossrail project, few UK local authorities have ventured into the bond markets. Bond issuance requires an entity to possess a credit rating, which can cost up to £50,000 to acquire, and demands expertise in packaging up bonds at a scale, risk and maturity profile attractive to investors. Drawing upon the experience of Sweden, the local government associations of England and Wales have undertaken feasibility studies to develop a new municipal bond agency in response to the increased cost of PWLB loans, and to co-ordinate and support smaller local authority financial engagement and interaction with international capital markets (LGA, 2012).

Adopting a market and increasingly investment-led approach, local authorities and other public bodies have, at times, been compelled by national governments to embrace PPPs and PFIs in order to finance infrastructure investment. The move towards PPPs and PFIs, which can be positioned within the broader, historical process of urban entrepreneurialism (Harvey, 1989; Peck, 2014a), has sought to take capital spending off government balance sheet, but has proved controversial in parts of the health, local government and education sectors because of inefficient private sector delivery and operation, and increasing public sector liabilities (Pollock, 2005; Shaoul, 2007). In the late 1990s, the Labour government argued that a new PPP model would upgrade and deliver maintenance of a major tranche of the London Underground system. The collapse of the Metronet PPP in 2010, due to severe financial problems, has been well-documented (HoC, 2013). In 2007, Metronet – a consortium of Adtranz, WS Atkins, Balfour Beatty, Seeboard and Thames Water – faced a major overspend and was unable to access bank lending facilities. In 2008, the PPP entered administration, and in 2010, TfL with UK government cash took over the PPP from the private consortia. What began as a private and market-led solution to a critical infrastructure asset need ultimately ended up being bailed-out and salvaged by the state. Continued concerns, particularly in relation to value for money, led the UK Coalition government to review PFI and PPPs in 2010, resulting in the creation of a 'new' PF2 scheme in 2013 (HMT, 2012). In a reflection of the devolved nature of UK territorial public policy, the Scottish government has been pursuing a 'non-profit distributing' variant of PFI in Scotland (SFT, 2015), separate to the UK government.

Since 1999, 'city-region-wide' governance has shaped infrastructure planning and investment in London, with the Greater London Authority (including the Mayor) adopting a visible role in overseeing transport infrastructure (such as London Underground and buses) through the co-ordinating role of TfL (Tomaney, 2014). London has stood alone amongst global cities in not having an infrastructure investment plan. Following a recommendation from the London Finance Commission (LFC) (2013), a new London infrastructure investment plan will identify and prioritize projects, and help leverage public and private funding and financing (GLA, 2014). The plan is designed to help London manage the implications of a rising population (London's population in January 2015 reached 8.615 million – the highest in its history – and is set to grow to 10 million by 2030), economic growth (London constitutes 20 per cent of total UK GDP) and environmental challenges, such as congestion, flood mitigation and energy security and sustainability. A funding gap of £135 billion has been calculated between current resources and the new investment needed in London's housing and transport infrastructure (Arup, 2014). Multiple actors have become embroiled in the debate, often reframing London's infrastructure needs as a 'national' imperative given its economic weight and importance in the UK economy (GLA, 2014; London First, 2010). The identified funding gap is giving succour to arguments for greater fiscal autonomy for London (LFC, 2013).

In addressing broader infrastructure needs, governance actors in London and other UK cities have had to confront the legacies of privatization of energy, communications and water industries in the 1980s and 1990s, which heralded a further detachment of local democratic accountability from the governance and operation of urban infrastructure (Martin, 1999). Privatization resulted in the creation of the regulated asset-based model (RAB) in which a regulator sets a framework for privatized investment that is 'offset' by user charges (Helm, 2013). The private sector will continue to have a major role in future UK infrastructure financing, with 64 per cent of investment in economic infrastructure up to 2020 expected to be wholly owned and financed by the private sector (HoC, 2013). However, state will remain active in the funding, financing, ownership, regulation and governance of national and local infrastructure provision in the UK (Helm, 2013), and, in particular, the emergent ways in which the state underwrites private sector investment.

Different places are engaged in various practices and mechanisms of infrastructure funding and financing, with some approaches increasingly of a hybrid nature, involving a continued role for the state but one that is to greater or lesser degrees financialized. In London, for example, large-scale infrastructure projects, such as Crossrail or the Northern Line Underground extension to Battersea, have required direct state investment or sovereign guarantees to underpin private capital financing. Crossrail, currently the largest construction project in Europe costing an estimated £24 billion, will not be funded entirely by the private sector because of the scale and risks involved in the project. Consequently, the national and local state is providing significant grant funding, as well as undertaking borrowing against hypothecated taxation. The UK government has also provided a standby refinancing facility worth £750 million to enable TfL and the GLA to borrow up to £1 billion to meet the cost of the Northern Line extension.

Reflecting the investment-led approach identified above (Table 10.4), there is growing evidence of state funding for infrastructure, deployed through grants, being articulated, represented and distributed in the guise of financialized investment funds. Here, investors provide resources in the form of revolving infrastructure funds (RIF), made via loan or equity. Examples include the London energy efficiency fund and the growing places fund (GPF), which forms part of a national (England-wide) infrastructure and regeneration funding programme that is designed to provide debt or equity funding for local projects that have stalled due to credit difficulties, but can demonstrate economic impact and provide an early return on investment.

As a city prominent in the international urban hierarchy, stable political economy and buoyant commercial and residential property markets, London is an appealing proposition for overseas investors (London First, 2013). The UK government is keen to attract pension and insurance fund investment, alongside sovereign wealth fund financial backing, for infrastructure projects in London and other UK cities (HMT, 2013; HMT/UKTI, 2014). Pooling resources in the pursuit of scale, London and Greater Manchester local authority pension schemes have created a joint pension fund of over £500 million, and a £10 billion strategic partnership has been created by the pension authorities in London and Lancashire. The mayor of London, Boris Johnson, has called for UK local authority pension schemes to aggregate by merger to match the largest global pension funds. There are nearly 2,500 pension funds in the UK, but only 190 funds have assets of over £1 billion (Delacroce et al., 2011).

Reaching out beyond national government grants toward wider sources of international finance has been an emergent practice of UK cities. The Greater Manchester local authority pension scheme has made a significant investment in housing development in Manchester, whilst other local pension schemes are considering investments in transport projects that offer stable, long-term returns. Sovereign capital (in particular Chinese and Emirati) has also been coveted, with Birmingham City Council publishing a prospectus, and Manchester City Council announcing a £1 billion finance deal with Abu Dhabi United Group to build 6,000 new homes in east Manchester (Manchester City Council, 2014). In 2013, two UK government agencies – UK Trade and Investment and Infrastructure UK – established the Regeneration Investment Organization to attract foreign investment into UK infrastructure (HMT/UKTI, 2014). Sovereign wealth funds have viewed London real estate as a major opportunity to capture value and generate high returns (WEF, 2014). The challenge for national and local state actors in the UK is to ensure that infrastructure is as attractive a proposition to international investors as property, or at least link infrastructure projects to real estate investment. Figure 10.2 compares Chinese investment in London real estate, between 2005 and 2014, with investment in UK infrastructure over the same period. The Malaysian government, for example, is a major investor in the Northern Line London Underground extension project in Battersea, focusing primarily around real estate development. The River Thames tideway tunnel in London is being partly designed, constructed and financed by a new regulated utility company, Thames Tideway Tunnel Ltd, which is seeking up-front private capital from pension funds and sovereign wealth funds. The project will be funded entirely through consumer charges, but the financing will be underpinned by a UK government support package designed to help mitigate construction risk (GLA, 2014). Other hybrid financialized initiatives and institutions include the emergence of TfL as a property developer to fund £1 billion of transport improvements in London (Allen, 2015).

The National Audit Office (NAO, 2015a) – a national public spending and accountancy

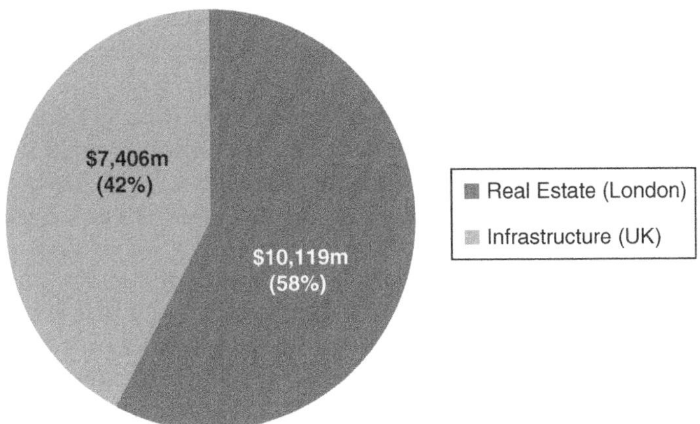

Source: Authors' research adapted from CEBR/Pinsent Masons (2014).

Figure 10.2 Chinese foreign direct investment in the UK (2005–14)

auditor – has been critical of the UK state guarantee scheme for infrastructure projects, which provides a sovereign-backed guarantee to encourage private lending. So far, the scheme has supported £1.7 billion of investments in seven projects. The UK treasury issues an unconditional and irrecoverable guarantee to lenders that scheduled interest and principle payments will be paid in full, irrespective of performance, thus transferring project and financing risk to the government in return for a fee. The NAO has questioned the value of the scheme compared to direct government lending, and the fact the arrangement provides stronger 'protection' for private lenders than any other comparable scheme in Europe.

Since 2010, the development of 'city deals', with a specific focus on infrastructure funding and financing mechanisms, couched within regional and urban governance reforms, has signified a further illustration of hybrid UK financialized infrastructure investment. Twenty eight city deals have been agreed between local authorities and UK government, including one deal between Glasgow city region, the Scottish government and UK government. City deals involve the largest cities in England and Scotland (not including London) preparing growth strategies, and identifying practical measures that national government could introduce to help deliver the plans. Early analysis suggests that the city deals are resulting in cities being compelled into finding new sources of private (including international) capital, developing innovative business models for infrastructure provision and establishing new institutional and governance arrangements (O'Brien and Pike, 2015). The efforts to devise new funding and financing practices and mechanisms for local infrastructure are situated within the context of the UK's highly centralized state, and the current wave of austerity. To what extent cities have been able to introduce speculative funding and financing arrangements remains questionable. The development of tax increment financing (TIF) projects in three city deals (Newcastle, Sheffield and Nottingham), coupled with TIF-type arrangements across enterprise zones, is predicted on local authorities engaging in securitization, and investing in up-front infrastructure (often through borrowing) to unlock development that forecasts suggest will generate additional business tax income – a proportion of which would then be retained by local authorities to repay initial borrowing. This variant of TIF is smaller and less comprehensive than TIF models in the United States, and is tightly controlled by the UK government.

Financialized models are a feature of the city deals and the broader local growth agenda in England. In 2012, the Greater Manchester city region agreed, as part of its city deal, an earn-back 'invest to earn' mechanism. Under this scheme, Greater Manchester would invest in infrastructure – mainly transport – and evaluate the impact of investments on economic growth with a view to assessing what uplift (if any) had accrued above and beyond an initial baseline. Growth is then measured in terms of additional tax take, which Greater Manchester would receive a share of to cover the cost of initial investments and to use as funding for new infrastructure. This mechanism represents an attempt to shift the incentive structure for local authorities from focusing on increasing the potential business rate tax base by encouraging investment and provision of commercial property, irrespective of likely demand, towards growing economic output and employment.

United States

Infrastructure in the United States has traditionally been supplied by federal, state and local governments because of their unique abilities to raise capital in a decentralized federal governance system. The majority of publicly owned infrastructure is funded by tax revenues, and the public sector continues to play an integral and active role in the planning, funding, financing and operation of infrastructure. Like most urban areas across the world, many US cities are looking to upgrade infrastructure to support growth and development (Manyika et al., 2012). President Obama's 2013 federal budget proposed to renew America's infrastructure using $50 billion of up-front investment connected to a $476 billion six-year transport programme, alongside the creation of a National Infrastructure Bank (US Treasury, 2014). 'Build America bonds' (BABs) were also introduced following the global financial crisis in order to attract private capital for infrastructure projects, and to stimulate economic recovery. The bonds invested over $180 billion in new infrastructure. Approximately half of all issuances (47 per cent) were for projects in the 100 largest metropolitan areas, whereas 8 per cent were in metros outside the 100 largest cities and city regions, and 5 per cent were outside 'metropolitan America'. The remaining 40 per cent were issued by the states, with the largest issuances in California, Illinois, New York and Texas (Puentes et al., 2013).

For over two hundred years, state and federal governments have issued bonds to finance infrastructure (US Treasury, 2014), a process that has extended the power and reach of financial markets into the urban environment as governments issued and purchased large amounts of debt. Municipal bond issuance has steadily declined since 2005, although total municipal debt stands at $3.7 trillion (SEC, 2012). Fiscal crisis and self-imposed debt caps have restricted the ability of states and local government to issue new bonds, whilst the Obama administration has toyed with changing the system of tax-exemptions on bonds.

Federal government investment in national infrastructure has declined, whilst states and local governments, some facing acute fiscal crisis (Peck, 2014b), have sought to introduce new mechanisms to generate revenues to either supplement or replace declining federal resources (Brasuell, 2015). In some cases, state governments have gained electoral mandates to use business and commercial taxes to fund infrastructure. Texas, for example, plans to use oil and gas production taxes to raise $1.7 billion towards transport infrastructure (*Economist*, 2014). The search for new mechanisms and practices forms a contribution towards the increased financialization of urban infrastructure as local and state governments seek to leverage in private capital by monetizing existing infrastructure assets and their future revenue streams (Farmer, 2014). Infrastructure privatization and financialization are recent phenomena in US cities – although Chicago has been a pioneer of initiatives such as TIF (Farmer, 2014; Strickland, 2014; Ward, 2012). The effects of TIF, which are highly uneven, have shaped and reshaped urban spaces and institutional arrangements in metropolitan areas (Weber, 2010; Katz and Bradley, 2013). TIF is used by municipalities in 49 states and is the most widely-used programme for financing local economic development (Briffault, 2010). TIF has been controversial, however, with evidence suggesting that financialization, through mechanisms such as TIF, can produce damaging impacts on cities, particularly those in peripheral and underperforming areas with less buoyant and dynamic property markets (Byrne, 2005; Strickland, 2011, 2014). This means that the 'intensification' of financialization (Lee et al., 2009: 727), through TIF and other processes, is contributing towards uneven economic development. Under these and other similar approaches, infrastructure (including international) investors (Farmer, 2014) have been prioritized to such an extent that they exercise direct influence on city governance and decouple urban infrastructure items and systems from their local context (Torrance, 2008). The risks, costs and unintended consequences for cities and local governments engaging in financialized activity are now understood (Schäfer and Streeck, 2013). There is a growing disconnect between the historic low cost of long-term financing – around 3 per cent interest per annum – and new investment in US infrastructure, which stands at its lowest level since 1950. The problem of legislative 'gridlock' in Washington DC, with a Democratic president and Republican-majority senate and congress at odds is fuelling a set of circumstances where national politicians are extremely reluctant to raise new revenues (including increasing taxes) to back infrastructure bonds. For example, the federal gas tax, which funds the US federal highway trust fund (that is, the inter-state road network), was last raised in 1993. Amidst this impasse, President Obama issued a memorandum in 2014 on expanding public–private collaboration on infrastructure development and financing, and tasked an expert group with presenting new proposals on how the private sector could increase its financial contribution to US national and local infrastructure (US Treasury, 2014).

In terms of private infrastructure investment and provision, over 75 per cent of US households rely on privately-owned electricity supplies regulated by public utility commissions. Telecommunications networks are owned by the private sector, which also owns oil, natural gas and railroad freight. Obama has called on local government to lead on providing high-speed broadband provision to create more competition for privatized monopolies (Hirschfield-Davis, 2015). Google has announced plans to work with US cities to expand super-fast broadband and the global giant is seeking greater access to local physical telecommunications infrastructure.

As well as encouraging local state involvement in communications infrastructure, the Obama administration has also sought to increase private involvement in infrastructure financing and operation, based on (re)emergent interest in PPPs, which to date has been a relatively small part of US infrastructure investment (Sabol and Puentes, 2014). PPPs have played a limited role due to their higher financing costs compared to municipal bonds. Recent examples of PPP arrangements, such as the leasing of Chicago's parking meters, have also been criticized for the liabilities incurred by city administrations and the excess influence that investors were given over spatial planning and urban development strategies (Farmer, 2014). Although most infrastructure in the US is financed on balance sheet through government taxes – echoing the financialized shift toward investment-led approaches – the US government is keen for more infrastructure investments at the local level to operate on a project finance basis in order to attract additional private capital and management expertise, and to limit tax-payer risk and indebtedness. The US government claims that access to low cost, tax-exempt bond financing for projects exclusively owned and operated by state and local governments has discouraged the public sector from turning to private equity financing (US Treasury, 2014). Furthermore, the decline of bond insurance markets because of high cost and risk factors stemming from the financial and banking crisis in 2007–08 has led senior debt lenders to be more cautious about investing in local infrastructure.

Given their relative autonomy in a decentralized federal system and traditions in circumscribing the bounds of the market, some US states do not permit PPPs because state tax law does not allow bond issuance for financing infrastructure owned by private interests. The US government believes that the most significant obstacle to developing and expanding the PPP market are the decentralized legal and regulatory frameworks that exist across the fifty states. This begs the question of how the US government should intervene to encourage greater PPP regulatory uniformity and adoption. Partly in response to this challenge, the federal government, in January 2015, announced proposals to integrate bond finance and PPPs, and enable greater private engagement in infrastructure financing. Qualified public infrastructure bonds (QPIBs) would be the first municipal bonds available for PPPs and would not be subject to tax. They would have no expiry date and no limits would be set on the total amount that could be issued.

Faced with a yawning investment gap, and political impasse on raising taxation or user fees, the federal government is looking to introduce mechanisms that encourage greater private sector finance and urban infrastructure investment, planning and operation alongside existing and long-standing financialized practices. However, despite concerns about the consequences of these practices, some states, such as Minnesota, are actively considering introducing new financialized land value capture mechanisms to facilitate investment in road transportation infrastructure.

Australia

Australia has a highly urbanized environment, with the vast majority of the population, which is rising, living in five coastal cities (Department of Infrastructure and Transport, 2013). Local and urban infrastructure assets, such as ports, airports, rail, road and other transport networks, matter given the density and location of Australia's metropolitan environments (Office of the National Infrastructure Coordinator, 2013). Like the UK and US, the demand for national and local infrastructure investment in Australia is outstripping 'available' public and private resources.

Local government does not have a formal role under the Australian constitution. The federal government, states and territories have separated powers, with individual states and territories governing the legislative and regulatory frameworks (and funding, some of which is pass-ported from the national government) for local government, which creates an uneven pattern of local authority roles, functions, powers and responsibilities, which in turn shapes the distinct form and function of local government interaction and engagement with infrastructure provision. The states play a leading role in metropolitan spatial planning and investment strategies.

Federal, state and local governments share responsibility for most publicly owned infrastructure (Grimsey et al., 2012), whilst major infrastructure assets, such as energy, have been funded by state governments. The federal government, like its US equivalent, funds the national inter-state road network. Local government is responsible, in the main, for the maintenance of local roads and bridges. A large number of assets are still owned and operated by the public sector, despite large-scale privatization in the 1980s and 1990s (Haughton and McManus, 2012), and individual states retain a key role in the operation and function of critical infrastructure. Some states have established 'sovereign wealth fund' bodies (for example, the Queensland investment corporation) to manage state investments, which have financed infrastructure projects both at home and abroad. Infrastructure bonds were introduced in the 1990s but failed to gain traction because of tax concerns and perceived fiscal implications for the federal government. However, they have re-emerged as a possible financing model due to rising demands for new investment in urban infrastructure build and maintenance. The main political parties have been reluctant to sanction direct long-term public borrowing by governments for capital expenditure (Grimsey et al., 2012); a position consolidated recently by the Liberal Coalition government as it implements fiscal consolidation in an attempt to reduce the national budget deficit, and move the country towards budget surplus (Australian Government, 2014). This has sparked criticism that Australian cities are being compelled into putting short-term financial considerations ahead of longer-term direct investments in infrastructure that could deliver sustainable economic outcomes (Committee for Melbourne, 2012).

Local government, which is responsible for infrastructure assets worth AUS$301 billion (Grimsey et al., 2012), has been exploring value capture mechanisms for funding infrastructure provision. Unlike the UK, cities in Australia have a wide range of taxes they can levy directly to raise revenue (Grimsey et al., 2012). Melbourne and Sydney operate a workplace parking levy, which is a fee-based mechanism that issues charges for the use of parking bays in a defined zone or zones. Typically, the revenue is a funding source for public transport investment (Committee for Melbourne, 2012). Other initiatives include local authorities in New South Wales forming formal city region coalitions in and around the Sydney metropolitan area to create a larger pool of assets and increase borrowing power (Grimsey et al., 2012). Policy transfer and learning, such as PPPs, have seen a rapid expansion over the last 25 years, with Melbourne and Sydney at the forefront of market-led models and regulatory regimes that have enabled infrastructure projects to remain 'off balance sheet' (Haughton and McManus, 2012). As with the London Underground PPP, however, there have been high profile casualties. Haughton and McManus (2012), for example, provide a detailed account of the background, operation and ultimate collapse of the Sydney Cross City tunnel PPP, and the cross-boundary, international institutional investment and financialized linkages the project enveloped and snared, stretching across the globe to the now nationalized (that is, UK government-owned) Royal Bank of Scotland.

Like the UK and US, Australian national and subnational governments face financial and public service delivery pressures. The federal government is making reductions in the local government federal assistance grants programme, as part of a package of spending reductions totalling AUS$36 billion over four years (Smith, 2014). These grants maintain local infrastructure and services, including roads and bridges (ALGA, 2014). Federal government funding will continue through the roads to recovery programme and a new renewal programme for bridges will be initiated, funded, in part, by receipts from the new Infrastructure Asset Recycling scheme.

The 2014 federal budget announced a AUS$11.6 billion infrastructure growth package, which aims to lever in an additional AUS$125 billion of private infrastructure investment. The scheme includes incentives to encourage asset recycling to generate receipts to fund new infrastructure, where individual states and territories sell or lease assets and in return receive a percentage of the sale price from the federal government to reinvest in infrastructure. Proponents, such as the Office of the National Infrastructure Coordinator, support the transfer of assets to the private sector (2013), whilst the Australian infrastructure reform working group has been pushing for states to monetize existing assets and implement privatization reforms in return for national government investment (IRWG, 2012). This initiative forms part of a broader set of objectives of federal, state and local governments to identify and introduce new financialized mechanisms and practices without adding directly to on balance sheet public debt and risking existing credit ratings (Haughton and McManus, 2012). Critics suggest that the asset recycling scheme will further splinter urban infrastructure (O'Neill, 2014). Other concerns centre on the public sector under-valuing and under-charging for infrastructure by underestimating how investors will package and plan future revenues (O'Neill, 2013), and that the financialized arrangements that will emerge out of the scheme will be opaque and difficult to scrutinize. The expectation is that assets will be bundled-up and sold to pension or insurance funds, sovereign wealth funds or private investment companies, attracted by guaranteed long-term stable revenue streams (O'Neill, 2009). Where complex PPP models materialize, the challenge for national and local states, across different countries, is how to regulate and share experiences and knowledge across different territories and sectors when so many privatized infrastructure contract arrangements are tightly governed by non-disclosure agreements (NAO, 2015b).

The 'Macquarie Infrastructure Model', with specialist infrastructure funds under management, originated in Australia in the mid-1990s, following changes in domestic pension law and the privatization of infrastructure assets. O'Neill (2009) argues that Macquarie led the mobilization and securitization of earnings from public utilities in Australia, UK and Canada, and that the bank's approach towards risk explains its success in creating, selling and managing financialized infrastructure assets. In an attempt to maximize fee income, Macquarie has shifted into new infrastructure products and geographical markets to derive benefits from localized infrastructure, and to overcome the limited investment opportunities in Australia. Whilst other global infrastructure funds have become rivals, few have been successful as Macquarie and their bespoke approach to tailoring funding and financing needs to local contexts (O'Neill, 2009).

There has been recent interest in Australia in the UK city deals (Property Council of Australia, 2013), with KPMG, which has advised some UK cities, publicizing the city deal model to Australian stakeholders (Atter, 2013). How these one-off, ad hoc arrangements fit within a formal federal governance system requires further investigation. The relatively informal position of local government in Australia, although it has a power of general competence, similar to local government in England, might lend itself to a transactional, business-type network relationship between different tiers of government and the private sector. In a sign of the geographical reach of financialization, the interest in city deals has been accompanied by federal government moves towards an incentivized, investment-led model that seeks economic and financial returns on investment. But as with developments in the UK, these changes do not imply a linear transition toward financialization. Rather, the process is hybridized, negotiated and implemented in particular contexts with the state at different scales playing pivotal roles.

The three cases reviewed in this section (United Kingdom, United States and Australia) illustrate the changing role of the state in infrastructure financialization and governance. Politics and financial constraints are directing national governments, to varying degrees, to encourage alternative funding and financing mechanisms and practices. Governments are also mindful of the geography of infrastructure, and the supply and demand implications of investment upon local and regional development. Infrastructure is seen as a critical tool of growth and competitiveness, which national governments want to retain sufficient regulatory control of in order to maintain tight fiscal management, under conditions of austerity, and to steer specific investments into particular places. The uneven geography of infrastructure financialization and governance, with its different funding and financing practices and mechanisms illustrates the evolving and complex nature of how national, subnational and local states, and private capital, interact with each other to generate and leverage in infrastructure investment. There is no binary transition between state and market-led funding and financing mechanisms, but instead actors in different nations and cities are adopting arrangements that best suit local circumstances, and are often hybrid (that is, state, market and financialized) in nature. There is evidence of different places learning from each other or willing to engage in policy translation, but sometimes without sufficient recourse to context or local geography. This means that the practical application of infrastructure financialization and governance, in specific local environments, may not endure beyond the short-term.

10.5 CONCLUSIONS

This chapter has attempted to contribute towards the growing conceptual and policy interest in the financialization of local and urban infrastructure. The two main arguments in the chapter have been, first, that financialization is an uneven, negotiated and messy process unfolding in differentiated ways in different geographical contexts; and second, the role of the state at different scales has been reinforced rather than reduced in the context of the financialization of infrastructure because of its particular form and nature. These points are derived from existing analysis and emergent evidence, which suggests that there has been a continued relationship between the state, in its different guises and at different scales, and the private sector, throughout the different stages of the infrastructure life-cycle, which has widened and deepened due to the advent of infrastructure as a new investment class.

Whilst the state retains a pivotal role, national, subnational and local governments nevertheless are looking to lever in private capital, using different mechanisms and practices, some of which are increasingly financialized and hybrid in nature. The process of financialization, which gained traction prior to the global financial crisis, and has retained influence through the great recession and beyond, now pervades everyday practices, and has given rise to infrastructure being defined as an alternative asset class. This model has gained further currency with governments struggling to deal with fiscal stress amidst rising state indebtedness and budget deficits. As a model, financialized infrastructure does not answer the question of where and how infrastructure is funded, as opposed to where and how it is financed. With an apparent wealth of international global capital waiting to invest in infrastructure, how the state and/or consumers ultimately pay – either through taxation or user fees – for infrastructure is often hidden or given limited attention, in the main because of political concerns about raising taxes or user fees.

As infrastructure becomes funded and financed in increasingly financialized ways, different practices, tools, instruments and governance arrangements are being modified or constructed in order to provide funding and finance. Geography remains an integral feature of the complex processes of infrastructure financialization and governance. National and local states, together with intermediary actors in capital markets, are shaping and reshaping how financialization takes place on the ground. The examples of the United Kingdom, United States and Australia illustrate how national, subnational and local governments are willing to adopt and utilize different mechanisms and practices, some state or market-led, but others hybrid, complex and at times ad hoc. The analysis finds that context matters in relation to local and regional development, and that policy transfers can be problematic and may not deliver the desired outcomes that policymakers intend.

In conclusion, we want to raise some research challenges in this area, and to encourage further empirical investigations into the financialization and governance of urban infrastructure to help strengthen understanding of the symbiotic relationship between local environments and institutional ensembles and public and private infrastructure funding and financing mechanisms and practices. In particular, there are two issues worth highlighting. First, scholars may find it useful to undertake studies that explore the continued tension between co-ordination and integration versus fragmentation and the splintering of urban infrastructure funding, financing and governance. And second, additional data and analysis, drawing upon both extensive and intensive research methods, would help to inform existing and emergent conceptual frameworks that are seeking to interpret the increasing interplay between the process of deepening financialization and the continued role for the state in constructing, developing and re-making local and urban landscapes in a comparative international context.

ACKNOWLEDGEMENTS

This chapter has been written as part of a project within the Infrastructure Business models, valuation and Innovation for Local Delivery (iBUILD) research centre funded by the UK Engineering and Physical Sciences Research Council (EPSRC) and Economic and Social Research Council (ESRC) (https://research.ncl.ac.uk/ibuild/).

REFERENCES

ALGA (2014), *Federal Budget 2014–15 Analysis*, Deakin, Australian Local Government Association.

Allen, J. and M. Pryke (2013), 'Financializing household water: Thames Water, MEIF, and "ring-fenced" politics', *Cambridge Journal of Regions, Economy and Society*, **6** (3), 419–439.

Allen, K. (2015), 'TfL turns property developer to help fund the capital's transport', *Financial Times*, 28 January.

Arup (2014), 'The cost of London's long-term infrastructure: a final report for the Greater London Authority', London: Arup.

Ashton, P., M. Doussard and R. Weber (2014), 'Reconstituting the state: City powers and exposures in Chicago's infrastructure leases', *Special Issue of Urban Studies on Financialization and the Production of Urban Space*: 1–17.

Atter, L. (2013), 'Making the future a success city strategies in an age of austerity – recent UK reforms', *AHURI National Urban Policy Conference*, Sydney, 17 May.

Australian Government (2014), *Budget Strategy and Outlook: Budget Paper No.1 2014-15*, Canberra, Commonwealth of Australia.

Bailey, S. (2013), *Innovations in Funding and Financing Public Sector Infrastructure*, Glasgow: Caledonian Business School, Glasgow Caledonian University.

Benner, C., C. Berndt, N. Coe, E. Engelen, J. Essletzbichler, J. Glassman, J. Glückler, M. Grote, A. Jones, R. Leichenko, D. Leslie, P. Lindner, M. Lorenzen, B. Mansfield, J. Murphy, J. Pollard, D. Power, E. Stam, D. Wòjcik, and M. Zook (2011), 'Editorial: Emerging themes in economic geography: Outcomes of the Economic Geography 2010 Workshop', *Economic Geography*, **87**, 111–126.

Brasuell, J. (2015), 'Needed: A fresh approach to funding US infrastructure', *Planetizen*, 11 February. Retrieved on 17 October 2016 from www.planetizen.com/node/73734/needed-fresh-approach-funding-us-infrastructure.

Briffault, R. (2010), 'The most popular tool: Tax increment financing and local government', *University of Chicago Law Review*, **77** (1), 65–95.

Byrne, P. (2005), 'Strategic interaction in the adoption of tax increment financing', *Regional Science and Urban Economics*, **35**, 279–298.

CBI (2012), *An Offer they Shouldn't Refuse: Attracting Investment to UK Infrastructure*, London: Confederation of British Industry.

Christopherson, S.R.L., R. Martin and J.S. Pollard (2013), 'Financialisation: roots and repercussions', *Cambridge Journal of Regions, Economy and Society*, **6**, 351–357.

Clark, Gordon, Adam Dixon and Ashby Monk (eds) (2009), *Managing Financial Risks: From Global to Local*, Oxford: Oxford University Press.

Committee for Melbourne (2012), 'Moving Melbourne: A transport funding and financing discussion paper', Melbourne, Committee for Melbourne.

Dawson, R. (2013), *Bridges n'that: A Definition of Infrastructure for the IBUILD Centre*, Newcastle upon Tyne: Newcastle University.

Delacroce, R., R.A Schieb and B. Stevens (2011), 'Pension funds investment in infrastructure: A survey', International Futures Programme Project on Strategic Transport Infrastructure to 2030, Paris: OECD.

Department of Infrastructure and Transport (2013), *State of Australian Cities 2013*, Canberra: Australian Department of Infrastructure and Transport.

Economist (2012), 'Maple revolutionaries: Canada's public pension funds are changing the deal-making landscape', Montreal and Toronto, *The Economist*, 3 March. Retrieved on 17 October 2016 from www.economist.com/node/21548970.

Economist (2014), 'Going their separate ways: States and cities seize the initiative on transport funding', Washington DC, *The Economist*, 22 November. Retrieved on 17 October 2016 from www.economist.com/news/united-states/21633848-states-and-cities-seize-initiative-transport-funding-going-their-separate-ways.

Engelen, E. and J. Faulconbridge (2009), 'Introduction: financial geographies – the credit crisis as an opportunity to catch economic geography's next boat?' *Journal of Economic Geography*, **9**, 587–595.

Farmer, S. (2014), 'Cities as risk managers: The impact of Chicago's parking meter P3 on municipal governance and transportation planning', *Environment and Planning A*, **46** (9), 2160–2174.

French, S., A. Leyshon and T. Wainwright (2011), 'Financializing space, spacing financialization', *Progress in Human Geography*, **35**, 798–819.

GLA (2014), 'Draft London Infrastructure Investment Plan 2050', London: Greater London Authority.

Graham, S. (2000), 'Constructing premium network spaces: Reflections on infrastructure networks and contemporary urban development', *International Journal of Urban and Regional Research*, **24** (1), 183–200.

Graham, Stephen and Simon Marvin (2001), *Splintering Urbanism: Networked Infrastructures, Technological Mobilities and the Urban Condition*, London: Routledge.

Grimsey, D., B. Carlton-Jones and G. Hemingway (2012), *Strong Foundations for Sustainable Local Infrastructure: Connecting Communities, Projects, Finance and Funds*, Melbourne: Ernst & Young.

Hall, S. and A.E.G. Jonas (2014), 'Urban fiscal austerity, infrastructure provision and the struggle for regional transit in "Motor City"', *Cambridge Journal of Regions, Economy and Society*, **7**, 189–206.
Harvey, David (1989), *The Urban Experience*, Baltimore, MD: Johns Hopkins University Press.
Harvey, David (2006), *Spaces of Global Capitalism: Towards a Theory of Uneven Geographical Development*, New York: Verso.
Harvey, David (2010), *The Enigma of Capital and the Crises of Capitalism*, Oxford: Oxford University Press.
Haughton, G. and P. McManus (2012), 'Neoliberal experiments with urban infrastructure: The cross city tunnel, Sydney', *International Journal of Urban and Regional Research*, **36** (1), 90–105.
Hebb, T. and R. Sharma (2014) 'New finance for America's cities', *Regional Studies*, **48** (3), 485–500.
Helm, D. (2013), 'British infrastructure policy and the gradual return of the state', *Oxford Review of Economic Policy*, **29** (2), 287–306.
Hirschfield-Davis (2015), 'Obama announces moves to encourage expansion of public broadband networks', *New York Times*, 14 January.
HMT (2012), *A New Approach to Public Private Partnerships*, London: HM Treasury.
HMT (2013), *The UK Insurance Growth Action Plan*, London: HM Treasury.
HMT/UKTI (2014), *Investing in UK Infrastructure*, London: HM Treasury/UK Trade and Industry.
HoC (2013), *Infrastructure Policy Standard Note: SN/EP/6594* Last updated: 11 October 2013, London: House of Commons.
Hodge, G.A., C. Greve and A.E. Boardman (eds) (2010), *International Handbook on Public–Private Partnerships*, Cheltenham, UK and Northampton, MA, USA: Edward Elgar Publishing.
iBUILD (2015), *Alternative Infrastructure Business Models to Improve Economic Growth and Well-Being: A Mid-Term Review and Manifesto from the iBUILD Research Centre*, Newcastle upon Tyne: Newcastle University.
Inderst, G. (2010), 'Infrastructure as an asset class', *EIB Public and Private Financing of Infrastructure, EIB Papers*, **15** (1), 70–104, Luxembourg: European Investment Bank.
Inderst, G. (2011), 'Infrastructure: A new asset class for investors?' in K. Uppenberg, H. Strauss and R. Wagenvoort (eds), *Financing Infrastructure: A Review of the 2010 EIB Conference in Economics and Finance*, Luxembourg: European Investment Bank, pp. 18–25.
Inderst, G. and D.R. Croce (2013), 'Pension fund investment in infrastructure: A comparison between Australia and Canada', OECD Working Papers on Finance, Insurance and Private Pensions, No.32, Paris: OECD.
IRWG (2012), *Infrastructure Finance and Funding Reform*, Canberra, Australian Infrastructure Reform Working Group, Infrastructure Australia.
Jonas, A.E.G. (2013), 'City-regionalism as a "contingent geopolitics of capitalism"', *Geopolitics*, **18** (2), 284–298.
Katz, B. and J. Bradley (2013), *The Metropolitan Revolution: How Cities and Metros are Fixing our Broken Politics and Fragile Economy*, Washington, DC: Brookings Institution Press.
KPMG (2012), *Insight: The Global Infrastructure Magazine*. Retrieved on 17 October 2016 from www.kpmg.com/global/en/issuesandinsights/articlespublications/insight-magazine/pages/default.aspx.
Lee, R., G.L. Clark, J.S. Pollard and A. Leyshon (2009), 'The remit of financial geography – before and after the crisis', *Journal of Economic Geography*, **9**, 723–747.
Leyshon, A. and N. Thrift (2007), 'The capitalization of almost everything: The future of finance and capitalism', *Theory, Culture and Society*, **24**, 97–115.
LFC (2013), *Raising the Capital: The Report of the London Finance Commission*, London: London Finance Commission.
LGA (2012), *Local Authority Bonds: A Local Government Collective Agency*, London: Local Government Association.
Llewellyn Consulting (2013), *Pension Insurance Corporation White Paper UK Infrastructure: The Challenges for Investors and Policymakers*, London: Llewellyn Consulting.
London First (2010), *World Class Infrastructure for a World Class City: The London First Infrastructure Commission*, London: London First.
London First (2013), *Ten Infrastructure Projects for London*, London: London First.
Manchester City Council (2014), 'Major new partnership will deliver thousands of new Manchester homes', press release, 24 June 2014. Retrieved on 17 October 2016 from www.manchester.gov.uk/news/article/6909/major_new_partnership_will_deliver_thousands_of_manchester_homes.
Manyika, J., J. Reemes, R. Dobbs, J. Orellan, and F. Schaer (2012), *Urban America: US Cities in the Global Economy*, Washington, DC: McKinsey Global Institute.
Martin, R. (1999), 'Selling off the state: Privatisation, the equity market and the geographies of private shareholding', in Ron Martin (ed.), *Money and the Space Economy*, London: Wiley, pp. 260–283.
Martin, R. (2011), 'The local geographies of the financial crisis: From the housing bubble to economic recession and beyond', *Journal of Economic Geography*, **11**, 587–618.
Martin, R. and P. Sunley (1997), 'The post-Keynesian state and the space economy', in Roger Lee and Jane Wills (eds), *Geographies of Economies*, London: Arnold, pp. 278–289.

Martínez-Lacambra, A. (2013), 'Governance in public and private management', *Local Government Studies*, **39** (3), 455–459.
NAO (2015a), *HM Treasury UK Guarantee Schemes for Infrastructure: Report of Comptroller and Auditor General*, London: National Audit Office.
NAO (2015b), *The Choice of Finance for Capital Investment*, London: National Audit Office.
O'Brien, P. and A. Pike (2014), 'The governance of infrastructure funding and financing: A literature review', iBUILD Working Paper, Newcastle upon Tyne: CURDS, Newcastle University.
O'Brien, P. and A. Pike (2015), 'City deals, decentralisation and the governance of local infrastructure funding and financing in the UK', *National Institute Economic Review*, **233** (1), R14–R26.
OECD (2012), *Economic Outlook No. 91*, Paris: OECD.
OECD (2013), *Annual Survey of Large Pension Funds and Public Pension Reserve Funds: Report on Pension Funds' Long-Term Investments*, Paris: OECD.
OECD (2014), *Private Financing and Governmental Support to Promote Long-Term Investments in Infrastructure*, Paris: OECD.
Office of the National Infrastructure Coordinator (2013), *Submission to the Productivity Commission Inquiry into Public Infrastructure*, Canberra: Infrastructure Australia.
OFT (2010), *Infrastructure Ownership and Control Stock-take: Final Report*, London: Office of Fair Trading.
O'Neill, P. (1997), 'Bringing the qualitative state into economic geography', in R. Lee and J. Wills (eds), *Geographies of Economies*, London: Arnold, pp. 290–301.
O'Neill, P. (2009), 'Infrastructure investment and the management of risk', in G. Clark, A. Dixon and A. Monk (eds), *Managing Financial Risks: from Global to Local*, Oxford: Oxford University Press, pp. 163–188.
O'Neill, P. (2013), 'The financialisation of infrastructure: The role of categorisation and property relations', *Cambridge Journal of Regions, Economy and Society*, **6** (3), 441–454.
O'Neill, P. (2014), 'Power play: Matter of trust', *Newcastle Herald*, 8 December.
Ottaviano, G. (2008), 'Infrastructure and economic geography: An overview of theory and evidence', *EIB Papers* **13** (2), *Infrastructure investment, growth and cohesion*, Luxembourg: European Investment Bank.
Peck, J. (2014a), 'Entrepreneurial urbanism: Between uncommon sense and dull compulsion', *Geografiska Annaler*, **96** (4), 396–401.
Peck, J. (2014b), 'Pushing austerity: State failure, municipal bankruptcy and the crises of fiscal federalism in the USA', *Cambridge Journal of Regions, Economy and Society*, **7**, 17–44.
Peck, J., N. Theodore and N. Brenner (2013), 'Neoliberal urbanism redux?', *International Journal of Urban and Regional Research*, **37** (3), 1091–1099.
Pike, A. and J.S. Pollard (2010), 'Economic geographies of financialization', *Economic Geography*, **86**, 29–51.
Pollock, A. (2005), *NHS Plc: The Privatisation of Our Health Care*, New York: Verso.
Preqin (2012), *Pension Funds Investing in Infrastructure*. Retrieved on 17 October 2016 from www.preqin.com/docs/newsletters/INF/Preqin_Infrastructure_Spotlight_July_2012.pdf.
Property Council of Australia (2013), *Submission to the Productivity Commission Public Infrastructure Inquiry*, Sydney: Property Council of Australia.
Puentes, R., P. Sabol and J. Kane (2013), 'Cut to invest: Revive Build America Bonds (BABs) to support state and local investments', Brookings Metropolitan Infrastructure Paper No. 63, Washington, DC: Brookings Institute.
PwC (2014), *Crossrail 2: Funding and Financing Study*, London, PwC.
Reuters (2013), 'Analysis: Austerity threatens EU's competitive edge in infrastructure', 28 March. Retrieved on 17 October 2016 from www.rzd-partner.com/press/analysis--austerity-threatens-eu-s-competitive-edge-in-infrastructure/.
RSA (2014), *Connected Cities: The Link to Growth*, London: RSA Cities Growth Commission.
Sabol, P. and R. Puentes (2014), *Private Capital, Public Good: Drivers of Successful Infrastructure Public–Private Partnerships*, Washington, DC: Brookings Institute.
Schäfer, A. and W. Streeck (2013), 'Introduction: politics in the age of austerity', in W. Streeck and A. Schäfer (eds), *Politics in the Age of Austerity*, Cambridge: Polity Press, pp. 1–25.
SEC (2012), *Report on the Municipal Securities Market*, Washington, DC: US Securities and Exchange Commission.
SFT (2015), *NPD Model: Explanatory Note*, Edinburgh: The Scottish Futures Trust.
Shaoul, J. (2007), 'PFI: the evidence', in C. Talbot and M. Baker (eds), *The Alternative Comprehensive Spending Review*, Manchester: Manchester University Press.
Sleeman, John (1953), *British Public Utilities*, London: Issac Pitman.
Smith, A. (1976), *An Inquiry into the Nature and Causes of the Wealth of Nations*, vol. 2, in R.H. Campbell, A.S. Skinner and W.B. Todd (eds), Oxford: Oxford University Press.
Smith, J. (2014), 'Buoyant economy fails to brighten Australia's gloomy outlook', *Financial Times*, 4 June.
Smith Institute (2012), *Local Authority Pension Funds: Investing for Growth*, London: The Smith Institute.
Solomon, Lewis (2009), *The Promise and Perils of Infrastructure Privatization*, New York: Palgrave.

Spackman, M. (2002), 'Public–private partnerships: Lessons from the British approach', *Economic Systems*, **26**, 283–301.
Standard & Poor's (2013), *Out of the Shadows: The Rise of Alternative Financing in Infrastructure*, London: Standard & Poor's Ratings Services.
Strickland, T. (2011), *The Financialisation of Urban Development: Tax Increment Financing in Newcastle upon Tyne*, unpublished MA dissertation, Newcastle upon Tyne: CURDS, Newcastle University.
Strickland, T. (2014), *The Financialisation Infrastructure Funding and Financing in the UK and the US*, unpublished PhD thesis, Newcastle upon Tyne, CURDS: Newcastle University.
Tomaney, J. (2014), 'Governing London', *Utzon Lecture*, University of New South Wales, Sydney, 3 September.
Torrance, M.I. (2008), 'Forging glocal governance? Urban infrastructures as networked financial products', *International Journal of Urban and Regional Research*, **32** (1), 1–21.
US Treasury (2014), *Expanding our Nation's Infrastructure through Innovative Financing*, Washington, DC: US Department of the Treasury.
Vammalle, C., C. Hulbert and R. Ahrend (2014), 'Creating fiscal space for investment by sub-national governments: the role of institutions', OECD Regional Development Working Papers, 2014/02, Paris: OECD.
Wall, A. and C. Connolly (2009), 'The private finance initiative', *Public Management Review*, **11** (5), 707–724.
Ward, K. (2012), 'Mobilities and mutations: Financing urban infrastructure in the twenty first century', *Human Geography Seminar Series*, London, UCL, November 2012.
Weber, B. and H.W. Alfen (2010), *Infrastructure as an Asset Class: Investment Strategy, Project Finance and PPP*, Chichester: Wiley.
Weber, R. (2010), 'Selling city futures: The financialization of urban redevelopment policy', *Economic Geography*, **86** (3), 251–274.
WEF (2014), *Accelerating Infrastructure Delivery: New Evidence from the International Financial Institutions*, Davos: World Economic Forum.
Whitfield, D. (2010), *Global Auction of Public Assets*, Nottingham: Spokesman.
Wójcik, D., J.V. Beaverstock and J. Sidaway (2007), 'European financial geographies', *Growth and Change*, **38**, 167–173.
World Bank (2012), *World Bank Group Innovations for Leveraging the Private Sector for Development: A Discussion Note*, Washington, DC: The World Bank.

11. The geography of local public finance

Enid Slack[1]

11.1 INTRODUCTION

The primary role of local government is to provide goods and services to residents and businesses within their geographic boundaries – roads, transit, clean water, sewage treatment, refuse collection and disposal, police and fire protection.[2] In some countries, local governments also deliver health, education, and social services. If the benefits of these services are confined to the local government jurisdiction (and do not spill over into neighbouring jurisdictions), efficiency is enhanced by local provision because the level and mix of services varies with local preferences. In short, local governments are better equipped to respond to differences in what people want in different locations than are other levels of government.

To pay for services, local governments raise their own revenues through user fees and taxes (property, sales, and income taxes, for example) as well as relying on transfers from other levels of government. Although efficient, local government provision of services may be inequitable because not all local governments are able to provide an adequate level of service at reasonable tax rates. In particular, richer jurisdictions are generally able to provide a high level of service at low tax rates whereas poorer ones are only able to provide a low level of service and often at very high tax rates.

This chapter explores the geography of local public finance – the provision and payment for public services in different locations – and highlights some of the ways in which local fiscal disparities in taxing and spending have been tackled among local governments within countries (through equalization transfers) and within metropolitan regions (through municipal restructuring). The first section provides a general discussion of how geographic location influences the amount of public goods and services an individual will receive and why disparities might result across jurisdictions. Because the structure of government (in particular, the relationship between central and local governments) has an important impact on the geography of public finance, the second section briefly describes different models and the extent of fiscal decentralization (responsibilities and fiscal resources assigned to local governments). The third section compares expenditures and revenues of local governments at the country level for selected OECD countries. The fourth section sets out how central or provincial/state equalization transfers are used to address fiscal inequities among local jurisdictions within a country (in a unitary system) or within a state or province (in a federal system). The fifth section reviews alternative governance structures that can address inequities among local governments within a metropolitan area. The concluding section summarizes the issues around equalization and metropolitan governance.

11.2 GEOGRAPHY AND LOCAL PUBLIC FINANCE

Public finance is concerned with who derives benefits from publicly provided goods and services and who pays for them. The geography of public finance is also concerned with who benefits and who pays but adds another dimension – how tax burdens and expenditure benefits vary by geographic location: "who gets what, where, at what cost?" (Bennett, 1980: ix). The geography of public finance emphasizes the imbalance between the spatial patterns of revenue-raising, on the one hand, and the geographic distribution of expenditure benefits, on the other hand.

The quantity and quality of public goods and services that individuals enjoy depend on where they choose to live because each local government makes different choices about what services to deliver and how to pay for them. As Tiebout (1956) hypothesized, if there is a large number of communities each with its own tax-expenditure package and consumers are mobile between communities, consumers will reveal their preferences for local public goods by moving to the jurisdiction that has the tax and expenditure package that most closely resembles their preferences. The result of "voting with their feet" is a large number of homogeneous communities that reflect the preferences of their residents and, in this sense, a market-like solution would yield an efficient allocation of resources.

There are many reasons why local government decisions about what services to provide and what revenues to collect are not the same everywhere. As noted above, preferences for local services vary by location. In some communities, people may want sidewalks; in others, they may not. In some communities, there may be a preference for more policing; in others, more parks. Another reason is that the need to provide services differs among communities. For example, the need for affordable housing and social services will be higher for municipalities with a high proportion of low-income households. The cost to deliver services will also vary with geographic location according to factors such as the size of the population, population density, climate, or other factors. For example, wages and rents are usually higher in cities with high population density and the cost per unit to provide services increases with increasing population because of congestion (Fenge and Meier, 2001). Costs are generally higher in cold climates where heating and electricity costs are high. Of course, expenditures per capita could also be higher because of inefficient spending by some municipalities (Kim and Lotz, 2008). Finally, the ability to raise revenues to pay for local services is different. Revenue-raising capacity is unevenly distributed across municipalities because of differences in the size of the tax base.

Geography will also have an impact on the level of goods and services that individuals receive because of "tapering" (Bennett, 1980). The extent to which consumers can make use of a service (such as a school, library, recreational facility, and so on) depends on the distance they have to travel to get there. Because use tends to decline with distance from the facility, individuals who are far away may be excluded from enjoying the benefits of the public service. Moreover, where services are delivered to the individual (such as fire protection), distance may mean that some residents will receive a lower level of service than others. In the case of fire protection, for example, response times climb with distance from the fire station.

The amount of goods and services individuals receive will also depend on the extent to which the provision of some services results in externalities – where the benefits (or costs) of a specific service in one local government jurisdiction are not confined within the local government boundaries and spill over to residents of another jurisdiction who do not pay for them. For example, a road in one municipality can provide benefits to residents of neighbouring municipalities who also drive on it but do not pay for it. Although these external effects are not reflected in costs or prices, they do have an impact on the wellbeing of residents (Pacione, 2001). Moreover, some taxes are exported to other jurisdictions. A tax on non-residential property, for example, can be shifted on to the price of the goods produced on that property and these goods may be sold to residents of other jurisdictions who bear the burden of the tax.

All of these factors – differences in needs, costs, and fiscal capacity plus tapering and externalities – mean that individuals will receive a different level of service and pay different amounts of taxes depending on their geographic location. If some local governments are unable to provide an adequate level of services at reasonable tax rates, the resulting fiscal disparities across local jurisdictions can be addressed in at least two ways – equalization grants and municipal restructuring. Both of these options are discussed further below after a brief discussion of central–local relations and the differences in expenditure responsibilities and revenue-raising tools in local jurisdictions in selected OECD countries.

11.3 STRUCTURE OF GOVERNMENT AND FISCAL DECENTRALIZATION

The extent to which there will be fiscal disparities among local jurisdictions depends, at least in part, on the structure of government and the extent to which expenditures and revenues have been decentralized to local governments. In a centralized model, the central government retains all of the powers within a single unitary government (Bennett, 1980). Under a model of local autonomy, at the other extreme, local governments have control over taxes and spending for their citizens within clearly defined spheres of authority (Bird, 2011).

In most countries, the reality is a mixed central-local system. At the more centralized end of the spectrum, for example, territorial administration (sometimes referred to in the literature as "deconcentration") is a model under which local governments carry out centrally directed functions at the local level and have no autonomy. They are simply local lines in the central budget. Examples of this model in Europe are the Czech and Slovak Republics. Under administrative federalism, the welfare state is administered by a system in which both the central and local governments work almost as one unit even though they have different constituencies and responsibilities (Bird, 2011). In Denmark and Sweden, for example, most redistributive spending is locally administered and funded through central grants and local taxes. Local governments do have some flexibility to experiment, however. Under the agency model, local governments are viewed as agents to whom the central government has delegated specific functions (Bird, 2011). The main assumption underlying this model is that local and central interests are not the same and that national welfare will be better off if national interests prevail.

The extent of central versus local control is reflected in the degree to which expenditures and revenues have been devolved to local governments. Fiscal decentralization is about who collects what taxes and who makes expenditures as well as how to deal with any fiscal imbalance which results from the devolution of expenditure responsibilities and taxes. Fiscal decentralization has been a popular notion in many countries for the last 30 years.

A number of benefits have been attributed to fiscal decentralization of which the most often cited is efficiency. As government moves closer to the people, services more closely reflect local preferences rather than being provided uniformly across regions. Responding to local preferences is especially important when there are variations among regions in terms of language, geography, climate, and the split between urban and rural areas (Slack, Spicer and Montacer, 2014). Decentralization can also result in greater accountability because with increased responsibility for providing services, locally elected officials are held to account to a greater degree by the local population (Bahl, 2008). When local politicians are unable to shift responsibility and blame to central authorities, responsiveness inevitably increases. As a consequence of these local changes, citizen participation also increases, largely because local populations feel they have more control over service delivery in their area and more of a say in how they are governed (Bahl, 2008). Fiscal decentralization can also increase overall revenue mobilization by broadening the aggregate tax base and, by doing so, result in reduced intergovernmental transfers (Bahl, 2008). Local governments have a much better understanding of local economies and can more easily identify a tax base. For example, local administrators would be best positioned to establish and manage a property tax because they have information on individual properties and their characteristics.

Nevertheless, fiscal decentralization does have drawbacks. By providing more fiscal authority to local governments, it could potentially increase macroeconomic instability if sub-central revenues decline or if local borrowing becomes excessive (Bahl, 2008). Poor administration at the local level could also result in greater instability for fragile central economies. Most significantly for this chapter, there is a belief that the potential for equalization is greater under revenue centralization (Bahl, 2008; OECD, 2013). With greater decentralization, it is expected that there will be more responsibilities and taxing authority at the local level and a greater likelihood that there will be disparities among local governments in their ability to deliver services. Variations in fiscal conditions among local jurisdictions will mean that some local governments are unable to provide an adequate level of services without levying unduly high tax rates. The strong tradition of Home Rule in the United States, for example, has meant a higher tolerance for fiscal disparities than one might see in many parts of Europe (Bahl, 2010).

The extent of fiscal decentralization can have an impact on local governments in times of fiscal austerity. In general, one might expect that in a decentralized system, fiscal austerity at the national level will affect local governments less than under a more centralized system where local governments are highly dependent on transfers (which would presumably be cut back in bad economic times). On the other hand, if local governments have access to volatile tax sources, they may face more fiscal stress. In the United States, for example, Chernick and Reschovsky (2013) found that the fiscal health of most US cities has suffered as a result of the 2008 recession and housing crisis both in terms of own-source revenues (mainly taxes and user fees) and federal and state transfers. In Canada where local governments depend largely on the property tax, on the other hand, there was little impact on municipalities. Kitchen (2013), for example, concluded that municipalities in the largest province (Ontario) were not as hard hit by the recession as municipalities in other countries, even though the provincial economy, which relies heavily on manufacturing, was affected. He even suggested that the recession might have had a positive long-term impact by driving municipalities to use more funding instruments for operating and capital projects. Federal government stimulus funding also assisted municipalities in funding needed infrastructure.

Some authors have argued that it is in times of central fiscal stress that changes in the central-local relationship are most likely to occur (Côté and Fenn, 2014) and, in particular, with a tendency towards greater decentralization. When the central government is facing mounting deficits, it might be more interested in empowering local governments to raise their own revenues rather than providing them with transfers. In other words, periods of fiscal austerity can be catalysts for reform.

11.4 MUNICIPAL EXPENDITURES AND REVENUES IN SELECTED OECD COUNTRIES

The extent of fiscal decentralization varies considerably across countries as can be seen in Table 11.1 for 26 OECD countries. Local government expenditures range from a low of 3 per cent of GDP in Greece to a high of 38 per cent in Denmark. In eleven countries, the local government sector is less than 10 per cent of GDP; in eleven countries, it is between 10 and 20 per cent, and only in three Nordic countries, all of which rely heavily on local governments to deliver health, education, and social protection services, does the local government sector account for more than 20 per cent of GDP.

Countries with larger local government sectors assign a wider range of expenditure responsibilities to their local governments, as can be seen in Table 11.1. In most countries, local governments are responsible for public order and safety (fire and police protection), local transit and roads (included under economic affairs), environmental protection (including waste and wastewater), housing and community services (including water supply and street lighting), recreation and culture, education, and social protection. There is considerable variation, however, in the extent to which local governments in different countries are responsible for these services. For example, education represents more than 20 per cent of total local expenditures in 15 of the 26 countries but less than 10 per cent in three countries (Greece, Italy, and Spain). Similarly, although social protection represents more than 20 per cent of local expenditures in nine countries it accounts for less than 10 per cent in seven countries. Local expenditures on health, education, and social protection account for an astounding 87 per cent of all general government expenditures in Denmark, 75 per cent in Sweden, 72 per cent in Finland, and 65 per cent in Norway.

Services are financed in different ways by local governments in different countries, as Table 11.2 shows. Local taxes account for less than 15 per cent of local government revenues in some countries such as the United Kingdom and Ireland but for more than 60 per cent in Austria. In the three countries in Table 11.1 that limit local government taxing authority to the property tax – Australia, UK and Ireland, the local government sector in the two countries for which information is available (UK and Ireland) is heavily dependent on transfers. Local government revenues in these two countries also represent a fairly small share of GDP compared to countries such as Denmark, Sweden, and Finland where local governments depend relatively more heavily on taxes.

Transfer dependence is significant in all countries and transfers are more important

Table 11.1 Local government expenditure by function, selected OECD countries, 2012

Country	Local Governments spending as a percentage of GDP	Function as a percentage of total local government expenditure								
		General Public Services	Public Order, Safety and Defence	Economic Affairs	Environment Protections	Housing and Community Amenities	Health	Recreation, Culture and Religion	Education	Social Protection
Austria*	8%	21%	2%	–	15%	5%	3%	23%	8%	23%
Belgium	7%	18%	13%	11%	5%	2%	1%	9%	19%	22%
Czech Republic	10%	13%	2%	22%	10%	4%	3%	8%	32%	6%
Denmark	39%	4%	0%	4%	1%	1%	22%	2%	10%	55%
Estonia	11%	8%	0%	13%	3%	7%	18%	8%	35%	8%
Finland	24%	14%	1%	7%	0%	1%	30%	4%	17%	25%
France	12%	16%	3%	13%	8%	15%	1%	10%	15%	18%
Germany	8%	18%	3%	13%	5%	4%	2%	6%	16%	33%
Greece	3%	35%	1%	17%	16%	4%	0%	7%	2%	19%
Hungary	10%	21%	0%	12%	5%	6%	8%	6%	29%	13%
Iceland	14%	12%	1%	8%	2%	3%	1%	15%	35%	23%
Ireland	5%	6%	3%	20%	11%	13%	0%	5%	23%	19%
Israel**	–	15%	3%	8%	8%	4%	0%	12%	35%	15%
Italy	15%	14%	2%	13%	5%	4%	48%	2%	7%	5%
Korea*	13%	16%	2%	19%	4%	7%	6%	4%	31%	10%
Luxembourg	5%	25%	2%	13%	14%	8%	0%	13%	16%	8%
Netherlands	16%	8%	7%	17%	10%	3%	2%	9%	29%	15%
Norway	16%	10%	1%	10%	4%	4%	14%	5%	24%	27%
Poland	14%	11%	2%	16%	3%	5%	14%	7%	29%	13%
Portugal	6%	32%	1%	17%	7%	8%	6%	10%	12%	7%
Slovak Republic	7%	14%	1%	15%	8%	8%	0%	6%	40%	8%
Slovenia	9%	10%	1%	11%	5%	5%	11%	9%	37%	11%
Spain	6%	36%	8%	16%	9%	5%	1%	12%	4%	9%
Sweden	26%	12%	1%	6%	1%	3%	27%	3%	21%	27%
Switzerland	8%	15%	6%	15%	6%	2%	4%	7%	25%	19%
United Kingdom	14%	9%	9%	7%	4%	11%	0%	3%	27%	30%

Notes: *Figures are for 2011; **GDP not provided.
Source: OECD (2014a).

Table 11.2 Sources of revenue for local governments, selected OECD countries, 2012

Country	Revenues as a percentage of GDP	Source of revenue for local government as a percentage of total local government revenues			
		Taxes	Transfers	User fees	Other revenues*
Austria	1%	62%	19%	10%	9%
Czech Republic	0%	41%	42%	16%	1%
Denmark**	13%	34%	57%	–	3%
Estonia**	4%	45%	45%	–	2%
Finland	10%	46%	30%	21%	3%
Germany	3%	40%	41%	16%	4%
Hungary	2%	21%	67%	10%	1%
Ireland**	1%	13%	67%	–	10%
Italy	7%	40%	51%	7%	2%
Luxembourg	2%	31%	49%	18%	2%
Norway	5%	41%	42%	13%	4%
Portugal	2%	34%	43%	13%	10%
Slovenia	4%	42%	45%	11%	1%
Spain	3%	45%	44%	9%	2%
United Kingdom	2%	13%	72%	13%	3%

Notes: *Social contributions are included in this category; **Figures for user fees for these countries are missing. As a result, the percentage of total revenues does not sum to 100%.

Sources: OECD (2014a, 2014b).

than taxes in all but a few countries. Transfers (earmarked and non-earmarked combined) account for more than 50 per cent of local government revenues in five of the 15 countries in Table 11.2 and over 70 per cent in the UK. In contrast, with the sole exception of Finland, user fees provide less than 20 per cent of local government revenues in each of the 15 countries in Table 11.2.

Table 11.3 provides more detailed information on local taxes for a greater number of countries. Local taxes account for more than 25 per cent of total taxes (central, regional, and local governments) in Denmark, Iceland, and Sweden but 5 per cent or less in eight of the 26 countries. As a per cent of GDP, local taxes range from a high of over 10 per cent in the Nordic countries (Denmark, Finland, Iceland, and Sweden) to 1 per cent or less in six countries (Australia, Czech Republic, Greece, Ireland, the Netherlands, and Slovak Republic).

The types of taxes that local governments levy also have an impact on the extent of fiscal disparities across jurisdictions because the variability in the tax base across local jurisdictions will be greater for some taxes than others. The taxes available to local governments vary, as does the degree of autonomy they have to set the tax rates. Income taxes are the largest source of local tax revenue in 12 countries, especially the Nordic countries.[3] Indeed, in each of the 12 income tax countries, such taxes account for more than 50 per cent of local taxes. Goods and services taxes are the most important local tax source in six countries and provide 10 per cent or more of local taxes in 11 countries. Although local governments in all 28 countries levy property taxes, such taxes account for more than 10 per cent of local taxes in only 22 countries, and are the most important local tax source only in 11 countries.

Table 11.3 Sources of taxation for local governments, selected OECD countries, 2012

Country	Local tax revenues as a percentage of total tax revenues	Tax revenues as a percentage of total local government taxation				
		Income and payroll taxes	Property taxes (recurrent taxes on immovable property)	Property related taxes (others)	Taxes on goods and services	Other taxes
Australia*	3%	0%	100%	0%	0%	0%
Austria	3%	64%	14%	0%	10%	12%
Belgium	5%	34%	58%	0%	8%	0%
Canada	9%	0%	91%	7%	2%	1%
Czech Republic	1%	0%	56%	0%	44%	0%
Denmark	27%	89%	11%	0%	0%	0%
Estonia*	13%	86%	14%	0%	0%	0%
Finland	23%	93%	7%	0%	0%	0%
France	13%	7%	43%	9%	24%	17%
Germany	8%	79%	15%	0%	6%	0%
Greece*	4%	0%	76%	20%	4%	0%
Hungary	6%	0%	18%	2%	80%	0%
Iceland	27%	82%	17%	0%	2%	0%
Ireland	3%	0%	100%	0%	0%	0%
Israel	8%	0%	95%	0%	5%	0%
Italy	17%	26%	13%	2%	30%	29%
Korea	16%	19%	17%	28%	26%	11%
Luxembourg*	4%	100%	0%	0%	0%	0%
Netherlands*	4%	0%	52%	0%	47%	2%
Norway	13%	88%	5%	6%	1%	0%
Poland*	12%	59%	29%	0%	8%	4%
Portugal	7%	29%	32%	11%	29%	0%
Slovak Republic	3%	0%	50%	0%	50%	0%
Slovenia	11%	80%	13%	0%	7%	0%
Spain	10%	19%	33%	6%	36%	5%
Sweden	37%	97%	3%	0%	0%	0%
Switzerland	15%	82%	3%	12%	2%	0%
United Kingdom	5%	0%	100%	0%	0%	0%

Note: *2011 figures are used.

Source: OECD (2014a).

On the other hand, the property tax accounts for over 90 per cent of local taxes in Canada and Israel (and New Zealand which is not included in this table) and is the only local tax levied in Australia, Ireland, and the UK. The only countries with a balanced local revenue structure in the sense that it is not dominated by just one tax (that is, no tax accounts for 50 per cent or more of total taxes) are Italy, Korea, Portugal, and Spain.

A key conclusion that emerges from this section is that countries have considerable discretion in deciding how large a role that local governments play, the extent to which local activities are financed from local revenues, the types of taxes which local governments can levy, and the degree of autonomy they have in determining tax bases and tax rates. Not surprisingly, there are differences across countries in the expenditures made by local governments and the taxes levied to pay for them. One would expect that fiscal disparities would be greatest in those countries where local governments are tasked with delivering a wide range of services and have significant local autonomy to raise taxes. As will be noted below, for example, where local governments rely on income taxes (as they do in many countries), there tend to be greater disparities among local governments in their ability to provide services and a greater need for equalization.

Although there has been much talk about fiscal decentralization over the last 30 years, it is not clear that much has actually changed in that time. At the beginning of the twenty-first century, regional and local governments combined accounted for about 18 per cent of taxes and 33 per cent of expenditures. The same was true 30 years earlier (Bird, 2011). Moreover, these numbers show that expenditure decentralization has been greater than revenue decentralization leading to vertical fiscal imbalance everywhere meaning that the fiscal capacity of local governments is not sufficient to meet their spending responsibilities while, at the same time, the fiscal capacity of other levels of government is greater than is needed to meet their spending responsibilities. The result has been that intergovernmental transfers have increased both in size and complexity.

11.5 EQUALIZATION TRANSFERS TO ADDRESS LOCAL FISCAL DISPARITIES WITHIN COUNTRIES

The main role of equalization is to provide equity to residents of different local jurisdictions.[4] As noted earlier, when services are funded at the local level, there will inevitably be differences in the ability of local governments to deliver them because of differences in needs, costs, and fiscal capacity. Horizontal fiscal imbalance refers to the difference in resources among governments at the same level – some municipalities cannot provide an adequate level of service at reasonable tax rates whereas other municipalities can. One way to address horizontal fiscal imbalance is to provide equalization transfers to local governments which are designed to ensure that each local jurisdiction can provide a standard level of service by levying comparable levels of taxation.

A good equalization transfer distributes funds on the basis of a formula which includes measures of expenditure need and revenue-raising capacity. It is important that the grant formula be designed in a way that the amount of the grant received cannot be manipulated by local governments. To estimate expenditure need, for example, it is necessary to separate actual expenditures into the portion that is attributable to the costs of the service from local preferences or inefficiencies in spending (Chernick and Reschovsky, 2013). Actual expenditures are not recommended for use in an equalization formula because their inclusion would discourage revenue-raising efforts and local expenditure restraint – those with the highest expenditures and lowest tax rates would receive the largest transfers. In terms of the measurement of revenue capacity, it is not advisable to include actual revenues in the equalization formula to avoid creating an incentive to reduce revenues to increase the size of the grant.

The effort expended to determine expenditure need and revenue-raising capacity using factors that cannot be manipulated by local governments has resulted in very complicated formulas that are difficult for governments and citizens to understand or replicate. In an effort to get the formula right, the resulting complexity can greatly reduce the transparency of the grant system. As one author notes, it is all too easy to turn a simple formula into a complicated one that can be manipulated by donor and recipient governments by introducing too many refinements (Smart, 2007).

In the case of vertical equalization, the central government in a unitary country or a provincial/state government in a federal country transfers funding to local governments. With horizontal equalization, transfers are made from local governments with high fiscal capacity to local governments with low fiscal capacity (Dafflon, 2007). Horizontal equalization provides a disincentive to raise local taxes because local governments can only keep a portion of what they raise and the rest is distributed to other local governments. Where tax rates are set locally, there is a disincentive to raise rates. Where tax rates are set centrally, rates of tax collection may be low (Smart, 2007). It is possible, however, that municipalities can influence a vertical equalization system more easily than a horizontal system because it is less clear who receives the benefits and who pays the costs.

Fiscal equalization is shaped by the institutional framework of each country and is thus very country-specific. It will be influenced by factors such as size, the number of local governments and their geographic distribution, local responsibilities and sources of revenue, and the division of powers among levels of government (Blöchliger et al., 2007). The following sets out examples of local equalization programmes in five countries: three are federal countries where equalization is from the provincial or state government to local governments (Australia, Canada, and Germany); two are unitary countries (UK and Finland). In the UK, transfers go from the central government to local governments. Finland uses horizontal equalization for revenues but vertical equalization for cost differences.

Australia has a very complex system of equalization and uses local grants commissions to calculate the transfers; Canada is an example of a federal country where local equalization systems exist in only some provinces; and both Canada and Australia are countries where local governments depend largely on property taxes as their only tax revenue. Germany, on the other hand, provides an example of equalization in a system with heavy reliance on more volatile revenue sources at the local level such as business taxes which fluctuate with changes in the economy. The UK equalization programme is part of a very centralized system where local governments rely largely on the residential property tax (council tax) but where recent changes have allowed them to retain a portion of non-residential property taxes. Lastly, Finland is an example of a highly decentralized system with one of the largest local equalization schemes in the OECD. Equalization is significant in large part because local governments supply a wide range of social, health, and education services and have access to income taxes.

Australia

Funding for state transfers to local governments is provided by the Commonwealth government under the *Local Government (Financial Assistance) Act, 1995.*[5] Grants are distributed by each state government through a local government grants commission, an institution that is unique to Australia. The stated advantage of independent commissions is that there is less likely to be political interference in the determination of grant amounts. Others have argued, however, that decisions on the standard of equalization should not be divorced from politics (Shah, 2007).

Although each state has its own formula, they are all required to follow national principles so differences across states are minimal. The main principle is horizontal equalization – each local government body has to be able to function by reasonable effort, at a standard not lower than the average standard of other local governing bodies in the State or Territory. Other principles include (1) effort neutrality whereby individual local government expenditure and revenue decisions do not impact the grant amount; (2) the minimum grant in any year can be no less than it would be entitled to if 30 per cent of the total amount the state/territory grants were distributed on a per capita basis; (3) other grant support to local governments should be taken into account when assessing expenditure needs; (4) the grant should be allocated in a way that recognizes the needs of Aboriginal peoples and Torres Strait Islanders residing in their jurisdiction; and (5) if two local authorities amalgamate, their grant entitlements for the next four years should be equal to the total that would have been provided to each of them separately if they had not amalgamated.

General-purpose grants are allocated on the basis of expenditure need and an assessment of the ability of local governments to raise revenues from property taxes (rates). All municipalities in a state receive grants but poor, small, and rural municipalities receive more on a per capita basis than larger, urban municipalities. Local roads grants are separate grants designed to help local authorities pay for the cost of maintaining roads, even though the grants are unconditional. For the local roads grant, National Principles dictate that the grant should be allocated on the basis of the relative need for road expenditures to preserve road assets. In assessing need, factors such as length, type, and use of the road should be considered.

The general-purpose grant is calculated on the basis of detailed expenditure need and revenue capacity measures, weighted by a broad range of indicators, to account for differences in local conditions (known as "disabilities" or "cost adjustors"). Expenditure needs are defined as "differential costs, relative to standard, that a council needs to provide a standard level of service" (Worthington and Dollery, 2000b: 30). The basic concept behind calculating expenditure need is disability – an influence beyond the local government's control that requires it to spend more money per capita than the standard. In other words, a disability is an exogenous factor that influences the cost of providing services and may include demand factors (for example, influences that stem from socio-economic characteristics such as age, sex, income levels, and so on) or cost factors (such as economies of scale, population dispersion, and so on).

An overall disability factor is calculated for each local government by combining the different disabilities and this factor is used to estimate the standardized expenditure. The formula for the standardized expenditure is the number of units (usually measured by population) multiplied by the standard cost per unit (usually the average state expenditure) and the disability factor (a measure of the local government's disadvantage which is measured by the underlying factors that may lead councils to spend more (or less) per capita than the state average).

Revenue needs are defined as the "differential revenues a council would raise if the standardized revenue effort was applied to its revenue base" (Worthington and Dollery, 2000b: 30). Revenue capacity is calculated by a standardized property tax rate multiplied by the municipality's assessment base averaged over three years. Revenue capacity can also include standardized revenues from user fees and charges (as it does in the State of Victoria, for example, but not in all states). As with expenditures, disabilities can be applied to the standard revenue to account for differences among municipalities that are beyond their control. Examples of disabilities might include household income or socio-economic measures.

Perhaps the most common criticism of the Australian system is its complexity, especially with respect to how expenditure need is estimated. In an effort to determine the exogenous factors that influence expenditures, the formula includes a very large number of variables. The resulting complexity reduces transparency for both local councils and the public.

Although it is generally accepted that equalization grants in Australia reduce fiscal disparities among local governments, studies on the impact of these grants on efficiency are less conclusive (Dollery et al., 2013). For example, it has been argued that the equalization grants may reduce the efficiency of local governments because they provide the largest per capita grants to local governments who are experiencing revenue-raising difficulties and who face high expenditure needs (Dollery et al., 2013). Nevertheless, councils that are cost effective may be rewarded through unit cost adjustments up to the standard.

One study of local equalization grants in New South Wales estimated the impact of equalization grants on technical and scale efficiency for library services, waste management, and planning and regulatory services (Worthington and Dollery, 2000a). Their findings suggest that minimum grant requirements and the failure to calculate non-positive disabilities may exert a negative influence on efficiency. A minimum grant means that some local governments receive expenditure allowances in excess of notional requirements (because they received that amount in the previous year), thus promoting inefficient behaviour. The authors also found that the influence of grants on efficiency varies significantly across local governments and government functions.

It has also been argued that the use of local government expenditures to estimate a state's standard cost masks the impact that several efficient or inefficient councils have on grant allocation (Dollery et al., 2013). For example, an efficient local government would mean a lower standard cost for that function putting strong pressure on councils to improve efficiency to the state standard. If the overall standard is broadly inefficient, meaning a higher standard cost, however, the incentive for councils to remove inefficiency is reduced.

Canada – Nova Scotia

Under the Canadian Constitution, local governments are creatures of the provinces. As a result, provincial–municipal equalization grants are different in each province and, unlike in Australia, there are no national principles for provincial–municipal equalization. In most provinces, the vast majority of transfers are conditional (have to be spent on specific functions) but seven out of ten provinces also provide some form of equalization grants to municipalities.

Equalization grants explicitly recognize both expenditure need and fiscal capacity in only two provinces (Nova Scotia and New Brunswick); the other provinces only take explicit account of fiscal capacity. The two provinces that include measures of expenditure need in the grant formula differentiate their equalization grants by classes of municipalities because of wide divergences in expenditures and revenue-raising capacities of different types of municipalities. Without these groupings, expenditure levels and revenue-raising capacity would over-emphasize fiscal needs and fiscal capacity in the formula because of the significantly higher expenditure levels and tax base in the largest cities.

Under Nova Scotia's equalization programme, each municipality receives an entitlement that is determined by a formula that reflects the community's expenditure need and its fiscal capacity.[6] The formula is applied separately to two classes of communities – Class I which comprises regional municipalities and towns (the larger municipalities) and Class II which comprises mainly county and district municipalities (smaller municipalities). Municipalities are grouped so that cities and towns are equalized against each other rather than against all municipalities in the province. Grouping municipalities to reflect similar circumstances (for example, municipalities could be grouped by population size, urban versus rural, expenditures or revenues) makes sense because similar municipalities (for example, larger municipalities) can be equalized against each other rather than against very different municipalities (for example, smaller municipalities).

The equalization entitlement is determined by a formula that calculates the difference between the "standard expenditure" for the community and its corresponding "standard revenue". Standard expenditures do not include all municipal expenditures but rather are limited to expenditures on police protection, fire protection, transportation services (excluding public transit and operating grants from the provincial government for public works), and 50 per cent of expenditures on environmental services.[7]

Standard revenue is determined by multiplying the standard property tax rate by the uniform assessed value of property. The standard tax rate is calculated by the aggregate standard expenditure (for all municipalities in the group) divided by the aggregate uniform assessment. In other words, it represents the value of the tax rate that if applied to the aggregate uniform assessed value would in theory generate sufficient revenues to cover the standard expenditure. Uniform assessment (after adjusting for certain exemptions) is the assessed value of all residential and commercial property for tax purposes. Assessment is not weighted to reflect differential tax rates between residential and commercial assessment even though commercial tax rates are generally twice the rate on residential properties.

Although the Nova Scotia equalization programme is a fairly standard equalization programme, it only equalizes over less than half of municipal expenditures. It is not clear how these expenditures were chosen but one possibility is that they are considered to be non-discretionary in the sense that councils have little discretion over the levels of service and that these are the services that are essential to the functioning of municipalities (Locke, 2011). By including only some categories of expenditure, an incentive is created to use accounting practices to manipulate expenditure categories and the distribution of equalization entitlements. The grant pool is determined independently of the value of total entitlements so municipalities only receive a fraction of total entitlements. The consequence of scaling back the grant entitlements in this way is that recipient municipalities are left with standardized revenues per dwelling unit that are unequal to standardized expenditures per dwelling unit. There are also provisions to ensure that the equalization grant received by each local government is not less than what it received in 2001–02. This provision means that a municipality that no longer needs equalization will still receive it. Of course, it also means that those municipalities which are entitled to equalization will receive less than the formula would dictate.

Germany

Unlike local governments in Canada and Australia, German municipalities depend heavily on business income taxes and, to a much more limited extent, on property taxes. Moreover, German local governments have the ability to set their own tax rates (on business income and property taxes) and the average statutory rate for the business tax tends to be very high (Buettner and Holm-Hadulla, 2008). Given the revenue sources available to German local governments and the autonomy they have to set tax rates, the need for local equalization is probably greater in Germany than in the other two countries: the more tax autonomy local governments have, the greater will be the disparities and the greater the need for equalization (Blöchliger and Petzold, 2009).

As in Australia and Canada, local equalization in Germany is vertical in the sense that funds are distributed by the *Länder* (state governments) to local governments.[8] The formula generally takes account of expenditure need and revenue-raising capacity but there are differences among the *Länder*. The basic measure of expenditure need is population to which a weighting factor which increases with population size is applied. In North Rhine-Westphalia, for example, weights vary from 1.0 for municipalities with 25,000 people to 1.57 for municipalities with more than 634,000 people (Buettner and Holm-Hadulla, 2008). On the revenue side, the major taxes (local business taxes, property taxes, and share of personal income tax and value added tax) are included in the measure of fiscal capacity. The equalization system ranks all municipalities that are entitled to equalization grants according to the ratio of fiscal capacity to fiscal need – the lower the ratio, the higher the equalization grant. Where fiscal needs are less than or equal to fiscal capacity, no grant is received.

United Kingdom

Local authorities in the UK receive funding from government grants, council tax (residential property tax), business rates (non-residential property taxes), and fees and charges. Because the UK is a unitary state, the central government distributes grants to local councils. Prior to 2013–14, the central government levied and collected business rates and distributed the funds to local authorities roughly on a per capita basis. Local authorities are now permitted to retain 50 per cent of business rate revenues (the local share) and only 50 per cent goes to the central government (the central share). The central share provides most of the funding for the central equalization grant to local authorities.

Central government support of local councils is through the Settlement Funding

Assessment which includes the Revenue Support Grant and the Business Rates Retention Scheme, both of which have elements of equalization built into them. The calculation of the Revenue Support Grant has four components: relative needs, relative resources, central allocation, and a floor damping block (Department for Communities and Local Government, 2013).

The Revenue Support Grant to each authority is calculated by scaling the previous year's allocations in line with how much the total Revenue Support Grant has either increased or decreased. At the local level, the grant is based on an assessment of the needs of the authority (the Relative Needs Amount) and the ability to raise income through means other than business rates (the Relative Resources Amount) (Department for Communities and Local Government, 2012).

For the relative needs amount, the formula is split into seven components reflecting the seven main local service areas (children's services; adults' personal social services; police; fire and rescue; highways maintenance; environmental, protective and cultural services; and capital financing). The formula is not designed to measure the actual need but rather to recognize the factors which affect local costs. The grant formula is built on a basic amount per client plus additional top ups to reflect local circumstances (for example, deprivation, area costs). Because the formula is intended to reflect the relative differences in the cost of providing services, needs are expressed through a weighted per-capita measure.

The calculation of the relative resources amount uses each authority's council tax base to generate a minimum potential level of local income. The authority's tax base is divided by the projected population and this amount is subtracted from the lowest result for all authorities, generating a negative figure which is used to reduce grants to wealthier authorities. Once the relative needs and relative resources have been calculated, there is still money left for distribution. The central government distributes this remaining amount on a per capita basis based on the minimums for each authority already calculated for the needs/resources blocks.

Because it is intended that local authorities receive a reasonable grant increase from year to year, there is a guaranteed minimum increase in the grant on an annual basis. As there is a finite pool of funds, grant increases above the floor are scaled back and used to pay for the floor guarantee. A fundamental change in equalization occurred after 2013–14 when allocations to local authorities were no longer calculated on an annual basis to reflect changes in relative needs. Rather, local authorities with increasing service needs and low or negative growth in their business rates are now required to manage these changes within their individual budgets.

Redistribution also occurs through the Business Rates Retention Scheme. A baseline level of funding is calculated which is essentially the expected baseline of business rates within the local authority. If an authority's business rates exceed the baseline, the excess amount is paid to the central government as a tariff; if the revenues are less than the baseline, central government provides a top up. This scheme provides equalization by ensuring that no local authority is a winner or loser as a result of the change to 50 per cent retention of business rates. Changes as a result of the new retention policy only reflect changes arising from new development rather than pre-existing businesses. This change to 50 per cent retention suggests a move to some decentralization in the UK which has historically been one of the most centralized systems in the OECD.

Finland

Unlike the UK, Finland is highly decentralized and ranks near the top of OECD countries in terms of local tax autonomy with 23 per cent of total tax revenue collected at the local level (see Table 11.3). Finnish municipalities are responsible for a wide range of local services that includes health, education, and social welfare and Finland has one of the largest cost and revenue equalization systems in the OECD as a percentage of GDP (Blöchliger et al., 2007). Equalization comprises a series of unconditional, block grants (André and García, 2014).

As in the other countries that apply local equalization, Finnish municipal equalization operates through two mechanisms: cost adjustment and revenue equalization. Cost adjustment has three components: health and welfare services, education, and a general grant to account for rural and urban cost factors. Previously three separate grants, they were combined into one unified system of grants in 2010 (Lyytikäinen and Moisio, 2009).

The health and welfare grant uses a formula to calculate the cost per capita for each municipality and includes factors such as the population and age structure as well as factors that measure need and circumstances. These factors are combined to determine the national average per capita cost for a municipality's health and welfare services. Sixty-five per cent of this average cost is applied to each municipality and each municipality is expected to finance this figure from its own revenues, with any excess costs funded by the central government grant. The result is to standardize the costs that municipalities face at 65 per cent of the national average (Moisio, 2012).

A similar method is used to calculate the education grant. Cost indicators such as the number of pupils, their characteristics, and external factors are taken into account and used to define a benchmark per capita cost. In the same manner, this benchmark of 58 per cent is applied to each municipality, with the extent to which each municipality's costs exceed the benchmark forming the education element of the grant. Lastly, the general grant is very small (at only approximately 2 per cent of the total grant) and is calculated using several indicators including rural and urban cost factors. These grants are then combined into the single grant.

Revenue equalization is designed to compensate municipalities for disparities in revenue-raising capabilities. Because, as noted earlier, municipalities have significant tax autonomy in Finland, the need for equalization is perhaps stronger than in countries that have less autonomy. Revenue equalization accounts for differences by calculating how much revenue each municipality could raise if it applied average tax rates to its tax base. This amount is used to calculate per capita national average tax revenue. If a municipality has less than 91.86 per cent of the national average tax revenue, it receives the difference in the form of added transfers which are funded by municipalities with tax revenue above the national average whose share of state transfers is reduced by 37 per cent of their excess tax revenues (André and García, 2014).

Municipalities below the threshold do not benefit from increasing their tax base because any gains are offset by reduced grants but those above the threshold are permitted to keep 63 per cent of the gains (André and García, 2014). Minor reforms to equalization were pursued in 2010, but since that time the focus has been on amalgamation and efficiencies to address fiscal disparities rather than further reforms to the equalization system (Moisio, 2002).

Final Comments on Local Equalization

In terms of taxing powers, Australian, UK, and Canadian municipalities rely almost exclusively on property taxes (a fairly stable source of revenue) whereas German municipalities rely more heavily on business income taxes (a more volatile revenue source) and Finnish municipalities on income taxes (also relatively volatile when compared to the property tax). Local equalization has been particularly important in countries with significant tax autonomy and volatile taxes. It has been argued, however, at least in the case of Germany, that equalization transfers give local governments an incentive to levy more of these highly volatile taxes because the grant provides insurance against economic shocks (Buettner and Holm-Hadulla, 2008). It has also been suggested that local business tax rates are high in Germany because the transfers provide an incentive to increase tax rates.[9] The reason is that the revenue consequences of a change in the local tax base are partially compensated by the transfer so if a municipality raises its tax rate and the base falls, it will receive more grants. Equalization transfers reduce the marginal cost of levying business income taxes.

Who benefits most from equalization? In all five countries, transfers are distributed to municipalities on the basis of a formula that includes both cost and revenue equalization. Including both cost and revenues in the formula tends to help metropolitan areas and rural areas more than if just revenues are equalized. If only revenues are equalized, metropolitan areas tend not to benefit from equalization because, on average, they have greater fiscal capacity than other local jurisdictions. Rural and remote areas benefit from revenue equalization because they have limited revenue-raising capacity. In terms of costs, metropolitan areas have relatively greater costs because they have major transit systems to fund, more complex policing, larger social problems, and so on (Bird and Slack, 2013). Rural and remote areas have higher costs because they are unable to take advantage of economies of scale in service provision and face higher transportation costs (Kitchen and Slack, 2006).

Although in most countries large cities and metropolitan areas are seldom treated much differently than other local governments, in practice their expenditures are often both much higher and different in nature (Bahl, 2010; Shah, 2013). Moreover, in principle, their greater ability to pay and other unique characteristics suggest that big cities should generally have more fiscal autonomy than other areas in terms of being more responsible both for delivering local services and for levying and collecting the revenues to pay for such services (Bird and Slack, 2013). In other words, they are probably less in need of equalization, especially where local governments rely solely on property taxes.

Equalization has generally been successful at reducing fiscal disparities: disparities in fiscal capacity have been reduced by two-thirds, on average and, in some countries, disparities have been reduced to zero (Blöchliger et al., 2007).[10] In many countries, however, there tend to be provisions that prevent local governments from receiving fewer grants than in the previous year. Presumably the justification for doing so is to provide some stability and predictability for local governments but it means that the full effects of equalization will not be felt.

There are also potentially some downsides to equalization. In particular, equalization can reduce efforts on the part of local jurisdictions to develop their own tax base because it will reduce their grant funding. A high "equalization tax" (the rate at which additional own-source revenue is equalized away) can reduce the effort of local governments to develop their tax base especially in poor jurisdictions where the equalization rate is high with the result that regional convergence will be less likely (Blöchliger et al., 2007). In designing an equalization transfer, the incentives it creates need to be taken into account. In particular, the transfer should not discourage municipalities from collecting their own revenues or finding other ways to balance their budget.

11.6 GOVERNANCE CHANGES TO ADDRESS FISCAL DISPARITIES WITHIN METROPOLITAN AREAS

Fiscal disparities also exist among jurisdictions within metropolitan areas, especially those metropolitan areas that are characterized by a large number of small local government units.[11] When there are many local government jurisdictions in a metropolitan area, some are likely to be rich communities (in terms of the size of their tax base) and some are poor. Rich communities have a more adequate tax base with which to provide services and may not have as high a level of demands for some services (such as education or social services). Poor communities, on the other hand, may require more services but have only a small tax base on which to levy taxes. The more municipalities within a metropolitan area, the greater is the likelihood that the problem of fiscal disparities will arise.

As noted earlier, properly designed equalization transfers can redistribute funds to poorer municipalities with greater expenditure needs but, unless municipalities are grouped by type as in the Canadian example, each municipality will be compared with other municipalities across a province or nation. To address inequities within metropolitan areas, one option is to consolidate rich and poor areas and, in effect, tax the richer municipalities to help subsidize poorer municipalities. With sufficient financial flexibility, metropolitan governments could be large enough in scale to raise and redistribute revenue within their own region (City Growth Commission, 2014).

Inequities are often greatest between the central city and suburbs. In the US, for example, suburbanization of the population and industry has eroded the tax base of the central cities (the recent bankruptcy of the City of Detroit provides a good example of a declining central city surrounded by some of the richest suburbs in the country). Central cities have lost tax base as middle and high-income households have exited but the need for public services has increased. In some metropolitan areas, however, central cities have greater ability to levy higher tax rates due to agglomeration economies resulting from highly productive firms, skilled labour, and good infrastructure (Blöchliger and Piñero-Campos, 2011). Municipalities that benefit from agglomeration economies have higher tax rates and lower tax base mobility than those located outside of the agglomeration. Examples of higher tax rates in the central city compared to suburban municipalities can be found in countries such as the United States, Spain, and Switzerland (Blöchliger and Piñero-Campos, 2011).

To address fiscal disparities among local jurisdictions in a metropolitan region, two governance models are appropriate – a one-tier consolidated government model and a two-tier government model.[12] Table 11.4 provides examples of cities around the world that have opted for one of these models. Many local jurisdictions opt for voluntary cooperation to address regional issues and, although they rarely cooperate on redistribution, there are a few tax base sharing models whereby municipalities in a region voluntarily

Table 11.4 Metropolitan governance models in selected metropolitan areas

Metropolitan area	Details
One-tier consolidated model	
Toronto	Amalgamation of metropolitan level and 6 lower tiers in 1998
Bergen	Moved from two-tier to one-tier in 2004
Cape Town	Amalgamation of two-tiers in 2000; political boundaries coincide with boundaries of economic region
Madrid	Strong role for regional (autonomous community) government
Berlin	City-state
New York	Metropolitan area extends beyond New York City to include 29 counties in 4 states
Auckland	Merger of 8 municipalities in 2010; political boundaries coincide with economic region
Two-tier model	
Tokyo	Tokyo Metropolitan Government plus 23 special wards, 26 cities, 5 towns, and 8 villages
Barcelona	Metropolitan government plus 36 lower-tier municipalities
Vancouver	Regional district plus 22 municipalities
Seoul	Metropolitan government plus 25 districts and 522 neighbourhoods

Sources: Slack and Côté (2014) which is based on Slack and Chattopadhyay (2013); Zimmermann (2009); Fimreite and Aars (2007); Tokyo (2012); Travers (2005).

cooperate to pool commercial and industrial property taxes or the growth in those taxes. These arrangements are also summarized at the end of this section.

One-tier Consolidated Model

A one-tier consolidated government model involves a single local government with a geographic boundary that covers the entire metropolitan area.[13] It is responsible for providing the full range of local services. Large single-tier governments have generally been formed by amalgamation (the merger of two or more lower-tier municipalities within an existing region) or by annexation (appropriation of a portion of a municipality by an adjacent municipality).

Under a consolidated model, there is a wider tax base for sharing the costs of services that benefit taxpayers across the region so that the quality of service is not tied to the wealth of each constituent jurisdiction. If some local jurisdictions were previously unable to afford an adequate level of service at a reasonable tax rate because they did not have adequate fiscal resources, amalgamation may allow for the provision of a level of service comparable to richer localities in the region.

In addition to addressing fiscal inequities, the consolidated model can provide better regional service coordination, clearer accountability, more streamlined decision-making, and greater efficiency than a series of small, fragmented government units (Bahl and Linn, 1992). Large metropolitan governments may also have the ability to be more competitive in the global economy (Meloche and Vaillancourt, 2013). The larger taxable capacity of a consolidated one-tier government increases its ability to raise revenues, charge user fees, and borrow and thereby allows it be financially more self-sufficient than smaller government units. Metropolitan governments can be given access to more broad-based taxes because capital and labour are less mobile across metropolitan boundaries compared to smaller, local boundaries. Larger, consolidated governments may also have an inherent advantage in tax administration because of their size (Bahl, 2010). Large one-tier governments can also take advantage of economies of scale in service provision and internalize externalities.

On the downside, amalgamation can reduce competition among municipalities and thereby weaken incentives to deliver services efficiently. The consolidation of the upper-tier government and six lower-tier municipalities in Toronto in 1998, for example, was designed to save costs but the evidence suggests that it is unlikely that cost savings were actually achieved (Slack and Bird, 2012). The Toronto amalgamation did result, however, in some redistribution within the metropolitan area, increasing equity among residents in service levels and tax burden. Another downside is that reduced competition may lead to higher tax rates. Charlot, Paty, and Piguet (2012), for example, estimated a model of tax-rate setting for the local business tax in French urban municipalities from 1993 to 2003 and concluded that a reduction in the number of municipalities limits tax competition and increases local business tax rates.

A directly elected, consolidated one-tier government has the advantage that voters can elect decision makers who can be held accountable for their decisions. Yet, a large-scale one-tier government may reduce access and accountability because the jurisdiction becomes too large and bureaucratic and citizens do not feel that they can easily access their government. To overcome this problem, some metropolitan governments have established community committees to address local issues, or satellite offices have been set up across the municipality where people can pay tax bills, apply for building permits, or perform other municipal functions.

A major challenge with a one-tier consolidated structure is determining the appropriate geographic boundary for the metropolitan government. Looking around the world, we find that geographic boundaries of metropolitan governments rarely coincide with the boundaries of the economic region. Even where the geographic boundary does cover the economic region at the time of the consolidation, it will not continue to do so as economic boundaries expand over time – economically dynamic regions, by their nature, eventually outgrow their local political boundaries. Yet, government boundaries are difficult to alter and boundary expansions are rarely attempted by state or national governments simply because they are politically unpopular, involve substantial adjustments, and are difficult to get right (Clark and Clark, 2014).

Consolidation of municipalities through amalgamation, merger, or annexation to one tier turns out not to be very common. Nevertheless, there have been some noteworthy examples. The City of Cape Town was established as a one-tier municipality in 2000 by amalgamating the two-tier structure that was created following apartheid. The rationale for the amalgamation was to reduce the substantial inequities in services between the rich and poor local authorities by creating "one city one tax base" (Steytler, 2013). There was also recognition of the need for regional coordination of services. The boundaries of Cape Town, drawn by the Municipal Demarcation Board (an independent authority responsible for determining categories of municipalities, outer boundaries, and boundaries of wards), have resulted in a metropolitan city that is "truly bounded" in the sense that the entire metropolitan area falls within the political boundaries with little or no spillovers in service delivery (Steytler, 2013).

To improve local responsiveness in a one-tier consolidated structure, Cape Town has 24 sub-councils which exercise only those powers delegated by the municipal council. Sub-councils can supervise the expenditure of ward allocation budgets (there are 116 wards) and deal with building and planning applications, as well as other matters. They are not elected but they do allow the metropolitan city to devolve some decision-making to a level closer to the people without giving up any power. The metropolitan government has also adopted a system of ward forums with 20 members from community organizations but their effectiveness is questionable (Steytler, 2013).

The history of municipal amalgamation in Toronto spans more than fifty years beginning in 1954 with a system of one-tier municipalities, the subsequent creation of a two-tier metropolitan government (a metropolitan tier and 13 lower-tier municipalities) in 1954, and the most recent amalgamation in 1998 which saw the merger of the metropolitan and six lower tiers to create a single-tier City of Toronto. It has been argued that the amalgamation created a city that, at the same time, is too big and too small. It is too big to be responsive to local residents and too small to address the regional issues that plague the region. Nevertheless, as noted earlier, one of the successes of the Toronto amalgamation is that it resulted in a more equitable sharing of costs across the metropolitan area (Slack and Bird, 2013).

Two-tier Model

Another way to address fiscal disparities in a metropolitan region is by implementing a two-tier government model where there is an upper-tier governing body (usually a region, district, or metropolitan area) that encompasses a fairly large geographic area and two or more lower-tier or area municipalities (such as cities, towns, or villages). Under this model, redistribution happens at the upper-tier level which is also responsible for services that provide region-wide benefits, generate externalities, and display economies of scale. Services that provide local benefits are the responsibility of the lower tier.

Redistribution is achieved at the upper-tier level through a combination of tax and spending policies. Taxes are generally levied at uniform rates across the region, with the contribution of each lower-tier municipality to the upper-tier municipality dependent on the size of its tax base. The upper-tier government makes expenditures on services that benefit the entire city-region and those benefits are not necessarily distributed among the lower-tier municipalities in the same way as revenues are collected. A uniform tax at the upper-tier level combined with region-wide expenditures serves to redistribute resources from municipalities with larger tax bases to those with smaller tax bases. Nevertheless, there may still be differentiation in service levels and tax rates with respect to services provided by lower-tier municipalities.

Two-tier structures potentially have important advantages over the one-tier model in terms of accountability, efficiency, and local responsiveness. Critics of the two-tier model, however, commonly argue that costs will be higher because of waste and duplication in service provision. There is, however, little evidence to support this argument. It has also been criticized for being less transparent and more confusing to taxpayers than a one-tier model because they can seldom determine precisely who is responsible for which services.

Two-tier governance in London is generally regarded as a successful model. Greater London, with a population of 8.7 million, comprises 32 boroughs and the Corporation of London. The Greater London Authority (GLA) with a directly elected Mayor came into being in 2002. The GLA is responsible for region-wide services. Transport for London is responsible for roads, buses, trains, subways, traffic lights, regulation of taxis. The London Development Agency coordinates economic development. The Metropolitan Police Authority and the London Fire and Emergency Planning Authority are also included under the GLA umbrella. The boroughs retain primary planning responsibility as the local planning authority and are responsible for housing, education, social, and health services. Redistribution occurs at the upper-tier level because the geographic distribution of council taxes does not necessarily match the geographic distribution of spending at the upper-tier level. Disparities may still remain at the local level, however.

Barcelona is a more recent example of the formation of a two-tier structure. Legislation passed by the regional Parliament in 2010 significantly modified the governance of Barcelona through the creation of an upper-tier metropolitan government with 36 lower-tier jurisdictions. This new metropolitan body, which came into existence in 2011, replaced three previous metropolitan bodies: the Metropolitan Entity of Hydraulic Services and Waste Management (EMSHTR) which covered 33 municipalities, the Metropolitan Transport Entity (EMT) which covered 18 municipalities and the Association of Municipalities of the Metropolitan Area of Barcelona (MMAMB) which was a voluntary body made of 31 municipalities. Not only was the metropolitan area greater than that covered by these metropolitan bodies but it replaced three different entities in the same metropolitan area (each made up of a different number of municipalities). The new structure reduces the substantial (and unproductive) complexity of the previous system (Bosch et al., 2013). It also permits redistribution among municipalities at the upper-tier level.

Examples from the United States are rare but include Miami-Dade which is a two-tier metropolitan government that was introduced in Dade County in 1957. The upper-tier government (the county) covers 27 municipalities. Louisville, Kentucky provides an example of a fairly recent city–county consolidation, the first successful consolidation in more than 30 years in the US. However, the merger focused only on the city and one county government and there remains little cooperation at a regional level.[14]

Tax Base Sharing

In the absence of creating a metropolitan structure (one-tier or two-tier), some jurisdictions have implemented tax base sharing on a voluntary basis. Perhaps the most well-known example is the tax base sharing programme in Minneapolis-Saint Paul in the United States. Minneapolis-Saint Paul is a metropolitan area with about three million people that includes two central cities, seven counties, 143 cities, 43 townships, and 48 school districts. The Minnesota Fiscal Disparities Act, passed in 1971, was designed to address increasing property tax rates, tax base and rate disparities, and inter-jurisdictional competition for development in the metropolitan region.

Under the tax base sharing scheme, each municipality in the metropolitan area contributes 40 per cent of the growth in its commercial/industrial tax base to a regional pool and receives money from the pool based on the size of its population and the market value of all property in the community compared to the metropolitan average (for example, if a community is below the average market value, they receive a larger share of the pool). Commercial/industrial property is taxed at local rate and area-wide rate; the area-wide rate reduces differences across the region.

Recent changes in the financing of local authorities in the UK have also resulted in a voluntary tax base sharing programme for business rates. By allowing local authorities to retain 50 per cent of the business rates collected at the local level, 111 local authorities have come together on a voluntary basis to pool business rates (in 18 pools) and allow them to benefit from economic growth across the regions and smooth the impact of rates volatility across a wider geographic area (Department for Communities and Local Government, 2014).

Tax base sharing is a voluntary way for communities to share in the community's growth, reduces competition for the tax base, and encourages regional cooperation without altering the structure of local governments or removing local control over tax rates and collection. It reduces disparities across regions but, in these two examples, only for commercial and industrial properties and not for residential properties.

11.7 CONCLUDING COMMENTS

In a decentralized system, it is inevitable that there will be fiscal disparities among local governments – there will be differences in preferences for local services, costs and needs, and ability to pay for services. Some local governments will be able to deliver a broad range of high-quality services at reasonable tax rates; others will not. To address the resulting inequities, this chapter has looked into two broad approaches – central or state/provincial equalization programmes and reorganization of local government structure.

Equalization is designed to ensure that local governments can deliver a standard level of services by levying a standard tax rate. It has largely been successful at reducing or even eliminating fiscal disparities across local governments but, to get it right, often involves the design of a very complex formula. Equalization can also have an impact on the size of the local tax base (providing a disincentive to increase it), the level of tax rates (again, reducing the incentive to increase them), and the amount of expenditures (providing an incentive to increase them). Although equalization can be justified on equity grounds, it should not discourage local governments from collecting their own revenues or finding other ways to balance their budget.

Municipal reorganization can also serve a redistributive purpose by combining rich and poor municipalities within one taxing jurisdiction. A review of governance models around the world does not provide a clear indication of which model works best because the choice of model depends on the context and history of central-local relations in each jurisdiction. Yet, when it comes to reducing fiscal disparities, some form of regional governance structure is needed. Nevertheless, most metropolitan areas are characterized by fragmentation and voluntary cooperation is the most popular model. In some cases, municipalities within a metropolitan region will choose to share a portion of their tax base, but this type of redistribution is only partial and it is voluntary. Otherwise, redistribution does not tend to happen in metropolitan areas voluntarily.

As Pacione (2001) notes, it is unrealistic to expect that local politicians and bureaucrats would promote the common good of the metropolitan area at the expense of their own jurisdiction. For this reason, redistribution is likely to be most successful if achieved through equalization transfers from central or provincial/state governments or through consolidation of local governments within a metropolitan area imposed by senior governments. In this time of fiscal austerity, it is unclear how long central or provincial/state governments will be able to continue to fund local equalization programmes and these transfers may decline. If that is the case, an alternative might be greater empowerment of local governments to levy their own taxes coupled with municipal restructuring that will allow for equalization within large metropolitan areas.

NOTES

1. The author would like to thank Guy Miscampbell for research assistance and Almos Tassonyi for comments on an earlier draft of this chapter.
2. The public finance literature assigns three roles to government – stabilization, income redistribution, and resource allocation but only resource allocation is appropriate for local governments. For more details, see Bird and Slack (1993).
3. Countries that have the highest degree of fiscal decentralization tend to rely more heavily on personal income taxes followed by property taxes (Brülhart, Bucovestsky and Schmidheiny, 2014).
4. Other reasons for equalization include fiscal externalities and insurance (Blöchliger et al., 2007). In a decentralized fiscal system, unequal tax bases can provide incentives to locate in high tax base regions and thereby distort the location decisions of mobile factors. Equalization grants can equalize tax bases across regions and eliminate the source of inefficiency arising from fiscal externalities. Equalization grants can also provide regions with insurance against negative shocks on income or employment.
5. For a more complete description and analysis of the Australian system, see Worthington and Dollery (2000a) and Slack (2014a).
6. The information on equalization grants in Nova Scotia comes largely from the *Municipal Grants Act* and (Locke, 2011). An earlier version of this description also appears in Slack (2014a).
7. The expenditures not included in the formula are: general government services, protective services other than fire and police, public transit services, public health and welfare, environmental development, recreation and culture, fiscal services.
8. An earlier, more detailed, version of this description can be found in Slack (2014a).
9. The average business tax rate is 13 per cent (Buettner and Holm-Hadulla, 2008).
10. It should be noted that this study looked at both federal–provincial and federal–local equalization and not provincial–local equalization.
11. Urban areas in OECD countries tend to be very fragmented. On average, urban areas with more than 500,000 people contain 74 municipalities and there are 4.9 municipalities per 100,000 residents (Brülhart et al., 2014).
12. For a more detailed discussion of metropolitan governance models, see Slack (2014b) and Slack and Côté (2014).
13. A one-tier model is also referred to in the literature as the metropolitan reform tradition (Kübler and Heinelt, 2005) or the metropolitan model (Bahl, Linn and Wetzel, 2013).
14. The one exception is the Kentuckiana Regional Development Agency (crossing two states), that covers the nine core urban counties.

REFERENCES

André, Christophe and Clara García (2014), *Local Public Finances and Municipal Reform in Finland*, Paris: OECD.

Bahl, Roy (2008), 'Opportunities and risks of fiscal decentralization: a developing country perspective', in Gregory K. Ingram and Yu-Hung Hong (eds), *Fiscal Decentralization and Land Policies*, Cambridge, MA: Lincoln Institute of Land Policy, pp. 19–37.

Bahl, Roy (2010), 'Financing metropolitan cities, in United Cities and Local Governments', *Local Government*

Finance: The Challenges of the 21st Century, Second Global Report on Decentralization and Democracy, Barcelona: UCLG.

Bahl, Roy and Johannes Linn (1992), *Urban Public Finance in Developing Countries*, New York: Oxford University Press.

Bahl, Roy W., Johannes F. Linn and Deborah Wetzel (2013), 'Governing and financing metropolitan areas in the developing world', in Roy W. Bahl, Johannes F. Linn and Deborah Wetzel (eds), *Financing Metropolitan Governments in Developing Countries*, Cambridge, MA: Lincoln Institute of Land Policy, pp. 1–30.

Bennett, Robert, J. (1980), *The Geography of Public Finance: Welfare under Fiscal Federalism and Local Government Finance*, London: Methuen.

Bird, Richard, M. (2011), 'Are there trends in local finance? A cautionary note on comparative studies and normative models of local government finance', IMFG Papers on Municipal Finance and Governance, No. 1, Toronto: Institute on Municipal Finance and Governance, University of Toronto.

Bird, Richard, M. and Enid Slack (1993), *Urban Public Finance in Canada*, Toronto: John Wiley and Sons.

Bird, Richard, M. and Enid Slack (2013), 'Metropolitan public finance', in Roy Bahl, Johannes Linn and Deborah Wetzel (eds), *Financing Metropolitan Governments in Developing Countries*, Cambridge, MA: Lincoln Institute of Land Policy, pp. 135–158.

Blöchliger, Hansjörg and Oliver Petzold (2009), *Taxes or Grants: What Revenue Source for Sub-Central Governments? Economics Department Working Paper*, Paris: OECD Publishing.

Blöchliger, Hansjörg and José Piñero-Campos (2011), *Tax Competition between Sub-central Governments*, Paris: OECD Publishing.

Blöchliger, Hansjörg, Olaf Merk, Claire Charbit and Lee Mizell (2007), *Fiscal Equalisation in OECD Countries*, Paris: OECD Publishing.

Bosch, Nuria, Marta Espasa and Joaquim Solé-Vilanova (2013), 'Governance and finance of large metropolitan areas in federal systems: the case of Spain', in Enid Slack and Rupak Chattopadhyay (eds), *Governance and Finance of Metropolitan Areas in Federal Systems*, Toronto: Oxford University Press, pp. 223–253.

Brülhart, Marius, Sam Bucovetsky and Kurt Schmidheiny (2014), 'Taxes in cities', Munich: CESifo Working Paper Series No. 4951.

Buettner, Thiess and Fédéric Holm-Hadulla (2008), *Fiscal Equalization: The Case of German Municipalities*, Munich: CESifo DICE Report.

Charlot, Sylvie, Sonia Paty and Virginie Piguet (2012), *Does Fiscal Cooperation Increase Local Tax Rates in Urban Areas?*, Grenoble: Institut National de la Recherche Agronomique.

Chernick, Howard and Andrew Reschovsky (2013), *The Fiscal Health of US Cities*, Toronto: Institute on Municipal Finance and Governance.

City Growth Commission (2014), *Powers to Grow: City Finance and Governance*, UK, September.

Clark, Rt Hon Greg and Greg Clark (2014), *Nations and the Wealth of Cities: A New Phase in Public Policy*, London: Centre for London.

Côté, André and Michael Fenn (2014), 'Provincial–municipal relations in Ontario: approaching and inflection point', IMFG Papers on Municipal Finance and Governance, Number 17, Toronto: Institute on Municipal Finance and Governance, University of Toronto.

Dafflon, Bernard (2007), 'Fiscal capacity equalization in horizontal fiscal equalization programs', in Robin Boadway and Anwar Shah (eds), *Intergovernmental Fiscal Transfers: Principles and Practice*, Washington, DC: The World Bank, pp. 361–396.

Department for Communities and Local Government (2012), *Business Rates Retention Technical Consultation – Equality Statement*, London: UK Government.

Department for Communities and Local Government (2013), *Business Rates Retention and the Local Government Finance Settlement*, London: UK Government.

Department for Communities and Local Government (2014), *Business Rates Retention – Pooling Prospectus 2015–16*, London: UK Government.

Dollery, Brian, Michael Kortt and Bligh Grant (2013), *Funding the Future: Financial Sustainability and Infrastructure Finance in Australian Local Governments*, Sydney: The Federation Press.

Fenge, Robert and Volker Meier (2001), *Why Cities Should Not be Subsidized*, Munich: CESifo.

Fimreite, Anne Lise and Jacob Aars (2007), 'Tensions and cooperation in a multilevel system: integrating District Councils in city government in Bergen', *Local Government Studies*, **33** (5), 677–698.

Kim, Junghun and Jorgen Lotz (2008), *Measuring Local Government Expenditure Needs*, Copenhagen: The Korea Institute of Public Finance and The Danish Ministry of Social Welfare.

Kitchen, Harry (2013), 'Canadian municipalities and the recent recession: what have we learned?' Unpublished paper.

Kitchen, Harry and Enid Slack (2006), 'Providing public services in remote areas', in Richard M. Bird and François Vaillancourt (eds), *Perspectives on Fiscal Federalism*, Washington, DC: World Bank Institute.

Kübler, Daniel and Hubert Heinelt (2005), 'Metropolitan governance, democracy and the dynamics of place',

in Hubert Heinelt and Daniel Kübler (eds), *Metropolitan Governance: Capacity, Democracy and the Dynamics of Place*, Abingdon, Oxon: Routledge, pp. 8–28.
Locke, Wade (2011), *Municipal Fiscal Sustainability: Alternative Funding Arrangements to Promote Fiscal Sustainability of Newfoundland and Labrador Municipalities – The Role of Income and Sales Taxes*, St. John's: Municipalities Newfoundland and Labrador.
Lyytikäinen, Teemu and Antti Moisio (2009), 'Aiming to offset local cost disadvantages: The case of Finland', Presented at the Copenhagen Seminar on Designing Grants to Subcentral Governments, Copenhagen: VATT, 17–18 September.
Meloche, Jean-Philippe and François Vaillancourt (2013), 'Public finance in Montréal: in search of equity and efficiency', IMFG Papers on Municipal Finance and Governance, No. 15, Toronto: Institute on Municipal Finance and Governance, University of Toronto.
Moisio, Antti (2002), *Determinants of Expenditure Variation in Finnish Municipalities*, Helsinki: Government Institute for Economic Research.
Moisio, Antti (2012), 'Municipal partnerships: the experience of Nordic countries', in Nuria Bosch and Albert Solé-Olle (eds), *IEB Report on Fiscal Federalism 2011*, Barcelona: IEB, pp. 20–27.
OECD (2013), *Fiscal Federalism 2014: Making Decentralisation Work*, Paris: OECD Publishing.
OECD (2014a), *National Accounts, 2011–2012*, Paris: OECD Statistics.
OECD (2014b), *Revenue Statistics, 2011–2012*, Paris: OECD Statistics.
Pacione, Michael (2001) 'Geography and public finance: planning for fiscal equity in a metropolitan region', *Progress in Planning*, **56**, 1–59.
Shah, Anwar (2007), 'Institutional arrangements for intergovernmental fiscal transfers', in Robin Boadway and Anwar Shah (eds), *Intergovernmental Fiscal Transfers: Principles and Practice*, Washington, DC: The World Bank, pp. 293–317.
Shah, Anwar (2013), 'Grant financing of metropolitan areas', in Roy Bahl, Johannes Linn and Deborah Wetzel (eds), *Financing Metropolitan Governments in Developing Countries*, Cambridge, MA: Lincoln Institute of Land Policy, pp. 213–242.
Slack, Enid (2014a), 'Local finances and fiscal equalization schemes in a comparative perspective', paper presented to a Conference on Making Fiscal Equalization Work, Freie Universität Berlin, 27 June.
Slack, Enid (2014b), 'Innovative governance approaches in metropolitan areas in developing countries', paper presented to UN Habitat Global Expert Group Meeting on Urban Development Financing: The Challenge of Local Governments in Developing Countries, Barcelona, 25 June.
Slack, Enid and Richard M. Bird (2012), 'Merging municipalities: is bigger better?', in Antti Moisio (ed.), *Rethinking Local Government: Essays on Municipal Reform* (Vol. Publication 61), Helsinki: Government Institute for Economic Research, pp. 83–130.
Slack, Enid and Rupak Chattopadhyay (eds) (2013), *Governance and Finance of Metropolitan Areas in Federal Systems*, Toronto: Oxford University Press.
Slack, Enid and André Côté (2014), 'Comparative urban governance', Future of Cities working paper, London: Foresight, UK Department for Business Innovation and Skills.
Slack, Enid, Zachary Spicer and Makram Montacer (2014),'Decentralization and gender equity', Occasional Paper Series 14, Ottawa: Forum of Federations.
Smart, Michael (2007), 'The incentive effects of grants', in Robin Boadway and Anwar Shah (eds), *Intergovernmental Fiscal Transfers: Principles and Practice*, Washington, DC: The World Bank, pp. 203–223.
Steytler, Nico (2013), 'Governance and finance of two South African metropolitan areas', in Enid Slack and Rupak Chattopadhyay (eds), *Governance and Finance of Metropolitan Areas in Federal Systems*, Toronto: Oxford University Press, pp. 189–222.
Tiebout, Charles, M. (1956), 'A pure theory of local expenditures', *Journal of Political Economy*, **64**, 416–424.
Tokyo (2012), Tokyo Metropolitan Government (2006–2010) Overview of Tokyo – Tokyo's Financial System.
Travers, Tony (2005), *International Comparisons of Local Government Finance: Propositions and Analysis*, London: London School of Economics and Political Science.
Worthington, Andrew and Brian Dollery (2000a), 'Productive efficiency and the Australian local government grants process: an empirical analysis of New South Wales local government', *Australasian Journal of Regional Studies*, **6** (1), 95–121.
Worthington, Andrew and Brian Dollery (2000b), 'The debate on Australian federalism: local government financial interrelationships with State and Commonwealth governments', *Australian Journal of Public Administration*, **59** (4), 25–35.
Zimmermann, Horst (2009), 'Berlin, Germany', in Enid Slack and Rupak Chattopadhyay (eds), *Finance and Governance of Capital Cities in Federal Systems*, Montreal: McGill-Queen's University Press, pp. 101–125.

12. The state as institutional investor: unpacking the geographical political economy of sovereign wealth funds

Adam D. Dixon

12.1 INTRODUCTION

In the last decade there has been a proliferation of state-sponsored institutional investors (Monk, 2011). Although state-sponsored investors are not necessarily a novelty, this massive growth in the number of funds and the total assets under management, coupled with their growing visibility in the global political economy and global financial markets, has led many to classify them as a new class of institutional investors (Rozanov, 2005). Now commonly referred to as sovereign wealth funds (SWF), these institutional investors can be found in nearly all different types of political regime, from social democracies to autocracies, and in high-income developed economies and low-income developing economies. Rough estimates place the number of SWFs at 60, with total assets under management between US$5 and US$6 trillion.[1] Even though total assets under management are still a small proportion of total global financial assets, the largest SWFs are big enough to sway markets or take massive positions in companies and other asset classes. And even where moving markets is impossible, as in the case of smaller funds, SWFs notionally bring the tools and opportunities of modern finance into the economic toolkit available to government (Balding, 2012; Clark, Dixon, and Monk, 2013).

If a reflection of the financialization of state and economy (Dixon, 2014; Dore, 2008; Pike and Pollard, 2010), governments around the world have been seduced by the SWF, even in countries where there is no substantial surplus capital to fund a SWF. For example, in sub-Saharan Africa there are around 10 SWFs depending on what definition is used. However, there are at least another nine SWFs under consideration across the continent, as governments look to potential future commodity revenues (Dixon and Monk, 2014a). In this respect, SWFs may simply represent a current fashion or fad, where the SWF is more of a status symbol for governments, rather than a necessary policy tool (Chwieroth, 2014). This may explain some of the more illogical or impetuous cases of SWF development, or why some governments seem to be taken by the promises of modern finance. But, this does not completely discount that SWFs may provide important policy options for governments, and that their emergence reflects developments in the global political economy.

Although emulation and institutional mimesis are to be expected in the context of increasing flows of capital, people, and ideas, within globalization are different causal explanations for the emergence of SWFs on the world stage. Put simply, there are structural drivers that make SWFs possible, limiting agential explanations. There are two primary types of SWF whose growth and development are partly related: commodity-based SWFs and reserve-based SWFs. Commodity-based SWFs have become an important tool for resource-rich countries, particularly in the Middle East, in seeking to manage and diversify resource revenues. Over the last decade commodity prices have been higher than the historical average, leading to significant growth in the number of these funds and in their assets under management. High commodity prices reflect, in part, the rapid growth and expansion of East Asian emerging market economies, namely China. The rapid growth of many of these economies reflects an export-led development model, which has resulted in the accumulation of massive foreign exchange reserves. As there is a cost to holding, some governments have chosen to establish a SWF to invest these funds in order to achieve higher returns.

One of the most consequential social developments of the twenty-first century will be demographic aging. While sub-Saharan Africa will remain relatively young, most other high-income and middle-income regions of the world will experience considerable demographic aging, with Western Europe and Japan aging the most. Social security systems have been reformed considerably in the last few decades to encourage the capitalization of retirement-income to reduce the demands on state-sponsored pay-as-you-go pension systems, which will come under increasing strain as more people begin to draw pensions and fewer people are contributing (Holzmann and Hinz, 2005). Failing increases in productivity, the economic consequences can be significant for the economy (Barr, 2012; Nyce and Schieber, 2005). Notwithstanding such reform, some countries, such as New Zealand, have moved to partially prefund state pension obligations through a pension reserve fund. Pension reserve funds, like other SWFs, are supposed to be able to diversify assets and tap the higher returns available on global financial markets, rather than leaving the financing of public pensions exclusively to the returns from national economic growth.

By this logic, the emergence of SWFs seems to be reactionary; they are a response to economic and social change at various scales from the nation-state to the global economy. But the agency of SWFs should not be discounted. Notwithstanding there direct role in certain policy domains, SWFs provide certain intangible power resources in the global political economy, if one agrees that financial power is an important resource for nation-states in the ebb and flow global capitalist market formation. Yet the agency of SWFs should not be overstated in geopolitics. Institutional investors of any kind and any size are limited in what they can do as financial institutions. By that same logic, the capacity of SWFs to shape economic growth and development at different scales is also limited.

In this chapter we consider the rise of SWFs and their place in the global political economy and their role in national and regional economic development, unpacking their different forms and functions as institutional investors and as policy tools. As such, this chapter is a work of political economy and economic geography. In the next section we consider the growth of SWFs as a power resource for some states to engage the global financial economy, while providing a source of resistance against the predations of the market and global economic and social change. The following three sections considers the origins and political-economic foundation and effects of the different aforementioned types of SWF. The penultimate section considers the scope and limits of SWFs in shaping economic growth and development at different scales. The final section concludes.

12.2 SWFS AND THE DOUBLE MOVEMENT

Even though SWFs have gained increased notoriety in the last decade, not least because there are so many new ones, the SWF is not actually a recent phenomenon. The contemporary organizational form of the SWF has developed in line with global financial integration and the dissemination of common asset management techniques, but the sovereign sponsorship of wealth funds has a long history. For example, at the state level in the United States, government-sponsored wealth funds have existed since the nineteenth century. Some consider the first SWF to be the Texas Permanent School Fund, which was founded in 1854 and whose investment income is used to supplement the funding of primary and secondary education in the state (Rose, 2011). But subnational SWFs are less significant in terms of geopolitics and the international political economy than SWFs sponsored by nation-states. The latter's history is more recent. One of the first still existing SWFs is the Kuwait Investment Authority, which was founded in London in 1954 as the Kuwait Investment Board while the country was still a protectorate of Great Britain. In that respect, the SWF was a creation of western financial capitalism and not a sui generis creation derivative of some form of statist non-liberal capitalism (Clark, Dixon, and Monk, 2013).

The map in Figure 12.1 shows SWFs with assets under management of at least US$1 billion at year-end 2013. As is evident, the largest SWFs in the world are concentrated in the Middle East and East Asia, save for the Norwegian GPF-G. In the western hemisphere there are few SWFs in comparison and the size of assets under management pales in comparison. This reflects, arguably, the limited scope national governments have in accumulating capital in the form of a SWF. In the United States, for example, the federal government would have great difficulty in legitimizing a government-sponsored institutional investor, notwithstanding the legitimate role of public-sector pension funds and the Social Security Trust Fund – the latter of which is simply an accounting entry that the government owes itself. If the federal government were to accumulate capital surpluses in any form, it would likely be forced to redistribute such surpluses, probably through lower taxation, or it would likely be forced to retire national debts. Ultimately, the politics of sponsoring an institutional investor is contentious where state intervention is already problematic and where financial markets and the financial services sector are already well-developed. This feature of the US political economy is in many respects shared across other advanced economies, hence the few SWFs present in Europe. But the limited incidence of SWFs in the advanced economies is not simply a function of domestic political economy. It is, rather, explained by the relative economic and political power of the advanced economies in the global political economy. In short, there is little demand for their creation, even if there was the means to do so.

Although western financial capitalism appears biased against more statist and interventionist forms of capitalism, the state is still a crucial actor in the construction and maintenance of the global capitalist market economy (Wallerstein, 1983). As such, states in various ways engage with global capitalism, such as through supporting industrial development, financing R&D, or protecting intellectual property. The SWF can be classed as another tool for engaging the global political economy (Dixon and Monk, 2012; Hatton and Pistor, 2012; Haberly, 2014). Notwithstanding the underlying intent of the engagement via the SWF, the engagement ensures, in abstract terms, a certain degree of

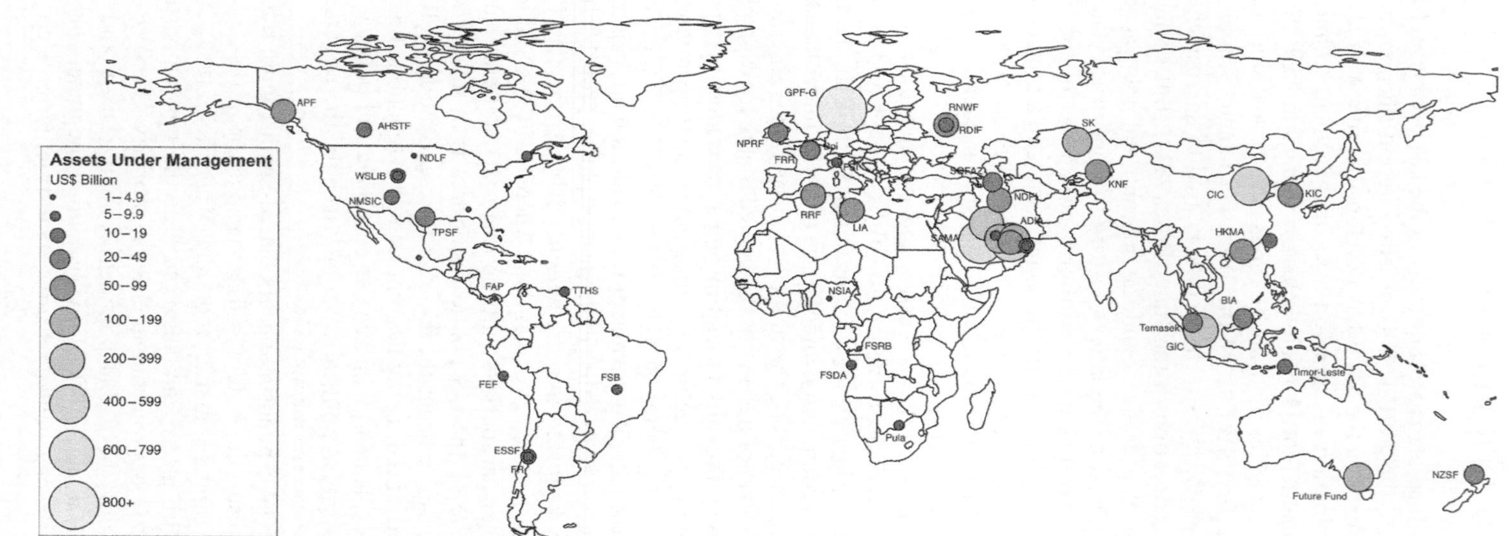

Source: Author's compilation.

Figure 12.1 The geography of sovereign wealth funds

proximity for the state (cf. Boschma and Frenken, 2010).[2] Put slightly differently, states have various ways of engaging and following the leading edge of global capitalist development, largely through regulation, supervision, and macroeconomic management exercised through fiscal and monetary authority. The SWF provides another avenue through which the state can participate (which does not necessarily entail active influence) in what is ostensibly private market activity.

Recognizing that global capitalist development is a powerful force, with its expansionary logic driven by the search for new markets, technological change, the profit motive, and the political ambitions of individuals and entire populations, engagement for the nation-state is by default a necessity (Rodrik, 2011). Some may argue that there is a choice (Gibson-Graham, 1996), but the collapse of alternative economic systems, namely the fall of communism, appears to limit the choice not to engage. Despite the necessity to engage, engagement does not me that states are not sensitive to the predations and risks associated with global markets and the rapid changes and uncertainty they may bring. States employ a variety of tools to resist or tame the potential negative consequences of the market (Polanyi, [1944]1975). Welfare state institutions and social insurance are the most obvious form of resistance. Others include anything from nontariff barriers to the projection of military power and non-market industrial policy underwritten by a military-industrial complex, as the United States exhibits. Obviously, many states around the world are very limited in their ability to resist the incursions of global market forces, in comparison to the high-income advanced economies of North America, Europe, and Japan.

The SWF offers a tool of resistance. There are obvious limits to resisting the pressures of the market, at least in the medium to long term. The force of the market will force change eventually. But in the short term a SWF can provide a country the means to withstand an external shock, such as a balance of payments crisis. In that respect, the SWF can be utilized as a lender of last resort, underwriting a fledgling economy through the worst moments of a crisis. The SWF is therefore an insurance policy at the disposal of a country's economic managers. More importantly, the SWF is an insurance policy over which they have control and direction. Calling on the economic resources of the country's SWF does not come with conditionalities, as a country would face, for example, if it were to seek help from the International Monetary Fund – conditionalities that may be politically undesirable and injurious to some in society.

If resisting the economic and social consequences of short-term economic crises is important, particularly for sustaining higher potential economic growth and a more stable developmental trajectory, it is perhaps even more important to resist capitalist crises of long duration. These are the crises that result from the accumulation of change in social structures, such as demographic aging, and the evolutionary technological change the reshape, and in some cases ultimately eliminate, entire industries. They are also the crises that are produced by capitalist geographic expansion and consolidation of markets for products and services (Storper and Walker, 1989), when certain forms of resistance and protection a country can yield become unviable or helplessly inadequate. Without overstating the capacity, competence, and power of any institutional investor and its financial resources to shape possibilities for resisting crises of a long duration, the SWF may still be an important component of a polity's answer to future economic and demographic contingencies. Perhaps the most obvious, an SWF, in the form of a pension reserve fund, functions to mitigate the effects of demographic aging by buffering a pay-as-you-go social security system.

If the language of engagement and resistance provides a useful, yet partial, means to conceptualize the SWF as a policy device at the disposal of the sovereign state, it does not provide an adequate explanation for the conditions that make the creation of a SWF possible in the first instance. Nor does it provide sufficient clarity as to the different types of SWF. To understand the foundations of any SWF, it is necessary to consider its source capital. Although the source capital does not necessarily determine the mandate of a SWF in all cases, source capital is frequently correlated with its stated policy function. Source capital, as indicated previously, generally comes from three different sources: commodity revenues, balances of payments surpluses, and fiscal surpluses. In each case, there is a wider connection to developments in the global economy.

12.3 A WEALTH OF COMMODITIES

Over much of the twentieth century the price of basic commodities, particularly petroleum, was relatively stable. Aside from the two oil shocks of the 1970s, the price of petroleum for consuming countries and regions was relatively low, and therefore so were the revenues received by producers. As Figure 12.2 shows, the 2013 adjusted price of crude oil in 1900 was US$33 per barrel. In 1950 the 2013 adjusted price was US$16 per barrel. For much of the post-Second World War economic boom years in the advanced countries, prices remained below this. The first oil shock in 1973 saw the real (2013 dollars) price

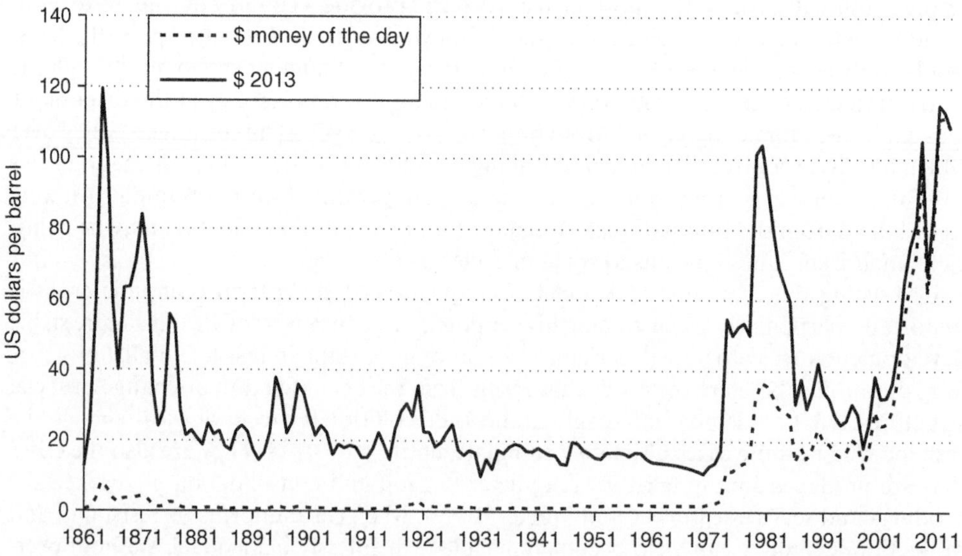

Source: BP Statistical Review of World Energy 2014, www.bp.com/en/global/corporate/energy-economics/statistical-review-of-world-energy.html.

Figure 12.2 Crude oil prices 1861–2013

increase from US$17 per barrel to US$54 per barrel in 1974. The second oil shock in 1979 saw prices increase again to over US$100 (2013 dollars) in 1980. During that period oil producing countries, particularly in the Middle East, received huge windfalls from the crisis, enriching them (and their leaders) in the process. It was this period that set the groundwork for some of the world's largest current SWFs (see Figure 12.1).

After the 1970s oil shocks petroleum prices decreased back toward their historical average. For petroleum producing countries this still represented positive cash flow, but not to the degree experienced during the oil shocks. Yet, this stability in oil prices would be short-lived. At the turn of the century prices would resume an upward trajectory, fueled by increasingly strong demand from fast growing emerging market economies like China and India coupled with an insatiable thirst for oil in the rich countries, as well as the decreasing availability of easily extractable petroleum resources. Consequently, higher prices and increasing resource exhaustion in certain geographies has pushed production out to new countries and regions, bringing possibilities for wealth generation to countries not generally associated with the oil-rich producing states (namely members of OPEC) that dominated the markets and the headlines in the twentieth century. Not surprisingly, this has resulted in the establishment or planned establishment of new SWFs. This is particularly the case in Africa, which has seen an expansion of oil and gas production as well as other primary commodities. Although estimates vary, the number of SWFs in Africa ranges from the low- to mid-teens. Add to that the number of countries considering or constructing new SWFs, the Africa region could soon have upwards of 20 or more SWFs (Barbary, Monk, and Triki, 2011).

Considering global population growth and an expanding middle class in emerging markets it would seem cogent to assume a trend of high long-term commodity prices, at least at levels higher than the long-term average of the twentieth century. This provides a strong incentive for governments controlling access to natural resources to exploit them and utilize the resource to finance government spending. If commodity prices are high and stable, this is a feasible fiscal policy. If commodity prices are more volatile or collapse in the short term, as they were following the subprime financial crisis of 2007–08, then this fiscal policy is unsustainable.

The other problem for commodity-producing economies is the problem of Dutch disease (Corden, 1984; Corden and Neary, 1982). This occurs when the booming extractive sector contributes to upward pressure on the value of the national currency on foreign exchange markets. Consequently, the traded manufacturing sector, inasmuch as one exists, becomes uncompetitive on global markets. The non-extractive sectors are furthermore under pressure as a larger proportion of economic resources flow to the extractive sector. Economic growth and development becomes highly asymmetric, which may be detrimental to the economy and society over the medium and long runs, as natural resources are extinguished or as prices collapse (Auty, 2001; Auty and Mikesell, 1998).

For sponsors of commodity-based SWFs, the ideal short-term economic function of the SWF is to provide stability to government resource revenues from one year to the next, while also serving as a buffer in the event of a collapse in prices (Collier et al., 2010; Das et al., 2009; Davis, Ossowski, and Fedelino, 2003). In turn, by holding some of the proceeds of commodity production in foreign assets instead of injecting them in the domestic economy, the SWF limits appreciation of the national currency and thus the effects of Dutch disease. Once these functions are covered, the ideal long-term economic function of the SWF, or more appropriately a separately sponsored SWF than that of a revenue stabilization fund, is to save for future generations when commodity exploitation and resource revenues will have decreased or have come to an end.

For developing countries, however, saving for the future is not necessarily the most beneficial route (Dixon and Monk, 2014a; Gylfason, 2011). A diverse and modern economy that provides economic opportunities and well-being to current generations, underwritten by accessible and comprehensive education and healthcare systems, and basic provision of infrastructure, for example, is arguably a more effective way of ensuring the prosperity of future generations. To give an example, the strategy taken by Norway in the accumulation and saving of its petroleum wealth as an economic resource for future generations is not necessarily the best strategy for a capital-starved low-income country in Africa blighted by poverty, poor infrastructure, and inadequate public services. For the former, there is a clear economic case for saving for future generations. For the latter, there is a clear case for putting the capital to work now by way of a sovereign development fund; a type of SWF devoted to purely developmental goals (Santiso, 2009).

There are few active sovereign development funds in the developing world, even though interest in them is growing. Moreover, such funds are not a replacement for parliamentary decision-making as to the allocation of state resources. Put simply, sovereign development funds, as institutional investors akin to a private equity fund, have limited influence. They may be able to engage in pump priming activities to support industrial and infrastructural development, but such pump priming is likely only to be sustainable in the long term if operationalized in an explicitly commercial manner. In other words, they must generate financial returns in the first instance to justify their existence. This does not negate possible double or triple-bottom lines, and an explicit emphasis to find them. Rather, if financial returns are not a core operational and mandated concern, a different type of organizational form (for example, a charity) is more appropriate.

Although the economic rationale behind the commodity-based SWF is fairly obvious for resource-rich economies, the underlying political rationale may be driven by a variety of reasons that have little to do with improving the prospects for the country's citizenry at-large. The structure of political authority of sponsoring governments in the Middle East is generally that of an absolute monarchy (for example, Saudi Arabia; Qatar; Oman; United Arab Emirates) or a constitutional monarchy with some notionally democratic institutions (for example, Kuwait). In these countries vast natural resource wealth has produced a rentier social contract (Ross, 2012; Karl, 1997). As governments do not rely on popular taxation to finance the institutions of government, the government is essentially free from popular accountability. In modern democracies, in contrast, the power to tax and the legitimacy surrounding that power rests on government accountability and the existence of popular representation in the functions of the state. In a rentier state governments have limited incentive to be accountable and to share decision-making across the citizenry. Moreover, resource revenues can be used to influence or implicitly suborn different interests groups inasmuch as they exist.

As this state of affairs implies, the resilience of resource revenues is of critical importance to maintaining the existing structure of political power. Consequently, there is an incentive for the ruling elites to effectively manage resource wealth over the long term. Understanding this incentive provides a more nearly complete explanation for some commodity-based SWFs, particularly those associated with autocratic or oligarchic regimes (Dixon and Monk, 2012). In establishing a commodity-based SWF, the state can diversify resource revenues into public and private securities and real assets around the world. Instead of relying on current and future commodity production alone, the state is relying on the performance of the global economy.

With many resource-rich developing countries rushing to establish new commodity-based SWFs it is questionable whether this development is universally beneficial for the country. Although a SWF may provide a tool for managing resource revenues that is more in-line with the realities of investing in the twenty-first century global economy, a SWF should not necessarily be seen as an institutional innovation that necessarily counteracts the resource curse and the concentration of power in the hands of a few. SWFs are still creations of the sovereign authorities that sponsor them. While their economic effects as a policy tool managing resource revenues may prove beneficial for the wider economy, they may simply reinforce the existing balance of political power.

12.4 EXPORT-LED GROWTH AND RESERVE ACCUMULATION

To explain the source capital of a second variant of SWF, the reserve fund or those funds derivative of reserve funds, we need to understand the structure of the global political economy and how it developed over the latter half of the twentieth century, and the importance of export-led growth. At the end of the Second World War, the economies of Europe and Japan were in shambles on the whole – save for a few isolated pockets that had avoided conflict (for example, Sweden; Switzerland). Productive capital (that is, factories and machinery) and major infrastructure had been destroyed or was in need of re-modification to civilian uses. Europe and Japan were reliant on imports of goods and capital from the United States to cover consumption and reconstruction efforts, quickly exhausting their foreign exchange reserves and leading to a balance of payments crisis in need of correction (Eichengreen, 2008; Scammell, 1980).

The international monetary system established at Bretton Woods, New Hampshire in 1944, set to stabilize the international economy, establishing a system of fixed exchange rates centered on the US dollar pegged at 35 dollars to an ounce of gold. The US economy, acting as an open mass consumer market and a major supplier of capital, would become the core of the first-world global economy supporting the reconstruction and development of Japan and Western Europe (Dooley, Folkerts-Landau, and Garber, 2004). The dollar peg, in effect, allowed Western Europe and Japan to rebuild and redevelop through an export-led growth model, underpinned by undervalued currencies. Whereas at the end of the Second World War the United States was a major creditor with a large trade surplus, the three decades after the war completely reversed this position, with Europe (primarily West Germany) and Japan having accumulated large trade surpluses and large foreign currency reserves. By the middle of the 1960s the United States began to have trouble maintaining the peg that was set at Bretton Woods, as its balance of payments deficit continued to grow. US gold reserves declined and surplus dollars held abroad multiplied. The system was in significant disequilibrium; and during the presidency of Richard Nixon the United States left the Gold Standard, in part to force a revaluation of the Yen and the Deutsch Mark.

This major change in US policy represented the recognition that the destroyed economies

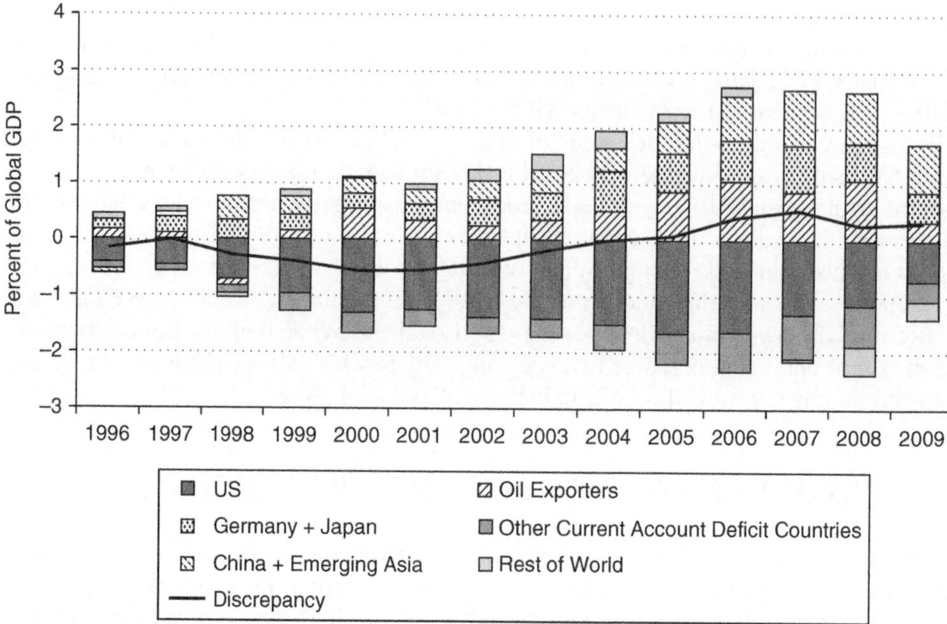

Source: International Monetary Fund (2010), World Economic Outlook: Crisis and Recovery. Washington, DC: International Monetary Fund.

Figure 12.3 Global imbalances 1996–2009

of Europe and Japan had been rebuilt. Put simply, Europe and Japan returned from the periphery back to the core. An argument for supporting undervalued currencies in support of an export-led reconstruction and development model ceased to be logical. This does not mean that West Germany, in particular, and Japan ceased to be export-driven economies, amassing huge surpluses vis-à-vis the United States and other economies. Despite the collapse of the Bretton Woods exchange rate regime in the early 1970s, the core–periphery structure that characterized it is still present albeit with a different membership. The periphery now includes predominantly emerging economies in East Asia, who are following a growth and development model based on undervalued currencies and exports. This has supported rapid economic growth and prosperity for many in the region.

The core, as during Bretton Woods, continues to provide unfettered goods and capital markets that support growth and development in the periphery. As Figure 12.3 shows, this created significant global current account imbalances in the last decade, which only subsided as the global financial crisis took hold. Consequently, emerging Asian economies, particularly China, have amassed huge foreign exchange reserves, primarily held in US Treasuries. For example, China's foreign exchange reserves, managed by the State Administration of Foreign Exchange, topped US$3.31 trillion at the end of 2012.

Notwithstanding the key role of the export-led growth model in driving reserve accumulation, some have suggested that emerging economies in Asia have accumulated reserves in response to the 1997 Asian Financial Crisis. That crisis sapped growth and created generalized social hardship, particularly among the poor. Some countries, such as South Korea and Thailand, required assistance from the IMF to rectify their balance of payments problems. Yet, as mentioned in a previous section, help from the IMF comes with conditions that are not always politically and socially popular. Following that experience, reserve accumulation has become arguably a form of insurance that governments can utilize in the event of a crisis, thus eliminating (or seriously reducing) their need for external support (Griffith-Jones and Ocampo, 2011).

There is problem, however, with reserve accumulation. On the one hand, the rate of return on foreign exchange reserves is usually below the rate of inflation of the domestic economy. In effect, there is a cost to holding reserves (Rodrik, 2006). On the other hand, as accumulating reserves is part of a strategy to hold back currency appreciation, the rate of return will be further depressed if currency appreciation is allowed to take hold (which would happen if the currency were allowed to float freely on the market). Considering that the reserves are held in foreign currency (primarily US dollars), the value of the reserves in the domestic currency would, in other words, be lower as they mature. Realizing this implicit cost of reserve accumulation – notwithstanding the benefits it brings to export-led growth and the implied lender-of-last resort insurance function – governments have typically sought to diversify the asset base of their reserves into higher yielding securities and real assets.

This diversification of reserve assets has coincided with the establishment of new SWFs. South Korea, for example, established the Korea Investment Corporation in 2005 to manage funds entrusted to it by the government, the Bank of Korea, and other public funds. China, likewise, established the China Investment Corporation with the intent of maximizing the returns on the country's staggeringly and increasingly large reserves. Initially allocated approximately US$200 billion, assets under management at the CIC have continued to grow, reaching US$575 billion by the end of 2012. But recent SWF development is not new to the region. In 1981 Singapore launched the Government of Singapore Investment Corporation to manage the city-state's reserves. Now called GIC Private Limited, the fund has offices around the world and is active in public and private markets. Whereas the largest SWFs were the almost exclusive reserve of commodity producers, export-led growth in East Asia has brought the region much higher in the ranks of SWFs (see Figure 12.1).

While not necessarily unique to SWFs from the East Asian region, the conduct and comportment of SWFs in the region appears to follow the developmental logic of the export-led growth model. There are those SWFs like Singapore's Temasek and Malaysia's Khazanah Nasional Berhard, which began as the asset owner of state assets and state-owned enterprises, that have explicit mandates as strategic investment funds that make investments in national and foreign companies in support of nation-building and national economic development (Yeung, 2011). These SWFs are not simply in pursuit of adjusted returns. In effect, they are in search of a double-bottom line, one that makes a return on investment and another that produces beneficial externalities that spill over into wider national economic development. Then there those SWFs, like the CIC, whose mandate is not as explicit, but whose actions suggest otherwise. For example, the CIC has made strategic investments in the extractive sector, which appear geared toward supporting Chinese state-owned enterprises and ensuring stable energy and mineral supplies for the country's resource-intensive growth (Haberly, 2011).

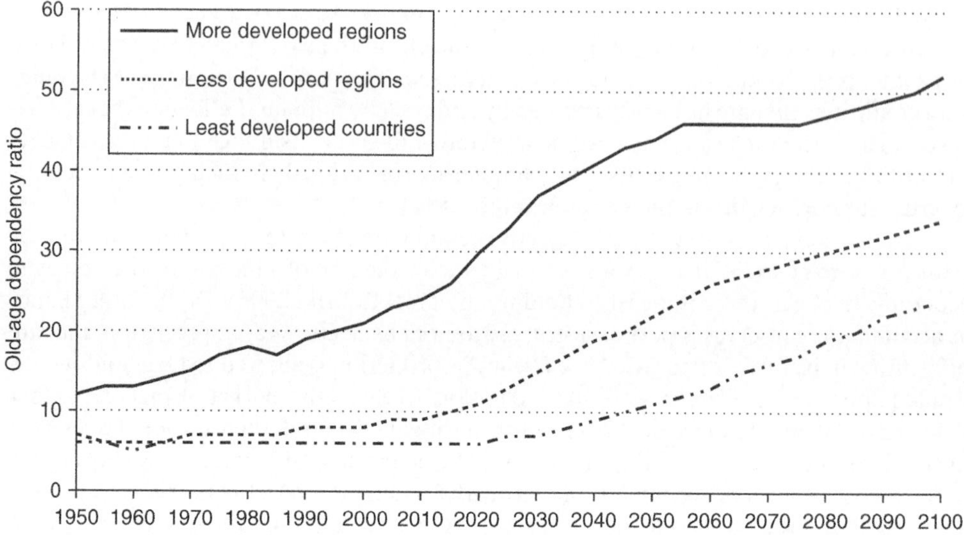

Source: Population Division of the Department of Economic and Social Affairs of the United Nations Secretariat, *World Population Prospects: The 2012 Revision*. New York: United Nations.

Figure 12.4 Global demographic aging 1950–2100

12.5 THE CONSEQUENCES OF DEMOGRAPHIC AGING

One of the biggest challenges of the twenty-first century will be demographic aging, particularly in the advanced and middle-income economies. Japan and some countries in Europe, such as Italy, are already seeing significant demographic aging due to low birth rates and increased longevity. Even though China has made major strides in economic growth and development compared with a generation ago, there is still a concern that the country will get old before it gets rich (Golley and Tyers, 2012). Figure 12.4 shows the medium variant projections of the old-age dependency ratios for more developed regions, less developed regions, and the least developed countries. This is the ratio of the population aged 65 and older to the population aged 15–64. Old-age dependency ratios will increase in all regions, but rapidly for more developed regions after 2020. Less developed and the least developed countries will see increases more toward the middle of the century.

Increasing longevity is normally considered an achievement. It is now largely an outcome of advancements in medicine and public health. Decreased fertility, which is a factor contributing to demographic aging, is a consequence of greater educational attainment of the female population, which is also normally considered a positive achievement. These triumphs of modern civilization are, however, still unevenly distributed around the world. In the advanced and middle-income economies where these achievements are most felt, they bring with them additional economic and, therefore, policy implications (Auerbach, Kotlikoff, and Leibfritz, 1999; Barr, 2012). Most industrialized countries have some form of pay-as-you-go pension system, where transfers of income from current workers are made to retirees. With demographic aging the burden for current workers increases, unless significant gains are made in national productivity. For advanced economies, however, productivity gains are slower as compared developing economies. Reducing the accumulated claims by the retired population is politically contentious, as is asking the working population to contribute more.

Over the last two decades all advanced welfare states have reformed their pension systems in various ways, with some more significantly than others. For the most part reform consists of increasing the age at which a full state pension can be claimed, making adjustments to benefit formulae and cost-of-living adjustments, while incentivizing private capitalized pension arrangements (George, Taylor-Gooby, and Bonoli, 2000). Notwithstanding the variation of reform among the advanced economies, in all cases there is a greater reliance on the performance of financial markets that are global in scope, as a means of diversifying the pool on which retirement-income security is founded away from current transfers that are contingent on national economic performance alone (Dixon and Sorsa, 2009). Even though reform has engendered increasing individualization with ostensibly diminishing opportunities for collective solidarity, neoliberalism is not necessarily triumphant. On the contrary, a number of countries have moved to prefund future state pension obligations by setting aside reserves in a state-sponsored pension reserve fund charged with employing the capital in markets for public and private assets.

There is some debate as to whether pension reserve funds, such as France's *Fonds de réserve pour les retraites* (FRR), should be classified as SWFs like the aforementioned commodity-based and reserve-based SWFs, and the strategic investment SWFs like Temasek. The FRR was set up in the last decade and financed with proceeds from the sale of state privatizations and other fiscal surpluses, and given a mandate to grow the capital through the period 2020–40 when it will be drawn down to cover the large deficits of the state pension that will occur when the post-Second World War baby boom generation is in retirement (Dixon, 2008). Another is the Australia Future Fund, established to cover the long-term unfunded defined benefit pension obligations promised to federal government civil servants. In 2006 these obligations were estimated to be AUS$140 billion by 2040. Yet, an argument could be made that the Future Fund is like any other commodity-based SWF, as its creation coincided with the increasingly positive fiscal position of the Australian government due to surging demand for Australia's natural resources. Although the Future Fund was endowed with shares of the privatized telecoms provider Telstra and growing tax receipts, the positive fiscal position provided by the booming extractive sector arguably made the Future Fund a macroeconomic necessity to store excess national wealth (Clark, Dixon, and Monk, 2013: Chapter 4).

The primary difference between pension reserve funds and other types of SWFs is that the former are geared toward covering a specific long-term liability. In that respect, pension reserve funds are not dissimilar to other defined benefit pension funds, public or private. Ideally, the asset management of defined benefit pensions should take into account the liability structure of the obligations. Put simply, the risk–return profile of the asset portfolio should reflect the risk profile of the liabilities. Although asset-liability matching is not employed with rigor across all defined benefit pension funds, the principle still holds. Asset-liability management is, in effect, a disciplinary device that shapes portfolio allocation. It brings to the fore the liabilities that will come due in the investment decision-making process. As a result, investment decision-making is constrained in ways that an investment fund operating without such liabilities is not. A pension reserve fund that has clearly defined liabilities does not have the same freedom of movement as do other SWFs. Such freedom of movement, unsurprisingly, has created a cause for concern among some over the power this bestows on sponsoring governments (Truman, 2010).

12.6 SWFS AND GROWTH AND DEVELOPMENT

In each of the analyses above there is an implicit, if not explicit, recognition that SWFs have a part in the growth and development trajectory of national economies. It has also been argued that SWFs, particularly the largest, are a power resource for the nation-state in an increasingly globalized and financialized international political economy. Given the role and significance of financial markets and the financial services industry in contemporary political economies, one can be forgiven in thinking that the agency of SWFs is considerable. Put simply, SWFs allow the state to access the tools of modern finance. By this logic, one would expect that SWFs can play an active role in shaping economic growth and development. While such logic stands to reason, it is important not to overstate the influence of SWFs, or any institutional investor for that matter. Although many SWFs have no mandate to foster economic growth and development beyond managing the proceeds from national economic growth, as in the case of reserve-based funds, or sectoral growth, as in the case of commodity-based funds, some SWFs have a specific mandate to foster national economic development.

Some have argued that focusing on economic development at home and abroad should be a key competency and focus for SWFs of any kind (Santiso, 2009). SWFs with a strategic focus, such as Singapore's Temasek, Malaysia's Khasanah, or Abu Dhabi's Mubadala, are taken as models to follows. Mubadala, for example, has actively invested in aerospace firms to develop production and services capabilities in the UAE region (Haberly, 2011). In that respect, Mubadala is aiming to lead development, rather than following in the wake of entrepreneurs. Temasek, likewise, is charged with nurturing economic development, industrialization, and financial diversification of Singapore by making commercially driven strategic investments in and around the region (Yeung, 2011). Again, it would seem that Temasek leads economic development, rather than following it. But, and notwithstanding the fact that it follows an active investment strategy, Temasek began as a financial holding company of the Singapore government's shares in state-owned enterprises, start-ups, and joint ventures. In that respect, Temasek could be seen as following developments in the national economy, rather than being a direct catalyst thereof. Hence, when arguments are made regarding the catalyzing effects that SWFs can bring to economic growth and development, caution is required.

This caution reflects an ongoing debate in the social sciences and geography on the role of finance in economic growth and development. The origins of this debate are not new (Levine, 1997; Patrick, 1966). On one side there are those that contend that finance leads development. Associated with the work of Joseph Schumpeter (1934), the financial services industry, as a real sector in the economy, are seen as fundamental to economic and technological development, as it underwrites the capabilities of entrepreneurs. Put simply, financial intermediaries promote development by actively seeking out and allocating capital to certain sectors and entrepreneurs in the economy. Hence, the quality and capability of financial intermediaries matters. If one takes this Schumpeterian view, a SWF with sufficient capital and human resources capabilities should be able to shape growth and development possibilities at home and abroad. Finance in this perspective can be seen as supply-leading.

In contrast, there are those that see financial intermediaries as passive agents in growth and development. Instead of leading development, finance follows. This view is associated with post-Keynesian economist Joan Robinson (1952) who argued that where enterprise leads, finance follows. Finance in this perspective can be seen as demand-following. In short, financial intermediaries emerge to meet the needs of savers and borrowers (firms) as the economy grows and develops. This does not mean that financial intermediaries are not important to growth and development. A poorly functioning financial system or poorly organized financial intermediaries could constrain growth and development. If one takes this Robinsonian view seriously, a SWF is unlikely to be seen as a crucial agent catalyzing economic growth and development by investing in particular firms or sectors. This does not mean, however, that a SWF cannot be an important aggregate source of capital for growing sectors of the economy. It does mean that expectations about what a SWF is capable of achieving as an institutional investor is measured. This should not be confused with the contribution a SWF makes to other policy objectives, such as returning higher risk-adjusted returns on reserves, managing resource revenues, or covering state pension obligations.

But one not need take either extreme in this debate. In reality, particularly in more developed economies, financial systems have elements of both, but to varying degrees and spatial structure (on the latter, see Martin et al., 2005; Martin, Sunley, and Turner, 2002). This would suggest that SWFs, at least in certain forms, could play a role in catalyzing economic growth and development. The SWF operates in a model akin to a venture capital or private equity firm, assuming that there are no political-economic barriers to it doing so (that is, it is deemed legitimate for the state to invest in the local economy in the same manner that a private investor would). Yet, there is an important caveat. In the Schumpeterian view the quality and capabilities of the financial intermediary matter. In short, the financial intermediary, or a strategic SWF in this case, can make poor decisions that lead to failure. Although no organization is immune to making poor decisions, organizations with limited capabilities and limited human resources expertise are likely to have a higher probability of doing so. As many SWFs are located far from major financial centers or in countries with underdeveloped financial industries, attracting talent and investment expertise is a palpable dilemma. Consequently, many SWFs have yet to adopt more aggressive investment mandates, with many continuing to rely on external managers to place capital in the markets. Yet, many large SWFs are investing in their organizational capabilities and human resources expertise (Dixon and Monk, 2014b).

Ultimately, there is insufficient information or the examples too immature to conclude that SWFs are a viable vehicle for fomenting economic development, notwithstanding an aggregate contribution to capital deepening at different scales. Singapore's Temasek, an oft-mentioned exemplar of a strategic SWF, exists in parallel with a national (city-region) economy that has been highly attractive to foreign capital and where there is a developed financial system and financial services industry. Accordingly, it is difficult to disentangle its role in and significance to Singapore's development. The effect may be insignificant. The policy implication for other countries, particularly for less developed economies, is substantial. The city-region's connections with the larger global economy and its large and expert financial labor market provide conditions for a highly capable SWF. To be sure, Singapore's SWFs are considered to be among the most sophisticated. Hence, if Singapore's Temasek follows entrepreneurial development, it is harder to expect that SWFs elsewhere will be successful economic development catalysts – especially in places where access to organizational and human resources capabilities is limited. This is an empirical question that future research needs to answer.

12.7 CONCLUSIONS

The emergence of SWFs on the world stage in greater numbers in the last decade has rekindled a long-standing interest in the state vs. market dichotomy and the intersection of politics and finance (Balding, 2012). It would suggest that there are limits to neoliberalization. The state is not so easily extricated from the market. The SWF is one way in which states have sought to engage with global market capitalism, but also a way of resisting its predatory tendencies (Clark, Dixon, and Monk, 2013). At the same time, the rise of SWFs reflects the significance of finance and financial markets in contemporary capitalism. In that sense, the rise of SWFs can be considered part and parcel of what some refer to as financialization (Engelen and Konings, 2010). The SWF brings the tools and opportunities of modern finance to the state's capabilities and its decision-making schema. The geography of capitalism has moved from an international economy distinguished by national borders to a global economy driven by powerful cities and regions interconnected through complex global production networks and global value chains, and where value is captured by and concentrated in the spaces and places of finance (Dixon, 2014). The SWF, in providing a means of accessing financial markets, is a response to this changing geography.

It is important, however, to not overstate the above explanation for the rise of SWFs. SWFs increase the agency of the state in providing opportunities to access financial markets, but the creation of most SWFs reflect a reaction to some other structural change in the global economy and national societies. They reflect the significant growth in commodity prices in the last decade, the residual effects of export-led growth and managed currencies, or the aging of societies. But none of these will last forever. Commodity prices may collapse, as they frequently have in the past. Countries following an export-led growth model, such as China, may be pressured increasingly to allow their currencies to appreciate, as has occurred in the past. And states may find other means of mitigating the impacts of demographic aging, such as facilitating work opportunities in later life. In addition, the geopolitical and regulatory environment could turn hostile toward SWFs (Truman, 2010). Ultimately, none of this means that SWFs will disappear. It means, rather, that this period of sovereign fund capitalism could be temporary.

In the short to medium term SWFs will continue to offer a compelling area of empirical study for the social sciences in general and economic and political geography in particular. First, how and whether SWFs are used to enhance and influence at country's standing in international relations is still a subject of debate, despite most evidence pointing to SWFs as relatively benign institutions (Kirshner, 2009; Langland, 2009). Second, it is unclear how, whether, and to what extent SWFs and other large asset owners can challenge the power of the financial services industry and thus shape the geography of financial power (Clark and Monk, 2013; Dixon and Monk, 2014b). Finally, it is unclear whether SWFs in general and sovereign development funds in particular are able to influence economic development at home and abroad (Dixon and Monk, 2014a; Haberly, 2011, 2014; Santiso, 2009).

NOTES

1. There are several, mostly commercial, organizations that track the number of SWFs in operation and their assets under management, such as Institutional Investor's Sovereign Wealth Center (www.sovereignwealthcenter.com). Academic organizations tracking SWFs include: ESADEgeo-Center for Global Economy and Geopolitics (www.esadegeo.com/global-economy) and the Sovereign Investment Lab at Bocconi (http://www.baffi.unibocconi.it/wps/wcm/connect/Cdr/Centro_BAFFIen/Home/Sovereign+Investment+Lab/). [Websites active as of 13 October 2014.]
2. It is useful to consider Boschma and Frenken's (2010) delineation of proximity along cognitive, organizational, social, and institutional dimensions. Although they are writing about innovation networks, the concepts still apply. In this respect, the SWF, adopting the practices, organizational forms, and human resources of western financial institutions, provides a conduit through which cognitively, organizationally, socially, and institutionally distinct political economies can access the global (western-dominated) political economy and financial markets.

REFERENCES

Auerbach, A., L. Kotlikoff and W. Leibfritz (1999), *Generational Accounting Around the World*, Chicago, IL: University of Chicago Press.

Auty, R.M. (2001), *Resource Abundance and Economic Development*, Oxford: Oxford University Press.

Auty, R.M. and R.F. Mikesell (1998), *Sustainable Development in Mineral Economies*, Oxford: Clarendon.

Balding, C. (2012), *Sovereign Wealth Funds: The New Intersection of Money and Politics*, New York: Oxford University Press.

Barbary, V., A. Monk and T. Triki (2011), 'The new investment frontier: SWF investment in Africa', in V. Barbary and B. Bortolotti (eds), *Braving the New World: Sovereign Wealth Fund Investment in the Uncertain Times of 2010*, London: Monitor Group, pp. 54–60.

Barr, N.A. (2012), *Economics of the Welfare State*, 5th edition. Oxford: Oxford University Press.

Boschma, R. and K. Frenken (2010), 'The spatial evolution of innovation networks: a proximity perspective', in R. Boschma and R. Martin (eds), *The Handbook of Evolutionary Economic Geography*, Cheltenham, UK and Northampton, MA, USA: Edward Elgar Publishing, pp. 120–135.

Chwieroth, J.M. (2014), 'Fashions and fads in finance: the political foundations of sovereign wealth fund creation', *International Studies Quarterly*, **58** (4), 752–763.

Clark, G.L. and A.H.B. Monk (2013), 'The scope of financial institutions: in-sourcing, outsourcing and off-shoring', *Journal of Economic Geography*, **13** (2), 279–298.

Clark, G.L., A.D. Dixon and A.H.B. Monk (2013), *Sovereign Wealth Funds: Legitimacy, Governance, and Global Power*, Princeton, NJ: Princeton University Press.

Collier, P., R. Van Der Ploeg, M. Spence and A.J. Venables (2010), 'Managing resource revenues in developing economies', *IMF Staff Papers*, **57** (1), 84–118.

Corden, W. (1984), 'Booming sector and Dutch disease economics: survey and consolidation', *Oxford Economic Papers*, **36** (3), 359–380.

Corden, W. and J. Neary (1982), 'Booming sector and de-industrialisation in a small open economy', *The Economic Journal*, **92** (368), 825–848.

Das, U., Y. Lu, C. Mulder and A. Sy (2009), 'Setting up a sovereign wealth fund: some policy and operational considerations', IMF Working Paper.

Davis, J.M., R. Ossowski and A. Fedelino (2003), *Fiscal Policy Formulation and Implementation in Oil-producing Countries*, Washington, DC: International Monetary Fund.

Dixon, A.D. (2008), 'The rise of pension fund capitalism in Europe: an unseen revolution?' *New Political Economy*, **13** (3), 249–270.

Dixon, A.D. and A.H.B. Monk (2012), 'Rethinking the sovereign in Sovereign Wealth Funds', *Transactions of the Institute of British Geographers*, **37** (1), 104–117.

Dixon, A.D. and V. Sorsa (2009), 'Institutional change and the financialisation of pensions in Europe', *Competition & Change*, **13** (4), 347–367.

Dixon, A.D. and A.H.B. Monk (2014a), 'Financializing development: toward a sympathetic critique of sovereign development funds', *Journal of Sustainable Finance & Investment*, **4** (4), 357–371.

Dixon, A.D. and A.H.B. Monk (2014b), 'Frontier finance', *Annals of the Association of American Geographers*, **104** (4), 852–868.

Dixon, A.D. (2014), *The New Geography of Capitalism: Firms, Finance, and Society*, 1st edition, Oxford: Oxford University Press.

Dooley, M., D. Folkerts-Landau and P. Garber (2004), 'The revived Bretton Woods system', *International Journal of Finance & Economics*, **9** (4), 307–313.

Dore, R. (2008), 'Financialization of the global economy', *Industrial and Corporate Change*, **17** (6), 1097–1112.

Eichengreen, B. (2008), *Globalizing Capital: A History of the International Monetary System*, 2nd edition. Princeton, NJ: Princeton University Press.

Engelen, E. and M. Konings (2010), 'Financial capitalism resurgent: comparative institutionalism and the challenges of financialization', in G. Morgan, John L. Campbell, Colin Crouch, P.H. Kristensen, O.K. Pedersen and R. Whitely (eds), *Oxford Handbook of Comparative Institutionalism*, Oxford: Oxford University Press, pp. 601–624.

George, V., P. Taylor-Gooby and G. Bonoli (2000), *European Welfare Futures: Towards a Theory of Retrenchment*, Cambridge: Polity Press.

Gibson-Graham, J.K. (1996), *The End of Capitalism (As We Knew It): A Feminist Critique of Political Economy*, Cambridge, MA and Oxford: Blackwell.

Golley, J. and R. Tyers (2012), 'Population pessimism and economic optimism in the Asian giants', *The World Economy*, **35** (11), 1387–1416.

Griffith-Jones, S. and J.A Ocampo (2011), 'The rationale for sovereign wealth funds: a developing country perspective', in P. Bolton, F. Samama and J. Stiglitz (eds), *Sovereign Wealth Funds and Long-term Investing*, New York: Columbia University Press, pp. 60–66.

Gylfason, T. (2011), 'Natural resource endowment: a mixed blessing?' CESifo Working Paper Series (3353).

Haberly, D. (2011), 'Strategic sovereign wealth fund investment and the new alliance capitalism: a network mapping investigation', *Environment and Planning A*, **43** (8), 1833–1852.

Haberly, D. (2014), 'White knights from the Gulf: sovereign wealth fund investment and the evolution of German industrial finance', *Economic Geography*, **90** (3), 293–320.

Hatton, K.J. and K. Pistor (2012), 'Maximizing autonomy in the shadow of great powers: the political economy of sovereign wealth funds', *Columbia Journal of Transnational Law*, **50** (1), 1–81.

Holzmann, R. and R.P. Hinz (2005), *Old-age Income Support in the 21st Century: An International Perspective on Pension Systems And Reform*, Washington, DC: World Bank.

Karl, T.L. (1997), *The Paradox Of Plenty: Oil Booms and Petro-states*, Berkeley, CA; London: University of California Press.

Kirshner, J. (2009), 'Sovereign wealth funds and national security: the dog that will refuse to bark', *Geopolitics*, **14** (2), 305–316.

Langland, E. (2009), 'Misplaced fears put to rest: financial crisis reveals the true motives of sovereign wealth funds', *Tulane Journal of International & Comparative Law*, **18**, 263.

Levine, R. (1997), 'Financial development and economic growth: views and agenda', *Journal of Economic Literature*, **35** (2), 688–726.

Martin, R., P. Sunley and D. Turner (2002), 'Taking risks in regions: the geographical anatomy of Europe's emerging venture capital market', *Journal of Economic Geography*, **2** (2), 121–150.

Martin, R., C. Berndt, B. Klagge and P. Sunley (2005), 'Spatial proximity effects and regional equity gaps in the venture capital market: evidence from Germany and the United Kingdom', *Environment and Planning A*, **37** (7), 1207–1231.

Monk, A.H.B. (2011), 'Sovereignty in the era of global capitalism: the rise of sovereign wealth funds and the power of finance', *Environment and Planning A*, **43** (8), 1813–1832.

Nyce, S.A. and S.J. Schieber (2005), *The Economic Implications of Aging Societies: The Costs of Living Happily Ever After*, Cambridge: Cambridge University Press.

Patrick, H. (1966), 'Financial development and economic growth in underdeveloped countries', *Economic Development and Cultural Change*, **14** (2), 174–189.

Pike, A. and J. Pollard (2010), 'Economic geographies of financialization', *Economic Geography*, **86** (1), 29–51.

Polanyi, Karl ([1944]1975), *The Great Transformation*, New York: Octagon Books.

Robinson, J. (1952), *The Rate of Interest, and Other Essays*, London: Macmillan & Co.

Rodrik, D. (2011), *The Globalization Paradox: Why Global Markets, States, and Democracy Can't Coexist*, Oxford: Oxford University Press.

Rodrik, Dani (2006), 'The social cost of foreign exchange reserves', *International Economic Journal*, **20** (3), 253–266.

Rose, P. (2011), 'American sovereign wealth', Ohio State public law Working Papers (161). doi:http://dx.doi.org/10.2139/ssrn.1960706.

Ross, M.L. (2012), *The Oil Curse: How Petroleum Wealth Shapes the Development of Nations*, Princeton, NJ: Princeton University Press.
Rozanov, Andrew (2005), 'Who holds the wealth of nations?', *Central Banking Journal*, **15** (4), 52–57.
Santiso, J. (2009), 'Sovereign development funds: key actors in the shifting wealth of nations', *Revue d'Économie Finacière*, **9** (1), 291–315.
Scammell, W.M. (1980), *The International Economy Since 1945*, London: Macmillan.
Schumpeter, J. (1934), *The Theory of Economic Development: An Inquiry into Profits, Capital, Credit, Interest, and the Business Cycle*, Cambridge, MA: Harvard University Press.
Storper, M. and R. Walker (1989), *The Capitalist Imperative: Territory, Technology, and Industrial Growth*, Oxford: Basil Blackwell.
Truman, E.M. (2010), *Sovereign Wealth Funds: Threat or Salvation?* Washington, DC: Peterson Institute for International Economics.
Wallerstein, I. (1983), *Historical Capitalism*, London: Verso.
Yeung, H. (2011), 'From national development to economic diplomacy? Governing Singapore's sovereign wealth funds', *The Pacific Review*, **24** (5), 625–652.

13. Geographies of mortgage markets

Manuel B. Aalbers

13.1 INTRODUCTION: THE CENTURY OF THE MORTGAGE MARKET

The twentieth century could easily be called the century of the mortgage market.[1] Over the course of that century, the share of mortgage loans in banks' total lending portfolios doubled from 30 to 60 per cent in a group of countries including the US, Canada, Australia, Japan and 13 European states (Jordà et al., 2014). Between 1870 and 2010 the ratio of mortgage-lending-to-GDP increased from less than one to around seven (Jordà et al., 2014). At the end of 2004, there was €4.5 trillion of outstanding mortgage loans in the European Union (EU) and €6.1 trillion in the United States (US). Eight years and a severe crisis later, these figures stand at €6.7 trillion and €7.8 trillion respectively (EMF, 2014). It is worth noting that the figures for the EU continue to rise, while the US figure is down from €8.6 at the end of 2007. And while the mortgage-debt-to-GDP ratio in the US rose from 61 to 86 per cent between 2003 and 2007, and subsequently dropped to 72 per cent in 2012, the same figure for the EU rose from 41 to 47 and then 51 per cent. In the most extreme case, the Netherlands, the figures are 84, 100 and a 105 per cent for the same years, although the last figure actually represents a drop of 4 percentage points compared to the maximum two years previously (Figure 13.1).

At the other end of the spectrum, figures in Romania and Bulgaria stay well below 10 per cent. In relative terms, small Cyprus saw the biggest increase in mortgage-debt-to-GDP: from 10 to 72 per cent in the scope of eight years, even though the homeownership rate dropped from 91 to 74 per cent (EMF, 2014). Housing prices declined in many OECD countries, most notably in Ireland where they almost halved since the end of 2007 (Figure 13.2). Other notable declines in house prices were recorded in Spain, Romania and Greece. On the other hand, house prices continued to increase with more 30 per cent in Norway, Turkey and Austria.

Mortgage markets are not just important due to their sheer volume, but also because most homeowners depend on them, because they fuel the economy both directly and indirectly (through equity withdrawal), and because they serve an ideological purpose in the neoliberal age. Mortgage markets – and credit markets more generally – have been de- and re-regulated in order to widen access to mortgage markets and thus to fuel economic growth and increase homeownership rates. That is, this 'regulated deregulation' (Aalbers, 2016) of mortgage markets is not just a goal in itself, but also a means to further the neoliberal agenda of private property, firms and growing profits. It comes as no surprise then that this neoliberalization of the mortgage market took place earlier in the US than in the United Kingdom (UK), and earlier in the UK than in most of continental Europe and elsewhere.

In this chapter, I will discuss the geographies of mortgage markets. These are located at different scales: as already noted, the expansion and decline of the mortgage market are

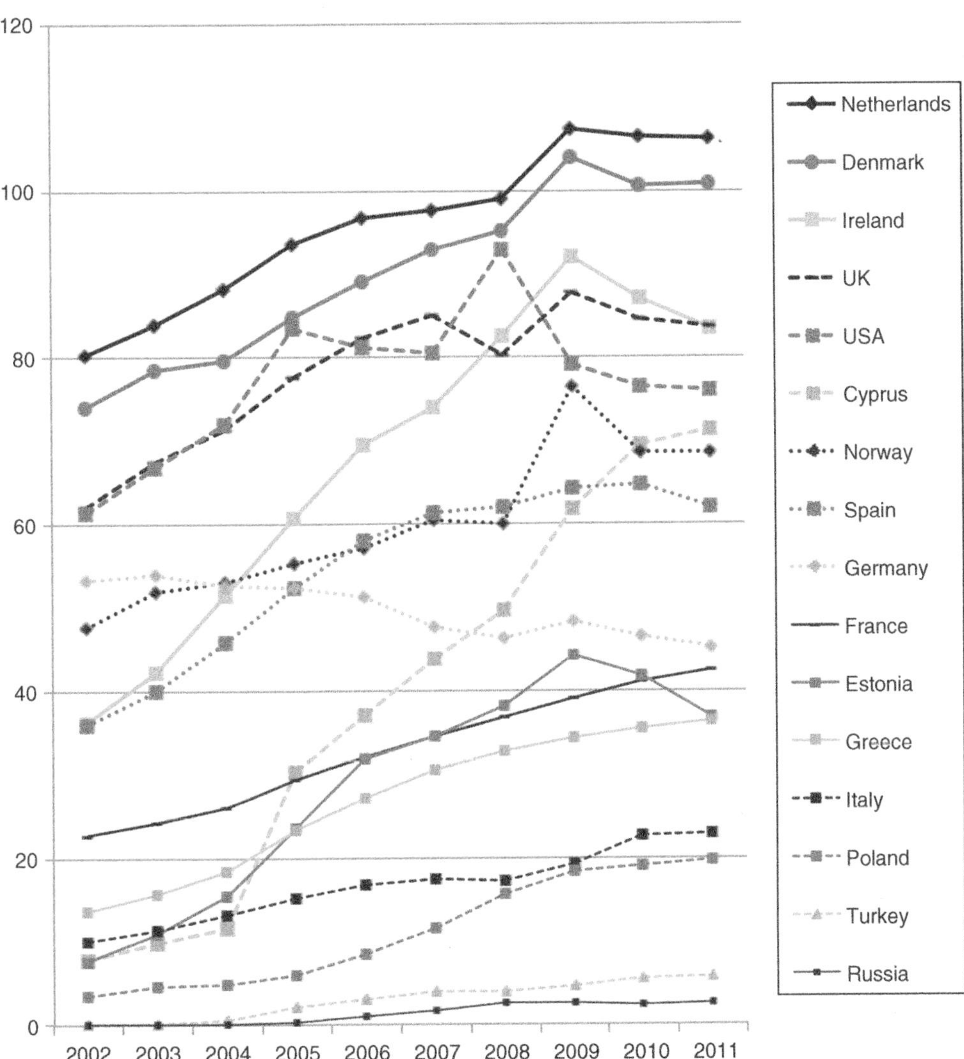

Sources: European Mortgage Federation National Experts, European Central Bank, National Central Banks, Eurostat, Bureau of Economic Analysis, Federal Reserve.

Figure 13.1 *Residential mortgage debt to GDP ratio*

uneven in international terms, but of course they are uneven within countries and cities as well. The patterns and structures of mortgage lending reflect uneven socio-economic geographies but also contribute to re/producing uneven development and this takes place at different scales. I focus specifically on two scales: the urban geographies of mortgage lending and the international geography of mortgage funding. Once we start looking at the interaction of these geographies, we can begin to understand the crucial role of the mortgage market and its geographies in the origins and spread of the global financial

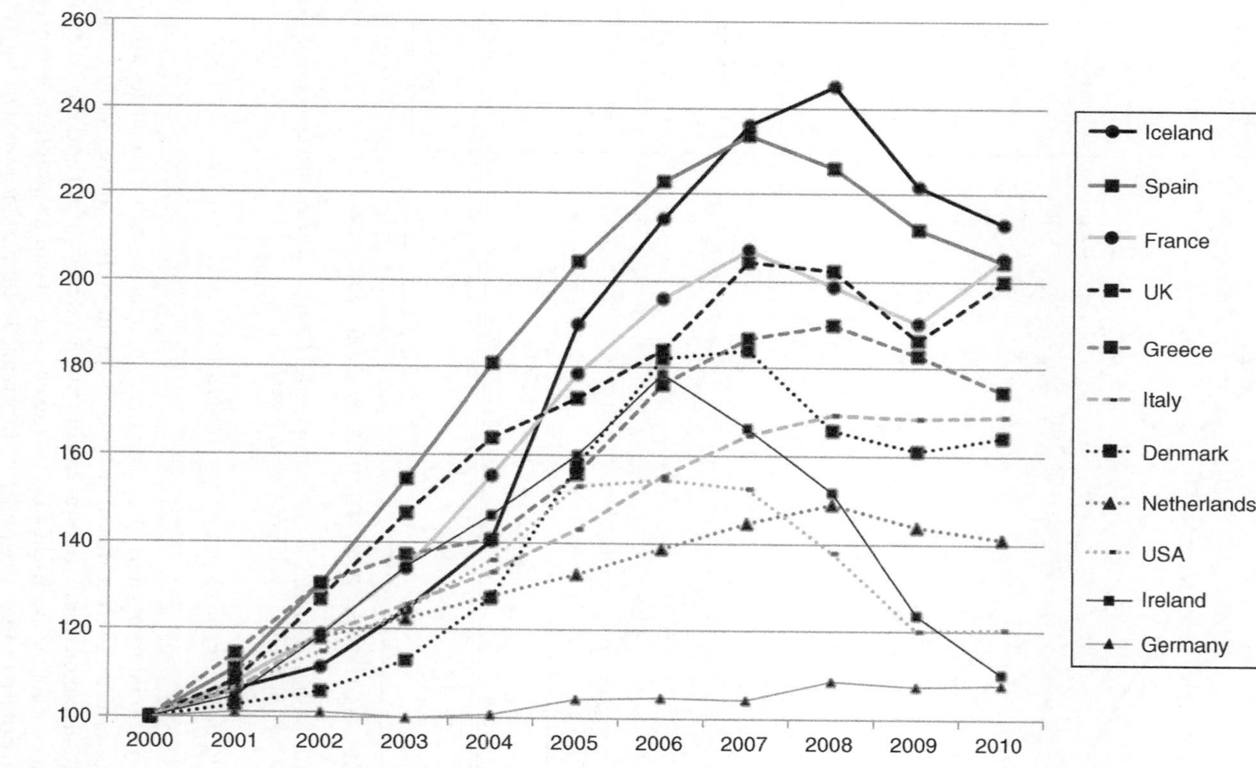

Sources: European Mortgage Federation, National Statistics Offices, OECD, ECB (for the euro area), US Bureau of Census.

Figure 13.2 Nominal house prices, 2000 = 100

crisis. These geographies and the ensuing crisis will be discussed in terms of the financialization of home, which was enabled though regulated deregulation, securitization and credit scoring. But before we can delve into the urban and international geographies of mortgage markets, we need to introduce the nature of mortgage lending and summarize its history.

13.2 THE NATURE OF MORTGAGE LENDING

Land underlies all real estate. The use of land, the desire to acquire it, and the need to regulate its transfer were among the fundamental reasons for the development of states. Land is at the base of both power and wealth. Because land transaction administration and land surveys established the security and value of land, not only did land become a secure investment, it also became possible to borrow money on the basis of the value of one's land. This is the basis for the formation of mortgage markets. A mortgage 'gives a lender contingent property rights over an asset of the debtor, and in the event of default the lender may activate those rights. Collateral reduces the creditor's vulnerability and bolsters the debtor's willingness to repay' (Carruthers, 2005: 365). Although the mortgage system has changed tremendously throughout the centuries, and continues to change, the idea of the mortgage loan is still the same as it was hundreds of years ago. The state secures property rights, including landownership and homeownership, and owners can get relatively cheap loans (that is, low interest rates) because in case of default the lender can take possession of the property (collateral).

Mortgage markets were originally designed to facilitate households who wanted to buy a house, but they also fuelled house prices (Aalbers, 2008). Homeownership has always been dependent on finance, but today investment in housing markets is more than ever before dependent on the development of financial markets. The push for homeownership has increased its importance, both at the individual and the societal level. The expansion of the mortgage market is not just meant to increase homeownership, but is also intended as a means to further the neoliberal agenda of private property, firms and growing profits. In this process, homeowners become more dependent on financial markets. Old arrangements of social rights have been replaced and continue to be replaced by new arrangements in which social rights and guarantees are transferred from the state to financial markets. Indeed, the restructuring of welfare states has resulted in a 'great risk shift' in which households are increasingly dependent on financial markets for their long-term security (Hacker, 2006). Boyer (2000) speaks of a finance-led regime of accumulation. Financialization is a pattern of accumulation in which profit making occurs increasingly through financial channels rather than through trade and commodity production (Arrighi, 1994; Krippner, 2005). It signifies that the financial industry has been transformed 'from a facilitator of other firms' economic growth into a growth industry in its own right' (Engelen, 2003).

Due to the financialization of homeownership, housing risks are increasingly financial market risks these days – and vice versa (Aalbers, 2008). The financialization of homeownership forces more and more households to see acquiring a house not just as a home, as a place to live, but as an investment, as something to put equity into and take equity from – the popular image of the home as an ATM or cash dispenser. This can be a financially gainful experience, but is not necessarily so. As homeownership has increased primarily among low-income groups, there are also more groups that have become vulnerable to the risks of homeownership. It is these groups that experience the most insecurity because of changes in the labour market, the welfare state and the mortgage market crisis. It is also these groups that are hit disproportionally hard by predatory lending.

The neoliberalization and financialization of housing is not limited to western countries but has rapidly spread throughout the developed and developing world (Rolnik, 2013). Mortgage lending and securitization may remain very limited in most of the Global South, but there is a significant increase in the more developed among them. Since the global financial crisis we see that emerging economies, notably China, Turkey and Brazil, seem to be amassing more and more mortgage debt, and have recorded rising price-to-income and price-to-rent levels. In May 2014 the IMF issued a warning of the re-appearance of housing bubbles, largely related to the global context of 'excess liquidity', the search for 'safe havens' and 'cheap money', and focused on new countries. The global house price index (constructed by residential property weighted by GDP) declined from 2007 onwards, but has been on the rise since 2011 and reached the 2006 level in 2013 (IMF, 2014). We need to take notice of how excess liquidity tries to find ways to financialize systems of housing finance around the globe (Fernandez and Aalbers, 2016).

Financialization has resulted in an increase in the number of homeowners, but also, and more importantly, in a rapid and huge increase in the price of homes. It is not recent homeowners who benefit most, but those who have been property owners for decades. The financialization of homeownership is of course the most beneficial for those who invested earlier and who were able to invest more: the 'upward pressure on house prices restricts access to homeownership and adds to the wealth of the "insiders" at the expense of the "outsiders"' (Stephens, 2007: 218). More available and, in particular, bigger mortgage loans may, at first sight, seem to benefit people who want to buy a house, but since it has resulted in dramatic increases in house prices, homeownership has paradoxically become both more accessible and more expensive.

13.3 THE HISTORY OF MORTGAGE LENDING

The origin of mortgage lending goes back to Egyptian and Roman times (Henry, 2002). After vanishing from the global scene, mortgage loans were reintroduced in some European countries in the Middle Ages. The English *mortgage* comes from the French *mort*, referring to the land that was 'dead', and from the German *gage*, meaning 'pledge'. A mortgage was thus a pledge on property. The Catholic Church stated that charging interest for money loaned was usury and as a result people in Catholic-dominated countries had to rely mostly on Jewish bankers. (The word *bank* originates in the Venice of the late Middle Ages where lenders would sit in a public square on a little bench, or *banca* in Italian.) In north-western Europe, where the Catholic Church was not as influential, lending slowly became more institutionalized and the first specialized mortgage lenders developed. A good example is Amsterdam, where many of the famous canal houses were initially financed by mortgages. Typically, masons and carpenters took out mortgage loans to buy the land and building material, selling the finished houses to merchants and others who could afford them. Subsequently, the loan was paid off and the masons and carpenters moved on to build new houses with new loans.

The colonization of the 'New World' and later also the independence of the US was also enabled by mortgage lenders, in particular, by land development banks that borrowed money in the 'Old World' to enable land acquisition for westward expansion. Land development banks, modelled after European examples, supplied mortgage loans for the purchase of land, but many of them went bankrupt as a result of speculative use of loans. Rich individuals were also important mortgage lenders, perhaps more so in the US than in Europe. In addition, small non-depository lenders were active, usually backed by one or a few wealthy investors. A large share of mortgage loans was given to farmers. This is another example of the fact that mortgages were focused on the acquisition of land rather than buildings.

In the late eighteenth century, we see the rise of all kinds of thrift institutions such as building societies, savings and loans institutions, building and loan associations, (mutual) savings banks, credit unions, trustee savings banks, homestead associations (for example, Louisiana), savings and credit cooperative organizations (some English-speaking countries in Africa), *cooperativas de ahorro y crédito* (credit unions in several Spanish-speaking countries), *realkreditobligationer* (mortgage bonds [literally: real estate credit obligations] in Denmark), and *Bausparkassen* (building societies in German-speaking countries). Throughout the first 100 years of their existence, most of these lenders were small institutions that would often teach people to be 'thrifty' – hence the name 'thrifts', in particular used in the US – that is, to save before spending. People who had been thrifty, and saved according to a particular savings scheme, were then entitled to use this money for a down payment and get a mortgage loan to finance the remainder of the cost of buying a house.

These mutual savings banks and building societies only started granting mortgage loans on a significant scale at the end of the nineteenth century. Around that time, national mortgage banks – some public, others private – were set up. In the Netherlands, for example, Samuel Sarphati – a doctor, economist and politician – in 1864 founded the *Nationale Hypotheekbank* (National Mortgage Bank) to finance the development of his urban plan for the surroundings of the *Paleis voor Volksvlijt*, a combination of a Palace of National Industry and a sort of People's Palace. The *Nationale Hypotheekbank* was modelled after the French *Crédit Mobilier* (Real Estate Credit Bank), founded to finance Baron Haussmann's reconstruction plans for Paris.

The late nineteenth century was also the time that more specialized mortgage banks were set up in the US; these companies originated loans and sold their portfolios only to investors such as insurance companies, often from Europe (Dennis and Pinkowish, 2004; Immergluck, 2004). In those days most loans covered 40 per cent of the value (loan-to-value ratio of 40); hence, purchasing real estate required a very large down payment. In addition, most loans had very short terms of five years or less. Since most loans were either not paid off or did not have any provision for loan amortization (repayment of the loan in equal instalments of principal and interest), mortgage loans were usually refinanced after five years.

In many countries, the law had excluded commercial banks from lending money on real estate. In 1913, the Federal Reserve Act in the US authorized federally chartered banks to lend money on real estate. Many other developed countries began to allow commercial banks to do so only decades after the Second World War. In the US, the boom of the

1920s was followed by the Wall Street Crash of 1929 and the crisis of the 1930s. In this crisis many homeowners lost their houses in one of two different ways. First, widespread unemployment made it impossible for many homeowners to pay off their mortgage loans, resulting in foreclosures and tax sales. Second, people who retained their jobs were often unable to refinance their loan after five years because of the withdrawal of financial institutions from the mortgage market, and therefore also lost their homes. In the early 1930s, the average number of foreclosed mortgage loans was 250,000 per year and at one point exceeded 1,000 per day (Dennis and Pinkowish, 2004; Immergluck, 2004). Half of all residential mortgages in the US were in default. Many financial institutions failed and went bankrupt along with their borrowers, partly as a result of the massive withdrawal of savings.

As a response to the crisis, the US government began to more significantly involve itself with the market. In 1931, President Hoover organized a conference on home building and homeownership, which generated four key recommendations: the creation of long-term, amortized mortgages; the encouragement of low interest rates; the institution of government aid to private efforts to house low-income families; and the reduction of home construction costs (cited in Jackson, 1985: 194). Hardly ever has any policy conference recommendation been so quickly or comprehensively implemented. As a result, the details of the mortgage contract and therefore of the mortgage loan changed a lot, replacing the non-amortizing five-year loans with the self-amortizing loan of 25–30 years. This practice was first adopted in the US and later elsewhere. Nonetheless, lenders did not change that much: in Europe and elsewhere, thrifts continued to dominate the mortgage market; while in the US, thrifts and commercial banks split the market between them.

In the late 1960s, the US government enabled the government-sponsored enterprises that were erected in the post-Great Depression years to buy up mortgages. The secondary mortgage market was born. Although this influenced mortgage lending – money could now revolve, resulting in more available mortgage credit and lower interest rates – it did not directly lead to a major change in the type of mortgage lenders. In the late 1980s, investment banks also became active in the secondary mortgage market. This fuelled a steep rise in the number of non-depository and non-bank lenders and also increased the number of loans by commercial banks sold in the secondary market. Funding and origination, two activities that most mortgage lenders had traditionally combined, became increasingly separated.

With the rise of mortgage brokers and mortgage servicers, two other traditional roles of many lenders – selling loans and administrating loans – also became increasingly separated. In countries where mortgage brokers became popular (not only in the US, but also in countries like the UK and the Netherlands), they quickly captured 40–70 per cent of the market for mortgage sales. Specialized mortgage servicers did not expand as fast, with most commercial banks working with in-house servicers and only smaller, usually non-depository lenders, working with external servicers, possibly a subsidiary of a big commercial bank or a big non-bank lender. As a result, many, but certainly not all, mortgage lenders retreated to their core business: lending money, that is, loan origination. Funding, sales, and servicing were either externalized or 'compartmentalized', that is, handled in separate departments or separate firms.

Another important development took place in the late 1980s. In the US, deregulation and hyperinflation undermined the savings and loans institutions. Many of them first got into a liquidity crisis, then into a solvency crisis and, finally, either went into bankruptcy or got bailed out by the federal government. For a short period of time, commercial banks became the most important source of mortgage credit. Then, non-bank lenders took over this role.

In the UK, traditionally building societies had had the monopoly on the supply of mortgage credit. However, from 1986 onwards, commercial banks were allowed to provide mortgage credit. At the same time, building societies were allowed to 'demutualize' and become banks – only ten of them did and those ten are now all owned by commercial banks or have been nationalized as a result of the financial crisis of 2007–09. Former building society Northern Rock is a case in point. In the 1990s, Northern Rock demutualized, followed by an extremely rapid expansion. In September 2007, Northern Rock received liquidity support from the Bank of England, although this was not enough to stop the rot, and a few months later (in February 2008), the bank was nationalized after two unsuccessful bids to take over the bank, with neither being able to fully commit to repayment of taxpayers' money (Marshall et al., 2012).

Similar developments took place in several other countries where the introduction of commercial banks to the mortgage market and deregulation sometimes undermined thrift-like institutions. While several building societies in the UK became banks, many others survived (often after mergers) and remain relatively successful as building societies. Only half of the savings and loans institutions in the US survived the crisis years and those that did generally lost market share. In both countries, many of those that survived the crisis of the 1980s and early 1990s did become active in the secondary mortgage market, sometimes even as buyers rather than sellers.

13.4 URBAN GEOGRAPHIES I: MORTGAGE REDLINING

Mortgage redlining is the policy of a mortgage lender to reject mortgage loan applications based on the neighbourhood. Many authors include uneven conditions such as higher transaction costs and higher interest rates than on other loans in their definition of redlining. For matters of clarity, we define such uneven home mortgage finance conditions as 'yellowlining' which is different from 'redlining' where a lender does not grant any mortgage loans at all. Redlining is a form of place-based financial and social exclusion. Through redlining mortgage applicants are excluded *from* obtaining housing by denying them mortgage loans. Homeowners are excluded *through* housing because they are unable to sell their house, thereby becoming trapped in their home.

Lenders reject mortgage applications for neighbourhoods where they have no trust in the financial dependability of potential customers or in the price development of houses in those neighbourhoods. The risk that a homeowner can only sell her/his home for a lower price than purchased, and as a result is unable to pay off the entire mortgage, is considered too big. Lenders assume that members of certain groups are on average less able to fulfil their financial commitments. For example, if lenders believe that minority applicants are more likely than majority applicants to default this creates an economic incentive to discriminate against minority applicants or minority neighbourhoods – whether this belief is founded on an empirical correlation or not.

The practice of redlining cannot exist without a notion of internal differentiation of geographical space: no internal differentiation – or to put it differently, no sub-markets – no redlining. The question of scale is central to any relevant explanation. We could say that redlining is a product of the uneven development of capitalism, of the application of credit scoring models, of prejudiced urban managers and gatekeepers, of the structure and regulation of the mortgage market, of statistical discrimination or of neighbourhood decline and the devalorization of capital invested in the built environment. It is, of course, in some way, a product of all these forces. This chapter is not the place to connect these different forces and scales at length. Alternatively, we look at the origins of redlining in the US, the development and evidence of redlining in the US, and redlining outside the US.

The origins of redlining policies are to be found in the 1930s economic and housing crisis in the US in which many homeowners lost their homes. As mentioned in the previous section, President Hoover took swift action in the early 1930s. I will focus here on the creation of the *Home Owners Loan Corporation* (HOLC). The HOLC was designed 'to provide emergency relief to homeowners by refinancing or purchasing defaulted mortgages' (Dennis and Pinkowish, 2004: 7) – in other words, to forestall foreclosures. Thanks to the HOLC tens of thousands of borrowers were kept from losing their homes in the mid- and late 1930s and, in addition, it refinanced more than one million mortgages, all on relatively low-interest rates (Gotham, 2002: 53). It also introduced 'the long-term, self-amortizing mortgage with uniform payments spread over the life of the debt' (Jackson, 1985: 196), thereby replacing the five-years, non-amortizing mortgage with a balloon payment at the end of the loan period. The HOLC set the standards for mortgage lending till this day, not only in the US but also elsewhere.

The HOLC was not only instrumental in developing and applying uniform, standardized appraisals, but it was also instrumental in implementing and institutionalizing redlining policies. The HOLC developed a neighbourhood rating and mapping system comprising of four colours corresponding to four different numbers and four different letter codes (see Table 13.1). Although the HOLC is often blamed for *introducing* redlining policies and practices, it is important to note that the HOLC was simply following dominant ideas in real estate and mortgage markets, already practised at the local level

Table 13.1 Redlining colour-coding scheme in the 1930s

Color	Grade	X	Description(summary)
Green	First-grade	A	Homogeneous neighborhoods, hot spots, in demand as residential locations in good times and bad, American business and professional men
Blue	Second-grade	B	Stable, still good, still desirable areas that had reached their peak
Yellow	Third-grade	C	Definitely declining, heterogeneous neighborhoods that attract undesirable elements and are infiltrated by a lower grade population
Red	Fourth-grade	D	Neighborhoods in which the things taking place in C areas have already happened as a result of detrimental influences in a pronounced degree and where houses have little or no value today, having suffered a tremendous decline in values due to the colored element now controlling the district

Sources: Adapted from and cited in Jackson (1985: 197–200); Hillier (2005: 216–217).

(Hillier, 2003). However, the HOLC did *implement* and *institutionalize* already existing policies of redlining into government policies by designing redlining maps for more than 200 American cities (Aalbers, 2011; cf. Crossney and Bartelt, 2005a, 2005b; Gotham, 2002; Hillier, 2005; Immergluck, 2004; Jackson, 1985; Stuart, 2003). Fourth-grade, red-coloured neighbourhoods were no exception, but more rare on some city maps than on others. While the map of St. Louis County, for example, only shows a small number of neighbourhoods coloured red, the map of the city of Newark, NJ is full of redlined neighbourhoods and no single neighbourhood in Newark is coloured green (Jackson, 1985). Figure 13.3, the map for the city of Baltimore, shows a classic pattern: inner-city

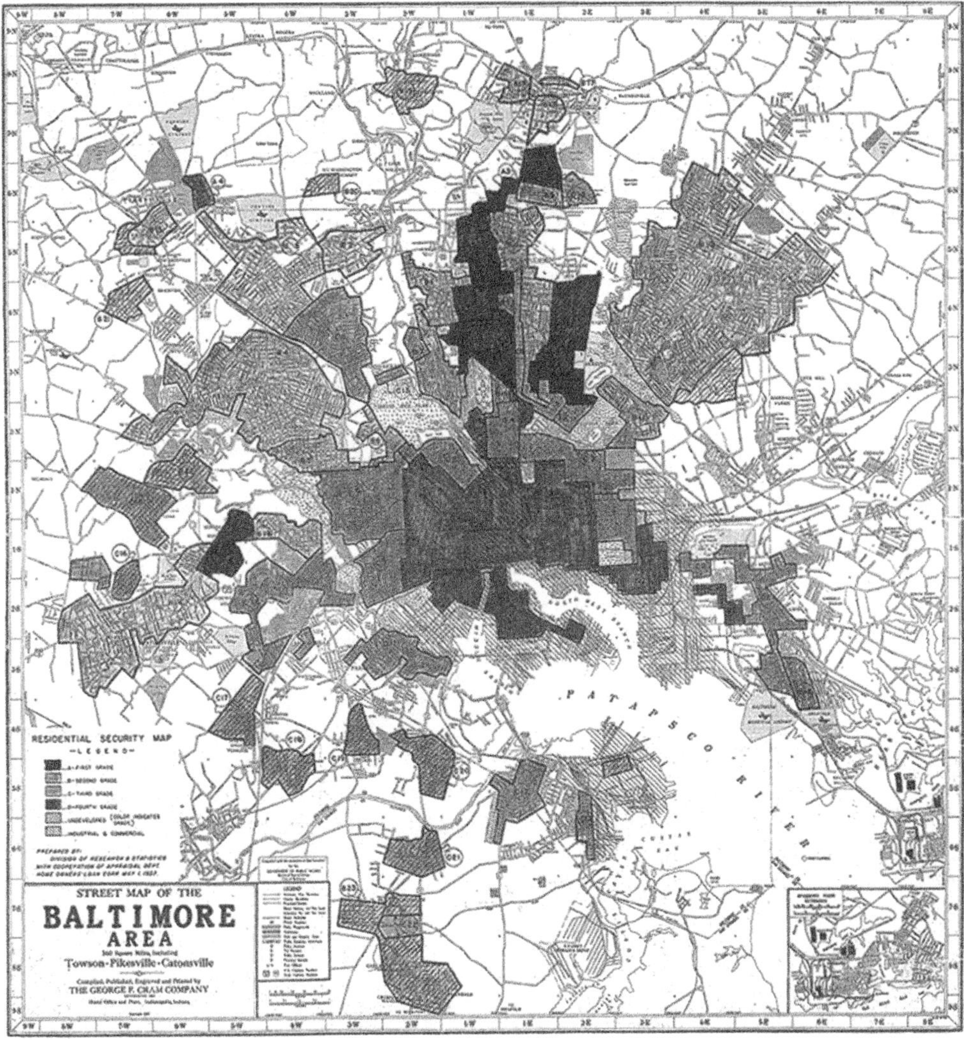

Source: US National Archives.

Figure 13.3 HOLC redlining map of Baltimore, 1937

neighbourhoods surrounding the central business district are coloured red, the next ring of neighbourhoods and the older suburbs are largely coloured yellow, while newer suburbs – albeit with a few exceptions – are coloured blue or, less common, green.

Redlining policies were adopted not only by the HOLC and private mortgage lenders, but also by the *Federal Housing Administration* (FHA). The FHA, established in 1934 under the Roosevelt administration, was created to insure private mortgage loans. The Veterans Administration (VA), created in 1930, started doing the same in the late 1930s. A borrower pays a loan premium for an FHA- or VA-insured home mortgage loan; the premiums are used as reserves and would flow to the lender in case an insured borrower defaulted. Like the HOLC, the creation of the FHA changed the mortgage market and set standards and practices that are followed to this day. By 1972, the FHA had insured about 11 million loans-for-purchase and about 22 million loans-for-home-improvement. FHA's standardization made it easier, less risky and cheaper to buy a home, thereby fuelling the development of the mortgage market.

The FHA helped to encourage suburbanization, but also 'hastened the decay of inner-city neighbourhoods by stripping them of their middle-class constituency', because 'in practice, FHA insurance went to new residential developments on the edges of metropolitan areas, to the neglect of core cities' (Jackson, 1985: 206). The inner city areas were overlooked partly because they had lower appraised values for housing and FHA simply did not grant insurance in many of these areas. Kenneth Jackson (1985: 213) concludes his ground-breaking work by claiming that the FHA 'helped to turn the building industry against the minority and inner-city housing market, and its policies supported the income and racial segregation of suburbia'. Kevin Fox Gotham (2002: 63) arrives at similar conclusions arguing that the FHA's 'insurance system and homeownership subsidies established a racially dual home financing market by refusing to insure mortgages in areas not covered with a racially restrictive covenant, thus denying mortgages to Black families, and channelling capital into suburban housing construction'. Indeed, discussions on redlining have been connected to debates on the causes of segregation and forms of racial discrimination: redlining is often seen as a form of (institutionalized) discrimination and as one of the causes of segregation. Together with many other mechanisms and policies, redlining is understood to be one of the causes of the erosion of cities, the decline of (inner-city) neighbourhoods and the mass exodus to the suburbs.

In the mid- and late 1960s the FHA was forced to change its policies and make mortgage insurance available in formerly redlined and yellowlined areas. Today, FHA loans are actually responsible for increasing homeownership among Black households. As research by Wyly and Holloway (1999) shows, even if controlled for income, Black households significantly more often rely on FHA-insured loans. The assumption is that Black households rely on FHA-insured loans because it is more difficult for them to acquire loans in the non-insured mortgage market.

In the wake of the social rights movement, redlining returned to political and research agendas in the late 1960s and 1970s. Community-based organizations in particular claimed that lenders were redlining large parts of American inner cities (Squires, 1992). In 1968, discrimination in housing – including mortgaging – became legally prohibited through the *Fair Housing Act*. In addition, the US government responded by implementing the *Home Mortgage Disclosure Act* (HMDA) in 1975, and the *Community Reinvestment Act* (CRA) in 1977. These laws require lenders to report granted loans by census tract and to provide credit to the local communities within the states in which they are active. Despite these laws and the related move of the FHA to the inner-city, research from the 1970s, 1980s and early 1990s clearly shows the existence of redlining policies, mostly in inner-city areas. Some of the earliest studies from the 1970s found evidence of redlining, but have been criticized for omitting important variables and for the use of aggregate level data. Studies from the 1980s have demonstrated that minority and inner-city neighbourhoods receive less credit, but these studies are susceptible to the criticism of pre-selection bias. Whatever the case may be, it is clear that community and legal struggles against redlining have been successful in diminishing redlining practices (Aalbers, 2011; Immergluck, 2004; Squires, 1992; Wyly and Holloway, 1999).

Even though most research on redlining is carried out in the US, there are also a number of studies documenting redlining processes in other countries. Research in the UK (Bassett and Short, 1980; Boddy, 1976; Weir, 1976; Williams, 1978), South Africa (Kotze and Van Huyssteen, 1990), Australia (Engels, 1994), Canada (Harris and Forrester, 2003; Murdie, 1986), the Netherlands (Aalbers, 2005, 2011) and Italy (Aalbers, 2007, 2011) has demonstrated the existence of redlining and/or yellowlining, whether in the 1970s and 1980s or in the 1990s and 2000s. Redlining is sometimes mentioned in other countries, but I am not aware of any redlining research elsewhere in Europe or in the Global South. The most recent unambiguous example of redlining comes from the city of Rotterdam where at one point all the major banks (who together dominate the Dutch mortgage market) redlined large parts of the city. Typically, redlined neighbourhoods in Rotterdam are areas with relatively high percentages of low-income people, ethnic minorities, rental housing, and low-priced housing (Aalbers, 2005, 2011).

13.5 URBAN GEOGRAPHIES II: SUBPRIME LENDING

Traditionally, mortgage lending was about trust. With the standardization of mortgage loans, starting in the 1930s in the US, mortgage lending became a 'one-size-fits-all' industry where people would either qualify for a certain type of loan or they would not. Borrower segmentation became more popular with the advent of credit scoring systems and risk-based pricing, the rise of securitization, and the entry of new types of lenders. The basic distinction is that between prime and subprime loans (see also the chapter by French), the latter including Alt-A loans (often considered an intermediate class between prime and subprime lending), predatory loans, NINJA loans (no income, no job or assets), no doc and stated income/stated asset loans (often called 'liar loans' because the information provided by the borrower is not verified and therefore susceptible to fraud), and other exotic loans. Lenders themselves use an endless variety of names for their loans, but this often has more to do with marketing than with real differences between loan types.

Subprime mortgage lending in the US had been growing fast, from about $35 billion (5 per cent of total mortgage originations) in 1994 to $600 billion (20 per cent) in 2006 (Figure 13.4; see also Avery et al., 2006), 75 per cent of which is securitized. In some states like Nevada, subprime loans accounted for more than 30 per cent of the loans originated in 2006. In 2006, 13 per cent of outstanding loans were subprime, but 60 per cent of the loans in foreclosure were subprime, up from 30 per cent in 2003 (Nassar, 2007). Neither

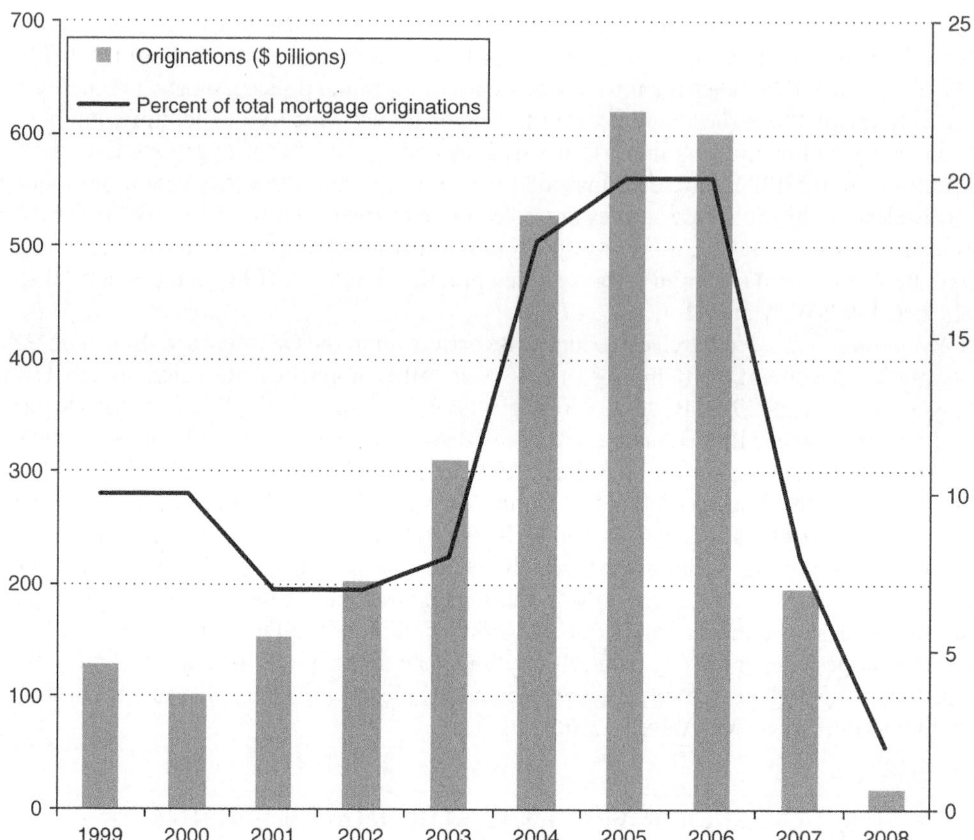

Source: Inside Mortgage Finance (2009).

Figure 13.4 Subprime mortgage origination in the US

the media nor economists ever pass an opportunity to point out that many borrowers took out loans they could not afford. This is correct, but in most cases this was not because borrowers were eager to take on large loans even though they had bad credit. A majority of the subprime loans went to borrowers with prime credit (Brooks and Simon, 2007; Dymski, 2012). This implies that lenders systematically overcharged borrowers. Subprime lending is often defined as lending to a low-income borrower with poor credit, but this would be a misrepresentation of the essence of subprime lending, which is lending at higher fees and interest rates whether or not the borrower actually has bad credit or a low income (Aalbers, 2009). Subprime loans were pushed on borrowers – low and moderate-income as well as middle and high-income – because they brought in more money, not just because lenders were pushed to sell them.

Selling subprime loans to prime borrowers was good business for both mortgage lenders and brokers. Lenders could charge higher interest rates on subprime loans and thus make more money. For this reason lenders gave brokers bigger sales fees for selling subprime loans. Brokers did not have negative results as a result of defaulting borrowers, as they only get paid for what they sell. And defaulting borrowers actually created a bigger market for refinancing, which implied that brokers could make more money on clients by selling them another loan (Aalbers, 2012; Immergluck, 2009; Squires, 2004; Wyly et al., 2006).

In addition, it is often argued that subprime lending enabled many people that were formerly excluded from homeownership, that is, low-income and ethnic minority groups, to buy a house and enjoy the benefits of homeownership. This is questionable for at least two reasons. First, many of these borrowers had bought properties at the low-end of the market that needed improvement work and because of the high interest rates their monthly expenses often went up much faster than their income and became unmanageable. Homeownership for many subprime homebuyers became a burden. Second, most subprime loans were not enabling homeownership as more than half of them were refinance loans and second mortgages – in other words, loans for people who already owned a mortgaged property. Most of the refinance loans were designed in such a way that they looked cheaper than the original loan, but would, in fact, turn out more expensive for the borrowers and more profitable for the mortgage broker and the lender. Adjustable Rate Mortgages (ARMs) are a good example: one type of ARM known as a 2/28 or 3/27 will start with a low interest rate, but after two or three years the interest rate resets to a much higher rate. Borrowers are shown the initial, low interest rate while the higher interest rate is hidden in the small print of the mortgage contract, which is typically unreadable.

A subset of subprime lending is known as predatory lending. Predatory lenders charge excessive fees and interest rates and originated loans that were not beneficial for borrowers (Squires, 2004). Originally predatory lending was seen as a small part of the subprime mortgage market, but research has demonstrated predatory lending has not an exception but rather something very common in subprime lending. Often homeowners do not have a full understanding of the mortgage lending process and fail to hire experts, not only at the time of mortgage origination, but also when the first payment problems arise (Engel and McCoy, 2002). There is mounting evidence that subprime and predatory lenders use sophisticated marketing techniques to reach people with little education or prior lending experience (Carr and Schuetz, 2001; Quercia et al., 2004; Newman, 2012). Predatory loans were sold mostly in neighbourhoods with ethnic minority populations. Almost half of the loans in minority areas were predatory compared to 22 per cent in white areas (Avery et al., 2007). African-Americans receive more than twice as many high-priced loans as Whites, even after controlling for the risk level of the borrower (Schloemer et al., 2006). It then comes as no surprise that foreclosures are concentrated in certain parts of the city. These problems are not new: in the years before the crisis researchers pointed out how subprime and predatory lending result in rising default and foreclosure rates (for example, Pennington-Cross, 2002; Squires, 2004; Wyly et al., 2009).

Some authors have argued that subprime lending and predatory lending replaced redlining. This is possible due to the increased use of credit scoring. Credit scoring enables lenders (often through credit agencies) to map the social characteristics of households, and by coupling those to financial characteristics and past financial behaviour, mortgage lenders try to predict the default risk of a borrower. Low-risk prospective borrowers can then be offered low-priced loans and while high-risk borrowers would have been denied a mortgage loan in the past, they can now get a high-priced loan. The problem is not only that some loans become too high-priced for households to handle, but also that several lenders in the subprime market offer mortgage loans with high prices that no longer hold any real correlation between risk and price. Predatory lending – sometimes referred to as 'reversed redlining' – causes more harm to homeowners than it does benefit.

But how does this relate to redlining? It may seem that credit scoring systems have been so well developed to accurately predict borrower behaviour that lenders no longer need such crude methods as redlining to limit risk. Although this may very well be the case, this does not necessarily mean that redlining has in fact become obsolete. First, redlining may still exist next to credit scoring: this way formal application procedures that generate the input for credit scoring systems have to make no mention of 'zip code policies', while lenders can still enact redlining policies. Second, lenders may use geographical location as an additional criterion, in particular when reassessing 'review cases'. Third, because geographical location may be included in credit scoring systems, redlining may take place through those credit scoring systems, as geographical location may be the decisive factor in turning down an application, in particular if geographical location gets a relatively large weight in a credit scoring system. Even though geographical location will not be the only factor predicting exclusion or inclusion, the result nonetheless is de facto or actual redlining (Aalbers, 2011). The new redlining builds on and reproduces the uneven development of the old redlining (Dymski, 2012; Squires, 2004).

13.6 THE INTERNATIONAL GEOGRAPHY OF MORTGAGE FUNDING

A mortgage lender is a firm that originates mortgage loans in the primary mortgage market, that is, the market where borrowers and mortgage originators come together to negotiate terms and complete a mortgage transaction. The term 'originator' is often used in the mortgage industry to indicate that the lender that made the loan is not necessarily the holder of mortgage debt. Some mortgage lenders hold most or all of the mortgage debt they originate in their portfolios, while other lenders sell most or all of the loans they originate in the so-called 'secondary mortgage market', where investment banks, financial institutions, and, particularly in the US, government-sponsored enterprises repackage mortgages as securities to sell to institutional investors in national and global capital markets.

Throughout the history of mortgage markets there have been different kinds of institutions that originate mortgage loans. Historically, most of these institutions have been 'depository institutions': lenders that not only make loans but also take deposits from savers. It may seem obvious that lenders need to accumulate deposits as a reserve from which to make loans, but this is not a necessity. It is also possible for a lender to acquire funding in other ways. 'Non-depository institutions' may only need a small amount of 'working capital' to originate loans if they sell these loans in the secondary mortgage market. Every time they sell a portfolio of loans they have freed up capital that they can use to originate new loans. Other non-depository lenders include insurance companies and pension funds. Most non-depository lenders are non-banks, which means nothing more than that they are, by law, not considered banks.[2] This does, however, not imply that depository lenders do not use the secondary mortgage markets to sell mortgage loans they originated. Many commercial banks in developed countries not only take deposits from savers, but also sell a significant share of the loans they originated in the secondary mortgage market.

Until a few decades ago most mortgage lenders were local or regional institutions. Today, most mortgage lenders are national lenders who tap into the global credit market. This is not so much the case because lenders are global financial institutions – most lenders are national in scope – but because they compete for the same credit in a global market. Before the financial crisis of the late 1980s, savings and loans institutions and the like granted loans based on the savings that got into the bank. Generally speaking, the savings and loans were made in the same geographical market. The fact that the S&Ls only worked in local markets was seen as a problem: what if savings are available in one area, but loans are needed in another; and what if a local housing market goes bust? The 'solution' was to connect local markets and to spread risk. The idea was that interest rates on loans would fall because there was now a more efficient market for the demand and supply of money and credit. Moreover, national lenders could more easily take the burdens of a local housing market bust because risk would be spread.

The trend from local to national mortgage lenders was one thing, but, it was argued, mortgage markets could be even more efficient if they were connected to other financial markets and not just to savings. In the wider credit market it would be easy for mortgage lenders to get funding as mortgages were considered low risk. Mortgages would be an ideal investment for low-risk investors and cheaper credit, in return, would lower interest rates on mortgage loans. In the US, securitization was already introduced in the 1960s by Fannie Mae and Freddie Mac, two government sponsored enterprises that were meant to spur homeownership rates for low- and middle-income households. Securitization enables mortgage lenders to sell their mortgage portfolios on the secondary mortgage markets to investors. Following the S&L crisis, deregulation favoured securitization, not only through Fannie Mae and Freddie Mac, but also through so-called 'private labels'. Gotham (2006, 2012) has studied the de- and re-regulation of the mortgage market and demonstrates how the federal government, step-by-step, has enabled securitization, for example, by the Financial Institutions Reform, Recovery and Enforcement Act (1989) that pushed portfolio lenders to securitize their loans and shift to non-depository lending. In other words, the state was at the origins of the current crisis.

'Regulated deregulation' (Aalbers, 2016) also removed the walls between the different rooms of finance, thereby enabling existing financial firms to become active in more types of financial markets and providing opportunities for new mortgage lenders. Securitization meant that mortgage lenders could work according to a new business model whereby mortgages are taken off-balance. This frees up more equity for more loans and enabled non-banks to enter the mortgage market. Many of these new, non-bank lenders had different regulators than traditional lenders and were also assessed by other, that is, weaker, regulatory frameworks. In addition, it is not always clear which regulator watches what, but even if this is clear, this is no guarantee that regulators actually execute their regulatory powers, sometimes due to a lack of interest and sometimes due to a lack of resources. In many cases, lenders can actually shop around for a regulator. It is obvious that they will not opt for the hardest regulator. Mortgage portfolios could now be sold to investors anywhere in the world and because these investors thought mortgage portfolios were low-risk and there was a lot of money waiting to be invested, especially after the dot-com bubble crash (2000–02), there was a great appetite for residential mortgage-backed securities

(RMBS). In other words, the S&L crisis, the following bank merger wave (Dymski, 1999), securitization, the entry of non-bank lenders and the demand for low-risk investments together shaped the globalization and financialization of mortgage markets (Aalbers, 2008).

Within geography and sociology there is now a growing body of literature that tries to trace the trajectories of different national structures of securitization (Aalbers et al., 2011; Aalbers and Engelen, 2015; Gotham, 2006, 2012; Wainwright, 2012). While strongly linked to the surge of financial innovation characteristic of post-Bretton Woods financial markets (see Engelen et al., 2011), securitization is in fact an old financial technique that can be traced back to the creation of proto-mutual funds in eighteenth-century Holland, which issued tradable shares on the back of aggregated life insurance premiums (Rouwenhorst, 2005). In essence, today's structured financial products are based on the same insights. Opaque contracts are pooled and sold to a separate legal entity or special purpose vehicle (SPV), which in turn issues bonds to end investors to pay for the underlying assets. The investors receive parts of the cash flow generated by these contracts. As a result, the amount of information needed to assess the bonds on offer is radically reduced. For example, in mortgage contracts investors do not have to assess the quality of the mortgaged property, the socio-economic expectations of the neighbourhood or the creditworthiness of the mortgagee (Aalbers and Engelen, 2015). They only have to assess the reliability of the originator (Is the mortgage granted by a prudential lender?), the sophistication of the structurer (Does the investment bank do a good enough job?), and the trustworthiness of the servicer (Is the servicer a reliable collector of the principal of the loan and interest?). As a result, it has become extremely uncommon for investors to look at the underlying portfolio of their securities, other than through aggregate data. Instead, all risk assessments have increasingly been delegated to rating agencies. These private organizations have a legal mandate to rate the creditworthiness of emitters of bonds and are remunerated for their work by the emitters on a fee-basis. The largest and best-known agencies are Standard & Poor's, Moody's and Fitch (see Chapter 20, this volume).

13.7 CRISIS: BRINGING TOGETHER THE URBAN AND INTERNATIONAL GEOGRAPHIES

The root of the mortgage crisis, according to some observers, is in the housing market: the rapid increase of house prices forced people to take out bigger loans (Shiller, 2008). The housing bubble, like all bubbles, depended on a constant inflow of liquidity to sustain the rising market as well as the illusion that all participants in the market are winners (Lordon, 2007; see also Chapter 2, this volume). Once the housing bubble burst, homeowners got in trouble, not just because their homes were worth less, but also because so many of them had taken out big loans with small down-payments and high interest rates. Negative equity, default and foreclosure were some of the negative results. Indeed, there was a strong housing bubble, but this did not so much fuel the mortgage market – the mortgage market, in the first place, fuelled the housing bubble. House prices increased first and foremost because mortgages allowed borrowers to buy more expensive homes, but since almost everyone could now afford a mortgage loan – and generally speaking a much bigger loan than a decade ago – the expansion of the mortgage market resulted in higher house prices forcing people to take out ever-bigger loans. In that sense, the mortgage market created its own expansion. Thus, mortgage and housing markets fuelled one another, but it is crucial to understand that the driving force here is the mortgage market. All this was enabled through regulated deregulation.

There were enough investors who had an appetite for RMBS, first in so-called conforming loans because of their low-risk that was considered to be comparable to state obligations. But since the late 1990s, and increasingly so after the dot-com bubble crash (2000–02), they also showed an interest in subprime loans issued as RMBS: in an ever more competitive search for yield 'each stage of market development replayed a dynamic of overspeculation based on competitive pressures to adopt riskier borrowers and loan products' (Ashton, 2008: 1425). Investors, in return, 'had concentrated risks by leveraging their holdings of mortgages in securitized assets, so [when the bubble burst] their losses were multiplied' (Mizen, 2008: 532). Subprime loans were considered riskier, but this was compensated by higher returns and since the rating agencies still supplied high ratings, such RMBS were seen as low-risk/high-return. Rating agencies saw the increased likeliness of default on such loans, but like the lenders they did not see this as a major problem, more as an inconvenience. In addition, rating agencies get paid by the firms whose securities they have to rate (see Chapter 20, this volume).

These RMBS were now traded on global markets that are localized in places like New York and London (Sassen, 2001). While in the past a mortgage bubble or a housing bubble would affect the economy through homeowners, the recent bursting of these bubbles affects the economy not just through homeowners, but also through financial markets. Because lenders are now national in scope this no longer affects only some housing markets, but all housing markets throughout the US and beyond. Housing markets may still be local or regional; mortgage markets are not. Since primary mortgage markets are national, the bubble in the national mortgage market affects all local and regional housing markets, although it clearly affects housing markets with a greater bubble more than those with a smaller bubble (Aalbers, 2009). In addition, secondary mortgage markets are global markets, which means that a crisis of mortgage securitization implies that investors around the globe, and therefore economies around the globe, are affected. The mortgage market crisis affects the US economy on both sides of the mortgage lending chain – through homeowners and through financial markets – while it affects other economies in the world mostly through financial markets, not just because investors around the globe have invested in RMBS, but also because the mortgage market has triggered a whole chain of events that have decreased liquidity and this affects even agents in financial markets that have never been involved in RMBS. Unsurprisingly, outstanding RMBS have declined in all EU countries except for the Netherlands and Belgium (EMF, 2014). In *absolute* terms, in Europe the Netherlands and the UK represent the largest markets for RMBS, but they are still dwarfed by the size of the RMBS market in the US (see Figure 13.5).

It is no coincidence that the securitization of mortgage loans went too far and created a mortgage bubble – and thereby also a housing bubble. Securitization may have started out for the sake of increasing homeownership, but in the last 15 to 20 years the growth in securitization had little to do with increasing homeownership – this was simply a by-product – and more with the dependence of the US economy – and increasingly also other

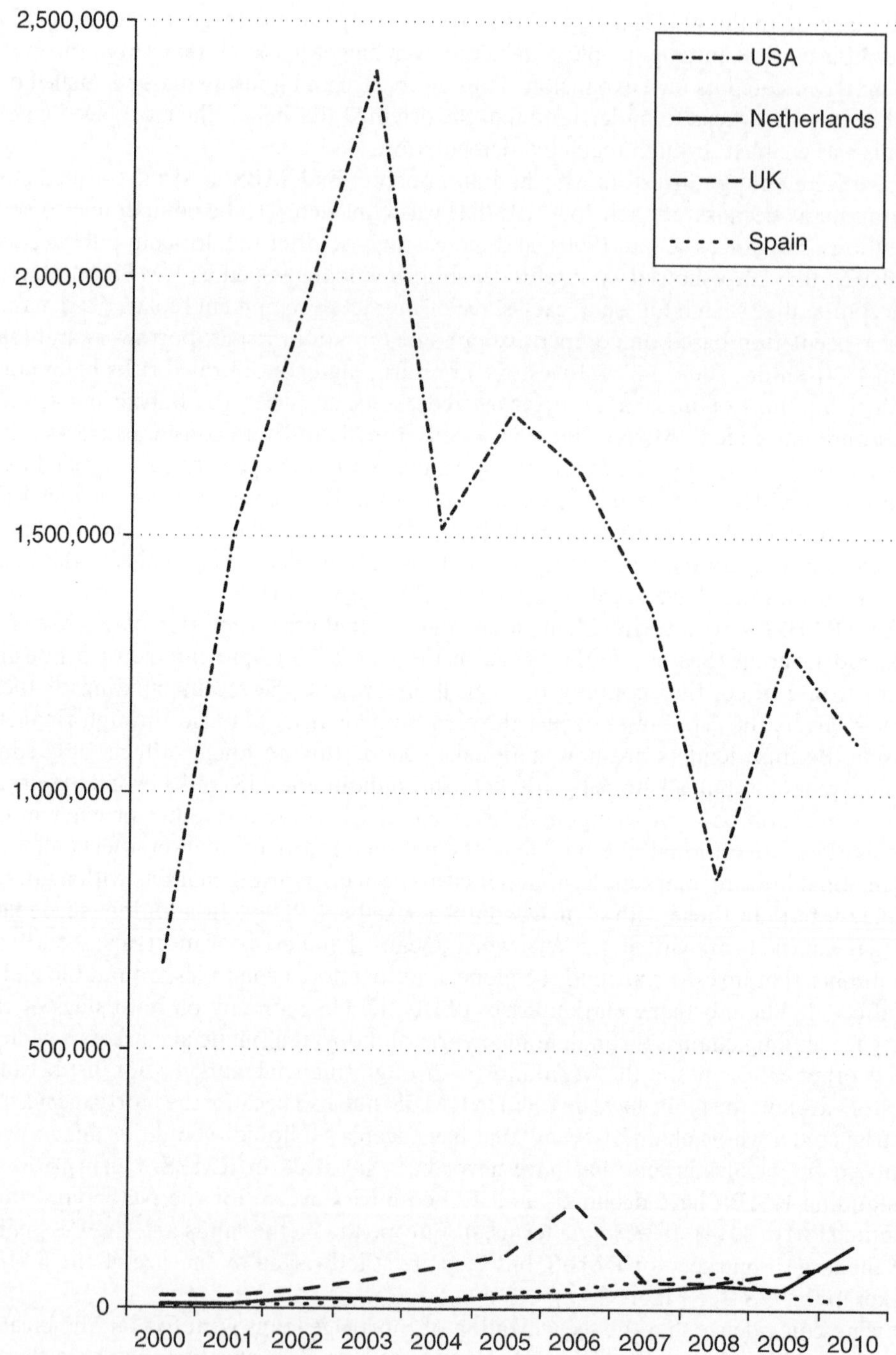

Source: Association for Financial Markets in Europe (AFME), Federal Reserve.

Figure 13.5 Total RMBS issuance per year, EUR million

economies – on the financial sector for economic growth. Due to the slowing down of the overall growth rate and the stagnation of the real economy, capitalism has increasingly become dependent on the growth of finance to enlarge money capital (Sweezy, 1995; Foster, 2007). Therefore the capital accumulation process becomes financialized: focused on the growth of finance not to benefit the real economy but to benefit actors within financial markets such as investors.

Some commentators (for example, Mizen, 2008) would argue that it is a coincidence that the financial crisis started in the mortgage market. They may argue that the whole financial system is so rotten that, sooner or later, it had to fail: the mortgage market is the trigger of the downturn, but the actual causes are much deeper and have affected all financial sectors. Other commentators (for example, Ashton, 2009) would alternatively argue that it is no surprise that the fall down of the financial sector was caused by the mortgage market. They may argue that the mortgage market was far more rotten than any other financial sector and that in no other financial sector was money provided as recklessly. In fact, the mortgage market was not unique in its financial excesses; other financial markets also showed developments that were getting out of hand. For example, at Lehman Brothers, the American investment bank that failed, it was possible to speculate on almost anything, including the weather. Investing in a house by taking out a mortgage loan, albeit a risky one, in that respect looks less risky; and also investing in RMBS, even in subprime RMBS, does not seem so excessive any more.

Nevertheless, the mortgage market is different from other financial markets in at least two important ways. First, the market for mortgage lending and the market for RMBS, not necessarily in turnover but certainly in outstanding volume, are simply much bigger than most other financial markets. If the market for weather speculation or even that for the securitization of car loans would fall apart, the impact would be far less reaching. Second, unlike many other financial markets, a downturn in the mortgage market hits not only agents active in the credit and securities markets, but also homeowners. Since a home is the most expensive thing most households will ever buy and because it is such a basic need, the impact of a mortgage crisis – in a country like the US that is heavily depended on mortgage loans to make the housing market work – could only be dramatic. In the sense that there were too many wrong incentives in the market, mortgages and RMBS were not so different from many other financial markets, but in its impact on both 'sophisticated' financial markets and ordinary citizens, the mortgage market is unique.

Crises have often been blamed on a lack of openness and transparency. Yet, the current credit crunch originates in a market *made open, liquid, and transparent*; located in a country that prides itself on its free, open markets. In addition, an analysis of financial crises since 1945 demonstrates that financial liberalization, whether de jure or de facto, precedes the majority of crises (Kaminsky and Reinhart, 1999) – the current crisis is no exception. Liberalization-enabled securitization and financialization, by embracing risk rather than avoiding it, act against the interests of long-term investments. Though securitization was designed to limit risk by spreading it over a wider area and to increase efficiency as a result of economies of scale, the spread of risk gives the crisis wider latitude, not only affecting subprime loans, but also prime loans; not only affecting mortgage markets, but also other credit markets; and not only affecting the US, but also other places around the globe. Through financialization, the volatility of Wall Street has entered not only companies off-Wall-Street, but increasingly also individual houses – homeownership and finance are more entangled than ever before (Aalbers, 2008). It could be argued that the state has facilitated the privatization of profit and the socialization of risk (Aalbers, 2013).

The current credit crunch exemplifies how the fate of homeowners is increasingly tied to the fate of financial markets. In its origins, this is not because rising default rates and foreclosures trouble financial markets, but because the financialization of mortgages and homeowners has led to the extraction of capital from homeowners to financial investors. In other words, the mortgage crisis is a direct result of the financialization of both mortgage markets and homeowners. The financialization of homeownership is not just another example of financialization but a crucial one, as mortgage markets are crucial markets in the present economy, while homes are as crucial as ever for households, but have increased their importance as indicators of the economy (Aalbers, 2008).

13.8 THE END OF THE GREAT EXCESS

The years between the crisis of the late 1980s and the recent/current global financial crisis were the decades of the great excess in which income and wealth inequality in many countries increased rapidly (for example, Piketty, 2014). In western countries the lack of (or in some countries, very limited) real income growth was matched with a rapid rise in household debt, and in particular mortgage debt for the middle – and in the US also for the lower – classes. What respectively Crouch (2011) and Watson (2010) have dubbed 'privatized Keynesianism' and 'house price Keynesianism' is essentially a way both to fuel the economy by propping up consumption and to 'compensate' labour for decades of negligible or even negative real income growth. Indeed, many western economies have become so addicted to high and increasing house prices that it seems difficult for governments and households alike to deal with a situation of declining prices, which are seen as lowering people's economic perceptions and therefore as having a negative influence on the economy at large. Even in times of crises and austerity, the housing and mortgage sectors are still seen as key vehicles to foster economic growth (Aalbers and Christophers, 2014; Forrest and Yip, 2011).

In many western countries, younger cohorts are now less likely to be or become homeowners than the cohorts before them when they were the same age (cf. Forrest and Yip, 2011). For decades, the trend was towards increasing home-ownership amongst younger cohorts. Widely available mortgage credit had enabled their homeownership pursuits, but since the 1980s in some places, and since the 1990s in others, young people also had less choice: social housing was reduced in size and increasingly hard to get access to, even in countries where social housing previously tended to be more widely available, of higher quality and less stigmatized (Aalbers, 2015). The social housing sector remains barred to most young households, so the alternatives are private rented housing – which is again on the rise in some countries, in particular English speaking ones (for example, Forrest and Hirayama, 2015) – but it is often under-maintained, overpriced or both. This results in delaying leaving the nest or even returning to one's parents, to doubling up, house sharing and prolonged room renting. Renting a room has for decades been considered a typical condition for both students and young people everywhere and in particular for many people, including professionals in their thirties, in global and other high-priced cities, but it is increasingly becoming normalized as employment, in particular of the permanent kind, is harder to obtain (for example, Laparra and Pérez, 2011). Since current younger generations have seen less income growth than the younger generations before them, the only way they could afford to become homeowners was to take on massive amounts of debt (see also Chapter 14, this volume). For many people the entry into homeownership was less of a choice than a necessity (Aalbers, 2015).

Although the dominant policy response has been to restore 'business as usual' in housing and mortgage lending (Smith, 2010), the current crisis has the potential to be a game-changer as well – 'the good old days' are unlikely to return. So far, we have seen a decline in homeownership rates in selective countries and a decline in home-buying younger households in most western countries. It remains to be seen whether this is a conjunctural development that will soon be reversed. The shift towards a casualized workforce suggests homeownership rates are unlikely to start rising again, but the lack of affordable and accessible alternatives also casts doubt on an accelerated decline in homeownership rates. As long as states are undermined discursively as well as materially (austerity, tax flight, and so on), and as long as the financialized regime of accumulation is not rolled back, households that can get mortgage credit are destined to be indebted while those who cannot will remain on social housing waiting lists, in sub-standard housing or doubled up (Aalbers, 2015). A decommodified housing alternative is needed more than ever before, but it would already be a great improvement if existing decommodified housing were allowed to subsist and are not commodified any further.

NOTES

1. This chapter relies heavily on Aalbers (2008, 2011: Chapter 4, 2015).
2. Confusingly, non-bank lenders are also known as mortgage banks although often they are, legally speaking, not banks.

REFERENCES

Aalbers, M.B. (2005), 'Who's afraid of red, yellow and green?: Redlining in Rotterdam', *Geoforum*, **36** (5), 562–580.

Aalbers, M.B. (2007), 'Geographies of housing finance: the mortgage market in Milan, Italy', *Growth and Change*, **38** (2), 174–199.

Aalbers, M.B. (2008), 'The financialization of home and the mortgage market crisis', *Competition & Change*, **12** (2), 148–166.

Aalbers, M.B. (2009), 'Geographies of the financial crisis', *Area*, **41** (1), 34–42.

Aalbers, M.B. (2011), *Place, Exclusion, and Mortgage Markets*, Oxford: Wiley-Blackwell.

Aalbers M.B. (2012), *Subprime Cities: The Political Economy of Mortgage Markets*, Oxford: Wiley-Blackwell.

Aalbers, M.B. (2013), 'Neoliberalism is dead . . . long live neoliberalism!', *International Journal of Urban and Regional Research*, **37** (3), 1083–1090.

Aalbers, M.B. (2015), 'The great moderation, the great excess and the global housing crisis', *Journal of Housing Policy*, **15** (1), 43–60.

Aalbers, M.B. (2016), 'Regulated deregulation', in S. Springer, K. Birch and J. MacLeavy (eds), *Handbook of Neoliberalism*, London: Routledge, pp. 549–559.

Aalbers, M.B. and B. Christophers (2014), 'Centring housing in political economy', *Housing, Theory and Society*, **31**, 373–394.

Aalbers, M.B. and E. Engelen (2015), 'The political economy of the rise, fall, and rise again of securitization', *Environment and Planning A*, **47**, 1597–1605.
Aalbers, M.B., E. Engelen and A. Glasmacher (2011), '"Cognitive closure" in the Netherlands: mortgage securitization in a hybrid European political economy', *Environment and Planning A*, **43** (8), 1779–1795.
Arrighi, Giovanni (1994), *The Long Twentieth Century: Money, Power, and the Origins of our Times*, London: Verso.
Ashton, P. (2008), 'Advantage or disadvantage? The changing institutional landscape of underserved mortgage markets', *Urban Affairs Review*, **43**, 352–402.
Ashton, P. (2009), 'An appetite for yield: the anatomy of the subprime mortgage crisis', *Environment & Planning A*, **41** (6), 1420–1441.
Avery, R.B., K.P. Brevoort and G.B. Canner (2006), 'Higher-priced home lending and the 2005 HMDA data', *Federal Reserve Bulletin*, **92**, 123–166.
Avery, R.B., K.P. Brevoort and G.B. Canner (2007), 'The 2006 HMDA data', *Federal Reserve Bulletin*, **93**, 73–109.
Bassett, K.A. and J.R. Short (1980), 'Patterns of building society and local authority mortgage lending in the 1970s', *Environment & Planning A*, **12** (3), 279–300.
Boddy, M.J. (1976), 'The structure of mortgage finance: building societies and the British social formation', *Transactions of the Institute of British Geographers*, **1** (1), 58–71.
Boyer, R. (2000), 'Is a finance-led growth regime a viable alternative to Fordism? A preliminary analysis', *Economy and Society*, **29** (1), 111–145.
Brooks, R. and R. Simon (2007), 'Subprime debacle traps even very credit-worthy', *Wall Street Journal*, 3 December: A1.
Carr, James and Jenny Schuetz (2001), *Financial Services in Distressed Communities: Framing the Issue, Finding Solutions*, Washington, DC: Fannie Mae Foundation.
Carruthers, B.G. (2005), 'The sociology of money and credit', in N.J. Smelser and R. Swedberg (eds), *The Handbook of Economic Sociology*, 2nd edition, Princeton, NJ: Princeton University Press, pp. 355–378.
Crossney, K.B. and D.W. Bartelt (2005a), 'The legacy of the Home Owners' Loan Corporation', *Housing Policy Debate*, **16** (3/4), 547–574.
Crossney, K.B. and D.W. Bartelt (2005b), 'Residential security, risk, and race: the Home Owners' Loan Corporation and mortgage access in two cities', *Urban Geography*, **26** (8), 707–736.
Crouch, Colin (2011), *The Strange Non-Death of Neoliberalism*, Cambridge: Polity.
Dennis, M.W. and T.J. Pinkowish (2004), *Residential Mortgage Lending: Principles and Practices*, 5th edition, Mason, OH: Thomson South-Western.
Dymski, Gary (1999), *The Bank Merger Wave: The Economic Causes and Social Consequences of Financial Consolidation*, Armonk, NY: Sharpe.
Dymski, G.A. (2012), 'The reinvention of banking and the subprime crisis: on the origins of subprime loans, and how economics missed the crisis', in M.B. Aalbers (ed.), *Subprime Cities: The Political Economy of Mortgage Markets*, Oxford: Wiley-Blackwell, pp. 151–184.
EMF (2014), *Hypostat 2014*, Brussels: European Mortgage Federation.
Engel, K. and P. McCoy (2002), 'Tale of three markets: the law and economics of predatory lending', *Texas Law Review*, **80**, 1255–1381.
Engelen, E. (2003), 'The logic of funding European pension restructuring and the dangers of financialization', *Environment and Planning A*, **35** (8), 1357–1372.
Engelen Ewald, Ismail Erturk, Julie Froud, Adam Leaver and Karel Williams (2011), *After the Great Complacence; Financial Innovation and the Politics of Finance*, Oxford: Oxford University Press.
Engels, B. (1994), 'Capital flows, redlining and gentrification: the pattern of mortgage lending and social change in Glebe, Sydney, 1960–1984', *International Journal or Urban and Regional Research*, **18** (4), 628–657.
Fernandez, R. and M.B. Aalbers (2016), 'Housing and the variations of financialized capitalism', *Competition and Change*, **20** (2), 71–88.
Forrest, R. and Y. Hirayama (2015), 'The financialisation of the social project: embedded liberalism, neoliberalism and home ownership', *Urban Studies*, **52** (2), 233–244.
Forrest, R. and N-M. Yip (eds) (2011), *Housing Markets and the Global Financial Crisis*, Cheltenham, UK and Northampton, MA, USA: Edward Elgar Publishing.
Foster, J.B. (2007), 'The financialization of capitalism', *Monthly Review*, **58** (11), 1–12.
Gotham, Kevin (2002), *Race, Real Estate, and Uneven Development. The Kansas City Experience, 1900–2000*, Albany: State University of New York Press.
Gotham, K.F. (2006), 'The secondary circuit of capital reconsidered: Globalization and the US real estate sector', *American Journal of Sociology*, **112** (1), 231–275.
Gotham, K.F. (2012), 'Creating liquidity out of spatial fixity: the secondary circuit of capital and the restructuring of the US housing finance system', in M.B. Aalbers (ed.), *Subprime Cities: The Political Economy of Mortgage Markets*, Oxford: Wiley-Blackwell, pp. 25–52.

Hacker, Jacob (2006), *The Great Risk Shift: The Assault on American Jobs, Families, Health Care and Retirement – and How You Can Fight Back*, New York: Oxford University Press.
Harris, R. and D. Forrester (2003), 'The suburban origins of redlining: a Canadian case study, 1935–54', *Urban Studies*, **40** (13), 2661–2686.
Henry, J.F. (2002), *The Social Origins of Money: The Case of Egypt*, Sacramento: California State University Press.
Hillier, A.E. (2003), 'Redlining and the Home Owners' Loan Corporation', *Journal of Urban History*, **29** (4), 394–420.
Hillier, A.E. (2005), 'Residential security maps and neighbourhood appraisals: The Home Owners' Loan Corporation and the case of Philadelphia', *Social Science History*, **29** (2), 207–233.
IMF (2014), *Global Housing Watch*. International Monetary Fund. Retrieved on 18 October 2016 from www.imf.org/external/research/housing/.
Immergluck, Daniel (2004), *Credit to the Community: Community Reinvestment and Fair Lending Policy in the United States*, Armonk, NY: Sharpe.
Immergluck, Daniel (2009), *Foreclosed*, Ithaca, NY: Cornell University Press.
Jackson, Kenneth (1985), *Crabgrass Frontier. The Suburbanization of the United States*, New York: Oxford University Press.
Jordà, Oscar, Moritz Schularick and Alan Taylor (2014), 'The great mortgaging: housing finance, crises, and business cycles', NBER Woking Paper No. 20501, Cambridge, MA: National Bureau of Economic Research.
Kaminsky, G.L. and C.M. Reinhart (1999), 'The twin crises: the causes of banking and balance-of-payment problems', *American Economic Review*, **89** (3), 473–500.
Kotze, N.J. and M.K.R. Van Huyssteen (1990), 'Rooi-omlyning in die behuisingsmark van Kaapstad', *South African Geographer*, **18** (1–2), 97–122.
Krippner, G. (2005), 'The financialization of the American economy', *Socio-Economic Review*, **3**, 173–208.
Laparra, M. and B. Pérez (2011), 'The impact of the crisis on social cohesion or Spanish households surfing a "liquid" model of integration', *Revista de Asistență Socială*, **9** (3), 21–51.
Lordon, F. (2007), 'Spéculation immobilière, ralentissement économique. Quand la finance prend le monde en otage', *Le Monde diplomatique*, Septembre.
Marshall, J.N., A. Pike, J.S. Pollard, J. Tomaney, S. Dawley and J. Gray (2012), 'Placing the run on Northern Rock', *Journal of Economic Geography*, **12** (1), 157–181.
Mizen, P. (2008), 'The credit crunch of 2007–2008: a discussion of the background, market reactions, and policy responses', *Federal Reserve Bank of St. Louis Review*, **90** (5), 531–567.
Murdie, R.A. (1986), 'Residential mortgage lending in metropolitan Toronto: a case study of the resale market', *The Canadian Geographer*, **30** (2), 98–110.
Nassar, J. (2007), *Foreclosure, predatory mortgage and payday lending in America's cities*. Testimony before the US House Committee on Oversight and Government Reform, Washington, DC.
Newman, K. (2012), 'The new economy and the city: foreclosures in Essex County, New Jersey', in M.B. Aalbers (ed.), *Subprime Cities: The Political Economy of Mortgage Markets*, Oxford: Wiley-Blackwell, pp. 219–241.
Pennington-Cross, A. (2002), 'Subprime lending in the primary and secondary markets', *Journal of Housing Research*, **13**, 31–50.
Piketty, Thomas (2014), *Capital in the Twenty-First Century*, Cambridge, MA: Harvard University Press.
Quercia, R.G., M. Stegman and W.R. Davis (2004), 'Assessing the impact of North Carolina's anti-predatory lending law', *Housing Policy Debate*, **15**, 573–602.
Rouwenhorst, K.G. (2005), 'The origins of mutual funds', in W.N. Gotzmann and K.G. Rouwenhorst (eds), *The Origins of Value: The Financial Innovations that Created Modern Capital Markets*, Oxford: Oxford University Press, pp. 249–270.
Rolnik, R. (2013), 'Late neoliberalism: the financialization of homeownership and housing rights', *International Journal of Urban and Regional Research*, **37** (3), 1058–1066.
Sassen, Saskia (2001), *The Global City: New York, London, Tokyo*, 2nd edition, Princeton, NJ: Princeton University Press.
Schloemer, E., W. Li, K. Ernst and K. Keest (2006), *Losing Ground: Foreclosures in the Subprime Market and their Cost to Homeowners*, Washington, DC: Center for Responsible Lending.
Shiller, Robert (2008), *The Subprime Solution*, Princeton, NJ: Princeton University Press.
Smith, S.J. (2010), 'Housing futures: a role for derivatives', in S.J. Smith and B.A. Searle (eds), *Companion to the Economics of Housing*, New York, NY: Wiley, pp. 585–607.
Squires, Gary (ed.) (1992), *From Redlining to Reinvestment: Community Response to Urban Disinvestment*, Philadelphia, PA: Temple University Press.
Squires Gary (ed.) (2004), *Why the Poor Pay More. How to Stop Predatory Lending*. Westport: Praeger.
Stephens, M. (2007), 'Mortgage market deregulation and its consequences', *Housing Studies*, **22** (2), 201–220.
Stuart, G. (2003), *Discriminating Risk: The US Mortgage Lending Industry in the Twentieth Century*, Ithaca. NY: Cornell University Press.

Sweezy, P.M. (1995), 'Economic reminiscences', *Monthly Review*, **47** (1), 1–11.

Wainwright, T. (2012), 'Building new markets: transferring securitization, bond-rating, and a crisis from the US to the UK', in M.B. Aalbers (ed.), *Subprime Cities: The Political Economy of Mortgage Markets*, Oxford: Wiley-Blackwell, pp. 97–119.

Watson, M. (2010), 'House price Keynesianism and the contradictions of the modern investor subject', *Housing Studies*, **25** (3), 413–426.

Weir, S. (1976), 'Red line districts', *Roof*, **1** (July), 109–114.

Williams, P. (1978), 'Building societies and the inner city', *Transactions of the Institute of British Geographers*, **3** (1), 23–34.

Wyly, E.K. and S.R. Holloway (1999), '"The color of money" revisited. Racial lending patterns in Atlanta's neighborhoods', *Housing Policy Debate*, **10**, 555–600.

Wyly, E., M. Atia, H. Foxcroft, D. Hammel and K. Philips-Watts (2006), 'American home: predatory mortgage capital and neighbourhood spaces of race and class exploitation in the United States', *Geografiska Annaler B*, **88**, 105–132.

Wyly, E., M. Moos, D. Hammel and E. Kabahizi (2009), 'Cartographies of race and class: mapping the class-monopoly rents of American subprime mortgage capital', *International Journal of Urban and Regional Research*, **33** (2), 332–354.

14. Geographies of assets and debt

Beverley A. Searle and Stephan Köppe

14.1 INTRODUCTION

This chapter focuses on individual and household debt.[1] Rising household debt has become of increased concern across many nations. We consider two important contributing factors. First, the global rise in financial services and institutions seeking to expand their market share of consumer credit. Second, the dismantling of public welfare provision and the shift towards individualisation and personal asset-building.

Historical accounts suggest that debt actually appeared much earlier than money (Graeber, 2011). Though our focus is on contemporary societies, the anthropological history of debt underscores the central social role of debt observed today, such as facilitating economic exchange, creating interdependencies and social ties, and exerting political power through debt obligations. In modern times prior to the 1980s the use of debt, or consumer credit, was deemed to be beneficial, enabling consumption smoothing and providing a coping mechanism in response to sudden and temporary loses of income (Valins, 2004). The idea is that over the life course an individual's debt and savings balance each other out; debt concentrated in the early stage, is repaid during middle-age and savings and assets are accumulated in later life stages – something referred to as the life-cycle model (Modigliani and Brumberg, 1954). Using credit or borrowing therefore was perceived as normal consumer behaviour, with a certain level of debt being inevitable for most people (Betti et al., 2001).

Household debt became a concern to economists and policymakers at national and international levels following the relaxing of financial constraints in many western nations during the 1980s and 1990s. This opened up credit access to households lower down the income stream whilst also providing favourable rates to higher income earners (Valins, 2004). In the decades following the de-regulation of financial services household debt levels increased, reaching historically high levels across many OECD nations by the mid-2000s (La Cava and Simon, 2005; Girouard et al., 2006; Valins, 2004). The expansion of financial services also spread credit and debt to previously excluded developing countries (Soederberg, 2014, 2013a). As a result turning modern capitalism into a 'debt economy' (Lazzarato, 2012).

Sokol (2013: 505) argues that 'credit–debt relationships have been contributing a great deal to the exacerbation of socio-spatial inequalities in the run up to, and during, the 2008 global financial crisis'. In this context, debt becomes a key analytical focus in understanding the geographies of money and finance. Sutherland et al. (2012) show how debt migrates and cascades across sectors (household, non-financial corporate, financial, government), high debt especially amplifies risks and weakens economic recovery after recessions. From a geographical perspective external sovereign debt crises – that is state obligation to another jurisdiction, usually in another currency (Reinhart and Rogoff, 2009) have a stronger spatial element as they are linked to global economic interdependencies and inequalities of wealth. External debt crises can affect single countries (for example, Greek or Argentinian credit crises in the 2000s) and regions (Latin America in the 1980s; Cline, 1995). On a global scale it is also related to inequalities between developing and advanced economies, fuelled by loans from the International Monetary Fund and the World Bank, which led to the debt crisis of several developing countries around the early 2000s, especially sub-Saharan Africa (Millet and Toussaint, 2004). On the other hand there is also increasing concern on reversing trends (Wang and Walters, 2013). Developed nations are increasingly indebted to developing nations who hold large foreign exchange reserves (for example, the US and China).

The global financial crisis (GFC) of 2008 demonstrated the causal link between spiralling household debt and sovereign debt within Lazzarato's (2012) new 'debt economy'. The default of several private banks and anticipated collapse of the global banking system had allegedly been prevented through public bailout programmes in almost all western societies (see Priemus and Whitehead, 2014).

Notwithstanding these links to the spatial distribution of debt our focus is on the geography of household debt. Traditionally problems of indebtedness had focused on households in lower socio-economic groups. Debt most often arose as a consequence of missed utility (for example energy and water) or housing payments (EQLS, 2013), or a change in personal circumstances for example following the birth of a child, illness, unemployment or breakdown of a relationship (Valins, 2004). Whilst such concerns are still important in understanding and dealing with financial problems and financial exclusion (for example see Hartfree and Collard, 2014), the crisis in the banking system during 2006–7 marked a turning point. Personal debt had become caught up in financial systems which operated on an international scale. Servicing debt, especially mortgage debt, was no longer a national concern of low income groups, but spread across the whole social spectrum and the globe (EQLS, 2013; Faber, 2011; Oxfam, 2013).

Although much academic and political attention was focused on financial vulnerability to interest rates and income shocks, two key elements had been overlooked. First, the changing nature of debt and the financial systems which fed into it had been neglected. This was particularly in respect of home purchase and the globalisation of mortgage finance. The unsustainability of this new mortgage market, as noted above, being directly linked to the GFC (Mian and Sufi, 2014). Second, the move towards a system of asset-based welfare had increased the exposure to debt and financial markets. Households were encouraged to build up their own resources in the form of financial (savings and pensions) and non-financial (housing) assets. But what had been overlooked was how much of this asset-based welfare was in fact underpinned by growing household debt.

This chapter will address these issues in turn. First, we provide a definition of assets and debt. Second, we conceptualise debt and assets over the life course. Third, we set out the extent of household debt drawing international and regional comparisons and also within different household and individual characteristics. Fourth, we point out the politics of debt and policy responses to increasing personal indebtedness. Fifth, we discuss why debt has become so important by reflecting on the theoretical shift towards asset-based welfare and the drive to increase individuals' savings and wealth accumulation, which in practice has contributed to rising debt levels and increased vulnerability. We conclude the chapter in the final section. Throughout the chapter we will focus on housing, arguably the key contributing factor to rising household debt, and through its inextricable connection to place demonstrates how the geography of mortgage debt connects local property assets with global financial markets and has inherently turned into a socio-spatial issue of global dimension (Aalbers, 2009).

14.2 DEFINITIONS OF ASSETS AND DEBT

Assets are also referred to as capital. They can be physical (such as a car, house), financial (stocks and shares or other investments), social (the network of people we know) or human (skills, level of education). Assets provide a stock of wealth which can provide a return or income flow, for example interest earned on savings, rental income or services provided from housing (Searle and Köppe, 2014).

Defining debt is more problematic due the different forms it takes, and the difficulty of distinguishing between debt and credit. Indeed some scholars refer to credit/debt arguing they are an 'inseparable dyadic unit' (Peebles, 2010: 126). There are also different types of debt which often fall under different regulation adding further complexity to its definition. Examples of debt and their definitions are given in Box 14.1.

The terminology of debt includes other notions such as secured and unsecured loans, credit, indebtedness and liabilities often with fuzzy distinctions. For some a defining feature of 'credit/debt' is its ability to link time and space: 'credit is a method of lending resource in the present and demanding (or hoping for) a return in the future' (see Peebles, 2010: 226–227). It can also be underpinned by a moral stance creating a hierarchy between beneficial and liberating credit, and burdensome debt (Peebles, 2010). Credit implies an arrangement for borrowing that people want to enter into, whereas debt is a financial

BOX 14.1 DEFINITIONS OF DEBT

Student loans are available to students at higher education institutions to pay for fees and/or maintenance. They are often managed by public bodies with no or very low interest rates, but also private banks offer student credit at market prices. Repayment of student loans may be taken directly from the payroll.

Later life loans. The new German *caregiver leave (Pflegezeit)* is to our knowledge the first nationwide policy that provides interest-free loans to care for elderly relatives (BMFSFJ, 2015). While student loans are common in many countries, government supported loans for specific social purposes later in life are a new policy development.

Mortgages are used to finance property purchases and have a long-term investment horizon. Usually offered by banks, some countries have dedicated mortgage lenders. Public regulation can fuel or limit the access of mortgage credit through loan-to-value ratios, tax deductions and other means. Mortgages traditionally were used only to purchase a home. More recently, they can be used to withdraw equity from the home (Smith and Searle, 2008). Flexible mortgages for example allow the home owner to increase existing mortgage debt, whereas reverse mortgages enable outright home owners to release equity by borrowing against the value of their property.

Consumer credit is a form of debt which can be used on a long-term basis (for example leasing a car or other consumer goods such as TVs or white goods), or short-term basis such as credit cards or pay day loans to cover short-term income and expenditure needs.

commitment that people are struggling to repay and can be a cause of financial stress (Berthoud and Kempson, 1992; Lea et al., 1993).

In this chapter we use both terms – credit and debt – and refer to negative and positive connotations that different forms can take. Generally 'good' debt or credit, assumes agency and control over the liabilities. Debt can be considered positive where it gives households the financial flexibility needed to meet consumption needs at a point in time when saving would take too long. From a macroeconomic perspective debt can be positive where it fuels consumption growth which benefits the economy. Positive aspects of debt are also often associated with long-term investments that have a guaranteed rate of return or are used as an investment, such as student loans (investing in human capital), mortgages (investing in property), car leasing (facilitating or investing in wider employment opportunities). Debt is also perceived as good when it is secured through an investment or physical asset (for example, mortgage or business).

Negative aspects arise when the debt becomes a burden and in the case of over-indebtedness becomes unmanageable and spirals into increasing levels of debt. Some scholars associated debt, or over-indebtedness with a lack of self-discipline, or even carelessness which constrains consumption and is bad for the economy (Marron, 2012; Weinberg, 2006). Debt can be perceived as bad where it is associated with imposed debt (for example, court-imposed fees) and high cost short-term lending (such as pay day loans; see Valins, 2004).

Difficulties arise when debt starts out being good, where it is manageable and in some instances encouraged, but due to a change in circumstances or behaviour, can turn bad and become unmanageable. For example, unsecured credit card loans can be managed very well, without incurring any interest payments. As long as individuals can serve their monthly credit card bill, a free credit card loan buys enough time to access fixed savings (for example, with 30 days notice) to pay for emergency expenses (for example, broken washing machine). However, credit card loans can turn bad if they are used for other purposes such as long-term loans for example to buy a car, or meeting general living costs such as paying rent or mortgages, which would then incur additional interest charges. They can also turn bad where low or postponed monthly payments incur interest charges or late payment penalties, or where excessively high interest rates quickly exceed the size of the original loan, thereby increasing the debt burden.

14.3 DEBT OVER THE LIFE-CYCLE

Savings and debt fluctuate over the life course. Debt tends to be higher during the earlier stages of the life-cycle when incomes and savings are lower. Debt tends to reduce during later stages of the life-cycle, when income is reduced as people reach retirement age, and savings have accumulated. This connection of saving and debt over different life stages has been formalised in the life-cycle hypothesis (Modigliani and Brumberg, 1954). The assumption being that people maintain more or less constant consumption during their life by adjusting their borrowing and saving behaviour in line with income changes. This hypothesis has been criticised on many grounds (Japelli, 2001; Kuehlwein, 1995). As Kotlikoff (1986) and Rubaszek and Serwa (2014) note, before young adults earn any income they acquire a huge debt both in financial terms but also in-kind benefits from their family. Moreover, saving is assumed to be linear, not taking into account interruptions such as unemployment, child care or illness, where people have to dip into their savings or in the absence of savings accrue debt. In addition, consumption is far from constant over time. For instance, health care consumption is concentrated on the final years or months of life, when income is declining as well.

These fluctuations of income and consumption have been studied empirically and globally with the National Transfer Account (NTA) framework to estimate the life-cycle deficit for 23 countries (Lee and Mason, 2011; see Figure 3.1; www.ntaccounts.org).

Looking only at income and consumption most people in their early 20s have accrued substantial nominal deficit. During their active working life their income outweighs their consumption until their income declines around 65 and their consumption increases even further. These general trends can be observed both in developed and developing nations. Overall these estimations suggest that people would accrue a huge life-cycle deficit as consumption seems to outweigh income. However, when returns of savings and strategic debt are included the life-cycle deficit becomes balanced. 'Relying on assets generates the additional resources required to fund lifecycle deficits' (Lee and Mason, 2011: 10).

Figure 14.1 depicts this life-cycle balance. In the figure private and public transfers refer to pay-as-you-go exchanges of money (and time as monetised in-kind transfers). Asset-based reallocations are net asset income (income from assets minus saving). Positive asset

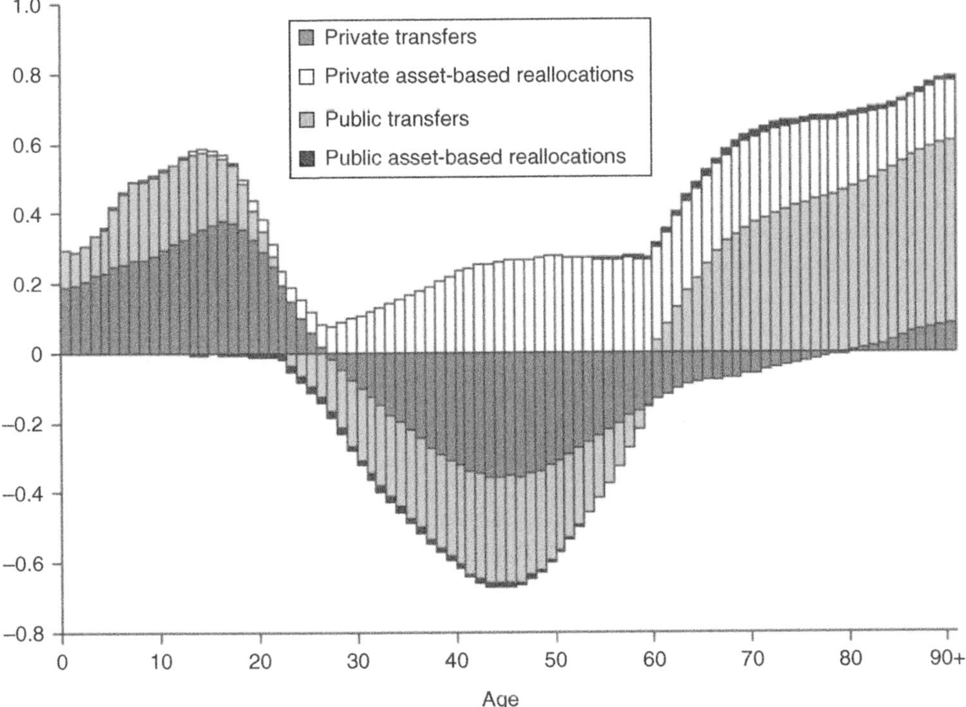

Source: Lee and Mason (2011: 58, figure 3.2).

Figure 14.1 Per capita age reallocations: average of 17 economies around 2000

income, or an inflow in the NTA terminology, includes among others interest, income, profits, dividends, imputed rent from owner-occupied housing. Negative asset income is measured, for instance, as interest expense, losses, dividend paid. Dissaving contributes to a positive asset income, while saving reduces the net income.[2] The disaggregation into age groups reveals the accumulation and usage of assets over the life-course.

Generally speaking Figure 14.1 underscores the relevance of private asset-based reallocations to finance consumption over the life-course. Most of these returns are generated through taking up mortgage debt early in life (Lee and Mason, 2011). Assets are also far more relevant in developing countries and liberal welfare states than in societies with generous and well developed public transfer systems (reliance on assets varies between two-thirds to less than 1 per cent). In middle-income countries especially, the elderly rely heavily on asset income. Moreover, these figures underscore earlier results that the elderly are not dissaving, especially non-annuitised wealth (Rowlingson, 2006; Spilerman, 2000).

In sum, over the life course individuals acquire positive net assets not only through saving, but also through taking on debt, mainly mortgage debt. The relevance of these asset-based reallocations varies considerably between countries and is inversely related to public transfers. Although the data overall show that on average there is a positive accumulation of assets at the end of a lifecourse, nonetheless debt has increasing relevance in financing personal consumption.

14.4 THE RISE IN DEBT

During the twentieth century access to finance had become an important element of economic development and growth (Claessens, 2005). Improving access to credit and finance was deemed beneficial to the economy as a whole. Increasing access to borrowing, it was argued, provided individuals with greater control and flexibility in governing their own finances, enabling consumption thus facilitating economic growth (Marron, 2012). Widening access to credit was deemed beneficial to individuals through reducing inequality and poverty, and facilitating consumption smoothing (Claessens, 2005). This belief in the benefits of the financial system and the role of credit underpinned the relaxation of financial regulations by many western states during the 1980s and 1990s. Deregulation liberated and expanded the financial sector, creating new competitive credit markets. In the decades that followed financial companies actively pursued excluded and vulnerable sectors of the population, permeating into each strata of society to the extent that virtually every household and individual borrowed (Stenning et al., 2010). In consequence there was a notable increase in households debt across many nations worldwide (La Cava and Simon, 2005; Girouard et al., 2006; Pinsloo, 2002; Valins, 2004; World Bank, 2010). For example in the US credit card debt spread spatially and towards low income households from the 1970s, fuelled by the ability to bypass stricter state laws when banks were allowed to borrow across state borders (Soederberg, 2013b). Furthermore, geographers increasingly acknowledge the cross border implications of personal household debt. For instance, remittances, that is payments of immigrants to their home country, are used as a source for welfare expenses instead of credit (Ambrosius and Cuecuecha, 2013). Other examples show that migra-loans are used to cover the upfront costs of migration in the hope for future remittances or to smooth consumption of irregular remittances

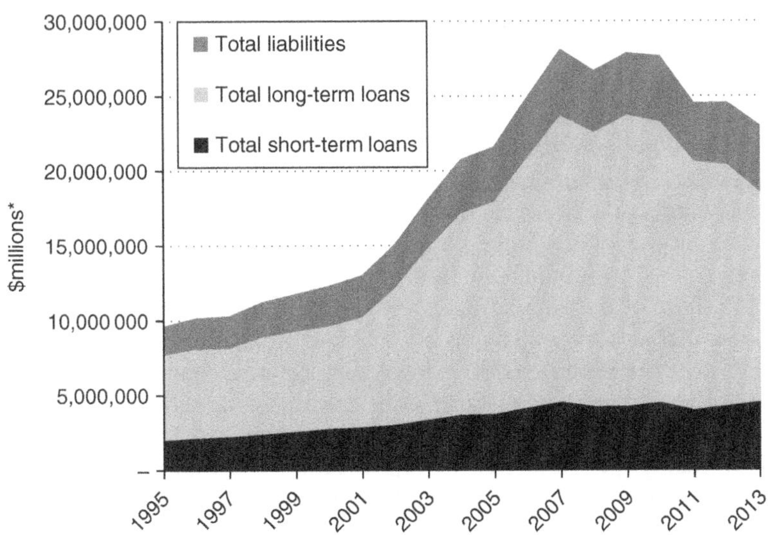

Notes: Countries included where information is available across all three measures: Australia, Austria, Belgium Canada, Chile, Czech Republic, Denmark, France, Germany, Greece, Hungary, Italy, Netherlands, New Zealand, Norway, Portugal, Slovak Republic, Spain, Sweden, Turkey, UK, US; *Current US-Dollar prices, current exchange rate.

Source: OECD Economic Outlook: Households' financial and non-financial assets and liabilities.

Figure 14.2 Total household financial liabilities: 22 OECD nations 1995–2013

(Bylander, 2014). Both examples point out new private cross border debt that is not recorded in official international debt surveys.

Acknowledging the limitations of national debt records, Figure 14.2 shows total household financial liabilities using data from the 22 OECD nations where full information is available. Total long-term loans (mostly consisting of mortgage debt) saw a threefold increase from $7.7 trillion peaking in 2009 at around $23.6 trillion, since then there has been a noticeable decline. Short-term household liabilities (such as credit cards and other short-term credit) rose steadily from $1.9 trillion in 1995, and continued to rise through the global recession reaching $4.5 trillion in 2013.

Although overall debt levels began to fall after 2010, the debt burden on households remained high (see also World Bank, 2010). Where information is available, average household debt as a proportion of net household income rose from 83 per cent in 1999 to 140 per cent in 2010, but had only fallen to 127 per cent by 2012 (OECD, 2014). The debt to income ratio increased between 1999–2012 across nearly all the OECD nations (Germany and Japan saw a fall of 23 per cent and 7 per cent, respectively). Although the highest ratios achieved during the period were in some of the richer OECD countries, they spanned a diverse range of welfare regimes such as Denmark (356 per cent), the Netherlands (312 per cent), Ireland (238 per cent), Norway (214 per cent) and Switzerland (201 per cent). Substantial increases to their peak ratio were also seen across several Eastern European countries (Estonia from 18 per cent to 112 per cent, Hungary 13 per cent to 79 per cent, Czech Republic 21 per cent to 67 per cent, Poland 11 per cent to 61 per cent and Slovak Republic 17 per cent to 55 per cent, see Figure 14.2).[3] The highest household debt levels are rooted in expanded mortgage markets. Countries who liberalised lending practices, encouraged home ownership and provided mortgage tax relief showed the highest levels and increases in debt (Andrews, 2010; Howard, 1997).

Analysis by Girouard and colleagues (2006) show that although household debt levels vary across nations, the characteristics of debtors are fairly consistent. Household debt patterns loosely reflect the life-cycle theory of consumption. They find that the proportion of indebted households is highest among younger households (under 35 years) who are borrowing against future income. Indebtedness reaches the lowest point in nominal terms and as a share of the population by the time households reach the age of 64 when relatively higher incomes are used to pay off debt and build up savings. After the age of 65 net assets fall when people are spending down savings rather than incurring further debt.

The shift from short-term consumer debt towards long-term mortgage debt also extended the average duration of loans (Sutherland et al., 2012). Extreme cases were Portugal and Finland where mortgage maturities could extend to 50 and 60 years, respectively (Schich and Jung-Hyun, 2007). From a life course perspective this underscores that debt levels not only increased, but that debt extends to all life stages. Girouard and colleagues (2006) also find that debt levels increase with income. Although low income households are therefore the least likely to have debt, time-series analysis (for nations where data is available) showed indebted households among this group increased the most since the 1980s, reflecting the easing of credit constraints for lower income households.

The systems put in place to aid the flow of finance across global markets, however, have not always been effective in catering for the needs of individuals. Banking systems often favour wealthier customers (Claessens, 2005), with the position of poorer households remaining marginal and weak (Stenning et al., 2010). The expansion of credit down the income scale was considered a risker practice, reflected in the rise of credit scoring and identification 'at a distance of good and bad risk' (Leyshon and Thrift, 1999: 441). Targeting and identifying this risk resulted in higher costs and interests rates charged to low-income households (Claessens, 2005; Kempson and Paxton, 2002). Across developed and developing nations low-income households faced many institutional and cultural barriers to accessing financial services generally (Claessens, 2005; Stenning et al., 2010), leading to the development of new high cost, subprime lending markets in many nations (Consumer Focus, 2011). There also developed a black market for illegal and predatory lending practices which exploited the vulnerable situation that some lower income and indebted households were facing (Carr and Kolluri, 2001). Although interest rates may not have been unduly high, the abusive and threatening practices were not only 'financially destroying' individuals, but the use of violence and intimidation put psychological pressure on people, leaving households and communities scared and a 'veil of silence allowed such activities to go on undetected' (Carr and Kolluri, 2001: 4; CSJ, 2013: 29). As a consequence such debt is absent from national records meaning the true level of problem debt is under-recorded.[4]

Widening access to credit meant that most people held some sort of 'normal debt', such as a mortgage, credit card or an overdraft facility on their bank account (CSJ, 2013). The rise in household debt, particularly among poorer households, however, gave rise to concerns that acceptable 'good' credit could easily become 'bad' debt, where households were moving away from credit as a deliberate vehicle to smooth incomes, to over-indebtedness where it became difficult to meet repayment terms. Survey data from 2009 for example

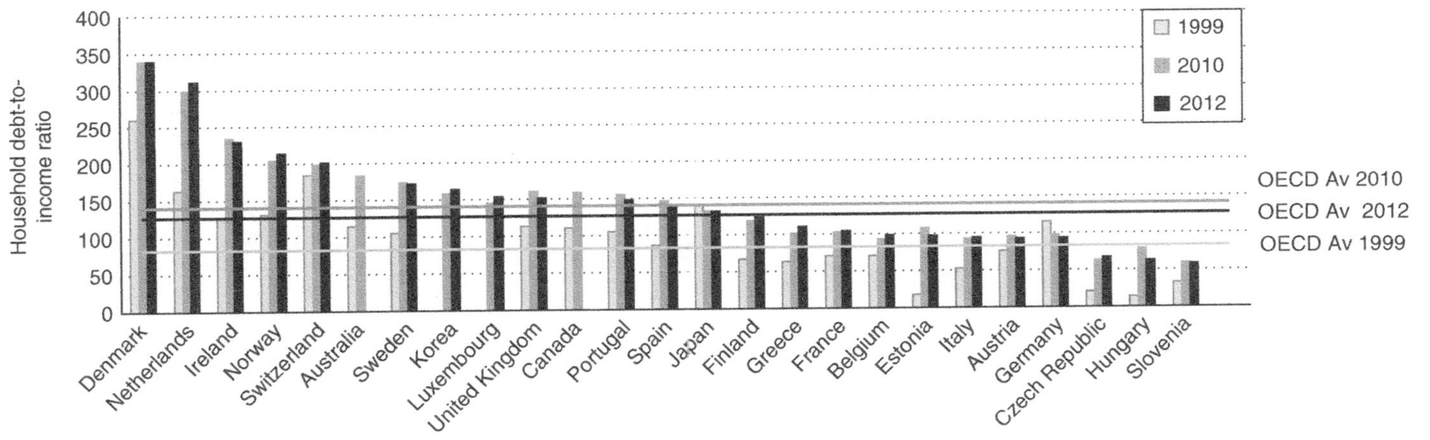

Notes: *Austria 2000, 2008; Australia 1999, 2010; Canada 1999, 2010; Denmark 2003, 2010, 2011; Greece 2005, 2010, 2011; Ireland 2002, 2010, 2012; Korea and Luxembourg 2010, 2012; Slovenia 2001, 2010, 2012; Spain 2000, 2010, 2012; Switzerland 1999, 2010, 2011.

Source: OECD (2014, Table 20.1 Household debt).

*Figure 14.3 Household debt-to-income ratio in 28 OECD countries: 1999, 2010 and 2012**

showed that in some European Member States half of respondents felt they were at risk of becoming over-indebted (Hungary (53 per cent), Latvia (51 per cent) and Spain (49 per cent)). Such fears were matched by a reported increase in the use of debt services across several different countries (Eurofound, 2010). Overall, individual over-indebtedness continued to increase throughout the early decades of the 2000s in most affluent societies (Heuer, 2014).

14.5 INDIVIDUAL AND INSTITUTIONAL RISK FACTORS OF INDEBTEDNESS

Over-indebtedness was for many years more likely to be associated with long-term unemployment (Eurofound, 2010). Other 'at risk' groups included people living in urban areas, families with children or single parents, young adults, benefit recipients, people with a long-term illness or disability and those living in privately rented accommodation (see Eurofound, 2010). These groups generally accounting for those on lower-incomes or the working poor. The accumulation of debt mainly arose from missed payments on utility bills (water and energy) or rent (EQLS, 2013). Over-indebtedness was also associated with lack of financial management skills, with people running up large debts over time, without fully realising the consequences. Following the GFC the characteristics of over-indebtedness changed, incorporating those recently unemployed, particularly the lower-middle class who had been laid off from well-paid jobs but still had large mortgage or other debts (Eurofound, 2010; EQLS, 2013).

Marron (2012) notes that another potential site of risk lies within the credit market itself. Although credit markets were opened up, and costs reduced, the system became complex, with increasingly specialised products, confusing terminology and an array of interest rates. This made it difficult for consumers to make the appropriate calculations and inhibit their ability to choose the appropriate financial product. Demand for debt was created by 'excited creditors' who pushed potential debtors to take on more credit (see Peebles, 2010: 227). Consumers were subject to aggressive marketing of cheap credit and inducements to borrow more, such as 0 per cent interest on balance transfers or automatic increase of credit limits, encouraging consumers to overspend. This deliberate mis-selling of products to protect or accumulate assets resulted in several financial institutions being fined and further regulated (see Marron, 2012; Searle and Köppe, 2014). Seen in this way indebtedness was not so much a problem of a lack of individual agency and self-governance of needy debtors, but of institutional risk factors making consumers 'vulnerable and victims of market inequalities' (Marron, 2012: 414; Peebles, 2010).

The consequences of being in debt extend beyond financial difficulties and was associated with many negative aspects including: financial exclusion; stigma or severe stress (CSJ, 2013; Finch et al., 2007; Jenkins et al., 2008; Valins, 2004). The relationships however remain complex and cause and effect can be difficult to determine (Brown et al., 2005); does problem debt lead to financial exclusion, or financial exclusion lead to problem debt?

A parallel concern about increasing consumer credit (and household debt) was the implications for psychological well-being (Worthington, 2005). Within this field of research, however, mortgage debt, compared to other forms of consumer debt, was seen as generally unproblematic with little or no relationship with mental illness (Brown et al.,

2005; Jenkins et al., 2008). However, research has shown there are detrimental psychological effects associated with unsustainable housing commitments and fear of repossession (Ford et al., 1995; Nettleton, 1998; Nettleton and Burrows, 2000; Taylor et al., 2007). Although this literature recognised the importance of measuring households total wealth resources (income, assets and debt) – the negative implications of being in debt still tended to exclude mortgages. This was because mortgages fell into the 'good credit' definition. They enabled the smoothing of the consumption of housing services across the life course (Weinberg, 2006), and represented an investment rather than 'consumer debt' (Park and DeVaney, 2007). This is despite the diversity of consumption wants and needs that mortgages could and were increasingly facilitating during the latter part of the twentieth century (Searle et al., 2009; Smith and Searle, 2008).

14.6 HOUSING DEBT

It is now well established that borrowing for home ownership accounts for a major proportion of the growth in household and individual debt (Worthington, 2005). Rising mortgage debt was therefore linked to the rise in owner-occupation, however, it was also a reflection of how much easier it had become to withdraw housing wealth (Hurst and Stafford, 2004; Smith and Searle, 2008). Housing debt, namely mortgages, therefore provides an interesting case study where it has become simultaneously a source of credit and debt across the life course.

The deregulation of the financial services was part of an ideological shift towards individual responsibility and away from state support within a neoliberal framework, initiated in the US and UK towards the end of the 1970s (Harvey, 2005; Soederberg, 2014). This line of policy thinking rippled out across many nations, who sought in the first instance to reduce or rid their state's responsibility for the provision of housing. A variety of policy initiatives were implemented which saw public housing being sold off across the USA as well as in many European and Asian nations, leading to a rise in the level of home ownership (Jones and Murie, 2006; Ronald, 2008).

In the decades that followed, household net wealth rose mainly due to the increase in house prices, however, mortgage debt was also on the rise in some nations. Higher economic development, urbanisation and well developed financial markets contributed to higher mortgage debt and penetration among the population (Badev et al., 2014). By 2011 most developing countries had hardly any mortgage markets, while most OECD countries had the highest outstanding mortgage debt relative to GDP; among 118 countries between 2006 and 2010 this ranged from 1 per cent in Rwanda to 109 per cent in Denmark. A similar pattern emerges when the percentage of the adult population with a mortgage, is compared; less than 1 per cent in most African countries rising to 60 per cent in Sweden (Figure 14.4). By 2012 mortgage debt accounted for more than 80 per cent of total household debt in 26 OECD countries, compared to on average only 5 per cent being due to credit cards (OECD, 2014).

The credit system through which much of this mortgage debt was supplied grew into a complex and opaque securitised product on a global scale, and was a key contributing factor to the GFC of 2008 (Kiff and Mills, 2007; and see Smith and Searle, 2010). Nonetheless not all nations felt the negative impact to the same extent and the

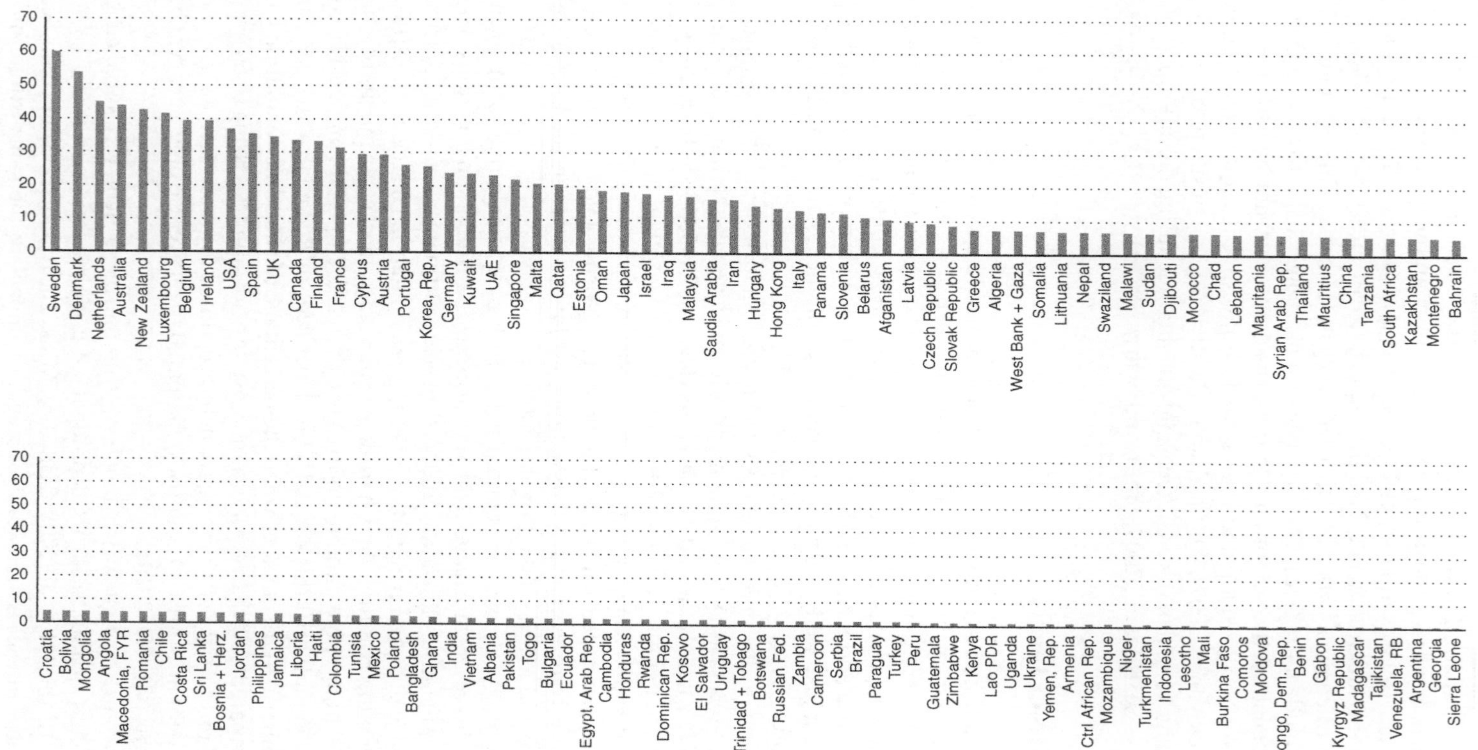

Source: Data sourced from Badev et al. (2014).

Figure 14.4 Percentage of adult population with an outstanding loan to purchase a home, 2011

2008 crisis and subsequent recession highlighted national variations in the resilience of regions (Martin and Sunley, 2015), mortgage systems, and mortgaged households. Nonperforming loans (loans that are 90 days or more in arrears), as a proportion of total gross loans, soared in the aftermath of the crisis in European nations – notably in Greece reaching 34 per cent in 2014 from 5 per cent in 2005. However, not all countries in Europe were similarly affected; in Sweden (with the highest penetration of mortgage loans) nonperforming loans remained below 1 per cent between 2005 and 2014. Some individual nations in Central and South Asia (Kazakhstan rising from 2 per cent in 2006 to 31 per cent in 2013) and sub-Saharan Africa (Nigeria peaking at 37 per cent in 2009) were also more exposed to the collapse in the banking and finance system than other nations in these regions. East Asia and Latin America were hardly affected by the turmoil on the credit markets in North America and Western Europe (Figure 14.5).

Differences in mortgage products, policy and taxation, and local economies contribute to this geographical variation in mortgage resilience. For example, countries with high proportions of flexible interest mortgages (exceeding 90 per cent in Spain, Portugal and Finland) were immediately exposed to the wider financial market risks, unlike those in Germany or Belgium where variable interest mortgages accounted for 10 per cent of the market. Dealing with the problems of household indebtedness therefore became an issue of monetary policy with interest rates lowered sharply close to zero in most advanced economies (turning negative for some government bonds) and tighter regulation of the credit industry (*The Economist*, 2013).

Further evidence shows the importance of local and regional geographies in concentrations of problem debt and repossessions (see UK: FIC, 2012; Germany: SCHUFA, 2014). For example, in the United States mortgage delinquency rates and foreclosures generally increase the further east and south that households are located. Mortgage delinquency levels (90 days or more in arrears) at the end of 2007 were under 1.7 per cent in Alaska (in the north west), whereas they generally exceeded 1.8 per cent in Florida (south east) (FRS, 2008) (Figure 14.6). Similarly, by 2015 the proportion of foreclosures ranged from 0.3 per cent (Alaska) to 5.2 per cent (New Jersey) (CoreLogic, 2015) (Figure 14.7). Among UK regions the proportion of households having mortgage payment problems ranged from around 15 per cent in the south west to 32 per cent in Northern Ireland; whilst repossessions ranged from less than 1 per cent in the south east and south west to 2 per cent in the north east (FIC, 2012) (Figure 14.8).

These regional variations arise from a complex mix of socio-economic factors affecting local housing and labour markets, cost of living and inequalities arising from financial policies and initiatives which tend to benefit those who are better off (SCHUFA, 2014; Searle and Köppe, 2014). Mortgage tax relief contributed to the rise in prices, and subsequent rise in debt, while also being more beneficial to higher rather than lower income earners (Andrews, 2010). Low cost home ownership initiatives also tended to benefit better off households (see Searle and Köppe, 2014). Regional studies also suggest that socio-spatial factors influence mortgage choices. For instance, UK evidence shows that lower incomes and higher unemployment rates increase the likelihood to opt for a variable mortgage rate, exposing regions with these characteristics to interest rate fluctuations (Koblyakova et al., 2013).

The existence of regional discrepancies however is a much more complex process and demonstrates how the consequences of major economic shocks, such as recession, play

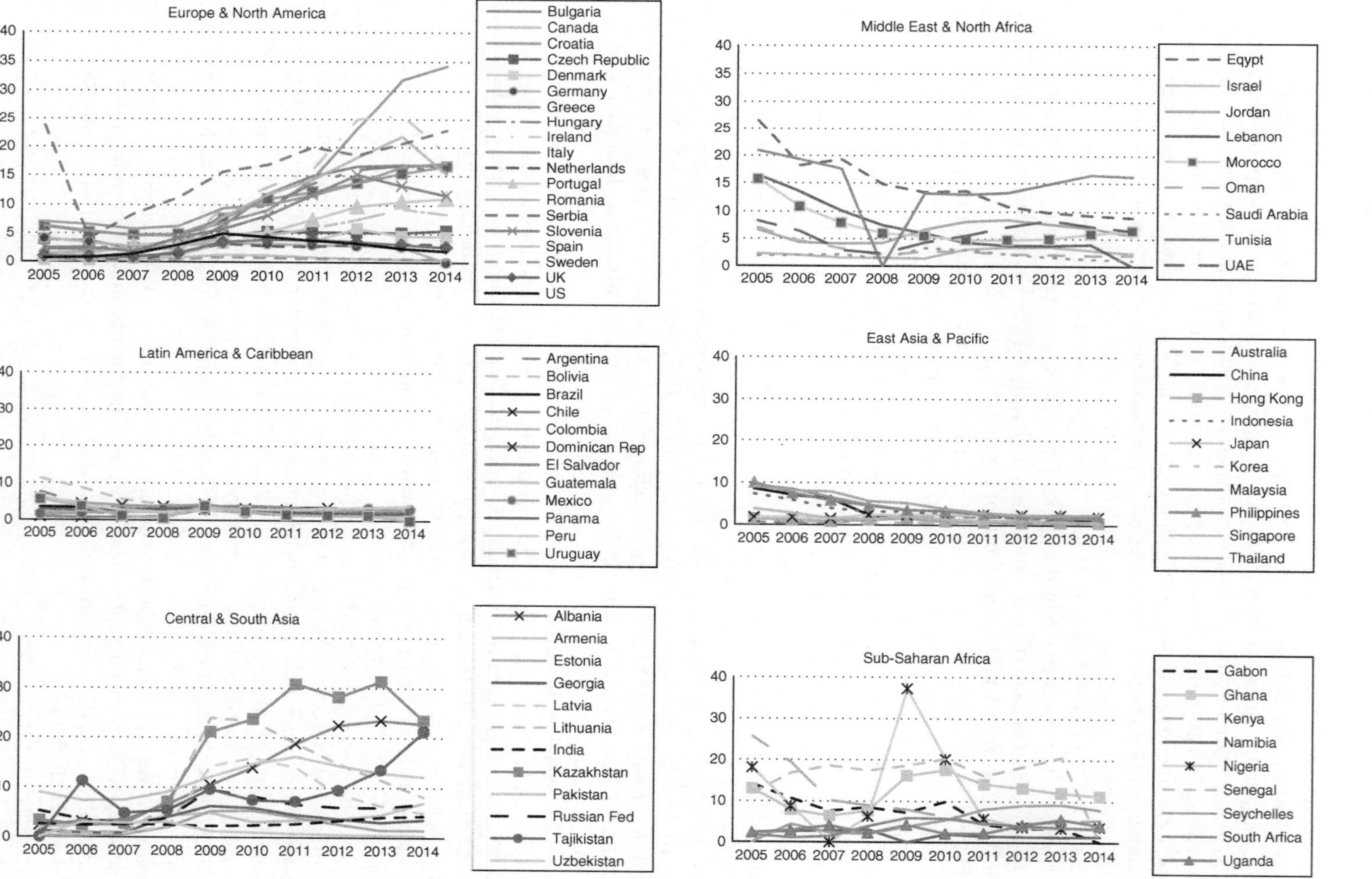

Source: The World Bank, series code FB.AST.NPER.ZS.

Figure 14.5 Bank nonperforming loans to total gross loans (%): 2006–14

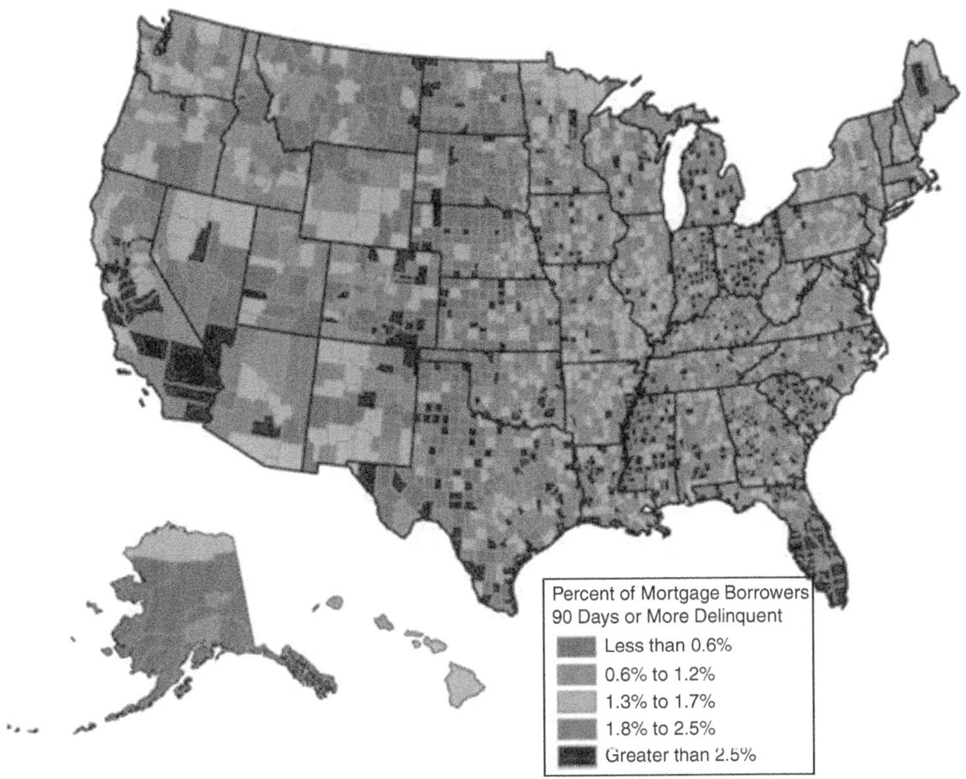

Source: TrenData from TransUnion, LLC, found in FRS (2008).

Figure 14.6 Mortgage delinquency rates: US 2007

out within local economies, reflecting path dependencies of population growth, economic development, housing and financial markets among other components (Martin and Sunley, 2014). Understanding these local geographies of debt therefore require in-depth analysis of the inter-dependencies of the multi-scalar components that make up local financial systems including the reactions and needs of individuals and local economic agents, local or national political interventions and other external linkages at the global scale (Martin and Sunley, 2014), but are beyond the scope of this chapter.

(Geo)Politics of Debt

Exploring the geography of debt at the macro, meso and micro levels demonstrates that 'while the deregulation of *who* could offer housing finance expanded on a global scale the regulatory framework as to *how* this was provided was slower to respond' (Searle, 2012: 2, original emphasis). The circumstances surrounding the expansion of credit and the subsequent rise in over-indebtedness raises questions about the power imbalance, in particular who should be responsible for the financial difficulties households were facing,

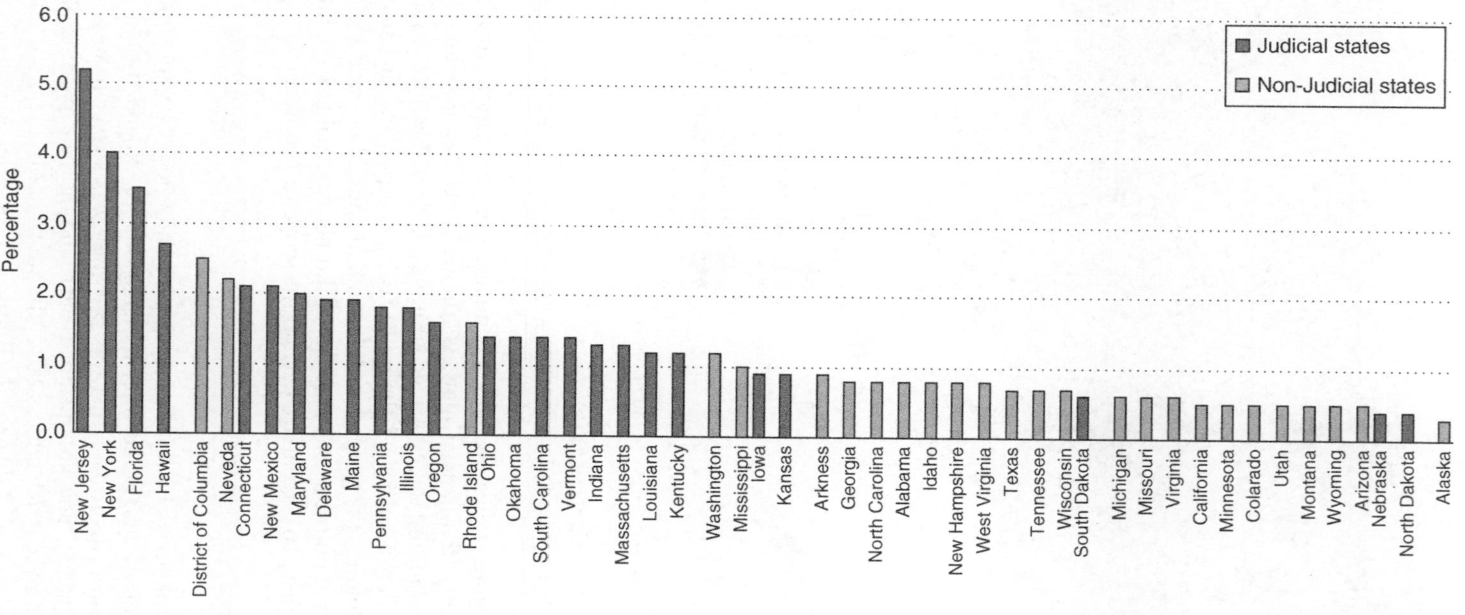

Source: CoreLogic (2015).

Figure 14.7 Foreclosures as a percentage of all homes with a mortgage, USA 2015

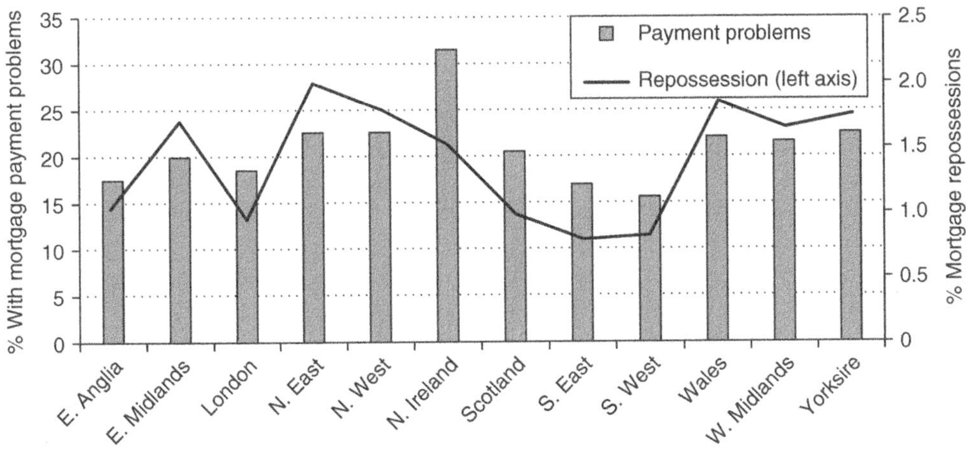

Source: FIC (2012: figures 3 and 4).

Figure 14.8 Problems with mortgage payments and repossessions: UK regions

given the challenging economic circumstances were a direct consequence of the actions of the banks and financial institutions who would seek repossession, or foreclosure, in the event of non-payment of mortgage debt (Searle, 2012).

The fallout of the economic crisis gave rise to a turn to the geopolitics of debt, and the power relations around creditors and debtors (Montgomerie et al., 2014; Soederberg, 2013a, 2014). The key argument is that existing power imbalances in the 1970s and a neoliberal reform agenda spread the 'debt economy' (Lazzarato, 2012) across the world. Liberalisation of credit regulation fuelled the spread of credit towards households, alongside protecting banks from arrears and defaults. This development shifted all the risks associated with debt on to individuals and households, while increasing profits of financial intermediaries such as banks and other investors (Soederberg, 2013b). With over-indebtedness, personal bankruptcies and defaults on payments increased, leading to increased costs for lenders, financial intermediaries (banks) and debtors (court fees) (BBC, 2014; SJPG, 2007). Despite this increase in defaults, however, revenue and profits of lenders still increased through widening access to credit (Soederberg, 2013b).

This affected both developed and developing nations. While consumer and mortgage debt spread mainly in developed and affluent societies (World Bank, 2010), developing nations had already become exposed to sovereign debt prior the GFC (Cline, 1995; Millet and Toussaint, 2004). These power imbalances were hardly questioned in public discourse (Graeber, 2011), although there is some tentative evidence that grass-roots movements and civil society began to fill the vacant political and policy void through small-scale initiatives at the household and community-level (for example, in the UK see Montgomerie et al., 2014).

14.7 POLICY RESPONSES AND DEBT CLEARANCE

National policy responses to the rise in individual debt and over-indebtedness have ranged from soft policies such as raising consumer awareness and financial literacy to various personal bankruptcy legislations. Key responses can be broadly grouped into six approaches:

First, education initiatives to increase financial literacy and consumer awareness of the risks of debt. Though cheap and popular among politicians, showed only limited success in overcoming over-indebtedness, in part due to methodological problems in measuring educational effects (Atkinson, 2008; Collins and O'Rourke, 2010).

Second, debt advice and support was provided through various channels including public authorities, charities, legal services and financial institutions. Debt support contributed to effective reduction in debt, and also increased incomes to repay debt more effectively, mainly through increasing welfare benefit claims (Hartfree and Collard, 2014).

Third, insurances could help prevent the need to acquire credit or secure debt against social risks. Public and private insurances that maintain an income after economic and social shocks (such as unemployment/health/life insurance) enable debtors to continue their loan repayments, whilst loans could be secured with payment protection insurances (PPI), although these were not always effective particularly amongst those with the highest need (Ford and Quilgars, 2001). The mis-selling of mortgage-related insurances to those who were ineligible to make an insurance claim if in need, led to one of the biggest fines for the insurance sector and £3 billion being repaid to costumers (FSA, 2009; Robertson, 2010).

Fourth, policymakers could implement stricter credit regulation and demand more responsible lending. Policy options included stricter credit checks, lower mortgage/value-ratios or interest ceilings (Priemus and Whitehead, 2014). However, in Europe tighter regulation created greater opportunities for illegal credit markets with the associated problems discussed above (Iff/ZEW, 2010). Consumer protection (in respect of financial products and services) was among the 'shared pillars of financial adjustments' embraced by a coordinated approach to financial reform by the European Union and the US (Masera, 2011: 333). The US took the lead in detailing independent, macro-prudential oversight across all aspects of finance and economic policies, although mortgages remained a notable exception (Masera, 2011).

Fifth, to break the vicious cycle of high-interest payday loans and credit card bills, affordable small sum loans were suggested for low-income households. While such schemes had only been piloted in some countries (for example, DWP growth fund – UK, Small-Dollar Loan Pilot Program – US), they had been in place for several years in others (the Australian small loans schemes (NILS/StepUP) had been in place for more than 30 years; UK's Discretionary Social Fund operated between 1988 and 2013).

Sixth, often as a last resort, over-indebted borrowers could use personal bankruptcy solutions to break the cycle of debt. Heuer (2014) revealed four distinct clusters of personal insolvency policies in 15 advanced economies. A 'market model' (US and Canada) enabled those who were over-indebted a fresh start after a relatively short waiting period to clear commercial debt. Similarly the 'restrictions model' (UK, Australia, NZ) allowed a relatively quick discharge of debt (one to three years), but imposed more economic and behavioural restrictions on debtors during and after bankruptcy. The 'liability model'

(Germany and Austria) with long waiting periods (six to seven years), strict obligations on the debtors and strong rights for the creditors until debt clearance. Finally, the 'mercy model' (France, Belgium and Scandinavian countries (Denmark, Finland, Norway and Sweden)) where officials had significant discretion in when and under which circumstances debts were cleared, the main criteria being deservingness.

As highlighted with the personal bankruptcy clusters, credit policies strongly complemented other existing welfare support schemes and cannot be understood in isolation. At the time of writing, little research had been conducted to understand competing institutional incentives for the take-up of credit, safety-nets and behavioural responses in a comprehensive policy framework. Yet, a recent World Bank report highlighted issues of personal bankruptcy and its wider social and political implications, serving as a White Paper that will shape future global policy debates on this topic (Insolvency and Creditor/Debtor Regimes Task Force, 2014).

14.8 THE TURN TO ASSETS

As noted above household indebtedness is inextricably linked with financial exclusion. As everyday lives became financialised (Langley, 2008), there was a parallel concern that those on low incomes would become increasingly financially excluded. A key theory developed to address this was asset-based welfare (ABW) (Sherraden, 1991). The premise of ABW is that investment in initial assets (for example, savings, pensions, business or education) will provide returns (through interest payments or better earnings opportunities) and a base from which further asset accumulation can flow (Sherraden, 1991, 2002).

Savings represent one effective means of buffering against unexpected expense and preventing debt acquisition, particularly among low-income households. Borrowing, or being in debt, has been identified as a key barrier to regular saving among low-income households, although it was not necessarily borrowing that was the problem but as noted above unsecured credit (see Kempson and Paxton, 2002). Having savings prevents the need for adopting risk management strategies (Harrison, 2013; Lusardi et al., 2011). It also prevents the need for taking out unsecured debt, resorting to alternative expensive credit solutions which are more likely to lead to a spiral into further debt and long-term financial problems (Hartfree and Collard, 2014) or borrow from family or friends which puts a strain on family relationships (Lusardi et al., 2011). So whilst household debt was rising, a parallel concern was that people were saving less. Across the OECD net saving rates on average declined from the 1990s, although huge country differences remained (OECD, 2014). Even Japan who had been known for a relatively high household saving rate for decades turned negative in 2009, as households were on average dissaving and acquiring debt.

Although initially positioned as being complementary to existing welfare provision, access to personal savings, assets and wealth increasingly became part of national and international government policy, especially in Anglo-Saxon and East Asian welfare states where in some instances it replaced traditional welfare schemes. Personal saving embodied the resilience, reliability and integrity of individuals and households, although evidence for most claims is weak. National schemes were developed to encourage saving, but evidence showed they disproportionately benefitted middle-income households rather than the poorest in society (Searle and Köppe, 2014). However, access to assets (notably housing) lead to the financial inclusion into credit, but also ultimately debt. So although household net wealth was increasing as noted earlier, much of this wealth was underpinned by a growth in debt among those already financially included (Girouard et al., 2006). *Asset*-based welfare was turning into risky *debt-financed* welfare (Searle and Köppe, 2014).

Housing Wealth

As everyone needs a place to live, arguably housing is a natural asset to hold. The implementation of a range of policies would seem to support this view, including discount schemes for home purchase among sitting tenants of social housing, mortgage tax relief or house deposit saving schemes which have been implemented in many countries (Searle and Köppe, 2014).

The relaxing of credit constraints on mortgage finance not only facilitated increased access to funds to enable home purchase, but also opened up a market for new forms of credit (and debt) through mortgage equity borrowing. The practice of equity borrowing reached unprecedented levels in some countries, for example average quarterly withdrawals of $80 billion in the US in 2006 (Searle, 2011), and was common in Canada, UK, Australia and New Zealand (Hurst and Stafford, 2004; and see Smith and Searle, 2010).

National studies showed that home owners were using the wealth reserves in their home to fund a range of consumption wants and welfare needs (Smith, 2010; Wood et al., 2013), boost retirement income or pay off other debts (Overton, 2010; Smith, 2005; Smith, 2010). The geography of this form of credit and debt is also evident. In some nations home owners were more reluctant to tap into housing wealth, preferring to save any equity for later life or pass on as inheritance (Toussaint and Elsinga, 2009).

The nature of mortgage debt and extended borrowing was generally seen as a relatively low risk form of credit. Because mortgage debt is secured against a physical asset, it reduces the risk of loss for the lender if the borrower becomes unable to repay the loan (Weinberg, 2006). Such assumptions were brought into question during 2005 and 2006 in the US when those who borrowed via the subprime mortgage market and existing home owners who had over-stretched themselves through borrowing equity from their homes, defaulted on their loans. House values started to fall leading to the GFC which followed (Mian and Sufi, 2014).

Research from the UK also demonstrated the fine line between good credit and bad debt. Home owners who struggled to manage household budgets and meet housing payments, were twice as likely to access further credit through withdrawing equity (Searle, 2011). However, this placed them at greater risk of falling behind with mortgage payments and of being repossessed (Searle, 2012). Analysis of mortgage rescue applicants also revealed that half of applicants in 2009–10 had additional charges, other than their initial mortgage, secured against their home (Wilcox et al., 2010). The changing role of housing wealth and home owners' willingness to engage in equity borrowing across several nations served to challenge the previously held assumption that mortgage debt could be considered a safe and unproblematic form of credit, instead drawing attention to its potential to become a burden and source of problematic debt.

14.9 CONCLUSIONS

Throughout the twentieth century debt became as an acceptable part of household budget management. It provided the means to smooth gaps in income, savings and expenditure across the life course. More importantly from a macroeconomic perspective, debt enabled people to sustain their consumption behaviour, thus fuelling economic growth. The relaxing of constraints on the system to supply credit was seen as a legitimate contribution to national progress, resulting in debt finance spreading spatially across the globe.

Although consumer credit under these conditions was deemed to be good debt, the shift towards an individualised asset-based welfare approach meant that the risks, previously born by the nation state or other broader collectives, were increasingly being taken on by the individual. Saving and investing remained a viable strategy for accumulating wealth and assets, however, most households needed to take out debt in order to finance major life-time investments. So even during a period when net wealth was on the increase, fuelled by rising house prices and a booming economy, concerns were being raised about historical high levels of household debt, and mortgage debt in particular and the extent to which debt obligations were sustainable.

Such concerns were realised when the global financial crisis exposed the extent to which individual and national welfare provision was underpinned by insecure forms of debt finance. The problem of indebtedness not only affected groups traditionally deemed 'at risk', but spread to include households across the socio-economic spectrum, and indeed to entire nation states. Paradoxically, the system implemented to enhance welfare and protect against social risks through greater access to financial assets and wealth, was not only at the heart of the greatest recession since the Depression of the 1930s, but failed to give the security it was set up to provide. When the mortgage finance system collapsed, house values – the largest asset holding for most households, and increasingly a source of income through equity borrowing – fell drastically. Whilst lowering interest rates to historic lows, significantly reduced the income returns on individual savings and investments.

The policy response to the GFC also reinforced historical power relations embedded in the supply of credit and debt obligations. Creditors were protected first through implementation of rescue packages and plans, whilst regulation of the financial sector to protect vulnerable debtors did not come until later. On the one hand this reinforces the moral hierarchy of credit as power and debt as weakness; the consequences of the financial collapse were borne by the debtors rather than the creditors (Mian and Sufi, 2014; Soederberg, 2014). On the other hand it challenges this notion where indebtedness had arisen in response to a political and economic push towards a credit economy. The limited alternatives for appropriate and affordable credit, the need to accumulate expensive assets to provide for welfare; and the lack of public safety nets, left individuals vulnerable to the social and economic costs of the collapse in the financial system. The inability of individuals to accumulate income and service debt payments was arguably less about poor self-governance or weakness and more about institutional failings.

Exposing the geographic differences in credit finance and regulation therefore provides an important contribution to understanding the global rise in household debt and subsequent financial recession. Notwithstanding the complexity of interdependencies at multi-scalar levels, this chapter demonstrates how global connections provide the channel through which credit (and debt) flows; regional differences demonstrate welfare ideologies and judicial responses, whilst local divisions draw out the distinct geographies of financial booms, and socio-economic factors which feed into the resilience (or not) of people, regions and nations in the face of economic busts.

NOTES

1. This chapter has focused mainly on formal credit and debt, it does not address the informal finance mechanisms that operate in many sectors in society, or indeed is still prevalent in many nations (Stenning et al., 2010).
2. Bequests are not included in the calculations. Furthermore, the national accounts calculations assume a steady state where saving and dissaving should balance out in a society.
3. Further in-depth national accounts data support these observed trends. It is also worth noting that private credit bureaus (also known as consumer reporting agencies as in the US, or credit reference agencies in the UK) can provide a wealth of regional level data for the countries they are operating in, based on their client databases (for example, for Germany see Creditreform 2014, SCHUFA 2014; for the US see TransUnion's *Credit Report Studies* www.transunion.com/corporate/about-transunion/credit-studies.page, Experian's *White Papers* www.experian.com/consumer-information/white-papers.html; for the UK CallCredit's *Define* Consumer Database www.callcredit.co.uk/products-and-services/consumer-marketing-data/define). However, while some research reports are available to the public, most databases are only accessible through a paywall for marketing research and not easily available for academic research.
4. The introduction of real time databases in some states in the United States provided the way forward for better monitoring and potential regulation of the sector (CfRC, 2011).

REFERENCES

Aalbers, M. (2009), 'Geographies of the financial crisis', *Area*, **41** (1), 34–42.

Ambrosius, C. and A. Cuecuecha (2013), 'Are remittances a substitute for credit? Carrying the financial burden of health shocks in national and transnational households', *World Development*, **46**, 143–152.

Andrews, D. (2010), 'Real house prices in OECD countries: The role of demand shocks and structural and policy factors', OECD Economics Department Working Papers, No. 831.

Atkinson, A. (2008) 'Evidence of impact: an overview of financial education evaluations', Financial Services Authority, Consumer Research Report 68.

Badev, A., T. Beck, L. Vado and S. Walley (2014), *Housing Finance Across Countries: New Data and Analysis*, Washington, DC: World Bank.

BBC (2014), 'Wonga to write off £220m of customer debts', *BBC News Business*, 2 October. Retrieved on 1 November 2014 from www.bbc.co.uk/news/business-29457044?print=true.

Berthoud R. and E. Kempson (1992), *Credit and Debt: The PSI Report*, London: Policy Studies Institute.

Betti, G., N. Dourmashkin, M. Rossi, V. Verma and Y. Yin (2001), 'Study of the problem of consumer indebtedness: statistical aspects final report', Contract no.: B5–1000/00/000197, London: ORC Macro.

BMFSFJ (2015), 'Better reconciliation of family, care and work. New statutory provisions since 1 January 2015', Berlin: Federal Ministry for Family Affairs, Senior Citizens, Women and Youth. Retrieved 7 December 2015 from www.wege-zur-pflege.de/fileadmin/daten/Infomaterialien/BMFSFJ_WegeZurPflege_Flyer_en_RZ6_bb.pdf.

Brown, S., K. Taylor and S. Wheatley Price (2005), 'Debt and distress: evaluating the psychological cost of credit', *Journal of Economic Psychology*, **26** (5), 642–663.

Bylander, M. (2014), 'Borrowing across borders: migration and microcredit in rural Cambodia', *Development and Change*, **45** (2), 284–307.

Carr, J.H. and L. Kolluri (2001), *Predatory Lending: An Overview*, New York: Fannie Mae Foundation.

CfRC (Centre for Responsible Credit) (2011), 'How to regulate payday lending: learning from international best practice', Policy Briefing December 2011. Retrieved on 1 November 2014 from www.responsible-credit.org.uk/uimages/File/how%20to%20regulate%20payday%20lending%20final%2014th%20December%202011.pdf.

Claessens, S. (2005), 'Access to financial services: a review of the issues and public policy objectives', World Bank Policy Research Working Paper 3589, Washington: World Bank. Retrieved on 23 December 2014 from http://hdl.handle.net/10986/8958.

Cline, W.R. (1995), *International Debt Reexamined*, Washington, DC: Institute for International Economics.
Collins, J. and C. O'Rourke (2010), 'Financial education and counseling – still holding promise', *The Journal of Consumer Affairs*, **44** (3), 483–498.
Consumer Focus (2011), 'Affordable credit: lessons from overseas', Report prepared for Consumer Focus by the Personal Finance Research Centre (PFRC) University of Bristol. London: Consumer Focus.
CoreLogic (2015), *National Foreclosure Report: January 2015*, Irvine, CA: CoreLogic.
Creditreform (2014), *SchuldnerAtlas Deutschland 2014*, Neuss: Creditreform.
CSJ (Centre for Social Justice) (2013), 'Maxed out: serious personal debt in Britain', Policy Report by the CJS Working Group, November 2013. London: Centre for Social Justice.
EQLS (European Quality of Life Surverys) (2013), 'Household over-indebtedness in the EU: the role of informal debts', EQLS Policy Brief, Dublin: European Foundation for the Improvement of Living and Working Conditions.
Eurofound (2010), 'Managing household debts: social service provision in the EU working paper', Dublin: European Foundation for the Improvement of Living and Working Conditions.
Faber, H.S. (2011), 'Job loss in the Great Recession: historical perspective from the displaced workers survey, 1984–2010', NBER Working Paper Series, Working Paper 17040, Cambridge, MA: NBER.
FIC (2012), Debt and the Family Series: Report 3: 'Debt and the regions', London: The Financial Inclusion Centre. Retrieved 1 December 2015 from www.stepchange.org/Portals/0/Documents/media/reports/additionalreports/Report_Debt_and_the_Regions.pdf.
Finch, C., A. Simpson, S. Collard and M. Teasdale (2007), 'Mental health and debt: challenges for knowledge, practice and identity', *Journal of Psychiatric and Mental Health Nursing*, **14** (2), 128–133.
Ford, J. and D. Quilgars (2001), 'Failing home owners? The effectiveness of public and private safety-nets', *Housing Studies*, **16** (2), 147–162.
Ford, J., E. Kempson and M. Wilson (1995), *Mortgage Arrears and Possession; Perspectives from Borrowers, Lenders and the Courts*, London: HMSO.
FRS (Federal Reserve System) (2008), Mortgage Delinquencies and Foreclosures, Speech by B.S. Bernanke at the Columbia Business School's 32nd Annual Dinner, New York, 5 May 2008. Retrieved on 8 December 2015 from www.federalreserve.gov/newsevents/speech/Bernanke20080505a.htm.
FSA (Food Standards Agency) (2009), *MPPI Premium Variation Clauses: Industry-wide Agreement. CEO-Letter 07 October 2009*, London: FSA.
Girouard, N., M. Kennedy and C. Andre (2006), 'Has the rise in debt made households more vulnerable?' OECD Economics Department Working Papers No 535, Paris: OECD Publishing.
Graeber, D. (2011), *Debt. The First 5,000 Years*, New York: Melville House.
Harrison, E. (2013), 'Bouncing back? Recession, resilience and everyday lives', *Critical Social Policy*, **33** (1), 97–113.
Hartfree, Y. and S. Collard (2014), *Poverty, Credit and Debt: An Expert-led Review*, Bristol: University of Bristol. Retrieved on 18 October 2016 from www.bristol.ac.uk/media-library/sites/geography/migrated/documents/pfrc1404.pdf.
Harvey, D. (2005), *A Brief History of Neoliberalism*, Oxford: Oxford University Press.
Heuer, J.-O. (2014), 'Rules and norms of consumer insolvency and debt relief: a comparison and classification of personal bankruptcy systems in 15 economically advanced countries', PhD thesis (microfiche), Bremen: University of Bremen.
Howard, C. (1997), *The Hidden Welfare State. Tax Expenditures and Social Policy in the United States*, Princeton, NJ: Princeton University Press.
Hurst, E. and F. Stafford (2004), 'Home is where the equity is: mortgage refinancing and household consumption', *Journal of Money, Credit and Banking*, **36** (6), 987–1014.
Iff/ZEW (2010), 'Study on interest rate restrictions in the EU', Final report. Brussels: European Commission.
Insolvency and Creditor/Debtor Regimes Task Force (2014), *Report on the Treatment of the Insolvency of Natural Persons*, Washington, DC: World Bank.
Japelli, T. (2001), 'Comment on the International Savings Comparison Project', *Research in Economics*, **55** (2), 173–184.
Jenkins, R., P. Bhugra, P. Bebbington, T. Bruha, M. Farell, J. Coid, T. Fryers, S. Weich, N. Singlton and H. Meltzer (2008), 'Debt, income and mental disorder in the general population', *Psychological Medicine*, **38**, 1485–1493.
Jones, C. and A. Murie (2006), *The Right to Buy: Analysis and Evaluation of a Housing Policy*, Oxford: Blackwell.
Kempson, E. and W. Paxton (2002), 'Saving among people on low to moderate incomes: the barriers and how they might be overcome', in W. Paxton (ed.), *Equal Shares? Building a Progressive and Coherent Asset-based Welfare Policy*, London: IPPR, pp. 57–71.
Kiff, J. and P. Mills (2007), 'Money for nothing and checks for free: recent developments in US subprime mortgage markets', IMF Working Paper WP/07/188.

Koblyakova, A., N. Hutchison and P. Tiwari (2013), 'Regional differences in mortgage demand and mortgage instrument choice in the UK', *Regional Studies*, **48** (9), 1499–1513.
Kotlikoff, L.J. (1986), 'Is debt neutral in the life cycle model?', National Bureau of Economic Research Working Paper Series, No. 2053.
Kuehlwein, M. (1995), 'A close look at dissaving in the longitudinal retirement history survey', *Review of Income and Wealth*, **41** (2), 161–176.
La Cava, G. and J. Simon (2005), 'Household debt and financial constraints in Australia', *The Australian Economic Review*, **38** (1), 40–60.
Langley, P. (2008), 'Financialization and the consumer credit boom', *Competition and Change*, **12** (2), 133–147.
Lazzarato, M. (2012), *The Making of the Indebted Man. Essay on the Neoliberal Condition*, Los Angeles: Semiotext(e).
Lea, S., P. Webley and R. Levine (1993), 'The economic psychology of consumer debt', *Journal of Economic Psychology*, **14**, 85–119.
Lee, R.D. and A. Mason (2011), *Population Aging and the Generational Economy*, Cheltenham, UK and Northampton, MA, USA: Edward Elgar Publishing.
Leyshon, A. and N. Thrift (1999), 'Lists come alive: electronic systems of knowledge and the rise of credit-scoring in retail banking', *Economy and Society*, **28** (3), 434–466.
Lusardi, A., D.J. Schneider and P. Tufano (2011), 'Financial fragile households: evidence and implications', NBER Working Paper No. 17072, Cambridge, MA: National Bureau of Economic Research.
Marron, D. (2012), 'Producing over-indebtedness', *Journal of Cultural Economy*, **5** (4), 407–421.
Martin R. and P. Sunley (2015), 'On the notion of regional economic resilience: conceptualisation and explanation', *Journal of Economic Geography*, **15** (1), 1–42.
Masera, R. (2011), 'Reforming financial systems after the crisis: a comparison of EU and USA', *PSL Quarterly Review*, **63** (255), 297–360.
McKillop, D., P. Goth and N. Hyndman (2006), *Credit Unions in Ireland. Structure, Performance & Governance*, Dublin: Institute of Chartered Accountants.
Mian, A. and A. Sufi (2014), *House of Debt. How They (and You) Caused the Great Recession, and How We Can Prevent It from Happening Again*, Chicago, IL: University of Chicago Press.
Millet, D. and E. Toussaint (2004), *Who Owes Who? 50 Questions about World Debt*, London: Zed Books.
Modigliani, F. and F. Brumberg (1954), 'Utility analysis and the consumption function: an interpretation of cross-section data', in Kenneth K. Kurihara (ed.), *Post Keynesian Economics*, New Brunswick: Rutgers University Press, pp. 388–436.
Montgomerie, J., C. Packman, J. Deville, A. Simpson and G. Warren (eds) (2014), *The Politics of Indebtedness in the UK. A Public Interest Report*, London: Goldsmiths University of London.
Nettleton, S. (1998), 'Losing homes through mortgage possession: a "new" public health issue', *Critical Public Health*, **8**, 53–63.
Nettleton, S. and R. Burrows (2000), 'When a capital investment becomes an emotional loss: the health consequences of the experience of mortgage possession in England', *Housing Studies*, **15** (3), 463–479.
OECD (2014), *National Accounts at a Glance*, Paris: OECD.
Overton, L. (2010), *Housing and Finance in Later Life: A Study of UK Equity Release Customers*, London: Age UK.
Oxfam (2013), 'A cautionary tale: the true cost of austerity and inequality in Europe', Oxfam Briefing Paper 174. Oxford: Oxfam GB for Oxfam International.
Park, M.J. and S.A. DeVaney (2007), 'Examining a model of economic well-being based on financial ratios', *Consumer Interests Annual*, **53**, 131–145.
Peebles, G. (2010), 'The anthropology of credit and debt', *Annual Review of Anthropology*, **39**, 225–240.
Pinsloo, J.W. (2002), 'Household debt, wealth and saving', *Quarterly Bulletin December 2002*. South Africa: SA Reserve Bank.
Priemus, H. and C. Whitehead (2014), 'Interactions between the financial crisis and national housing markets', *Journal of Housing and the Built Environment*, **29** (2), 193–200.
Reinhart, C.M. and K.S. Rogoff (2009), *This Time is Different: Eight Centuries of Financial Folly*, Princeton, NJ: Princeton University Press.
Robertson P. (2010), 'PPI reimbursement will cost up to £3bn – Defaqto', *Cover Magazine*. Retrieved on 18 October 2016 from www.covermagazine.co.uk/cover/news/2147225/ppi-reimbursement-cost-gbp3bn-defaqto.
Ronald, R. (2008), *The Ideology of Home Ownership. Homeowner Societies and the Role of Housing*, Basingstoke: Palgrave Macmillan.
Rowlingson, K. (2006), '"Living poor to die rich?" or "Spending the kids' inheritance"? Attitudes to assets and inheritance in later life', *Journal of Social Policy*, **35** (2), 175–192.
Rubaszek, M. and D. Serwa (2014), 'Determinants of credit to households: an approach using the life-cycle model', *Economic Systems*, **38** (4), 572–587.
Schich, S. and A. Jung-Hyun (2007), 'Housing markets and household debt', *Financial Market Trends*, 2007/1.

SCHUFA (ed.) (2014), *SCHUFA Kredit-Kompass 2014. Empirische Untersuchung der privaten Kreditaufnahme in Deutschland. Konsum und Finanzen in der Rushhour des Lebens*, Wiesbaden: SCHUFA.
Searle, B.A. (2011), 'Recession and housing wealth', *Journal of Financial Economic Policy*, **3** (1), 33–48.
Searle, B.A. (2012), 'Recession, repossession and family welfare', *Child and Family Law Quarterly*, **42** (1), 1–23.
Searle, B.A. and S. Köppe (2014), 'Savings, assets, wealth and poverty: a review of evidence', Final report for the Joseph Rowntree Foundation. Bristol: Personal Finance Research Centre. Retrieved on 18 October 2016 from http://www.bristol.ac.uk/media-library/sites/geography/pfrc/pfrc1405-assets-savings-wealth-poverty.pdf.
Searle, B.A., S.J. Smith and N. Cook (2009), 'From housing wealth to well-being?' *Sociology of Health and Illness*, **31** (1), 112–127.
Sherraden, M. (1991), *Assets and the Poor: A New American Welfare Policy*, New York: M.E. Sharpe.
Sherraden, M. (2002), 'Assets and the social investment state', in W. Paxton (ed.), *Equal Shares? Building a progressive and coherent asset-based welfare policy*, London: IPPR, pp. 28–41.
SJPG (Social Justice Policy Group) (2007), *Breakthrough Britain: Eding the costs of social breakdown. Volume 5: Serious Personal Debt*, London: SJPG.
Smith, M. (2010), 'What do we know about equity withdrawal by households in New Zealand?', in S.J. Smith and B.A. Searle (eds), *The Blackwell Companion to the Economics of Housing: The Housing Wealth of Nations*, Chichester, UK: Wiley-Blackwell, pp. 176–200.
Smith, S.J. (2005), 'States, markets and an ethic of care', *Political Geography*, **24** (1), 1–20.
Smith, S.J. and B.A. Searle (2008), 'Dematerialising money: the ebb and flow of wealth between housing and other things', *Housing Studies*, **23** (1), 21–43.
Smith, S.J. and B.A. Searle (eds) (2010), *A Blackwell Companion to the Economics of Housing: The Housing Wealth of Nations*, New York and Oxford: Wiley-Blackwell.
Soederberg, S.(2013a), 'The politics of debt and development in the new millennium: an introduction', *Third World Quarterly*, **34** (4), 535–546.
Soederberg, S. (2013b), 'The US debtfare state and the credit card industry: forging spaces of dispossession', *Antipode*, **45** (2), 493–512.
Soederberg, S. (2014), *Debtfare States and the Poverty Industry: Money, Discipline and the Surplus Population*, London: Routledge.
Sokol, M. (2013), 'Towards a "newer" economic geography? Injecting finance and financialisation into economic geographies', *Cambridge Journal of Regions, Economy and Society*, **6** (3), 501–515.
Spilerman, S. (2000), 'Wealth and stratification processes', *Annual Review of Sociology*, **26** (1), 497–524.
Stenning, A., A. Smith, A. Rochovská and D. Świątek (2010), 'Credit, debt, and everyday financial practices: low-income households in two postsocialist cities', *Economic Geography*, **86** (2), 119–145.
Sutherland, D., P. Hoeller, R. Merola and V. Ziemann (2012), 'Debt and macroeconomic stability', OECD Economics Department Working Papers, 1003.
Taylor, M.P., D. Pevalin and J. Todd (2007), 'The psychological costs of unsustainable housing commitments', *Psychological Medicine*, **37** (7), 1027–1036.
The Economist (2013), 'Monetary policy after the crash. Controlling interest 21 September 2013', retrieved 23 December 2014 from www.economist.com/news/schools-brief/21586527-third-our-series-articles-financial-crisis-looks-unconventional.
Toussaint, J. and M. Elsinga (2009), 'Exploring "housing asset-based welfare", can the UK be held up as an example for Europe?', *Housing Studies*, **24** (5), 669–692.
Valins, O. (2004), *When Debt Becomes a Problem: A Literature Study*, New Zealand: Ministry of Social Development.
Wang, X. and B. Walters (2013), 'The real origin of global financial imbalances', *Journal of International Development*, **25** (8), 1050–1060.
Weinberg, J.A. (2006), 'Borrowing by US households', *Economic Quarterly*, Federal Reserve Bank of Richmond, **92** (3), 177–194.
Wilcox S., A. Wallace, G. Bramley, J. Morgan, F. Sosenko and J. Ford (2010), 'Evaluation of the mortgage rescue scheme and home-owners mortgage support', London: Communities and Local Government.
Wood, G., S. Parkinson, B.A. Searle and S.J. Smith (2013), 'Motivations for equity borrowing: a welfare switching effect', *Urban Studies*, **50** (12), 2588–2607.
World Bank (ed.) (2010), *Crisis Hits Home: Stress Testing Households in Europe and Central Asia*, Washington, DC: World Bank.
Worthington, A.C. (2005), 'Debt as a source of financial stress in Australian households', *International Journal of Consumer Studies*, **30** (1), 2–15.

15. The financial legacy of pension fund capitalism

Gordon L. Clark

15.1 INTRODUCTION

Pension fund capitalism is a set of institutions and conventions pertaining to the nature and value of pension benefits *and* financial market institutions and asset management practices, which came to dominate Anglo-American economies over the second half of the twentieth century (Clark, 2000). These institutions and practices owe their origins to English common-law principles regarding fiduciary duty and the deference claimed by intermediaries by virtue of expertise and skill (Clark, 2014). The rise of pension fund capitalism can be explained with reference to two issues. First, the emerging power of industrial unions over the twentieth century, and second, the incorporation into statute of entitlements to wage-related benefits previously negotiated through the employment contract at the level of the plant, the firm, or the industry (Ghilarducci, 1992; Sass, 1997). Pension fund capitalism is also an expression of what some writers have referred to as 'modern capitalism' (Shonfield, 1965) or 'managerial capitalism' (Galbraith, 1967).[1]

In this chapter I argue that pension fund capitalism has been undercut by the transformation of corporate form and functions. The long-term decline of employer-sponsored benefit systems matches the transformation of managerial capitalism and the relative decline of manufacturing and industrial employment (if not their value-added in relation to gross domestic product). It is not surprising that defined contribution (DC) pension systems have become important *and* could yet be eclipsed by other types of contingent compensation. The administrative costs involved in providing pension benefits have grown enormously over the past 30 years, accelerating the decline of private pension plans. Even if governments reduced the regulatory costs and the liabilities associated with these systems, the changing nature of the Anglo-American corporation is such that there can be no return to the past.

Company-sponsored pension benefit systems have had their day. This does not necessarily mean that pension funds as institutional investors need be less important over the coming decades than they have been over the past forty years. The overhang of accumulated financial assets and obligations is such that Anglo-American economies will continue to derive enormous value from these third-party financial and beneficial institutions, long after their relevance for the average person has passed. Much has been written about the positive consequences of these institutions for the liquidity of Anglo-American securities markets (Clowes, 2000). More recently, these institutions have played vital roles in prosecuting poor corporate governance and in promoting higher standards of corporate disclosure domestically and internationally (Hebb, 2006). At the limit, pension funds could take on the responsibility for the performance of capitalism at home and abroad (Hebb and Wójcik, 2005).[2]

At one level, this chapter is an exercise in comparative institutional analysis, providing an account of the evolution of Anglo-American capitalism in relation to continental

Europe and the gathering forces of globalization (compare Strange, 1997). Equally, it provides an account of the rise of what contemporary writers term as 'financialization': the increasing importance of financial markets in pricing the current and expected value of institutions and relationships (see Jameson, 1997; Boyer, 2000; Froud et al., 2006). The chapter also resonates with recent research on long-term patterns of income inequality (Piketty, 2014), the bifurcation of labour markets into high income and low-income sectors (Weil, 2014) and patterns of inequality evident in global financial centres (McDowell et al., 2008, 2009). There appears to be a premium on certain types of expertise and skills – whether 'cognitive' as suggested by Scott (2008), or function- and task-specific to certain types of occupations in certain types of industries that have distinctive urban, regional, national and international footprints (see early work by Rosen, 1981, 1986 in conjunction with Florida, 2002 and Lucas, 2009).

To sustain my argument, I focus upon the corporation. Whatever the virtues of providing retirement benefits in terms of individual and social welfare, my reading of the past 100 years would have it that private pension systems were first and foremost mechanisms for managing labour resources (Clark, 2000). Over the past few decades, governments have 'bolted-on' to private institutions expectations and requirements as to equitable treatment and due process for different classes of employees within firms. A firm-focused perspective is an essential ingredient in better understanding apparent trends in the provision of retirement benefits and, most importantly, future prospects regarding the nature and value of corporate benefits systems. We need to think again about the purpose of employment benefits from the perspective of sponsoring institutions, eschewing normative conceptions about the proper purpose of the corporation for a better appreciation of its current and prospective economic interests (see Babchuk and Roe, 1999).

In the next section, I summarize the logic of my argument with respect to institutional evolution and innovation. Thereafter, I consider the nature and transformation of Anglo-American capitalism, beginning with Shonfield (1965) and Galbraith (1967) and linking to Jensen (1993), Zingales (2000) and Roberts (2004). These writers conceptualize capitalism through the lens of the modern corporation, noting the changing significance of compensation systems that once benefited insiders (managers and employees) over outsiders (customers and shareholders). Even so, Shonfield was aware of the growing power of institutional investors shorn of close alliances with corporate managers and other shareholders. Reference to Jensen drives home the point that the modern corporation has become beholden to financial markets. Later sections of the paper are devoted to conceptualizing the emerging firm of the twenty-first century, focused upon a typology of compensation practices with reference to company-sponsored benefits. The concluding section summarizes the arguments of the paper and its implications for retirement income over the twenty-first century.

15.2 GEOGRAPHY OF PENSION SYSTEMS

As originally conceived, the institutional formation termed 'pension fund capitalism' traded on a related argument made by Drucker (1976) to the effect that the growth of large pension funds in the US was likely to result in the concentration of ownership of major corporations. Being beneficial institutions rather than banks or related holding companies whose overriding interest is, or was, the flow of profits, Drucker believed that large pension funds would represent the interests of workers (pension fund participants) in the allocation of income. He suggested, in fact, that this would remake US corporate capitalism of the first half of the twentieth century into pension fund socialism over the second half of the twentieth century. While it is not entirely clear how or why he believed that large pension funds would be active owners of major corporations and would extract benefits on behalf of their contributors he suggested that pension fund socialism would tame American corporate capitalism.

A rather different view was expressed in the 1970 UK government review of pension funds and investment (the Wilson Report). This Report announced that the growth in pension fund assets through to the end of the twentieth century would transform the UK economy and its place in the world. At the time, sections of the Labour Party had hoped that pension fund assets could be used to underpin the faltering UK economy and its industries. As well, those on the left that sought further nationalization and state control of broad sections of the UK economy looked to the emerging pension funds as a ready source of 'social' capital to be deployed on behalf of industrial unions. The Wilson Report dashed these hopes, rejecting arguments that government should direct pension fund investment to certain sectors of the UK economy or indeed the UK economy. Rather, the Wilson Report embraced the liberalization of capital markets and the role that pension funds could play in fostering economic growth at home and abroad. Chaired by the previous Labour Prime Minister, the Wilson Report was readily accepted by the Thatcher government.

The growth and significance of pension funds over the second half of the twentieth century was largely an Anglo-American phenomenon. As an institution with express powers and responsibilities, it was 'located' in the second-tier or pillar of many countries' pension saving systems. Recall that pension systems are typically cast in terms of three separate pillars: pillar 1 pensions are government funded or provided social security benefits, pillar 2 pensions are employer funded or provided retirement benefits and pillar 3 pensions are individual saving programmes sometimes tax preferred and sometimes not (World Bank, 1994). As such, it was possible to distinguish between countries and groups of countries on the basis of the significance attributed to each of the pillars of pension saving and the combination of those pillars in terms of expected total retirement income (Dixon, 2008). So, for example, French retirement income was (and still is to some extent) dominated by pillar 1, whereas British retirement income was underwritten by a modest pillar 1 social welfare benefit but supplemented by a significant pillar 2 component. By classifying countries according to the relative contribution of each pillar to total retirement income it was possible to talk of different 'worlds of welfare' and, ultimately, varieties of capitalism (Esping-Anderson, 1999; Hall and Soskice, 2001).

There was, by this assessment, a distinctive geography of pension systems. This type of classification pitted Anglo-American pension systems against European pension systems and even East Asian and Latin American pension systems. It was also, though less recognized as such, a classification of nation-states according to their reliance of stock markets (Anglo-American countries) as opposed to banking systems (continental European countries) for financing economic growth (Dore, 2000). It was a conversation or debate about institutional formation and path dependence amongst developed and developing economies buttressed by reference to nation-state traditions and cultural expectations as to the respective roles of markets and states, employers and individuals, and social solidarity in saving for retirement. It was also an argument about what type of pension saving system was best suited to the twenty-first century (Clark, 2003). Around 1995, it was possible to argue that the UK model of modest state retirement benefits combined with employer-sponsored income-related pension savings was more sustainable in terms of the expected welfare burden of an ageing population. This assessment, however, was based on an assumption that workplace pensions would remain a significant element of total employee compensation in the private and public sectors for the foreseeable future. This assumption was not to be realized.

The post-war growth in pension fund assets across the Anglo-American world can be explained by three factors (Sass, 1997). First, the spread of workplace pension benefits from the public sector to large manufacturing companies and then to smaller companies inside and outside of manufacturing dramatically increased the numbers of pillar 2 participants and, most importantly, accommodated the baby-boom generation as they entered the workforce. Second, because pension contributions are tied to earned income and are funded at the time of salary payment, as employment increased and as salaries increased, the inflow of assets to pension funds far outweighed paid benefits. Third, as the occupational structure of Anglo-American countries shifted from manufacturing to service sectors, and as the average employee entered into professional employment rather than waged-work, average salaries increased and with that came increased pension contributions. By the turn of the twenty-first century, is was clear that the benefits of further education were not likely to pay-off in quite the same way as had been the case from the 1960s through to the first decade of the twenty-first century. This issue is discussed in subsequent sections of the chapter.

In effect, the growth of pension fund assets transformed the financial structure of Anglo-American societies, introducing a financial sector that, in effect, bypassed existing banks and trust companies. Furthermore, these institutions owe little if anything to the companies and sectors that sponsored these savings institutions. For continental European countries, heavily reliant upon established banks whether national or regional in origin, the apparent vitality of Anglo-American pension funds and their significance for financial market liquidity at home and abroad was nothing short of a direct challenge to the established order. Not surprisingly, through the 1980s and 1990s there was a vigorous debate about the respective virtues of bank-led versus stock market-led modern capitalism, with proponents on both sides debating probable consequences of finance capitalism in Anglo-American societies as opposed to bank-dependent corporate capitalism in European societies. This argument has been framed and reframed in a number of ways, its most recent expression found in the debate over financialization (Dixon, 2012).

Less obvious, however, is the fact that many continental European countries have recognized that continued reliance upon pillar 1 pay-as-you-go pension systems and, in some instances, unfunded or underfunded pillar 2 pension schemes is likely to result in unsustainable long-term pension liabilities. In a related vein, estimates of the rate of growth needed to sustain European pension systems have been in the order of 2–4 per cent (real) per annum through to about 2050. This appears to be out-of-reach for almost all developed economies, let alone continental Europe beset by stagnation and economic crisis (Clark et al., 2015). Paying promised pension benefits will not be possible unless retirement promises are systematically discounted, or those retired or about to be retired are protected by discounting the future entitlements of younger workers, or new modes of pension saving are introduced so as to take the weight off pay-as-you-go pillar 1 schemes. Nation-states have tackled the problems of long-term funding in these ways and other ways. In some countries, pay-as-you-go pension assets have been partially allocated to institutions that have sought to gain a premium through stock market investment (as in Sweden and France). In other countries, 'voluntary' employer-sponsored funded pensions have been introduced (as in Germany).

The irony is that as other countries have sought to emulate Anglo-American countries' multi-pillar model of retirement income provision and, in particular, introduce retirement saving institutions like pension funds, there are significant doubts about the viability of this model. This chapter explains how and why this might be case, focusing on the transformation of private corporations over the past 25 years and what appears to be the emerging economic model of the twenty-first century. In part, this is an argument about corporate capitalism. But it is also an argument about the segmentation of labour markets within and without companies paying particular regard to the forces of globalization and competition and the spatial and functional dissembling of major companies. Nonetheless, there remains an enormous legacy from pension fund capitalism which is to be found in the volume of financial assets invested in public and private financial markets.

These assets are, of course, not the only source of market liquidity in London, New York and other linked markets around the world. Markets such as London and New York draw together public and private assets from around the world including the assets of sovereign investment institutions, resource-rich economies, insurance companies, and families and individuals. Indeed, over the past 25 years, the relative share of total assets flowing through these markets owned by pension funds has declined even though the total volume of assets circumnavigating the world each day has grown enormously in volume over the same period. Some of these pools of assets are less predictable than others, being responsive to shifts and changes in market sentiment quite unlike the long-term investments associated with pension funds and sovereign wealth funds. Even so, it is arguable that pension fund capitalism remains a fact of life in the sense that these institutions underwrite the financial capitalism of the twenty-first century.

15.3 POST-WAR 'MODERN CAPITALISM'

Andrew Shonfield's (1965) book was an exercise in political economy, integrating macroeconomic trends with the changing structure of corporate capitalism while blurring the boundaries between the private world of industry and the public world of macroeconomic management. Most importantly, his book was published at the height of the Cold War wherein the economic and political prospects of Europe in relation to the United States were widely debated. It was an era of open hostility between NATO and the Soviet Union, fought over the corpse of Central and Eastern Europe. It was also an era of political rivalry between European right-wing and left-wing political parties. Few foresaw the collapse of the Soviet system, and it was commonplace to suppose that capitalism would mutate into a 'mixed' system of large industries and large governments.

Shonfield began his book astonished at the remarkable growth of Western economies over the 1950s and 1960s, comparing and contrasting the post-war era with the dark days of the Great Depression and the rise of fascism prior to the Second World War. One of his objectives was to explain how and why capitalism survived and then prospered in the UK and Western Europe considering, in particular, the circumstances of France and Germany. But there was a second element to his project; he sought to explain the success of European capitalism in contrast with the rather indifferent economic record of the United States over the same period. His book was a story of economic management by European governments that provided the context for a set of mutually reinforcing economic trends and the transformation of capitalism into managerial capitalism reliant upon the stability of prices. By his account, Europe had created new institutions and innovative mechanisms for economic management in contrast with the laissez-faire United States.[3]

Basically, his intellectual framework was an expression of economic policies and evolving institutions, just as it was an expression (albeit implied) of a political economy committed to the European project of accommodating competing political interests within public and private institutions. In this sense, his story was as much about an empirical world measured and formalized as it was about the proper organization of the economy, both public and private. By his account, private pensions played a crucial role in the success of post-war capitalism, combining the interests of corporations in the management of labour with a collective commitment to social welfare. Still to come, however, was the stagflation of the 1980s, confrontations between UK unions and governments through the 1970s and 1980s, and episodes of significant financial turmoil that brought forth political 'solutions' that were less about accommodation and mutual coexistence, and more about the resolution of conflict in favour of the rigours of market competition (the Thatcher revolution).[4]

Shonfield argued that UK and Western European governments had learnt the lessons of the Great Depression including the dangers of liquidity 'traps'. Active economic management became the cornerstone of government policies promoting short-term economic stability and high levels of employment. With the significance of economic stability in mind, Shonfield compared the UK and Western European records of macroeconomic stability with the US, arguing that the relatively poor record of the latter could be explained by the unwillingness or inability of the US federal government to deploy an active economic policy regime. He noted, however, that there was some debate about the importance of short-run economic management as opposed to long-term trends. For example, he discounted arguments to the effect that the UK and European housing boom would eventually falter and carry those economies to recession. Even if there were long-term trends to be considered, there were countervailing forces that would produce stable economic growth.[5]

With governments committed to full employment, companies could plan for an increasing rate of return on investment, thereby encouraging technological innovation and labour productivity, which in turn would drive higher incomes, which in turn would contribute to the demand for labour across the economy (full employment). There was a danger, of course, of prosperity becoming unsustainable if higher incomes fed an escalating cycle of consumption and economic instability, through wage and price inflation. By his account, UK and European governments had avoided this pitfall by converting a significant portion of higher worked incomes into savings, either through the formation of private pension institutions or through a commitment to maintaining the real value of retirees' incomes through wage-indexed social security pensions. This policy recipe was the basis of the introduction of compulsory superannuation in Australia in the late-1980s (Clark, 2012).

Most importantly, Shonfield suggested that active economic management combined with longer-term corporate pricing practices had dampened short-term volatility, while contributing to greater predictability in earned income. Underpinning his model of success were policies – or at least preferences – in favour of the consolidation of capacity, higher levels of industry concentration and the increasing size of corporations. He suggested that industry consolidation was in the interests of long-term economic growth because the vertical integration of production promoted technological innovation. Managing markets, setting prices and controlling the process of production were claimed to provide a degree of stability that had been missing in the first 50 years of the twentieth century. Indeed, Shonfield suggested that the growth of large businesses had effectively tamed 'the traditional violence of markets' (Shonfield, 1965: 368). Policymakers were 'committed to keeping [large businesses] alive, just as surely as if they were nationalized undertakings' (Shonfield, 1965: 369).

The remnants of industrial capitalism inherited from the Depression and the Second World War had been transformed into managerial capitalism: the insulation of corporate managers from their immediate owners, the rise of institutional investors such as insurance companies and pension funds and the creation of industry-wide corporations. These factors had given rise to firms of considerable complexity requiring management through hierarchies.[6] The scale and scope of the modern corporation necessitated teams of managers at the interstices of tasks and functions for the creation of added value and for the reconciliation of rival claims on corporate resources for innovation. With innovation came the management of production and the discounting of direct labour input, as capital intensity increased with each round of innovation. One consequence was the transformation of employment across society and within large firms in favour of salaried workers and away from hourly production workers.[7]

15.4 THE TWENTIETH-CENTURY CORPORATION

If we believe Shonfield, European commitment to public and private pension systems was to be found in the active economic management strategies of governments and in the public interest in dampening incipient tendencies towards economic instability. Given the fact that the Cold War was close at hand and entrenched in domestic politics, it is arguable that economic stability and the equitable distribution of income between social classes and between working and retired were vital elements underpinning post-war social stability. By this logic, expanding public and private pension systems were elements in a much larger commitment to social and political solidarity.[8] At the same time, Shonfield had an argument about the nature and management of the modern corporation. It is difficult, however, to conceptualize that argument without looking across the Atlantic.

John Kenneth Galbraith's (1967) *The New Industrial State* appeared two years after the publication of *Modern Capitalism*. His argument focused upon the increasing significance of modern corporations and the consequences of these institutions for the political economy of employment, the distribution of power and the distribution of income. Galbraith's book focused almost exclusively on the United States. But when he did mention another country, arguing that it shared similar circumstances and common corporate structures, it was the United Kingdom. Quoted a number of times were similar industry concentration ratios, the growing importance of institutional investors relative to banks and the size of dominant corporations. Galbraith might also have pointed to common legal traditions, especially as regards the formation of joint stock companies in the eighteenth and nineteenth centuries, as well as common law expectations as regards the nature and purpose of corporations that persist even now – as compared to continental Europe.[9]

Galbraith's point of departure was a set of observations comparing the modern corporation (circa 1970) with the corporation of the late-nineteenth and early-twentieth centuries. He noted that corporations were once the 'instruments' of individual financiers. By 1970, the modern corporation was owned by large numbers of dispersed owners whose individual votes on matters of corporate policy were virtually irrelevant. The separation between ownership and control first noted by Berle and Means (1933) was now complete. He noted that the corporation, once limited to just a few industrial sectors, had spread throughout industry and into many service sectors. Corporations were once a relatively unusual organizational form compared to the myriad of small enterprises that were subject to market discipline. By 1970, corporations dominated markets and controlled prices using their size, control of the production process and command of economic resources.

Having established the role and significance of the modern corporation, Galbraith suggested that being of a large size was desirable because it allowed corporate managers a significant role in setting prices, and also because size enabled corporate managers to reap economies of scale. In the first instance, he noted that there were many examples of corporations colluding to set market prices such that firms were able to plan their activities without being penalized by price volatility. In the second instance, he noted that large-scale production gave corporate managers control over unit costs, while controlling the costs of inputs and ultimately the prices charged for outputs. Most importantly, Galbraith argued that size enabled the modern corporation to manage time and space.[10] He suggested that the planning process had been extended in time by virtue of technological innovation and the scale of capital investment required to apply innovation to production processes. In effect, large size allowed corporate managers the luxury of planning both short-term and long-term rates of return across the world.

Like a number of his colleagues, Galbraith suggested that the modern corporation sought a rate of return that would satisfy shareholders while minimizing scrutiny of corporate decision-making by outsiders. By his account, there was a high premium on retained earnings: on one hand, the cost of capital from that source was nominally lower than that available in financial markets; on the other hand, avoiding stock markets enabled corporations to discount the interests of shareholders when planning for future investment over the long-term. Most importantly, Galbraith argued that the modern corporation hardly ever maximizes profit but instead maximizes growth, measured as the flow of revenue over expenditure. It does so having first satisfied the interests of shareholders and then governments whose political fortunes relied, as they still do, on the growth of domestic economies. A considerable portion of the book was devoted to justifying this model of the modern corporation against theoretical versions of the firm subject to the discipline of competitive markets.

Like Shonfield, Galbraith observed that the modern corporation employed many thousands of people. He also observed that the composition of employment was changing, such that 'white-collar' employees were increasingly important in relation to 'blue-collar' employees. Because of the significance he attached to longer-term planning consistent with the time horizons of investment and technical innovation, Galbraith suggested that the modern corporation had been taken over by a technocracy. Because of the increasing capital intensity of production, labour productivity grew rapidly and discounted demand for labour; at the same time, demand for unskilled labour was declining concurrently with increased demand for skilled production workers capable of operating at the interface between production and technological change. Labour, expressed in terms of the quantity of hours, was transformed into an issue of human capital over both the short term and over the long term, foreshadowing contemporary writers such as Florida (2002) and Scott (2008).

Galbraith suggested that expertize was necessary for the design and implementation of production whether manufactured or otherwise. Growing numbers of employees were required to have technical skills; specific knowledge related to the production process and a capacity to work in teams of related tasks and functions. Given the foresight required to plan and implement corporate strategy, and given the time horizons of investment and technical innovation, skilled employees were necessary to carry through strategies that required commitment and organization-specific knowledge (in the manner suggested by Gertler, 2001, 2004). Accordingly, there was a high premium on coordination between tasks and functions and between the units of complex organizations. Coordination required information, defined hierarchies and monitoring of those responsible for the execution of tasks and functions – thus economic performance was deemed a function of embedded knowledge.[11]

For all the significance of talent and the premium placed on coordination, the modern corporation requires mechanisms for governing conflict between tasks and functions (employees). One of the advantages of a high level of retained earnings was the opportunity to distribute those earnings down through the corporation in the form of higher wages and salaries and benefits. Conflict between different classes of employees could be managed by sharing income from higher corporate earnings. Pursuing a systematic policy of sharing benefits across tasks and functions and down the corporate hierarchy fosters control, commitment and constituency building among disparate groups and locations. This did mean, however, the spreading of benefits according to general criteria: compensation became *part* of the technocracy outside of the potentially arbitrary discretion of supervisors.

15.5 FINANCING THE THIRD INDUSTRIAL REVOLUTION

Rereading Shonfield and Galbraith is instructive. They believed that capitalism had found a settled organizational form of management and production that would last another century (or so). Notwithstanding the popular acclaim that greeted their assessment of the then-current form of capitalism, they had simply captured a point in time an evolving type of capitalism that was to dramatically change form and functions through the 1980s and 1990s. It is arguable that 'modern' capitalism was to become the object of corporate and industrial restructuring. Systems of management and compensation, such as corporate pensions, that had played important roles in buying industrial peace in the years following the Second World War were put in play in financial markets (Clark, 1993).

Representing this changing world is quite a challenge (see Baumol, 2002). Many writers have tried to date the crisis of managerial capitalism beginning with the first oil price shock, circa 1973, and the onset of a decade of macroeconomic instability. For Anglo-American economies, however, there were other forces at work coincident with the decade of stagflation. These included the rise to prominence of institutional investors, especially pension funds whose commitment to the inherited configuration of production was discounted by their fiduciary duties to beneficiaries (Hawley and Williams, 2005). Paradoxically, the post-war development of private pension benefit systems within and across major corporations had fuelled the growth of financial assets and the gathering momentum behind financial markets. Financial innovation and successive waves of mergers and acquisitions turned managerial capitalism inside and out and ultimately discounted the value of benefits as important elements in corporate management systems. This is one of the implications to be drawn from the past 30 years of asset management and financial engineering.

To provide an overview of the motive forces behind this transformation, we rely on a paper published by Michael Jensen (1993) about what he termed as the 'modern industrial revolution'. He began by arguing, 'fundamental technological, political, regulatory and economic forces are radically changing the worldwide competitive environment. We have not seen such a metamorphosis of the economic landscape since the industrial revolution of the 19th century' (Jensen, 1993: 831). He suggested that the modern industrial revolution had parallels with the Industrial Revolution of the late-nineteenth century that had profoundly affected the US and the UK (the home of the Industrial Revolution). Of the issues identified by Jensen as crucial to the new industrial revolution, two overlapping drivers were emphasized. On one side, he suggested that investment in technological innovation had driven the organizational transformation of modern corporations. The nature and structure of production systems were transformed, reducing the demand for low-skilled employment.

On the other side of the equation, the modernization of production and technological innovation prompted growth in capacity. He suggested that the 1970s and 1980s were dominated by an 'investment mania', involving the substitution of capital for labour – which inevitably carried with it changes in the unit size of production. Investment in technological innovation added greater productive capacity as many corporations and industries held-in-place plant and equipment that had been made obsolete by technological innovation. Furthermore, technological innovation in other industries changed the demand for inputs and outputs, such that industries became more economical in how they used inputs relative to the volume of outputs. In some industries, moreover, new competitors came to Anglo-American and Western European markets with very different cost configurations and technological qualities. Jensen argued that firms and industries were slow to respond to excess capacity, carrying large numbers of under-employed workers, enormous legacy costs associated with retiring or firing those workers and the prospect that, if sold, excess capacity could be used by new entrants with different cost structures.

In manufacturing industries with a significant union presence and an historical commitment to defined benefit pensions, these benefit systems became mechanisms for the early retirement of older employees. Benefits were enhanced for those short of the required age and years of service just as benefits were enhanced for workers retained in order to buy their cooperation.[12] There were three problems associated with this kind of strategy of restructuring. First, precedents were set in terms of benefits for those offered early retirement in successive rounds of restructuring. Second, management became preoccupied with the process of restructuring rather than competitive strategy and global prospects. Third, accumulating enormous numbers of early retirees in their defined benefit pension systems threatened the solvency of the corporations themselves. In a number of cases, corporate and industry-wide defined benefit pension systems took on the attributes of underfunded pay-as-you-go pension benefits (Clark, 1993).

Jensen suggested that the development of new sources of funding enabled financial institutions to focus upon the rationalization of capacity, mergers and acquisitions, and leveraged buyouts. As noted above, these financial institutions came to the market for capacity rationalization shorn of alliances with corporate elites and communities. In doing so, they began a process of pricing past commitments with respect to anticipated higher rates of return, in the context of the expected rates of return available in publicly-traded securities markets. Through the 1980s, corporate and industrial restructuring was made possible by new kinds of financial intermediaries, an experience not shared by the continental European industry. Through the 1990s and the early years of the twenty-first century, however, the costs attributed to past commitments were increasingly realized in the expected prices of traded corporate securities (Bergstresser et al., 2004). By this stage, pension benefits systems were conceptualized as financial liabilities rather than labour-management systems and were set against expected stock market prices (Orszag and Sand, 2006).

Accentuating these trends were developments in the ownership and regulation of industry and financial markets (Hansmann and Kraakman, 2004). This was most pronounced in the UK, where a number of large firms and industries were nationalized in the late 1940s and early 1950s, and were denationalized in the 1980s and 1990s. Most obviously, this included companies such as British Steel and British Telecom that claimed near-monopolies in the domestic market. When denationalized, these firms claimed a significant place in public securities markets and attracted institutional and individual investors from the UK, Europe and the rest of the world. However, they came to market as expressions of Shonfield's 'modern capitalism', rather than of Jensen's 'modern industrial revolution'. In doing so, they carried bureaucratic structures, benefit systems and pricing practices that were to be revolutionized over the next 20 years. Their financial structures were, at best, rudimentary.

Jensen (1993) suggested that the relatively slow response of modern corporations to technological change and excess capacity was due to the escalation of prior commitments, and the fact that prior commitments were constraints on structural change, rather than mechanisms for mobilizing internal constituencies to confront external threats to their survival. Financial institutions attacked the entrenchment of managers, their lack of responsiveness to shareholders and their myopia (in the context of global standards of performance, and so on). One response was to link the compensation of senior managers with external investors rather than their colleagues. By this sleight-of-hand, senior executives became a cadre of structural engineers whose responsibility it was to redesign the corporation rather than lead its adjustment to changing circumstances. The modern corporation as a 'community of interest' was attacked by its own leaders so as to introduce greater responsiveness to financial imperatives. Galbraith's technocracy was dismantled, and with it, the commitment to comprehensive benefit systems and income equality.

The deregulation of financial markets, especially in London and to a lesser extent in continental Europe, was an essential ingredient in the process of discounting the legacy costs of denationalized industries. Much has been written about financial deregulation and the subsequent growth of financial markets in London and across Europe. What is striking about the development of these markets is the fact that they owed their liquidity, in large part, to the financial assets of domestic and foreign institutional investors. The growth and development of defined benefit pension systems in UK private industry after the Second World War created a large pool of assets to be invested according to norms and conventions quite different to those that guided the management of industrial corporations over the same period of time. Institutional investors and pension funds fuelled the market for corporate control. These same institutions have since fuelled corporate and industrial restructuring in the EU single market (Clark and Wójcik, 2007).

15.6 RETHINKING CORPORATE FORM AND FUNCTIONS

In an essay devoted to reconceptualizing the theory of the firm, Zingales (2000) observed that economics and finance are preoccupied with 'traditional' firms. The firm represented in academic research was large, publicly traded, owed its origins to twentieth century industries and – though not explicitly noted as such – had a national identity and certainly a national significance, even if it traded in financial markets around the world. He sketched the most important theories of the firm, recognizing their underlying principles as well as their limits in terms of providing an adequate representation of contemporary circumstances. For example, he noted that the 'firm as a nexus of contracts' loses some of its sheen when those contracts are implicit, specific to certain sets of tasks and functions, and rely upon the continuity of relationships within the firm. If contracts are explicit and subject to renegotiation over the short-term, Zingales wondered why there would be firms at all.

Referencing Chandler (1990) and others, the archetypal firm was deemed asset rich and vertically integrated so as to exploit the available economies of scope and scale. As a consequence of being large and complex, these firms were highly structured with extensive systems of control. Most importantly, size, asset specificity and complexity implied high levels of recurrent investment so as to reproduce the firm's capital base and pay for management and coordination. For Zingales, the traditional firm sought outside investors because of the sheer volume of capital needed to reproduce the firm. Given the risks of concentrating investments in a small group of firms, investors limited their holdings in any one firm. Consequently, the agency problem became between managers in control of the corporation and the financial institutions that provided the capital to reproduce the firm. He assumed that agency problems between managers and workers had been solved by the distribution of current and expected income.

In part, Zingales's argument relied upon the juxtaposition of the model firm with the new realities of the twenty-first century. He identified four such 'realities' which are important for my argument in this section and in the following sections. These new realities should not come as a surprise to the informed reader (see Dixon, 2014). However, like Zingales, I believe that these new realities, when confronted by the twentieth-century corporation, prompted significant innovation in its form and functions such that there are important lessons to be learnt about the likely nature and distribution of income over the coming 25 years.[13]

Price Competition

One of the observations made about market competition 50 years ago was that price competition could be managed either directly through collusion, or indirectly through corporate pricing strategies that sought to converge upon and maintain a stable market price for goods and services. Over the past 30 years, however, Anglo-American governments have reinvigorated competition policy, making consumer welfare measured in terms of the real price of commodity bundles one of the litmus tests of policy effectiveness. At the same time, national markets have become increasingly subject to the discounted pricing practices of competitors located in the rest of the world. This has been apparent in North America and Europe: competitors based in cheaper jurisdictions combined with lower costs of bringing products from distant shores to market have made a substantial difference to the ability of incumbent firms to control market prices or maintain their pricing practices. This is one expression of globalization.

Another expression of globalization has been outsourcing by incumbent producers (Dicken, 2011). This involves the use of spatially elongated production networks to sustain competitiveness in home markets by matching the price structures of competitors from outside those markets (Grossman and Helpman, 2005). In effect, the slow but profound incursion of price competition into domestic markets has forced 'traditional' firms to reassess the competitiveness of every part of their inherited configuration of production. At one level, this has resulted in the horizontal segmentation of the 'traditional' firm by task and function in ways unanticipated by Shonfield, Galbraith, or even Jensen. At another level, the merits of vertical integration have come under scrutiny such that the production process has also become increasingly segmented both within and without the firm (Scott, 1983).

Market Segmentation

Just as market competition has become much more important than was previously the case, it appears that market segmentation has also accelerated. In part, market segmentation has been driven by consumers and their demand for products that are differentiated by taste and attributes of otherwise homogeneous products. Even if consumer markets are dominated by recognized branded products, for every market-leading product there are overlapping rival products designed to siphon off consumer loyalty into their own niches. Furthermore, the premium attributed to brand value is vulnerable to the introduction of related but generic products for sale at heavily discounted prices. Whereas large firms use branded products sold at a premium to manage the core value of markets, they can also produce generic products sold at a discount into market segments that would otherwise be served by rivals. This has been made possible by the fact that the optimal scale of production has been declining and sites of production have been relocating to cheaper sites than those available in Western countries.

Product and Process Innovation

By this logic, markets are increasingly unstable in the sense that consumer attachment to the market-leading products of the largest firms is more uncertain than ever before. One consequence has been that large firms cannot stand still – not only must they develop a broad array of products that are able to compete across segments of Western consumer markets, they must do so in ways that allow for differential pricing for more or less cost conscious consumers. It has proven difficult for single-site production facilities to accommodate this diversity and, in particular, to accommodate the variable market pricing profiles, given stable and homogeneous compensation practices. Another consequence has been heavy investment in maintaining the design qualities of premium-priced consumer products, as well as heavy investment in maintaining the quality of production process consistent with the price charged to consumers.

This kind of investment requires human capital as much as it requires tangible assets such as plant and equipment. Moreover, human capital comes at a price, resistant to the conventional systems of control through the hierarchies of tasks and functions that characterized the corporation 40 years previously. Not only is rent-seeking common in these circumstances, but also different types of compensation, like stock options, have come to rival conventional forms of compensation such as wages and salaries. At the other end of the spectrum, however, the only way to discount the price of generic products is to discount the price of the embodied labour. Inevitably, segmentation (dividing the corporation within and without) is one way senior executives are able to retain control over the flow of reported earnings against capital market expectations.

Capital Market Options and Prospects

One of the advantages of conglomerates built upon different businesses and production processes was the opportunity to use excess revenue from one side of the business to sustain investment and growth opportunities in other parts of the business. This enabled large firms to discount the cost of capital relative to the price charged by capital markets, while holding at bay the scrutiny of financial analysts. Of course, in companies that nevertheless require enormous volumes of tangible assets, access to capital markets is a crucial means of sustaining successive rounds of investment. However, over the past 20 years or so new kinds of financial intermediaries – including private equity investors – have developed. These are at once more specialized in terms of their expertise and are more willing to take positions in highly leveraged firms without immediately seeking an exit to capital markets.

One consequence of these developments has been the proliferation of spin-out firms from large corporations led by entrepreneurs with an eye towards exploiting a niche or opportunity in consumer markets that is often at odds with the interests of large firms. Another consequence has been the realization that innovation is sometimes best developed outside the walls of large corporations. At the limit, the traditional corporation has become an 'incubator' for ideas that rely upon the interaction between tangible assets and human capital, providing the milieu for interaction, if not the milieu for development of innovations through to their capitalization in the market.

Responsiveness to financial market imperatives has become the litmus test of senior executives in a world where managing expectations for current and future flow of revenue has enormous implications for volatility of stock prices. But the challenges facing the modern corporation are more profound than market expectations; at issue is whether the focus on mechanisms governing the distribution of income is consistent with promoting the long-term growth of the modern corporation. It is doubtful whether being listed on publicly traded financial markets is consistent with responding to the market imperatives transforming twenty-first century capitalism.

15.7 CORPORATE FORM, COMPENSATION AND GLOBALIZATION

The lessons to be learnt from the previous discussion are twofold: the modern corporation is neither a constant, nor is it necessarily a homogeneous organization. The challenge is to design and implement compensation systems that are consistent with survival and growth of the modern corporation, recognizing that its form and functions are becoming ever more differentiated. To illustrate this argument, let us work through a set of four models of the modern corporation and their implications for the nature and value of corporate compensation. As we shall see, there are winners *and* losers in the new world of the modern corporation (compare Weil, 2014).

Consider Firm A, a large market-leading corporation with two types of assets: those which are tangible, including plant and equipment, and those which are intangible such as a portfolio of brand-name products and an enviable corporate reputation (Clark and Hebb, 2005). Assume that Firm A has been around for many years having dominated its home market before spreading its wings into the rest of the world. Also assume that Firm A was known as a progressive firm in providing its employees with a wide range of benefits whatever their tasks or functions. Yet now, consider some points of contention: with the momentum behind the market for corporate control, senior managers took up stock options as part of their compensation packages; the management of brand-name products moved from the traditional home of the corporation to London and New York, and into very different labour markets for talent; and new production technologies radically increased productivity while decreasing the demand for skilled labour.

Having sponsored a well-funded pension system, Firm A introduces early-retirement pension benefits to encourage home-based product managers and blue-collar employees to retire rather than be permanently laid off. There could be three effects from this strategic move. First, the internal market for pension benefits shrinks as home-based tasks and functions are rationalized; second, the market for pensions shrinks as tasks and functions move to external service providers in other labour markets, characterized by higher turnover and defined contribution or personal pension plans; third, the national 'market' shrinks for certain financial services as other forms of compensation become more attractive – particularly for senior managers who no longer expect to remain with the firm or industry for their careers. Within a decade, the ratio of active to deferred and retired plan participants dramatically declines, with a funding problem compounded by lower-than-expected returns in securities markets (Clark and Monk, 2017).

To complicate the picture, consider Firm B, a rival to Firm A. Firm B also has tangible assets and intangible assets – however, the former do not include plant and equipment, but rather large outlet stores; the latter are not branded products but include its reputation for generic products at highly competitive prices. Firm B produces its products by contract, relying upon an extensive network of suppliers that are governed according to specific performance criteria of price and quality. Renewal of contract is dependent upon continuous improvement in quality and continuous discounting in the price to Firm B. As for the management of its reputation, Firm B outsources the supply of those services and, as Firm A does, draws on talent from London and New York. The value of the firm, according to industry analysts, is its reputation for price and quality across a wide range of generic products that firms like A produce. Indeed, walking down the aisles of Firm B's outlets, the consumer is likely to come across generic products with packages that look very similar to the packages of Firm A's products sold at twice the price.

Firm B leaves to its product providers issues of compensation. However, given the premium placed by Firm B on lower costs, B's suppliers face a trade-off between investment and wages and benefits. This is resolved, in almost all cases, in favour of the former such that suppliers seek sites of production that are relatively cost-effective and carry with them little in the way of long-term commitments to wages and benefits. To the extent that these suppliers do offer pension benefits, most offer benefits based upon employee contributions rather than employer contributions. Likewise, in its giant distribution centres, Firm B employs predominantly part-time workers, many of who are women and many of who have no long-term commitment to the firm. Few are eligible for participation in the company's benefit systems. At the senior level, managers participate in incentive-based compensation schemes that include highly lucrative termination benefits. Indeed, over time, senior executive benefits offered to both Firm A and Firm B employees begin to converge.

Firm B's strategies have numerous implications for the nature and value of offered benefits. Defined benefit (DB) plans hardly exist, except in some suppliers by virtue of inherited firm-specific and, perhaps, union-specific productivity agreements. At the limit, the costs of managing such schemes may be so prohibitive, relative to the continuous pressure to improve quality and discount costs, that even the unions involved agree to close DB schemes in favour of more limited defined contribution (DC) schemes. More importantly, Firm B has no incentive to offer any benefits to its thousands of relatively unskilled employees. While turnover may be a problem, affecting the quality of in-store consumer responsiveness, it is not so significant that benefits need be offered to hold employees in place for more than a couple of years at a time. In any event, if offered, the rate of employee pension contributions is likely to be low relative to that required to ensure an adequate retirement income (Clark et al., 2012). Few employees deem these benefits valuable; recognizing this, unions use low wages – but not the lack of benefits – as a weapon in their attempts to unionize Firm B's workforce.

To complicate matters further, imagine that a new Firm C enters the market. This firm is rather different to Firms A and B in that it is privately owned, being a partnership between a group of private equity investors and senior executives from Firm A who left to create Firm C. For simplicity's sake, we shall assume that this company was formed to take advantage of the gap in the market between Firms A and B, as neither is focused on new products. Firm C's products are designed to latch on to emerging tastes and fashions otherwise ignored by existing branded products and unfulfilled by generic products. Given the premium attached to taste and fashion, neither the price of the product nor the costs of production are essential to Firm C's claims in the marketplace. Rather, its place in the market depends upon continuous innovation of the nature, design and image of products.

Here, then, is the hard-case. What kinds of compensation and benefit systems are consistent with the interests of Firm C's principals?[14] In the first instance, it would seem that human capital is the cornerstone of Firm C's competitiveness between Firms A and B. In buying the market knowledge and quality control experience of Firm A's senior executives, investors place bets on the capacity of those executives to conceive of and implement a competitive strategy that cannot be replicated by large competitors. The time horizon for such a bet is longer than many public capital market investors would accept, but a series of sign-posts indicating positive progress could result in investors being carried through to an IPO. To get that far, however, requires a governance regime and a set of incentives integrating the short-term with the long-term between the partners and within the firm.

There are a variety of options. For example, firms could offer a standard defined contribution pension to all employees regardless of status. This would have the advantage of treating all employees as equal whatever their tasks and functions, thereby building solidarity and commitment around teams of individuals who are committed to the long-term growth of the firm. Of course, the success of Firm C is open to question; a defined contribution pension plan with an external service provider may provide an exit option for individuals who are unwilling to carry the risk of the firm's success in terms of their long-term retirement income. Given the contingent nature of funding, it is unlikely that Firm C would match individual contributions to the DC scheme. But the firm could hold out the promise of significant wealth through stock options should the company succeed and be floated through an IPO (Teece, 2000). Employees are required to trade off short-term insecurity with the prospect of wealth in the medium-term. If Firm C was an IPO success, one way of integrating a DC scheme with the accumulated growth of the firm would be for Firm C to make contributions to employee pension plans using company stock.[15]

Finally, there is Firm D. It comes to market from another country that has neither private benefit schemes nor well-developed, comprehensive social security entitlements. Its costs of production are a fraction of incumbent firms, although it has access to the most recent generation of production technologies that dominate the industry. It is able to enter the market, in the first instance, through Firm B's supply chain. However, once established, Firm A recognizes opportunities to outsource component manufacturing of brand-name products, and Firm C gambles on a relationship with Firm D in order to cover short-term limitations in its own capacity (Coe et al., 2008). The unit of income insurance, in this case, is neither the firm nor the state. It is the family, the village or the lifetime opportunities of urban life.

15.8 PENSION FUND CAPITALISM (REPRISED)

I have argued that pension fund capitalism as a set of corporate labour-related management practices is in decline. Throughout, I have sought to show that the initial conditions underpinning growth and development of comprehensive corporate benefit systems have been eroded by a combination of changing market conditions, as well as changes in the form and function of corporations themselves. In this context, DB pension systems and even DC systems are at best irrelevant to the corporations we might otherwise imagine committed to the provision of long-term income. At worst, these systems are antithetical to the current and future performance of corporations in highly contested markets. By this logic, pension fund capitalism is the legacy of a bygone era when corporations dominated markets and managed labour resources in ways that are unimaginable today.

Pension fund capitalism is, nonetheless, an ever-present fact of life, a dominant force in Anglo-American and global financial markets. The financial institutions of pension fund capitalism exercise a significant degree of power and control over the market price of traded corporations and the careers of senior executives. This was barely thought possible 50 years ago, except by those knowledgeable of the competition for power and control in the modern corporation (see Shonfield, 1965 and Drucker, 1976, and compare Roe, 1994). Even as firms have closed pension systems and introduced other forms of compensation, these same corporations had been held to account by the institutions and agents representing pension plan participants. Moreover, as the public sector has become the last bastion for DB pension systems, some of the most active institutional investors in the market for corporate control and the regulation of senior executives' perquisites have come from public sector pension systems with boards of trustees including union and member-nominated representatives. By this account, pension fund capitalism is alive and well in financial markets.

It has become commonplace to acknowledge the significance of institutional investors and their pension fund clients in publicly traded securities markets. In some countries, notably the UK, pension funds allocate the majority of assets to domestic and international equities, affecting the depth of liquidity of public markets and their relative efficiency. The nature and shape of domestic and global stock markets owes a great deal to the enormous growth of pension fund assets over the past 50 years in countries that have had a significant commitment to funded pension systems. This has been described by numerous authors: some have documented the rise of new kinds of financial institutions and intermediaries (Davis and Steil, 2001), some have focused upon the development of innovative financial products and instruments (Clowes, 2000) and some have emphasized the role of these institutional investors in driving the performance of financial markets, for good and for bad (Shiller, 2000, 2002). It is clear that financial markets dominated by institutional investors and their pension fund clients have had significant effects on the growth and development of their national economies.

Whereas Anglo-American institutional investors have focused upon short-term rates of return relative to widely accepted benchmarks, traditional investors in continental European markets have been less concerned with short-term performance than long-term performance. The former trade in and out of company securities according to short-term investment objectives, whereas the latter tend not to trade securities but rather affect corporate strategy and ultimately long-term rates of return, by virtue of their voice on supervisory boards. In recent years, as Anglo-American pension funds have sought higher rates of return in other financial markets, portfolio managers have become more aggressive in seeking to affect the form and function of the corporations themselves. Furthermore, as these investors have made incursions into previously stable and settled financial relationships, long-term investors have also begun to change their investment strategies to take advantage of the developments initiated by Anglo-American institutional investors. By this logic, pension fund capitalism as a set of financial institutions, principles and practices, has been exported to the rest of the world (see Clark and Wójcik, 2007).

Institutional investors and their pension fund clients rely upon the principles of modern portfolio theory, including the diversification of investment portfolios. As a consequence, few such investors would take a controlling stake in publicly traded companies; ownership is incredibly diffuse. Nonetheless, over the past 20 years, institutional investors have begun to use even small stakes in large corporations to lobby senior executives in public and not so public ways, so as to affect corporate competitive strategy and corporate responsibilities. Elsewhere, we refer to this development as the fifth stage of capitalism: an era of active engagement with corporate management by institutional investors with respect to a range of issues and policies – some of which are intimately related to corporate economic performance and some of which are more related to corporate reputation (Clark and Hebb, 2004). The strategy of engagement varies by institution and by country: some of the largest US public-sector pension funds deliberately use public forums to voice their concerns, whereas in the UK, lobbying efforts may not be disclosed to the public at large at any point. Pension fund engagement of corporate management is an exercise in prompting entrenched managers to be responsive to investor concerns, especially in circumstances where investors are unable to divest their (relatively low) stakes (Bauer et al., 2014).[16]

At one level, it might be contended that public sector pension funds that engage corporate executives do so for political reasons, such as the enhancement of corporate behaviour with respect to social, labour and environmental standards at home and abroad. But in many respects what might appear to be political interests at work in affecting corporate management are more plausibly interpreted as a commitment to enhancing corporate economic performance in circumstances where intangible assets like brand image and reputation affect the market price of the firms concerned. In these circumstances, pension fund corporate engagement is a contest for power involving legitimate claims by corporate executives for the right to pursue approved competitive strategies, set against the legitimate claims of institutional investors for recognition where competitive strategies are believed to be antithetical to investor interests. It is simultaneously a contest for corporate value, involving the interests of corporate executives set against the expectations of institutional investors as regards the likely market value of the firm. Large corporate pension funds hardly ever become involved in contests for power and value in other firms.

15.9 IMPLICATIONS AND CONCLUSIONS

Twentieth-century pension fund capitalism was a remarkable combination of large public and private institutions bound together in a shared commitment to certain standards of retirement income and a mechanism for funding future income through the investment of deferred wages and salaries of employees. Looking back over the past 50 years, the enormous growth in financial assets can be explained by the nature of pension benefits, the commitment to the forward-funding of those benefits, the diffusion of these benefit systems into small and medium enterprises and the growth of employment. It was an era characterized by some as the golden age of capitalism (Webber and Rigby, 1996).

Shonfield and Galbraith thought they had captured the essence of 'modern capitalism'. They had, in fact, caught it at a moment in time and space. Their large corporations were assumed to be bound together with the nation-state, but were about to disassemble for different reasons. The past 25 years have seen dramatic changes in the fortunes of large corporations, being turned inside and out by technological change and market competition driven by forces outside their control. Changing consumer tastes and habits, technological change and globalization have separately and together put enormous pressures on the nature and value of offered corporate benefits. It is not surprising the integration of large firms has given way to greater differentiation in internal tasks and functions; this kind of differentiation discounts homogeneous corporate compensation practices (Roberts, 2004).

As a consequence, large and small corporations have introduced various kinds of contingent compensation systems that put a premium on short-term employee job performance rather than employee loyalty to the company. As internal and external labour markets have become increasingly differentiated with respect to expertise and skills, at home and abroad, so too have companies sought to vary the mix of total compensation, paying particular regard to wages and salaries, bonuses, productivity enhancements and savings instruments. While there remain significant barriers to the individualization of compensation in many countries, the shift from DB to DC pension savings schemes has effectively 'individualized' three decisions as regards long-term retirement saving: whether to join or remain with such a scheme, how much to contribute and how to invest the accumulated assets in individual retirement accounts. By contrast, in Shonfield and Galbraith's world, these decisions were taken on behalf of employees by employers and/or by employers and union representatives in collective-bargaining agreements.

In fact, whereas DB pensions were conceptualized as a reward for long-term commitment to the employer, DC pensions and related savings instruments can be conceptualized as rewards for job performance as indicated by employee's month-to-month, quarter-to-quarter and year-to-year account balances. Just as importantly, DB pensions are paid by the employer as a discounted income stream upon retirement whereas, in some instances and in some countries, the individualization of retirement savings accounts means that the individuals concerned have responsibility for translating their accumulated assets into a long-term income. On the DB side, the employer takes responsibility thereby fulfilling an obligation – whether implicit or explicit – in the employment contract that binds the employee and the employer together over the long term. On the DC side, however, the employer has no responsibility, other than that imposed by regulatory agencies, to ensure that employees' savings decisions are not compromised by employer agreements with service providers that could compromise employees' abilities to make effective financial decisions.

More generally, the transition from DB to DC and related savings instruments has transformed the employee (Langley, 2008). He or she is no longer someone who earns long-term savings credits that are paid in retirement as an income, just as income was paid when he or she was an employee. Instead, they are now an 'investor', responsible for the accumulation of an investment fund and also responsible for the investment of those assets through to retirement and beyond (Preda, 2009). The distinction here is between being a saver and an investor, a distinction fostered by the financial services industry which is segmented into different types of institutions. Banks provide savings products which promise a certain rate of return on a minimum volume of deposits; others such as asset managers provide investment products in the guise of savings products. By convention, it is assumed that saving is risk-free, whereas investing is subject to market risk and uncertainty (Clark et al., 2012). If plausible in the circumstances of financial stability and prudential regulation, it is apparent that financial deregulation and the concentration of the financial services industry effectively blurred this distinction. Knowingly or unknowingly savers became investors and investors are not always savers.

Fundamental to the individualization of compensation and the investment of retirement savings, is the assumption that individuals are well placed to take on these responsibilities. In the vernacular of conventional economic theory, it is assumed that individuals are rational agents, are fully informed about the nature and scope of their responsibilities and able to realize their retirement objectives through investment decisions that are sensitive to, and can adapt to, market risk and uncertainty. So much has been written about this theory of individual behaviour that it is pointless, at this stage, to rehearse the logic and assumptions underpinning the argument. It is more important to recognize that the rise to hegemony of this claim about the nature of individual decision-making over the past 50 years was very helpful in discounting of the roles and responsibilities of companies to their employees. Just as companies found it very difficult to maintain unified and comprehensive compensation systems in the face of economic imperatives, the idealization of individual sovereignty effectively undercut legislation and regulation that would have held the private sector to such commitments.

The significance of individual sovereignty in many developed economies has been widely documented and discussed. For some, it is a matter of ideology and the formation of a hegemonic discourse around the notion of neoliberalism. For others, less convinced about the power and significance of a 'universal' conception of society and economy when confronting specific political and social formations (Weller and O'Neill, 2014), the individualization of income and employment in many developed economies is nonetheless important and requires explanation. This is a vibrant research theme in many disciplines, combining an interest in the structural transformation of capitalist economies with an appreciation of the emerging importance of human capital in explaining the economic and social differentiation of the landscape (Scott, 2008). As such, this chapter is a contribution to that research programme, in that I have sought to explain the differentiation of employment practices and hence the individualization of income and future well-being in terms of the transformation of the modern corporation.

Equally important, however, is the larger question about the nature of individual decision-making. Whereas conventional economic theory carried the day for much of the second half of the twentieth century, the behavioural revolution inspired by Simon (1956) and Kahneman and Tversky (1979), amongst others, has provided both a fundamental critique of rational agent model and has provided the building blocks for a research programme which is less about rationality and/or irrationality and more about the nature and scope of individual behaviour in the context of market risk and uncertainty. This logic is as much applicable to how we should understand organization behaviour as it is applicable to individual behaviour in time and space (Clark 2014). Recognition of the significance of context for understanding institutional formation and evolution as well as individual behaviour is one of the key building blocks of this research programme, demanding a more nuanced understanding of time and space than that which is found in standard critiques of financialization.

ACKNOWLEDGEMENTS

This chapter is taken from a paper which was sponsored by the French government's Ministère des Solidarités de la Santé et de la Famille. I am grateful for the interest and advice of Michele Lelièvre and Najat El Mekkaoui de Freitas in relation to the project. It bears the imprint of conversations with a number of colleagues including Tessa Hebb, Ashby Monk and Teresa Ghilarducci. Research assistance was provided by Yu-Wei Hu and help on data sources was provided by the UK government Actuary, Office of National Statistics, the Institute of Fiscal Studies, the Pensions Policy Institute and the US Employee Benefits Research Institute. Alice Chautard, Amanda Diener and Sarah-Jane Littleford helped with the preparation of this manuscript and related material. None of the above should be held responsible for any errors or omissions or for that matter my opinions contained herein.

NOTES

1. There is a veritable industry in critical theory that disputes the terms modern, modernity and post-modernism, referencing their cultural and political significance when considered over a century or so (Eagleton, 1996). Here, I simply use the term in relation to contemporary analysts and commentators recognizing that each generation probably think of themselves as 'modern', in the sense of being a development of the past with their own institutions and practices.
2. See Hawley and Williams (2000) on the idea (and practice) of the 'universal investor', and their notional responsibilities for the efficiency and standards of capital markets at home and abroad.
3. Shonfield's views about the management of the economy were representative of the success in the UK of the Keynesian revolution and the less secure status of Keynes's prescription for macroeconomic policy in the US. Difference in status can be attributed to the emerging hegemony of a new generation of US economic theorists transfixed by Walrasian general equilibrium theory and the greater involvement of leading UK economists with the practicalities of Treasury policymaking. The tensions between UK and US economists on this issue are played out in a set of papers and discussions in Worswick and Trevithick (1983).
4. The stability and growth prospects of the 'mixed economy' were widely debated in the late 1970s and early 1980s. Samuelson (1983: 215) believed that, 'the mixed economy was sick' and that its problems (including wage and price inflation with increasing unemployment) could be attributed to the inflexibility of inherited institutions. Samuelson noted, 'stagflation is a basic feature of the humane welfare state that replaced ruthless capitalism. It changes drastically the behavioural equations of the modern macro world'.
5. For example, Shonfield stressed the positive contribution of increasing volumes of European and global trade to the performance and stability of the UK economy. In circumstances where full employment threatened price stability, imports of finished and raw materials dispersed the effects of increased demand, while contributing to the welfare of Europe (and elsewhere) as a whole.
6. One reflection of the managerial transformation of the corporation was to be found in subsequent academic debate over the 1980s and 1990s, about the relative merits of markets and hierarchies for firm-specific and economy-wide economic efficiency (as indicated by the success of Williamson's 1975 transaction cost economics and its incorporation into economic geography see Scott, 1983).
7. Notwithstanding the logic of Shonfield's argument, it is apparent that 'old' model of work and employment persisted alongside of the new realities of dominant corporations. So, for example, Hayek's (1937) depiction of the small-scale, segmented work practices characteristic of building and construction remained relevant throughout the post-war era prompting governments to become concerned about the fate of these types of workers not eligible for workplace pensions and reliant upon a very basic state pension.
8. If rarely considered in Anglo-American economies, social solidarity remains an important reference point for pension and welfare policy in many continental European countries (see van De Deken et al., 2006). While disputed by those who do not share its social democratic ideals, and even if it is subject to discounting by the largest European global corporations, any solution to current problems of funding social insurance obligations must find a way of addressing the issue of solidarity (Clark, 2003).

9. This is, of course, a large topic. For recent research mapping the distribution of various legal traditions with relevance to finance and corporate form see La Porta et al. (1997, 1999).
10. Research by Schoenberger (1997, 2000), amongst others, suggests that large corporations found it hard to conceptualize and execute such grand visions, particularly in situations where the lack of a common internal culture combined with poorly conceived incentives and bureaucratic procedures have paralysed decision-making. Even so, I would suggest along with Galbraith and others that size gave corporate managers the *opportunity* to plan in a systematic and global fashion. There is, of course, a vast difference between recognizing an opportunity and realizing its advantages.
11. This remains the mantra of many industrial sociologists and economic geographers (see Grabher, 1993). In a global economy, there may be some jurisdictions with firms able and willing to persist with this organizational logic, especially if the firm is vertically and horizontally segmented by form and function.
12. In this section, I cannot do justice to the complexity of negotiations involved in the rationalization of US and UK industry over this period. See Blackburn (2003) on the UK and Ghilarducci (2006) for a broad perspective on the interaction between unions, pensions and management in the US. Jensen (2003) was largely antagonistic to the idea of 'negotiating' with stakeholders over the changing form and function of the modern corporation.
13. The distinctions drawn here between the twentieth-century corporation and its current form are widely discussed across the social sciences. Some analysts distinguish between Fordism and post-Fordism, some emphasize mass production as opposed to flexible accumulation and others refer to globalization. Along these lines, Roberts (2004: Chapter 2, Tables 1 and 2, 48–49) provides a useful summary of the differences between mass production and modern manufacturing.
14. The issue is motivation: how can employer-sponsored pension systems play a role in motivating specific classes of employees, while rewarding them according to their respective contributions to short-term and long-term corporate performance? Fifty years ago, this was an important element in the design of company-sponsored pension schemes – but was washed out by virtue of public policy commitments. Even so, according to Roberts (2004), motivation remains a crucial organizing principle for corporate performance and growth.
15. This kind of benefit policy and funding strategy may not be in the best interests of plan participants. By agreeing to company stocks as the company contribution in place of money invested in a diversified portfolio, should Firm C fail, employees would be exposed to the risks of default twice-over. This may be entirely consistent with corporate strategy – but may be antithetical to the public interest in protecting benefits from current exigencies (Benartzi et al., 2004).
16. It should be noted that there are significant differences between jurisdictions in the status attributed to corporate managers as opposed to shareholders, especially as regards the rights of the former to carry through their plans unimpeded by the scrutiny of the latter. Bebchuk (2005) developed this point comparing the relative insulation of US corporate managers compared to UK corporate managers from institutional investors. He argued, in fact, that US corporate governance procedures that insulate corporate executives are imperfect, and that 'increased shareholder power would be desirable' in relation to improved 'corporate performance and value' (Bebchuk, 2005: 842–843).

REFERENCES

Bauer, R., G.L. Clark and M. Viehs (2014), 'The geography of shareholder engagement: evidence from a large British institutional investor'. Retrieved on 4 November 2014 from http://papers.ssrn.com/sol3 /papers.cfm?abstract_id=2261649.

Baumol, W.J. (2002), *The Free-Market Innovation Machine: Analysing the Growth Miracle of Capitalism*, Princeton, NJ: Princeton University Press.

Bebchuk, L.A. (2005), 'The case for increasing shareholder power', *Harvard Law Review*, 118: 833–914.

Benartzi, S., R.H. Thaler, S.P. Utkas and C.R. Sunstein (2004), 'Company stock, market rationality and legal reform', University of Chicago Law & Economics, Olin Working Paper No. 218. Retrieved on 4 November 2014 from http://papers.ssrn.com/sol3/papers. cfm?abstract_id=573504.

Bergstresser, D., M. Desai and J. Rauh (2004), 'Earnings manipulation and managerial investment decisions: evidence from sponsored pension plans', Working Paper 10543, Cambridge, MA: National Bureau of Economic Research.

Berle, A.A. and G.G.C. Means (1933), *The Modern Corporation and Private Property*, New York: Harcourt, Brace and World.

Blackburn, R. (2003), *Banking on Death: Or, Investing in Life: The History and Future of Pensions*, London: Verso.

Boyer, R. (2000), 'Is a finance-led growth regime a viable alternative to Fordism? A preliminary analysis', *Economy and Society*, **29** (1), 111–145.
Chandler, A.D. (1990), *Scale and Scope: The Dynamics of Industrial Capitalism*, Cambridge, MA: Harvard University Press.
Clark, G.L. (1993), *Pensions and Corporate Restructuring in American Industry: A Crisis of Regulation*, Baltimore, MD: Johns Hopkins University Press.
Clark, G.L. (2000), *Pension Fund Capitalism*, Oxford: Oxford University Press.
Clark, G.L. (2003), *European Pensions and Global Finance*, Oxford: Oxford University Press.
Clark, G.L. (2012), 'From corporatism to public utilities: workplace pensions in the 21st century', *Geographical Research*, **50**, 31–46.
Clark, G.L. (2014), 'Roepke lecture in economic geography – financial literacy in context', *Economic Geography*, **90** (1), 1–23.
Clark, G.L. and T. Hebb (2004), 'Pension fund corporate engagement: the fifth stage of capitalism', *Relations Industrielles/Industrial Relations*, **59**, 142–171.
Clark, G.L. and T. Hebb (2005), 'Why should they care? The role of institutional investors in the market for corporate global standards', *Environment and Planning A*, **37** (11), 2015–2031.
Clark, G.L. and Monk, A.H.B. (2017), *Institutional Investors in Global Markets*, Oxford: Oxford University Press
Clark, G.L. and D. Wójcik (2007), *The Geography of Finance: Corporate Governance in the Global Marketplace*, Oxford: Oxford University Press.
Clark, G.L., S. Christopherson and J. Whiteman (2015), 'The euro crisis and the future of Europe', *Journal of Economic Geography*, **15** (5), 843–844.
Clark, G.L., K. Strauss and J. Knox-Hayes (2012), *Saving for Retirement: Intention, Context and Behaviour*, Oxford: Oxford University Press.
Clowes, M.J. (2000), *The Money Flood: How Pension Funds Revolutionized Investing*, New York: Wiley.
Coe, N.M., P. Dicken and M. Hess (2008), 'Global production networks: realizing the potential', *Journal of Economic Geography*, **8**, 271–295.
Davis, E.P. and B. Steil (2001), *Institutional Investors*, Cambridge MA: MIT Press.
Dicken, P. (2011), *Global Shift*, London: Sage.
Dixon, A.D. (2008), 'The rise of pension fund capitalism in Europe: An unseen revolution?', *New Political Economy*, **13** (3), 249–270.
Dixon, A.D. (2012), 'Function before form: Macro-institutional comparison and the geography of finance', *Journal of Economic Geography*, **12** (3), 579–600.
Dixon, A.D. (2014), *The New Geography of Capitalism: Firms, Finance, and Society*, Oxford: Oxford University Press.
Dore, R. (2000), *Stock Market Capitalism: Welfare Capitalism: Japan and Germany versus the Anglo-Saxons*, Oxford: Oxford University Press.
Drucker, P.F. (1976), *The Unseen Revolution: How Pension Fund Socialism Came to America*, London: Heinemann.
Eagleton, T. (1996), *The Illusions of Postmodernism*, Oxford: Blackwell.
Esping-Anderson, G. (1999), *Social Foundations of Postindustrial Economies*, Oxford: Oxford University Press.
Florida, R. (2002), *The Rise of the Creative Class*, New York: Basic Books.
Froud, J., S. Johal, A. Leaver and K. Williams (2006), *Financialization and Strategy: Narrative and Numbers*, London: Routledge.
Galbraith, J.K. (1967), *The New Industrial State*, London: Andre Deutsch.
Gertler, M.S. (2001), 'Best practice? Geography, learning and the institutional limits to strong convergence', *Journal of Economic Geography*, **1** (1), 5–26.
Gertler, M.S. (2004), *Manufacturing Culture: The Institutional Geography of Industrial Practice*, Oxford: Oxford University Press.
Ghilarducci, T. (1992), *Labor's Capital: The Economics and Politics of Private Pensions*, Cambridge, MA: MIT Press.
Ghilarducci, T. (2006), 'Organized labor and pensions', in G.L. Clark, A. Munnell and M. Orszag (eds), *The Oxford Handbook of Pensions and Retirement Income*, Oxford: Oxford University Press, pp. 381–398.
Grabher, G. (ed.) (1993), *The Embedded Firm: On the Socio-economics of Industrial Networks*, London: Routledge.
Grossman, G.M. and E. Helpman (2005), 'Outsourcing in a global economy', *Review of Economic Studies*, **72** (1), 135–159.
Hall, P.A. and D. Soskice (eds) (2001), *Varieties of Capitalism: The Institutional Foundations of Comparative Advantage*, Oxford: Oxford University Press.
Hansmann, H. and R. Kraakman (2004), 'The end of history for corporate law', in J.N. Gordon and M.J. Roe

(eds), *Convergence and Persistence in Corporate Governance*, Cambridge: Cambridge University Press, pp. 33–68.
Hawley, J.P. and A.T. Williams (2000), *The Rise of Fiduciary Capitalism: How Institutional Investors Can Make Corporate America More Democratic*, Philadelphia: University of Pennsylvania Press.
Hawley, J.P. and A.T. Williams (2005), 'Shifting ground: global corporate governance standards and the rise of fiduciary capitalism', *Environment and Planning A*, **37** (11), 1995–2013.
Hayek, F.A. (1937), 'Economics and knowledge', *Economica*, **4** (13), 33–54.
Hebb, T. (2006), 'The economic inefficiency of secrecy: pension fund investors' transparency concerns', *Journal of Business Ethics*, **63** (4), 385–405.
Hebb, T. and D. Wójcik (2005), 'Global standards and emerging markets: the institutional investment value chain and the CalPERS' investment strategy', *Environment and Planning A*, **37** (11), 1955–1974.
Jameson, F. (1997), 'Culture and finance capital', *Critical Inquiry*, **24**, 246–265.
Jensen, M.C. (1993), 'The modern industrial revolution, exit, and the failure of internal control systems', *Journal of Finance*, **48** (3), 831–880.
Jensen, M.C. (2003), *A Theory of the Firm: Governance, Residual Claims, and Organizational Forms*, Cambridge, MA: Harvard University Press.
Kahneman, D. and A. Tversky (1979), 'Prospect theory: An analysis of decision under risk', *Econometrica*, **47** (2), 263–291.
La Porta, R., F. Lopez-de-Silanes and A. Shleifer (1999), 'Corporate ownership around the world', *Journal of Finance*, **54** (2), 471–518.
La Porta, R., F. Lopez-de-Silanes, A. Shleifer and R.W. Vishny (1997), 'Legal determinants of external finance', *Journal of Finance*, **52** (3), 1131–1150.
Langley, P. (2008), *The Everyday Life of Global Finance: Saving and Borrowing in Anglo-America*, Oxford: Oxford University Press.
Lucas, R.E. (2009), 'Ideas and growth', *Economica*, **76** (301), 1–19.
McDowell, L., A. Batnitzky and S. Dyer (2008), 'Internationalization and the spaces of temporary labour: the global assembly of a local workforce', *British Journal of Industrial Relations*, **46**, 750–770.
McDowell, L., A. Batnitzky and S. Dyer (2009), 'Precarious work and economic migration: emerging immigrant divisions of labour in Greater London's service sector', *International Journal of Urban and Regional Research*, **33**, 3–25.
Orszag, M. and N. Sand (2006), 'Corporate finance and capital markets', in G.L. Clark, A. Munnell and M. Orszag (eds), *The Oxford Handbook of Pensions and Retirement Income*, Oxford: Oxford University Press, pp. 399–414.
Piketty, T. (2014), *Capital in the 21st Century*, Cambridge, MA: Harvard University Press.
Preda, A. (2009), *Framing Finance: The Boundaries of Markets and Modern Capitalism*, Chicago, IL: University of Chicago Press.
Roberts, J. (2004), *The Modern Firm: Organizational Design for Performance and Growth*, Oxford: Oxford University Press.
Roe, M.J. (1994), *Strong Managers, Weak Owners: The Political Roots of American Corporate Finance*, Princeton, NJ: Princeton University Press.
Rosen, S. (1981), 'The economics of superstars', *American Economic Review*, **71** (5), 845–858.
Rosen, S. (1986), 'Prizes and incentives in elimination tournaments', *American Economic Review*, **76**, 701–715.
Samuelson, P.A. (1983), 'Comment', in G.D.N. Worswick and J.A. Trevithick (eds), *Keynes and the Modern World: Proceedings of the Keynes Centenary Conference*, Cambridge: Cambridge University Press, pp. 212–217.
Sass, S.A. (1997), *The Promise of Private Pensions*, Cambridge, MA: Harvard University Press.
Schoenberger, E. (1997), *The Cultural Crisis of the Firm*, Oxford: Blackwell.
Schoenberger, E. (2000), 'The management of time and space', in G.L. Clark, M. Feldman and M.S. Gertler (eds), *The Oxford Handbook of Economic Geography*, Oxford: Oxford University Press, pp. 317–332.
Scott, A.J. (1983), 'Industrial organization and the logic of intra-metropolitan location: I. Theoretical considerations', *Economic Geography*, **59** (3), 233–250.
Scott, A.J. (2008), *Social Economy of the Metropolis: Cognitive-Cultural Capitalism and the Global Resurgence of Cities*, Oxford: Oxford University Press.
Shiller, R.J. (2000), *Irrational Exuberance*, Princeton, NJ: Princeton University Press.
Shiller, R.J. (2002), 'Bubbles, human judgement, and expert opinion', *Financial Analysts Journal*, **58** (3), 18–26.
Shonfield, A. (1965), *Modern Capitalism: The Changing Balance of Public and Private Power*, Oxford: Oxford University Press.
Simon, H.A. (1956), 'Rational choice and the structure of the environment', *Psychological Review*, **63** (2), 129–138.
Strange, S. (1997), 'The future of global capitalism; or, will divergence persist forever?', in C. Crouch and W. Streeck (eds), *Political Economy of Modern Capitalism: Mapping Convergence and Divergence*, London: Sage, pp. 182–191.

Teece, D.J. (2000), *Managing Intellectual Capital*, Oxford: Oxford University Press.
van De Deken, J.J., E. Ponds and B. van Reil (2006), 'Social solidarity', in G.L. Clark, A. Munnell and M. Orszag (eds), *The Oxford Handbook of Pensions and Retirement Income*, Oxford: Oxford University Press, pp. 141–160.
Webber, M.J. and D.L. Rigby (1996), *The Golden Age Illusion: Rethinking Postwar Capitalism*, New York: Guilford Press.
Weil, D. (2014), *The Fissured Workplace: Why Work Became so Bad for So Many and What Can Be Done to Improve It*, Cambridge, MA: Harvard University Press.
Weller, S. and P. O'Neill (2014), 'An argument with neoliberalism Australia's place in a global imaginary', *Dialogues in Human Geography*, **4** (2), 105–130.
Williamson, O.E. (1975), *Markets and Hierarchies: Antitrust Analysis and Implications*, New York: Free Press.
World Bank (1994), *Averting the Old Age Crisis: Policies to Protect the Old and Promote Growth*, New York: Oxford University Press.
Worswick, G.D.N. and J.A. Trevithick (eds) (1983), *Keynes and the Modern World: Proceedings of the Keynes Centenary Conference*, Cambridge: Cambridge University Press.
Zingales, L. (2000), 'In search of new foundations', *Journal of Finance*, **55** (4), 1623–1653.

PART III

SPACES OF FINANCIAL AND MONETARY REGULATION

16. Regulatory space and the flow of funds across the hierarchy of money

David S. Bieri

It is well that the people of the nation do not understand our banking and monetary system, for if they did, I believe there would be a revolution by tomorrow morning. (Henry Ford, n.d.)

Capitalism is essentially a financial system, and the peculiar behavioral attributes of a capitalist economy center around the impact of finance upon system behavior. The behavior of the financial system in turn depends upon the behavior of its component parts; and a complex set of financial intermediaries is central to the financial system of an advanced capitalist economy. (Hyman Minsky, 1967: 33)

16.1 INTRODUCTION

This chapter emphasizes the regulatory linkages between the institutional evolution of money, credit and banking and the spatial structure of the flow of funds, both from a theoretical and from an empirical perspective. In the first part of the chapter, I treat the trajectory of spatial development and the advancement of the monetary-financial system as a joint historical process.[1] Specifically, I adopt an "evolutionary" (or institutional) perspective in documenting how different regulatory regimes in the United States have shaped the international and interregional flow of funds across space. In doing so, the theoretical perspective of this chapter engages with the fact that the modern monetary system is not only inherently hierarchical in *finance*, but it is also hierarchical in *power*. Funds are transferred across space through the purchase and sale of direct financial assets and through the purchase and sale of claims against financial intermediaries. As a whole, the structure of the regulatory system shapes in important ways the roles played by the various components of the monetary-financial system (financial instruments, financial markets, monetary intermediaries, private non-bank financial intermediaries, publicly sponsored intermediaries) in promoting the interregional mobility of funds and, by extension, the mobility of funds among the various sectors of the *space economy*. Focusing on the US banking sector before and after the recent crisis, the second part of the chapter then empirically quantifies how the interplay between structural changes in financial intermediation and shifting regimes of US banking regulation give rise to a distinct unevenness of spatial capital flows and depository agglomeration – a combination that ultimately co-determined the spatial impact of the fall-out from the financial crisis.

From the historical origins of modern money to the rise of "shadow banking", this chapter contends that the *political economy of regulation* creates specific geographies of flows of funds – a set of spatial circuits that has come to be typified by the rapid evolution in bank complexity and a growing prominence of "murky finance", whereby market-based credit intermediation via minimally regulated entities plays an increasingly central role. Recognizing the importance of real-financial linkages, my argument connects the political economy of regulation with the process of spatial development. Across different historical regimes, the intrinsic instability of the financial system governs a dialectical relationship between financial regulation and government intervention, in turn leading to financial innovation which opens up new frontiers across financial space.

Overall, then, this chapter explores how regulatory developments in the financial system interact with the local and regional elements of the real economy. The remainder of this chapter proceeds as follows. Section 16.2 engages with the intrinsic instability and hierarchy of the monetary-financial system, highlighting that both of these characteristics are directly linked to the institutional realities of regulation. This implies that both *monetary hierarchy and financial instability have important spatial implications*. Specifically, I engage with heterodox economic paradigms that do not accept the neutrality of money, particularly in connection with the broader phenomenon of financialization.[2] As part of this argument, I revisit a hitherto neglected aspect of spatial monetary thinking in August Lösch's (1940, 1949) economic geography and demonstrate that it ties in directly with central elements of a spatial view of the flow of funds – an equally neglected aspect of regional analysis that saw some attempts of integrating Morris Copeland's (1947, 1952) pioneering work on a balance sheet view of the economy into the core of post-war location theory (for example in Isard, 1956, 1960).

Section 16.3 proceeds by examining the process of financial regulation as part of a larger evolutionary process of regulatory governance of the economic system. In this setting, all regulation is deeply path-dependent and every action of a given regulatory regime creates a (financial) reaction, the consequences of which – both spatial and non-spatial – have lasting effects on the configuration of activity in the financial sector and the real sector alike. In addition to an evolutionary perspective, this section of the chapter touches on to the specific historical circumstances of financial regulation in the US, emphasising the link between functional (as opposed to institutional) aspects of regulation and their spatial consequences that range from the integration of financial markets and financial agglomeration to the process of suburbanization. Section 16.4 empirically documents specific spatial patterns of the flow of funds across each layer of the US monetary hierarchy. From liquidity injections into the banking system via the Federal Reserve's Discount Window to the securitisation of mortgage credit, this section renders legible how the historical trajectory of financial regulation had become inscribed into the economic landscape, producing a variety of spatial effects in the run-up, during and in the aftermath of the recent crisis. Section 16.5 traces out elements of future research on the geography of financial regulation and offers some concluding considerations.

16.2 INSTABILITY AND HIERARCHY OF THE MONETARY-FINANCIAL SYSTEM

The recent financial crisis was a powerful reminder that the inherent instability of the monetary-financial system can entail serious consequences for the real economy. At the same time, the crisis has also highlighted that the deeply integrated nature of the global economy by no means implies an end to the relevance of spatial economic thinking with regard to money and finance. To the contrary, the lasting consequences of the recent financial and real sector upheavals were anything but uniformly spread across space. In this sense, the 2007–08 crisis was a "very geographical crisis" (French et al., 2009) – an unprecedented example of the "glocalization" nature of financialized capitalism, where locally varying origins and global consequences create complex interdependencies and asymmetric feedbacks (Bieri, 2009; Martin, 2011).

In responding to the crisis, both national and international policymakers have identified several gaps in the perimeter of financial regulation as the main culprits for the severe bouts of systemic instability that had dislocated the global financial system; not only did regulatory checks fail to prevent the financial meltdown, but the regulatory system itself appears to have amplified the reverberations from the financial fallout across the global economy. Yet any new regulation – be it the Dodd–Frank Wall Street Reform at the local level or the most recent set of capital adequacy and liquidity standards for banks under Basel III (BCBS, 2013a, 2013b) at the global level – is unlikely to completely rid the financial system of the so-called "boundary problem of regulation", that is the problem that institutions in the regulated sector and those in the unregulated sector face different incentives (Goodhart, 2008a, 2008b). During the Great Moderation, the boundary problem profoundly misaligned incentives across agents in the financial sector as systemic financial imbalances accumulated in the run-up to the crisis. This induced regulatory arbitrage on a large scale, for example in the form of securitization, offsetting some or all of the intended regulatory effects, while simultaneously exposing the financial system to new forms of systemic risk.

The Inherent Instability of the Monetary-financial System

In the aftermath of the crisis, far-reaching disenchantment with the intellectual underpinnings of the conventional regulatory apparatus has led to a dramatic (re)discovery of the importance of Hyman Minsky's work on financial instability (Minsky, 1977, 1993, 2008) and, perhaps in a more subtle way, to a wider appreciation of post-Keynesian thinking on the "non-neutrality of money".[3] Common to all of this work is the special attention that it pays to the role of the financial sector as a source of fluctuations in the real sector and – of particular importance to our discussion – as an influence over the spatial structure of regional economies. In keeping both with its Schumpeterian and Keynesian intellectual roots, there is the fundamental belief at the core of the Minskian system that the inherent instability of the economy under finance-led capitalism can be stabilized or fine-tuned via a specific set of technical adjustments and policies.[4]

In order to achieve such regulatory control over a capitalist economy, we must obtain a detailed understanding of the financial linkages that drive economic activity, both between economic agents and – as I argue in more detail elsewhere (Bieri, 2014a) – also across space. As Minsky put it:

> to analyze how financial commitments affect the economy it is necessary to look at economic units in terms of their cash flows. The cash flow approach looks at all units – be they households, corporations, state and municipal governments, or even national governments – as if they were banks. (Minsky, 2008: 221)

With the increasing globalization of the monetary-financial system, funds are transferred across space through the purchase and sale of direct financial assets and through the purchase and sale of claims against financial intermediaries. In an evolutionary sense, financial regulation has played a crucial role in shaping the historical process by which the monetary-financial system grew into a hybrid arrangement of public and private credit creation that is both bank-based and market-based ("shadow banking") – a point that is explored in more detail below. In the context of the recent crisis, this hybridity of the system has influenced in important ways the shift of policy goals away from monetary stability towards financial stability, the quest for which has seen a considerable emphasis on an institutional and functional redesign of the regulatory framework that monitors systemic risk. In this regard, institutional responses to the crisis have begun to unify both "micro-prudential" and "macro-prudential" principles of financial regulation to enhance overall financial stability (Goodhart, 2008b; Hanson et al., 2011; Bieri, 2015a, 2015b).

The intensified pursuit of financial stability as a post-crisis policy target is closely linked to regulatory control and governance which, in turn, directly relate to the idea of monetary non-neutrality by ascribing systemic importance to the monetary-financial system for all sectors of the space economy. With the crisis dealing a devastating blow to the notion of self-regulating and self-stabilizing markets in the policy mainstream, the re-regulation of financial markets has rapidly emerged as a new paradigm – a "new normal" that is frequently couched in a rapidly proliferating policy discourse around notions of resilience and complexity.[5] As part of this new thinking comes a renewed acceptance of the idea that – across different historical regimes – the intrinsic instability of the financial system is a by-product of financial regulation and government intervention, in turn leading to financial innovation which opens up new frontiers across financial space (Bieri, 2013). As part of such a narrative of regulation as a dynamic politico-economic process, much of the blame for the financial crisis has been attributed to a general breakdown in the (financial) regulatory system, both in the US and elsewhere (Tropeano, 2011; Litan, 2012).[6]

The Spatial Non-neutrality and Monetary Hierarchy in the Löschian System

The geographical nature of the financial crisis has not only challenged the standard view that globalization implied the "end of geography for finance", it has also added a new tenor to theoretical debates that were deemed silenced by the spatial flattening of the global financial system. From the specific vantage point of our discussion of regulatory space, the dissenting positions vis-à-vis the orthodoxy of the classical dichotomy and, by implication, the notion of monetary neutrality, are the most relevant of these debates. Because the neoclassical mainstream ascribes no economic importance to the interaction between real and financial variables, standard theory views money as the proverbial veil, such that "real" factors determine "real" variables. Yet, as we have seen, the financial crisis has systematically challenged the concept of neutral money, even in the aspatial setting of standard macroeconomics and finance.

At the same time, however, the canon of contemporary regional economic theory, by and large, continues to uphold the classical dichotomy in that it treats the spheres of money and production as analytically distinct. In fact, much of regional analysis is formulated in terms of the mechanics of a pure exchange economy which relegates money and financial interrelations, at best, to being a source for short-term frictions, but not fundamentally relevant to the determination of regional market (dis)equilibria. In short, real factors determine real regional variables. Or, put differently, regional money is neutral in the long run. Despite the fact that the recent crisis so powerfully reminded us that money and finance are also – always and everywhere – local phenomena with real effects, little theoretical progress has been made in the analysis of spatial monetary and financial phenomena.[7]

In advancing new perspectives on the spatial non-neutrality of money, it may thus be helpful to examine various schools of economic thought regarding the different theoretical explanations they provide as to the origins of economic cycles. For this purpose, Table 16.1 summarizes the treatment of the real-monetary nexus across different economic paradigms, along with the corresponding view on the nature of booms and busts. Table 16.1 also highlights that – with the notable exception of a spatialized version of the Marxian system pioneered by David Harvey (1978, 1985a, 1985b) – conventional economic doctrine either deals with monetary non-neutrality or spatial economic effects, but not both.

In related work elsewhere (Bieri, 2016), I propose an alternative to the dominant Marxist view of the real–monetary nexus, highlighting that important theoretical insights in this regard are contained in August Lösch's (1940, 1949) pioneering analysis of the spatial consequences of monetary-financial arrangements and of the flow of credit money across space. Specifically, I argue that these lesser-known aspects of Lösch's work are broadly consistent with a spatialized version of post-Keynesian monetary theory (Dow and Earl, 1982; Arestis, 1988, 1996; Chick and Tily, 2014). At its core, this literature questions the sanctity of the money multiplier and acknowledges that regional money creation happens endogenously by commercial banks "at the stroke of a pen", while the central bank retains ultimate control through monetary policy, particularly by setting the interest rate. In addition to the regional effects of endogenous money, place-based credit

Table 16.1 Money matters across different schools of economic thought

Economic paradigm	Origins of economic cycles	Real-monetary sector relationship	Nature of crises	Spatial consequences
Classics	Real sector	Neutral	Resources	Not considered
Marxism	Real sector	Non-neutral	Over-accumulation	Urbanization
(Post) Keynesianism	Both sectors	Non-neutral	Investment bubble, effective demand, financial instability	Not considered
Neoclassical (RBC)	Real sector	(Super)neutral	Exogenous shocks (technology)	Not considered
Monetarism	Monetary sector	Non-neutral	Inflation	Not considered
Urban economics (NUUE-NEG)*	Real sector	Neutral	Cumulative causation	Agglomeration

Notes: *"New neoclassical urban economics" (NNUE) and new economic geography (NEG)/geographical economics.

Source: Bieri and Schaeffer (2015).

allocations are an (re-)emergent core competency of the state which, in turn, is tied to a long historical arc of institutional and regulatory changes. In the US, the origins of these changes can certainly be traced back to the Great Depression, and perhaps even as far back as the new monetary order of the post-civil war Reconstruction Era (Bieri, 2015b).

At the same time, post-Keynesian monetary theory also implies what can be considered a "hierarchy of monies" in that the modern monetary system is a hybrid which is part public ("outside money", a net asset to the private sector) and part private ("inside money").[8] It has both public and private liabilities that circulate as money (Bell, 2001; Mehrling, 2013). Indeed, two specific aspects of Lösch's analysis of the spatial consequences of monetary-financial arrangements provide a useful lens for linking the hierarchy of money to the spatial structure of the financial system.

First, Lösch (1949, 1954) recognizes that money and credit are always and everywhere fundamentally hierarchical in nature and that all money is credit money, even state money. The modern monetary system is not only hierarchical in finance, but it is also hierarchical in power (for example, in the Federal Reserve's *ex post* definition of what is adequate collateral and its inherent role as the "market maker of last resort", Mehrling, 2011). Table 16.2 illustrates the hierarchy of money in the Löschian system as a spatial monetary order where money and credit are created by different financial institutions at separate levels of the hierarchy. The Löschian monetary pyramid can be read both institutionally and, perhaps more importantly, in a functional manner, that is in terms of what constitutes money and credit as an accepted mean of settlement. A central feature of this monetary hierarchy is the fact that the distinctions between money and credit are not strict and largely depend on the specific vantage point from within each layer of the system. In this system, gold and deposits at the Bank for International Settlements are the ultimate money because they are the ultimate means of international payment.[9] Currencies, both international money and national money, are deemed a form of credit in so far as they are promises to pay gold. Similarly, further down the hierarchy, bank deposits are viewed as a form of private credit money, effectively promises to pay currency on demand and thus twice removed from the promises to pay ultimate money. Private money in the form of debt obligations or securities is then a promise to pay currency or deposits over some specific time horizon. A second crucial feature of this hierarchical view of money lies in the fact that at each layer the "moneyness of credit" depends on the credibility of the promise by a given issuer to convert a specific form of credit into the next higher form of money. In other words, what counts as money and what counts as credit depends on the layer of the hierarchy under consideration, on what counts as ultimate means of settlement.

The translated and augmented version of Lösch's original table in the bottom panel of Table 16.2 reveals that the Löschian monetary hierarchy maps directly into a post-Keynesian perspective of monetary hybridity according to which the credit pyramid oscillates between a condition where money is "scarce" and one where credit is "elastic" (Bell, 2001; Wray, 2009; Mehrling, 2013; Mehrling et al., 2013). In fact, one of Minsky's (2008) key insights was that the hierarchy of money shifts across the economic cycle through three distinct phases, namely hedge finance, speculative finance and Ponzi schemes. Money and credit are thus fluctuating between states of elasticity and states of discipline. In this context, it is then precisely the role of financial regulation, broadly conceived, to determine the institutional plane within which the monetary-financial pendulum swings

Table 16.2 Hierarchical money in the Löschian system

Ordnung			
1. Geld höchster Ordnung	Weltgeld		(Bargeld: Gold; Buchgeld: BIZ)
2. Geld hoher Ordnung:	Teilgeld	Großraumgeld	(£, *RM*)
3. Geld mittlerer Ordnung:	Teilgeld	National geld	(Banknoten, Zentralbankguthaben, mitunter entsprechendes Regionalgeld)
4. Geld unterer Ordnung:	Teilgeld	Privatbuchgeld	(der Groß-, Regional-, Lokalbanken)
5. Geld unterster Ordnung:	Teilgeld	Privatbargeld	(private oder fiskalische Schuldurkunden, besonders Wechsel)

Translated (and augmented) version

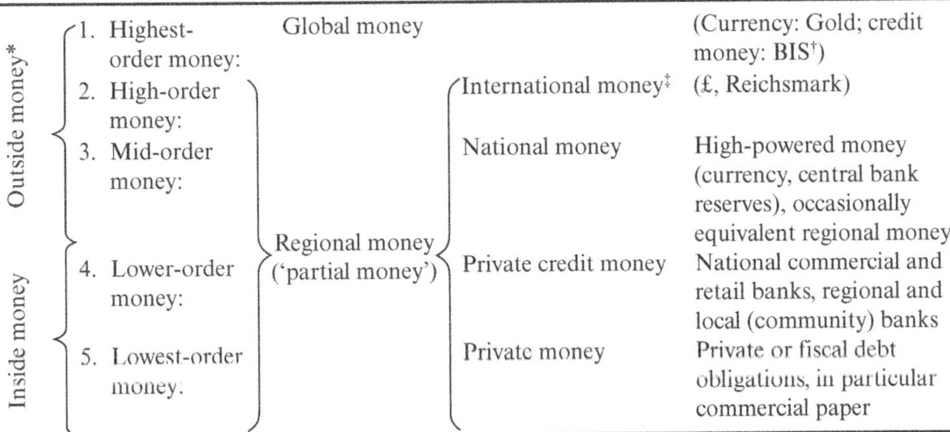

	Order			
Outside money*	1. Highest-order money:	Global money		(Currency: Gold; credit money: BIS[†])
Outside money*	2. High-order money:	Regional money ('partial money')	International money[‡]	(£, Reichsmark)
Outside money*	3. Mid-order money:	Regional money ('partial money')	National money	High-powered money (currency, central bank reserves), occasionally equivalent regional money
Inside money	4. Lower-order money:	Regional money ('partial money')	Private credit money	National commercial and retail banks, regional and local (community) banks
Inside money	5. Lowest-order money:	Regional money ('partial money')	Private money	Private or fiscal debt obligations, in particular commercial paper

Notes: This "monetary order" links the hierarchy of money on the left-hand side to the spatial structure of the financial system on the right-hand side. * "Outside" money is either of a fiat nature or backed by some asset that is in positive net supply within the private sector, whereas "inside" money is an asset backed by any form of private liabilities (credit) that circulate as a medium of exchange, an analytical distinction first introduced by Gurley and Shaw (1960). † BIZ/BIS: Bank für Internationalen Zahlungsausgleich/Bank for International Settlements, Basel, Switzerland. ‡ corresponds to both "top currency" and "patrician currency" in the terminology of Cohen's (1998, 2003) currency pyramid.

Source: Original table with monetary hierarchy in Lösch (1949: 59). Author's translation and adaptation.

between different states. Beyond mere institutional design, the influence of regulatory governance thus also deeply determines the extent to which the system's oscillations spill over to the real sector – all of which is inextricably linked to the spatial structure of economic activity.

Second, Lösch's (1940) work on financial markets acknowledges the importance of capital flows throughout the urban hierarchy, highlighting the spatial relationship between financial variables and institutional functions, such as financial regulation. Indeed, post-Keynesian monetary thought counts functional and institutional variation as among the most influential pathways for change in real-financial linkages (Chick and Dow, 1988, 1996). Another important, related perspective that is consistent with Lösch's work comes from Minsky's (1991, 1993) re-emphasis of Keynes's (1930) fundamental insight that the non-neutrality of money needs to be a "deep part of the system, not an afterthought" in a capitalist economy. In contrast to the orthodoxy of the classical dichotomy, monetary and financial variables thus enter different parts of the system in different ways, most importantly, perhaps, via two distinct price levels where the proximate determinants of these price levels are quite different. One price level is that of current wages and output, which – when combined with financing conditions – yields the supply conditions for investment goods and consumption goods. The other is that of capital and financial assets, which is determined by economic agents' relative preferences for income later versus liquidity now.[10]

16.3 THE FLOW OF FUNDS PERSPECTIVE AND POST-CRISIS MONETARY SPACE

In what follows, it will be useful to relate the discussion of the spatial aspects of financial regulation to both an *institutional view of regulation* (that is the regulation of financial institutions) and a *functional view of regulation* (that is the regulation of funding flows and asset flows). These different perspectives are illustrated in Figure 16.1 which encompasses two schematic representations of the flow of funds across different sectors of the space economy. The upper portion of the figure – reproduced a from Isard's (1960) seminal text on regional analysis – underlines the importance of interregional moneyflows across different sectors of the space economy. The lower portion of the figure provides a circular flow-of-funds representation of economic activity that – in addition to the two price levels mentioned above – is consistent with the moneyflow accounting pioneered by Copeland (1947, 1952).

In particular, the focus on the sources and uses of funds in the lower schematic of Figure 16.1 helps to emphasize the two key elements of Löschian monetary system introduced above, namely the hierarchical relationships between different forms of money and credit on the one hand, and the (spatial) non-neutrality of money via the price level of output and the price level of financial assets on the other hand. In this setting, the non-neutrality of money arises from the simple fact that, for each sector, real transactions and financial transactions are closely linked as investment (I) and increases in financial assets (A) equal saving (S) and increases in financial liabilities (L) such that for each sector i we have $I_i + A_i = S_i + L_i$. The spatial consequences of this perspective and its linkages to the regulatory complex are examined next.

Broadly speaking then, financial regulation encompasses all governance that shapes the flow of funds within the price level of financial assets. While financial regulation provides the institutional and functional vector that undermines the spatial neutrality of money, flow-of-funds accounts are the accounting lens through which its outward appearance becomes empirically tractable. As Figure 16.1 illustrates, the financial accounts follow funds as they move from sectors, such as households or firms that serve as sources of funds (net lenders), through intermediaries (financial institutions) or financial markets, to sectors that use the funds to acquire physical and financial assets. Indeed, the financial crisis has driven home the importance of financial flows and the composition of sectoral balance sheets for an understanding of real–financial linkages. A good six decades since

Panel (a): Money flows across sectors

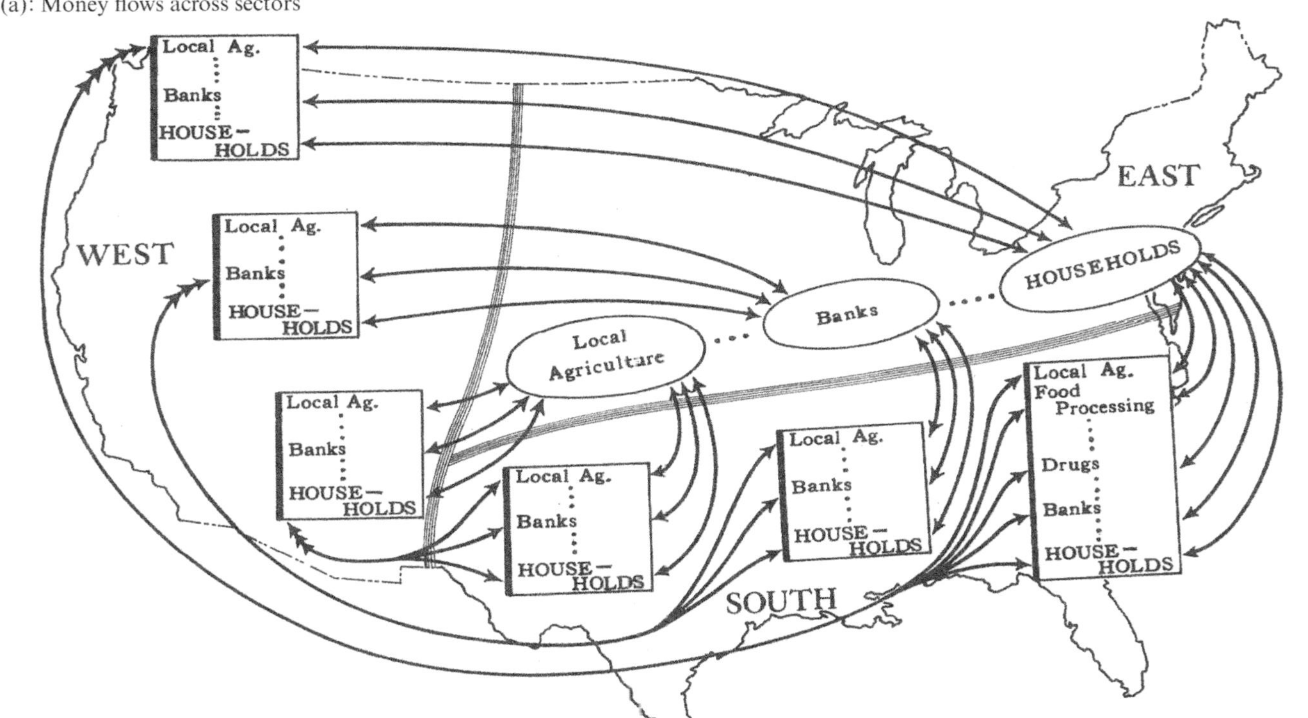

Notes: Panel (a) illustrates a set of hypothetical interregional money flows across different sector of the economy (Isard, 1960). Panel (b) presents a schematic representation of the flow of funds across different sectors of the economy, paying particular attention on the hierarchical relationships between different forms of money and credit. The lower portion of the panel presents a sectoral flow-of-funds table that is consistent with the moneyflow accounting pioneered by Copeland (1947, 1952). See main text for more details.

Source: Bieri (2014a).

Figure 16.1 Money flows across the space-economy

Panel (b): Circular flow of funds

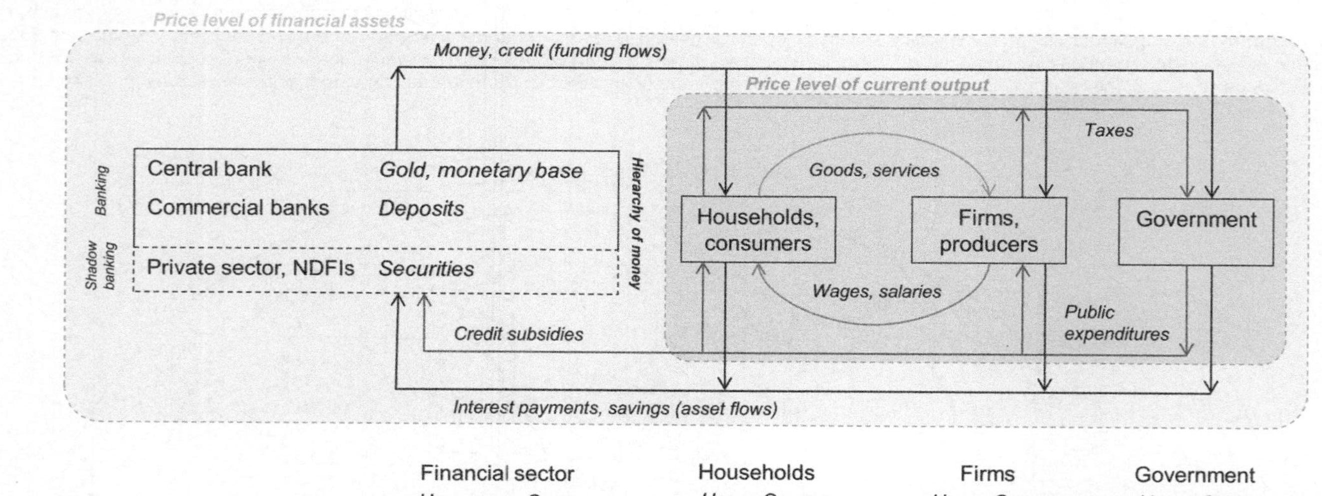

	Financial sector		Households		Firms		Government	
	Use	*Source*	*Use*	*Source*	*Use*	*Source*	*Use*	*Source*
Real transactions	I_{fin}	S_{fin}	I_h	S_h	I_f	S_f	I_g	S_g
Financial transactions	A_{fin}	L_{fin}	A_h	L_h	A_f	L_f	A_g	L_g

for each sector, $I_i + A_i = S_i + L_i$ such that:

Surplus	$S_i - I_i = A_i - L_i$	: non-financial sources → net financial savings	*Money outflow*	$A_i - L_i > 0$
Deficit	$L_i - A_i = I_i - S_i$	: financial sources → product expenditures	*Money inflow*	$L_i - A_i > 0$

Figure 16.1 (continued)

its conception, the flow-of-funds analysis has seen a flurry of renewed academic and policy interest in understanding central aspects of the financial crisis that the conventional equilibrium-based mainstream models were not able to capture by design (Palumbo and Parker, 2009; Bezemer, 2010; Winkler et al., 2013).

As the quote from Minsky (2008) at the beginning of the previous section stresses, the key to the flow of funds perspective is to look at all actors in the economy (households, firms, governments and the financial sector) "as if they were banks", each with a balance sheet of cash inflows and cash outflows and each bound by the "survival constraint" (that is the requirement that cash outflow not exceed cash inflow). The money flow economy then arises in aggregate from the interconnection of all balance sheets which, in turn, gives rise to the "fundamental instability of a credit economy" (Hawtrey, 1919; Minsky, 1977, 1993). The money flow economy is the basis for the flow-of-funds accounting which – as an analytical approach – provides a unique characterization of how financialization has progressively been reshaping the modern macroeconomy through the process of financial globalisation and deregulation.[11]

Over the past forty years or so, the process of financialization has completely intertwined the monetary system with the financial system such that we cannot talk about money without talking about finance. This raises the importance of several institutional hallmarks of the current system. At its core, there are the wholesale money markets as the central funding mechanism, with "shadow banks" as key institutions that facilitate short-term funding of long-term lending.[12] Given the importance of these flow-based changes to the relevance of the inner workings of the monetary-financial system, the need arises for refocusing the discussion in conceptual terms. In this process, increased emphasis ought to be placed on the changing nature of the monetary-financial system in terms of increasing complexity and spatial reach.

The Regulatory–Spatial Dialectic

A central feature of such a re-conceptualization of the geography of money lies in distinguishing between physical and functional notions of space, a distinction that draws on Perroux's (1950) re-theorization of economic space around a set of "field forces". Privileging "spaces of flows" over the more conventional notion of "spaces of places", discourses on the monetary geography are centred around a what Cohen (1998) terms a "flow-based model of currency relation", where networks and hierarchies form the primary units of analysis, all within a largely de-territorialized spatial organization of monetary-financial relations. At the regional level, early aspects of such "flow-based hierarchical monetary spaces" are illustrated in Figure 16.2 where panels (a) and (b) trace regional money flows through the Federal Reserve Districts, which represent in many ways a prototypical functional monetary-financial space, albeit one with distinct territorial boundaries. Similarly, panel (c) shows the spatial hierarchy of retail banking networks in Switzerland from Labasse's (1974) novel work on the spatial dimensions of finance.[13]

In many ways, the reconfiguration of spatial relations because of monetary-financial globalization can be read as being consistent with what Thrift and Olds (1996: 314) envisage – in the Perrouxian sense described above – as a "transformative re-conceptualisation of the remit of the economic". Much in the same spirit, French et al. (2011) suggest that research on financialization has been insufficiently attentive to

Panel (a): Flows of funds from and to the St. Louis Federal Reserve District

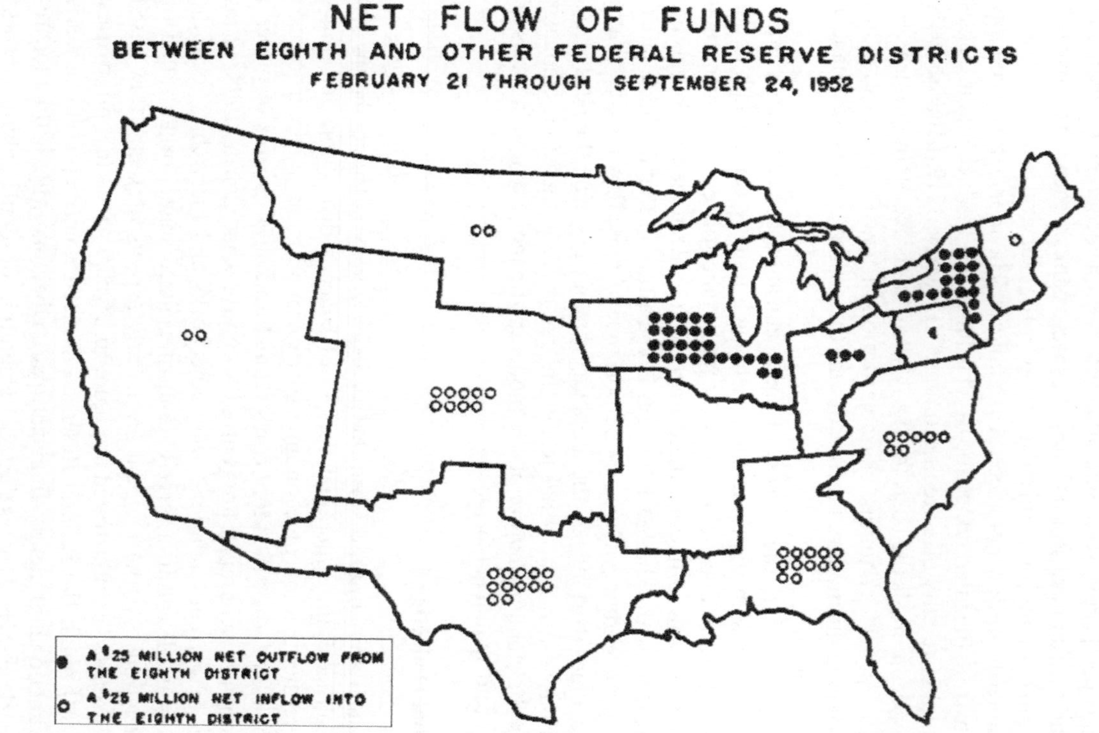

Notes: Panel (a) illustrates the net flow of funds between the Eight Federal Reserve District (St. Louis) and other districts in the Federal Reserve System through the Interdistrict Settlement Account (IDSA) in February 21 through September 24, 1952. Panel (b) shows the net regional inflows through the IDSA to the Federal Reserve offices in Detroit, Pittsburgh and Atlanta for two months in 1954. Panel (c) illustrates the spatial hierarchy of the banking network of regional offices and local branches of Union Bank of Switzerland and Credit Suisse across Switzerland.

Sources: Bowsher (1952), Bowsher et al. (1958), and Labasse (1974).

Figure 16.2 The monetary hierarchy and the spatial flow of funds

Panel (b): Interdistrict flow of funds

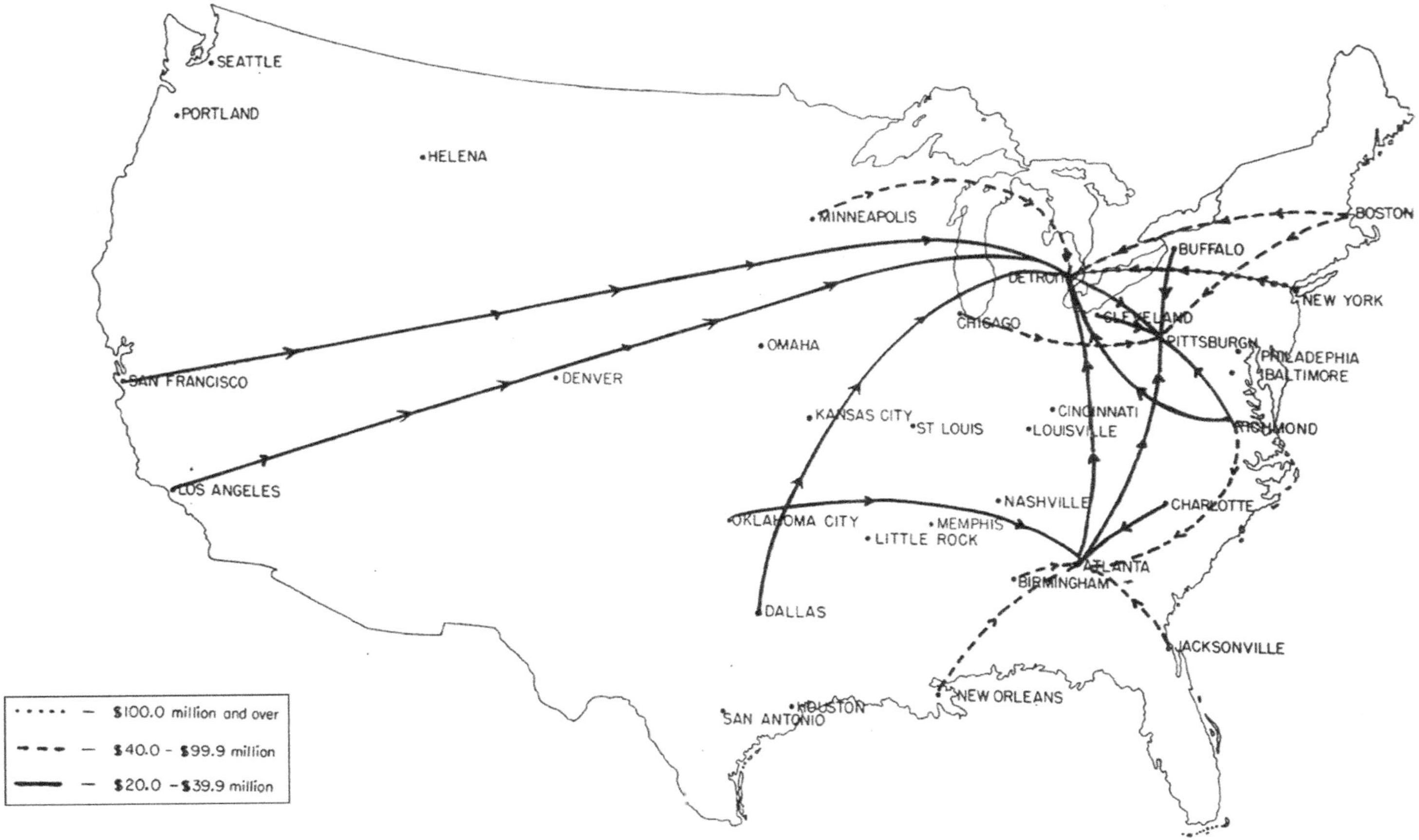

Figure 16.2 (continued)

Panel (c): Spatial network of banking branches in Switzerland

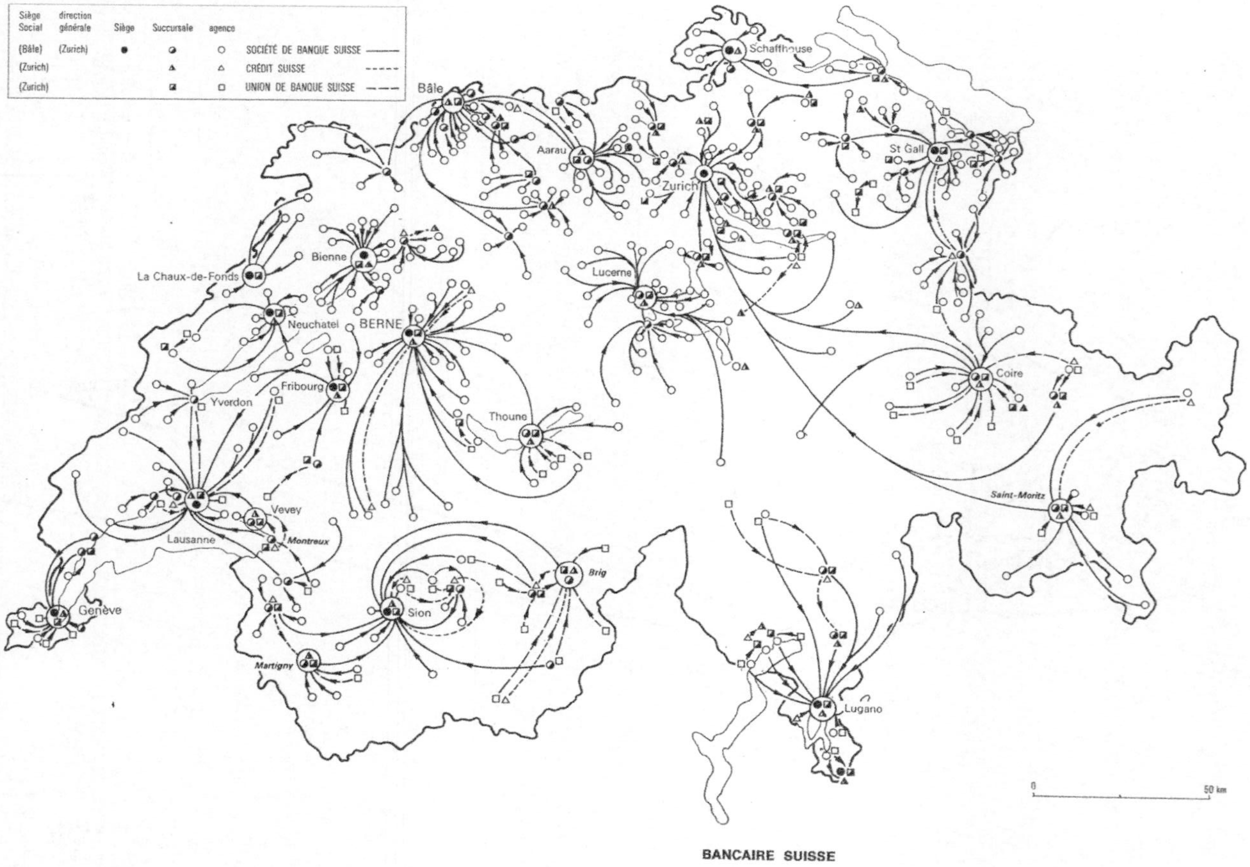

Figure 16.2 (continued)

network- or flow-based notions of economic space. In fact, of all abstract economic spaces, Perroux (1950: 98) places particular emphasis on monetary space – a field of forces "seen more easily in terms of a network of payments, or by means of the description of monetary flows". In Perroux's analysis, monetary space is simultaneously delocalized, yet inherently hierarchical, operating at several levels of "banal space" (regional, national, and global scale), much like the spatial flow of funds at different levels of the hierarchy of money in Figure 16.2.[14]

At the same time, the financial crisis has also lead to a certain amount of re-territorialization of the discourse on the spatial consequences of finance as regulatory responses to the crises – from bailouts to the creation of new regulatory arrangements – almost invariably took place within the institutional framework of nations. In this theoretical sense, the current section is motivated by the broader theoretical consideration to lay the groundwork for spatializing the analysis of money and finance in the post-Keynesian tradition within the larger setting of a Löschian economic geography of money and finance. Indeed, I contend that – in contrast to the mainstream view in monetary thought – both Lösch's economic geography and post-Keynesian monetary theory emphatically challenge the notion of monetary neutrality and both assume that money is created endogenously.

The regulatory process and the political economy of its institutions are central to the view that money and finance are non-neutral with regard to space, principally because the institutional arrangements of finance matter for how the space economy evolves. Furthermore, the geographical consequences of the recent crisis have challenged the "old geography" with competing nation-states and clear urban hierarchies as the key spatial units of interest. Instead, a new geography is emerging, where globally dispersed creditors and debtors are the main actors (Bieri, 2009). Within this new geography, the traditional roles and interactions between borrowers and investors are being reconstituted with regard to both their spatial and their institutional organization. While the monetary and financial aspects of this new spatial order still assign states significant regulatory control over currency, money has become de-territorialized and the political governance of the Westphalian system has been replaced by a new geography of globalised currency relations (Cohen, 2007).

In light of the modern regulatory arrangements that have shaped the US financial system since the civil war (beginning with watershed moments such as the National Currency Act of 1863 and the National Bank Act of 1864), it becomes clear that a general theory of uneven spatial development must establish explicit regulatory linkages between money, credit and banking and economic spatial structure. Against the background of a hierarchy of globalized money that has the US monetary-financial system at its core, the structure and function of the American space economy must be seen as one that is closely linked to the institutional evolution of its regulatory functions. At the heart of this process lies the "regulatory–spatial dialectic" of the US regulatory complex, the institutional elements and linkages of which are discussed in more detail elsewhere (Bieri, 2015b).

Indeed, the historical trajectory of regulatory regimes and financial innovation creates a dynamic force field in the sense of Perroux (1950) – a force field that is spanned by the vectors of financial integration, agglomeration and suburbanization, setting in motion spatio-temporal processes that continuously reconstitute monetary space across the economic cycle. The evolutionary interplay between markets, institutions and the state thus initiates a dialectical process of adjustments and counter-adjustments with respect to monetary governance and financial regulation.

The Scope and Spatial Limits of Financial Regulation

Financial regulation is of course not an end in itself, but rather an essential means to the larger end of promoting monetary and financial stability, both of which are key policy goals for national authorities. Conventional, neoclassical economic theory of the public sector generally rationalizes any form of government regulation – and intervention, for that matter – as a response to market failures that, by and large, arise because of a variety of market imperfections, ranging from adverse selection, moral hazard to incomplete markets.[15] Specifically focusing on bank regulation, orthodox theories of modern banking explain the asset transformation function of intermediaries and optimal bank liability contracts, while focusing on coordination problems associated with bank failures as the central motivation for regulatory interventions. As such, standard theory focuses on regulations aimed primarily at ameliorating deposit-insurance-related moral hazards, such as cash-asset reserve requirements, risk-sensitive capital requirements and deposit insurance premia, and bank closure policy (Bhattacharya et al., 1998).

The monetary thinking at the centre of my argument here, on the other hand, presents a different view on the economic rationale for financial regulation – one that is consistent with the theoretical underpinnings of a credit theory of money. As we have seen in the previous section, money is endogenous and hierarchical according to this approach. Furthermore, the financial system is essentially a public–private institutional arrangement where government yields the exclusive right to provide the means of payment in return for the acceptance of regulatory restrictions that ensure the stability and soundness of financial institutions and the financial system as a whole. According to this more heterodox approach to financial regulation, financial entities should be regulated according to their function in providing different types of liquidity to the financial system, not because of the presence of "spatial frictions" that interfere with the process of financial intermediation. (Goodhart, 2010; Kregel and Tonveronachi, 2013).

In the context of our analysis, understanding the nature of financial instability among mature economies relies critically on the path-dependent nature of the regulatory process and the temporal irreversibility of some of its institutional consequences. This is particularly true with regard to one central aspect of the process of financial intermediation, namely the causality between savings and investments, long a source of confusion, contention and debate among different schools of economic thought. Specifically, a central insight in Chick (1983), Chick and Dow (1988) and Dow (1999) is the historical fact that the reversal of causality between savings and investments – that is the textbook version of the loanable funds theory where savings and deposits create loans – and the modern reality where banks create credit "at the stroke of a pen" depends on the maturity of the banking system. In other words, the historical evolution of the monetary-financial system determines its operational realities. As such it is helpful to distinguish between different stages of banking, each implying a different type of theory for financial instability.

From an historical perspective, financial functions appear to be more stable than the institutional form of the financial system (Merton, 1995). Yet the (spatial) link between the financial system's most basic function – to facilitate the allocation and deployment of economic resources across time and space – and its optimal institutional form remains an issue of much debate (Bieri, 2013). Overcoming the constraints of a spatial mismatch between borrowers and lenders, different participants in the financial system have never been more geographically dispersed. As a result, the operation of global financial entities in local markets means that – financial risks taken in one region can have consequences for another. Undeniably, the recent dislocations in the housing market have highlighted the paradox that financial innovation can lead to a concentration, rather than a diversification, of risks among market participants (Bieri, 2010). Against this institutional setting and functional realities of US post-crisis financial regulation, the following section now aims to illustrate the emergence and change of specific spatial patterns in the flow of funds across each layer of the US monetary hierarchy.

16.4 US REGULATORY SPACE AND THE CHANGING NATURE OF FINANCIAL INTERMEDIATION

From liquidity injections into the banking system via the Federal Reserve's Discount window, the geography of crisis-related bank failures to the spatial patterns of securitisation of mortgage credit, financial regulation influences the spatial flow of funds at each layer in the monetary hierarchy. This section empirically documents a wide variety of these regulatory-driven spatial effects that took place in the run-up, during and in the immediate aftermath of the recent crisis. In order to set the conceptual stage for this analysis, it is useful to recall the different financial functions across our highly simplified hierarchy of money in panel (b) of Figure 16.1. In what follows, I do not attempt to formally establish any causal connections between specific spatial aspects of the US monetary-financial system and its regulatory arrangements, but rather I present a rich set of visualizations to illustrate the empirical content of the preceding discussion in terms of the relevance of the flow of funds across the hierarchy of money within the broader context the geography of money and finance.

At the highest layer in the hierarchy, the Federal Reserve fulfils part of its lender of last resort function by providing temporary liquidity to depository institutions in need for emergency funding via the Discount Window. Figure 16.3 documents the uneven spatial pattern of liquidity strains among US banks in the wake of the financial crisis from 2010 to 2012. Specifically, the extrusions for individual metro areas are proportional to the cumulative borrowing by depository institutions in a given location via the Federal Reserve's Discount Window, expressed as a percentage of local GDP. In order to distinguish between access to Discount Window access for "window dressing purposes" and access for more pressing liquidity needs, the area shading reflects the amount of reserve fund credit obtained as share of total collateral pledged. The intuition for interpreting this loan-to-value ratio (LTV) is that, analogous to households using home equity to smooth consumption, a higher LTV is indicative of more severe liquidity problems.

Perhaps the most notable spatial feature for this period of exceptional access to reserve funds is the fact that the most extreme liquidity strains of the banking system occur outside of the major financial centres – where short-term borrowing reaches as much as

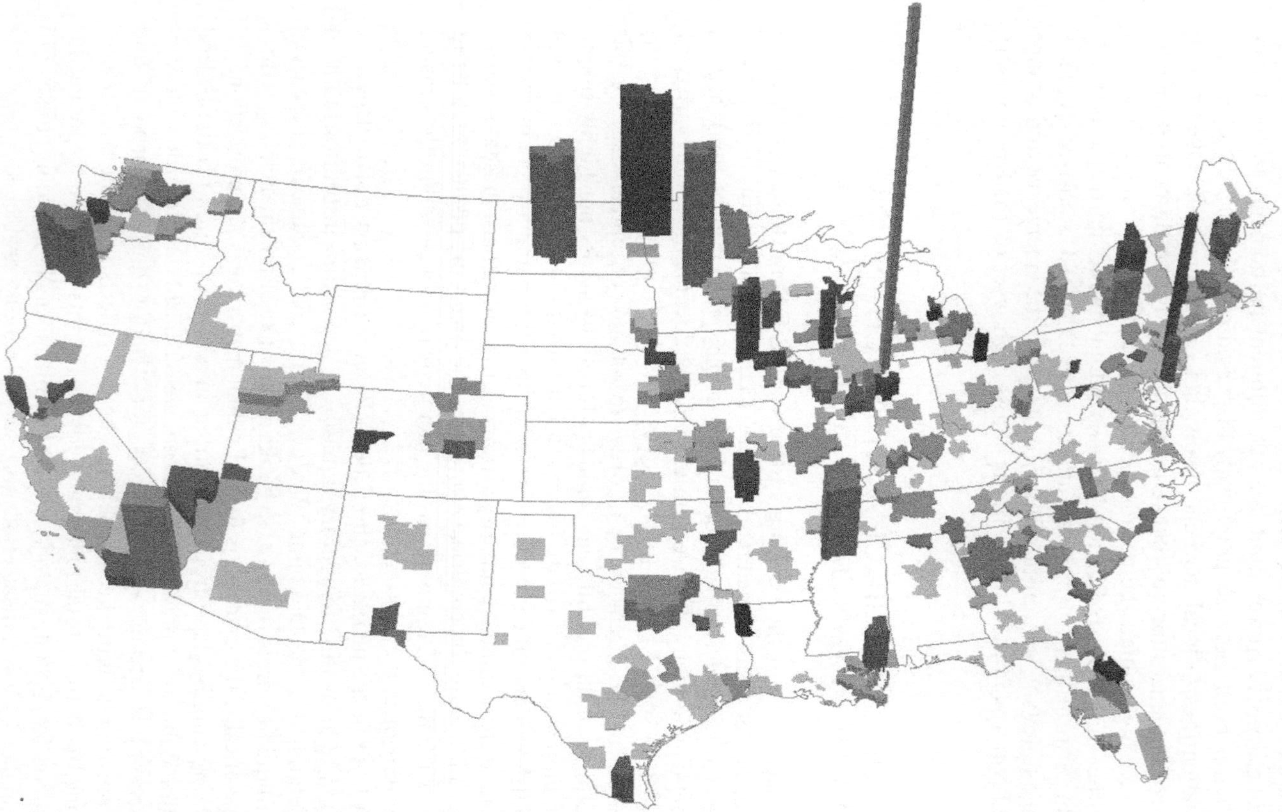

Notes: Metro area extrusions are proportional to cumulative borrowing by depository institutions via the Federal Reserve's Discount Window as a percentage of metropolitan GDP. Area shading reflects the average loan-to-value ratio for banks (credit outstanding as share to total collateral pledged) per metro area (ranging from light grey: 3–5% LTV to black: 70–85% LTV).

Source: Author's calculations from Federal Reserve data on discount window lending and BEA data.

Figure 16.3 Liquidity strains and the spatial flow of reserve funds, 2010–12

15 per cent of local GDP with LTVs as much as 70–85 per cent. This suggests that access to the Federal Reserve's Discount Window plays an important role in keeping the financial periphery integrated into to the broader fabric of the US monetary-financial system.

Moving down one layer in the hierarchy, the next section documents the profound structural change that the US banking industry has experienced in the two decades since the abolition of spatial impediments to bank branching under the Riegle–Neal Interstate Banking and Branching Efficiency Act of 1994, one of the most defining pieces of post-war US banking regulation.

Regulatory Governance and the Structural Change of US Banking

The gradual reduction of spatial barriers to the activity of banks in the United States culminated in 1994 with the passing of the Riegle–Neal Act which repealed interstate bank branching restrictions and allowed interstate bank mergers and was complete in 1999 when the Gramm–Leach–Bliley Act repealed additional restrictions on bank consolidations. Like most of the efforts to deregulate financial markets, the relaxation of the bank branch restrictions in the United States was motivated in part by the belief that financial markets can – by reducing frictions to the circulation of capital – directly affect economic growth and in part by the political self-interest of financial lobby groups (Kane, 1996). In both instances, there is strong evidence that the deregulation of interstate banking activity had a number of important structural effects, significantly changing the face of depository institutions during the two decades since the Riegle–Neal Act was passed. First, while banking deregulation did not increase the volume of bank lending, improvements in the quality of bank lending appear to be responsible for faster economic growth (Jayaratne and Strahan, 1996). At the same time, the gains from deregulation were highly unevenly spread across the institutional spectrum, largely a result of interest group factors related to the relative strength of potential winners (large banks and small, bank-dependent firms) and losers (small banks and the rival insurance firms). Furthermore, the post-Riegle–Neal environment has been characterized by a substantial amount of spatial reconfiguration and intensified competition of retail banking (Pollard, 1999).

Figure 16.4 captures the nature of these structural changes in the banking industry through the lens of the institutionally fragmented US regulatory complex. Grouping the number of regulated depository entities by activity across their respective regulators, the left panel quantifies the dramatic consolidation and concentration among banks with the total number of depository institutions roughly halving from almost 13,000 in 1994 to fewer than 6,700 in 2014. With around two thirds of all banks under its supervision, the Federal Deposit Insurance Corporation (FDIC) remains the regulator responsible for the largest number of depository institutions. In 2011, Title III of the Dodd–Frank Act prompted the merger of the Office of Thrift Supervision (OTS) with the Office of the Comptroller of the Currency (OCC) which has also led to some redistribution of regulatory responsibility between the OCC and the Federal Reserve.

In addition to a high degree of regulatory fragmentation, the US regulatory complex is also characterized by an unusual amount of competition between the main regulatory agencies – the FDIC, the Federal Reserve and the OCC – whereby banks are able to switch among three options for a primary federal regulator. While there is some evidence

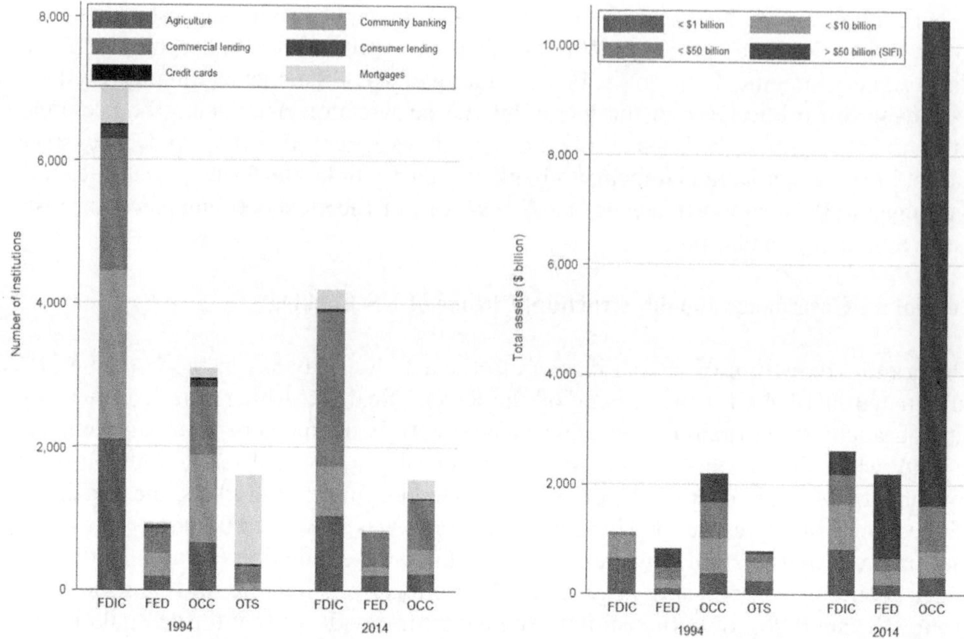

Notes: Depository institutions are grouped by balance sheet size using the groups defined in Section 165 of Dodd–Frank, including the designation of "systemically important financial institutions" (SIFI) for institutions with assets above $50 billion (Tarullo, 2014). "OCC": Office of the Comptroller of the Currency, US Department of the Treasury; "Fed": Federal Reserve System; "FDIC": Federal Deposit Insurance Corporation; "OTS": Office of Thrift Supervision, US Department of the Treasury (merged with OCC in 2011, Title III of Dodd–Frank Act); "NCUA": National Credit Union Association; "HUD": US Department of Housing and Urban Development; "CFPB": Consumer Financial Protection Bureau (created via Title X of Dodd–Frank Act, effective in 2011).

Source: Author's calculations from FDIC data and Federal Reserve data.

Figure 16.4 Regulatory governance and structural change of US banking, 1994 and 2014

of efficiency benefits to regulatory specialization (Rosen, 2003), over the same period, however, there has been a clear and persistent shift in preference by newly regulated banks away from national bank charters and in favour of state bank charters, largely because of the lower regulatory cost of state regulation compared to its federal equivalent (Whalen, 2010). The left panel of Figure 16.4 also highlights the changing nature of lending activities covered by the three main regulators, both in terms of the distribution of activities by depository institution and the regulatory coverage of these activities among regulatory agencies. In the right panel Figure 16.4, depository institutions are grouped by balance sheet size using the groups defined in Section 165 of Dodd–Frank, including the designation of "systemically important financial institutions" (SIFI) for institutions with assets above $50 billion (Tarullo, 2014). The uneven distribution of the US banking assets across different regulators is clearly visible, including the striking concentration of assets under the regulatory control of the OCC, covering approximately four times as many assets of SIFIs than the FDIC and Fed combined. By the end of

2014, total assets of US depository institutions had reached close to $27.9 trillion, or about 175 per cent of US GDP, but only 37 institutions, less than 1 per cent of all regulated entities, accounted for almost 40 per cent of all industry assets. By contrast, 90 per cent of small banks (entities is with a balance sheet size of less than $10 billion) were controlling a mere 5 per cent of all assets.

The extreme increase and concentration of banking assets in the two decades from 1994 to 2014 is the combined result of a steady process of global consolidation and the disruption of the financial crisis. In particular, the expansion of the regulatory control in terms of assets under supervision is to a large part the outcome of seemingly technical, but structurally important regulatory changes in the aftermath of the crisis. First, a number of near financial implosions of non-depository institutions such as Bear Stearns and Merrill Lynch were absorbed into the balance sheets of existing, large bank holding companies (BHC) such as J.P. Morgan and Bank of America. Second, former Wall Street icons Goldman Sachs and Morgan Stanley, the last two independent investment banks, were converted into BHCs, also giving them access to important government liquidity subsidies via the Federal Reserve's Discount Window.

The spatial dimensions of this concentration of banking assets across different regulatory agencies are illustrated in Figure 16.5. The upper panel of the figure shows the extent of the regulatory space for the FDIC, the Federal Reserve and the OCC on a banking assets per capita basis, whereas the lower panel depicts the high degree of spatial concentration for the three agencies with regard to the assets controlled by SIFIs.

One of the most remarkable features of Figure 16.5, perhaps, is the decidedly uneven and intensely clustered nature of US regulatory space expressed in terms of the balance sheet strength of its regulated depository institutions. Unsurprisingly, SIFIs are highly clustered in the traditional US financial centres along the coasts and the primary cities of the Midwest. At the same time, the lower panel of Figure 16.5 also illustrates the asset concentration by regulatory agency, spatially replicating the large concentration of large financial institutions under the oversight of the OCC. Indeed, among this class of financial institution, the OCC's regulatory space has the largest "geographic reach" regarding its absolute spatial coverage.

By contrast, the span of regulatory space – visualised in terms of country-level banking assets per capita in the upper panel of Figure 16.5 – presents a different feature of the geographical extent of regulatory influence for the three main banking regulators: the FDIC is the undisputed regulator of middle America, covering the depository activities of most of America's Heartland more densely than either the Fed or the OCC. In many ways, this pattern is fully consistent with US regulatory history and the evolution of its financial frontier from the coasts to the rapidly developing urban system in Midwest and the Sunbelt (Conzen, 1975; Calomiris, 2000; Barth et al., 2010; Bieri, 2014b). In other words, the institutional divides of US regulatory space thus trace out the frontiers of past financial crises. I show next that this phenomenon of a historical imprinting of the particularities of regulatory arrangements onto the financial landscape by no means is an exception.

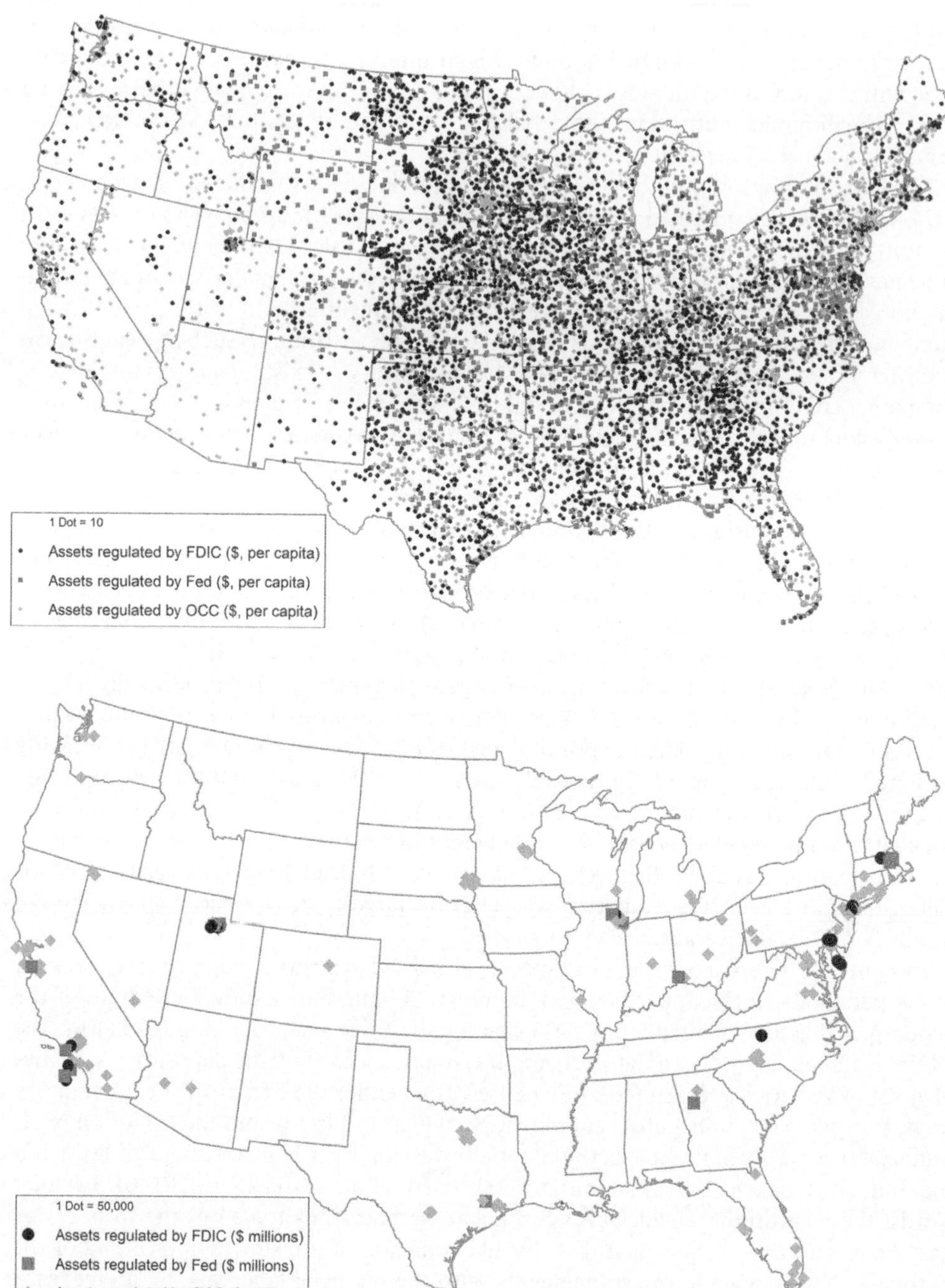

Source: Author's calculations from FDIC, Federal Reserve and Census Bureau data.

Figure 16.5 Banking asset concentration across US regulatory space, 2014

Financial Agglomeration, Path-dependency and the Geography of Banking Failures

Contrary to the common belief the Riegle–Neal Act of 1994 completely removed regulatory barriers to the interstate flow of deposits and loans, section 109 of the Interstate Act still restricts the spatial distribution of credit across the US banking system today.[16] While the Riegle–Neal legislation allows banks to branch across state lines, it contains a little-known regulatory provision that still affects the flow of funds across space today. Specifically, Section 109 of the Act "prohibits a bank from establishing or acquiring a branch or branches outside its home state, pursuant to the act, primarily for the purpose of deposit production" (Federal Reserve Board, 2002). Indeed, the political reasoning behind the enactment of Section 109 (which became effective in 1997) was to ensure that interstate branches would not "take deposits from a community without the bank's reasonably helping to meet the credit needs of that community". Regulatory enforcement of this provision takes place via the "host state loan-to-deposit ratio (LTD)" and requires the lending and deposit activities of a given bank's interstate branches to lie within a certain fraction of the host state LTD ratio.[17] The temporal evolution of this provision is shown in Figure 16.6 where the left panel shows the upper and lower bounds for the host state LTD ratio (the dashed line is the US average LTD). One implication of this regulatory requirement is that credit creation by out-of-state banks is tied to differences in the structure of the local banking industry which, in turn, is a function of the funding models of individual banks. LTD ratios are highest in (more peripheral) states where home banks are particularly risk averse, focusing almost entirely on traditional banking services for a regional customer base. By contrast, the lowest LTDs are in states where there is a substantial local presence of large BHCs with diversified international loan portfolios for which regulatory requirements force them to keep more of their deposits liquid.

In other words, because LTDs are endogenously determined by the conditions of the local banking industry, the regulatory provisions of section 109 of the Riegle–Neal Act create some form of "regulatory lock-in" effect whereby local conditions in the banking industry are reinforced to the extent that outside banks have to comply with local funding models and lending practices. In the context of another industry, this is functionally equivalent to imposing the regulatory requirement that a high-tech company wanting to establish operations, say, in Silicon Valley, must adopt the same average technology that all other local high-tech companies in the State of California deploy. While disentangling the qualitative economic effects of this regulatory provision is beyond the scope of our discussion here, it is clear that such regulation – at a very minimum – accentuates and accelerates the cumulative causation of agglomerative forces in the banking industry. The right panel of Figure 16.6 adds further emphasis to this point by documenting a robust connection between interstate capital flows – approximated by the difference between gross state income and gross state product (see Kalemli-Ozcan et al., 2010) – and LTDs, whereby low LTD states, that is states with more globally active banks, tend to experience the largest capital outflows.

Another dimension of the intensely agglomerated nature of the US banking industry was revealed by the spatial incidence of banking failures during the financial crisis. Figure 16.7 depicts the uneven geography of these banking failures across US metro areas from the beginning of the crisis in 2007 to the end of 2014. The metro area extrusions in

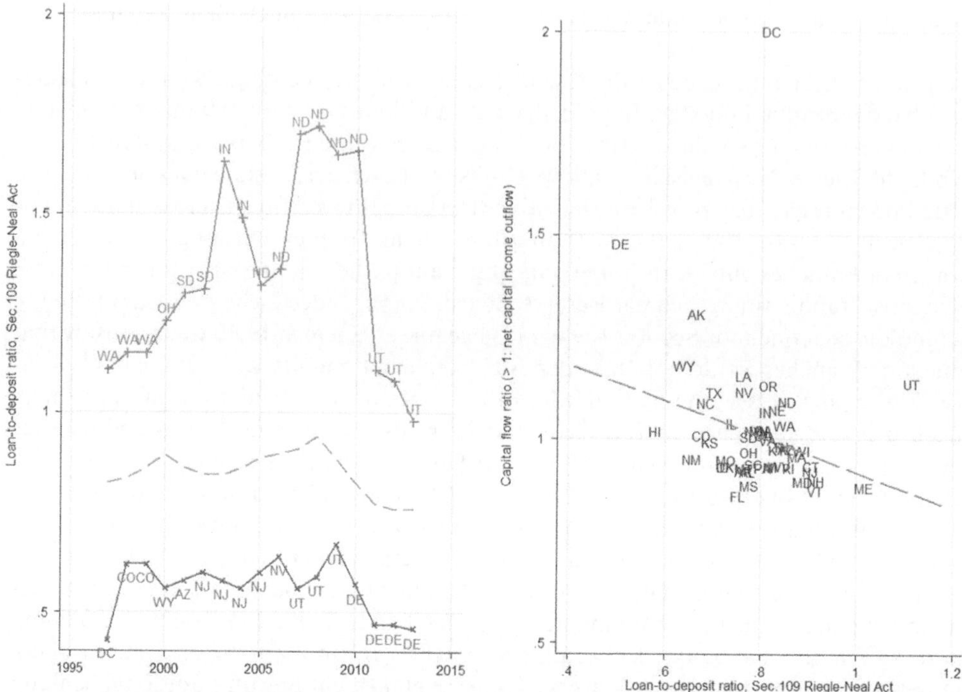

Notes: Section 109 of the Riegle–Neal Act "prohibits a bank from establishing or acquiring a branch or branches outside its home state, pursuant to the act, primarily for the purpose of deposit production". Regulatory enforcement of this provision takes place via the "host state loan-to-deposit ratio (LTD)" and requires the lending and deposit activities of a given bank's interstate branches to lie within a certain fraction of the host state LTD ratio. The right panel uses the 2013 cross section. Capital flows are approximated by the difference between gross state income and gross state product (see Kalemli-Ozcan, Reshef, Sørensen and Yosha, 2010).

Source: Author's calculations from FDIC, Federal Reserve and Census Bureau data.

Figure 16.6 Regional capital flows and the legacy of interstate banking regulation

this graph are proportional to total losses from FDIC-supervised depository institutions as a percentage of metropolitan GDP and area shading reflects the total number of failed institutions per metro area (ranging from light grey: 1–5 failures to black: 20–59 failures). Remarkably, the number of failed depository institutions and the relative economic magnitude of these failures are inversely distributed between the financial cores of the large urban centres and the more remote periphery. In other words, while more institutions failed in large metro areas, the cumulative economic impact of these failures was relatively modest in terms of local GDP, not exceeding for 2 per cent for the ten MSAs with the largest number of banking failures. By contrast, a few catastrophic failures of local depository institutions lower down in the urban systems had much more devastating impacts that were tallying up costs of as much as 30 per cent of GDP in Montgomery, AL – almost exclusively due the collapse of just three banks, including Alabama's second largest community BHC, Superior Bancorp (Table 16.3).

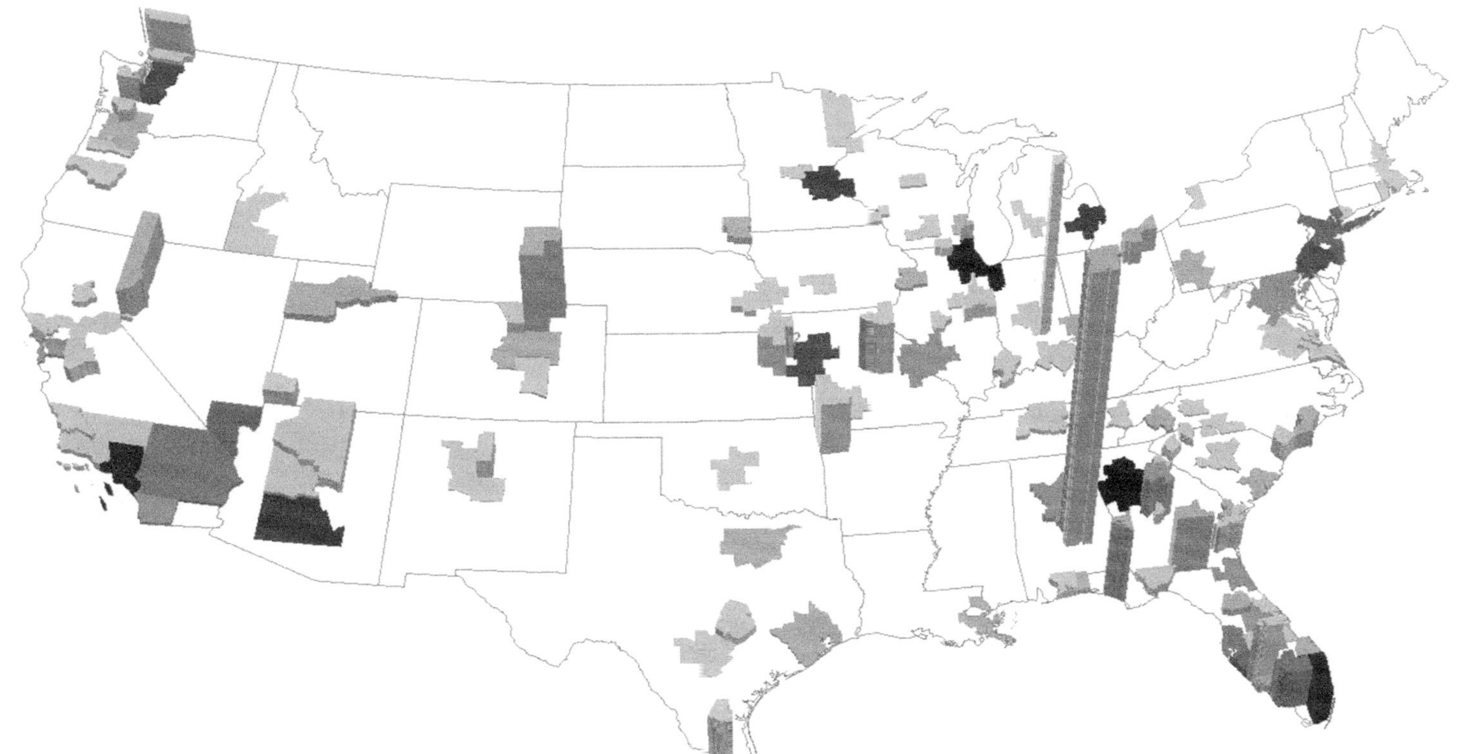

Notes: Metro area extrusions are proportional to total losses from FDIC-supervised depository institutions as a percentage of metropolitan GDP. Area shading reflects the total number of failed institutions per metro area (ranging from light grey: 1–5 failures to black: 20–59 failures).

Source: Author's calculations from FDIC Historical Statistics on Banking and BEA data.

Figure 16.7 Geography of banking failures across US metro areas, 2007–14

Table 16.3 Failures of depository institutions across US metro areas, 2007–14

Metro areas with the largest number of bank failures

Metro area	Loss as % GDP	Loss as % total deposit base	Loss as % FI's assets	Deposit-to-asset ratio	Deposit-to-asset ratio MSA	Loss ($ mn)	Deposits ($ mn, 2013)	Failed FIs
Atlanta, GA	0.1%	6.5%	32%	90%	76%	8,253	127,439	56
Chicago, IL-IN-WI	0.0%	1.3%	16%	91%	71%	4,501	357,573	42
Los Angeles, CA	0.8%	3.9%	23%	69%	74%	1,5281	391,348	14
Miami, FL	1.6%	3.7%	36%	72%	74%	6,681	182,613	13
Minneapolis-St. Paul, MN-WI	0.0%	0.3%	25%	94%	78%	551	211,213	13
Phoenix, AZ	0.0%	0.8%	24%	88%	74%	530	70,460	13
Detroit, MI	0.1%	1.3%	28%	90%	72%	1,320	100,909	12
Kansas City, MO-KS	0.2%	1.8%	21%	89%	77%	855	46,853	11
Seattle, WA	0.2%	1.6%	19%	88%	74%	1,289	78,560	10
Las Vegas, NV	0.0%	3.5%	1%	28%	75%	1,635	47,294	8

Metro areas with the most sizeable bank failures in terms of economic magnitude

Metro area	Loss as % GDP	Loss as % total deposit base	Loss as % FI's assets	Deposit-to-asset ratio	Deposit-to-asset ratio MSA	Loss ($ mn)	Deposits ($ mn, 2013)	Failed FIs
Columbus, IN	18.8%	77.1%	29%	79%	73%	831	1,078	1
Montgomery, AL	30.1%	62.5%	18%	79%	78%	4,542	7,268	3
Greeley, CO	8.8%	35.4%	39%	85%	74%	1,054	2,974	2
Macon, GA	4.1%	34.4%	42%	90%	78%	962	2,798	4
Panama City, FL	8.7%	27.6%	37%	95%	79%	796	2,886	2
Valdosta, GA	6.4%	15.6%	33%	86%	78%	301	1,933	2
Fayetteville, AR-MO	5.7%	12.7%	54%	96%	78%	1,032	8,095	1
Naples-Marco Island, FL	4.4%	11.3%	31%	87%	75%	1,387	12,251	7
Bellingham, WA	3.8%	10.8%	26%	88%	74%	313	2,901	1
Olympia, WA	2.7%	9.0%	24%	95%	73%	235	2,609	1

Source: Author's calculations from FDIC and BEA data.

In the remaining part of this section, I now turn to the lowest layer in the hierarchy of money, namely the world of market-based credit intermediation where "shadow banks" are most active. In what follows, I examine the spatial realities of the institutionally and functionally fragmented US regulatory complex in the context of the stunning growth and decline of housing credit during the Great Housing Boom and Bust.

Housing Credit, Regulatory Arbitrage and the Geography of Shadow Banking

Perhaps more than anywhere in the US financial system, the intensely regulated domain of housing credit was – and continues to be – the venue for a substantial amount of regulatory arbitrage, whereby BHCs directly attempt to circumvent costly regulatory requirements or specific financial activities get driven into the least regulated areas of the monetary-financial system, namely the opaque realm of "shadow banks". Indeed, the severity of the regulatory tax on traditional banking entities has arguably played an active role in pushing these activities beyond the perimeter of financial regulation into the world of "murky finance" (see for example Demyanyk and Loutskina, 2016).

Figure 16.8 illustrates the large volumes of mortgage origination by regulatory agency over the two decades that marked the largest rise and fall of house prices in modern US financial history. Two regulatory aspects of these developments are particularly worth highlighting. First, in addition to the three main banking regulators – the FDIC, the Fed and the OCC – the US Department of Housing and Urban Development (HUD) has regulatory oversight over all mortgage-related activities of non-depository institutions that can originate housing credit. This includes online mortgage originators, some of which play important roles in the long chains of the vertically disintegrated shadow banking machinery (Adrian and Ashcraft, 2012). At several points during the Great Housing Boom, up to one quarter of all mortgage originations – some $1 trillion in housing credit – took place outside of the conventional regulatory remit of the FIDC, the Fed and the OCC.

Second, Figure 16.8 also documents the strong amount of "regulatory sorting" that reveals itself with regard to another stylised fact of lending during the housing bubble, specifically the very distinct pattern of secondary-market loan sales (including sales for the purposes of securitization) to the GSEs (Fannie Mae, Freddy Mac) on the one hand, and sales and securitisation activities of private-sector entities.[18] The middle and bottom graphs of Figure 16.8 document that, while the bulk of GSE-related loan sales were originated by traditional depository entities under the regulatory control of the either the FDIC, the Fed or the OCC, up to a third of all secondary-market loan sales into private portfolios were originated by entities under the oversight of HUD. Indeed, on eve of the financial meltdown in 2006 when loan sales into private portfolios reached a historic peak, more HUD-regulated mortgages were sold to private sector securitizers than all the portfolio purchases by the GSEs combined.

Put differently, the "origination-to-distribute" (OTD) patterns of mortgage activities in the secondary market displayed a significant amount of variation not only over the course of the housing cycle, but also across different regulatory agencies. For example, loans originated by HUD-supervised entities had the highest likelihood of being sold for investment purposes (including securitization) in almost every year between 1994 and 2013. At the same time, the financial crisis also led to another instance of regulatory sorting in that there was an immense transfer of regulatory responsibility for the (functional) oversight of housing credit away from the pre-Dodd–Frank regulators to the newly created Consumer Financial Protection Bureau (CFPB) – to a large part, this shift in regulatory jurisdiction affected depository entities that were hitherto covered by the OCC. In this sense, the creation of the CFPB in 2011 under the Dodd–Frank Act marks an important departure from the US regulatory tradition of decentralized agencies whereby

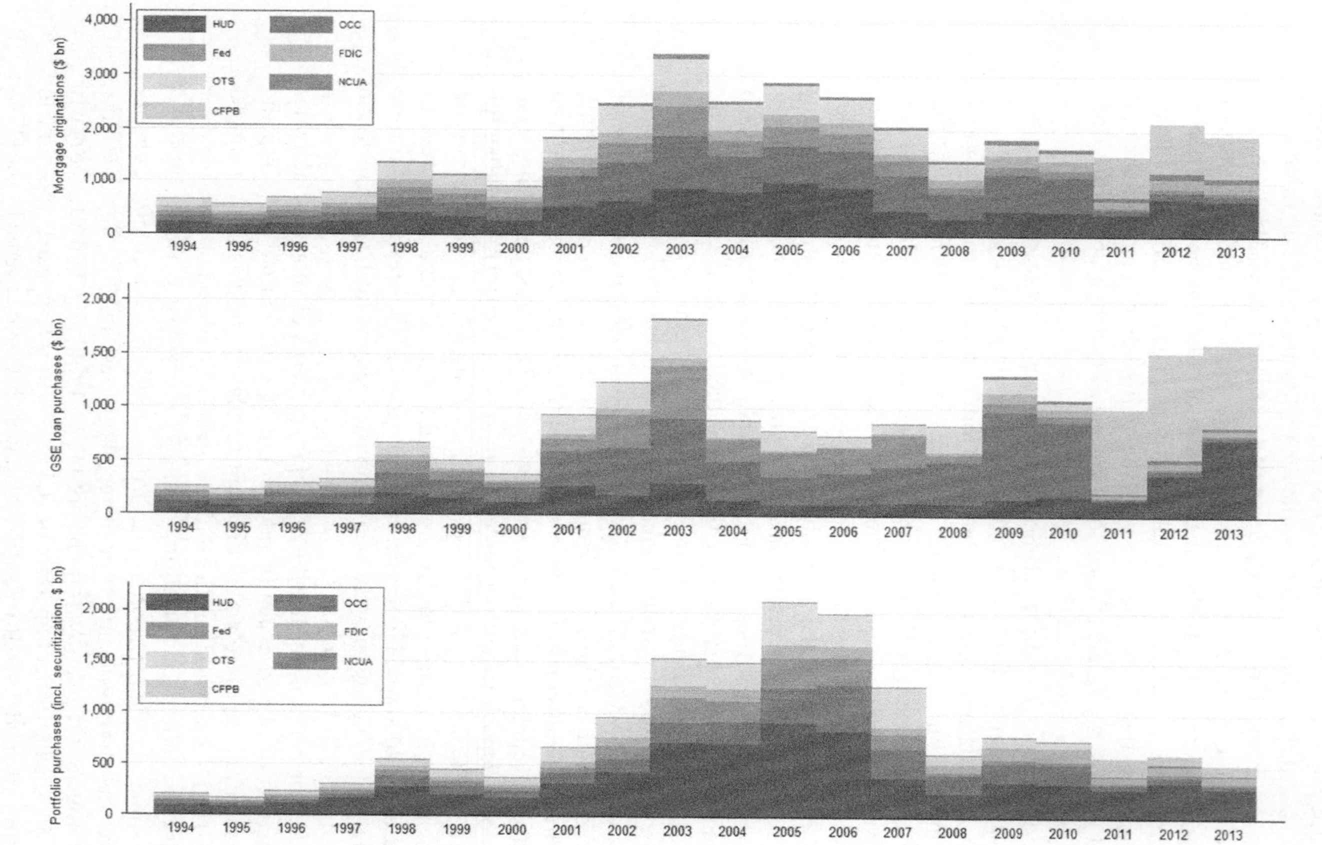

Notes: "OCC": Office of the Comptroller of the Currency, US Department of the Treasury; "Fed": Federal Reserve System; "FDIC": Federal Deposit Insurance Corporation; "OTS": Office of Thrift Supervision, US Department of the Treasury (merged with OCC in 2011, Title III of Dodd–Frank Act); "NCUA": National Credit Union Association; "HUD": US Department of Housing and Urban Development; "CFPB": Consumer Financial Protection Bureau (created via Title X of Dodd–Frank Act, effective in 2011).

Source: Author's calculations from HMDA microdata.

Figure 16.8 *Regulatory competency across the US housing credit cycle: volume of mortgage originations, loan sales by purchaser type, 1994–2013*

the institutional locus of financial oversight depended on the precise nature of the legal structure of and business activities pursued by individual financial intermediaries (Bieri, 2015a, 2015b).

For the purposes of the final part of our analysis, it is useful to retain the broad distinction between depository financial institutions (banks, savings institutions, credit unions and their affiliated mortgage subsidiaries (MBS)) and non-depository financial institutions (NDFIs). The systematic spatial variation in securitization patterns of banks and NDFIs over the course of the housing credit cycle is documented in Figure 16.9. As we have seen above, regulatory arbitrage by financial institutions outside the regulatory perimeter manifested itself in particular in the large differences in the loan purchase (and securitisation) activities of the GSEs versus those of the private sector. While GSEs tended to purchase and securitise bank-originated conventional loans that met the underwriting standards established by those entities, a large share of private-label purchases were originated by NDFIs.

Panel (a): Loan sales by banks and non-banks (NDFIs), 2006 and 2013

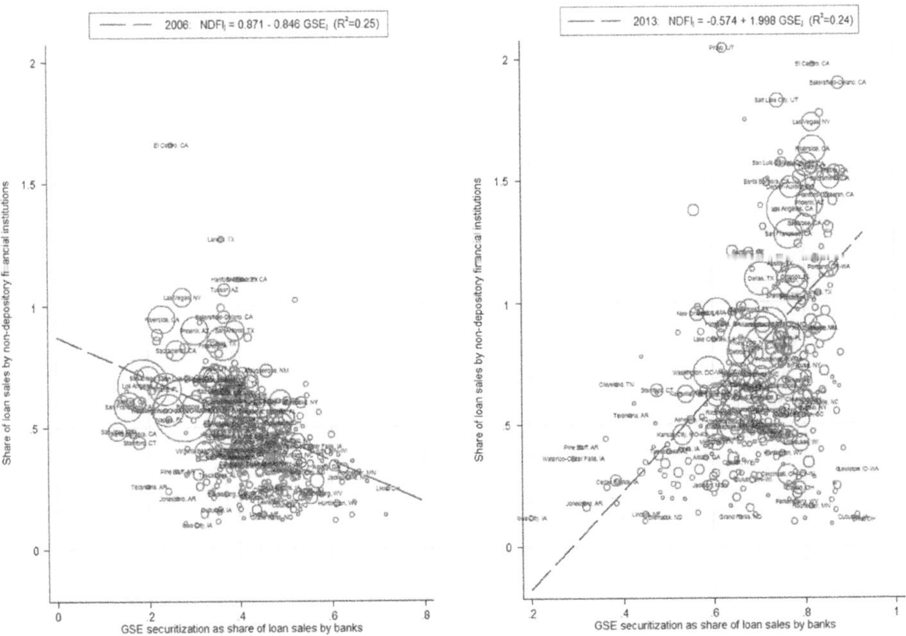

Notes: In panel (b), metro area extrusions are proportional to the share of total loan sales by NDFIs – this is the y-axis variable in panel (a). Area shading reflects the relative share of securitisation by GSEs (this is the x-axis variable in panel (a) – ranging from light grey: 15–20% to dark grey: 60–70%). In panel (c), extrusions are proportional to the volume of loan sales/securitisation by NDFIs as a percentage of MSA GDP. Area shading reflects the relative share of private label securitisation by NDFIs (ranging from light grey: 40–50% to dark grey: 95–99%).

Source: Author's calculations from HMDA microdata, BEA and Census Bureau data.

Figure 16.9 Securitization, regulatory arbitrage and the geography of shadow banking

Panel (b): GSE loan sales by banks, 2006

Panel (c): Private loan sales by NDFIs, 2006

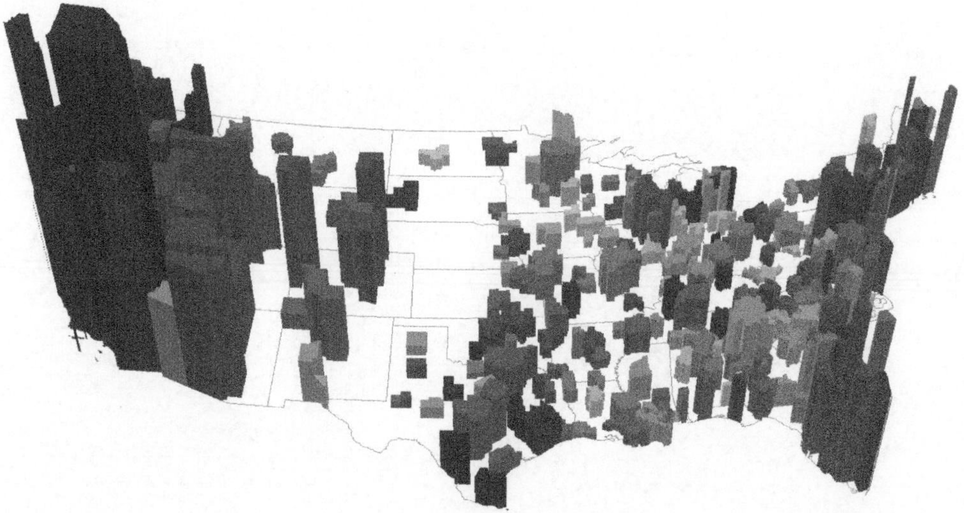

Figure 16.9 (continued)

Panel (a) in Figure 16.9 shows the remarkable change in the spatial relationship between this government-sponsored secondary market activity and private-sector secondary market activity. At the peak of the securitization boom in 2006, those US metro areas of the Sunbelt and on the coasts where housing markets were heating up the most also saw the highest amount of activity regarding the amount securitization conducted by NDFIs. In fact, in areas where NDFI were aggressively pursuing their OTD strategies, GSE secondary market activities were comparatively muted, while at the same time MSAs with the highest share of GSE-driven loan sales generally saw less private-sector securitization.[19]

As local housing markets were increasingly getting overheated, there appeared to have been a veritable "spatial crowding in" of mortgage credit whereby bank-originated loans sold to the GSEs were being displaced by a glut of NDFI-originated mortgages destined for private-label securitisation. The very distinct spatial patterns of GSE loan sales by banks and private loan sales by NDFIs is illustrated in panels (b) and (c) of Figure 16.9. In panel (b), metro area extrusions are proportional the share of total loan sales by NDFIs – this is the y-axis variable in panel (a). The area shadings reflect the relative share of securitization by GSEs (this is the x-axis variable in panel (a) – ranging from light grey: 15–20 per cent to dark grey: 60–70 per cent). In panel (c), by contrast, extrusions are proportional to the volume of loan sales/securitization by NDFIs as a percentage of MSA GDP and area shading reflects the relative share of private label securitisation by NDFIs (ranging from light grey: 40–50 per cent to dark grey: 95–99 per cent). While these distinct spatial patterns do not permit any causal inference about the regulatory origins of the housing bubble, they emphasize the intensely geographical nature of financialization in the housing market – a rapidly expanding, promising area of research (Hall and Leyshon, 2013; Immergluck and Law, 2014).

By early 2014, with private-label securitization activities at only a fraction of their pre-crisis levels, the pre-crisis relationship between government-led and private securitization appeared to have subsided completely – to the contrary, now, in the metro areas where the GSEs were most active in terms of their loan purchases, private sector financial institutions followed suit (see right section of panel (a) in Figure 16.9). The spatial effects of regulatory arbitrage in the lowest layer of the monetary hierarchy had all but vanished.

16.5 CONCLUSION AND OUTLOOK

In very broad terms – as the global economy no longer stares into the abyss of a financial market fallout – the principal regulatory lesson of the recent crisis seems to suggest excessive risk taking by global financial actors outside the perimeter of regulation as the main cause for the current meltdown. Going forward, this implies both expanding the scope of regulation of institutions (improved disclosure, limits on leverage, liquidity requirements, and governance standards) and a tighter regulation for markets and individual financial products. Thus what are the implications of the financial crisis for the regulatory spaces of the global financial system? In some ways, the crisis has highlighted the disruptive potential of the regulatory–spatial dialectic, putting a preliminary stop to market forms of regulation. Before the crisis, the preferred mode of regulation was "market-based" in the sense that private organizations such as credit rating agencies and international regulatory governance standards – codified by the internal-risk management standards of the Basel framework – would allow financial institutions to deploy and decipher price-based risk signals which in turn would exert sufficient regulatory pressure as to avoid any serious financial disasters, both at the institutional and at the systemic level (Lee et al., 2009).

For now at least, the crisis has debunked the idea that markets can effectively be understood as rational or efficient. Both nationally and at an international level, this has led to a significant strengthening of the political argument for greater levels of regulatory intervention and much stronger international co-ordination, tackling in particular the issue of regulatory arbitrage that so deeply dominated the dynamics of regulatory competition, both among financial centres (French et al., 2009) and, as this chapter argues, among different sectors of the monetary-financial complex. The scale of relevant activities outside the formal regulatory perimeter depends on the definition of regulation. For the United States, it has been estimated that the total assets of the "shadow banking system" – that is, bank-like entities not subject to bank-like prudential regulation – were roughly US$10 trillion in late 2007, about the same size as those of the banking system.[20] By 2015, assets of the US shadow banking industry had grown further to reach just under US$15 trillion, corresponding to almost 90 per cent of US GDP. Indeed, the regulation of the shadow banking system has been one of the most active areas of regulatory reform efforts since the financial crisis. Despite some improvements in strengthening the stability of the shadow banking system, progress to date has been uneven, at best (see for example Gorton and Metrick, 2010; Tarullo, 2012; Adrian et al., 2013).[21]

From the historical origins of modern money to the rise of shadow banking, this chapter has attempted to illustrate how the political economy of regulation creates new geographies of flows of funds – a set of spatial circuits that has come to be typified by the rapid evolution in bank complexity and a growing importance of "murky finance", that is the role of market-based credit intermediation. Recognizing the importance of real-financial linkages, my argument connects the political economy of regulation with the process of spatial development. Across different historical regimes, the intrinsic instability of the financial system governs a dialectical relationship between financial regulation and government intervention, in turn leading to financial innovation which opens up new frontiers across financial space.

Disciplinary debates about the future direction of the economic geography project call for an engaged pluralism. In this spirit, I have tried to argue the relevance of post-Keynesian monetary thinking for the economic geography of money and finance, as a complement to rather than substitute for a long-standing analytical tradition following the Marxian political economy in economic geography (Scott, 2000). While Sheppard and Barnes's (1990) seminal work has laid the foundations for a rich spatializing of post-Keynesian thought, their work is primarily focused on the real sector, that is production and consumption in a cash or barter setting that abstracts from the challenges of a modern monetary system that is dominated by the role of finance. I argue that a successful spatial theorizing of the monetary-financial system must complement the dominant Marxian view of money among geographers with heterodox monetary theories.

Overall, then, this chapter recognizes that regulatory developments in the financial system interact with the local and regional elements of the real economy. By demonstrating that the institutional arrangements of financial regulation matter for how the spatial economy evolves, I contend that money and finance are strongly non-neutral with regard to space, contrary to the central tenet of monetary neutrality in orthodox economics. In doing so, this work also seeks to contribute to an emergent literature on the spatial dimensions of financialization (Lee et al., 2009; French et al., 2011; Sokol, 2013). Perhaps a more subtle implication of the evidence presented here is the implicit relevance of post-Keynesian monetary thinking for the rapidly evolving literature on economic geography of money and finance. In this sense, Löschian economic geography implicitly contains essential spatial elements of post-Keynesian monetary theory, including the notion of a hierarchical credit theory of money and the assumption that money is created endogenously.[22]

NOTES

1. The term "monetary-financial system" reflects the view that monetary institutions and financial markets now overlap to such a degree that they are best viewed as parts of a larger whole (cf. Chandler, 1979; Davidson, 2003).
2. Economists generally distinguish between two separate approaches to monetary theory. The first develops monetary theory from the transactions, store-of-value and unit-of-account needs of a basic exchange economy with an exogenous amount of high-powered government money. The second approach, which includes Chartalism, views money as a hierarchical form of credit which renders it essentially endogenous to the economic system. See Godley and Lavoie (2007) and Wray (2012) for comprehensive primers on this literature and its importance for the finance–macroeconomy nexus.
3. The notion of "monetary neutrality" is a central tenet of neoclassical mainstream economics, suggesting that the spheres of money and production are analytically distinct. By contrast, heterodox monetary theories – from the German Historical School to post-Keynesianism, and in the case of the latter, most prominently and explicitly perhaps in the work of Hyman Minsky – emphasize the importance of the financial sector as a source of fluctuations in the real sector, thus opening up a pathway for the non-neutrality of money. See Cottrell (1994) for a good review of monetary analysis in the Post Keynesian tradition. Dow and Earl (1982), Arestis (1988) and Davidson (2003) provide a more detailed treatment of this material.
4. A student of Schumpeter's at Harvard and prominent biographer of Keynes (Minsky, 1975), much of Minsky's monetary thinking contains important elements that are common to both the views of Keynes and Schumpeter. See Whalen (2001) and Bertocco (2007) for elaborations on the theoretical importance of the Keynes–Schumpeter connection for the non-neutrality of money. See also endnote 10 below.
5. The rapidly expanding literature on spatial aspects of "economic resilience" is most relevant for our discussion here. See Martin and Sunley (2015) for a comprehensive review of this literature. Bieri (forthcoming) examines how "financial resilience" relates to conceptualizations of resilience that implicitly adhere to the classical dichotomy of treating real and monetary phenomena as analytically distinct.
6. The structural inadequacies of the US regulatory system, in particular, might actually extend beyond just financial regulation and are seen by some as affecting the entire scope of US regulation. From a series of recent environmental regulatory failures – including the BP Deepwater Horizon oil spill in the Gulf of Mexico – to the financial meltdown, the US regulatory complex appears to be plagued by administrative complexity, institutional sclerosis, budgetary austerity and policy uncertainty due to bipartisan polarization (for example Carrigan and Coglianese, 2012; *Economist*, 2012).
7. This dearth of regional monetary analysis notwithstanding, periodic attempts have been made to incorporate monetary and financial variables into regional economic models (for example Dow, 1988, 1999; Klagge and Martin, 2005). At the same time, the burgeoning literature on financialization remains "spatially anaemic" (Christophers, 2012).
8. The distinction between "outside money" and "inside money" goes back to seminal work of Gurley and Shaw (1960). In this context, "outside money" is either of a fiat nature or backed by some asset that is not in zero net supply within the private sector, whereas "inside money" is an asset backed by any form of private credit that circulates as a medium of exchange.
9. See Toniolo (2005) and Yago (2013) for historical details of the BIS as a precursor to the International Monetary Fund and on the creation of the BIS Currency Unit (BCU), linked to the Gold Swiss Franc, as a global reserve currency that was eventually overtaken by the IMF's Special Drawing Rights (SDR).
10. The similarities between Lösch's monetary thought and that of Minsky are far from coincidental, as both were students of Joseph Schumpeter's (Lösch at Friedrich-Wilhelms-Universität Bonn, and Minsky at Harvard). The Lösch-Minsky relationship and its deep connection to the misadventures of Schumpeter's *Treatise on Money* (1970) and its much more successful Keynesian counterpart are discussed in more detail elsewhere (Bieri, 2016).
11. See Epstein (2006) and Palley (2013) for a comprehensive theoretical framing of how financialization has been transforming the global economy.

12. In the present context, I use the conventional definition of "shadow banks" as financial institutions that conduct credit intermediation without direct, explicit access to public sources of liquidity and credit guarantees, largely emerging as the result of regulatory arbitrage. See Adrian and Ashcraft (2012) and Adrian, Ashcraft and Cetorelli (2013) for detailed discussions of the regulatory challenges associated with the shadow banking system.
13. Lösch (1938) explicitly recognized what – in more modern language – might be referred to as the complex network nature of regions, whereby "a clear economic region is a fortunate accident rather than a natural subdivision of state [. . .] a region is a system of various areas, an organism rather than just an organ" (Lösch, 1938: 71).
14. In a related sense, Taylor et al. (2010) underline the increasing importance of global flows within networks, proposing "central flow theory" as a complement to conventional location choice models anchored by Central Place Theory.
15. See, for example, Stiglitz (2000) for a prominent instance that captures the canon of this approach to theorizing government intervention. This literature views regulation as the public economics face of industrial organization, exploring the various ways in which governments interfere with industrial activities (Laffont, 1994).
16. For example, Section 106 of the Gramm-Leach-Bliley Act of 1999 further expanded the coverage of Section 109 by changing the definition of an "interstate branch", also applying the coverage to any bank or branch of a bank controlled by an out-of-state BHC. Interagency regulations implementing this amendment are still effective today.
17. A loan-to-deposit ratio of 1 indicates that a bank lends a dollar for each dollar in deposits. Note that the reasoning behind this regulatory provision – that is to "keep deposits local" – is inconsistent with the mechanics of modern banking where the arrow of causality runs from loans to deposits and not the other way around. See also Chick and Dow (1988), Dow (1999).
18. Among the information included in the annual Home Mortgage Disclosure Act (HMDA) data is the type of purchaser for loans that are originated and sold during the year. Although one of the few sources of information on loan sales, the HMDA data tend to understate the importance of the secondary market. See Avery et al. (2007) for more technical details on this point.
19. The literature on the spatial distribution of foreclosures is most directly related to this point. See, for example, Immergluck (2011) for a discussion of the spatial consequences of high-risk mortgage lending that came with greater financialization.
20. However, it is important to recognize that this total includes the assets of entities such as investment banks, which were subject to a degree of regulation, although this was often focused mainly on ensuring investor protection and appropriate business conduct (Carvajal et al., 2009).
21. In the context of shadow banking regulation, a key challenge is the potential for regulatory overlap when regulated banks actively participate in a shadow financial system (Schwarcz, 2012; Tarullo, 2013a, 2013b).
22. I discuss the theoretical aspects of the relevance of Post Keynesian monetary theory for economic geography in more detail elsewhere (Bieri, 2014a).

REFERENCES

Adrian, T. and A.B. Ashcraft (2012), 'Shadow banking regulation', *Annual Review of Financial Economics*, **4**, 99–140.

Adrian, T., A.B. Ashcraft and N. Cetorelli (2013), 'Shadow bank monitoring', in A.N. Berger, P. Molyneux and J.O.S. Wilson (eds), *The Oxford Handbook of Banking*, 2nd edition, New York: Oxford University Press, pp. 378–407.

Arestis, P. (ed.) (1988), *Post-Keynesian Monetary Economics: New Approaches to Financial Modelling*, New Directions in Modern Economics, Aldershot, UK and Brookfield, VT, USA: Edward Elgar Publishing.

Arestis, P. (1996), 'Post-Keynesian economics: towards coherence', *Cambridge Journal of Economics*, **20** (2), 111–135.

Avery, R.B., K.P Brevoort and G.B. Canner (2007), 'Opportunities and issues in using HMDA data', *Journal of Real Estate Research*, **29** (4), 351–379.

Barth, J.R., T. Liy and W. Luy (2010), 'Bank regulation in the United States', *CESifo Economic Studies*, **56** (1), 112–140.

BCBS (2013a), 'Global systemically important banks: updated assessment methodology and the higher loss absorbency requirement', Basel, Switzerland: Basel Committee on Banking Supervision, Bank for International Settlements.

BCBS (2013b), 'International regulatory framework for banks (Basel III)', Basel, Switzerland: Basel Committee on Banking Supervision, Bank for International Settlements.

Bell, S. (2001), 'The role of the state and the hierarchy of money', *Cambridge Journal of Economics*, **25** (2), 149–163.

Bertocco, G. (2007), 'The characteristics of a monetary economy: a Keynes–Schumpeter approach', *Cambridge Journal of Economics*, **31** (1), 101–122.

Bezemer, D.J. (2010), 'Understanding financial crisis through accounting models', *Accounting, Organizations and Society*, **35** (7), 676–688.

Bhattacharya, S., A.W.A. Boot and A.V. Thakor (1998), 'The economics of bank regulation', *Journal of Money, Credit and Banking*, **30** (4), 745–770.

Bieri, D.S. (2009), 'Financial stability, the Basel process and the new geography of regulation', *Cambridge Journal of Regions, Economy and Society*, **2** (2), 303–331.

Bieri, D.S. (2010), 'Regulation and financial stability in the age of turbulence', in R.W. Kolb (ed.), *Lessons from the Financial Crisis: Causes, Consequences, and Our Economic Future*, Hoboken, NJ: John Wiley & Sons, pp. 327–336.

Bieri, D.S. (2013), 'Form follows function: on the interaction between real estate finance and urban spatial structure', *CriticalProductive*, **2** (1), 7–16.

Bieri, D.S. (2014a), 'Hamlet without the prince? Economic geographies of money and finance without monetary theory', Mimeograph, University of Michigan.

Bieri, D.S. (2014b), *Moonlights, Sunspots and Frontier Finance: The Historical Nexus between Money, Credit and Urban Form*, Ann Arbor, MI: Political Space Economy Lab.

Bieri, D.S. (2015a), 'Financial stability rearticulated: institutional reform, post-crisis governance, and the new regulatory landscape in the United States', in P. Iglesias-Rodrigues (ed.), *Building Responsive and Responsible Regulators in the Aftermath of the Financial Crisis*, Cambridge, UK: Intersentia Publishers, pp. 213–232.

Bieri, D.S. (2015b), 'On the road again to Oz: a brief history of financial (in)stability and the regulatory–spatial dialectic of the US monetary-financial system', Mimeograph, Global Forum on Urban and Regional Resilience, Virginia Tech.

Bieri, D.S. (2016), 'August Lösch's monetary theory and its implications for the spatial neutrality of money', Mimeograph, Global Forum on Urban and Regional Resilience, Virginia Tech.

Bieri, D.S. (forthcoming), 'Conceptualizing financial resilience', in J. Bohland and J. Harald (eds), *The Resilience Challenge: Looking at Resilience through Multiple Lenses*, Springfield, IL: Charles Thomas Publishers.

Bieri, D.S. and P. Schaeffer (2015), 'The treatment of money in regional economics: a review', Mimeograph, University of Michigan and University of West Virginia.

Bowsher, N.N. (1952), 'Bank reserves and the flow of funds', *Federal Reserve Bank of St. Louis Monthly Review*, **34** (11), 155–165.

Bowsher, N.N., J.D. Daane and R.S. Einzig (1958), 'The flows of funds between regions of the United States', *Journal of Finance*, **13** (1), 1–20.

Calomiris, C.W. (2000), *US Bank Regulation in Historical Perspective*, Cambridge, UK and New York: Cambridge University Press.

Carrigan, C. and C. Coglianese (2012), 'Oversight in hindsight: assessing the US regulatory system in the wake of calamity', in C. Coglianese (ed.), *Regulatory Breakdown: The Crisis of Confidence in U.S. Regulation*, Philadelphia, PA: University of Pennsylvania Press, pp. 1–20.

Carvajal, A., R. Dodd, M. Moore, E. Nier, I. Tower and L. Zanforlin (2009), 'The perimeter of financial regulation', IMF Staff Position Note No. SPN/09/03, International Monetary Fund, Washington, DC.

Chandler, L.V. (1979), *The Monetary-Financial System*, New York: Harper & Row.

Chick, V. (1983), *Macroeconomics after Keynes: A Reconsideration of the General Theory*, Cambridge, MA: The MIT Press.

Chick, V. and S.C. Dow (1988), 'A post-Keynesian perspective on the relation between banking and regional development', in P. Arestis (ed.), *Post-Keynesian Monetary Economics: New Approaches to Financial Modelling*, Aldershot, UK and Brookfield, VT, USA: Edward Elgar Publishing, pp. 219–250.

Chick, V. and S.C. Dow (1996), 'Regulation and differences in financial institutions', *Journal of Economic Issues*, **30** (2), 535–541.

Chick, V. and G. Tily (2014), 'Whatever happened to Keynes's monetary theory?' *Cambridge Journal of Economics*, **38** (3), 681–699.

Christophers, B. (2012), 'Anaemic geographies of financialisation', *New Political Economy*, **17** (3), 271–291.

Cohen, B.J. (1998), 'Currency competition and hierarchy', in B.J. Cohen, *The Geography of Money*, 1st edition, Ithaca, NY: Cornell University Press, pp. 92–118.

Cohen, B.J. (2003), *The Future of Money*, Princeton, NJ and New York: Princeton University Press.

Cohen, B.J. (2007), 'The new geography of money', in B.J. Cohen, *Global Monetary Governance*, London: Routledge, pp. 207–224.

Conzen, M.P. (1975), 'Capital flows and the developing urban hierarchy: state bank capital in Wisconsin, 1854–1895', *Economic Geography*, **51** (4), 321–338.
Copeland, M.A. (1947), 'Tracing money flows through the United States economy', *American Economic Review*, **37** (2), 31–49.
Copeland, M.A. (1952), *A Study of Moneyflows in the United States*, Cambridge, MA: National Bureau of Economic Research.
Cottrell, A. (1994), 'Post-Keynesian monetary economics', *Cambridge Journal of Economics*, **18** (4), 587–605.
Davidson, P. (2003), *Financial Markets, Money and the Real World*, Cheltenham, UK and Northampton, MA, USA: Edward Elgar Publishing.
Demyanyk, Y. and E. Loutskina (2016), 'Mortgage companies and regulatory arbitrage', *Journal of Financial Economics*, **122** (2), 328–351.
Dow, S.C. (1988), 'Incorporating money in regional economic models', in F.J. Harrigan and P.G. McGregor (eds), *Recent Advances in Regional Economic Modelling*, London Papers in Regional Science No. 19, London: Pion Limited, pp. 208–218.
Dow, S.C. (1999), 'The stages of banking development and the spatial evolution of financial systems', in R.L. Martin (ed.), *Money and the Space Economy*, Chichester: John Wiley & Sons, pp. 31–48.
Dow, S.C. and P.E. Earl (1982), *Money Matters: A Keynesian Approach to Monetary Economics*, London: M. Robertson.
Economist (2012), 'Over-regulated America', *The Economist*, **396** (8786), 27–30, Print edition.
Epstein, G.A. (ed.) (2006), *Financialization and the World Economy*, Cheltenham, UK and Northampton, MA, USA: Edward Elgar Publishing.
Federal Reserve Board (2002), *Regulation H, Membership of State Banking Institutions in the Federal Reserve System*, Washington, DC.
French, S., A. Leyshon and N. Thrift (2009), 'A very geographical crisis: the making and breaking of the 2007–2008 financial crisis', *Cambridge Journal of Regions, Economy and Society*, **2** (2), 287–302.
French, S., A. Leyshon and T. Wainwright (2011), 'Financialising space, spacing financialisation', *Progress in Human Geography*, **35** (6), 798–819.
Godley, W. and M. Lavoie (2007), *Monetary Economics: An Integrated Approach to Credit, Money, Income, Production and Wealth*, New York: Palgrave Macmillan.
Goodhart, C.A.E. (2008a), 'The boundary problem in financial regulation', *National Institute Economic Review*, **206** (1), 48–55.
Goodhart, C.A.E. (2008b), 'The regulatory response to the financial crisis', *Journal of Financial Stability*, **4** (4), 351–358.
Goodhart, C.A.E. (2010), 'How Should we regulate the financial sector?' in *The Future of Finance: The LSE Report*, The London School of Economics and Political Science, pp. 153–176.
Gorton, G. and A. Metrick (2010), 'Regulating the shadow banking system', *Brookings Papers on Economic Activity*, **41** (2), 261–312.
Gurley, J.G. and E.S. Shaw (1960), *Money in a Theory of Finance*, Washington, DC: Brookings Institution Press.
Hall, S. and A. Leyshon (2013), 'Editorial: financialization, space and place', *Regional Studies*, **47** (6), 831–833.
Hanson, S.G., A.K. Kashyap and J.C. Stein (2011), 'A macroprudential approach to financial regulation', *Journal of Economic Perspectives*, **25** (1), 3–28.
Harvey, D. (1978), 'The urban process under capitalism: a framework for analysis', *International Journal of Urban and Regional Research*, **2** (1–4), 100–131.
Harvey, D. (1985a), *Money, Time, Space, and the City*, Cambridge, UK: Denman Lectures. Granta Editions.
Harvey, D. (1985b), *The Urbanization of Capital: Studies in the History and Theory of Capitalist Urbanization*, Baltimore, MD: Johns Hopkins University Press.
Hawtrey, R.G. (1919), *Currency and Credit*, London: Longmans, Green & Company.
Immergluck, D. (2011), 'The local wreckage of global capital: the subprime crisis, federal policy and high-foreclosure neighborhoods in the US', *International Journal of Urban and Regional Research*, **35** (1), 130–146.
Immergluck, D. and J. Law (2014), 'Speculating in crisis: the intrametropolitan geography of investing in foreclosed homes in Atlanta', *Urban Geography*, **35** (1), 1–24.
Isard, W. (1956), 'Location and space-economy: a general theory relating to industrial location', *Market Areas, Land Use, Trade, and Urban Structure*, vol. 1 of *Regional Science Studies Series*, 1st edition, Cambridge, MA: MIT Press.
Isard, W. (1960), 'Interregional flow analysis and balance of payment statements', *Methods of Regional Analysis*, vol. 4 of *Regional Science Studies Series*, 1st edition, Cambridge, MA: MIT Press, pp. 122–179.
Jayaratne, J. and P.E. Strahan (1996), 'The finance–growth nexus: evidence from bank branch deregulation', *Quarterly Journal of Economics*, **111** (3), 639–670.
Kalemli-Ozcan, S., A. Reshef, B.E. Sørensen and O. Yosha (2010), 'Why does capital flow to rich states?', *Review of Economics and Statistics*, **92** (4), 769–783.

Kane, E.J. (1996), 'De jure interstate banking: why only now?', *Journal of Money, Credit and Banking*, **28** (2), 141–161.
Keynes, J.M. (1930), *A Treatise on Money: The Pure Theory of Money and The Applied Theory of Money*, New York: Harcourt, Brace and Company.
Klagge, B. and R.L. Martin (2005), 'Decentralized versus centralized financial systems: is there a case for local capital markets?' *Journal of Economic Geography*, **5** (4), 387–421.
Kregel, J.A. and M. Tonveronachi (2013), 'Fundamental principles of financial regulation and supervision', Working Paper No. 29, Financialisation, Economy, Society and Sustainable Development, Leeds, UK.
Labasse, J. (1974), *L'Éspace Financier: Analyse Géographique*, Paris: Armand Colin.
Laffont, J.-J. (1994), 'The new economics of regulation: ten years after', *Econometrica*, **62** (3), 507–537.
Lee, R., G.L. Clark, J. Pollard and A. Leyshon (2009), 'The remit of financial geography – before and after the crisis', *Journal of Economic Geography*, **9** (6), 723–747.
Litan, R.E (2012) 'The political economy of financial regulation after the crisis', in A.S. Blinder, A.W. Lo and R.M. Solow (eds), *Rethinking the Financial Crisis*, New York: Russell Sage Foundation, pp. 269–303.
Lösch, A. (1938), 'The nature of economic regions', *Southern Economic Journal*, **5** (1), 71–78.
Lösch, A. (1940), 'Geographie des Zinses', *Die Bank*, **33**, 24–28.
Lösch, A. (1949), 'Theorie der Währung: Ein Fragment', *Weltwirtschaftliches Archiv*, **62**, 35–88.
Lösch, A. (1954), *The Economics of Location*, New Haven, CT: Yale University Press.
Martin, R.L. (2011), 'The local geographies of the financial crisis: from the housing bubble to economic recession and beyond', *Journal of Economic Geography*, **11** (4), 587–618.
Martin, R.L. and P. Sunley (2015), 'On the notion of regional economic resilience: conceptualization and explanation', *Journal of Economic Geography*, **15** (1), 1–42.
Mehrling, P.G. (2011), *The New Lombard Street: How the Fed Became the Dealer of Last Resort*, Princeton, NJ: Princeton University Press.
Mehrling, P.G. (2013), 'The inherent hierarchy of money', in P.G. Mehrling, *Social Fairness and Economics: Economic Essays in the Spirit of Duncan Foley*, New York: Festschrift, Routledge Frontier of Political Economy, Routledge, pp. 394–404.
Mehrling, P., Z. Pozsar, J. Sweeney and D.H. Neilson (2013), 'Bagehot was a shadow banker: shadow banking, central banking, and the future of global finance', Discussion paper, Institute for New Economic Thinking.
Merton, R.C. (1995), 'A functional perspective of financial intermediation', *Financial Management*, **24** (2), 23–41.
Minsky, H.P. (1967), 'Financial intermediation in the money and capital markets', in G. Pontecorvo, R.P. Shay, P. Robert and G. Hart (eds), *Issues in Banking and Monetary Analysis*, New York: Columbia University Graduate School of Business. Holt, Rinehart and Winston, pp. 33–56.
Minsky, H.P. (1975), *John Maynard Keynes*, New York: Columbia University Press.
Minsky, H.P. (1977), 'The financial instability hypothesis: an interpretation of Keynes and an alternative to "standard" theory', *Challenge*, **20** (1), 20–27.
Minsky, H.P. (1991), 'The financial instability hypothesis: a clarification', in M. Feldstein (ed.), *The Risk of Economic Crisis*, Chicago, IL: University of Chicago Press, pp. 158–166.
Minsky, H.P. (1993), 'On the non-neutrality of money', *Federal Reserve Bank of New York Quarterly Review*, **18** (1), 77–82.
Minsky, H.P. (2008), *Stabilizing an Unstable Economy*, New York: McGraw Hill.
Palley, T.I. (2013), *Financialization: The Economics of Finance Capital Domination*, London and New York: Palgrave Macmillan.
Palumbo, M.G. and J.A. Parker (2009), 'The integrated financial and real system of national accounts for the United States: does it presage the financial crisis?' *American Economic Review*, **99** (2), 80–86.
Perroux, F. (1950), 'Economic space: theory and application', *Quarterly Journal of Economics*, **64** (1), 89–104.
Pollard, J. (1999), 'Globalisation, regulation and the changing organisation of retail banking in the United States and Britain', in R.L. Martin (ed.), *Money and the Space Economy*, Chichester: John Wiley & Sons, pp. 49–70.
Rosen, R.J. (2003), 'Is three a crowd? Competition among regulators in banking', *Journal of Money, Credit and Banking*, **35** (6), 967–998.
Schumpeter, J.A. (1970), *Das Wesen des Geldes*, F.K. Mann (ed.), Göttingen: Vandenhoeck und Ruprecht.
Schwarcz, S.L. (2012), 'Regulating shadow banking', *Review of Banking and Financial Law*, **31**, 619–642.
Scott, A.J. (2000), 'Economic geography: the great half-century', *Cambridge Journal of Economics*, **24** (3), 483–504.
Sheppard, E. and T.J. Barnes (1990), *The Capitalist Space Economy: Geographical Analysis after Ricardo, Marx and Sraffa*, London: Unwin Hyman.
Sokol, M. (2013), 'Towards a "newer" economic geography? Injecting finance and financialisation into economic geographies', *Cambridge Journal of Regions, Economics and Society*, **6** (3), 501–515.
Stiglitz, J.E. (2000), *Economics of the Public Sector*, 3rd edition, New York: W.W. Norton & Company.

Tarullo, D.K. (2012), 'Shadow banking after the financial crisis', Speech, Board of Governors of the Federal Reserve System.

Tarullo, D.K. (2013a), 'Macroprudential regulation', Keynote Address at Yale Law School Conference on Challenges in Global Financial Services, Board of Governors of the Federal Reserve System, New Haven, CT.

Tarullo, D.K. (2013b), 'Shadow banking and systemic regulation', Speech, Board of Governors of the Federal Reserve System, Washington, DC.

Tarullo, D.K. (2014), 'Regulating large foreign banking organizations', Speech, Board of Governors of the Federal Reserve System, Armonk, NY.

Taylor, P.J., M. Hoyler and R. Verbruggen (2010), 'External urban relational process: introducing central flow theory to complement central place theory', *Urban Studies*, **47** (13), 2803–2818.

Thrift, N. and K. Olds (1996), 'Refiguring the economic in economic geography', *Progress in Human Geography*, **20** (3), 311–337.

Toniolo, G. (2005), *Central Bank Cooperation at the Bank for International Settlements, 1930–1973*, Cambridge and New York: Cambridge University Press.

Tropeano, D. (2011), 'Financial regulation after the crisis: where do we stand?', *International Journal of Political Economy*, **40** (2), 45–60.

Whalen, C.J. (2001), 'Integrating Schumpeter and Keynes: Hyman Minsky's theory of capitalist development', *Journal of Economic Issues*, **35** (5), 805–823.

Whalen, G. (2010), 'Why do de novo banks choose a national charter?', Working Paper, Office of the Comptroller of the Currency, Washington, DC.

Winkler, B., A. Van Riet and P. Bull (eds) (2013), 'A flow-of-funds perspective on the financial crisis: money, credit and sectoral balance sheets', vol. 1 of *Palgrave Studies in Economics and Banking*, Basingstoke and New York: Palgrave Macmillan.

Wray, L.R. (2009), 'The rise and fall of money manager capitalism: a Minskian approach', *Cambridge Journal of Economics*, **33** (4), 807–828.

Wray, L.R. (2012), *Modern Money Theory: A Primer on Macroeconomics for Sovereign Monetary Systems*, London and New York: Palgrave Macmillan.

Yago, K. (2013), *The Financial History of the Bank for International Settlements*, Abingdon and New York: Routledge.

17. Regulatory spaces in global finance

Sabine Dörry

17.1 GEOGRAPHIES OF FINANCE

Global finance has been significantly transformed from a 'Main Street model', that finances innovation and product manufacturing, so as to increase wages and stimulate demand, into a global capital-accumulating 'Wall Street model' whose innovative capacity creates ever more sophisticated financial instruments and contracts that nurture financial speculation rather than material production. This transformation, among others, entails both a shift from banking to shadow banking, that is, an upsurge of the sources of credit supply and the continual reshaping of the geographies of finance across all scales. Financial markets vary significantly in their geographies, marked by dynamics of both concentration and dispersion. Sophisticated technological infrastructures have greatly amplified the speed, volume and spatial reach of financial transactions. New demand for financial services, governments' thirst for funding and corporations' trawls for cheap financing fuelled the physical, virtual and economic expansion of the global financial markets. All this happened not least 'on the back of competition between financial centers' (Story and Lawton, 2010: 103), well-equipped with particular sets of regulations to attract and channel flows of money within the world economy, thus, creating and recreating 'regulatory spaces' (Hancher and Moran, 1989) of finance.

All these observations are of course only fractions that depict snapshots of changes in financial markets. This chapter engages with the binding power of capital flows, financial firms' strategies and the resulting shifting landscapes of finance. At the heart of this ongoing process is the problem of regulation. Financial innovation is often generated to offset and avoid it, that is, to respond to regulatory structures' intended or unintended effects on incentives for financial market participants. Financial markets and regulation are, however, inseparably bound together in their making (Pollard and Samers, 2011). Finance is deeply encoded in law and the states' decisions to outsource their control over legal privileges to the financial industry over time are deeply engrained social processes between market and regulatory forces. This chapter repeatedly refers to this argument and – in situating regulatory processes and practices in space – encourages a wider conversation between regulation and geography.

Finance has always been among the most regulated industries. Traditionally, nation states hardly trusted high finance to produce outcomes of common interests (Polanyi, [1944] 1978) and were proved right in their caution. The rise of the Euromarkets' 'stateless monies' (Martin, 1994) since the late 1950s, ideologically supported by the US and the UK (and especially the Bank of England), marked the emergence of truly integrated international financial markets that have since 'coexisted' with the national financial markets. This process – together with the breakup of the Bretton Woods system discussed later in this chapter – literally decoupled the US dollar from US territorial regulation (Hudson, 1998) and paved the way for a competitive race among international financial centres (IFCs) to attract more financial business by relaxing their tax and business environments. In 1985, the annual report of the Bank for International Settlements (BIS) alertly pointed towards vital structural changes in international finance: that new financial techniques and instruments had soared to minimize taxation and regulations costs; that the authorities had 'deliberately' moved towards deregulation, thus, triggering not only the emergence of new categories of financial institutions but also encouraging the new role of international financial markets; and that (western) banks' international exposure had increased dramatically (Bank for International Settlements (BIS), 1985). Within this historically unprecedented situation and challenging period of transition, BIS advocated a prudential supervision model – about techniques of risk management and focused on institutions to protect their solvency and viability – thus, moving away from forms of an economic or product regulatory regime. Prudential supervision impacted fundamentally on the behaviour of financial institutions. Under economic regulation – based on basic rules of disclosure and focusing on standards of customer service – banks were passive investors who simply took what the market offered them (Thompson, 1996). In contrast, prudential regulation offered banks a new degree of operational freedom to 'behave as *market-oriented economic agents* and interact with market forces' (Casu et al., 2010: 118, emphasis added).

This chapter approaches the concept of regulatory spaces from a broad range of empirical examples. It takes the altering international physiognomies of modern finance to engage with contemporary regulations. In doing so, it applies a range of illustrative examples from the global securities markets, banking and lending operations and foreign exchange (Forex) trading in order to tackle the question, how and to what extent have (new) regulatory spaces solidified and reinforced the (prevailing) uneven geographies in international finance? Uneven regulation is the very foundation of the contemporary globalizing financial system, of which the states take advantage (Christophers, 2013) as well as private arbitrageurs and financial speculators. As this chapter will show, the asymmetric power relations associated with institutions, regulatory myopia (Clark, 2011), institutional innovation and intense competition between spaces across geographical scales solidify and reinforce patterns of the (prevailing) uneven geographies in international finance. Financial instability is only one result. A second, arguably somewhat contradictory, outcome is the increasing integration and mutual interdependence between regulatory spaces. Their interconnectedness, manifested in the boundary spanning geopolitics and geoeconomics of finance, the complex web of competing, yet interconnected specialized and (therefore often even) cooperating spaces of finance (Dörry, 2015) and the perilous power of a few financial institutions (Wójcik, 2013), define the binding ties that hold the manifold rivalling spaces together. This chapter encourages the joined-up thinking of the varying regulatory spaces, shaped by conflicting legal foundations, business cultures and geographical reach. It hopes to direct new conceptual thinking on how regulatory capacities could capture the fluid character of increasingly 'hybrid' and 'transitory' regulatory spaces and how institutional regimes interact to negotiate the nature, scope and depth of emerging regulatory spaces of finance.

The fundamental contradiction of regulation is the second key theme of this chapter. On the one hand, the state and other 'public' authorities have a profound interest in a stable and growth oriented macroeconomy that produces widespread prosperity. On the other hand, the financial capitalist economy at various scales is dependent upon a fluid banking system and fluid financial markets that are able to innovate new products to deal with all sorts of micro-, meso- and at worst macroeconomic changes. This fluid system is, however, at best a tool for capitalists to avoid tax and at worst subject to wild fluctuations and crises which disrupt the macroeconomy, which sparks a second collision of financial regulation: private actors seek to circumvent regulations and to exploit the potential of market forces yet at the same time seek protection from the very same system whose rules they try to avoid.

Hence, the second section recalls how the states have indeed addressed the de- and re-regulation of their financial markets on the example of the Euromarkets. Section 17.3 alludes to this historical evolution and genealogy of the global regulatory landscape over the post-war period and suggests the conceptual foundations of the shaping and making of regulatory spaces in order to study the organizational complexities of spatially interconnected financial markets more distinctly. The fourth section illustrates a range of regulatory spaces in order to stimulate discussion on the outcomes of distinct politico-economic settings and legal environments, dissimilar legal traditions as found in the juxtaposition of common law and civil law countries and their resulting degrees of liberty for financial innovation, market integration dynamics and emerging virtual spaces as a potential new stage of 'financial liberty' and stateless monies. The chapter's final section reflects on these examples conceptually and identifies potential future research agendas of geographical research into money and finance.

17.2 THE EVOLUTION OF A NEW GLOBAL REGULATORY LANDSCAPE

From the late 1990s onwards, de-regulation heavily conditioned the restructuring of the banking sector, which also altered the level of international capital mobility (Eichengreen, 2008). Both the US and the UK played a leading role in the abolition of capital controls and a 'competitive deregulation' in the 1970s and 1980s, with many European states following suit in the 1980s. The 1990s saw 'an almost fully liberal financial order [. . .] in the OECD region, giving market operators a degree of freedom they had not since the 1920s' (Helleiner, 1994: 9). This drawback triggered 'geographical discontinuities and gaps in [. . .] regulatory spaces' (Martin, 1999: 9) and paved the way for market participants' global regulatory arbitrage and other exploiting strategies (Laulajainen, 2003). Fundamental ideological shifts and the almost unconditional political support for the Euromarkets lastingly reconfigured the highly regulated post-war national financial markets and boosted the well-being of a number of emerging IFCs as the following brief genealogy of the global regulatory landscape shows.

Still encumbered with the appalling experience of the Great Depression, the Bretton Woods Agreement dramatically rejected the prominent liberal financial policies from before 1931 (Helleiner, 1994). With the dollar crisis in 1966 and the collapse of the Bretton Woods system in 1973, the rapid growth and transformation of the international financial markets, along with the shifts in state economic policies towards neoliberal forms, and the rise of new global financial centres, went hand in hand to create new realities in global finance. One crux of the matter was the success of the Euromarket, which was unregulated and truly international and was both an outcome and instrument of a financial liberalization in the US and the UK. The Kennedy and Johnson administrations sought to curb the growing US fiscal deficit and the progressive speculation against the US dollar when the market lost confidence in the dollar's gold convertibility. A series of capital controls complemented by tax impositions since the early 1960s was introduced to discourage the dollar export by American banks and corporations (Helleiner, 1994). Whilst such capital control programmes continued to subordinate 'the interests of US bankers [. . .] to the priorities of New Deal economics and global strategic objectives' (Helleiner, 1994: 87), the 1960s clearly marked a transition period.

The development in the UK was similar. Just like the US, the chronic deficit country UK imposed a series of capital controls to stop capital outflows, whilst chronic surplus countries such as Germany used capital controls to stop capital inflows. The 1957 sterling crisis, however, forced London's heavily battered international bankers to shift their business to a dollar basis on the emerging Euromarket. It presented a viable way to preserve their international businesses without being burdened by the existing British capital controls. British financial authorities, especially the Bank of England, actively supported the Eurodollar market because it represented 'a solution to the problem of how to reconcile the goal of restoring London's international position with the Keynesian welfare state and Britain's deteriorating economic position' (Helleiner, 1994: 84). Although western European states and Japan initially resisted these liberalization initiatives and instead pressed for tighter capital controls, they failed 'to move toward a more closed financial order in the early 1970s' (Helleiner, 1994: 121). Their failure marked the beginning of the end of the Bretton Woods financial framework.

When the US catalysed a capital controls programme in July 1963, that is, the interest equalization tax, London was well-equipped to replace New York as the leading international capital market. In the early 1970s, a general disillusionment with the post-war regulatory environment corresponded to growing frustrations from high unemployment, rising inflation and economic slowdown. Further, new competitors increasingly threatened the US's post-war economic supremacy. These dynamics dramatically reversed the US international economic policy in August 1971, which continued under the presidencies of Nixon and Ford (Bergsten, 1996: 320). It also provided an ideal breeding ground for a new alignment of economic neoliberalism and financial liberalization. Henceforth, the industrial nations' financial interests, multinational businesses and officials encouraged the financial markets' disciplining power over government policy and sacrificed stable exchange rates in their hopes to stimulate international and domestic competitiveness (Helleiner, 1994: 116).

In 1961, the new born OECD Code of Liberalisation of Capital Movements still conveyed the idea of the Bretton Woods architects White and Keynes to strictly discriminate desirable flows of productive capital [from] undesirable flows of speculative capital (OECD, 2015). With the departure from the Keynesian welfare system and the rise of economic neoliberalism, however, the power of financial capital also prevailed over the power of industrial capital (Hampton, 1996). The new speculative capital flows were a 'new source of trouble' because they 'responded not just to economic fundamentals but also to the sometimes volatile and irrational judgements of currency traders and asset holders' (Helleiner, 1994: 123). The thriving Eurodollar and – equivalently – Asian dollar markets also created opportunities for new places to participate in and steer the international financial flows. Offshore financial centres added to the necessary infrastructure. They functioned as markets in which financial operators would collect deposits in US dollars from and lend US dollars to non-residents, 'free from most regulations and taxes'

(Palan, 2012). Prominent examples besides the City of London-centred archipelago of the Channel Islands, BVI and Cayman Islands are Luxembourg and Singapore. Over time, these highly specialized centres also formed new growth coalitions between private and public elites (Dörry, 2016), thus further encouraging the flows of speculative capital. Overall, the Euromarket served the purpose of two powerful interests, which nourished and nurtured its growth. The financial industry exploited the Euromarket as a powerful means to circumvent restricting national economic policies, and the US government hoped to encourage foreign governments and private investors to finance its growing state deficit. However, Eric Helleiner (1994) demonstrates convincingly the fundamental contradiction: that at the same time as the Bretton Woods system was trying to limit financial flows, it was also trying to encourage a healthy level of international trade – at least to the extent that it promoted national economic development, benevolently referred to as an 'even' development. In so doing, Helleiner establishes a genealogy of financial globalization, for which the seeds were already planted in the 1940s.

17.3 IDIOSYNCRASIES OF FINANCE AND IMPLICATIONS FOR REGULATION

Finance stands out against other industries for the following reasons (White, 1999). First, it is all-pervasive as the well-established body of financialization literature illustrates. Second, finance is vital to the development of any economy because it is the instrument for transforming and transferring the savings of an economy into its investment. The degree of efficiency of the funds' reallocation, however, determines an economy's growth and depends on financial regulation. Financial regulation facilitates a third characteristic of finance, that is, information asymmetries between borrowers and lenders. Information asymmetries inevitably result in time sequencing and vulnerabilities of borrowers. These vulnerabilities are amplified by the consequential social externalities from (shadow) banks' moral hazard behaviour such as privatizing profits and socializing costs and risks (The Warwick Commission, 2009). Hence, financial regulation aims primarily at maintaining market confidence, stabilizing the financial systems, protecting retail investors and reducing financial crime. Regulation also covers many financial markets and activities. Banking regulation, for example, defines only one part of contemporary banking supervision, with the second important pillar being securities regulation.

The term 'regulation' itself is, however, a misnomer (Fagan and Heron, 1994) as it is often solely associated with strong forms and discrete modes of governance activity (Holton, 2012). More subtle meanings of the terms regulation and deregulation relate to strong forms of external control and state actions, including economic incentive setting, prohibition and radical restriction. It distinguishes a 'red light' concept that restricts certain behaviour and prevents the occurrence of certain undesirable activities from a 'green light' concept, which enables and facilitates other behaviour (Baldwin and Cave, 1999). More informal notions of regulation refer to forms of social control and influence delivered by different kinds of organization and embodied in a variety of rules and practices. Undoubtedly, effective market operation necessitates rules and preconditions. The notion of deregulation, however, does not refer to the abolition of regulations but to 'lighter forms of control, which may be delivered by private as much as public bodies'

(Holton, 2012: 13). Regulatory authorities implement financial regulations and legal procedures, whereas independent industry associations coordinate standard practices and facilitate industry supervision. Financial subsectors are regulated separately. All this has given rise to a highly fragmented regulatory authority whose responsibilities overlap and create gaps, which, as critics argue, causes financial instability (Haldane and May, 2011). The most recent financial meltdown bluntly revealed the inadequate regulatory oversight in financial markets (Mattli and Woods, 2009) and the incapability of nation states to align interests and achieve international consensus on matters such as banking and securities regulation due to their differing national needs and policies regulation (Haldane and May, 2011). In a similar vein, federal states such as the US also face regulatory failure as a result of historically deployed 'patchwork' systems (for the example of the US, cf. Konings, 2011), a point that is discussed below in more detail.

Overall, global financial history has repeatedly shown sequences of market de- and re-regulation, powerful enough to provoke serious juridical and spatial consequences beyond national borders. For example, the foreign exchange (FX) markets were taken by surprise when the Swiss National Bank suddenly abandoned its policy of capping the Swiss franc against the euro in January 2015. Among the casualties of this bombshell decision were brokerage websites, some allowing individuals, others institutions to speculate on FX, banks and other financial agents holding short contracts in Swiss currency, and numerous European communes who simply borrowed loans in the previously more economical Swiss franc (*The Economist*, 2015). Finance was and remains a key political actor and regulation does not simply happen. Regulation is a contested and continuously renegotiated process between actors from the private sector, the public and the civil society. Originating in the literatures of international political economy (IPE), yet for many reasons contested, the claimed consequential shifts in power from the state to market authority (Strange, 1996) reshaped the role of the state towards being more like 'the *servant* of the market and of business than its controller' (Coen et al., 2010). Strange herself warned against the rising power of financial markets relative to the political power (Strange, [1988] 1994) and pointed to the strategic weakness of nation states in their power struggle with market authorities. The shifting 'market–authority nexus' would discriminate against the state due to its territorial inflexibility, whilst, in contrast, markets would be able to reign free from spatial boundaries. Collateral to the increased capital mobility, intermediaries such as global banks enhanced their capacity to engage in regulatory arbitrage.

Although appealing, this approach to market liberalization is contested among IPE scholars for several reasons. First, it fails to explain the initial decision to increase capital mobility (Cerny, 2000). Second, the 'clear-cut victory of "markets" over "states"' (Fernandez, 2011) is at least questionable with regard to the actual decision-making processes across different markets. The example of London's *Big Bang* from 1986, when the Bank of England lowered the prevailing protectionist walls of the City's 'gentlemanly capitalism', illustrates that public actors were often vanguards in their push for market liberalization and as such 'often directly conflicted with the interests of private actors' (Fernandez, 2011). Explanations for the states' motivation for these types of policy reforms range from 'regulatory capture' (Dal Bó, 2006) to the 'competitive state' (Vogel, 1996). Controversially discussed is also whether states act autonomously or on behalf of private interest groups (Mattli and Woods, 2009) and whom the new formation and functioning of regulation on both national and supranational levels would serve best: the predominantly narrow vested interest groups (Stiglitz, 2008) or – more optimistically – larger groups benefitting from a more efficient market allocation mechanism when dismantling inefficient regulations (Bhagwati, 2007). Common ground, however, is that financial elites directly influence financial and monetary government policies although this neither implies that their policy objectives are the same nor does the public–private relationship always agree in unanimity. Regulation is integral to market mechanisms. By historically linking the agricultural markets with the emergence of financial derivative markets in the US, Muellerleile takes the argument further and suggests that, in fact, 'markets and regulations are often one and the same' (Muellerleile, 2015: 1). Fellow geographers also promote the performative nature of law and regulation on financial markets (Brenner et al., 2010) and illustrate how 'competition law constitutes markets' (Christophers, 2015) because regulation is a critical factor 'in the reproduction of the [financial] system itself' (Tickell, 2000: 236).

The next section develops the key point that regulation is integral to market mechanisms and includes a range of examples showing the distinctiveness of regulatory spaces. It brings their geographical, sequential, and institutional mismatches, overlaps and gaps to the fore. Hence, the fifth section summarizes and conceptualizes the varieties of the regulatory spaces introduced in the following.

17.4 MAKING NEW MARKETS AND SHAPING NEW REGULATORY SPACES

Three key themes of making and reshaping regulatory spaces are discussed in the remainder of this chapter in order to understand the defining powers of the interactions between regulatory activity and space. The *first theme* engages with the legal, cultural and business manifestations of particular regulatory spaces. Examples include financial centres in their role as the 'chief points of surveillance and scripting for the global financial services industry' (Thrift, 1994: 335) and strategic meeting places where industry and state actors of both national and international origin negotiate and reshape regulatory frameworks. In this sense, the first theme engages with 'cultural spaces of finance'.

A *second theme* discusses the dynamics of regional integration of financial markets. Building on neoliberal traditions, such expanding regulatory spaces also reflect the influential powers of high finance. Regulatory resources implemented by hegemonic powers, that is, the US and the European Union (EU), are typically of strategic character. As such they are important means of foreign politics (Cohen, 1998) and gateways to a new global 'financial imperialism' (Christophers, 2013). We can hence title this approach as 'new hegemonic spaces of finance'.

The *third theme* alludes to and canvasses the emerging 'virtual spaces of finance' as another form of territory-transcending regulatory spaces. Such spaces, however, could not have emerged without practices and processes that have formed around a 'regulation–technology nexus'. Rapid technologization has created unprecedented 'opportunity spaces' representing leverage opportunities for finance. Financial activities such as 'dark' electronic trading platforms and cryptocurrency markets most often challenge regulations based on 'typical regulatory jurisdictional territories' (Hudson, 1999: 139).

Amalgamating these three conceptual ideas, the term 'regulatory space' defines a jurisdiction that is in principle territorial, yet, rules and regulations may allude to only 'a particular set of activities and/or a particular geographical territory' (Hudson, 1999: 139). Situations like the early 'extraterritorial' Euromarkets and the current 'virtual' cryptocurrency markets exemplify that international finance activities can easily slip across regulatory borders, thus, presenting vivid prospects for regulatory arbitrage and shifting 'spatialities of power' (Allen, 1997).

Legally Defined Cultural Spaces

Law and economics scholars analyze the effects and efficiencies of corporate law as this is indeed a central building block of national economies. The overall structure of corporate law is traditionally supplemented by further legal sources such as tax law, securities law, stock exchange rules and – for example in the case of the UK – the City's Code on mergers and takeovers. Competing law families encourage varying degrees of financial liberalism and innovativeness. Relating the underlying legal system, their scope of regulation, and the place's resulting 'innovativeness' with one another may help to better comprehend processing of shifting and reshaping of regulatory spaces in international contemporary finance.

The opposing legal traditions of the Anglo-American common law and the French civil code – two extremes of a whole spectrum of law in between, that is, the Scandinavian civil law and the German civil law – differ vitally in understanding and interpreting the law, which, hence, influences the strategic behaviour of financial firms. Broadly speaking, the common law tradition accepts broad interpretation and therefore expensive legal battles, in which corporate lawyers constantly challenge the law to make small amendments. Common law permits everything except that is listed in the statutes (*negative-list regulation*), suggesting 'that investment banking and the capital markets are deeper and more advanced in these countries than those that follow the civil law tradition' (Choi et al., 2009: 23). In contrast, civil law operates on the basis of a *positive-list regulation* (Beck and Levine, 2008: 255ff.). Its codified law enforces a high degree of both predictability and protection of property rights, yet, permits less freedom for innovation.[1] This framing, however, suggests a highly paradoxical situation in Europe's financial market. London is arguably the largest financial centre within the EU; the City's commercial law builds on the common law tradition. The EU, however, is currently the world's largest integrated financial market with the majority of its member states' commercial laws building on more restrictive civil code principles. Both – in many aspects contrasting – regulatory spaces form a political (although not a currency) union that makes it a challenging task to find common ground in financial regulation. The complexities not only comprise technical law, but especially the embodied mentalities of financial actors towards financial activities.

English, French and German legal traditions colonized the world (Porta et al., 1998). Asian-Pacific financial centres such as Hong Kong, Singapore, Sydney and Wellington have adopted the legal framework of the common law tradition similar to that of the UK and the US. Other Asian jurisdictions such as Japan and Korea and, to some extent, China show a strong fingerprint of the European law traditions. The Japanese commercial code of 1899 squarely originates from the German civil code, although their public law was influenced by the common law during the post-Second World War occupation period (Beck and Levine, 2008). Japan is a particularly interesting case. In its endeavour to strengthen Tokyo's competitiveness and Japan's financial markets more generally, in 2006, the Koizumi administration transformed Japan's securities law from a positive- into a negative-list in order to attract more 'innovative' financial activities. Korea's financial centres Seoul and Bussan and also Europe's financial centre Luxembourg acted in a similarly pragmatic way and shaped increasingly more hybrid spaces of regulation. When, for example, the EU-wide AIFMD[2] was introduced, Luxembourg concurrently revised its corporate law. Among others, it incorporated the limited liability partnership (LLP), an established corporate structure borrowed from common law, which is hoped will strengthen the country's competitiveness in the alternative fund business.

Linking Competing Spaces of Financial Business Culture

Further no less important institutions, that is, language and business culture, characterize fundamental traits of financial 'cultural spaces'. Some regulatory spaces are more closely connected than others. A much higher degree of cultural commonality, for example, exists in London and New York City for Europe and North America than for Southeast Asia and the Middle East (Arner, 2009). This is not only based on the underlying legal understanding of doing business but relations between these cultural spaces can also be drawn on the basis of colonial heritage (Haberly and Wójcik, 2015). Casablanca, for example, represents Morocco's current attempt to create its own financial centre. In so doing, it has invited advice from both Switzerland and Luxembourg. The choice of selecting advisers from these two countries seemingly draws on cultural similarities and the common French language and is in line with Casablanca's primary aim to serve the French-speaking markets in Africa.

Language and cultural commonalities/proximities also form particularities of regulatory spaces as they incentivize distinct geographies of financial flows. In hindsight of Dublin's rise as an emerging competitor of Luxembourg's financial centre in the investment fund industry in the early 1990s, in which many US suppliers domiciled their funds for the EU market, a high-ranking industry professional identified cultural and legal differences between both countries as key success factors and a significant element that meant Dublin never seriously challenged Luxembourg in its position as the world's largest cross-border investment fund centre:

> The self-image of the Englishmen concerning continental-European business was marked by a certain arrogance. [. . .] But they know very little about how continental Europe works. Germany works differently, France works differently, and the mentalities are absolutely different. The English believe that in finance all they do is standard par excellence. [. . .] The self-image of the Englishmen considers the financial world their own: Finance comes from Britain. For cultural and language reasons some Americans may have gone to Dublin, or maybe even to London, because from there one could also distribute the UCITS,[3] but the industry there has never properly developed. [. . .] The understanding of continental Europe from an English perspective is not one you develop when being on-site in continental Europe. (Interview, 12 August 2013, author's translation)

Global networks of advanced business services (ABS) professionals, that is, bankers, lawyers, auditors/accountants and other advisers, act as boundary spanners between these culturally distinct spaces of finance and inherently link them with each other. The wide-ranging ABS complex holds considerable power (Wójcik, 2013) by siphoning off arbitrage profits from at least two prevalent manifestations. First, they pursue 'epistemic arbitrage' strategies by deploying opportunities between different bodies of professional knowledge (Seabrooke, 2014), that is, advising regulatory authorities on how to design regulations and businesses on how to circumvent it (Miller, 1986); second, they operate 'legal, accounting and financial vehicles designed partly to escape the control of governmental or intergovernmental organizations through the use of offshore jurisdictions' (Wójcik, 2013: 331). The list of damaging consequences includes financial instability and inequity as well as harmful tax competition. A vital building block for the finance's successful retreat from the regulators' grip is, however, a highly specific type of regulatory space: offshore jurisdictions (OJs), established with acquiescence of the financial superpowers US and UK.

Offshore finance is based upon a territory's sovereign rights and high degree of flexibility to create a financial centre through lax regulations (Hudson, 1998), 'competitive interest rates [and a] freedom from regulation over the movement of offshore money controlled by and on the books of their resident bank' (Reed, 1988: 58). A 'British Empire-centred economy' continues to exist until today (Palan et al., 2010: 126). Offshore jurisdictions are usually either independent small jurisdictions or former colonies and remaining dependent territories whose former colonial powers act as (politically stabilizing) patrons. Onshore–offshore jurisdiction relationships are shaped by a common language, similar legal institutions and often shared business cultures and a small circle of elites who bridge both spaces (Wójcik, 2013). Definition details on whether an offshore centre is indeed an OJ and whether an OJ is always a 'tax efficient jurisdiction' (Reed, 1988), or whether an OJ is rather a functional, a compound or a notional offshore centre (Hampton, 1995) are secondary to the argument at hand. The consequences of the ABS complex's powerful interventions alongside the OJs' tight integration in the global financial architecture, however, are of utmost importance to understand the circuits of financial capital. This ABS–offshore nexus (Wójcik, 2013) defines a specific kind of regulatory space that operates with the fundamental techniques and instrumentalities of securitization, tax planning, and the exertion of soft power strategies like persuasion and intellectual leadership rather than corruption and coercion (Arrighi, 1994); processes, which – ironically – place offshore finance both at the margin and at the centre of global financial capitalism (Roberts, 1994). In harnessing such power, the ABS-offshore complex utilizes an international mesh of an offshore–midshore–onshore infrastructure that also enables it to surmount barriers for their financial activities. Hence, it does not only pursue the systemic dislocation of national and international governing mechanisms but also distresses the existing order of regulatory spaces of finance.

Whilst this section has thus far set its sight on the legal geographies between territories, the functional, competing and partly overlapping regulatory spaces *within* large markets ought not to be neglected. Examples of such regulatory spaces include federal systems such as the US, Germany, Switzerland and – considering the creation of the pan-European financial services market – the EU. A remarkably resilient core debate revolves around controversy of whether state competition fosters a regulatory 'race to the bottom' (Cary, 1974) or a 'race to the top' (Winter, 1977). Whilst the latter argues for the maximization of shareholders' wealth, the former claims that state competition serves managers and not necessarily shareholders' interest (Bebchuk et al., 2002). European policymakers indeed 'face the pressing question of how to allocate regulatory authority between the institutions of the European Union and its member national governments in the area of corporate law' (Bebchuk et al., 2002: 1778), yet, evidence emerges that 'the ECJ [European Court of Justice] rulings are leading to regulatory competition between EU Member States to provide low-cost corporate law' (Becht et al., 2008: 242). This would be due to the power of yet another particularly influential group, that is, corporate managers. They would 'have substantial influence over where companies are incorporated, a state that wishes to maximize the number of corporations chartered in [. . .] will have to take into account the interest of managers. As a result, state competition pushes states to give significant weight to managerial interests' (Bebchuk et al., 2002: 1780). The very same logic applies to incorporation decisions by highly mobile financial actors. Banks, asset managers and other finance companies are free in choosing their domiciliation country, specifically designed for federal communities of states such as the EU. An acknowledged principle that overcomes potentially inefficient legislation is the instrument of passporting (mutual recognition). It is based on 'bargaining between member state governments and special interest groups' (Griffin, 2001: 350), which – as a reciprocal agreement among jurisdictions – 'accept[s] the other's regulatory standards that govern the creation and conduct of companies and businesses' (Griffin, 2001: 337). European UCITS funds, for example, apply the passporting scheme and are among Europe's largest financial export hits.

Regional Market Integration

Financial systems have adopted organizational forms and logics from the manufacturing industry (Dörry, 2015). Similar to industrial clusters, financial centres – embedded in their particular jurisdictions – serve as key financial 'production sites'. They are hence nodes embedded in a globalized system of finance originating in the key territories of the US, the UK and the EU. Contrasting dynamics of inclusion and exclusion form the global financial industry of today. Whilst many states have been pushing for regional market integration, other emerging financial markets are only cautiously opening their domestic financial markets. China's (Renminbi) Qualified Foreign Institutional Investor (RQFII and QFII) programmes are perhaps the most prominent examples of a largely closed financial market that carefully selects foreign investors for admission into its capital markets.

Other regions have comprehensively embraced the idea of regional financial market integration. In 1992, the formation of the Economic and Monetary Union marked an instrumental step towards the implementation of the European Capital Markets Union and the European Banking Union, launched under the umbrella of the EU Single Market. It heralded not only the integration of 12 separate national financial markets into a larger market with a single currency but also marked an unprecedented shift towards the formation of a much larger regulatory space with the capacity to counteract the dominant currencies of the US dollar and Japanese yen. This particular politically driven project also laid the foundations for a number of so-called 'passporting schemes' for financial products and services.

Asia's significance as the new investment Mecca mirrors its ability to attract flows of investment capital. As counterweight to the EU's and the US's large single markets, several Asian countries in altering alliances have been seeking to establish a fiscal union although without forming a political union. The ASEAN (Association of Southeast Asian Nations) Economic Community represents a current example to reap higher benefits from scale economies in the future. Current preconditions are favourable as the investment fund industry shows. A number of Asian countries are endeavouring to copy the EU-UCITS passporting scheme and attempting to establish regulatory spaces that would contribute to create a favourable environment for a common Asian investment fund market. Besides the expected benefits from creating a larger market, governments' motives for fostering regional economic integration is also driven by a simple fear of being left behind in regional competition. Asia hosts several competing financial powers. The competition between the two IFCs Hong Kong/China and Singapore is especially fierce, and the conflicting political interests as well as the fight for economic supremacy are still obstacles yet to be overcome. However, despite these political differences, regional market integration in Asia is proceeding apace as the example of the investment fund industry illustrates. There are currently three competing passporting schemes at the stage of implementation: first, the Hong Kong–China Mutual Recognition of Funds established in 2014, a long-term initiative which due to its market size attracts the main commercial interest; second, the Asia Region Funds Passport within the Asia-Pacific Economic Cooperation (APEC) framework to promote a potential EU-UCITS substitute across those countries, primarily driven by Australia and comprising New Zealand, Singapore, South Korea, Thailand and the Philippines; third, the ASEAN/CSI (Confederation of Service Industry), specifically promoted by Singapore which hopes to leverage primarily Southeast Asia with its fellow union members Malaysia and Thailand, although the potential extension to the fast growing economies such as Indonesia, the Philippines and Vietnam would attract even greater economic interest.

However, all these emerging regulatory spaces compete with each other and their 'making' confronts foreign asset managers and investors with fundamental dilemmas. First, whilst the Hong Kong–China mutual recognition has been rapid, uncertainty about a future legal expansion of the scheme impedes foreign asset managers' decisions to set up their funds in Hong Kong. Their caution builds on previous experiences with the RQFII scheme that sets quotas and initially started with Hong Kong. China then extended the scheme to Singapore and some European countries, however, so that initial investments in Hong Kong did not always pay off. Second, the fragmented cooperation frameworks so far contradict the idea of scale economies, and high returns like that of a UCITS fund with a potential market distribution to 28 European markets remain politically ambitious. Problematic for the future shaping of one Asian regulatory space may also be the differences in the development and maturity of the Asian financial markets and their regulators. Third, passporting schemes are still highly contested issues in practice and require high levels of mutual trust between regulators. Singapore and Hong Kong, for example, adopt different approaches of regulation. Broadly speaking, the Monetary Authority Singapore adopts the EU approach and approves European UCITS for sale in Singapore within a timeframe of about a month.[4] The Hong Kong authority, in contrast, reviews a European UCITS investment fund from the ground up, which extends the approval period to as long as 12 months (with an official approval period of six months). The length of approval periods is, however, fundamental for the competitiveness of a jurisdiction as long approval times contradict opportunistic fund strategies.

Libertarian Cyberspaces?[5]

The significance of regulation and regulated spaces becomes most obvious at their porous boundaries. New financial subsystems have created financial spaces largely outside regulation and surveillance. Certain kinds of shadier spaces comprising shadow banks, digital or cryptocurrencies and so-called 'dark pools' exemplify how several parts of the financial system have indeed migrated and created new spaces outside traditional, territory-based regulation. These spaces are orchestrated by their own, partially informal, rules and are positioned largely outside the regulators' immediate access, thus, generating novel strategic opportunities for (technologically well-equipped) financial actors in factually stateless spaces. Overall, shadow banking, cryptocurrency investing and dark trading platforms present a range of examples that endeavour to cloud transparency, a key pillar to financial stability, yet with different motives and motivations as discussed in the following. These three micro-regulatory spaces define a technology-regulation complex. Technology comprises instruments and activities such as securitization and taxation vehicles, sophisticated information technologies, but in most cases a combination of both. Regulation is most often a cost driver for the newly regulated activities and vehicles and in this sense also a key driver for financial innovation, responding to intended and unintended regulatory effects. The interplay of both technology and regulation on a micro level spills over into the larger financial system not least by transferring risks; risks include run risks, agency problems, opacity and complexity, leverage and procyclicality, and spillovers (cf. IMF, 2014: 68–69), and makes an interrogation in these spaces sensible.

Shadow banking comprises 'financing of banks and nonbank financial institutions through noncore liabilities [. . .] regardless of the entity that carries it out' (IMF, 2014: 68). Although scholars have not yet agreed on a single definition, the IMF definition starts from the performed financial activity and includes, for example securitization, irrespective of being conducted 'directly on balance sheet by a bank or indirectly through a special purpose vehicle (SPV)' (IMF, 2014: 68). Shadow banking, ingloriously tied to the last financial crisis, is probably among the most prominent outcomes of a transition 'from an antiquated hold-to-maturity loan-based system to a modern originate-and-distribute securitization-based system more fully able to exploit the advances in information and communication offered by the technology revolution' (Dymski and Kaltenbrunner, 2017: 363). The shadow banking sector's estimated size equals, if not exceeds, the one of the traditional banking system. It peaked close to US$20 trillion in 2007 and shrank to about US$15 trillion in 2010 (Noeth and Sengupta, 2011: 8). Its prominence traces back to a reaction of different regulations which increased compliance costs and legal risks for traditional banking. One key area of concern is specifically important for the argument at hand in its exemplification of the technology-regulatory complex. Other than traditional banking, which involves a simple process of deposit-taking and originating loans held to maturity, shadow banking employs a highly complicated process to achieve maturity transformation. Shadow bank credit intermediation thus includes the transfer of funds (fees, and so on) in exchange for securities along a long chain of intermediaries and – among them – a proliferation of private contractual agreements via a range of SPVs and securities. Originally designed to help shore up stability, to disperse risk and to help protect banks by moving liabilities off their balance-sheets, shadow banks, in essence, were 'accounting gimmicks', as one commentator from *The Economist* recently pointed out. Regulators thus far could only control the entities in their own regulated territories. Shadowy financial activities and instruments like SPVs were able to shift the huge number of private agreements among the complex intermediary chains into the realms of less strict regulatory spaces, that is, offshore territories. It precisely fitted into the legal gaps and empowered them to arbitrage regulations.

Dark pool trading is yet another example of the regulation–technology nexus. The pools' original purpose to handle big trades, so-called 'block transactions' by large institutional investors like pension funds, provided 'a simple solution to an old problem for investors: how to buy or sell lots of shares without moving their price?' (*The Economist*, 2011). Dark pool trading, sustained by technological and regulatory changes, conceals the volume and price of each transaction from the public as it is settled in private venues (Levinson, 2014: 185). Hedge funds and other investors seized the new opportunity of the growing algorithmic and high frequency trading (HFT) (cf. Zook and Grote, 2014). In doing so, they increasingly interfered with the large block transactions and, as a consequence, adversely affected price movements for institutional investors. The first Markets in Financial Instruments Directive (MiFID I), implemented in 2007, 'revolutionised share-trading in the EU' (*The Economist*, 2014a: 71). MiFID I opened the market of stock exchanges for new competitors. To date, at least three major types of dark pools exist: independent companies, broker-owned dark pools (crossing networks, which investment banks use to match orders in-house), and dark pools owned by public exchanges. Depending on the precise way a dark pool operates and interacts with other electronic platforms, that is, whether the venues' liquidity is fully or partially hidden, it may be considered a 'grey' or dark pool (The TABB Group, 2015). These linguistic nuances also indicate the subtle differences in how these particular regulatory spaces can be defined in terms of their proneness to mechanisms of price manipulation, predatory trading and information leakages (Mittal, 2008) as opposed to the trading activities within regulated spaces of traditional stock exchanges. The operator's massive information advantage makes the problem of moral hazard most apparent. On 11 August 2015, the US Securities and Exchange Commission (SEC) imposed a record US$20 million fine on a London-based dark pool (POSIT) for running a secret trading desk that used knowledge of customer's dark-pool orders to trade for its own benefit (Robinson and Mamudi, 2015).

These processes reveal a fundamental dilemma of the financial industry. As they want to leave the system, they also want to enforce their rights. The Regulation National Market System (RegNMS), a series of US financial regulations, the European Market Infrastructure Regulation (EMIR) that sets clearing rules for derivatives, and MiFID II, which endeavours to make equity trading less opaque, are current attempts to regulate dark trading but regulators need to deal with the fundamental tension between institutional and retail investors.

Last but not least, there are *cryptocurrencies*, virtual currencies not (yet) taxed that – if used carefully – enable anonymous transactions. The latter trait is also a reason that Bitcoin, presently one of the most prominent cryptocurrencies at the market, was the currency of choice for paying at shadow websites like Silk Road. Nonetheless, some economists see Bitcoin as a part of our future economy and even the next best alternative to the Gold Standard (Hern, 2013) and banks have started to explore opportunities to use Bitcoin's underlying sophisticated technology (*The Economist*, 2014b). Until now, however, Bitcoin still lacks essential network externalities and is far from being a stable store of value. These major shortcomings, however, do not hinder Bitcoin from appealing to users because of its secrecy and attracting speculators – the *Financial Times* even calls Bitcoins 'the tulips of modern times' (Landau, 2014). Current discussions suggest the probability of banning cryptocurrencies not least in order 'to prevent virtual money from slipping into a legal grey zone' (Schwartzkopff, 2013) or to avoid a situation where cryptocurrencies 'replace tax havens as the weapon-of-choice for tax-evaders' (Marian, 2013: 1).

17.5 REFLECTIONS

The landscape of money and finance is clearly in motion. This chapter offered a broad spectrum of views on how to approach and characterize the considerable variety of spaces across financial subsectors, offering conceptual starting points to define the term 'regulatory space'. Motivated by fuelling the dialogue between geography and regulation, this chapter has reflected on the intersecting workings of finance across scales. It considered the conflicting interests and powers between regulators and regulated groups by introducing the technology-regulation complex, and it incorporated space as an outcome and driver to define new financial activities, instruments, and markets. There is much inconsistency among the regulatory spaces in finance, and their distinct legal, cultural and technological demarcations suggest that it is vital to intellectually combine the scale, scope and nature of each financial regulatory space in question. A way to summarize the mosaic of fragmented regulatory spaces discussed in this chapter is to visualize it as a 'Game of Zones' that represents the asymmetric relationships between regulators, technology firms, and financial intermediaries.

Whilst existing national regulatory spaces become more and more mottled, new virtual, supranational and extra-regulatory financial spaces are emerging, superseding regulatory spaces that are 'never fixed, but are perpetually redefined, contested and restructured' (Swyngedouw, 1997: 141). Geographical mismatches come to the fore when territorially based law clashes with the new realities of a financial sector that operates truly cross-boundaries, supported by a mosaic of light and dark spaces, with much grey in between, thus creating a 'complex intertwining of the digital and the physical' (Zook, 2012: 2). Global integration and financial growth are, nevertheless, opposed by the continuing existence of a fragmented piecemeal of national interests and attempted trials of supranational regulators to operate a 'complicated patchwork of metrics' (Braithwaite, 2015: 18) across this colourful mosaic of financial spaces. Time and technical mismatches are only one outcome of the diluted and often delayed regulations after intense lobbying activities, and institutional mismatches originate in fragmented regulatory authority and also opposing incentivizing by the financial activities based in the spaces of different law families. In their interaction, these mismatched regulatory spaces also create overlaps and gaps.

An often neglected part in the academic discussion is cultural proximity as a key shaper of financial spaces. Culture is indeed an important factor that serves as a category for regulation. Financial centres, for example, are concrete places where global flows of mobile finance physically 'touch down' to adopt the chosen regulatory environment that match their needs best and wherefrom local financial practices, technologies, and instruments are injected into the global financial system. Financial centres are also spaces for a geocultural positioning within the global world of finance. The emergence of Casablanca's financial centre is strategically situated along a francophone axis, linking Switzerland and Luxembourg with the francophone Africa; another example is Malaysia's increasing recognition as an Islamic finance centre within a financial space defined by religious principles. All these examples suggest that cultural proximity between markets shape regulatory spaces in an often overlooked key dimension, that is, the interconnected legal and business cultures, which are relatively resistant to change.

This is but one perspective from which the inseparability of financial markets and regulation become evident. The example of the regional integration dynamics within Asia's investment fund industry further suggested that the idea of passporting regulated funds across national (and hence regulatory) borders is a matter of fundamental trust between regulators themselves. This is difficult to achieve when investor protection is based on vastly differing underlying cultures of business and regulation between neighbouring economies, also driven by an underlying prudential supervision model that accelerates competition between financial spaces.

The asymmetric power relations associated with institutions, regulatory myopia, institutional innovation and intense competition between spaces across geographical scales solidify and reinforce patterns of the (prevailing) uneven geographies in international finance. Financial instability is only one result. A second, although somewhat contradictory, outcome is the increasing integration and mutual interdependence between regulatory spaces. Their interconnectedness, manifested in the boundary spanning geopolitics and geoeconomics of finance, the complex web of competing, yet interconnected specialized and (therefore often even) cooperating spaces of finance and the perilous power of a few financial institutions, define the binding ties that hold the manifold alleged rivalling spaces together. The joined-up thinking of the varying regulatory spaces, shaped by conflicting legal foundations, business cultures and geographical reach, could direct new conceptual thinking on how regulatory capacities could capture the fluid character of increasingly 'hybrid' and 'transitory' regulatory spaces and how institutional regimes interact to negotiate the nature, scope and depth of emerging regulatory spaces of finance. This chapter attempted to provide a flavour of the manifold regulatory spaces produced and ingrained by agents of divergent powers.

ACKNOWLEDGEMENTS/FUNDING

This book chapter has benefited from valuable insights of finance industry representatives in London, Luxembourg and Singapore, whom I would like to thank for their time and invaluable insights. Interviews were conducted between June 2013 and December 2015. I am very grateful for the constructive comments on previous versions of this chapter by Jane Pollard, Ron Martin and Chris Muellerleile, which helped to improve and sharpen its argument. The responsibility for any errors is, however, mine alone.

This research is funded by a Marie Curie Intra European Fellowship within the 7th European Community Framework Programme (EC Grant Agreement No. 326740), whose support is gratefully acknowledged.

NOTES

1. The example of the US-based car-pooling company Uber illustrates this principle. The company's legality has been challenged by governments and taxi companies in primarily civil law countries. Whilst in civil law countries the company is accused of violating existing safety and licensing issues, in common law countries such issues are legally negotiated in the event of damage only.
2. AIFMD is the abbreviation for the Alternative Investment Fund Managers Directive.
3. UCITS (Undertakings for Collective Investment in Transferable Securities) are regulated investment funds, primarily designed for the retail sector.
4. Interviews with industry representatives in Singapore and Hong Kong, November 2014.
5. Jamie Peck and colleagues (2012) coined this term.

REFERENCES

Allen, J. (1997), 'Economies of power and space', in R. Lee and J. Wills (eds), *Geographies of Economies*, London: Arnold, pp. 59–70.

Arner, D.W. (2009), 'The competition of international financial centres and the role of law', in K. Meesen (ed.), *Economic Law as an Economic good, its rule Function and its Tool Function in the Competition of Systems*, München: Sellier, pp. 193–210.

Arrighi, G. (1994), *The Long Twentieth Century: Money, Power, and the Origins of Our Times*, Brooklyn, NY: Verso.

Baldwin, R.E. and M. Cave (1999), *Understanding Regulation. Theory, Strategy, and Practice*, Oxford: Oxford University Press.

Bank for International Settlements (BIS) (1985), *Fifty-Fifth Annual Report*, Basle: BIS.

Bebchuk, L.A., A. Cohen and A. Ferrell (2002), 'Does the evidence favor state competition in corporate law?', *California Law Review*, **90**, 1775–1821.

Becht, M., C. Mayer and H.F. Wagner (2008), 'Where do firms incorporate? Deregulation and the cost of entry', *Journal of Corporate Finance*, **14**, 241–256.

Beck, T. and R. Levine (2008), 'Legal institutions and financial development', in C. Ménard and M.M. Shirley (eds), *Handbook of New Institutional Economics*, Berlin: Springer, pp. 251–278.

Bergsten, F.C. (1996), *Dilemmas of the Dollar. The Economics and Politics of United States International Monetary Policy*, New York: Council on Foreign Relations.

Bhagwati, J. (2007), *In Defense of Globalization*, Oxford: Oxford University Press USA.

Braithwaite, T. (2015), 'When finance meets pornography expect 50 trades of grey', *Financial Times*, 24 February, p. 18.

Brenner, N., J. Peck, and N.I.K. Theodore (2010), 'Variegated neoliberalization: geographies, modalities, pathways', *Global Networks*, **10**, 182–222.

Cary, W.L. (1974), 'Federalism and corporate law: reflections upon Delaware', *The Yale Law Journal*, **83**, 663–705.

Casu, B., A. Ferrari and T. Zhao (2010), 'Financial reforms, competition and risk in banking markets', in F. Fiordelisi, P. Molyneux and D. Previati (eds), *New Issues in Financial and Credit Markets*, London: Palgrave Macmillan, pp. 111–120.

Cerny, P.G. (2000), 'Political agency in a globalizing world: toward a structurational approach', *European Journal of International Relations*, **6**, 435–463.

Choi, D., J. Seade, S. Shirai and S. Young (2009), 'Competition among financial centres in Asia Pacific: prospects, benefits, risks and policy challenges', in S. Young, D. Choi, J. Seade and S. Shirai (eds), *Competition among Financial Centres in Asia-Pacific. Prospects, Benefits, Risks and Policy Challenges*, Singapore: ISEAS Publishing, pp. 3–57.

Christophers, B. (2013), *Banking Across Boundaries. Placing Finance in Capitalism*, Chichester: Wiley-Blackwell.

Christophers, B. (2015), 'The law's markets', *Journal of Cultural Economy*, **8**, 125–143.

Clark, G.L. (2011), 'Myopia and the global financial crisis: context-specific reasoning, market structure, and institutional governance', *Dialogues in Human Geography*, **1**, 4–25.

Coen, D., W. Grant and G. Wilson (2010), 'Overview', in D. Coen, W. Grant and G. Wilson (eds), *The Oxford Handbook of Business and Government*, Oxford: Oxford University Press, pp. 1–5.

Cohen, B.J. (1998), *The Geography of Money*, Ithaca, NY, London: Cornell University Press.

Dal Bó, E. (2006), 'Regulatory capture: a review', *Oxford Review of Economic Policy*, **22**, 203–225.

Dörry, S. (2015), 'Strategic nodes in investment fund global production networks: the example of the financial centre Luxembourg', *Journal of Economic Geography*, **15**, 797–814.
Dörry, S. (2016), 'The role of elites in the co-evolution of international financial markets and financial centres: the case of Luxembourg', *Competition and Change*, **20**, 21–36.
Dymski G.A. and A. Kaltenbrunner (2017), 'How finance globalized: a tale of two cities', in I. Ertürk and D. Gabor (eds), *The Routledge Companion to Banking Regulation and Reform*, London: Routledge, pp. 351–372.
Eichengreen, B. (2008), *Globalizing Capital*, Princeton, NJ: Princeton University Press.
Fagan, R.H. and R.B.L. Heron (1994), 'Reinterpreting the geography of accumulation: the global shift and local restructuring', *Environment and Planning D: Society and Space*, **12**, 265–285.
Fernandez, R. (2011), *Explaining the Decline of the Amsterdam Financial Centre: Globalizing Finance and the Rise of a Hierarchical Inter-city Network*, Amsterdam: University of Amsterdam.
Griffin, P.B. (2001), 'Delaware effect: keeping the tiger in its cage – the European experience on mutual recognition in financial services', *Columbian Journal of European Law*, **7**, 337–354.
Haberly, D. and D. Wójcik (2015), 'Tax havens and the production of offshore FDI: an empirical analysis', *Journal of Economic Geography*, **15**, 75–101.
Haldane, A.G. and R.M. May (2011), 'Systemic risk in banking ecosystems', *Nature*, **469**, 351–355.
Hampton, M.P. (1995), 'Exploring the offshore interface', *Crime, Law and Social Change*, **24**, 293–317.
Hampton, M.P. (1996), 'Sixties child? The emergence of Jersey as an offshore finance centre 1955–71', *Accounting, Business & Financial History*, **6**, 51–71.
Hancher, L. and M. Moran (1989), 'Organizing regulatory space', in L. Hancher and M. Moran (eds), *Capitalism, Culture, and Economic Regulation*, Oxford: Oxford University Press, pp. 271–299.
Helleiner, E. (1994), *States and the Reemergence of Global Finance. From Bretton Woods to the 1990s*, Ithaca, NY: Cornell University Press.
Hern, A. (2013), 'Partial payment for future transactions', *The Guardian Weekly*, 20 December.
Holton, R.J. (2012), *Global Finance*, London: Routledge.
Hudson, A.C. (1998), 'Reshaping the regulatory landscape: border skirmishes around the Bahamas and Cayman offshore financial centres', *Review of International Political Economy*, **5**, 534–564.
Hudson, A.C. (1999), 'Off-shore on-shore: new regulatory spaces and real historical places in the landscape of global money', in R. Martin (ed.), *Money and the Space Economy*, Chichester: Wiley, pp. 139–154.
International Monetary Fund (IMF) (2014), *Global Financial Stability Report*, Washington, DC: International Monetary Fund.
Konings, M. (2011), *The Development of American Finance*, New York: Cambridge University Press.
Landau, J.-P. (2014), 'Beware the mania for Bitcoin, the tulip of the 21st century', *Financial Times*, 17 January.
Laulajainen, R. (2003), *Financial Geography: A Banker's View*, London: Routledge.
Levinson, M. (2014), *Guide to Financial Markets. Why They Exist and How They Work*, London: The Economist in association with Profile Books.
Marian, O.Y. (2013), 'Are cryptocurrencies "super" tax havens?'. Retrieved on 15 June 2015 from http://ssrn.com/abstract=2305863.
Martin, R. (1994), 'Stateless monies, global financial integration and national autonomy: the end of geography?' in S. Corbridge, R.L. Martin and N. Thrift (eds), *Money, Power and Space*, Oxford: Blackwell, pp. 253–278.
Martin, R. (1999), 'The new economic geography of money', in R. Martin (ed.), *Money and the Space Economy*, Chichester: John Wiley & Sons, pp. 3–27.
Mattli, W. and N. Woods (eds) (2009), *The Politics of Global Regulation*, Princeton, NJ: Princeton University Press.
Miller, M.H. (1986), 'Financial innovation: the last twenty years and the next', *The Journal of Financial and Quantitative Analysis*, **21**, 459–471.
Mittal, H. (2008), 'Are you playing in a toxic dark pool? A guide to preventing information leakage', *The Journal of Trading*, **3**, 20–33.
Muellerleile, C. (2015), 'Speculative boundaries: Chicago and the regulatory history of US financial derivative markets', *Environment and Planning A*, **47**, 1805–1823.
Noeth, B.J. and R. Sengupta (2011), 'Is shadow banking really banking?', *The Regional Economist*. St. Louis: Federal Reserve Bank of St. Louis.
Organisation for Economic Co-operation and Development (OECD) (2015), *OECD Code of Liberalisation of Capital Movements. Promoting Orderly Capital Flows: the Approach of the Code*, Paris: OECD.
Palan, R. (2012), 'Tax havens and offshore financial centres', *Academic Foresight*, **4** [online journal].
Palan, R., R. Murphy and C. Chavagneux (2010), *Tax Havens: How Globalization Really Works*, Ithaca, NY: Cornell University Press.
Peck, J., T.J. Barnes and E. Sheppard (2012), 'Editors' introduction: regulation and governance', in T.J. Barnes, J. Peck and E. Sheppard (eds), *The Wiley-Blackwell Companion to Economic Geography*, Chichester: Blackwell, pp. 291–297.

Polanyi, K. [1944] (1978), *The Great Transformation*, Frankfurt am Main: Suhrkamp.
Pollard, J. and M. Samers (2011), 'Governing Islamic finance: territory, agency, and the making of cosmopolitan financial geographies', *Annals of the Association of American Geographers*, **103**, 710–726.
Porta, R.L., F. Lopez-De-Silanes, A. Shleifer and R.W. Vishny (1998), 'Law and finance', *Journal of Political Economy*, **106**, 1113–1155.
Reed, A.P. (1988), *Money and the Global Economy*, Cambridge: Woodhead Publishing.
Roberts, S. (1994), 'Fictitious capital, fictitious spaces: the geography of offshore financial centres', in S. Corbridge, R.L. Martin and N. Thrift (eds), *Money, Power and Space*, Oxford: Blackwell, pp. 91–115.
Robinson, M. and S. Mamudi (2015), 'ITG pays record dark pool fine for secret trading desk', 12 August, Bloomberg.
Schwartzkopff, F. (2013), 'Bitcoins spark regulatory crackdown as Denmark drafts rules', 17 December ed.: Bloomberg.
Seabrooke, L. (2014), 'Epistemic arbitrage: transnational professional knowledge in action', *Journal of Professions and Organization*, **1**, 49–64.
Stiglitz, J.E. (2008), 'Making globalisation work – the 2006 Geary Lecture', *The Economic and Social Review*, **39**, 171–190.
Story, J. and T. Lawton (2010), 'Business studies. The global dynamics of business-state relations', in D. Coen, W. Grant and G. Wilson (eds), *The Oxford Handbook of Business and Government*, Oxford: Oxford University Press, pp. 89–120.
Strange, S. (1996), *The Retreat of the State. The Diffusion of Power in the World Economy*, Cambridge: Cambridge University Press.
Strange, S. [1988] (1994), *States and Markets*, London/New York: Pinter.
Swyngedouw, E. (1997), 'Neither global nor local: "glocalization" and the politics of scale', in K. Cox (ed.), *Spaces of Globalization. Reasserting the Power of the Local*, New York: Guilford Press, pp. 137–166.
The Economist (2011), 'Some like it not', *The Economist*, 20 August, pp. 60–61.
The Economist (2014a), 'A bigger bang', *The Economist*, 26 April, pp. 71–73.
The Economist (2014b), 'Hidden flipside', *The Economist*, 15 March, p. 75.
The Economist (2015), 'Swiss miss', *The Economist*, 19 January, p. 71.
The TABB Group (2015), 'At the dark liquidity crossroads in Canada'. Retrieved on 23 March 2015 from www.tabbforum.com/opinions/at-the-dark-liquidity-crossroads-in-canada?print_preview=true&single=true.
The Warwick Commission (2009), *The Warwick Commission on International Financial Reform: In Praise of Unlevel Playing Fields*, Warwick: The University of Warwick.
Thompson, G.J. (1996), *Prudential Supervision and the Changing Financial System*, Sydney: Reserve Bank of Australia Bulletin.
Thrift, N. (1994), 'On the social and cultural determinants of international financial centres: the case of the City of London', in S. Corbridge, R. Martin and N. Thrift (eds), *Money, Power and Space*, Oxford: Blackwell, pp. 327–355.
Tickell, A. (2000), 'Finance and localities', in G.L. Clark, M.P. Feldman and M.S. Gertler (eds), *The Oxford Handbook of Economic Geography*, Oxford: Oxford University Press, pp. 230–247.
Vogel, S.K. (1996), *Freer Markets, More Rules: Regulatory Reform in Advanced Industrial Countries*, Ithaca, NY: Cornell University Press.
White, L.J. (1999), *The Role of Financial Regulation in a World of Deregulation and Market Forces*, Washington, DC: International Monetary Fund.
Winter, R.K., Jr. (1977), 'State law, shareholder protection, and the theory of the corporation', *The Journal of Legal Studies*, **6**, 251–292.
Wójcik, D. (2013), 'Where governance fails: advanced business services and the offshore world', *Progress in Human Geography*, **37**, 330–347.
Zook, M. (2012), 'The virtual economy', in T.J. Barnes, J. Peck and E. Sheppard (eds), *The Wiley-Blackwell Companion to Economic Geography*, Chichester: Blackwell, pp. 298–312.
Zook, M. and M.H. Grote (2014), 'The microgeographies of global finance: high frequency trading and the construction of information inequality'. Retrieved on 15 July 2015 from http://ssrn.com/abstract=2401030.

18. Emerging onshore–offshore services: the case of asset-backed finance markets in Europe

Thomas Wainwright

The recent global financial crisis (GFC) has highlighted the fragility of Anglo-American economies, ending strong periods of growth throughout the 1990s and 2000s. However, it has been particularly notable in that this was the first major crisis to substantially disrupt new finance-led growth regimes, which were pursued by capitalist economies in the 1990s. Since the early 2000s, scholars in economic geography and the social sciences have sought to gain deeper insight in the growing role of financial markets in contemporary capitalist systems (Boyer, 2000; Aglietta and Breton, 2001; Froud et al., 2006; French et al., 2011), while more recently, they have begun to uncover the spatial effects of the subsequent financial crisis (Aalbers, 2009a; Aalbers et al., 2011; Wainwright, 2015). The outcome of these efforts has been the growth of a diverse body of research which has begun to successfully interrogate how the politics of finance have begun to permeate the 'real' economy and everyday life. For example, research has uncovered how finance has become important in driving corporate decisions (Pike, 2006; Erturk, 2008; Wainwright, 2012) and those of financialized subjects in households (Langley, 2007; Finlayson, 2009).

However, one shortcoming in privileging 'finance' over political institutions is that academic analysis is frequently limited to the study of private actors, whether they are banks or households. Subsequently, the role of regulatory, political and offshore spaces in governing and facilitating finance-led growth regimes has been broadly overlooked in recent studies, breaking from earlier analyses which integrated financial and political institutions within space (cf. Leyshon and Thrift, 1997). This trend may be underpinned by the theoretical framings of financialization, which have had a tendency to view the deepening of finance's politics as being entwined within the wider processes of neoliberalism (French et al., 2011). These framings highlight the roll-back of nation-state institutions, which may have led researchers to prematurely overlook the role that state power and institutions have in supporting contemporary financial institutions and elites. This is problematic in seeking to understand the architecture of international finance, which underpins financialization, as the flows of capital connecting, national, regional, local and household spaces are facilitated through a complex mosaic of offshore and onshore spaces (Clark and Monk, 2013), which have been developed through both financial and state institutions. Due to the growth of financialization throughout the 2000s, these spaces became increasingly important to the global financial system, yet it is surprising that the study of these spaces appears to have fallen outside of the research agenda of economic and financial geographers in recent years (Wójcik, 2013).

Earlier work from economic geography has often viewed offshore financial spaces (OFCs) as locations to hide and 'clean' the proceeds of crime, or to evade tax, casting them as illegitimate spaces which deprive nation-states of tax revenue (Roberts, 1995; Hudson, 2000). This analysis has detracted from the other important 'legal' functions of offshore spaces; including their role in managing double taxation risks for organizations engaged in global trade, to situate the ownership of mobile assets such as aircraft and ships (*Economist*, 2013; Wainwright, 2013; Haberly and Wójcik, 2013), or to locate business ownership in spaces which have a strong legal system, to protect them from the illegitimate activities of corrupt state institutions (Karhunen and Ledyaeva, 2013). The preoccupation with the illegal and dubious activities undertaken in offshore spaces has also obscured the roles of financial institutions in facilitating the tax planning activities, which seek to legally reduce tax liabilities, as opposed to evading tax altogether (Picciotto, 1992). As such, more detailed studies of offshore spaces, and their connection to onshore space are required to provide critical insight into how these spaces function, how they facilitate the flow of global capital, and how they are reliant on the role of state regulation to facilitate the flow of capital across and between onshore and offshore spaces. This is particularly important as the growth of financialization and the associated enlargement of debt capital markets have seen the emergence of new 'onshore–offshore' financial spaces, where low tax, low regulation spaces associated with OFCs are found in developed economies (Hudson, 2000; *Economist*, 2013). This chapter seeks to address these shortcomings by providing a nuanced narrative which sheds light into the growth of new onshore–offshore spaces, through the case of asset-backed securities (ABS) markets.

This chapter has three specific aims: First, it seeks to provide novel insight into the role of onshore–offshore spaces, to highlight the heterogeneity of tax related space and to move beyond rudimentary debates on avoidance and evasion. Structured finance transactions stretch across national spaces, with asset ownership held in one jurisdiction, with the physical assets in another, and bond holders with the rights to asset revenue located in other spaces. This exposes multiple stakeholders to different types of taxation across different onshore and offshore locations, which problematizes simplistic distinctions between offshore or onshore spaces. Examining the functions that onshore–offshore spaces and industries play in the case of ABS transactions will enable a much more fine grained analysis of tax space heterogeneity, how it is created and how it is used. Second, the chapter investigates the emergence of new ABS markets and how their participants developed new demand for tax neutral spaces. While offshore spaces have previously been used to avoid double taxation, or to evade tax entirely, the development of a new asset class in the 1990s required the development of new spaces that facilitate tax minimization to support new finance products. This provides insight into how tax spaces are not existing opportunities to be exploited, but are instead deliberately constructed. Third, the chapter will examine how new onshore–offshore spaces began to emerge in established financial centers, assisted through state intervention, to support European ABS bond markets and to provide states with opportunities to capture taxable revenue. While financial elites are often viewed as being particularly adept at exploiting 'loopholes' in tax regulation, governments have been active in producing the opportunities for financers to minimize taxation. This will enable the chapter to provide more insight into how political and financial elites work together to facilitate financial political economies. This chapter is structured as follows: First, it will explore recent research on OFCs, before turning to briefly review research on theories of emergence. This body of research will be used to frame the analysis and investigate how new ABS markets and onshore–offshore spaces developed in Europe. The chapter then turns to examine how this new market became reliant on special-purpose vehicles (SPV), how new market participants were required to manage them, and how chains of SPVs required tax neutral space to operate. The development of onshore–offshore spaces is then examined, with particular attention being focused on the role of European policymakers in re-regulating space, to create competitive advantages in SPV servicing. The final section concludes the chapter.

18.1 UNCOVERING EMERGENT SPACES OF ONSHORE AND OFFSHORE FINANCE

Understanding Offshore Spaces

Research on economic and financial geographies is arguably experiencing a 'boom' period, with abundant scholarship focused on uncovering the triggers of the recent global financial crisis (GFC) and its uneven effects across space (Immergluck, 2008; Gotham, 2009; Aalbers, 2009a; French and Leyshon, 2010; Marshall et al., 2011; Wainwright, 2012). Despite the loss of momentum in OFC research over the past decade, interest into the spatialities of offshore activities has recently begun to undergo a slow resurgence. On the one hand, this renewed interest could potentially be attributed to the increasingly visible impact of tax minimization plans on developed nation-states, struggling to manage their politics of austerity. For example, OFCs have long been criticized for their negative impact on developing economies and vulnerable communities (Cameron, 2008; Maurer, 2008), but new light has also been shed by media commentators and politicians as to how corporate tax minimization programs are undermining the ability of indebted European governments to balance their spending in the recovery (Wainwright and Rodgers, 2013), while driving inequalities within those centers (Christensen and Shaxson, 2013). In many ways, this has perhaps brought the issues and impacts associated with OFCs and tax minimization closer to home for both policymakers and citizens outside of the developing world. On the other hand, increased scrutiny into the functioning of financial networks, after the latest crisis of contemporary capitalism, has called into question how and where money flows and what role OFCs play in managing global capital circulations (Clark and Wójcik, 2007; Clark and Monk, 2013; Bryan et al., 2013), setting the agenda for further research in this area.

According to Haberly and Wójcik (2013), OFCs deliberately engineer their geo-economic space to make it easy to store assets within legal entities, known as special purpose vehicles (SPVs), where a range of corporate service providers, accountants and lawyers provide administrative, financial and legal expertise to manage and account for the assets. As such, SPVs often hold assets on behalf of organizations and high-net-worth individuals (HNWIs) who undertake their activities in different countries, where it can be useful for the assets to be based in a different jurisdiction, to enable the beneficial owners to participate in regulatory arbitrage, or to facilitate tax minimization programs (Wainwright, 2011). SPVs are important to a diverse range of owners, including corporations, mutual funds, trusts and family estates, which hold intellectual property rights, aircraft, and shipping assets (Bardouille, 2001), in addition to more 'regular' equities, bonds and derivatives. However, the diverse characteristics of OFCs and the services they provide has made it difficult to define exactly which financial centers fall into under this categorization (Wójcik, 2013).

One notable trend, by both geographers and social scientists, has focused on the physical geography of OFCs, mainly that they are small island economies. These studies have paid particular attention to the social construction of small island economy space, to create political economies that are compatible with the demands of professional service providers, global organizations and HNWIs in order to attract mobile capital (Hudson, 1999, 2000; Cobb, 1999; Beaverstock et al., 2013). The initial aim of state re-regulation was to stimulate the growth of financial services sectors on small, resource poor islands as a mode of development. However, one issue which has remained underdeveloped in research on OFCs is the role of professional service providers, specifically corporate service providers, law and accountancy firms, who wield substantial power in the management of these assets and how they circulate through the global economy.

In particular, Eden and Kudrle (2005) have suggested that there is a lack of understanding about the role of professions in managing financial transactions within OFCs. This is surprising on two counts. First, corporate service providers (CSPs) manage and control large volumes of SPVs and global assets connecting them to different owners, beneficiaries and funds located in other offshore and onshore jurisdictions (Engelen and Fernandez, 2013). Therefore, it is striking that such an important and powerful role in global finance is absent from research on OFCs and global finance more broadly. Second, recent research in economic geography has become increasingly attentive to the role of professions and elites in economic networks (cf. Faulconbridge, 2010a, 2010b; Beaverstock et al., 2010), complementing work on the trend of global organizations to outsource and offshore particular specialist functions to form global production chains (Coe, 2012; Coe and Hess, 2013). Again, while recent research in the context of OFCs has turned to examine the stretched networks of assets and SPVs which operate across space and outsource financial transactions in global fund management (Clark and Monk, 2013), it is still surprising that researchers studying professional global networks have bypassed the opportunity to provide much needed analysis into the role of professions in controlling and managing OFC flows across networks of onshore–offshore space.

The role of global financial networks needs to be positioned more centrally within future research on OFCs, because earlier studies emphasized the secrecy and illegitimate nature of these spaces, implying that they are part of a shadow economy. This is a misnomer, as the functions of OFCs and professional service providers cannot be quietly resigned to corners of the global economy. For example, Haberly and Wójcik (2013) highlight how 30 percent of foreign direct investment (FDI) alone passes through OFCs, including funding from OECD nations, which demonstrates how both developing and developed economies frequently use OFCs. As such, it could be argued that existing studies of OFCs are problematic in that their exclusive focus on offshore space obscures and separates their wider relationships with 'traditional' onshore spaces with which they are deeply entwined. This is significant as although the role of tax minimization planning has been viewed as a key characteristic of OFCs, it has deflected attention from the widespread use of tax planning activities in associated onshore spaces too (Wainwright, 2011).

One unique exception to this is Hudson (1999) who explains how 'traditional' global financial centers underwent reregulation in the 1970s and 1980s to provide New York, London and Tokyo with a more liberal financial environment with which to attract offshore business from small island economies, although clients had to be based outside of these respective nation-states. In this sense, the 1970s witnessed the emergence of 'offshore' spaces within 'traditional' onshore financial centers, where tax minimization activities were no longer the preserve of small island economies. Ironically, OECD economies that have been active in criticizing OFCs for their role in tax minimization plans have also been quietly developing their own onshore–offshore spaces (Haberly and Wójcik, 2013), which hold and control considerable volumes of capital (Meinzer and Cobham, 2013). These spaces are sometimes less well known and include more mundane spaces such as Delaware and Nevada (*Economist*, 2013). This chapter will refer to European onshore financial spaces which have overlapping low regulation, low taxation spaces as 'onshore–offshore' space throughout the analysis.

Towards Theories of Emergence

This chapter's analysis will be framed through theories of emergence, in order to gain insight into how onshore–offshore spaces have developed since the 1990s, in the context of ABS bond markets. Theories of emergence have been gaining interest over the last two decades within the social sciences (Clayton and Davies, 2006). However, a lack of understanding remains as to how and why emergence operates in practice (Martin and Sunley, 2012). Part of this lacuna is due to the wide interest in emergence across the social sciences, which has introduced ambiguities and various interpretations from different disciplines, often giving way to disagreement and controversy (Clayton and Davies, 2006). Despite this, theories of emergence still provide a useful framework to explore how individual actors form new market sectors and practices.

Martin and Sunley (2012) have identified two broad issues that drive researcher interest in emergence. First, it is an approach which can provide insight into how complex adaptive systems undergo self-organization. Second, it examines hypotheses of emergence which investigate ontology and problems with reductionism. This chapter will focus on the first point of interest. Earlier criticisms of emergence as a framework have often focused on its use of biological metaphors, which may not be particularly useful to understanding socio-economic self-organization and the development of new structures (Martin and Sunley, 2012). In order to depart from the biological metaphors used in theories of emergence, the chapter will draw specifically on the emergence literature that has stemmed from institutional theory.

Institutional theory has been used in the fields of sociology, management and innovation studies to examine the development of new industrial and product sectors (cf. Di Maggio, 1998; Rao, 2004; Giarrantana, 2004; Geroski, 2003; Benner and Tripsas, 2012). The benefits of drawing on emergence within this context over other theoretical frameworks, is that it places a strong focus on the development of particular codes of practice and an evolving series of relationships between a range of different actors (Deacon, 2006). This assists the chapter in providing new understandings into how the relatively unknown market sector of CSPs became organized, functional, and eventually a lynchpin in the creation of new onshore–offshore spaces that would facilitate a global securitization market.

In the field of organizational sociology, emergence has been used as a conceptual tool to problematize previous research on industry sectors, which often focuses exclusively on phases of growth, celebrating 'successful' innovations or markets, where the implicit assumption is that nascent industries are guaranteed success and how different actors organize to form new micro and macro structures. Instead, theories of emergence seek to provide deeper insight into the development of new industries in their proto-sector stages, giving precedence to the role of local culture, histories and institutions in shaping how new markets emerge (Giarrantana, 2004; Agarwal and Bayus, 2002; Geroski, 2003). Given the lack of research into the development of CSPs and tax minimization professionals, and its recent evolution since the late 1990s, a framework such as this that provides a historical lens on the organization of a new industry sector is particularly useful.

This develops further complementarities between existing studies on emergence and OFCs, as one area of research which has been neglected by researchers of emergence are new innovations in the services sector. As such, it is unclear as to how new service sectors develop, using untested processes with an absence of accepted standards and structures, or knowledgeable market participants and stakeholders (Navis and Glynn, 2010, 2011). In the context of onshore–offshore spaces that have emerged within established onshore financial spaces, there was a lack of compatibility with existing tax regulation and structures for ABS transactions, which required the formalization of new legislation and cultural codes borrowed from existing markets to create new micro-structures in the CSP sector.

Deacon (2006) has drawn attention to three types of emergence. First-order emergence refers to the self-organization of previously unaligned agents who begin to exhibit micro-behaviors. This creates a new socio-economic system, which can be viewed as a new emerging market sector. Second-order emergence refers to the development of macro-structures within the new sector that begin to establish new patterns and norms which crystalize the nascent socio-economic system. This has downward and upward causal effects as the macro-structure begins to self-reinforce and lock in behaviors and routines of other actors within the socio-economic system. Third-order emergence sees the macro-structure beginning to adapt to fit its changing environment (Goodenough and Deacon, 2003), changing lower order structures, and tailoring the emergent sector to wider forces and institutions.

Subsequently, this provides a useful lens with which to examine how agents including accountants, fund administrators, and legal professionals began to develop a new community and socio-economic system of CSPs to manage ABS transactions. While these professions originally undertook a different series of activities, some novel actors began to develop a new loosely organized micro-structure of CSP providers. As will be demonstrated later, the nascent sector's macro-structure was reconfigured by policymakers, who became closely involved in redesigning new legislation that would assist CSPs in tax minimization practices.

As such, drawing upon existing research from the field of emergence is useful to interrogate how political and legal determinants shaped the third order of emergence in the CSP sector. This is important as previous research has emphasized how new market participants cultivate legitimacy and industry standards through trust government approval (Aldrich and Fiol, 1994; Kennedy et al., 2010; Rao, 2004), to obtain legal recognition for new products and services which support participants and protagonists in establishing and growing their sector (Kennedy et al., 2010). In this sense, the theories of emergence literature have parallels with earlier research on OFCs, which highlighted how small island states re-regulated their economies to attract international capital (Hudson, 1999, 2000; Cobb, 1999; Palan, 1998).

Onshore–offshore spaces are unique in that they emerge alongside financial institutions in existing financial centers (cf. Hudson, 2000). In many cases, they make use of the services of domestic financial service providers, and in doing so, intermesh deregulated 'offshore-style' activities with domestic banking systems. An additional feature of using emergence as a conceptual tool to unpick the development of onshore–offshore spaces, is that it highlights how new markets and industries borrow from existing institutions, norms and standards which are re-used, morphing existing knowledge and artifacts for use in new activities, and in doing so, creating new spaces (Aldrich and Fiol, 1994; Benner and Tripsas, 2012; Martin and Sunley, 2012).

Methodology

This chapter draws upon semi-structured in-depth interviews conducted with London-based financial professionals between 2007 and 2008. Each interview lasted for between 45 minutes and two hours and was recorded and transcribed before being thematically coded. The research participants included individuals working for mortgage lenders, investment banks, law firms, bond-rating agencies, investors and corporate service providers. In total, 40 interviews were conducted. Although the participants were UK based, many of the senior executives worked for companies which operated across Europe and had worked on ABS transactions involving European financial institutions. These participants had been engaged in securitizing residential and commercial mortgages and consumer credit assets. In several cases, respondents had been key protagonists in the development of emergent onshore–offshore tax spaces throughout the 1990s and early 2000s through their corporate service provision and management of SPVs. The research participants were identified from searches of the financial press (for example, *Financial Times* and *Euromoney*) and by exploring the websites of financial organizations and professional bodies. The research also used snowballing to identify important participants working across different networks of financial services providers, including investment banks, law firms and the corporate service providers.

18.2 EMERGING SERVICES AND THE USE OF OFFSHORE SPACE

The emergence of securitization markets in Europe was an important financial innovation for both investors and European corporate borrowers. Securitization transactions were particularly popular amongst European mortgage lenders (Aalbers, 2009b; Blommestein et al., 2011), but lenders later sought to reengineer revenue streams from other assets including credit card portfolios, car loans, small- and medium-sized enterprise (SME) loans, whole business securitizations (WBS), commercial mortgages (CMBS) and collateralized debt obligations (CDOs) (see Figure 18.1). This chapter will refer to all of the former as ABS securitizations, to cover the multiple types of assets that have been securitized. European securitization origination grew steadily throughout the early 2000s as new participants entered the market, helping the emergent sector to develop further legitimacy (Figure 18.2), although volumes began to decrease rapidly after the GFC (Table 18.1). Despite the overall reduction in European securitization origination, EUR1.71 trillion of assets were still outstanding in 2012 (AFME, 2013), indicating that

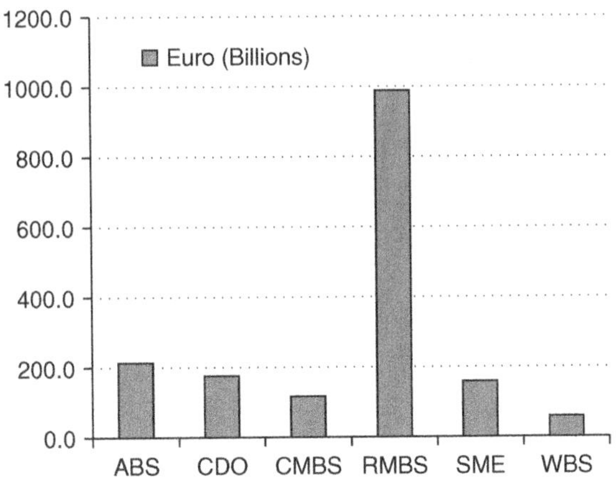

Source: AFME (2013).

Figure 18.1 European securitization, outstanding collateral in 2012

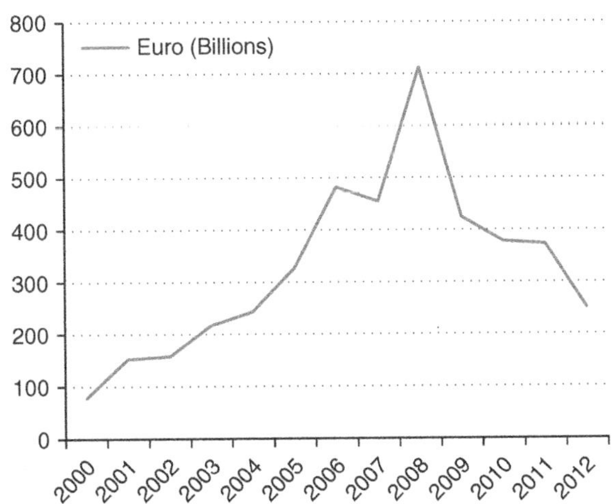

Source: AFME (2013).

Figure 18.2 Total European securitization issuance

ABS markets will remain important for European corporations that are seeking cheaper capital market funding (Blommestein et al., 2011; AFME, 2012).

Previously, many corporations and finance houses had gained access to credit through corporate loans or medium-term note (MTN) issues. However, ABS bond markets were able to overcome the main drawbacks of these two funding modes (Blommestein et al., 2011). On the one hand, large long-term loans can be viewed as high-risk lending by commercial banks, which in turn command higher interest rates. On the other hand, MTNs

Table 18.1 Issuance by country of collateral (euro, billions)

	2012	2011	2010	2009	2008
Belgium	15.4	19	14.1	27.4	34.9
Denmark	0	0	1.5	0	0
France	14.9	16.4	9	6.9	14.2
Germany	10	12.9	13.4	18.4	50.1
Greece	2	6.4	1	22.5	12.7
Ireland	1.2	0	6.6	25.1	40.7
Italy	58.3	48.1	16	69.2	82.2
Netherlands	48.7	85.6	137.6	44.2	72.6
Portugal	1.4	9.9	16.9	10.5	14.8
Spain	18.6	61.7	54.9	64.9	80.7
UK	76.5	99.5	101.5	88.7	271.9
PanEurope	0.4	3	2.6	20.3	0
Other Europe	3	3.4	1.6	1.8	0
Multinational	0.5	6	0.7	23.7	36.3
European Total	250.9	372	377.4	423.6	711.1
US Total	1,551.60	1,013.70	1,276.70	1,358.90	933.6

Source: AFME (2013).

provide cheaper credit and longer term credit than corporate loans, but the coupon rates are dependent upon the overall bond rating of a company, as the stability of its income streams and balance sheet affect its ability to repay bond holders (AFME, 2012). Unsurprisingly, corporations which are viewed as being less stable are required to pay investors a higher return.

The main advantage of ABS securitization over MTNs is that it enables a corporation's revenue producing assets to be financially reengineered, creating high-quality assets with low funding costs through the use of SPVs. To achieve this, pools of assets are transferred from the balance sheet of an organization to an SPV, which makes these assets 'bankruptcy remote' where they are legally separated from the original parent (Wainwright, 2009), as highlighted below:

> If you want to deal with the [SPV's] financial trustee, you send it to those offices, care of [Corporate service provider 1 . . .] they have an office in London, so for the directors, we have, I think there's one [Bank B] director, which is our treasurer, and the rest are directors from the trustees, so any changes go through there, so there's no recourse to [Bank B] in court at all, it's a separate legal entity, the assets of which are [Bank B] mortgages, which they have bought from [Bank B]. (Securitization Manager 1, July 2007)

Subsequently, the diverse risks and liabilities which faced the parent corporation, whether a commercial landlord, bank or leasing company, are no longer relevant to the assets, so the ABS bonds produced from the asset revenue streams are typically of lower risk, making the ABS bonds cheaper in comparison to MTN notes. The success of this practice is contingent on the use of SPVs, and as highlighted earlier, SPVs need to be registered and located within financial spaces, in order to hold the bankruptcy remote assets which underpin bonds (cf. Wainwright, 2011; Haberly and Wójcik, 2013).

As such, the growth of ABS issuance in Europe stimulated an expansion in the number of SPVs, but this required the emergence of a new group of specialist professional service providers to manage them. As SPVs are separated from the parent, they are not created with a sophisticated management team to control them as they do not undertake the usual, complex functions of organizations which produce goods and services. Despite this, SPVs still need to arrange audits and comply with local regulations while repaying investors. The result was the emergence of a new type of market participant known as corporate service providers (CSPs) who act as caretakers, providing formal, yet passive management functions for large numbers of orphaned SPVs. CSPs provide directors and trustees to ensure that SPVs are fulfilling their legal obligations, while providing book keeping and secretarial services:

> I'm a director of around 100 companies, which is meaningless . . . I'm a director of companies that don't do anything, I'm not deliberately playing it down, but the whole point of them is they shouldn't be complicated . . . we provide company directors, we could still be sued if [the SPV] doesn't deliver its reporting accounts, you can still be sued in a civil court if you haven't filed the various returns on time, it still has to do tax returns so, as a service provider in those situations we would set up a company . . . it exists as a company, it has shareholders, a company secretary, then those roles are transferred to us, there's a series of forms that have to be filled out. (Director of Corporate Service Provider, June 2007)

The growth in the number of ABS bond issuances unsurprisingly corresponded in a rise in demand for SPVs, which led to emergence of the CSP industry which provided services specifically aimed at ABS markets. However, single ABS transactions require the formation and management of multiple chains of SPVs, where each SPV provides a unique task, such as holding assets, or issuing notes to investors. As centralized mortgage lenders make several securitizations a year (Wainwright, 2011), for example, this requires the registration of new multiple chains of SPVs which need to be managed. Research from studies on emergence has noted that prototype markets often lack specialized participants and professions with stabilized knowledge and skills (Navis and Glynn, 2011). Similarly, in the case of ABS SPV administration, specialist firms did not exist in the nascent stages of this industry, which still lacked a coherent identity (cf. Rao, 2004). It has been argued that new participants in emergent markets often borrow labels, norms and knowledge, and in doing so, some of the legitimacy of established professions in order to function (Benner and Tripsas, 2012). This also occurred in the context of emergent ABS markets, where ABS CSPs initially grew out of existing firms which provided legal or trustee services to fund managers. In other cases, experienced staff from the legal, accountancy and financial professions began to create new entrepreneurial CSP ventures to seize these new market opportunities. For professionals with legal and accountancy experience and entrepreneurial flair, the widespread growth of ABS markets, in terms of bond issue volumes and geographical production, produced a growing pan-European market for the new ABS CSP sector:

> they all needed special purpose vehicles, which comes back to us, and they're so busy making deals, Morgan Stanley needs SPVs, Barclays needs SPVs, Goldman Sachs needs SPVs, RBS need SPVs, what do we sell, SPVs [. . . ABS] are now a massive market, a huge field, and then of course these asset classes have started to move geographically, we're now seeing securitization, in France, Spain, Germany, Italy, Greece, Turkey. (Ex-commercial bank director, July 2007)

The development of the ABS market became increasingly important in funding European corporations and financial institutions, and as will be demonstrated later, policymakers actively created new legislation to accommodate and legitimize the emergence of ABS. In the earlier years when this emergent market developed, ABS transactions were found to be incompatible with European financial spaces and existing tax regulation. This was because the market stability and credit quality of ABS bonds is reliant on SPVs being structured in a way so that they do not generate income, and effectively become 'tax neutral'.

The main issue facing financiers is that ABS transaction volumes are measured in millions of euros and if the SPVs begin to make profits, revenue flowing through the SPVs to investors can be taxed. Additional uncertainty is introduced as tax rates can vary, which would have a substantial impact on the revenue streams being paid to bond investors, potentially creating significant shortfalls, hence the argument for tax neutrality. Interestingly, while tax planning is often used to facilitate evasion, avoidance, and the minimization of tax on profits (Roberts, 1995; Maurer, 2008), SPV chains in ABS transactions are designed to not be profitable in the first instance, as highlighted below:

> It's not because it's terrible or sinful, it's because they don't make any money, you don't want the company, the whole process, the drivers behind this transaction is not that the SPV makes money, it has to be transparent, and two dimensional if it has anything more in substance, it starts to generate tax, and that tax is cash that is not going through to the investors, and it reduces the return . . . you would, only ever pay tax on net income, you wouldn't pay tax on the cash flow. (Director of Corporate Service Provider, June 2007)

Ensuring that ABS SPVs could become tax neutral was a difficult task under the existing legislation of European countries, posing new difficulties for emergent market participants, such as legal advisors and CSPs. As ABS bond issues are complex and multifaceted, it was particularly difficult to determine which different taxes would apply to various aspects of the transactions and how they would be treated under existing legislation. Initially, this brought into question whether ABS markets would be feasible outside of the US, as legal frameworks in Europe were at odds with ABS structures. The answer to overcoming ambiguous and complex tax legislation was to simply register and domicile the SPVs in offshore spaces. One notable example was the UK's Northern Rock, which was a substantial securitizer prior to its demise in 2007 (Marshall et al., 2011) and deliberately located its main asset holding SPV, named the Granite Mastertrust, in Jersey. The main advantage of using OFCs was that their light regulation made it easier for legal experts and CSPs to ensure that the chains of SPVs would be tax neutral, as outlined below:

> essentially the easiest thing to do was to have your SPV locate in an offshore jurisdiction because on the whole it got around a lot of problems, it didn't get around them all, because sometimes when you own the assets abroad it makes life incredibly more complicated later, maybe withholding tax problems, with getting flows from an offshore jurisdiction. (Ex-commercial bank director, July 2007)

> [A] lot of SPVs moved offshore because the tax regime here [UK] was fairly unclear in terms of how they were treated, I think it's been made clearer, not transparent, but it means people are quite happy to have English SPVs now. (Director of Corporate Service Provider, June 2007)

However, as ABS markets began to grow, European governments became aware that more assets, and indeed market opportunities, would be lost to OFCs. This later led to the design of new tailor-made legislation by policymakers, or the re-regulation of existing legal frameworks, to create new tax environments which would be compatible with ABS transactions, enabling SPV assets to remain in Europe, culminating in new onshore–offshore spaces.

18.3 EMERGENCE, RE-REGULATION AND ONSHORE–OFFSHORE COMPETITION

Earlier research on OFCs revealed how low levels of transparency and light regulation were central to their strategy in attracting international capital and assets (Palan, 1998; Hudson, 1999, 2000; Cobb, 1999, 1995; Hampton and Levi, 1999). As such, small island economies actively sought to remove layers of regulation, to enable the domicile of SPVs within their jurisdictions. Similarly, the complexity of ABS securitizations in Europe also required SPVs to be located in lightly regulated spaces, which stimulated the restructuring of European financial centers and culminated in the creation of new bespoke onshore–offshore spaces to accommodate ABS SPVs. While earlier work has suggested that capital flows to OFCs with the lowest rates of taxation (cf. Hampton and Levi, 1999), the extract below highlights how non-economic considerations became important, too:

> What I refer to as 'grown up' jurisdictions, tend to be more sophisticated . . . a lot of the offshore jurisdictions like Cayman and some of the weirder and wackier ones don't care [about transparency], as long as they get their money . . . historically, Germany and Benelux, and German investors will look to stuff in Luxembourg, sometimes there is a genuine bona fide tax reason why you choose that jurisdiction, but often it is the comfort level, Cayman for example is dearly beloved of the US, and the Far East, the Japanese are very happy with Cayman structures, European investors will look at erm Luxembourg or maybe Dublin, they have these strange EU offshore–onshore jurisdictions, Jersey, Channel Islands . . . so it's a combination of a historical understanding of the legal system plus geographical locality . . . there's some very heavy hitters who wouldn't want to spend 26 hours on a flight to go to a 1.5 hour board meeting. (Director of Corporate Service Provider, June 2007)

In this sense, European financial centers already had a spatial competitive advantage over OFCs, for two key reasons. First, European financial centers are viewed to be more familiar, professional and legitimate to ABS bond issuers and investors. This is due to the prevalence of similar legal systems, banking structures and shared cultures. Second, the creation and administration of SPV chains requires legal advisors, investment bankers, bond issuers and CSPs to meet and plan the transactions. Subsequently, face-to-face interaction is important, making regular and extensive travel to OFCs for senior managers and consultants for administrative purposes impractical. These two factors ensured that European financial centers would be a preferable location for the location of ABS SPVs, in contrast to established OFCs.

This finding is consistent with more recent research on OFCs, which has emphasized how SPV and investor activity is clustered as a result of cultural complementarities, shared histories and language, in addition to the constraints of travel times and time zones (Clark and Wójcik, 2007; Haberly and Wójcik, 2013). As the European ABS securitization market continued to emerge, policymakers became increasingly aware of its importance in reducing the regulatory capital reserves of financial institutions, but it also became viewed as a key technology in widening the private sector's access to finance, to fund business growth (European Investment Bank, 2013). Studies from the field of emergence have identified the important role of state recognition in providing legitimacy to new market sectors (Aldrich and Fiol, 1994; Kennedy et al., 2010), which is often primed by the work of lobbyists and protagonists seeking to gain wider recognition from potential market participants. As such, the early successes of the emerging European ABS market were contingent on recognition from policymakers, who sought to enhance its legitimacy. This moved beyond the simple approval and recognition of the market and resulted in the active development of new regulation to accommodate ABS SPVs, developed in collaboration between policymakers and key industry stakeholders. This new legislation began to initiate the emergence of new onshore–offshore spaces in existing financial centers. In this sense, European governments effectively came to mimic the earlier behavior of small island economy OFCs by re-regulating their spaces to become compatible with securitization:

> we were asked by the [Italian] banks to help them lobby for as flexible a framework as possible when they knew the law was going to be changed . . . at that point we got involved in persuading the regulators and legislators, that to produce a framework that was going to be not difficult to comply with and get the flexibility they were looking for to get those objectives. (Partner, law firm, July 2007)

> Some countries have set up a securitization law, that says the government allows, the state has set up a framework, more for Anglo-Saxon countries . . . we don't have many problems with SPVs, we just track the credit performance. (Securitization Research Analyst, investment bank, November 2008)

The introduction of SPV friendly laws also brought governments an additional advantage, with regard to governance. This issue has been identified by Wójcik (2013), who has argued how OFCs have the potential to trigger governance failures, where asset and ownership rights are hidden in SPVs that are positioned beyond the control and surveillance of regulators. In the context of ABS securitization, the control and ownership of 'real' assets such as equipment and infrastructure could be controlled and hidden offshore, which governments were uncomfortable with. This potential risk was mitigated through the development of onshore–offshore spaces as European assets could be made bankruptcy remote, but domiciled closer to home. In addition to this, policymakers also recognized that they could benefit from the creation of onshore–offshore space, as the clustering of large numbers of SPVs in their financial centers would require growing CSP, legal and accountancy sectors:

> When you start to put tax legislation in place that says, hey, we'll allow an SPV here, you have to be extremely precise in what it is you're defining, which has caused governments a lot of headaches, now to move on, the Irish, 7 or 8 years ago, thought actually, it would be a bloody good idea if they passed legislation to make life incredibly easy in Ireland, why, because they suddenly realized if they could capture huge flows of capital, [they could] charge infinitesimally small amounts of tax on it . . . they produced the lowest corporate tax rate in Europe 12.5 per cent, they then went on to say everything was deductible against everything else which meant

you pay virtually no tax at all, as the profit was very small, they then changed VAT legislation that said, VAT on servicing was virtually non-existent, they made sure that all the withholding tax, double tax agreements all were extremely fluid, so virtually any sort of assets could go into Ireland as Eurobonds, and they became certain that the Irish stock exchange would turn around documentation in 48 hours with a guarantee, they said if you want to set up an SPV, we're in the European community, were virtually tax free by the way, its set up, you can get anything in here, it can be synthetic, non-synthetic, multiple tranches, options on this, things on that, bells, whistles, everything else, used some wonderful blanket legislation that said anything goes, so what happens, the Irish cornered the market for SPVs, they now employ huge armies of people in Dublin, accountants, SPV managers, asset managers, a phenomenal industry. (Ex-commercial bank director, July 2007)

This point problematizes literatures that argue how governments take a negative view against aggressive tax minimization, where policymakers seek to close loopholes that deprive them of fiscal revenue. However, as indicated above, and away from the gaze of the media, the development of offshore–onshore spaces was quietly welcomed by policymakers as they could attract SPVs from international financial firms, stimulating new job creation and growth in supportive professional services, which in turn generated taxable income. The creation of Irish onshore–offshore space was also welcomed by financers, as highlighted in the extract below. The financial space's light regulation enabled SPV tax neutrality, which in turn reduced the time required to complete the legal and administrative paperwork of SPVs, making it faster and more convenient to launch ABS securitizations:

Where SPVs are domiciled . . . we have a few in Jersey, England, we like the Irish stock exchange because it turns documents around faster and we like the Irish SPV management, it was easier to work with than anyone in the UK, but the UK guys use England and Wales plc, they vary the regions for withholding tax, it's all tax . . . yeah, so what stock exchange you're listing on, Luxembourg, UK, Ireland, some of them leave stuff and it takes 3 or 8 weeks to turn a document around, some will do it in two. (Securitization Structurer, investment bank, July 2007)

Previous studies have suggested that OFCs have been engaged in a 'race to the bottom' seeking to offer the lowest tax rates in order to attract more capital from their competitors (cf. Sharman, 2005). However, OFCs in small island economies have often chosen to strategically position themselves as specialist centers as well, developing technical competencies and social capital which aligns them with particular types of clients and assets. For example, the Cayman Islands attract vehicles associated with captive insurance and hedge funds, whereas collective investment funds are often situated in Luxembourg and Ireland (Roberts, 1995; Palan et al., 2010). Ironically, European countries have frequently criticized small island economy OFCs for their activities in the past, but they have also begun to mimic their behavior through rounds of competitive re-regulation to create SPV compatible onshore–offshore spaces:

So what happened, Luxembourg who for years had done financing transactions had gone to sleep about securitization and volumes of business went to Ireland, and the Commission de Surveillance du Secteur Financier (CSSF), which is the regulatory authority out there said, what are they doing in Ireland, all we have to do is pass legislation and get it right and we can take our business back and we can have a great business here. It took 5 years to get their securitization law passed, about 18 months, 2 years later and what's happened exactly, that business has gone to Luxembourg, and now whose jealous, the Dutch, you know, lots of finance companies

> there, we must get up to speed, so now it's a competitive game . . . now most of the developed European countries are setting up their own domestic SPVs . . . its entirely employment driven and the fact that the government realizes that there is some money that can be extracted, why give it to someone else. (Ex-commercial bank director, July 2007)

The design of onshore–offshore spaces enabled emergent ABS markets to become more stable and legitimate, as the legal landscape had been altered to support asset holding SPVs. However, the creation of different onshore–offshore spaces within existing European financial centers resulted in the development of a competitive pan-European market of onshore–offshore spaces, where financiers could pick and choose jurisdictions that provided an expedient service in SPV management with lower management fees, or a regulatory regime which provides a more favorable treatment for particular ABS assets:

> Typically [UK] residential mortgage transactions use a UK vehicle, however other assets you're not so limited, trade receivables use Irish vehicles, commercial mortgages, you could use Irish vehicles, Luxemburg, Belgium, Netherlands vehicles, and with some assets you can use Cayman and Bermuda . . . we would often set them up erm, depending on the jurisdiction and it varies depending on the cost effectiveness of it. (Partner, law firm, July 2007)

One particularly interesting observation of this chapter is how European members of the OECD, have chosen to partially emulate the strategies of small island economy OFCs, despite their criticism of low regulatory regimes which are seen as facilitating tax avoidance and evasion (Haberly and Wójcik, 2013). This effectively created offshore spaces for ABS SPVs within existing onshore financial centers, which stimulated the growth of new professional service providers, to enable the retention of assets in Europe and to facilitate more transactions.

This raises interesting questions as to where the balance of power sits between policymakers and financiers in the development and management of onshore–offshore space. Throughout the 2000s, financiers pushed for greater transparency and regulatory change that would minimize the tax liabilities of structured finance SPVs and enable the ABS market to grow. While power was initially wielded by financiers, regulators began to realize that creating new economic spaces for SPVs led to growth in supportive professional services which could be taxed. After the GFC in 2008, this power relationship shifted to become more complex, with policymakers seeking to protect and promote onshore–offshore space.

Due to market uncertainty and weakened demand for ABS assets since the GFC, there have been fewer transactions, leading to a reduction in demand for SPVs, and the importance of onshore–offshore space. However, the Bank of England and European Central Bank (2014) have been keen to understand how securitization markets could be re-stimulated. In this sense, European governments view ABS securitization as an important technique that can add liquidity to European financial markets and fund growth in the economic recovery, where governments and the industry could introduce new steps to promote securitization. As such, the power relations have begun to shift, where policy elites are becoming increasingly concerned about supporting the ABS community, particularly onshore–offshore spaces. This in turn, demonstrates how governments have maintained an important role in the development of securitization and its relationship with tax planning.

18.4 CONCLUSION

This chapter has sought to contribute to the existing body of research on OFCs, while also adding to calls for a new research agenda to reignite economic and financial geographers' interest in onshore–offshore spaces. Earlier work on OFCs provided much needed insight into the role that they play in facilitating the flows of international financial networks, particularly regarding their role in facilitating tax avoidance and evasion (Hudson, 1999, 2000; Cobb, 1999, 1995; Cameron, 2008). These earlier endeavors provided deeper understandings into the processes of globalization, but even though there has been an increased focus on the financialization of capitalist economies, scholars have turned their attention away from the importance of OFCs in contemporary financial systems (Haberly and Wójcik, 2013). Despite this slowdown, some momentum is returning in the study of OFCs. Recent research has begun to investigate the wider roles of OFCs and the multiplicity of onshore–offshore spaces (Clark and Monk, 2013; Clark and Wójcik, 2007; Karhunen and Ledyaeva, 2013; Haberly and Wójcik, 2013; Wainwright, 2011).

This chapter has sought to extend the limited OFC literature through its novel findings. First, it has highlighted how onshore spaces in established European financial centers underwent restructuring to create new onshore–offshore financial spaces, modeled on the earlier activities of small island economies (cf. Roberts, 1995). The chapter drew upon interdisciplinary research which uses theories of emergence (Aldrich and Fiol, 1994; Agarwal and Bayus, 2002; Rao, 2004) to develop insight into how this new European sector developed. The chapter uncovered how new market actors and participants became organized to form new macro-structures and onshore–offshore spaces by developing new standards and practices (cf. Aldrich and Fiol, 1994; Benner and Tripsas, 2012) through communities of practice from law and accountancy to administer chains of ABS SPVs.

One particularly interesting finding was how the structures of ABS securitization require SPVs to engage in tax neutral transactions, a feature which was not compatible with existing European legal systems. The consequence of this was that earlier European securitization assets were domiciled in OFCs. However, due to cultural complementarities, transparency, social capital, and physical constraints such as travel times, as recently highlighted by Haberly and Wójcik (2013), ABS financiers preferred the idea of domiciling assets closer to European financial centers. The early re-regulation of Dublin's financial space enabled ABS SPVs to become domiciled within Europe. Shortly after this time, European policymakers and regulators had begun to recognize securitization was a useful financing mechanism, which would lower costs to corporate borrowers and potentially fund growth (EIB, 2013). As such, ABS markets became legitimized as bespoke regulation was designed (cf. Rao, 2004; Kennedy et al., 2010) to facilitate the tax neutral functioning of SPVs.

This enabled the growth of ABS markets, CSPs, legal and accountancy providers in existing European financial centers, who began to benefit from the government sponsored legitimization of the market. This was created in part by the successful lobbying of key protagonists from professional services providers, to develop and promote ABS markets. Policymakers decided that the domiciling of SPVs in existing European financial centers could be beneficial in potentially creating employment and taxable revenue for European states, a debatable argument often used to legitimize the formation of OFCs (Christensen and Shaxson, 2013). While the development of onshore–offshore spaces in London, New

York and Tokyo have previously been identified (Hudson, 2000; *Economist*, 2013), analysis of the emergence of ABS markets in Europe illustrates how European governments have also adopted the strategies of small island economies.

Turning to summarize the chapter's theoretical considerations, this chapter presented a novel case on the emergence of a service industry, its new market participants and its legitimization through new regulation. However, while studies on emergence often focus on the impact of institutions, history and knowledge in new market emergence (Giarrantana, 2004; Agarwal and Bayus, 2002; Geroski, 2003), this chapter has shown how space is deeply implicated in market development, spatialities which can initially prohibit new innovations, but which can be altered to accommodate new professional services.

This chapter has also sought to demonstrate how OFCs cannot be viewed primarily as small island economies, nor can offshore space be viewed as being isolated from wider financial networks. Subsequently, this study has shown how traditionally 'offshore' activities have become integrated within onshore space to create new hybrid spaces, which are compatible with new financial products (cf. Engelen and Fernandez, 2013). In addition to exploring the emergence of new ABS markets, this study has also shown how securitization, just one of the many mechanisms of financialization (French et al., 2011), is firmly rooted and dependent on the existence of onshore–offshore spaces.

Economic and financial geographers should no longer neglect the importance of offshore and onshore spaces, and their associated institutions, as they are key to enabling the function of international financial networks (cf. Haberly and Wójcik, 2013). Subsequently, this chapter calls for future work to scrutinize the roles of new market specific professional services providers and interdisciplinary project teams to understand how elites manage assets and SPVs. There is an increasing literature on financial elites such as investment bankers and other capital market intermediaries (Savage and Williams, 2008), and although there is a growing body of research on the legal profession (for example Faulconbridge and Muzio, 2015, 2016), there is a surprising lack of study into how financiers, legal professionals and accountants function as interdisciplinary project groups. It therefore comes as no surprise that while the role of legal and accounting professions are missing from studies of finance, they are absent from research which examines analysis of onshore–offshore spaces. This chapter has brought to light the central role that these professions play in international finance and tax affairs, highlighting how more research is needed to understand their roles in facilitating the production of tax neutral transactions and space.

REFERENCES

Aalbers, M.B. (2009a), 'Geographies of this financial crisis', *Area*, **41**, 34–42.

Aalbers, M.B. (2009b), 'The globalization and Europeanization of mortgage markets', *International Journal of Urban and Regional Research*, **33**, 389–410.

Aalbers, M.B., E. Engelen and A. Glasmacher (2011), '"Cognitive closure" in the Netherlands: mortgage securitization in a hybrid European political economy', *Environment and Planning A*, **43**, 1779–1795.

Agarwal, R. and A. Bayus (2002), 'The market evolution and take-off of new product innovations', *Management Science*, **38**, 1024–1041.

Aglietta, M. and R. Breton (2001), 'Financial systems, corporate control, and capital accumulation', *Economy and Society*, **30**, 344–466.

Aldrich, H. and M. Fiol (1994), 'Fools rush in? The institutional context of industry creations', *The Academy of Management Review*, **19**, 645–670.
Association for Financial Markets in Europe (AFME) (2012), *The Economic Benefits of High Quality Securitization to the EU Economy*, London: AFME.
Association for Financial Markets in Europe (AFME) (2013), *Securitization Data Report Q2:2013*, London: AFME.
Bank of England and European Central Bank (2014), *The Case for a Better Functioning Securitization Market in the European Union*, London: Bank of England.
Bardouille, N. (2001), 'The offshore services industry in the Caribbean: a conceptual and sub-regional analysis', *Economic Analysis and Policy*, **31**, 111–124.
Beaverstock, J., S. Hall and J. Faulconbridge (2010), 'Professionalization, legitimization and the creation of executive search markets in Europe', *Journal of Economic Geography*, **10**, 825–843.
Beaverstock, J., S. Hall and T. Wainwright (2013), 'Servicing the super-rich: new financial elites and the rise of the private wealth management retail ecology', *Regional Studies*, **47**, 834–849.
Benner, M. and M. Tripsas (2012), 'The influence of prior industry affiliation on framing in nascent industries: the evolution of digital cameras', *Strategic Management Journal*, **33**, 277–302.
Blommestein, H., A. Keskinler and C. Lucas (2011), 'Outlook for the securitization market', *OECD Journal: Financial Market Trends*, **2011**, 1–18.
Boyer, R. (2000), 'The political in the era of globalization and finance: focus on some regulation school research', *International Journal of Urban and Regional Research*, **24**, 274–322.
Bryan, D., M. Rafferty and D. Wigan (2013), 'Intangible assets, profit shifting and unbundling the (multinational) corporation: towards an understanding of capital in motion', *Deconstructing Offshore Finance Seminar*, St Peter's College Oxford, August 2–3, 2013.
Cameron, A. (2008), 'Crisis? What crisis? Displacing the spatial imaginary of the fiscal state', *Geoforum*, **39**, 1135–1154.
Christensen, J. and N. Shaxson (2013), 'The Finance Curse: exploring the possible impacts of hosting an oversize offshore financial centre', *Deconstructing Offshore Finance Seminar*, St Peter's College Oxford, 2–3 August 2013.
Clark, G. and A. Monk (2013), 'The scope of financial institutions: in-sourcing, outsourcing and off-shoring', *Journal of Economic Geography*, **13**, 279–298.
Clark, Gordon and Dariuz Wójcik (2007), *The Geography of Finance: Corporate Governance in the Global Marketplace*, Oxford: Oxford University Press.
Clayton, Philip and Paul Davies (eds) (2006), *The Re-Emergence of Emergence*, Oxford: Oxford University Press.
Cobb, S. (1999), 'The role of corporate, professional and personal networks, in the provision of offshore financial services', *Environment and Planning A*, **31**, 1877–1892.
Coe, N. (2012), 'Geographies of production II: a global production networks A–Z', *Progress in Human Geography*, **36**, 389–402.
Coe, N. and M. Hess (2013), 'Global production networks, labour and development', *Geoforum*, **44**, 4–9.
Deacon, T. (2006), 'Emergence: the hole at the wheel's hub', in Phillip Clayton and Paul Davies (eds), *The Re-Emergence of Emergence: The Emergentist Hypothesis from Science to Religion*, Oxford: Oxford University Press, pp. 111–150.
Di Maggio, P. (1998), 'The new institutionalisms: avenues of collaboration', *Journal of Institutional and Theoretical Economics*, 696–705.
Economist (2013), 'Onshore financial centres: not a palm tree in sight', *Economist*, 16 February.
Eden, L. and R. Kudrle (2005), 'Tax havens: renegade states in the international tax regime?', *Law and Policy*, **27**, 100–127.
Engelen, E. and R. Fernandez (2013), 'Institutional conversion or how the infrastructure for fiscal arbitration was "discovered" by TBTF banks for regulatory arbitrage purposes – the case of Lehman Brothers Treasury BV', *Deconstructing Offshore Finance Seminar*, St Peter's College Oxford, August 2–3, 2013.
Erturk, Ismail, Julie Froud, Sukdev Johal, Adam Leaver and Karel Williams (eds) (2008), *Financialization at Work: Key Texts and Commentary*, Abingdon: Routledge.
European Investment Bank (EIB) (2013), *Increasing Lending to the Economy: Implementing the EIB Capital Increase and Joint Commission–EIB initiatives*, Brussels, Belgium: EIB.
Faulconbridge, J. (2010a), 'Global architects: learning and innovation through communities and constellations of practice', *Environment and Planning A*, **42**, 2842–2858.
Faulconbridge, J. (2010b), 'TNCs as embedded social communities: transdisciplinary perspectives', *Critical Perspectives on International Business*, **6**, 273–290.
Faulconbridge, J. and D. Muzio (2015), 'Transnational corporations shaping institutional change: the case of English law firms in Germany', *Journal of Economic Geography*, **15** (6), 1195–1226.
Faulconbridge, J. and D. Muzio (2016), 'Global professional service firms and the challenge of institutional complexity: "field relocation" as a response strategy', *Journal of Management Studies*, **53** (1), 89–124.

Finlayson, A. (2009), 'Financialization, financial literacy and asset based welfare', *The British Journal of Politics and International Relations*, **11**, 400–421.
French, S. and A. Leyshon (2010), '"These f@#king guys": the terrible waste of a good crisis', *Environment and Planning A*, **42**, 2549–2559.
French, S., A. Leyshon and T. Wainwright (2011), 'Financializing space, spacing financialization', *Progress in Human Geography*, **35**, 798–819.
Froud, Julie, Sukdev Johal, Adam Leaver and Karel Williams (2006), *Financialization and Strategy: Narrative and Numbers*, Abingdon: Routledge.
Geroski, Paul (2003), *The Evolution of New Markets*, Oxford: Oxford University Press.
Giarrantana, M. (2004), 'The birth of a new industry: entry by start-ups and the drivers of firm growth: the case of encryption software', *Research Policy*, **33**, 787–806.
Goodenough, U. and T.W. Deacon (2003), 'From biology to consciousness to morality', *Zygon*, **38**, 801–819.
Gotham, K. (2009), 'Creating liquidity out of spatial fixity: the secondary circuit of capital and the subprime mortgage crisis', *International Journal of Urban and Regional Research*, **33**, 355–371.
Haberly, D. and D. Wójcik (2013), 'Tax havens and the production of offshore FDI: an empirical analysis', Working Papers in Employment, Work and Finance, no.13–02: University of Oxford.
Hampton, M. and M. Levi (1999), 'Fast spinning into oblivion? Recent developments in money-laundering policies and offshore finance centres', *Third World Quarterly*, **20**, 645–656.
Hudson, A. (1999), 'Offshores onshore: new regulatory spaces and real historical places in the landscape of global money', in Ron Martin (ed.), *Money and the Space Economy*, Oxford: Wiley, pp. 139–154.
Hudson, A. (2000), 'Offshoreness, globalisation and sovereignty: a postmodern geo-political economy?', *Transactions of the Institute of British Geographers*, **25**, 269–283.
Immergluck, D. (2008), 'From the subprime to the exotic: excessive mortgage market risk and foreclosures', *Journal of the American Planning Association*, **74**, 59–76.
Karhunen, P. and S. Ledyaeva (2013), 'Offshore jurisdictions (including Cyprus), corruption money laundering and Russian round-trip investment', Deconstructing Offshore Finance Seminar, St Peter's College Oxford, August 2–3, 2013.
Kennedy, Mark, Jade Lo and Michael Lounsbury (2010), 'Category currency: the changing value of conformity as a function of ongoing meaning construction', in Greta Hsu, Giacomo Negro and Ozgecan Koçak (eds), *Categories in Markets: Origins and Evolution*, London: Emerald, pp. 369–397.
Langley, P. (2007), 'Uncertain subjects of Anglo-American financialization', *Cultural Critique*, **65**, 67–91.
Leyshon, Andrew and Nigel Thrift (1997), *Money/space: Geographies of Monetary Transformation*, London: Psychology Press.
Marshall, J., A. Pike, J. Pollard, J. Tomaney, S. Dawley and J. Gray (2011), 'Placing the run on Northern Rock', *Journal of Economic Geography*, **11**, 1–25.
Martin, R. and P. Sunley (2012), 'Forms of emergence and the evolution of economic landscapes', *Journal of Economic Behavior & Organization*, **82**, 338–351.
Maurer, B. (2008), 'Re-regulating offshore finance?', *Geography Compass*, **2**, 155–175.
Meinzer, M. and A. Cobham (2013), 'The financial secrecy index: shedding new light on the geography of secrecy?', Deconstructing Offshore Finance Seminar, St Peter's College Oxford, August 2–3, 2013.
Navis, C. and M. Glynn (2010), 'How new categories emerge: the temporal dynamics of legitimacy, identity and entrepreneurship in Satellite Radio 1990–2004', *Administrative Science Quarterly*, **55**, 439–471.
Navis, C. and M. Glynn (2011), 'Legitimate distinctiveness and the entrepreneurial identity: influence on investor judgments of new venture plausibility', *Academy of Management Review*, **36**, 479–499.
Palan, R. (1998), 'Trying to have your cake and eat it: how and why the state system has created offshore', *International Studies Quarterly*, **42**, 625–643.
Palan, Ronen, Richard Murphy and Christian Chavagneux (2010), *Tax Havens: How Globalization Really Works*, New York: Cornell University Press.
Picciotto, S. (1992), 'International taxation and intrafirm pricing in transnational corporate groups', *Accounting, Organizations and Society*, **17**, 759–792.
Pike, A. (2006), '"Shareholder value" versus the regions: the closure of the Vaux brewery in Sunderland', *Journal of Economic Geography*, **6**, 201–222.
Rao, H. (2004), 'Institutional activism in the early American automobile industry', *Journal of Business Venturing*, **19**, 359–384.
Roberts, S. (1995), 'Small place, big money: the Cayman Islands and the international financial system', *Economic Geography*, **71**, 237–256.
Savage, Mike and Karel Williams (2008), 'Elites: remembered in capitalism and forgotten by social sciences', in Mike Savage and Karel Williams (eds), *Remembering Elites*, Oxford: Blackwell, pp. 1–24.
Sharman, J. (2005), 'South Pacific tax havens: from leaders in the race to the bottom to laggards in the race to the top', *Accounting Forum*, **29**, 311–323.
Wainwright, T. (2009), 'Laying the foundations for a crisis: mapping the historico-geographical construction of

residential mortgage backed securitization in the UK', *International Journal of Urban and Regional Research*, **33**, 372–388.
Wainwright, T. (2011), 'Tax doesn't have to be taxing: London's 'onshore' finance industry and the fiscal spaces of a global crisis', *Environment and Planning A*, **43**, 1287–1304.
Wainwright, T. (2012), 'Number crunching: financialization and spatial strategies of risk organization', *Journal of Economic Geography*, **12**, 1267–1291.
Wainwright, T. (2015), 'Circulating financial innovation: new knowledge and securitization in Europe', *Environment and Planning A*, **47** (8), 1643–1660.
Wainwright, T. and P. Rodgers (2013), 'Which crisis? The need to understand spaces of (non)tax in the economic recovery', *Environment and Planning A*, **45**, 1008–1012.
Wójcik, D. (2013), 'Where governance fails: advanced business services and the offshore world', *Progress in Human Geography*, **37**, 330–347.

19. Banking reform in China: a balancing act between financial viability and financial security

Godfrey Yeung

19.1 INTRODUCTION

China is an interesting case in the banking industry as her economy is moving towards (some forms of) capitalism after three decades of economic reform and rapid economic growth, but the state still plays an important role in the economy. Along with the market-oriented reforms in the manufacturing sector, there has been a massive restructuring of the Chinese banking industry during the last few decades. The change in the ownership structure of banks reflects the changing role of the state in the economy and thus the institutional environment in China.

High street banking in China is still effectively controlled by five former wholly state-owned commercial banks (SOCBs) even after joining the World Trade Organization (WTO) in 2001. As bad debts accumulated by SOCBs had reached nearly 50 per cent (4 trillion *yuan*) of the nation's gross domestic product (GDP) in 1999, and the non-performing loan (NPL) ratio of SOCBs reached 31 per cent in 2001, critics pointed out that SOCBs, with their ambiguous property rights, are obliged to grant loans to moribund state-owned enterprises (SOEs), largely as a result of political pressure from the local governments (Lardy, 1998; OECD, 2005). Lardy (1998) went further and claimed that the banking sector in China would be technically insolvent if western benchmarks for the liquidity ratio and non-performing loans (NPLs) were used in the Chinese system.

The existing literature in financial geography focuses on major financial centres in developed countries (Leyshon and Thrift, 1995; Leyshon and Pollard, 2000; Morrison and O'Brien, 2001; Clark and Wójcik, 2003; Faulconbridge et al., 2007; Grote, 2007; Wójcik, 2011) or emerging markets (Wójcik and Burger, 2010; Lai, 2012) rather than banking in transitional economies where the state still has a strong influence on socio-economic development. Much of the literature emphasizes the geographical aspect of financial exclusion, with exceptions like Kempson and Whyley (1999a, 1999b) and Kempson et al. (2000). The consolidation of the financial markets (Avery et al., 1999) and significant structural changes in the financial sector (Devlin and Wright, 1995) have led to the 'desertification' of banking services in low income areas (Kempson et al., 2000; McKillop and Wilson, 2007).

The pertinent literature on China has two major related but separate strands: the expansion of foreign banks in China and the potential impact of banking reforms on Chinese banks. Examples of the former approaches are Lu and Dewhurst (2007), Zhang and Yang (2007), He and Fu (2008), Chen (2009), He and Yeung (2011) and Lai (2011). Other discussions in the literature have focused on the potential impact of banking reforms on Chinese banks, for example, Pei (1998), Berger et al. (2009), Jia (2009), Yeung (2009a), McGuinness and Keasey (2010). Bonin and Huang (2002) examined the implications of

China's accession to the WTO for domestic banks, while Yeung (2009a) examined the lending criteria of SOCBs, and McGuinness and Keasey (2010) investigated the competitiveness of SOCBs after their public listing.

The mainstream theories on banking geographies may not be fully applicable in non-Anglo-Saxon banking and financial industries (Pollard and Samers, 2007). This is the case of the transitional economy of China, where a functioning market does not exist and the state plays an even more important role in the opening up of retail banking. To examine the roles of the state in banking reform, this chapter focuses on the two specific regulatory objectives of China Banking Regulatory Commission (CBRC): the financial viability of the banking industry, especially that of SOCBs, and the financial security of the general public.

The existing theories on Anglo-American banking geographies have highlighted the decentralization of banking operations and subsequent market segmentation and financial exclusion. These theories, however, have not emphasized the institutional environment of a transitional economy where the transformation of the property structure blurs the conventional boundaries between public and private property while the state still plays an important role in the regulation and operation of a significant portion of these 'hybrid properties'. To fulfil the short-term need for regulation and to ensure the long-term financial viability of the banking industry and the financial security of the general public, the CBRC is performing a balancing act of aiming for multiple and potentially conflicting objectives. On the one hand, the CBRC has to ensure its reforms will facilitate the development of a modern formal banking system in China, given the increasing competition from the overseas banking giants and the local non-bank financial institutes (including the informal banking sectors, which take various forms from trust accounts and wealth management products marketed to the general public to micro-credit institutes and informal lending). The piecemeal approach of reform adopted by the CBRC has its costs, notably perpetuating the moral hazard of the formal banking system by local government officials and the general public whereby their NPLs expect to be bailed out by the central government and investments are expected to be safe under the CBRC's regulations.[1] On the other hand, the CBRC has to ensure that the formal and informal banking sectors are properly regulated during the transitional period and any reforms in the sector will not lead to an increased risk of financial crisis and the consequent loss of public confidence and the possibility of political upheavals.

A brief overview of the theories of Anglo-American banking geographies and the debates on property rights in transitional economies, together with the role of the regulatory authority in China in the next two sections provide the context of the discussions on the reforms in Chinese banking industry, with specific focus on the recapitalization, centralization, and commercialization of SOCBs. The balancing act of the CBRC in maintaining both the financial viability of the banking industry and the financial security of the general public will be discussed.

19.2 CONVERGENCE OF THE ANGLO-AMERICAN BANKING INDUSTRY AND THE INSTITUTIONAL RIGIDITY IN TRANSITIONAL ECONOMIES

The structural deregulation of Anglo-American commercial banks has prompted industrial consolidation through mergers and acquisitions (Berger et al., 1999; Dymski, 1999; Martin, 1999).[2] To improve economic efficiency, banking operations are centralized and the provision of banking services through bank branches has become marginalized. This is illustrated by the widespread use of automated telephone and electronic banking rather than face-to-face interaction for the provision, assessment and processing of banking services (Pollard, 1996; Leyshon et al., 1998; Leyshon and Thrift, 1993, 1999; Leyshon and Pollard, 2000; Wills, 1996). Market segmentation and financial exclusion are two specific features of the converged banking industry, whereby banks provide tailor-made services for their high value customers while they withdraw the full range of services to poorer customers, charge fees to maintain low balance accounts under the 'user pays' principle or even close branches in deprived neighbourhoods to reduce costs and improve their overall competitiveness (Dymski and Veitch, 1996; Leyshon and Thrift, 1995, 1996; Fuller, 1998). People without bank accounts are unable to access the wide range of services for which bank accounts provide gateways, and are thus financially excluded and have to settle all their transactions in cash.

Consequently, a particular group of people may experience one or more forms of financial exclusion from the formal banking services (Kempson and Whyley, 1999a, 1999b; Kempson et al., 2000). Specifically, they could be excluded geographically due to branch closures; they could also be excluded due to the conditions attached to financial products, for example, failing to qualify because minimum deposits are required, not meeting identity requirements, or having a poor credit history. Furthermore, their lack of access to formal banking services could be due to the cost of financial products, such as the relatively high costs of unauthorized overdrafts and insurance premiums being beyond their reach or being unaware of the available financial services as they are not targeted by banks' marketing and sales, and so on.

The state played an important role in the deregulation and the subsequent convergence of the Anglo-American banking industry. The role of the state in the transitional economy of China, where a fully functioning market does not exist and the state plays an even more important role in the opening up of retail banking, consequently requires greater in depth study.

Scholars of the formerly planned economies in Eastern Europe and China have debated the role and mix of plans and markets for decades (Stark and Nee, 1989). Instead of a 'socialist mixed economy' with well-defined public and private sectors (Szelényi, 1988), Stark (1989: 167–168) argued that the institutional reforms implemented in these formerly planned economies resulted in 'hybrid mixtures of public ownership and private initiative' that crossed and blurred the conventional boundaries between public and private property. Based on his field surveys of 220 of the largest Hungarian enterprises and banks, Stark (1996) further argued that the blurring of conventional boundaries between public and private property suggests the emergence of a distinctively Eastern European capitalism in post-socialist Hungary. Stark (1996: 997) coined the term 'recombinant property' to explain a distinctive form of organizational hedging through the diversification, redefinition and recombination of assets by actors. This form of organizational hedging has resulted from actors responding to the uncertainty created by institutional reforms in Hungary.

Similar ideas were also expressed in scholarly research in China. For instance, Oi (1992) introduced the concept of 'local corporatism' to explain the fiscal reforms of taxation that had allowed local governments to be involved in the establishment of township and village enterprises in China. Based on the transaction costs and new institutional economics, Nee (1992: 2) argued that the ownership reforms implemented in China resulted in 'hybrid organizational forms' (a mixed form of public and private property) rather than a simple mixed economy. When the structure of property rights is poorly defined in a transitional economy, actors can use their personal connections (*guanxi*) to lower the transaction costs of 'hybrid organizational forms' and be more responsive to market demands (see also Nee and Young, 1991). Based on the property rights school of thought, Walder (1994) argued that the property reform implemented in China was not equivalent to privatization (transformation from public to private ownership). It is the clarification of property rights in Chinese fiscal reforms (which thus define the reward recipients) that has contributed to the rise of township and village enterprises in China. Therefore, there can be a transformation of property without privatization (from the fully publicly-owned to hybrid property) and economic efficiency can be improved in this way. This chapter uses the term *hybrid property*, proposed by Nee (1992) and further conceptualized by Stark (1996), to explain the blurring of boundaries between public and private property rights in the Chinese banking industry.

19.3 THE CHINESE BANKING INDUSTRY IN REFORM AND THE CREATION OF HYBRID PROPERTY

After the establishment of the People's Republic of China in 1949, the central bank basically monopolized almost all the banking services in the Chinese banking system. This situation remained unchanged for almost three decades until economic reforms were implemented in China in 1979. There was still no direct competition between the commercial banks due to the 'sector-specific segmentation' policy in China: industrial enterprises dealt with the China Construction Bank (CCB), peasants banked with the Agricultural Bank of China (ABC), while trade or foreign-financed companies had to channel their foreign exchange through the Bank of China (BOC). This policy literally created three monopolies in each of the agricultural, industrial, and trade sectors (Yeung, 2009b). This institutional setting was too rigid and unable to fulfil the needs of the economy.

The retail banking industry in China exhibits features typical of a transitional economy, with some of the largest publicly listed banks in the world co-existing with hundreds of thousands of rural co-operative institutions. The present Chinese banking industry, regulated by the People's Bank of China (PBoC, the central bank) and the CBRC, includes the SOCBs, joint-stock commercial banks (JSCBs), city commercial banks, rural financial institutions, foreign banks, and the three policy banks. The PBoC is responsible for formulating and implementing monetary policy to ensure the stability of the financial system. Specifically, the PBoC is responsible for the setting of minimum reserve requirements and interest rates for inter-bank lending and inter-bank bond markets, and setting the targets for money supply and exchange rates – including issuing the *Renminbi* and administering its circulation – and the holding and managing the state foreign exchanges and gold reserves, and so on (PBoC, 2014).

Established in 2003, the CBRC formulates the rules and regulations governing the banking institutions, and supervises all banking institutions and their business activities in China. Specifically, the CBRC's major supervisory roles are (CBRC, 2013):

- To assess, monitor and mitigate the risks of banking institutions;
- To improve the governance of banking institutions; and
- To improve the transparency and adopt international standards and practices for bank supervision.

Through prudential and effective supervision, the CBRC aims to achieve the following regulatory objectives (CBRC, 2013):

- To maintain confidence in the banking industry and to maintain financial stability;
- To facilitate financial innovation and improve the competitiveness of the banking industry;
- To promote fair and orderly competition;
- To protect the interests of both depositors and consumers;
- To educate the general public in modern finance, its services and products; and
- To combat financial crimes.

The SOCBs include the 'Big Four' – the Industrial and Commercial Bank of China (ICBC); Bank of China (BOC); China Construction Bank (CCB) and the Agricultural Bank of China (ABC) – and also the Bank of Communications (BOCOM) (Table 19.1). Rural co-operative institutions include all legitimate financial institutions based in rural China: rural credit co-operatives, rural co-operative banks, and rural commercial banks. The three policy banks are China Development Bank, the Export–Import Bank of China, and Agricultural Development Bank of China.

The Chinese government is under tremendous pressure to reform the banking system. On the one hand, the state is under internal economic pressure to improve governance and thus reduce the financial burden on the Ministry of Finance. The State Council allows a number of Chinese SOCBs and SOEs to issue initial public offerings (IPOs) of minority equities in local and/or overseas stock markets. SOCBs became, by definition, international financial holding institutions once their IPOs were on the Stock Exchange of Hong Kong in 2005–06 and 2010, in the case of ABC. The state is still the majority equity holder in all SOCBs, with at least 54 per cent of equity (in the case of BOCOM). In 2013, the SOCBs controlled 43 per cent of the 151.35 trillion *yuan* banking assets in China (CBRC, 2013: 128). With the exception of 12 JSCBs, both SOCBs and SOEs are ultimately owned by the central or local governments. A number of other city commercial banks are also partly owned by foreign investors but local governments are the majority shareholders. As China is still undergoing a series of institutional reforms to create a functioning market economy, the transformation of the property structure from wholly publicly owned to a mixture of public and private property in the Chinese banking industry has created a hybrid property: a mixed public–private ownership structure that has

Table 19.1 Four major types of banking institutions in China

Types of banks	Names	Remarks
Market-oriented banks	State-owned commercial banks (Industrial and Commercial Bank of China, ICBC; Bank of China, BOC; China Construction Bank, CCB; Agricultural Bank of China, ABC; Bank of Communications, BOCOM) & 12 joint-stock commercial banks	Largely state-owned but listed on stock markets
Policy-oriented banks	China Development Bank, The Export–Import Bank of China, Agricultural Development Bank of China	State-owned
City commercial banks	City commercial banks & city credit co-operatives	Local governments & privately owned, but some are partly owned by foreign investors
Rural financial institutions	Traditional rural financial institutions: rural credit co-operatives, rural co-operative banks, rural commercial banks, postal savings institutes New rural financial institutions: village-township banks, lending companies, & rural mutual co-operatives	Local governments & privately owned

Source: Compiled by the author.

been adopted for previously wholly SOCBs (Yeung, 2009b; see also Oi, 1992; Nee, 1992) illustrating how, the boundaries between public and private property rights in the Chinese banking industry are blurred.

On the other hand, the state had to open up the banking market to foreign banks as stipulated in the WTO accession treaty, signed in 2001. Foreign banks have been allowed to provide local currency services to Chinese companies since 11 December 2003 and had full market access (including individual customers) all over China from 11 December 2006, when all non-prudential market access constraints against foreign financial institutions were removed. The CBRC pushed the SOCBs to restructure their operations to strengthen their capital adequacy ratios to prepare for the implementation of Basel II and Basel III (He and Yeung, 2011). SOCBs are under pressure from their shareholders to maximize profits, and yet the state is still the majority shareholder. Again, SOCBs can be seen to be hybrid properties; the boundaries between public and private property rights are blurred (Yeung, 2009b; Yeung, He and Liu, 2012). How this may impact on the roles and functions of SOCBs, given the CBRC's need to reform the banking industry while maintaining the financial security of the general public is an interesting question.

19.4 SOCBS AS HYBRID PROPERTIES

To improve competitiveness and reduce financial dependency, the state recapitalizes SOCBs and revitalizes its finances through asset management corporations (AMCs), and the CBRC pushes SOCBs to centralize their operation and formalize lending practices.

Recapitalization and Centralization of SOCBs

The NPL ratio of SOCBs had reached a staggering 31 per cent in 2001, partly as a result of the bad debts with SOEs (the so-called 'triangle debts' where both lenders and borrowers are ultimately owned by the state). To insulate SOCBs from the vicious circle of refinancing bad debts, the Chinese state established four AMCs (Orient, Huarong, Cinda, and Great Wall) to take over 1.4 trillion *yuan* (US$169.1 billion) of their pre-1996 NPLs, in addition to an injection of 270 billion *yuan* (US$32.61 billion) into the banking system in 1998. By taking over bad debts before the IPOs of SOCBs, AMCs played a vital role in the restructuring of the Chinese banking industry. After the capital injection into the system, the CBRC estimated that the NPL ratio of the 'Big Four' was reduced significantly to 8.2 per cent (1.06 trillion *yuan*) at the end of March 2007 (CBRC, 16 May 2007). In other words, SOCBs became 'good banks' while the four AMCs became 'bad banks' (Yeung, 2009a).[3]

In addition to recapitalization, the centralization of banking operations is vital to revitalize the finances of SOCBs. The scale of centralization of banking operations is best illustrated by the transformation of the ABC. The ABC adopted the commercialization strategy of 'large banks, large markets and large industries' from the mid-to-late 1990s by withdrawing from the agricultural banking market at county-level to access the more profitable business of commerce and industries in cities. ABC separated from the Agricultural Development Bank of China (ADBC) operations and delinked rural credit corporates from its management in 1996 and subsequently reduced its outlets from about 65,900 (538,800+ employees) to 36,100 (511,400+ employees) in 2003 (Ong, 2006, 2011). To prepare for the IPO on the Stock Exchange of Hong Kong in 2010, the ABC underwent massive restructuring to improve its balance sheet, transferred billions of NPLs to the Great Wall AMC, and further centralized its banking operations after 2004, that is, reduced its outlets from 31,000+ units and 489,400+ employees in 2003 to 24,000+ outlets and 441,000+ employees in 2010 (ABC, 2004; CBRC, various years). Different from the Anglo-American banking industry, the drive for centralization of banking operations at the ABC focuses on the reduction of outlets (a reduction of 64 per cent between 1996 and 2010) rather than redundancy (only 18 per cent), presumably due to the hybrid nature of its property where massive redundancies would be a politically sensitive issue for the state.

Although originally established to support agricultural and rural development, the Executive Vice-President of ABC, Mr Pan Gongsheng, differentiated their mode of business from the rural financial institutions by pointing out that large and medium-sized enterprises based in various counties are their major customers. As the only SOCB with service outlets and an electronic banking network reaching every county in China, the balance of loans in ABC's County Area Banking Business unit had reached 1505 billion *yuan* by the end of 2010. Subsequently, the ABC had reduced its NPLs at an unprecedented scale and pace, from 30.62 per cent in 2003 to 23.43 per cent in 2006, then experienced a massive decrease to 4.32 per cent in 2008, which further fell to 2.03 per cent in 2010 (ABC, 2004, 2006, 2010).

In addition to reducing operational costs through centralization, the CBRC formalized lending criteria to enhance the financial viability of the banking sector.

The Political Economy of the Commercialization of Lending Practices in SOCBs

To improve competitiveness, the SOCBs began to restructure their loan portfolios by adopting the strategy of commercial lending between 1998 and 2003. All Chinese banking institutions have been adopting the international five-tier risk-based classification system according to the CBRC's *Guiding Principles on the Classification of Loan Risk Management* to rank loans as either 'pass', 'special mention', 'sub-standard', 'doubtful', or 'loss' since 2004 (CBRC, 2007: 72–73; OECD, 2005: 42, 145).[4] All SOCBs in China have used a credit score to assess every loan application since the establishment of the CBRC in 2003. Irrespective of the amount of a loan and its purpose, credit managers evaluate and grade every loan application based on the verified business report and three years of audited financial statements submitted by the loan applicant (Yeung, 2009a).[5]

Unless it is demonstrated that they have followed the loan assessment procedures fully, credit managers are individually responsible for new NPLs incurred under their tenure. According to the CBRC (2013: 136), 38 senior managers (involved in a total of over 2.3 trillion *yuan*) were sacked for violation of CBRC's regulatory policies in the banking industry in 2013. The CBRC also warned that a lifetime ban from senior financial management posts would be imposed upon bankers responsible for large-scale irregularities (Yeung, 2009a).

It is generally argued that SOCBs positively discriminate in favour of SOEs and are biased against private enterprises (Wei and Wang, 1997). Although contributing to 60 per cent of industrial output in China, private enterprises only accounted for 22.5 per cent (16.5 trillion *yuan*) of the total loan balance by the end of July 2013 (CBRC, 5 September 2013). The perceived lending bias of SOCBs is actually due to a combination of factors, from the lack of a nationwide risk assessment database of private borrowers and the limited formalized channels of credit risks mitigation to the corresponding high transaction costs of risk assessment.[6]

It is well-known among credit managers at SOCBs that a number of private enterprises used falsified financial statements in loan applications. Moreover, the opaque ownership structure (a number of so-called private firms are actually controlled by local government officials) and 'unsystematic management' (that is, run like a family business and the business founders treat the companies' accounts as personal/family bank accounts) of private firms in China explains why credit managers are normally reluctant to embrace lending to private enterprises enthusiastically (Yeung, 2009a). This strong argument is partially supported by a series of high profile scandals and embezzlement involving Chinese private enterprises listed in overseas stock markets. The US Securities and Exchange Commission opened 40 cases of possible fraud by Chinese listed firms, including the allegation that Puda Coal Inc.'s chairman sold off its coal mines and turned it into an empty shell company before the IPO (Mosk et al., 2013; see Zhu and Gao, 2011).

SOCBs generally prefer to lend to SOEs, partly due to the (much) lower transaction costs in the assessment of credit worthiness. Importantly, the hybrid property rights of SOCBs facilitate the financing of industrial and economic development and thus contribute to political stability in China.

The transaction costs incurred by SOCBs in assessing the credit worthiness of SOEs is lower due to the stricter regulations by the relevant government bureaux. Moreover, part of the default risk of lending to SOEs is reduced by the guarantees of the corresponding 'guarantee institution': a company, normally funded by the local government but unregulated by the CBRC, acts as a guarantor for a loan applicant. Such companies were commonly used for loan applications in the 1990s, when the official criteria for loan assessment had not been fully formulated.[7] Although the usages of these 'guarantee institutions' has been highly regulated since 2000s, SOCBs still lend to SOEs as these loans maintain their profitability and serve a specific function within the economy (Yeung, 2009b).

To maintain political stability in its quest for a 'moderately prosperous society', the CBRC has to implement policies that maintain the legitimacy of the Chinese Communist Party leadership.[8] This is especially the case given the increasingly frequent mass demonstrations about inequality and other major concerns, from unlawful land acquisition to corruption. As policymakers are fixated on socio-economic and political stability (or 'social stability' in the official documents), the hybrid nature of SOCBs' property rights provides a convenient channel for the state to inject capital into the economy indirectly, although this is precisely what the CBRC originally tried to avoid (see Yeung, 2009b).

To respond to the adverse effects of the global financial crisis on the economy, the Chinese government initiated a series of massive infrastructure-oriented projects accounting for 46.75 per cent of the 4 trillion *yuan* (US$586 billion) stimulus plan in November 2008. As the central government only contributed 29.5 per cent of the total budget, local governments had to secure the remaining 2.82 trillion *yuan* using various forms of finance, from bond issuance to bank lending (Dunford and Yeung, 2011). SOCBs, especially the CCB, are willing to grant preferential loans to the various SOEs involved in infrastructure projects.

Parts of such lending could be interpreted as an indirect capital injection by the state through the SOCBs to stimulate local demand and offset the adverse effects of the global financial crisis. Although providing financial support to the local economy is not part of the official policy remit of either PBoC or CBRC, support of national 'key infrastructure projects' and 'industrial upgrading' by SOCBs were actually highlighted in a recent *CBRC Annual Report* (CBRC, 2012: 46, 2013: 27), and further emphasized in State Council Document number 67 in 2013.[9] China's economic growth has been capital-intensive, and the gross fixed capital formation has accounted for at least one-third of GDP in China since the late 1970s. Partly the results of the 4 trillion *yuan* stimulus plan, gross fixed capital formation accounted for more than 48 per cent of GDP for the first time in 2009 (an increase of 4.3 percentage points at current prices over 2008), and maintained that level until reaching an all-time high of 49.3 per cent in 2013. This massive monetary injection along with the expansionary monetary policies has stabilized the shock from the global financial crisis, with the real GDP per capita growth rate at 9.3 per cent in 2009, 13.7 per cent in 2010, and 11.8 per cent in 2011 (National Bureau of Statistics, various years).[10]

SOEs are the major clients of SOCBs partly because the state banking system was originally established to serve the fiscal arm of the state, and funneled funds to and from SOEs, particularly SOEs in prioritized industrial sectors. Laurenceson and Chai (2001:

214) argued that SOCBs in China have the strong characteristics of development banks, so the conventional evaluation criteria of commercial banks, such as return rates to assets and liquidity ratios, are not applicable. They further argued that SOCBs have an overall positive and sustainable impact on China's economic development, despite their poor commercial performance.[11] Most SOEs, especially in the coastal provinces, are profitable (partly because they have regional monopolies) higher value-added clients and have well-organized management (partly due to the intense competition and learning by doing with foreign joint ventures). Credit managers at SOCBs have the incentive to allocate credit to profitable endeavours so that they can qualify for bonuses, which are dependent on the bank's profitability.

Given the fact that the rural peasantry still accounts for more than 57 per cent of the total population, 200 million (82.49 million at the national poverty line) of whom live below the poverty line of US$1.25/day (constant 2005 purchasing power parity prices), it is a great challenge to fulfil the CBRC objectives of providing basic formal banking services to everyone and yet improve the competitiveness of SOCBs by enhancing their financial viability.

19.5 THE DILEMMA OF REGULATORY AUTHORITIES: FINANCIAL VIABILITY AND/OR FINANCIAL SECURITY?

To facilitate the development of a modern banking system in China, the CBRC has to ensure its regulations will not 'stunt' the growth of the banking industry while lowering the chances of financial crises and issues that could lead to political upheaval. It is argued that the CBRC's twin goals of ensuring the financial viability of the banking industry as well as the financial security of the general public are not always compatible.

Financial Viability of the Banking Industry and the Rising Hidden Debts

The Chinese formal banking industry in general is *profitable* and financially viable, partly due to the hybrid properties of SOCBs and their subsequent domination of domestic banking. According to the CBRC, the return on average assets (ROA, defined as net profit-asset ratio) of the banking industry improved significantly, from 0.12 per cent in 2003 to 0.68 per cent in 2005, before increasing further to 1.15 per cent in 2013 (Table 19.2). The ROA of SOCBs has mirrored the trends in the banking industry since 2005 in China: it improved significantly from the loss-making −0.02 per cent in 2003, to profit-making a year later, before increasing consistently from 0.74 per cent in 2005, to 1.28 per cent in 2013.[12] The ROA of SOCBs has not only been much higher than that of foreign banks (0.45–0.78 per cent) since 2010 in China, but also consistently higher than that of joint-stock commercial banks (0.91–1.09 per cent) (CBRC, 2006, 2013). As a comparison, the ROA of the banking industry in the US ranged between −0.1 in 2009 to 1.41 in 2003 (1.06 in 2013 and 1.0 in 2014). The ROA for the Bank of America, one of the big four in the US, was 0.37 in 2013, lower than that of foreign banks incorporated in China (FRED, 2015a; YCharts, 2015).

Moreover, the financial sector is most profitable among large corporations in China.

Table 19.2 The return on assets of selected Chinese and American commercial banks, 2003–13, per cent

Year	Chinese banks				American banks	
	All commercial banks	SOCBs	JSCBs	Foreign banks	All commercial banks	Bank of America
2003	0.12	−0.02	0.49	0.40	1.41	–
2004	0.33	0.26	0.48	0.40	1.33	–
2005	0.68	0.74	0.65	0.51	1.30	–
2006	0.77	0.81	0.80	0.62	1.34	–
2007	0.84	0.87	0.78	0.49	0.94	–
2008	0.92	1.09	0.95	0.89	0.16	–
2009	0.84	0.98	0.78	0.48	−0.10	0.31
2010	0.94	1.10	0.91	0.45	0.63	0.08
2011	1.11	1.24	1.09	0.78	0.88	−0.21
2012	1.13	1.26	1.07	0.69	0.99	0.24
2013	1.15	1.28	1.09	0.55	1.06	0.37

Notes: For Chinese banks, 2003–06 data are based on gross profits due to the unavailability of net profits. The data is estimated based on the end of year aggregation method, and without seasonally adjusted.

Sources: Compiled from 2006–13 issues of *CBRC Annual Report*, FRED (2015a), and YCharts (2015).

Fortune estimates that 29 financial institutions, with a combined profit of 1.27 trillion *yuan*, account for more than half the total profits of 500 companies. The 'Big Four' are the most profitable companies in China, all recording double-digit profit growth in 2013: 262.6 billion *yuan* by the ICBC, 214.6 billion *yuan* by the CBC, 166.3 billion *yuan* by the ABC, and 156.9 billion *yuan* by the BOC, well ahead of the 129.5 billion *yuan* of profit recorded by the fifth most profitable company (China National Petroleum Corporation, with a monopoly in the petrochemical industry) (*Fortune*, 2015).[13]

The de facto monopoly of property mortgaging contributes to the profitability of SOCBs. Both Chinese and western banks have adopted collateral-based lending, but there are two major differences in their loan portfolios. First, the NPLs in western banks are largely tied to private individuals with mortgages in residential properties, while a large proportion of debts in the Chinese formal banking system is loans for infrastructure projects, and the borrowers are local governments rather than private individuals, partly due to the hybrid nature of SOCBs' property, where lending to local governments is perceived by credit managers as low risk. Although up to 34 per cent of China's debt was related to real estate in 2014, property mortgages for private individuals accounted for only 19 per cent (US$1.8 trillion) of US$9.5 trillion of real estate-related debts, and household debt was equivalent to 58 per cent of disposable household income. The corporate sectors and local governments accounted for the lion's share of the debts in real estate: US$3 trillion in real estate sector, US$2.5 trillion in real estate-related sectors, and US$2.2 trillion in local governments (MGI, 2015: 78–79).[14] Second, the property-related loans to private individuals in China are largely prime loans with a lower chance of default as a down payment of 20 per cent (or more for non-primary residences) is required vis-à-vis

Table 19.3 The NPL ratios of selected Chinese and American commercial banks, 2006–13

Year	Chinese banks				American banks
	All commercial banks	SOCBs	JSCBs	Foreign banks	All commercial banks
2006	7.1	7.5	–	0.8	0.78
2007	6.2	8.0	2.1	0.5	1.34
2008	2.4	2.8	1.3	0.8	2.97
2009	1.6	1.8	1.0	0.9	5.63
2010	1.1	1.3	0.7	0.5	4.98
2011	1.0	1.1	0.6	0.4	4.29
2012	1.0	1.0	0.7	0.5	3.66
2013	1.0	1.0	0.9	0.5	2.67

Note: The data is estimated based on the end of year aggregation method, and without seasonally adjusted.

Sources: Compiled from 2006–13 issues of *CBRC Annual Report* and FRED (2015b).

subprime home buyers, with no down payment for self-certified mortgages in the west. Although the issuing of asset-backed securities increased significantly to 326 billion *yuan* in 2014, residential mortgages only accounted for 3.6 per cent of collateralized loan obligations (CLO) in China (*Financial Times*, 20 January 2015).[15]

In addition to the formalization of lending criteria, whereby credit managers have become responsible for the NPLs since the mid-2000, the massive drive to centralize banking operations and capital injection by the state has contributed to a significant improvement in the financial performance of the Chinese banking industry (see Yeung, 2009b; Yeung et al., 2012). The NPL ratio of the Chinese banking industry has improved significantly, from 7.1 per cent in 2006 to 1.0 per cent in 2011 and is staying at this level (Table 19.3). A similar trend is mirrored by the SOCBs, city commercial banks, and rural commercial banks. As expected, the most dramatic improvement in NPLs is by the SOCBs. After the capital injection into the system, the NPL ratio of SOCBs was 8 per cent in 2007, but fell significantly to 2.8 per cent in 2008, and further reduced to 1.1 per cent (299 billion *yuan*) in 2011. In 2013, the NPLs of SOCBs was at the very low level of 1 per cent (compared with the 0.5 per cent of foreign banks incorporated in China, 0.9 per cent of joint-stock commercial banks and city commercial banks, and 1.7 per cent of rural commercial banks). As a comparison, the NPL ratio of American commercial banks deteriorated significantly during the financial crisis: it increased from 0.78 per cent in 2006 to reach its peak of 5.63 per cent, before decreasing back to 2.67 per cent in 2013 (and 1.96 per cent in 2014) (FRED, 2015b). Partly as a response to the global financial crisis, the provision coverage ratio (loan loss provision divided by gross NPLs) of Chinese SOCBs increased significantly, from less than half the value of NPLs in 2007 to about three times their value in 2013, which was much higher than the international norm of 40 per cent and the CRBC's threshold of 150 per cent (CBRC, 2013: 133). The provision coverage ratio of the American commercial banks has, however, been decreasing consistently, from 183 per cent in 1998 to 92 per cent in 2007, and then further down to 63 per cent in 2011 (FRED, 2015b).

Notwithstanding the fact that the official NPLs ratio (1 per cent) in China is below that of banks in the US (2.67 per cent) and the EU (3.8 per cent) (Table 19.3, FRED, 2015b), the *hidden debts* in the form of off-balance-sheet finance through the arms-length financial institutions of local governments could still be potential lightning rods of financial instability. SOCBs can disguise the true magnitude of their NPLs by various means, from rolling over debts to offering new loans to cover mature ones, normally with the involvement of short-term bridging loans with informal banking institutions. Moreover, SOCBs could classify some of these loans as 'special mention' loans as long as repayments are not overdue – where the loans are questionable but not yet 'non-performing' (Shi and Xu, 2014). For the ICBC, 1.98 per cent of its loans are classified under 'special mention', and the 231 billion *yuan* of special mention loans is more than double the 106 billion *yuan* of NPLs (Anderlini and Wildau, 2014). The NPL ratio for commercial banks increased over 11 consecutive quarters and reached 1.1 per cent by June 2014, and the corresponding overdue loan ratio also increased from 1.06 per cent to 1.63 per cent, which was particularly contributed by the rising trend of joint-stock commercial banks, from 0.6 per cent in 2011 to 1 per cent in June 2014 (PwC, September 2014: 11–13).

The frantic rate of credit expansion during the implementation of 4 trillion *yuan* of stimulus projects could have led to an increase in the hidden debts of SOCBs as some local governments may not have been able to repay their debts. Although the total debt in China tripled from US$2.1 trillion in 2000 to US$7.4 trillion in 2007, such a rise in debt was partially offset by rapid economic growth, that is, its debt-to-GDP ratio only increased from 121 to 158 per cent (Table 19.4). Partly due to the stimulus projects implemented by the central government during the financial crisis, China's debt had quadrupled to US$28.2 trillion by mid-2014, and accounted for 37 per cent of the US$57 trillion increase in global debts since 2007. Financial and non-financial institutions accounted for a significant proportion of the rising debt: debt-to-GDP ratios increased from 24 to 65 per cent for financial institutions and 72 to 125 per cent for non-financial corporations (this is higher than the 105 per cent of non-financial corporations recorded in South Korea) (Figure 19.1). Researchers at the National Development and Reform Commission (the state planning agency) estimate that almost half of the investment projects between 2009 and 2013 are cost ineffective and this could impact on the ability of local governments to repay

Table 19.4 Debt-to-GDP ratios of China in 2000, 2007 and the second quarter of 2014

	Debt–GDP ratio					Total debt (in US$ trillion)
	Government	Financial institutions	Non-financial corporate	Households	Total	
2000	23	7	83	8	121	2.1
2007	42	24	72	20	158	7.4
2Q, 2014	55*	65	125	38	282	28.2

Notes: *The debt-to-GDP ratio for the central government was 27 per cent. The summation of 2Q of 2014 data is equal to 283 due to rounding.

Source: MGI (2015: 75, 86).

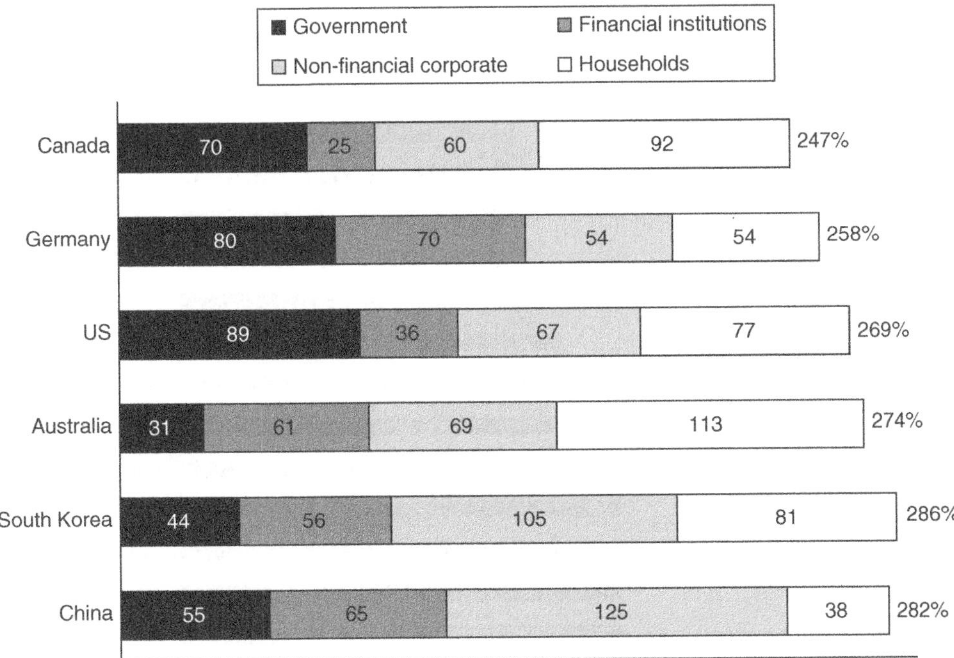

Figure 19.1 Debt-to-GDP ratios of selected countries in the second quarter of 2014

their debts (Anderlini, 2014). According to the latest reports issued by the National Audit Office (2013: 4), the debts incurred by local governments surged by 67 per cent over two years, reaching 17.9 trillion *yuan* (US$3 trillion) by the middle of 2013. Out of the 17.9 trillion *yuan* of debt, 10.12 trillion *yuan* are financed through the formal banking system, including various local government financing platforms (LGFPs), while other means of off-balance-sheet financing borrowed 6.97 trillion *yuan* (39 per cent of the total debts).[16] Local governments are fully responsible for 10.89 trillion *yuan* of debts and are guarantors of another 2.67 trillion *yuan* (Zheng, 2014; Reuters, 27 January 2014). Two-thirds of Chinese provinces had debt-to-revenue ratios of higher than 100 per cent, and Guizhou and Yunnan, the two poorest provinces in China, also recorded the highest debt-to-GDP ratios at 79 and 51 per cent in 2012 respectively (Figure 19.2).[17] As the average pay-out ratio for debts guaranteed by local governments is 23 per cent in China, the expected costs of these guarantees are (much) lower than their full face value; for example, Chongqing's debt burden has decreased from 59 to 38 per cent (*Economist*, 22 February 2014). With an overall 5.4 per cent of debts overdue, local government debts per se will not have a significant impact on the viability of the formal banking system in China as the central government could raise fresh capital due to its relatively low level of debt-to-GDP ratio of 27 per cent (total government debt at 55 per cent of GDP) (MGI, 2015: 86).

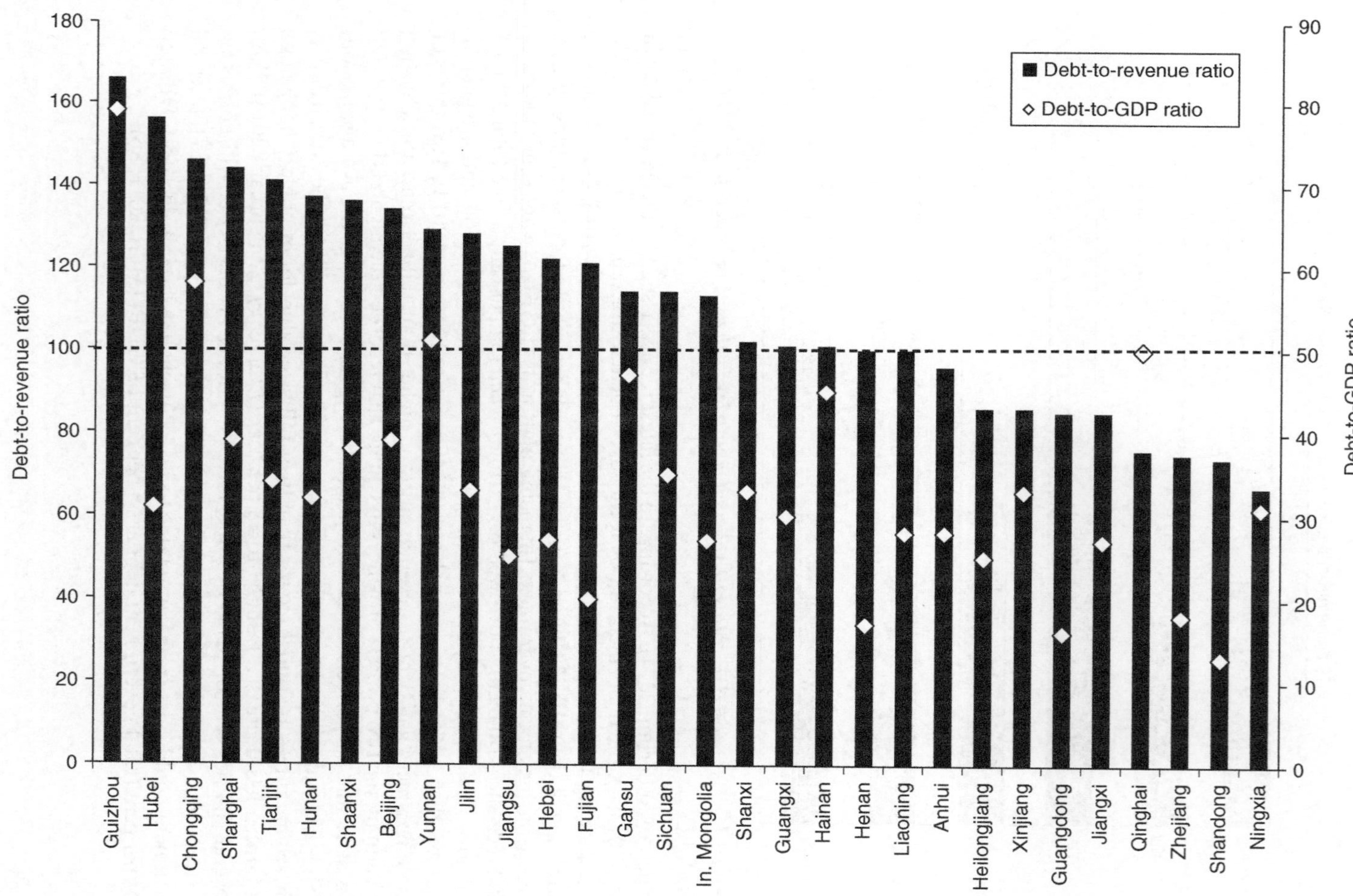

Figure 19.2 Debt ratio and fiscal performance in Chinese provinces, 2012

Financial Security of the General Public and the Moral Hazard of (In)formal Banking Systems

The financial security of the general public could be undermined by the risk whereby financial products are 'guaranteed' by the formal banking institutions, and the boom in informal banking. The hybrid nature of SOCBs has created a *moral hazard* for the formal banking system in China: there is a widespread misconception by the general public that Chinese banks, especially the SOCBs, are trustworthy and safe as (almost) all banks are owned directly or indirectly by the local or central government. In other words, the savings and investment products marketed by these banking institutions are ultimately guaranteed by the central government.

Instead of using inter-bank lending facilities (which are subject to a higher level of regulatory money supply policy implemented by the PBoC), commercial banks increasingly utilize structured financial products to raise funds and improve their profitability. Some such (highly) popular investment products are actually off-balance sheet financial transactions and products marketed by SOCBs as high-yielding alternatives to bank deposits. This has led to a proliferation of 'wealth management products': 87,718 of these new products (with 49.41 trillion *yuan*) were launched by commercial banks in the first quarter of 2014. The top 10 listed commercial banks have issued a total of 14.48 trillion *yuan* of such products, a massive increase of 48 per cent of funding over the same quarter in the previous year, with ICBC and CCB being the top two issuers. There were 51,560 non-maturing wealth management products by June 2014 (PwC, September 2014: 51).

The credibility of SOCBs has been dented in recent cases of the de facto default of several popular structured financial products. There are about 60 reported cases of trust product bailouts, including the 3 billion *yuan* trust product called 'China Credit Equals Gold #1', marketed by the ICBC to investors as a high-yielding financial product with a 10 per cent interest rate per annum. The bailout was carried out by an ICBC 3 billion *yuan* bridging loan to Huarong AMC (which itself was transformed into a joint-stock asset management company in 2012 prior its IPO), and then Huarong purchased the loans backing the trust product with a 5 per cent 'haircut' (discount) (Anderlini and Wildau, 2014).[18] The state's indirect bailout via bridging loans to AMCs could increase the moral hazard by 'nationalizing the losses and privatizing the gains' of such financial products. As the credit default option (CDO) and similar instruments are not used as collateral for new funds in China, the potential danger of hidden debts is still relatively low compared with the US or the EU, but there could be a time bomb in the making should economic growth slow down significantly and local governments and lenders be unable to service their debts.

The recent relaxation of control over interest rates for loans (in 2013), the opening of the sector to private banks by the PBoC, and the rise in Internet-based financing are signs of further reforms in the banking sector in China. The BOC and China Merchants Bank were the pioneers of Internet-based banking in China, offering Internet banking and an online payment system in 1996 and 1997 respectively. As expected, the SOCBs were the major providers of the 382.7 trillion *yuan* (US$63 trillion) of transactions conducted through Internet banking in the second quarter of 2014; for example, ICBC accounted for 34 per cent and CCB accounted for another 15.3 per cent of transactions (Hu and Moody, 2014).

A significant development in Internet banking in China is the rapid growth of *non-bank financial institutions*, especially online commerce companies (Alibaba) and Internet service providers (Tencent and Baidu), and even peer-to-peer lending companies. With the expectation of the opening up of private banks by the CBRC, these Internet giants started to offer alternative financial products and finance to their clients through their innovative online and mobile banking products from 2010. The most innovative and aggressive players are Alibaba and Tencent. Alibaba, the fastest growing e-commerce company in the world, with its popular consumer-to-consumer portal (Taobao) and online payment escrow service (Alipay, with 300 million users and US$248 billion online transactions in 2013, more than eBay and Amazon.com combined) launched a financial product platform called Yu'e Bao in June 2013.[19] This online money market fund already had US$81 billion assets (accumulated from 81 million investors at the end of February 2014) under its management, making it the fourth largest money market fund in the world (Hu and Moody, 2014).[20] Tencent using its massive client base and its instant messaging platform, WeChat, has developed mobile payment tools. The conglomerates lead by Tencent and Alibaba were also awarded two of the first five licenses for private banks in China by the CBRC in July and September 2014 respectively (*Mingpao*, 30 September 2014).

Furthermore, the proliferation of informal financial products and institutions (in various forms, from trust accounts and wealth management products marketed to the general public, to micro-credit institutions and informal lending, including the traditional rotating savings and credit associations) in China could contribute to a significant increase in hidden NPLs. The PBoC's ceiling on deposit interest rates created the demand for higher yield financial products, and this contributed to the rise in informal banking at 36 per cent per annum, which reached US$6.5 trillion and accounted for 30 per cent of total loans accumulated since 2007 (MGI, 2015: 83–84). Internet banking provides a platform for a massive expansion of peer-to-peer lending, including lending to small and medium-sized enterprises. Credit Ease, based in Beijing, established eight years ago, the leading peer-to-peer lending company in China, has grown rapidly and is now twice the size of its US counterpart (Lending Club) (Hu and Moody, 2014). The IMF has estimated that financial products and the informal banking sector now account for around 18 and 40 per cent respectively of GDP (US$3 trillion) in China (IMF, 2014: 28). MGI (2015: 84) has estimated that informal lending accounted for an even higher figure of 65 per cent of GDP in 2014. These informal financial institutions are not regulated by the CBRC or local government and the acceptance of mutual guarantees on a personal basis (borrowers act as guarantors for each other's loans) could plant a time-bomb within the financial system and create instability in the wider economy. The high profile bankruptcies of established companies involved with informal financial institutions with hundreds of million *yuan* of loans in Wenzhou in 2011 drew the attention of the central government to the importance of the financial gap in the formal banking system in China.

Rising Leverage Ratio and the State's Counter-measures

An examination of the leverage ratio in China reveals the financial costs to the Chinese central government for performing a balancing act by attempting to improve the competitiveness of the banking system while maintaining the financial security of the general public. With a significant increase in the corporate debt of both financial and non-financial institutions (including informal banking), China's debt-to-GDP ratio has increased to 282 per cent, much higher than in developing countries and even higher than the 269 per cent in the US and 258 per cent in Germany, but lower than the 401 per cent in Spain and 517 per cent in Japan (Figure 19.2). Local government debt in China reached US$2.9 trillion (US$1.7 trillion from LGFPs) and accounted for 53 per cent of US$5.5 trillion of total government debts in 2014 (MGI, 2015: 81). Given the government's debt account of 55 per cent of GDP and its US$4 trillion foreign exchange reserves, the Chinese government has the financial capacity to cope with a potential financial crisis. If half of the property-related loans defaulted, the MGI (2015: 87) estimates that the government debt ratio could rise to 79 per cent, which is still much lower than the average figure of 101 per cent in developed countries. Nonetheless, this is cause for concern as similar rapid debt run-ups have led to financial crises in other countries (Reinhart and Rogoff, 2013).

Sensing the potential danger of the increase in public debt, the central government imposed new restrictions on local government debts in October 2014. Any new loans can only be used for capital investment and have to be approved by the central government (Wildau, 2014). Moreover, the State Council issued the *Circular Regarding Enhancing Supervisory Risks in Shadow Banking Operations* (Circular No. 107), drafted by the PBoC, CBRC, China Securities Regulatory Commission (CSRC), and China Insurance Regulatory Commission (CIRC), on 11 December 2013 to detail the regulations and regulatory responsibilities of the shadow banking sector. In addition to defining and specifying the shadow banking responsibilities of each regulatory authority – in the same way that CBRC regulates financial products in the formal banking sector and CSRC deals with security products – it outlines the regulations for the provision of financial products through other informal financial vehicles, for example, guarantee companies (including LGFPs) and online financing.

To further improve the supervision of inter-bank transactions and the proliferation of wealth management products, the PBoC, CBRC, CSRC, CIRC, and State Administration of Foreign Exchange (SAFE) jointly issued the *Circular Regarding Improving Supervision in Inter-bank Operations of Financial Institutions* (Circular No. 127) in 2014. This states that only eligible and authorized financial institutions can collect and manage inter-bank deposits and loan businesses, and defines the scope of inter-bank investment in the form of structured products, including wealth management products, trust investment schemes and funds, and so on (see also PwC, September 2014: 44–45).

19.6 CONCLUSIONS

The building of a 'moderately prosperous society' implies the provision of basic financial and social services for the general public. China's central government is facing the challenges of a 'new normal' stage of economic development, including the risks of bubbles in the real estate sector, the uncertainties of local government and other hidden debts and their potential domino effects in the finance and banking industry.[21] The twin goals of maintaining the financial viability of banking institutions and the financial security of the general public under the post-WTO banking reforms implemented by the CBRC are *intrinsically contradictory*.

To maintain the financial viability of the banking industry, the Chinese government implemented 'tried and tested' strategies by establishing four 'bad banks' in the form of AMCs to absorb the NPLs and recapitalized the SOCBs before their IPOs, and established the CBRC to formalize lending criteria and regulate banking operations. Under these reforms, SOCBs and other banking institutions in China have adopted the expected strategies for restructuring the industry: the centralization of banking operations and the resultant redundancies (although at a much lower scale than their Anglo-America counterparts), market segmentation and the financial exclusion of low value-added clients. All these phenomena can be explained clearly by the existing theories on Anglo-American banking geographies (Leyshon and Thrift, 1999; Leyshon and Pollard, 2000; Leyshon et al., 1998).

Based on the assessment criteria of Anglo-American banking, the reforms in the Chinese banking system could be argued to be like 'one step forward, two steps back'. The reforms of the Chinese banking system have served China well in terms of economic growth during the last three decades. However, a piecemeal approach to reform is not without costs, notably the perpetuation of the moral hazard of local government officials and the general public in the formal banking system. This is especially the case when the state used SOCBs as an instrument to inject capital into the economy through the massive construction projects of physical infrastructures during the 4 trillion *yuan* stimulus policies (the de facto Chinese version of quantitative easing monetary policy). There are signs of massive lending by SOCBs, including a significant rise in debts accumulated by local governments and hidden debts through off-balance-sheet financing by local governments, normally through arms-length LGFPs to avoid regulatory control of such borrowing. As a proportion of these loans may not be based on commercial decisions and some projects are economically inefficient, it is argued that the hybrid properties of SOCBs creates a moral hazard for the formal banking system in China and this partially contributed to the significant rise of debt-to-GDP ratio from 158 per cent in 2007 to 282 per cent in 2014.

Nonetheless, the mainstream theories based on Anglo-American banking geographies have not emphasized the institutional environment of the Chinese transitional economy, where the transformation of the property structure blurs the conventional boundaries between public and private property and the state still plays an important role in the regulation and operation of a significant portion of these hybrid properties, and the financial security of the general public.

If the CBRC's banking reforms are considered in terms of the Chinese socio-economic context, the development of the Chinese banking system could be argued as being like taking 'two steps forward one step back'. Given that the NPL ratio of SOCBs was 31 per cent in 2001 and 200 million people still live under the poverty line of US$1.25/day in constant 2005 purchasing power parity (PPP) prices, it is a great challenge to fulfil the CBRC's objective of providing basic formal banking services to everyone in China. Notwithstanding the recent boom in local government debts and the proliferation of informal finance and its potential hidden bad debts, the single-digit NPLs of the Chinese banking system is well below the 31 per cent reached in 2001. Partly due to the hybrid nature of SOCBs, the CBRC can bail out structured financial products marketed by SOCBs indirectly through AMCs rather than allowing them to create further uncertainties that could impact the wider economy. The CBRC is clearly aware of the potential moral hazards of such decisions and playing a balancing act between stepping forward to reform the formal and informal banking systems while stepping back from sensitive issues that could be a lightning rod for a public crisis of confidence in the banking industry and/or issues that could lead to political upheavals. The recent CBRC restrictions on the usage of LGFPs and other means of off-balance-sheet financing, and the regulations on informal banking suggest the state intends to rein in such practices.

The experience of banking reform in China clearly highlights the importance of the state's role in the operation of a transitional economy, partly due to the path dependency of the planned economy that was in operation for decades. Without a fully functioning market economy, the state has to improve the economic efficiency of the banking system and yet has to keep a check on the moral hazard that could be created by the hybrid properties of SOCBs. This is especially the case where the general public still perceives SOCBs as the fully state-owned institutions they were during the pre-reform era and where their money was safe. Although the Chinese experience should not be a 'model' that other developing countries should simply try to replicate, economic geographers could be in a strong position to unpack the empirical and pragmatic implications, including the specific political and socio-economic circumstances crucial for the development of the banking industry in any transitional economy. In addition to the centralization-marginalization thesis of Anglo-American economic geographies, the experience of Chinese banking reforms along with other developments in the banking industry in non-market economies provide rich empirical evidence for an alternative thesis for the economic geographical study of banking where the state plays a pro-active role in the regulation and even operation of commercial banks.

NOTES

1. Moral hazard is the perception of too big or too safe to fail due to information asymmetry, that is, the SOCBs will be bailed out by the state.
2. This section relies heavily on Yeung (2009b).
3. Cinda AMC was listed in the Stock Exchange of Hong Kong in 2013, while Huarong AMC has been transformed into a joint-stock asset management company and is ready for the IPO. Refer to Dobson and Kashyap (2006) for more details about the NPLs, and Shih (2004) for an interesting analysis of the political considerations of central government for the management of NPLs.
4. Loans classified in the 'sub-standard', 'doubtful', and 'loss' categories are regarded as NPLs (CBRC, 2006: 72–73).
5. The formal criteria of the loan granting mechanism in SOCBs have features of both transaction and relationship lending. See Boot and Thakor (2000) and Berger and Udell (2002) for relationship banking, and Rajan (1992) for transaction lending.
6. China is scheduled to launch a nationwide online credit database for citizens and corporations in the second half of 2014, after pilot tests in Jiangsu and Sichuan provinces and Chongqing city since March 2013 (PBoC, 2014).
7. Guarantee institutions proliferated all over China after the pilot programme in 1998. By June 2004, there were 2,136 guarantee institutions of various forms and ownership structures, with 200 billion *yuan* of loans carrying guarantees (OECD, 2005: 152).
8. 'Moderately prosperous society' was used by Deng Xiaoping to describe the goal of Four Modernization in 1979 to justify the economic reforms. The goal of relative equality in economic growth by the year 2020 was also used by then Premier Wen Jiabao.
9. In the PBoC and CBRC websites, one of the duties of both institutes is to perform 'other functions prescribed by the State Council' (CBRC, 2014; PBoC, 2014).
10. The PBoC lifted credit quotas and lowered SOCBs' reserve ratios from 17.5 per cent to 14–15 per cent (World Bank, 2009) which, along with the lowering of the equity requirement of fixed asset investments by the central government in May 2009, contributed to a frantic rate of credit expansion. SOCBs lent 7.37 trillion *yuan* (US$1.08 trillion) in the first half of 2009, nearly double the total loans for the whole of 2008 (CBRC, 2009).
11. In fact, the solvency ratio of SOCBs in terms of NPLs to GNP did not deteriorate rapidly during the 1990s,

for example NPLs of SOCBs accounted for 13.8 per cent of GNP in 1993, with the ratio increased to 18 per cent in 1997 (Laurenceson and Chai, 2001: 220–221).

12. SOCBs, joint-stock commercial banks, city commercial banks, and rural commercial banks accounted for 74–77 per cent of the asset value of the Chinese banking system between 2003 and 2013 (CBRC, 2013).
13. In addition to the massive pre-IPO US$560 billion recapitalization and capital injection, including the transfer of 1.4 trillion *yuan* of NPLs to AMCs, the profitability of SOCBs is at least partly due to their oligopolistic large-scale lending with well-funded capital bases (by controlling the largest share of deposits) and the inconvertibility of the Chinese currency, so that foreign banks have to secure their capital in *Renminbi* from the Chinese banking system. Although it is still an inconvertible currency, the usage of *Renminbi* for global payment has increased significantly and ranked as seventh (accounting for 1.6 per cent of global payments, higher than the Swiss franc or Hong Kong dollar) in 2013 due to the bilateral trade settlements and the issuance of offshore Chinese-currency bonds (the so-called 'dim sum bonds') (Moore, 2014).
14. As local governments are responsible for their budgets, a proportion of local governments' loan is used for speculative real estate projects which may generate higher returns.
15. Various forms of securitization, including collateralized loan obligations, are regarded as instruments used by western banks to 'over leverage' their loans before the global financial crisis. In China, the outstanding securitized products account for 0.5 per cent GDP, which is much lower than the 60 per cent in the US, 3.6 per cent in Japan, and 2.8 per cent in Germany (*Financial Times*, 20 January 2015).
16. As local governments were responsible for 80 per cent of public spending but only received 48 per cent of fiscal income in 2010, they have to find other means of finance to make up their budgetary deficits, normally through selling of land use rights and indirect borrowing through LGFPs. Under the *1994 Budget Law*, they are not allowed to borrow directly from banks or individuals (Reuters, 27 January 2014).
17. Eight provinces were in fiscal deficit of at least 15 per cent of revenue (MGI, 2015: 81).
18. Shortly afterwards, another off-balance-sheet credit product defaulted under the 4 billion *yuan* guarantee of a small Chinese joint-stock commercial bank, Evergrowing Bank.
19. Alibaba focuses on individual investors (with small-scale financial products at below 200,000 *yuan*) and small and medium-sized enterprises (with small-scale loans of below 5 million *yuan*). Alibaba's US$25 billion IPO in the New York Stock Exchange in 2014 was the largest in the world. Alipay accounted for 77.8 per cent of the 1.63 trillion *yuan* of transactions through third-party Internet payment tools in the first quarter of 2014 (although the value was inflated due to the Chinese New Year holiday) (*Mingpao*, 30 September 2014).
20. For comparison with the popularity of Yu'eBao, there are only 77 million active equity trading accounts in China (Hu and Moody, 2014). These funds normally invest in the inter-bank and domestic bond markets.
21. The 'new norm', first referred to by President Xi Jinping on a visit to Henan in May 2014, refers to a new developmental stage characterized by more sustainable, efficiency-oriented and innovation-driven growth at 7–8 per cent per annum rather than the cost-oriented and production investment-driven growth rate of 10 per cent per annum during the first three decades of reforms.

REFERENCES

Anderlini, J. (2014), China has 'wasted' $6.8tn in investment, warn Beijing researchers, *Financial Times*, 27 November.

Anderlini, J and G. Wildau (2014), 'China's "bad banks" back in the spotlight', *Financial Times*, 31 August.

Agricultural Bank of China (ABC) (various years), *Annual Report of Agricultural Bank of China*, accessed 15 October 2014 at www.abchina.com/en/about-us/annual-report/.

Avery, R.A., R.W. Bostic, P.S. Calem and G.B. Canner (1999), 'Trends in home purchase lending: consolidation and the Community Reinvestment Act', *Federal Reserve Bulletin*, **85**, 81–102.

Berger, A.N. and G.F. Udell (2002), 'Small business credit availability and relationship lending: the importance of bank organisational structure', *The Economic Journal*, **112** (477), F32–F53.

Berger, A.N., R.S. Demsetz and P.E. Strahan (1999), 'The consolidation of the financial services industry: causes, consequences, and implications for the future', *Journal of Banking & Finance*, **23** (2–4), 135–194.

Berger, A.N., I. Hasan and M. Zhou (2009), 'Bank ownership and efficiency in China: what will happen in the world's largest nation?', *Journal of Banking & Finance*, **33** (1), 113–130.

Bonin, J.P. and Y. Huang (2002), 'Foreign entry into Chinese banking: does WTO membership threaten domestic banks?', *The World Economy*, **25** (8), 1077–1093.

Boot, A.W.A. and A.V. Thakor (2000), 'Can relationship banking survive competition?', *Journal of Finance*, **55** (2), 679–713.

Chen, M. (2009), *Multinational Banking in China: Theory and Practice*, Cheltenham, UK and Northampton, MA, USA: Edward Elgar Publishing.

China Banking Regulatory Commission (CBRC) (2007), *NPLs of Commercial Banks as of end-March 2007*, accessed 16 May 2007 at www.cbrc.gov.cn/english/info/statistics/index.jsp.

China Banking Regulatory Commission (CBRC) (2013), *The CBRC Issued Guidelines on Further Enhancing Financial Services for Small- and Micro-Sized Enterprises*, 5 September, accessed 23 September 2014 at www.cbrc.gov.cn/chinese/home/docView/FDA6DF57EFF74AE0989FE303C4186FAF.html.

China Banking Regulatory Commission (CBRC) (various years), *CBRC Annual Report* (in Chinese), accessed 23 September 2014 at www.cbrc.gov.cn/chinese/home/docViewPage/110007.html.

China National Audit Office (2013) *Introduction to Local Government Debt*, **174** (32), 30 December, accessed 13 March 2015 at www.audit.gov.cn/n1992130/n1992150/n1992500/n3432077.files/n3432112.pdf.

Clark, G.L. and D. Wójcik (2003), 'An economic geography of global finance: ownership concentration and stock-price volatility in German firms and regions', *Annals of the Association of American Geographers*, **93** (4), 909–924.

Devlin, J.F. and M. Wright (1995), 'The changing environment of financial services', in C. Ennew, M. Wright and T Watkins (eds), *Marketing Financial Services*, 2nd edition, Oxford: Heinemann, pp. 1–32.

Dobson, W. and A.K. Kashyap (2006), 'The contradiction in China's gradualist banking reforms', *Brookings Papers on Economic Activity*, **2**, 103–148.

Dunford, M. and G. Yeung (2011), 'Towards global convergence: emerging economies, the rise of China and western sunset?', *European Urban and Regional Studies*, **18** (1), 22–46.

Dymski, G. (1999), *The Bank Merger Wave: The Economic and Social Consequences of Financial Consolidation*, New York: M.E. Sharpe.

Dymski, G.A. and J. Veitch (1996), 'Financial transformation and the metropolis: booms, busts, and banking in Los Angeles', *Environment and Planning A*, **28** (7), 1233–1260.

Faulconbridge, J., E. Engelen, M. Hoyler and J. Beaverstock (2007), 'Analysing the changing landscape of European financial centres: the role of financial products and the case of Amsterdam', *Growth and Change*, **38** (2), 279–303.

Economist (2014), 'Bridging the fiscal chasm: fancy infrastructure is one example of local-government largesse. Which province is deepest in debt as a result?', 22 February. accessed 17 April 2015 at http://www.economist.com/news/china/21596991-fancy-infrastructure-one-example-local-government-largesse-which-province-deepest-debt.

Financial Times (2015), 'Sliced and diced loans take off in China', 20 January.

Fortune (2015), *Fortune Global 500*, accessed on 17 April 2015 at beta.fortune.com/global500/list/filtered?hqcountry=China&sortBy=profits.

FRED (2015a), *Return on average assets for all US banks*, Federal Reserve Bank of St. Louis, Economic Data, accessed 4 April 2015 at www.research.stlouisfed.org/fred2/series/USROA.

FRED (2015b), *Nonperforming Loans (Past Due 90+ Days Plus Nonaccrual) to Total Loans for all US Banks*, Federal Reserve Bank of St. Louis, Economic Data, accessed 4 April 2015 at http://research.stlouisfed.org/fred2/series/USNPTL.

Fuller, D. (1998), 'Credit union development: financial inclusion and exclusion', *Geoforum*, **29** (2), 145–157.

Grote, M.H. (2007), 'Mobile marketplaces – consequences of the changing governance of European stock exchanges', *Growth and Change*, **38** (2), 260–278.

He, C.F. and R. Fu (2008), 'Foreign banking in China: a study of 279 branch units in 32 cities', *Eurasian Geography and Economics*, **49** (4), 457–480.

He, C.F. and G. Yeung (2011), 'The locational distribution of foreign banks in China: a disaggregated analysis', *Regional Studies*, **45** (6), 733–754.

Hu, H. and Moody, A. (2014), 'Internet banking a game changer', *China Daily*, 17 November, accessed 31 October 2016 at http://europe.chinadaily.com.cn/epaper/2014-11/07/content_18883045.htm.

IMF (2014), *Global financial stability report: moving from liquidity- to growth-driven markets*. April 2014. Washington, DC: IMF, accessed 31 October 2016 at www.imf.org/External/Pubs/FT/GFSR/2014/01/index.htm.

Jia, C. (2009), 'The effect of ownership on the prudential behavior of banks – the case of China', *Journal of Banking and Finance*, **33** (1), 77–87.

Kempson, E. and C. Whyley (1999a), 'Kept out or opted out? Understanding and combating financial exclusion', The Policy Press with the Joseph Rowntree Foundation, Bristol, accessed 14 October 2011 at www.jrf.org.uk/sites/files/jrf/jr060-understanding-financial-exclusion.pdf.

Kempson, E. and C. Whyley (1999b), 'Understanding and combating financial exclusion', *Insurance Trends*, **21**, 18–22.

Kempson, E., C. Whyley, J. Caskey and S. Collard (2000), 'In or out? Financial exclusion: a literature and research review', Financial Services Authority, London, accessed 14 October 2011 at www.fsa.gov.uk/pubs/consumer-research/crpr03.pdf.

Lai, K.P.Y. (2011), 'Marketisation through contestation: reconfiguring China's financial markets through knowledge networks', *Journal of Economic Geography*, **11** (1), 87–117.
Lai, K.P.Y. (2012), 'Differentiated markets: Shanghai, Beijing and Hong Kong in China's financial centre network', *Urban Studies*, **49** (6), 1275–1296.
Lardy, N.R. (1998), *China's Unfinished Economic Revolution*, Washington, DC: Brookings Institution Press.
Laurenceson, J. and J.C.H. Chai (2001), 'State banks and economic development in China', *Journal of International Development*, **13** (2), 211–225.
Leyshon, A. and J. Pollard (2000), 'Geographies of industrial convergence: the case of retail banking', *Transactions of the Institute of British Geographer*, **25** (2), 203–220.
Leyshon, A. and N. Thrift (1993), 'The restructuring of the UK financial services industry in the 1990s: a reverse of fortune?', *Journal of Rural Studies*, **9** (3), 223–241.
Leyshon, A. and N. Thrift (1995), 'Geographies of financial exclusion: financial abandonment in Britain and the United States', *Transactions of the Institute of British Geographer*, **20** (3), 312–341.
Leyshon, A. and N. Thrift (1996), 'Financial exclusion and the shifting boundaries of the financial system', *Environment and Planning A*, **28** (7), 1150–1156.
Leyshon, A. and N. Thrift (1999), 'Lists come alive: electronic systems of knowledge and the rise of credit scoring in retail banking', *Economy and Society*, **28** (3), 434–466.
Leyshon, A., N. Thrift and J. Pratt (1998), 'Reading financial services: texts, consumers and financial literacy', *Environment and Planning D: Society and Space*, **16** (1), 29–55.
Lu, Q. and J. Dewhurst (2007), 'Factors influencing the growth of foreign banks' branches in China', *Journal of Contemporary China*, **16** (52), 517–534.
Martin, R. (1999), 'The new economic geography of money', in Ron Martin (ed.), *Money and the Space Economy*, Chichester: Wiley, pp. 3–27.
McGuinness, P.B. and K. Keasey (2010), 'The listing of Chinese state-owned banks and their path to banking and ownership reform', *The China Quarterly*, **201** (March), 125–155.
McKillop, D. and J. Wilson (2007), 'Financial exclusion', *Public Money and Management*, **27** (1), 9–12.
McKinsey Global Institute (MGI) (2015), *Debt and (Not Much) Deleveraging*, February 2015, accessed 13 March 2015, www.mckinsey.com/insights/economic_studies/debt_and_not_much_deleveraging.
Mingpao (2014), 'Jack Ma secures private bank license', 30 September (in Chinese).
Moore, E. (2014), 'The renminbi's place in the FX world', *Financial Times*, 3 November, accessed 31 October 2015 at https://www.ft.com/content/51e2a5d2-59f0-11e4-8771-00144feab7de.
Morrison, P.S. and R. O'Brien (2001), 'Bank branch closures in New Zealand: the application of a spatial interaction model', *Applied Geography*, **21** (4), 301–330.
Mosk, M., B. Ross and S. Johnson (2013), 'US officials: China refuses to help stop investment scams', *ABC News*, 9 January 2013, accessed 8 October 2015 at http://abcnews.go.com/Blotter/us-investors-lose-billions-alleged-chinese-stock-schemes/story?id=18164787.
National Bureau of Statistics (NBS) various issues of *Statistical Yearbook of China* (*Zhongguo tongji nianjian*), Beijing: China Statistics Press.
Nee, V. (1992), 'Organizational dynamics of market transition: hybrid forms, property rights, and mixed economy in China', *Administrative Science Quarterly*, **37** (1), 1–27.
Nee, V. and F.W. Young (1991), 'Peasant entrepreneurs in China's 'second economy': an institutional analysis', *Economic Development and Cultural Change*, **39** (2), 293–310.
Oi, J.C. (1992), 'Fiscal reform and the economic foundations of local state corporatism in China', *World Politics*, **45** (1), 99–126.
Ong, L.H. (2006), 'The political economy of township government debt, township enterprises and rural financial institutions in China', *The China Quarterly*, **186** (June), 377–400.
Ong, L. H. (2011), 'Greasing the wheels of development: rural credit in China', in Björn Alpermann (ed.), *Politics and Markets in Rural China*, London: Routledge, pp. 48–68.
Organisation for Economic Co-operation and Development (OECD) (2005) *OECD Economic Surveys: China*, 2005/13 (September 2005), OECD, accessed 25 November 2014 at http://www.oecd.org/.
Pei, M.X. (1998), 'The political economy of banking reforms in China, 1993–1997', *Journal of Contemporary China*, **7** (18), 321–350.
People's Bank of China (PBoC) (2014), 'The roll out of online personal credit database', Notice distribution by the People's Bank of China, 28 May 2014 (in Chinese), accessed 28 May 2014 at www.pbc.gov.cn/publish/goutongjiaoliu/524/2014/20140527181453169810486/20140527181453169810486_.html.
Pollard, J. and M. Samers (2007), 'Islamic banking and finance: postcolonial political economy and the decentring of economic geography', *Transactions of the Institute of British Geographers*, **32** (3), 313–330.
Pollard, J.S. (1996), 'Banking at the margins: a geography of financial exclusion in Los Angeles', *Environment and Planning A*, **28** (7), 1209–1232.
PriceWaterhouseCoopers (PwC) (2014) *Banking Newsletter: Analysis of China's Top 10 Listed Banks Results*

for the First Half of 2014, September 2014, accessed 24 October 2014 at www.pwchk.com/home/eng/banking_newsletter.html.
Rajan, R.G. (1992), 'Insiders and outsiders: the choice between informed and arm's length debt', *Journal of Finance*, **47** (4), 1367–1400.
Reinhart, C. and K. Rogoff (2013), 'Financial and sovereign debt crises: some lessons learned and those forgotten', IMF Working Paper No. 13/266, December 2013, accessed 20 November 2014 at www.imf.org/external/pubs/ft/wp/2013/wp13266.pdf.
Reuters (2014), 'China details $3-trillion local public debt risk', 27 January, accessed 30 October 2015 at http://www.reuters.com/article/us-china-economy-debt-idUSBREA0Q0LA20140127.
Shi, Q.W. and S.S. Xu (2014), 'A reflection on the management of NPLs', CBRC Working Paper 2014, Vol. 5 (in Chinese), accessed 23 September 2014 at www.cbrc.gov.cn/chinese/files/2014/B8EE111EC1234E23A065481D292ABBBB.pdf.
Shih, V. (2004), 'Dealing with non-performing loans: political constraints and financial policies in China', *The China Quarterly*, **180** (December), 922–944.
Stark, D. (1989), 'Coexisting organizational forms in Hungary's emerging mixed economy', in Victor Nee and David Stark (eds), *Remarking the Economic Institutions of Socialism: China and Eastern Europe*, Stanford: Stanford University Press, pp. 137–168.
Stark, D. (1996), 'Recombinant property in East European capitalism', *American Journal of Sociology*, **101** (4), 993–1027.
Stark, D. and V. Nee (1989), 'Toward an institutional analysis of state capitalism', in Victor Nee and David Stark (eds), *Remarking the Economic Institutions of Socialism: China and Eastern Europe*, Stanford: Stanford University Press, pp. 1–31.
Szelényi, I. (1988), *Socialist Entrepreneurs: Embourgeoisement in Rural Hungary*, Madison: University of Wisconsin Press.
Walder, A. (1994), 'Corporate organization and local government property rights in China', in Vedat Milor (ed.), *Changing Political Economies: Privatization in Post-Communist and Reforming Communist States*, Colorado: Lynne Rienner, pp. 53–66.
Wei, S.J. and T. Wang (1997), 'The Siamese twins: do state-owned banks favor state-owned enterprises in China?', *China Economic Review*, **8** (1), 19–29.
Wildau, G. (2014), 'China to cap local government debt', *Financial Times*, 2 October.
Wills, J. (1996), 'Uneven reserves: geographies of banking trade unionism', *Regional Studies*, **30** (4), 359–373.
Wójcik, D. (2011), 'Securitization and its footprint: the rise of the US securities industry centres 1998–2007', *Journal of Economic Geography*, **11** (6), 925–947.
Wójcik, D. and C. Burger (2010), 'Listing BRICs: issuers from Brazil, Russia, India and China in New York, London and Luxembourg', *Economic Geography*, **86** (3), 275–296.
World Bank (2009), *China Quarterly Update*, June 2009, accessed 15 October 2014 at www.worldbank.org/china.
YCharts (2015) *Bank of America Return on Assets (TTM)*, accessed 4 April 2015 at http://ycharts.com/companies/BAC/return_on_assets.
Yeung, G. (2009a), 'How banks in China make lending decisions', *Journal of Contemporary China*, **18** (59), 285–302.
Yeung, G. (2009b), 'Hybrid property, path dependence, market segmentation and financial exclusion: the case of the banking industry in China', *Transactions of the Institute of British Geographers*, **34** (2), 177–194.
Yeung, G., C.F. He and H. Liu (2012), 'Centralization and marginalization: the Chinese banking industry in reform', *Applied Geography*, **32** (2), 854–867.
Zhang, H. and C. Yang (2007), 'Locational choice of foreign banks in China and their investment motives', *Financial Research*, **9**, 160–172 (in Chinese).
Zheng, Yangpeng (2014), 'PBOC sets sights on "zombie" financing vehicles', *China Daily*, 18 January.
Zhu, J.Y. and S.S. Gao (2011), 'Fraudulent financial reporting: corporate behavior of Chinese listed companies', in S. Susela Devi and Keith Hooper (eds), *Accounting in Asia* (Research in Accounting in Emerging Economies, Volume 11), Bingley: Emerald Group Publishing, pp. 61–82.

20. Credit rating agencies are poorly understood and the rules developed for them will not work

Ginevra Marandola and Timothy J. Sinclair

20.1 INTRODUCTION

Credit rating agencies such as Moody's and S&P (Standard and Poor's) have been subject to close examination by policymakers since the Enron bankruptcy of 2001.[1] Enron operated through a complex set of companies linked by carefully timed payments. The agencies did not spot the precarious financial engineering lurking behind Enron's books, and lost credibility when the company collapsed without any warning. Concerns about what the agencies do and how well they do it were subsequently greatly heightened by the onset of the global financial crisis in 2007. Concerns focused on the role of the agencies in the mortgage market and the transformation of illiquid housing loans into liquid securities. This market seemed to allow for the disconnection between the supply of housing lending to home owners and the financial markets built around the housing market. This is what at the time was called the 'originate and distribute' model. Initially, this seemed to be just a US issue, but the global reach of the agencies and of the securitization mania spread the affect around the globe. Many observers have blamed the agencies for the elaborate financial engineering involved and have questioned both their competence and motives. The public panic about the agencies gave rise to new demands for regulation of what until recently has been a largely ungoverned industry.

In this chapter we argue these efforts to regulate rating agencies have been largely ineffective, bringing more heat than light to the challenge of governing the credit rating agencies. The current regulation of credit rating agencies is more in the nature of a tax than a carefully designed framework of rules which shape what the rating agencies do in the direction of desired outcomes that expand societal welfare. Indeed, the process of building a regulatory approach has been so drawn out that it now threatens to throw any future agenda of credit rating agency reform into disrepute. Why have governments not been able to regulate credit rating agencies like they regulate other institutions in the financial markets? Why is the regulation we have, or that may be contemplated, seemingly so insubstantial? What is missing in our understanding of the agencies that would allow for effective intervention? What is the problem and what could and should be done about the rating agencies?

We argue that some of the reasons for this failure stem from the nature of rating itself, which seems to be poorly understood by regulators and by the financial industry. Rating agencies are not banks. Indeed, they are not financial institutions. But their specific characteristics seem lost on many trying to understand them and what they do. Beyond this important question about understanding what the agencies actually are and how they function we argue that rule-making has focused on superficial regulative governance. Normally, this sets the boundaries on what the agencies can do, prohibits specific activities and sets penalties for infractions, although in rating it largely amounts to a licensing system. Most regulation is of this rule-making type. It works well in many areas. But it works badly for banks because of banks' ability to engage in regulatory arbitrage (Rethel and Sinclair, 2012). Banks tend to side-step the intent of the law and pursue their ends via other means the law has not prohibited. We think similar problems pervade rating, perhaps even more so because the agencies are not involved in financial transactions (which can be identified specifically for regulatory purposes). In this context, regulation needs to take a different form, which we call constitutive, and address the very purpose of the credit rating businesses. We claim this broader and deeper form of regulation has some hope of reforming credit rating agencies.

The following section of the chapter considers what rating actually is and how it works. The subsequent section examines different approaches to rating agency regulation. This is followed by an explanation of why the traditional approach to regulation does not work well in relation to the rating agencies. Last, we set out our case for a constitutive framework for rating regulation before concluding with some thoughts on prospects for rating agency governance.

20.2 WHAT RATING ACTUALLY IS AND HOW IT WORKS

Credit ratings are opinions on the creditworthiness of financial and non-financial corporations, local, provincial, and state governments, countries, and the securities issued by these entities (Sinclair, 2005; Abdelal, 2007; Paudyn, 2013). A credit rating consists of a letter that corresponds to a given probability of default, usually accompanied by a text rationale. Credit ratings may be publicly available or require subscription. Credit rating agencies may charge investors or issuers according to their business model. The three principal credit rating agencies – Moody's, Fitch and S&P – adopted an issuer-pays model in the late 1960s and early 1970s, and provide free access to their ratings, although they charge for additional information.

The process through which ratings are assigned by internal rating committees was tradi-

Table 20.1 Credit rating scales

Moody's Investors Service	Fitch/S&P
Aaa	AAA
Aa	AA
A	A
Baa	BBB
Ba	BB
B	B
Caa	CCC
Ca	CC
C	C
N/A	RD*/D

Note: *Fitch uses the category Restricted Default or RD to refer to the circumstance where non-payment is selective or partial.

tionally obscure. In the last twenty years or so this has changed with more market and regulatory demands for transparency. Regulatory pressure since the Enron bankruptcy has made the process more publicly accessible, although the specific deliberations of rating committees remain entirely confidential. Ratings are not mere calculations. They are judgments made by committees and it is not clear if quantitative or qualitative data prevail in the assignment of ratings by these committees. All the agencies follow more or less the same procedure. A credit rating may be solicited or unsolicited. The former is sought by the issuer and implies cooperation between the two parties. The latter is issued at a credit rating agency's initiative and relies mostly on public information and information internal to the agency. When the rating is solicited, the agency analyses the environment in which the issuer operates and considers firm-specific information obtained through the interaction with managers. Rating analysts recommend a rating to a rating committee of senior agency staff, who determine the rating. The process lasts around a month and the rating is revised once a year or earlier if any particular developments occur.

In principle, ratings have an important function: they allow investors to get to know issuers and their plans. Ratings reduce the asymmetry of information between investors and issuers and encourage the allocation of funds to the best entrepreneurs thanks to economies of scale in gathering and diffusing information. Credit rating agencies' work is convenient to investors because it allows them to make investment decisions based on information which would otherwise be costly for them to gather. Furthermore, rating agencies provide a constant monitoring of managers and government officials (or at least the possibility of monitoring). The threat of a ratings downgrade may encourage officials to act in the interests of bondholders rather than themselves. Finally, ratings may act as a governance tool by influencing issuers' financing strategies. Evidence suggests that when evaluating debt issuance decisions firms take into account the potential impact of those decisions on their credit ratings (Kisgen, 2006; Hovakimian et al., 2009). Indeed, the cost of debt is highly correlated with credit ratings, making firms generally eager to maintain their ratings at the highest possible level.

Anyone who is familiar with the rating business has probably skimmed through the above paragraph, waiting for the interesting part of this chapter. However, misunderstandings of what ratings are and what they are not are more common than one might expect. Fitch states that 'Ratings, including Rating Watches and Outlooks, assigned by Fitch are opinions based on established criteria and methodologies. . . . Ratings are not facts, and therefore cannot be described as being 'accurate' or "inaccurate"' (Fitch, 2014: 4). On the other hand, in the section of the Dodd–Frank Act dedicated to rating reform the words 'ratings' and 'accurate' are associated more than once. Notwithstanding its relevance, a rating is not a formal certification of a corporation's financial statements. Credit rating agencies are not liable for their opinions and do not audit the information they use. As will be clearer in the next part of the chapter, the mismatching of perceptions about ratings among market participants is one of the causes of the misuse of ratings. The market and regulators often seem to forget that credit rating agencies are actually private entities operating to maximize their profits. Credit rating agencies' authority in the market has increased over time as disintermediation has become a secular trend in global financial markets. Those looking to raise funds increasingly bypass relatively expensive bank borrowing, which bears the costs of bank overheads including failed loans, and seek funding in the capital markets directly by issuing bonds. Ratings are the tools through which credit rating agencies perform their institutional role and they seem to have acquired a value which goes beyond economic efficiency. Ratings represent an accepted and reliable reference point for financial practitioners just as school grades represent a reference for parents, employers or university admissions offices. Even though the educational system may be criticized on different levels, professors' authority to give grades is rarely questioned.

There is a remarkable affinity between credit rating agencies and the rating of restaurants. This comparison helps with understanding the role of credit ratings by showing that the epistemic authority obtained by the rating agencies over time and its consequences are not due to the particular sector in which they operate or to the regulation they are subject to, but are inherently rooted in markets of a specific form. These are markets characterized by the asymmetry of information between customers and providers, scope for subjectivity in product or services' evaluation, and the high costs of product comparison by the consumer. In other words, these are markets in which knowledge intermediation in some form is needed.

The *Michelin Red Guide* is the world's most famous restaurant rating book. It awards one to three stars to selected restaurants according to quality. Restaurants included in the guide, but not awarded with a star, are deemed to be good restaurants. Unworthy restaurants are not included at all. Credit rating works in a similar way. The big three agencies assign creditworthiness symbols to financial securities around the world. Safer securities are assigned higher investment grade ratings, while the risky ones are considered speculative grade. This latter sort of restaurant is not included in the Michelin guide. There are no 'junk' grade restaurant ratings. In the rating world speculative or junk bonds are included and investors are not told to avoid trading in them. However, if they do buy and sell them, they bear higher risk in exchange for the higher return. A customer may prefer to have dinner in a cheaper restaurant not included in the Michelin Guide, bearing the risk they will consume food they may come to regret.

The Michelin Guide covers 23 countries in Asia, North America and Europe. For each restaurant the guide provides a short description written in the language of the corresponding country, but the symbols are universal. Some American food critics have suggested the guide is biased in favor of French cuisine. Steven Kurutz (2005) of the *New York Times* alleged that in New York more than half of the restaurants with stars 'could be considered French'. The big three are not exempt from similar criticism. As Sinclair (2005: 120) suggests: 'Even if rating is increasingly transnational, the mental framework of rating remains largely American'. A typical example is the Japanese case. Japanese managers and financial institutions complain about judgments made about the unique Japanese corporate governance system by the US credit rating agencies. According to them, this leads to lower ratings. The Japan Center for International Finance (JCIF), in a 1999 survey of 175 financial institutions and 89 industrial firms, found 90 percent partly or totally disagreed with the following statement: 'the rating standards of the US rating agencies (Moody's and S&P) appropriately reflect specifically Japanese factors in areas like corporate governance' (Shin and Moore, 2003: 329).

The US domination of credit rating is part of a wider phenomenon in which US knowledge producers such as accounting firms hold sway as makers of global standards and norms. This is why changes in US law, such as the Sarbanes–Oxley Act of 2002, which limited the scope of accounting firms in the wake of the Enron scandal, have global effects. Even where local interests try to set up new credit rating firms it is always the major American companies with which they compare themselves. These local upstarts try to convince possible clients in countries such as China and Russia that their interests are not served by the US firms and that they should support the counter-hegemony represented by the new agency. These initiatives have had little impact so far because credit rating as a mental process and set of behaviors continues to be headquartered in the US and it is this to which all newcomers are compared. As long as this mental framework persists there is a strong incentive for all new firms to adopt these norms as this is what customers expect. But the adoption of 'global' US norms denies the new firms any substantial claim to adding value to this US-dominated industry.

Although the Michelin guide is one of the most famous and consulted restaurant guides in the western world, being French-oriented is only one of many criticisms of the guide. These are collected by Pascal Rémy (2004), a former Michelin inspector, in *L'Inspecteur se Met à Table* ('The Inspector Spills the Beans'). We will discuss some of the criticisms of the guide due to their similarity to those of the credit rating agencies.

Rémy alleged that the Guide has loosened its standards, favoring profits at the expense of customer needs. According to him, Michelin has reduced the number of inspectors and their restaurant visits in France over the previous ten years. In the same way, congressional investigations have accused Moody's of being more focused on market share and short-term profits than rating accuracy, after being spun off as a stock market listed corporation in 2000. Kedia et al. (2014) find empirical evidence that Moody's ratings were more favorable than S&P's both for new corporate bond issues and outstanding bonds after 2000. The authors also show that the loosening of Moody's credit rating standards is more the case for structured finance products and financial firms' ratings that represent the most profitable activities for credit rating agencies. We assume that for both restaurant guides and credit rating agencies the primary aim of their businesses is profit maximization, and if laxer standards and less monitoring (fewer restaurant visits) do not weaken their reputation, it is optimal to cut costs. Both Michelin and the big three have gained significant market power over time. Their reputations are deep-rooted and this allows them to engage in profitable strategies and operations that may reduce the quality of their services compared to provision in the past.

The agencies' and Michelin's market power also derive from the inability of users to effectively evaluate rating performance. According to Rémy, the results of research conducted by Michelin showed that 90 percent of customers could not tell the difference between a three star and a two star restaurant. Exploiting customers' lack of 'taste', managers assigned the stars to restaurants regardless of inspectors' suggestions, according to criteria other than food quality, related to marketing strategies. It may be that credit rating agencies could be similarly accused of having exploited investors' lack of expertise when rating CDOs (collateralized debt obligations) and other complex financial products prior to the onset of the global financial crisis in 2007. Indeed, the relatively new nature of these products and their complexity prevented investors from critically evaluating their creditworthiness, and this gave ratings huge value, but also much more scope for subjectivity. Moreover, credit rating agencies increased their involvement in complex financial products well beyond the mere examination of creditworthiness. They participated in the design of the products themselves. However, their subsequent ratings were stronger than might have been expected because of a lack of experience and resources specific to the new products, and perhaps because of the desire to boost the business of rating structured products and especially ancillary services. Similar tendencies can be observed with Michelin. In 2011, Japan had the highest number of restaurants in the world awarded Michelin stars. This generated concern about whether the Michelin guide was adopting lower standards in Japan in order to enter the market and undertake promotion for the parent auto tire manufacturing company.

Concerning conflict of interests, Rémy accuses the Guide of being influenced by lobbying activities and by chefs that use the media to threaten Michelin's reputation. The guide's publication director Derek Brown replied: 'There's no possible way that we can be influenced like that because we are not working for the profession. We're working for the customers and I can't insist on that enough' (Lee, 2004). The issue of lobbying is even more of a concern in the case of credit rating agencies given their issuer-pays business model. Are credit rating agencies really working in the interests of investors? Do they, instead, favor issuers' needs? Investors' needs should be the first concern for credit rating agencies because investors are the final users of ratings and issuers have no incentive to want ratings if they do not matter to investors. In practice, issuers have asymmetric information about the degree to which ratings really matter to investors. Empirical literature shows that there is a significant market response to rating changes (Hand et al., 1992; Holthausen and Leftwich, 1986; Dichev and Piotroski, 2001; Bannier and Hirsch, 2010). However, a direct causal effect cannot be clearly identified. For example, market reaction to rating changes may be explained by regulatory investment constraints or by contemporaneously released information. Given this asymmetry, issuers are likely to continue to demand ratings even if they do not have any ascertainable information content for investors. In this sense, an issuer-pays model creates the potential for market distortions, suggesting returning to the investor-pays model would be preferable if practical. Investors would be more demanding about rating standards if they paid, and would have greater incentives to find alternatives, placing a constraint on credit rating agencies' market power. However, as is the case with well-known chefs and the Michelin Guide, governments and big corporations might still retain lobbying power in relation to the credit rating agencies despite a return to the pre-1970 investor-pays model. Their bargaining power is generated by the information they possess about their own businesses, as credit ratings would be less useful if they were not based on private information from inside issuers. Moreover, if the investor-pays model, which is vulnerable to the free rider problem because investors may obtain ratings information freely from issuers or news sources, hampers credit rating agencies' business model and profits, as was the case in the busy bull market of the 1960s, this might lead to lower quality ratings and the decline of the sector. This discussion of the best business model to adopt is far from comprehensive, but it shows regulatory intervention into how the rating business is funded may be useless or even detrimental, given the complexity of the issues. Mutual trust between issuers, investors and rating agencies is the key element irrespective of business model.

Besides the business model, another difference between the Michelin Guide system and the credit rating agencies is the anonymity of the restaurant inspectors and the randomness of the restaurant visits. This procedure guarantees the performance of the chef on the day of the visit to be average, other things being equal. This is difficult to translate to the credit rating business, in which cooperation with managers and private information represents value added to agencies and investors. At the same time, as is the case with restaurants if they knew the inspector was visiting, issuers are keener to provide positive information than negative to the raters. The only condition under which the rating business would be perfectly informative is one in which investors are able to exactly evaluate rating performance and consequently adapt their own behavior. In that case, issuers would have no incentive to give biased information if they want ratings to work for them. However measures of rating performance are necessarily long-term in nature and historical data is not readily available to investors. Unless regulators find a way to reconcile anonymity and private information, or to prevent issuers from giving biased information, possible regulatory provisions seem to be weak in this context.

Many authors and credit rating agency experts attribute the privileged position of the big three to the regulatory framework in which credit rating agencies operate. The necessity to be recognized by the SEC (US Securities and Exchange Commission) and references to ratings in financial regulation are thought to be the causes of undeserved power on the part of the credit rating agencies. However, the parallel with Michelin shows that the same privileged position leading to the same problems may occur without any regulatory intervention. For example, White (2010), Partnoy (1999, 2007) and Cornaggia and Cornaggia (2013) among others think that rules that limit institutional investors to investment in investment grade securities rated by the big three may have enhanced credit rating agencies' market power, by forcing investors to make use of ratings. However, the heavy reliance on ratings by investment managers is easily explained by reference to the restaurant example without regulation. If you plan a dinner with your boss, you may not want to take the risk of taking him or her to a bad restaurant, and so you may consult the Guide before making a reservation. Even if the restaurant turns out to be disappointing, you can always blame the Guide. This is why an investment manager may choose to invest in securities rated by the big three rather than other competing agencies. They are guaranteed by the credit rating agencies' reputation. If failure does occur the agent may not be condemned because he or she has relied on globally recognized credit rating agencies. The *Red Guide* has existed for more than 100 years, selling 30 million copies in France alone, without any regulatory intervention. The guide acts as a certification and information provider. Even though the criticisms highlighted here may suggest the Guide's information quality has decreased over time, its certification value has become so important that this suffices to maintain its market power. Given the similarities between restaurants and the ratings market, it seems reasonable to think the credit rating regulatory framework has only played a subordinate role in strengthening the rating agencies' market power.

20.3 FORMS OF RULE

We argue attention to rules governing behavior is actually mistaken when it comes to finance and rating agencies. The global financial crisis occurred not because of rule-breaking but because some relatively simple but crucial social relationships came apart and prevented market actors from transacting with each other, as they had prior to the crisis. This breakdown involves quite different sorts of rules to those normally considered by regulators. What fell apart are what we call the constitutive rules of global finance. These are the rules that make financial markets work. Following John Searle, these rules are the social practices, like trust, that make transactions possible between market participants (Searle, 2005). Without these rules there can be no markets. Regulation, in the sense of rules governing behavior, was not the primary issue behind the crisis, and so changing the regulative rules of finance will not prevent crises of similar seriousness in future. Searle suggested it is possible to distinguish regulative rules that 'regulate antecedently or independently existing forms of behaviour' from a much more architectural form of rule (Searle, 1969: 33). These other 'constitutive rules do not merely regulate, they create or define new forms of behaviour'. He goes on to suggest that chess and football are only possible with rules. The rules actually make or constitute the game. The point which follows is that the public and elite panic has focused specifically on the regulative form of rules and on those who allegedly broke these. But we argue that this is not the problem. Constitutive rules were damaged in the crisis, the basic social foundations of market interaction, such as trust and confidence in transactions, and this is why the crisis was so profound. Finding bad guys is not the answer.

The regulative approach is associated with the hegemonic way of understanding finance. This has dominated economic thought about finance for at least 30 years or more and has had a major influence on policymakers. This tradition we label the exogenous approach (Sinclair, 2009). Exogenous accounts of finance assume market participants are constantly adjusting their behavior – for example, whether they buy or sell bonds and stocks – based on new information. In this context, market prices are assumed to always reflect what other market participants are prepared to pay. If this is the case, reason exogenous thinkers, prices are never inflated or false. They must always be correct. So the idea of a 'bubble economy', in which assets like houses, stocks and oil futures deviate from true value to a higher, false value, is rejected. Similarly, regulation is an external imposition by institutions and governs activities in markets which they conceive to be natural interactions.

The exogenous tradition was championed by the New York financial interests that opposed the Bretton Woods agreement in the 1940s. Although subordinated to notions of a 'mixed economy' during much of the post-war era until the mid-1970s, the notion of a self-regulating market never went away. When the United States fell into a low growth and inflationary crisis in the 1970s these ideas became an increasingly powerful narrative. The growing weight of financial imperatives in a relatively low growth environment has empowered ways of thinking like economics, finance ministries, and the credit rating agencies. The exogenous view was exported from the developed core, where growth is low, by these and many similar institutions and disciplines, to the periphery where growth is higher, potentially forestalling the sort of social and political benefits in these countries that have been enjoyed by large segments of the population in the rich countries. The credit rating agencies are a key part of this institutional reduction in the transformative effects of growth.

The endogenous account, by contrast, says that financial crises begin primarily inside finance and that markets are social institutions with a history of their own. For Keynes, the 'animal spirits' or passions of speculation, give rise to risky activity. Typical of the endogenous perspective is the idea that market traders do not merely integrate information coming from outside the markets in the wider, real economy, but are focused on what other traders are doing, in an effort to anticipate their buy/sell activities, and thus make money from them (or at least avoid losing more money than the average).

Keynes provided what remains perhaps the best intuitive illustration of the importance of this internal, social understanding of finance in his tabloid beauty contest metaphor, first published in 1936 (Keynes, 1936: 156; Akerlof and Shiller, 2009: 133). Keynes suggested that the essence of finance is not, as most suppose, a matter of picking winners, based on an economic analysis of which assets should rise (or fall) in value in future. More relevant was anticipating what others in the market were likely to do. Keynes compared finance to beauty contests that ran in the popular newspapers of his time. These contests were not, as might be assumed, about picking the most attractive face. Success was achieved by estimating how *others* would vote and voting with them. So, for Keynes, markets are driven not by the fundamental analysis of commodities and companies, but by the much more immediate social dynamics of anticipating the future actions of others.

The exogenous-regulative approach to understanding finance, crises and by extension the rating agencies, suggests the solution to the problems created by the agencies can be found by tinkering with the rules that regulate the agencies. But the confidence financial markets had, prior to 2007, reached such a frenzy that it became an episode of 'irrational exuberance', like so many financial manias in history. The 'bad news' about subprime lending was actually quite modest in summer 2007, but in the context of the preceding mania this was enough to act as a tripwire and cause panic. The panic created widespread uncertainty about the quality of financial institutions and their balance sheets. It is this uncertainty that effectively brought the financial markets to a halt, forcing government intervention.

The financial panic started as a local phenomenon. The house pricing bubble burst that led to the default of many subprime borrowers originally involved a small number of states in the north-east of the United States (for example, Massachusetts, New York, Rhode Island and District of Columbia) and some in the west and the south (that is, California, Nevada and Florida).[2] However, the existence of an intense financial network made this local crisis global. The mechanism was the following. The risky mortgage originated by a local bank in California is sold to a Federal National Mortgage Association (for example, Fannie Mae and Freddie Mac), that in turn sells it to an investment bank; the investment bank bundles the asset with others and creates a mortgage-backed security (MBS) or a collateralized debt obligation (CDO) which is divided into tranches by the degree of riskiness of the assets. An investor in US buys these tranches deeming them safe given their high credit ratings. The assets continue to be traded until they end up on the balance sheet of a small town in Norway. As long as housing prices were increasing, borrowers could refinance their debt using the house as collateral and any party involved earned profits. When the housing bubble burst, borrowers started to default generating a general loss of trust. Pooling assets did not effectively protect investors as expected. MBSs and CDOs became worthless despite their high ratings. It became difficult for banks to get rid of these risky assets and fire-sale prices reduced the value of their capital. Wholesale funding decreased and credit followed. The fall in bank credit to firms and the negative effects on stock prices made the crisis hit the real economy in the US and in the rest of the world. The real estate bubble in some parts of the US became a global turmoil. Banks were rescued in the UK (for example, Royal Bank of Scotland and Lloyds TSB Group); Belgium, the Netherlands, Luxembourg (for example, Fortis NV); Germany (for example, Commerzbank); Switzerland (for example, UBS). Greece, Spain, Portugal and Italy suffered large increases in their bond spreads. Iceland almost went bankrupt due to the collapse of the three biggest banks in the country. Hungary and Latvia also risked default.

Even countries not directly affected by the financial crisis like China suffered the decline in demand from the US and Europe in 2009. Moreover, banks and other investors reduced their exposure in emerging markets that also had to deal with pressure on exchange rates. 'Virtually no country, developing or industrial, has escaped the impact of the widening crisis', the World Bank reported (World Bank, 2008: 2).

This alternate account of the origins of the global financial crisis points the finger at euphoria and dysphoria rather than rule-breaking as the source of eventual breakdown. Given this, simply amending the rules of behavior is not the right remedy to the problems of banks or credit rating agencies. The problems are not regulative but constitutive, and change needs to be pursued at this much more architectural level. In the next section we discuss the rules-based approach to governing the agencies, and show how it failed. After this we will suggest possible constitutive solutions based on an endogenous understanding of credit rating agencies.

20.4 RULES FOR THE RATING AGENCIES HAVE FAILED

Since their appearance in the US financial market, state and federal regulators have considered credit ratings a convenient tool for determining credit worthiness and have employed ratings to set banks' capital requirements[3] and to regulate the securities' market.[4] In the municipal bond market they were essential as early as the 1920s as bonds issued without ratings increasingly would not sell without the issuer offering higher interest. Initiatives to use ratings in regulation in the United States started during the Great Depression in the early 1930s, and expanded up to the Enron crisis in 2001. On the one hand, the recourse to credit ratings has enabled state and federal regulators to protect investors against credit risks while keeping the regulatory framework flexible and dynamic. On the other, the reliance on ratings may have enhanced the market power of the incumbent credit rating agencies. The formal adoption of ratings in regulation could be understood to have conferred on credit rating agencies a 'regulatory license' as suggested by Partnoy.[5] However, we identify a different mechanism through which regulation has affected the rating industry. In our view, the use of ratings in financial regulation has *certified* the reliability of ratings, encouraging the market to rely on them more than it would have given a different regulatory approach.

Ratings are heavily employed in private contracts, as governance tools to solve or ameliorate principal–agent conflicts, and by banks in their internal risk evaluations. Demanding one or more ratings has become a standard practice in the market. Investors may base their decisions on information sources other than ratings but securities issued without a rating may be deemed 'suspect' or 'problematic' and be discarded in favor of rated ones. Indeed, ratings seem to be recognized as necessary market 'standards' by participants (Kerwer, 2005). This is confirmed by a survey by Cantor et al. (2007), in which fund managers were asked about their use of ratings (see Table 20.2). The survey shows that ratings are used mostly because they are mandated by clients and far less because relying on ratings is deemed to be a good investment strategy by the professionals. Other reasons cited for the use of ratings are herding behavior and regulatory requirements.

After the Enron collapse in 2001 and the subsequent strong attacks on the agencies by market participants, the press, politicians and regulators became more critical of the

Table 20.2 Use of ratings in investment management

Motivation (percentages)	Fund Managers	Plan Sponsors
Mandated by regulation	20	4
Mandated by clients or internal guidelines	80	56
Most other managers (plan sponsors) do it	14	20
Good investment strategy	12	20

Source: Survey by Cantor, Gwilym and Thomas (2007).

agencies and started to investigate the industry. This led to the International Organization of Securities Commissions (IOSCO) code of conduct in 2004 and the US Credit Rating Agency Reform Act of 2006. IOSCO's Code of Conduct focused on the quality of ratings and on credit rating agencies' independence, conflicts of interest, and responsibilities to the public. Several investigations subsequently reported that on balance credit rating agencies complied with the IOSCO code with a few exceptions (Committee of European Securities Regulators, 2006a, 2006b; the French securities regulator, Autorité de Marchés Financiers, report, 2006). One issue was thought problematic: the provision of ancillary services to issuers by the agencies. For example, credit rating agencies may give advice on the structure of debt issues in order to help the issuer obtain higher ratings from themselves and other agencies. But this practice puts the rating agency in the position of 'auditing its own work' (Mishkin, 2003: 8). Credit rating agencies may in these circumstances have incentives to issue more favorable ratings than they would have done otherwise in order to expand their consulting business. The fact that credit rating agencies decided not to abandon the provision of ancillary services such as this in order to comply with the IOSCO code of conduct should have set alarm bells ringing at the SEC. Instead, the SEC seems to have underestimated the significance of the issue.

The US Credit Rating Agency Reform Act became law September 29, 2006 with the aim of fostering competition in the credit rating industry together with establishing accountability of credit rating agencies and increasing the transparency of the rating process. Specifically, the act establishes a new registration process to create a clear route for a rating agency wishing to gain Nationally Recognized Statistical Rating Organization (NRSRO) status with the SEC. Any rating agency with at least three years of experience and meeting certain quality requirements can register with the SEC according to the new system.[6] However, the introduction of a formal process of recognition of NRSROs has had little substantial effect. Even though the number of NRSROs has increased after the reform, new entrants have mainly focused on niche markets and rate a relatively small number of issues.[7] The oligopoly of the 'big three' has not been threatened by the new NRSRO process. Indeed, the market shares of Moody's, S&P and Fitch (based on revenues) were still about 40 percent, 40 percent and 15 percent respectively as of 2008 (Caouette et al., 2008: 82). Reducing regulatory barriers has not been enough to increase competition because the historical advantages of the major agencies and economic barriers are still at work. In order to compete with the 'big three', significant financial resources and expertise are needed, given the degree of internationalization of the rating business. In fact, the key element in the rating business is global reputation, which represents a very significant barrier for new entrants. Incumbents' reputation also negatively affects investors' demand for the product of start-up credit rating agencies. For example, portfolio managers, who do not directly bear the risk of debt defaults, seem to prefer to stick to the 'big three' even at the expense of quality. Indeed, they would incur some costs if they had to justify recourse to minor (and thus non-standard) agencies' ratings.

This attempt to reform the system failed because it did not address a fundamental issue: understandings of the role of ratings differ between the credit rating agencies themselves, and issuers and investors. Credit rating agencies state that their ratings are merely opinions. Issuers actually want them because they represent a market 'certification', irrespective of any specific regulatory requirements. But issuing an opinion does not necessitate the same amount of effort, responsibility and caution as certification in say, maritime or aviation safety. Credit rating agencies do not, as we have noted, audit the information they use. Ratings are based on public information mixed with private data, and in the case of unsolicited ratings only public information. Moreover, as the number of clients increases, fewer resources are devoted to a single rating.

> Certainly the relationship between an issuer and the credit analyst is nothing like the relationship the issuer has with the engagement partner of its external audit firm or with the corresponding attorney at its outside law firm. The credit analyst only has very infrequent personal meetings with company management, is responsible for the ratings of dozens of issuers, and is not paid based on any relationship with any issuer. (Frost, 2007: 17)

New regulatory provisions can be effective only if they challenge the differing understandings of the role of ratings between issuers and investors on one side and credit rating agencies on the other. Similarly, there is a gap between how rating agencies understand their role and the expectations of policymakers and regulators. For example, US Senate committee staff have at times characterized credit rating agencies as 'outside watchdogs', although the agencies have never portrayed themselves as such.

Heightened criticism of credit rating agencies emerged as a consequence of the global financial crisis which started in 2007. This criticism suggested the credit rating agencies should be held responsible for the crisis, having enhanced and expanded the market for complex financial products with their ratings. The complexity of structured finance products together with its spectacular growth in terms of relative market value is acknowledged to have played an important role in increasing the business of credit rating agencies. 'From 2000 to 2007 Moody's rated nearly 45,000 mortgage-related securities as triple-A. . . . In 2006 alone, Moody's put its triple-A stamp of approval on 30 mortgage-related securities every working day' (*US Financial Crisis Inquiry Commission*, 2010, Conclusions: XXV). This process, in which favorable ratings were issued to senior tranches of structured products, means that the underlying non-investment grade assets went to the market with very high ratings. These ratings determined not only the ability and incentives of 'regulated' investors to buy risky products, but also made them more attractive for non-regulated investors reassured by the good reputation of 'the big three'. Credit rating agencies participated closely in the creation of these investment opportunities by supplying preliminary feedback on the rating of the tranches. As became apparent in the summer of 2007, credit rating agencies had failed to manage the ratings of structured products effectively, possibly due to weakened reputational incentives, perhaps because of weak resources, or both. 'Moody's . . . relied on flawed and outdated models to issue erroneous ratings on mortgage-related securities, failed to perform meaningful due diligence on the assets underlying the securities, and continued to rely on those models even after it became obvious that the models were wrong' (*US Financial Crisis Inquiry Commission*, 2010: 125–126).

In response to the problems of the financial system that led to the financial crisis, in 2010, President Obama signed the Dodd–Frank Act into law. The Act also addresses issues related to credit rating agencies, focusing on the level of public oversight and accountability, standards of liability and concerns about conflicts of interest. The intention was to reform the rating system, but the measures suffer from the haste needed to repair past inertia. The most representative example of the lack of foresight and thoughtfulness in the Act is the repealing of Rule 436(g). After the repeal, credit rating agencies would be potentially exposed to 'expert' liability when, with their consent, ratings were included in Asset-Backed Security registration statements. This was a liability to which they were not exposed before having always been protected as opinion-givers by the First Amendment to the US Constitution. The immediate reaction of credit rating agencies was to not allow debt issuers to include their ratings in prospectuses or debt registration statements. This reaction by the credit rating agencies was not anticipated by Congress. Agency reaction, which led to the 'repeal of Rule 436(g) prompted severe dislocation in the trillion dollars asset-backed securities market' (Ishmael, 2011). Rule 436(g) of the Dodd–Frank Act was repealed by the Asset-Backed Market Stabilization Act of 2011. This episode reveals the continuing leverage of credit rating agencies and the limited ability of regulators to reform the rules governing the system. The use of ratings is so deep-rooted in financial markets that even if substitutes to ratings exist, they find it hard to compete against ratings. This circumstance, more than favorable regulation, gives credit rating agencies strong bargaining power. As Sinclair (1994) anticipated, rating agencies have become more socially and economically powerful than their 'bean counter' image suggests. An increase in transparency, accountability and competition may be achieved only by substantially changing the rules of the rating business itself, starting with greater understanding of ratings amongst market participants.

20.5 MORE EFFECTIVE RULE

Attending to a new framework of regulative rules for credit rating agencies could provide some short-term political relief to politicians but is unlikely to make credit rating more effective. We think there is another approach to the rating agency problem. This approach addresses the core purposes of credit rating agencies rather than just trying to limit their actions. The broad aim must be to make the agencies self-regulating, in the sense that they come to organize themselves around the broad purpose of their work, which should be determined by regulation. The justification for prescribing what business credit rating agencies are in is that their work has systemic implications. Physicians are licensed and are disciplined by self-regulating professional bodies because the consequences of their misbehavior are very serious. While lives are not at stake here, livelihoods are, and potentially on a global scale. Rethel and Sinclair (2012: 26) considered the same issue in banking. Drawing on Searle (2005), Cox (1987) and Sinclair (2005), they looked at the problem along two axes. On one axis they considered the logic of bank practice, distinguishing between a synchronic approach and a diachronic one. Drawing on Cox, the synchronic mentality is concerned with short-term instrumentalities and the diachronic with understanding linkages, longer-term implications and the complexities of creating and producing. The synchronic mentality is characteristic of financial speculation and the diachronic of investment for growth. On the other axis they considered regulation, distinguishing between regulative rules which limit behavior, and constitutive rules, which make institutions and behaviors, like the game of chess, what it is. Rethel and Sinclair (2012) suggested that contemporary banks are typically synchronic and regulative in character. We argue this is a fair characterization of the credit rating agencies today too. But historically, from their origins until some point around the new millennium, the agencies could instead have been characterized as diachronic and constitutive in outlook. Indeed, this was their very purpose, what gave them a role in the otherwise synchronic world of finance. Their role was traditionally to act as a disciplinary agent, as a mechanism of governance, as a restraint on the narrow and short-term motivations of finance. The transformation of this mentality into a synchronic and regulative one is what needs to be reversed if the agencies are to make an effective contribution to financial market governance in the future. The puzzle is, how is this return to the traditional credit rating agency mentality to be achieved?

The first step is to clarify the business of the agencies and make them stick to this work. Because of the systemic risks attached to the agencies we cannot allow them to engage in any business activities that threaten the integrity of their core business. Such activities might undermine the quality and reputation of their core business. Like a banking license, a license to provide credit rating services should prohibit other work such as advising, or force divestment, where associated units have undertaken other work in the past. Sarbanes–Oxley had this effect, forcing accounting firms to sell their other non-audit businesses, such as their legal units. Prescribing the business they are in will make the agencies less likely to focus on non-core, potentially more profitable activities that might compromise their reason for existing.

We argue that the second element in bringing about a constitutive transformation of the rating agencies back into what they traditionally were and what they need to be in future is much greater clarity and openness about the subjectivity and limits of credit ratings. Because ratings combine quantitative data and qualitative information they are not objective, replicable forms of knowledge, even if issuers and investors want them to be this. They are subjective judgments about what might probably happen in the future. Occasionally, observers express shock when they realise ratings have this standing. This may be because the agencies, although always acknowledging that ratings are judgments in the small print, are happy to take advantage of the authority that can be derived from the production of knowledge people mistake for science.

Open and direct acknowledgment of the subjectivity of ratings could take a similar form to that required of home lenders who typically have to state directly and without qualification that 'your home is at risk of foreclosure if you do not keep up your payments', or similar. Requiring all ratings websites and contracts to undertake ratings to display a similar warning that 'ratings are subjective judgments about the future' would make all parties more aware of the challenges inherent in rating, encouraging parties – issuers, investors and the rating agencies – to be more judicious. We think the repeated acknowledgment of subjectivity will help to reposition rating back to where it was before the explosion in structured finance stimulated hubris about the scientific possibilities of financial knowledge.

Our third major mechanism through which to push rating agencies back toward a diachronic and constitutive way of operating is to encourage community norms amongst credit rating agencies. Such norms have always existed, even if rating agency officials were eager to deny they were even aware of the activities of other rating firms. But membership in a professional society or industry association would make scrutiny of these norms possible, enable their enforcement, and help to systematically socialize industry participants into good and bad ways of operating. We envisage this as a self-regulating organization, but one that like those for medical practitioners and other professionals, is compulsory for firms and their employees. While professional and industry bodies have elements that are rent-seeking about them as they can exclude rivals, we think the self-interest in improving standards, in training, and in promoting the work of the agencies is likely to outweigh these costs.

The idea of a self-regulating organization with compulsory participation is not very far from some already observable phenomena. One example is the ACRAA (Association of Credit Rating Agencies in Asia). ACRAA was born in 2001 at the Asian Development Bank headquarters with the participation of 15 Asian credit rating agencies from ten countries. As of 2015, the association counts 28 members. ACRAA's members must abide by certain minimum requirements. The association organizes training for its analysts with the aim of reaching higher standards in the rating process. Agencies are asked to adopt high ethical standards and to regularly participate at forums 'in a constant exercise of benchmarking each other's performance and against international practices' (ACRAA website). The sort of communities we have in mind will be similar to the ACRAA. They should be regional or national communities as geographical proximity may facilitate communication and the sharing of norms and best practices among members. The regional focus would not exclude membership by the global agencies. Moody's, S&P and Fitch have branches in 46 countries, thus they may be members of different communities through their local offices. This approach would also partly address the criticism that the global agencies, being of US origins, are unable to adapt their standards and assessment benchmarks to different economies, showing a tendency to underrate non US businesses (see the Japanese case mentioned in the first section).

This is not an exhaustive view of how to turn around the agencies, but we think these points focus squarely on the root causes of the problems with rating agencies. Those problems will not be solved by rules governing the behavior of rating agencies. Nor do we consider other ideas such as the creation of a public sector allocator of ratings or even a new international organization to do this work addresses the issues effectively. The proposal of entrusting the supervisory authority with choosing the rating agencies responsible for issuing ratings for structured products has been considered but not yet adopted in the European Union and in the US. Although this system may mitigate conflicts of interest implied by the issuer-paid business model and may help smaller agencies to increase their market share, the introduction of a non-market model may also have negative and unexpected effects. First, this system does not prevent the issuer from obtaining a rating from another agency of its choice, thus leaving the problem of rating shopping unsolved. Moreover, government involvement in the rating business may create the wrong perception that ratings are approved by the regulatory authority, reinforcing the issue of over reliance on ratings by investors. The process through which a public agency could assign ratings is unclear. The level of discretion of the authority members and the question of whether all the agencies should be assumed to issue ratings of the same quality are among the issues that may arise. Finally, forcing issuers to obtain ratings from agencies that they do not trust would be a problematic interference in business. The external assignment of ratings may also reduce competition and agencies' incentives to increase the quality of their ratings. Finally, it may lead some potentially profitable agencies to leave the market or to operate without seeking national recognition. The logic of this last proposal seems to rest on the idea that random allocation or forced reallocation of rating contracts will somehow improve the quality of ratings but we think it risks negative and unexpected consequences. For this reason we think it a suboptimal approach.

20.6 CONCLUSIONS

Credit rating agencies are very poorly understood institutions and thus far the efforts to govern them through regulation have been weak and ineffective. Although based in the United States, the work of the agencies is global. Governments and other observers have taken a regulative approach to governing the credit rating agencies, and this is where they have produced weak interventions. If we want to produce better ratings and rating agencies we need to approach the challenge like a driving instructor does. The first task here is to train the new driver to control the car effectively. Only after this has been achieved are the minutiae of a specific jurisdiction's road rules relevant. It is the same with rating. The global financial crisis revealed that the credit rating agencies were no longer operating within conservative, diachronic constitutive norms. Devising the means through which these norms can be rewritten in an organic way, via self-regulation, is necessary for making the agencies the wise watchers of the capital markets once again. We argue this can be done by prescribing the business the agencies are in, and proscribing peripheral activities. Acknowledgment of the limits of rating will reduce hubris by all parties. Encouraging the development and enforcement of community or professional norms in the rating industry is also required in the United States and Europe. None of these will turn rating into science. Nor need it. But the diachronic and constitutive approach advocated here will help to prevent credit rating agencies becoming the catalyst to another global financial crisis in the foreseeable future.

NOTES

1. An earlier version of this chapter appeared as a working paper of the Sheffield Political Economy Research Institute in October 2014.
2. Martin (2011).
3. In 1973 the US Securities and Exchange Commission (SEC) adopted new broker-dealer net capital requirements based on bond ratings issued by credit rating agencies registered as Nationally Recognised Statistical Rating Organizations (NRSROs). Since 2001, banking capital regulations under the Recourse Rule have enabled banks to hold lower capital for purchases of higher-rated securities. Basel II makes use of credit ratings for bank portfolios in one of three alternative frameworks for assessing capital requirements.
4. For example, credit ratings were used as eligibility criteria for companies seeking to use 'short form' registration when registering securities for public sale. In 1936, the US Comptroller of the Currency formally

prohibited banks from buying speculative securities. To identify eligible securities banks were explicitly instructed to rely on at least two 'recognized' bond rating manuals. Immediately, credit spreads between investment grade and speculative grade bonds widened, and issuers started to seek ratings before issuance of their bonds.

5. Partnoy (1999, 2007) argues that the most successful credit rating agencies have benefited from an oligopoly market structure that is reinforced by regulation.
6. Before the reform, the national recognition of NRSROs was based on a 'No Action' letter, a document the SEC sent to NRSROs to authorize them implicitly (by committing to no action against them by the SEC).
7. On its website the SEC states that ten credit rating agencies are currently registered as NRSROs, eight of which are registered for issuers of asset-backed securities.

REFERENCES

Abdelal, Rawi (2007), *Capital Rules: The Construction of Global Finance*, Cambridge, MA: Harvard University Press.

Akerlof, George and Robert J. Shiller (2009), *Animal Spirits: How Human Psychology Drives the Economy and Why it Matters for Global Capitalism*, Princeton, NJ: Princeton University Press.

Autorité de Marchés Financiers (2006), 'AMF 2005 report on Rating Agencies' pursuant to the Financial Security Act of 2003 which requires the French Financial Authority to publish an annual report on Credit Rating Agencies. Retrieved on October 20, 2016 from www.amf-france.org/en_US/Publications/Rapports-etudes-et-analyses/Agences-de-notation.html?docId=workspace%3A%2F%2FSpacesStore%2Fce1aa5e3-b3ac-4c9e-b0de-72191cf3d223.

Bannier, C.E. and C.W. Hirsch (2010), 'The economic function of credit rating agencies: what does the watch list tell us?', *Journal of Banking & Finance*, **34**, 3037–3049.

Cantor, R., O. Gwilym and S. Thomas (2007), 'The use of credit ratings in investment management in US and Europe'. Retrieved on October 20, 2016 from http://ssrn.com/abstract=996133.

Caouette, John. B., Edward I. Altman, Paul Narayanan and Robert Nimmo (2008), *Managing Credit Risk*, New York: John Wiley & Sons.

Committee of European Securities Regulators (CESR) (2006a), 'Update on CESR's dialogue with credit rating agencies to review how the IOSCO code of conduct is being implemented', CESR/06-220, July.

Committee of European Securities Regulators (CESR) (2006b), 'CESR's report to the European Commission on the compliance of audit rating agencies with the IOSCO code', 06/545, December.

Cornaggia, J. and K.J. Cornaggia (2013), 'Estimating the costs of issuer-paid credit ratings', *Review of Financial Studies*, **26** (9), 2229–2269.

Cox, Robert W. (1987), *Production, Power and World Order. Social Forces in the Making of History*, New York: Columbia University Press.

Dichev, I.D. and J.D. Piotroski (2001), 'The long-run stock returns following bond ratings changes', *The Journal of Finance*, **56**, 173–204.

Fitch Ratings (2014), 'Definitions of ratings and other forms of opinion'. Retrieved on October 10, 2013 from www.fitchratings.com/creditdesk/public/ratings_defintions/index.cfm.

Frost, C.A. (2007), 'Credit rating agencies in capital markets: a review of research evidence on selected criticisms of the agencies', *Journal of Accounting, Auditing & Finance*, **22** (3), 469–492.

Hand, J.R.M., R.W. Holthausen and R.W. Leftwich (1992), 'The effect of bond rating agency announcements on bond and stock prices', *The Journal of Finance*, **47**, 773–752.

Holthausen, R.W. and R.W. Leftwich (1986), 'The effect of bond rating changes on common stock prices', *Journal of Financial Economics*, 17, 57–89.

Hovakimian, A., A. Kayhan and S. Titman (2009), 'Credit rating targets'. Retrieved on September 15, 2013 from http://ssrn.com/abstract=1098351 or http://dx.doi.org/10.2139/ssrn.1098351.

Ishmael, S.M. (2011), Post published on the blog 'ft.com/alphaville' on July 22. 'What's the SEC to do about 436(g)? Call a time out'. Retrieved on February 25, 2013 from http://ftalphaville.ft.com/blog/2010/07/22/295376/whats-the-sec-to-do-about-436g-call-a-time-out/.

Japan Center for International Finance (1999), 'Characteristics and appraisal of major rating companies: focusing on ratings in Japan and Asia', Tokyo: JCIF.

Kedia, S., S. Rajgopal and X. Zhou (2014), 'Did going public impair Moody's credit rating?, *Journal of Financial Economics*', **114** (2), 293–315.

Kerwer, D. (2005), 'Holding global regulators accountable: the case of credit rating agencies', *Governance*, **18** (3), 453–475.

Keynes, John Maynard (1936), *The General Theory of Employment, Interest and Money*, London: Macmillan.

Kisgen, D.J. (2006), 'Credit ratings and capital structure', *The Journal of Finance*, **61**, 1035–1072.
Kurutz, S. (2005), 'She's a belle of the city, but the French are blasé', *The New York Times*, November 13.
Lee, J.J. (2004), 'Dishing the dirt – former Michelin inspector lifts the lid on Red Guide's practices', *South China Morning Post Sunday Morning Post Magazine*, Sunday, May 2. Retrieved on August 24, 2014 at www.scmp.com/article/454148/dishing-dirt.
Martin, R. (2011), 'The local geographies of the financial crisis: from the housing bubble to economic recession and beyond', *Journal of Economic Geography*, **11** (4), 587–618.
Mishkin, F.S. (2003), 'Policy remedies for conflicts of interest in the financial system'. Paper presented to the Macroeconomics, monetary policy and financial stability conference. Ottawa: Bank of Canada.
Partnoy, F. (1999), 'The Siskel and Ebert of financial markets: two thumbs down for the credit rating agencies', *Washington University Law Quarterly*, **77** (3), 619–712.
Partnoy, F. (2007), 'Second-order benefits from standards', *Boston College Law Review*, **48**, 169–191.
Paudyn, B. (2013), 'Credit rating agencies and the sovereign debt crisis: performing the politics of creditworthiness through risk and uncertainty', *Review of International Political Economy*, **20** (4), 788–818.
Rémy, Pascal (2004), *L'inspecteur se met à table*, Paris: Editions des Equateurs.
Rethel, Lena and Timothy J. Sinclair (2012), *The Problem with Banks*, London: Zed Books.
Searle, John. A. (1969), *Speech Acts: An Essay in the Philosophy of Language*, Cambridge: Cambridge University Press.
Searle, J.A. (2005), 'What is an institution?', *Journal of Institutional Economics*, **1** (1), 1–22.
Shin, Y.S. and W.T. Moore (2003), 'Explaining credit rating differences between Japanese and US agencies', *Review of Financial Economics*, **12** (4), 327–344.
Sinclair, T.J. (1994), 'Passing judgement: credit rating processes as regulatory mechanisms of governance in the emerging world order', *Review of International Political Economy*, **1** (1), 133–159.
Sinclair, T.J. (2005), *The New Masters of Capital: American Bond Rating Agencies and the Politics of Creditworthiness*, Ithaca, NY and London: Cornell University Press.
Sinclair, T.J. (2009), 'Let's get it right this time! Why regulation will not solve or prevent global financial crises', *International Political Sociology*, **3** (4), 450–453.
US FCIC (Financial Crisis Inquiry Commission) (2010), 'The financial crisis inquiry report', Final Report of the National Commission on the Causes of the Financial and Economic Crisis in the United States, submitted Pursuant to Public Law 111-21, January 2011.
White, L. (2010), 'Markets. The credit rating agencies', *Journal of Economic Perspectives*, **24** (2), 211–226.
World Bank (2008), 'Global financial crisis and implications for developing countries', G-20 Finance Ministers Meeting.

PART IV

NEW AND EMERGING MONEY SPACES

21. Alternative circuits of capital: parallel economies of environmental finance

Janelle Knox-Hayes

21.1 INTRODUCTION

In 2009, one of the worst financial crises in modern history unfolded in the United States and Europe with the collapse of the US mortgage market. At the end of the same year academics (scientists and economists), NGOs, advocates, interest groups and world leaders gathered in Copenhagen to try to generate a binding international response to climate change. The two events are seemingly independent, and yet deeply interconnected. The crises of capitalism and the crises of the natural environment have the same roots in a crisis of spatial and temporal production and representation of value. The financial crisis stems from a system of borrowing credit, or the promise of future earnings, to maintain consumption and production in the present. Climate change represents the fundamental dis-entrainment of the rate and scale of production of socio-economic systems from natural systems.

Although the 2008 financial crisis was the worst since the Great Depression, it was only one of a series of crises in the recent history of modern capitalism. Kettell (2006) outlines a series of crises since the late 1970s that have shaken world markets. Like the 2008 crisis, these events were marked by a similar set of circumstances. Namely, in each of these crises the overproduction of goods and services (particularly within the agricultural, primary producing and high technology sectors) led to a decline in profit, the stagnation of real wages, and as a consequence increasing rates of individual and national debt to maintain consumption. Kettell explores the ways in which these circumstances operate not only within specific domestic contexts but across the global economy, as emerging economies, for example, service their debt by becoming more dependent on export-led growth. Meanwhile, the growth in demand for cheap consumer goods in places like the United States and Europe is fueled not by wage growth, but by access to cheap credit. Indeed the 2008 crisis in its most simple form was a by-product of the false representation of financial profits from mortgages, and mortgage-based derivatives, when nothing more than credit was in fact backing these financial products (Reinhart and Rogoff, 2008).

The nature of the 2008 and prior crises lies at long-standing debates within economics about the nature and source of value and productivity in the economy. In the twentieth century two prominent political economists, John Maynard Keynes and Friedrich von Hayek, set the tone of these debates. Both scholars were profoundly influenced by the Great Wars and the Great Depression, and sought to derive theories that would bring Europe and the United States into a period of lasting peace and prosperity, but they held fundamentally different beliefs about the role of states and markets in generating growth. Keynes (1937) argues that economies are circular, crises stem from a failure to adequately supply consumers with the means of consumption. The government can therefore intervene in a variety of ways to stimulate the economy with a focus on generating consumption. In contrast, Hayek (2014) argues that markets create and steer value and that individuals must save in order to generate the investments needed for meaningful production. Government intervention to stimulate the market only leads to creation of debt. In other words, the means of production must be addressed in a meaningful way. The argument about whether economies should generate production through saving or stimulate consumption with government spending revolves around circuits of exchange or how best to keep capital circulating through the economy. Associated with the issue of capital circulation is a more fundamental question about the nature and source of value, and specifically how and when value is produced. Keynes solution has governments borrow from the future to maintain consumption in the present. Hayek's solution has people save and withstand downturn in the present so that they can make productive investments in the future.

Keynes and Hayek's theories of consumption and production both recognize that the behavior of people, acting independently as well as collectively across time shapes economic productivity. But another critical ingredient is the resources that are also required to supply and fuel the means of production. In other words, another critical circuit of consideration is the natural environment. Production is sustained through the extraction of materials from the natural environment. Consumption is sustained by the deposition of waste back into the natural environment. A variety of natural crises, from biodiversity loss, resource depletion, to ecological degradation have resulted from human production. Climate change, which results from the release of greenhouse gases generated by virtually every sector of every economy into the atmosphere, is likewise a crisis of the over productivity of capitalism. Each of these crises signal that the Earth is diminishing in its capacity to produce the resources that sustain the growth of every economy, and for that matter every living system on the planet, and to sink and recycle the waste generated from production.

The solution to crises like climate change increasingly seems to be to treat environmental pollution as an externality (costs accrued from economic activities that are not accounted for in economic transaction) and to create systems that can price the externalities. For example, a range of markets have been created around the world to price greenhouse gases. The solution, however, fails to engage with the critical issue of how and where value is generated in space and time. Much as political economists such as Keynes and Hayek have sought to address financial crises by aligning circuits of production and consumption, so too must policymakers find ways in which to bring the scale and rate of socio-economic production into alignment with the scale and rate of natural systems of production. Critical to this process is an understanding of how economies generate value through socio-economic as well as socio-natural circuits of capital, as well as within circuits in time.

This chapter explores the source of value and the ways in which its production utilizes various spatial as well as temporal circuits of capital. In Section 21.2 I examine the spatial and temporal nature of value through the concepts of use and exchange. In Section 21.3 I examine the relationship between socio-economic and social-natural circuits of capital and introduce the idea of a parallel economy, which seeks to use environmental finance as a means of balancing economic productivity in space and time. In Section 21.4 I examine the operation of markets for pricing externalities and elaborate on the extension of these markets to other systems of environmental finance. The final section concludes with the implications of environmental finance for financial and environmental crises, and suggest ways in which the parallel economy can be made more successful.

21.2 SOCIO-ECONOMIC AND SOCIO-NATURAL CIRCUITS OF CAPITAL

The term 'circuits of capital' refers to Marx's famous equation for the function of economies M-C-M' or the process through which capital circulates from money to commodities transformed through production (a combination of labor power and means of production – land, equipment, organizational forms, and so on), to surplus capital. Within the global economy, the ceaseless drive for the expansion of capital therefore leads to the growth of both the extent and the scale of production (Kettell, 2006). The great paradox of the capitalist system is that its growth requires the generation of a large mass of commodities, which cannot be adequately consumed by either the laboring class (who produce more value than they accumulate in wages) or the capitalist class (whose ultimate objective is the accumulation of capital rather than commodities). The government must either periodically intervene by issuing various forms of credit to perpetuate the circuit of consumption, then production, or downturns and recession must be withstood until sufficient saving can restart production (Kettell, 2004). The dual crises that arise out of the very nature of capitalism are therefore always both socio-economic (the imbalance of capital between circuits of production and consumption) as well as environmental (the use and degradation of limited natural resource to produce commodities in excess of what can even be consumed).

The sources of value as well as the nature of crises are long-debated topics within economic geography and related disciplines (see for example Mol and Spaargaren, 2000). In the classical and Marxist traditions, value is believed to stem from the productivity of labor. Surplus accumulation after all accrues from the transformation of commodities according to the formula M-C-M': money transformed into commodities transformed (through the labor of the proletariat) into surplus value (Marx, 1867). Thus, the wealth of capitalism is built through social labor. However, Marxist thinking on value also asserts a relationship to natural resources through the concepts of historical materialism and metabolic rift. Historical materialism is the idea that social history is the story of the evolution of the means of production; the development of new technologies, and greater productive capacity eventually advance to the point where they revolutionize the relations of production (changing the structure of society) (Marx, 1993; Marx and Engels, 1965). From this standpoint, understanding the evolution of political economy therefore requires understanding the transformation of the social relations of production, how labor is coerced or brought into service. Marx eventually realized that societies do not evolve a variety of systems of production in a linear matter, but rather that the paths to development are plural and also reflect the conditions of the natural environment (Marx, 1993).

From this standpoint, scholars like Jared Diamond (2005) begin to explore the specific socio-environmental contingencies under which various productive forms have evolved. It follows that civilizations must either learn to balance the use of the natural environment in their productive activities or experience systematic collapse (Diamond, 2005). Although

Marx rejected natural determinism as an explanation for the function of capitalism (Harvey, 2011) he also directly addressed the decline of the natural environment with concepts like 'the metabolic rift' – the idea that increasing the productivity of large-scale agriculture and industry ultimately leads to a decline of the long-term fertility and productivity of the soil (Foster, 1999). Nevertheless, the ways in which ecological conditions impact the evolution of the forces and relations of production, as well as the implications of production on environmental decline were secondary to the concerns and issues of the social relations of production in Marx's scholarship.

Environmental historians such as William Cronon (1990, 1993) take issue with the overemphasis on labor in neo-Marxist conceptions of the production of value and seek to instead integrate both the natural environment, and cultures of ecological interaction into the understanding of production and consumption decisions at various points in time. Cronon (1993) in particular highlights the ways societies make production decisions based on both the ecology of the environment in which they live as well as culturally driven perceptions of society–environment relations. Cronon (1990) argues that the evolution of social history can be understood from the standpoint of 'modes of consumption' rather than modes of production. The value of economic processes is a product of both socio-economic relations of production, as well as socio-natural relations of consumption. In this view circuits of production revolve around socio-economic systems, whereas circuits of consumption revolve around socio-environmental systems.

The distinction between socio-economic and socio-environmental systems is spatial. Space here does not refer specifically to place, but rather to a frame of reference from which relationships between subjects and objects can be understood (Lefebvre, 1991). Socio-economic space references socio-material relationships, particularly relationships that are built around economic transactions (a laborer paid a wage for performing a service or constructing a good is a relationship that can be framed from the standpoint of socio-economic space). In contrast, socio-environmental space refers to the relationship between humans and environmental resources (the felling of timber or the consumption of energy are relationships that can be framed from the standpoint of socio-economic space). These relationships are about physical materiality, the consumption and use of physical resources (for a more comprehensive overview of the distinction between socio-material and physical materiality see Bansal and Knox-Hayes, 2013).

Crises have a spatial nature in that they can result from a failure to bring together the sufficient ingredients for production (the necessary labor, materials and even the capital to initiate production) or from a failure to consume sufficient goods and services so as to create a space or need for additional production. Circuits of capital are spatial but also temporal. Crises can also have temporal dynamics. Part of the failure to bring together the means of production can be a failure to bring enough capital to bear in time. Likewise, a failure to supply sufficient levels of consumption to make room for the production of new goods and services can be a failure to procure sufficient capital in time. Credit seeks to solve crises in the present by borrowing capital from the future. Saving seeks to address crises in the future, by building capital today.

The mobility of capital in space as well as time raises questions about the nature and reality of value. Hayek's (1931) emphasis on saving is backed by claims that credit capital does not generate 'real' value. Keynes (1937) counters these arguments with terms like 'animal spirits', his emphasis on the ways in which the instincts, proclivities and emotions influence and guide human behavior, and as a consequence the function of markets. The issue is not whether or not capital is 'real' but whether or not people believe capital is real and are motivated to act by that belief. To understand the circulation of capital – how, when and where it exists – it is important to first understand the nature of the value of capital, and in particular its spatial and temporal connotation.

21.3 SPATIAL AND TEMPORAL DYNAMICS OF VALUE

Contemporary definitions of value within economics are derived from a common understanding of two primary forms of value, use value and exchange value. Adam Smith (1776: 32) elaborated the dichotomy of value: 'The word value . . . has two different meanings, and sometimes expresses the utility of some particular object, and sometimes the power of purchasing other goods which the passion of that object conveys. The one may be called "value in use"; the other, "value in exchange."'[1] Clarifying the relationship of space and time to these forms of value elucidates and helps to synthesize the various conceptions of value and valuation.

Use value is objective in the sense that it is value that is fixed in space and time. It is embedded in both the object and the activity that uses it. In other words, the use value of any thing requires a specific set of actors, at a determined location, performing a particular activity for a defined duration. The spatial and temporal dimensions of use value can be identified on a Cartesian grid and located in a specific frame of time. It is perhaps these characteristics that led Marx to refer to use value as 'singular' (Harvey, 1982; Marx, 1867). Exchange, in contrast, is a process of liberating or moving value in space and time. The very purpose and nature of exchange is to move value. Capital in the Marxian sense is 'value-in-process' (Marx and Nicolaus, 1973: 536), or value in circulation. In other words, capital is exchange value. However, exchange does not guarantee that use will occur nor that value will actually be produced. For example, an exchange contract for wheat can represent the value of wheat in multiple cities and on different time horizons (a wheat futures contract might guarantee a future price for a certain quantity of wheat exchange). The contract can even be used as capital, exchanged for other sources of financial value. But the contract cannot guarantee the production of wheat. In this regard, exchange value is potential rather than realized value because it is subject to judgment and future use.

Potential value is the benefit or advantage that accrues from the exchange of resources while realized value is the benefit or advantage accruing from the use of a resource (Ramsay, 2005). Realized value is value that has already been brought to use. To illustrate these examples Ramsay (2005) provides the following example:

> Imagine a firm with a warehouse full of a product that enjoys high sales demand. Now suppose that one of the company's competitors launches a clearly superior and cheaper alternative on the market. The value that the firm and its stored product previously appeared to "possess" evaporates or "moves" to the competitor in an instant. (Ramsay, 2005: 558)

Before the value of an object is realized through its use, it is subjective; it is a product of perception or belief. Reframed in spatial and temporal terms, before the use of a resource grounds it in space and time, the resource has only potentially existing value. It may be exchanged or it may be useful at some point in time, but until it is exchanged, and until it is put to use, its value is subjective. Keynes' emphasis on animal spirits focuses attention on subjective human value or valuation. If individuals believe something is valuable it has subjective value. But to be objectively valued (actually existing in space and time) that something must be put to use (sold, from the company's perspective) or consumed (from the consumer's perspective). This is not to suggest that subjective value does not exist, but rather that it is fluid, subject to perception and does not solidify until it is made objective.

In an exploration of the place of property in the dynamics of value creation under modern capitalism, Brett Christophers (2010) makes a similar point. He suggests that property is increasingly being exchanged for the value that can be extracted from it. However, the value of the property cannot be separated from the activities that occupy the property. Any apparent 'economic growth' located in the property rental market must ultimately be grounded in, and sustained by, growth in real economy of productive activity. If such growth is not occurring, if the property is not being put to use, any rent or exchange value circulating in the property market will eventually crash, because the value or property is the value of the industry utilizing it (Christophers, 2010: 106). In other words, the exchange value of a property cannot be truly removed from its use value, and furthermore the 'real' value of the property is its use value.

Another way to consider this facet of property value is Hernando de Soto's 'mystery of capital' (2000). De Soto argues that capitalism has failed to flourish in non-western nations because the assets citizens and entrepreneurs control are exercised outside of the 'formal economy.' In other words, capitalism does not flourish in countries where property rights are not granted. For example, in China property cannot be owned, only leased from the government. Without the rights to property, it is not possible to turn 'assets into capital' (de Soto, 2000: 5–7). Without a title it is not possible to transform the use of a property into exchange value. Furthermore, de Soto suggests that property systems are 'crucial vehicles for the enhancement of exchange value' and as such 'property can produce surplus value' (de Soto, 2000: 215). As de Soto recognizes, the title of a property can only produce surplus exchange value or profit by serving as a means to liberate the use value of a property from objective space and time by converting it into an instrument of exchange. Yet, as Christophers point out, without the use value (the productivity of the property) embedded in objective space and time, the exchange value derived from it is meaningless.

21.4 VALUE IN TIME: FINANCIALIZATION

Finally, within the dynamics of use to exchange conversion, there is an issue of the temporal movement of value that arises from systems of financialization. Finance serves to move capital not only in space but also in time. Financialization is the process of reducing value that is exchanged (whether tangible, intangible, future or present) into financial instruments or derivatives of financial instruments (Krippner, 2010). Financialization is also a process of accelerating the rate and profit accumulation from the exchange of financial instruments (Epstein, 2005; Krippner, 2005). Financial instruments such as derivatives (instruments whose value is derived from the exchange rather than directly related to an underlying commodity) are compressed representations of the space and time in which commodities exist (Knox-Hayes, 2013). Financial derivatives in particular, bring future potential value into the present.

The exchange of these instruments accelerates the rate at which economic transactions occur (Castells, 1996; Harvey, 1990; Leyshon and Thrift, 2007). Even if finance relies on derivatives or future representations of value, it is still related to real social conditions (Thrift, 2005). As such the dematerialization of money through processes such as the creation of derivatives increases the vulnerability to crisis (Harvey, 1990). Financial capital can be used to represent future value that does not yet objectively exist (Bryan and Rafferty, 2006). In the process of representing future value, finance can create demand to accelerate the rate of production that underlies commodity exchange. In other words, by accelerating the rate at which future value is represented, finance creates demand to accelerate the rate at which value is actually produced.

21.5 A SPATIAL AND TEMPORAL VIEW OF THE CIRCUITS OF CAPITAL

The use of finance to move capital involves not only social systems of exchange, but also material systems of resource production. Additionally, it involves at least two frames of spatial reference: socio-economic relationships, and socio-environmental relationships. Taken together these views suggest the various circuits described by political economists are spatially and temporally connected. The connections are illustrated in a typology that considers the space and time of production and consumption processes as well as their material constitution (Figure 21.1).

The matrix in Figure 21.1 represents the spatial and temporal dynamics of circuits of capital. The vertical axis divides space into socio-economic – symbolizing social interaction and economic structuring or socio-materiality – and socio-environmental – symbolizing the interaction of human and environmental systems or physical materiality. The horizontal axis divides time into present (symbolic of realized economy) and future (symbolic of potential economy). Four distinct circuits of capital result: consumption, commerce, finance and environmental finance. Associated with each circuit is a distinct type of value (use, exchange, derived and external). The lower left quadrant, socio-environmental transaction in present time, is where use value is created and consumption takes place. The upper left quadrant, present socio-economic transaction, is where exchange value is created and commerce takes place. The upper right quadrant, future or potential socio-economic transaction, is where derived value (value derived from goods and services, for example, derivatives like wheat options or repackaged home mortgages) is created and where finance exists. Finance derives its value from underlying resources and services (or commodities and social relations). Finally, the lower right quadrant, future or potential socio-environmental transactions, is where external value (the value of externalities, or value 'external' to present use and exchange) is created and where environmental finance is being created. I will discuss this alternative circuit of capital in greater detail in subsequent sections.

At the center of the diagram, the transition of value according to Marx's cycle of production (M-C-M') is represented. Additionally, a cycle of what I term 'internalization of externalities' (M'-C'-C) is represented. This cycle results from the creation of the fourth, and hereto missing, circuit of capital – environmental finance. Internalization is considered here as the process of pricing externalities to change production decisions. For example,

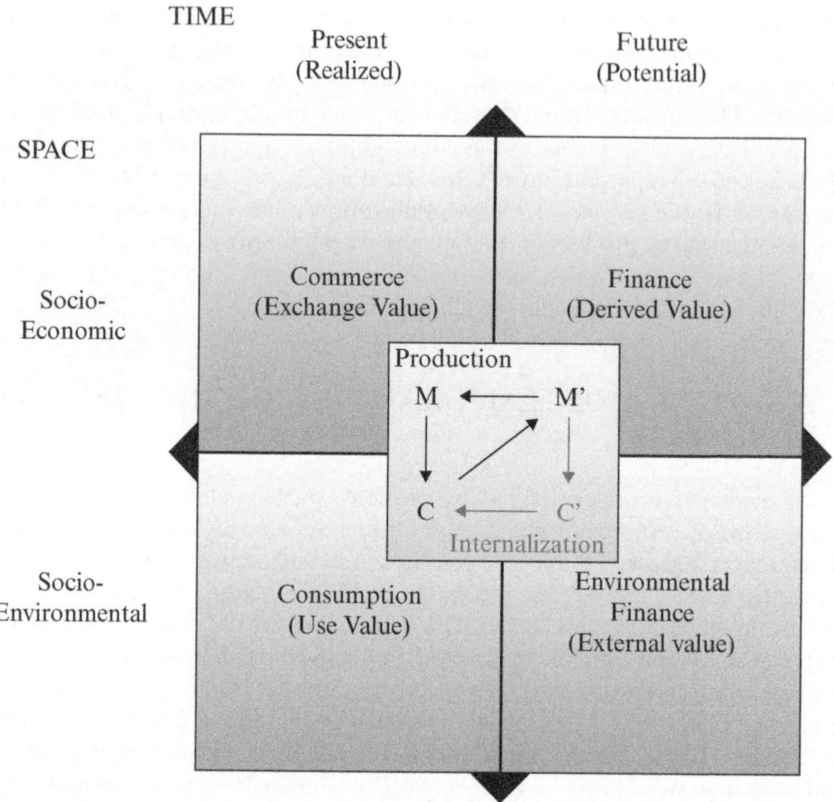

Figure 21.1 Typology of the spatial and temporal dynamics of circuits of value

accounting for the price of carbon dioxide released from the burning of fossil fuels might lead to the production of solar panels due to new relative price competiveness of solar energy over conventional thermal energy combined with a carbon price. The concept of the inverse commodity (C') is introduced to represent the certificates and other commodities such as carbon credits that are used to price externalities. Priced externalities are considered inverse commodities because rather than being built from the existence of something tangible, they are structured out of its absence (see for example Knox-Hayes, 2010). A carbon credit represents the absence rather than presence of 1 ton of carbon dioxide equivalent.

Crisis can be identified by a breakup of the flow (spatially and temporally) of value between types and circuits of capital in the equation M-C-M'. From Keynes' view, crises result from a failure to generate sufficient consumption of commodities (C). From Hayek's perspective, crisis is an issue of commerce, a failure to generate adequate means of production (M). Crisis can result from either of these disruptions to production, or simply from short-circuiting production by using finance to represent value that has not yet been created. In the diagram, production is denoted by the black arrows moving in a clockwise rotation from money (M) to commodities (C) to surplus money (M'), each situated with its associated type of value. Arguably, the circuit could also be short-circuited (M-M', as with some forms of derivatives trading) and money can be used to directly generate surplus value without ever mobilizing physical commodities. However, in both circuits (M-C-M' and M-M') the ultimate goal is to accumulate value in finance.

The surplus value is extracted both from natural resources as well as social labor. As Marx acknowledged with concepts like 'metabolic rift,' the production cycle by its very nature depletes the natural resources and social production systems upon which it relies. The pricing of externalities is designed to balance this circuit by forcing value from finance through externalities (inverse commodities) into the creation of environmentally beneficial technologies like renewable energy. This cycle is represented in the center of the diagram by the grey arrows moving from surplus value (M') to priced externalities (C') back to commodities (C). In theory, this circuit should close the loop and return value from finance or surplus accumulation to improve the quality of the natural environment or at the least to improve socio-environmental relations.

In this framework, environmental finance generates a parallel economy (parallel to the economy of production) that internalizes externalities and transforms production decisions to return value to the natural environment (Figure 21.2). In the subsequent sections I will explore the meaning and function of parallel economies.

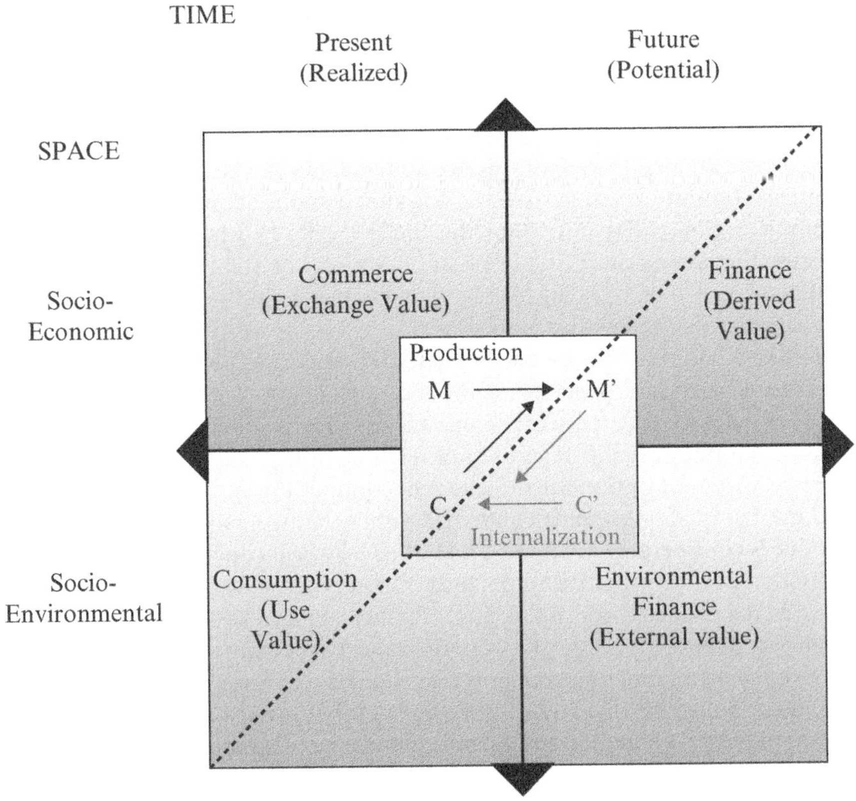

Figure 21.2 Parallel economies: the use of internalization to return value to the natural environment

21.6 ALTERNATIVE CIRCUITS OF CAPITAL: ENVIRONMENTAL FINANCE AND THE PARALLEL ECONOMY

The notion of parallel economies indicates several issues at play. First, parallel economies refer to the creation of externality pricing economies intended to balance the environmental impact of economic production. The notion of parallel economies also represents the ability to extend the value of physical resources from their present objective spatial and temporal connotation across space and time. Figure 21.2 illustrates both present and future or potential value with individual columns. While present value is singular (commodities and services exist in particular places and have value either in use or exchange at any given moment), future or potential value is unlimited. Figure 21.2 could therefore illustrate future value with innumerable columns moving to the right across time. Because future or potential value is subjective, within finance (and indeed even environmental finance) there exists the potential to create numerous layers of value from singular physical resources through the structuring of potential value (Knox-Hayes, 2013).

For example, returning to the consideration of a commodity such as a bushel of wheat, the bushel can be used through consumption to generate use value (lower left quadrant). It can also be first exchanged (upper left quadrant) and then consumed to generate use value – sold to a baker and baked into bread. However, as long as the value of the bushel of wheat is located with its physical existence it generates single sources of value (it can either be used or exchanged), but its value is very much in its present place and time. In contrast, the subjective value of the bushel of wheat can exist in numerous places and times. For example, finance can derive value from the wheat through the creation of a variety of 'options' to buy or sell the wheat at a specified price at various points in time. Multiple options (derivatives) for the single bushel of wheat can exist simultaneously because they represent future or potential sources of value spread across time. As suggested before, each of these instruments themselves have financial value, even if the underlying commodity is singular in its use.

The subjective nature of future and potential value creates concerns for the accounting of financial value and particularly for the ways in which financial value becomes represented in present time. Modern economic systems recognize all types of value as commensurate through pricing, regardless of qualifications of how, when and where value actually exists. A wheat option might generate a quantitatively similar price to a bushel of wheat, but the quality of value contained within the two as well as the consequence of their value is considerably different. The bushel of wheat can feed hungry people. The wheat option merely provides the opportunity for a potentially advantageous economic transaction in the future. This is not to say a financial option is without value, but rather that its value is qualitatively different from the value of a commodity itself. Therefore, in addition to offering an understanding of the relations of various economic spheres and processes, the topology in Figure 21.1 also suggests that the spatial and temporal nature of value is significant. Economic crises can result from a misrepresentation of the quality and scale of value operating across the circuits of capital.

In practice, there are several challenges with the ability of externality pricing to balance the social and environmental detriments of production. In order to operate effectively, environmental finance must create a truly parallel economy, of similar scale and scope, which internalizes the externalities of production and operates according to the specified pathway of finance accounting for externalities and generating environmentally beneficial commodities. The problem is that just as finance can short-circuit the cycle of production, creating paths for money to generate surplus value irrespective of underlying physical commodities, so too can environmental finance shortcut the cycle of externality pricing that should generate new technologies. Environmental finance can instead derive surplus value solely from the circulation of environmental externalities through financial transactions. In the subsequent sections, the structure of environmental finance is further detailed and some of the concerns for accounting the value of environmental assets are outlined.

21.7 ENVIRONMENTAL FINANCE: PATHWAYS, OPPORTUNITIES AND CHALLENGES

While natural resources have always been incorporated as productive inputs in economic systems, environmental finance has the potential to transform the way in which natural resources are valued in economic systems. Environmental finance manages natural resources through the pricing and trading of positive and negative externalities – environmental benefits or costs accrued from economic activities that are not accounted in economic transactions. For example, the burning of fossil fuels results in the emission of carbon dioxide and other greenhouse gases which are not accounted for in the price of energy unless a carbon-pricing scheme is put in place. To price externalities, the value of environmental resources is shifted from use value – the value of using a good or service, which is grounded in objective space and time – to external value derived from the good or service, which is value liberated in subjective space and time. The conversion of the use value of the natural environment (which is deeply embedded in physical-materiality) to financial or external value (value external to the consumption or exchange of the resource) through the pricing of the externalities presents some concerns that environmental finance will ultimately serve to devalue and destabilize – rather than preserve – natural environmental systems (Knox-Hayes, 2013). These concerns primarily stem from the mismatch between the scale of financial productivity that markets achieve and the material impacts they generate for natural resources. Environmental finance will undoubtedly have profound implications for energy and environment use in coming decades, particularly as financial markets are adapted to manage new sets of environmental asset classes.

21.8 EFFORTS TO RESOLVE CLIMATE CHANGE THROUGH THE PRICING OF EXTERNALITIES

The idea that market mechanisms utilizing well-defined property rights could be used to price and overcome the problem of negative externalities is a theory derived from Ronald Coase (1960). Early applications of Coase's theory of externalities, particularly the EPA's Acid Rain Trading Program in the United States, demonstrated the ability of markets to successfully control levels of pollution from sulfur (SO_x) and nitrogen (NO_x) oxides. Under the EPA program, yearly caps on SO_x and NO_x were established and heavy emitters were allocated a limited set of allowances to emit SO_x and NO_x (also called permits). The emitters could meet the cap either by reducing their emissions of SO_x and NO_x pollution in line with the permits they had been allocated or by buying additional permits from more efficient emitters who had reduced their levels of pollution below their established targets. The acid rain trading program was seen by many to be a success in the United States because SO_2 levels fell. The perhaps unintended consequence of the program however was the rise in coal use as electricity generation increased.

The general success of the Acid Rain Trading Program established the viability of using market-based approaches for addressing negative externalities. The precedent the program set established the foundations for treaties addressing climate change under the United Nations Framework Convention on Climate Change (UNFCCC). Climate change is framed first and foremost as an economic problem rooted in the failure to correctly commodify environmental externalities. The 1998 Kyoto Protocol introduced market mechanisms through which countries could cooperate to meet their national emissions reduction targets. Emissions trading in the Kyoto Protocol functions along lines similar to the trading systems set up under the Acid Rain Trading Program, wherein economic actors can buy and sell emissions permits under an overall emissions cap.

Both within and without the framework of the Kyoto Protocol, the cap and trade of emissions has become a common policy response around the globe to mitigating climate change. This policy response is again designed to create parallel economic activity that internalizes the cost of externalities through the creation and transaction of inverse commodities (C') such as carbon emissions credits (Knox-Hayes, 2010; Bumpus, 2011). Emissions trading systems have been set up in the European Union, in California and the Northeastern United States, in Australia (although the system was repealed a few years after initiation), China, Japan and South Korea. Additional systems are planned in the Ukraine, Turkey, Brazil, and Thailand. For a comprehensive overview in the development of emissions trading schemes see for example the World Bank's annual State and Trends of Carbon Pricing Report (Kossoy et al., 2014).

Environmental finance will eventually encompass a range of environmental externalities. The system has been initiated through market-based efforts to address climate change (Goodland, Daly and El Serafy, 2009; Newell and Paterson, 2010). Since the Kyoto Protocol came into force in 2004, a number of regulated and voluntary carbon management systems have been set up around the world aiming to achieve CO_2 emissions reductions, largely through cap and trade mechanisms (Michaelowa and Michaelowa, 2007). The oldest of these systems is the European Union Emissions Trading System (EU ETS), which caps the emissions of more than 10,000 industrial facilities in Europe. Additionally, regulated markets have been created in Australia, China, Japan, New Zealand, and South Korea. Finally, trial emissions markets are being established in a range of countries including Brazil, Chile, Mexico, Indonesia, and Thailand (Kossoy et al., 2014).

Each system is structured with its own unique rules and procedures, but all carbon markets operate in a similar way. Regulators or market authorities in each system place a cap on the amount of carbon that can be emitted by various greenhouse gas emitters, such as power plants, heavy industrial corporations, waste management facilities and so on. If the carbon emitted by a capped entity exceeds its cap, the entity must purchase credits to offset its emissions. Entities that do not reach their cap, can sell excess permits onto the carbon market. In theory, the cap is ratcheted down in time, and emitters either become more efficient or go out of business. The system is meant to be more flexible than command and control regulation or even taxes because emitters have greater flexibility in how they meet their targets. Either way the systems should reduce the total amount of emissions under the cap as well as send a price signal through the markets that benefits carbon-alternative fuel sources and technologies.[2] Much of the challenge and uncertainty of the markets resides in the details of the design as well as the enforcement of rules (Lohmann, 2009). One of the biggest challenges is the nature of the construction of the carbon credits as inverse commodities, based on the absence rather than physical presence of something (Knox-Hayes, 2010).

Although there are differences across the schemes, all carbon markets trade two main types of credits: allowances and offsets, which are measured in units equivalent to 1 ton of CO_2 (Michaelowa, 2004). Both products are constructed purely from information. Allowances are essentially permits, which allow regulated entities to emit a certain amount of greenhouse gases. Offsets serve as reduction credits and mark the absence of an emissions occurrence in one location for transfer to another. Both credit types are constructed through a system of measurement that creates baselines or projection scenarios of the levels of greenhouse gas emission that would occur without intervention (see for example Bansal and Knox-Hayes, 2013). As such the reality of emissions reduction through carbon markets cannot be proven, only presented through arguments of 'additionality' (additional greenhouse gas reductions) both within and external to each system (Mason and Plantinga, 2013).

Because the markets trade commodities that are measured against otherwise assumed realities it becomes very difficult to assess whether the markets are reducing emissions. A number of scholars have highlighted design flaws, failures, and pervasive weaknesses in implementation of emissions markets (Knight, 2008; Lohmann, 2009; MacKenzie, 2009). However, there arguably have also been positive developments from the emissions markets, such as the establishment of the carbon disclosure project, an initiative that asks some of the world's largest companies to voluntarily disclose their emissions. In measuring their carbon liabilities, companies have suggested they identify inefficiencies and reduce carbon emissions (Plambeck, 2012). As a consequence of initiatives such as these, the business community is becoming increasingly aware of carbon liabilities, and policy responses to climate change are beginning to assume a business logic (Knox-Hayes and Levy, 2011).

Nevertheless, the challenge with the carbon markets is that they do not fully accommodate the spatial and temporal scale at which carbon dioxide and other greenhouse gases actually cycle within the ecosphere, and particularly the rate of actual removal from the atmosphere (Bansal and Knox-Hayes, 2013; Knox-Hayes, 2013). The valuation and trade of a highly abstract commodity constructed from compressed information (compressed in the sense that the information of instruments is reduced to a serial number, quantity, price, and so on) does not fully capture the ecological complexity of the system the credits are designed to represent. In particular, there is a disjuncture in the rate and scale of greenhouse gas pollution that is not fully accounted for in carbon markets, which create instruments that are absent in space and time.

Regardless of their potential inability to have a material impact, carbon credits are exchanged as financial instruments, and they carry financial value. As such they can circulate as a system of capital that never directly leads to changes in technological or energy usage. Furthermore, through the creation of carbon derivatives such as collateralized carbon obligations (Lotay, 2009), they can generate a perverse economy through which C' generates M' short-circuiting the intended return of value to the natural environment (Figure 21.1). Ironically, the emissions markets and the environmental markets that will follow from them are intended to grant value to undervalued services, but through financialization they diminish environmental value. The application of these markets to the management of environmental systems may suggest adverse consequences for environmental systems by undervaluing the rate at which environmental systems operate and reproduce themselves.

21.9 THE CREATION OF ENVIRONMENTAL FINANCE

In addition to mitigating greenhouse gases, carbon emissions markets also serve as demonstration markets: if greenhouse gases can be successfully regulated through market mechanisms, then so too can virtually every positive and negative externality. Pilot programs have been trialed to manage other negative externalities, including water pollution. Further, a series of markets to manage positive externalities such as forestry and biodiversity are being created. For example, a program called Reducing Emissions from Deforestation and Degradation (REDD) is being negotiated under the UNFCCC. This program would finance the positive externalities (including carbon syncing and biodiversity preservation) of the world's forests (particularly rainforests) with funding from emissions trading programs and private and public environmental funds. The establishment of markets to trade carbon emissions, forestry and biodiversity demonstrate the widespread belief in the potential of environmental finance to manage negative externalities.

Gretchen Daily (1997) coined the term 'ecosystem services' to describe the ways in which the positive externalities generated by the world's ecosystems are capital assets. The logic of pricing environmental externalities can be extended to suggest that the function of the biosphere itself could be priced. According to Daily et al. (2000), for example, ecosystems can be priced to manage the flow of vital services, including the production of goods (such as seafood and timber), and life support processes (such as water filtration and pollination). Moreover, ecosystems have value in terms of the conservation of future use options (such as preserving genetic diversity for future medicinal use). Despite these potential benefits, it is challenging to directly price ecosystems. Relative to other forms of capital, ecosystems are poorly understood, scarcely monitored, and (in many cases) undergoing rapid degradation and depletion. Market prices often do not reflect the full social costs of production, and most ecosystem services are presently not traded on markets. Additionally, methods of indirect revealed preference (for example, valuing clean air by comparing land rents in clean versus polluted areas) are not relevant to setting a value on the existence of certain assets (such as the satisfaction derived from contemplating the existence of a tropical rainforest). Finally, measuring the value of ecosystem services based on avoidance of costs provides only partial, lower bound indications of value, especially for services without adequate substitutes.

Undeterred by these challenges, Robert Costanza et al. (1997) have estimated the financial worth of the biosphere to be in the range of US$16–54 trillion per year. To put this in perspective, they highlight the fact that the global gross national product in 1997 was

US$18 trillion. In other words, the unaccounted economic functions of the biosphere (the sum of positive externalities) are on a yearly average twice the size of the global economy. The pricing of ecosystem services suggests that there is tremendous untapped value to be gained from the pricing of the functions of the ecosphere. In combination with programs such as sulfur trading and carbon trading which value the avoidance of negative externalities, these efforts to price the value of ecosystem services demonstrates the scale and potential at which environmental finance could operate.

The inclusion of the full sum of ecosystem services into financial services would at the least double the size of the economy. However, the productivity arising from integrating ecosystem services is not really based on the creation of new avenues of resources but rather on the valuation of existing environmental resources in parallel ways (Figure 21.1). First, natural resources are valued in the conventional sense of economic inputs (lower left quadrant in Figure 21.1); second, the generation of positive and negative externalities from the environmental resources are valued (lower right quadrant in Figure 21.1). In other words, the valuation and integration of ecosystems services into financial systems has the potential to create parallel economies (economies of use and economies of quality of natural resources), increasing not only the scope, but also the scale of financial incursion into environmental resources. For environmental finance to achieve its full potential, however, it must transform the natural environment into new sources of assets. Ecosystem service pricing demonstrates the value of environmental positive externalities and the potential for the marketization of externalities to create parallel economies that magnify financial value.

In addition to carbon emissions markets, a series of markets to value positive externalities such as forestry and biodiversity are being created. For example, a program called Reducing Emissions from Deforestation and Degradation (REDD) would finance the positive externalities (including carbon sinking and biodiversity preservation) of the world's forests (particularly rainforests) with funding from emissions trading programs and private and public environmental funds. The establishment of markets to trade carbon emissions, forestry and biodiversity demonstrate the widespread belief in the potential of environmental finance to manage externalities.

21.10 CONCLUSION

Real world events, notably the recent financial crisis, exemplify the importance of efforts within economic geography to understand capitalism's institutions. In this chapter I argue that circuits of capital can be used to understand relationships between socio-economic and environmental systems, as well as the ways in which value is mobilized across time. The issues of spatial and temporal circulation are essential to the function of production, to the nature of both economic and ecological crises, and finally potentially to the solution as well. As an alternative circuit of capital, environmental finance can either serve to produce a parallel economy to the productive economy, which returns value to the natural environment, or it can work to further destabilize the natural environment by enhancing the logic of financialization.

Carbon markets are a representation of the logic of financialization. They are designed to mitigate the physical impacts of anthropogenic climate change by coordinating the global reduction of greenhouse gas production. To do this they must build an extensive network with the aim of changing collective behavior. By transforming the material problem of CO_2 emissions into financial instruments, the markets can communicate value to disparate places. Carbon emission reduction in Europe can be linked to clean energy production in China. Such a connection could have the potential to reduce the global emissions impact as well as to communicate and share the philosophical as well as exchange value of reducing emissions across national boundaries.

Indeed the process of financialization has benefits. Despite the multiple shortcomings of carbon markets, they have arguably had an impact on raising market awareness for the need and potential value of reducing emissions. Finance can be useful in translating aspects of the natural world into economic systems in a language that permeates national and cultural boundaries (Knox-Hayes and Hayes, 2014). Finance also creates mobility through the compression of a spatially and temporally embedded resource into a financial instrument that enhances the mobilization of exchange value. The greater the extent that a product is composed of information the greater its reach or ability to be mobilized and accessed in different places and across time (Marx and Engels, 1965). It is difficult to mobilize a physical resource, a bushel of wheat for example, because it is bound to a specific place and exists in a temporal frame, whereas a financial certificate representing wheat, or even the future existence of wheat, in contrast has tremendous spatial and temporal mobility. Likewise carbon credits can be accessed from the portals of traders all over the world, and individuals around the world may come to value the absence of carbon emissions because of the existence and communication through the markets of a price signal.

However, financialization also presents dangers in the way it represents the natural world. Finance transforms the physical process of reducing emissions into compressed representations. The exchange value of the credits becomes disconnected from the process or reducing emissions. There is considerable doubt whether emissions markets produce material use value, because it is uncertain as to whether or not emissions reductions are achieved through the construction of the credits (Ellerman, Joskow, Harrison, and Pew Center on Global Climate Change, 2003; Lohmann, 2005, 2009). The markets are producing exchange value that can be represented in financial capital; recent estimates suggest the markets were worth $144 billion in 2009 (Knox-Hayes, 2010), but the question remains are they really producing use value by reducing emissions? If the value of carbon markets is representative primarily of intermediary financial services and derivatives trading, the emissions markets arguably are not producing real use value. To be meaningful value must be useful; it must be connected to material impact, which is inevitably embedded in space and time. As I argue here, there is reason to be skeptical that managing environmental processes by removing them from their spatial and temporal contexts by way of financialization can be successful. Furthermore, distortions of space and time in the representation of value may lead to the mismanagement of resources and ultimately can produce financial crises.

The construction of financial markets to serve as systems of governance challenges environmental processes, which are embedded in physical materiality (Daly, 1992; O'Neill, 2007). While the productivity of economic (the rate of good and service production for example) and social systems (the rate and scale of communication for example) can be accelerated through the operation of digital networks, environmental systems cannot withstand the pressures to accelerate their rate of productivity in line with financialization. Overconsumption of these systems will lead to collapse. Markets to conserve forests can trade the exchange value of the trees around the globe instantaneously, but the trees still require decades if not centuries to reproduce themselves. Their use value, if not their intrinsic value, is deeply embedded in space and time. In divorcing the spatial and temporal scale of use value from exchange value, financial markets are unlikely to address the very real and material demands our society places on the natural environment.

To be made more effective the systems of environmental finance, and perhaps even finance, must be made to account for spatial and temporal scale. There are a number of ways in which this could be envisioned, including having instruments that have geographic limits on the extent to which they can be traded, forcing accountability and linkage between the revenue of projects and the credits to which they belong. Additionally, there could be temporal restrictions placed on the exchange of environmental instruments such that their rate of turnover is slowed to better represent the underlying physical processes of the natural environment valued by the instruments. It might even be possible to imagine a system through which property rights could be transformed such that instruments of environmental finance could have fixed use but flexible exchange parameters. In such an instance, the instruments would allow for the generation of exchange value, but guarantee a specific type and quality of use value to the natural environment. In any case, to better accommodate the function of environmental systems, the parallel economy must seek to entrain the spatial and temporal scale of production and reproduction between the socio-economic, and socio-environmental worlds.

Climate change is a multifaceted problem, which signals the dangers of current economic activities and of the increasing disconnect between socio-economic and environmental productivity (Newell and Paterson, 2010). Environmental finance accomplishes several things. It accelerates the evolution of information governance, and creates a digital monitoring and valuation network for the natural environment that is becoming global in scope. It also serves to communicate the potential value of priced positive and negative externalities to communities around the globe, but in so doing it may fail to address the underlying problem; human systems have become over-productive undermining the spatial and temporal regenerative requirements of environmental systems. Environmental finance is almost certainly capable of generating exchange value, but to be meaningful it must make real the promise of a parallel economy capable of countering the ecological waste and destruction of an economic system that is designed only to extract and never to return value.

NOTES

1. It should be noted that the concept of use and exchange value has a much longer history. For example Aristotle expounds on the concept of use and exchange value in *The Politics* (Barker, 1952).
2. For a more detailed description of the operation and tension within several of the regulated carbon markets see for example Knox-Hayes and Hayes (2014).

REFERENCES

Bansal, P. and J. Knox-Hayes (2013), 'The time and space of materiality in organizations and the natural environment', *Organization & Environment*. doi: 10.1177/1086026612475069.

Barker, E. (1952), *Aristotle: Politics*, London: Oxford University Press.

Bryan, D. and M. Rafferty (2006), *Capitalism with Derivatives*, New York: Palgrave Macmillan.

Bumpus, A.G. (2011), 'The matter of carbon: understanding the materiality of tCO_2e in Carbon offsets', *Antipode*, **43** (3), 612–638.

Castells, M. (1996), *The Rise of the Network Society*, Oxford: Blackwell.

Christophers, B. (2010), 'On voodoo economics: theorising relations of property, value and contemporary capitalism', *Transactions of the Institute of British Geographers*, **35** (1), 94–108.

Coase, Ronald H. (1960), 'The problem of social cost', in *Classic Papers in Natural Resource Economics*, London: Palgrave Macmillan, pp. 87–137.

Costanza, Robert et al. (1997), 'The value of the world's ecosystem services and natural capital', *Nature*, **387**, 253–260.

Cronon, W. (1990), 'Modes of prophecy and production: placing nature in history', *The Journal of American History*, 1122–1131.

Cronon, W. (1993), 'The uses of environmental history', *Environmental History Review*, **17** (3), 1–22.

Daily, Gretchen (1997), *Nature's Services: Societal Dependence On Natural Ecosystems*, Washington, DC: Island Press.

Daily, Gretchen C. et al. (2000), 'The value of nature and the nature of value', *Science*, **289** (5478), 395–396.

Daly, H.E. (1992), 'Allocation, distribution, and scale: towards an economics that is efficient, just, and sustainable', *Ecological Economics*, **6** (3), 185–193.

de Soto, H. (2000), *The Mystery of Capital: Why Capitalism Triumphs in the West and Fails Everywhere Else*, New York: Basic Books.

Diamond, J. (2005), *Collapse: How Societies Choose to Fail or Succeed*, London: Penguin.

Ellerman, A.D., P.L. Joskow, D. Harrison and Pew Center on Global Climate Change (2003), *Emissions Trading in the US: Experience, Lessons, and Considerations for Greenhouse Gases*, Arlington, VA: Pew Center for Global Climate Change.

Epstein, G.A. (2005), *Financialization and the World Economy*, Cheltenham, UK and Northampton, MA, USA: Edward Elgar Publishing.

Foster, J.B. (1999), 'Marx's theory of metabolic rift: classical foundations for environmental sociology: 1', *American Journal of Sociology*, **105** (2), 366–405.

Goodland, R.J.A., H.E. Daly and S. El Serafy (2009), 'The urgent need for rapid transition to global environmental sustainability', *Environmental Conservation*, **20** (4), 297–309.

Harvey, D. (1982), *The Limits to Capital*, Chicago: University of Chicago Press.

Harvey, D. (1990), *The Condition of Postmodernity*, Oxford: Blackwell.

Harvey, D. (2011), 'The enigma of capital'. Retrieved on 11 November 2016 from https://global.oup.com/academic/product/the-enigma-of-capital-9780199758715?cc=us&lang=en&.

Hayek, F.A. (1931), *Prices and Production*, New York: Augustus Kelly.

Hayek, F.A. (2014), *The Road to Serfdom: Text and Documents: The Definitive Edition*, London: Routledge.

Kettell, S. (2004), 'The political economy of exchange rate policy-making', in *The Political Economy of Exchange Rate Policy-Making*, London: Palgrave Macmillan, pp. 10–32.

Kettell, S. (2006), Circuits of capital and overproduction: a Marxist analysis of the present world economic crisis, *Review of Radical Political Economics*, **38** (1), 24–44.

Keynes, J.M. (1937), 'The general theory of employment', *The Quarterly Journal of Economics*, 209–223.

Knight, E.R.W. (2008), 'The economic geography of carbon market trading: how legal regimes and environmental performance influence share performance under a carbon market', SSRN Working Papers. Retrieved on 20 October 2016 from http://ssrn.com/abstract=1302982.

Knox-Hayes, J. (2010), 'Constructing carbon market spacetime: climate change and the onset of neo-modernity', *Annals of the Association of American Geographers*, **100** (4), 953–962.

Knox-Hayes, J. (2013), 'The spatial and temporal dynamics of value in financialization: analysis of the infrastructure of carbon markets', *Geoforum*, **50**, 117–128.

Knox-Hayes, J. and J. Hayes (2014), 'Technocratic norms, political culture and climate change governance', *Geografiska Annaler: Series B, Human Geography*, **96** (3), 261–276.

Knox-Hayes, J. and D.L. Levy (2011), 'The politics of carbon disclosure as climate governance' Available at SSRN 1830401.

Kossoy, A., K. Oppermann, A. Platonova-Oquab, S. Suphachalasai, N. Höhne, N. Klein and Q. Wu (2014), 'State and trends of carbon pricing 2014', *World Bank*. Retrieved on 20 October 2016 from https://wdronline.worldbank.com/handle/10986/18415.

Krippner, G. (2005), 'The financialization of the American economy', *Socio-Economic Review*, **3** (2), 173–208.
Krippner, G.R. (2010), 'The political economy of financial exuberance', *Research in the Sociology of Organizations*, **30**, 141–173.
Lefebvre, H. (1991), *The Production of Space*, Oxford: Blackwell.
Leyshon, A. and N. Thrift (2007), 'The capitalization of almost everything: the future of finance and capitalism', *Theory, Culture & Society*, **24** (7–8), 97.
Lohmann, L. (2005), 'Marketing and making carbon dumps: commodification, calculation and counterfactuals in climate change mitigation', *Science as Culture*, **14** (3), 203–235.
Lohmann, L. (2009), 'Toward a different debate in environmental accounting: the cases of carbon and cost–benefit', *Accounting, Organizations and Society*, **34** (3–4), 499–534.
Lotay, Jessie S. (2009), 'Subprime carbon: fashioning an appropriate regulatory and legislative response to the emerging us carbon market to avoid a repeat of history in carbon structured finance and derivative instruments', *Houson Journal of International Law*, **32**, 459.
MacKenzie, D. (2009), *Material Markets: How Economic Agents Are Constructed*, Oxford: Oxford University Press.
Marx, K. (1867), *Capital, Volume I*, Harmondsworth: Penguin/New Left Review.
Marx, K. (1993), *Grundrisse*, London: Penguin.
Marx, K. and F. Engels (1965), *The German Ideology (1845)*, London: International Publishers Co. (1970).
Marx, K. and M. Nicolaus (1973), *Grundrisse: Foundations of the Critique of Political Economy*, Harmondsworth: Penguin/New Left Review.
Mason, C.F. and A.J. Plantinga (2013), 'The additionality problem with offsets: optimal contracts for carbon sequestration in forests', *Journal of Environmental Economics and Management*, **66** (1), 1–14.
Michaelowa, A. (2004), 'CDM incentives in industrialized countries-the long and winding road', *International Review for Environmental Strategies*, **5** (1), 217–231.
Michaelowa, A. and K. Michaelowa (2007), 'Climate or development: is ODA diverted from its original purpose?', *Climatic Change*, **84** (1), 5–21.
Mol, A.P.J. and G. Spaargaren (2000), 'Ecological modernisation theory in debate: a review', *Environmental Politics*, **9** (1), 17–49.
Newell, P. and M. Paterson (2010), *Climate Capitalism: Global Warming and the Transformation of the Global Economy*, Cambridge: Cambridge University Press.
O'Neill, J. (2007), *Markets, Deliberation and Environment*, London: Routledge.
Plambeck, E.L. (2012), 'Reducing greenhouse gas emissions through operations and supply chain management', *Energy Economics*, **34**, S64–S74.
Ramsay, J. (2005), 'The real meaning of value in trading relationships', *International Journal of Operations and Production Management*, **25** (6), 549–565.
Reinhart, C.M. and K.S. Rogoff (2008), 'Is the 2007 US sub-prime financial crisis so different? An international historical comparison', National Bureau of Economic Research.
Smith, A. (1776), *The Wealth of Nations* (E. Cannan, ed., 1937 edition), New York: Modern Library.
Thrift, N. (2005), *Knowing Capitalism*, New York: Sage Publications.

22. Geographies of alternative, complementary and community currencies

Peter North

22.1 INTRODUCTION

Recent years has seen a mushrooming of alternative, complementary and community currencies, established by subaltern and community groups and NGOs as an alternative to or as a complement to state-created money (the pound, dollar or euro). Examples include community-based exchange networks such as Local Exchange Trading Schemes (LETS) established in the 1990s, electronic and paper-based currencies denominated in time (Ithaca Hours, Time Banks), and more recently local scrip circulating in small towns (BerkShares, Lewes, Stroud or Bristol Pounds). The economic crisis of 2001 that devastated Argentina's economy led to mass use of community and NGO created scrip, as cash points jammed up in an attempt to limit the effects of a bank run on the Argentine Peso (Gómez, 2008; North, 2007). The advent of the Eurozone crisis meant they later emerged in Greece (Sotiropoulou, 2011; Thanou et al., 2013) and Spain (Cha, 2012).

As the chapters in this Handbook show, money has always been diverse and evolves over time from cowries and tally sticks through silver and gold to paper and electronic money (Ingham, 2004). It has had different geographies (Cohen, 1998), being at times attached to and performing a key role in constructing the legitimacy of nation states, while at other times weak states have used currency of another state (Croatia using the German mark in the 1990s, contemporary Panama and Ecuador using the US dollar). Sometimes this works well, sometimes it can be disastrous (Argentina in 2001) or lack credibility (proposals for an independent Scotland to keep the UK pound). As Viviana Zelizer (1997, 2005) has shown, we have different attitudes to the acceptability of using money in some social settings, not in others. At times, states favour strong, limited currencies to enforce contracts and labour discipline, at others easy access to credit is felt appropriate to facilitate economic development: see the 'great compromise' in the nineteenth century for hard money in the eastern United States, and a looser arrangement involving notes issued by local (sometimes fraudulent) banks in the west (Galbraith, 1975). This diversity in the form of money is reflected in the late twentieth- and early twenty-first-century effervescence of community and alternative currencies.

How to make sense of such a bewildering diversity? Advocates of alternative currencies have a variety of critiques of the way bank-created fiat money works. This chapter will first examine the rationales for creating alternative currencies before painting some pen pictures of contemporary alternative currencies and analysing the strengths and weaknesses of the different models. This analysis can, very simply, be organized around a consideration (a) of complementary currencies that enable calculations to be undertaken about value to be enumerated in relation either to time or in alignment with conventional currencies; (b) those that are manifested in paper (or scrip) forms, and those that are purely

Table 22.1 Typology of alternative currencies

Name of currency	Valuation	Physical form	Extent of area in which it circulates
Local exchange trading schemes	Aligned to national currency with an hourly rate	Electronic, accounts on a personal computer, pay by cheque	Neighbourhood or small town
Time banks	One credit for one hour's work, non-negotiable	Electronic, accounts on a personal computer	Network around an organization
Ithaca and other Hours	Hours	Scrip	Small town and its hinterland
Transition currencies and BerkShares	Aligned to, convertible with, and backed by national currency	Scrip, mobile phone app	Small town or borough of London and its hinterland
Bristol Pound, German regional currencies	Aligned to, convertible with, and backed by national currency	Scrip, debit card, mobile phone app	City region

electronic, and (c) the geographic scale in which they circulate. Table 22.1 summarizes the differences between Local Exchange Trading Schemes or LETS, Time Banks, Ithaca and other hours, the Transition Currencies and BerkShares, and more recent currencies that operate at a city region (the Bristol Pound) or regional level (German regional currencies).

22.2 THE RATIONALE FOR ALTERNATIVE CURRENCIES

There is a long, perhaps hidden history of contestation over the form of money (see North, 2007) which rather died out during that period in the twentieth century when the battle between visions of possible futures was between competing state strategies – consumer-led capitalism within a regulated mixed economy in the Global North and West, state-led socialism in the USSR and China, and state-led developmentalism in the Global South. All focused on the state as the engine of development, but rarely considered the form of money. The state issued and regulated money, and the debate about it was about how much should be issued, and who should get it. Alternatives to 'money as it is' were considered either utopian or suspect. As Galbraith (1975: 51) put it, money reformers were considered to be either fools or thieves:

> Those who supported sound money and the gold standard were good men. Those that did not were not. If they knew what they were about, they were only marginally better than thieves. If they did not, they were cranks. In neither case could they be accepted into the company of reputable citizens.

At this time, even socialists agreed: they wanted to be revolutionaries, not knaves. The dominance of what J.K. Gibson-Graham (2006a) call 'capitalocentric' thinking meant that examining the form of money, outside 'precapitalist' societies in the Global South, was limited even by anthropologists who wanted to think outside the formal conceptions of how complex market economies work (Peck, 2013: 1557). Money was a rather uninteresting part of the wider capitalist system, what Schumpeter called a '"garb" or "veil" over things that really matter'. For Schumpeter, 'not only can (money) be discarded when we are analysing the fundamental features of the economic process but *it must be discarded just as a veil must be drawn aside to see what is behind it*' (Schumpeter, 1954 quoted by Ingham [2004: 17] – emphasis added). This conceptually constrained way of thinking about (or not thinking about) money continued even past the historical defeat of state socialism and 'the end of history' (Fukuyama, 1992) after the fall of the Berlin Wall in 1989. Socialists debated ways to overthrow capitalism, not experiment with the form of money (or with different types of markets).

The green and environmental movement was, though, more open to thinking about money as part of their wider critique of growth as fundamentally unsustainable in a finite 'spaceship earth' (Douthwaite, 1999; Kennedy, 1996). In particular, they objected to, and continue to object to, the ability of banks to create fiat money out of thin air in the form of loans and mortgages, which will have to be paid back with interest, thereby inevitably fuelling growth (Dittmer, 2015; Jackson and Dyson, 2012). They objected to the way that globalization enables money to flow to where it is able to gain the highest reward, perhaps in the process devastating local economies that are experiencing these disadvantageous changes in global trade flows and investment patterns, advocating ecolocalization – the building of locally owned and controlled economies – as a response (Douthwaite, 1996; Shuman, 2001; Woodin and Lucas, 2004). They objected to the cyclical nature of market capitalism, where periodic economic crises can similarly devastate local communities. As part of their strategy for economic community-led localization, they advocated the use of local currencies to help build what Dauncey in an influential book published in 1988 called a 'harbour in the storm'. For Dauncey (1988), the 'rainbow economy' would emerge from the crises of the newly deregulated global capitalism. This locally owned, convivial, sustainable rainbow economy would value the done by working people, especially people working in areas that market economies poorly reward such as care-based work commonly undertaken by women, childcare, work done by children or older people, work done perhaps imperfectly or more slowly by people unable to compete on price, speed of delivery or quality alone, or work remunerated less well than that done by elites (for example, lawyers, bankers, advertising executives).

A key tool for this community-led eco-localization would be local or community-created currencies. A number of studies of the first wave of these currencies, Local Exchange Trading Schemes, examined their potential for providing new forms of work and employment for those who were excluded from it (Williams, 1996a, 1996b; Williams et al., 2001), for remoralizing (Lee, 1996) and, in a Polanyian sense, re-embedding money within the everyday practices through which people meet their needs, and as a way for those who felt isolated to meet new people and build a sense of community (Seyfang, 2003a, 2003b). Meeting practical needs and meeting new people was a strong draw to many who joined Local Exchange Trading Schemes, and later time banks. Pacione (1997) and North (1999a, 2006) examined the motivations of those activists who joined LETS schemes for more overtly political reasons. North (1999a) argued that LETS schemes could be seen as a micropolitical resistance to the systems of domination associated with capitalism, through which members of LETS tried to live by different codes around the place of money in wider economies (as a thing of value of itself, or as a way to measure, calculate, facilitate exchange, and store value over time). LETS facilitated debates about what sorts of work should be valued, and about the role of community in economic lives. Pacione (1997) saw them as islands of resistance to globalization.

In his ethnographic study of Manchester LETS, a network of over 500 traders in the 1990s, North (2006) differentiated between activists who saw local currencies as an apolitical innovation in the form of money that has no more significance than air miles or paying by debit card as opposed to cash, and those who took a more overtly political stance. The latter he divided into 'humanisers' who wanted a complementary currency that would operate alongside conventional money but which would value those that market economies do not value or under reward. They wanted an economy where the relationships between people mattered. Greeners supported Dauncey's rainbow economy which would, in time they hoped, replace unsustainable and crisis ridden fossil fuel capitalism. For greeners, LETS were a precursor of this coming transformation as, later, were the scrip based local currencies like Ithaca Hours and the transition currencies (North, 2010c). Finally, North identified green anarchists who wanted to develop islands of co-operation as demonstrators of what a more liberated economy could look like and as a place where co-operative skills could be developed. They had less faith than the greeners that the transition to a rainbow economy could be as smooth as the latter suggested it would be.

Alternative currencies raise a number of issues for geographical theory. First, how alternative are they (Jonas, 2010)? To what extent do they enable Dauncey's (1988) 'harbours in the storm' of globalization to be constructed? Are ordinary people able to enact forms of money that are not issued by states, and if so, are they able to reform the substantive nature of economies through changed practices; or do they remain as visions of what could be, critiques of what is wrong with 'money as is', and of market economies? Are they manifestations of, or ways of manifesting, Gibson-Graham's (2006a, 2006b) diverse economies, economies constructed by a far wider range of motivations and practices than work for a capitalist employer and exchange based on profit and utility maximization? Second, what scale do these localized economies operate at? How 'local' is local – the neighbourhood, town, city, city region or region? Given that geographers know that regions are relational and intertwined, rather than distinct and cut off from each other and that economic activities operate at a range of intersecting and cross-cutting scales (Massey, 1992, 1994), does it make sense to try to cut off or privilege one scale (the local) above others, or is this an example of what geographers call the 'local trap', assuming that the 'local' is an appropriate scale in which to confront global problems (Brown and Purcell, 2005; North, 2005, 2010a)? These are issues we return to below, after a series of pen pictures to help the reader understand more concretely how alternative currencies work.

22.3 CONTEMPORARY ALTERNATIVE CURRENCIES

From Brixton LETS to the Brixton Pound, London

Local Exchange Trading Schemes (in the UK), Talente (in Germany, Hungary), and Grains of Salt (France) use a local currency based on a number of units per hour, sometimes with a locally significant name such as ('Tales' in Canterbury, 'Brights' in Brighton, or 'Bobbins' in Manchester) (Williams, 1996a, 1996b; North, 2006). Members advertise their wants and needs in a directory, and then trading takes place lubricated by this local currency, preferably without the use of any national currency (although this is not prohibited). LETS units have no physical form: users write a cheque in the local money units to pay for goods and services. Account balances showing how much everyone has exchanged with each other are kept on a computer, and start with an opening balance of zero – the member can spend LETS units they don't yet have from day one which they back with a 'commitment' to earn, at a later date, sufficient local money to return their account to zero. The person commissioning the work has their account debited, and the person doing the work is credited the same amount; so the totality of credits paid in and out of all accounts across the network balances out at zero. All members' balances and turnovers are publicly available, and members are expected to take their accounts back to zero before they leave the network to prevent a member running up a large negative balance and then absconding. These latter facets are designed to facilitate trust, and to ensure that the currency acts as an effective store of value over time. Some LETS networks now have over 20 years trading experience under their belt (North, 2010b).

Brixton LETS was a typical LETS scheme in the 1990s. The Brixton LETS currency was the Brick, with one Brick equivalent to one pound. There was a recommended rate of five Bricks for an hour's work. Like many other LETS schemes, Brixton LETS was a conscious attempt to materialize a green, community-based economy from out of south London's vibrant and environmentalist and do-it-yourself (DIY) networks. By the mid-1990s Brixton LETS had grown to some 350 members who had collectively traded some 47,000 Bricks. Like many LETS schemes, Brixton LETS was also not without its problems. The network covered the whole of the borough of Lambeth which, being long and thin, is not a natural economic area for trading day-to-day services, but is also too small to include a large variety of goods and services. While its founder members came from a vibrant activist community, their militantly anti-hierarchical ethos meant that organization was somewhat chaotic. Accounts were done manually, LETS cheques were kept in a box on someone's floor, and cash in a jam jar. While this worked for a small network of like-minded people, it struggled to cope with the volume of transactions generated by a network of 350 members, and in time the network atrophied. In time, however, the idea of a local currency was resurrected in the form of the Brixton Pound, discussed below.

Time Banks: From Walnut Creek, San Francisco to Catford, London and Athens, Greece

Time Banks connect people who exchange services rewarded with time-based credits called time or service credits (Cahn, 2000; Seyfang, 2003a). One time credit is paid for one hour's work. Members needing help contact a broker who finds someone to meet the request, arranges for the service to be provided, and records the transaction in a time bank account which stores the accumulated credits on a computer. Although members are encouraged to both give and receive, there is no obligation for this to be in balance. Rather, the philosophy is that members contribute to and receive from the time bank as collective, and if a member needs to receive more support than she can realistically ever give back, that is not a problem. The advantage of this model over LETS is that vulnerable people are helped more effectively as they are not left to find someone to meet their needs, perhaps making a number of phone calls to members of a LETS network in which people's commitment to the idea of sharing their skills with others is greater than their willingness, or ability, to actually do it given other day-to-day calls on their time.

Time banks are often run by NGOs in the health and social services sectors as part of a wider portfolio of services for vulnerable people. The broker takes responsibility for making sure that needs are met, and if this is not from within the network, then they will make alternative arrangements which might be statutory support. This means both that time banks are integrated with wider social services provision, and the services provided will be more reliable and of a higher quality than those run on a DIY basis by a group of (admittedly well meaning) activists. The agency also ensures that the value of the credits will be maintained over time. Time banks thus have the potential to be a better store of value than LETS (North, 2003). Time money is enthusiastically supported by advocates of a mixed economy of welfare through which service users and professionals co-produce services which, they argue, will be more effectively targeted on need and more democratically delivered than would be the case from a perhaps bureaucratic, unresponsive, one-size-fits-all state delivered welfare system (Cahn, 2000). For some, this is a worryingly neoliberal approach (North, 2011). Time banks have flourished in communities as diverse as the Rossmore gated retirement community outside San Francisco to the Rushy Green doctor's surgery in Catford, South London (North, 2010c: 88–102). As a result of the Eurozone crisis, Athens Time Bank, the first Greek alternative currency network was established in 2006 (Sotiropoulou, 2011). By 2013 Thanou et al. (2013) had identified 11 Time Banks operating across Greece alongside 20 LETS schemes. By 2015 Stephanides (personal correspondence) had identified 59 LETS schemes, time banks, and bartering and exchange networks in Greece.

Ithaca and Other Hours

An alternative, perhaps more radical vision for currency denominated in time is that found in Ithaca, a university town in upstate New York with a long tradition of attracting the hippies, artists, intellectuals and environmentalists who flocked to the district in the 1960s and 1970s in a quest for self-sufficiency. Local activist Paul Glover created Ithaca Hours in 1991, and they continue to circulate to this day (North, 2014; Maurer, 2003; Glover, 1995). 'Hours' are a paper currency that are spent like cash, denominated in a tenth, eighth, quarter, half, one and two hours. The notes are decorated with locally significant images (a local salamander, waterfalls, a tramcar) and emblazoned with the slogan 'In Ithaca we trust'. Unlike the transition currencies discussed below, hours are not backed by national currency on deposit. The community decides collectively how much of the currency should be printed at a monthly potluck meal. The notes are then issued to merchants who advertise in a local newspaper (Hourtown), are given out in change, and can be bought for and exchanged back into US dollars at the rate of ten dollars an hour, the average local wage in 1991. More local currency is issued in the form of one year, zero-interest loans to local community groups and businesses. By 2009 some 900 businesses and individuals accepted Ithaca Hours, which have become a familiar and accepted part of the local economy. Other towns in the US and Canada have experimented with hour-based currencies.

Local Paper Currencies: From the Berkshires to Transition Towns

In the Berkshires, western Massachusetts, as an alternative to Ithaca Hours, the EF Schumacher Society established a local paper currency denominated in BerkShares, with one BerkShare equivalent to one dollar (North, 2014). News of BerkShares and Ithaca Hours spread across the Atlantic to the transition movement, a network of local community-led initiatives that aim to relocalize economies to build in (or we should say, rebuild) resilience to economic shocks, to the changing price of oil and in response to concerns about Peak Oil, and to cut down on the emissions and fossil fuel consumption associated with globalization that is contributing to dangerous climate change (Hopkins, 2011; North, 2010a). In 2007 members of Transition Town Totnes launched the Totnes Pound (Longhurst, 2012), closely followed by transition currencies in Lewes, Brixton, Stroud and later Bristol. The transition currencies are local notes denominated in local pounds, at parity with sterling, and backed by sterling. People wanting to support their local economy buy transition pounds, and the money held on deposit can later be used to redeem them. For reasons we discuss in more detail below, the transition currencies have been more successful than LETS at involving locally businesses in their project.

Regional Money: Chiemgauer

Chiemgauer regional money circulates in an area 100km around the Chiemsee, the lake in the centre of the Chiemgau district in south Bavaria (North and Weber, 2013). The aim is for Chiemgauer to circulate in an area small enough to be considered 'local' but large enough to facilitate enough exchange to make a material difference to the local economy and reduce emissions associated with transporting goods needlessly from place to place (for example, selling Danish bacon in the UK and British bacon in Denmark: see Woodin and Lucas, 2004). The currency, linked at parity to the Euro, exists as scrip (again adorned with local images) and in electronic form. Users of Chiemgauer buy them from issuing offices or NGOs, spending them with participating businesses either using the scrip or a debit card. The NGOs that act as issuing agents can buy 100 Chiemgauer for 97 euros, keeping the balance when they issue them to others. Businesses can spend them with other businesses or community groups, pay suppliers, give them out in change, donate them, or redeem them for euros. If they do the latter, they get 95 cents back for every Chiemgauer. Since the introduction of a debit card an average of 35 per cent of Chiemgauer transactions are electronic, with some popular businesses processing 80 per cent of their Cheimgauer transactions electronically. The Chiemgauer website[1] claims that that as of July 2015 just under a million Chiemgauer were in circulation, accepted by 588 businesses.

22.4 THE GEOGRAPHIES OF ALTERNATIVE CURRENCIES: MAKING SENSE OF THE DIVERSITY

Our analysis is built around a discussion of the strengths and weaknesses of a range of organizational and design features of the different complementary currency models and the implications of these features. We discuss: (1) valuation, (2) currency design and physical form, (3) convertibility, (4) supply management, (5) disciplining and commitment building mechanisms, and (6) the geographical reach of the alternative exchange network.

Valuation

Alternative currencies can be denominated in time (time banks, Ithaca Hours), with reference to national currency (transition currencies, BerkShares, Regiogeld), or as a hybrid of the two. Until the recent rise of the transition currencies, the majority of complementary currencies have tended to stress their dissimilarity with national currency values. For example, many UK LETS schemes argued that a LETS unit is 'like' a pound, and that a recommended hourly rate should be charged that is considered to be a 'fair' rate.[2] Others argued for a rate that specifically does not align with sterling: for example the Bright Exchange's (Brighton, UK) rate of 12 units to the hour was felt to be specifically non-decimal and therefore discouraged valuations aligned to sterling. Belfast used the pint.[3] Ideal LETS, in Bristol, set a rate of 20 Ideals an hour, reflecting a desire by many of its well-paid members for rates that reflected their expected sterling hourly rates.

The arguments for and against various rates give rise to different geographies, and are as follows. Time-based money mainly appeals to those who want to value work in ways un-connected to the capitalist nexus whereby, for example, a lawyer is paid more than a cleaner. A strict hourly rate appeals to those for whom equality and equity in trading relations is of major importance, that is, as a technique of resistance to capitalist commodification. Local money advocates here are engaging with arguments developed by Robert Owen, Proudhon and Marx that the basis of all wealth is labour, not the skills or qualities of the entrepreneur. They reject the economics of austerity, arguing for problems to be solved and needs to be met above the need for money to be in existence in advance to meet these needs, for money to be just the lubrication needed to facilitate work, which is what matters (North, 1999a). Third, there is an engagement with feminist analyses of labour markets that want to properly recognize, value and reward work often attributed to and carried out by women (Waring, 1990).

Of course, valuations of what constitutes fair recompense for labour time can be contested. If one person works harder or more efficiently than another, should they be paid the same given that one person has produced more than the other, and worked harder to do it? Elites argue that one person's time is worth more than another's as, for example, an hour of a lawyer's time is actually twenty years' experience and training concentrated into an hour. Having a time-based currency potentially restricts its appeal to those with whose political views are aligned with those of the exchange network, framing the currency as a radical, countercultural experiment aiming to revalue work and time in favour of those that market capitalism does not remunerate well (North, 1999a). Consequently, while is not adequate to assume that all businesspeople think in purely instrumental terms (North and Nurse, 2014; North, 2016), a time-based currency generally is less appealing for those unfamiliar with the politics behind time money, and who consequently will not take it seriously in purely economic terms – and this is likely to be an issue for business owners. Second, the absence of any national currency referent led to confusion in pricing goods in time-based money. How many hours for a fridge? Here, time money could work well as unit of exchange for people with aligned values, but was a poor measurement of value between incommensurable goods and services (Maurer, 2003).

The practical issues involved in attracting businesses who wanted to support their local economy, perhaps for instrumental reasons, and who did not share LETS members' resistant values suggested a move away from equality of valuation of members' time. This is why BerkShares and the transition currencies decided to denominate their currency in units aligned to the dollar and the pound. The downside of this was that aligning the local currency directly to national currency was seen by more radical members as replicating the inequalities of the conventional economy (North, 2006). For LETS, the dilemma was solved with a (perhaps very British) fudge and in practice, LETS members developed a range of diverse values for the currency. These valuations included:

- A LETS unit would be worth exactly a pound, and hourly rates would be calculated directly translating members expectations of their worth at mainstream prices. Members were free to bargain and exchange goods and services in a free market, and those who charged too much would need to adjust their prices according to market signals.
- A LETS unit is 'like' a pound, and a recommended hourly rate was set. This would be a more moral market (Lee, 1996).
- A gesture: One LETS unit would be paid, irrespective of the time taken to provide a service. In Manchester, advocates of this called themselves the 'bob-a-jobbers'.
- Distrusted: Others distrusted complementary currencies which they saw as commodification of co-operation that would have happened irrespective of the existence of the currency. They used the network to share without using the currency.
- Variable valuation: All or some of the above, depending on the quality of the relationship between traders, how much or little a trader wished to or enjoyed providing a service, or the relative account balances of the respective traders.

The problem with this early diversity was that the currency failed to act as either an effective measure of value or an accepted means of exchange (North, 2006). It did not fulfil one of the key roles of money in Simellian terms, building trust and providing a framework for exchange between people who did not know each other and who struggled to value incommensurable goods and services (Simmel, 1978/1908). Second, we value money differently (Zelizer, 1997). Problems arose when traders with essentially different value systems interacted with each other, tried to come to an agreement, but struggled to resolve wildly differing expectations. For example, cleaners could feel that an accepted rate of ten LETS an hour compared favourably with the going rates in the pre-minimum wage UK, while a homoeopathist could feel that her hourly rate should include recompense for her hours of training. This differential meant that LETS failed to act as an effective store (or measure) of value if a trader who charged above the odds could then buy more labour per hour than someone earning a lower rate. Others felt that as they had access to unlimited currency, the fact that one person charged more than another seemed irrelevant as all that is traded is points. They felt that an unlimited currency did not need to function as a store of value, while others felt that they had worked hard to build up a sizeable balance in the alternative currency that they now wanted to enjoy spending. In a third scenario, market mechanisms worked and the trader charging above the odds began to store up unspendable credits and lowered their prices. The problem was that strong bonds of trust were not developed in the absence of a universally accepted currency valuation, either imposed on the network by a strong organizational structure running the network, through rules, regulations and/or penalties, or through the construction of a shared and accepted ethos.

Design and Physical Form

The physical manifestation of the currency can communicate the ethos and politics of the currency. The physical form of alternative currencies varies from the immaterial to beautifully designed scrip that compare favourably with banknotes produced by nation states. Believing that money is 'just information', and should not be valuable in its own right, Michael Linton's original 1984 LETS design the LetSystem did not give the currency any physical form: users recorded transactions on an answerphone which were then logged onto the computer database. While this had the advantage of being simple and easy to set up, in large LETS schemes the central administration team often struggled to keep track of large numbers of transactions. In a financial crisis they would be overwhelmed, so if a LETS scheme was to be a harbour in a financial storm (Dauncey, 1988) this lack of resilience was problematic.

A second, big problem with a virtual currency with transactions recorded on a database specific to the United States was that any organization offering a computer-based currency scheme was subject to the same regulations as business-to-business barter and the organizers were legally responsible for notifying members' details to the Internal Revenue Service for tax purposes. This was a major structural barrier, which led to the innovation of moving to a paper currency. The issuance of scrip notes, like Ithaca Hours did not come up against either the IRS or volume problem as no central records are kept. Notes are also quicker and easier to take in and out of tills and wallets, speeding up transactions immeasurably – of crucial importance to businesses. This is why the Argentines who set up that country's barter networks used paper currencies, not LETS.[4]

Third, a virtual currency is so far removed from common understandings about money that new members found the concept difficult to grasp (North, 1996). Money, especially in the 1990s before the widespread use of cashless payments, is a physical 'thing', like a banknote, many felt. The lack of corporeality of LETS meant it was often not taken seriously by elite actors. Worse, if all money is, is a balance on a computer printout, people often displayed an over-casual attitude both to the value of the currency and to the need to return accounts to zero (Aldridge and Patterson, 2002). Banknotes and credit cards are designed with suitably historic or patriotic images to bestow grandeur on and communicate the solemnity and timeless value of a currency issued by a nation state that can enforce its use for paying taxes and settling disputes (Ingham, 2004). They use colour, ink and watermarks, declarations of value and the signature of an eminent person within the system of financial governance such as the Governor of a central bank or treasury to convey an element of 'moneyness' (Cohen, 1998) in contrast to 'Monopoly' money. This sense of 'moneyness' communicates subliminally that, even though fiat money is just a piece of paper, you should take it seriously and pay back debts, irrespective of the unethical activities of bankers that were revealed by the crisis of 2008, the LIBOR scandal, and questionable financial practices. The alternative is the trope of the 'irresponsible' Greek people who do not submit to this financial disciplining. Live within your means, or it will be 'as bad as Greece' (Knight, 2013).

Given that fiat currencies are disconnected from any relation to a tangible value base such as gold, currencies backed just by the personal commitment to repay by those who issue them are intellectually tenable (Ingham, 2004; Dodd, 1994). However, a currency with no method of demonstrating its credibility beyond trust in the issuer might (and often does) work for a small community of people who share the same value system, but will have problems in gaining usage and respect beyond those who accept and these values and who agree to be governed by them (North, 1999a). Those who have more conventional understandings of money, who see it as in some way 'hard', limited, connected to something tangible in the real world, will be less attracted to forms of money that diverge too strongly from uncontested or unconsidered attitudes about it.

The activists who established the transition currencies attended to the design, look and feel of the notes to ensure they had this quality of 'moneyness'. Well-designed and nicely produced local currencies that looked and felt like money resonated with accepted views of what money should do. If backed by national currency on demand then very few businesspeople continued to violently object to at least experimenting with a local currency given that there were no obvious dis-benefits. This is one of the reasons for the relative success of the transition currencies in involving businesses and thereby widening the resources that members of the network can access when compared with the more modest penetration of LETS. For advocates of the transition currencies, they are a significant step forward in their goal of transitioning to a localized, sustainable, convivial economy. LETS purists, though, can feel that as they are denominated in pounds and backed not by a personal promise to pay but by national currency on deposit, their potential for enacting economies based on changed values is less strong than LETS. Ithaca Hours, well designed local notes that look like money but are denominated in time, are a midway between these competing conceptions.

Regulating the Use of and the Circulation of the Currency

The supply of any new currency and how it circulates must be managed in some way. There are two approaches. With 'personal credit' money like LETS and time money, currency issue is governed by the users of the currency themselves with the simple act of commissioning work and paying for it with local credits, backed with their labour in the future, their personal 'promise to pay the bearer on demand'. Here a second set of power relations relate to the management of individual accounts. To what extent are there credit or debit limits? Are members expected to earn as much as they spend, periodically returning their account to a zero balance as in LETS; or should needs be met irrespective of the existence of otherwise of credits to pay for received services (the case with time banks)? Can an account with a growing debit be tolerated? Should balances be made public, proactively or otherwise, and what are the cultural mores of the community concerned about what many regard as private, personal information about spending habits, indebtedness, and account balances? How important is it that account statements are accurate – do members care or not what others are doing, or do they regard this as inappropriate surveillance over other people's private affairs?

The geometries of power in LETS pay close attention to accurate account management. Members are expected to periodically balance their accounts. Some LETS schemes impose credit or debit limits, and actively enforce them either through the proactive publication of balances or through the oversight by the management group. Green Dollar schemes in New Zealand are particularly proactive in this regard, and have gone as far as taking members to small claims courts to enforce payment of debts they don't feel are being repaid (North, 2002). LETS schemes often go out of their way to regularly provide account statements, and pay considerable attention to their accuracy. These account management systems are, it is argued, necessary to maintain the integrity of the currency and confidence in it. Public access to account balances is necessary to ensure that all traders are contributing to the scheme, and that a member who takes more from others than they contribute will find that opportunities to trade reduce when the depth of the imbalance is known.

In reality, the extent that individual members do check up on the credit balances of others and regulate their trading relations to ensure equitable contributions is questionable, especially in the absence of regularly published balances. The publication of individual balances can cut against cultural conceptions of privacy. In New Zealand, Green Dollar committees involved themselves in the management of individual accounts in ways that a UK audience might find intrusive, yet felt that the open publication of accounts would invade member's privacy. Regulatory practices balance close attention to cultural conceptions of what should or should not be made public with the need for feedback mechanisms. The publication of account balances and surveillance by a management committee creates to some extent a financial panopticon where financial practices can be monitored either by other community members, or by the committee. In practice community regulation does not happen.

With time banking the emphasis is on meeting needs and on people making whatever contribution they feel they can, irrespective of whether the volumes of services given and received are in balance in any individual case. Accounts statements are often not provided, to avoid putting those whose needs outweigh their ability to reciprocate feeling beholden to the community, or holding back from asking for the support they are entitled to as they are unwilling to go into what they see as 'debt'. In time banking the concept of 'debt' does not exist in the same way as in the conventional economy; participants collectively contribute and withdraw 'time' from 'the bank', rather than manage an individual account. The ethos is of 'co-production', of people meeting their needs collectively, of providing as well as receiving help (Cahn, 2000).

With scrip such as 'Hours', the Argentine Red Global de Trueque, the transition currencies and German Regional Currencies, a central issuing authority decides how much scrip to issue. If this currency issuance is through new users converting national currency into local currency and then spending it into circulation, the market decides how much currency is in existence. If too many unbacked notes are issued, as we saw in Argentina, they may (perhaps catastrophically) lose value in an inflationary cycle as too many notes are chasing too few trading opportunities (Gómez, 2008). If too few are issued, needs may still be unmet for lack of money, recreating the pathologies of the conventional currency. How many notes to issue is a delicate decision, and it is unclear who has the right, or knowledge, to make a decision that affects the fundamental integrity of the system. Some of the currency networks driven by activists with more radical objectives decide collectively at open meetings how much currency should be issued. Regiogeld and BerkShares, which do involve significant numbers of businesses, are formally organized by NGOs, with the support and participation of local banks.

In the UK, some of the transition currencies have suffered from a perception that they are not professionally organized and managed. Users exchanging limited volumes of personal services or buying the odd hand-made card or homebaked cake are likely to be more relaxed about the professionalism and accountability of the network when compared with what is necessary to facilitate business-to-business exchange and the tax and (potentially) regulatory liabilities associated with that. With the latter businesses and livelihoods are on the line, and people affected need ways in which they can hold the currency system accountable and change the rules if the currency is affecting their livelihood adversely (North, 2014). In time, the transition currencies began to formalize their management structures and develop explicit channels to enable them to get feedback from users of the currency and to involve them in decision-making about the rules that governed exchange and the way the exchange network was developed.

Convertibility

To maintain the distinctiveness of the complementary currency system, few LETS schemes actively facilitated their exchange into national currency. Time banks specifically prohibited it, and refused to make any points of connection or valuation with state money. The result is that traders with popular services could often be left with a store of unspendable credits. While participants in time banks saw themselves as people helping each other out and had a relaxed view about their account balance (with the result that some did not distinguish between purely voluntary and time bank-funded work, and did not want to spend their accumulated time credits), in LETS, an inability to spend what some saw as hard-earned cash could, in time, become problematic. This was a particular problem for those able to earn large amounts of a local currency, especially businesses and skilled, high demand workers like plumbers or carpenters, and acted as a disincentive to their continued participation in the exchange network. They would stop taking on new work until they had spent their balances, or drop out, writing their credit balance off. If enough people did this, the network would atrophy. Sometimes, for example in Ithaca, the organizer of the currency spent a considerable amount of time working with participants to help them find new ways to recirculate the currency. In time, it became clear that this was a previously underemphasized managerial requirement for an alternative currency network: while a bank does not need to help account holders to spend their money, there is, in the form of advertising, a considerable infrastructure already in place that does this, and which enables the currency to be spent. A local currency that lacked these wider 'enabling' institutions could suffer (North and Longhurst, 2013).

Two more solutions were utilized to facilitate the circulation of the currency. Both Chiemgauer and the Stroud Pound are experimenting with demurrage, whereby a currency depreciates, or 'rusts', over time unless a stamp or voucher is periodically purchased which revalidates it so it can be spent again (North and Weber, 2013). The notes are periodically withdrawn from circulation, so they cannot be hoarded over long periods. The advantage of demurrage is that holders of currency are incentivized to spend it before the validation date, boosting the performance of the currency as a means of exchange rather than as a store of value. Conversely, the problem is that demurrage can exacerbate the unattractiveness of complementary currencies to those providers of in-demand services who are willing to spend their accumulated credits, but lack opportunities to do so. A balance losing value over time is likely to ensure that providers of such services quickly cease accepting the currency, disproportionately penalizing those who have provided the most services. Interestingly though, recent evidence from Germany suggests that in an environment where there are many opportunities to trade demurrage can incentivize recirculation to avoid having to revalidate the notes (North and Weber, 2013).

The second solution to the problem of encouraging recirculation is to have a local paper currency that is fully backed by national currency, which those who struggle to spend can easily exchange back into national currency if they have to, reducing the likelihood that local businesses will be left with an unspendable balance. There being few downsides to participation, more businesses are likely to join with the result that the need to convert back to national currency reduces; they can spend it with their suppliers, other businesses, and give it out in change. However, solving one problem can, in turn, create three new ones. First, why would anyone refuse universal money in favour of a more limited form of money, unless they had a political or affective commitment to their local economy? Second, those who do not have enough spare national currency to convert into the local scrip are still excluded from participation in the network: this is not new money boosting spending power for those without much money (which LETS and time banks both do). People on a budget who live from one payday to the next, perhaps reliant on family credit or even a foodbank or payday loans (in the UK) are not likely to convert universal money spendable anywhere, and especially in budget supermarkets, into a local currency that cannot be used for everyday non-discretionary purchases. Third, what is the benefit of a currency that does not circulate widely through the local economy, but is just banked after one exchange? A wider alternative circuit of capital is not created; the hoped-for 'structuring' elements of a local currency, supporting ethical local business that support each other and penalize exploitative businesses who do not contribute to their community or remit all their profits to a head office elsewhere, are missing (North, 2005).

BerkShares and the transition currencies consequently incentivize new users by offering a favourable exchange rate between local and national currencies: for example, nine dollars bought ten BerkShares, giving users a 10 per cent boost to their spending power. They also dis-incentivized businesses from banking rather than recirculating BerkShares as businesses that did this only received nine dollars for ten BerkShares that they banked, while businesses that recirculated them were not similarly penalized. Many businesses could absorb this effective 10 per cent discount to customers: offering discounts is a normal business practice. Further, as the local currency featured prominently in the media and provided good publicity for the town, many businesses felt this was a price worth paying as the benefits to town pride outweighed the costs of absorbing the discount. But businesses that were popular with many users and whose business was characterized by large volumes of low value-added transactions, and who could not recirculate the local currency in the volumes they accepted, struggled. They began to describe the cost of banking BerkShares as a taking a 10 per cent 'hit' which they described as the cost of doing business in that community (North, 2014). The E.F. Schumacher Society responded to this by reducing the discount to 5 per cent, a practice replicated by the transition currencies. This seems more sustainable.

Commitment-building Mechanisms

A debate that goes back to the beginning of the modern wave of complementary currencies centres on the question: is this a tool for anyone to use, for whatever they want, or a community, a social movement arguing for a different form of money that will help to build a sustainable, convivial, low carbon world (North, 1999a)? Is it a form of protest, a strategy for local economic development (North, 1998, 1999b), or a mix of the two? This has implications for ways of organizing the currency network. Those who see the local currency as a tool for building communities or experimenting with different economic values are more likely to be interested in a complementary currency that is organized by a democratically accountable management group, that does not have too many members so community feeling is maintained, and which operates within a geographically tight area or homogenous community. They are likely to favour mechanisms that facilitate community and commitment such as directories and newsletters with a strong 'alternative' or 'community' feel, organized trading days so the community can come together, and a brokerage service which actively puts members in touch with each other on the time bank model. They will enjoy and appreciate strong boundaries with the outside world, a feeling that the community that uses the currency is distinct or special and 'doing things in a different way'. They will actively want to feel part of that community. Time banks are especially strong in providing the support necessary so that vulnerable members are looked after, their needs are met, and they are protected by a duty of care (Seyfang, 2003b). Research on alternative communities that achieve longevity suggests these commitment and community building mechanisms, and boundaries with the outside world, are important (Kantor, 1972).

Simmel (1978/1908) famously argued that 'money is freedom': you don't need to like someone or feel in community with them to trade with them. Those who prefer to use a complementary currency as a ladder into mainstream employment or as a way to strengthen or relocalize economies may prefer a larger, more diverse, more anonymous community, and feel stifled by commitment building mechanisms that those with a stronger commitment to community may appreciate. They like the idea that their money, which they have earned, is as good as anyone else's. Here, how prospective members find out about the opportunities to use a complementary currency, and what value systems govern how the money should and should not be used, matters. Which groups in society do those organizing the currency target to get them to participate, and why do they target some groups not others? How does the management group go about developing the range of services available within the network – if at all?

LETS groups rarely identified target markets or systematically attempted to explain the benefits of complementary currencies to potential new users. Promotional materials were, and still are, are often poorly produced, if at all. Many LETS groups did little more than rely on their directory to convey the flavour of what sort of skills and goods were exchanged. Others simply relied on word of mouth to recruit new members. Often this could be deliberate. Many more radical members of LETS specifically set out to be part of a hidden network of tranquillity and fair exchange, and actively sought to create a border against a wider world 'gone mad'. Community-based complementary currency networks relied on significant levels of trust in the absence of methods of enforcing payment, and the personal or home-based nature of many services meant that many users sought assurances that they will feel 'comfortable' with their fellow traders, and networks developed through word of mouth are often homogenous as people recruit 'people like us'. Time banks managed who would and who would not be allowed into the network, often insisting on Criminal Records Bureau (CRB) checks. These processes all build a shared identity, but beyond obvious problems with equal opportunities also restricted the size of the network, kept the benefits to a small group, and could cut off new blood, skills and energy from the network. Critics wanting more engagement with local businesses and a wide exchange network disparaged small homogenous LETS schemes and Time Banks as 'cosy clubs', not the rainbow economy they wanted to see.

Some alternative currency networks did attempt to grow into a local economy, beyond cosy club, by including local businesspeople in the exchange network. The problem was that adopting promotional approaches that focused on the economic benefits to a business did not inspire activists to do the hard work necessary to build a more diverse exchange network. It was only when NGOs such as the US E.F. Schumacher Society, Argentina's Programma de Autosuficiencia Regional or the UK's New Economics Foundation put organizational resources behind business-focused currency networks, and the need to relocalize economies to avoid dangerous climate change was identified as a new rationale for local currencies, that networks involving local businesses were built to any extent.

The Geographical Extent of Alternative Circuits of Exchange

Local currency activists are attempting to develop a localized 'politics of scale' that they find ethically appropriate, as a counter to what they regard as an unethical scale – globalization (North, 2005). Thus alternative currency networks have both a moral geography (Lee, 1996) and an economic geography. The question then arises: what is an 'optimum currency area' (Mundell, 1961) in terms of economic efficiency that both maximizes the amount of goods and services that can be exchanged with the currency and facilitates opportunities for supply networks to be developed that can extend the amount of goods and services while maintaining a sense of the 'local' either in terms of community feeling or minimizing avoidable emissions and resource consumption through localization? Does this economically optimal area map onto, or clash with, socially or ecologically constructed conceptions of the local? How far 'away' is 'too far', when do 'we' end, and 'they' begin? Can these conflicting drivers be reconciled (North, 2010a)?

LETS and time bank users wish to locate economic relations at a specific geographical scale – the very local, a village or small town, or at the largest a district in a city. It is not likely that people will travel more than a few streets to provide low value personal services like DIY or babysitting. A larger scale, such as city, might provide a wider range of services, but still be too small for businesses either to be able to exchange with each other or secure local suppliers of the goods they sell. Thus German Regiogeld operate at a regional level, while BerkShares circulate in the western part of a US state: these seem to be scales that mix an ethical attachment to the 'local' at a scale that enough businesses join to make circulation possible. Generally, the UK transition currencies, at a town level, have struggled to generate much recirculation. Their borders are too tight. But conversely, regional currencies are likely to operate at too big a scale for LETS and time bank members. Thus the scale of currencies is not given, but both created and contested. Certain scales are regarded as more appropriate than others, but they may not facilitate another objective of local currency activists. What is local might not facilitate enough exchange, while what facilitates access to a wider range of goods and services may no longer feel 'local' (North, 2005, 2010a).

For some critics, this advocacy of localization can be problematic (North, 2010a), suggesting a desire to look back perhaps rather wistfully to a simpler world of localized economies where everyone lived in small towns surrounded by market gardens and which may seem faintly xenophobic. Does it mean a toll booth on every road out of town (for example, see Wolf, 2005: 194–199)? This critique does not stand up to examination. The emergence of local currencies in global cities, in places like Brixton, suggests that local currency activists are producing more than a nostalgic, autarchic conception of the local. Brixton LETS and later the Brixton Pound emerged within London, a globally connected metropolis, the powerhouse of the financial colossus (Sassen, 1996) that almost brought the global economy crashing down in 2008, a city with huge global 'geographies of responsibility' for the impact in other places of financial decisions made in the metropolis (Massey, 2004). But London is also famously Patrick Abercrombie's city of villages. The global is produced locally in London (Massey, 1994), and the local can be produced in London's communities in ways that are more than a nostalgia with a hint of xenophobia. Members of alternative currency networks are using a local currency as both a symbol of the sort of communities they want to live in, and a tool for enacting it. The existence of a successful alternative currency network in a particular locality suggests that this is a place where large numbers of people who feel that way congregate (Longhurst, 2013).

Here we find debates about the production of scale. Geographers have argued that it is inadequate to view scales as set, solid, hierarchically nested; rather, they are actively produced by conscious political, cultural and economic actors (Delaney and Leitner, 1997) acting through relational networks constructed at a variety of spatial scales (Massey, 1992). Actors engage in 'rescaling' processes to defend 'locality' (Escobar, 2001) or 'community' (Imbroscio, 1997) while the powerful use a 'spatial fix' to move production to places with low labour and employment rights in order to maximize their profits (Harvey, 2001: 324–344). This rescaling can be at a rhetorical level as actors make claims about the value of specific scales (usually local/good, global/bad), but also in terms of material practices as through their actions, actors create scale by developing economic, social and political networks. This suggests that the processes of scale creation are diffuse, multiple, and thus larger numbers of people will have access to scale construction, not just the powerful. The effervescent connections of subaltern groups are as important for scale construction as say economic forces controlled by business elites. Local currency networks are such a politics of scale constructed by subaltern actors.

22.5 CONCLUSION

Geographers have debated the extent that alternative currencies, especially LETS, constitute micro-political practices shedding light on the 'disciplining' processes of money and of calls for financial stability (Bonefield and Holloway, 1996). They are attempts to construct alternative circuits of capital that enable those who use them to enact different conceptions of the role of money, of work, and of livelihood (North, 1999a; Lee, 1999). Research suggests that these alternative circuits of exchange do enable those who use them to explore different values of the role of money, of the importance of community, and the need to develop alternatives: as such they are producers of different knowledges (Eyerman and Jamison, 1991) about money, work and livelihoods, especially in the context of the need to avoid dangerous climate change and develop an economic ethics for the Anthropocene (Gibson-Graham and Roelvink, 2010). Lee (1996) and Thorne (1996) see them as attempts to re-moralize money and, in a Polanyan sense, re-embed economies in communities, especially as part of the reaction of the anti-globalization movement to neoliberalization (Pacione, 1997).

Can we say more? Through alternative currency networks, can we go beyond resistance and the creation of new knowledges about work and money and enact a heterotopian diversity of currencies operating to changed rules as part of a community economy such as that advocated in the diverse economies perspectives of geographers such as J.K. Gibson-Graham (2006a, 2006b, 2008)? Can these networks act as what Seyfang and Smith (2007) call 'grassroots innovation niches' developing alternative ways of living? Through an examination of the experiences of subaltern actors in their attempts to construct alternative circuits of value, we can understand the extent that it is possible to construct alternative practices that are more than precapitalist hangovers or doomed utopian experiments that are unable to compete with capitalism as the world historic system, with capitalism associated with progress and modernity (Engels, 1892[1968]). They do more than survive in the interstices, hidden places where capitalism has yet to penetrate and where everyday life has yet to become fully commodified, or as the survival strategies of the surplus proletarians that capitalism has no need of (Samers, 2005).

Actors with alternative values and visions of how economies and worlds should be brought into being have experimented with a range of diverse or alternative economic practices based on solidarity rather than competition (Fuller et al., 2010; Leyshon et al., 2003). Alternative forms of currency are now a well-established part of the community economy armoury, enabling those who use them to experiment with alternative visions of convivial localized economies, and, within the limits of their productive capacity, experiment with alternative visions of work, livelihood and economy (North, 2007). There were hopes that alternative currencies might be fecund sources of new forms of less commodified and regulated forms of work and of livelihoods that did operate by alternative rhythms than that of capitalist disciplining (Williams, 1996b; Williams et al., 2001). They might, it was hoped, provide an alternative to having to work to neoliberal rhythms, to the nine-to-five. However, the reality of what these alternative networks could concretely achieve without access to means of production beyond those held up ordinary people was limited (Aldridge and Patterson, 2002). Few alternative currencies networks have facilitated a move out of an alternative circuit of consumption to an alternative site of production (North, 2014). As yet no local currencies have significantly contributed to the localization of an economy to the extent that emissions and resource throughputs have been significantly reduced at levels necessary to avoid dangerous climate change (Dittmer, 2013). In the Chiemgau and Bristol we are now starting to see the emergence of something about which we can perhaps be more hopeful that we are beginning to enact more robust local circuits of exchange using local money. The growth of the sharing economy based on the Internet, and of peer-to-peer lending has extended the range of this new rainbow economy in ways that were not possible in the early days of LETS experimentation. There has been a rise in interest in co-operation, workplace democracy, and other forms of commoning (Cato and North, 2016). The full potential of this new sharing economy will need to be uncovered through future research that focuses less on alternative visions, and more critically on concrete alternative practices, including both alternative circuits of exchange and of production facilitated by alternative currencies (Jonas, 2010; Fickey, 2011).

NOTES

1. See www.chiemgauer.info/.
2. In this, LETS (and Ithaca Hours) prefigure later debates about 'minimum', 'fair' and 'living' wages. Rather than argue for and wait for legislation, local currency activists attempted to implement fair pay from below.
3. ('I'll buy you a pint if you . . . .').
4. Interestingly, at the time of writing this lesson had not been taken on board in Greece, in the face of a similarly severe economic crisis.

BIBLIOGRAPHY

Aldridge, T. and A. Patterson (2002), 'LETS get real: constraints on the development of Local Exchange Trading Schemes', *Area*, **34** (4), 370–381.

Bonefield, Werner and John Holloway (eds) (1996), *Global Capital, National State and the Politics of Money*, London: Macmillan.

Brown, J. and M. Purcell (2005), 'There's nothing inherent about scale: political ecology, the local trap, and the politics of development in the Brazilian Amazon', *Geoforum*, **36** (5), 607–624.

Cahn, E. (2000), *No More Throw Away People*, London: Harper Collins.

Cha, A.E. (2012), 'Spain's crisis spawns alternative economy that doesn't rely on the euro', *Washington Post*, Washington, DC. Retrieved on 21 October 2016 from www.theguardian.com/world/2012/sep/04/spain-euro-free-economy.

Cohen, Benjamin (1998), *The Geography of Money*, Ithaca: Cornell University Press.

Cato, M.S. and P. North (2016), 'Rethinking the factors of production for a world of common ownership and sustainability: Europe and Latin America compared', *Review of Radical Political Economics*, **48** (1), 36–52.

Dauncey, G. (1988), *Beyond the Crash: The emerging rainbow economy*, London: Greenprint.

Delaney, D and H. Leitner (1997), 'The political construction of scale', *Political Geography* **16** (2), 93–97.

Dittmer, K. (2013), 'Local currencies for purposive degrowth? A quality check of some proposals for changing money-as-usual', *Journal of Cleaner Production*, **54**, 3–13.

Dittmer, K. (2015), '100 percent reserve banking: a critical review of green perspectives', *Ecological Economics*, **109**, 9–16.

Dodd, N. (1994), *The Sociology of Money*, New York: Continuum.

Douthwaite, R. (1996), *Short Circuit: Strengthening Local Economies for Security in an Uncertain World*, Totnes: Green Books.

Douthwaite, R. (1999), *The Ecology of Money*, Totnes: Green Books.

Engels, F. (1892[1968]), *Socialism: Utopian and Scientific*, London: Lawrence and Wishart.

Escobar, A. (2001), 'Culture sits in places: reflections on globalism and subaltern strategies of localization', *Political Geography*, **20** (2), 139–174.

Eyerman, R. and R. Jamison (1991), *Social Movements: a Cognitive Approach*, Cambridge: Polity.

Fickey, A. (2011), '"The focus has to be on helping people make a living": exploring diverse economies and alternative economic spaces', *Geography Compass*, **5** (5), 237–248.

Fukuyama, F. (1992), *The End of History and the Last Man*, Harmondsworth: Penguin.

Fuller, Duncan, Andrew Jonas and Roger Lee (eds) (2010), *Interrogating Alterity: Alternative Spaces of Economy, Society and Politics*, London: Ashgate.

Galbraith, John (1975), *Money: Whence It Came, Where It Went*, London: Andre Deutsch.

Gibson-Graham, J.K. (2006a), *The End of Capitalism (as we knew it): A Feminist Critique of Political Economy*, Minneapolis: University of Minnesota Press.

Gibson-Graham, J.K. (2006b), *A Post Capitalist Politics*, Minneapolis: University of Minnesota Press.

Gibson-Graham, J.K. (2008), 'Diverse economies: performative practices for "other worlds"', *Progress in Human Geography*, **32** (5), 613–632.

Gibson-Graham, J.K. and G. Roelvink (2010), 'An economic ethics for the anthropocene', *Antipode*, **41** (1), 320–346.

Glover, P. (1995), 'Ithaca Hours', in S. Meeker Lowry (ed.), *Invested in the Common Good*, New York: New Society Publishers, pp. 72–80.

Gómez, Georgina (2008), *Making Markets: The Institutional Rise and Decline of the Argentine Red de Trueque*, The Hague: Institute of Social Studies.

Harvey, David (2001), *Spaces of Capital: Towards a Critical Geography*, Edinburgh: Edinburgh University Press.

Hopkins, Rob (2011), *The Transition Companion*, Totnes: Green Books.

Imbroscio, Davis (1997), *Reconstructing City Politics: Alternative Economic Development and Urban Regimes*, London: Sage.

Ingham, Geoffrey (2004), *The Nature of Money*, Cambridge: Polity.

Jackson, A. and B. Dyson (2012), *Modernising Money: How our Monetary System is Broken and How it can be Fixed*, London: Positive Money.

Jonas, A. (2010), '"Alternative" this, "alternative" that . . .: interrogating alterity and diversity', in Duncan Fuller, Andrew Jonas and Roger Lee (eds), *Interrogating Alterity: Alternative Economic and Political Spaces*, Farnham: Ashgate, pp. 3–30.

Kantor, Rosabeth Moss (1972), *Commitment and Community: Communes and Utopia in Sociological Perspective*, Cambridge, MA: Harvard University Press.

Kennedy, Margrit (1996), *Interest and Inflation-free Money*, Philadelphia, PA: New Society Publishers.

Knight, D.M. (2013), 'The Greek economic crisis as trope', *Focaal*, **65**, 147–159.

Lee, R. (1996), 'Moral money? LETS and the social construction of local economic geographies in southeast England', *Environment and Planning A*, **28** (8), 1377–1394.

Lee, R. (1999), 'Local money: geographies of autonomy and resistance', in R. Martin (ed.), *Money and the Space Economy*, Chichester: Wiley, pp. 207–224.

Leyshon, Andrew, Roger Lee and Colin Williams (eds) (2003), *Alternative Economic Spaces*, London: Sage.

Longhurst, N. (2012), 'The Totnes Pound: a grassroots technological niche', in A. Davies (ed.), *Enterprising Communities: Grassroots Sustainability Innovations*, Bingley: Emerald, pp. 163–188.

Longhurst, N. (2013), 'The emergence of an alternative milieu: conceptualising the nature of alternative places', *Environment and Planning A*, **45** (9), 2100–2119.

Massey, D. (1992), 'Politics and space/time', *New Left Review*, **196**, 65–84.

Massey, D. (1994), 'A global sense of place', in D. Massey (ed.), *Space, Place and Gender*, Cambridge: Polity Press, pp. 146–156.

Massey, D. (2004), 'Geographies of responsibility', *Geografiska Annaler*, **86B** (1), 5–18.

Maurer, B. (2003), 'Uncanny exchange: the possibilities and failures of "making change" with alternative money forms', *Environment and Planning D: Society and Space*, **21** (3), 317–340.

Mundell, R. (1961), 'A theory of optimum currency areas', *American Economic Review*, **51**, 657–665.

North, P. (1996), 'LETS: a tool for empowerment in the inner city?', *Local Economy*, **11** (3), 284–293.

North, P. (1998), 'LETS, Hours and the Swiss Business Link: local currencies and business development programmes', *Local Economy*, **13** (2), 114–132.

North, P. (1999a), 'Explorations in heterotopia: LETS and the micropolitics of money and livelihood', *Environment and Planning D: Society and Space*, **17** (1), 69–86.

North, P. (1999b), 'LETS get down to business!: problems and possibilities of involving the small business sector in CED using local currencies', in G. Haughton (ed.), *Community Economic Development*, London: The Stationary Office/Regional Studies Association, pp. 139–148.

North, P. (2002), 'LETS in a cold climate: Green Dollars, self-help and neo-liberal welfare reform in New Zealand', *Policy and Politics*, **30** (4), 483–500.

North, P. (2003), 'Time Banks: learning the lessons from LETS?', *Local Economy*, **18** (3), 267–270.

North, P. (2005), 'Scaling alternative economic practices? Some lessons from alternative currencies', *Transactions of the Institute of British Geographers*, **30** (2), 221–233.

North, Peter (2006), *Alternative Currencies as a Challenge to Globalisation?: A Case Study of Manchester's Local Money Networks*, Aldershot: Ashgate.

North, Peter (2007), *Money and Liberation: The Micropolitics Of Alternative Currency Movements*, Minneapolis: University of Minnesota Press.

North, P. (2010a), 'Eco-localisation as a progressive response to peak oil and climate change – a sympathetic critique', *Geoforum*, **41** (4), 585–594.

North, P. (2010b), 'The longevity of alternative economic practices: lessons from alternative currency networks', in D. Fuller, A. Jonas and R. Lee (eds), *Interrogating Alterity: Alternative Spaces of Economy, Society and Politics*, London: Ashgate, pp. 31–46.

North, P. (2010c), *Local Money*, Totnes: Green Books.

North, P. (2011), 'Geographies and utopias of Cameron's Big Society', *Social & Cultural Geography*, **12** (8), 817–827.

North, P. (2014), 'Ten square miles surrounded by reality? Materialising alternative economies using local currencies', *Antipode*, **46** (1), 246–265.

North, P. (2016), 'The business of the Anthropocene? Substantivist and diverse economies perspectives on SME engagement in local low carbon transitions', *Progress in Human Geography*, **40** (4), 437–454.

North, P. and N. Longhurst (2013), 'Grassroots localisation? The scalar potential of and limits of the "transition" approach to climate change and resource constraint', *Urban Studies*, **50** (7), 1423–1438.

North, P. and A. Nurse (2014), '"War stories": morality, curiosity, enthusiasm and commitment as facilitators of SME owners' engagement in low carbon transitions', *Geoforum*, **52** (2), 32–41.

North, P. and K. Weber (2013), 'The alternative economy at the regional scale?: lessons from the Chiemgau', in S. Hilebrand and H-M. Zademach (eds), *Alternative Economies and Spaces. Space for Alternative Economies*, Bielefeld: Transcript, pp. 43–69.
Pacione, M. (1997), 'Local exchange trading systems as a response to the globalisation of capitalism', *Urban Studies*, **34** (8), 1179–1199.
Peck, J. (2013), 'For Polanyian economic geographies', *Environment and Planning A*, **45** (7), 1545–1568.
Samers, M. (2005), 'The myopia of "diverse economies", or a critique of the informal economy', *Antipode*, **37** (5), 875–886.
Sassen, S. (1996), 'The global city', in S. Fainstein and S. Campbell (eds), *Readings in Urban Theory*, Oxford: Blackwell, pp. 61–71.
Seyfang, G. (2003a), 'Growing cohesive communities one favour at a time: social exclusion, active citizenship and time banks', *International Journal of Urban and Regional Research*, **27** (3), 699–706.
Seyfang, G. (2003b), 'With a little help from my friends. Evaluating time banks as a tool for community self help', *Local Economy*, **18** (3), 257–264.
Seyfang, G. and A. Smith (2007), 'Grassroots innovations for sustainable development: towards a new research and policy agenda', *Environmental Politics*, **16** (4), 584–603.
Shuman, Michael (2001), *Going Local: Creating Self Reliant Communities in a Global Age*, London: Routledge.
Simmel, Georg (1978/1908), *The Philosophy of Money*, London, Routledge.
Sotiropoulou, I. (2011), 'Alternative exchange systems in contemporary Greece', *International Journal of Community Currency Research*, 27–31.
Thanou, E, G. Theodossiou and D. Kallivokas (2013), *Local Exchange Trading Systems (LETS) as a response to Economic Crisis: The Case of Greece*, Geneva: United Nations Non-Governmental Liaison Service.
Thorne, L. (1996), 'Local exchange trading systems in the UK – a case of re-embedding?' *Environment and Planning A*, **28** (8), 1361–1376.
Waring, Marilyn (1990), *If Women Counted: A New Feminist Economics*, London: Harper Collins.
Williams, C.C. (1996a), 'Informal sector responses to unemployment: an evaluation of the potential of LETS', *Work, Employment and Society*, **10** (2), 341–360.
Williams, C.C. (1996b), 'Local exchange trading systems: a new source of work and employment?', *Environment and Planning A*, **28** (8), 1395–1415.
Williams, C.C., T. Aldridge, R. Lee, A. Leyshon, N. Thrift and J. Tooke (2001), *Bridges into Work: An Evaluation of Local Exchange Trading Schemes*, Bristol: The Policy Press.
Wolf, Martin (2005), *Why Globalization Works*, New Haven, Yale Nota Bene.
Woodin, M. and C. Lucas (2004), *Green Alternatives to Globalisation: A Manifesto*, London: Pluto.
Zelizer, Viviana (1997), *The Social Meaning of Money*, Princeton, NJ: Princeton University Press.
Zelizer, Viviana (2005), *The Purchase of Intimacy*, Princeton, NJ: Princeton University Press.

23. 'Mainstreaming' the 'alternative'? The financialization of transnational migrant remittances

Kavita Datta

23.1 INTRODUCTION

Few financial flows have attracted as much academic and political attention as migrant remittances. Part of this interest is attributable to – or perhaps more precisely created by – the apparent exponential 'growth' of these transfers which is painstakingly and regularly documented at global, regional and national scales (Bakker, 2015). Emphasizing particular geographies and volumes of remittance flows, the data presented suggests a dominant upward trajectory with transfers to the Global South alone, for example, rising from US$2 billion in 1970 to US$31.2 billion in 1990 to US$414 billion in 2016, with an average annual growth rate of 8 per cent between 2013 and 2016 (World Bank, 2006, 2013, 2015, 2016). Such figures are all the more impressive when measured against other declining, unstable and/or fluctuating development finance such as official development assistance (ODA) and foreign direct investment (FDI). In terms of the corresponding geographies of remittances flows, despite the significance of transfers within and between countries in the Global South, as well as those which leave the Global South for the Global North, it is the movement of capital from the 'richer' to the 'poorer' parts of the world which have captured the greatest attention (World Bank, 2015). The more recent estimates suggest that in 2016, the top four migrant destination countries were the USA, Saudi Arabia, Germany and the Russian Federation while the largest remittance recipient countries were India (US$72 billion); China (US$64 billion); Philippines (US$30 billion) and Mexico (US$26 billion) (World Bank, 2016).

Alongside this empirical focus, the scrutiny of remittances is also undoubtedly shaped by the fact that they appeal to a broad range of stakeholders (Datta, 2009a). As such, remittances are simultaneously positioned as 'alternative', 'bottom up' and 'third way' finance as well as an 'ideal neoliberal currency' and 'new development finance' appealing to both grass-root communitarians as well as neoliberal economists (Adams and Page, 2005; Datta, 2009a; Hernandez and Coutin, 2006; Kapur, 2003; Ratha, 2003; Wimaladharma et al., 2004). For the former, they are private intra-household transfers – 'aid which reaches its destination' (Cross, 2013: 161) – utilized to fulfill the basic welfare needs of poor recipient families and operating as an informal internationalized welfare system (Cross, 2015). As such remittances facilitate grass-root based sustainable development initiatives. For the latter, remittances are a significant source of development funding particularly within the context of insufficient if varied flows to the Global South, trends which have worsened in recent years of recession (Datta, 2012; Hudson, 2008; IDS, 2009). As Hernandez and Coutin (2006: 188) state: 'neo-liberal economic policies [have] focused new attention on the possibility that remittances might play a significant role in national development, or at least national solvency'. Correspondingly there is a growing argument that remittances can be leveraged or harnessed to fund macroeconomic development initiatives as part of a technocratic response to the management of poverty *and* migration (Datta et al., 2007; World Bank, 2005).

Arising from this consensus, the last decade has witnessed the emergence of a 'global remittance agenda' whereby remittance senders and recipients, the remittance process and remittance landscape have been progressively financialized (Kunz, 2011; also Datta, 2012; Hudson, 2008; Zapata, 2013). Spearheaded by a loose coalition of International Financial Institutions (most notably the World Bank and the Multi-Lateral Fund of the Inter-American Development Bank), national governments, civil society organizations and the commercial financial sector, this agenda is animated by diverse concerns ranging from poverty alleviation, expanding commercial financial markets and fighting financial crime (Kunz, 2011). Financial access is increasingly identified as central to satisfying these priorities with initiatives underway to link households to financial markets by providing access to a range of credit, savings, micro-insurance and mortgage products, and nation states to investment markets via the securitization of remittances (Cross, 2008; Soederberg, 2013). Considerable attention is also focused on creating the 'right financial conditions' in receiving countries to facilitate a shift in remittance expenditure from consumption to investment related activities. As a critical part of finance-led capitalism, migrants and remittance recipients are themselves being financialized or cast as 'investor' subjects disciplined to act in economically rational ways (Datta, 2012; Page and Mercer, 2012; Zapata, 2013).

While these processes of financialization may be interpreted as entailing the 'mainstreaming' of an 'alternative' financial flow, the deployment of these terms has to be problematized. Debates on the accuracy of remittance data notwithstanding, the depiction of a long-standing and endemic migrant practice and a significant financial flow as 'alternative' is problematic. Two interrelated arguments are important here: first, these terms are embedded within long-standing academic divisions which are perhaps particularly apparent in the remarkably multidisciplinary field of migration studies which spans from (development) economics through to geography, sociology and anthropology (Lindley, 2013). Within this context, understandings of what is rendered 'alternative' or 'mainstream' is dependent upon disciplinary perspective. Arguably remittances have entered the 'mainstream' in recent years partly due to their growing significance which has rendered them visible to development economists who, in the words of Page and Mercer (2012: 7) 'rule the roost'. Second, these same interdisciplinary boundaries have led to partial understandings of remittances. On the one hand, economic research focuses explicitly upon remittances rather than remittance sending/giving/taking, interprets these predominantly as a monetary resource and represents them as curiously divorced from the everyday lived practices of migrant men and women (Carling, 2014; Kunz, 2011). On the other hand, anthropological interpretations, which have highlighted the significance of social relations underpinning remittance transactions, have tended to downplay the economic agency of migrant men and women. As such, more holistic interpretations are urgently needed whereby remittances are recognized as compound transactions which extend beyond the material to encompass the emotional and the relational, and which vary within and across space and time in terms of their nature and logic (Carling, 2014).

Drawing upon empirical research conducted with diverse migrant communities in London, this chapter will begin by documenting the financialization of remittances focusing in particular on how this process has unfolded and its multi-scalar impacts particularly in relation to how finance is penetrating into the intimate spaces of everyday lives before offering a critique of these processes. This will lead onto a discussion on the understanding of remittances as 'alternative' illustrating the ways in which these transfers are economic transactions which are embedded within social relations. This section will highlight the diverse financial, social, political and cultural forms remittances assume, the norms shaping these practices and how they correspond to 'alternative' visions of development. The final part of the chapter will problematize understandings of remittances as either 'mainstream' or 'alternative' identifying the heterogeneity of migrant communities' everyday lived practices of remitting. The chapter is based upon a project, *Migrants and their Money*, which explored migrants' diverse everyday formal and informal financial practices – including those related to remittances – in London (Datta, 2012, 2009b). The project entailed 319 questionnaire interviews, 81 in-depth interviews and three focus groups conducted with migrant men and women drawn from five different communities.[1]

23.2 'MAINSTREAMING' REMITTANCES: THE FORMALIZATION AND FINANCIALIZATON OF MONEY TRANSFERS

> Migration and remittances offer a vital lifeline for millions of people and can play a major role in an economy's take-off. They enable people to partake in the global labour market and create resources that can be leveraged for development and growth. But they are also a source of political contention, and for that very reason deserving of dispassionate analysis. (Basu, 2013, World Bank's Chief Economist and Senior Vice President for Development Economics)

Defined as the 'money sent home by immigrant workers', the mainstreaming of remittances has to be understood within the context of broader debates on development, and the specific relationship between migration and development (Ratha, 2003: 157). The 'migration–development nexus', a term coined by scholars in the 1990s, encompasses diverse perspectives on this relationship ranging from largely negative to more positive views first advanced by the 'new economics of labour migration' (NELM) approach in the 1980s and 1990s (Bracking, 2003; Carling, 2004; Robinson, 2004; Taylor, 1999). Focusing explicitly on remittances, NELM advocates argued that the 'capital-gain' associated with migration outweighed concerns relating to development losses attributed, for example, to the exit of skilled workers from the Global South.

Inspiring subsequent 'money-based' or 'remittances for development' discourses, monetary concerns have come to dominate migration–development debates (Kunz, 2011; Bakker, 2015). Proponents emphasize the positive relationship between money transfers and poverty alleviation, and the potential multiplier effects of remittances which augment disposable incomes, stimulate demand for local goods and services including food, clothing, education and health and energize local, national and global economies (Ballard, 2003; Ratha, 2003; Skeldon, 2002). A well-cited study in this respect presents evidence from a World Bank commissioned study of 71 developing countries which reported that a 10 per cent increase in remittances from each migrant potentially led to a 3.5 per cent decline in the share of people living in poverty as well as reducing income inequality (Adams and Page, 2005).

Yet, the initial euphoria surrounding remittances as evidenced by its identification as a 'new development finance' has dissipated to an extent as empirical evidence illustrating that the impacts of remittances at the household, national and global levels, and on poverty, growth and in/equality, are highly variable and context specific, has mounted (Bracking, 2003; Brown, 2006; De Haas, 2005; Gamlen, 2014; Ratha, 2003; Robinson, 2004). Despite efforts to the contrary, for neoliberal proponents the fact that the majority of migrant remittances continue to be devoted to meeting the subsistence needs of migrants' families with only 10 per cent being invested in entrepreneurial activities is problematic (Orozco and Fedewa, 2005). This critique has been accompanied by revived debates about the 'brain-drain' partly attributable to the adoption of points based immigration systems by a number of host countries including the UK which privilege and facilitate skilled migration, and the dependency which remittances potentially induce in countries of emigration as (young) people aspire to be migrants over and above other productive activities (Cross, 2008).

As a consequence there have been subtle shifts in money based strategies as Kunz (2011: 57) argues: 'initially it [money based discourse] emphasized the intrinsic benefits of migration and remittances for development, and now, it acknowledges that the potential for remittances and migration for development can only be achieved under certain conditions'. From the early 2000s, these conditions have been explicitly related to a broader financial inclusion agenda (Roy, 2010; Soederberg, 2013; Schwittay, 2011). With roughly 2.8 billion people identified globally as lacking access to formal financial services (including banking, micro-credit, savings, housing loans and insurance), poverty alleviation is increasingly positioned as being dependent upon financial access which, it is posited, will raise individual and household productivity, stabilize livelihoods and protect against emergencies (Datta, 2012; Schwittay, 2011). Importantly, financial inclusion has been adopted as a core development strategy in the wake of the 2008 financial crisis, embraced by the G20 as potentially aiding global economic recovery while stabilizing the financial system and also featuring in the Sustainable Development Goals which will define the post-2015 development agenda (see below; also Soederberg, 2013).

Even while the microfinance industry has been both the target of, and the vantage point from which, processes of the financialization or marketization of development have been critically investigated, more recent research has been attentive to the ways in which transnational migrant remittances are being incorporated into global financial systems (Cross, 2015; Datta, 2012; Hudson, 2008; Roy, 2010; Zapata, 2013).[2] Hudson (2008) identifies two mechanisms through which this agenda is being pursued: first a greater attention to the ways in which money travels from migrants to recipients which is mediated by a remittance marketplace, and second the expansion of the financial outreach of formal financial institutions to peoples and places which have hitherto been excluded. To this, one can add a third dimension which entails the reconstitution of migrants and remittance recipients as 'investors' with attempts being made to 'improve' migrants' behaviour primarily in relation to what they do with their money (see Datta, 2012; Page and Mercer, 2012).

Considering these briefly in turn, initiatives regarding the mechanisms by which remittances travel from migrants to beneficiaries have rotated around the financial intermediation of money transfers and reduction of transaction costs. The case for formalizing remittance transfers is shaped by two intertwined agendas: the expansion of financial markets and the securitization of migration in the aftermath of 9/11 due to an (erroneous) association of informal money transfers with terrorist financing and money laundering (see Atia, 2007; De Goede, 2003, 2008; Farrant et al., 2006; Fugfugosh, 2006).[3] Formalization initiatives have been spearheaded by the World Bank which has worked in conjunction with a special task force on retail payment systems, the Committee on Payment and Settlement Systems, to identify key principles upon which the international remittance service edifice should rest.[4] Endorsed by the G8, G20 and the Financial Stability Forum, these principles seek to render the formal remittance industry more competitive, transparent and accessible so that it emerges as a viable option for a greater number of migrants across different remittance corridors and have been adopted and implemented through a series of public–private partnerships.[5]

This priority has entailed an engagement with the multi-billion dollar remittance 'marketplace' which has emerged in response to the global demand for remittance services and is comprised of 'various actors, institutions and procedures through which money is transferred from migrants to their families' (Pieke et al., 2005: 14; also Maimbo, 2004; Lindley, 2009; Orozco, 2004). Alongside remitters and recipients, remittance service providers (RSPs) (and/or their agents) who operate in both host and home countries are crucial in relaying information and money up and down the remittance mile (see Carling et al., 2007; Orozco, 2004). At the formal end of the spectrum, these financial intermediaries include banks, post offices and credit unions and non-bank financial intermediaries (NBFIs) of which money transfer organizations (MTOs) are the most important. The latter can be subdivided into large global enterprises such as Western Union and MoneyGram[6] and specialist MTOs which concentrate on specific remittance corridors and which, in certain contexts, may be more usefully identified as semi-formal institutions. At the informal end, remittances are hand carried as cash or transmitted using *hawaala*, an informal value transfer system, with the latter generating the most political anxiety in relation to tracking money as it travels across borders (De Geode, 2003, 2008).

Public policy identifies high transaction costs as the main barrier to formalization endeavours which rest upon encouraging account to account transfers utilizing formal RSPs.[7] An increased appreciation that even a small decrease in transaction costs can translate into noteworthy increases in remittance receipts has led to concerted efforts to reduce these costs with the global average cost declining from 9.8 per cent to 8.72 per cent[8] of the principle value in recent years (Carling et al., 2007; Hugo, 2010; World Bank, 2015). However, this decline falls short of the ambitious '5 + 5' target adopted by the G20 Global Remittance Working Group which has promulgated the reduction of the global average of transaction costs from 10 to 5 per cent over a period of five years. Indeed, transaction costs have remained stubbornly high in some corridors, such as for example, in the African continent where the average transaction cost stands at 12.06 per cent (Cross, 2015; Watkins and Quattri, 2014). Banks are particularly identified as 'non-transparent' costly remittance service providers, with the majority of these located in Europe including France, Germany, Italy and the Netherlands, partly due to their failure to offer dedicated remittance services such that migrants use the same costly infrastructure put in place for high volume transfers. Differences between official and 'black' market foreign exchange currency rates further render informal transfers more attractive. The World Bank (2015) also acknowledges that concerns over money laundering are keeping costs high by increasing compliance costs for commercial banks and money transfer operators, and delaying the entry of new players and the use of mobile technology.

Notwithstanding these difficulties, a second and interrelated mechanism by which financialization is unfolding, is via the financial inclusion of migrants in host countries and remittance recipients in home countries. Toxopeus and Lensink (2007) argue that remittances foster relationship building between banks, remitters and recipients due to their informational and direct value. Even while remittance services offered by banks may be unprofitable 'loss leaders', the argument is that that once banked, both remitters and recipients can be 'cross-sold' financial products which complement remittance sending, and 'up-sold' more sophisticated financial services including credit thus enabling banks to expand their financial reach and market share (Yujuico, 2009). Research conducted in the US suggests that banked migrants are able to save more, remit more and acquire credit and assets in both home and host societies (Ameudo-Dorantes and Bansak, 2006). Further, if remittances are paid out via formal institutions at the receiving end then this process can also engender the financial incorporation of remittance beneficiaries (see below; also Ballard, 2003; Farrant et al., 2006). Thus, regular remittance receipts give banks an opportunity to accumulate information about new (recipient) clients who are able to build up a financial history which, checked against present and future remittance receipts, enables similar cross- and up-selling. Remittances can also potentially act as a form of (informal) insurance against loan defaults while enabling low income households to move into higher income brackets which are more appealing to banks (Toxopeus and Lensink, 2007). Formal transmission ticks another key public policy priority relating to how remittances are spent. Remittance recipients who are unable to access appropriate financial products and services are reported as finding it difficult to accumulate savings with a higher proportion of transfers subsequently spent on more 'unproductive' items (Connell and Conway, 2000). The argument then is that formally accumulated remittances potentially promote entrepreneurship with both present and future remittances acting as collateral for loans thus enabling a transnational accumulation of assets.

Formal remittance receipts also potentially promote broader financial depth and development in home countries through the accumulation of foreign exchange reserves, enlargement of tax bases and improved national credit rating via securitization. As the 2009 UNDP Human Development Report points out, transnational migration is an increasingly costly affair comprising of official fees charged for issuing documents such as passports, clearances including visas, and costs related to travel expenses which include departure taxes. While some of these revenues may disappear into the pockets of officials as bribes, a proportion does potentially contribute to an expanded tax base. There is also a link between remittances and improved national credit rating arising from the securitization of money transfers (Hudson, 2008). Traditionally focused on the conversion of mortgages, loans and credit card receipts, the securitization market has diversified considerably and now extends to the securitization of future flows of remittances as an income stream. The advantages of this become apparent where they achieve high credit ratings, enabling poorer governments to secure low-cost but long-term credit which is often in short supply particularly in periods of economic downturn (although see Soederberg, 2013). Thus, financial flows which start off as intra-household transfers can potentially emerge as a new development finance.

There is some evidence that the banking sector is showing greater interest in remittances in both sending and receiving countries, spurred on no doubt by the size of these financial flows, even while their penetration in this market remains fairly modest[9] (Toxopeus and Lensink, 2007). Milligan (2009) documents the activities of *Banco Solidario*, a microfinance institution in Ecuador, which has formed partnerships with Spanish banks in an attempt to encourage migrants to remit using their products. Such initiatives are part of a wider strategy to foster broader financial relationships with migrants who are also offered short term credit to meet their financial needs in Spain as well as savings, insurance and mortgage products in Ecuador. Other banks such as the Indian ICICI, Andhra Bank and State Bank of India all provide free money transfers if minimum balance requirements are met. Meanwhile in host countries like the US, Wells Fargo have facilitated the financial inclusion of Mexican migrants by accepting Mexican identification documents, the *Matricula Consular*, in order to open accounts. Once banked, migrants are offered remittance products through the bank's *ExpressSend* service which waives service fees in conjunction with other financial services.

A third strand of financialization initiatives revolve around reconstituting migrant and beneficiaries identities. Scholars have noted the fact that the monetized migration–development discourses ascribe a particular identity and agential capacity to migrants who are variously positioned as 'development agents' and 'national heroes' (Datta, 2009a). Page and Mercer (2012) argue that this nexus rests upon the key discursive figure of the hard working migrant who maintains an active and meaningful relationship with the place from which s/he came and who is driven by a desire to aid these communities. Information is seen as being key to changing migrants' values in the belief that in so doing migrant behaviour towards remittance sending and expenditure will 'improve'. Thus, for example, a lack of information about available investment opportunities is identified as the key barrier resulting in, for example, an over-investment of remittances in service based micro-enterprises which are at best 'marginally productive' (Potter and Phillips, 2006: 587).

Critical analysis of this global remittance agenda – or financialization of development and remittances – has emerged in recent years. Cross (2015: 307) points to the dangers of the incorporation of 'financial stakeholders in policy-making and development practice' which is leading, in the words of Roy (2010: 386) to a 'mission drift from poverty alleviation to profit maximization'. The speculative tendencies of financial inclusion strategies are interpreted as an articulation of wider strategies of capital accumulation with a powerful transnational capital sector and the state working in collusion (Soederberg, 2013).

New neoliberal subjectivities and narrowly defined market-centred constructions of citizenship are criticized for resulting in the careful integration of responsibilized citizens into global financial markets. Charting this process, Roy (2010: 5, 64) argues that poor people and their communities are being transformed into what she terms a 'frontier market' built on a consensus that 'poor people do not only possess assets but are assets'. Finally, the presumption that migrants act the way that they do (in economically irrational ways leading to a lack of development specific action) due to dearth of information is deemed erroneous (Page and Mercer, 2012). In fact migrants' diverse behaviours in relation to the motivations shaping remittance sending, how remittances are spent, saved and/or invested and how they are transmitted are critically shaped by the social relations in which they are embedded.

23.3 PUTTING THE SOCIAL BACK INTO THE ECONOMIC: REMITTANCES AS 'ALTERNATIVE'

> Placing money in a global context also transforms its use and meaning . . . the value of money changes across borders according to the way people perceive the connection between work, money earned and sent and physical caring for families. Often the dollar sent is not the dollar received. (Singh, 2013: ix)

Running parallel with dominant economic understandings of remittances which underpin the financialization process, a more critical geographical, anthropological and ethnographic transnational literature explicates remittances in significantly different ways in relation to the forms that they take, the norms which underwrite these and the 'alternative' types of development which they support. A key argument of much of this work is the need to be attendant to the social values and relations which underpin economic transactions, and correspondingly to recognize remittances as both economic and social resources (Cliggett, 2005; Ferguson, 1999; Levitt, 1998; Levitt and Lamba-Nieves, 2011). The starting premise is that privileging the economic is problematic as is the (false) dichotomy between economic and social realms (Levitt and Lamba-Nieves, 2011). Challenging economistic renditions which present remitting as normal, unchanged and therefore unchangeable, Page and Mercer (2012) argue for the need to recognize that remittances are fundamentally a social practice embedded within socially inscribed everyday practices. As such '[remittance] exchanges contain a bundle of meanings that cannot be polarised into formalised economic *or* social value; they must be understood as intertwined' recognizing specifically that material exchanges alone cannot foster social relations and networks (Cliggett, 2005: 38; Ferguson, 1999).

Tellingly, perhaps, the focus of this research is not explicitly on remittances but rather a more holistic consideration of migrant/ion practices of which remitting is just one aspect (Carling, 2014). A key argument is that remittances are inherently varied and diverse such that they are not embodied simply or only as money but also as gifts, ideas and knowledge which transcend the economic to encompass the social and cultural (Cliggett, 2003, 2005; Levitt, 1998; Levitt and Lamba-Nieves, 2011). Levitt's (1998: 5) deployment of the term 'social remittances' captures some of this diversity. Defining these as 'ideas, behaviours, identities and social capital' that flow 'continuously and iteratively' in transnational social spaces, she argues migrants arrive in host communities with sets of social and cultural tools which, depending on the nature and the extent of their integration, are reconstituted (see also Levitt and Lamba-Nieves, 2011). Travelling back and forth between home and host communities, social remittances have a significant bearing upon normative structures (ideas, values and beliefs), systems of practice (in relation to, for example, household labour, religious practices) and social capital. Thus, for example, remittance sending may be predicated upon strategic decisions on which social relations are important and which can be let go of, and these are often judged against anticipated future need (see below). Viewed as such, economic transfers have demonstrable positive and negative social outcomes in relation to attitudes towards gender norms and relations, political values, cultural norms and religious practices.

Just as remittances are recognized as taking varied form, a second strand of this body of work has problematized the motivations which shape remittance sending, recognizing that these are also context specific and shaped by sociocultural foundations

(Carling, 2014). An influential economic framework explains remittance sending in relation to a broad continuum ranging from 'altruism' at one extreme to 'self-interest' at the other, with positions of 'enlightened self-interest/tempered altruism' located in between these extremes (Lucas and Stark, 1985; also Brown, 2006; Datta et al., 2007). In turn, insurance – either individual or family based co-insurance – influences remittance sending to varying extents enabling migrants to shore up their positions in their households and communities (Carling, 2008). Importantly, this framework also suggests that while remittances sent for altruistic reasons are often used for consumption/subsistence purposes, those guided by self-interest are likely to be invested in physical asset accumulation (such as land and housing) and/or financial assets (in savings accounts, pensions and so on). Transnational approaches have revisited the narrow economic thesis of 'cooperative households' highlighting more complex transnational households and families. These more critical accounts have borrowed from anthropological theories of the 'gift economy' whereby remittances are understood as creating and/or strengthening social bonds between the giver and recipient and where the act of giving and receiving is structured by an interplay of altruism and reciprocity (see Lucas and Stark, 1985; also Cliggett, 2005; Lindley, 2013; Mawdsley, 2012).

Integrating the social, material and symbolic aspects of remitting, such perspectives challenge economic interpretations which view money as being about the market to stress the fact that it is in fact embedded within social worlds. Cliggett's research among the Gwembe Tonga in Zambia exemplifies this in that not only does it further problematize the nature of the 'thing' being given[10] – in her case study gifts (sugar, *chitenges*), small sums of cash and/or transfer of resources (gendered labour) – but also the motivations underwriting these exchanges. The gifts, she argues, while seemingly insignificant in terms of market value hold much greater symbolic value as they convey affection and remembrance, recognition, the interdependency of both remitters and recipients and an investment and maintenance of social networks which operate on the basis of mutual reciprocity. As such, while the intrinsic value of the actual gift maybe inconsequential, the process of 'giving creates, represents and reinforces social relationships' and sustains connections between people and places (Cliggett, 2005: 38). Mata Codesal (2015) further argues that remittances need to be deconstructed to acknowledge the diverse meanings which underpin different types/uses of remittances which range from savings, debt repayment and emergency money to maintenance and gift money. The latter three, she contends, reflect nurturing and 'materializations of affection' (Codesal, 2015: 58). More holistic understandings of these transfers depend upon their contextualization within the frame of receivers' needs and resources, migrants expenses and income and negotiations between members of transnational families.

This critical scholarship deploys more nuanced complex understandings of agency which challenge the depiction of migrants as primarily 'development agents', the lack of agential capacity ascribed to remittance recipients as well as the investing of agency in the individual as opposed to the social group (Cliggett, 2003, 2005; Datta, 2009a; Page and Mercer, 2012). Taking these in turn, Kunz (2011) argues that economistic accounts tend to present remittances as de-personalized and abstract practices paying little attention to the costs involved in generating these remittances. These costs are evidenced in research on low paid migrants in London which documents both how remittances are funded as well as the considerable economic, social and emotional sacrifices that migrants make in order to remit (Datta et al., 2007; Datta, 2009a; Datta, 2012). Remittance recipients are also afforded agential capacity such that they are not represented as mere 'beneficiaries' of transfers (a label ascribed to them in neoliberalized migration–development policy literature) or indeed broader financial inclusion initiatives. Instead, the instrumental role they play is highlighted. Returning back to Cliggett's (2005) research in Zambia, remitting is linked to 'place-holding' among migrants who wish to return back to their home villages which entails a mutual recognition by migrants of their rural kin by the giving of gifts and the recipients acknowledgement of migrants' investment in social networks which enables a successful return to home villages. As such migrants and recipients are inter-dependent challenging a common representation of the former supporting the latter. A third dimension of agency which this scholarship explores is the ascription of agency to the social group as opposed to the individual (Page and Mercer, 2012). My research with Somali migrants illustrates the collective familial and clan effort which goes into the migration of a family member to advanced economies such as the UK and the considerable sacrifice that this entails in relation to the erosion of scarce assets and the operationalization of transnational migrant networks (Datta, 2012). These context-specific insights explicate the subsequent obligation that migrant men and women experience to remit.

Finally, these discourses also challenge the rendering of development as primarily an economic process. In elaborating upon a 'new' migration–development nexus, academics have highlighted the importance of adopting alternative development optics including rights based and gendered perspectives, identifying 'new' actors in the form of transnational civil society organizations and 'new' forms of knowledge transfer from the Global South to Global North (Faist, 2008; Kunz, 2011; Petrozziello, 2013; Piper, 2008, 2009). Such perspectives are themselves more in line with radical understandings of development as grass-root based, sustainable and alternative. Within this context, critics have questioned how and why private intra-household transfers are being subjected to 'public scrutiny', why certain expenditures are condemned as 'frivolous consumption' and why poor households are expected to save and/or invest remittances rather than spend (Cross, 2008; Horst et al., 2014). They have particularly challenged the classification of remittance expenditure as having either 'productive' or 'unproductive' outcomes given that the latter often entail significant subsistence purchases relating to food, health and education. These, in turn, are arguably critical for the well-being and welfare of households and families, and cognizant with both sustainable livelihood and capabilities perspectives on development (Chappell and Sriskandarajah, 2007). Indeed, as Connell and Conway (2000) point out, higher levels of consumption are an indication of major welfare gains and improvements in basic needs (Carling, 2004; De Haas, 2005).

While this scholarship has contributed significantly to more critical understandings of remittances, and the migration–development nexus, it is perhaps overly attentive to the social at the expense of the economic which the final section of this chapter addresses.

23.4 STRADDLING THE ECONOMIC AND THE SOCIAL: REMITTANCE SENDING AS LIVED EVERYDAY PRACTICES

The preceding discussion has highlighted the emergence of largely dichotomous understandings of remittances. Drawing upon research which interrogated the remittance practices of Bulgarian, Polish, Turkish, Somali and Brazilian migrant men and women, this section of the chapter seeks to bridge this distance between 'mainstream'–'alternative', economic–social, readings of remittances so as to frame them more holistically as everyday lived economic and social practices. Beginning with a broad overview of migrant men and women's remittance practices, the discussion proceeds to focus on the ways in which remittances travel from migrants to recipients, partly because this is the predominant site in which processes of financialization are unfolding but also because it has received relatively little critical academic attention to date (although see Datta, 2012; Lindley, 2009).

Immediately problematizing the categorization of remittances as 'alternative', the majority of migrant men and women (67 per cent, or 214 of 319 survey participants) who participated in this research identified themselves as remitters, albeit with some variation across the five research communities.[11] Indeed, money transfers were an integral component of the everyday financial practices – a routine item in weekly/monthly outgoings – of a significant number of London based migrants with over half remitters sending money on a monthly basis and a further 6 per cent remitting two or three times a month. In turn, both the prevalence and regularity with which remittances were sent was perhaps surprising given that even while the majority of migrants were employed (82 per cent), they were predominantly working in low paid jobs (see Table 23.1). Again, employment rates varied across the five migrant communities reflecting broader research which documents high levels of employment among East and Central European migrants (both in relation to the UK-born population and other migrant communities) with lower rates of employment associated with asylum and refugee populations (Sumption and Sommerville, 2010).

Correspondingly, just under 60 per cent of the participants worked in London's low wage – and some would argue migrant-dependent – economy, concentrated in the hospitality, construction, care and cleaning sectors (see also Wills et al., 2010). This said, gender, racial and national divisions of labour interrelated with a migrant division of labour such that, for example, while the majority of Brazilian women were domestic cleaners and/or nannies, their male compatriots tended to work in catering, construction and office cleaning. Or to take another example, while the majority of Polish and Bulgarian research participants were concentrated in the building/construction trades (dominated by men), followed by retail, cleaning and hospitality (in kitchens, and as bar tenders), all but two of the Turkish migrants were employed in an ethnic economy working for co-national employers in a variety of low paid occupations ranging from cashiers and general shop assistants in Turkish supermarkets, in pitta bread factories, as butchers and as cooks in Turkish takeaways. Reflecting the 'low skilled' status ascribed to the work that they did, wages earned from these occupations were low with over half of migrants (54 per cent) earning £1,000 or less a month, and wage levels particularly poor in the Turkish and Somali communities (see Table 23.1). In order to augment their wages, a number of research participants worked long hours, held down two or more jobs (14 per cent of all employed migrants), with additional jobs also often held in the low wage – and at times an

Table 23.1 Economic circumstances of migrant households in London

	Brazilian (n=119)	Bulgarian (n=54)	Polish (n=36)	Somali (n=80)	Turkish (n=30)	TOTAL (n=319)
Employment status						
Employed	96	96	100	50	60	82
Unemployed	4	4	0	50	40	18
Wages per month	(n=114)	(n=52)	(n=36)	(n=40)	(n=18)	(n=260)
Less than £200	2	0	0	5	0	2
£201–400	5	0	0	18	6	5
£401–600	11	4	6	5	17	8
£601–800	8	12	17	17	32	13
£801–1,000	29	26	22	20	27	26
£1,001–1,200	18	23	19	22	0	19
£1,201–1,400	10	23	3	2	0	10
£1,401–1,600	7	10	8	5	6	7
£1,601–1,800	2	0	3	3	6	2
£1,801–2,000	4	2	14	3	0	5
£2,001–2,200	0	0	0	0	0	0
Over £2,201	3	0	0	0	0	1
No response	1	0	8	0	6	2

Source: Questionnaire survey.

informal – economy. Furthermore, amongst Turkish and Somali migrants, whose employment rates were lower in comparison to the other three communities, research participants reported being in receipt of various welfare payments including job seekers allowance, working tax credit and child benefit. Average monthly benefit income at the time of the research ranging from £451 in the Somali community to £629 in Turkish households.

Given their economic circumstances, interviews with migrant men and women revealed that remittances were funded through a mixture of wages (37 per cent of migrants), savings (29 per cent) and even benefits payments (10 per cent) such that sending remittances arguably eroded migrants' financial assets. Migrants were saving, for example, for others, or stretching their benefit income to meet the needs of their transnational family members. Furthermore, unanticipated expenses in home countries – particularly those related to medical emergencies but also the payment of debts – pressurized migrants even further. Often involving larger sums of money than normally sent, these were met by acquiring loans, usually from family and friends in order to remit. To this end, Rosana borrowed £1000 from a friend in order to send money home to her mother in Brazil at short notice.

Verifying that these transfers were predicated upon and reinforced social relations, the main remittance recipients were close family members including spouses, parents and children. It was only among the Somali community that remittances were likely to be sent to a much wider group (comprising 15 people in the case of one migrant man) reflecting the clan based organization of social relations in this community. The underlying motivations for these transfers were diverse and contingent upon migrants' own and their family's circumstances, their position in the life course, the nature of their obligations back home, and their financial situation in London. It was this contextualization which explicated why migrants remitted, namely that even while transferring money on a regular basis was eroding their economic and financial capital, it augmented stocks of social capital. Furthermore, some migrant men and women articulated remittance sending practices as a moral duty. Depending on their national origins, migrants remitted back to family members who were living in communities in which political conflict was rife and economic restructuring had disrupted lives and livelihoods. To this end, Zahra, a Somali woman, who could only afford to send £50 every month or two, felt that her remittances were critical as 'it's important to help the people left behind. The international community does not give them anything. People in Somalia have nothing, they cannot work, there are so many problems and [they are] needy people, nor can we support them. But they need help'.

Yet significantly, remitting was not only in response to need, and driven by altruism, but also reflected economic agency being exercised by migrants who sought to cement their own financial position through the transnational accumulation of financial and physical assets as well as the disposal of financial liabilities including debts. This was more evident among those migrants who originated from middle income countries such as Brazil with 45 per cent of migrant men and women remitting to pay bills and debts accrued in their home country (including utility payments, outstanding credit card bills, mortgage payments and pension contributions), 17 per cent contributing towards the upkeep of their families, 12 per cent investing in land, housing or businesses and the remainder utilizing remittances for a combination of the above. Fleshing this out further in in-depth interviews and highlighting intra-community differences, Rita, a Brazilian woman, reported that her remittances were contributing to mortgage payments for a flat she was buying and while 'if there is a need, I may send to relatives, but everybody in Brazil is doing fine, they don't need it . . . I am tight-fisted anyway! And as I said before, our profile [class position] is slightly different from that of the majority of Brazilians here'.

In relation to remittance expenditure, some migrants felt that they had little control over how money received was spent highlighting in these cases the extent to which remittances were seen as 'shared money' – Amina, a Somali woman, argued that her money 'has to stretch' as her mother was entitled to a share of this income. In a majority of cases it was clear that remittances were spent on subsistence related items particularly in the Somali (98 per cent) and Bulgarian (65 per cent) communities. These remittances enabled family members to pay for food, basic utility bills, school fees as well as medical bills. Other migrants highlighted that they were paying towards the education costs of children with Svetla from Bulgaria, sending money home every month to support her ill and unemployed husband, pay for her son's school fees and support her daughter who was employed in a low wage job. In her words, 'it is not a matter of investment, it is a matter of survival'.

This said, other migrants identified a lack of investment opportunities in home countries as determining the expenditure of their remittances. In part at least, Somali migrants' remittances were used for subsistence purposes both because they were insufficient to fund investment, as well as the fact that opportunities to invest were far and few between. Asha, from Somalia, sent money to her sister's children for their daily subsistence needs and said that she would need to send at least 'US$2,000' in order to set up a business for her relatives to run which was beyond her means given that she herself was dependent on benefit income. Interestingly some migrants argued that relatives were more eager to receive these subsistence-related remittances rather than being pushed to set up businesses illustrating the dependency which remittances can engender. In turn, the dearth of investment opportunities in home villages and towns also prohibited investment related remittance expenditure. Asha's compatriot Ahmed who sent money to his wife argued that 'she can't invest, because she lives in a small village, you can't open a shop there is no one but her family so there is no point in her investing'. Such findings lend weight to money based discourses on remittances which attribute a lack of investment of remittances to the absence of the 'right' financial conditions in home countries.

Having provided an overview of migrant men and women's remittance sending practices which are shaped by an interplay of economic and social 'rationalities', the discussion now turns to consider the institutions which migrants engage with in order to send money to remittance recipients. Such an interrogation is instructive as this is a key site in which the financialization of remittances is unveiling even while, as discussed above, it has received relatively limited academic attention. Table 23.2 illustrates the key remittance service providers utilized by migrants across the five researched communities with distinct patterns

Table 23.2 RSPs utilized across five migrant communities, per cent

	Brazilian (n=85)	Bulgarian (n=23)	Polish (n=27)	Somali (n=61)	Turkish (n=19)	TOTAL (n=215)
Banks/ Post Office	2 (Banco de Brasil; Post Office)	30 (NatWest)	0	0	11 (Turkiye is Bankasi)	5
Large MTOs	4 (Western Union)	22 (Western Union; MoneyGram)	11 (Western Union)	2 (Western Union and Dahabshiil)	0	6
Specialist MTOs	94 (LCC; Intertransfer; Speedfast; Moneyone Express; Money transfer; Safe Transfer; Easy Transfer; Transfast; Other*)	0	74 (Sami Swoi; LCC; Gosia Travel; Hascobar; Cheque-point)	98 (Dahabshiil; IFTIN; Qaran Express; Mustaqbal; Amal; Somalia hawala)	0	74
Hand carry By migrants, family members and friends	0	48	15	0	89	15

Note: *Including a hair salon and travel company.

Source: Questionnaire surveys.

evident in each of the remittance corridors. While remitting via banks and hand carrying (as the two extremes of the formal-informal RSP continuum) were active in two of the five communities (Bulgarian and Turkish), it was the MTO sector which emerged as the most significant remittance intermediary in the other three (Polish, Brazilian and Somali). In part this reflects the size and diversity of the UK MTO sector with approximately 3,750 UK registered MTOs in mid-2009 operating through some 30,000 outlets as compared to 60 MTOs in Spain, 30 in Germany and three in France (see below; Financial World, 2008; Vargas-Silva, 2011). With 80 per cent of all remittances sent through this sector, a further distinction could be made between the larger global MTOs and the more specialist remittance corridor specific organizations with the latter capturing the lion's share of remittances. Thus, for example, while all Somali migrants and 98 per cent of Brazilians remitted via MTOs, of these 98 per cent and 94 per cent respectively used specialist agencies with migrants identifying a number of agencies specifically serving their communities.

What factors account for these remittance sending practices? Migrants' agential capacity is clearly tempered by broader structural factors which determine the choices available to them. I elaborate on two here, the first being the number of RSPs operational in specific remittance corridors. Of the five researched communities, the remittance marketplace was much less diversified for Somali and Turkish migrants then it was for Brazilian, Polish and Bulgarian migrants. Focusing on the Somali case, banks and larger MTOs including MoneyGram did not offer remittance services to this community largely due to the decimation of the financial industry in Somalia and the consequent lack of suitable partner payout institutions. Furthermore, while bank based remittance services were theoretically available for migrants drawn from the other researched communities, they were actively targeting some while redlining others. The use of UK banks to remit among Bulgarian migrants, for example, was in direct response to a specific initiative put in place by a high street bank which encouraged Bulgarian men and women to open a bank account in London from which funds could be transferred into a 'remittance' account which recipients could access via debit cards issued in their names. By the same token, Brazilian migrants were construed as risky particularly in relation to the extension of credit. For these and Turkish migrants, their own national banks provided a service which appeared to be more tailored to their needs.

Beyond RSPs, migrants' immigration status also played a key role in shaping available choices. Here the critical factor related to requirements to produce identity verification documents so as to engage in foreign transfers about which irregular migrants were particularly cautious. The sorting of migrants remittance sending patterns along the lines evidenced in Table 23.2 is partly the result of the hitherto two-tier regulatory stance adopted by the UK government in relation to payment services organizations dealing with foreign exchange payments. This framework defines and structures the ways in which money transfers take place, the institutions authorized to engage in international payments and the conditions under which foreign currency transfers are allowed. Key areas of concern include anti-money laundering requirements, 'know-your-customer' (KYC) requirements, level of enforcement and compliance types and remittance transfer processing. Even while banks (supposedly) comply with these regulations and face significant fines if they fail to do so, MTOs were not subjected to same regulatory rigour prior to the late 2000s. Yet, coinciding with the timing of this research, this situation began to change partly due to the Financial Action Taskforce's (an intergovernmental agency) remit to address variance across the EU in terms of the treatment of remittance service providers and to subject NBFIs to the same level of licensing and supervision applied to retail banking which was evident in a number of European nations including Germany (Carling et al., 2007; Pieke et al., 2005; Vleck, 2006). In an effort to comply, the UK government set up the UK Remittance Taskforce which formulated a Remittance Charter aimed at spreading 'best practice' among RSPs as well as the establishment of a remittance price comparison website (*Send Money Home*[12]) (Datta, 2009a). In turn, the oversight of RSPs shifted from Her Majesty's Revenue and Customs Department to the (former) Financial Services Authority (FSA) which phased in a twin system of 'registration' (applicable to smaller NBFIs) and 'authorization' with the critical distinction being that the latter required a safeguarding of clients' money as well as FSA checks on all associated agents. The clear intention was that all financial intermediaries would be required to obtain the latter status over a period of time. Further, following the introduction of the Payment Services Directive in the UK, more pressure has been brought to bear upon MTOs particularly with regard to 'KYC' requirements which has particular implications for irregular migrants (see below).

Situated within these structural constraints, migrant choices reflected an interplay of financial and economic considerations (which given the hardship that they endured in order to remit was understandable), alongside social reasoning. For a start and reinforcing the World Bank's mantra, the cost of remitting mattered to migrants. This was perhaps best expressed by Jacinto, a Brazilian migrant, who argued that migrants who worked in the low wage economy had to 'sweat a lot to earn money here and send it over to Brazil' and were therefore very mindful of the 'tips' or transaction costs associated with remittance sending. Formal RSPs including banks and the large MTOs, often came off worst in price comparisons not only due to high transaction costs but also poor exchange rate spread. Among UK based banks, while the cost charged by SWIFT for account to account transfers is low (which constitute a small minority of all transfers), banks charge a flat fee to cover their administrative charges which starts at £20 (Isaacs, 2008). Furthermore, among migrants' own national banks, the exchange rate offered was identified as being poor. The latter was evidenced in a focus group held with Brazilian migrants in which all the participants agreed that the exchange rate offered by the Brazilian state bank, *Banco de Brasil* was 'not so good, the exchange rate of remittance agencies is much better'. Importantly, remittances transferred over a bank counter were also perceived as running the risk of being picked up by tax authorities in home countries. Jacinto reflected that a number of his compatriots avoided using *Banco do Brasil* in case the Inland Revenue in Brazil taxed these. In his words, one did want to 'work hard here to pay the layabouts over there'.

In contrast to the rather inflexible service that they encountered in banks, MTOs were identified as being much more competitive. Given the fierce competition within this diverse sector, it is not surprising that many niche MTOs offer a number of incentives to attract customers. In many cases these amounted to financial incentives such as special introductory offers for new customers and lower transaction fees for regular customers. Mimicking sales tactics found in large retail industries, Dahabshiil which served a significant proportion of the Somali participants in this research was reported as offering customers a loyalty card, the 'Dahabcard', whereby customers are able to collect points which they could redeem against lower transaction costs in the future and the partial or complete waiving of the transfer fee. Other specialist services were identified by a Polish participant who had 'tried the LCC and Western Union, but Sami Swoi are the best – the best exchange rate, they text the family that money has been sent, the service is really very helpful'.

Yet, importantly, it was not only cost – or economic rationality – which drove migrant choice. This was perhaps most clearly evidenced by the fact that only a small number of migrants had changed their RSP in the year preceding the research despite an awareness of cheaper services available elsewhere. Security and trust emerged as crucial factors in shaping remittance practices. In the same focus group discussion identified above, the participants agreed that while specialist MTOs offered more competitive prices:

> [It] is dangerous [to use these], like with *Banco do Brasil* it is all above board, so you send your money and you know it will arrive, but the exchange rate is no good, whereas with the agencies it is dangerous but their exchange rate is much better, you really risk [losing your money] in the remittance agencies.

Given that personal experiences of remittances not arriving at their destination were restricted to an extremely small number of research participants, such perceptions were undoubtedly shaped by a wider discourse on the insecurity that 'informal' remittance sending entailed. A number of migrants cited media reports of MTOs which had collapsed leaving migrants out of pocket (see also Saini, 2007).

Equally, however, other migrants were sceptical about the amount of faith one could place in banks. Given the timing of this research which coincided amidst actual and perceived fears of banking failure in the UK at the start of the financial crisis, it was not uncommon for research participants to question the security of banks both in relation to providing secure remittance services as well as banking services. The hand carrying of remittances was partly understandable in this context. Largely prevalent among Turkish and Polish migrants who originated from geographically proximate countries thus enabling more frequent visits either by migrants themselves or by their friends and family members, hand carrying was clearly predicated upon trust and faith that remittances would arrive where intended. As expressed by Andrez, a Polish man: 'of course the best way is to give to your family in person or to give to someone to hand over . . . my brother in law took some cash some time ago and this is a safe way, you know one must trust the family'.

The retail strategies of MTOs identified above also reflected an understanding and operationalization of the social relations which underpin economic transactions. At least part of the attraction of (especially specialist) MTOs is undoubtedly related to the fact that they are tailored to a migrant client base. The physical presence of these MTOs in the communities in which migrant communities dominate as well as longer opening hours are particularly suited to migrants long and irregular working hours. Further, many provided language specific services to their clients, were familiar with the places left behind and had a wider presence in their communities engaging in organizing and funding diverse diaspora events. Importantly, even while at the time of the research MTOs did not require identity verification for transactions below £600 as well as for repeat transaction customers, informal discussions with several representatives from the MTO sector revealed the incidence of what may be termed 'front of shop' and 'back of shop' services whereby the latter could be used to remit sums in excess of £600 without having to produce the pre-requisite identification documents. This was explained in terms of the intense competition endemic in this sector and the consequent importance of retaining clients. Banks would be hard pressed to compete with the services that MTOs offer.

While remittance agencies are often seen as 'transaction based' businesses as opposed to 'relationship based' banks, it could be argued that these agencies are more in the business of building relationships with migrant communities by re-inscribing social relations into financial transactions. Yet, many of these operators are themselves identified as 'high risk' businesses and face considerable hurdles in opening business bank accounts in high street retail banks. These tensions were brought to the fore in 2013 when Barclays Bank announced its intention to shut the business accounts of 250 small and medium size remittance Money Transfer Organizations in the UK. Judging MTOs to be 'high risk' yet low value migrant businesses, the Bank's increased vigilance was influenced by the US$1.9 billion fine levied on HSBC by US regulators for its purported involvement in facilitating money laundering. Barclays Bank's 'hit list' included the MTO, Dahabshiil, which as highlighted above transmits a significant proportion of UK originating money transfers to Somalia. Interestingly, it was the swift mobilization of London's East End Somali community and its *Save Remittance Giving Campaign* which underpinned Dahabshiil's ongoing legal challenge resulting in a temporary postponement of the closure of its bank accounts.

23.5 CONCLUSION

This chapter has sought to illustrate the ways in which what may be considered an 'alternative' financial flow has been 'mainstreamed' through processes of financialization. Arguing that this is partly the result of migrants' remittances coming into the purview of 'mainstream' discourses which have tended to obscure sites, flows and places outside of the hegemonic west, it has highlighted how the marketization of remittances has progressed. Mapping the ascendency of money based discourses on migration and development, it has illustrated that remittances are increasingly viewed in narrow monetary terms, as a financial resource which can be leveraged as development finance both at the household and nation-state level. Following on from this, the chapter has highlighted the limitations of the global remittance agenda drawing attention to broader critical debates which have elaborated upon remittances sending *practices* which are embedded in social relations in terms of the forms that they take and the values which underpin these exchanges. Such understandings of remittances resonate with alternative understandings of development. The chapter has argued that the dichotomous thinking which underpins remittance discourses prohibits more holistic understandings. Drawing upon research interrogating the diverse everyday remittance practices of five migrant communities in London, it has attempted to address these tensions illustrating the myriad ways in which economic and social values, norms and relations intertwine to produce particular context specific patterns of remitting. This discussion particularly focuses upon an emerging and under studied aspect of the marketization of remittances relating to the institutions which mediate transfers. Here too there is evidence that migrant men and women deploy a range of economic, social and cultural rationales and financial knowledge when engaging with these intermediaries.

Yet, on the global stage, dichotomous renditions of remittances look set to continue, and perhaps more importantly, money based discourses on remittances and development remain dominant. 2015 is a (seemingly) watershed year for D/development as it marks the transition from the millennium development goals (MDGs) to the sustainable development goals (SDGs). Indeed, as scholars such as Hudson (2008) point out, it was a 'crisis in development' – and more specifically the recognition that a number of MDGs could not be met due to a severe shortfall in development finance – which led to the initial focus on remittances as a financial flow which could be leveraged for development purposes. In the run up to the adoption of the 17 SDGs and 169 targets against which progress will be measured at a UN summit in September 2015, there has been a flurry of activity on the international scene to make sure that the significance of migration and the financial flows that it generates – including but not restricted to only remittances – is acknowledged. In relation to the financing of the SDGs, the World Bank's Migration and Development Brief of April 2015 identified 'a few under-exploited market-based financing options that are directly connected to migration. As much as $100 billion, or more, could be raised annually by developing countries' (World Bank, 2015: 12).[13] Setting aside the continued implication that it is the responsibility of migrants and their home countries to fund development endeavours (see Datta et al., 2007), in relation to remittances these options include – and to a large extent echo those identified above – reducing remittance costs and leveraging remittances for development financing via future-flow securitization of remittances, enhancing sovereign credit ratings and linking remittances to financial savings and insurance. Significantly, recent discussions also hint at what might tentatively be labelled a post-remittance agenda as possibilities for leveraging diasporic savings and philanthropic giving are also articulated (World Bank, 2015). Premised perhaps on a realization that remittances alone are an insufficient source of development finance, attention is being afforded to other more mature financial flows associated with migration such as diaspora bonds. As such, migrants' money – increasingly in all its diverse forms – continues to be framed as a vital source of development finance.

ACKNOWLEDGEMENT

The author is grateful to Policy Press for permitting use of material from her book entitled *Migrants and their Money: Surviving Financial Exclusion in London* (2012).

NOTES

1. I would like to acknowledge the Friends Provident Foundation which funded this research.
2. Arguably the financialization of remittances is not a new or recent process with historical analysis illustrating a long-standing ambition to shift migrant remittance expenditure from 'frivolous' and 'conspicuous' consumption to productive uses.
3. As Lindley (2009) argues, notwithstanding broader tendencies towards the deregulation of the financial sector, the drive for powerful states to regulate certain global financial flows after 9/11 including informal remittances which are depicted as something of a 'loose cannon' has been substantially reinvigorated on the grounds that these may undermine the stability of global financial, economic and political systems (see also Robinson, 2004: 5).
4. These principles include transparency and consumer protection, improvement of payment system

infrastructure, sound and proportionate legal and regulatory environment, competitive market conditions and appropriate governance and risk management practices (Committee on Payment and Settlement Systems and World Bank 2006).

5. The World Bank has created an institutional apparatus which focuses on research and forecasting of global remittances (the Migration and Remittances team); advice on financial regulation as it relates to global payment systems (the Financial Integrity Group) as well as the explicit connection of remittances to microfinance initiatives (the Consultative Group to Assist the Poor (CGAP). In addition it operates a Remittance Price Database, set up in 2008, designed to enable migrants to compare remittance costs within remittance corridors. In 2013, the Bank also announced a new unit, KNOMAD, the Global Knowledge Partnership on Migration and Development.
6. Both of these MTOs have extensive geographic coverage: Western Union has 470,000 agent locations across 200 countries while MoneyGram has 233,000 agents working in 191 countries with money transfer services offered through Wal-Mart stores in the US and the Post Office network in the UK (www.moneygram.com; www.westernunion.com). The large market share of these MTOs in certain 'light traffic' remittance corridors gives them near monopoly status which can result in higher transaction fees (Yujuico, 2009).
7. Remittance transaction costs comprise of three elements namely a transaction fee, foreign exchange spread and profit margins.
8. In comparison, informal channels as a whole have an average cost of between 3 to 5 per cent of the principle value while the cost of *hawaala* sending is less than 2 per cent and remittances sent by hand are often free (Hugo, 2010; Sander, 2003).
9. Banks only serve 5 per cent of the remittance market in the US with the main hurdle being limited banking penetration in home countries through which remittances could potentially be paid out (Yujuico, 2009).
10. Cliggett (2003) argues that in the context of her research migrants do not *send* but rather *give* or *take* gifts illustrating the importance of personal contact in the act of remitting.
11. Seventy-six per cent of Somalis, 75 per cent of Polish, 71 per cent of Brazilian, 63 per cent of Turkish to 43 per cent of Bulgarian migrant men and women identified themselves as remitters.
12. Similar services are offered in Spain (via the www.remesas.org website), the Netherlands (www.geldnaarhius.nl) and Norway (www.sendepenger.no) (Carling et al., 2007). Price comparison websites are partly in response to wide variations in remittance fees. For example, Isaacs (2008) reports that the fees charged for a £100 remittance from the UK to Nigeria ranges from £3 to £21.
13. The recommendations of this Brief have since fed into a series of international conferences and forums including a conference organised by the Global Migration Group, *Harnessing Migration, Remittances and Diaspora Contributions for Financing Sustainable Development* in May 2015, and the Finance for Development Meeting in July 2015 (Plaza, 2015).

REFERENCES

Adams, R. and J. Page (2005), 'Do international migration and remittances reduce poverty in developing countries?', *World Development*, **33**, 1645–1666.

Ameudo-Dorantes, C. and C. Bansak (2006), 'Money transfers among banked and unbanked Mexican immigrants', *Southern Economic Journal*, **73** (2), 374–401.

Atia, M. (2007), 'In whose interest? Financial surveillance and the circuits of exception in the war on terror', *Environment and Planning D*, **25**, 447–475.

Bakker, M (2015), 'Discursive representations and policy mobility: how migrant remittances became a "development tool"', *Global Networks*, **15** (1), 21–42.

Ballard, R. (2003), 'Remittances and economic development', Paper submitted to the House of Commons Select Committee for its inquiry into Migration and Development, 2003–2004.

Basu, K. (2013), 'World Bank launches new initiative on migration', accessed 10 February 2015 at www.worldbank.org/en/news/press-release/2013/04/19/world-bank-launches-initiative-on-migration-releases-new-projections-on-remittance-flows.

Bracking, S. (2003), 'Sending money home: are remittances always beneficial to those who stay behind?', *Journal of International Development*, **15**, 633–644.

Brown, S. (2006), 'Can remittances spur development? A critical survey', *International Studies Review*, **8**, 55–75.

Carling, J. (2004), 'Policy options for increasing the benefits of remittances', Working Paper 8, Oxford: COMPAS.

Carling, J. (2008), 'The determinants of migrant remittances', *Oxford Review of Economic Policy*, **24** (3), 582–99.

Carling, J. (2014), 'Scripting remittances: making sense of money transfers in transnational relationships', *International Migration Review*, **48** (S1), 218–262.

Carling, J., M.B. Erdal, C. Horst and H. Wallacher (2007), 'Legal, rapid and reasonably priced? A survey of remittance services in Norway', PRIO Report 2007/3, Oslo: International Peace Research Institute.
Chappell, L. and D. Sriskandarajah (2007), 'Mapping the development impacts of migration: development on the move', Working Paper 1, London: IPPR.
Cliggett, L. (2003), 'Gift remitting and alliance building in Zambian modernity: old answers to modern problems', *American Anthropologist*, **105** (3), 1–10.
Cliggett, L. (2005), 'Remitting the gift: Zambian mobility and anthropological insights for migration studies', *Population, Space and Place*, **11**, 35–48.
Connell, J. and D. Conway (2000), 'Migration and remittances in island microstates: a comparative perspective on the South Pacific and the Caribbean', *International Journal of Urban and Regional Research*, **24** (1), 52–78.
Cross, H. (2008), 'Migration, remittances and development in West Africa: the case of Senegal', *Global Development Studies*, **5** (3–4), 133–164.
Cross, H. (2013), *Migrants, Borders and Global Capitalism: West African Labour Mobility and EU Borders*, Oxford, UK and New York, USA: Abingdon and Routledge.
Cross, H. (2015), 'Finance, development and remittances: extending the scale of accumulation in migrant labour regimes', *Globalizations*, **12** (3), 305–321.
Datta, K. (2009a), 'Transforming south–north relations? International migration and development', *Geography Compass*, **3** (1), 108–134.
Datta, K. (2009b), 'Risky migrants? Low paid migrants coping with financial exclusion in London', *European Urban and Regional Studies*, **16** (4), 331–344.
Datta, K. (2012), *Migrants and their Money: Surviving Financial Exclusion in London*, Bristol: Policy Press.
Datta, K., C.J. McIlwaine, J. Wills, Y. Evans, J. Herbert and J. May (2007), 'The new development finance or exploiting migrant labour? Remittance sending among low-paid migrant workers in London', *International Development Planning Review*, **29** (1), 43–67.
De Goede, M. (2003), 'Hawala discourses and the war on terrorist finance', *Environment and Planning D: Society and Space*, **21** (5), 513–532.
De Goede, M. (2008), 'The politics of pre-emption and the war on terror in Europe', *European Journal of International Relations*, **14** (1), 161–184.
De Haas, H. (2005), 'International migration, remittances and development: myths and facts', *Third World Quarterly*, **26**, 1269–1284.
Faist, T. (2008), 'Migrants as transnational development agents: an inquiry into the newest round of the migration–development nexus', *Population, Space and Place*, **14**, 21–42.
Farrant, M., A. MacDonald and D. Sriskandarajah (2006), 'Migration and development: opportunities and challenges for policymakers', IOM Migration Research Series no 22, Geneva: International Organisation for Migration.
Ferguson, James (1999), *Expectations of Modernity: Myths and Meanings of Urban Life on the Zambian Copperbelt*, Berkeley: University of California Press.
Financial World (2008), 'Money on the move', accessed 13 November 2008 at www.financialworld.co.uk/archive/2008/2008_11nov.
Fugfugosh, M.A. (2006), 'Informal remittance flows and their implications for global security', GCSP Brief no 11, Program on the Geopolitical Implications of Globalization and Transnational Security, Geneva: Geneva Centre for Security Policy.
Gamlen, A (2014), 'The new migration-and-development pessimism', *Progress in Human Geography*, **38** (4), 581–597.
Hernandez, E. and S.B. Coutin (2006), 'Remitting subjects: migrants, money and states', *Economy and Society*, **35** (2), 185–208.
Horst, C., M.B. Erdal, J. Carling and K. Areef (2014), 'Private money, public scrutiny? Contrasting perspectives on remittances', *Global Networks*, **14** (4), 514–532.
Hudson, D. (2008), 'Developing geographies of financialisation: banking the poor and remittance securitisation', *Contemporary Politics*, **14** (3), 315–333.
Hugo, S. (2010), 'Remittance sending costs', Paper presented at ICBI Money Transfers and Workers' Remittances Conference, June 2010, Barcelona.
IDS (Institute of Development Studies) (2009), Institute of Development Studies Bulletin, Special Issue: *Policy Responses to the Global Financial Crisis*, **40** (5).
Isaacs, L. (2008), 'Research on migrant remittances and linkage to broader access to financial services', Report to UK Remittance Taskforce, London.
Kapur, D. (2003), 'Remittances: the new development mantra?', Paper delivered to the G-24 Technical Group Meeting.
Kunz, Rahel (2011), *The Political Economy of Global Remittances: Gender, Governmentality and Neolibralism*, London, UK and New York, USA: Routledge.

Levitt, P. (1998), 'Social remittances: migration driven local-level forms of cultural diffusion', *International Migration Review*, **32** (4), 926–948.
Levitt, P. and D. Lamba-Nieves (2011), 'Social remittances revisited', *Journal of Ethnic and Migration Studies*, **37** (1), 1–22.
Lindley, A. (2009), 'Between dirty money and development capital: Somali money transfer infrastructure under global scrutiny', *African Affairs*, **108** (433), 519–539.
Lindley, A. (2013), 'Diaspora and transnational perspectives on remittances', in A. Quayson and G. Daswani (eds), *Companion to Diaspora and Transnationalism*, Oxford: Blackwell, pp. 316–329.
Lucas, R.B. and O. Stark (1985), 'Motivations to remit: evidence from Botswana', *Journal of Political Economy*, **93** (5), 901–918.
Maimbo, S. (2004), 'The regulation and supervision of informal remittance systems: emerging oversight strategies', Paper presented at the Seminar on Current Developments in Monetary and Financial Law.
Mata Codesal, D. (2015), 'Are all dollars equal? The meanings behind migrants financial transfers', *Migraciones Internacionales*, **8**, 39–64.
Mawdsley, E. (2012), 'The changing geographies of foreign aid and development cooperation: contributions from gift theory', *Transactions of the Institute of British Geographers*, **37**, 256–272.
Milligan, M. (2009), 'The welfare effects of international remittance income', PhD Dissertation, Department of Economics, University of New Mexico.
Orozco, M. (2004), 'The remittance marketplace: prices, policy and financial institutions', Washington, DC: Institute for the Study of International Migration, Georgetown University.
Orozco, Manuel and Rachel Fedewa (2005), *Regional integration? Trends and Patterns of Remittance Flows within South East Asia*, Washington, DC: Inter-American Dialogue.
Page, B. and C. Mercer (2012), 'Why do people do stuff? Reconceptualizing remittance behaviour in diaspora-development research and policy', *Progress in Development Studies*, **12** (1), 1–18.
Petrozziello, Allison (2013), *Gender on the Move: Working on the Migration–Development Nexus from a Gender Perspective*, New York: UN Women.
Pieke, F., N. Van Hear and A. Lindley (2005), 'Synthesis study: part of the report on informal remittance systems in Africa, the Caribbean and Pacific (ACP) countries', Oxford: COMPAS (ESRC Centre on Migration, Policy and Society), University of Oxford.
Piper, N. (2008), 'The "migration–development nexus" revisited from a rights perspective', *Journal of Human Rights*, **7** (3), 282–298.
Piper, N. (2009), 'The complex interconnections of the migration–development nexus: a social perspective', *Population, Space and Place*, Special Issue: *Rethinking the migration–development nexus – bringing marginalized visions and actors to the fore*, **15** (2), 93–101.
Plaza, S. (2015), 'Will there be policy coherence between the FfD Action Agenda and the Post 2015 Development Agenda on migration, remittances and diaspora', blog, 22 July, blogs.worldbank.org/peoplemove/frontpage?page=4, accessed July 2015.
Potter, R.B. and J. Phillips (2006), 'Both black and symbolically white: the 'Bajan-Brit' return migrant as post-colonial hybrid', *Ethnic and Racial Studies*, **29** (5), 901–27.
Ratha, D. (2003), Workers remittances: an important and stable source of external development finance, in World Bank (2003) *World Bank Global Development Finance Report 2003*, Washington, DC: World Bank, pp. 157–175.
Robinson, R. (2004), 'Globalization, immigrants transnational agency and economic developments in their homelands', Policy Paper, Ontario: Canadian Foundation for the Americas.
Roy, Ananya (2010), *Poverty Capital: Microfinance and the Making of Development*, New York: Routledge.
Saini, A. (2007), *First Solution's last stand*, BBC Online, accessed September 2007 at www.bbc.co.uk/london/content/articles/2007/07/03/towerhamlets_transfer_video_feature.shtml.
Sander, C. (2003), *Migrant Remittances to Developing Countries, a Scoping Study: Overview and Introduction to Issues for Pro-Poor Financial Services*, London: Bannock Consulting.
Schwittay, A.F. (2011), 'The financial inclusion assemblage: subjects, technics, rationalities', *Critique of Anthropology*, **31** (4), 381–401.
Singh, Supriya (2013), *Globalization and Money: A Global South Perspective*, Plymouth: Rowman and Littlefield.
Skeldon, R. (2002), 'Migration and poverty', *Asia-Pacific Population Journal*, **17**, 67–82.
Soederberg, S. (2013), 'The US debtfare state and the credit card industry: forging spaces of dispossession', *Antipode: Radical Journal of Geography*, **45** (2), 493–512.
Sumption, Madeline and Will Sommerville (2010), *The UK's new Europeans: Progress and Challenges Five Years after Ascension*, London: Equality and Human Rights Commission.
Taylor, J. (1999), 'The new economics of labour migration and the role of remittances in the migration process', *International Migration*, **37**, 63–88.
Toxopeus, H.S. and R. Lensink (2007), 'Remittances and financial inclusion in development', Research Paper no 2007/49, World Institute for Economic Development Research, United Nations University.

Vargas-Silva, C. (2011), 'Long-term international migration flows to and from the UK', Migration Observatory Briefing, accessed 21 October 2016 at www.migrationobservatory.ox.ac.uk.
Vleck, W. (2006), 'Development versus terrorism: migrant remittances or terrorist financing, challenge', Working Paper, accessed 21 October 2016 at www.lse.ac.uk/internationalRelations/centresandunits/EFPU/EFPUpdfs/EFPUchallengewp6.pdf.
Watkins, K. and M. Quattri (2014), *Lost in Intermediation: How Excessive Charges Undermine the Benefits of Remittances for Africa*, London, ODI Research Reports and Studies.
Wills, Jane, Kavita Datta, Yara Evans, Joanna Herbert, Jon May and Cathy McIlwaine (2010), *Global Cities at Work: New Migrant Divisions of Labour*, London: Pluto Press.
Wimaladharma, J., D. Pearce and D. Stanton (2004), 'Remittances: the new development finance?', *Small Enterprise Development*, **15** (1), 12–19.
World Bank (2005), Remittances a powerful tool to reduce poverty if effectively harnessed analysts say', accessed 30 January 2015 at http://web.worldbank.org/WBSITE/EXTERNAL/NEWS/0,,contentMDK:20571102~menuPK:34463~pagePK:34370~piPK:34424~theSituPK:4607,00.html.
World Bank (2006), *Global Economic Prospects: Economic Implications of Remittances and Migration*, Washington, DC: World Bank.
World Bank (2013), 'Migration and remittance flows: recent trends and outlook, 2013–2016', Migration and Development Brief 21, Migration and Remittances Team, Development Prospects Group, accessed 30 January 2015 at http://siteresources.worldbank.org/INTPROSPECTS/Resources/334934-1288990760745/MigrationandDevelopmentBrief21.pdf.
World Bank (2015), 'Migration and remittances: recent developments and outlook: Special topic: Financing for Development', Migration and Development Brief 24, Migration and Remittances Team, Development Prospects Group.
World Bank (2016), *Migration and Remittances Factbook 2016*, Third Edition, Washington, DC: World Bank.
Yujuico, E. (2009), 'All modes lead to home: assessing the state of the remittance art', *Global Networks*, **9** (1), 63–81.
Zapata, G.P. (2013), 'The migration–development nexus: rendering migrants as transnational financial subjects through housing', *Geoforum*, **47**, 93–102.

24. The imaginary landscapes of Islamic finance and the global financial crisis

Lena Rethel

24.1 INTRODUCTION

The global financial crisis has fundamentally challenged beliefs in the efficiency and self-regulatory capacity of international financial markets. It has also given new momentum to the search for alternatives to the existing global financial order. One such alternative that has been put forward is Islamic finance. Cast in both moral and economic terms, Islamic finance is a rapidly growing segment of international financial markets. Conservatively estimated, it has reached a market size of around US$1.8 trillion, roughly 1 per cent of global financial assets. Current growth rates of around 15 per cent per year suggest that it may play a more significant role in the future. Indeed, Islamic finance has very much become part of the 'variegated financial landscape' of twenty-first century capitalism (Pollard and Samers, 2013: 2).

Prima facie, Islamic finance offers distinct notions about debt, creditworthiness and the relationship between the 'financial' and the 'real' economy as will be outlined in the following. Indeed, its advocates suggest that Islamic finance is a means to create a financial order based on risk-sharing, not risk-transfer as epitomized by the current global financial system. However, despite these claims to a moral high-ground, Islamic finance has not been left unscathed by the global financial crisis. The crisis has affected Islamic finance in both material and ideational terms and challenged some of its core assumptions. Yet, it would be wrong to understand Islamic finance as a coherent whole. Islamic finance is a 'project under construction' (Pollard and Samers, 2007), whose meanings and boundaries are subject to continuous processes of negotiation. This makes it an interesting lens through which to explore the imaginary landscapes of finance more generally – and the socio-political fault lines that underpin it – and to study how they have been impacted and possibly transformed by the global financial crisis. In so doing, Islamic finance offers an entry point for the social (re-)imagination of finance as a whole.

Whilst setting out Islamic finance's claims to distinctiveness, the chapter demonstrates that rather than being a set of fixed and universally agreed principles, Islamic finance emphatically illustrates the social nature of financial practice. To substantiate this claim, this chapter conducts an investigation into attempts to construct a specific image of Islamic finance. It identifies three such images and uses them to explore the contested imaginary landscapes of Islamic finance and how it has been affected by the global financial crisis. In so doing, it builds upon Arjun Appadurai's (1996: 31) work on 'the image, the imagined, the imaginary' as 'central to all forms of agency' and thus offers a tool for rethinking finance as social practice. Here, it is of central importance to understand that finance as a whole is much more amorphous, less clearly bound and more open to contestation than often is acknowledged.

Following on from the above, this chapter takes its examination of Islamic finance as a vantage point from which to think about the political possibilities of reimagining finance and its moral underpinnings in the aftermath of the crisis. The global financial crisis has provoked much debate about specific financial practices (most notably perhaps securitization) as well as the democratic elusiveness and tenuous morality of finance more generally. Indeed, generations of political economists have pointed out the fictitious character of capital. However, its imaginary nature places finance in an elevated analytical position. To paraphrase Arjun Appadurai (2013), finance is a 'cultural fact', a product of our imagination. Thus, it becomes imperative to scrutinize the normative content and bounded moralities of the multiple imaginations associated with finance. In so doing, the social construct of finance can be made (to be seen as) amenable to change.

To substantiate its claims, this chapter will investigate competing imaginary landscapes of Islamic finance and their relationship with contemporary financial practices more broadly. In so doing, it will primarily focus on the United Kingdom, the United States and Malaysia as sites of image construction (cf. Samers, 2015). Those first two countries were at the core of the crisis that hit financial markets in 2007–08 and their elevated role in the global financial system also has important implications for the post-crisis reform agenda, whilst Malaysia aspires to be the global Islamic finance hub. The next section will look at Islamic finance and how it compares to conventional finance.[1] It identifies three competing images of Islamic finance: Islamic finance as 'business as usual', Islamic finance as 'other' and Islamic finance as 'socio-economic project'. In the second part of the chapter, the argument will then move on to using these three images as lenses through which the impact of the global financial crisis and its transformative potential are explored.

24.2 IMAGINARY LANDSCAPES OF ISLAMIC FINANCE

The advent of fully-fledged interest-based financial systems played a significant role in the emergence and expansion of the modern economy. In so doing, the acceptance of receiving and paying interest as legitimate economic practice was part of the transformation of European social epistemologies in the transition from a medieval economic and political system to modernity (Maurer, 2006; Sen, 1991). Like medieval Christian economic thought, Islamic finance forbids interest. Nevertheless, in its current guise it is a distinctively modern phenomenon. Local Islamic savings schemes emerged in a number of former British colonies after independence in the 1960s (Warde, 2010). Private Islamic banks were established in the Middle East following the increase in oil prices in the early 1970s (Henry and Wilson, 2004). Other parts of the world followed swiftly. As a consequence, over the last twenty or so years, Islamic finance has made considerable inroads in both Muslim and non-Muslim societies and has spread to more than 75 countries (Zeti, 2012). Not only has the number of specialist Islamic financial institutions proliferated, but major international banks such as HSBC and Citibank have launched Islamic subsidiaries. At the same time, the range of Shariah-compliant financial products, that is, those that comply with the religious teachings of the *Quran*, the *Sunnah* and the *Hadith*, has also expanded.

Interest – or *riba* (literally: increase) – constitutes what Maurer (2005: 39) calls 'the absent center of [Islamic finance] today'. The prohibition of riba can be found in the

Quran. For example, the *Surah Al-Baqarah* sets out a number of principles with regard to charity and money-lending. Lending is not considered a legitimately profitable activity. According to Islamic financial thought, the prohibition of riba precludes conventional borrower–lender relationships in which borrowers are exposed to all sorts of risk, whilst the lender only risks the borrower's default. Islamic finance therefore has a strong preference for equity finance over debt finance. For example, bank accounts – unless funds are kept with a bank purely for safekeeping purposes – typically take the form of profit and loss sharing accounts, where the account holder enters into a partnership arrangement with the bank. Likewise, while interest-based instruments such as conventional bonds are deemed Islamically not acceptable, *sukuk* present a class of Shariah-compliant financial products that are functionally very similar. Sukuk are typically structured in the form of claims on assets that generate an income stream, such as land/rental income or leased assets, whilst not being interest-based. Some scholars argue that banning the risk-free accumulation of capital, and the concentration of wealth in the hands of only a few, is part of Islam's concern for greater economic and social justice. They see 'economic viability and profitability' as crucial determinants of a project's fundability (Al-Harran, 1995: xii). Along these lines, Islamic finance also forbids *gharar* (contractual uncertainty) and *maisir* (gambling). Moreover, certain products and practices such as pork, alcohol or prostitution are deemed *haram* (prohibited), which extends to their funding. Thus – with certain exceptions – Islamic financial products have to be tied to clearly specified economic assets whose delivery can be guaranteed.

Given these stipulations, what makes Islamic finance distinct? Prima facie, Islamic finance promotes distinctive ideas about debt, creditworthiness and the relationship between the financial and the real economy. Debt – no matter if sovereign, corporate or household – is not a legitimately profitable activity. Creditworthiness is based on the 'worthiness' (in terms of economic profitability but in some interpretations also social desirability) of the project, and not primarily the repayment capacity of the borrower. Islamic finance is asset-oriented in that financial products have to be linked to the 'real' economy, which rules out many of the synthetic financial innovations that were so heavily implicated in the recent financial crisis. In so doing, Islamic finance is thought to embrace the mutually constitutive roles of the financial and the productive dimensions of the economy. Indeed, from this perspective the primary purpose of finance is seen as serving the needs of the latter. Thus, the social epistemology upon which Islamic finance is built is distinct from that which underpins contemporary conventional finance.

Nevertheless, rather than presenting a unified alternative to mainstream financial practice, Islamic finance exhibits great variation both in the ways it is understood, enacted and reacted to. The imaginary landscapes of Islamic finance are a product of ongoing negotiation and contestation. Indeed, this is not just about how Islamic finance and its conventional counterpart have been framed in various professional, popular and media discourses before and after the global financial crisis (cf. Thompson, 2009). It goes to the very heart of a financial reality that only acquires meaning through the practices to which it gives rise and the ways in which it is acted upon. In this regard, it is particularly striking how different imaginaries of Islamic finance have responded to the global financial crisis in very different ways with significant implications for the kind of financial practices they (de-)legitimize; the possibilities for progressive financial change they entail and foreclose.

This has a significant analytical implication: it necessitates an agency-centred approach to Islamic finance. In this regard, a number of recent contributions have engaged specifically with the agency of Shariah scholars and Shariah boards in legitimising Islamic financial practices. For example, Pollard and Samers (2013: 722–723) explore 'how an Islamic economic rationality is being constructed . . . through the work of Shariah scholars who are able to bridge and meld diverse legal and religious codes'. Their study focuses expressly on two non-Muslim majority countries, the United Kingdom and the United States. Similarly, Bassens et al. (2012: 343) suggest that 'Shariah scholars remain crucial gatekeepers for Islamic circuits'. However, whilst Shariah scholars certainly play a pivotal role in legitimising Islamic financial practices to religiously conscious investors and borrowers, a wider range of actors needs to be considered to better understand the economic, political and cultural significance of how the imaginary landscapes of Islamic finance have emerged and are acted upon. This includes not only the agency of elites such as professional economists, international bankers and global standard-setters (of both Muslim and non-Muslim variants), but also the everyday practices of financial subjects such as savers and homebuyers. This chapter identifies three prevailing images of Islamic finance.[2] Image 1 emphasizes its similarity with conventional finance. Image 2 highlights its alterity. The third image conceives of Islamic finance as part of a wider socio-economic project that seeks to reconnect finance to its social relations.

Image 1: Islamic Finance as Business as Usual

The most common understanding of Islamic finance sees it as financial practice constrained by what is deemed as not permissible according to the Shariah. This understanding of Islamic finance as conventional finance minus those elements that are clearly prohibited in Quran and Shariah is illustrated, for example, by the construction of Islamic stock market indices such as the Dow Jones Islamic Market Indexes and the FTSE Global Islamic Index Series (Rethel, 2011). They reflect the constitution of the secular indices compiled by these companies, from which non-Islamic stocks such as breweries (alcohol) and conventional banks (riba) are then excluded (see for example, Dow Jones, 2007). Similarities with conventional finance are emphasized. Here, Islamic finance is couched in rather neutral terms and often emulates the technical discourses and pseudo-scientific practices of mainstream economics and financial theory. Indeed, a significant strand of the Islamic finance literature seeks to develop Islamicized versions of the mainstream models of financial economics, such as the capital asset pricing model (CAPM) (Selim, 2008; Hanif, 2010).

Importantly, considerations of power relations, which are so crucial to our understanding of the constitution of the economic sphere, are largely absent. As long as the Islamic principles are adhered to, it is back to business as usual. This understanding of Islamic finance emphasizes the role of the market mechanism, albeit subjected to certain, cultural–religious constraints. While it is at a remove from the *acultural* understanding of neoclassical economics, it nevertheless largely shares its principled beliefs in the equilibrium economics of the abstracted market model and its efficiency. It is marked by a concern about what Hegazy (2007) terms the 'legalistic' approach to Islamic finance that seeks to adapt conventional financial services and products to the principles of the Shariah.

This image is also reproduced through a proliferating number of Islamic finance degree programmes, hosted by UK (and to a somewhat lesser extent US) Business Schools that are typically structured so that students take the standard modules on accounting and finance, in addition to a more custom-made element on Islamic finance. It has been maintained in recent rulings on cross-jurisdictional Islamic financial contracts made by UK and US courts (most Islamic financial contracts are governed by English commercial law), which deem the enforcement of Shariah-compliance outside their competence according to current legal practice (Foster, 2006). This practice is mirrored in the judgements which the two major US-based ratings agencies Standard & Poor's and Moody's make, in that they do not take into account compliance with the Shariah in their assessment of Islamic financial products, but use their standard models. It is also expressed in more critical academic work that questions the 'Islamicness' of Islamic finance, conducted by both Muslim and non-Muslim scholars (Khan, 2010).

Moreover, in recent years the focus has increasingly been put on promoting this image of Islamic finance. This is closely linked to attempts to 'professionalize' the industry. Indeed, it has been one of the most remarkable aspects of the recent expansion of Islamic finance that it is also specifically targeted at non-Muslims. The involvement of big international market players such as HSBC and Citibank is taken as an indicator that Islamic finance is increasingly moving away from the margins. Financial elites in both Muslim and non-Muslim countries have pointed to the similarities between Islamic finance and conventional finance, especially so as Islamic finance increasingly mirrors the product range of conventional financial products and services. They emphasize the mainstream capability of Islamic finance. In developing Islamic financial products, they derive their inspiration mainly from the conventional financial system and it is the big international financial players that are seen as having the strongest capacity to move Islamic finance forward (DeLorenzo, 2005). Here, Islamic finance is legitimized as conventional finance minus those characteristics that fail to comply with the principles of the Shariah. Islamic finance as business as usual is an elite project in which what Fang and Foucart (2014) term 'Western financial agents' play an increasingly significant role.

Image 2: Islamic Finance as Other

Yet while this first image highlights the similarities between Islamic and conventional finance and effectively constitutes an effort to assimilate it within the contemporary global financial order, it struggles to come to terms with its difference. Drawing on the distinct social epistemology underlying Islamic finance, at least two other understandings of Islamic finance can be discerned. They both emphasize the alternative character of Islamic finance, although for different reasons. The first 'other' understanding of Islamic finance fully draws on its alterity. Islamic finance is portrayed as something radically different from the existing conventional financial order. Here, Islamic finance is seen as challenging conventional financial practice, invented in and promulgated by the west to highly exclusionary effects. In so doing, this image exposes dynamics of inclusion and exclusion in the financial system, the withins and withouts of the global financial order. This image draws specific attention to the localities of Islamic finance, not just in spatial terms but also within hierarchies of power. This image of Islamic finance is negotiated by both devout Muslims seeking alternatives to financial systems that often fail to engage them in a meaningful way (Maurer, 2006) and by outsiders, in this instance mainly non-Muslims that link Islamic finance to shady and non-transparent practices and illegal activities (discussed in de Goede, 2003; Warde, 2007). It is constructed from both the inside and the outside as external to the mainstream.

With regard to the first category of attempts to demarcate Islamic finance as 'other', in this articulation it is portrayed as a means to escape western financial domination and to address the lack of adequate banking services by constructing an Islamic alternative. Indeed, the emergence of this image is strongly related to the exclusionary impact of conventional finance, both temporally and spatially (cf. Leyshon and Thrift, 1995). Along these lines, Pollard and Samers (2007) propose the frame of 'postcolonial political economy' to grasp the complexities of modern Islamic finance, and in particular to address questions of exclusion. For example, historically in the west, areas with significant Muslim minorities have often been under-banked with less access to financial retail services such as bank branches and automatic teller machines. In these instances, alternative financial spaces emerged in response to financial marginalization and exclusion. This includes both localized practices such as mutual savings schemes and housing finance and transnational networks such as hawala money transfer systems. Again, it is important to emphasize the distinctively modern character of these practices – intimately bound up with postcolonial migratory flows. Thus, for example, in cities such as Birmingham in Britain, migrant groups established mutual savings schemes, granting loans to their members (personal communication, 21 March 2009). Similarly in both the UK and the US, the creation of Islamic financial institutions providing non-interest based housing finance was a response to both a lack of access to finance *in general* and to Shariah-compliant funding *in particular*.

As Maurer (2006) demonstrates, the emergence of Islamic housing finance in the US created a space for those who not only were barred from buying a house due to their religious principles, but who in so doing were excluded from wider socio-economic and socio-political participation in an 'American way of life' premised upon being a home owner. Along these lines, hawala networks can be seen as satisfying the needs of in particular migrant groups with little access to conventional financial services, or for whom conventional financial services do not serve their particular needs, such as transferring money to relatives abroad.

As this brief overview of localized and transnational Islamic financial projects – at one remove from those captured by the first image – has shown, these initiatives often oscillate between deliberate attempts to construct alternative financial spaces and forms of economic belonging, and the desire just to achieve any form of economic belonging at all; some sort of greater inclusion through different means. On the one hand, this hints at the hybrid entanglement of Islamic finance and the mainstream as 'mutual frames of reference' (Maurer, 2005: 41). On the other hand, it has entailed further exclusion and marginalization as these constructions from the inside are replicated from the outside. The difference is that while from the inside Islamic finance is constructed as an alternative to the current financial order that can be occupied by the community of Muslims (*umma*) and thus evokes a strong sense of togetherness and inclusivity (for those inside) here the focus is to exclude, to marginalize, to 'other' Islamic finance as something beyond – outside – normal financial practice (de Goede, 2003). This also ties in with more recent historical trajectories, in particular the US-led 'war on terror' and its initially rather indiscriminate clampdown on Islamic financial assets (Warde, 2007). However, it had a significant impact on low-income Muslim migrant communities whose financial choices and opportunities were limited to begin with. For example, as Marieke de Goede (2007) argues, the portrayal of hawala networks as a 'criminal other' of conventional finance, in particular in the mid-2000s, has led to their further marginalization and 'made it more difficult and expensive for migrants in the West to send remittances' (de Goede, 2007: 148).[3]

Image 3: Islamic Finance as Socio-economic Project

In between these two images we can locate a third approach to Islamic finance. This third image also emphasizes the alterity of Islamic finance. Nevertheless, it does so not so much on the grounds of its religious character – its Islamic subjectiveness one may say, but in taking Islamic finance seriously as an alternative approach to contemporary financial practice. Here, Islamic finance is seen as part of a wider socio-economic paradigm that is very explicit about its normative commitment to greater economic fairness and social justice as well as the groundedness of economic practice. Islamic finance is thus contrasted with conventional financial practice which seeks its legitimacy in the theoretical constructs of neoclassical economics and modern finance theory and the profit motive. It is portrayed as being fundamentally concerned with and very articulate about embedded elements of morality and ethics. Not only is economic activity – in contrast to the efficient market model of conventional finance theory – seen as deeply enmeshed in social relations, but the link of Islamic finance to the productive economy is not just a regulative principle but a constitutive feature.

Moreover, in this image this is not so much due to Islamic finance's specific religious prescriptions but due to its commitment to a financial order of greater social justice, based on the (not only Quranic) principles of equity, mutuality and sustainability. Thus, El-Gamal (2006: xii) rejects the 'legalistic' approach to Islamic finance discussed in relation to its first image, and argues that 'the "Islamic" in "Islamic finance" should relate to the social and economic ends of financial transactions, rather than the contract mechanics through which financial ends are achieved'. Similarly, Hegazy (2007) identifies this as the 'socio-economic approach' that underpinned early Islamic financial thought, seeing Islamic economics as an alternative to both capitalism and socialism (see also Siddiqi, 2006). On this reading, Islamic finance derives its legitimacy not solely from its religious dimension, but from its emphasis on reconnecting with the social relations that underpin financial activity. However, this social connectivity of finance is not just an analytical claim but very much a political project. Thus, Islamic finance becomes significant as part of a broader effort towards creating a more responsible investment culture (along the lines of socially responsible investment), resting on a moral/ethical base with the overarching goal to achieve a socially embedded financial system that includes – if not actively promotes – ethical and moral dimensions for productive purposes (Pitluck, 2008).

Against this backdrop, the prohibition of financing *haram* products and services endows Islamic financial practice with a 'moral filter' of what is 'socially desirable' (Rice, 1999). The emphasis on equity finance over debt finance has been construed in a similar light. Indeed, the focus on economic outcomes – in basing financing decisions on the viability and profitability of a project – represents a significant departure from recent developments in financial markets where credit decisions have become more and more reliant on increasingly abstract constructions of creditworthiness such as credit scores (for an early elaboration, see Leyshon and Thrift, 1999). However, this presupposition of project knowledge does not necessarily mandate the same types of localized knowledge – and trust – assumed by certain aspects of the second image. What is of importance here is the link of Islamic finance to the real/productive – although not necessarily localized – economy. Nevertheless, the relevance of this image is clearly demonstrated by ongoing debates within Islamic finance about the respective merits of image 1-type (Shariah-compliant) versus image 3-type (Shariah-based) financial structures.

While this chapter has identified three co-existing images of Islamic finance, it is important to realize that these images are simultaneously both competing and overlapping in producing the rather diverse Islamic financial landscape. For example, Malaysian financial policy elites communicate all three images to different stakeholders. This is important as, by many accounts, Malaysia has the most advanced Islamic financial system, at least in terms of product innovation and legal framework, and is an important global Islamic financial player. The Malaysian government has successfully played off the different meanings associated with Islamic finance to increase its salience. To market players, such as big international corporations, investors and multilateral financial institutions it has pointed out the similarities of Islamic finance with conventional finance. To Muslims, whose strict belief prevented a participation in the conventional financial system, it has emphasized the alterity of Islamic finance (and it actively promotes the spread of anecdotes, for example of the small stallholder who always used to struggle, and who can now expand his business rapidly due to the availability of Islamic financing). Government officials employ a similar rhetoric towards their counterparts in other Muslim nations. Finally, Malaysian financial elites seek to attract both Muslim and non-Muslim investors and borrowers with the (supposedly) ethical and socially responsible character of Islamic finance and its potential developmental role (see for example, Zeti, 2012).

In sum, the emergence of the modern Islamic finance landscape is a complex phenomenon and its underlying principles are by no means uncontested. While Islamic finance draws on a distinctive social epistemology, effectively its practices exhibit strong similarities with existing conventional financial products and services. Specifically for this reason, the imaginary landscapes of Islamic finance can be used as lens to better understand the heterogeneous, evolving and contested practices of finance more broadly. This is what the second part of the chapter turns to. Indeed, accounts that unproblematically assume that Islamic financial practice can be assimilated into mainstream practice ignore the imaginary nature of finance and its contested politics. Yet, in so doing, the phenomenon of Islamic finance also highlights the possibility of reimagining finance more generally and in different ways. Especially at the current juncture, this is an alluring feature.

24.3 THE IMAGINARY LANDSCAPES OF ISLAMIC FINANCE AFTER THE GLOBAL FINANCIAL CRISIS

When it comes to exploring the significance of the global financial crisis for Islamic finance, we can distinguish between first-order analyses and second-order analyses. First-order analyses focus on Islamic finance and its technical dimensions. They include comparisons of the effects of the global financial crisis on Islamic and conventional finance as well as investigations into regulatory responses to the crisis on both the national and transnational level and their implications for Islamic finance. Thus, for example, Hasan and Dridi (2010) explore the performance of Islamic and conventional banks during the global financial crisis, looking at their profitability, credit and asset growth and external ratings. They conclude that overall Islamic banks fared better than conventional banks, especially with regard to asset and credit growth. According to Hasan and Dridi (2010: 33), this was at least partially due to the asset-orientation of Islamic finance and its focus on risk-sharing, which, according to the authors 'make their activities more closely related with the real economy and tend to reduce their contribution to excesses and bubbles'.

The differential impact of the crisis on conventional finance and Islamic finance is also highlighted in comparing how retail and wholesale markets have fared. Conventional financial institutions that heavily relied on money markets for their funding strategies suffered badly in the global financial crisis as vividly demonstrated by the collapse of the UK's Northern Rock (Rethel and Sinclair, 2012; see also Dawley et al., 2014 on the geographical dimension of Northern Rock's business model and collapse). Unlike conventional banks, Islamic banks typically have more deposits than assets. This made them relatively less vulnerable when money markets froze. Yet, the crisis has shown that the stronger link to the real economy has not necessarily made Islamic finance crisis-proof. Indeed, its significant exposure to real estate turned out to be highly problematic. While the impact of the collapse of Dubai World's property arm Nakheel on the wider Islamic financial industry could be contained, it has nevertheless caused unease about the substantial exposure of the industry to the property sector as was the case with the property bubble in Dubai (Hassler, 2011). Many industry observers deem the diversification of the range of assets underlying Islamic capital market products as being of the utmost importance. Despite these challenges, Islamic capital market resilience has been bolstered by its relatively limited exposure to structured finance, derivatives and toxic assets. This is somewhat qualified by the relatively lesser degree of 'financialization' of the market segment of Islamic finance (cf. Pike and Pollard, 2010).

In addition to analyses of the direct impact of the global financial crisis on the Islamic finance industry, there has also been interest in its indirect effects, most notably through efforts to reregulate finance in its wake. A key concern for the Islamic financial industry is to ensure that current regulatory reforms do not create new discriminatory barriers. This is especially relevant with regard to the impact of prudential regulation and changing capital requirement rules. Thus, for example, Mohieldin (2012) explores the challenges that Islamic financial institutions face in complying with the Third Basel Capital Accord (Basel III) (see also Parker, 2011). In terms of shaping the global reform agenda, Islamic finance has played only a muted role. For example, it is only at the time of writing and with the assumption of a Muslim-majority country (Turkey) of its presidency, that Islamic finance has made it onto the G20 agenda.

First-order analyses thus provide important insights into the challenges and opportunities that confront Islamic finance in the aftermath of the global financial crisis. Second-order analyses, however, look both at the subject – Islamic finance – as well as its social and political dimensions seen here as the imaginary landscapes of Islamic finance. In so doing, second-order analyses allow not only for a better understanding of the (differential) impact of the global financial crisis on Islamic finance but also for studying the transformational (or not) potential of the crisis more generally. They draw attention to socio-political trends that have been made visible by the global financial crisis or in whose emergence the crisis has played a significant role, provoking questions about the extent to which the global financial crisis has both challenged and further entrenched contemporary financial practices and knowledges. The remainder of this section will pursue these questions. It will look at how the three images of Islamic finance have been affected by the global financial crisis and the implications this has for the future imagination of finance.

The First Image and the Mainstreaming of Islamic Finance

With regard to the first image that emphasizes the similarity of Islamic finance with conventional finance, it seems as if the crisis presented only a temporary disturbance, since when things have returned to business as usual. Surprisingly, this image of Islamic finance has perhaps been least challenged by the global financial crisis. Like conventional finance, Islamic finance was heavily exposed to the crisis, even if for slightly different reasons. Given the prohibitions discussed above, Islamic financial institutions were prevented from buying into those highly complex structured financial products that Warren Buffett so aptly called 'financial weapons of mass destruction' (BBC News, 4 March 2003). However, its asset-orientation actually meant that Islamic finance suffered from the collapse of the property bubble. Yet, in response to what Randall Germain (2010) has called the 'Great Freeze' of global capital markets, the global financial crisis actually accelerated the expansion of Islamic finance to new (non-Muslim) jurisdictions, attracting new borrowers keen to tap still liquid segments of global financial markets, in particular petrodollars. For example, since the outbreak of the global financial crisis, a growing number of non-Muslim majority countries have begun to issue sukuk – including the UK and Luxembourg. Thus, whilst Islamic finance had already made inroads in western financial systems before the US subprime bubble broke in 2007, the crisis certainly gave new impetus to such efforts, in particular with regard to capital market finance – 'high finance'.

Along these lines, there was also an intensification of efforts to standardize Islamic finance in line with the current international financial architecture, again with the aim to broaden its appeal, especially amongst non-Muslim constituencies. An example of this trend was the completion of the Tahawwut (Hedging) Agreement in 2010. The 42-page Tahawwut Master Agreement is based on the 2002 (1992) ISDA Master Agreement, a framework governing hedging transactions between conventional (that is, non-Islamic) parties. However, in consultation with both market practitioners and Shariah scholars, it was adapted to be Shariah-compliant. The Tahawwut (Hedging) Agreement was developed by the International Islamic Financial Market (IIFM) in collaboration with the International Swaps and Derivatives Association (ISDA). IIFM, created in Bahrain in 2002, is a global standard-setting body for Islamic finance. Its principal objectives are to establish, develop and promote Islamic money and capital markets. For this purpose, it focuses on the development of common platforms and standards for Islamic financial markets. It is a state-sponsored institution (counting the Central Bank of Bahrain and the Islamic Development Bank amongst its members) that endorses and promotes in particular the issuance of sukuk and increasingly Islamic derivatives. IIFM activities are overseen by its Shariah Advisory Panel to ensure compliance with the principles of the Shariah (Rethel, 2011).

Like conventional finance, Islamic finance is not a risk-free endeavour. However,

Shariah stipulations against excessive risk-taking and uncertainty pose major constraints on the development of hedging instruments for Islamic financial institutions. At the same time, the increasing popularity of profit and loss sharing investment accounts makes it more problematic for Islamic financial institutions to leave risky positions unhedged. Constraints on the mitigation of liquidity risk were identified as a major disadvantage for Islamic banks vis-à-vis their conventional competitors. Similarly, currency risk had come to be seen as an increasingly important issue as transnational Islamic financial activity gathers momentum. The lack of standardized documentation added to the complexity and cost of Islamic hedging instruments. Against this background, the Tahawwut Master Agreement was heralded as a breakthrough in providing Islamic banks with such a framework.[4] In so doing, it contributes to efforts at greater standardization in the Islamic finance industry. As a result of these developments, we have witnessed a further 'mainstreaming' of Islamic finance and the broader acceptance of this image of Islamic finance. At least on the surface, it is back to business as usual.

However, the development process was not just so straightforward. In Islamic finance, the prohibition of profiting from uncertainty is meant to prevent the taking of excessive risk and the entering into a commercial venture without sufficient knowledge. The underlying rationale is that one party should not unfairly benefit from the other party's ignorance. Accordingly, the Tahawwut Master Agreement clarifies that the hedge must be linked to an underlying transaction (that is, be asset-based) and that trades must be entered for hedging and not speculative purposes as making money from money is not acceptable according to the Shariah (unlike, for example, the 'naked' short-selling of certain financial instruments in the EU whose temporary ban by Germany and other countries in 2010 caused much furore). A certain degree of ambiguity persists with regard to the enforceability of contracts negotiated within the framework of the Tahawwut Master Agreement. The Tahawwut Master Agreement is targeted at private parties negotiating Islamic derivative contracts. Its adoption rests on a voluntary basis. Certain provisions (for example, close-out netting) will be enforceable only after changes to the national bankruptcy law in some of the places where Islamic financial institutions operate, such as Dubai.[5] This indicates that there may remain tensions between national practices and the standards developed by international standard-setting institutions when it comes to making binding the agreements that contracting parties enter into.

Perhaps ironically, the global financial crisis has given rise to a greater diversity of financial market practices as both investors and borrowers were trying to cope with frozen asset markets. Islamic finance has certainly benefited from this. At the same time, however, the aftermath of the crisis has seen a boost to efforts at the standardization of Islamic finance such as creating a framework for Shariah-compliant hedging transactions. On the one hand, the ISDA/IIFM Tahawwut Master Agreement is the result of the 'legalistic approach' criticized by Hegazy (2007), especially so as the ISDA Master Agreement served as a template. On the other hand, a certain reflexivity of the process of adaptation cannot be denied, given that it took 24 drafts and a consultation process that lasted three and a half years for the Agreement to be concluded (Clark, 2010; for a discussion of the inherent reflexivity of Islamic financial products, see Maurer, 2008; Pitluck, 2013). However, according to industry observers the availability of standardized documentation should alleviate the necessity of Shariah approval for individual product structures and will thus spur product development and reduce cost and time. As such, the

Agreement is deemed to result in a certain convergence of financial practices within the industry. Moreover, it is thought that the new documentation, being a Shariah-compliant version of the ISDA conventional framework, is especially attractive for western-based internationally active conventional banks that operate Islamic subsidiaries.

The Second Image and the Wall Street–Jihad Nexus

Post-crisis dynamics have played out quite differently with regard to the second image of Islamic finance, namely that which highlights its alterity. To reiterate, this image is constructed from both the inside and the outside. Thus, from the inside a significant challenge to Islamic financial practices arose in 2007, when the Accounting and Auditing Organization for Islamic Financial Institutions (AAOIFI) claimed that a large share of sukuk issued in the GCC (amounting to over 60 per cent) were not actually in compliance with the Shariah. With a strong sense of déjà vu – given that the crisis had exposed the close cooperation between rating agencies and issuers in the design of highly rated financial products – it was suggested that these sukuk were primarily structured so that they could be rated by the international rating agencies, leaving doubts about whether sukuk were debt or equity. Indeed, this clearly shows some of the frictions that are papered over in the first image, given genuine questions about the suitability of standard rating methodologies for Islamic financial products. Clarifying this position, Sheikh Usmani, presiding over the AAOIFI Shariah Board, argued that deals where the repurchase is guaranteed in advance cannot be reconciled with the risk-sharing intentions of Islamic financial principles (Usmani, 2007). In the short-term, the response to his announcement was a decline in sukuk issuance. Since then, however, a number of new sukuk structures have emerged that lay claim to Islamic finance's innovative potential.

On the other hand, we also have more intense efforts to marginalize Islamic finance from without. This is clearly visible in the vitriolic responses to Islamic finance on blogs such as shariahfinancewatch.org, and familitysecuritymatters.org. In articles and film clips hatred of bankers and hatred of Muslims has become fused, creating a new threatening image of a 'Wall Street–Jihad' nexus (see for example, Act4America, 2008). And these sentiments are becoming increasingly popularized. Thus, for example, in April 2011, Tea Party-supporting TV moderator Glenn Beck used his show on Fox News to give viewers an 'Introduction to Shariah Finance'. In addition to having the editor of shariahwatch.org as one of his guests, during the show Beck actually rehearsed many of the arguments and dubious connections that had been put forward previously in fringe online discussion fora and YouTube clips. Islamic finance, as it is referred to by the financial industry, is here turned into 'Shariah finance'. In these representations, (Islamic) finance is portrayed as the threatening 'other', endangering life, family, and national security.

Here, the global financial crisis has accelerated the vilification of Islamic finance. When Marieke de Goede (2003, 2007) could argue in the aftermath of 9/11 that discourses surrounding hawala networks served to normalize and legitimize conventional finance vis-à-vis its Islamic other and in so doing deflect from demands for the greater regulation of investment banking, then this fusion of Wall Street-type investment banking with Islamic finance as a joint threat represents a significant departure. That this is more than just a mere fringe phenomenon became clear in the summer of 2010 during the confirmation hearings for Elena Kagan's appointment to the US Supreme Court. During these hearings a 'controversy' emerged over her 'support for Shariah law'. It was based on the fact that during her time as Dean of Harvard Law School Elena Kagan oversaw the introduction of Harvard's Islamic Finance Project, internationally renowned and amongst others attended by US Treasury Officials. In Britain, there are similarly hostile discourses about 'Shariah law' (for example, the response drawn by the Archbishop of Canterbury's comments on Shariah law (*The Telegraph*, 7 February 2008) and 'greedy bankers' (*The Telegraph*, 7 July 2012), although they have not yet been fused.

Rather ironically, both Islamic finance and its portrayal as threatening other by self-declared defenders of Christian faith and American values are part of a religious resurgence that does not see the economic as outside its purview. Islamic finance thus becomes an integral part of a postsecular international landscape where religion is increasingly politicized and polarizing (Toft et al., 2011). However, taking this image seriously also shows some of the political limitations that are faced by attempts to rethink the social purpose of finance and the modalities of its delivery in the aftermath of the global financial crisis.

The Third Image and the Political Possibilities for Progressive Change

With regard to the third image, Islamic finance understood as socio-economic project, again the picture is mixed. The crisis has challenged the widely held belief that the asset-orientation of Islamic finance and its resulting proximity to real economic activity make it less crisis-prone and thus more stable than conventional financial instruments (cf. Zeti, 2007). Indeed, during the global financial crisis, this turned out to be a double-edged sword. The link to the real economy also meant a heavy exposure to the property bubble in a place such as Dubai (Hassler, 2011). This caused problems for Islamic finance, such as for example the collapse of Nakheel, the property arm of Dubai World. Social connectivity through asset-orientation is not a good on its own, especially so if the range of assets upon which Islamic financial products are based is very limited or if they represent a rather tenuous reality as in the case of Nakheel's investment in human-made palm-shaped islands off the coast of Dubai. Wholesale Islamic financial markets did suffer not only from the global economic turmoil, but also from uncertainty caused by differing interpretations of Shariah principles and doubts that were raised about the Shariah-compliance of certain sukuk structures. In particular, the claim that certain sukuk were structured so that they were rateable by external rating agencies and effectively not in compliance with the Shariah not only highlights concerns about the involvement of rating agencies in the design of products similar to those voiced with regard to conventional securitization techniques, but also points to the fact that Islamic finance struggles with developing its own financial knowledge base in greater independence from the current global financial system.

Nevertheless, in particular Islamic housing finance fared much better than its conventional counterpart, specifically so from a borrower's perspective. Since the US subprime credit bubble burst in 2007, 'negative equity' has emerged as a significant problem for both borrowers and lenders. It refers to a situation where the mortgage on a house exceeds its market value, following the decline in house prices. Borrowers are thus doubly hit: not only are their houses worth less, but they also still owe the bank the full amount of the mortgage they have taken out. Banks were also negatively affected by this as people in

US states such as Florida just walked away from their houses/mortgages ('walking away' from mortgages is possible in some US states as unlike in other countries such as Spain, the borrower's obligation to the lender either ceases with the lender's repossession of the house or because banks have to demonstrate that they have undertaken all 'reasonable steps' to sell the property at market rates if they want to go after other assets; see also Martin (2011) on geographical variations in US 'subprime' lending). It could be argued that this system thus has a certain degree of flexibility (borrowers can cut their losses and walk away), yet it is neither economically efficient nor socially desirable (borrowers would still lose the money they have put in the house). While there exist different contractual arrangements for Shariah-compliant housing finance, they all typically entail the bank owning at least part of the house. In so doing, the lender is directly exposed to fluctuating property values. Advocates of Islamic finance suggest that this type of financing – as lenders and borrowers have to genuinely share the risk of fluctuating values – would also make the emergence of property bubbles, fuelled by the rather indiscriminate disbursal of credit, less likely.

Given the general market uncertainty, Islamic finance could not profit as much from its supposedly moral high-ground as its supporters were hoping for. However, the correspondence of Islamic financial thinking with recent reform proposals means that financial ideas and practices that until recently were very much at the margins of global financial markets have made stronger inroads into mainstream financial thought. The global financial crisis has stimulated greater international interest in Islamic finance, its focus on risk-sharing and its emphasis on the social purpose of finance. Some of the shortcomings of the conventional financial system that were pointed out in relation to the global financial crisis – and resonate well with advocates of Islamic finance – include: the risks posed by fractional reserve banking, especially in combination with inadequate capital reserve requirements; the volatility of fiat currency systems; and the economic and moral limitations of a debt-based economy. What Islamic finance certainly cannot do is to provide a comprehensive template for the reform of global finance. In its current guise, it is too intimately bound up with the conventional financial system and its knowledge structures (Rethel, 2011). It sometimes also exhibits a distinct lack of imagination and a tendency to romanticize an imaginary past such as in proposals of a return to gold money.

Nonetheless, Islamic finance offers some ideas about how to move away from a debt-based economy. There are a range of Islamic concepts that have been – both implicitly and explicitly – taken forward in discussions about how to reform the current financial system. One such example would be Robert Shiller's (2008) proposal of home equity insurance to foster greater risk-sharing between mortgage lenders and borrowers. Similar sentiments were recently voiced by then-Bank of England Monetary Policy Committee external member David Miles in his endorsement of a greater role for equity in housing finance (Bank of England, 2013). Another example would be post-crisis calls to reconsider banking practices such as Laurence J. Kotlikoff's (2010) suggestion of 'limited purpose banking' which bears a close resemblance to Islamic profit and loss sharing accounts.

Yet, Islamic finance can do more than just provide examples of alternative financing techniques and thus informing debates about how finance can be 'fixed'. Islamic finance offers an important point of departure for debating and reimagining finance as a whole. Combining consequentialist and deontological elements, Islamic finance highlights that it is possible to take a principled approach to finance.[6] Such a principled approach to finance does not have to be restricted to, or even based upon the religious principles of the Shariah. One could imagine a whole catalogue of ethical principles that would endow finance with a socially meaningful purpose and allow to better harness its socio-economic potential.

24.4 CONCLUSION: REIMAGINING FINANCE

> This apparent consensus that 'everything is constructed', however, is accompanied by the moral imperative that we can and must construct these worlds at will. (Maurer, 2005: 167)

Compliant with Shariah principles, Islamic finance offers distinct ideas about debt, creditworthiness and the relationship between the 'financial' and the 'real' economy. Over the last decade, it has been a rapidly growing segment of international financial markets. However, at the same time it struggled both with internal disagreements about the interpretation of Islamic financial principles with regard to the permissibility of certain product structures and the external ramifications of the global credit crunch. This chapter used the imaginary landscapes of Islamic finance as an entry point to exploring the constructed nature and bounded moralities of finance more generally. It has identified three images of Islamic finance that prevail in contemporary discourses: Islamic finance as business as usual; Islamic finance as alterity; and Islamic finance as a socio-economic project. These three images cast different lights on the emancipatory (or not) potential of finance more broadly and how it can be harnessed to a socially meaningful purpose.

These images were then employed to assess the transformative impact of the global financial crisis of 2007–08. Despite a heightened concern with rethinking finance and its moral underpinnings that was provoked by the crisis, it has not led to a negation of mainstream financial practice on both global and local levels. Looking at the imaginary landscapes of Islamic finance in the aftermath of the global financial crisis clearly shows the limited impact of the crisis in changing current financial practice. Indeed, the existing images of Islamic finance have been deepened. Islamic finance as business as usual has made further progress down the road of mainstream capability; at the same time, there have been attempts to broaden Islamic finance as 'other' as a threat image along the lines of a Wall Street–Jihad nexus. Ironically enough, these two images of Islamic finance seem to reinforce each other. On the one hand, a more mainstream capable Islamic finance seems to provide its detractors with ample ammunition as even a cursory reading of blogs such as shariahfinancewatch.org emphatically demonstrates. On the other hand, this vilification of Islamic finance is countered by efforts to demonstrate its 'normalcy', even leading some of its advocates to suggest dropping the 'I' word and focusing on its 'value-proposition' instead (personal communication, 14 March 2013).

Are there any possibilities left for reimagining finance as a means of engendering and engaging progressive change? What about the third image of Islamic finance as socio-economic project? The recent expansion of Islamic finance clearly demonstrates the multifaceted, uneven and contested character of global finance. What the global financial crisis has done is that it has brought the fault lines underpinning financial ideas and practices to the fore. It has made more visible the cracks within global finance that for the last two decades or so were papered over by visions of self-regulating markets. Against this backdrop, Islamic finance can offer some ideas for rethinking finance. While it falls short of providing a comprehensive template for an alternative financial system, it nevertheless shows that finance is a creature of the social world – an economy of our making – and therefore amenable to change. Thus, the imaginary landscapes of finance (re-)emerge as a site of struggle over the meaning of modern life.

ACKNOWLEDGEMENTS

I would like to thank Aaron Z. Pitluck, Sebastian Botzem, the participants of the 2012 AGORA workshop and the editors of this volume for their critical reading of earlier versions of this chapter.

NOTES

1. The terms 'conventional finance' and 'mainstream finance' are used interchangeably in this chapter.
2. These three images of Islamic finance are by no means exhaustive. Their boundaries are blurred.
3. Similarly, Islamic practices of zakat (mandatory alms-giving) and the activities of Islamic charities have been castigated as means of supporting terrorism (de Goede, 2012: Chapter 5; de Goede, 2007: 150–151).
4. It also levels the playing field between Malaysia, an important Islamic financial centre where the development of Shariah-compliant risk management tools has been relatively advanced, and other parts of the Islamic finance world.
5. Close-out netting is a process whereby two parties settle multiple claims by agreeing to offset the values of their various positions and settle the remainder as net payment.
6. The 'principled' is understood here not as in 'rules-based' versus 'principles-based' regulation, but in *categorical terms*.

REFERENCES

Act4America (2008), 'Shariah finance', accessed 24 November 2012 at www.youtube.com/watch?v=VmRbum9x0nU.

Al-Harran, Saad (ed.) (1995), *Leading Issues in Islamic Banking and Finance*, Petaling Jaya: Pelanduk Publications.

Appadurai, Arjun (1996), *Modernity at Large. Cultural Dimensions of Globalization*, Minneapolis and London: University of Minnesota Press.

Appadurai, Arjun (2013), *The Future as Cultural Fact. Essays on the Global Condition*, London and New York: Verso.

Bank of England (2013), 'News release – housing, leverage and stability in the wider economy – speech by David Miles', accessed 3 March 2014 at www.bankofengland.co.uk/publications/Pages/news/2013/132.aspx.

Bassens, D., B. Derudder and F. Witlox (2012), '"Gatekeepers" of Islamic financial circuits: analysing urban geographies of the global Shari'a elite', *Entrepreneurship & Regional Development*, **24** (5–6), 337–355.

BBC News (2003), 'Buffett warns on investment "time bomb"', 4 March, accessed 1 November 2016 at http://news.bbc.co.uk/2/hi/2817995.stm.

Clark, Joel (2010), 'Islamic tahawwut master agreement arrives at last', *Risk Magazine*, 1 March, accessed 22 November 2012 at www.risk.net/risk-magazine/news/1593967/islamic-tahawwut-master-agreement-arrives.

Dawley, S., N. Marshall, A. Pike, J.S. Pollard and J. Tomaney (2014), 'Continuity and evolution in an old industrial region: the labour market dynamics of the rise and fall of Northern Rock', *Regional Studies*, **48** (1), 154–172.

de Goede, M. (2003), 'Hawala discourses and the war on terrorist finance', *Environment and Planning D: Society and Space*, **21**, 513–532.

de Goede, M. (2007), 'Underground money', *Cultural Critique*, **65** (4), 140–163.

de Goede, M. (2012), *Speculative Security. The Politics of Pursuing Terrorist Monies*, Minneapolis: University of Minnesota Press.

DeLorenzo, Y.T. (2005), 'The Shari'a scholar's view of Islamic consumer finance and retail products', in S. Jaffer (ed.), *Islamic Retail Banking and Finance. Global Challenges and Opportunities*, London: Euromoney Books, pp. 5–17.

Dow Jones Indexes (2007), *Guide to the Dow Jones Islamic Market Indexes*, Princeton, NJ: Dow Jones Indexes.

El-Gamal, Mahmoud A. (2006), *Islamic Finance. Law, Economics and Practice*, Cambridge: Cambridge University Press.

Fang, Eddy S. and Renaud Foucart (2014), 'Western financial agents and Islamic ethics', *Journal of Business Ethics*, **123** (3), 475–491.

Foster, Nicholas H.D. (2006), 'Encounters between legal systems: recent cases concerning Islamic commercial law in secular courts', *Amicus Curiae*, **68** (November/December), 1–9.

Germain, Randall (2010), *Global Governance and Financial Politics*, Basingstoke: Palgrave Macmillan.

Hanif, Muhammad (2010), 'Risk and return under Sharia framework: an attempt to develop Sharia Compliant Asset Pricing Model-SCAPM', *Pakistan Journal of Commerce & Social Sciences*, **5** (2), available at SSRN: http://ssrn.com/abstract=1716821.

Hasan, Maher and Jemma Dridi (2010), 'The effects of the global crisis on Islamic and conventional banks: a comparative study', IMF Working Paper WP/10/201.

Hassler, Olivier (2011) 'Housing and real estate finance in Middle East and North Africa countries', Financial Flagship Report, the World Bank.

Hegazy, W.S. (2007), 'Contemporary Islamic finance: from socio-economic idealism to pure legalism', *Chicago Journal of International Law*, **581** (Winter), 581–603.

Henry, Clement M. and Rodney Wilson (eds) (2004), *The Politics of Islamic Finance*, Edinburgh: Edinburgh University Press.

Khan, Feisal (2010), 'How "Islamic" is Islamic banking?', *Journal of Economic Behaviour & Organization*, **76**, 805–820.

Kotlikoff, Laurence J. (2010), *Jimmy Stewart Is Dead: Ending the World's Ongoing Financial Plague with Limited Purpose Banking*, Hoboken, NJ: John Wiley and Sons.

Leyshon, Andrew and Nigel Thrift (1995), 'Geographies of financial exclusion: financial abandonment in Britain and the United States', *Transactions of the Institute of British Geographers*, **20** (3), 312–341.

Leyshon, Andrew and Nigel Thrift (1999), 'Lists come alive: electronic systems of knowledge and the rise of credit-scoring in retail banking', *Economy and Society*, **28** (3), 434–466.

Martin, Ron (2011) 'The local geographies of the financial crisis: from the housing bubble to economic recession and beyond', *Journal of Economic Geography*, **11** (4), 587–618.

Maurer, Bill (2005), *Mutual Life, Limited. Islamic Banking, Alternative Currencies, Lateral Reasons*, Princeton, NJ: Princeton University Press.

Maurer, Bill (2006), *Pious Property. Islamic Mortgages in the United States*, New York: Russell Sage Foundation.

Maurer, Bill (2008), 'Resocializing finance? Or dressing it in mufti? Calculating alternatives for cultural economies', *Journal of Cultural Economy*, **1** (1), 65–78.

Mohieldin, Mahmoud (2012), 'Realizing the potential of Islamic finance', *Economic Premise*, **77** (March), Poverty Reduction and Economic Management (PREM) Network, accessed 22 November 2012 at https://openknowledge.worldbank.org/bitstream/handle/10986/10051/676440BRI0econ00Box367885B00PUBLIC0.pdf?sequence=1.

Parker, M. (2011), 'Issues in regulating Islamic finance', *Central Banking*, **21** (3), 60–69.

Pike, A. and J.S. Pollard (2010), 'Economic geographies of financialization', *Economic Geography*, **86** (1), 29–51.

Pitluck, Aaron Z. (2008), 'Moral behavior in stock markets: Islamic finance and socially responsible investment', in Katherine E. Browne and Lynne B. Milgram (eds), *Economics and Morality: Anthropological Approaches*, Lanham, MD: AltaMira Press, Rowman & Littlefield Publishers, pp. 233–255.

Pitluck, Aaron Z. (2013), 'Islamic banking and finance: alternative or façade?', in Karin Knorr Cetina and Alex Preda (eds), *Handbook of the Sociology of Finance*, Oxford: Oxford University Press, pp. 431–449.

Pollard, J.S. and M. Samers (2007), 'Islamic banking and finance: postcolonial political economy and the decentring of economic geography', *Transactions of the Institute of British Geographers*, **32** (3), 313–330.

Pollard, J.S. and M. Samers (2013), 'Governing Islamic finance: territory, agency, and the making of cosmopolitan financial geographies', *Annals of the Association of American Geographers*, **103** (3), 710–726.

Rethel, L. (2011), 'Whose legitimacy? Islamic finance and the global financial order', *Review of International Political Economy*, **18** (1), 75–98.

Rethel, Lena and Timothy J. Sinclair (2012), *The Problem with Banks*, London: Zed Books.

Rice, Gillian (1999), 'Islamic ethics and the implications for business', *Journal of Business Ethics*, **18** (4), 345–358.

Samers, Michael (2015), 'A marriage of convenience? Islamic banking and finance meet neoliberalization', in S. Brunn (ed.), *The Changing World Religion Map*, Berlin: Springer, pp. 1173–1187.

Selim, Tarek H. (2008), 'An Islamic capital asset pricing model', *Humanomics*, **24** (2), 122–129.

Sen, Amartya K. (1991), *Money and Value: On the Ethics and Economics of Finance* [Denaro e Valore: Etica ed Economia della Finanza], Rome: Bank of Italy.

Shiller, Robert (2008), *The Subprime Solution. How Today's Global Financial Crisis Happened, and What to Do about It*, Princeton, NJ: Princeton University Press.

Siddiqi, Mohammad N. (2006), 'Shariah, economics and the progress of Islamic finance: the role of Shariah experts', Concept Paper presented at the Pre-Forum Workshop on Select, Seventh Harvard Forum on Islamic Finance, accessed 22 November 2012 at www.siddiqi.com/mns/Role_of_Shariah_Experts.htm.

The Telegraph (2008), 'Adopt Sharia law in Britain, says the Archbishop of Canterbury Dr Rowan Williams', by Jonathan Petre and Andrew Porter, 8 February, accessed 22 November 2012 at www.telegraph.co.uk/news/uknews/1578017/Adopt-sharia-law-in-Britain-says-the-Archbishop-of-Canterbury-Dr-Rowan-Williams.html.

The Telegraph (2012), 'The law cannot curb greedy bankers, but morals might', Janet Daley, 7 July, accessed 22 November 2012 at www.telegraph.co.uk/finance/newsbysector/banksandfinance/9383114/The-law-cannot-curb-greedy-bankers-but-morals-might.html.

Thompson, G. (2009), 'What's in the frame? How the financial crisis is being packaged for consumption', *Economy and Society*, **38** (3), 520–524.

Toft, Monica D., Daniel Philpott and Timothy S. Shah (2011), *God's Century: Resurgent Religion and Global Politics*, New York: W.W. Norton.

Usmani, M.T. (2007), 'Sukuk and their contemporary applications', AAOIFI Working Paper, accessed 12 February 2008 at www.failaka.com/downloads/Usmani_SukukApplications.pdf.

Warde, Ibrahim A. (2007), *The Price of Fear*, London and New York: IB Tauris & Co.

Warde, Ibrahim A. (2010), *Islamic Finance in the Global Economy*, 2nd edition, Edinburgh: Edinburgh University Press.

Zeti Akhtar Aziz (2007), 'The international dimension of Islamic finance', *BIS Review*, 95/2007.

Zeti Akhtar Aziz (2012), 'Internationalisation of Islamic finance – bridging economies', welcoming address by the Governor of the Central Bank of Malaysia at the Global Islamic Finance Forum 2012, Kuala Lumpur, September 19, accessed 22 November 2012 at www.bis.org/review/r120920d.pdf.

25. Crowdfunding: understanding diversity

Mia Gray and Bryan Zhang

25.1 INTRODUCTION

Since the 2008 financial crisis, crowdfunding has grown into a small but significant global industry, which has largely by-passed the traditional banking sector. Crowdfunding is estimated to have reached €3 billion worth of transactions across Europe in 2014 (Zhang et al., 2015). Crowdfunding allows individuals to pool resources to provide capital to firms, ideas, places and projects. For some commentators, crowdfunding represents a real alternative to a discredited banking sector. Crowdfunding supporters claim the sector represents an alternative to the traditional banking sector which facilitates new ways to accumulate and allocate capital (Kim and Hann, 2013; Shiller, 2012). Shiller applauds the rise of crowdfunding as part of the 'democratization of finance', which enables individuals to determine where and how their savings and investments are made (Shiller, 2013).

The mainstream banking system was profoundly implicated in the 2008 financial crisis as banks created sophisticated financial tools which functioned to encourage excessive speculation and risk on a global scale (Blyth, 2013; Aalbers, 2015). The global banking crisis in 2007–08 was transformed into a sovereign debt crisis and the widespread adoption of austerity policies on both national and urban scales (Kitson et al., 2011; Donald et al., 2014). This led many individuals to search for alternatives and, in particular, less financial intermediation between the saver and borrower, the investor and investee. Aalbers (2015) argues that this growth has created a significant increase in the sources of credit supply and a reshaping of financial geographies across all scales. Whether this trend should be celebrated or condemned is debatable. While Shiller applauds the 'democratization of finance', Erturk and his colleagues are critical of the 'broadening and deepening' of access to capital markets for ordinary individuals (Erturk et al., 2007).

Although crowdfunding has received much popular press, it remains on the fringes of academic scrutiny. There has been little systematic academic attention paid to the levels and areas of growth, the behaviour of the industry, and the spatial and financial implications of this growth. We conceptualize crowdfunding as technology-enabled online financial channels, instruments and activities that allow individuals and organizations to participate in capital formation and allocation processes, which have emerged *outside* of the traditional financial system (for example, regulated banks and capital markets). This chapter explores a multitude of different crowdfunding financial models utilizing primary survey data from over 15,000 respondents, as well as a primary transactional dataset containing over a million micro-transactions totalling £1 billion. To date, very little quantitative work has been conducted on this burgeoning phenomenon and there exist few qualitative studies; thus, this chapter will fulfil an important function in providing a critical and systematic analysis of an emerging industry.

The term crowdfunding covers a diverse set of practices, from supporting emerging art projects to lending and borrowing money, to investing in new business ventures and supporting local charities. The term is used to understand the financial support of friends and family to complete strangers making each other short-term loans, and to institutional actors finding new investment opportunities. However, by conflating all these phenomena into one, the term hides as much as it reveals. We argue that, to understand the phenomena, the term must be broken down into its constituent parts, which display different dynamics and geographies. This chapter explores the different models emerging in the crowdfunding sector – its diversity and its spatial patterns.

25.2 GEOGRAPHY AND THE FINANCIAL SECTOR

One crucial question is the extent to which these emerging financial phenomena may change the geography of the mainstream financial system. Almost 25 years ago, O'Brien claimed that 'geographical location no longer holds sway in finance . . . money, being fungible, will continue to try to avoid and will largely succeed in escaping the confines of geography' (O'Brien, 1992: 1). O'Brien argued that deregulation, financial innovation, and the adoption of enabling ICT deemphasized the importance of geography and location for financial firms, financial flows and access to financial services. However, geographers have long critiqued this argument and emphasized the mainstream financial sector's overconcentration of capital and power in financial centres such as London and New York, its distinct locational biases in the distribution of capital, and strong spatial patterns of financial exclusion (Klagge and Martin, 2005). If anything, Garretsen and his colleagues argue that the 'spatial concentration of banks, investment houses and other financial institutions in the major national (and global) financial centres has not dramatically lessened: indeed in many respects it has increased, as has the financial specializations of those centres and the competition between them' (Garretsen et al., 2009: 144).

In the UK, the nation's highly centralized finance sector – the main financial institutions, capital markets, and financial service firms – is firmly entrenched in London and the South East of the country. London's dominance in finance arises from and is reinforced by its function as a 'portal through which global financial developments and perturbations are diffused – directly and indirectly – across domestic and capital markets' (Klagge and Martin, 2005: 389). Klagge and Martin show that the level of financial concentration in London is cumulative and leads to a spatial bias in the flows of equity capital to firms in other regions of the UK. The argument is that the information-gathering and monitoring functions necessary for banks to lend to small firms are spatially sensitive and this results in funds being biased towards firms in close proximity to the banks. The cumulative nature of the growth resulting from the centralized and concentrated finance industry is highlighted by Wójcik (2009). He shows that firms that are located in financial centres, such as London, are more likely to go public than firms in other regions. Thus, these firms find funds for expansion and growth in a manner less likely for firms in other regions.

Likewise, there is a great deal of literature which shows that other parts of the finance industry, such as venture capitalists, also display a similar spatial pattern. Mason and Harrison (2002) show that, like the mainstream financial institutions, venture capitalists are concentrated in London and the South East, as are their investments. Likewise, Martin et al. (2003) find a strong regional bias in the UK's venture capital industry. They find that venture capital investments are highly concentrated in London and the

South East, reinforcing existing patterns of regional concentration of economic activity. Proximity enables a 'hands on' business model, where financial support is accompanied by higher levels of engagement and monitoring of the funded firm. Smaller firms, in regions further away from London, are likely to find it more difficult to raise venture funds.

Therefore, the mainstream financial industry has a clear locational bias that is producing a large regional gap in funding for small firms outside of London and the South East. To what extent might this locational bias be challenged by new financial intermediaries represented by crowdfunding? To answer this, we explore the rise of the newest segment of the financial industry, its diversity and its spatial patterns.

25.3 UNDERSTANDING THE RISE OF NEW FINANCIAL INTERMEDIARIES

There exists a large amount of established literature on the economic geography of money and finance (Martin, 1999; Leyshon and Thrift, 1997; Clark, 2005). Broadly, these studies explore the variation of financial systems across and through space and, in particular, the tensions between the national and regional organization of finance and financial systems' global tendencies. Although few geographers explored the scale and scope of crowdfunding as an emerging form of finance, they have contributed to our understanding of the crowdfunding phenomena by stressing the importance of space to contemporary capital formation.

David Harvey's work has focused for decades on Marxist interpretations of the financial system (Harvey, 1982, 1989, 2010). He has continued to argue that capital is a *process of circulation* and that to understand the process we must understand the logic, structure and organization of the circuits of capital. Harvey's political economy approach leads him to emphasize the classic split between productive and finance capital. He analyzes capital's tendency to switch circuits, or to move investments from capital's primary circuit of investment in industry to the secondary circuit of the built environment. In later works, Harvey (1989, 2010) expands this point to include switching into the financial circuit, and the complex relationship between the different circuits as illiquid forms of capital seek more liquid forms through financialization and securitization. However, all financial circuits tend to be homogenized in Harvey's treatment. Additionally, Harvey's theory of capital switching is difficult to show empirically (see Beauregard, 1994; Gotham, 2009), and it is often unclear to what extent investment is actually withdrawn from one circuit of capital to another. Although crowdfunding is not explicitly addressed in this debate, we argue that the expansion of these alternative forms of capital formation might, at least conceptually, represent another circuit for capital. Further, its potential as an alternative to the traditional banking system means it has the potential to create different financial, social and spatial consequences compared with other financial circuits. However, to understand this fully, the processes and practices which shape these circuits must be examined.

Another important contribution of economic geographers that helps us to understand the phenomena of crowdfunding is the continued emphasis on the *social* nature of capital (Martin, 1999; Leyshon and Thrift, 1997). Martin (1999: 11) argues that financial markets are 'structured networks of social relations, interactions and dependencies'. Leyshon and

Thrift (1997), however, stress the set of social practices which create and recreate financial spaces on different scales. They argue that, although money has the potential to be placeless as part of global flows of capital, monetary practices are forged in particular places. New forms of money and capital formation produce new social practices, which combine with older forms of monetary practice into innovative combinations. They examine the culture of money – the shared norms, practices and conventions which uphold and extend the system of money. Pollard and Samers (2013) illustrate this in their work on Islamic finance, which brings together Western and Islamic financial rules, practices and norms not often articulated in finance – such as fairness, justice and transparency.

One of the strengths of the financial geography literature is the importance it gives to institutional and regulatory changes, which constantly reshape and structure the industry. As part of this, Leyshon and Thrift discuss the social practices of regulation and argue that established regulatory boundaries continue to link money to place and social practice. In their discussion of virtual forms of money, they highlight the importance of trust and its maintenance through expert systems and knowledge structures (state regulation, monitoring, surveillance) which act to guarantee expectations across space (Giddens, 2013). This is particularly important in new sectors; Leyshon and Thrift, for example, argue that the actors in novel markets can often benefit from monopoly profits because the area is not yet regulated. Martin (1999) makes a similar point that firms will escape regulatory oversight by moving between regulatory spaces and seeking regulatory gaps. However, neither Martin nor Leyshon and Thrift expand upon the conditions under which new market agents may actually promote regulation as part of an expert system that will function to enhance trust.

The focus on the changing role of institutional actors is a useful one for understanding the role of the crowdfunding *platforms*. Martin and Turner (2000) detail the regulatory changes in the UK in the 1980s, which resulted in the demutualization of Building Societies and the decline of Building Societies as a financial alternative to the traditional banking sector. Martin and Turner highlight how the regulatory changes promoted the political agenda of 'popular capitalism'. Likewise, Clark (2005) and Dixon and Monk (2012) highlight the rise of institutional investors, such as the large pension and sovereign wealth funds, who have become important actors in understanding the importance of institutional investors in contemporary capital formation and distribution. Clark (2005: 99) argues, 'If we are to understand the economic landscape of twenty-first century capitalism, it should be understood through global financial institutions, its social formation and investment practices'. The rise of crowdfunding has created new institutional intermediaries – crowdfunding platforms – which shape the processes and practices of this new form of capital formation. Understanding these platforms, the role they play in capital formation, and how they create certain practices and conventions of crowdfunding, requires more research.

Other disciplines have been quicker to examine the rise of crowdfunding. Most of the academic attention given to crowdfunding comes from the fields of business, finance (Colombo et al., 2015; Belleflamme et al., 2014; Mollick, 2014) and law (Griffin, 2012; Schwartz, 2013; Bradford, 2012). This literature is predominantly focused on the motivations for crowdfunding, the determinants of success and the legal restrictions of equity-based crowdfunding. However, some spatial issues also feature strongly in this literature. One important debate in the business literature is focused on the extent to which crowdfunding functions to eliminate the importance of distance between investors and the projects or firms that receive funding. Focusing on Kickstarter, a large US-based platform which specializes in cultural projects, Mollick (2014) argues that geography is important in understanding crowdfunding in two ways. First, Mollick shows that crowdfunding results in an uneven distribution of funds to cultural projects around the US. Second, Mollick finds geographic patterns in the production of the cultural product itself. For example, that regional specialization (for example, country music in Nashville, Tennessee) is reflected in the Kickstarter projects. Agrawal and his colleagues in the US have conducted one of the larger studies of the industry, exploring crowdfunding's ability to eliminate the 'friction of distance' between investors and small, early-stage artistic projects that successfully receive funding. Agrawal et al. (2011) followed musicians seeking funding to see if crowdfunding relaxes geographic constraints on fundraising. They found that, although funders of successful projects were geographically dispersed, *local* investors still played an important role – they invested relatively early (often having a personal connection with the artist-entrepreneur), which served to signify the quality of the project to other potential investors. Agrawal et al. conclude that crowdfunding does not remove, but does relax, geographic constraints among funders.

Unlike the studies discussed above, Lin and Viswanathan (2014) focus on a debt-based crowdfunding platform to see if investment behaviour is different from the support or donation models discussed in the arts-based examples above. Lin and Viswanathan explore the extent to which the 'home bias' documented in traditional finance continues to be displayed in debt-based crowdfunding, where the crowd invests in an early-stage firm. Lin and Viswanathan point out that home bias, where transactions are more likely to occur between parties in the same geographical area, is considered a sub-optimal behaviour in economics, leading to inefficiencies in the market. They find that, although crowdfunding has the potential to make home bias less relevant, lenders still favour investors in their own state.

These studies all suggest that spatial factors remain important in understanding how crowdfunding functions as a mechanism to distribute finance and the extent to which it might vary from, or reinforce, more traditional sources of finance. However, Mollick and Agrawal et al.'s findings are based on platforms which specialize in cultural projects. They assume the findings hold for other parts of the crowdfunding sector, but we do not know the extent to which the same patterns might hold over other burgeoning parts of the industry. Lin and Viswanathan's study is interesting in its focus on a debt-based platform, but is limited by the large spatial scale of their data. That is to say that measuring home bias on a state scale in the US might lose meaning in large and diverse states, such as California or New York.

25.4 HISTORY OF CROWDFUNDING

Different forms of crowdfunding – where individuals pool resources to provide capital to firms, ideas, places and projects – have a longer history than we might initially think, but how we view crowdfunding fundamentally affects *which* antecedents are held up as precursors of the contemporary crowdfunding phenomena. One early and often-cited example of a donor-based crowdfunding campaign is Joseph Pulitzer's drive to fund the pedestal of the Statue of Liberty in 1885. As editor of the New York daily newspaper, *The World*, Pulitzer started a campaign encouraging individuals to make small donations, which successfully raised over $100,000. However, what made this campaign interesting was the fact that not only were many donors encouraged to participate, no matter how small the donation, but that the methods used to garner support, in many ways, mirror today's technologically mediated crowdfunding campaigns. Davies (2014) highlights that Pulitzer's newspaper campaign promoted a mutual awareness and collective identity of supporters by publishing the name of every single backer, often accompanied by quotes and personal stories. The paper also published daily updates on the progress of the campaign, which created an 'in-time' dynamic and charted progress towards the fundraising goal. Both methods still feature prominently in many contemporary crowdfunding campaigns and remind us that the technological infrastructure of modern campaigns allows, but does not determine, the phenomena (Davies, 2014).

However, we need to look further afield for antecedents for other types of crowdfunding. We can see elements of the lending crowdfunding models in the rise of different alternative financial institutions such as building societies, credit unions and micro-loan funds (Martin and Turner, 2000; Fuller, 1998; Morduch, 1999). For example, Martin and Turner (2000) detail the growth of building societies in the UK – mutual societies owned by their members, or savers, who invested in local mortgages. They show that, while confined by law to providing first-time mortgages and to the retail savings which financed the mortgages, the building societies provided non-profit financial institutions that were often anchored in localities. Thus, building societies allowed many small savers to lend their money to fund local mortgages for first-time buyers. However, regulatory change in the guise of the 1986 Building Society Act led the sector to restructure, to break the link with local members and function more like traditional banks (Leyshon and Thrift, 1997). In a similar vein, Fuller and Jonas (2003) critically examined the role played by credit unions as a cooperative form of local banking, whereby savings of the community are pooled in order to lend to other members of the community or workplace. Fuller and Jonas highlight regulatory and competitive changes which mitigated against the model functioning as a real alternative to the mainstream financial institutions.

Finally, many scholars have often looked to the venture capital industry as a precursor for equity-based models of crowdfunding and argue that crowdfunding functions to democratize the seed capital funding model (Mollick, 2014; Schwienbacher and Larralde, 2012). Mollick contends that much of the venture capital model, such as the search for indicators of quality of the project and team, can be used equally well by crowdfunding backers. He finds that high-quality projects tend to get funded and that quality signals are magnified through a network of backers. Thus, the 'crowd' of supporters can function like the networks supplied by venture capitalists.

25.5 UNDERSTANDING CROWDFUNDING DIVERSITY THROUGH EMPIRICAL STUDIES

We argue that, while the burgeoning literature on contemporary crowdfunding highlights a broad interest in the phenomena, our conceptual and empirical understanding of crowdfunding is hampered by the many studies which treat the industry as one homogeneous whole. This literature suffers from the tendency to examine one particular *model* (for example, donation-based crowdfunding or peer-to-peer lending) or one particular industry vertical or subsector (for example, arts- or music-based investment), with the assumption that their findings apply to the entire crowdfunding field. Thus, the emerging crowdfunding literature often suffers from the fallacy of composition (for example, Mollick, 2014) and the lack of a clearly-defined taxonomy.

We argue that, in order to understand the motivations and the effects of 'the crowd' as types of financial flows through alternative financing channels, academic studies must examine the diversity of crowdfunding. This chapter explores the different models hidden by the term 'crowdfunding'. To accomplish this, we examine donation-, reward- and equity-based crowdfunding models, debt-based crowdfunding models including peer-to-peer consumer and business lending, debt-based securities as well as invoice trading and community shares. We argue that each of these market segments of crowdfunding has different funding mechanisms, characteristics, motivations, and manifest varying geographies of financial transactions.

To understand the diversity and dynamics of the crowdfunding sector, we enlisted the support of the largest 26 UK-based crowdfunding platforms, which function to mediate between funders and fundraisers. Besides surveying platform operators directly, we also worked with the platforms to conduct surveys of funders and fundraisers based on their database between May and September 2014. Although it is difficult to know our response rate, since the universe of all potential respondents is unknown, we received survey responses from 15,685 individuals and businesses that have participated in one of the different crowdfunding models above. Our surveys produced quantitative data across eight models of crowdfunding, from equity-based crowdfunding to peer-to-peer business lending, in order to understand the distinct mechanisms and dynamics driving each specific model. In addition, with cooperation from these leading crowdfunding platforms, we also collected and analyzed a million granular-level micro-transactions totalling £1 billion. These one million micro-transactions were extracted from the platforms' sanitized operating database (that is, after deleting personal and financial information) and contained detailed information in regard to the crowdfunding transactions that took place. Besides the loan/equity offering information, auction/bidding data and repayment information, the funders and fundraisers' four-digit postcode data were also captured. Relying upon this largest academic crowdfunding database to date, we were able to derive, capture, analyze and aggregate important information for each crowdfunding model, such as the average amount of fundraising, average number of funders per deal and average contribution per funder.

25.6 DIVERSITY IN MARKET FUNCTION AND SIZE

As argued above, one of the problems with the academic treatment of crowdfunding is that many scholars use the term broadly to refer to distinct, if related, models. In this section, we examine the market function and size of various models of crowdfunding. When people mention crowdfunding, both in popular culture and academic studies, they often refer to either donation- or reward-based crowdfunding, which have risen in prominence with the success of platforms such as Kickstarter and GoFundMe. However, as clearly shown in Figure 25.1, the two largest models of crowdfunding in the UK are both

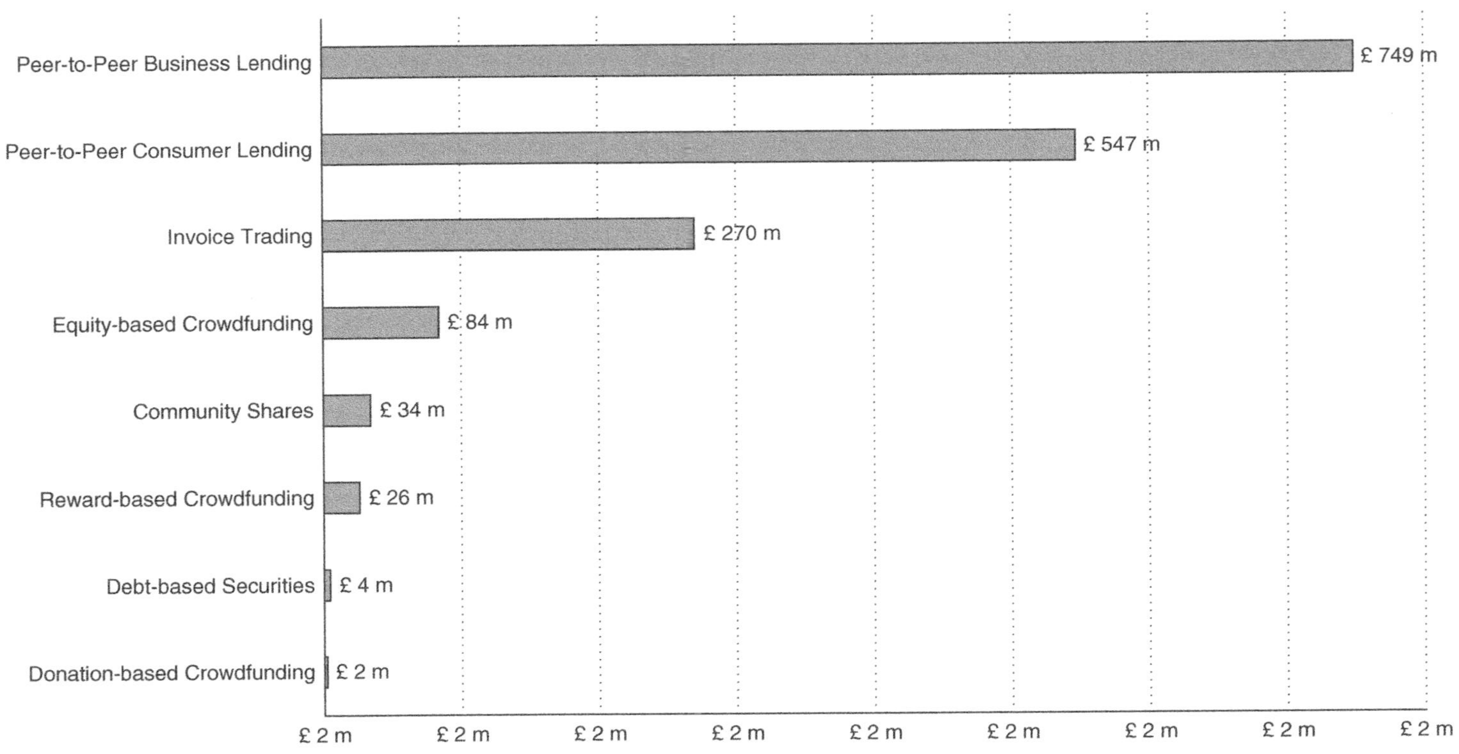

Figure 25.1 *2014 UK alternative finance market volume by model*

debt-based crowdfunding models. The largest is the peer-to-peer business lending sector. Peer-to-peer business lending comprises secured or unsecured debt-based transactions between individuals and businesses with an established trading history, most of which are SMEs.

Crucially, peer-to-peer business lending has emerged as an alternative source of SME funding, which allows some small firms to sidestep traditional bank lending. This segment of the crowdfunding market has grown rapidly since the 2007–08 banking crisis, as borrowers try to find alternatives to the traditional bank loans. Our data show that the majority of SMEs who obtained finance in this way had sought funding from sources such as banks (79 per cent), public funders (19 per cent), and venture capitalists (12 per cent) before obtaining finance through crowdfunding. The model allows many individual lenders to contribute to any one loan, usually through an auction process, thus 'pooling' investment and risk amongst a large number of lenders. In 2014, peer-to-peer business lending accounted for £749 million worth of loans and makes up around 43 per cent of the total crowdfunding market volume. Although an important phenomenon to understand, to put this in perspective, traditional bank lending to SMEs in the UK during the same period totaled £53.4 billion (Bank of England, 2015). Despite this, supporters see signs of Shiller's 'democratization of finance' in the rise of this crowdfunding model (Shiller, 2013).

As Table 25.1 demonstrates, the average peer-to-peer business loan size in the UK is £73,222. It typically takes 796 individual lenders to fund one loan with an average contribution of £92. It is important to note that the data on peer-to-peer business lending also includes secured loans in the real estate sector, which provides finance capital for small and mid-sized real estate developers. This particular segment of peer-to-peer business lending had a much larger average loan of roughly £662,000 (Shiller, 2013) and is dominated by fewer investors per loan. Paradoxically, as many borrowers try to find alternatives to the large finance firms, we can also see that many of the funders for peer-to-peer *real estate* business lending are already dominated by large *institutional* investors, such as hedge and pension funds, attracted to the returns in peer-to-peer business lending, which can range from 8 per cent to 18 per cent depending on the loan risk profiles and maturity.

The second largest model of crowdfunding also has the potential to challenge the role of the traditional banking sector. The peer-to-peer *consumer* lending model is another debt-

Table 25.1 Crowdfunding model in numbers

	Average Amount Raised (£)	Average Number of Funders	Average Contribution Amount (£)
Debt-based Securities	730,000	587	1,243.61
Equity-based Crowdfunding	199,095	125	1,592.76
Community Shares	174,286	474	367.69
Peer-to-Peer Business Lending	73,222	796	91.99
Invoice Trading	56,075	7	8,010.71
Donation-based Crowdfunding	6,102	55	110.95
Peer-to-Peer Consumer Lending	5,471	201	27.22
Reward-based Crowdfunding	3,766	77	48.91

based model of crowdfunding, which accounted for over £547 million worth of loans in the UK in 2014. This crowdfunding model is growing rapidly; however, at this point, peer-to-peer consumer lending only represents 2 per cent of the £26 billion worth of personal unsecured loans made in the UK in 2014 (Nostrum, 2015). Like its business counterpart, peer-to-peer consumer lending is a model where individuals borrow money from an amalgamated lender, comprising hundreds of individual micro-loans, thus spreading the risk of lending over a large number of lenders. Similar to the traditional bank lending models, borrowers used the loan to purchase cars (46 per cent), fund home improvements (26 per cent) and to consolidate existing debt (25 per cent). However, sole traders and small firms also used the consumer loans to start or finance micro-businesses (3 per cent). Thus, the distinction between consumer and business lending on these peer-to-peer platforms can be overdrawn. Crucially, a number of peer-to-peer consumer platforms are now seeing substantial volumes of unsecured lending to these businesses.

The crowdfunding platforms function as intermediaries in peer-to-peer consumer lending. The platforms, in an increasingly automated fashion, reject or accept applications for unsecured loans from borrowers. Studies find rejection rates as high as 90 per cent as the platform algorithms weed out all but the lowest risk borrowers with the highest credit scores (Zhang et al., 2014: 40). Clearly, this does not function as a lending model for the economically marginalized. Conversely, the majority of successful borrowers had other offers of loans from the mainstream financial industry. The result is a very low default rate of less than 1 per cent for the crowdfunding platforms that provide peer-to-peer consumer lending (Zhang et al., 2014: 40).

Lenders and borrowers are not only attracted by competitive interest rates than that offered by the traditional banks, but are also motivated by a pronounced anti-bank sentiment. Reflecting the continued resentment some respondents felt about the banking crisis of 2007–08 and its lasting effect on public finances, many respondents wrote comments in their survey expressing anger and frustration with the banks. Unsolicited comments, such as 'deliberately taking my business away from the big banks' and 'supporting a real alternative to the traditional finance sector' were volunteered in a significant proportion of survey returns. Again, this suggests that, for some, the peer-to-peer consumer lending platforms offer an alternative financial mechanism worth pursuing for symbolic as well as financial reasons.

However, it remains very unclear the extent to which we can consider these peer-to-peer models as alternatives to traditional financial sources, as their success attracts major financial players. The crowdfunding industry has seen an influx of institutional funding from traditional financial institutions, such as pension funds, hedge funds, mutual funds, and asset management firms either lending through or buying equity stakes in crowdfunding platforms. In addition, governmental and non-governmental organizations such as the British Business Bank and county councils are investing through platforms as lenders, particularly in peer-to-peer business lending, thus blurring the boundaries of traditional and alternative finance.

The other rapidly growing type of crowdfunding is equity-based crowdfunding, which is based on buying equity shares in early-stage start-up or growth-stage firms. This model entails selling registered securities to investors (retail, professional, and institutional) and is often promoted as a type of 'democratized' version of venture capital (Mollick, 2014; Schwienbacher and Larralde, 2012). The majority of our respondents (62 per cent of the

290 investors) identified themselves as retail investors, with no previous experience of investing. This type of crowdfunding seems to attract investors with no pre-existing social ties, but also functions to formalize the financial support of friends and family. The rest, roughly 38 per cent, were either wealthy individuals or institutional investors. These investors were professional investors with previous experience investing in early-stage firms or high-net-worth individuals.

In 2014, this equity-based crowdfunding model accounted for over £84 million worth of capital for small firms in the UK. To give this context, this compares to £874 million of total seed stage and venture stage equity investment in the UK according to Beauhurst (2015). As shown in Table 25.1, the average equity fundraising deal on the crowdfunding platforms are much bigger than the average peer-to-peer business loan at £199,095. Typically speaking, around 125 investors would invest in a typical equity crowdfunding offering with £1,592 being the average investment amount per investor.

Although the platforms perform a number of 'due diligence' procedures on the fundraising firms, this model is inevitably riskier than the debt-based models mentioned above, as the rate of failure for new ventures is high. These investors are often long-term investors, or 'patient capital', as there is not always a secondary market for these shares and 'exits' (either through IPO or merger and acquisition) are hard to come by. This makes it impossible at this point to measure any return on investment at an aggregate level given there are only two known 'exits' in the UK thus far. From the fundraisers' perspective in our research, it seems that, besides funding, they also value the non-financial benefits associated with the crowdfunding process, such as marketing, branding, product testing, concept validation and user engagement.

Like the peer-to-peer business models, there is a large and growing segment of the equity-based model exclusively focused on the property industry. Equity-based crowdfunding for real estate enables investors to obtain ownership of a property by purchasing shares of a single property or a portfolio of properties through a special purpose vehicle (SPV). The risk of investing in real estate crowdfunding is typically lower than in pure equity-based crowdfunding with properties acting as collaterals for securities. However, the potential upside of investment could be smaller as well.

Crucially, the equity model of crowdfunding is heavily promoted by the state in the UK, who have created specific schemes to encourage investment in start-up firms. In particular, the great majority of the funded equity-based crowdfunding investments (90 per cent) were eligible for large income tax concessions through either the Enterprise Investment Scheme (EIS) or the Seed Enterprise Investment Scheme (SEIS). By allowing large tax deductions, these government schemes function to reduce risk for investors and encourage venture investing through crowdfunding.

Reward-based crowdfunding, although often perceived as being synonymous with crowdfunding itself, is actually very small in comparison with equity-based crowdfunding. In the UK, this model only reached £26 million in 2014. Reward-based crowdfunding is a model in which individuals donate towards a specific project or firm with the expectation of receiving a tangible, but non-financial, return or reward for their support. As Table 25.1 shows, reward-based crowdfunding has the smallest average fundraising amount at just £3,766, which is typically funded by 77 backers each with a donation of £49. Akin to equity-based crowdfunding, in addition to providing funding, this model can enable fundraisers (particularly within the creative industries) to test their ideas, obtain a proof of concept, engage with their users and supporters as well as aid marketing efforts.

In the beginning of its development, reward-based crowdfunding was often employed as a fundraising alternative for unestablished artists, budding entrepreneurs, independent movie makers and unsigned singers and dancers. However, this model has also seen the introduction of large institutional players. In recent years, big brands and corporations, from Sony, Microsoft, AXA to Ben & Jerry's, are leveraging the reward-based crowdfunding channels – not to raise funds, but to test their products, create 'social buzz' and engage with their consumers.

Donation-based crowdfunding is another small segment of the total crowdfunding phenomena, comprising less than 1 per cent of the total volume. Unlike the reward crowdfunding model, donors in donation-based crowdfunding do not expect any returns – financial or non-financial. They are typically making contributions to support charities or good causes. The historical antecedent here comes from the traditional charity sector rather than a segment of the finance industry. According to our data, a typical donor will donate on average £111 on the crowdfunding platforms and it takes 55 donors to fund a donation-based crowdfunding campaign.

Invoice trading is another crowdfunding model that has emerged in the UK, which allows firms to quickly raise capital without resorting to either debt or equity. Invoice trading enables firms, which are mostly SMEs, to sell their invoices at a discount, in return for immediate working capital. This model accounts for £270 million in 2014, thus accounting for around 16 per cent of total crowdfunding market volume. Firms using invoicing trading are attracted by the speed of raising capital, which averaged only a few hours in an online auction of invoices. The average firm using this model to raise funds was small, at less than 50 employees, and raised an average of £56,075. This particularly model functions to test the boundaries of 'crowdfunding' as, again, the large institutional investors dominate this form of capital formation. It is mostly institutional investors who are funding the auction of invoices rather than 'a crowd' of smaller retail investors. On average, this model only takes seven institutional investors or high-net-worth individuals to finance a typical invoice. The main reason firms gave for using invoice trading was to improve cash flow – cited by an overwhelming 92 per cent of respondents. Like the peer-to-peer business model, the majority of these firms had approached the traditional banking sector first and 80 per cent of those firms had been turned down by the banks. Thus, the speed and flexibility of invoice trading made it a useful funding mechanism for small firms.

In contrast, one of the most locally oriented types of crowdfunding is the community shares model. In this model, individuals invest in a withdrawable share of a community project. The projects range from renovating a village hall, to creating renewable energy projects, to major construction projects for a new arts centre. In 2014, this crowdfunding model raised roughly £34 million in the UK. This is perhaps the model that best fits a democratized model of funding. The funding model is based on UK legislation from the cooperative and community benefit societies. Funders' investments are amalgamated to support the community project, and supporters choose which individual projects to support. In 2014, successfully funded community projects combined funds from an average of 474 investors, each investing an average of £368.

The majority (55 per cent) of community supporters chose a local project which they are able to access themselves. Some revenue-generating community projects have the potential of repaying the supporters if they wish to cash-in their shares, although many funders are motivated by 'investing in my local community' (89 per cent) rather than 'financial returns' (24 per cent). Perhaps, in a reflection of this, funders in this model also often became personally involved in the running and monitoring of the community project. A sizeable proportion of funders thought it was important to get directly involved with the project (33 per cent), and to attend shareholders' meeting and AGMs (37 per cent), as well as to get their investment back (30 per cent). Overall, the community-based model of crowdfunding allows social, community, and environmentally oriented investing to flourish.

Finally, the debt-based securities sector is a niche section of the crowdfunding market, which only recorded £4 million in total volume in 2014. However, as demonstrated by Table 25.1, a typical crowdfunding campaign in this model on average raises over £730,000 from 587 investors. The large sum of investment is a reflection of its market function, which is to provide long-term 'patient capital' for relatively large-scale renewable energy projects in the UK such as wind farms and solar panel installation. The debt-based securities, such as bonds and debentures, are issued by renewable energy companies with a fixed majority and interest rate. Most debt-based securities issued, unlike that of the community shares, are fully tradable and transferrable. This crowdfunding model taps into investors' social and environmental affinity to renewable energy and offers long-term investment opportunities which can have 20 or 25-year maturity, far longer than the three to five year loan terms offered by peer-to-peer business lending platforms.

This section introduced an array of distinctive models of crowdfunding. We argue that it is vital to delineate each model to understand their differing market sizes, highly differentiated funding mechanisms, composition of investors, fundraising dynamics and funding outcomes. It is evident that crowdfunding is an ambiguous and often convoluted umbrella term which lacks conceptual and empirical clarity. It includes an array of financial flows including charitable giving, for-profit, lending, high risk seed-capital investing, and community building. To conduct a critical and in-depth analysis of crowdfunding, one must adopt a more nuanced approach in order to appreciate the characteristics of these highly diverse models.

25.7 DIVERSITY IN GEOGRAPHY

In the UK, the concentration of the financial services industry in London and the South East and the centralization of its financial power has long been a hallmark of the institutional geography of traditional finance (Klagge and Martin, 2005). This concentrated and centralized geography of finance is pronounced both in regard to SME financing (Martin, 1999) and venture capital financing (Mason and Harrison, 2002; Martin et al., 2003), with resulting locational biases, often against the SMEs and start-ups in the areas and regions outside London and the South East. Therefore, it is pertinent to examine whether the economic geography of crowdfunding, which facilitates funding through online alternative channels (that is, platforms), exhibits different kinds of geography, both in terms of funding (where the money comes from), fundraising (where the money goes) and the regional patterns of flow (whether a region has a higher or lower proportion of fundraisers in relation to funders). More importantly, will different crowdfunding models demonstrate varied or even contrasting spatial patterns?

In this section, we investigate the geography of funding and fundraising for the four most prevalent crowdfunding models in the UK. They are peer-to-peer business lending, peer-to-peer consumer lending, and equity- and reward-based crowdfunding. Combined together, these four models account for over 80 per cent of the total crowdfunding market volume in the UK. As discussed above, peer-to-peer business and consumer lending are debt-based crowdfunding, whilst equity-based crowdfunding relies upon the sales of securities or shares and reward-based crowdfunding facilitates donations from backers for tangible, but non-financial, returns.

For peer-to-peer consumer lending, where consumers borrow money from other individuals through highly automated online platforms, the survey findings depict a 'decentralized' geography of crowdfunding with more funding outflow from London and the South East (the centre) to the rest of the regions in the UK. As Figure 25.2 demonstrates, based on over 10,000 survey responses, it seems that there are higher proportions (as percentage of surveyed sample) of lenders than borrowers in London and the South East when compared to the rest of the UK regions. Nearly 15 per cent of the surveyed lenders and 8 per cent of surveyed borrowers in peer-to-peer consumer lending are based in London, while 22 per cent of surveyed lenders and 17 per cent of surveyed borrowers are from the South East. Furthermore, 7 per cent of the surveyed lenders and 5 per cent of surveyed borrowers are from the East of England. We assume that the average lending amount per lender and borrowing amount per borrower do not vary significantly across regions (as validated by our granular-level transaction dataset). Given this, our findings suggest a spatial outflow of funding from London and the South East to the rest of the

Figure 25.2 Funder and fundraiser location by region – P2P consumer lending (n=10308)

UK regions. London seems to be the biggest net exporter of funding (7 per cent difference between the surveyed lenders and borrowers), followed by the South East (5 per cent) and the East of England (2 per cent). This, in turn, depicts a 'decentralizing' geography for the peer-to-peer consumer lending model of crowdfunding. Indeed, in most of the regions outside of London and the South East, there is a higher percentage of surveyed borrowers than lenders. For instance, in Scotland, there are 5 per cent more surveyed borrowers than lenders; in the North West, the difference is 4 per cent, whilst the gap is 2 per cent in the North East and Northern Ireland regions.

Our survey data from 1,654 lenders and borrowers of peer-to-peer *business* lending also depicts a decentralized geography of crowdfunding, albeit to a smaller degree. As illustrated in Figure 25.3, there are 2 per cent more surveyed lenders than surveyed SME borrowers in London. In the South East, the gap is 1 per cent, while in the East of England the difference is 6 per cent, with 9 per cent of all surveyed funders for peer-to-peer business lending being located in this region in contrast to 3 per cent of surveyed SME borrowers. Again, assuming the average lending amount per funder and borrowing amount per fundraiser do not vary significantly across regions, which is supported by our transactional dataset, it seems that London, the South East and the East of England are all net exporters of funding in online peer-to-peer business lending. In contrast, the percentage of surveyed SME borrowers seems to be higher than the percentage of surveyed lenders in the West Midlands (5 per cent difference), North West (3 per cent), East Midlands (2 per cent), Wales (2 per cent), Northern Ireland (1 per cent) and North East (1 per cent), indicating a net inflow of funding for SMEs through peer-to-peer business lending online channels for these regions. Although the regional pattern differences are less pronounced in peer-to-peer business lending than in peer-to-peer consumer lending, the findings

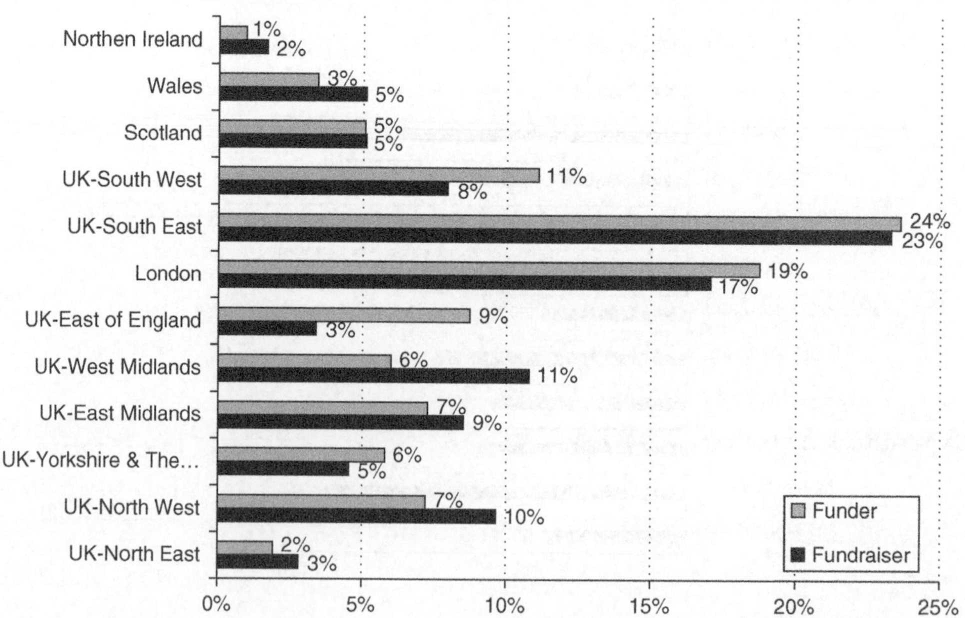

Figure 25.3 Funder and fundraiser location by region – P2P business lending (n=1654)

still illustrate a decentralizing geography of debt-based crowdfunding, where funding is flowing disproportionately from London and the South East to the rest of the UK. This is very different to the centralized geography of traditional finance, where London and the South East are usually attracting disproportionately higher levels of funding than the rest of the UK.

However, other models of crowdfunding show a very different geography. Equity- and reward-based crowdfunding show signs of the centralization of funding, which closely resemble those of traditional venture finance. Clearly, London still dominates equity-based crowdfunding, which facilitates mostly seed-stage and early-stage venture capital for start-ups, with 41 per cent of surveyed fundraisers/entrepreneurs and 31 per cent of surveyed investors located in the region (Figure 25.4). Assuming the average equity investment amount per investor (that is, averaging £1,592) and the fundraising amount per fundraiser (that is, averaging £199,095) do not vary significantly between regions, London benefits from being the main 'net importer' of venture capital funding channelled through equity-based crowdfunding platforms in the UK. Many other UK regions are the 'net exporters' in this particular crowdfunding model, with the South East (8 per cent difference between the percentage of investors and fundraisers), Wales (4 per cent), Yorkshire and the Humber (3 per cent), the East of England (1 per cent) and the North East (1 per cent) all seemingly contributing net outflow of funding to London. Nevertheless, it is worth noting that both Northern Ireland and the South West regions have a higher percentage of fundraisers than the percentage of investors in equity-based crowdfunding, which indicate a net inflow of funding from equity-based crowdfunding. In the case of the South West, it has 15 per cent of surveyed fundraisers and 12 per cent

Figure 25.4 Funder and fundraiser location by region – equity-based crowdfunding (n=205)

of surveyed investors in the survey sample. Correspondingly, the South West also has a disproportionately higher level of funding volumes and number of equity-based crowdfunding deals which originated in the region, according to our transactional dataset. This could be explained by the fact that one of the largest and most successful equity-based crowdfunding platforms in the country is based in the South West. Therefore, the region has benefited from this particular institutional geography anomaly accordingly with heightened equity-based crowdfunding activities and funding volume in the region. Nevertheless, overall, equity-based crowdfunding is exhibiting a centralized geography very similar to that which we have seen in the traditional venture capital paradigm, with London gaining a much higher proportion of funding than the rest of the UK regions.

In a similar vein, although reward-based crowdfunding has been applauded in the press and academic studies alike for its potential to 'democratize finance and make it more accessible' (Shiller, 2013), at least in terms of regional geography, it has failed to break the mould according to our survey data. Our findings show London is still the dominant region in the UK in this model, with 26 per cent of surveyed fundraisers/campaign owners and 19 per cent of surveyed funders/backers. Again, assuming average donation and fundraising amounts for reward-based crowdfunding do not vary significantly between regions, London seems to be a 'net importer' of funding flows from the reward-based crowdfunding online channels. The South East is also prevalent, with 14 per cent of surveyed fundraisers and 11 per cent of surveyed funders. However, many other regions have a disproportionately higher percentage of surveyed funders than percentage of surveyed fundraisers, such as the South West (3 per cent difference), Wales (2 per cent), West Midlands (2 per cent) and North East (1 per cent), which indicate funding outflow. Interestingly, given the global nature of reward-based crowdfunding and the proliferation of international reward-based crowdfunding platforms such as Kickstarter, 9 per cent of the surveyed funders and 6 per cent of the surveyed fundraisers are actually from outside of the UK. Notwithstanding the similarities to equity-based crowdfunding, our findings suggest that reward-based crowdfunding is demonstrating a more centralized geography akin to that of traditional finance.

Overall, it seems that equity- and reward-based crowdfunding reinforce, if not exacerbate, the centralized geography of finance by channelling more funding inflow than outflow to London and the South East. In contrast, debt-based crowdfunding models, such as peer-to-peer consumer lending and business lending, exhibit a more decentralized geography of crowdfunding by channelling more funding inflow to the rest of UK regions from London and the South East. Therefore, when it comes to geographical and spatial analysis of crowdfunding, it is imperative to examine each distinctive crowdfunding model in detail and appreciate the extent to which they challenge or reinforce the geographies of investing and lending in the mainstream financial institutions.

25.8 DIVERSITY IN THE CROWD: GENDER AND INCOME

One of the problems of the existing literature on crowdfunding is that people tend to treat 'crowd' as a homogenous entity without developing a more nuanced understanding of who comprises the crowd and their demographic and socio-economic characteristics. This applies to both funders, who are sources of funding and fundraisers, who are the

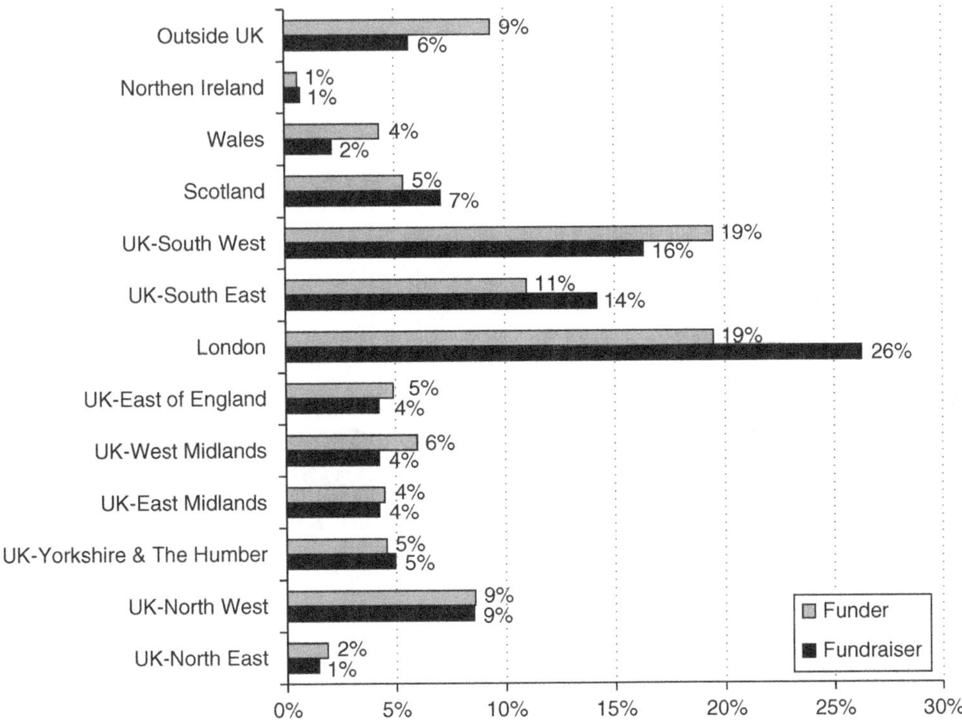

Figure 25.5 Funder and fundraiser location by region – reward based crowdfunding (n=1343)

recipients of funding. Furthermore, we need to examine whether the dynamics and composition of the 'crowd' vary from crowdfunding model to crowdfunding model in order to understand the socio-economic implications and impact of crowdfunded capital; for instance, on widening access to finance in terms of gender and income equality in comparison with the traditional finance paradigm.

There are long-standing gendered patterns of funding in the traditional finance sector, which disadvantage female entrepreneurs (Brush et al., 2014; Marlow and Patton, 2005). We explored the extent to which these might be challenged or reversed by the different crowdfunding models. From this perspective, it is evident that female participation levels in fundraising through online crowdfunding channels, as an entrepreneur, a campaign owner or a borrower, are highly varied from model to model (Figure 25.6). At first, it seems striking that 64 per cent of fundraisers in donation-based crowdfunding are women, far higher than that of any other crowdfunding models. This is probably not too surprising, however, considering around two-thirds (66 per cent) of the voluntary sector workforce are women in the UK (NCVO, 2014). Therefore, it is expected that a higher percentage of fundraisers in donation-based crowdfunding, which is primarily catering for charitable and voluntary sector fundraising, would be women. Reward-based crowdfunding has the second highest percentage of women fundraisers among all crowdfunding models at 51 per cent. This finding is interesting, as reward-based crowdfunding is popularly utilized

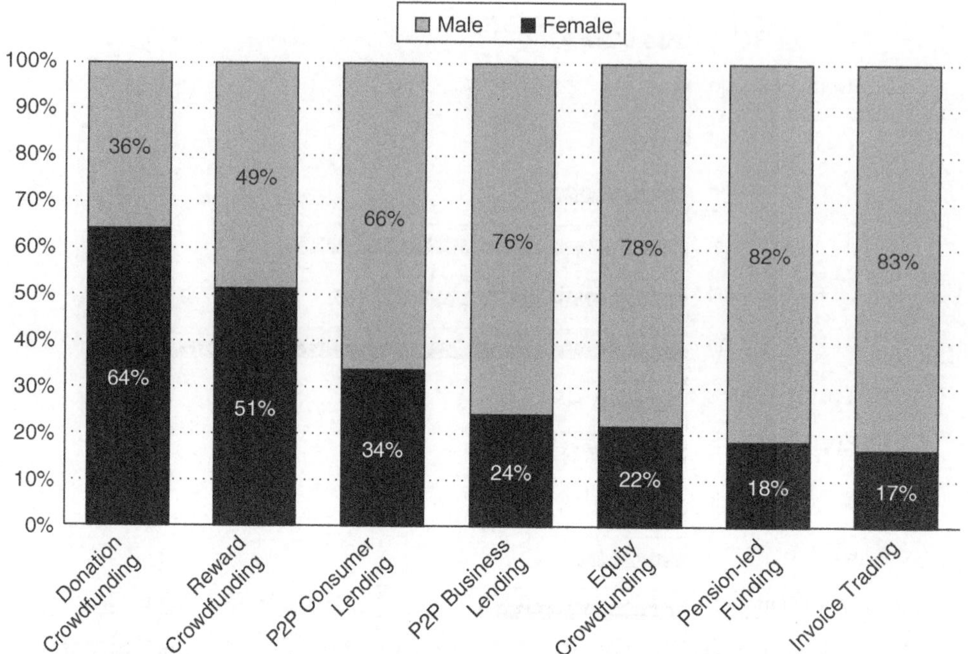

Figure 25.6 Gender variations across crowdfunding models – fundraisers' perspective

by fundraisers who are working in the digital and creative industries such as filmmaking, video games, design and fashion. According to the UK Commission for Employment and Skills, just one quarter (26 per cent) of the workforce in the digital and creative sector in the UK are female (UKCES, 2015). Reward-based crowdfunding seems to be offering more fundraising opportunities to women who work in the digital and creative industries.

As discussed above, equity-based crowdfunding facilitates seed-stage and early-stage venture capital funding for entrepreneurs. Traditionally speaking, female entrepreneurs are less likely than men to acquire venture capital from either business angels or venture capitalists (Brush et al., 2014). During an extensive study, which surveyed 6,517 companies that received venture capital funding in the USA between 2011 and 2013, only 2.7 per cent of the companies had a woman founder or CEO (Brush et al., 2014). In addition, women only make up a small percentage (1–3 per cent) of high-tech entrepreneurs, which is an active group vying for venture capital funding (Robb and Coleman, 2009). Our survey findings show that 22 per cent of the fundraisers in equity-based crowdfunding in the UK are women, which seems to be significantly higher than statistics gathered under the traditional venture capital paradigm. The much higher percentage of female fundraisers in this model may indicate that they were unable to access funding through traditional financial institutions.

Access to credit from banks is one of the greatest and most prevalent challenges female entrepreneurs and borrowers face (Gatewood et al., 2004). Our survey findings show that 24 per cent of business borrowers on peer-to-peer lending platforms are women.

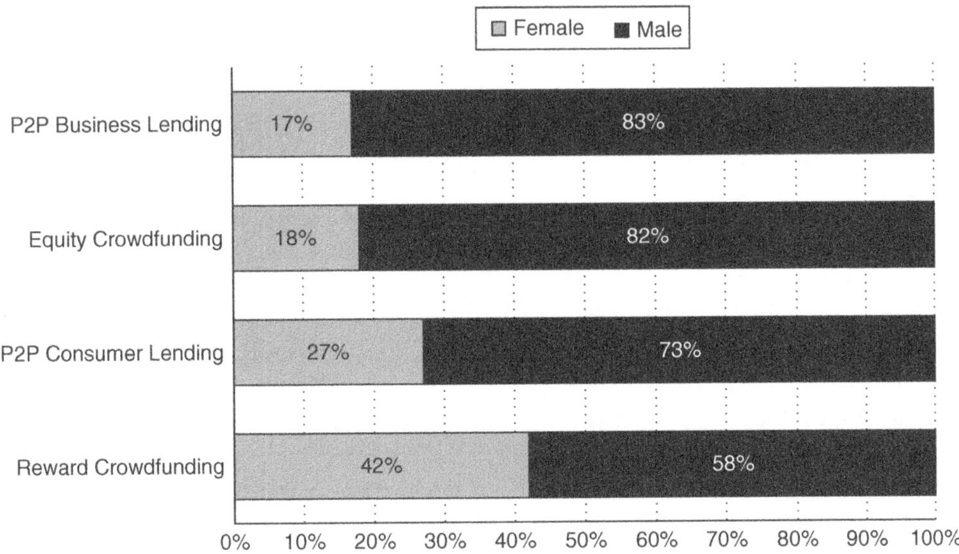

Figure 25.7 Gender variations across crowdfunding models – funders' perspective

In addition, 17 per cent of the SME borrowers who auction invoices or receivables on crowdfunding platforms are women. Our data also shows that 34 per cent of *consumer* borrowers are women, some of which may be using consumer credit to finance activities as sole traders. Taken in total, this suggests that the different models of crowdfunding may function to open up alternative channels of finance for female owners of SMEs.

From the funders' perspective, there is also a significant variation in gender composition across crowdfunding platforms. Figure 25.7 illustrates that 17 per cent of the lenders on peer-to-peer business lending platforms and 18 per cent of investors on equity-based crowdfunding platforms are women. The percentage of female funders is higher in peer-to-peer consumer lending at 27 per cent and reward-based crowdfunding at 42 per cent. These findings show that female participation in the crowdfunding market from the funding side is significant and varied across models.

To investigate whether crowdfunding can truly 'democratize finance', it is also important to examine the income profiles of both funders and fundraisers. Our data shows significant income variations among fundraisers across five prevalent crowdfunding models (Figure 25.8). It is striking that borrowers on peer-to-peer consumer lending platforms seem to be occupying the higher end of the income spectrum, with 46 per cent of the borrowers earning more than £35,000 per year and 18 per cent earning more than £50,000 per year. Around 3 per cent of the borrowers on peer-to-peer consumer lending platforms are actually earning more than £100,000 per year, with only 25 per cent of the borrowers earning less than £25,000 per year. These findings coincide with our earlier discussions that the vast majority of approved borrowers on peer-to-peer consumer lending platforms are relatively well-off people, who are either prime or super-prime borrowers with excellent credit ratings. Most of them can easily access credit and borrow money from the banks. The primary reasons for them to opt to borrow on peer-to-peer lending

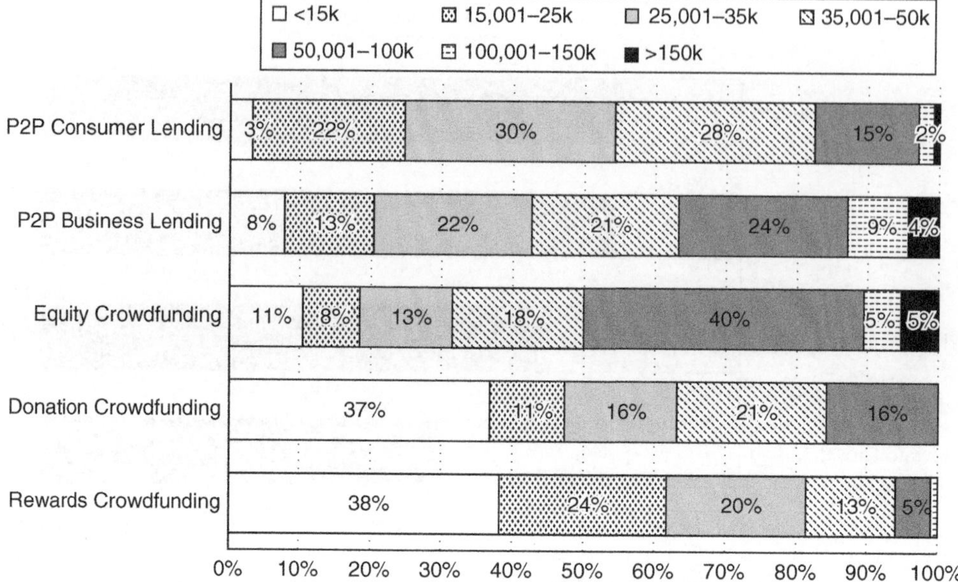

Figure 25.8 Income variations by crowdfunding models – fundraisers

platforms are 'better interest rates' (71 per cent rated as a very important factor), 'more flexible terms' (56 per cent), 'ease of use' (52 per cent), 'transparency' (50 per cent), 'speed' (50 per cent), 'more control' (45 per cent) and 'better services' (42 per cent) (Zhang et al., 2014: 45). These results question the extent to which crowdfunding is 'broadening and deepening' access to capital markets for ordinary individuals (Erturk et al., 2007).

In a similar vein, significant numbers of SME owners who are borrowing on peer-to-peer business lending platforms and entrepreneurs who are fundraising on equity-based crowdfunding platforms also belong to the higher end of the income strata according to our survey data. A large proportion (37 per cent) of the SME borrowers on peer-to-peer business lending platforms are earning more than £50,000 per year. The pattern is similar for equity-based fundraisers. Just over 50 per cent of the fundraisers on equity-based crowdfunding are also earning more than £50,000 a year, with 11 per cent earning more than £100,000 a year. Only 19 per cent of the fundraisers on equity-based crowdfunding platforms and 20 per cent of borrowers on peer-to-peer business lending platforms are earning less than £25,000 a year. Therefore, the data shows that these models of crowdfunding are serving a significant number of people who already have access to credit and have the ability to obtain capital from traditional channels, albeit more efficiently, speedily and on better terms.

However, when it comes to non-investment models such as donation- and reward-based crowdfunding, the income profiles of fundraisers do alter remarkably. For instance, 37 per cent of the fundraisers on donation-based crowdfunding platforms have income levels lower than £15,000 per year, 63 per cent of the surveyed fundraisers have annual earnings less than £35,000 and only 16 per cent are earning more than £50,000 per year. Similarly, 39 per cent of the fundraisers on reward-based crowdfunding platforms are earning less than £15,000 per year and 81 per cent of the fundraisers are earning less than

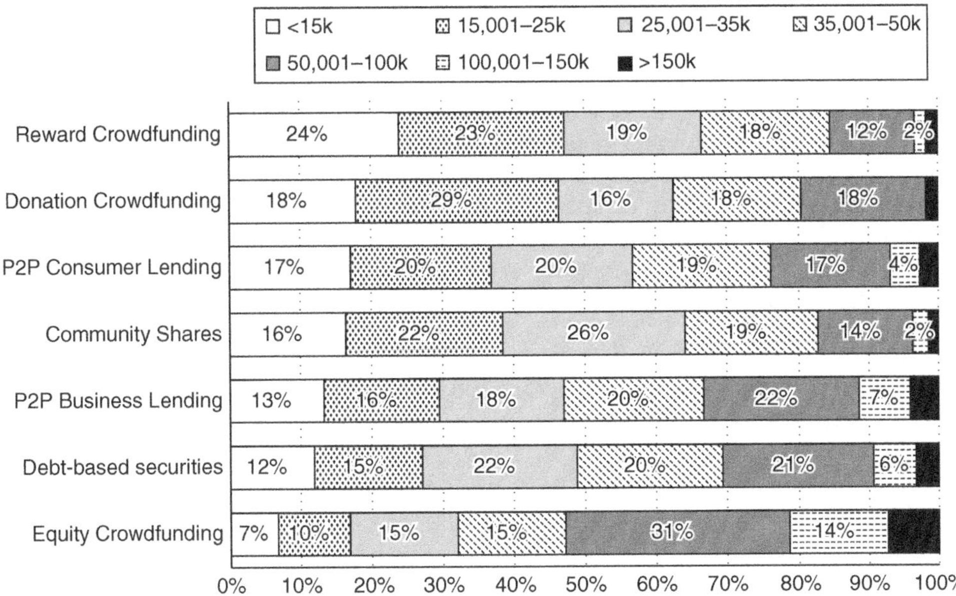

Figure 25.9 Income variations by crowdfunding models – funders

£35,000 a year. Therefore, we also argue that particularly models of crowdfunding, such as donation- and reward-based crowdfunding, can function as effective and alternative capital accumulation channels for people who come from lower income backgrounds and who might have difficulty in raising capital or accessing credit through traditional means.

When it comes to funders, there are also important variations in the income profiles of investors, backers and lenders (Figure 25.9). The backers and donors of reward- and donation-based crowdfunding seem to have relatively lower income levels. Roughly 66 per cent of the backers for reward-based crowdfunding and 63 per cent of the donors for donation-based crowdfunding are earning less than £35,000. This seems to support the thesis that people from the lower income groups tend to donate disproportionately more than well-off people (NewTithing Group, 2004). On the other end of the spectrum, the investors for equity-based crowdfunding seem to be more well-off, with only 32 per cent of them earning less than £35,000 per year. The majority of investors (53 per cent) on equity-based crowdfunding earn more than £50,000 per year, with 21 per cent of them earning more than £100,000. If angel investing and venture investing have always been a more privileged financial activity for the rich and well-off, equity-based crowdfunding's investor base doesn't seem to be a radical departure from that paradigm.

Nevertheless, it is also interesting to note that, for the other two prevailing investment crowdfunding models – peer-to-peer consumer and business lending – a significant number of lenders/funders have an annual income of less than £35,000. In fact, 57 per cent of the lenders in peer-to-peer consumer lending are earning less than £35,000 per year, with 17 per cent reported earning less than £15,000 per year. Similarly, 47 per cent of the lenders in peer-to-peer business lending are earning less than £35,000 annually, with 13 per cent reported earning less than £15,000 per year. From our qualitative studies, it was apparent that, although some of these lenders do come from lower income groups and intend to invest a small amount of money (for example, £20–£50) to test the water with peer-to-peer lending and 'taking a punt', a significant proportion of the lenders are 'cash-poor' but 'asset-rich' pensioners over the age of 65. In this sense, from the funding side at least, some crowdfunding models such as peer-to-peer lending do offer new opportunities and access to new asset classes (for example, peer-to-peer loans) for people who are normally not involved in, or able to participate in, these investment marketplaces. Therefore, to have a detailed and nuanced analysis about crowdfunding, one needs to be aware of the diverse income and gender profiles associated with each of the distinctive crowdfunding models.

25.9 DIVERSITY IN FUNDING AND FUNDRAISING MOTIVATIONS

To begin to understand if crowdfunding offers an alternative circuit of finance, which allows capital to be accumulated and distributed differently to traditional finance, either socially or economically, we need to examine the motivations for both funders and fundraisers to use crowdfunding.

Community shares, debt-based securities, equity-based crowdfunding and peer-to-peer business lending are all forms of investment crowdfunding where investors or lenders are expecting financial returns for their capital. However, as the data in Figure 25.10 clearly demonstrates, financial motivation is a much more important factor in some of the crowdfunding models than in others. The overwhelming majority of investors and lenders in equity-based crowdfunding and peer-to-peer business lending state that 'making a

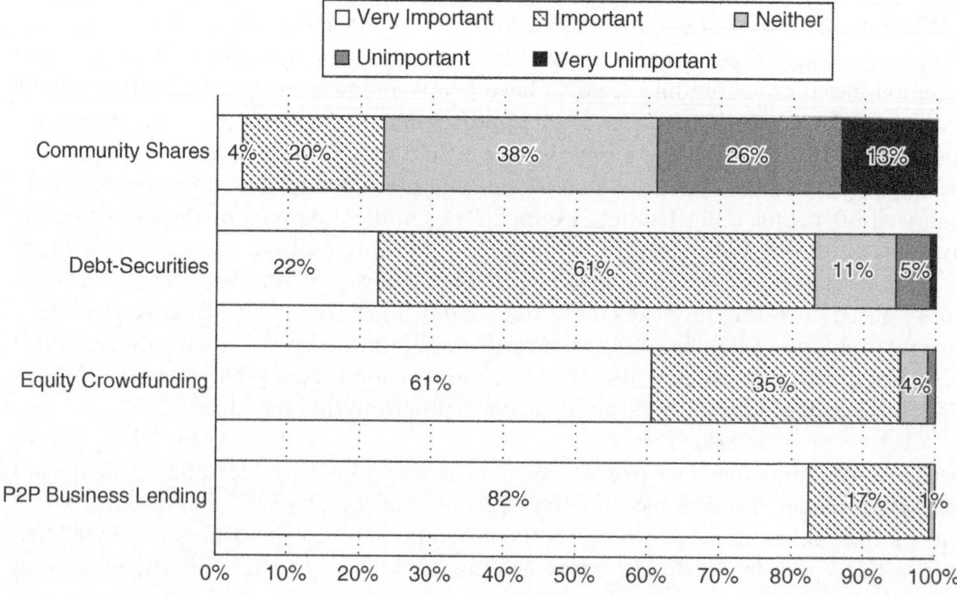

Figure 25.10 Funders' motivation – 'making a financial return'

financial return' is a very important motivational factor for them to invest through crowdfunding platforms. Indeed, 99 per cent of the surveyed lenders in peer-to-peer business lending rate 'making a financial return' as either a very important or important factor. Similarly, 95 per cent of the investors in equity-based crowdfunding made the same claim. However, for investors in community shares and debt-based securities, only 3.5 per cent and 22 per cent of them rate 'making a financial return' as a 'very important' motivational driver for making investments. Indeed, in community shares, only 23 per cent of the investors think making a financial return is either very important or important. Some 39 per cent of the total surveyed investors regard making a financial return as either 'unimportant' or 'very unimportant'.

This discrepancy in funders' motivation across crowdfunding models is further validated and, at least partially, explained by Figure 25.11, which depicts the perceived importance of 'doing social and environmental good' as a motivational factor for investing in some models of crowdfunding. Unsurprisingly, given the importance of making a financial return, investors and lenders in peer-to-peer business lending and equity-based crowdfunding give relatively low importance to this factor. Only 7 per cent of the lenders and 10 per cent of the investors in these two crowdfunding models state that doing social and environmental good is a 'very important' factor in their decision to invest in crowdfunded loans or start-ups. In contrast, 44 per cent of the lenders in debt-based securities and 53 per cent of the investors in community shares claim that 'doing social and environmental good' is a very important factor for them, definitely more so than 'making a financial return'. Backers and donors in reward- and donation-based crowdfunding also exhibited a higher level of affinity with 'doing social and environmental good'.

From the fundraiser's perspective, our data illustrates the variations in perceived

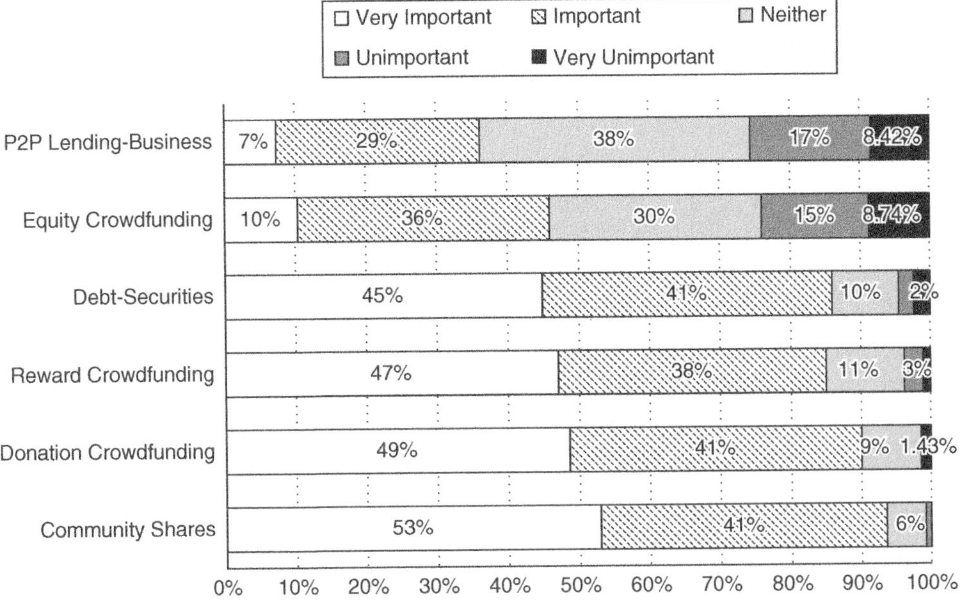

Figure 25.11 Funders' motivation – 'doing social and environmental good'

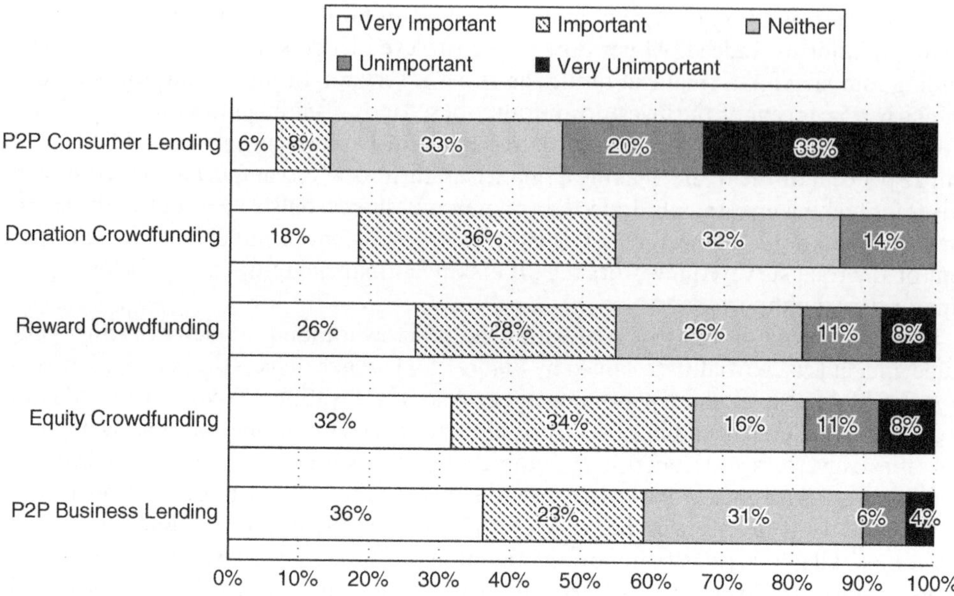

Figure 25.12 Fundraisers' motivation – 'unable to source funding locally'

importance of 'unable to source funding locally' as a motivational factor for crowdfunding. For both equity-based crowdfunding and peer-to-peer business lending, there seem to be a real challenge for fundraisers to raise capital locally (Figure 25.12). We find 59 per cent of the SME borrowers in peer-to-peer business lending and 66 per cent of the entrepreneurs in equity-based crowdfunding state that 'unable to source funding locally' is either a 'very important' or 'important' determining factor for them to choose raising capital through crowdfunding. From our qualitative research, it seems that 'unable to source funding locally' can either imply difficulties in fundraising in a particular locality (for example, raising venture capital in Newcastle) *or* through traditional financing channels (for example, a consumer product start-up raising angel investment in London). Around 55 per cent of the fundraisers in reward- and donation-based crowdfunding also cited this factor as either important or very important. However, it is interesting to note that only 6 per cent of the borrowers in peer-to-peer consumer lending feel 'unable to source funding locally' is a key motivational factor. This correlates with and further validates our previous observation, that borrowers in peer-to-peer consumer lending are mostly well-off individuals with excellent credit ratings and have no great difficulties in accessing bank credit. Speed of funding is another important motivation for fundraisers in various crowdfunding models (Figure 25.13). Clearly, for most of the models, the 'speed of raising finance' was an important factor offered by crowdfunding when compared to traditional channels of finance. Around 85–90 per cent of fundraisers in most of the crowdfunding models consider it either 'very important' or 'important' as a motivational factor. It is worth noting that this factor was less an issue for fundraisers in reward-based crowdfunding (only 18 per cent of them rating it as a 'very important' factor).

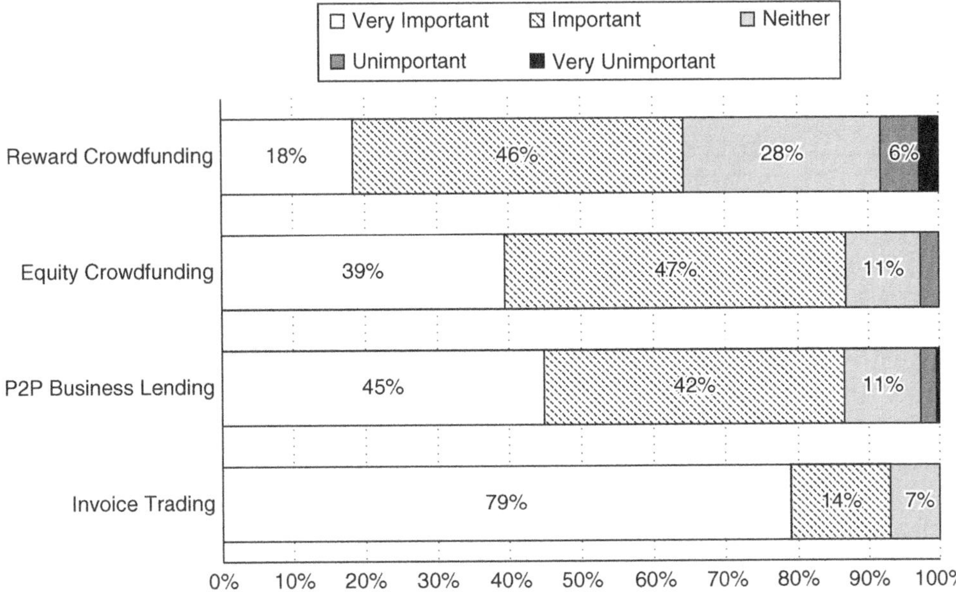

Figure 25.13 Fundraisers' motivation – 'speed of raising finance'

Finally, as mentioned earlier, the 2008 banking crisis, the mis-selling of financial products, and corrupt practices in some high-profile banking houses have also clearly affected the motivations of some users of the peer-to-peer lending models. Although our survey did not include a question on borrowers' and lenders' attitudes towards the mainstream finance industry, a significant proportion of respondents in the peer-to-peer crowdfunding models wrote comments on the survey which indicated a pronounced anti-bank sentiment. The comments suggested respondents consciously used peer-to-peer models as an alternative form of finance in order to sidestep the traditional banking system.

This analysis of the varied motivations of crowdfunding users highlights the importance of developing a nuanced understanding of different models. Financial motivation is clearly pronounced in the equity-based and business-lending models, while promoting social and environmental good motivates users in many other models. Avoiding mainstream financial institutions seems to motivate others – particularly in the peer-to-peer lending models.

25.10 TOWARDS A WORKING TAXONOMY FOR CROWDFUNDING

Our data and analysis have shown that it is imperative to distinguish various crowdfunding models and to examine them systematically and critically in academic studies. Crowdfunding is not homogeneous, but rather a spectrum consisting of highly differentiated models exhibiting an array of social, economic and geographical characteristics. Some of the models are akin to charitable giving, others function like venture capital;

Table 25.2 Crowdfunding models

Crowdfunding Model	Definition	Terms to describe those who provide funding and receive funding
Peer-to-Peer Business Lending	Secured and unsecured debt-based transactions between individuals/institutions and SMEs with trading history.	Lenders and Borrowers
Peer-to-Peer Consumer Lending	Mostly unsecured debt-based transactions between individuals/institutions to a consumer borrower.	Lenders and Borrowers
Invoice trading	Businesses sell their invoices or receivables to a pool of primarily high-net-worth individuals or institutional investors at discount.	Investors and Borrowers
Equity-based Crowdfunding	Sale of registered securities, by mostly start-ups or early-stage firms, to both retail, sophisticated and institutional investors (e.g. VCs).	Investors and Fundraisers
Community Shares	Withdrawable share capital unique to cooperative and community benefit society and organizations.	Investors and Fundraisers
Reward-based Crowdfunding	Backers have an expectation that fundraisers (or campaign owners) will provide non-financial reward(s) or product(s) in exchange for their contributions.	Backers and Campaign Owners
Donation-based Crowdfunding	Donations are made by donors usually for charities and good causes without an expectation for financial or non-financial rewards.	Donor and Fundraisers
Debt-based securities	Individuals purchase debentures or long-term bonds at a fixed interest rate. Lenders receive full repayment plus interest paid at maturity.	Lenders and Borrowers

the gender and income profiles of fundraisers in peer-to-peer consumer lending is very distinct to that of the reward-based crowdfunding; funders are motivated differently in community shares than in peer-to-peer business lending. We should be wary of any academic claim that conflates these distinct models or discusses them all in the same breath.

Thus, it is useful to develop a clearly defined taxonomy of prevalent crowdfunding models to aid further academic studies. Our working taxonomy (Table 25.2) has been gradually developed and refined in the last three years from both academic and industry research (for example, Zhang et al., 2013). It encompasses the eight crowdfunding models we have explored in this chapter, which are defined in a simple language and with suggestions for appropriate terms to describe 'funders' and 'fundraisers' in each model. This taxonomy is meant to be a work in progress and, of course, will evolve with the development of the industry and the progress of the academic studies associated with it. It is by no means an end product, but a method by which to begin our understanding of a growing phenomenon and to crystallize our conceptualization of this fluid landscape.

We also argue that the language used in this taxonomy to describe the different crowdfunding actors, for example, lender or donor, fundraiser or borrower, is important as it functions to remind analysts and academics of the distinctions, the antecedents, and the processes involved in each distinct model.

25.11 CONCLUSION

This chapter has sought to demystify, delineate and deconstruct crowdfunding, whilst demonstrating its diversity in a geographical context. We situate crowdfunding within the literature of financial and economic geography and set out to examine an array of highly distinctive crowdfunding models from peer-to-peer consumer lending, equity-based crowdfunding to community shares. We argue that, to truly understand crowdfunding and effectively research this fast-evolving phenomenon, it is important to appreciate that various crowdfunding models have different market functions, volume sizes, funding mechanisms, user dynamics and socio-economic impacts.

Specifically, we examined crowdfunding models' diversities and variations in a spatial and regional geography that they manifested, in gender and income profiles, as well as in funder and fundraiser's motivations. We found that, whilst peer-to-peer consumer and business lending models tend to facilitate a more decentralized spatial geography by channelling more funding outflow from London and the South East to the rest of the UK, equity- and reward-based crowdfunding actually reinforces if not exacerbate the centralized geography of funding, as evidenced in traditional finance by attracting funding inflows to London from other regions. The gendered patterns of several models of crowdfunding, in particular peer-to-peer business lending and equity-based crowdfunding, suggest an increasing level of access to new finance for female entrepreneurs. However, the income distribution of fundraisers for the same two prevailing crowdfunding models indicate that the crowdfunding marketplace is predominately serving a section of the population that is already well-off and has access to credit from traditional finance channels. The motivations for funders and fundraisers are also highly varied in crowdfunding, with more investment-orientated crowdfunding models attracting funders driven by financial motives, whilst more socially orientated models such as community shares, debt-based securities and donation-based crowdfunding having more funders motivated by doing social and environmental good.

Each model has the potential to either challenge or reinforce the status-quo, contributing to the formation of an alternative circuit of finance or merely entrenching the old channels and flows. The extent of 'democratization' of finance represented by crowdfunding is certainly stronger in some models than others. These channels and flows can be further teased out through analyzing the geography, accessibility, and institutional structure of crowdfunding, while one pronounced feature of many of the different models is the large and growing presence of the mainstream financial players. These may be different financial circuits, but clearly they are not always alternative.

ACKNOWLEDGEMENTS

The authors would like to thank Mingfeng Lin, Peter Baeck and Liam Collins for their generous help and input in making this chapter possible.

BIBLIOGRAPHY

Aalbers, M.B. (2015), 'The great moderation, the great excess and the global housing crisis', *International Journal of Housing Policy*, **15** (1), 43–60.

Agrawal, A., C. Catalini and A. Goldfarb (2011), 'The geography of crowdfunding', NBER Working Paper (w16820).

Bank of England (2015), 'Credit conditions review', 14, accessed 15 May, 2016 at www.bankofengland.co.uk/publications/Documents/creditconditionsreview/2016/ccrq415.pdf.

Beauhurst, (2015), 'Total seed stage and venture stage equity investment statistics, the deal 2014–2015', London: Beauhurst.

Beauregard, R.A. (1994), 'Capital switching and the built environment: United States, 1970–89', *Environment and Planning A*, **26** (5), 715–732.

Belleflamme, P., T. Lambert and A. Schwienbacher (2014), 'Crowdfunding: tapping the right crowd', *Journal of Business Venturing*, **29** (5), 585–609.

Blyth, M. (2013), *Austerity, History of a Dangerous Idea*, Oxford: Oxford University Press.

Bradford, C.S. (2012), 'Crowdfunding and the federal securities laws', *Columbia Business Law Review*, **1** (1), 1–150.

Brush, C., P. Greene, L. Balachandra and A. Davis (2014), 'Women entrepreneurs 2014: bridging the gender gap in venture capital', Arthur M. Blank Center for Entrepreneurship Babson College, Wellesley, Massachusetts.

Clark, G.L. (2005), 'Money flows like mercury: the geography of global finance', *Geografiska Annaler: Series B, Human Geography*, **87** (2), 99–112.

Colombo, M.G., C. Franzoni and C. Rossi-Lamastra (2015), 'Internal social capital and the attraction of early contributions in crowdfunding', *Entrepreneurship Theory and Practice*, **39** (1), 75–100.

Davies, R. (2014), 'Civic crowdfunding as a marketplace for participation in urban development', Working Paper, Center for Work, Technology and Organization, Stanford University, Stanford.

Dixon, A.D. and A.H. Monk (2012), 'Rethinking the sovereign in sovereign wealth funds', *Transactions of the Institute of British Geographers*, **37** (1), 104–117.

Donald, B., A. Glasmeier, M. Gray and L. Lobao (2014), 'Austerity in the city: economic crisis and urban service decline?', *Cambridge Journal of Regions, Economy and Society*, **7** (1), 3–15.

Erturk, I., J. Froud, J. Sukhdev, A. Leaver and K. Williams (2007), 'The democratization of finance? Promises, outcomes and conditions', *Review of International Political Economy*, **14**, 553–575.

Fuller, D. (1998), 'Credit union development: financial inclusion and exclusion', *Geoforum*, **29** (2), 145–157.

Fuller, D. and A. Jonas (2003), 'Alternative financial spaces', in A. Leyshon, R. Lee and C. Williams (eds), *Alternative Economic Spaces*, London: Sage, pp. 55–73.

Garretsen, H., M. Kitson and R.L. Martin (2009), 'Spatial circuits of global finance', *Cambridge Journal of Regions, Economy and Society*, **2** (2), 143–148.

Gatewood, E., C. Brush, N. Carter, P. Greene and M. Hart (2004), 'Women entrepreneurs, growth, and implications for the classroom', Coleman Foundation White Paper series, United States Association for Small Business and Entrepreneurship.

Giddens, A. (2013), *The Consequences of Modernity*, Cambridge: Polity Press.

Gotham, K.F. (2009), 'Creating liquidity out of spatial fixity: the secondary circuit of capital and the subprime mortgage crisis', *International Journal of Urban and Regional Research*, **33** (2), 355–371.

Griffin, Z.J. (2012), 'Crowdfunding: fleecing the American masses', *Journal of Law, Technology and the Internet*, **4**, 375–410.

Harvey, David (1982), *The Limits to Capital*, Oxford: Blackwell.

Harvey, David (1989), *Condition of PostModernity*, Oxford: Blackwell.

Harvey, David (2010), *The Enigma of Capital*, London: Profile Books.

Kim, K. and I.H. Hann (2013), 'Does crowdfunding democratize access to capital? A geographical analysis', in *INFORMS Conference on Information Systems and Technology (CIST)*.

Kitson, M., R.L. Martin and P. Tyler (2011), 'The geographies of austerity', *Cambridge Journal of Regions, Economy and Society*, **4** (3), 289–302.

Klagge, B. and R.L. Martin (2005), 'Decentralized versus centralized financial systems: is there a case for local capital markets?', *Journal of Economic Geography*, **5** (4), 387–421.

Leyshon, Andrew and Nigel Thrift (1997), *Money Space. Geographies of Monetary Transformation*, London: Routledge.

Lin, M. and S. Viswanathan (2014), 'Home bias in online investments: an empirical study of an online crowdfunding market', *Management Science*, **62** (5), 1393–1414.

Marlow, S. and D. Patton (2005), 'All credit to men? Entrepreneurship, finance, and gender', *Entrepreneurship Theory and Practice*, **29** (6), 717–735.

Martin, R.L. (1999), *Money and the Space Economy*, London: John Wiley & Sons.
Martin, R.L. and D. Turner (2000), 'Demutualization and the remapping of financial landscapes', *Transactions of the Institute of British Geographers*, **25** (2), 221–241.
Martin, R.L., P. Sunley, B. Klaage and C. Berndt (2003), *Regional Venture Capital Policy in Germany and the UK*, London: Anglo-German Foundation.
Mason, C. and R.T. Harrison (2002), 'The geography of venture capital investments in the UK', *Transactions of the Institute of British Geographers*, **27**, 427–451.
Mollick, E. (2014), 'The dynamics of crowdfunding: an exploratory study', *Journal of Business Venturing*, **29** (1), 1–16.
Morduch, J. (1999), 'The microfinance promise', *Journal of Economic Literature*, **37** (4), 1569–1614.
NCVO (2014), *UK Civil Society Almanac 2014 – the Voluntary Sector and People*, London: NCVO & the Third Sector Research Centre (TSRC).
NewTithing Group (2004), *The Generosity of Rich and Poor – How the Newly Discovered 'Middle Rich' Stack Up*, Toledo: The Toledo Community Foundation.
Nostrum Group (2015), 'Unsecured lending market – April 2015', accessed 25 April 2016 from www.nostrumgroup.com/insights/lending/unsecured-lending-market-april-2015/.
O'Brien, Richard (1992), *Global Financial Integration: The End of Geography*, London: Royal Institute of International Affairs, Pinter Publishers.
Pollard, J.S and M. Samers (2013), 'Governing Islamic finance: territory, agency, and the making of cosmopolitan financial geographies', *Annals of the Association of American Geographers*, **103** (3), 710–726.
Robb, A.M. and S. Coleman (2009), *Sources of Financing for New Technology Firms: A Comparison by Gender*, Kansas City: The Kauffman Foundation.
Schwartz, A.A. (2013), 'Crowdfunding securities', *Notre Dame Law Review*, **88**, 1457.
Schwienbacher, A. and B. Larralde (2012), 'Crowdfunding of small entrepreneurial ventures', in D. Cummings (ed.), *The Oxford Handbook of Entrepreneurial Finance*, Oxford: Oxford University Press, Chapter 13, pp. 369–391.
Shiller, R.J. (2013), 'Capitalism and financial innovation', *Financial Analysts Journal*, **69** (1), 21–25.
Shiller, R.J. (2012), 'Democratize Wall Street, for social good', *New York Times*, 7 April.
UKCES (2015), UK Commission for Employment and Skills, UK Labour Market Projections: 2014–2024, accessed 4 May 2016 at www.gov.uk/government/organisations/uk-commission-for-employment-and-skills.
Wójcik, D. (2009), 'Financial centre bias in primary equity markets', *Cambridge Journal of Regions, Economy and Society*, **2** (2), 193–209.
Zhang, B., L. Collins and P. Baeck (2014), *Understanding Alternative Finance – the UK Alternative Finance Industry Report*, London: Nesta.
Zhang, B., L. Collins and R. Swart (2013), *The Rise of Future Finance – the UK Alternative Finance Benchmarking Report*, London: Nesta.
Zhang, B., R. Wardrop, R. Rau and M. Gray (2015), 'Moving mainstream: benchmarking the European alternative finance market', *The Journal of Financial Perspectives*, **3** (3), 60–77.

26. Bitcoin through the lenses of complexity theory

Marc Pilkington

There are three eras of currency: commodity-based, politically based, and now math based.
(Chris Dixon, Technology Investor, 2013)

26.1 INTRODUCTION

Since 2009, a virtual and stateless currency has emerged in the world economy in the form of an unprecedented transnational monetary phenomenon, which has aroused the interest of commentators, regulators and monetary theory specialists. Bitcoin is a crypto-currency created in 2009 by a mysterious pseudonymous developer named Satoshi Nakamoto. Its existence is dependent on the workings of a distributed IT system taking the form of a vast peer-to-peer network, connecting programmes (that is, Bitcoin clients) implementing the Bitcoin protocol on individual computers worldwide. Once the programme is running on the computer, Bitcoin-related information is saved on a file called the wallet, thereby enabling Bitcoin to perform the traditional functions of money.[1] Of course, whether Bitcoin, a non-fiat currency, is on par with standard fiat currencies, and performs the functions of money, should be the subject of passionate discussions amongst specialists, seeking answers to the fascinating and fundamental questions posed by Bitcoin. Yet, as pinpointed by the European Central Bank (ECB, 2012: 9), such a reflection 'has been absent, at least to some extent, from the existing literature'.

In this chapter, we wish to define the Bitcoin ecosystem as a community formed by heterogeneous and autonomous entities in complex interaction. Section 26.2 examines the context that presided over the emergence of Bitcoin in a pluridisciplinary fashion. In Section 26.3 we show that the preferred framework for analyzing this complex distributed system is not the mainstream paradigm that revolves around equilibrium, rationality and self-interest. Rather, the insights of complexity economics will help us define the salient features of a new approach in terms of dynamics, emergence, self-organization and non-predictability. Another objective of this chapter is to show that, in spite of its virtual nature, Bitcoin is not a placeless phenomenon devoid of spatial considerations. In Section 26.4 we therefore try to articulate our arguments with a reflection on the new geography of money and finance.

26.2 BITCOIN IN CONTEXT: A PLURIDISCIPLINARY APPROACH

As Rescher (1998: xiv–xv) notes, we all live in several different worlds. There is the real world of human experience that includes the 'social world – the realm of our interrelationships among fellow human beings – and also the inner world, the world of human thoughts, interacting with the natural one'. Likewise for Sornette (2003: xv), '"world" is taken with several meanings, as it can be the physical world, the natural world, the biological, and even the inner intellectual and psychological worlds'. Of course, Bitcoin, though virtual in essence, is a new feature of the technological, the socio-economic and the political arenas, with its manifold complex interactions. Hereafter, we consider the different contexts within which Bitcoin has emerged.

Technological Context

Bitcoin is a peer-to-peer, client-based, completely distributed currency that does not depend on any centralized issuing bodies to operate; the value is created by the users (it is therefore a pure market-driven currency), and the operation is distributed using an open source client installed on a computer running Windows, Mac or Linux. It is simply a non-fiat, non-centralized digital currency, which is not issued by any government (or central bank), and does not have any physical manifestation in the real world. Bitcoins are nothing less than digital files that sit in a distributed peer-to-peer database using electronic signatures. At the heart of the Bitcoin protocol, primarily, there is the Blockchain (Blundell-Wignall, 2014: 8):

> Transactions are recorded in the 'Blockchain' which is the key innovation in this technology – that is, a technology that removes the need for a trusted third party and the intermediary costs associated with such institutions (banks, credit card companies, payment companies, non-bank financial intermediaries). The Blockchain is a public database (giant ledger book), openly maintained by computers all over the world – it is a sequential record of all transactions and current ownership.

The coding of Bitcoin is a secret kept by pseudonymous developer 'Satoshi Nakamoto'. The whole set of instructions needed to generate Bitcoin, and enable its transfer from one account to the other, is characterized by a high degree of complexity. The amount of time needed to produce a single unit of Bitcoin draws on the functioning of the open-source cryptographic protocol.

Socio-economic Context

Bitcoin is a technological, sociological and anthropological phenomenon. How many people use Bitcoin worldwide? The answer to this question is unclear; several million probably. Yet, the number of users must be distinguished with potential ones, the latter figure being equated to the world population of Internet users. The widespread use of the Internet has had dramatic societal consequences: '[t]he impact has been so significant that it could reasonably be considered a structural change in social behavior, affecting the way people live, interact with each other, gather information and, of course, the way they pay' (ECB, 2012: 11). There are more unbanked people than people with no Internet access in the world: '[f]ully 2.5 billion of the world's adults don't use formal banks or semiformal microfinance institutions to save or borrow money, our research finds. Nearly 2.2 billion of these unserved live in Africa, Asia, Latin America, and the Middle East' (Chaia et al., 2010).

Granularity is the extent to which a system can be broken down into small parts. Yet, in spite of undeniable weaknesses and persisting uncertainty surrounding its acceptance and further use in international economic transactions, Bitcoin is now a potential challenger on the international currency market, and is acquiring an unexpected global dimension: it is now traded for the principal currencies within the international monetary system. Ron and Shamir (2012) explain that 'the network is programmed to increase the money supply in a slowly increasing geometric series until the total number of Bitcoins reaches an upper limit of about 21 million BTC's'. By mid-2013, there were between 11 and 12 million units in circulation (Rickards, 2014: 254), while the total value in circulation had risen to $1.25 billion. Market capitalization grew continuously throughout 2013, experiencing a huge increase between November and December, when it reached a stunning $14 billion. Bitcoin price reached a high of $1,040 in January 2014, but the rest of the year was disappointing with a decline to circa $350 in December. Cryptologist Courtois (2014) dates back the birth of Bitcoin as a mainstream financial instrument to April 2013 when *The Economist* (2013) magazine named the crypto-currency 'digital gold'. Courtois (2014) argues that the Bitcoin ecosystem acquired a professionalized dimension after April 2013, with an explosion of Bitcoin infrastructure, industrial mining and Bitcoin-backed start-up companies. By September 2014, cumulative trading (measured in Bitcoins) was closing on 100,000,000 BTC (CoinDesk, 2014).

Just a few years after its creation, is this evolution a surprise? Through pre-crisis lenses of economic theory, it arguably is. However, the insights of complexity theory shed light on this phenomenon: 'complexity has the tendency to make for a destabilization that tends toward potentially surprising results' (Rescher, 1998: 13). Concerns spurred by Bitcoin are a surprise, but surprises, namely unpredicted outcomes, do occur in a complex world. Economists have tried since 2008 to come to terms with a post-crisis world: '[w]e've entered a brave new world in the wake of the crisis; a very different world in terms of policy making and we just have to accept it' (Blanchard, 2011). Once the circulatory nature of Bitcoin has been ascertained, it is given an extrinsic market value on the foreign exchange market through the workings of virtual exchange schemes. Bitcoin then becomes a tradable currency within the prevailing system of floating exchange rates.

Political Context

As Mill argued (1894: 176), in order to affirm their sovereignty, national governments have an incentive to create a unit of account by force of law, and enable its effective circulation for economic purposes. The path towards a transnational unit of account indeed resembles an unavoidable Tower of Babel. It is true that international politics has historically stood in the way of a global currency. Hegemonic powers, such as Britain in the nineteenth century, and the USA in the twentieth century, played a decisive role in this regard (Mundell, 2003: 4). Yet, after 2008, the world witnessed massive bailout plans and the implementation of QE policies translated into the injection of huge amounts of liquidities into the banking system, resulting in a sheer resizing of central bank balance sheets. These spectacular policy moves raised fears about the possibility of long-term inflation, and therefore the legitimacy of centralized payment systems functioning under the aegis of central bank authority to maintain a stable standard of value throughout the crisis. It is at this juncture in history that Bitcoin was born as an open source cryptographic protocol not managed by any central authority. Prior to the global crisis, the idea of a global currency emerging from a complex set of micro interactions through peer-to-peer networking on the Internet, would have been rejected out of hand by monetary economics experts. In August 2013, however, the definition of Bitcoin as a private unit of account was acknowledged by Germany (Ferrara, 2013), thereby making transactions in the virtual currency subject to sales tax, and profits on transactions to income tax.

In the tradition of Austrian economics (Hayek, 1976; Matonis, 2012; Murphy and Barta, 2013), Bitcoin espouses the idea that the governmental monopoly in the supply of money should be abolished, and the provision of money left to unfettered markets, with private entities being free to issue units of account, whose acceptance will be established on competition grounds. So far, Bitcoin has not required regulatory legitimacy and/or coercion by law to gain acceptance (ECB, 2012). Banking regulation is seemingly irrelevant to Bitcoin, because of the inherent design properties of its peer-to-peer distributed computing system. Quoted by Forbes, self-proclaimed expert Michael Parsons (Libros. tel, 2016) states that:

> Bitcoin is 'regulated' by its peers and mathematics. And Bitcoin is not a currency like fiat money. It is a value transfer system which is given value only by its users. So the ECB, FED, etc. have no mandate to control a 'virtual currency' just because they call it (bitcoin) that! It will just go underground. Bitcoin is like Light and Air. Free to use and transfer. Owned and issued by the people and NOT the State!

Yet, this sense of impunity is not shared by all the actors on the regulatory scene: 'Fraudsters are not beyond the reach of the SEC just because they use Bitcoin or another virtual currency to mislead investors and violate the federal securities law' (Andrew Calamari cited in US Securities Exchange Commission, 2013). The Office of Investor Education and Advocacy of the SEC seems to be taking the matter very seriously as it issued an investor alert pointing to the risk of Ponzi schemes and even 'fraudulent schemes that may involve Bitcoin and other virtual currencies' (US Securities Exchange Commission, 2016).

The FinCEN (US Treasury, 2007)[2] has recently redefined currency in an interpretative Guidance (FinCEN, 2013):

> FinCEN's regulations define currency (also referred to as 'real' currency) as 'the coin and paper money of the United States or of any other country that [i] is designated as legal tender and that [ii] circulates and [iii] is customarily used and accepted as a medium of exchange in the country of issuance'. In contrast to real currency, 'virtual' currency is a medium of exchange that operates like a currency in some environments, but does not have all the attributes of real currency. In particular, virtual currency does not have legal tender status in any jurisdiction.

Following this clarification, at least three virtual currency exchanges (that is, BTC Buy, Bitfloor and Bitme) have been shut down. In Poland, Bitcoin-24 experienced the same fate after the government froze its bank account, after a German bank had signaled several compromised accounts transferring stolen money without identification to Bitcoin-24 (Röhl Dehm and Partner, 2013).

The ECB (2012: 27) has pointed to regulatory agitation:

> In June 2011 two US senators, Charles Schumer and Joe Manchin, wrote to the Attorney General and to the Administrator of the Drug Enforcement Administration expressing their

worries about Bitcoin and its use for illegal purposes. Mr Andresen was also asked to give a presentation to the CIA about this virtual currency scheme. Further action from other authorities can reasonably be expected in the near future.

The legal framework is a complex one (Cohn, 2011). As far as the safeguarding of digital rights are concerned, non-profit digital rights group *Electronic Frontier Foundation* states that it does not 'fully understand the complex legal issues involved with creating a new currency system. Bitcoin raises untested legal concerns related to securities law, the Stamp Payments Act, tax evasion, consumer protection and money laundering, among others'. Bitcoin raises a number of issues that pertain to data protection, privacy, consumer protection, e-commerce law, international contract law. The European Parliament Directive 2009/110/EC of the European Parliament and the Council of 16 September 2009 aims to enable new, innovative and secure electronic money services, provide market access to new companies, foster real and effective competition between all market participants. The EU favours 'the emergence of a true single market for e-money services and the development of such user-friendly services'. For the European Commission's Information Society and Media Directorate-General (European Commission, 2009: 4), '[t]he legal treatment of electronic money services – particularly platform payment and mobile payment systems – is still not entirely clear, although precisely these types of services seem to be the future of online payments'. Currently, Bitcoin is exempted from the scope of the e-money directive. If this situation were to evolve under the impact of widespread acceptance, the exemption would no longer be warranted. Yet, legal sustainability in the EU is dependent on its exemption from the e-money directive. Without it, issuers must obtain a license, comply with prudential rules, hold capital requirements, and be able to redeem Bitcoins in fiat currency at any time upon request of depositors. Finally, a law on e-money was passed in France in May 2013, fixing the minimal capital requirement of issuers of e-money at 350,000 euros (Gouvernement Français, 2013).

26.3 BITCOIN AND COMPLEXITY THEORY: SOME IMPORTANT ISSUES

At the heart of the new complexity paradigm, we find the following question: 'How do the behaviours, relationships, institutions, and ideas that underpin an economy form, and how do they evolve over time (Beinhocker, 2007: 80)?' The issues of the emergence and the evolution of (actual) complex systems are therefore paramount in our endeavour to shed new light on Bitcoin through complexity theory.

Defining Complexity Theory

First and foremost, complexity theory entails a plurality of underlying conceptions of complexity. As a complex system, Bitcoin lends itself to complex theory investigation. Yet, complexity itself is a complex matter, and without a single definition,[3] there are several modes that shed light on our present object of study. Beinhocker (2007: 17–18) argues that the dominant paradigm in economics for more than a century has been structured around the idea of equilibrium, one that portrays 'the economy as a system that moves from equilibrium point to equilibrium point over time, propelled along by shocks from technology, politics, changes in consumer tastes, and other external factors' (Beinhocker, 2007: 17–18). Since the 1970s, social scientists have pursued an alternative research programme that views the economy as evolutionary, adaptive and dynamic in essence. So-called complex systems are made of 'many dynamically interacting parts' wherein 'the micro-level interactions of the parts or particles lead to the emergence of macro-level patterns of behavior' (Beinhocker, 2007: 18). This research programme that Martin and Sunley (2010: 94) date back to at least the mid-twentieth century was given a new impetus under the impulse of physicists and mathematicians (Nicolis and Prigogine, 1989; Prigogine and Nicolis, 1977). These authors set out to go beyond the second law of thermodynamics that dominated the study of elementary particles in physics and chemistry throughout the major part of the twentieth century. In his 1977 Nobel lecture, Prigogine explains that most types of organizations, such as cities or living organisms, do not obey the principle of thermodynamic equilibrium. This is so, because irreversible processes are conducive to dynamic states known as dissipative structures. The resulting order of a new type is the outcome of non-equilibrium (Prigogine, 1977, 1989).

Complexity theorists have built on these profound insights, so as to focus on self-organizing, complex adaptive and evolutionary systems in social science (Pavard and Dugdale, 2000). In spite of this major breakthrough (both conceptual and epistemological), no consensus on a universal theory of complexity has emerged to date (Lewin, 1992), due to the nature of the approach under scrutiny: 'complexity is one of those ideas whose definition is an integral part of the problems that it raises' (Nicolis and Prigogine, 1989: 36).

Bitcoin through the Lenses of Complexity Theory

Table 26.1 presents a summary of the salient features of mainstream, as opposed to complexity economics. In the last column, some of the implications for conceptualizing the new Bitcoin ecosystem are singled out.

The single most important lesson of the Bitcoin experiment is that non-intuitive macro-results may be derived from a set of microeconomic interactions involving complex technology. This amounts to the old Aristotelian idea that, in any system, 'the whole is more than the sum of its parts' (Aristotle, Metaphysica 10f-1045a in Aristotle, 1924 [1953]). Complex systems can be the object of simulations (Gilbert and Troitzsch, 2005) wherein complexity is captured by agent-based models: 'The modeler . . . only observes the generated macro dynamics of the simulation, while he designs the model solely on the basis of individual behaviors and interactions. Basically, this approach is related to the theory of "complex systems"' (Oeffner, 2008: 2). The emergence of macro-properties out of numerous micro-interactions should occupy a central role in the new orientation of macroeconomic theory. Oeffner (2008: 5) regrets that, while other disciplines have engaged in the study of the complex interaction of heterogeneous and autonomous entities, dynamic monetary macroeconomics has not embraced the complexity paradigm to date. This is most unfortunate, as our economies are precisely complex, adaptive and dynamic systems (Oeffner, 2008: 5). However, promising economists, such as Seppecher (2011, 2012) with his agent-based model JAMEL, have begun to fill this void. For Seppecher (2012: 1, our translation), 'the macroeconomic properties of [his] model are not assumed, they

Table 26.1 Features of mainstream and complexity economics and some implications for Bitcoin

	Mainstream economics	Complexity economics	Bitcoin (BTC) translation
Dynamics	Static linear systems, equilibrium paradigm	Open systems, non-linearities, non-equilibrium paradigm, path-dependence	Market BTC dynamics cannot be modeled in a static framework; equilibrium models are irrelevant and even misleading
Agents (methodology)	Representative agent, Substantive rationality, Homo oeconomicus, predetermined preferences, omniscience of agents	Use of agent-based computer simulations, rules of thumb, learning from interactions, decision under uncertainty. 'The mainstream models smart people in unbelievably simple situations while complexity theory involves simple people coping with incredibly complex situations' (Leijonhufvud quoted by Beinhocker, 2007:52)	Mining and investment decisions are subject to uncertain outcomes. The system is mainly based on trust. Miners and market participants form an experimental protocol. Learning processes characterize the agents. Black swan events are possible (e.g. the MtGox breakdown in February 2014)
Networks	The market (i.e. the price system) is the only interface between agents	Complex interactions prevail. Size and scope of networks will change over time	The BTC community exchanges knowledge and non-price information. Cooperative behaviour is an important feature of the system
Emergence	Although macro-analysis may be micro-founded, regularities do not stem from micro-interactions; the two remain separated	Macro-patterns are emergent, and result directly from complex micro-interactions	BTC prices and transaction volumes cannot be understood without the integration of micro and macroanalysis. BTC market participants engage in feed-back loops (i.e. individual / systemic behaviour display positive and negative feed-back effects)
Evolution	Endogenous growth is illdefined. Complexity is alien to the system that is constantly bombarded by	The system is fundamentally evolutionary, due to its intrinsic complexity. In-built/endogenous mechanisms are	Since its inception, Bitcoin has grown into an ecosystem (miners, market participants, IT entrepreneurs, regulators etc.), whose behavioural

Table 26.1 (continued)

	Mainstream economics	Complexity economics	Bitcoin (BTC) translation
	exogenous shocks that determine its evolution	paramount in the workings of the system	characteristics are reminiscent of living organisms
Predictability	Closed system: stochastic calculus leads to reliable predictions An objective distribution of probabilities can be determined	No omniscient planner exists. The future is uncertain. Emergent properties are *not* captured by stochastic calculus. Probabilities are subjective	No Bitcoin mastermind /omniscient planner. The BTC ecosystem is evolutionary and non-deterministic
Relation to the environment	Boundaries between agents and the environment are fixed and well-identified	Boundaries between agents and the environment are not fixed and hard to identify	Soros' reflexivity concept is relevant for all BTC decisions. The interface between the BTC ecosystem and its environment is difficult to pin down
Role of space	Space is oft-neglected. The efficient market hypothesis is tantamount to the end of geography (Dymski, 2009: 268–269)	Economic geography and complexity theory are likely to join forces. Spatially oriented relations and self-organized structures emerge out of micro-scale behaviours	Virtualization prevails, but geography and space remain relevant. Emergence of spatial structures in the BTC ecosystem. Spatial structures tend to self-organize

are emerging properties of the complex system formed by the interaction of agents'. Likewise, the functioning of an open source cryptographic protocol arguably amounts to a complex agent-based system (agents being Bitcoin miners and users). It follows that unexpected properties of the system may arise as a result of the complex interaction of its users. Another important application is the enhanced understanding of systematic risk in finance. This research programme was undertaken by physicist and complexity scientist Didier Sornette in his book *Why Stock Markets Crash – Critical Events in Complex Financial Systems*: 'stock market crashes provide an excuse for exploring the wonderful world of self-organizing systems. Market crashes exemplify in a dramatic way the spontaneous emergence of extreme events in self-organizing systems' (Sornette, 2003: xv). Systematic risk, paramount in the chain of events that led to the global crisis, is a risk common to an entire class of assets or liabilities. It is located at the interface between the micro and macro spheres of the financial system (Aglietta and Moutot, 1993). The value of investments declines over a given time period, because of economic changes or other events that impact large portions of the market. In many ways, systematic risk reflects the increase in aggregate complexity of a given system.

Dimensions of Complexity

What are the different modes of complexity that pertain to Bitcoin? Let us begin with a wide-ranging epistemic mode that may be descriptive, generative or computational (Rescher, 1998). Descriptive complexity pertains, in the case at hand, to the required length for a faithful account of all relevant Bitcoin-related phenomena, so as to provide an adequate description of the overall system under scrutiny. Generative complexity refers to the coding of Bitcoin. This is still a secret kept by pseudonymous Japanese developer 'Satoshi Nakamoto'. Here, we surmise that the whole set of instructions needed to generate Bitcoin and enable its transfer from one account to the other, is characterized by a high degree of generative complexity.

Third, computational complexity refers to the amount of time needed to produce a single unit of Bitcoin. Akin to the generative mode, it draws on the functioning of the open-source cryptographic protocol at the heart of Bitcoin.

In terms of its compositional complexity, the Bitcoin protocol requires five building blocks: hashes, merkle trees, digital signatures, transaction verification and signatures. A sixth constituent consists of a combination of the five building blocks, and is referred to as the Blockchain (Blundell-Wignall, 2014: 8).

The structural complexity of Bitcoin can be broken down into organizational and hierarchical complexity. The organizational complexity of Bitcoin refers to the numbers of ways of arranging components in different modes of interrelationships. Here the possibilities are infinite. Any economic agent can download the Bitcoin client from the website http://bitcoin.org/, install the client server on his or her PC, and immediately engage in transactions denominated in Bitcoins. The number of possible transactions (that is, transactional arrangements between economic agents) is infinite. Hierarchical complexity is more subtle. Bitcoin functions without a central bank, and is not controlled by anybody. This does not mean that the system is a-hierarchical. We identify hereafter three subsystems in order of importance.

1. *The Bitcoin generating system*, namely the mining process: this fundamental money-creation process conditions all others.
2. *The Bitcoin payment system*: this essential feature of any currency system amounts to the *effective and secure transfer between accounts*.
3. *The currency exchange system*: once the circulatory nature of Bitcoin has been ascertained, it is given an extrinsic market value on the foreign exchange market through the workings of virtual exchanges schemes such as Currency Connect. Bitcoin then becomes a tradable currency within the prevailing system of floating exchange rates.

In terms of the functional complexity of Bitcoin, this mode can be broken down into nomic and operational complexity. Nomic complexity refers to the elaborateness at the stage of the original design, such as the complex laws governing the production of Bitcoins (that is, its mining process) through a secret algorithm. As the Bitcoin community grows, so does operational complexity. Operational complexity is linked to compositional complexity, as the two modes grow in concert. Let us note that the current level of operational complexity of the booming Bitcoin economy is indeterminate, because the mass of real-world economic operations generated by Bitcoin is independent of its initial design.

As argued by Rescher (1998: 173), operational complexity is increased by technological progress, which lies in 'the realm of human artifice'. Although, Bitcoin functions without any central authority, it has grown into an artifact currently threatening the management of standard payments systems. Hence, the whole payments system's complexity management 'becomes shifted from operating the system itself to managing the functioning of its cybernetic governance' (Rescher, 1998: 175). Further, operational complexity is exemplified by growing concerns over the security of the system. An ever larger number of Bitcoin holders engaging in increasingly significant transactions require a more secure functioning of the payment systems, so as to prevent attempts by hackers. In this regard, Bitcoin Savings and Trust (BTCST) was a virtual Bitcoin-based hedge fund that offered and sold Bitcoin-denominated investments through the Internet that promised a 7 per cent return per week. BTCST shut down in August 2012, and the Securities and Exchange Commission (SEC) formally charged its founder with running a Ponzi scheme. This scam was enabled through enhanced operational complexity, along with rising compositional complexity giving rising to regulatory loopholes identified by fraudulent investors. In order to apprehend operational complexity of Bitcoin, we investigate the interrelationships between the real and the (virtual) Bitcoin economy:

> One possible way to overcome this situation and obtain some quantitative information on the magnitude of the funds moved through these virtual currency schemes could be to focus on the link between the virtual economy and the real economy, i.e. the transfer of money from the banking environment to the virtual environment. Virtual accounts need to be funded either via credit transfer, payment card or PayPal and therefore a possibility would be to request this information from credit institutions, card schemes and PayPal. (ECB, 2012)

Bitcoin's aggregate complexity is best explained through '[a] key set of interrelated concepts that define a complex system: relationships between entities; internal structure and surrounding environment; learning and emergent behavior; and the different means by which complex systems change and grow' (Manson, 2001: 409). Manson gives the example of an economy, whose components merely exchange information, matter and energy. Interestingly enough, the Bitcoin system entails highly complex exchanges of information through 'an electronic payment system based on cryptographic proof' (Nakamoto, 2009: 1). Yet what is money? It is merely '[t]he monetary form where matter and energy are moulded into according to the project devised by human beings and implemented within the productive sphere' (Rossi, 1998: 9). Therefore, Manson's definition involves the exchange of information, energy and matter within the confines of the Bitcoin economy. Acknowledging aggregate complexity foretells future modeling endeavours. The number of potential arrangements explains why interrelationships that define the Bitcoin system 'extend beyond simple feedback into higher order, non-linear processes not amenable to modeling with traditional techniques' (Manson, 2001: 409).

Finally, discursive complexity is an oft-overlooked aspect of complexity science. The power of thinking about reality is shaped by the terms we employ for describing it, as shown by the sometimes misleading notion of the local as a container in geography (Byrne and Callaghan, 2013: 137). Discursive inertia confined to a non-complex world impedes scientific understanding. This also applies to the geography of money: 'in many respects the vocabulary has remained trapped within a framework that attempts to identify new territorial settlements, even if the size and nature of territories has changed' (Allen and Cochrane, 2007: 1162).

26.4 HOW IS BITCOIN BREAKING AWAY FROM THE MAINSTREAM PARADIGM?

Chen (2010: xxiii) explains how the global crisis has brought about a paradigm shift in economic theory:

> But the physics concepts of nonequilibrium, complexity, and chaos imply not only the destruction of an old order, but also the emergence of a new structure. From this perspective, the current Grand Crisis may bring about a new world of economic order and a new era of economic thinking. 'The whole intellectual edifice collapsed in the summer of last year,' the perplexed former Federal Reserve Chairman Alan Greenspan confessed in congressional testimony on October 23, 2008. Changing historical currents demand changes in economic paradigm.

Why have mainstream approaches to economic theorizing utterly failed? For Chen (2010), two failed mainstream theories account for this failure, namely the efficient market hypothesis in finance and the microfoundations theory in macroeconomics. In a famous 'Letter to the Queen: Why No One Predicted the Crisis', Hodgson et al. (2009) remind us that 'some leading economists – including Nobel Laureates Ronald Coase, Milton Friedman and Wassily Leontief – have complained that in recent years economics has turned virtually into a branch of applied mathematics, and has been become detached from real-world institutions and events'. Hodgson et al. (2009) point to 'the highly questionable belief in universal "rationality" and the "efficient markets hypothesis" (hereafter EMH) both widely promoted by mainstream economists'. Interestingly, the EMH has been equated by Dymski (2009: 268–269) to the phantasmagoric claim of the end of geography put forward by O'Brien (1992). Yet, from a methodological standpoint, the critique of the mainstream should not come down to that of formal modeling. For Hodgson et al. (2009), the complexity of the global economy requires 'a broader range of models and techniques governed by a far greater respect for substance, and much more attention to historical, institutional, psychological and other highly relevant factors'. Among these other factors, the present chapter argues that geographic and spatial considerations are paramount in the definition of a new paradigm.

At first glance, currencies traded on international currency markets are fiat currencies, to wit, units of account that Governments have declared to be legal, although they have no intrinsic value, and are not backed by reserves. Although the value of any fiat currency is based on faith (Aglietta and Orléan, 1982) rather than physical commodities, it is puzzling to think of an accepted unit of account, which would not be backed by any central authority. Before it becomes a pure market-based currency, what would its initial value be derived from? Unless Bitcoin was originally a virtual commodity before becoming a virtual currency, the entry point of Bitcoin market value is indeterminate,[4] at least, it cannot be fully grasped rationally. When and why did rational agents start to exchange Bitcoins for *something*, thereby providing it with a monetary value? Of course, Bitcoins had to be accepted by someone, but who and what conferred the original acceptability of the crypto-currency other than the market itself? As Victoria Chick (2011, italics added) argues, 'to the depositor [a bank deposit] is . . . a transferable asset with wide acceptability. *It is this acceptability that makes it money*'. Bitcoin is an intangible asset that performs the traditional functions of money outside the banking system. Whereas transferability is ensured by Internet-based technology, its acceptability can only be explained by pure market behaviour. Hence, Bitcoin is defining anew the source of monetary value by circumventing the traditional anchor to commodities and fiat power to which it poses a political challenge of a new kind (Rickards, 2014: 254). For Colander et al. (2004: 490), rationality and equilibrium are intertwined concepts in neoclassical economics: 'Neoclassical economics is an analysis that focuses on the optimizing behavior of fully rational and well-informed individuals in a static context and the equilibria that result from that optimization'.

Chen (2010) elaborates upon this idea by equating the core belief of neoclassical economics to efficient markets and rational expectations. The economy follows a long-term growth trajectory occasionally perturbed by exogenous random shocks. Yet these disturbances do not question the self-stabilizing forces of the market best captured by methodological individualism and the representative agent. Yet, the focus on short-term market fluctuations leads Chen (2010) to characterize this approach as econometrically flawed, thereby giving rise to an 'equilibrium illusion'. We try hereafter to shed light on this long drawn-out debate in the history of economic thought.

The Bitcoin price is a market-determined equilibrium price. At a given moment in time, the Bitcoin spot price is determined by the law of supply and demand, with buyers and sellers continuously placing orders featuring a price and a quantity. The Bitcoin price is thus a classic example of market-determined equilibrium price. For instance, the website http://bitcoin-analytics.com/ describes the near real-time development of the bid-ask spread along with the last clearing price. The charts help feel the overall direction of the market. A series of small trades often make a better average price than one larger trade, even with a higher commission. Market transparency is ensured, which is a sine qua none for the determination of a market-determined equilibrium price even in the absence of a regulatory body.

For Chen (2010: xxiv), the equilibrium school comes in sharp contrast with disequilibrium economics, whose:

> [c]entral theme is a fragile market, which frequently collapses under irrational panic or historical events. Known scholars in this camp include John Maynard Keynes, Hyman Minsky, Benoît Mandelbrot and behavioural economists. Their main effort is introducing social psychology into economic behaviour (Akerlof and Shiller, 2009). However, they have not yet developed a consistent theoretical framework. They experiment with various mathematical models, ranging from Levy distribution, fractal Brownian motion, unit roots, co-integration, sunspot, sand-pile, to power law in econophysics. Monetary and fiscal policies are the main tools for restoring market confidence from time to time. Their weakness is a lack of structural analysis and historical perspective.

Hereafter, we list a set of reasons why Bitcoin is inherently unstable, and might pertain to the disequilibrium school of economics:

I. Bitcoin is Deflationary

Until the end of 2013, the continuously rising price of Bitcoin was spurring long-term deflationary fears, because prices expressed in BTC would necessarily fall. The risk of a deflationary spiral has been pinpointed by the ECB (2012) and Grinberg (2011), as Bitcoin supply is exogenous (that is, the number of Bitcoins is capped at 21 million), with a periodically declining rate of supply growth until 2140. What would happen if, say, more than fifty million people started using Bitcoin on a regular basis? Because of the in-built declining supply growth, Bitcoin's spot market price would soar vertiginously, as a consequence of its rising purchasing power. If Bitcoin becomes widely adopted, and even displaces some of the market power of sovereign fiat currencies, the deflationary risk could propagate to fiat currencies, and ultimately pose a major issue to the global economy. Finally, deflation could hamper the function of Bitcoin as a medium of exchange: 'if the value of a currency is increasing – that is, there is deflation – currency owners have an incentive to hold it to realize the appreciation' (Evans, 2014: 7). Bitcoin as currency has indeed very little utility as a medium of trade if it is hoarded. Yet, deflationary risks posed by its finite supply may result in a liquidity trap (Keynes, 1936: 207).

II. Bitcoin is Ill-suited to Credit-based Monetary Economies of Production

As we were painfully reminded of in 2008, credit is the lubricant oil that keeps the wheels of modern economies turning smoothly. Yet, Bitcoin's exogenous supply poses deflationary risks that prevent lenders from taking up risks to finance real-world projects as loans become harder to pay back due to Bitcoin scarcity. Operators on currency markets may face risks that outweigh the benefits: margins insufficient to cover open positions will trigger margin calls. In a volatile environment, failure to meet the latter, by either deposit of additional funds or reduction of open positions, will inevitably disrupt activity.

III. Bitcoin is Volatile

The Bitcoin real exchange rate experiences 10 to 30 per cent single-day fluctuations. Bitcoin is capable of volatility in the form of 10x changes in price versus the US dollar, in a relatively short period of time (Barker, 2014). The website https://btcvol.info/ is powered by CoinDesk, the world leader in news on Bitcoin, and features the Bitcoin Volatility Index in real time (see Figure 26.1).

IV. Bitcoin Mining is Subject to Tail Risk

What are the tail risks of a massive cryptographic breakthrough (for example, a quantum computer mining Bitcoins, or a breach in a key cryptographic hash)? For Taleb (2007), a black swan event must (1) be a surprise to observers, (2) have major effects on the currency, (3) be rationalized *ex post*, had the relevant data been properly accounted for. Somehow, the collapse in February 2014 of Tokyo-based MtGox Exchange, which was handling 70 per cent of all Bitcoin trading by 2013, was arguably a black swan event that could have precipitated the crypto-currency into the abyss (Vigna, 2014).

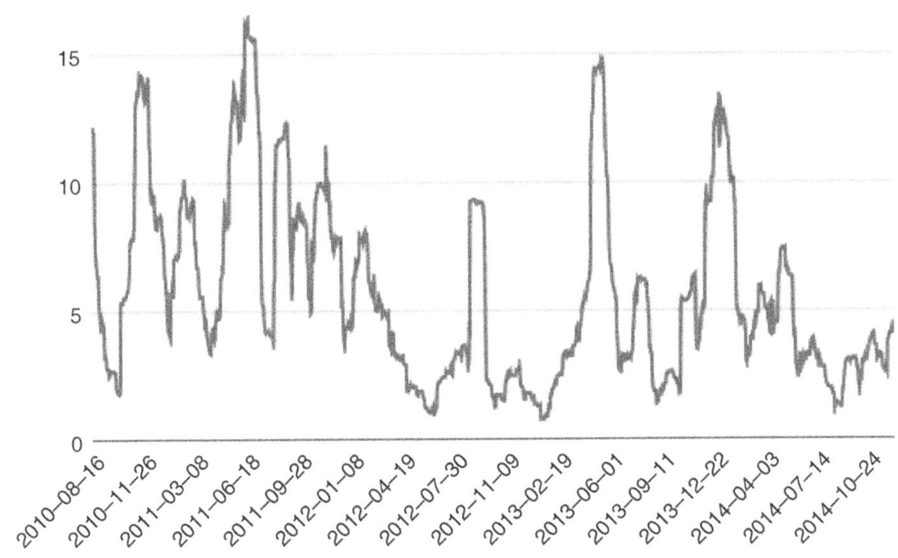

Source: CoinDesk (2014).

Figure 26.1 The Bitcoin volatility index

V. Bitcoin Granularity

Granularity is the extent to which a system can be broken down into small parts. Ron and Shamir (2012) explain that 'the network is programmed to increase the money supply in a slowly increasing geometric series until the total number of Bitcoins reaches an upper limit of about 21 million BTC's'. In 2014, the dollar value of world merchandise trade amounted to US$18.93 trillion (World Trade Report, 2015). Current global trade is closing in on 100 trillion dollars per year. Therefore, there is a big disconnect between 21 million BTC and global trade turnover.

VI. Transaction Volumes are Low Compared to Major Providers of Electronic Payments Providers

According to Fitch ratings (Grossman et. al., 2014):

> In February 2014, total Bitcoin transactions averaged $68 million per day, up over 10 fold from February 2013. As of end-2013, Western Union and PayPal averaged $225 million and $492 million in transaction volume per day, up 4% and 24% respectively during 2013. Despite these increases, Bitcoin's transaction volumes are insignificant compared to the major credit card

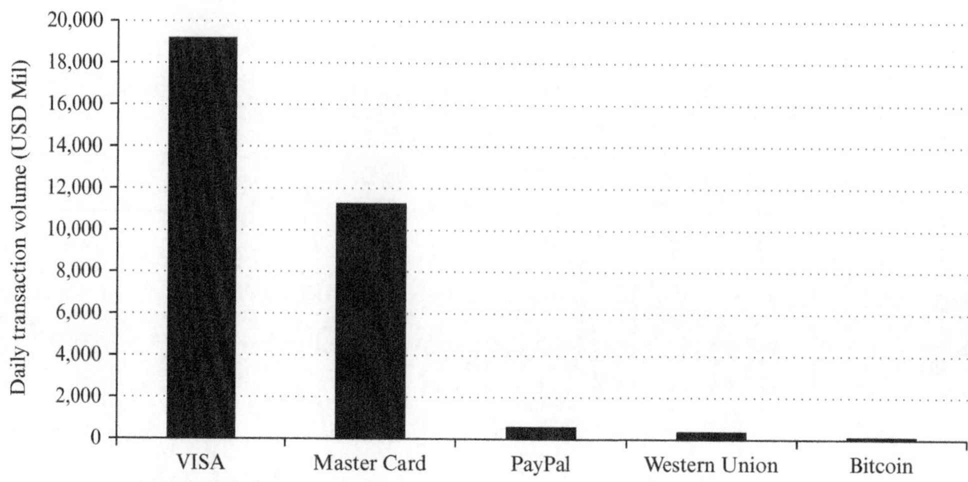

Source: Fitch, company Filings, blockchain.info, CoinDesk, found on Fitch Ratings, http://thewhyforum.com/articles/sizing-up-bitcoin/.

Figure 26.2 Transaction volumes for major providers of electronic payment

companies such as Visa and MasterCard, whose transaction volumes averaged $19 Billion and $11 billion per day in 2013 respectively.

Figure 26.2 clearly shows that Bitcoin's transaction volumes, in spite of the newly acquired global notoriety of the crypto-currency, remains low compared to major electronic payments providers. In short, Bitcoin has not yet entered the mainstream of global payments.

VII. Bitcoin is Not a Geopolitical Contender

Currency hegemony is apprehended through the lenses of history and geopolitics. The reason for the dollar hegemony after WW2 was essentially the acceptance of the exorbitant privilege accrued to the United States by virtue of its role as the key currency. This configuration was the expression of a shifting geopolitical balance of power wherein 'a leader, or "hegemon", is a direct reflection of the distribution of interstate power' (Cohen, 2010: 296). Yet, without any sovereign power to back up its value in times of turmoil, Bitcoin remains a geopolitical dwarf.

VIII. Bitcoin's Use is Circumscribed to a Limited Number of Market Participants

One sees no end in sight to the long road to acceptance for Bitcoin beyond the sphere of private individuals and select corporations (see Table 26.2).

Table 26.2 Market participants in the Bitcoin versus conventional currency markets

	Bitcoin	Conventional Currency
Market Participants	– Miners – Bitcoin exchanges – Online wallet services – Companies accepting Bitcoin – Bitcoin exchange-traded funds (ETF), such as the Winklevoss Bitcoin Trust	– Financial institutions: central banks, commercial banks, deposit insurance institutions etc. – Financial regulators – Payment services providers – Auditing/consulting firms – Non-financial corporations

IX. The Commodification of Bitcoin and its Ban by Some Countries

In Singapore, Bitcoin is treated as a market commodity and authorities have imposed a tax whenever it is used for trading on in payment of goods and services. In Russia, the Prosecutor General's office outlawed all Bitcoin transactions in 2014 (see Figure 26.3); although the situation has changed recently (Rizzo, 2016)! Likewise, in October 2014, the Payment Systems Management Department of Kazakhstan's central bank announced a ban on Bitcoin for all financial institutions, arguing that it might cause a threat to financial stability (Tengrinews, 2014). The 5 December 2013 memo from the People's Bank of China warned all national financial institutions not to trade in Bitcoin. China had first given the impression it was going to outlaw Bitcoin within its national boundaries in late 2013. Yet, a few months later, transactions had regained momentum with a new sense of legitimacy (China Briefing, 2014).

Are Bitcoin users driven by mere self-interest? The Bitcoin experiment only exists because miners form a community (though virtual). It is unsure whether the latter is populated by individual agents maximizing their utility under constraint with disregard for the holistic dimension of the project. Miners are arguably self-interested in the sense that they hope to derive a future gain from their mining endeavour. Yet, the viability of the crypto-currency implies a sense of altruism amongst miners, ensured when individual and systemic incentives are aligned. Notwithstanding the existence of personal motives, there might exist a cooperative behavioural dimension in sharp contrast with a neoclassical economic arena dominated by Darwinian principles. Experimental economists have gathered overwhelming evidence in recent years that cooperation is a widespread human trait in human interactions throughout the world. Grund et al. (2013) lay the foundations for an evolutionarily grounded theory of other-regarding agents, explaining individually different utility functions and conditional cooperation. The legacy of Darwinism on economic methodology, exemplified by the infamous homo economicus, is evident. Mainstream models are designed with rational agents competing with one another. What is less known is that Darwinism can, under certain circumstances, account for group dynamics deemed altruistic. This result was shown by Trivers in 'The Evolution of Reciprocal Altruism' in the *Quarterly Review of Biology* in 1971. Trivers demonstrated how reciprocal altruism evolves between unrelated individuals in the natural environment, even between individuals of entirely different species. It is understood that a majority of participants in the Bitcoin ecosystem are driven by self-interest. Yet, from a holistic

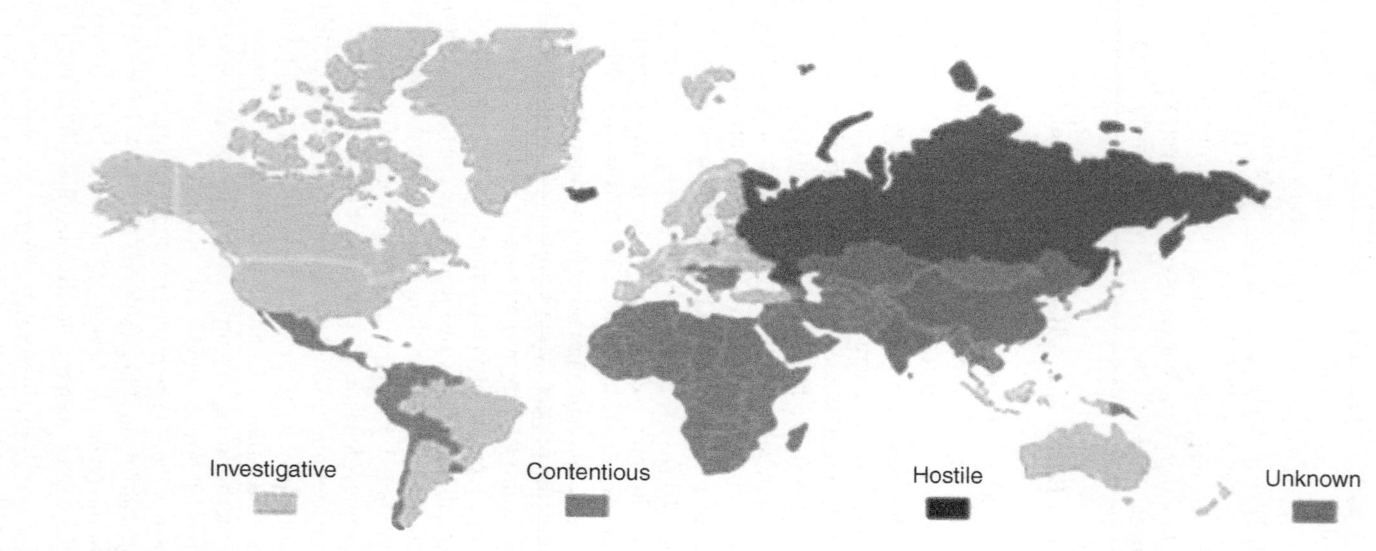

Source: CoinDesk (2014).

Figure 26.3 Bitcoin regulatory heat map

perspective, the cooperative dimension, notably in the initial stages, might have been overlooked in explaining the viability of this highly complex system.

26.5 CONSEQUENCES FOR THE NEW GEOGRAPHIES OF MONEY AND FINANCE

How Does Bitcoin Fit into Conventional Monetary Theory?

Complexity is the by-product of history and anthropology. Conventional wisdom states that currencies were invented as a means to transfer value, with barter systems preceding metal coins deemed valuable for their scarcity. Coins were followed by paper notes, giving the bearer the equivalent value in gold, and eventually fiat money, delinked from the available quantity of reserves. Following this line of thought, virtual currencies are the ultimate stage in the history of money with digital supports performing all textbook functions of money. Commenting on Graeber (2011), Tett (2011, italics added) writes that:

> However, Graeber asserts this sequencing [that money emerged as a medium of exchange to replace barter, while virtual credit developed after that] is wrong: his reading of history suggests that *complex* debt relations, in the widest sense, emerged before coins circulated (and before complex systems of barter, too). Back in 3,000BC in Mesopotamia, people were keeping records of who owed what to whom – but were barely using coins. And today, numerous non-western societies operate with fiendishly complex debt systems, which blur social and economic obligations, even if they barely use 'currency'. Indeed, anthropologists spend a considerable amount of time looking at how these 'debts' bind groups together. '*There is nothing new about virtual money*. Actually this was the original form of money,' Graeber argues. 'Credit systems were interspersed with a period of bullion, but credit came first'.

The idea that barter systems preceded the emergence of monetary economies has been given theoretical pretense in standard monetary theory, but was nonetheless criticized by Innes (1913). Notwithstanding the high degree of technological innovation in the design of the Bitcoin protocol, its novelty is subject to caution.

The Anthropological and Socio-psychological Approaches to Money

Hoffer (1951) offers an explanation of mass movements originating in a desire for change from human communities discontented by the prevailing cultural artifacts and traditions. Interestingly, Bitcoin features elements of the psychology of mass movements. Hoffer offers insight into what drives the mind of the fanatic and the dynamics of mass movements. Regarding Bitcoin, viewed as a mass movement, the coexistence of virtual currencies bears testimony that 'all mass movements are competitive' (Hoffer, 1951: 17). Likewise, drawing on the philosophical and anthropological insights of René Girard about the mimetic rivalry, contagious in essence, originating from the struggle for the possession of goods in ancient societies, thereby leading to the threat of violence, the mimetic nature of money was explored by Aglietta and Orléan (1982) in their landmark book *La Violence de la Monnaie*. Weigand (2009: 64) lists the characteristic features of complex systems:

- Nonlinear effects: a small perturbation may have a large effect.
- Feedback loops: the effects of an element's behaviour are fed back to it in some way. The feedback can be positive (amplification, runaway) or negative (damping).
- Openness: a typical complex system interacts with its environment.
- Memory: the history of a complex system may be important. Prior states may have an influence on present states.
- Nesting, hierarchy: a complex system may itself be an element of a larger complex system. For example, clans in a tribal society, nation-states in an international system, or divisions in a company.
- Topology: the interactions of the elements are enabled and constrained by the network, or grid, of relationships between them.

Weigand presents a special version of complex adaptative systems called complex mimetic systems (CMS), building on Girardian mimetic theory. Although the strengths of Bitcoin are acknowledged by the ECB (2012),[5] its mimetic nature is conditioned by its worldwide acceptance. Yet, the path towards full acceptance hinges on three market-based developments (ECB, 2012), namely robust and liquid global exchanges similar to national currencies that can offer risk management via futures and options; more user-friendly applications that mask the complexities of cryptography from users and merchants, and a paradigm shift towards 'closing the loop': receiving source payments and wages in Bitcoins to eliminate the need for conversion from or to national fiat.

Bitcoin with Regard to the Claims of Chartalism

Money, just like words in linguistics, is a sign (de Saussure, 1916) as well as a quasi-universal and institutionalized mass illusion (in this sense, it has no intrinsic value substance, as its value is conferred by its acceptance, which extends to the entire payments community through mere mimetic behaviour). The existence of Bitcoin runs counter to the ideas propounded by Lerner (1947).[6] Proponents of the Bitcoin-is-money view would agree with Lerner's premises (1947: 313): 'money, as I have said . . . is what we use to pay for things. The basic condition for its effectiveness is that it should be generally acceptable'. Lerner (1947: 313) makes a formidable prediction of what the post-1971 world of fiat currencies and State-controlled illusions[7] will look like: 'the modern state can make anything it chooses generally acceptable as money and thus establish its value quite apart from any connection, even of the most formidable kind, with gold or with backing of any kind'. The following quotation is hardly compatible with the Bitcoin-is-money view: 'but if the state is willing to accept the proposed money in payment of taxes and other obligations to itself *the trick is done*' (Lerner, 1947: 313, italics added). But what trick is Lerner referring to? It is nothing less than bringing closure to his conceptual attempt to reach a universal definition of money. Contrariwise, Bitcoin is a market-driven currency. The cryptographic unit of account is gaining legitimacy worldwide through the free and open marketplace. Therefore, a market-based illusion with a decentralized modus operandi may prove just as valid (if not more) than a State-controlled one. The chartalist view of money has thus come under attack with the advent of Bitcoin.

Money Without a Central Bank and Without Monetary Policy

Bitcoin supply is pre-determined by a complex mathematical algorithm, and its growth model runs counter to the recent QE experiments ran by the Federal Reserve, or more generally, to all 'helicopter money' conceptions (Friedman, 1969, *Financial Times*, 2012). The creation of new units is capped at 21 million with eight current decimal places. There is no need for a central authority to manage the supply thereof, which is determined by technological factors on a decentralized basis, whilst demand is guided by market forces. Toporowski (2010: 13) acknowledges that, 'bank credits and debits replaced paper money or coins for all but the smallest transactions'. This configuration is contingent on fiat currencies and organized banking systems. As a product of Hayekian free choice, Bitcoin contrasts with century-old practices of central bank monetary manipulation. For Hayekians, central banks are an undesirable form of centralized planning. Contrariwise, Bitcoin represents an intangible mathematical puzzle for economic planners as its legal existence is restricted to transfer rights on a cloud-based public ledger. Bitcoin is 'a good starting point to end the monopoly central banks have in the issuance of money' (ECB, 2012), as exemplified by its recent use in Venezuela to bypass currency controls in this socialist-run country (Gupta, 2014).

Why Bitcoin Rehabilitates Geography

The idea of an exogenous and predictable money supply *à la* Friedman (1974: 27) runs counter to the idea of complexity. Yet, the latter may be sneaking through the back door with the new geography of money and finance. Global monetarism was once advocated by McKinnon (1984), who called for 'a coordinated money supply on the part of the United States, Germany and Japan, the three countries that account[ed] for nearly two-thirds of the industrial world's output' (Corbridge and Thrift, 1994: 12). Three decades later, a study from the COFACE shows that the market capitalization/GDP ratio of BRICS has caught up with advanced economies (Briant and Marcilly, 2014: 8). Therefore, any yet-to-be designed world governance protocol for virtual money, with subsequent organizational, hierarchical and aggregative complexity levels, could hardly be geographically circumscribed to developed countries. Attention has been placed in the literature since the 1990s on the relation between money and space (Cohen, 1998; Corbridge and Thrift, 1994; Dow, 1990; Eichengreen and Flandreau, 1996; Laulajainen, 1998; Leyshon and Thrift, 1997; Martin, 1994, 1999). O'Brien (1992) put forward the thesis of the annihilation of space under the impulse of technological progress (ICT), financial deregulation and innovation in Anglo-Saxon countries, and world financial integration. Likewise, Grote (2009: 280) investigates virtualization understood 'as the substitution of virtual proximity, through the use of electronic systems, for spatial proximity'. For Gehrig (1998: 13), virtual agglomerations, the agglomeration of traders, 'take place within electronic communication networks', thereby rendering locational factors obsolete. For Bergstra and Leeuw (2013: 23), geography is not a relevant dimension to the analysis of Bitcoin: 'The bundle of existing monies may be moving away from horizontally juxtaposed monies of the same type, each featuring geographical universality in geographically disjoint areas. Newly created informational monies (e.g. Bitcoin and DigiCash to mention some) are increasingly geography insensitive and are combined by way of vertical juxtaposition'.

We disagree with the claim of geographic irrelevance, and endorse the opposite stance: 'money remains highly geographical, even in today's globalized world' (Garretsen et al., 2009: 145); we abide by the view that 'the geographical circuits of money and finance are the "wiring" of the socio-economy, as it were, along with the "currents" of wealth creation, consumption and economic power are transmitted' (Martin, 1999: 6).

As argued by Corbridge and Thrift (1994: 22), 'money is also a social and cultural relation bound up with asymmetries of power, which must vary from place to place'. Henning (1996: 93) noted in the 1990s that several factors 'reinforce[d] the gradual historical decline in the role of the dollar exhibited over the last decades'. In the aftermath of the global crisis, this hegemony is questioned more than ever with countries, such as post-Sotchi Russia, threatening to suspend dollar settlement in exports of oil and gas products: 'Russian bankers and big business, in light of recent threats from the west, may break the dollar peg of the world market' (Pravda.ru, 2014). In the light of this growing climate of defiance, a perceptible shift in the geography of money and finance is taking place with the creation, under the aegis of the BRICS countries, of a New Development Bank, based in Shanghai: '[t]he five-nation bloc also said it would create a $100 billion fund of currency reserves for members to use during balance of payments crises' (Romero, 2014).

The New Development Bank carries the seeds of a new approach to the governance of world money, along with shifting geographical boundaries. In this sense, McKinnon's proposal should be reassessed in the light of both Bitcoin's exogenous money supply, and the fact that emergent powers entail novel spatially oriented governance for transactions occurring within BRICS' financial systems. Future geographical analysis of money is likely to be centred on the most fertile regions for Bitcoin (see Figure 26.4), and shaped by the governance mechanisms of the embryonic New Development Bank.

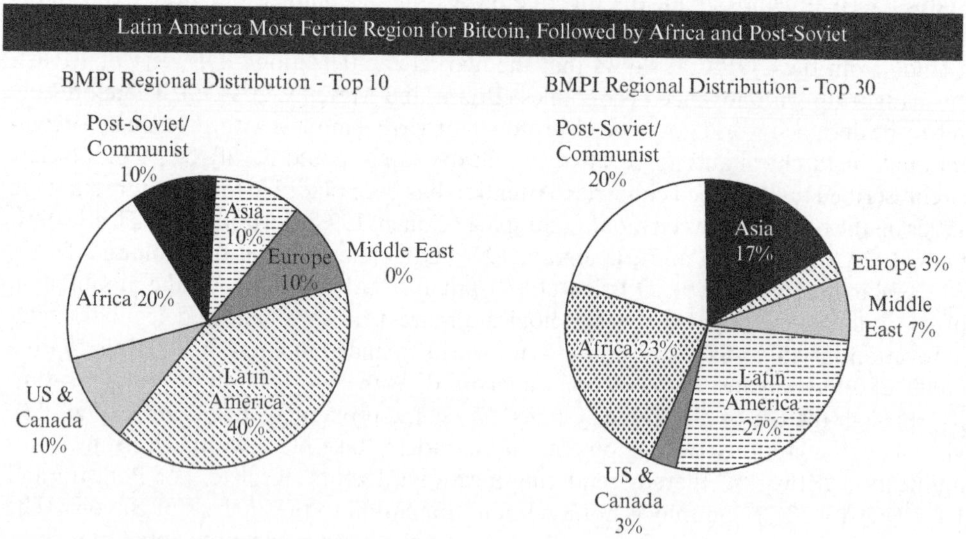

Source: CoinDesk (2014).

Figure 26.4 The most fertile regions for Bitcoin

a) Regional analysis

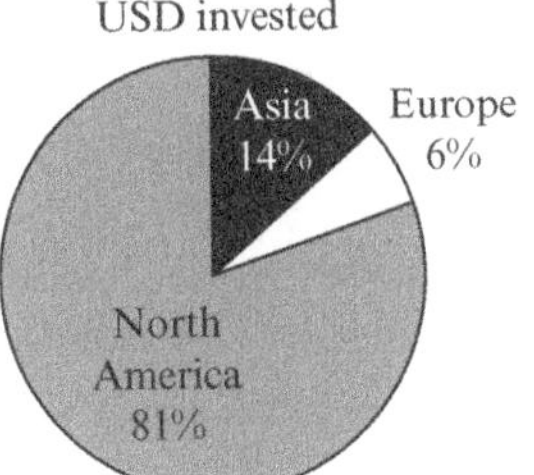

Regions	Value ($ m)	No. of companies
Asia	13.3	9
Europe	5.6	3
N. America	78.6	18
Total	97.5	30

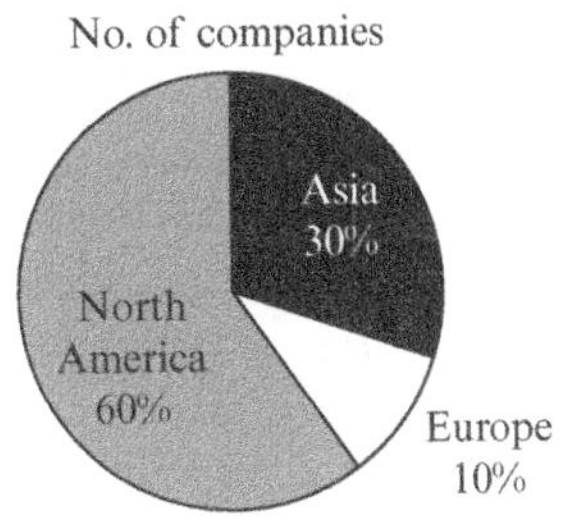

81% of all Bitcoin VC $s have been invested in North America to date, but only 60% of the companies are based there

b) Country analysis

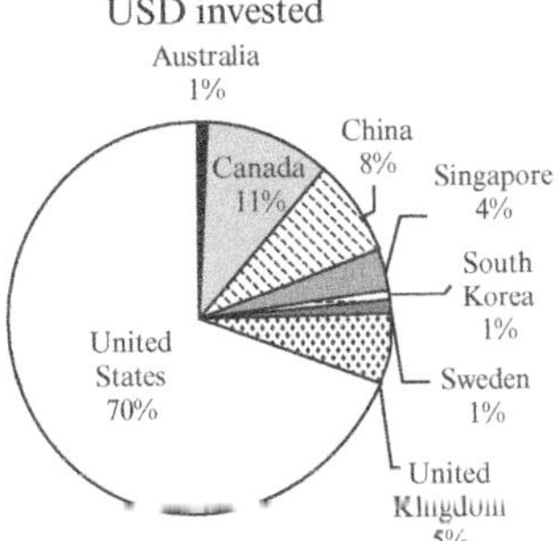

Countries	Vlaue ($ m)	No. of companies
Australia	0.7	2
Canada	10.5	2
China	8.0	3
Singapore	3.8	2
South Korea	0.8	2
Sweden	0.6	1
United Kingdom	5.0	2
United States	68.1	16

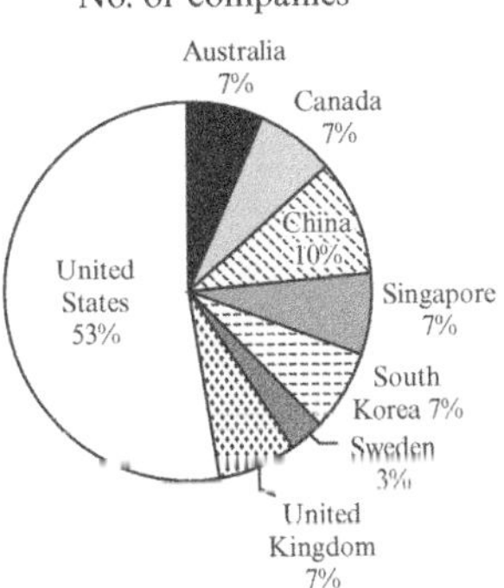

Greatest number of Bitcoin companies are in the US and China, over two-thirds of all Bitcoin VC investment is in the US

Source: CoinDesk (2014).

Figure 26.5 Geographic distribution of Bitcoin venture-capital investment

Another shifting pattern pertains to the geography of venture-capital (VC) backed Bitcoin companies. In 2014, North America was the largest recipient of VC investment inflows, but Asian and European VC investment outflows were picking up (see Figure 26.5). The spatial dimension of VC backed Bitcoin firms is paramount. As Martin (1999: 6) argues, these more specialized financial institutions 'are typically much more spatially concentrated'.

26.6 CONCLUSION

As argued by Robinson (2004: xv), 'the twenty-first century world is a complex place in which change takes place so quickly that meaningful participation, indeed survival, requires that we grasp the essential dynamics of our times and gain an understanding of how this global society works'. In this chapter, we have shown how Bitcoin may be apprehended through the lenses of complexity theory, thereby offering original research paths for understanding the nature of this complex object of study, while simultaneously breaking away from the holy trinity of the mainstream. Bitcoin first appeared as an innovative technological breakthrough in 2009. Since then, its foundations have helped launch a fierce attack on the holy trinity of the mainstream. The latter was widely criticized for causing the academic community to cover their eyes in the run-up to the global crisis. Yet, triumph cannot and should not be prematurely proclaimed. The ruins of the mainstream do not necessarily make room for an alternative paradigm geared at socio-economic progress. Complexity should not conceal the deceptive nature of Bitcoin, the ultimate artifact of technology-driven capitalism, blinding our eyes and distracting our minds with a mere smokescreen, ignoring the unfolding destructive tendencies of present times. However, in spite of the prevailing scepticism surrounding the transformative long-term socio-economic impact of Bitcoin, its potential for a novel spatial reorganization of virtual money schemes should not be neglected. As regards the future of the ongoing, yet uncertain, institutional rivalry between crypto and fiat currencies, let us conclude by this audacious prediction by security expert and Bitcoin entrepreneur Andreas Antonopoulos (Bundrick, 2015):

> You put an open, decentralized ecosystem: open source, open standards, open networking and the intelligence and innovation pushed all the way to the edge – put that against a closed system, controlled by a central provider, whose permission you need in order to innovate and who will only innovate at the exclusion and competition of all of the other companies – and we will crush them.

NOTES

1. These functions are the following:
   (i) Medium of exchange (Bitcoins are transferable over to Internet from one party to the other, in order to make payments and acquire goods and services),
   (ii) Measurement of value (the numbers in the Bitcoin wallet are the measure of its value),
   (iii) Store of value (Bitcoins are storable on electronic media).
2. The Financial Crimes Enforcement Network (FinCEN) was established in April 1990 by Treasury Order Number 105–08. Its original mission was to provide a government-wide, multi-source intelligence and analytical network to support the detection, investigation, and prosecution of domestic and international money laundering and other financial crimes. FinCEN was made a Treasury bureau by the USA Patriot Act of October 2001.
3. Seth Lloyd has identified 45, see Horgan (1996: 303, footnote 11).
4. This is confirmed by Blundell-Wignall (2014: 10): 'Unlike gold, there is no intrinsic value for a Bitcoin'.
5. (a) 'higher degree of anonymity compared to other electronic payment instruments',
   (b) 'lower transaction costs compared with traditional payment systems', and
   (c) 'more direct and faster clearing and settlement of transactions' from the absence of intermediaries (ECB, 2012).
6. Of course, Keynes (1930) and Knapp (1924) were the first proponents of this view. More recently, let us mention Randy Wray (2000).
7. Until the advent of the euro, of course, that one may label a supranational institution-controlled illusion . . .

REFERENCES

Aglietta, M. and P. Moutot (1993), 'Le risque de système et sa prévention', *Cahiers économiques et monétaires*, Banque de France, **41**, 38–39.

Aglietta, Michel and André Orléan (1982), *La Violence de la monnaie*, Paris: PUF.

Akerlof, G.A. and R.J. Shiller (2009), *Animal Spirits: How human psychology drives the economy, and why it matters for global capitalism*, Princeton, NJ: Princeton University Press.

Allen, J. and A. Cochrane (2007), 'Beyond the territorial fix: regional assemblage, politics and power', *Regional Studies*, **41** (9), 1161–1175.

Aristotle (1924 [1953]), 'Greek text with commentary: Aristotle's Metaphysics', W.D. Ross, 2 vols, Oxford: Clarendon Press.

Barker, J.T. (2014), 'Why is Bitcoin's value so volatile?', accessed 31 March 2015 at www.investopedia.com/articles/investing/052014/why-bitcoins-value-so-volatile.asp.

Beinhocker, E.D. (2007), *The Origin of Wealth: Evolution, Complexity and the Radical Remaking of Economics*, London: Random House.

Bergstra, J.A and K. Leeuw (2013), 'Bitcoin and beyond: exclusively informational monies', accessed 31 March 2015 at http://arxiv.org/pdf/1304.4758.pdf.

Blanchard, O. (2011), 'The future of macroeconomic policy: nine tentative conclusions', 14 March, *Huffington Post*, accessed 31 March 2015 at www.huffingtonpost.com/olivier-blanchard/the-future-of-macroeconom_b_835653.html.

Blundell-Wignall, A. (2014), 'The Bitcoin question: currency versus trust-less transfer technology', OECD Working Papers on Finance, Insurance and Private Pensions, No. 37, OECD Publishing, accessed 31 March 2015 at http://dx.doi.org/10.1787/5jz2pwjd9t20-en.

Briant, L. and J. Marcilly (2014), 'Quels pays émergents prendront le relais des BRICS?' *Panorama, Les Publications Economiques de Coface*, Printemps, 2–9, accessed 31 March 2015 at www.coface.fr/Actualites-Publications/Publications/Quels-pays-emergents-prendront-le-relais-des-BRICS.

Bundrick, H. (2015), 'Andreas Antonopoulos: "Give Bitcoin Two Years"', insidebitcoins.com/news, accessed 31 March 2015 at http://insidebitcoins.com/news/andreas-antonopoulos-give-bitcoin-two-years/29708.

Byrne, D. and G. Callaghan (2013), *Complexity Theory and the Social Sciences – The State of the Art*, Abingdon: Routledge.

Chaia, A., T. Goland and R. Schiff (2010), 'Counting the world's unbanked', *McKinsey Quarterly*, March, accessed 31 March 2015 at www.mckinsey.com/insights/financial_services/counting_the_worlds_unbanked.

Chen, P. (2010), *Economic Complexity and Equilibrium Illusion: Essays on Market Instability and Macro Vitality*, London: Routledge.

Chick, V. (2011), 'Money defined by its acceptability', *Financial Times*, 22 August, accessed 31 March 2015 at www.ft.com/intl/cms/s/0/ddc029f0-ca68-11e0-a0dc-00144feabdc0.html#axzz2hgqRFie0.

China Briefing (2014), 'Bitcoin exchange BTC China resumes RMB-based deposits', 4 February, accessed 8 July 2016, www.china-briefing.com/news/2014/02/04/bitcoin-exchange-btc-china-resumes-rmb-based-deposits.html.

Cohen B.J. (1998), *The Geography of Money*, Ithaca: Cornell University Press.

Cohen, B.J. (2010), *The Future of Global Currency: The Euro Versus the Dollar*, London: Routledge.

Cohn, C. (2011), 'EFF and Bitcoin', Electronic Frontier Foundation, 20 June, accessed 15 August 2015 at www.eff.org/fr/deeplinks/2011/06/eff-and-bitcoin.

CoinDesk (2014), 'State of Bitcoin Q3 2014', accessed 31 March 2015 at www.coindesk.com/state-of-bitcoin-q3-2014-report-maturing-ecosystem-price-pressure/.

Colander, D., R. Holt and B. Rosser (2004), 'The changing face of mainstream economics', *Review of Political Economy*, **16** (4), 485–499.

Corbridge, S. and N.J. Thrift (1994), 'Money, power and space: introduction and overview', in Stuart Corbridge, Ron Martin and Nigel Thrift (eds), *Money, Power and Space*, Oxford: Blackwell, pp. 1–25.

Courtois, N. (2014), 'On the longest chain rule and programmed self-destruction of crypto currencies', Cornell University Library, Working Paper, accessed 31 March 2015 at http://arxiv.org/abs/1405.0534.

de Saussure, Ferdinand (1916), *Course in General Linguistics*, London: Duckworth.

Dixon, C. (2013) cdixon tumblr, blogpost, accessed 22 October 2016 at http://nonchalantrepreneur.com/post/46485623457/three-eras-of-currency.

Dow S.C. (1990), *Financial Markets and Regional Economic Development*, Aldershot: Avebury.

Dymski, G.A. (2009), 'The global financial customer and the spatiality of exclusion after the "end of geography"', *Cambridge Journal of Regions, Economy and Society*, **2** (2), 267–285.

Eichengreen B. and M. Flandreau (1996), 'The geography of the Gold Standard', in Jorge Braga Braga de Macedo, Barry Eichengreen and Jaime Reis (eds), *Currency Convertibility: The Gold Standard and Beyond*, London: Routledge, pp. 113–143.

European Central Bank (ECB) (2012), 'Virtual currency schemes', October 2012, accessed 31 March 2015 at www.ecb.europa.eu/pub/pdf/other/virtualcurrencyschemes201210en.pdf.
European Commission (2009), 'EU study on the New rules for a new age? Legal analysis of a single market for the information society', European Commission's Information Society and Media Directorate-General, accessed 31 March 2015 at http://ec.europa.eu/information_society/newsroom/cf/dae/document.cfm?doc_id=842.
European Parliament (2009), 'Directive 2009/110/EC of the European Parliament and of the Council of 16 September, the e-money directive', on the taking up, pursuit and prudential supervision of the business of electronic money institutions amending Directives 2005/60/EC and 2006/48/EC and repealing Directive 2000/46/EC, Official Journal of the European Union, 10 October, accessed 31 March 2015 at http://eur-lex.europa.eu/LexUriServ/LexUriServ.do?uri=OJ:L:2009:267:0007:0017:EN:PDF.
Evans, D. (2014), 'Economic aspects of Bitcoin and other decentralized public-ledger currency platforms', Coase-Sandor Institute for Law and Economics Working Paper 685, April.
Ferrara, P. (2013), 'The Federal Government's reaction to Bitcoin is an acknowledgement of the dollar's vulnerability', *Forbes*, 25, accessed 15 August 2016 at www.forbes.com/sites/peterferrara/2013/08/25/the-federal-governments-reaction-to-bitcoin-is-an-acknowledgement-of-the-dollars-vulnerability/#2fd3d0d3e9e7.
Financial Times (2012), 'Time for helicopter money?' 1 November, accessed 8 July 2016 at http://video.ft.com/1938690861001/Time-for-helicopter-money-/Markets.
FinCEN (2013), 'Guidance – application of FinCEN's Regulations to Persons Administering, Exchanging, or Using Virtual Currencies', 18 March, accessed 9 July 2016 at http://www.fincen.gov/statutes_regs/guidance/html/FIN-2013-G001.html.
Friedman, M. (1969), 'The optimum quantity of money', in Milton Friedman (ed.), *The Optimum Quantity of Money*, Chicago: Aldine Publishing Company, pp. 1–50.
Friedman, M. (1974), 'A theoretical framework for monetary analysis', in Robert J. Gordon (ed.), *Milton Friedman's Monetary Framework: A Debate with his Critics*, Chicago: Chicago University Press, pp. 1–61.
Garretsen, H., M. Kitson and R. Martin (2009), 'Spatial circuits of global finance', *Cambridge Journal of Regions Economy and Society*, **2** (2), 143–148.
Gehrig, T. (1998), 'Cities and the geography of financial centres', June, CEPR Discussion Paper Series No. 1894, accessed 31 March 2015 at http://ssrn.com/abstract=125529.
Gilbert, N. and K.G. Troitzsch (2005), *Simulation for the Social Scientist*, Maidenhead: Open University Press.
Gouvernement Français (2013), 'Arrêté du 2 mai 2013 portant sur la réglementation prudentielle des établissements de monnaie électronique', accessed 31 March 2015 at www.legifrance.gouv.fr/affichTexte.do?cidTexte=JORFTEXT000027385232.
Graeber, D. (2011), *Debt: The First 5,000 Years*, New York: Melville House Publishing.
Grinberg, R. (2011), 'Bitcoin: an innovative alternative digital currency', *Hastings Science and Technology Law Journal*, **4** (1), 159–208.
Grossman, R., A. Mitropoulos and J. Boise (2014), 'Sizing up Bitcoin', The Why? Forum, Fitch Ratings, accessed 31 March 2015 at http://thewhyforum.com/articles/sizing-up-bitcoin/.
Grote, M.H. (2009), 'Financial centers between centralization and virtualization', in Pietro Alessandrini, Alberto Zazzaro and Michele Fratianni (eds), *The Changing Geography of Banking and Finance*, Dordrecht: Springer, pp. 277–295.
Grund, T., C. Waloszek and D. Helbing (2013), 'How natural selection can create both self- and other-regarding preferences, and networked minds', *Scientific Reports*, **3**, Article number: 1480, accessed 31 March 2015 at www.nature.com/srep/2013/130319/srep01480/full/srep01480.html.
Gupta, G. (2014), 'Venezuelans turn to bitcoins to bypass socialist currency controls', Reuters, 8 October, accessed 22 October 2016 at www.reuters.com/article/2014/10/08/us-venezuela-bitcoin-idUSKCN0HX11O20141008.
Hayek, F.A. (1976), *Denationalisation of Money*, London: Institute of Economic Affairs.
Henning, C.R. (1996), 'Europe's Monetary Union and the United States', *Foreign Policy*,**102** (Spring), 83–100.
Hodgson, G. et al. (2009), Open Letter to the Queen, 14 August, accessed 31 March 2015 at http://transitionculture.org/2009/09/07/an-open-letter-to-the-queen/.
Hoffer, E. (1951), *The True Believer: Thoughts on the Nature of Mass Movements*, New York: Harper & Row Publishers.
Horgan, J. (1996), *The End of Science – Facing the Limits of Knowledge in the Twilight of the Scientific Age*, New York: Broadway Books.
Innes, A.M. (1913), 'What is money?', *Banking Law Journal*, May, 377–408.
Keynes, J.M. (1930), *Treatise on Money, Volume II*, London: Macmillan.
Keynes, J.M. (1936), *The General Theory of Employment, Interest, and Money*, New York: Harcourt Brace.
Knapp, G.F. (1924), *The State Theory of Money*, London: Macmillan and Company.
Laulajainen, R. (1998), *Financial Geography*, Göteborg: School of Economic and Commercial Law.
Lerner, A.P. (1947), 'Money as a creature of the state', *American Economic Review*, **37** (2), 312–317.
Lewin, R. (1992), *Complexity – Life at the Edge of Chaos*, New York, NY: Macmillan.
Leyshon A. and N. Thrift (1997), *Money/Space: Geographies of Monetary Transformation*, London: Routledge.

Libros.tel (2016) 'Michael Parsons Bitcoin expert', accessed 8 July 2016 at http://michaelparsons.europa.expertos.bitcoin.libros.tel/.
Manson, S.M. (2001), 'Simplifying complexity: a review of complexity theory', *Geoforum*, **32** (3), 405–414.
Martin, R.L. (1994), 'Stateless monies, global financial integration and national economic autonomy: the end of geography?', in Stuart Corbridge, Ron Martin, Nigel Thrift (eds), *Money, Power and Space*, Oxford: Blackwell, pp. 253–278.
Martin, R.L. (1999), *Money and the Space Economy*, London: Wiley.
Martin, R. and P. Sunley (2010), 'Complexity thinking and evolutionary economic geography', in R. Boschma and R. Martin (eds), *The Handbook of Evolutionary Economic Geography*, Cheltenham, UK and Northampton, MA, USA: Edward Elgar Publishing, pp. 93–119.
Matonis, J. (2012), 'Roots of Bitcoin can be found in the Austrian School Of Economics', *Forbes*, 3 November, accessed 9 July 2016 at www.forbes.com/sites/jonmatonis/2012/11/03/ecb-roots-of-bitcoin-can-be-found-in-the-austrian-school-of-economics/.
McKinnon, R. (1984), *An International Standard for Monetary Stabilization*, Washington, DC: Institute for International Economics.
Mill, J. Stuart (1894), *Principles of Political Economy*, New York: D. Appleton and Company.
Mundell, R.A. (2003), 'The international monetary system and the case for a world currency', Distinguished Lecture Series No. 12, Leon Kozminski Academy of Entrepreneurship and Management, 23 October.
Murphy, R.P. and S. Barta (2013), 'Bitcoin from an Austro-libertarian perspective', Part I, personal blog of Robert. P. Murphy, accessed 31 March 2015 at http://consultingbyrpm.com/blog/2013/04/bitcoin-from-an-austro-libertarian-perspective-part-i.html.
Nakamoto, S. (2009), 'Bitcoin: a peer-to-peer electronic cash system', accessed 31 March 2015 at http://bitcoin.org/bitcoin.pdf.
Nicolis, G. and I. Prigogine (1989), *Exploring Complexity: An Introduction*, New York: Freeman.
O'Brien, R. (1992), *Global Financial Integration: The End of Geography*, London: Pinter/RIIA.
Oeffner, M. (2008), 'Agent-based Keynesian macroeconomics – an evolutionary model embedded in an agent-based computer simulation', Doctoral dissertation, Bayerische Julius – Maximilians Universitat, Wurzburg, accessed 31 March 2015 at http://mpra.ub.uni-muenchen.de/18199/1/MPRA_paper_18199.pdf.
Pavard, B. and J. Dugdale (2000), *An Introduction to Complexity in Social Science*, Toulouse: GRIC-IRIT.
Pravda.ru (2014), 'Can Russia break dollar's spine?', 8 April, accessed 31 March 2015 at http://english.pravda.ru/russia/economics/08-04-2014/127297-russia_dollars-0/.
Prigogine, I. (1977), 'Time, structure and fluctuations', Nobel Lecture, 8 December.
Prigogine, I. (1989), 'The behavior of matter under nonequilibrium conditions: fundamental aspects and applications: progress report, April 15, 1988–April 14, 1989', Center for Studies in Statistical Mathematics at the University of Texas-Austin, United States Department of Energy, October.
Prigogine, Ilya and Grégoire Nicolis (1977), *Self-Organization in Non-Equilibrium Systems*, New York: Wiley.
Rescher, N. (1998), *Complexity: A Philosophical Overview*, New Brunswick: Transaction Publishers.
Rickards James (2014), *The Death of Money: The Coming Collapse of the International Monetary System*, New York: Portfolio Penguin.
Rizzo, P. (2016), Report: 'Russian government to abandon penalties for Bitcoin use', CoinDesk, 12 August, accessed 30 October 2016 at www.coindesk.com/russian-bitcoin-penalties-abandon-report/.
Robinson, W.I. (2004), *A Theory of Global Capitalism: Production, Class and State in a Transnational World*, Baltimore and London: Johns Hopkins University Press.
Röhl Dehm and Partner (2013), Letter to the clients of bitcoin24.com, 22 April, accessed 9 July 2016 at https://docs.google.com/file/d/0B5oMV-mCjuNlcnlwNkN2Tlg5b1k/edit?usp=sharing.
Romero, S. (2014), 'Emerging nations bloc to open development bank', *New York Times*, 15 July.
Ron, D. and A. Shamir (2012), 'Quantitative analysis of the full Bitcoin – transaction graph', Department of Computer Science and Applied Mathematics, accessed 31 March 2015 at http://eprint.iacr.org/2012/584.pdf.
Rossi, S. (1998), 'Endogenous money and banking activity: some notes on the workings of modern payment systems', University of Friburg, Working Paper No. 309, November.
Seppecher, P. (2011), 'Modélisation multi-agants d'une économie monétaire – Un système dynamique et complexe d'interactions réelles et monétaires entre des agents multiples, hétérogènes, autonomes et concurrents', PhD thesis, December, accessed 31 March 2015 at http://hal.archives-ouvertes.fr/docs/00/69/31/51/PDF/these_SEPPECHER_modelisation_multi-agents.pdf.
Seppecher, P. (2012), 'Flexibility of wages and macroeconomic instability in an agent-based computational model with endogenous money', *Macroeconomic Dynamics*, **16** (S2), 284–297.
Sornette, D. (2003), *Why Stock Markets Crash: Critical Events in Complex Financial Systems*, Princeton, NJ: Princeton University Press.
Taleb, N. (2007), *The Black Swan: The Impact of the Highly Improbable*, London: Random House.
Tengrinews (2014), 'Kazakhstan's financial institutions banned from using Bitcoin-institutions-banned-from-

using-Bitcoin', 15 October, accessed 9 July 2016 at http://en.tengrinews.kz/finance/Kazakhstans-financial-institutions-banned-from-using-Bitcoin-256880/.

Tett, G. (2011), 'Debt: it's back to the future', *Financial Times*, 9 September, accessed 31 March 2015 at www.ft.com/intl/cms/s/2/04e44606-d9a0-11e0-b16a-00144feabdc0.html#axzz2hgqRFie0.

The Economist (2013), 'Mining digital gold', from the print edition: *Finance and Economics*, 13 April.

Toporowski, J. (2010), *Why the World Economy Needs a Financial Crash and Other Critical Essays on Finance and Financial Economics*, London and New York: Anthem Press.

Trivers, R.L. (1971), 'The evolution of reciprocal altruism', *Quarterly Review of Biology*, **46** (March), 35–57.

US Securities Exchange Commission (2013), 'SEC charges Texas man with running Bitcoin-denominated Ponzi scheme', Press Release, accessed 23 July at www.sec.gov/News/PressRelease/Detail/PressRelease/1370539730583#.UlZ6zRDer_B.

US Securities and Exchange Commission (2016), 'investor alert – Ponzi schemes using virtual currencies', SEC Office of Investor Education and Advocacy, SEC Pub. No. 153 (7/13), accessed 8 July 2016 at www.sec.gov/investor/alerts/ia_virtualcurrencies.pdf.

US Treasury (2007), 'Financial crimes enforcement network', last updated 8 March 2007, accessed 9 July 2016 at www.treasury.gov/about/history/Pages/fincen.aspx.

Vigna, P. (2014), '5 things about Mt. Gox's crisis', *Wall Street Journal*, accessed 31 March 2015 at http://blogs.wsj.com/briefly/2014/02/25/5-things-about-mt-goxs-crisis/.

Weigand, H. (2009), 'Complex mimetic systems. Contagion', *Journal of Violence, Mimesis, and Culture*, **1** (15/16), 63–87.

World Trade Report (2015), 'Speeding up trade: benefits and challenges of implementing the WTO Trade Facilitation Agreement', accessed 8 July 2016 at www.wto.org/english/res_e/publications_e/wtr15_e.htm.

Wray, R. (2000), 'The neo-chartalist approach to money', Working Paper No. 10, Center for Full Employment and Price Stability, University of Missouri – Kansas City.

Index